Sisson's Synonyms

An Unabridged Synonym and Related-Terms Locater

By the Same Author:

SISSON'S WORD AND EXPRESSION LOCATER
THE UNABRIDGED CROSSWORD PUZZLE DICTIONARY

Sisson's Synonyms

An Unabridged

Synonym and Related-Terms

Locater

A. F. SISSON

PARKER PUBLISHING COMPANY, INC., West Nyack, N.Y.

PRINTED IN THE UNITED STATES OF AMERICA
B & P—13-810630-4

TO RUTH

Without whom this book would
never have been completed

ABOUT THIS BOOK

Sisson's Synonyms should be invaluable to any individual who is seeking to communicate more effectively and precisely, whether orally or in writing. In addition to the business and professional audience generally, both college and high school students will find this book helpful in the preparation of term papers and other special projects, as well as an all-around, useful tool to consult in their pursuit of an improved vocabulary. Whether the reader refers to this book in connection with his vocational activities, formal or informal educational endeavors, or for sheer pleasure of learning more about our language, the compiler hopes and trusts that he will be well rewarded.

Attempt has been made in this work to assemble, following each entry or lead word, as many synonyms and suggested related words and terms as could be obtained from any and every available source. Included are applicable foreign words and expressions, acceptable slang, short words, long words, simple words, abstruse words, and technical, legal, medical and other scientific nomenclature suited to the subject involved. This will enable the user to locate terminology appropriate to the idea he wishes to express, regardless of his educational level. The completeness of this compilation is exemplified by the fact that there are over 19,000 entry or lead words, and over 324,500 synonyms and related terms, making it one of the most complete and modern books of its kind.

A study of the groupings of words and expressions would seem to shed considerable insight into the social history of mankind, and to reveal many of man's predilections, weaknesses, fears, etc., using as a criterion the number of words and expressions for particular ideas, desires and fears. One finds that there are more words for the forces inimical to man, the forces of calamity, evil, destruction, war, fear and the like, than for those of good, peace, and general well-being. For example, there are in this book 465 words or expressions for "bad," 64 for "evil," 111 for "cruel," and 76 for "brutal," but only 150 for "good." There are 110 words for "sad" but only 27 for "glad." There are 124 for "attack" and 67 for "calamity," but only 28 for "peace."

That man is a contentious animal would seem to follow from the fact that there are 96 words for "argue," and a recalcitrant one, as shown by 167 for "stubborn." He has a spirit of helpfulness (180 "to aid") but is still contemptuous of his fellow beings as evidenced by 87 for "fool," 87 for "stupid," 55 for "blockhead," and

110 for "belittle." Over the centuries, man has become accustomed to fakery, to being duped, and to having advantage taken of his credulity, as shown by 110 words for "trickery," 143 for "deception," 70 for "to cheat," 109 "to fool," and 121 for "false." Still he has faith in the future, there being 33 for "hope," 120 for "begin" and 147 for "beginning," yet he abandons easily, and finishes much less than he begins, as there are only 14 for "finish" in sense of completion. He prefers to destroy rather than build (186 for "break" and 159 for "waste" but only 26 for "to build" and 46 for "to make"). Man is conditioned to severity and to being the underdog, as there are 146 words for "austere," 155 for "beat" and 113 for the verb "defeat." He is accustomed to submission to superior force (144 for "authority").

He is comfortable and smug in his preference for what he considers the correct inclinations and beliefs (his own), as there are 54 words for "biased" and 208 for "certain." He likes to take chances and glorifies those that do (136 for "bold"), has a love for the aesthetic (79 for "beautiful") and strives for perfection (91 for "perfect"), but makes many mistakes (102 for "error"). He is given to exaggeration and showiness (45 for "boastful" and 166 for "showy"), is a great charmer, flatterer and seeker after favors (91 for "charm" as a verb, and 124 for the noun), is gregarious (60 for "assemble" and 181 for the noun "group") and likes to talk (105 for "speak" and 118 for "speech"), but is easily bored (102 for "commonplace" and 75 for "nonsense"). Lastly, he has a proclivity for dodging obligations as evidenced by 139 words for "avoid," 52 for "lazy," and 96 for "apathetic."

Many additional analogies such as the foregoing could be cited, as can be observed by an examination of the various groupings in the book, but it is felt that sufficient examples have been given to support a theory that there may be a correlation between the vocabulary and the inherent nature of the people and their social and political history.

A. F. SISSON

Dr. Sisson's new book, *Sisson's Synonyms*, is a real masterpiece in the study of words, their ways and uses. It surpasses similar works which I have examined in its scholarly approach and completeness. Writers, educators, businessmen, college students, politicians, and laymen in general who wish to express themselves with force and exactness should consult *Sisson's Synonyms* when in search for words that best convey their thoughts. It will be an invaluable aid which I recommend without reservation.

Susan E. Harman, Ph.D.
Professor Emeritus
English Language and Literature
University of Maryland

ABBREVIATIONS

a. ....adjective
abb. ....abbreviated
adv. ....adverb
conj. ....conjunction
fem. ....feminine
n. ....noun
pl. ....plural
prep. ....preposition
v. ....verb

A

ABANDON: **v.** abdicate; abjure; abnegate; abrogate; abscond; absent; absquatulate; annul; apostatize; banish; bench; betray; cast (off); cease; cede; chuck; clear (out); decamp; defect; demit; depart; desert; desist; disappear; discard; discharge; discontinue; dismiss; dispose; disuse; ditch; divorce; double-cross; drop; dump; eject; eliminate; elope; emit; empty; enisle; erase; evacuate; exhaust; expel; expunge; flee; fling; fly; forego; forsake; forswear; go; isolate; jettison; junk; leave; maroon; move; nullify; omit; oust; part; purge; quit; rat; recant; reject; release; relieve; relinquish; remove; renege; renounce; repeal; repudiate; requite; resign; retire; retreat; scrap; scrub; scuttle; shed; shipwreck; shoot; shuck; slough; stop; strand; surcease; surrender; throw over; toss; unload; vacate; void; waive; withdraw; yield; ABANDON(MENT) **n.** abdication; abjuration; abrogation; abscondence; absentation; absquatulation; aloneness; banishment; betrayal; cessation; defection; defenestration; departure; depravity; desertion; desistance; despoliation; discarding; discontinuance; discontinuation; dismissal; dissipation; disuse; divorce(ment); ejection; elimination; elopement; enthusiasm; evacuation; exuberation; forsakenness; isolation; move; nullification; omission; ouster; quittance; recantation; recreancy; rejection; release; relinquishment; removal; renege; renunciation; repeal; repudiation; resignation; retirement; retreat; self-surrender; solitariness; stop; surcease; tergiversation; vacation; waiver; withdrawal; yielding; ABANDONED: abdicated; alone; annulled; apostate; apostatic; bereft; carefree; comfortless; corrupt; degraded; departed; depraved; deprived; derelict; deserted; desolate; destitute; detested; discarded; discontinued; dismal; disreputable; dissipated; ditched; dropped; enisled; fled; forgotten; forlorn; forsaken; forsworn; friendless; Godforsaken; helpless; hopeless; isolated; jettisoned; junked; left; lewd; lone(some); lost; low; marooned; native; quiet; recanted; rejected; relinquished; renounced; renunciative; renunciatory; repealed; repudiated; resigned; retired;

scrapped; scuttled; shipwrecked; solitary; stopped; stranded; surrendered; unalleviated; unbridled; vacant; vacated; waived; wild; withdrawn; yielded

ABASE: **see** "degrade" and "lower"

ABASH: (**see** "embarrass") awe; chagrin; confound; confuse; cow; daunt; discomfit; discompose; disconcert; discountenance; dishearten; humble; humiliate; intimidate; mortify; overawe; shame; ABASHMENT: (**see** "embarrassment") chagrin; discomfiture; discomposure; humiliation; mortification; shame; ABASHED: **see** "embarrassed"

ABATE: (**see** "check") abort; abridge; allay; ameliorate; annul; curtail; decay; decline; decrease; deduct; degenerate; demolish; deprive; detract; dim(inish); dissipate; drain; drip; dwindle; ebb; end; exhaust; fade; fail; fall; fritter; lessen; let up; lower; mitigate; moderate; modify; narrow; nullify; omit; peter; pine; quash; recede; reduce; reflux; regress; relieve; remit; restrain; retard; retire; retreat; shorten; shrink; sink; slack(en); slake; slow (up); subside; taper; thin; void; wane; waste; ABATEMENT: (**see** "check") amelioration; annulment; curtailment; declination; decline; decrease; deduction; degeneration; demolishment; deprivation; diminishment; dissipation; drain(age); drip; dwindle; dwindling; ebb; end; exhaustion; failure; fall; lessening; letup; lowering; mitigation; moderation; modification; narrowing; nullification; omission; rebate(ment); recision; reduction; refluence; reflux; regression; relief; remission; rescission; restraint; retardation; retirement; retreat; shortening; shrinkage; slack(ening); subsidence; thinning; waning; waste

ABBREVIATE: (**see** "brief") abate; abridge; bind; bobtail; clip; close; compress; concentrate; condense; constrict; constringe; contract; crowd; curtail; cut; digest; diminish; dock; elide; epitomize; lessen; limit; lop; pack; pare; pinch; press; prune; reduce; repress; restrain; retrench; shorten; shrink; simplify; slash; squeeze; stop; syncopate;

1

synopsize; top; trim; truncate; ABBREVIA-TION: (**see** "brief" and "summary") abridgement; condensation; contraction; curtailment; decrease; epitome; narrowing; narrowness; reduction; shortening; shrinkage; symbol; synopsis; ABBREVIATED: abridged; bobtailed; brief; compressed; condensed; contracted; curt(ailed); cryptic; cut; digested; diminished; short(ened); simplified; synopsized; topped; truncated

ABDICATE: (**see** "abandon") cede; demit; discard; disown; disinherit; forgo; forsake; leave; quit; relinquish; remit; renounce; retire; surrender; ABDICATION: abandonment; cessation; leave; quittance; relinquishment; remission; remittance; renunciation; resignation; retirement; surrender; ABDICATED: **see** "abandoned"

ABDOMEN: belly; middle; paunch; pleon; tharm; venter

ABDUCT: capture; draw (away); kidnap; lure; ravish; seduce; separate; snatch; snitch; steal; take

ABERRATION: (**see** "deviation") anomaly; change; error; failure; fault; foible; hallucination; insanity; lapse; mania; oddity; sin; slip; twist; unsoundness; variation; wandering; warp(age); ABERRANT: **see** "erratic"

ABET: (**see** "aid") advance; advocate; assist; back; boost; coach; countenance; countersign; egg (on); embellish; embolden; encourage; endorse; espouse; expedite; favor; foment; foster; further; hasten; help; incite; instigate; nurse; promote; sanction; second; stake; stimulate; subscribe; subsidize; substantiate; succor; support; sustain; uphold; ABETTING: (**see** "aiding") adjuvant; ancillary; contributory; sanctionative; subsidiary; ABETTOR: **see** "accessory"; ABETMENT: (**see** "assistance") adjuvancy; boost; countenance; encouragement; endorsement; espousal; favor; fostering; furtherance; help; incitement; promotion; sanction; succor; support; sustenance

ABEYANCE: abeyancy; cessation; cold storage; hold; inactivity; lapse; latency; storage; suppression; suspension

ABHOR: abominate; anathematize; avoid; berate; cloy; condemn; contemn; curse; damn; denounce; despise; detest; disapprove; disdain; disgust; dislike; disprize; disrelish; disrespect; execrate; grudge; hate; imprecate; loathe; mind; nauseate; objurgate; rate; reject; repel; reprehend; repulse; revile; revolt; scout; shock; shun; sicken; spurn; ABHORRENT: (**see** "bad") abject; abominable; annoying; antipathetical; averse; beastly; conflicting; contemptible; contemptuous; contumelious; despicable; despisable; despised; detestable; discordant; disdainful; disgustful; disgusting; dislikable; dispiteous; disrespected; execrable; foul; fulsome; hateful; loathsome; nasty; nauseating; *nauséeux*; nauseous; odious; offensive; outrageous; rancorous; rank; repellant; repelling; reprehensible; repugnant; repulsive; revolting; scornful; shocking; unbeloved; unenvied; unloved; unpalatable; unsavory; vile; villainous; ABHORRENCE: abomination; annoyance; antagonism; antipathy; aversion; *bête noire*; detestation; disaffection; disapprobation; disapproval; discountenance; disesteem; disfavor; disgust; disinclination; dislike; displeasure; disregard; disrelish; disrepute; disrespect; distaste; enmity; execration; grudge; hate; hatred; horror; hostility; loathing; nastiness; nausea; odium; offense; opposition; rancor; repellancy; repugnance; repugnancy; repulsion; repulsiveness; resentment; revolt; scorn(fulness); shock; squeamishness; trial: unsavoriness; vexation; wantonness

ABIDE: accept; anticipate; await; bear; bide; brook; continue; dally; dawdle; delay; drag; dwell; endure; exist; expect; face; house; inhabit; last; lie; linger; live; lodge; occupy; pause; perch; remain; reside; rest; sojourn; stand; stay; stomach; stop; submit; suffer; tarry; tolerate; wait; watch; withstand; ABIDING: **see** "fixed" and "lasting"

ABILITY: **see** after "able"

ABJECT: base; contemptible; cringing; degraded; depressed; despicable; despised; dispirited; downcast; downtrodden; execrable; fawning; forlorn; groveling; helpless; hopeless; ignoble; low; mean; miserable; paltry; sad; servile; shrinking; sordid; squalid; supine; sycophantic; vile; villainous; underfoot; wretched

ABJURE: (**see** "abandon") abhor; annul; avert; avoid; deny; disclaim; dodge; elude; escape; eschew; evade; flee; forswear; give (up); hedge; recall; recant; reject; renounce; repudiate; resign; retract; revoke; shirk; shun; sidestep; spurn

ABLE: (**see** "competent") ace; accomplished; adapted; adept; adequate; adroit; ambidextrous; apt; *au fait*; capable; clever; consummate; conversant; crack; deft; dext(e)rous; doughty; dynamic; effective; efficient; eligible; endowed; excellent; experienced; expert; facile; fit; forceful; free; ingenious; knowing; knowledgeable; licensed; masterful; masterly; mighty; notable; outstanding; potent; powerful; practised; professional; proficient; qualified; qualitied; skilled; skillful; smart; strong; tactful; talented; tested; trained; useful; versatile; versed; virtuosic; ABILITY: (**see** "capacity") access; accomplishment; adaptation; adeptness; adequacy; adroitness; ambidexterity; aptitude; aptness; art(fulness); attainment; bore; brains; breadth; caliber; capability; capableness; capacity; cleverness; competence; competency; consummation; craft (iness); deftness; degree; dexterity; diameter; doughtiness; *dynamis*; dynamism; ease; easiness; effectiveness; efficiency; eligibility; endowment; energy; excellence; experience; expertise; facilitation; facility; faculty; fitness; flair; force; freedom; gauge; gift; ingeniosity; ingenuity; knack; knowledge; leadership; magnitude; mastery; means; measure; might; panurgy; perfection; pliancy; poise; potency; potentiality; power; practice; professionalism; proficiency; qualification; quality; quickness; readiness; skill(fulness); stature; strength; sufficiency; tact(fulness); talent; training; usefulness; versatility; virtuosity; wisdom; wit

ABLUTION: baptism; bath(ing); cleansing; lavation; purge; purification; washing

ABNEGATE: (**see** "abandon") abjure; abstain; deny; disavow; forgo; refuse; reject; relinquish; renunciate; restrain; surrender; ABNEGATION: (**see** "abandonment") abjuration; abstention; denial; disavowal; humility; refusal; rejection; relinquishment; renunciation; restraint; self-denial; surrender

ABNORMAL: aberrant; aberrative; adventitious; adventive; anomalistic; anomalous; atypic(al); bizarre; cantankerous; capricious; comical; cranky; crazy; crotchety; curious; deficient; departing; deviating; different; dotty; droll; eccentric; erratic; exceptional; excessive; extraordinary; fantastic(al); freak(ish); grotesque; heteroclite; heterodox; heterogeneous; idiocratic; idiosyncratic; improper; irregular; lawless; nonnatural; nutty; odd(ball); paranormal; pathological; peculiar; phenomenal; preternatural; prodigious; quaint; queer; rare; singular; strange; subnormal; substandard; supernatural; supernormal; teratogenic; uncommon;

unconventional; unique; unnatural; unorthodox; unseasonable; unusual; vagarious; wayward; whimsical; ABNORMALITY: aberrance; aberrancy; aberration; abnormalcy; anomalism; anomaly; atypicism; bizarrerie; brainstorm; caprice; characteristic; curiosity; deficiency; deformity; departure; deviant; deviate; deviation; difference; dottiness; drollery; eccentricity; error; exception; foible; freak; grotesquerie; haecceity; heterodox(y); idiasm; idiocrasy; idiosyncrasy; imperfection; impropriety; individuality; irregularity; kink; lawlessness; lunacy; macula; malformation; mannerism; nuttiness; oddity; oddness; particularity; pathology; peculiarity; phenom(enality); phenomenon; prodigality; queer(ness); quiddity; quirk; rarity; singularity; stigma; trait; trick; twist; unconventionality; uniquity; unorthodoxy; unusualness; vagary; whim(sicality)

ABODE: (**see** "house") address; aerie; caravansary; castle; city; country; domicile; dwelling; encampment; estate; habitat(ion); hearth(stone); igloo; ingleside; inn; location; lodging; nest; quarters; residence; residency; rookery; seat; sojourn; tent; town; village; xenodochium

ABOLISH: (**see** "cancel" and "eliminate") abate; abrogate; annihilate; annul; block; blot (out); check; choke; close; collapse; countermand; crumble; crush; decimate; decompose; dele(te); demolish; deracinate; destroy; disappear; discontinue; disestablish; dismantle; dissolve; douse; drop; drown; efface; effect; eliminate; end; eradicate; erase; expel; expunge; expurgate; exterminate; extinguish; extirpate; invalidate; kill; murder; neutralize; nullify; obliterate; obscure; offset; ostracize; out; override; overthrow; quash; quell; quench; recall; relinquish; remit; remove; repeal; repress; repudiate; rescind; retract; revoke; root (out); ruin; scratch; scrub; slay; smother; snuff (out); starve; stifle; strike; supersede; supplant; suppress; terminate; undo; uproot; upset; upturn; vacate; vitiate; void; ABOLISHMENT: abatement; abolition; abrogation; annihilation; annulment; cancellation; countermand; decimation; deletion; demolishment; deracination; destruction; discontinuance; disestablishment; dismantlement; drowning; effacement; elimination; end(ing); expunction; expurgation; extermination; extinction; extinguishment; extirpation; invalidation; killing; murder; neutralization; nullification; obliteration; ostracism; overthrow; recision; remission; repeal; repression;

rescission; retraction; reversal; revocation; scratch; smothering; supersedence; termination; undoing; vitiation

ABOMINATE: (see "abhor") detest; hate; loathe; ABOMINABLE: (see "accursed") detestable; distasteful; God-awful; hateful; loathsome; unnatural; ABOMINATION: abhorrence; annoyance; antipathy; aversion; bother(ation); crime; curse; detestation; disgust; distaste; evil; execration; hate; hatred; horror; iniquity; loathing; loathsomeness; pest; plague; repugnance; repugnancy; shame; villainy; wickedness

ABORIGINAL: **a.** beginning; first; inborn; indigenous; inherent; innate; natural; native; primary; primeval; primitive; ABORIGINAL **n.** or ABORIGINE: autochthon; Indian; indigene; native; primitive; savage

ABORT: see "check"; ABORTIVE: (see "fruitless") barren; futile; idle; incomplete; irresultive; miscarrying; rudimentary; unsuccessful; useless; vain

ABOUND: flourish; flow; luxuriate; overflow; prevail; revel; swarm; swell; teem; ABOUNDING: (see "abundant") epidemic; everywhere; far-reaching; flourishing; flowing; overflowing; pandemic; prevalent; replete; rife; scopic; swollen; teeming; widespread; worldwide

ABOUT: abroad; almost; approximate(ly); anent; around; astir; circa; circiter; close; concerning; encircling; *in re*; near(by); nearly; re; round; some; throughout

ABOVE: aloft; astral; atop; before; beyond; celestial; exalted; exceeding; excelling; farther; heavenly; heavenward; high(er); o'er; over(head); past; skyward; superior; superjacent; supernal; supra; surpassing; ultra; up(on); upstairs

ABRADE: abrase; anger; annoy; cavitate; chafe; censure; consume; eat; erase; erode; excoriate; file; flay; fray; fret; gall; gnaw; grate; graze; grind; irritate; lash; rasp; revile; roughen; rub; ruffle; score; scrape; scratch; skin; wear; ABRADED: cavitated; chafed; consumed; eaten; erased; eroded; erose; excoriated; filed; flat; flayed; frayed; galled; gnawed; grazed; irritated; level; raspy; raw; roughened; rubbed; scored; scraped; scratched; skinned; smooth; worn; ABRASIVE: abradant; corundum; emery; erodent; pumice; quartz; sand(paper); ABRASION: attrition; cavitation; chafing;

erosion; excoriation; friction; gall; gnawing; grating; grinding; intertrigo; irritation; rage; rasp(ing); roughness; rub; scoring; scrape; scratch; sore; vexation; weakening; wear

ABREAST: (see "beside" and "modern") alongside; equal; even; knowing; neck-and-neck; tied; up-to-date

ABRIDGE: (see "brief") abstract; analyze; concentrate; condense; curtail; cut; digest; diminish; distill; dock; limit; outline; pare; prune; retrench; shorten; shrink; simplify; synopsize; ABRIDGEMENT: (see "brief") abbreviation; abreviature; abstract; analysis; breviary; compend(ium); condensation; contraction; curtailment; digest; diminishment; distillation; embodiment; epitome; essence; outline; preçis; retrenchment; schema; shortening; simplification; sketch; synopsis

ABROAD: (see "out") about; apart; astir; astray; away; off; overseas; roving; traveling; vagrant; voyaging; wandering

ABROGATE: see "annul"

ABRUPT: (see "rude") bluff; blunt; brazen; brusque; coarse; craggy; cross; crusty; curt; dead; disconnected; discourteous; explosive; fast; frank; gruff; hasty; impetuous; impolite: impulsive; instantaneous; outspoken; plain; precipitant; precipitate; precipitous; quick; rapid; rude; rugged; sharp; sheer; short (ened); staccato; steep; subitaneous; sudden; surly; swift; terse; tumultuous; unceremonious; uncivil; unexpected; unmannerly; violent; ABRUPTNESS: (see "haste") bluntness; brazenness; brusquerie; curtness; discourtesy; expedition; explosiveness; frankness; gruffness; hastiness; impetuosity; impoliteness; impulsivity; incivility; instantaneity; precipitancy; quickness; rapidity; rapidness; rudeness; sharpness; shortness; suddenness; surliness; swiftness; terseness; unmanneliness; violence

ABSCESS: see "sore"

ABSCOND: (see "depart") blow; bolt; break; decamp; deport; desert; disappear; elope; elude; escape; evade; flee; fly; hide; hie; jump; lam; leave; quit; scram; shun; steal (away); withdraw

ABSENCE: abscondence; absentation; absenteeism; defect; deficiency; desertion; escape; failure; furlough; impairment; lack; leave;

loss; nonappearance; nonattendance; nonexistence; preoccupation; privation; vacancy; vacuum; void; want; withdrawal; ABSENT: absconded; absentaneous; abstracted; A.W.O.L.; deserted; elsewhere; escaped; gone; inattentive; lacking; left; missing; nonexistent; oblivious; off; preoccupied; vacant; void; withdrawn

ABSOLUTE: **a.** (**see** "certain") absolutist; arbitrary; arithmetical; arrant; arrogant; assertive; austere; authentic; authoritative; autocratic; categoric(al); clear; coercive; commanding; complete(ly); compulsory; concrete; confident; confirmed; consummate; dead; decisive; despotic; dictatorial; direct; dogmatic(al); domineering; downright; entire; errant; exacting; exclusive; extreme; fair; final; firm; fixed; free; full; fundamental; genuine; gross; harsh; haughty; imperative; inperious; imprescriptible; inalienable; inclusive; incomparable; inconceivable; incontestable; indefeasible; independent; indubitable; inexorable; inflexible; intrinsic; invincible; irrefutable; masterful; mathematical; notorious; obstinate; official; oppressive; out-and-out; outright; peremptory; perfect; plenary; plenipotent(ial); plenipotentiary; positive; powerful; precise; preemptory; pure (and simple); *pur et simple*; real; relentless; resolute; right; rigid; rigorous; self-assured; self-contained; self-sufficient; shameless; sheer; simple; sole; stern; supreme; sure; sweeping; thorough(-going); total; true; tyrannic(al); tyrannous; ultimate; unalienable; unconditional; unconditioned; unequivocal; unknowable; unlimited; unmitigated; unqualified; unquestionable; unreserved; unrestrained; unrestricted; unsparing; unswerving; utter; very; whole(hearted); wholly; ABSOLUTE: **n.** concretum; positive(ness); positivity; totality; unconditionality

ABSOLUTION: (**see** "acquittal" and "pardon") cleansing; penance; remission

ABSOLVE: (**see** "acquit") cleanse; clear; discharge; emancipate; exculpate; excuse; exempt; exonerate; finish; forgive; free; liberate; overlook; pardon; redeem; release; remit; shrive

ABSORB: abstract; adapt; allure; apply; assimilate; assume; attract; bewitch; blend; bury; busy; buy; charm; coalesce; combine; conform; consume; deluge; devour; digest; drink; engage; engross; engulf; fascinate; flood; free; fuse; hold; imbibe; immerse; incorporate; infiltrate; interject; inundate;

invade; involve; merge; metabolize; mix; monopolize; occupy; osmose; overflow; overpower; overwhelm; penetrate; plunge; preoccupy; purchase; receive; rivet; sink; soak; sop; sponge (up); submerge; suck; swallow; swamp; take; unite; whelm; ABSORBED: abstracted; assimilated; busy; captivated; charmed; coalesced; combined; consumed; deep; devoured; digested; dreamy; employed; enchanted; engaged; engrossed; engulfed; enraptured; entangled; entranced; fixed; imbibed; immersed; incorporated; intent; involved; merged; metabolized; monopolized; occupied; penetrated; pensive; preoccupied; rapt; swallowed; thoughtful; united; ABSORBENT: absorptive; assimilative; assimilatory; bibulous; imbibitional; incorporative; monopolistic; osmotic; ABSORPTION: abstraction; alimentation; assimilation; assumption; bibulosity; coalescence; confirmation; consumption; digestion; engagement; eupepsia; eupepsy; imbibition; immersion; incorporation; infiltration; involvement; merger; metabolism; monopolization; occupation; osmosis; pepsis; preoccupation; rapture; raptus; study; summary; trance; unction; union; ABSORBING: **see** "fascinating"

ABSTAIN: (**see** "forbear") cease; deny; desist; disuse; fast; keep; refrain; refuse; reject; spare; spurn; waive; withhold; ABSTINENT: **see** "temperate"

ABSTRACT: **v.** (**see** "abridge" and "remove") abbreviate; absorb; appropriate; cite; compend; compile; condense; cull; cut; deplete; derive; detach; dig; distil(l); divert; draw; educe; elicit; epitomize; estreat; evoke; evulse; exact; excerpt; extirpate; extort; extract; extricate; grub; mine; obtain; pry; pull; purloin; render; select; separate; steal; summarize; take; withdraw; ABSTRACT (ED): **a.** absentminded; abstruse; acroamatic; apart; detached; distrait; distraught; dreamy; esoteric; formal; heedless; hermetic(al); ideal; impersonal; inattentive; inconcrete; incorporeal; metaphysical; moony; nebulous; notional; occult; preoccupied; pure; recondite; removed; separate(d); speculative; stratospheric(al); supernatural; theoretical; transcendental; ABSTRACT(ION): **n.** abbreviation; abbreviature; abridgement; absorption; abstractum; appropriation; brief; citation; compend(ium); compilation; concern; condensation; conspectus; cutting; deed; distillation; document; elicitation; epitome; excerpt; extract; lexicon; outline; *précis*; preoccupation; rapture; raptus; résumé; revelry; summarization; summary;

syllabus; synopsis; trance; universal; withdrawal

ABSTRUSE: (see "abstract") acroamatic; arcane; cabalistic; complex; concealed; cryptic(al); dark(ened); deep; Delphian; difficult; epoptic; esoteric; hard; hidden; inaccessible; inscrutable; intricate; involuted; involved; latent; metaphysical; mysterious; mystic(al); nebulous; obscure; occult; perplexing; profound; puzzling; rarefied; recondite; remote; secret; stratospheric(al); subtle; supernatural; tangled; undetached; undisclosed; unknown

ABSURD: *ad absurdum*; asinine; atypical; baroque; bizarre; brainless; burlesque; chimerical; clownish; comic(al); crazy; daedalian; daedalic(al); decipient; dotty; droll(ish); eccentric; egregious; fallacious; false; fantastic(al); farcical; fatuitous; fatuous; foolish; grotesque; hideous; idiotic; imbecilic; impracticable; imprudent; impuissant; inane; incongruous; inconsistent; incredible; indiscreet; inept; infeasible; insuperable; irrational; laputan; ludicrous; lunatic(al); macaronic; mad; misshapen; nonsensical; odd(ish); *opera-bouffe*; preposterous; quaint; queer; ridiculous; risible; self-contradictory; senseless; silly; simple; stupid; unbelievable; uncanny; unearthly; unintelligent; unrealistic; unreasonable; unsound; vacant; vacuous; wild; witless; ABSURDITY: absurdness; asininity; ate; *bêtise*; bizarrerie; brainlessness; brainstorm; chimera; comic opera; contradiction; craziness; decipience; drollery; fallacy; falsity; fantasy; farce; fatuity; folly; foolery; foolishness; grotesqueness; grotesquerie; idiocy; idiotcy; imbecility; imprudence; impuissance; inanity; incongruity; inconsistency; incredibility; indiscretion; ineptitude; insanity; irrationality; ludicrousness; lunacy; madness; maggotry; nonsense; nonsensicality; *non sequitur*; *opera bouffe;* ridiculosity; senselessness; silliness; stupidity; unreasonableness; unwisdom

ABUNDANT: (see "generous") abounding; affluent; *à gogo*; ample; aplenty; bounteous; considerable; copious; cornucopian; *de trop*; elaborate; exaggerated; excess(ive); exhaustless; exorbitant; extravagant; extreme; exuberant; fantastic(al); fat; feracious; full; galore; gaudy; hearty; hefty; immoderate; improvident; incredible; inexhaustible; inordinate; intemperate; irrational; lavish; liberal; lush; luxuriant; luxurious; magnanimous; many; measureless; melodramatic; much; niminous; numerous; opulent; overboard; overflowing; plenteous; plentiful;

plen(t)itudinous; plenty; pleonastic; plethoric; prodigal; profligate; profuse; prolific; rampant; rash; reckless; redundant; replete; rich; rife; showy; sufficient; sumptuous; superabundant; superfluous; teeming; thick; uncommon; unending; unmeasured; unreasonable; unrestrained; unsparing; unstinted; voluble; wasteful; ABUNDANCE: (see "superfluity") affluence; afflux(ation); amplitude; aplenty; bountifulness; bounty; circumlocution; copiosity; copiousness; cornucopia; excess; exorbitancy; extravagance; exuberance; fat; fecundity; fluency; fullness; galore; generosity; gobs; grandiosity; heap(s); immoderation; improvidence; intemperance; lavishness; liberality; loquaciousness; loquacity; lot(s); lushness; luxuriance; luxuriousness; magnanimity; magnificence; magnitude; nimiety; opulence; overflowing; plenteousness; plentifulness; plen(t)itude; plenty; pleonasm; plethora; prodigality; profligacy; profusion; prolificity; rampancy; rashness; redundance; redundancy; repletion; riches; richness; satiety; showiness; spate; store; sufficiency; sumptuosity; superabundance; superfluity; superflux; uberty; unreasonableness; unrestraint; volubility; wantonness; wastefulness; wealth

ABUSE: **v.** accuse; animadvert; asperse; assail; assault; attack; backbite; beat; belie; berate; blacken; blaspheme; calumniate; castigate; censure; chafe; chide; curse; damage; defalcate; defame; denigrate; denounce; depreciate; derogate; desecrate; detract; disparage; excoriate; execrate; expostulate; flay; harm; humiliate; hurt; illtreat; ill-use; impair; impute; injure; malign; maltreat; mar; maul; misapply; mishandle; misrepresent; mistreat; misuse; neglect; oppose; oppress; persecute; pervert; profane; prostitute; punish; rail; ravish; reproach; revile; ruin; scathe; scold; shame; slander; slur; spoil; taunt; traduce; tyrannize; victimize; vilify; violate; vituperate; wrong; ABUSE: **n.** abusiveness; anguish; animadversion; aspersion; attack; backbiting; billingsgate; blasphemy; calumniation; calumny; castigation; censure; condemnation; contumely; cruelty; damage; defalcation; defamation; denigration; denouncement; depreciation; derogation; desecration; detraction; diatribe; disparagement; epithet; excoriation; execration; expostulation; fault; harm; humiliation; hurt; ill-treatment; ill-usage; ill-use; infamy; injury; invective; license; malice; malignity; maltreatment; misapplication; mishandling; mistreatment; misuse; neglect; negligence; objurgation; obloquy; offense; opposition; oppression;

persecution; philippic; profanation; profanity; punishment; reprehension; reproach; revilement; sassiness; scalding; scurrility; shame; slander; tongue; torture; traducement; traduction; tyranny; viciousness; vilification; villainousness; villainy; vituperation; vulgarity; wrong; ABUSIVE: abhorrent; blasphemous; calumnious; captious; castigatory; caustic; censorious; clamorous; condemnatory; contemptuous; cruel; damaging; damnatory; defamatory; demanding; denunciative; denunciatory; despicable; detestable; dirty; disparaging; foul; harmful; hateful; hurtful; indecent; infamous; injurious; insulting; malicious; malign(ant); objurgatory; offensive; opposite; oppositional; oppositious; oppressive; opprobrious; overbearing; perverted; reproachful; reprobative; reviling; rough; ruinous; sarcastic; sardonic; satirical; scurrilous; shameful; slanderous; trenchant; vicious; vilifying; villainous; vituperative; vituperous; vulgar

ABUT: see "border"

ABYSS: abysm; avernus; breach; canyon; chaos; chasm; cleft; deep; fissure; gap; Gehenna; gorge; gulf; gully; hell; hiatus; hole; interval; omission; opening; pit; profundity; ravine; reft; rift; separation; void; vorago; ABYSMAL: bottomless; deep; dire; dreadful; great; profound; unending; wretched

ACADEMIC(AL): abstract; bookish; classic (al); collegiate; conjectural; conservative; conventional; didactic; doctrinaire; doctrinal; erudite; formal(istic); hypothetical; impractical; institutional; learned; lettered; literary; pedantic; Platonic; postulatory; professional; professorial; propa(e)deutic(al); quodlibetic(al); realistic; rigid; scholarly; scholastic; schoolish; speculative; suppositional; supposititious; teachery; theoretic(al); visionary; ACADEMICIAN: see "teacher;" ACADEMY: see "school"

ACCEDE: (see "accept") acquiesce; agree; allow; approve; assent; assume; attain; comply; concede; concur; consent; give; grant; join; let; permit; yield

ACCELERATE: (see "advance") catalyze; dispatch; drive; emphasize; enhance; escalate; excite; exhort; expand; expedite; force; forward; gain; gear; go; grow; gun; hasten; hurry; increase; inspire; move; precipitate; press; prod; provoke; push; quicken; rev; run; speed; spiral; spur;

stimulate; throttle; urge; ACCELERATOR: see "mover"

ACCENT: **v.** accelerate; accentuate; emphasize; enhance; exacerbate; force; hammer; highlight; hit; increase; inflict; insist; intensify; intone; maintain; mark; pound; press; pulsate; sharpen; stress; throb; underdraw; underscore; ACCENT: **n.** acceleration; accentuation; beat; brogue; burr; cadence; characteristic; emphasis; enhancement; exacerbation; force(fulness); ictus; impact; increase; inflection; insistence; intensification; intonation; mark; palpitation; pressure; prominence; pulsation; pulse; rhythm; sound; stress; stroke; swing; tap; tempo; throb; tick; tone; underlineation; underscore; underscoring; vehemence; vigor

ACCEPT: (see "accede" and "acquiesce") acknowledge; adapt; adhere; admit; adopt; agree; allow; annex; approve; assent; believe; buy; caress; cherish; choose; clasp; clinch; cling; comply; comprehend; comprise; conceive; conclude; concur; conform; consider; cooperate; credit; deem; defend; embosom; embrace; encircle; enclose; encompass; endorse; endure; engage; espouse; expect; fancy; feel; follow; fondle; gain; get; grasp; have; heed; hold; honor; hug; imagine; include; incorporate; join; judge; kiss; know; obey; marry; mind; receive; recognize; respect; respond; support; suppose; surmise; swallow; think; trow; understand; undertake; welcome; win; yield; ACCEPTABLE or ACCEPTED: (see "conventional") according to Hoyle; acknowledged; adaptable; adequate; admissible; admitted; adopted; agreed; allowable; allowed; approved; believed; canonical; compliant; conformable; corresponding; credited; embraceable; endorsed; endured; engaged; espoused; ethical; familiar; gained; honored; kosher; married; moral; normal; orthodox; pleasing; prevailing; prevalent; proper; received; recognized; sanctioned; satisfactory; standard; submissive; swallowed; tolerated; traditional; understood; unobjectionable; unprotested; welcome(d); widespread; ACCEPTANCE: acceptation; acclaim; acknowledgement; acquiescence; adaptation; adherence; agreement; annexation; approval; assent; belief; canonicity; caress; compliance; compliancy; compromise; concession; concurrence; conformance; conformation; conformity; conviction; cooperation; credence; credit; credo; creed; embrace (ment); encirclement; endorsement; espousal; expectation; faith; feeling; grasp; handshake; hug; *idée fixe*; inclusion; incorporation; kiss; marriage; observance; orthodoxy; persuasion; philosophy; position; prestige; principle; profession; reception; recognition; response; standing; support; tenet; theory; traditon; troth; trust; view; welcome; yield(ing)

ACCESS: ability; acquisition; addition; adit; admission; admittance; approach; arrival; attack; avenue; channel; corridor; door; entrance(way); *entrée*; entry; fit; foyer; freedom; gate; increase; liberty; outburst; pass; passage(way); path; permission; permit; portal; postern; road; route; street; use; way; ACCESSIBLE: admissible; approachable; available; communicative; comprehensible; comprehensive; easy; open; permissible; ready; ACCESSION: addition; adherence; admission; agglutination; approach; arrival; fit; increase; outburst; spell

ACCESSORY: **a. see** "additional"; ACCESSORY **n.** or ACCESSORIES: (**see** "adjunct") abettor; accompaniment; accomplice; addenda (pl.); addendum; additive; aide; ally; ancilla; ancillae (pl.); appendage; appurtenance; article; assistant; associate; attachment; auxiliary; buddy; chum; coadjutor; cohort; collaborateur; collaborator; colleague; companion; complementary; confederate; *confrère*; contributor; crony; device; equipment; fitting; furniture; hardware; helper; incidental(s); participator; partner; retainer; satellite; subordinate; subsidiary; substitute; substitution; succenturiate; tool

ACCIDENT: abomination; accidentality; adversity; affliction; bereavement; blow; calamity; casualty; catastrophe; circumstance; contingence; contingency; contretemps; crash; cross; curse; disaster; distress; event; evil; failure; fortuity; hap(pening); haplessness; happenstance; hardship; harm; hazard; hell; hitch; holocaust; ill(ness); inadvertence; inadvertency; incident; infliction; injury; misadventure; mischance; misery; misfortune; mishap; occasion; occurrence; ordeal; reversal; reverse; ruin; scourge; scrape; slip; situation; sorrow; trial; tribulation; trouble; unluck(iness); venture; ACCIDENTAL: (**see** "casual") adventitious; afflictive; aimless; calamitous; careless; catastrophic; causeless; chancy; circumstantial; contingent; disastrous; distressing; eventful; external; extrinsic; fortuitous; haphazard; heedless; inadvertent; inattentive; incidental; injurious; involuntary; irregular; misadventurous; misfortunate; negligent; nonessential; occasional; odd; random; serendipitous; sponta-

neous; sporadic; troublesome; uncertain; undeliberate; undesigned; undirected; unforeseen; unfortunate; unintended; unintentional; unlucky; unmotivated; unplanned; unpredictable; unpremeditated; unprepared; untoward; unwitting

ACCLAIM: **v.** applaud; approve; cheer; clap; extol; glorify; hail; honor; laud; plaudit; praise; revere; root; shout; ACCLAIM or **n.** ACCLAMATION: (**see** "accolade") applause; approbation; approval; attention; cheer; cry; distinction; éclat; glorification; glory; homage; honor; kiss; kudos; laudation; ole!; plaudit; praise; publicity; renown; reverence; shout

ACCLIMATIZE or ACCLIMATE: (**see** "adapt") accustom; acquaint; adjust; conform; discipline; drill; enure; familiarize; habituate; harden; indoctrinate; instruct; inure; prepare; season; steel; tolerate; toughen; train; ACCLIMATIZATION: **see** "adaptation"

ACCLIVITY: **see** "hill"

ACCOLADE: acclaim; acclamation; acknowledgment; applause; approbation; approval; attention; award; ceremony; cheer; commendation; cry; distinction; éclat; embrace; garland; glorification; glory; homage; honor; kiss; kudos; laudation; laurel; medal; merit; ole!; plaudit; praise; prestige; publicity; renown; reverence; shout (of approval); yell

ACCOMMODATE: adapt; adjust; agree; aid; alter; arrange; attend; blend; board; bow; comfort; conform; contain; convenience; defer; fashion; favor; fit; garrison; give; harbor; help; hold; house; lend; lodge; match; oblige; open; receive; reconcile; serve; suit; take; transform; yield; ACCOMMODATION: adaptation; adjustment; agreeableness; agreement; aid; alteration; arrangement(s); berth; board; comfort; conformation; convenience; deference; favor; gift; harbor(ing); help; housing; loan; lodgement; lodging; place; reconciliation; room; seat; service; settlement; space

ACCOMPANY: add; associate; attend; bring; chaperon(e); coexist; collaborate; come; concur; conduct; convey; convoy; escort; follow; foster; go; guard; guide; heed; join; lead; mind; participate; pilot; protect; see; serve; shepherd; squire; steer; support; tend; usher; ACCOMPANIMENT: agreement; association; background; circumstantiality; coexistence; collaboration; complement; concomitance; concomitancy; concomitant; concurrence; conveyance; corollary; following; guard; guide; melody; obbligato; participation; protection; support; time; ACCOMPANIED or ACCOMPANYING: see "associated" and "attended"

ACCOMPLICE: (see "accessory") abettor; associate; bait; buddy; chum; cohort; companion; confederate; crony; helper; participator

ACCOMPLISH: achieve; acquire; act(ualize); administer; answer; arrive; attain; climax; close; compass; complete; conclude; conduct; conquer; consummate; crown; discharge; dispatch; do; earn; educate; effect(uate); enact; encompass; end; enforce; execute; exhaust; finalize; finish; fructify; fulfill; gain; get; give; govern; grasp; implement; invoke; learn; make; manage; master; meet; merit; negotiate; obtain; occupy; perfect; perform; perpetuate; play; possess; procure; produce; prove; put (over); reach; realize; receive; rule; satisfy; score; secure; sell; sign; succeed; supply; swing; terminate; traverse; win; wrest; ACCOMPLISHED: (see "competent") adept; apt; artistic; attained; completed; consummate; discharged; done; educated; effected; effectuated; efficient; ended; established; executed; expert; exquisite; finished; fulfilled; gained; handy; implemented; managed; mastered; negotiated; perfect(ed); performed; produced; proficient; reached; realized; satisfied; secured; skilled; skillful; successful; talented; taught; terminated; trained; ACCOMPLISHMENT: ability; achievement; acquirement; act(ion); actuality; actualization; arrival; art(istry); attainment; closure; compass; completeness; completion; conclusion; consummation; craft; deed; discharge; doing; earning; education; effectualization; effectuation; effort; enactment; ending; entelechy; entireness; execution; exercise; exertion; expertise; exploit; fact; *fait accompli*; feat; finality; finalization; finish; forte; fructification; fruition; fulfillment; gain; gest(e); grasp; gymnastics; implementation; invocation; learning; maneuver; mastery; negotiation; occupation; perfection; performance; possession; procurement; production; proficiency; quest; reality; realization; record; satisfaction; skill; stunt; success; talent; temperance; temperateness; termination; texture; training; transaction; transfer; utterness; victory

ACCORD: **v.** accede; adapt; adjust; agree; allot; allow; approve; attune; award; be-

come; befit; behave; bestow; conform; coordinate; correspond; give; grant; harmonize; jibe; key; melodize; mesh; prepare; reconcile; render; sympathize; tally; temper; tolerate; tune; unite; ACCORD: **n.** accordance; accordancy; adaptation; adjustment; affinity; agreement; approval; assonance; attainment; attunement; balance; chorus; coherence; comparability; compatibility; compatibleness; concert; concord(ance); conformance; conformancy; congruence; congruency; congruity; consensus; consistence; consistency; consonance; consonancy; constantaneousness; coordination; correspondence; empathy; euphony; evenness; feeling; firmness; harmonization; harmony; homogeneity; honeymoon; identity; integrity; invariability; isogeny; lilt; melody; meter; mutuality; oneness; orchestration; persistence; persistency; plan; proportion; rapport; reciprocity; reconciliation; regularity; rhythm; singleness; suitability; sympathy; symphony; tolerance; tranquility; treaty; unanimity; understanding; uniformity; union; unison; unity; wholeness; ACCORDANT: see "agreeing"

ACCOST: (see "address") advance; approach; approximate; assail; assault; attack; challenge; confront; face; front; greet; hail; meet; salute; solicit; speak; welcome

ACCOUNT: **v.** answer; classify; compute; consider; deem; explain; narrate; rate; recite; reckon; regard; relate; report; respond; state; ACCOUNT: **n.** advantage; annal(s); answer; attention; business; chronicle; client; computation; consideration; customer; description; diary; esteem; explanation; hearsay; history; judgment; legend; money; narration; narrative; profit; recital; recitation; reckoning; record; register; report; response; score; statement; stewardship; story; summary; tale; value; words; worth; writeup; writing; ACCOUNTABLE: answerable; explainable; responsible

ACCOUTER: see "dress"

ACCREDIT: accept; allege; allot; appoint; approve; ascribe; assign; attribute; authorize; believe; blame; certify; charge; cite; commission; credit; depute; endorse; give; guarantee; honor; impute; license; recognize; refer; sanction; trust; vouch (for); warrant

ACCRETION: (see "accumulation" and "growth") accrescence; acquirement; addition; agglomeration; coating; coherence;

concretion; corruption; development; dirt; earning(s); exudate; increase; increment; oxidation; patina; riches; rust; sum; take; tarnish; verdigris; wealth; winnings

ACCROACH: (see "assume") approximate; trespass; usurp

ACCRUE: (see "accumulate") accresce; acquire; add; amass; arise; ascribe; attribute; collect; derive; earn; ensue; gather; grow; inure; issue; pile; redound; result; vest; win; ACCRUEMENT: (see "accretion" and "accumulation") accrual; increment

ACCUMULATE: (see "collect") accresce; accrete; accrue; acquire; add; agglomerate; agglutinate; aggregate; amass; arise; assemble; attain; cache; cluster; collect; conglomerate; congregate; drift; earn; gain; garner; gather; get; grow; harvest; heap; hide; hoard; increase; incrust; inure; lay away; lay up; mass; muster; pile; pool; pyramid; reap; result; save; scrape; stack; stock; store; win; ACCUMULATION: (see "collection") accrescence; accretion; accrual; accruement; acervation; acquirement; addition; agglomeration; agglutination; aggregate; aggregation; amassing; amassment; appreciation; assemblage; bloc; bulk; cache; cluster; congeries; conglomeration; congregation; debris; deposit; dividend; drift (age); earnings; fund; gain; gathering; group; growth; harvest; heap; hoard; increase; increment; incrustation; interest; inurement; mass; material(s); muster; nest (egg); pile; pool; pyramid; result; riches; saving(s); scrapings; stack; stock; store; supplies; supply; thrift; treasure; treasury; winnings; ACCUMULATED: see "acquired"

ACCURATE: according to Hoyle; actual; airtight; *au fait*; authentic; authoritative; authorized; candid; careful; certain; classic (al); clear; conforming; conventional; correct; decorous; definite; definitive; *de rigueur*; detailed; determinative; distinct; documentary; due; even; exact(ing); factual; flawless; genuine; honest; impeccable; just; lawful; legitimate; literal; meticulous; microscopic; minute; nice; objective; official; okay; orthodox; painstaking; particular; precise; proper; punctilious; punctual; real; rectitudinous; regular; reliable; right; rigid; rigorous; scrupulous; sincere; slavish; sound; staid; straight; strict; sure; true; trustworthy; truthful; unalterable; undeviating; unequivocal; unflattering; unquestionable; valid;

veracious; word-for-word; ACCURACY: (see "certainty") authenticity; authoritativeness; care(fulness); conformity; correctitude; correctness; decorum; definiteness; definitude; exactitude; exactness; fidelity; flawlessness; honesty; impeccability; legitimacy; literality; meticulosity; meticulousness; nicety; officiality; perfection; precision; properness; propriety; punctiliousness; punctuality; rectitude; regularity; reliability; rightness; rigidity; rigor(ousness); scrupulosity; sincerity; strictness; trustworthiness; truth(fulness); validity; veracity

ACCURSED: abominable; bad; damnable; deplorable; detestable; disagreeable; execrable; loathsome; revolting; stubborn; unbearable; vile; wicked; wrathful; wretched

ACCUSE: (see "blame") adduce; allege; arouse; arraign; ascribe; attribute; betray; blame; call; censure; challenge; charge; cite; command; criminate; declare; denounce; evoke; impeach; impute; incriminate; inculpate; indict; invoke; mention; name; plead; point; present; provoke; reproach; reveal; summon; tax; tell; warn; ACCUSATION: (see "blame") accusal; allegation; arraignment; ascription; attribution; betrayal; censure; challenge; charge; citation; crimination; declaration; delation; denouncement; impeachment; imputation; incrimination; inculpation; indictment; innuendo; presentation; reproach (ment); revelation; summons; ACCUSATORY or ACCUSING: accusable; accusatival; accusative; accusive; blameworthy; censurable; challenging; condemnatory; criminative; criminatory; demeritorious; guilty; imputable; imputational; incriminative; inculpative; inculpatory; peccable; reprehensible; reprovable; ACCUSER: accusant; accusatrix (fem.); betrayer; delator; denouncer; denunciator; incriminator; indictor; informer; namer; plaintiff; prosecutor; traitor(ess)

ACCUSTOM: acclimate; acclimatize; acquaint; adapt; addict; adjust; adopt; conform; discipline; drill; educate; enure; familiarize; habituate; harden; indoctrinate; instruct; inure; naturalize; orient(ate); popularize; prepare; season; steel; teach; tolerate; toughen; train; use; ACCUSTOMED: see "customary"

ACE: **a.** (see "able") adept; A-one; expert; outstanding; tops; virtuoso; ACE: **n.** see "expert"

ACERB: (**see** "sour") acerbic; acid; acrid; astringent; biting; bitter; critical; hard; harsh; ironic; sarcastic; sharp; tart; vinegary

ACHE: **v. see** "pain;" ACHE: **n.** affliction; agony; *angoisse*; angst; anguish; annoyance; anxiety; bereavement; consternation; cross; cruciation; desire; discomfort; discomfiture; disease; distress; dolor; dysphoria; excruciation; grief; hurt; longing; malaise; misease; misery; obsession; pain; pant; perturbation; pining; rack; regret; remorse; sorrow; stitch; suffering; symptom; throb; throe; torment; travail; trouble; uncomfort; uneasiness; woe; worry; yearn(ing)

ACHIEVE: (**see** "accomplish") attain; compass; complete; conclude; consummate; do; earn; effect(uate); end; find; finish; fulfill; gain; get; harvest; have; hit; make; obtain; pass; perform; produce; prosper; reach; realize; score; succeed; win; wrest; ACHIEVEMENT: accomplishment; act-(ion); attainment; completion; conclusion; consummation; deed; exploit; feat; fulfillment; gain; harvest; job; landmark; masterpiece; masterstroke; performance; production; prosperity; realization; record; result; score; standing; success; winnings; work; yield

ACID(ULOUS) **a.** acerb(ic); acescent; acetous; acidic; acidulated; acidulent; acrid; acrimonious; acute; astringent; biting; bitter; burning; caustic; corrosive; critical; cutting; destructive; dry; erodent; escharotic; harsh; incisive; keen; malevolent; offensive; penetrating; pungent; pyrotic; rigid; sarcastic; satirical; scathing; severe; sharp; shrewd; snappish; sour; tart; testy; trenchant; unyielding; vinegarish; vinegary; virulent; vitriolic; ACID: **n.** amino; citric; hydrochloric; nitric; sulfuric; vinegar; ACIDITY: acerbity; acidification; acor; acridity; acrimony; acuteness; causticity; incisiveness; pungency; sarcasm; satire; severity; sourness; tartness; trenchancy; virulence

ACKNOWLEDGE: accede; accept; acquiesce; admit; adopt; agree; allow; answer; approve; ascribe; assent; assert; attest; avow; capitulate; charge; concede; condescend; confess; confirm; countenance; credit; declare; disclose; embrace; endorse; espouse; grant; honor; impute; include; let on; nod; notice; observe; own; pledge; publicize; publish; ratify; receipt; receive; recognize; regard; repeat; reply; respect; reward; sanction; show; sign; support; testify; thank; trust; welcome; ACKNOWLEDGED: (**see** "accepted") welcomed; well-known; ACKNOWLEDGEMENT: (**see** "credit") acceptance; acceptation; accolade; admission; allowance; answer; approval; assent(ation); assertion; attention; avowal; award; capitulation; concession; condescension; confession; confirmation; declaration; disclosure; embrace(ment); endorsement; grant; handshake; honor; indulgence; kiss; medal; nod; obligation; observation; pledge; praise; protest; ratification; receipt; recognition; reply; reward; sanction; sign; support; testimony; thanks; welcome

ACME: absolute; ace; apex; apogee; apotheosis; cap(sheaf); capstone; climacteric; climacterium; climax; comble; completion; consummation; crest; crown; culmination; end; epi; epitome; excellence; extreme; finial; height; heyday; high tide; keystone; meridian; *ne plus ultra*; noon; peak; pinnacle; point; roof; spire; sublimity; summit; tip; top; turret; ultimate; vertex; zenith

ACOLYTE: (**see** "learner") altar boy; assistant; follower; helper; novice; satellite; server

ACQUAINT: apprise; educate; familiarize; inform; introduce; notify; school; teach; tell; train; ACQUAINTED: *au courant*; *au fait*; aware; cognizant; conversant; familiar(ized); informed; introduced; known; practiced; schooled; skilled; trained; versant; versed; ACQUAINTANCE: associate; awareness; experience; expertise; familiar-(ity); friend

ACQUIESCE: accede; accept; acknowledge; agree; approve; assent; bow; chime; comply; concede; concur; condescend; consent; endorse; espouse; obey; receive; resign; submit; unbend; yield; welcome

ACQUIRE: (**see** "accumulate") accrue; achieve; add; amass; annex; ascertain; buy; collect; derive; develop; draw; earn; gain; get; glean; grab; harvest; learn; obtain; procure; purchase; reach; realize; reap; receive; seize; snatch; succeed; steal; take; win; wrest; ACQUIRED: accrued; accumulated; achieved; added; amassed; annexed; bought; collected; derived; developed; earned; gained; gleaned; grabbed; harvested; innate; learned; native; obtained; procured; purchased; reached; realized; reaped; received; seized; snatched; stolen; taken; won; wrested; ACQUIREMENT or AC-

QUISITION: **see** "accumulation" and "gain"

ACQUIT: absolve; act; annul; behave; clear; comport; conciliate; condone; conduct; conform; countenance; defend; demean; deport; discharge; disculpate; dispense; disregard; emancipate; encourage; exculpate; excuse; exempt; exonerate; extenuate; favor; forget; forgive; free; ignore; indulge; justify; liberate; overlook; palliate; pardon; pay; quash; release; relieve; remit; sanction; treat; vindicate; ACQUITTAL: absolution; amnesty; annulment; clearance; conciliation; condonation; countenance; deliverance; demeanor; discharge; dispensation; disregard; emancipation; exculpation; excuse; exemption; exoneration; extenuation; forgiveness; freedom; indulgence; justification; liberation; palliation; pardon; release; relief; remission; sanction; vindication

ACRID: (**see** "tart") acrimonious; biting; bitter; caustic; corrosive; harsh; keen; pungent; rancorous; sour; strong; surly; unsavory; vinegary

ACRIMONY: acerbity; acidity; acridity; anger; asperity; bitterness; causticity; corrosion; corrosiveness; ferocity; fierceness; gruffness; harshness; irascibility; madness; malevolence; malignancy; right; severity; sharpness; sourness; surliness; virulence; ACRIMONIOUS: (**see** "biting") acerb; acid; acrid; angry; bitter; caustic; corrosive; cutting; fierce; gruff; harsh; irate; mad; malignant; rigorous; severe; sharp; sour; surly; tart; virulent; unkind

ACROSS: abroad; athwart; cater-cornered; crosswise; over; transverse(ly)

ACT: **v.** accomplish; administer; assume; behave; bestir; comport; conduct; counterfeit; decree; direct; dissemble; do; drive; effect; emote; endeavor; execute; exercise; exert; feign; force; function; grandstand; initiate; labor; move; operate; personate; play; ply; press; pretend; produce; pull; push; react; represent; run; serve; shift; stimulate; stir; strain; struggle; thrust; toil; transact; try; tug; wield; work; ACT: **n.** (**see** "action") accomplishment; attitude; award; bearing; behavior; comportment; conduct; course; decree; deed; demeanor; deportment; direction; discipline; doing; drama; drive; edict; effort; endeavor; ethics; ethos; etiquette; execution; exercise; exertion; exploit; feat; force; front; function; gest(e); gymnastic(s); gyration(s); habit;

judgment; karma; law; mien; move; operation; performance; play; posture; pretense; show; statute; step; transaction; treatment; way; work

ACTING: affected; delegated; dramatic; gymnastic; histrionic; melodramatic; operatic; pretending; showy; simulative; substitutionary; theatrical; vicarious

ACTION: (**see** "act") accomplishment; achievement; actification; activation; activity; ado; advance(ment); agitation; application; award; battle; bout; brouhaha; bustle; buzz; case; ceremony; coil; commotion; conduct; confusion; contention; coup; course; decision; deed; deportment; dint; direction; discipline; disturbance; drill; drive; edict; effort; emergency; endeavor; engagement; enterprise; etiquette; event; excitement; execution; exercise; exertion; fare; feat; fight; flurry; force; fray; frisk; function; fuss; gest(e); gesture; grind; gymnastics; gyration; harassment; haste; heroism; hubbub; hullabaloo; hurry; hustle; imbroglio; initiation; initiative; judgment; labor; liveliness; maneuver; manipulation; manner(s); mechanics; mechanism; motion; movement; occurrence; operation; pains; performance; play; plot; ploy; pother; power; practice; praxis; procedure; proceeding; process; production; progress; push; quest; reaction; rite; rush; rustle; scuffle; scutter; show; sprightliness; step; stir; struggle; suit; synergy; task; test; thrust; to-do; training; transaction; treatment; trouble; tumult; turmoil; vigor; vim; vivacity; way; whirl; work

ACTIVATE: (**see** "begin" and "start") abet; actify; activize; catalyze; detonate; enliven; excite; foment; incite; initiate; instigate; move; precipitate; progress; provoke; quicken; revive; rouse; spark; stimulate; stir; trigger

ACTIVE: abustle; abuzz; acute; advancing; aggressive; agile; alacritous; alert; alive; animated; aprowl; assiduous; astir; athletic; attentive; blithe; bold; brawny; breezy; brisk; bustling; busy; charged; *con brio*; constant; diligent; driving; dynamic(al); ebullient; effervescent; efficient; effective; employed; energetic; engaged; engrossed; enlivened; enterprising; expeditious; fast; fleet; flourishing; frantic; fresh; frisky; gymnastic; hard-hitting; hardworking; high-powered; high-spirited; humming; hustling; impetuous; indefatigable; industrious; intense; intent; keen; kinetic;

laborious; live(ly); living; meddling; mobile; muscular; nimble; noisy; occupied; officious; on-the-jump; open; operational; operose; painstaking; peppy; perky; persevering; pert; potent; powerful; prompt; puissant; purposeful; quick; rapid; ready; resolute; robust(ious); running; sedulous; sharp; sleepless; smart; snappy; solicitous; spirited; sprightly; spritely; spruce; spry; steadfast; sthenic; stout; strenuous; strong; supercharged; swift; trotty; unleisured; vigorous; violent; vital; vivacious; vivid; working; yare; zealous

ACTIVITY: (**see** "action and "business") activation; advance(ment); agency; aggression; agility; alacrity; alarums and excursions; animation; application; assiduity; athleticism; attention; briskness; bustle; buzz; celerity; constancy; diligence; drive; dynamics; ebulliency; effervescence; effort; energy; engagement; enterprise; event; exertion; expedition; field; flourish; force; function; gambit; happening; hustle; hyperkinesia; industriousness; industry; intentness; job; labor(iousness); life; line; liveliness; manufacturing; mobility; motion; move(ment); nimbleness; noise; occupation; operation; operosity; organization; pep; perseverance; persistency; phase; play; ploy; power; procedure; process; pursuit; rally; recreation; round; sedulity; sedulousness; shop; spirit; sprightliness; steadfastness; stir; storm; swing; tempest; tempo; toil; trade; traffic; undertaking; unit; vigor; vim; violence; vivacity; vortex; way; work; zeal

ACTOR(S): agent; barnstormer; cast; company; *corps dramatique*; deuteragonist; diva; doer; *dramatis personae*; facient; ham; histrio(n); ingenue(fem.); lead; mime; participant; performer; personae (pl.); player; protagonist; retinue; soubrette (fem.); stager; star; super(numerary); thespian; tragedian; tragedienne (fem.); tritagonist; troupe(r); vaudevillian; wrongdoer; ACTORISH: **see** "showy"

ACTUAL: (**see** "genuine") *au fait*; authentic; concrete; correct; current; *de facto*; definite; definitive; documentary; exact; existent; existing; factual; indisputable; intrinsic; legitimate; literal; material; objective; official; positive; present; real; right; substantial; sure; true; unadulterated; unquestionable; valid; veritable; ACTUALITY: accomplishment; animation; authenticity; being(ness); certainty; certitude; circumstance; concretum; continuity; corporality;

corporeity; correctitude; correctness; data (pl.); datum; death; definitude; duration; ens; entelechy; entity; esse(nce); event; evidence; exactitude; exactness; existence; existent(iality); facta (pl.); fact(s); factuality; factum; fait; *fait accompli*; fate; feat; grounds; happening; knowledge; life; maintenance; manifestation; materiality; objectivity; occurrence; particular(ity); phenomenon; proof; reality; right; state; statistics; status; substantivity; survival; truth; validity; veritability; verity; way

ACTUATE: (**see** "activate") initiate; release; stimulate; trigger

ACUMEN: acuity; acuteness; astucity; astuteness; brains; clearness; cleverness; criticality; discernment; discrimination; insight; intellect; intelligence; keenness; knowledge; learning; mind; penetration; perception; perspicacity; perspicuity; poignancy; sagacity; sharpness; shrewdness; smartness; trenchancy; wisdom

ACUTE: (**see** "crucial") active; astute; brisk; clear; clever; compelling; consequential; crisp; critical; crying; curt; cutting; dangerous; deadly; decisive; definitive; demanding; desperate; disastrous; discerning; discriminating; discriminative; edged; essential; exigent; extreme; fine; frantic; grim; high (-pitched); hopeless; hurrying; immediate; imminent; important; intelligent; intense; keen; mordant; outrageous; painful; penetrating; penetrative; perspicacious; poignant; pointed; pointing; pressing; quick; rushing; sarcastic; searching; sensitive; serious; severe; sharp(-witted); short; shrewd; shrill; snappish; solemn; telling; treble; trenchant; trying; urgent; vital; weighty; wise; ACUTENESS: (**see** "acumen") criticality; cruciality; danger; exigency; extremity; urgency

ADAGE: (**see** "witticism") aphorism; apothegm; axiom; *bon mot*; bromide; byword; catchword; dictum; epigram(mation); epithet; gnome; maxim; mot(to); phrase; precept; proverb; quip; saw; saying; sententia; truism; wisecrack

ADAMANT(INE): (**see** "stubborn") callous; chronic: deep-rooted; deep-seated; grim; hard; immovable; inveterate; militant; solid; strong; tough; unaffected; unmoved; unmoving; unyielding

ADAPT: acclimate; acclimatize; accommodate; accustom; adaptate; adjust; agree;

alter; apply; assimilate; change; climatize; coadjust; coincide; comply; condition; conform; conventionalize; convert; derive; edit; educate; equalize; fashion; fit; fix; gear; habituate; harmonize; hew; inure; keep; match; modify; mold; naturalize; orientate; reconcile; regularize; regulate; select; set; shape; square; stylize; suit; tailor; temper(ize); tolerate; train; translate; trim; ADAPTABLE: (see "changeable") acceptable; accepted; accommodating; adaptational; adjustable; agreeable; amenable; assimilable; compliant; conformable; corresponding; elastic; ethical; fitting; flexuous; labile; malleable; maneuverable; matched; mobile; modifiable; moldable; plastic; pliant; shapable; submissive; suitable; supple; tractable; ADAPTATION: assimilation; acclimatization; accommodation; adjustment; agreement; alteration; application; arrangement; assimilation; change; coadjustment; coaptation; conformation; conversion; copy; education; equalization; gearing; habituation; harmonization; inurement; lability; modification; orientation; reconciliation; selection; stylization; temporization; toleration; training; transition; version

ADD: accelerate; adjoin; advance; affix; aggrandize; aggravate; amplify; annex; append; attach; augment; broaden; calculate; cast; combine; compound; compute; deepen; delate; descant; develop; diffuse; dilate; distend; double; eke; elaborate; elevate; elongate; enhance; enlarge; enrich; enumerate; escalate; exacerbate; exaggerate; excite; expand; expatiate; explain; extend; fatten; feed; fertilize; figure; foot; further; gain; give, glue; grow; heighten; impose; include; incorporate; increase; intensify; introduce; intumesce; join; jut; lend; lengthen; luxuriate; magnify; multiply; mushroom; number; pad; pend; proffer; project; proliferate; prolong; protract; protrude; ramify; reckon; say; score; spread; sprout; stick; stretch; stuff; subjoin; sum; superimpose; surpass; swell; tabulate; tack; tally; tot(al); triple; triplicate; tumefy; tumesce; unfold; unite; widen; ADDITION: access (ion); accessory; accrescence; accretion; addenda (pl.); addendum; additament; adjunct(ion); advancement; affixation; affixture; agglutination; aggrandizement; aggravation; aggregation; amplification; annex(ation); appanage; appendage; appendix; attachment; augmentation; broadening; codicil; combination; computation; concretion; development; diffusion;

dilation; distension; elaboration; ell; elongation; encore; enhancement; enlargement; enrichment; escalation; exacerbation; exaggeration; expansion; expansiveness; expatiation; explanation; extension; furtherance; furthering; gain; growth; heightening; imposition; improvement; inclusion; incorporation; increase; intensification; intumescence; joining; lengthening; magnification; multiplication; mushrooming; padding; plus; prefix; proliferation; prolongation; protraction; protrusion; reckoning; rider; rise; spread(ing); sprouting; stretching; subjunction; suffix; sum; superimposition; tab; total; tumefaction; tumescence; tumidity; widening; ADDITIONAL: accessorial; added; adjunct(ive); aggrandizing; aggregative; also; ancillary; another; apart; augmentative; besides; developmental; different; dilative; elongative; else; exacerbative; expansive; extensional; extensive; extra; fresh; further; helpful; instead; more; new; odd; other(wise); prefixal; proliferative; prolongative; protractive; secondary; spreading; sprouting; subordinate; subsidiary; substitute; substitutionary; supplemental; supplementary; too; tumescent; withal

ADDICT: v. (see "adapt") crave; devote; dispose; give; habituate; incline; indulge; surrender; use; ADDICT; n. (see "follower") buff; captive; devotee; enthusiast; fan(atic); fiend; habituate; habitué; hound; user; zealot; ADDICTION: adoration; ardency; ardor; attachment; bent; craving; devotion; disposition; enslavement; habit(uation); inclination; indulgence; surrender; usage

ADDITIONAL: see under "add"

ADDLE: agitate; amaze; bewilder; confound; confuse; muddle; puzzle; spoil; upset; ADDLED: addlebrained; addlepated; agitated; asea; bewildered; confounded; confused; dizzy; fruitless; muddled; putrid; puzzled; rotten; spoiled; upset

ADDRESS: v. accost; aim; apostrophize; appeal; apply; approach; call; challenge; confront; consign; correct; court; direct; dispatch; front; greet; hail; meet; petition; point; pray; redress; salute; solicit; speak; spend; sue; woo; write; ADDRESS: n. abode; adroitness; allocution; appeal; attention; bearing; challenge; confrontation; delivery; deportment; dexterity; diplomacy; direction; dispatch; ease; greeting; home; ingenuity; petition; poise; prayer; preparation; residence; salutation; salute; skill (fulness); solicitation; speech; tact (fulness)

ADDUCE: advance; allege; assign; bear; cite; give; infer; mention; name; offer; present; quote; urge

ADEPT: **a.** (**see** "expert") able; adroit; apt; capable; competent; condign; consummate; dexterous; educated; nifty; proficient; qualified; skilled; skillful; suitable; trained; versed; ADEPT: **n.** (**see** "expert") artist(e); master; seer; virtuoso; ADEPTNESS: **see** "expertness"

ADEQUATE: able; abundant; adapted; adequative; ample; appropriate; apt; basta; bully; capable; clear; commensurate; competent; complete; copious; corresponding; decent; deserved; due; enough; enow; equal; equivalent; exemplary; fair; fit(ting); good; just(ifiable); justified; lawful; legal; licensed; meet; merited; plenteous; plentiful; plen-(t)itudinous; proper; qualified; reasonable; regular; representative; requisite; rich; right(ful); satisfactory; sufficient; suitable; suited; valid; warranted; worthy; ADEQUACY: ability; abundance; adequateness; adequation; amplitude; appropriateness; aptness; capability; competence; competency; completeness; copiosity; copiousness; equality; equivalence; meet; plentitude; propriety; qualification; satisfaction; sufficiency; suitability; superabundance; supererogation; worthiness

ADHERE: (**see** "bind") accrete; affix; agglutinate; associate; attach; cement; cleave; cling; coapt; cohere; combine; conform; conglutinate; embrace; follow; glue; glutinate; grasp; hang; hew; hold; hug; join; keep; knit; linger; link; maintain; mortar; paste; persevere; persist; practice; preserve; putty; remain; solder; solidify; stick; unify; unite; vine; ADHERENT: (**see** "follower") adamant; adherescent; adhesive; agglutinant; agglutinative; believing; clinging; coherent; cohesive; gluey; glutinous; gummy; persevering; persistent; sticky; tenacious; viscid; viscous; ADHERENCE: accretion; agglutination; attachment; clinginess; coaptation; coherence; fidelity; maintenance; stickiness; stick-to-itiveness; tenacity; union; viscosity

ADHESIVE: **a.** (**see** "adherent") dauby; emplastic; tacky; viscid; viscous; ADHESIVE: **n.** (**see** "stickiness") glue; gum; paste

ADHIBIT: admit; affix; apply; attach; summon; use

ADIPOSE: **see** "obese"

ADIT: access; aditus; admission; approach; door(way); entrance(way); opening; passage(way); stulm

ADJOIN: abut; add; append; attach; border; contact; impinge; juxtapose; meet; touch; ADJOINING or ADJACENT: (**see** "near") abutting; annexed; appended; attached; beside; bordering; close; coadjacent; contacting; conterminate; conterminous; contiguous; coterminous; immediate; juxtaposed; juxtapositional; juxtapositioned; meet(ing); nearby; neighboring; next; nigh; satellite; satellitic; tangent; touching; ADJACENCY: contiguity; contiguousness; immediacy; juxtaposition; tangency

ADJOURN: (**see** "end") cease; close; continue; defer; delay; disband; discontinue; postpone; procrastinate; prorogue; recess; stay; stop; suspend

ADJUDGE or ADJUDICATE: (**see** "adjust") allot; award; balance; categorize; decide; decree; deem; determine; find; give; grant; hear; hold; judge; ordain; pronounce; rate; regard; resolve; rule; set(tle); stamp; try; weigh

ADJUNCT: **a.** accompanying; added; adjective; adjunctive; attached; joined; secondary; subsidiary; tangent; ADJUNCT: **n.** accessory; accompaniment; addendum; additament; addition; additive; adjective; adjunction; aid; annex(ation); ap(p)anage; appendage; appendix; appurtenance; attachment; auxiliary; belonging(s); endowment; help; jewelry; ornament; part; perquisite; subsidiary; tangency

ADJURE: advise; appeal; ask; beg; beseech; bid; bind; charge; command; crave; entreat; plead; pray; request; urge; warn

ADJUST: (**see** "adapt" and "fit") accommodate; accustom; adjudicate; align; allot; amend; aright; arrange; attune; award; balance; better; change; check; collimate; compound; connate; conform; coordinate; correct; decide; decree; determine; doctor; ease; edit; emend; equal(ize); equate; find; fix; focalize; focus; form(ulate); frame; hammer; harmonize; improve; integrate; line; manipulate; mend; methodize; mitigate;

modify; modulate; organize; orient(ate); pacify; prepare; purify; rate; rearrange; rectify; regulate; remedy; renovate; repair; resolve; revamp; revise; right; rule; satisfy; set(tle); shake down; shape; solve; square; stabilize; straighten; suit; synchronize; systematize; temper; trim; true; tune; zero; ADJUSTABLE: accommodating; adaptable; amenable; amendable; fictile; malleable; mitigative; modifiable; modificatory; modulatory; plastic; pliable; regulatory; resolvable; ADJUSTMENT: acclimation; acclimatization; accommodation; adaptation; adjudication; agreement; alignment; arrangement; attunement; change; coaptation; collineation; composition; compromise; concinnity; conformation; conformity; coordination; correction; determination; equalization; equilibration; equilibrium; fit; focus; harmonization; improvement; integration; manipulation; methodization; mitigation; modification; modulation; organization; orientation; pacification; preparation; rearrangement; reconcilation; regulation; remedy; repair; reparation; resolution; satisfaction; settlement; settling; shakedown; solution; stabilization; synchronization; transaction; tuneup; tuning; understanding; warm-up

ADMINISTER: (**see** "govern") accomplish; act; apply; boss; conduct; control; deal; direct; dispense; dispose; distribute; do; dose; execute; furnish; give; husband; manage; master; mete out; minister; perform; pilot; police; regulate; reign; remedy; render; resolve; rule; run; superintend; supply; sway; tend(er); treat; use; ADMINISTRATION: accommodation; action; activity; applicaton; command; conduct; control; direction; dispensation; disposal; disposition; distribution; dosage; execution; furnishing; government; headquarters; husbandry; management; performance; policy; regime(n); regulation; rule; running; superintendence; supply; sway; treatment

ADMIRE: adore; adulate; apotheosize; applaud; appreciate; canonize; cherish; covet; deify; dote; embosom; enshrine; esteem; eulogize; exalt; extol; gloat; glorify; honor; idolize; indulge; like; love; marvel; mother; panegyrize; pedestal; pet; praise; prize; protect; regard; respect; revel; revere(nce); spiritualize; treasure; value; venerate; wonder; worship; ADMIRATION: adoration; adulation; apotheosis; applause; approbation; astonishment; awe; canonization; conceit; deification; esteem; eulogy; exaltation; glorification; glory; honor; idolatry; idolization; laudation; love; praise; regard;

respect; reverence; veneration; wonder; worship; ADMIRED: admiring; adored; adulated; apotheosized; applauded; canonized; deified; doted; esteemed; eulogized; exalted; extolled; fine; glorified; grand; honorable; honored; idolized; lauded; laureled; liked; loved; marveled; panegyrized; pedestalized; popular; praised; prized; regarded; respected; revered; valued; venerated; wonderful; worshipped; ADMIRING: adorable; adulatory; complimentary; encomiastic; eulogistic; idolatric; idolatrous; laudative; laudatory; panegyrical; praiseworthy; ADMIRABLE: (**see** "commendable") adorable; adulatory; approbatory; divine; excellent; gallant; good; great; lofty; marvelous; noble; surprising; wonderful; worshipful; ADMIRER: (**see** "follower") adorer; adulator; devotee; disciple; worshiper

ADMIT: accede; accept; acknowledge; acquiesce; adhibit; affirm; agree; allow; annex; assent; attest; avow; begrudge; capitulate; cede; certify; comprise; concede; concur; confess; confide; declare; disclose; divulge; embrace; enclose; enrol(l); entrust; give; grant; impart; include; induct; initiate; intromit; let; manifest; manipulate; own; permit; profess; receive; relieve; reveal; shrive; suffer; surrender; take (in;) tell; trust; unburden; waive; yield; ADMISSION: acceptance; access(ion); acknowledgment; acquiescence; adit; admittance; agreement; allowance; annexation; assent-(ation); attestation; avowal; capitulation; charge; communication; concession; concurrence; confession; consent; cost; declaration; disclosure; divulgence; embracement; enrollment; *entrée*; entry; fee; grant(ing); imparting; inclusion; induction; ingress; initiation; intromission; matriculation; permission; profession; reception; revelation; statement; sufferance; surrender; ticket; trust

ADMIXTURE: alloy; amalgam(ation); blend; compound; flavor; medley; mingling; potpourri; shade; soupçon; tinge

ADMONISH; advise; berate; blame; brawl; caution; censure; chastise; chide; clamor; complain; contend; counsel; direct; disapprove; encourage; exhort; rake; rate; rebuke; reprimand; reproach; reprove; scold; threaten; tongue-lash; upbraid; warn; wrangle; ADMONISHMENT or ADMONITION: advice; blame; caution; censure; chastisement; complaint; contention; counsel; direction; disapproval; encouragement;

exhortation; homily; lecture; rebuke; reminder; reproof; reproval; scolding; threat (ening); warning

ADO: (**see** "commotion") agitation; blather; blazonry; bother; brouhaha; bustle; coil; confusion; convulsion; difficulty; disorder; disturbance; effort; excitement; fanfare; ferment; flair; flourish; flurriment; flurry; fuss; hubbub; hullabaloo; imbroglio; ostentation; paroxysm; pother; show; stir; storm; to-do; trouble; tumult; turbulence; turmoil; uncertainty; unrest; work

ADOLESCENCE: juniority; minority; nonage; puberty; teens; transition; youth; ADOLESCENT: (**see** "young") immature; youngish; youthful

ADOPT: accept; acknowledge; appropriate; approve; assume; borrow; choose; embrace; employ; endorse; espouse; father; foster; introduce; maintain; mother; naturalize; pass; practice; steal; support; take

ADORE: (**see** "admire" and "cherish") honor; like; revere(nce); worship ADORATION: (**see** "worship") veneration

ADORN: add; award; beautify; become; bedeck; bedizen; befit; begem; behoove; bejewel; beseem; border; caparison; clothe; crown; deck; decorate; diamondize; dress; embellish; emblason; emboss; embroider; endow; enhance; enrich; fancy up; festoon; flourish; furbish; garland; garnish; gild; grace; gratify; gussy up; honor; improve; invest; lace; lard; ornament; paint; redo; refurbish; spangle; splendor; suit; tassel; trim; ADORNMENT: atmosphere; attraction; badge; beautification; beauty; bedizonment; caparison; citation; clothing; crown; cup; decor(ation); dress; edging; elegancy; embellishment; emblazonment; embossing; embroidery; endowment; enhancement; enrichment; fancification; festoon; flourish; frill; frippery; garland; garnish(ment); garniture; gaudery; gild; gingerbread; gold; honor; improvement; insigne; insignia (pl.); opulence; opulency; ornament(ation); ostentation; paint; panoply; polish; refinement; richness; rouge; scenery; setting; show; splendor; trim; trophy

ADRIFT: asea; astray; derelict; drifting; freed; loose; lost; pilotless; stray; unanchored; unloosened; unmoored; untied

ADROIT: (**see** "dexterous") adept; artful; clever; conciliatory; consummate; crafty; deft; delicate; diplomatic; discriminative; easy; expert; finished; good; habile; handy; neat; polished; polite; politic(al;) ready; resourceful; shrewd; skilled; skillful; slick; smart; smooth; suave; urbane; wily; witty; ADROITNESS: (**see** "dexterity") address; adeptness; art(fulness); assurance; cleverness; coolness; craft(iness); cunning; deftness; dexterity; dexterousness; diplomacy; ease; expertise; finesse; hability; knack; magic; poise; quickness; readiness; resolution; resourcefulness; *savoir-faire*; self-possession; skillfulness; stability; surety; tack; trickery; wit(tiness)

ADULATE: **see** "admire"

ADULT: (**see** "mature") developed; grown (up); manlike; mannish; matured; postpubertal; ripen(ed); womanish

ADULTERATE: alloy; conceal; corrupt; cut; debase; deceive; defile; denature; dilute; falsify; impurify; lessen; mix; simulate; taint; thin; vitiate; water(-down); weaken

ADVANCE: **v.** (**see** "elevate") accelerate; accentuate; accomplish; accumulate; achieve; add; age; aggrandize; aggravate; allege; ameliorate; amend; approach; assist; augment; benefit; better; boast; boost; breed; brighten; bud; burgeon; civilize; correct; crawl; create; creep; culminate; cultivate; cure; develop; differentiate; dig; dilate; drift; earn; educate; effect; effervesce; effloresce; elaborate; elevate; encourage; enhance; enlarge; ennoble; enrich; enter; escalate; establish; evolute; evolve; exacerbate; exalt; exhibit; expand; expedite; extend; fatten; flourish; flower; force; forge; forward; foster; freshen; further; gain; gather; generate; germinate; get; give; go; graduate; grow; hasten; heighten; help; hurry; husband; improve; inch; increase; incubate; intensify; interject; leap (frog); lend; live; loan; lobby; manifest; march; mass; materialize; maturate; mature; meliorate; mend; metastasize; mount; move; naturalize; net; nourish; nurse; obtain; pass; pay; penetrate; perfect; place; polish; prepare; prepay; proceed; procure; profit; progress; promote; propose; prosper; protect; purify; push; raise; reach; realize; reap; rear; receive; rectify; recuperate; refine; reform; refresh(en); revise; ripen; rise; rush; school; score; secure; serve; shape; speed; step(-up); strengthen; strive; succeed; supply; surge; swing; tame; teach; tend(er); thrive; till; train; transform; travel; traverse; tune; unfold; unroll; upgrade; walk; wave;

wax; win; worm; ADVANCE(MENT): **n.** (**see** "elevation") acceleration; accentuation; accession; accomplishment; accrescence; accretion; accrual; accruement; accumulation; achievement; acquirement; acquisition; additament; addition; agglutination; aggrandizement; aggravation; aid; amplification; anabasis; assist(ance); augmentation; benefit; boost; buildup; burgeoning; civilization; concrescence; consummation; crawl(ing); creeping; cultivation; culture; deepening; development; differentiation; dilation; education; elaboration; elevation; encouragement; enhancement; enlargement; enrichment; escalation; evolution; exacerbation; exacerbescence; exaggeration; exaltation; excrescence; expedition; extension; florescence; furtherance; gain; germination; graduation; growing; growth; haste; headway; help; improvement; inching; increase; increment; incubation; inflation; intensification; jump; leap; leaps and bounds; lengthening; lift; loan; magnification; majoration; manifestation; march; maturation; maturescence; maturity; metastasis; morphosis; move(ment); multiplication; offer; ontogeny; outgrowth; overflow; overture; payment; penetration; phenomenon; plus; preferment; preparation; process(ion); produce; profit; progress(ion); promotion; proposal; prosperity; push; raise; realization; refinement; return; ripeness; rise; schooling; service; speed; spread; step(-up); stride; study; surge; swing; tender(ing); training; wave; way; ADVANCED: (**see** "modern") accelerated; afar; deep; distant; far(-out); farthest; forane; front-line; furthest; metastatic; much; progressed; remote; removed; senior; superior; tramontane; ultramontane; upward; vanward

ADVANTAGE: (**see** "patronage") asset; avail; beachhead; benefit; chance; control; cut; edge; effect; excess; favor; favorableness; fluke; foothold; gain; handicap; handiness; help; importance; inprovement; interest; lead; leverage; likelihood; mastery; object; odds; opportuneness; opportunity; partiality; percentage; per centum; plus; point; precedence; preference; preferment; privilege; prize; probability; profit; purchase; sake; service; share; start; stead; superiority; surplus; upper hand; use; utility; weather gauge; whip hand; windfall; ADVANTAGEOUS: (**see** "favorable") auspicious; available; beneficent; beneficial; convenient; desirable; eligible; expedient; fit(ting); golden; good; handy; helpful; opportune; preferable; preferent(ial); profitable; pro-

pitious; remunerative; right; strategetic; strategic(al); tactical; useful

ADVENTITIOUS: accidental; acquired; casual; episodic; extrinsic; foreign; incidental; spontaneous; sporadic;

ADVENTURE: chance; danger; dare; daringness; dido; enterprise; escapade; event; experiment; frolic; gambade; gambit; gamble; gest(e); harlequinade; hazard; indiscretion; lark; peccadillo; peril; ploy; prank; quest; risk; vagary; venture; ADVENTUROUS or ADVENTURESOME: (**see** "bold") brash; cavalier; chancy; dangerous; daredevil(ish); daring; enterprising; errant; eventful; experimental; foolhardy; frolicsome; gambling; hasty; hazardous; Icarian; incautious; indiscreet; larkish; perilous; picaresque; precarious; precipitate; quixotic; rash; reckless; risky; speculative; temerarious; uncalculating; vagarious; venturesome

ADVERSARY: (**see** "antagonist") competitor; disputant; enemy; foe; foil; opponent; protagonist; Satan; unfriend

ADVERSE: adversitive; afflictive; antagonistic; antipathetic(al); antipathic; antithetical; calamitous; cataclysmic(al); catastrophic(al); condemnatory; conflicting; confronting; contrary; counter(active); critical; deplorable; derogatory; destructive; detrimental; difficult; dire; disadvantageous; disastrous; disparaging; distressful; distressing; doomed; evil; hapless; harmful; holocaustic; hostile; incompatible; inimical; injurious; irreconcilable; malevolent; malign(ant); misfortunate; ominous; opposed; opposing; opposite; portentous; prejudicial; repellant; repugnant; repulsive; sad; sinister; stubborn; tragic(al); troublesome; unfavorable; unfortunate; unfriendly; unlucky; unpropitious; untoward; ADVERSITY: (**see** "calamity") accident; affliction; bankruptcy; burden; catastrophe; conflict; death; difficulty; disaster; distress; drudgery; hardship; harm; grief; ill fortune; ill luck; illness; injury; injustice; malady; malevolence; malignancy; misadventure; misery; misfortune; opposition; oppression; peril; privation; rigor; sadness; sickness; sorrow; suffering; toil; trial; trouble; want; woe(fulness)

ADVERT: allude; attend; heed; refer; warn; ADVERTENCE: (**see** "attention") heed; notice; reference

ADVERTISE: acquaint; advocate; air; announce; apprise; bark; barnstorm; blazon; broadcast; bruit; bulletinize; circulate; communicate; convey; cry; declare; denote; diffuse; disclose; disseminate; divulge; emblazon; endorse; exploit; foretell; herald; indicate; inform; issue; notify; overrate; pitch; plug; proclaim; promulgate; pronounce; propagandize; publicize; publish; puff; reveal; sell; sow; specify; spread; tell; thump; tout; vent(ilate); ADVERTISEMENT: ad; advocacy; announcement; bill; blurb; broadcast; bulletin; commercial; dissemination; dodger; exploitation; notification; pitch; plug; propaganda; publicity; puff; spread; ADVERTISING: disseminative; exploitative; informational; informative; promotional; promulgative; propagandistic

ADVICE: adhortation; admonishment; advisement; caution; charge; consultation; counsel; deliberation; direction; discussion; exhortation; expostulation; guidance; guide; information; instruction; intelligence; news; notice; opinion; recommendation; rede; teaching; tidings; warning

ADVISE: acquaint; admonish; advocate; apprise; caution; charge; chide; conduct; consult; counsel; deliberate; direct; educate; expostulate; guide; inform; instruct; notify; preach; proctor; recommend; reveal; show; teach; tell; urge; warn; ADVISABLE: advisatory; counsel(l)able; desirable; expedient; opportune; politic(al); provident; prudent(ial); seemly; well; ADVISER: (see "advocate") aide; attorney; counselor; director; doctor; Egeria; instructor; lawyer; leader; mentor; minister; monitor; Nestor; physician; preacher; preceptor; priest; professor; teacher; ADVISORY: admonitory; cautionary; consultative; consultatory; directional; exhortative; exhortatory; expedient; expostulatory; hortative; hortatory; instructive; prudent; recommendatory; urging; ADVISEMENT: see "advice"; ADVISABILITY: see "expedience"

ADVOCATE: **v.** abet; advertise; argue; back; beg; champion; commend; defend; desiderate; endorse; espouse; expound; favor; plead; plug; promote; provoke; support; thump; urge; ADVOCATE: **n.** (see "adviser") agent; aide; angel; apologist; attorney; backer; barrister; champion; combatant; counsel(l)or; defender; exemplifier; explainer; exponent; expounder; fighter; guide; helper; hero; hierophant; ite; knight;

lawyer; mentor; paladin; paraclete; paranymph; partisan; patron; Perseus; preacher; proctor; propugnator; protagonist; scholar; solicitor; speaker; spokesman; squire; supporter; victor; warrior; winner; ADVOCACY: commendation; desideration; espousal; patronage; pleading; subscription

AFAR: (**see** "distant") abroad; afield; away; off; overseas; remote; removed; thence

AFFABLE: (**see** "genial") agreeable; benign (ant); charming; civil; complacent; conversable; cordial; courteous; easy; fair; frank; friendly; gallant; gracious; hospitable; ingratiating; kind; likable; merry; mild; nice; open; plausible; pleasant; polite; popular; smooth; sociable; suave; urbane

AFFAIR(S): action; amour; battle; business; care; career; case; concern; cup of tea; duty; event; experience; intrigue; liaison; life; lookout; matter; occasion; occurrence; palaver; party; ploy; procedure; rendezvous; romance; shebang; shindig; world

AFFECT: alter; assume; change; color; concern; condition; counterfeit; disturb; drive; entail; excite; fancy; feign; frequent; hit; impel; impress; influence; inspire; interest; involve; move; pose; pretend; shake (up); sham; simulate; stimulate; stir; strike; sway; thrill; touch; AFFECTATION: air; artificiality; display; foppery; hypocrisy; mannerism; *minauderie*; pietism; pose; pretense; pretension; religiosity; sanctimony; sham; simulation; AFFECTED: affectational; apish; assumed; assuming; artificial; conditioned; disposed; *distingué*; disturbed; dramatic; moved; pedantic; pietistic; *précieuse*; *précieux*; pretended; pretending; pretentious; puritanical; religiose; sanctimonious; sentimental; shammed; showy; simulated; staged; stirred; swayed; theatrical; thrilled; touched; AFFECTION: affliction; ailment; appreciation; approval; attachment; dispositon; emotion; esteem; feeling; fondness; inclination; liking; love; malady; motherliness; partiality; preciosity; predilection; prejudice; propensity; regard; AFFECTIONATE: amatory; amorous; ardent; attached; beloved; brotherly; cherished; darling; dear; devoted; devoting; doting; effusive; emotional; enamored; fond; foolish; friendly; indulgent; infatuated; kind; lovable; loved; loving; motherly; overindulgent; precious; priceless; sentimental; sisterly; sweet; tender; warm; zealous

AFFIANCE: (see "betroth") engage; pledge; plight

AFFILIATE: **v.** adopt; associate; attach; combine; connect; incorporate; join; merge; unite; AFFILIATE: **n.** (see "associate") branch; subsidiary

AFFINITY: accord; association; attraction; connecton; kinship; relation(ship); resemblance; sympathy; unity

AFFIRM: allege; approve; assert; asseverate; assume; attest; aver; avouch; avow; back; brace; certify; check; claim; confirm; corroborate; countersign; declare; depose; determine; endorse; establish; evidence; evince; fortify; guarantee; justify; notarize; predicate; profess; propose; ratify; reassure; sanction; say; seal; second; stamp; state; strengthen; support; sustain; swear; test(ify); uphold; validate; verify; vindicate; vouch; vow; witness; AFFIRMATION: affirmative; agreement; allegation; approval; assertion; asseveration; assurance; attestation; averment; avouchment; avowal; certification; check; confirmation; corroboration; declaration; deposition; endorsement; guarantee; justification; oath; predication; profession; ratification; reassurance; sanction; seal; stamp; statement; testimony; thesis; truth; validation; verification; vow; word; yes; AFFIRMATIVE: (see "positive") declarative; declaratory; favorable

AFFIX: (see "fasten") add; impale; seal; sign; stamp; subjoin; transfix

AFFLICT: abuse; ail; annoy; badger; beset; bother; burden; chafe; curse; damage; distress; disturb; eat; fret; gall; gnaw; grieve; grill; hamper; handicap; harass; harry; hector; hurt: incapacitate; infect; infest; inflict; injure; molest; nag; overrun; pain; persecute; pester; plague; press; rack; scourge; tease; torment; torture; trouble; try; twit; vex; worry; AFFLICTIVE: see "dire"; AFFLICTION: (see "plague") abuse; affection; ailment; anguish; annoyance; besetment; botheration; burden; calamity; cross; curse; damage; disease; disorder; distress; epidemic; grief; grievance; handicap; harassment; hurt; illness; incapacitation; infection; infestation; infliction; injury; nuisance; pain; pang; persecution; pest (ilence); plague; rack; scourge; sickness; torment; torture; trouble; vexation; worry

AFFLUENT: abundant; copious; flooded; flowing; flush; halcyon; opulent; over-flowing; plenteous; profuse; prosperous; replete; rich; sufficient; wealthy; AFFLUENCE: abundance; afflux(ation); copiosity; copiousness; ease; flood; fortune; influx; means; money; opulence; overflow; plenty; profusion; prosperity; riches; richness; sufficiency; wealth

AFFORD: bear; endure; furnish; give; grant; lend; manage; offer; pay; produce; supply; yield

AFFRAY: (see "contest") action; alarm; assault; battle; brawl; brouhaha; combat; disturbance; duel; engagement; feud; fight; fracas; fray; melee; quarrel; riot; scare; scuffle; strife; struggle; terror; war(fare)

AFFRIGHT: (see "scare") alarm; appall; frighten; intimidate; terrify

AFFRONT: **v.** abash; annoy; assault; confront; defy; displease; encounter; face; humiliate; insult; irritate; meet; nettle; offend; peeve; provoke; shame; slap; slight; taunt; tease; vex; wound; AFFRONT: **n.** abashment; anoyance; assault; confrontation; defiance; displeasure; encounter; humiliation; indignity; *infra dignitatem* (abb. infra dig.); insult; irritation; *lese majesty*; offense; provocation; slap; slight; taunt; vexation; wound

AFORESAID: above; aforementioned; antecedent; ditto; foregoing; previous; prior

AFRAID: affrightened; aghast; alarmed; anxious; apprehensive; averse; awestricken; awestruck; concerned; cowering; craven; disinclined; dismayed; fearful; frightened; gun-shy; jittery; nervous; reluctant; scared; terrified; timed; timorous; undaring

AFRESH: again; anew; anon; another; beginning; bis; commending; *de integro*; *de novo*; encore; more; new(ly); over; reappearing; recalling; recommenced; renewed; repeated; repetitious

AFTER: abaft; *après*; astern; behind; below; beyond; characteristic of; consequential; following; later; next; past; posteriad; posterior; postlimin(i)ary; residual; resultant; subsequent; seccedent; succeeding

AFTERMATH: backlash; backwash; consequence; culmination; echo; effect; end(ing); issue; loss; outcome; profit; repercussion; residual; residuum; result; rowen; sequel(a); stubble; termination; trial; upshot; wake; wave(s)

AFTERTHOUGHT: (see "memory") post-script (abb. P.S.); reflecton; regret

AGAIN: see "afresh"

AGAINST: (see "averse") anti; beside; contra; counter(active); counterclockwise; facing; opposed; opposite; resisting; resulting; touching; toward; versus(abb. vs.)

AGE: **v.** antiquate; change; decline; develop; grow; maturate; mature; mellow; ripen; season; senesce; wrinkle; AGE: **n.** advancement; aeon; anecdotage; antiquity; caducity; century; change; childhood; childishness; cycle; date; declination; decline; decrepitude; development; diminution; diuturnity; dotage; duration; eon; episode; epoch; era; eternality; eternity; event; eviternity; existence; feebleness; generation; growth; hoariness; immortability; immortality; infinitude; infinity; length; life(time); longevity; maturation; measurement; mellowing; oldness; period; perpetuality; perpetuity; primogeniture; ripeness; ripening; saeculum; sempiternity; senescence; senility; seniority; *siècle*; stage; superannuation; tenuity; time; venerableness; years; AGED: advanced; aging; ancient; anecdotal; anile; antediluvian; antiquated; bedridden; caducous; creaky; decayed; declined; decrepit; developed; dilapidated; doddering; elder(ly); enervated; feeble; first; former; fragile; frail; geriatric; gray; grown; hoary; ill; inane; infirm; maturated; mature; mellow(ed); Nestorian; old(er); patriarchal; prior; ripe(ned); seared; seasoned; senescent; senile; senior; superannuated; venerable; veteran; weak(ened); wobbling; worn(-out); wrinkled; yellowed; AGELESS: see "everlasting" and "unending"

AGENDA or AGENDUM: (see "calendar") business

AGENT: actor; advocate; attorney; broker; canvasser; catalyst; cause; channel; coefficient; commissionaire; commissioner; dealer; delegate; deputy; doer; dragoman; emissary; envoy; facient; factor; factotum; fiduciary; force; gene; go-between; guide; instrument; intermediary; investigator; legate; manager; mandatory; means; mediator; medium; messenger; middleman; minion; minister; mover; official; operant; operator; organ; performer; plenipotentiary; power; principal; principle; proctor; procurator; promoter; protector; proxy; reeve; representative; saleslady; salesman; salesperson; satellite; scout; senator; solicitor; spy; steward; vector;

vicar; worker; AGENCY: activity; administration; association; authority; board; branch; bureau; business; commission; committee; corporation; court; department; district; embassy; establishment; facility; faculty; firm; force; government; hand; headquarters; influence; instrument(ality); lever; means; media; medium; ministry; office(r); operation; organ; power; registry; section; service; station; unit

AGGLOMERATE: see "pile"

AGGRANDIZE: advance; agglutinate; aggravate; amass; augment; beautify; boost; diamondize; dignify; elevate; enhance; enlarge; ennoble; enrich; exacerbate; exalt; expand; greaten; increase; intensify; lift; magnify; pedestalize; promote; stellify

AGGRAVATE: add; affect; aggrandize; agitate; anger; annoy; arouse; augment; bestir; chafe; deepen; electrify; embitter; enhance; enlarge; enrage; exacerbate; exaggerate; exasperate; excite; expand; feed; fire; flush; fulminate; galvanize; goad; greaten; hearten; heat; hurry; impassion; incite; increase; induce; inflame; infuriate; inspirit; intensify; intoxicate; irk; irritate; kindle; lash; madden; magnify; nag; pique; precipitate; provoke; raise; rally; rankle; roil; shock; startle; stimulate; stir; taunt; tease; twit; vex; whet; worry; worsen; AGGRAVATION: additive; advancement; aggrandizement; agitation; alarm; anger; annoyance; arousal; augmentation; commotion; embitterment; encouragement; enhancement; enlargement; exacerbation; exacerbescence; exaggeration; exasperation; excitement; expansion; ferment; fever; fomentation; frenzy; fulmination; goad; heat; incitation; incitement; increase; inflammation; infuriation; instigation; intensification; irksomeness; irritation; magnification; precipitation; provocation; stimulation; stimulus; stir; vexation; worry; worsening; AGGRAVATING: see "annoying"

AGGREGATE: **v.** accumulate; add; agglomerate; agglutinate; amass; assemble; coacervate; collect; conglomerate; congregate; flock; gather; mass; muster; total; yield; AGGREGATE: **n.** or AGGREGATION: (see "group") accretion; accumulation; addition; agglomeration; agglutination; all; amount; army; assemblage; association; band; body; bulk; coacervation; cohort; collection; colony; combination; congeries; conglomeration; congregation; corporation; crowd; ensemble; extent; flock; force;

gallery; gang; gathering; gross; group; harvest; heaviness; hoard; intensity; largeness; legislature; magnitude; majority; mass; mob; multitude; muster; nest; number; organization; pile; pool; posse; pot; quanta (pl.); quantum; raft; settlement; size; society; suite; sum; swarm; thickness; total; tribe; unification; weight; whole; yield

AGGRESSIVE: assertive; bellicose; belligerent; bullish; combative; contentious; driving; enterprising; ferocious; fierce; fire-eating; forceful; gladiatorial; hard-hitting; hostile; intensive; martial; militant; military; provocative; pugilistic; pugnacious; pushful; pushing; pushy; rampant; self-assertive; self-confident; taurine; truculent; unbridled; unprovoked; unrestrained; warlike; AGGRESSIVENESS: bellicosity; belligerence; belligerency; combativeness; contentiousness; ferocity; fierceness; hostility; intensity; militancy; pugnacity; push; rampancy; truculence; truculency; war(fare); AGGRESSION: (see "aggressiveness") assault; attack; combat; destructon; fighting; hostility; invasion; offense; raid; war(fare)

AGGRIEVE: afflict; distress; harm; harry; hurt; injure; oppress; pain; persecute; provoke; trouble; try; wrong

AGHAST: afraid; agape; agog; amused; astonished; astounded; awed; bewildered; dazed; disgusted; frightened; horrified; humbled; numbed; petrified; scared; shocked; stunned; stupefied; surprised; terrified

AGILE: acrobatic; active; adept; adroit; alert; alive; athletic; brisk; bustling; catlike; catty; deft; dextrous; elastic; expeditious; expert; fast; gleg; graceful; light; limber; lissom(e); lithe; lively; nimble; prompt; quick; ready; resourceful; responsive; speedy; spright(ly); springy; spry; supple; swift; volant; AGILITY: acrobatics; action; activity; address; adeptness; adroitness; athleticism; briskness; deftness; dexterity; elasticity; flexibility; grace(fulness); legerity; lightness; limberness; lissomeness; liveliness; nimbleness; nippiness; promptitude; promptness; quickness; readiness; resourcefulness; responsiveness; sprightliness; springiness; suppleness; swiftness

AGITATE: activate; actuate; afflict; alarm; anger; animate; annoy; arouse; boil; bother; brew; bubble; change; churn; commove; concuss; convulse; coax; discompose; disconcert; discuss; disturb; drive; effervesce; engage; enliven; erupt; evoke; exasperate; excite; fire; fluster; foam; foment; fret; harry; hurry; impassion; impel; incite; inflame; inspire; inspirit; instigate; interest; irk; irritate; jar; jostle; kindle; liven; mix; move; pique; precipitate; prompt; provoke; rack; rage; rally; rile; rock; roil; rouse; rush; seethe; shake; simmer; steam; stew; stimulate; stir; swirl; toss; trouble; vex; vibrate; whip; work; AGITATED: (see¯ "unsettled") activated; actuated; alarmed; annoyed; anxious; ardent; aroused; bothered; bubbling; cyclonic; delirious; demoniacal; discomposed; distracted; disturbed; driven; ebullient; effervescent; emotional; enthusiastic; excited; exercised; febrile; fervid; feverish; fey; fidgety; flushed; flustered; foaming; fretful; fuming; hasty; hectic; hot; hurried; impassioned; inflammatory; intense; irked; jumpy; mad; maniac(al); moved; nervous; overwrought; passionate; perturbed; precipitant; quivering; restless; roiled; roused; seething; shaking; troubled; tumultuary; turbulent; unhappy; unpeaceable; unpeaceful; unquiet; unrestful; unstable; untranquil; violent; AGITATION: action; activation; activity; actuation; ado; affection; alarm; annoyance; anxiety; ardor; arousing; boiling; bother(ation); brew; brouhaha; calenture; change; commotion; conation; convulsion; craze; debate; delirium; desire; discomposure; disconcertion; disorder; distress; disturbance; dither; drive; ebullience; ebulliency; eddy; effervescence; emotion; energy; enthusiasm; eruption; excitement; fear; fever; fire; flurry; fluster; flutter; foam; foment(ation); fret; frustration; hate (mongering); hurry; impetuosity; incitement; intensity; instigation; irksomeness; irritation; jac(ti)tation; jar; jerk; jog; jolt; motion; movement; nervousness; orgasm; passion; perplexity; perturbation; precipitation; pyrexia; quake; quiver; racket; rage; raging; revolt; ripple; rush; seething; shake; shaking; stew; stimulation; stir(ring); swirl(ing); to-do; tremor; trouble; tumult; turbulence; turmoil; upheaval; uproar; vexation; vibration; AGITATOR: activator; actuator; agent; alarmer; arouser; catalyst; disturber; driver; firebrand; hatemonger; hothead; hotspur; incendiary; instigator; mixer; mover; prompter; provocateur; rabble-rouser; stimulator; troublemaker

AGNOSTIC: see "unbeliever"

AGO: after; agone; ancient; antiquated; before; buried; bygone; ci-devant; dead; distant; earlier; elapsed; eld; ended; erewhile; erst(while); ex; extinct; first; foregoing; former(ly); gone; heretofore; historical; obsolete; old(er); once; onetime; outmoded; over; passé; past; preceding; prior; quondam; since; sometime; spent; syne; then; through; up; whilom; yesteryear; yore

AGOG: (see "eager") afire; agitated; anticipative; ardent; enthusiastic; excited; inflamed; intense; roused; stirred; zealous

AGONIZE: ache; bear; contort; harrow; hurt; pain; rack; squirm; strain; suffer; torment; torture; twist; writhe; AGONIZING: see "painful"; AGONY: ache; affliction; *angoisse*; anguish; anxiety; calamity; convulsion; desolation; distress; dolor; excruciation; grief; heartache; hell; hurt; misery; misfortune; outburst; pain; pang; panic; penury; privation; purgatory; rack; squirm; stitch; struggle; suffering; throe; torment; torture; travail; trial; tribulation; twist; unhappiness; woe; writhe; writhing

AGREE: abide; accede; accept; accord; acquiesce; admit; allow; approve; arrange; assent; assure; certify; chime; click; coincide; combine; compare; complement; comply; compound; concert; concord; concur; conform; conjoin; consent; contract; cooperate; correlate; correspond; endorse; equal; equate; fit; fix; give; grant; harmonize; homologate; jibe; join; match; meet; overlap; parallel; quadrate; reciprocate; square; subscribe; symbolize; synchronize; syncretize; tally; unite; yield; AGREEABLE: accessible; accommodating; adaptable; affable; affirmative; agreeing; amiable; amicable; apolaustic; appetizing; charming; cheerful; choice; coinciding; companionable; compatible; complaisant; compliant; concordant; concurring; congruent; congruous; consentaneous; consentient; consistent; consonant; cooperating; cordial; correspondent; corresponding; delectable; delicate; disposed; dulcet; easy; engaging; favorable; fragrant; friendly; gay; gemütlich; good(-natured); gracious; gratifying; halcyon; harmonious; harmonizing; humorous; kind(ly); likely; obliging; palatable; plausible; pleasant; pleasing; popular; ready; resonant; quadrate; saccharine; sapid; satisfying; savory; seemly; sirupy; smiling; sociable; suave; sugary; suitable; sweet; sympathetic; synchronizing; syrupy; treacly; unisonal; unisonous; unobstinate; winsome; yielding; AGREEABLENESS: accessibility; acquiescence; adaptability; agreeability; amenity; amicability; amicableness; cheerfulness; compatibility; complaisance; concord(ance); concordancy; congeniality; delectation;

docility; gaiety; good-naturedness; goodwill; gratification; harmony; peace; pleasantness; pleasantry; sapidity; savoriness; suavity; suitability; sweetness; toleration; tractability; unanimity; winsomeness; AGREEING: accordant; acquiescent; assentaneous; associated; conformable; consentaneous; consentient; constant; *d'accord*; *en rapport*; synchronous; unanimous; *una voce*; unopposed; AGREEMENT: acceptance; accession; accompaniment; accord(ance); accordancy; acquiescence; adherence; adjustment; admission; affirmation; affirmative; alliance; allowance; amen; amity; approval; arrangement; assent(ation); assonance; assurance; band; bargain; bloc; cartel; coincidence; coinstantaneity; combination; commensality; communion; compact; compliance; compromise; concert; concomitance; concord(ance); concordancy; concordat; confederation; conformance; conformity; congeniality; congruence; congruity; conjunction; consent(ation); consolidation; consonance; contemporaneity; contract; convention; correspondence; covenant; deal; endorsement; euphony; entente; fit; grant; harmony; nod; pact; peace; pledge; promise; rapport; rapprochement; settlement; simultaneity; solidarity; stipulation; subscription; suit; synchroneity; synchronicity; synchronism; synchronization; term(s); tranquility; transaction; treaty; tune; unanimity; understanding; union; unison; unit(y); yea; yielding

AGRESTIC: (see "rural") bucolic

AGRICULTURE: agronomics; agronomy; farming; geoponics; horticulture; husbandry; tillage

AHEAD: (see "modern") above; accelerated; advanced; advancing; afore; along; ante; antecedaneous; antecedent; anterior; avant; *avant-garde*; before; ci-devant; confronting; earlier; early; ere; facing; former(ly); forth; forward; frontline; initial; leading; on(ward); over; precedent; preceding; preliminary; premature; premundane; prevenient; previous(ly); prior; progressing; senior; sooner; united; upward; vanguard

AID: v. abet; accommodate; add; administer; adopt; advance; advantage; advise; advocate; alleviate; animate; appropriate; approve; assist; associate; assuage; attend; augment; avail; back; befriend; benefit; bestow; better; bless; bolster; boost; calm; challenge; cheer; coach; coact; coadjute; coddle; collaborate; combine; comfort;

concur; condole; console; conspire; contribute; cooperate; corroborate; counsel; countenance; cultivate; cure; defend; defy; delight; dispense; divert; doctor; dole; donate; ease; elevate; embolden; encourage; endorse; enliven; escort; espouse; esteem; exalt; exhilarate; expedite; expostulate; extend; extricate; facilitate; father; favor; feed; fight; fix; flatter; foment; fortify; forward; foster; further; give; gladden; goad; grant; gratify; handle; harbor; harden; hasten; hearten; heave; heighten; help; hoist; house; humor; impel; improve; incite; increase; induce; indulge; inspire; inspirit; instigate; intensify; invigorate; invite; lodge; maintain; mend; mother; nourish; nurse; nurture; oblige; pamper; patronize; plan; play; please; plot; plug; prefer; produce; profit; promote; prompt; prop; protect; provide; push; quicken; quiet(en); raise; rally; rear; recommend; reinforce; relieve; remedy; rescue; rouse; sanction; satisfy; save; second; serve; share; signal; solace; soothe; speed; sponsor; spur; squire; steel; stimulate; stir; strengthen; subsidize; succor; supplement; supply; support; sustain; teach; tend; train; tranquilize; treat; tutor; unite; uphold; urge; welcome; AID(E): **n.** (**see** "assistance," "assistant" and "associate") abettor; accessory; accommodation; adjuvant; adminicle; administration; administrator; advantage; advocate; alleviation; allocaton; alms; amount; ancillary; ante; appropriation; approval; appurtenance; assist; assuagement; attention; augmentation; backer; balm; behalf; benefit; blessing; boom; boost(er); *bras*; calm; cheer; coach; coadjutor; cohort; condescension; condolence; consideration; consolation; consort; contribution; contributor; convenience; delight; dispensation; diversion; dole; donation; ease; encouragement; endorsement; endorser; escort; esteem; excitation; exhortation; facilitation; favor; fomentation; fortification; friend; furtherance; gift; goodwill; grace; gratification; hand; handmaid(en); help(er); helping (hand); incentive; inducement; indulgence; inspiration; instigation; interest; invitation; kindness; largesse; mediator; medication; meditation; minister; ministration; money; nerve; odds; partiality; participation; partnership; patronage; pay(ment); pledge; pony; preference; present; privilege; promoter; promotion; protection; quest; raise; recommendation; relaxation; relief; repose; rescue(r); resort; rest; sanction; satisfaction; second; secours; server; share; signal; sponsor(ship); stimulation; strength; subsidiary; subsidy; succor; support(er); sustenance; teacher; tutor;

welcome; welfare; AIDING: abetting; accessorial; accessory; adjuvant; adminicular; approbatory; assisting; auspicious; auxiliary; benevolent; contributory; encouraging; exhortative; exhortatory; favoring; fostering; helpful; helping; hortative; hortatory; inspirational; inspiring; inviting; ministrant; nursing; persuasive; propitious; protreptic (al); psychagogic; rescuing; sanctionative; serving; subsidiary; supplemental; supplementary; supporting; upholding

AIL: affect; afflict; decline; fail; falter; pain; pine; suffer; trouble; AILMENT: (**see** "disease") discomfort; trouble; uneasiness; unrest; AILING: (**see** "sick") unwell

AIM: **v.** (**see** "intend") aspire; assay; conceive; concept; covet; design; desire; determine; diagram; direct; dream; endeavor; essay; hold; hope; hunger; level; long; pant; pine; plan; plot; point; propose; purpose; seek; signify; soar; thirst; thrive; tower; wish; yearn; AIM: **n.** ambition; aspiration; bearing; bent; cause; choice; concept(ion); consideration; course; current; design; desire; destination; determinant; determination; diagram; direction; directive; doom; dream; drift; dynamics; education; effectiveness; end; endeavor; essay; fate; fillip; force; goal; ground(s); guidance; hope; horizon; idea(l); incentive; incitement; inclination; indication; instruction; intendment; intent(ion); lot; manner; mark; Mecca; motive; object(ive); order; path; philosophy; plan; plot; point; port; prescription; prospect; purpose; reason; role; scheme; significance; sphere; star; stream; tendency; tenor; terminal; termination; terminus; thirst; thought; training; try; use; view-(point); want; way; will; wish

AIMLESS: arrant; capricious; casual; chancy; chaotic; desultory; driftless; dysteleological; empty; erratic; erring; feckless; fickle; fitful; floating; foolish; goalless; haphazard; hit-or-miss; idle; inconstant; indefinite; indirect; indiscriminate; intentionless; intentless; irregular; lax; loose; maundering; meandering; meaningless; objectless; prodigal; purportless; purposeless; rambling; random; senseless; shifting; stochastic; stray; tumultuary; unaimed; undirected; undisciplined; unintended; unintentional; unpremeditated; unpurposed; unpurposeful; vagrant; wandering; wavering; wild

AIR: **v.** advertise; aerate; bare; broach; broadcast; debunk; declare; demonstrate;

denounce; denunciate; diffuse; disclose; display; disseminate; dramatize; evince; exercise; exhibit; explain; expose; flaunt; illustrate; manifest; offer; open; parade; picture; present; promote; publicize; radiate; represent; reveal; say; scatter; show; spread; stage; state; strew; televise; tell; uncover; unmask; unveil; utter; vent(ilate); voice; wear; AIR(S): **n.** act(ion); address; affectation; affectedness; aim; amyl; angle; appearance; approach; artificiality; aspect; atmosphere; attitude; attitudinization; aura; bearing; behavior; bias; blast; bluster; breeding; breeze; cachet; carriage; ceremony; character; color(ation); comportment; conduct; countenance; course; courtesy; culture; current; custom; decorum; deed; demeanor; deportment; direction; discipline; disposition; disturbance; eccentricity; effect; empyrean; environment; ergasia; essence; ester; ether; ethics; etiquette; exposure; expression; face; facet; facies; fashion; feature; feeling; flow; foible; formality; frill; front; gait; gale; grace; guise; gust; habit(us); heaven(s); idiosyncrasy; inclination; influence; look; manner(ism); means; melody; mien; mode; mood; motion; nature; nimbus; odor; ostent; ozone; pattern; peculiarity; phase; physiognomy; physique; pirr; poise; politeness; port; pose; position; posture; preciseness; precision; presence; pretense; pretension; propriety; publicity; quirk; radio; refinement; *savoir faire*; semblance; shape; showiness; significance; singularity; situation; sky; song; space; spirit; stage; stamp; stance; stand; stir; style; suavity; substance; superficies; tact; taste; television; temper; tempest; theatricality; tradition; tune; urbanity; vanity; ventilation; view (point); visage; walk; way; welkin; whimsicality; wind; zephyr; AIRING: see "disclosure"; AIRY: aerial; aery; affected; airified; airlike; animated; atmospheric; attenuated; birdlike; blithe(some); breezy; buoyant; celestial; cloud-built; cobwebby; dainty; debonair; delicate; diaphanous; disembodied; empty; empyreal; empyrean; ethereal; etheric; exquisite; fairy; fastidious; fine; flimsy; flippant; foamy; fragile; frivolous; frolicsome; frothy; gauzy; gossamer(y); graceful; heavenly; imaginary; immaterial; impalpable; imperceptible; incorporeal; insubstantial; intangible; lazy; light; misty; rare (fied); refined; riant; shadowy; shallow; sheer; soft; spiritual; sprightly; springy; superfine; supernal; tenuous; thin(ly); trifling; trivial; unpalpable; unreal; unsubstantial; urbane; vague; visionary; vivacious; zephyrean; zephyrous; AIRINESS: aereality; attenuation; blithesomeness; breeziness;

buoyancy; delicacy; diaphaneity; ethereality; etherealness; froth(iness); gauziness; immateriality; impalpability; incorporeality; incorporeity; insubstantiality; intangibility; loftiness; mistiness; spirituality; sprightliness; springiness; superficiality; tenuity; tenuousness; unsubstantiality; vivacity

AISLE: aisleway; alley; lane; passage(way); walk(way); way

AKIN: (**see** "alike") affiliated; agnate; agnatic; allied; analogous; cognate; colateral; compatible; congeneric; consanguineous; fraternal; germane; kin(dred); like; near; propinquitous; related; similar; sympathetic; synonymic; synonymous

ALACRITY: activity; acuteness; agility; alertness; animation; awareness; briskness; celerity; eagerness; energy; excitement; expedition; haste; hastiness; keenness; liveliness; nimbleness; perception; pertness; promptitude; promptness; quickness; rapidity; readiness; suddenness; swiftness; urgency; vigor; vivacity; zealousy; zest

ALARM: **v.** (**see** "daunt") affright; agitate; alert; appal(l); arouse; awaken; awe; disconcert; dismay; disquiet; disturb; electrify; excite; frighten; horrify; intimidate; overawe; panic; perturb(ate); petrify; rattle; rouse; scare; shock; startle; stir; surprise; terrorize; threaten; unnerve; upset; waken; warn; ALARM: **n.** affright; agitation; alert(ness); amazement; angst; anxiety; apprehension; arousal; awe; bell; *bête noir*; bogey; bugaboo; buzzer; call; clock; consternation; cowardice; din; dismay; distraction; disturbance; dread(fulness); exasperation; excitement; fear(fulness); fright; gong; horror; knell; larum; misgiving; noise; notice; panic; peril; perturbation; petrification; reverence; ring; scare; signal; siren; S.O.S.; surprise; terror; threat; timidity; tocsin; tremor; trepidation; trepidity; warning; wonder; ALARMING: **see** "fearful" and "frightful"

ALCOHOL: *aqua vitae;* ardent spirits; bottle; drink(s); ethanol; ethyl (hydroxide); gin; hard liquor; liquor; rum; spirituous liquors; stimulant; whiskey; ALCOHOLIC: **a.** intoxicating; liquorish; liquorous; liquory; spiritous; vinic; vinous; ALCOHOLIC: **n.** (**see** "drunkard") alcoholist; bacchanalian; bacchante; dipsomaniac; dram-drinker; oenophilist; winebibber; wino; ALCOHOLISM: bibacity; bibation; bibulosity; crapulence; dipsomania; ebriosity;

inebriation; inebriety; insobriety; intemperance; oenophlygia; temulence; winebibbing

ALERT: **v.** (**see** "warn") arouse; waken; ALERT: **a.** (**see** "diligent") active; acute; agile; agog; alive; appreciative; aroused; arrect; astir; attentive; awake; aware; brisk; bristling; careful; circumspect; conscious; considerate; considerative; dapper; eager; excited; exhilarated; gay; guarded; heads-up; heedful; judicious; keen; knowing; lively; moving; nimble; observant; perceptive; percipient; pert; prepared; prompt; quick(witted); ready; resourceful; roused; sharp; stirred; stirring; sudden; swift; vigilant; wary; watchful; wide-awake; zealous; ALERT: **n. see** "alarm"; ALERTNESS: **see** "alacrity" and "heedfulness"

ALIAS: allonym; epithet; hypocorism; hypocoristic; Lucy Stoner; name; *nom de guerre*; *nom de plume*; other; pen name; pet name; pseudandry; pseudogyny; pseudonym

ALIBI: (**see** "excuse") apology

ALIEN: **a.** (**see** "foreign") adventitious; adverse; conflicting; contradictory; different; distant; estranged; external; extraneous; extrinsic; forane; foreign-born; hostile; impertinent; inapplicable; inappropriate; inconsistent; irregular; irrelevant; nonnative; opposed; outside; peregrinate; peregrine; Philistine; Philistinic; remote; removed; repugnant; strange; ultramontane; ultramundane; unconnected; unfamiliar; unknown; unlike; unsympathetic; ALIEN: **n.** auslander; emigre; exoteric; foreign-born; foreigner; gringo; heathen; immigrant; invader; nonnative; nonresident; outlander; outsider; peregrine; Philistine; stranger; tramontane; ultramontane; ALIENATE: **see** "divide"

ALIGN: adjust; allineate; arrange; array; collimate; coordinate; dress; fix; focus; hierarchize; line; position; range; regiment; rig; set; square; straighten; true; ALIGNMENT: adjustment; allineation; arrangement; array; collimation; coordination; fixation; focus; hierarchization; plan; position(ing); range; regimentation; view

ALIKE: (**see** "akin" and "equivalent") analogical; analogous; comparable; congruent; congruous; consimilar; corresponding; duplicate; equal; equivalent; homogeneous; homologous; homonymous; identic(al); kin(dred); like; parallel; reciprocal; resembling; same; semblable; similar; synonymous; twin;

undistinguishable; uniform; unisonant; unisonous; ALIKENESS: **see** "uniformity"

ALIMENT: **see** "food"

ALIVE: above-ground; active; advised; affected; agile; alert; animate(d); apprehensive; apprised; astir; athletic; awake; aware; breathing; brisk; bustling; busy; certain; cognizant; concerned; conscient; conscious; effective; energetic; existent; existing; felt; fresh; glowing; green; informed; keen; knowing; live(ly); living; perceiving; perceptive; perspicacious; pullulant; pulsating; quick; rational; recognizing; sensible; sentient; spirited; spry; stirring; subsisting; sure; teeming thronged; unperished; vibrant; viral; virile; vital; vivacious

ALL: aggregate; alone; any; complete; each; entire; every(body); everyone; everything; full(y); greatest; gross; lion's share; plenary; quite; sum; thorough; together; total(ity); toto; unabridged; uncut; undivided; unexpurgated; whole(hog); wholly

ALLAY: (**see** "alleviate" and "appease") alloy; calm; check; diminish; ease; lull; pacify; qualify; quell; quench; settle; stay; still; weaken

ALLEGE: (**see** "maintain") advance; affirm; assert; asseverate; assure; attest; aver; avow; cite; claim; declare; depone; depose; feign; offer; plead; pretend; profess; recite; say; state; swear; testify; witness; ALLEGED: (**see** "supposed") assumed; pretended; unproved; ALLEGATION: **see** "statement"

ALLEGIANCE: (**see** "fidelity") constancy; constantness; devotion; duty; faith(fulness); fealty; homage; honor; humility; loyalness; loyalty; oath; obedience; obligation; respect; sta(u)nchness; steadfastness; tenacity

ALLEGORY: apologue; emblem; fable; legend; metaphor; myth; parable; simile; similitude; symbolization; tale

ALLEVIATE: (**see** "ease") abate; allay; appease; assuage; calm; comfort; compose; conciliate; console; cool; correct; cure; diminish; fix; help; lay; lessen; lighten; loosen; medicate; mitigate; moderate; modify; mollify; pacify; palliate; plaster; qualify; quench; quiet(en); relieve; remedy; remove; repair; slake; soften; soothe; still; temper; treat; weaken; ALLEVIATION: (**see** "ease") abatement; appeasement; assuagement; calm; comfort; composure;

consolation; correction; cure; diminishment; help; lessening; letup; lightening; loosening; medication; mitigation; moderation; modification; mollification; pacification; palliation; quiet(ness); quietude; relief; remedy; removal; repair; softening; solace; soothing; tempering; treatment

ALLIANCE: (see "association") accord; agreement; axis; band; body; bond; bund; coalescence; coalition; compact; company; confederacy; confederation; connection; consociation; consortion; contract; entente; federation; fusion; group; league; monopolization; monopoly; pact; partnership; party; society; treaty; understanding; undertaking; union

ALLIED: agnate; akin; analogous; ancillary; associated; coalesced; cognate; collateral; concomitant; concurrent; confederated; connatural; connected; federated; fused; grouped; inborn; inherent; joined; kin(dred); leagued; linked; one; parallel; related; secondary; similar; subordinated; subsidiary; tangential; unalienated; united

ALLNESS: completeness; entireness; entirety; omneity; omnitude; totality; unanimity; universality; wholeness

ALLOCATE or ALLOT: (see "distribute") allow; appoint; apportion; appropriate; assign; authorize; award; bestow; cut; deal; designate; direct; dispose; divide; dole; earmark; give; grant; impart; limit; measure; mete; ordain; parcel; partition; prescribe; rate; ration; regulate; set; share; slice; split; ALLOCATION or ALLOTMENT: see "distribution"

ALLOW: abide; accede; accept; accord; acknowledge; acquiesce; acquire; admit; agree; allot; apportion; approbate; appropriate; approve; assent; assign; authorize; bear; bide; charter; commission; comply; concede; concur; confer; confess; consent; cooperate; countenance; credit; defer; dispense; dole; empower; endorse; endure; entitle; favor; franchise; free; give; grant; have; hear; indulge; leave; legalize; lend; let; license; loan; ordain; order; pass; patent; permit; portion; provide; rate; ration; receive; recognize; sanction; set; share; stand; stomach; submit; suffer; tolerate; vouchsafe; warrant; yield; ALLOWED or ALLOWABLE: (see "permissive") acceptable; admissible; admissive; agreeable; authorized; bearable; dispensable; franchised; legal; legitimate; licensed; licit;

official; pardonable; permitted; sanctioned; tolerable; tolerated; unprohibited; ALLOWANCE: accord(ance); acknowledgment; acquiescence; admission; agreement; allotment; amen; amount; apportionment; approbation; approval; assent(ation); assignment; authorization; clearance; complement; compliance; concession; concurrence; confession; consent; cooperation; corroboration; countenance; deduction; deference; difference; dole; edge; emolument; franchise; freedom; gift; grant; honorarium; indulgence; license; loan; lulu; margin; mileage; odds; pass; permission; permit; perquisite; portion; privilege; provision; ratification; rating; ration; reception; recognition; reduction; sanction; share; size; solatium; stipend(ium); sufferance; sum; tare; tolerance; toleration; total; tret; unanimity; unison; warrant

ALLOY: see "mixture"; ALLOYED: amalgamated; base; mixed; moderated; spurious; tempered

ALLUDE: (see "hint") advert; chart; cite; concern; connote; denote; glance; imply; impute; indicate; insinuate; intimate; mention; name; point; refer; signify; suggest; touch; ALLUSION: (see "hint") complication; connotation; denotation; indication; inference; inkling; innuendo; insinuation; instance; intimation; reference

ALLURE: v. abduct; abstract; appeal; attract; bait; beckon; beg; beguile; bewitch; blandish; cajole; captivate; capture; charm; cheat; coax; decoy; delight; divert; dominate; draw; elicit; enamor; enchant; enrapture; enslave; ensorcel(l); enthral(l); entice; entrance; evoke; excite; extract; fascinate; flatter; gather; glamorize; incite; induce; infatuate; influence; infuse; ingratiate; instigate; inveigle; invite; lead; lure; magnetize; manipulate; mesmerize; move; overpower; permeate; persuade; please; prompt; provoke; pull; rouse; seduce; solicit; stimulate; subdue; sway; take; tantalize; tease; tempt; thrill; tole; tow; transfix; transport; trap; trick; tug; wheedle; wile; win; witch; woo; ALLURE(MENT): n. appeal; attraction; bait; beauty; beckon(ing); beguilement; bewitchingness; bewitchment; blandishment(s); cajole(ry); cajolement; captivation; charm; comeliness; come-on; conjuration; decoy; delight; diversion; enamor; ensorcelment; enticement; fascination; flattery; glamor; gramary(e); incantation; incitement; inducement; influence; instigation; inveiglement; invitation; lure; magic; mesmeration;

mesmerism; persuasion; power; provocation; seduction; siren; solicitation; song; sorcery; sortilege; spell; stimulation; temptation; transfixion; trap; trickery; wile; witchcraft; witchery; ALLURING: adorable; arresting; attractive; beckoning; beguiling; beautiful; bewitching; cajoling; captivating; catching; catchy; charming; Circean; coaxing; contagious; enticing; entrancing; fascinating; flattering; flavorful; florid; inciting; infectious; influential; instigative; inveigling; inviting; leading; liking; mesmeric; mesmerizing; personable; persuasive; prompting; provocative; seductive; sirenic(al); soliciting; stimulating; stimulative; suasive; taking; tantalizing; teasing; tempting; voluptuous; winning; wooing

ALLUSION: **see** under "allude"

ALLY: **v.** associate; confederate; connect; join; league; relate; unite; ALLY: **n.** (**see** "assistant") associate; auxiliary; backer; confederate; supporter

ALMIGHTY: all-powerful; authoritarian; autocrat; dictatorial; extreme(ly); great; Herculean; heroic; multipotent; omnipotent; plutocratic; powerful; puissant; strong; titanic; tyrannical; tyrannous

ALMOST: about; anear; approaching; approximate(ly); circa; close; greater; near(ly); nigh; nominal; quasi; roughly; semi; well-nigh

ALMS: (**see** "charity") benefaction; bounty; dole; donation; gift; grant; gratuity

ALOFT: (**see** "above") heavenward; high; overhead; skyward; up(ward)

ALONE: (**see** "exclusive") abandoned; aloof; apart; away; bypassed; derelict; desolate; detached; enisled; exclusive(ly); extinctive; forlorn; forsaken; Godforsaken; incomparable; individual; isolated; kinless; left; lone(ly); lonesome; lorn; lost; marooned; odd; one; only; particular; *per se*; rejected; renounced; scrapped; segregated; separate(d); sequestered; simple; single; sole; solitary; solo; solus; stag; unaccompanied; unaided; unapproached; unattended; unbefriended; unchaperoned; uncompanied; uncompanioned; unhelped; uninhabited; unique; untended; unvisited

ALONGSIDE: abutting; accompanied; attingent; contiguous; juxtaposed; juxtapositioned; tangent

ALOOF: (**see** "detached") alone; apart; apathetic; bashful; cautious; chary; circumspect; cloistered; cold; cool; coy; delitescent; demure; detached; distant; egocentric; exclusive; frosty; gelid; haughty; icy; impersonal; incommunicative; indifferent; indrawn; isolated; kept; modest; moodish; off(ish); only; proud; remote; removed; reserved; restrained; retarded; reticent; retiring; secluded; secretive; segregated; sequestered; shy; silent; standoffish; stately; taciturn; timid; unapproachable; uncommunicative; uncordial; undemonstrative; unemotional; unfriendly; uninvolved; unsociable; withdrawn; ALOOFNESS: **see** "detachment"

ALOUD: *à haut voix*; audible; distinct; vocal

ALPHABETICAL: **see** "consecutive"

ALSO: additional; and; as; besides; ditto; furthermore; likewise; plus; same; still; too; withal; yet

ALTAR: chancel; chantry; shrine

ALTER: abrogate; adapt; adjust; affect; agitate; alternate; amend; bend; blue-pencil; castrate; change; color; commutate; commute; condition; convert; correct; cut; decrease; deflect; deform; detour; deviate; distort; disturb; diversify; divert; edit; emasculate; emend; fashion; hedge; improve; increase; influence; lessen; limit; lower; main; manipulate; master; metamorphose; metastasize; moderate; modify; modulate; move; mutate; mutilate; overhaul; patch; qualify; rearrange; reconsider; rectify; redact; redo; reduce; reexamine; refashion; reform; remodel; renew; renovate; reorganize; repair; reshape; restore; reverse; revise; reword; rewrite; shape; shift; soften; spay; swerve; tamper; temper; tinge; transfigure; transform; transmogrify; transmute; trim; truncate; turn; twist; vary; veer; wheel; ALTERED: **see** "varied"; ALTERATION: adaptation; adjustment; amendment; castration; change; commutation; conditioning; conversion; correction; deformation; detour; deviation; distortion; disturbance; diversification; diversion; emasculation; emendation; emendment; improvement; influence; manipulation; mayhem; metamorphosis; metastasis; modification; modulation; movement; mutation; mutilation; overhaul; permutation; qualification; rearrangement; reciprocity; rectification; redaction; reduction; reformation; remodeling; renewal; renovation; reorganization; repair; restoration; reversal; revise; revision; rewording; shaping; shift; swerve; transfiguration; transformation; transmogrification; transmutation; turn; twist; variation; ALTERABLE: **see** "unstable" and "variable"

ALTERCATE: (**see** "quarrel") argue; bicker; brawl; caterwaul; cavil; clash; complain; contend; debate; disagree; dispute; dissent; feud; fight; fuss; jangle; row; rupture; scrap; spat; squabble; strive; struggle; tiff; tussle; wrangle; ALTERCATION: **see** "quarrel"

ALTERNATE: **v.** alter; change; counter (change); deviate; fluctuate; interchange; intermit; jump; oscillate; reciprocate; recur; rotate; shift; shuffle; stagger; stir; substitute; sway; swerve; swing; transfer; transpose; vary; waver; ALTERNATE: **n.** or ALTERNATION: alterance; alternant; alternative; backup; choice; detour; deviation; either; election; fluctuation; fork(ing); horns of a dilemma; interchange; intermission; option; oscillation; preference; reposition; second; shift; substitute; swerve; transfer; transposition; understudy; variance

ALTHOUGH: albeit; all told; e'en; even; notwithstanding; whereas; while

ALTOGETHER: all; collectively; completely; directly; *en banc*; *en bloc*; *en masse*; entire(ly); *entout*; ever(lasting); *in toto*; nude; pointblank; quite; thorough; unanimous(ly); whole; wholly

ALTRUISM: **see** "unselfishness"

ALWAYS: *ab aeterno*; *ad infinitum*; anyhow; aye; ceaseless(ly); constant(ly); e'er; endless; eternal(ly); ever(lasting); evermore; forever; habitually; *in adfinitum*; *in aeternum*; incessant(ly); in perpetuity; *in perpetuum*; *in saecula saeculorum*; invariable; invariably; lasting; perpetual(ly); unceasing(ly); uniform(ly)

AMALGAMATE: (**see** "combine") absorb; amalgamize; annex; blend; coalesce; compress; conjoin; fuse; integrate; intermarry; join; marry; merge; mingle; mix; pool; unite; AMALGAMATION: absorption; amalgam; annexation; blend; combination; conjunction; fusion; incorporation; integration; intermarriage; joint; marriage; merger; mingling; mix(ture); pool; union

AMASS: **see** "accumulate"

AMATEUR: (**see** "beginner") admirer; ap-

prentice; candidate; dabbler; devotee; dilettante; disciple; ham; initiate; layman; learner; neophyte; neoteric; nonprofessional; novice; novitiate; postulant; probationer; pupil; recruit; scholar; student; trainee; tyro; volunteer; votary; AMATEURISH: amateur; crude; dilettantish; elementary; incomplete; nonprofessional; primitive; rudimentary; undeveloped; unprofessional

AMATIVE or AMATORY: affectionate; amorous; anacreontic; ardent; brotherly; doting; enamored; erotic; fervent; fervid; fond; impassioned; indulgent; loving; motherly; overindulgent; passionate; sisterly; tender; warm

AMAZE: affect; affright; alarm; astonish; astound; awe; benumb; bewilder; confound; confuse; consternate; daze; dazzle; dumbfound; excite; flabbergast; frighten; impress; overwhelm; paralyze; perplex; rock; shock; stagger; startle; strike; stun; stupefy; surprise; AMAZEMENT: admiration; alarm; astonishment; astoundment; awe; bewilderment; confusion; consternation; dazzlement; dismay; fright; paralysis; perplexity; perturbation; petrification; shock; stupefaction; surprise; terror; wonder; AMAZING: (**see** "strange") alarming; astonishing; astounding; awesome; bewildered; confused; dumbfounded; exciting; extraordinary; flabbergasting; frightened; impressed; incredible; ineffable; goggle-eyed; marvelous; monstrous; paralyzed; petrifying; portentous; preposterous; prodigious; spectacular; staggering; stunning; stupendous; surprising; unlookedfor; wonderful; wondrous

AMBASSADOR: ablegate; agent; ambassadress; commissioner; deputy; diplomat; envoy; legate; messenger; minister; nuncio; plenipotentiary; representative; viceroy

AMBIDEXTROUS: **see** "versatile"

AMBIGUOUS: ambivalent; amphibolic; amphibologic(al); antonymous; aoristic; confused; contradictous; contradictive; contradictory; cryptic(al); dark; Delphian; Delphic; desultory; double-edged; doubtful; dubious; enigmatic(al); equivocal; erratic; evasive; hazy; homonymous; imprecise; incomparable; inconclusive; inconsistent; indefinite; infinitive; indeterminable; inexplicit; inscrutable; involved; lax; loose; mysterious; nebulous; obscure; opposite; paradoxical; perplexing; problematic(al); questionable; rambling; random; schizoid; sibylline; slippery; suspicious; uncertain; unclear;

undecided; undefined; unintelligible; vague; wavering; weasel-worded; AMBIGUITY: ambiguousness; ambivalence; amphibology; contradiction; double entendre; *double entente*; doubt; dubiosity; enigma; equivocality; equivocalness; incompatibility; inconsistency; inexplicitness; obscurity; paradox; uncertainty; vagueness

AMBIT: area; bounds; caliber; circuit; circumference; compass; comprehensiveness; course; degree; dimension; distance; extent; gauge; influence; intensity; jurisdiction; length; level; limit(s); magnitude; measure; precinct(s); proportion; range; reach; scope; size; space; span; sphere; sweep; thickness

AMBITION: aim; ardency; aspiration; ate; boldness; craving; desire; eagerness; energy; goal; hope; incentive; initiative; intendment; intention; longing; midnight oil; objective; overactivity; overanxiety; philosophy; pretention; purpose; rapacity; scope; solicitude; span; supererogation; thirst; yearning; AMBITIOUS: ardent; aspirant; aspiring; avid; bold; covetous; craving; desirous; eager; elaborate; emulative; emulous; energetic; extensive; fervent; high; hopeful; impetuous; intent; keen; overactive; overanxious; panting; pretentious; rapacious; sedulous; showy; solicitous; striving; thirsty; yearning

AMBLE: see "saunter"

AMBUSH: (see "snare") dry-gulch; lure; waylay

AMELIORATE: abate; adjust; advance; aid; amend; assuage; atone; bate; better; change; cleanse; correct; doctor; ease; emend; enlarge; fix; help; improve; lessen; medicate; mend; mollify; nurse; optionalize; palliate; promote; purify; rectify; reform; relieve; repair; restore; revise; temper

AMEN: assuredly; certainly; surely; truly; verily; yea; yes

AMENABLE: (see "pliable") and "pliant") accountable; addicted; addictive; agreeable; answerable; apt; arranged; biddable; coercive; complacent; compliant; conciliable; congenial; controllable; docile; dutiful; faithful; favorable; inclinable; inclinatory; inclined; liable; loyal; malleable; meek; obedient(ial); obeisant; obsequious; open; passive; prone; propendent; propense; ready; receptive; reconcilable; resigned; respectful;

set; sheeplike; suasive; subject; submissive; subservient; tame; tending; tractable; truckling; willing; yielding

AMEND: (see "ameliorate") adjust; atone; better; change; cleanse; correct; doctor; edit; enlarge; expiate; fix; improve; medicate; mend; mitigate; modify; patch; purify; reclaim; rectify; redress; reform; repair; revise

AMENDS: apology; atonement; compensation; expiation; penance; recompense; reconciliation; redress; repatriation; reward

AMENITY: agreeableness; amity; attractiveness; comforts; conveniences; conventionality; diplomacy; ease; geniality; joy; mildness; oiliness; pleasantness; policy; politeness; propriety; smoothness; suavity; unctuosity; urbanity

AMIABLE: (see "agreeable") amenable; amicable; amical; attractive; beneficent; benign(ant); charming; civil(ized); complaisant; congenial; cordial; courteous; easy; engaging; enjoyable; friendly; frictionless; genial; gentle; good-humored; good-natured; gracious; hospitable; indulgent; joyful; joyous; kind(ly); loving; mild; neighborly; obliging; pleasant; pleasurable; praiseworthy; smooth; sociable; suave; sweet; tender; unantagonistic; unctuous; urbane; warm; well-intentioned; winning; winsome; AMIABLENESS: see "amity" and "friendliness"

AMICABLE: (see "amiable") benign; friendly; unhostile

AMISS: (see "wrong") awry; erroneous; faulty; imperfect; improper; inaccurate; incorrect; indecorous; reprehensible; uncalled-for

AMITY: accord; aggreeableness; amenity; amiability; amiableness; cheer(fulness); docility; friendliness; friendship; goodwill; harmony; peace; pleasantness; pleasantry; suavity; suitability; sweetness; toleration; tractability; unanimity; unantagonism

AMMUNITION: ammo; arms; bombs; bullets; defense; explosives; matériel; munitions; ordnance; powder; power; resources; shells; shrapnel; weaponry

AMORAL: see "immoral"

AMOROUS: (see "amative") affectionate; enamored; fond; loving

AMORPHOUS: airy; chaotic; fluid; formless; heterogeneous; immaterial; inchoate; incorporeal; irregular; liquid; nebulous; shapeless; spiritual; unclassified; uncrystallized; unshaped; vague

AMOUNT: (see "bit") addition; aggregate; allotment; allowance; amplitude; apportion(ment); atom; bale; bindle; bole; bulk; bunch; bundle; capacity; catch; collection; compass; complement; cost; cubage; cut; degree; denomination; dimension(s); dividend; division; dole; dosage; dose; dower(y); draft; draught; due; entirety; equivalent; excerpt; extent; figure; formula; fraction; fragment; grain; harvest; helping; inheritance; intensity; kilo(gram); kind; lot; loudness; lump; magnitude; mass; money; morsel; number; ounce; pack(age); packet; parcel; part(icle); percent(age); percentum; piece; portion; potion; pound; prescription; price; purse; quanta (pl.); quantity; quantum; quota; quotient; ration; recapitulation; recipe; result(s); roll; sample; scrap; section; segment; selection; serving; share; sheaf; shot; side; size; slice; solidity; some; space; split; stipend; strength; substance; sum(mation); supply; task; ton; total (ity); tune; unit; vastity; vastness; volume; wad; wedge; whack; whole; worth; yield

AMPLE: abounding; abundant; affluent; aplenty; baronial; big; boundless; bounteous; bountiful; broad; buxom; capacious; cavernous; comfortable; commodious; comprehensible; copious; cornucopian; elaborate; enough; exhaustless; expansive; extensive; exuberant; fat; full; generous; good; great; hearty; hefty; huge; inexhaustible; large; lavish; liberal; lush; luxuriant; magnitudinous; measureless; much; opulent; overflowing; plenteous; plentiful; plentitudinous; plenty; plethoric; portly; profuse; prolific; prolix; rangy; replete; rich; rife; roomy; scopious; spacious; sufficient; suitable; sumptuous; teeming; uncrowded; vast; voluble; voluminous; wide; AMPLITUDE: see "abundance," "plenty" and "riches"

AMPLIFY: amass; augment; boom; broaden; compound; deepen; develop; dilate; distend; double; elongate; embellish; enlarge; escalate; exacerbate; exaggerate; expand; expatiate; explain; extend; fatten; gain; grow; heighten; hypertrophy; increase; inflate; intensify; jump; lengthen; magnify; maximize; mount; multiply; pad; pile; produce; promote; propagate; pullulate; pyramid; raise; recruit; rise; snowball; soar; speed; steepen; strengthen; stretch;

support; swell; triple; tumefy; tumesce; unfold; up; wax; widen

AMPUTATE: cut; excise; lob; lop; prune; truncate

AMULET: charm; fetish; grigri; periapt; phylactery; relic; symbol; talisman; token

AMUSE: beguile; charm; cheer; delight; disport; distract; divert; entertain; exhilarate; gratify; occupy; play; please; recreate; regale; sport; toy; tittivate; AMUSEMENT: beguilement; carnival; charm; cheer; delight; distraction; diversion; divertissement; enjoyment; entertainment; exhilaration; facetiosity; feast; festival; fiesta; frolic; fun; gaiety; game; glee; gratification; jest; joviality; laughter; merriment; merrymaking; mirth; occupation; picnic; play; pleasantry; pleasure; program; recreation; relaxation; relief; show; sport; tittivation; treat; AMUSING: amusive; antic; charming; clever; clownish; comic(al); delightful; distracting; diverting; divertive; droll; entertaining; exhilarative; facetious; fanciful; farcical; funny; gleeful; good; gratifying; humorous; impish; jocose; jocular; laughable; ludicrous; merry; mirthful; odd; queer; recreative; rich; risible; smart; tittivating; waggish; whimsical; witty; zany

ANALGESIC: see "anodyne"

ANALOGOUS: akin; alike; allied; cognate; commensurate; comparable; comparative; corresponding; equiponderant; equivalent; homeopathic; homogeneous; homologous; like; parallel; proportionate; related; same; similar; synonymous; uniform; ANALOGY: (see "likeness") collation; commensurability; contrast; correspondence; equivalence; homogeneity; parallelism; similarity; simulacra (pl.); simulacrum

ANALYZE: anatomize; answer; ascertain; assay; audit; break (down); catechize; clarify; clear; collate; comb; compare; consider; decide; decipher; decrypt; detect; determine; diagnose; diagnosticate; discover; discriminate; dissect; dissolve; divide; evaluate; examine; explain; explore; figure; identify; inquire; inspect; interpret; investigate; measure; observe; parse; part; perceive; probe; prove; pry; pursue; question; quiz; reduce; resolve; review; scan; scrutinize; search; separate; settle; sift; solve; study; test; titrate; undo; unfold; unravel; verify; weigh; work; ANALYTIC(AL): analogous; approximate; clarifying; clinical; collative;

determinative; exegetic(al); expositive; expository; interpretative; investigative; metaphorical; near; parallel; relative; tautological; tautologous; ANALYSIS: anatomy; ascertainment; assay; audit; autopsy; breakdown; catechism; clarification; close reading; collation; consideraton; critique; determination; dissection; dissolution; equating; equation; evaluation; examination; exegesis; exploration; exposition; inquiry; inspection; interpretation; investigation; likeness; measurement; metaphor; model; observation; parallel(ism); partition; perception; probe; proofreading; pursuit; question; quiz; reduction; review; scrutiny; search; separation; sifting; solution; study; synopsis; test; titration; trial; verification

ANARCHY: anarchism; chaos; confusion; disorder(liness); lawlessness; license; misgovernment; misrule; mutiny; revolt; riot; turbulency

ANATHEMATIZE: **see** "curse" and "denounce"

ANATOMY: analysis; anthropotomy; body; bones; cadre; frame(work); outline; phytotomy; plan; remains; skeleton; structure; support

ANCESTOR(S): Adam; antecedent; ascendant; creator; elder; family; father; forebear(er); forefather; forerunner; genitor; house; line; parent; precursor; primogenitor; procreator; progenitor; progenitress (fem.); progenitrix (fem.); sire; stock; ANCESTRAL: ancestorial; atavic; atavistic; aval; avital; derivational; familial; genealogical; hereditary; household; patrimonial; primogenitive; progenitor; traditional; ANCESTRY: background; birth; blood; bloodline; breed; caste; class; consanguinity; degree; derivation; descent; development; extraction; family; genealogy; genesis; grade; history; line(age); kin(dred); kinship; nativity; order; paternity; pedigree; prestige; progeny; provenance; race; rank; sib; source; status; stemma; stock; strain; succession; tradition; tree

ANCHOR: **v. see** "secure"; ANCHOR: **n.** grapnel; hook; kedge; support; ANCHOR-AGE: dock; harbor(age); haven; inlet; location; marina; moorage; port; refuge; roadstead; sanctuary; sanctum; seaport

ANCHORITE: **see** "hermit"

ANCIENT: (**see** "old") aged; age-old; antediluvial; antediluvian; antemundane; antiquated; antique; archaic; archaistic; dated; decrepit; eld; hoary; immemorable; immemorial; monolithic; neanderthalian; old(en); old-fashioned; paleolithic; paleozoic; patriarch(ic)al; preadamite; prehistoric; primal; primeval; primitive; pristine; protohistoric; remote; venerable; ANCIENTNESS: antiquity; oldness; venerability

AND: (**see** "also") ampassy; ampersand; ipseand; Tironian sign

ANECDOTE: event; joke; narrative; sketch; story; tale; yarn

ANEMIC: ashen; ashy; bloodless; etiolated; faded; faint; feeble; languid; lifeless; listless; livid; low; lusterless; pale; pallid; sickly; wan; watery; ANEMIA: bloodlessness; emptiness; lifelessness

ANESTHETIC: **a.** analgesic; anodynic; callous; cold(-blooded); comatose; dull; emotionless; frozen; impiteous; incompassionate; indurate; indurative; insensate; insensitive; numb(ed); obdurate; obtuse; sentimentless; stoic(al); stolid; torpid; unaffectionate; uncompassionate; unemotional; unfeeling; unimpressible; unresponsive; unstirred; unsympathetic; unyielding; ANESTHETIC: **n. see** "anodyne"; ANESTHETIZE: **see** "deaden"

ANEW: **see** "afresh"

ANGELIC: admirable; ambrosiac; ambrosial; beatific; blessed; canonized; celestial; cherubic; deific; deiform; divine; empyrean; ethereal; godlike; godly; good; heaven-born; heavenly; holy; Olympian; otherworldly; pietistic; pious; religious; sacred; saintly; sanctified; seraphic; spiritual; sublime; superhuman; supermundane; supernal; transcendental; unearthly; unprofane; ANGEL: backer; celestial; cherub; Egregor; guardian; harbinger; messenger; seraph; spirit

ANGER: **v.** acerbate; afflict; aggravate; agitate; annoy; antagonize; arouse; chafe; contend; craze; disgust; displease; dissatisfy; disturb; embitter; enrage; envenom; exacerbate; exasperate; excite; flare (up); fluster; foam; fret; froth; frustrate; fume; gall; goad; heat; incense; inflame; infuriate; ire; irk; irritate; kindle; madden; miff; nettle; offend; peeve; pique; poison; provoke;

rage; rankle; rile; roil; scorn; smoke; sour; stir; storm; vex; ANGER: **n.** acharnement; acrimony; afflatus; aggravation; agitation; angriness; animosity; animus; annoyance; antagonism; asperity; aversion; bellicosity; belligerence; belligerency; bile; bitterness; chaos; choler; confusion; crankiness; dander; deliration; delirium; dementia; derangement; disapproval; discomposure; disgust; dislike; displeasure; dissatisfaction; distraction; dudgeon; ebullition; embitterment; enmity; enragement; erinys; evil; exacerbation; exasperation; fanaticism; ferocity; fierceness; fire; fit; flare; frenzy; fret; froth; fume; furor; fury; gall; gloom; gorge; grievance; grudge; hate; hatred; heat; hostility; huff (iness); ill humor; ill will; impetuosity; incense(ment); indignation; inflammation; irascibility; irascibleness; irateness; ire; irksomeness; irritation; madness; malice; malignancy; malignity; melancholy; nettling; offense; outburst; outrage; passion; perturbation; petulance; pique; prejudice; provocation; rage; rancor; rashness; resentment; savagery; scorn; spite(fulness); spleen; sting; temper; tiff; truculence; truculency; umbrage; unsatisfaction; vehemence; vexation; virulence; wrath; ANGRY or ANGERED: acrimonious; aggravated; aggrieved; agitated; antagonized; bedlam(ite); bellicose; belligerent; berserk; bilious; blazing; boiling; bubbling; burning; chafed; choleric; cranky; crazed; crazy; cross; demented; deranged; disordered; displeased; distracted; distraught; distressed; enraged; evil; exasperated; excited; exercised; fanatical; ferocious; feverish; fey; fierce; fiery; flammable; flammatory; flashing; foaming; foolish; frantic; frenzied; fretful; fuming; furibund; furious; glowing; hostile; hot(-tempered); huffy; igneous; ill-humored; impassioned; impetuous; incensed; indignant; inflamed; infuriated; intense; intoxicated; iracund; irascible; irate; ired; ireful; irked; irritable; irritated; lunatic; mad(dened); maniac(al); merciless; nettled; nettlesome; outraged; passionate; petulant; piqued; provoked; psychotic; raged; raging; rancorous; rankled; rash; raving; red(-hot); roiled; roily; savage; seething; senseless; sore; spirited; splenetic; testy; touchy; turbulent; unrestrained; vehement; violent; vivacious; warlike; waspish; wild; wrathful; wroth

ANGLE: **v.** bend; crook; curve; deflect; deviate; diverge; flex; form; incline; predispose; tack; twist; warp; ANGLE: **n.** arcuation; arris; aspect; bend; bias; bow; buckling; bulge; catch; circumflexion; corner; crook; curvature; curve; deflection; deviation; divergence; effect; elbow; flexure; guise; inclination; incline; ingle; intersection; intrigue; kink; niche; nook; phase; pitch; point of view; position; quirk; sag; scheme; sinuosity; slant; slope; stoop; tortuosity; trend; turn(ing); twist; warp; wrinkle; ANGULAR: biased; bony; crooked; forked; gaunt; inclined; kinked; leaned; leaning; pointed; scrawny; sharp; slanted; slim; warped

ANGRY: **see** under "anger"

ANGUISH: abuse; ache; affliction; agony; *angoisse*; angst; anxiety; bereavement; consternation; cruciation; desire; distress; dole; dolor; excruciation; grief; hurt; longing; misery; pain; pang; pining; rack; regret; remorse; sorrow; stitch; suffering; throb; throe; torment; torture; travail; twinge; woe; worry; yearn(ing)

ANILE: aged; doddering; doting; flighty; foolish; old(-womanish); senile; simple

ANIMAL: **a.** (**see** "brutal") abominable; animalic; animalistic; animallike; base; bestial; bodily; brutal; brutish; carnal; coarse; corporeal; cruel; disgusting; distasteful; earthy; fell; fleshy; gross; indecent; lewd; lustful; mammalian; physical; savage; sensual; sexual; swinish; temporal; unspiritual; vile; vulgar; wild; worldly; zoological; ANIMAL(S): **n.** animalia (pl); beast; behemoth; being; biped; brute; creature; critter; fauna(pl.); human; mammal; Mammalia (pl.); mammalian; organism; person; quadrumane; quadruped; savage; thing; Vertebrata (pl.); vertebrate

ANIMATE: **v.** activate; actuate; amuse; applaud; arouse; brace; brighten; cheer; delight; divert; drive; elate; embolden; encourage; energize; enliven; ensoul; enthuse; evoke; excite; exhilarate; fire; flush; freshen; impel; importune; incite; induce; inflame; inspire; inspirit; instigate; instil(l); invigorate; liven; motivate; move; please; press; prompt; push; quicken; refresh; resuscitate; revivify; rouse; satisfy; smarten; stimulate; stir; suscitate; urge; vitalize; vivificate; vivify; waken; ANIMATE(D): **a.** (**see** "alive") activated; active; blithe(some); brightened; brisk; buoyant; cheerful; cheering; ebullient; ecstatic; elated; encouraging; enlivened; enthused; enthusiastic; euphoric; excited; exhilarant; exhilarated; festive; fired; flushed;

freshened; gay; happy; heady; impassioned; impelled; impelling; incited; inflamed; inspired; inspirited; intoxicated; invigorated; joyful; joyous; live(ly); livened; living; merry; mirthful; motivated; moving; organic; prompted; quick(ened); rapturous; refreshed; roused; spiritous; sprightly; springy; spunky; stimulated; stirred; stirring; titillated; vigorous; vital(ized); vivacious; vivid; vivified; zealous; zestful; ANIMATION: activation; actuation; applause; ardor; arousal; awakening; brightness; buoyancy; cheer; courage; dash; delight; dollop; drive; ebullience; ebulliency; éclat; ecstasy; effervescence; élan; elation; encouragement; energy; enlivenment; enthusiasm; eudaemonia; eudaemony; euphoria; excitement; exhilaration; exuberance; festivity; fire; flash; flush; force; gaiety; gladness; glee(fulness); happiness; headiness; hilarity; incitement; inspiration; instigation; intoxication; invigoration; joy(ousness); liveliness; merriment; mirth(fulness); motivation; movement; ostentation; pep(per); power; pressure; promptitude; promptness; push; race; refreshment; resuscitation; revivification; rush; sparkle; spirit(edness); splash; sprightliness; springiness; spunk; stimulation; stir; streak; suscitation; tantivy; tinge; titillation; touch; urge; vein; verve; vigor; vim; vitality; vitalization; vivaciousness; vivacity; vivification; wakening; zeal; zest(fulness)

ANIMOSITY: (see "anger") animus; antagonism; bellicosity; dislike; enmity; hate; hatred; hostility; ill will; pique; prejudice; rancor; resentment; spite(fulness)

ANNEX: (see "add" and "join") acquire; affix; append; attach; connect; get; grab; grasp; incorporate; obtain; unite

ANNIHILATE: abate; abolish; abrogate; bray; burden; burn; cancel; consume; crumble; crush; dash; decapitate; decimate; defeat; defenestrate; dele(te); demolish; deracinate; despoil; destroy; devastate; devitalize; devour; discard; discreate; dispatch; drop; efface; end; engulf; eradicate; erase; erode; exclude; exhaust; execute; expunge; expurgate; exterminate; extinguish; extirpate; grind; immolate; kill; mash; murder; neutralize; nullify; obliterate; omit; overcome; overpower; overrun; overthrow; overwhelm; poison; press; pulverize; quell; quench; raze; remove; ruin; sack; scrape; shatter; slash; slaughter; slay; smash; squash; stamp (out); steamroller; strike; strip; subdue; subjugate; suppress; uncreate; undo; uproot; vanquish; veto; weaken; wither;

wrack; wreck; ANNIHILATION: abatement; abolishment; abrogation; burning; cancellation; consumption; crushing; death; decapitation; defenestration; deletion; demolishment; demolition; deracination; destruction; devastation; devitalization; discreation; dispatch; dissolution; doom; eradication; erasure; erosion; evanishment; execution; exhaustion; extermination; extinction; extinguishment; extirpation; fatality; finis(h); immolation; killing; mortality; murder; neutralization; nothingness; nullification; obliteration; overthrow; poisoning; pulveration; quietus; ruin; slaughter; slaying; suppression; vanquishment; veto; wrack; wreck(age); wrecking

ANNIVERSARY: annual; birthday; celebration; commemoration; feast; festivity; fete; holiday

ANNOTATE: elucidate; explain; gloss; illustrate; note; ANNOTATION(S): addition; clarification; marginalia (pl.); postil

ANNOUNCE: advertise; air; annunciate; articulate; assert; asseverate; bare; begin; betray; blab; blaze; blazon; blurt; broach; broadcast; bruit; bulletinize; call; circulate; claim; clarify; clarion; communicate; confess; confide; cry; declaim; declare; demonstrate; denote; disburden; disclose; disseminate; divulge; enounce; evulgate; exclaim; explain; expose; express; forerun; foretell; formulate; gossip; herald; impart; indicate; inform; introduce; launch; manifest; name; notify; observe; open; praise; preach; proclaim; promulgate; pronounce; propagandize; propound; publicize; publish; relate; remark; repeat; report; reveal; say; show; sound; speak; spill; spread; spring; squeal; state; swear; talk; tattle; tell; trumpet; unbosom; unclose; uncover; unfold; unmask; unveil; unwrap; utter; vent (ilate); voice; ANNOUNCEMENT: acknowledgment; advertisement; affirmation; annunciation; apocalypse; articulation; assertion; asseveration; avowal; betrayal; bid; bill; blazon(ry); broadcast; bulletin; call; catalog(ue); circular; circulation; claim; clarification; communication; complaint; confession; cry; declamation; declaration; decree; demonstration; descrial; disclosure; discovery; dissemination; divulgation; divulgence; dodger; edict; explanation; exposition; exposure; fiat; flash; impartment; indication; informaton; introduction; law; leaflet; litter; manifestation; manifesto; memo(randum); message; notice; notification; observation; order; pamphlet; pledge;

poster; proclamation; promulgation; pronouncement; pronunciation; propaganda; prospectus; publication; remark; report; rescript; revelation; rule; sales pitch; saying; speech; spread; statement; utterance; ventilation; white paper; ANNOUNCING: annunciatory; assertive; communicative; declamatory; disseminative; enunciative; enunciatory; informative; informing; proclamatory; promulgative; pronunciative; publishing; revelatory

ANNOY: abash; affect; afflict; agitate; aggravate; aggrieve; ail; alarm; anger; arouse; badger; baffle; bait; bedevil; beg; beset; block; bore; bother; chafe; confuse; damage; derange; devil; disarrange; disarray; discomfit; discomfort; discommode; discompose; disconcert; disgust; dismay; displace; displease; disquiet; distress; disturb; eat; egg; embarrass; enrage; erode; exasperate; excite; faze; fluster; fray; frazzle; fret; frighten; fuss; gnaw; grate; harass; harry; heckle; hector; henpeck; hinder; hound; impede; importune; incommode; inconvenience; insist; interfere; interrupt; intrude; irk; irritate; jar; jostle; madden; maltreat; meddle; molest; move; nag; nettle; oppress; overwhelm; pain; peeve; perplex; persecute; perturb(ate); pester; pique; plague; provoke; pursue; puzzle; rag; rattle; ride; rile; rock; ruffle; scare; scold; shake; shift; shock; snipe; stir; tamper; tantalize; taunt; tease; thwart; tickle; torment; trouble; try; twit; unbalance; unnerve; unsettle; unstring; upset; urge; vex; wear(y); worry; ANNOYANCE: abomination; ado; affliction; agitation; ailment; alarm; altercation; bane; bedevilment; besetment; bore; bother; contretemps; controversy; derangement; din; discomfiture; discomfort; discomposure; disconcertion; disgust; disorder; displeasure; disquiet(ude); distress; disturbance; embarrassment; enragement; exasperation; excitment; evil; fight; fleabite; fluster; frenzy; furor(e); grief; harassment; hubbub; hurry; incitement; inconvenience; insect; interruption; intrusion; irritation; jar; kick (up); mischief; molestation; muss; nudnick; nuisance; offense; oppression; pain; pandemonium; persecution; perturbation; pest; plague; provocation; pursuit; puzzle(ment); quarrel; rabblement; racket; riot; ripple; rout; rush; shock; sting; tampering; thorn; torment; trial; trouble; tumult(uation); umbrage; uproar; vexation; vexedness; weed; whirl (wind); worry; ANNOYING: aggravating; agitated; agitating; ailing; boring; bothersome; calamitous; chafing; confusing; discomfiting; discomfortable; discommodious;

discomposing; disconcerting; displeasing; distressing; disturbing; embarrassing; enraging; exasperating; excruciating; execrable; flustering; fretsome; galling; grating; harassing; harsh; hateful; heckling; hectoring; hounding; inconvenient; invidious; irksome; irritant; irritating; maddening; meddlesome; mischievous; mortifying; nagging; nettlesome; nettling; oppressive; painful; perplexing; perturbative; pestering; pestiferous; pestilent(ial); plaguing; provocative; provoking; puzzling; rasping; raspy; repellant; repulsive; riling; roiling; scolding; tampering; teasing; tedious; thwarting; tiresome; tormenting; troublesome; unsettling; upsetting; vexing; wearing; wearisome; wearying

ANNUITY: income; payment; pension; perpetuity; tontine

ANNUL: (**see** "abolish") abrogate; cancel; cass; countermand; destroy; disaffirm; dismantle; eliminate; end; erase; invalidate; neutralize; nullify; obliterate; override; overrule; quash; recall; recant; repeal; rescind; retract; revoke; supersede; undo; withdraw; ANNULMENT: (**see** "abolishment") abrogation; cancellation; cassation; countermand; defeasance; destruction; disaffirmance; disaffirmation; disclaimer; disclamation; dismantlement; elimination; end(ing); erasure; invalidation; neutralization; nullification; obliteration; recall; recantation; recision; repeal; rescission; retraction; revocation; supersedence; vacation; withdrawal

ANNULAR: circular; cyclic; cylindrical; orbed; orbicular; ringed; round; spherical; spheroid(al)

ANODYNE: **a.** (**see** "anesthetic") acesodyne; bland; relaxing; somniferous; soothing; ANODYNE: **n.** analgesic; anesthetic; balm; hypnotic; narcotic; opiate; palliative; sedative; somnifacient

ANOINT: anele; choose; consecrate; crown; dedicate; grease; oil; rub; salve

ANOMALOUS: (**see** "abnormal") aberrant; adventitious; anomalistic; atypical; bizarre; eccentric; erratic; freak(ish); grotesque; heteroclete; heterodox; irregular; lawless; odd; pathological; peculiar; phenomenal; subnormal; teratogenic; unnatural; unorthodox; whimsical; ANOMALY: see "abnormality"

ANON: afresh; afterward; again; anew; by and by; early; erelong; forthwith; immediate(ly); later; prompt(ly); quickly; readily; shortly; soon; speedily; sudden(ly); thence

ANONYMOUS: alias; assumed; authorless; blank; disguised; feigned; hidden; incognito; masked; nameless; secret; unasked; unidentified; unknown; unrequested; unsolicited; unsought; veiled

ANOTHER: (see "afresh") alias; different; fresh; further; new; second

ANSWER: **v.** act; agree; ape; atone; bid; confirm; conform; confute; correspond; counter(act); defend; do; echo; explain; feel; fit; fulfill; imitate; meet; pay; react; rebut; rejoin; repeat; replicate; *réplique*; reply; report; resound; respond; retaliate; retort; return; reverberate; satisfy; serve; solve; speak; suit; write; ANSWER: **n.** action; agreement; antiphon; atonement; comeback; confirmation; conformation; conformity; confutation; correspondence; counteraction; counterstatement; defense; echo; explanation; fulfillment; letter; payment; plea; reaction; rebuttal; reception; rejoinder; repartee; replication; *réplique*; reply; report; response; result; retaliation; retort; return; reverberation; satisfaction; solution; speech; ANSWERABLE: accountable; adequate; amenable; chargeable; conformable; creditable; dependable; equal; equivalent; explainable; explanatory; fitting; liable; reliable; responsible; responsive; retaliative; satisfactory; subject; suitable; trusted

ANTAGONIZE: see "anger"; ANTAGONISM: (see "anger" and "opposition") antipathy; competition; conflict; contrariety; dissonance; enmity; friction; hostility; rivalry; unfriendliness; war(fare); ANTAGONISTIC: (see "unfriendly") abhorrent; a(d)verse; adversative; angered; antipathetic(al); antithetic(al); combating; combative; competitive; conflicting; contending; contradictory; contrariant; contrary; disagreeing; discordant; dissonant; hostile; immiscible; incompatible; incongruent; incongruous; inconsistent; inharmonious; inimical; irreconcilable; militant; opposing; opposite; oppositional; oppositious; oppositive; oppugnant; pitted; pugnacious; repugnant; resisting; resistive; uncongenial; unfriendly; unreconcilable; unsuitable; warring; ANTAGONIST: adversary; aggressor; agonist; anti; archenemy; assailant; attacker; candidate; challenger; combatant; competitor;

contender; contestant; corival; defendant; disputant; emulator; enemy; entry; fighter; foe; foil; gladiator; harm; invader; nemesis; opponent; opportunist; opposer; protagonist; rival; Satan; unfriend; wrangler; wrestler

ANTECEDENT: **a.** ancient; anterior; anticipatory; anticus; before; bygone; *ci-devant*; earlier; elapsed; erewhile; erstwhile; first; foregoing; former; heretofore; late; once; onetime; preceding; presumptive; previous; prior; quondam; redoubtable; sometime; whilom; ANTECEDENT **n.** or ANTECEDENCE: anteriority; background; cause; education; experience; foretaste; heredity; history; lineage; pedigree; precedence; priority; quondam; rank; reason; training

ANTERIOR: (see "antecedent") before; fore; front; previous; prior; van; ventral

ANTHEM: (**see** "song") chorus; hallelujah

ANTHOLOGY: adversaria (pl.); ana(lecta); book; collectanea (pl.); collection; compendium; corpus; crestomathy; garland; omnibus

ANTIC: **a.** absurd; clownish; comic(al); droll; extravagant; fantastic; fantastique; frolicsome; humorous; jocular; merry; mirthful; wild; witty; ANTIC: **n.** buffoon; caper; clown; comic; dido; fool; frolic; gambol; jest(er); prank; wag; wit

ANTICIPATE: abide; aim; analyze; antedate; appraise; apprehend; ascertain; aspire; assay; assess; assume; await; balk; bank; believe; bide; calculate; cast; cogitate; comprehend; compute; conjecture; consider; contemplate; count; dare (say); deduce; deem; design; desire; determine; develop; diagnose; diagnosticate; divine; envisage; establish; estimate; evaluate; evalue; evolve; examine; excogitate; expect; face; feel; figure; forecast; forerun; foresee; forestall; frame; gather; gauge; gaze; guess; hang; hope; hypothesize; imagine; impend; infer; intend; interpret; intuit; judge; jump; justify; look; measure; mediate; meditate; meet; muse; observe; opine; outguess; pend; perceive; plan; ponder; portend; pose; posit; postulate; predict; premise; prepare; presage; presume; presuppose; prevent; prognosticate; purpose; rate; realize; reason; recall; reckon; reflect; regard; rely; ruminate; see; sense; solve; specify; speculate; study; support; suppose; surmise; survey; suspect; suspend; test; theorize; think; thwart; trust; value; view; want; weigh; wish; ANTICIPATION:

aim; apprehension; aspiration; assumption; belief; cogitation; comprehension; confidence; conjecture; consideration; contemplation; deduction; design; desire; envisionment; excogitation; expectance; expectancy; expectation; forestallment; future; guess; hope; inference; intuition; meditation; muse; opinion; optimism; perception; plan; portent; postulate; postulation; predilection; premise; presumption; presupposition; promise; prospect; purpose; reliance; realization; reasoning; recognition; recollection; reflection; rumination; speculation; study; supposition; surmise; survey; suspension; suspicion; thought; trust; view; waiting; wish; ANTICIPATORY: abiding; anticipant; anticipated; anticipating; anticipative; apprehensive; awaited; awaiting; biding; comprehensive; contemplated; contingent; deemed; expectant; expected; expecting; foreseen; hoped; hopeful; impending; inchoate; inchoative; incipient; intuitive; obligated; pending; possible; potential; pregnant; prevenient; prospective; surprised; suspended; suspicious; wished

ANTIDOTE: counter(action); counter remedy; emetic; preventative; prophylactic; relief; remedy; restorative

ANTIPATHY: (**see** "hate") abhorrence; abomination; animus; annoyance; antagonism; detestation; disgust; dislike; distaste; enmity; hatred; horror; hostility; loathing; nausea; odium; offense; opposition; pique; rancor; repugnance; repugnancy; repulsion; revolt; shock; squeamishness; trial; unsavoriness; vexation

ANTIQUATED: (**see** "old") antique; chronic; deep-rooted; foggish; fusty; inveterate; moss-backed; mossy; musty; old-fashioned; outdated; outmoded; out-of-date; stale; worm-eaten; wornout

ANTIQUE: **see** "antiquated" and "curio"

ANTISEPTIC: **a.** aseptic; clean; disinfectant; germicidal; prophylactic; sterile; sterilized; ANTISEPTIC: **n.** alcohol; disinfectant; germicide; iodine; prophylactic

ANXIOUS: (**see** "fearful") afraid; agitated; agog; anguished; annoyed; apprehensive; careworn; champing at the bit; choleric; churning; concerned; desirous; desperate; disquiet; disturbed; doubtful; dreadful; dysphoric; eager; embarrassed; emotional; energetic; excited; expectant; feverish; fidgety; fitful; flurried; forward; frantic;

fretful; frightened; hasty; hectic; hurried; impatient; impavid; impetuous; indecisive; irascible; irritable; irritated; itching; itchy; nervous; neurotic; nightmarish; panicky; pettish; petulant; rattled; restive; restless; skittish; solicitous; solicitudinous; spasmodic; splenetic; strained; stricken; temperamental; terrified; terrorized; testy; timid; trembling; tremulous; troubled; turbulent; uncertain; uneasy; unpatient; unquiet; unsettled; untranquil; upset; waspish; wearied; wearisome; worried; worrying; ANXIETY: agitation; alarm; angst; anguish; annoyance; anxiousness; apprehension; besetment; care(fulness); choler; concern; desire; desperation; disquiet(ness); disquietude; disturbance; doubt; dread; dyspathy; dysphoria; eagerness; embarrassment; emotion; excitement; fear(fulness); ferment; fever; fretfulness; fright; haste; hurry; impatience; impetuosity; indecision; indecisiveness; inquietude; irascibility; irritability; itch; malaise; misgiving; nervousness; neurosis; nightmare; panic(kiness); petulance; phobia; restiveness; restlessness; solicitude; strain; suspense; tenterhooks; terror; timidity; trepidation; turbulence; uneasiness; unrest; vexation; worry

APART: (**see** "distinct") alone; aloof; aside; asunder; away; beyond; bifid; bifurcated; cleft; cloven; detached; dichotomous; different; discrete; distinct; divergent; divorced; else; enisled; estranged; excluded; exclusive; external; independent(ly); individual; isolated; otherwise; parted; partite; remote; removed; segregated; separate(d); severed; sole; solitary; solus; split

APATHETIC: (**see** "careless") adiaphorous; adynamic; ambitionless; blasé; cool; comatose; cursory; debilitated; *dégagé*; detached; dilatory; dispirited; dormant; dreamy; drooping; drowsy; dull; enervated; fatigued; feeble; glassy; hebetudinous; idle; immobile: impassive; imperturbable; impervious; inactive; inattentive; indifferent; indolent; inert; inexcitable; insipid; invertebrate; lackadaisical; lackluster; languid; languorous; Laodician; lassitudinous; latent; lax; lazy; leaden; lethargic; lifeless; listless; lukewarm; mechanical; mousy; negative; nonchalant; otiose; pachydermatous; passive; patient; perfunctory; phlegmatic; pliant; pococurante; prostrate; quiescent; quiet; receptive; reluctant; slack; sleepy; sluggish; spiritless; stoic(al); stupefactive; stupefying; stuporous; submissive; supine; tired; torpid; torporific; unconcerned; uneager; unenthusiastic; unfeeling; unimpressed; uninterested; unmoved; unresisting; unresistive; unresponsive; unstirred; weak; weary; vacuous; yielding; APATHY: (**see** "carelessness") abiotrophy; acedia; adiaphoria; adynamia; ambitiouslessness; anhedonia; blues; coma; coolness; debility; detachment; dispiritedness; doldrums; dreaminess; droop; drowsiness; dullness; dumps; enervation; ennui; exhaustion; fatigue; feebleness; hebetude; hypokinesia; idleness; immobility; impassiveness; impassivity; imperturbability; inaction; inactivity; inappetency; inattention; indifference; indolence; inertia; inertness; insipidity; lackadaisy; lackluster; languidness; languor; lassitude; laxity; laziness; lethargy; lifelessness; listlessness; melancholia; minauderie; nonchalance; otiosity; passiveness; passivity; perfunctoriness; phlegm(atism); prostration; quiet(ude); slackness; sleepiness; sloth (fulness); sluggishness; spiritlessness; stagnation; stoicism; stupefaction; stupor; submission; supineness; supinity; tenuity; torpidity; torpidness; torpor; unconcern(edness); unenthusiasm; unfeeling(ness); uninterestedness; unresponsiveness; vacuity; vegetation; weakness; weariness

APE: **v. see** "imitate"; APE: **n. see** "quadrumane"

APERÇU: (**see** "digest") breviary; brief; compendium; compilation; glance; insight; outline; preçis; prospectus; sketch; summation

APERTURE: (**see** "opening") chasm; cleft; crack; fenestra(tion); gap; hiatus; hole; mouth; orifice; os(tiole); perforation; pore; rent; slit; window

APEX: (**see** "crest") acme; apogee; *cacumen*; cap(sheaf); capstone; climacterium; climax; crisis; culmination; cusp; denouement; floodtide; focus; grand finale; head; meridian; noon(time); orgasm; peak; perihelion; pinnacle; point; scale; sublimity; summit; tidemark; tip; top; turning point; vertex; zenith

APHORISM: **see** "adage"

APLOMB: (**see** "assurance") address; adroitness; art(fulness); coolness; diplomacy; equilibrium; finesse; perpendicularity; poise; resolution; self-possession; stability; surety; tact(fulness)

APOGEE: **see** "apex" and "culmination"

APOLOGUE: allegory; fable; legend; metaphor; myth; parable; simile; similitude; story; symbolization; tale

APOLOGY: acknowledgment; alibi; *amende honorable*; amends; apologetic; apologia; atonement; defense; deprecation; excuse; exoneration; explanation; extenuation; justification; makeshift; pardon; plea; prayer; pretext; regret(s); vindication; APOLOGETIC: deprecating; deprecative; deprecatory; excusatory; justifiable; pardonable; regrettable

APOSTATE: **a. see** "disloyal"; APOSTATE: **n.** A.W.O.L.; backslider; betrayer; convert; defector; deserter; escapee; expatriate; heretic; pervert; rat; recreant; renegade; seceder; straggler; tergiversator; turncoat; turntail

APOSTLE: (**see** "follower") aficionada (fem.); aficionado; apprentice; devotee; disciple; fan; harbinger; ist; messenger; preacher; proselyte; satellite; scholar; sectary; sectator; student; supporter; teacher; votary

APOTHEGM: (**see** "adage") aphorism; precept; saying; witticism

APPAL(L): abominate; alarm; astonish; awe; daunt; disgust; dismay; fail; frighten; horrify; nauseate; offend; repel; revolt; scare; shock; sicken; terrify; terrorize; APPALLING: **see** "fearful" and "frightful"

APPARATUS: accessory; accoutrement(s); adjunct; appliance; appointments; appurtenance(s); armamentaria (pl.); armamentarium; armor; arrangement; artifice; badge; baggage; belongings; business; chattels; contraption; contrivance; design; device; dingus; effects; emblem; engine; equipment; fanglement; figure; fixture; gadget; garb; garments; gear; goods; guise; habiliment; habit; harness; implement; ingenuity; insigne; insignia (pl.); instrument(aria); invention; knickknack; machination; machine(ry); matériel; means; mechanism; motif; notion; outfit; paraphernalia; plan; procedure; project; property; regalia; rig(ging); robes; scheme; signal; stratagem; tackle; target; toggery; togs; tool(s); trappings; traps; trick; utensil; utility

APPAREL: **v. see** "dress"; APPAREL: **n.** accoutrement(s); apparatus; array; attire; caparison; clothes; clothing; costume; dress; equipage; equipment; garb; garments; guise; habiliment; habit; livery; outfit; paraphernalia; raiment; rig(ging); robes; tackle;

toga; toggery; togs; toilette; trappings; uniform; vestment(s); vesture

APPARENT: (**see** "clear") avowed; conspicuous; crystal(line); demonstrable; diaphanous; discernible; distinct; evident; exoteric; explicit; express; illusory; indubitable; intended; likely; lucid; manifest; obvious; open; ostensible; ostensive; overt; palpable; patent; perceivable; perceptible; phanic; plain; premeditated; presumable; presumed; presumptive; *prima facie*; probable; seeable: seeming; self-evident; semblable; shallow; specious; transparent; unconcealed; unmistakable; unobstructed; visible; vivid

APPARITION: (**see** "ghost") appearance; dream; ha(u)nt; image; phantasm(agoria); phantom; phenomenon; revenant; shade; specter; spectre; spectrum; spirit; spook; vision; wraith

APPEAL: **v.** address; apply; ask; attract; beg; beseech; call; charm; come out; cry; demand; enchant; entreat; implore; importune; invite; invoke; obsecrate; petition; plead; pray; propose; request; seek; solicit; speak; sue; supplicate; APPEAL: **n.** (**see** "request") address; adjuration; allure; attraction; attractiveness; call; charm; cry; demand; desire; enchantment; entreaty; imploration; importunity; imprecation; invitation; invocation; obsecration; petition; plea; plead (ing); popularity; prayer; proposal; request; rogation; solicitation; suit; supplication; urge; APPEALING; (**see** "alluring") beckoning; catchy; clever; cute; delicious; delightful; enchanting; invocative; invocatory; provocative; provocatory; supplicative

APPEAR: arise; arrive; attend; burgeon; come; dawn; debouch; develop; disembogue; effloresce; egress; emanate; emerge; energize; enter; flow; flower; grow; happen; hypostatize; issue; look; loom; manifest; materialize; objectify; occur; reify; rise; seem; shape; show; spring; stem; visit; APPEARANCE: air; apparition; arrival; aspect; attendance; bearing; burgeoning; cache; cast; character(istic); color; come-out; construction; countenance; dawn; debouchment; debut; debutant(e); demeanor; development; display; dress; eccentricity; efflorescence; egression; emanation; emergence; entrance; evolution; expression; face; facies; fashion; feature(s); flow; flower(ing); form(ality); front; *gestalt*; growth; guise; habitus; inspection; likeness; lineament; look; makeup; manifestation; mark; materialization; mien; occurrence; oddity; ostent;

peculiarity; perspective; phantasmagoria; phenomenon; physiognomy; physique; posture; profile; prospect; rise; scene; semblance; shape; show; sight; simulacrum; singularity; stamp; stemming; structure; style; surface; topography; trait; view; visage; visit; way

APPEASE: (**see** "calm") abate; allay; alleviate; assuage; compose; conciliate; content; dulcify; hush; lenify; lull; mitigate; moderate; modify; mollify; pacify; placate; propitiate; quiesce; quiet(en); reassure; reduce; sate; satiate; satisfy; settle; slake; smooth; soothe; stay; still; subdue; subside; suffice; tame; temper; tranquilize; APPEASING: (**see** "calm") alleviating; assuaging; calming; conciliatory; expiatory; lenitive; mitigative; mitigatory; moderate; moderative; mollifying: pacific; pacifying; peaceful; persuasive; piacular; placative; placatory; propitiative; propitiatory; satiating; satisfying; soothing; tranquilizing; APPEASEMENT: (**see** "calm") abatement; alleviation; assuagement; assuasion; atonement; composure; conciliation; contentment; dulcificaton; expiation; hush; lenity; lull; mitigation; moderation; modification; mollification; pacification; persuasion; placation; propitiation; reassurance; reduction; satiation; satisfaction; settlement; subsidence; tranquilization

APPELLATION: **see** "name"

APPEND: (**see** "add") adjoin; affix; annex; appendix; attach; augment; clip; compound; eke; fasten; hang; increase; intensify; join; pad; pend; pin; stick; subjoin; subscribe; suspend; tack; APPENDAGE(S): accessories; addition; adjunct; adnexa (pl.); annex; appendix; appurtenance; arm; attachment; attendant; augmentation; cauda; codicil; equipment; extension; hanger-on; hardware; increase; intensification; leg; limb; pendant; pedicle; P.S.; rider; subscription; suffix; supplement; stipel; tab; tail; APPENDED or APPENDANT: **see** "joined"

APPERTAIN: **see** "belong"

APPETITE: adephagia; anorexia; appetence; appetency; appetibility; *appétit*; appetition; aspiration; attraction; avarice; belly; bulimia; concupiscence; craving; delight; desiderata (pl.); desideration; desideratum; desire; disposition; edacity; envy; Eros; fancy; gluttony; greed; gust(o); hankering; heart; hope; hunger(ing); impulse; inclination; itch(ing); liking; longing(ness); love; lust;

need; obsession; orexis; passion; piquancy; pleasure; predilection; preference; proclivity; propensity; relish; sapor; stomach; striving; tang; taste; thirst; urge; voraciousness; voracity; want; yearning; yen; zest; APPETIZING: agreeable; ambrosiac; ambrosial; appealing; appetible; appetitious; apetitive; choice; dainty; delectable; delicate; delicious; delightful; desirable; edifying; enchanting; esculent; exquisite; flavorable; flavorful; flavorous; flavorsome; fragrant; good; gratifying; gustable; gustatory; gustful; luscious; luxurious; mint(y); nectarean; nectareous; nice; orexigenic; palatable; piquant; pleasant; pleasing; racy; rare; relishing; rich; salty; sapid; saporous; satisfying; savorous; savory; spicy; sweet; tangy; tasty; tempting; toothsome; wholesome; yummy; zestful; APPETIZER: aperitif; aperitive; *hors d'oeuvre*; liking; partiality; *paté*; pleasure; relish

APPLAUD: acclaim; approbate; approve; award; bespeak; boost; canonize; celebrate; charge; cheer; cite; clap; commend; commit; compliment; congratulate; deify; emblazon; endorse; enhance; enshrine; entrust; eulogize; exalt; extol; felicitate; fetishize; glorify; laud; macarize; magnify; panegyrize; pedestal; praise; proclaim; recommend; spiritualize; stellify; worship; APPLAUSE: acclaim; acclamation; accolade; approbation; approval; award; boost; bravo; canonization; celebration; cheer; citation; clap(ping); commendation; complement; congratulation; curtain call; deification; *éclat*; eloge; encomium; endorsement; enhancement; enshrinement; eulogium; eulogy; exaltation; felicitation; glorification; greeting; hand; hurrah; huzza; laudation; magnification; medal; ole!; palm; panegyric; pedestalization; plaudit(s); praise; recommendation; salvo; stellification; tribute; worship

APPLIANCE: (**see** "apparatus") accessory; application; fixture; implement; machine(ry); utilization

APPLICABLE: adaptable; apposite; apropos; appropriate; apt; commensurate; competent; congruent; consonant; deft; expert; fit(ted); fitting; germane; inclined; ingenious; likely; meet; opportune; pat; pertinent; prepared; prone; proper; proportional; qualified; relevant; right; suitable; suited; usable; useful

APPLY: act; add; addict; adhere; adjoin; affix; allot; append; appertain; apportion; appose; appropriate; ask; assign; attach;

attend; bear; belong; bind; clip; concern; conjoin; connect; consecrate; consign; dedicate; design; destine; devote; direct; do; effect; employ; exercise; exert; fasten; fit; fix; give; graft; grind; hitch; hold; honor; impose; inhere; join; labor; lay; link; nail; overlay; own; persevere; pertain; pin; place; provide; put; refer; regard; relate; request; secure; seek; set; solicit; stick; strive; study; suit; super(im)pose; tack; tie; toil; touch; use; utilize; work; worship; APPLICATION: activity; addiction; adherence; adhesion; adoration; allegiance; annexation; appeal; ardency; ardentness; ardor; attachment; attention; blank; conformation; congruency; consecration; consignment; dedication; devotedness; devotion; diligence; direction; doing; earnestness; effort; employment; engagement; enthusiasm; exercise; exertion; faith; fanaticism; fealty; fervency; fervor; fidelity; form; grind; labor; love; loyalty; motion; novena; perseverance; pertinence; pertinency; petition; plea; practice; pursuit; relation(ship); relevance; relevancy; request; solicitation; steadfastness; stick-to-itiveness; study; timeliness; toil; union; use; utilization; work; worship; zealotry

APPOINT: allot; allow; annex; apportion; arm; arrange; array; assign; authorize; award; bestow; call; capacitate; charge; choose; command; commission; create; crown; deck (out); declare; decree; delegate; denominate; denote; depute; deputize; designate; destine; determine; dictate; direct; earmark; elect; employ; empower; enable; enact; endow; engage; entrust; establish; fix; foreordain; formulate; franchise; furnish; give; grant; impose; inaugurate; induct; install; institute; invest; license; name; nominate; ordain; order; outfit; permit; pick; place; portion; predestine; prepare; prescribe; provide; sanction; schedule; select; send; set; signify; specify; stipulate; warrant; will; APPOINTMENT(S): (**see** "designation") accoutrements; allotment; annexation; apportionment; assignation; award; bestowal; call; charge; choice; command; commission; consultation; date; destination; direction; enactment; endowment; engagement; equipment; foreordination; inauguration; induction; installation; interview; job; meeting; order; ordination; portion; position; rendezvous; reservation; schedule; selection; specification; station; time; tryst; turn; warrant

APPORTION: (**see** "distribute") adjudge; admeasure; administer; allocate; allow;

appoint; appropriate; arrange; authorize; award; balance; bestow; budget; choose; consign; contribute; cut; deal; decide; designate; direct; discard; dispense; dispose; divide; dole; earmark; formulate; furnish; give; grant; help; lend; measure; mete; number; ordain; order; parcel; partition; place; plan; portion; prescribe; prorate; provide; rate; ration; regulate; release; set(tle); share; slice; split; stock; supply; APPORTIONMENT: (see "distribution") allocation; allotment; allowance; appointment; appropriation; arrangement; assignment; award; bestowal; budget; consignment; contribution; cut; deal; decision; designation; dispensation; disposal; disposition; distribution; dividend; division; dole; gift; grant; measure(ment); number; parcel; partition; plan; portion; prescription; provision; rate; ration; share; slice; split; stock; supply

APPOSITE: see "fit"

APPRAISE: (see "rate") adjudge; adjudicate; adjust; admire; analyze; appreciate; ascertain; assay; assess; average; budget; calculate; capitalize; charge; comprehend; compute; conclude; count; deem; determine; discriminate; esteem; estimate; evaluate; evalue; examine; figure; find; fix; forecast; gauge; guess; heed; hold; impose; interpret; judge; judicate; justify; levy; love; measure; mete; mise; number; ordain; regard; respect; rule; set(tle); solve; test; think; treasure; valuate; value; weigh; APPRAISAL: (see "estimation" and "opinion") computation; reckoning

APPRECIABLE: calculable; cognizable; cognoscible; cognoscitive; comprehensible; computable; determinable; discernable; essential; figurable; measurable; minimal; objective; observable; obvious; palpable; perceivable; perceptible; percipient; ponderable; recognizable; seeing; sensible; tangible

APPRECIATE: admire; appraise; approbate; approve; cherish; commendate; comprehend; dig; discern; discriminate; enjoy; esteem; evaluate; favor; feel; increase; judge; like; love; perceive; praise; prize; realize; recognize; respect; sense; treasure; understand; value; APPRECIATION: admiration; affection; approbation; approval; awareness; citation; commendation; comprehension; discernment; discrimination; esteem; estimation; evaluation; feeling; gratification; increase; judgment; liking; love; perception;

praise; realization; recognition; regard; respect; sense; taste; testimonial; understanding; value

APPREHEND: (see "catch") anticipate; arrest; ascertain; behold; believe; capture; conceive; cop; detail; detain; detect; discern; distinguish; dread; embrace; experience; fear; feel; foreknow; foresee; foreshadow; grasp; hear; hold; imagine; intuit; know; learn; nab; note; observe; perceive; realize; receive; recognize; regard; see; sense; suppose; swallow; take; understand; view; APPREHENSION: (see "detection") alarm; anticipation; anxiety; arrest; capture; cognition; cognizance; cold feet; conception; detention; discernment; disquiet(ude); distinguishment; doubt; dread; fear; feeling; foreboding; foreknowing; foreknowledge; foreshadowing; forewarning; grasp; idea; imagination; inquietude; intellection; intelligence; intuition; knowledge; misgiving; notion; opinion; pang; perception; prehension; premonition; presentiment; realization; reception; recognition; seizure; sentiment; supposition; suspicion; trepidation; trepidity; understanding; worry; APREHENSIVE: alarmed; all-overish; anticipating; anticipative; anxious; apt; cognizant; conspicuous; discerning; dreadful; fearful; foreboding; knowing; nervous; premonitory; presentient; solicitous; troubled; worried

APPRENTICE: see "learner;" APPRENTICED: articled; bound; contracted; indentured; learning

APPRISE: acquaint; advise; annunciate; articulate; asseverate; communicate; declare; disclose; divulge; enunciate; express; impart; inform; instruct; manifest; mention; narrate; notify; receive; recite; recount; relate; reveal; say; speak; squeal; talk; tell; utter; verbalize; warn

APPROACH: v. accost; advance; aproximate; assault; attempt; challenge; come; confront; equal; essay; face; front; greet; hail; impend; match; meet; near; salute; solicit; stalk; tackle; touch; trend; try; walk; APPROACH: n. access; adit; approximation; assault; avenue; challenge; commencement; confrontation; door; front; greeting; meeting; overture; road; salutation; salute; solicitation; street; walk(way); APPROACHABLE: see "friendly"; APPROACHING: forthcoming; oncoming; upcoming

APPROBATE: see "approve"; APPROBA-

TION: (**see** "approval") acclamation; accreditment; amen; assent; commendation; credit; dispensation; encomium; encore; esteem; favor; permission; permit; plaudit; praise; privilege; recognition; regard; repute; sanction

APPROPRIATE: **v.** (**see** "add" and "apportion") accroach; allot; annex; arrogate; assign; assume; award; borrow; claim; commandeer; condemn; confiscate; devour; engulf; formulate; grab; grasp; help; impound; pilfer; plan; preempt; provide; purloin; seize; sequester; steal; swallow; take; usurp; APPROPRIATE: **a.** (**see** "apt") applicable; apposite; apropos; becoming; befitting; classic; *comme il faut*; concordant; condign; conventional; comfortable; decent; decorous; due; felicitous; fit(ting); genteel; germane; happy; harmonious; ideal; idoneous; knowing; meet; opportune; orderly; pat; pertinent; proper; seemly; special; suitable; timely; worthy; APPROPRIATION: (**see** "funds") accroachment; allotment; annexation; arrogation; assignment; assumption; award; condemnation; confiscation; engulfment; grab; grasp; preemption; seizure; sequestration; theft; usurpation; APPROPRIATENESS: (**see** "fitness") applicability; applicableness; decorousness; decorum; germaneness; ideality; idoneity; relativity

APPROVE: (**see** "appreciate" and "value") abet; accept; accredit; acknowledge; affirm; agree; approbate; attest; authorize; award; beckon; buy; certify; cherish; cite; commend; compliment; condone; confirm; consent; corroborate; credit; dig; discriminate; elect; encourage; endorse; establish; esteem; exhibit; favor; homologate; license; like; notarize; O.K.; own; pass; permit; praise; ratify; rubber-stamp; salute; sanctify; sanction; seal; second; settle; sign; stamp; subscribe; substantiate; support; uphold; validate; verify; vote; welcome; APPROVAL: (**see** "applause" and "appreciation") acceptance; acclaim; acclamation; accolade; affirmation; amen; authorization; beckon(ing); bravo; certification; citation; clap; commendation; confirmation; consent; countenance; countermark; *éclat*; election; encouragement; endorsement; favor; fiat; franchise; grace; handclap; harmony; imprimatur; license; mark; nod; ole!; opinion; parole; password; permission; permit; plaudit; probation; ratification; reception; regard; rubber stamp; salute; sanction; seal; second; signal; signature; stamp; subscription; substantiation; sufferage; sufferance; support; unanimity; validation;

verification; vote; watchword; welcome; yes

APPROXIMATE: **v.** (**see** "approach" and "near") accost; advance; estimate; face; meet; APPROXIMATE(LY): **a.** or **adv.** about; almost; anear; approaching; circa; close; nearby; nearly; nigh; nominal; quasi; roughly; well-nigh

APROPOS: (**see** "apt") about; anent; appropriate; approximate; concerning; proper; regarding

APT: (**see** "appropriate" and "knowing") acute; adaptable; apposite; apropos; clever; commensurate; competent; congruent; consonant; decorous; deft; docile; easy; experienced; expert; fit(ted); fitting; germane; good; inclined; ingenious; liable; likely; meet; opportune; pat; pertinent; poignant; pointed; prepared; prone; proper; proportional; qualified; quick(-witted); ready; relevant; resourceful; right; seemly; skillful; smart; suitable; usable; useful; willing; APTNESS or APTITUDE: ability; appropriateness; art; bent; brains; capacity; cleverness; discernment; discrimination; ease; experience; faculty; felicity; flair; genius; gift; head; ingenuity; interest; instinct; knack; knowledge; leaning; learning; liking; opportunity; patness; penchant; poignancy; predilection; preparation; qualification; quick-wittedness; readiness; resourcefulness; skill(fulness); smartness; suitability; talent; taste; tendency; training; trend; willingness; wits

ARBITER: **see** "judge"

ARBITRARY: (**see** "arrogant") absolute; absolutist(ic); authoritarian; bigoted; capricious; captious; clever; despotic; determinated; determined; dictatorial; dogmatic; final; foxy; hierarchic(al); imperious; inexorable; irrational; irresponsible; nondemocratic; peremptory; positive; preferential; random; roguish; sassy; saucy; severe; sly; stubborn; thetic(al); totalitarian; tyrannical; tyrannous; willful

ARBITRATE: **see** "compromise"; ARBITRATOR: (**see** "judge") arbiter; conciliator

ARC: (**see** "range") curve; glow; path

ARCANE: **see** "mysterious" and "secret"

ARCH: **a.** artful; chief; clever; coquettish; coy; cunning; cute; fey; foxy; great; impish; pert; picaresque; playful; prime; principal;

roguish; sassy; saucy; shy; sly; timid; wary;
ARCH: **n.** arc; bend; bow; bridge; curvature;
curve; fornix; hance; ogive; sky; span;
support; vault; ARCHED: arcate; arcuate
(d); bowed; bulging; chamfered; circular;
concamerated; concave; convex; coped;
curved; domed; gibbous; rounded; rounding;
vaulted; ARCHNESS: **see** "coyness"

ARCHAIC: (**see** "ancient") antiquated;
old(-fashioned); unchanged; vintage

ARCHETYPE: (**see** "model") example; ideal;
original; pattern

ARCHIVE(S): annal; collection; document(s);
library; museum; record(s); repository

ARDOR: animation; ardency; assiduity;
blaze; brilliancy; burning; bustle; calenture;
combustion; compassion; concentration;
conflagration; dash; dedication; desire; devotedness; devotement; devotion; diligence;
drive; eagerness; ebullience; ebulliency;
ebullition; éclat; élan; emotion; energy;
enthusiasm; faithfulness; fanaticism; feeling;
ferment; fervency; ferventness; fervidity;
fervor; fever; fidelity; fire; flame; force;
ginger; glow; gusto; heart(iness); heat;
hustle; industry; inspiration; intensity; interest; light; love; loyalty; luminosity; nerve;
passion; pep; pressure; rabidity; rapture;
religiosity; rush; sparks; spirit; stimulation;
stir; strain; tension; vehemence; verve;
vigor; vivacity; voracity; warmth; zeal
(otry); zealousness; zest; ARDENT: agog;
animated; avid; beaming; burning; combustible; compassionate; crusading; devoted;
devout; dithyrambic; eager; earnest; ebullient; ecstatic; emotional; enraptured; enthusiastic; evangelical; evangelistic; excited;
extreme; faithful; febrile; feeling; fervent;
fervid; feverish; fiery; flammable; full-
blooded; glowing; great; high-spirited;
hot(-blooded); igneous; impassioned; intense;
keen; loving; loyal; passionate; perfervid;
pious; plutonic; rapturous; religious; romantic; sanguine; sentimental; shining; sincere;
tender; torrid; vehement; vigorous; volcanic;
warm; zealous

ARDUOUS: (**see** "hard" and "laborious")
difficult; exacting; lofty; onerous; rigorous;
steep; stiff; strenuous; trying; uphill

AREA: acre(s); acreage; activity; alentours;
ambience; ambient(e); ambit; areaway;
arena; arrondissement; atmosphere; authority; background; baron(r)y; beat; belt;
body politic; bounds; branch; breadth;

broadness; business; campgrounds; campus;
career; category; circuit; city; climate;
climature; clime; colony; command; commonalty; commons; commonwealth; commune; communion; community; compartment; compass; compound; confines; control; country; county; demesne; department; desert; distance; district; division;
domain; dominion; empire; entourage;
environment; environ(s); estate; expanse;
experience; extension; extent; farm; fief;
field; firmament; franchise; function; government; ground; habitat; haunt; hierarchy;
imperium; influence; jurisdiction; job; land
(scape); length; limit(s); locale; locality;
location; lordship; lot; margin; mass;
medium; metier; microcosm; milieu; mise-
en-scène; neighborhood; occupation; ocean;
orbit; outskirts; ownership; pale; place;
plot; portion; possession; power; precinct;
principality; property; province; purlieu;
radius; ranch; rand; range; reach; realm;
region; responsibility; right; room; rule;
scene; scope; sea; section; seign(i)ority;
setting; settlement; shire; site; size; society;
sovereignty; space; specialism; specialty;
sphere; spot; spread; stadium; stage; state;
stretch; subdivision; suburbia; suburbs;
superiority; supremacy; surface; surroundings; sway; sweep; system; terrain;
terrene; territory; topography; town(ship);
tract; trade; transcendency; venue; vicinage;
vicinity; village; vocation; volume; walk;
waste(land); way; width; wilderness; zone

ARENA: (**see** "area") circus; cockpit; contour;
court; field; hippodrome; oval; region;
ring; rink; scene; space; sphere; stadium;
state; terrain; topography

ARGUE: accuse; adduce; advocate; agitate;
altercate; arguify; back-talk; beef; bellyache;
bewail; bicker; brawl; carp; cavil; charge;
complain; conflict; contend; contest; controvert; criticize; debate; deny; deplore;
differ; disagree; disclaim; discourse; discuss;
disparage; dispute; dissent; dogmatize;
expostulate; expound; feud; fight; fret;
fuss; grieve; gripe; groan; grouse; growl;
grumble; grunt; haggle; howl; implicate;
imply; inveigh; keen; kick; lament; maintain;
moan; moot; mourn; murmur; object; orate;
persuade; pettifog; plead; press; protest;
prove; provoke; quarrel; question; quibble;
rail; reason; rebel; rebut; regret; remonstrate;
repine; resent; scrap; show; spat; squall;
squawk; squeal; talk; tangle; tiff; tilt; treat;
urge; wail; war; wrangle; yammer; yell;
ARGUMENT: (**see** "disagreement") advocation; agitation; altercation; appeal;

argumenta (pl.); argumentation; argumentum; back talk; battle; brannigan; brawl; case; cavil; competition; conflict; contention; contest; controversy; criticism; debate; dialectic(s); difference; difficulty; disagreement; discord(ance); discordancy; discourse; discussion; disparagement; disputation; dispute; dissent(ion); disturbance; divergence; entanglement; enthymeme; epagoge; expostulation; fight; feud; furor(e); fuss; go-round; ground; hassle; involvement; litigation; maintenance; objection; opposition; oration; plea; polemic(s); pressure; proof; protestation; provocation; quarrel; question; quibble; quodlibet; reason(ing); rebuttal; rift; skirmish; spat; squall; squawk; squeal; strife; struggle; suit; syllogism; tangle; text; theme; tiff; tilt; to-do; topic; trial; tumult; uproar; words; wrangle; ARGUMENTATIVE: agitative; agonistic; antagonistic; belligerent; carping; complaining; contential; contentious; contradictious; contradictory; controversial; cross; debatable; demagogic; dialectic; differing; disagreeable; disagreeing; discordant; discursive; discursory; disputable; disputatious; disputative; dissentient; dissentious; dissentive; dissident; divisive; dogmatic(al); eristic; expostulatory; factional; factious; forensic; fretful; heretical; hostile; indicative; insubordinate; mutinous; persuasive; perverse; pleading; polemic(al); pressing; presumptive; protestant; protesting; provocative; quarrelsome; querulous; quibbling; rebellious; recalcitrant; refractory; rhetorical; ructious; seditious; suggestive; turbulent; tyrannical; tyrannous; unruly; warring; wrangling

ARID: adust; anhydrous; bald; bare; barren; desiccated; dry; dull; jejune; lean; monotonous; parched; seared; shriveled; sterile; thirsty; torrid; uninteresting; unproductive; withered; ARIDITY: barrenness; desiccation; dryness; dullness; jejunity; monotony; sterility; unproductiveness

ARISE: accrue; appear; arrive; ascend; awake(n); begin; burgeon; cause; climb; debouch; deduce; derive; descend; disembogue; educe; effloresce; egress; emanate; emerge; emit; evolve; exist; flow; flower; gain; generate; get; happen; infer; issue; lift; loom; materialize; mount; obtain; originate; proceed; radiate; raise; reap; rear; return; rise; scale; soar; spread; spring; stand; stem; surge; tower; upspring; upswing; ARISING: ascendant; assurgent; budding; burgeoning; emerging; escalating; flowering; flowing; issuing; mounting; origi-

nating; proceeding; rising; soaring; springing; stemming; surging; towering

ARISTOCRAT(S): (see "elite") aristoi (pl.); *bas bleu*; blue blood; bluestocking (fem.); Brahmin; contessa; count(ess); grandee; grand seigneur; lord(ling); marquess; marquis; noble(man); parvenu; patrician; royalty; ARISTOCRATIC: anti-democratic; Brahminical; elite; exclusive; genteel; gentle; high(-hat); lordly; manor-born; noble; patrician; powerful; privileged; royal; snobbish; superior; thoroughbred

ARISTOPHANIC: (see "humorous") broad; comic(al); satirical; witty

ARM: **v.** see "provide"; ARM(S): **n.** accoutrement(s); armament(s); armamentaria (pl.); armamentarium; armor; bough; branch; bullets; defense; energy; equipage; fiord; firth; force(s); fortification(s); gun(s); inlet; instrument; limb; mail; matériel; member; might; munition(s); munitionment; musketry; offshoot; ordnance; outfit; paraphernalia; plate; power; projection; protection; ramification; ramus; saber(s); shield; sleeve; spur; strength; subdivision; subsidiary; support; sword; tentacle; tributary; weapon(s); weaponry; wing

ARMAMENT(S): **see** "arms"

ARMISTICE: abeyance; abeyancy; break; breather; cease-fire; cessation; closure; cloture; desition; discontinuance; end; halt; intermission; interruption; let-up; lull; moratorium; pause; peace; period; quiescence; quiet(ness); quietude; recess; reprieve; respite; rest; retardation; silence; stay; stop (page); surrender; suspension; truce; withdrawal

ARMOR: (**see** "arms") breastplate; panoply; shield

ARMY: (**see** "group") array(ment); assemblage; battalion; battery; brigade; crowd; force(s); hecatomb; horde; host; legion(s); military; militia; multitude; number; phalanx; soldiers; soldiery; supply; throng; troops

AROMA: (**see** "air") atmosphere; aura; balm; bouquet; cachet; dash; effluvia (pl.); effluvium; essence; fetor; flavor; fragrance; incense; inkling; intimation; nidor; nose; odor; perfume; piquancy; pungency; quality;

redolence; savor; scent; smell; sign; spice; stench; stink; AROMATIC: balmy; flavorful; fragrant; nidorous; odorous; piquant; pungent; redolent; savory; spicy

AROUND: about; almost; approximate(ly); astir; circa; circiter; close; concerning; encircling; near(by); nearly; through

AROUSE: activate; actuate; agitate; alarm; anger; animate; annoy; awake(n); bother; call; cause; discompose; disconcert; disturb; drive; educe; effect; egg; elicit; enliven; enrage; evoke; exact; exasperate; excite; exhort; fillip; fire; fluster; foment; force; fret; gain; galvanize; goad; hurry; impel; impress; incense; incite; induce; inflame; infuse; inspire; inspirit; instigate; interest; invoke; irk; irritate; jar; jostle; kindle; lash; liven; move; persuade; pique; precipitate; press; prevail; prompt; provoke; rack; raise; rally; recreate; revive; rile; rock; roil; rouse; shake; sow; spur; stimulate; stir; suggest; summon; sway; swirl; tempt; thrill; toss; trouble; urge; vex; vibrate; wake(n); whet; whip; AROUSING: (**see** "stimulating") galvanic; AROUSED: **see** "agitated"

ARRAIGN: accuse; attack; blame; censure; charge; cite; denounce; impeach; implicate; indict; prosecute; summon; try; ARRAIGN-MENT: accusation; censure; charge; citation; hearing; indictment; prosecution; summons; trial

ARRANGE: adapt; adjust; afford; agree; align; aline; alphabetize; arbitrate; array; assign; associate; assort; bequeath; bespeak; blazon; bracket; brew; build; catalog(ue); categorize; catenate; cause; chain; characterize; class(ify); code; codify; collate; collect; collimate; collocate; comb; combine; commit; compartmentalize; compass; compile; compose; compromise; concatenate; conceive; concern; concinnate; concoct; confect; conjure; consort; construct; contrive; control; conventionalize; cook (up); counterfeit; create; curry; decorate; departmentalize; design; determine; devise; display; dispose; distribute; divide; do; dress; edit; effect; employ; engage; engineer; enumerate; execute; exhibit; expose; file; find; fit; fix; forge; form(ulate); frame; get; grade; group; guide; harmonize; hatch; hierarchize; hire; imagine; improvisate; improvise; individualize; integrate; invent; invoice; invoke; label; lay; leave; line; list; machinate; make (up); manage; map; mark; marshal; match; methodize; mix; mobilize;

move; negotiate; orchestrate; order; organize; originate; pattern(ize); pigeonhole; pile; place; plan; plant; plat; plot; pose; position; predetermine; preen; premeditate; preordain; prepare; prime; primp; process; produce; project; range; rank; rate; ready; redact; register; regulate; request; scheme; score; segregate; select; separate; set(tle); shape; show; slate; smarten; sort; space; stack; stage; stamp; start; stock; store; stow; stratify; stylize; subjectify; succeed; surrender; synthesize; systematize; tabulate; think; ticket; trick; trim; type; typify; vamp; work; write; ARRANGED: adapted; adjusted; aligned; alphabetized; arrayed; assorted; bracketed; built; catalogued; categorized; characterized; classified; coded; codified; collated; collected; collimated; collocated; combined; compartmentalized; compiled; composed; concatenated; concerted; concinnate; concocted; conjured; contrived; conventionalized; departmentalized; designed; devised; displayed; disposed; distributed; done; engineered; enumerated; exhibited; farraginous; filed; fixed; formed; formulated; graded; grouped; harmonized; hierarchized; homogeneous; improvised; indexed; indexical; integrated; lined; listed; mapped; marshaled; matched; methodized; mobilized; orchestrated; ordered; orderly; organized; patterned; pigeonholed; planned; plotted; positioned; predeterminative; predetermined; prepared; primed; readied; ready; registered; regulated; schematic; segregated; selected; separate(d); set(tled); shaped; slated; sorted; spaced; stacked; staged; stocked; stored; straightened; stratified; stylized; synthesized; systematized; tabulated; trimmed; typed; ARRANGEMENT: (**see** "group") accretion; adaptation; adjustment; affair; agreement; alignment; alphabetization; ana; anthology; arbitration; array(ment); aspiration; assemblage; assembly; assignment; association; assortment; batch; blazonry; book; bracket; canon; carpentry; cascade; categorization; catalog(ue); catenation; census; chain; characterization; class(ification); code; codification; collation; collection; collocation; collimation; column; combination; commitment; committal; compartmentalizaton; compendium; compilation; composition; compromise; concinnity; concoction; constellation; constitution; construction; contour; contract; contrivance; copy; count; creation; department(alization); design; dictionary; digest; direction; display; disposition; distribution; division; document; drawing; effect; enumeration;

exhibition; exposure; expression; farrago; figure; file; form(at); formation; formulation; frame(work); group; guise; harmony; hierarchization; hierarchy; homogeneity; index; individualization; integration; invoice; layout; lineup; list; manner; method(ization); mixture; mobilization; mode; model; nature; negotiation; nomenclature; orchestration; order; organization; pageant; panoply; parade; pattern; permutation; plan; pose; position; preparation(s); range; rank; rate; recapitulation; registration; roster; rota; row; scene; schemata (pl.); scheme; score; segregation; selection; sequence; series; set(tlement); setup; shape; show; skeleton; slate; spectacle; spectacular; splash; splurge; spread; stack; stratification; structure; style; succession; suite; sum; surrender; synthesis; system(atization); table; tableau; tabulation; tariff; texture; thing; total; train; transcript(ion); treaty; type; understanding; version

ARRANT: (**see** "aimless") bad; confirmed; extreme; floating; itinerant; meandering; nomadic; notorious; out-and-out; roving; shameless; thoroughgoing; vagrant; wandering

ARRAY: **v.** (**see** "arrange") adorn; apparel; assemble; attire; bedeck; begem; clothe; deck; diamondize; dress; garb; marshal; muster; robe; throng; ARRAY(MENT): **n.** adornment; apparel; army; arrangement; assemblage; attire; battalion; battery; brigade; clothing; crowd; display; disposition; distribution; dress; exposition; finery; force; gamut; garb; group; hecatomb; horde; host; jury; legion(s); list; military; militia; multitude; number; order; panoply; parade; phalanx; pomp; rainbow; series; show; sight; soldiers; soldiery; spectrum; supply; throng; troops

ARREST: **v.** apprehend; balk; block; bridle; captivate; capture; catch; check; collar; contain; continue; control; cop; curb; dally; dawdle; defer; delay; detain; deter; dillydally; divert; drag; dwarf; ensnare; entangle; entrap; flag; get; grab; grasp; halt; hamper; hesitate; hinder; hold; hook; impede; intercept; interfere; interrupt; jail; lag; laten; lessen; linger; loiter; moderate; nab; nail; net; obstruct; pause; pinch; postpone; prevent; procrastinate; prolong; protract; quell; quench; restrain; retard; secure; seize; slacken; slow; snag; snare; snatch; sojourn; stall; stem; still; stop; stunt; suspend; take; tarry; temporize; thwart; trap; wait; ARREST: **n.** apprehen-

sion; armistice; arrestation; arrestment; blockage; captivation; capture; catch; cessation; check; containment; continuance; control; curb; cunctation; custody; deferment; delay; detention; entanglement; entrapment; forbearance; grab; halt; hampering; hesitation; hindrance; hold; impediment; imprisonment; interception; interference; intermission; interruption; lag; lessening; lingering; loitering; moratorium; obstruction(ism); pausation; pause; postponement; prevention; procrastination; prolongation; protraction; respite; rest; restraint; restriction; retardation; securement; seizure; slackening; snag; snare; sojourn; stasis; state; stay; stop(page); stopping; suspension; tarriance; temporization; termination; wait

ARRIVE: (**see** "appear") achieve; approach; arise; attain; become; befall; come; deplane; detrain; disembark; emanate; emerge; enter; finish; flow; gain; happen; hit; land; leave; occur; originate; reach; report; spring; stem; succeed; visit; ARRIVAL: (**see** "appearance") approach; attainment; avenue; emanation; emergence; entrance; origination; success

ARROGANT: aristocratic; audacious; autocratic; bold; bumptious; cavalier; commanding; compelling; contumacious; contumelious; despicable; despiteful; dictatorial; disdainful; disrespectful; distant; dogmatic; dominant; domineering; egocentric(al); egotistic(al); fastuous; forced; frosted; grandiloquent; grandiose; haughty; high; hubristic; huffy; imperative; imperial; imperious; impudent; insolent; lofty; lordly; magisterial; majestic; masterful; misproud; ostentatious; overbearing; overridden; overriding; patronizing; peremptive; peremptory; pompous; presumptuous; prideful; proud; queenly; sassy; saucy; scornful; snooty; stuck-up; supercilious; superior; swaggering; swaggish; toploftical; toplofty; uppish; uppity; vain; ARROGANCE: arrogancy; arrogantness; audacity; boldness; bumptiousness; conceit; contumacy; despicableness; dictatorship; disdain; disdainful(ness); disrespect; dogmatism; domination; effrontery; egocentricity; egotism; force(fulness); grandiloquence; grandiosity; haughtiness; hauteur; hubris; huff(iness); imperiousness; impudence; impudency; insolence; loftiness; lordliness; majesty; mastery; ostentation; peremptoriness; pomposity; pompousness; presumption; pride; queenliness; sass(iness); sauciness; scorn; snootiness; superciliousness; superiority; swagger; uppishness; vainglory; vanity

ARROGATE: (**see** "appropriate") ascribe; assume; attribute

ARROW: bolt; dart; hand; indicator; mark (er); missile; pointer; reed; shaft; weapon

ARSONIST: **see** "firebug"

ART(S): (**see** "business") ability; address; adeptness; adroitness; ambidexterity; aptitude; ars; artifice; artistry; calling; capacity; cleverness; competence; control; coordination; craft(iness); cunning; dexterity; ease; education; efficiency; esthetic(s); expertise; expertness; facility; finesse; fluency; hability; ingeniosity; ingenuity; knack; knowledge; learning; magic; method; occupation; practice; profession; proficiency; resource(s); *savoir faire*; science; skill; suavity; subtlety; tact; technique; touch; trade; training; trick; virtuosity; wit; work; ARTFUL: (**see** "skillful") adroit; ambidextrous; apt; clever; competent; crafty; cunning; deceitful; deceptive; designing; dext(e)rous; diplomatic; duplicitous; easy; efficient; esthetic; expert; facile; fluent; foxy; ingenious; ingenuous; knowing; magical; polite; politic(al); practic(al); practiced; professional; proficient; resourceful; sly; smooth; stealthy; suave; subt(i)le; tactful; trained; tricky; virtuosic; wily; witty; ARTFULNESS: **see** "skillfulness"

ARTERY: aorta; avenue; channel; conduit; course; medium; path; road; route; street; system; vessel; way

ARTFUL: **see** under "art"

ARTICLE(S): clause; commodity; condition; contrivance; detail; essay; feature; furnishings; furniture; gadget; gear; goods; implement(s); item(s); manner; merchandise; object; paper; paragraph; particular(ity); passage; person; plank; point; product(s); provision(s); proviso; report; section; segment; sentence; staple(s); stipulation; stock; story; stuff; the; theme; thing(s); tool; utensil

ARTICULATE: **v.** (**see** "speak") frame; join; link; say; sing; talk; unite; ARTICULATE(D): **a.** clear; distinct; enunciated; fluent; glib; joined; jointed; linked; meaningful; oral; said; talkative; united; uttered; vocal(ized)

ARTIFICE: (**see** "trick") art(fulness); artistry; astucity; astuteness; blind; canniness; caper; charlatanry; chicane(ry); cleverness; contrivance; coup; craft(iness); cunning; custom; deceit(fulness); deception; defraudation; design; device; dexterity; dido; dishonesty; dissimulation; dodge; duplicity; expedient; feint; finesse; forgery; fraud; gag; gambit; game; guile; imposture; ingenuity; ingenuosity; insincerity; intelligence; invention; inventiveness; knavery; knavishness; machination; maneuver; misrepresentation; perspicacity; plan; plot; prank; pretense; rascality; ruse; sagacity; scheme; shrewdness; skill(fulness); slyness; stratagem; suavity; subterfuge; subtility; subtlety; swindle; treachery; trick(ery); wile; wiliness; wisdom; wit(tiness)

ARTIFICIAL: (**see** "false") affected; apocryphal; artifactitious; bogus; Brummagem; contrived; conventional(ized); counterfeit; deceptive; dramatic(al); ersatz; fabricated; factitial; factitious; fake(d); false; falsified; feigned; fictitious; fictive; forged; fraudulent; histrionic; hollow; illegitimate; illusory; imitated; imitation; imitative; inauthentic; melodramatic; meretricious; *papier-mâché*; phony; poetic; postiche; pretended; pretentious; pseudepigraphic(al); pseudepigraphous; pseudo; quasi; shallow; sham; simulated; simulative; specious; spurious; stagy; stilted; synthetic(al); theatrical; tin(sel); unnatural; unreal; ARTIFICIALITY: (**see** "falseness") affectation; artifact; artificialness; factitiousness; fiction; simulation; staginess; theatricality

ARTISAN: artificer; craftsman; doer; fixer; hand(icrafter); handicraftsman; handyman; journeyman; laborer; mechanic; operator; smith; toiler; worker; workman

ARTIST: adept; etcher; expert; master; painter; sculptor; sketcher; virtuoso; wizard; ARTISTRY: **see** "craft"; ARTISTIC: (**see** "beautiful") aesthetic(al); arty; Bohemian; chic; cultured; discriminating; discriminative; elegant; esthetic(al); fashionable; fastidious; masterly; painterly; tasteful; virtuosic

ARTLESS: blunt; candid; crude; easy; forthright; forward; frank; gauche; genuine; guileless; honest; ignorant; inartistic; ingenuous; naif; naive; natural; open; outspoken; plain; rude; simple(minded); straight(forward); transparent; truthful; unaffected; unauspicious; unaware; undesigning; unexaggerated; unflattering; unskillful; unsophisticated; unsubtle; unvarnished; unwary; ARTLESSNESS: candidness; candor; crudity; frankness; gaucherie; guile (lessness); honesty; impartiality; ingeniosity; ingeniousness; naiveté; simplicity; unsophistication

ARTY: (see "showy") affected; artistic; *chichi*; frilly; theatrical

ASCEND: (see "arise") breast; clamber; climb; creep; elevate; escalate; gain; grow; increase; issue; lift; mount; raise; ramp; reach; rear; rise; scale; shin; slope; soar; spring; stem; surge; tower; transcend; twine; vine; ASCENDENCY or ASCENT: (see "rise") ascendant; authority; climb; control; domination; dominion; elevation; escalation; gain; glory; grade; gradient; growth; inclination; incline; increase; influence; leadership; leap; mastery; paramountcy; pitch; power; precedence; preeminence; prevalence; progress; raise; rise; slope; success; superiority; surge; sway; transcendency; upsurge; ASCENDING: (see "arising" and "rising") ascendant; transcendant

ASCERTAIN: (see "find") acquire; determine; estimate; examine; figure; gather; glean; measure; number; perceive; survey; trace; weigh

ASCETIC: **a.** (see "austere)" dour; drastic; Essenian; exacting; extreme; firm; fixed; hard; harsh; hermitic; inexorable; monkish; mortified; precise; relentless; rigid; rigorous; rugged; self-denying; self-disciplined; self-mortifying; severe; stark; stern; stiff; strenuous; strict; stringent; strong; unbending; ASCETIC: **n.** anchoret; anchorite; ascesis; Essene; friar; Heautontimorumenos; hermit; monk; nun; recluse; sabbatarian; Simon Stylites; solitudinarian; stoic; yogi

ASCRIBE: (see "charge") accredit; allege; arrogate; assign; associate; attribute; authorize; blame; certify; cite; commission; connect; credit; depute; give; guess; impute; license; place; recognize; refer; sanction; vouch (for); warrant; ASCRIBABLE: see "due"

ASEPTIC: antiseptic; barren; clean; germless; pure; sterile; undemonstrative; unfertile

ASHAMED: (see "embarrassed") abashed; chagrined; cowed; discomfited; discomposed; floored; flustered; hangdog; humbled; humiliated; shamed

ASHEN: (see "pale") anemic; cinereous

ASHES: see "cinders"

ASININE: (see "stupid") obsinate; silly; simple; unintelligent

ASK: (see "beg" and "beseech") adjure; analyze; appeal; beckon; bid; call; catechize; challenge; command; conjure; court; crave; cry; demand; direct; entice; entreat; examine; expect; implore; importune; inquire; interrogate; invite; lure; offer; order; petition; plead; pray; press; propose; pry; pump; pursue; query; question; quiz; request; seduce; seek; sift; solicit; speak; sue; summon; supplicate; tender; urge; welcome; woo

ASKEW: agee; akimbo; alop; amiss; angular; askant; atwist; awry; bent; bowed; circuitous; cockeyed; crooked; deformed; deranged; disheveled; distorted; frowsy; gnarled; meandering; messy; mussed; oblique; perverted; ratty; ruffled; seedy; shabby; sinuous; slipshod; tortuous; towsled; twisted; unkempt; untidy; warped; wry; zigzag

ASLEEP: (see "dormant") abed; comatose; dead; hypnotic; inactive; insensible; latent; lethargic; motionless; numb; out; quiescent; quiet; sleeping; slumbering; somniferous; somnolent; torpescent; torpid; unawake(ned)

ASPECT: affectation; affectedness; air; angle; apparency; appearance; arrangement; assurance; atmosphere; attitude; attitudinization; audacity; aura; bearing; behavior; bias; boldness; cachet; carriage; cheek; circumstance; cloak; color; complication; component; composure; condition; confidence; conjuncture; countenance; course; declaration; depiction; deportment; development; dignity; dilemma; direction; disguise; disposition; effect; effrontery; essence; exposure; expression; exterior; facade; face; facet; facies; feature; feeling; form; frill; front; garb; grimace; guise; habit(us); heart; impertinence; impudence; inclination; juncture; location; look; manifestation; manner(ism); map; mask; mien; mood; move; mug; nature; nerve; nimbus; obverse; occasion; occurrence; odor; opening; opinion; ostent; outside; pan; pass; pattern; persuasion; phase; philosophy; phizz; physiognomy; physique; picture; plight; pose; position; posture; preciseness; prediction; predilection; prestige; pretense; pretension; pretext; problem; property; propriety; puss; quality; quandary; scene; semblance; shape; side;

sign; signal; site; situation; slant; spirit; stage; stance; state; station; status; strait; style; substance; superficies (also pl.); surface; temper; tradition; view(point); visage; way

ASPERSE: abuse; assail; assualt; attack; baptize; belittle; berate; beset; besmirch; besplatter; blacken; blaspheme; bombard; buffet; calumniate; castigate; censure; charge; criticize; darken; defame; defile; degrade; denigrate; deprecate; depreciate; detract; dishonor; disparage; harass; harm; lampoon; lash; libel; malign; misrepresent; offend; revile; scandalize; slander; slur; traduce; vilify; vituperate; wrong; ASPERSION: abuse; assailment; attack; belittlement; calumniation; castigation; censure; charge; criticism; defamation; defilement; degradation; denigration; deprecation; depreciation; detraction; dishonor; disparagement; harassment; harm; lampoon; lash; libel; malignancy; misrepresentation; offense; oppugnation; revilement; scandal; slander; slur; traducement; traduction; vilification; vituperation; wickedness; wrong

ASPHYXIATE: see "suffocate"

ASPIRE: (see "aim") ascend; covet; crave; design; desire; dream; emulate; endeavor; essay; hope; hunger; intend; long; pant; pine; plan; propose; purpose; rise; seek; soar; strive; thirst; tower; try; want; wish; yearn; ASPIRATION: (see "aim" and "ambition") dream; endeavor; hope; hunger; intention; thirst; yearn; ASPIRANT: candidate; dreamer; hopeful; seeker; striver; yearner

ASSAIL: (see "asperse" and "attack") accuse; assault; batter; beat; berate; beset; bombard; buffet; castigate; censure; charge; confront; criticize; encounter; face; harass; invade; lash; libel; malign; offend; pelt; pound; press; raid; slug; smite; storm; strike; ASSAILMENT: (see "aspersion" and "attack") accusation; castigation; criticism; oppugnation

ASSAULT: v. see "attack"; ASSAULT: n. (see "attack") action; aggression; battery; bombardment; campaign; charge; invasion; libel; lunge; offense; offensive; onset; onslaught; push; raid; siege; thrust

ASSAY: v. see "analyze" and "try"; ASSAY: n. see "analyze" and "trial"

ASSEMBLE: accumulate; agglomerate; agglutinate; aggregate; appear; arrange; associate; band; call; categorize; caucus; club; cluster; collate; collect; collimate; compile; concentrate; confederate; confer; conflate; conglomerate; congregate; congress; consolidate; contact; convene; convocate; convoke; convoy; correlate; crowd; encamp; encounter; fit; flock; gather; group; heal; heap; herd; hold; huddle; join; levy; mass; meet; muster; organize; pack; press; rally; rendezvous; settle; summon; swarm; synthesize; teem; throng; troop; unite; ASSEMBLAGE or ASSEMBLY: (see "group" and "meeting") agglomeration; agglutination; aggregate; aggregation; agora; army; association; audience; band; bevy; body; brethren; bunch; caucus; church; club; cluster; clutch; collection; college; community; company; complement; concentration; confederation; conference; conglomeration; congregation; congress; constellation; convention; convocation; coterie; crew; crowd; denomination; fold; followers; following; gang; gathering; gobs; group; hands; herd; hookup; horde; host; huddle; legion; legislature; levee; mass; meeting; mob; multitude; organization; pack; parish; parliament; party; people; posse; press; resort; retainers; salon; sect; senate; session; set; society; staff; students; supporters; swarm; synod; team; throng; troop; union; workers

ASSENT: v. (see "allow") accede; accord; acquiesce; admit; agree; approbate; approve; concur; consent; cooperate; grant; receive; sanction; yield; ASSENT: n. accordance; acquiescence; admission; agreement; allowance; amen; approbation; approval; assentation; concurrence; consent; cooperation; grant; reception; sanction; unanimity; unison

ASSERT: (see "say") affirm; allege; announce; articulate; aver; avouch; avow; cite; confirm; declare; demonstrate; depose; emphasize; maintain; pose; posit; postulate; predicate; pretend; proclaim; profess; repeat; show; signify; state; swear; vindicate; voice; warrant; ASSERTIVE: affirmative; aggressive; articulate; assertative; assertorial; declarative; declaratory; enunciative; enunciatory; expository; positive; proclamative; promulgative; pronunciative; repetitive; ASSERTION: (see "statement") announcement; declaration; postulation; proclamation; say-so

ASSESS: (see "appraise" and "rate") adjudicate; analyze; cess; charge; determine;

estimate; evaluate; impose; judge; levy; measure; mise; price; reckon; tax; value; ASSESSMENT: adjudication; appraisal; cess; charge; duty; extent; impost; judgment; levy; measure; price; ratal; scot; scutage; tariff; tax(ation); tithe; toll; value; worth

ASSET(S): accounts; advantages; benefits; capital; credit; effects; estate; goods; honor; item(s); means; money; monies; potential (ity); property; resource(s); success; things; valuables

ASSEVERATE: (**see** "declare") affirm; aver; avouch; swear

ASSIDUOUS: (**see** "busy") attentive; obsequious; solicitous

ASSIGN: (**see** "appoint") alienate; allocate; allot; apportion; approximate; ascribe; award; bestow; budget; cede; charge; commission; concede; convey; deal; dedicate; deed; define; delegate; deliver; designate; destine; dole; endow; fix; give; grant; impute; leave; let; mark; ordain; order; place; portion; post; prescribe; rate; reckon; refer; relinquish; resign; schedule; seal; select; sell; set; specify; station; submit; surrender; transfer; waive; yield; ASSIGNMENT: (**see** "appointment") activity; allegement; allotment; amount; apportion(ment); appropriation; ascription; assignation; attribution; bestowal; commission; concession; conveyance; date; deal; deed; delegation; deliverance; designation; dole; duty; gift; grant; job; lesson; mission; order; placement; portion; post; pursuit; quota; reference; relinquishment; resignation; sale; statement; station; submission; surrender; task; transaction; transfer; waiver; warrant; work; yielding

ASSIMILATE: (**see** "absorb") adapt; appropriate; blend; compare; conform; digest; fuse; incorporate; introject; liken; merge; metabolize; mix; osmose; receive; resemble; take

ASSIST: **v.** (**see** "aid") abet; administer; attend; avail; back; befriend; benefit; board; boost; coach; escort; father; favor; feed; foster; further; grubstake; guide; hand; help; join; lead; minister; mother; nudge; nurse; nurture; prod; prompt; push; relieve; require; second; serve; speed; succor; support; sustain; wet-nurse; ASSIST(ANCE): **n.** (**see** "aid") abatement; alms; attention; backing; benefit; boost; coaching; coadjuvancy; cooperation; encouragement; favor;

food; furtherance; gift; grubstake; guidance; hand; help; helping hand; leadership; ministration; nudge; nursing; patronage; prod; push; relief; secours; service; succor; support; sustenance; ASSISTANT(S): (**see** "aide") abettor; acolyte; adjunct; adjutant; adjuvant; ally; ancillary; associate; auxiliary; clerk; coadjutant; coadjutator; coadjutress (fem.); coadjutrix (fem.); cohort; *collaborateur*; collaborator; colleague; confederate; confrere; co-worker; crew; deputy; followers; hand(s); handmaid(en); helper(s); mate; novice; nurse; pal; partner; satellite; second; servant; server; spouse; staff; subaltern(ant); subordinate; subsidiary; supporter; teammate; worker

ASSOCIATE: **v.** admix; affiliate; amalgamate; attach; attend; bind; blend; bond; bracket; coalesce; coalite; collect; combine; commix; confederate; conglomerate; conjoin; conjugate; connect; consolidate; consort; copulate; cotton; couple; entwine; fasten; fraternize; fuse; gather; herd; hobnob; identify; incorporate; infiltrate; integrate; interlard; intermix; intertwine; interweave; join; league; link; marry; match; mate; meld; melt; merge; mingle; mix; pair; relate; tie; travel; unite; yoke; ASSOCIATE(D): **a.** (**see** "united") accompanying; allied; attendant; concomitant; consociate; incidental; ASSOCIATE: **n.** (**see** "assistant") abettor; accompaniment; affiliate; aide; ally; associator; buddy; chum; coadjutor; cohort; colleague; companion; comrade; concomitant; confederate; confrere; consociate; consort; crony; deputy; entourage; fellow; follower(s); friend; helper; husband; mate; pal; partner; puisne; satellite; socius; spouse; subsidiary; supporter; traveler; wife; ASSOCIATION: affiliation; affinity; alliance; axis; band; body; brotherhood; bund; cabal; cartel; circuit; club; coalition; collusion; combination; comity; communion; compact; companionship; company; confederacy; confederation; conference; congress; connection; consolidation; consortium; contact; coterie; federation; firm; fraternity; fusion; group; guild; incorporation; league; legion; lodge; monopolization; monopoly; neighborhood; order; partnership; party; relationship; society; sodality; solidarity; sorority; togetherness; treaty; union; withness

ASSORT: (**see** "arrange") associate; class (ify); consort; distribute; file; grade; group; match; order; rank; separate; sort; type; ASSORTED: (**see** "arranged") alphabetized; classified; composite; disparate; distributed; diverse; diversified; farraginous; filed;

heterogeneous; matched; miscellaneous; motley; multiform; separate(d); variegated; varied; ASSORTMENT: (see "arrangement") batch; collection; farrago; hash; heterogeneity; lot; miscellanea (pl.); miscellaneity; miscellany; mixture; multiformity; olla podrida; set; suite; variation; variegation; variety

ASSUAGE: (see "calm") allay; ameliorate; anesthetize; appease; comfort; compose; cure; ease; lenify; mitigate; moderate; mollify; pacify; quench; quiet(en); reduce; relieve; remedy; slake; smooth; soothe; still; temper; ASSUASIVE: (see "calm") analgesic; anesthetic; calmative; comfortable; easeful; easing; easy; emollient; mitigative; mitigatory; moderating; mollifying; pacificatory; pacifying; quieting; remedial; smoothing; soothing

ASSUME: accept; accroach; adopt; affect; anticipate; appropriate; arrogate; ascribe; attribute; believe; cloak; clothe; conclude; confiscate; conjecture; consider; counterfeit; deduce; divine; don; educe; expect; fancy; feign; figure; gather; give; grab; grant; guess; hypothesize; imagine; impersonate; imply; incorporate; infer; judge; mask; opinionate; personate; portend; posit; postulate; posture; premise; presume; presuppose; pretend; reason; receive; regard; seize; sham; simulate; speculate; suppose; surmise; suspect; take (over); theorize; think; understand; undertake; usurp; ASSUMED: academic; accepted; adopted; affected; alleged; appropriated; arrogated; assumptious; conjectural; considered; derivative; factitious; false; feigned; fictitious; gratuitous; hypothesized; hypothetical; impersonated; implied; inferred; make-believe; masked; personated; postulated; postulatory; presumptuous; pretended; pretentious; simulated; soi-disant; speculated; stochastic; supposed; suppositional; supposititious; theoretical; unproved; usurpative; usurpatory; usurped; ASSUMPTION: acceptation; accroachment; adoption; affectation; anticipation; appropriation; arrogance; arrogation; ascription; attribution; audacity; belief; conception; confidence; confiscation; conjecture; consideration; deduction; expectation; fancy; feint; fiction; grab; guess(work); hypothecation; hypothesis; imagination; impersonation; implication; incorporation; inference; judgment; mask; opinion; personation; postulata (pl.); postulation; posture; premise; presumption; presupposition; pretension; principle; proposition; seizure; simulation; speculation; supposition; surmise; susception;

suspicion; take-over; theorem; theory; thesis; thought; view; understanding; usurpation

ASSURE: affirm; bind; certify; commit; contract; convince; covenant; encourage; enhearten; ensure; gage; guarantee; hearten; hypothecate; insure; mortgage; pawn; pledge; promise; prove; secure; strengthen; substantiate; swear; vouch; vow; warrant; ASSURED: (see "certain") adroit; artful; diplomatic; eager; expert; facile; firm; forward; hopeful; imperturbable; poised; proficient; quick; ready; self-possessed; skilled; skillful; stable; tactful; trustful; ASSURANCE: address; adroitness; affirmation; aplomb; arrogance; art(fulness); assertion; assumption; assuredness; audacity; avouchment; belief; boldness; brass; certainty; certification; certitude; cockiness; composure; confidence; contract; conviction; coolness; courage; covenant; credence; credit; diplomacy; eagerness; ease; effrontery; encouragement; enheartenment; equilibrium; faith; finesse; forwardness; guarantee; guaranty; hope; hypothecation; impudence; infallibility; insurance; mettle; mortgage; nerve; overconfidence; pawn; perpendicularity; positivism; presumption; promise; reliance; safety; savoir faire; securement; security; self-confidence; self-possession; self-reliance; spirit; stability; strength; substantiation; surety; tact(fulness); trust(fulness); vote; vow; warranty

ASTIR: (see "alert") about; active; afoot; alive; going; moving; stirring; up

ASTONISH or ASTOUND: affect; affright; alarm; amaze; awe; benumb; bewilder; confound; confuse; consternate; cow; daze; dazzle; dismay; dumbfound; excite; flabbergast; frighten; impress; overwhelm; paralyze; perplex; petrify; rock; shock; stagger; startle; strike; stun; stupefy; surprise; terrify; thunderstrike; ASTONISHMENT: admiration; alarm; amazement; awe; bewilderment; confusion; consternation; daze; dazzle; dismay; eye-opener; fog; fright; paralysis; perplexity; petrification; shock; show; splendor; stupefaction; surprise; terror; thunderstroke; wonder; ASTONISHING: (see "amazing," "marvelous" and "surprising") wondrous

ASTRAL: see "starry"

ASTRAY: abroad; afield; afraid; amiss; arrant; away; awry; dépaysé; deviating; devious; digressive; discursive; errant; erratic; erring; faulty; footloose; fugitive; lost; meandering;

migratory; nomadic; Odyssean; off; peripatetic; roaring; roving; sinning; straying; traveling; vagabond(ish); vagarious; vagrant; wandering; winding; wrong; wry

ASTRINGE: **v.** (**see** "sour") astrict; ASTRINGENT: **a.** (**see** "rigid") astrictive; austere; constricting; contradicting; restrained; restricted; severe; sharp; stern; styptic; tonic; ASTRINGENT: **n.** alum; astringence; astringency; styptic

ASTRONOMICAL: (**see** "immense") enorm(ous); inconceivable; magnitudinous; starry; uranic

ASTUTE: (**see** "clever") acute; artful; astucious; canny; cleverish; crafty; cunning; discriminating; foxy; intelligent; keen; learned; penetrating; penetrative; perspicacious; quick; sagacious; sharp; shrewd; skilled; sly; smart; subt(i)le; wily; witty; ASTUTENESS: **see** "cleverness" and "wit"

ASUNDER: (**see** "divided") apart; distinct; segregated; separated

ASYLUM: (**see** "refuge") altar; ark; bughouse; cover; covert; den; harbor; haven; home; hospital; lair; nest; retreat; sanctuary; sanitarium; shelter

ATHLETIC: acrobatic; active; agile; brawny; burly; gladiatorial; gymnastic; lissome; lithe; lusty; mesomorphic; muscular; nimble; physical; powerful; robust(ious); sinewy; stalwart; strapping; strong; vigorous; ATHLETE: contestant; gladiator

ATMOSPHERE: aesthetics; air; ambience; ambient(e); appeal; aroma; attitude; aura; background; cache; climate; condition(ing); decor(ation); effect; emanation; environment; esthetics; ether; exosphere; fascination; feel(ing); glamo(u)r; halo; influence; ionosphere; medium; mesosphere; miasma; milieu; mood; nimbus; odor; ornamentation; ozone; perfume; place; quality; savor; setting; stratosphere; tone

ATOM: (**see** "bit") corpuscle; dash; dot; fragment; granule; ion; iota; jot; minim; mite; molecule; monad; mote; particle; shade; speck; tinge; tittle; whim; whit; ATOMIC: minute; molecular

ATONE: (**see** "reconcile") agree; amend; appease; expiate; harmonize; pay; propitiate; purge; redeem; satisfy; shrive; ATONING: expiatory; piacular; propitiative; propitia-

tory; ATONEMENT: accord; amends; appeasement; cross; expiation; hair shirt; harmonization; harmony; penance; propitiation; purge; rapprochement; reconcilement; reconciliation; redemption; reparation; satisfaction; trial; understanding

ATROCIOUS: (**see** "bad") abhorrent; abominable; appalling; awful; barbaric; brutal; criminal; cruel; crying; detestable; evil; execrable; fierce; flagitious; flagrant; foul; grievous; gross; heinous; infamous; inhuman (e); monstrous; murderous; nefarious; notorious; odious; outrageous; painful; rank; revolting; savage; shameful; terrible; uncivil(ized); vile; villainous; wicked; ATROCITY: (**see** "badness" and "crime") calamity; flagrancy; savagery

ATTACH: (**see** "apply") add; adhere; adjoin; affix; annex; append; appoint; arrest; ascribe; associate; bind; clip; conjoin; connect; couple; entwine; fasten; fix; glue; graft; grip; hitch; hold; insert; join; link; love; moor; nail; peg; pend; pin; secure; seize; splice; stick; tack; take; tie; vest; ATTACHED: adherent; adnate; affixed; applied; associated; bound; coupled; fond; held; hitched; joined; linked; married; moored; sessile; stuck; tacked; umbilical; ATTACHMENT: (**see** "application") accessory; addition; adherence; adhesion; affection; affinity; alliance; alligation; annex(ation); codicil; devotion; engagement; esteem; fitting; fondness; infatuation; love; regard; tenderness; union

ATTACK: **v.** accrue; aggress; ambuscade; ambush; assail; assault; battle; beat; bedevil; beleaguer; berate; beset; besiege; blitz; bludgeon; bomb(ard); bruise; brush; buffet; burden; cannonade; castigate; censure; charge; clash; clinch; clutch; collide; combat; come to grips; compete; conflict; confront; contend; contest; cope; counter (act); cripple; criticize; damage; debate; decompose; demolish; denounce; dent; destroy; devil; dispute; dog; encroach; engage; envelop; experience; face; feud; fight; forage; grapple; grasp; grip; harass; harm; hit; hound; hurt; injure; invade; invest; jab; lash; libel; lunge; maim; malign; mar; maraud; meet; nibble; occupy; offend; oppose; oppugn; paste; pelt; pester; pillage; plague; plunder; pound; press; protest; push; raid; rake; ram; rape; ravage; riot; rummage; satirize; scorn; seize; shell; siege; skirmish; slug; smash; smite; storm; strafe; strike; struggle; surround; tackle; threaten; thrust; trouble; undergo; vituperate; war; worry;

wrestle; ATTACK: **n.** accusation; action; affair; affray; aggression; ambuscade; ambush(ment); assailment; assault; battery; battle; beating; blitz; bludgeon; bombardment; bout; brush; buffet; campaign; cannonade; castigation; censure; charge; clash; collision; combat; competition; conflict(ion); confrontation; contact; contest; controversy; counteraction; coup; *coup de plume*; criticism; crusade; debate; denunciation; diatribe; dispute; encounter; encroachment; engagement; envelopment; experience; feud; fight; fit; foray; fracas; fray; harassment; harm; hit; hurt; incursion; inroad; invasion; invective; jab; lash; libel; lunge; maraud; match; meet(ing); offense; offensive; onset; onslaught; oppugnation; outburst; paroxysm; philippic; pillage; plague; plunder; polemic; pounding; press; protest; push; raid; riot; round; sally; seizure; set-to; shelling; siege; skirmish; slug(fest); smite; sortie; spasm; spell; storm; strafing; strife; strike; struggle; tackle; thrust; tirade; trial; vituperation; war(fare)

ATTAIN: (**see** "accomplish" and "accumulate") accrue; achieve; acquire; add; amass; annex; arrive; buy; collect; compass; derive; develop; earn; effect(uate); encompass; end; gain; get; glean; go; grasp; grip; harvest; learn; make; master; obtain; occupy; pass; possess; procure; prove; purchase; reach; realize; reap; receive; secure; seize; snatch; steal; succeed; take; win; ATTAINMENT: accomplishment; accumulation; achievement; acquisition; addition; amassment; annexation; arrival; artistry; collection; earning(s); effectuation; end; endowment; experience; feat; finesse; fortune; gain; gleaning; grab; grasp; harvest; incorporation; knowledge; learning; mastery; obtainment; occupation; possession; procurement; purchase; reach; realization; reception; securement; seizure; skill; success; talent; winnings; wisdom

ATTEMPT: **v.** (**see** "begin") assay; beseech; endeavor; entreat; essay; explore; ferret; fish; hunt; probe; prosecute; pry; pursue; rummage; search; seek; solicit; start; strive; sue; supplicate; try; undertake; venture; ATTEMPT: **n.** (**see** "beginning") assay; conation; conatus; effort; endeavor; essay; go; shot; stab; start; test; trial; try; undertaking; venture; woo

ATTEND: (**see** "serve") accompany; administer; apply; associate; call; care (for); chaperone; coexist; collaborate; come; conduct; convoy; escort; favor; follow; foster; go; groom; guard; guide; hark(en); heed; help; inspect; lead; listen; maintain; mark; mind; mother; nurse; nurture; observe; participate; pilot; protect; receive; see; shepherd; shield; squire; steer; support; tend; treat; usher; visit; wait; watch; wetnurse; ATTENDED: accompanied; associated; attendant; chaperoned; escorted; favored; followed; fostered; fraught; guarded; heeded; mothered; nursed; squired; tended; visited; watched; ATTENDING: **see** "contemporary"

ATTENDANT(S): accompaniment; aide; appendage; appendant; auxiliary; conductor; chaperone; chasseur; cicerone; concomitant; convoy; corollary; duenna; entourage; escort; follower; governante; governess; guard(s); guardian; guide; handmaid(en); hireling; maid; man; matron; mercenary; messenger; minion; mother; myrmidon; nurse; observer; orderly; pilot; protector; retinue; scout; servant; server; squire; suite; supporter; surveillant; train; usher; valet; waiter; watch(man)

ATTENTION: (**see** "care") action; advertence; advertency; application; assiduity; attentiveness; awareness; caution; charge; circumspection; concern; consciousness; consideration; custody; defense; diligence; direction; discipline; ear; heed; favor; forethought; guardianship; intendence; interest; love; maintenance; mark; note; notice; nurturance; observation; order; pain(s); paternalism; patronage; perception; precaution; prudence; recognition; regard; respect; responsibility; scruple; solicitation; solicitude; spotlight; study; supervision; thought; tutelage; vigil(ance); wariness; watchfulness; worry; ATTENTIVE: (**see** "careful") active; advertent; alert; arrect; assiduous; astute; avid; brisk; busy; cautious; circumspect; civil; concerned; courteous; diligent; eager; heedful; inspective; intent; interested; keen; mindful; observant; observing; orderly; perceptive; polite; prevenient; prudent; regardful; sedulous; studious; thoughtful; vigilant; wary; watchful; wise; ATTENTIVENESS: **see** "carefulness" and "heedfulness"

ATTENUATE: (**see** "refine") decrease; dilute; draw (out); lessen; rarefy; reduce; sap; slenderize; thin; water; weaken

ATTEST: (**see** "testify") adjure; affirm; authenticate; certify; confess; evidence; evince; invoke; manifest; notarize; prove; reveal; seal; show; speak; swear; verify;

vouch; witness; ATTESTATION: **see** "evidence"

ATTIRE: **v. see** "dress;" ATTIRE: **n. (see** "apparel") accoutrement(s); array(ment); caparison; clothes; equipage; garb; guise; habiliment; habit; investment; livery; outfit; regalia; robes; toilette; uniform; vestment(s); vesture

ATTITUDE: (**see** "air" and "aspect") angle; arrangement; attitudinization; bearing; behavior; bias; coloration; complex; course; direction; disposition; feeling; front; heart; inclination; mien; mood; opinion; persuasion; phase; philosophy; pose; position; posture; predilection; slant; spirit; stand; style; temper; tradition; tune; view(point)

ATTRACT: (**see** "fascinate") allure; appeal; bait; bewitch; call; captivate; capture; charm; court; draw; enamor; enchant; enlist; entice; flaunt; gather; gravitate; influence; interest; invite; lure; magnetize; muster; obtrude; pull; seduce; solicit; summon; take; tempt; woo; ATTRACTIVE: (**see** "fascinating") alluring; amiable; appealing; appointed; arresting; beautiful; beguiling; bewitching; bonny; charming; Circean; comely; cute; decorative; decorous; delightful; desirable; enchanting; engaging; enjoyable; entrancing; excellent; fair; fetching; good(-looking); handsome; intriguing; lovely; luring; magnetic; mesmeric; nice; noticeable; palatable; personable; persuasive; photogenic; photographic; pleasing; prepossessing; pretty; psychagogic; ravishing; seductive; striking; stunning; sweet; taking; tasteful; tasty; tempting; winning; winsome; ATTRACTION or ATTRACTIVENESS: (**see** "fascination" and "grace") affinity; allure (ment); appeal; bait; bribe; carnival; charm; cynosure; diversion; encouragement; enticement; exhibition; fair; feature; fillip; force; glamo(u)r; goad; gravity; incentive; incitation; incitement; inducement; influence; invitation; lodestar; lodestone; lure; magnet (ism); offer; oomph; polestar; provocation; pull; seduction; sideshow; spell; spur; stimulant; stimulation; stimulus; temptation; urge; valence

ATTRIBUTE: **v.** accredit; allege; arrogate; ascribe; assign; associate; blame; certify; charge; cite; connect; credit; depute; give; impute; license; place; reckon; recognize; refer; sanction; set; vouch; warrant; ATTRIBUTE: **n.** (**see** "characteristic") accessory; appendage; property; proprium; quality; sign; symbol; token

ATTRITION: abrasion; anguish; chafing; erosion; friction; gnawing; grating; grief; grinding; intertrigo; irritation; loss; penitence; rasping; regret; rubbing; scraping; scratching; sorrow; weakening; wear

ATTUNE: accede; accord; adapt; adjust; agree; allow; conform; coordinate; correspond; harmonize; key; melodize; mesh; jibe; prepare; reconcile; tally; temper; tune; unite

ATYPICAL: (**see** "abnormal") irregular; unrepresentative

AUCTION: (**see** "sell" and "sale") outcry; venture

AUDACIOUS: adventuresome; adventurous; arrogant; bold; brash; brassy; brave; brazen (-faced); cheeky; courageous; cross; dangerous; daring; defying; fearless; fierce; forward; fresh; hardy; harsh; heroic; impertinent; imprudent; impudent; incautious; insolent; insulting; intrepid; intrusive; meddlesome; nervy; offensive; officious; pert; presumptuous; rash; rebellious; reckless; resolute; rude; sassy; saucy; shameless; unabashed; uncivil; unrestrained; unscrupulous; untrammeled; venturesome; venturous; wild; AUDACITY: (**see** "courage") arrogance; assurance; boldness; brashness; brass(iness); brazen(ness); cheekiness; crassness; crust (iness); danger; daring; disdain; effrontery; fearlessness; ferocity; fierceness; forwardness; fury; gall; guts; harshness; heedlessness; hubris; impertinence; impetuosity; impudence; indiscretion; insolence; intrepidity; mettle; nerve; presumption; pride; rashness; rebellion; resolution; rudeness; sand; sass(iness); sauciness; shamelessness; spirit; temerity; vanity; venture; wildness

AUDIBLE: **see** "aloud"

AUDIENCE: **see** "assembly"

AUDIT: **v.** (**see** "examine") check; hear; inquire; inspect; probe; prove; review; scan; scrutinize; verify; AUDIT: **n.** (**see** "examination") account; check; inquiry; probe; review; scrutiny; statement; verification

AUGMENT: add; aggrandize; aggravate; beef up; compound; deepen; dilate; double; eke; enhance; enlarge; escalate; exacerbate; excite; expand; feed; heighten; increase; intensify; magnify; multiply; swell; triple; AUGMENTATION: **see** "addition"

AUGUR: see "portend;" **AUGURY:** (see "omen") divination; handsel; indication; portent; sign(al); sortilege; token

AUGUST: (see "exalted") awesome; awful; courtly; dignified; elegant; eminent; ennobled; grand; imperial; imposing; kingly; lordly; magnificent; majestic; noble; princely; redoubtable; regal; royal; sedate; serene; stately; sublime; togated; venerable

AURA: (see "atmosphere") air; aroma; cachet; emanation; feel(ing); halo; mood; odor; perfume; savor; tone

AUSPICE: aid; care; favor; guidance; influence; omen; patronage; portent; sign; token; **AUSPICIOUS:** (see "favorable") apt; benign(ant); dexterous; fair; fortitudinous; fortunate; good; happy; hopeful; likely; lucky; opportune; promiseful; promising; propitious; **AUSPICES:** (see "protection") (a)egis; patronage; tutelage

AUSTERE: (see "ascetic") abandoned; acrimonious; asperous; astringent; barbarous; bare; barren; bleak; blue; calamitous; chaste; cheerless; chilly; cloudy; cold; colorless; cool; cruel; cutting; dark; dejected; desolate; dingy; dire(ful); dismal; dispirited; dispiriting; dispiteous; distressing; doleful; dolorous; dour; down; drab; Draconian; drastic; drear(y); dull; earnest; Essenian; exact(ing); extortionate; extreme; fell; feral; firm; fixed; flinty; formal; frightful; frigid; frozen; funebrial; funebrious; funerary; funereal; furious; gloomy; glum; granitic; grave; gray; hard; harsh; heavy; icy; imperative; implacable; inclement; inexorable; inflexible; inhuman(e); inquisitorial; intolerant; joyless; keen; lifeless; lugubrious; melancholic; melancholy; merciless; miserable; monotonous; mortified; mortifying; mournful; murky; Neronian; obdurate; ominous; precise; procrustean; raw; relentless; remorseless; rigid; rigorous; ruthless; sad(dened); scrupulous; serious; set; severe; sharp; sinister; sober; solid; sombre; sorry; Spartan(ic); stark; stern; stiff; stony; stormy; straight; strenuous; strict; stringent; strong; stubborn; sullen; tense; tough; unbending; unbent; unbowed; uncompromising; unembellished; unfeeling; unrelenting; unshakable; unsparing; unsympathetic; unyielding; vacuous; wanton; weak; wild; wintery; **AUSTERITY:** ascesis; austereness; bleakness; cheerlessness; coldness; cruelty; depression; desolation; difficulty; dismality; dismalness; dolor; dreariness; dullness; exaction; exactness; gloom(iness); glumness;

gravity; hardship; harshness; inclemency; inflexibility; loneliness; lornness; lugubriosity; melancholia; melancholy; monotonousness; rigidity; rigor; sadness; scrupulosity; sharpness; Spartanism; sternness; strenuosity; strictness; stringency; vicissitude; wearisomeness

AUTHENTICATE: see "confirm" and "verify;" **AUTHENTIC:** (see "authoritative") absolute; accepted; accredited; accurate; actual; approved; attested; authoritarian; authorized; bona fide; cathedral; cathedratic; certain; confirmed; convincing; correct; credible; definitive; demonstrable; endorsed; established; exact; factual; genuine; indisputable; kosher; legal; legitimate; letter-perfect; licensed; literal; notarized; official; original; positival; positive; prescribed; proper; proved; proven; pukka; pure; ratified; real; recognized; reliable; right; sanctioned; sealed; substantiated; sure; true; trustworthy; unquestionable; valid(ated); verified; veritable; worthy

AUTHOR: (see "writer") ancestor; begettor; compiler; composer; correspondent; creator; editor; father; informant; instigator; inventor; maker; mother; originator; parent; penman; procreator; producer; scribe; sire; source; **AUTHORSHIP:** instigation; origin(ation); paternity; writing

AUTHORITY: academy; adept; adjuration; administration; admonishment; armament; artist; ascendancy; author; authoritativeness; authorization; autonomy; basis; baton; behest; bid(ding); bureaucrat; call; canonicity; capacity; carte blanche; caveat; charge; chief; command(ment); competence; competency; compulsion; control; credit; critic; czardom; delegation; demand; dictation; dictum; direction; discipline; dispensation; domain; domination; dominion; dynasty; edict; efficiency; energy; enjoinder; exaction; expert; faculty; fasces; fiat; force; freedom; govenment; governor; headquarters; imperative; imposition; influence; injunction; intensity; interdiction; jurisdiction; king; law; license; mace; magisteriality; magistrate; main; majesty; management; mandament; mandarin; mandate; master(fulness); mastery; means; might; multipotence; office; officer; official(dom); officiality; omnipotence; opinion; order; ordinance; organization; orthodoxy; plenipotence; police; potency; power; power of attorney; precedent; precept; prerogative; prescription; prestige; puissance; pundit; purview; regent; regime; request; requirement; resources; responsibility; right;

rod; rule; Sanhedrin; say-so; scepter; shout; skill; source; sovereignty; specialist; speciality; state; stick; strength; summons; superiority; supremacy; suzerainty; sway; sword; territory; testimony; title; wand; warning; warrant; weight; whip; AUTHORITARIAN or AUTHORITATIVE: (see "autocratic" and "authentic") able; absolute; accredited; apostolic(al); arbitrary; authorized; bold; canonical; cathedral; cathedratic; certain; certified; classic(al); cogent; conclusive; convincing; despotic; dictatorial; documented; domineering; effective; efficacious; enormous; established; *ex cathedra;* extensive; genuine; great; hefty; Herculean; hierarchic(al); high; imperious; important; imposing; influential; invincible; judgmatical; legal; legitimate; magisterial; magistral; mighty; momentous; multipotent; official; omnipotent; oppressive; orthodox; plenipotent(iary); pompous; potent; powerful; preeemptory; prescribed; puissant; recognized; robust(ious); Samsonian; sanctioned; strong; sturdy; supreme; totalitarian; true; tyrannic(al); tyrannous; valid; vast; vigorous; violent

AUTHORIZE: accredit; admit; allot; allow; appoint; approve; award; bequest; bestow; cede; commission; concede; confer; confirm; consent; convey; charter; credit; decree; delegate; do; elect; employ; empower; enact; endorse; enjoin; entitle; establish; franchise; grant; guarantee; issue; justify; legalize; legislate; let; license; make; ordain; order; pass; patent; permit; portray; represent; sanction; suffer; vote; vouchsafe; warrant; AUTHORIZATION: (see "authority") accreditation; allotment; allowance; appointment; approval; award; certification; commission; decree; delegation; enactment; endorsement; entitlement; establishment; franchise; grant; justification; legalization; legislation; license; line of duty; order; ordination; pass; patent; permit; sanction; warrant

AUTOBIOGRAPHY: anamnesis; *curriculum vitae;* history; life; memoir(s); personalia (pl.); profile; prosopography; recollections; reminiscences; vita

AUTOCRATIC: (see "authoritative") absolute; absolutist(ic); arrogant; authoritarian; bigoted; capricious; captious; despotic; determinate; determined; dictatorial; dogmatic; domineering; hierarchic(al); imperious; inexorable; irrational; irresponsible; kingly; nondemocratic; positive; sassy; saucy; severe; totalitarian; tyrannical; tyrannous; willful;

AUTOCRAT: (see "despot") authoritarian; bigot; Caesar; czar; dictator; hierarch; mogul; monarch; sovereign; tyrant; AUTOCRACY: see "despotism"

AUTOMATIC: accidental; automatous; autonomic; inexorable; instinctive; involuntary; mechanical; reflex; self-acting; self-regulating; spontaneous; uncontrollable; uncontrolled; unintentional; unmotivated; unpremeditated; unthinking; unwilled; unwilling

AUTONOMY: see "freedom"

AUXILIARY: **a.** accessorial; accessory; added; additional; adjunct; adminicular; ancillary; assistant; augmentative; augmenting; collateral; consequential; dependent; derivational; derivative; epiphenomenal; etiological; extra; helpful; incidental; other; reserved; satellite; satellitic; secondary; subordinate; subservient; subsidiary; substitute; supplementary; tributary; AUXILIARY: **n.** (see "assistant") adjunct(ion); adjunctive; adminicle; aide; ally; appendage; appendix; augmentation; branch; coadjutor; confederate; incidental; mate; partner; satellite; sub(ordinate); substitute; tributary

AVAIL: (see "use") aid; advantage; apply; benefit; best; conquer; do; help; profit; serve; succeed; suffice; utilize; win; AVAILABLE: accessible; advantageous; agreeable; amenable; appropriate; around; attainable; close (by); compliant; convenient; deft; dispensable; disposed; eager; easy; expedient; expendable; facile; fair; favorable; feasible; fit(ting); flexible; free; handy; helpful; here; inclinable; inclined; near(by); obedient; obtainable; open; practicable; present; prone; ready; receptive; remittable; unforced; usable; utile; utilizable; valid; visible; voluntary; willing

AVARICE: (see "greed") avariciousness; avidity; covetousness; cupidity; desire; greediness; itch(ing); miserliness; parsimony; rapacity; stinginess; venality; AVARICIOUS: (see "greedy") acquisitive; avid; close; covetous; extortionate; grasping; gripping; miserly; parsimonious; pennypinching; rapacious; sordid; stingy; tight; venal

AVENGE: afflict; answer; chastise; pay; punish; reciprocate; repay; requite; retaliate; retort; return; revenge; vindicate; visit; AVENGER: Nemesis; retaliator; *vindex injuriae;* vindicator

AVENUE: (see "street") access; admittance; approach; artery; channel; corridor; door (way); entrance(way); entrée; entry; gate; mall; means; method; opening; passage (way); permission; permit; portal; road; route; way

AVER: (see "claim") affirm; allege; assert; avouch; avow; declare; depose; insist; postulate; protest; say; state; swear; testify; verify; voice

AVERAGE: **a.** acceptable; adequate; admissible; balanced; banal; between; betwixen; betwixt; *comme ci, comme ça*; common(place); conformable; conventional; *couci-couça*; customary; decent; even; everyday; fair; general; habitual; half-way; indifferent; intermediate; just; la-la; mean; medial; median; mediocre; medium; mesne; middle (-class); middle-of-the-road; middle-road; middling; midway; moderate; neutral; normal; orderly; ordinary; par; passable; plain; plebeian; presentable; prevalent; reasonable; regular; representative; routine; run-of-(the)-mill; run-of-(the)-mine; satisfactory; second-rate; so-so; standard; sufficient; tolerable; typical; undistinguished; unexceptional; uniform; usual; vernacular; vulgar; workaday; AVERAGE: **n.** convention; custom; mean; medial; medium; model; moderation; mold; norm(ality); orthodoxy; par; pattern; rule; standard; universal

AVERSE: abhorrent; abominating; afraid; against; anti(pathic); antithetical; apathetic; backward; balky; chary; counter(active); counterclockwise; demurring; discouraged; disinclined; disinterested; displeased; distasteful; doubtful; grudging; half-hearted; hated; hateful; hesitant; impassionate; indisposed; inertial; insufferable; lazy; loath (some); nauseating; noxious; obnoxious; obstinate; offensive; opposed; opposing; opposite; passive; recalcitrant; refractory; reluctant; remiss; repellant; repugnant; repulsive; resisting; shy; slack; slow; tardy; undisposed; uneager; unenthusiastic; uninterested; unpalatable; unpleasant; unresponsive; unsweet; unwelcome; unwilling; unwishful; wary; AVERSION: abhorrence; abomination; animosity; antipathy; *bête noir*; disgust; disinclination; dislike; displeasure; disrelish; distaste; hate; hatred; indisposition; inertia; loathsomeness; nausea; opposition; opprobrium; recalcitrance; reluctance; reluctation; repugnance; repugnancy; repulsion; resistance; revulsion; unwillingness

AVERT: (see "avoid") alienate; bend; bypass; deflect; depart; deter; detour; deviate; disgust; diverge; dodge; escape; estrange; expiate; fend; move; parry; prevent; reroute; retard; shield; thwart; turn; twist; ward (off); wind

AVID: afire; agitated; agog; animated; anticipative; anxious; ardent; athirst; avaricious; craving; desirous; eager; enthusiastic; esurient; excited; fond; gluttonous; greedy; hungry; inflamed; intense; keen; ravenous; roused; stirred; thirsty; vigorous; voracious; zealous

AVOCATION: calling; hobby; pastime; recreation; trade; vocation; work

AVOID: (see "avert") abhor; abjure; abstain; annul; baffle; bend; blacklist; blackmail; boycott; bypass; camouflage; cancel; change; cheat; circumnavigate; circumvent; cloak; cover; curve; deceive; decline; defeat; deflect; delude; deny; depart; detour; deviate; die; digress; disagree; disclaim; dissemble; divaricate; diverge; divert; divide; dodge; duck; elope; elude; equivocate; err; escape; eschew; evade; fear; fence; fend (off); fib; flee; fluctuate; fly; foil; forbear; forestall; forgo; frustrate; give up; hedge; hesitate; hinder; ignore; invalidate; lapse; lie; linger; malinger; maneuver; mislead; miss; move; neglect; nullify; obviate; omit; ostracize; outdo; outwit; overcome; palter; parry; prevaricate; prevent; quibble; recall; recant; recede; refrain; reject; renounce; repel; repudiate; resign; retract; revoke; rove; save; scorn; screen; shift; shirk; short-circuit; shove; shuffle; shun; shunt; shy; sidestep; sin; skid; skip; skirt; slack; slip; slue; spare; split; spurn; squint; stray; swerve; tack; tergiversate; thwart; trick; turn; twist; vacate; vary; veer; veil; vitiate; wander; ward (off); weasel; AVOIDANCE: (see "digression") adjuration; annulment; bypass; circumvention; deflection; detour; escape; eschewal; evasion; obviation; prevention; recall; rejection; renunciation; repudiation; resignation; retraction; revocation; shift; shunt; sidestep; skip; swerve; tack; trick; twist; veer

AVOUCH: (see "avow") accept; affirm; assert; confess; guarantee

AVOW: accept; acknowledge; admit; affirm; allege; assert; aver; avouch; claim; confess; declare; depone; depose; guarantee; insist; own; postulate; profess; protest; say; state; swear; testify; verify; voice; witness; AVO-

WAL: acceptance; acknowledgement; admission; affirmation; allegation; assertion; claim; confession; declaration; deposition; insistence; oath; postulation; profession; testimony; verification; AVOWED(LY): acknowledged; admitted; *ex professo*; sworn

AWAIT: (**see** "anticipate") abide; bide; expect; hang; hope; impend; look; pend; stay; suspend; tarry

AWAKE(N): **v. see** "waken;" AWAKE: **a.** active; acute; agile; agog; alert; alive; apprehensive; apprised; aroused; arrect; astir; attentive; aware; brisk; bristling; careful; cognizant; conscious; conversant; eager; excited; gay; heedful; hep; informed; intelligent; keen; knowing; lively; mindful; moving; nimble; observant; perceptive; percipient; perspicacious; pert; prompt; quick(-witted); ready; resourceful; roused; sensible; sensitive; sentient; sharp; sophisticated; stirred; stirring; sudden; sure; swift; unasleep; unblinded; undeceived; unsleeping; wary; watchful; zealous; AWAKENING: (**see** "awareness") acuteness; alertness; apprehension; burgeoning; disenchantment; disillusionment; quickening; realization; recognition; revival; vigilance

AWARD: **v.** (**see** "apportion") accord; add; adjudge; aid; allot; allow; apply; assign; authorize; bequeath; bestow; cite; commend; confer; consign; crown; deposit; designate; devise; devote; direct; dispense; distribute; divide; dole; donate; earmark; give; grant; ordain; parcel; partition; place; prescribe; present; rate; ration; regulate; render; reward; set; slice; split; AWARD: **n.** accolade; allotment; badge; bestowal; blue ribbon; bonus; boon; bounty; certificate; citation; coin; commendation; conferment; conferral; *cordon bleu*; crown; cup; decision; decoration; designation; diploma; dividend; emblem; flag; garland; gift; *grand prix*; grant; honor; keepsake; kiss; knighthood; largess; laurel(s); medal; medallion; meed; memorial; oscar; palm (leaf); patch; pin; plaque; premium; present(ation); prize; reward; ribbon; scalp; sentence; spoils; standard; subsidy; token; tony; trophy

AWARE: (**see** "alert") alive; apprised; cognizant; conscient; conscious; conversant; hep; informed; intelligent; keen; knowing; living; mindful; observant; perceptive; percipient; perspicacious; sensible; sensitive; sentient; sophisticated; sure; unblinded; undeceived; vigilant; watchful; AWARE-

NESS: (**see** "awakening") apprehension; attention; cognition; cognizance; comprehension; conscience; consciousness; control; conviction; discernment; ear; feeling; heed; insight; intelligence; intuition; jurisdiction; ken; knowledge; notice; observation; orientation; perception; percipience; recognition; sensation; sense; sentience; sentiency; surveillance; vigilance; vision; watchfulness

AWAY: (**see** "afar" and "distant") abroad; absent; afield; apart; aside; constantly; forthwith; fro; gone; hence; immediately; off; out(ward); remote; thence; uninterrupted

AWE: **v.** (**see** "daunt") petrify; scare; AWE: **n.** abasement; devotion; dread; esteem; fear; regard; respect; reverence; veneration; wonder; AWE-INSPIRING or AWESOME: (**see** "awful") august; doughty; dreadful; fearful; fell; formidable; illustrious; magnificent; malevolent; redoubtable; reverent; sinister

AWFUL: (**see** "outrageous") alarming; appalling; august; awe-inspiring; awesome; dangerous; deadly; diabolic(al); difficult; dire(ful); disagreeable; dread(ful); fearful; fell; formidable; frightening; frightful; ghastly; grand; horrendous; horrible; horrific; impressive; indescribable; ineffable; malevolent; morbid; morbific; mortal; ominous; outrageous; portentous; redoubtable; respectful; satanic; serious; shocking; sinister; stately; stupendous; terrible; terrific; undescribable; unpleasant

AWKWARD: (**see** "clumsy") bungling; coarse; contradictory; cumbersome; cumbrous; difficult; elephantine; embarrassed; feckless; fumbling; gawky; graceless; ill-adapted; ill-made; ill-proportioned; inapt; inconvenient; inelegant; inept; inexpert; infelicitous; inopportune; left-handed; loutish; lumbering; lumpish; maladroit; ponderous; rigid; rough; rude; rustic; shy; stiff; ugly; uncouth; uneasy; unfit; ungainly; ungraceful; unhandy; unhappy; unskilled; unskillful; unsociable; unwieldy; wooden; AWKWARDNESS: bungling; clumsiness; cumberousness; discomposure; embarrassment; fumblingness; gaucheness; gaucherie; gawkishness; inaptitude; inelegance; ineptitude; maladroitness; ponderosity; rigidity; rusticity; tension; unease; uneasiness; ungainliness; ungracefulness; unwieldiness; woodenness

AWRY: (**see** "crooked") askew; oblique(ly); wrong

AXIOM: (**see** "maxim") byword; canon; convention; law; motto; postulate; principle; proverb; rule; saw; standard; theorem; theorum; truism; truth; witticism; AXI-OMATIC: (**see** "self-evident") aphoristic; hypothetico-deductive; postulational; primitive; witty

AXIS: axle; center; core; focus; hub; league; nub; nucleus; pivot; point; rod; shaft; spindle; spine; spool; stem

B

BABBLE: **v.** blab; blather; blurt; chat(ter); gag; gibber; gossip; gurgle; jabber; palaver; prate; prattle; rave; say; speak; tattle; BABBLE: **n.** bavardage; blather; chatter; gab; galimatias; gibberish; gossip; harangue; jabber; jargon; palaver; prattle; raving; speech; stultiloquence; stultiloquy; talk; twaddle

BABEL: (**see** "confusion") din; noise; project; scheme; tower

BABY: **v.** caress; cherish; coax; coddle; comfort; console; cosset; encourage; favor; fondle; gratify; humor; indulge; love; mollycoddle; nurse; pamper; pet; placate; please; satiate; satisfy; spoil; BABY: **a** (**see** "small") diminutive; youngest; BABY: **n.** (**see** "child") babe; bairn; brat; darling; dear; doll; infant; toddler; tot(o); tyke; youngster

BACHELOR: agamist; celibate; Coelebs; misogynist

BACK: **v.** (**see** "abet" and "support") assist; boost; buttress; countersign; embolden; encourage; endorse; stake; substantiate; support; uphold; BACK: **a.** or **adv.** abaft; aft; ago; arear; astern; delayed; over(due); posterior; rear(ward); retarded; retroactive; BACK: **n.** chine; dorsum; hind; posterior(ity); rear; reverse; stern; tergum

BACKER: abettor; angel; cohort; collaborator; colleague; constituent; corroborator; exponent; follower; guarantor; insurer; proponent; reinforcer; subscriber; supporter; undersigner; underwriter

BACKFIRE: boomerang; bounce; echo; err; kick; miscalculate; miscarry; recoil; resile; ricochet

BACKGROUND: accompaniment; air; antecedent; arrangement(s); atmosphere; case; circumstances; composition; conditions; decor; details; distance; education; environment; experience; facts; family; heredity; history; information; lineage; milieu; *mise-en-scène*; music; ornamentation; particularity; particulars; past; pedigree; precedence; precedent; rear; setting; support; surroundings; training

BACKSLIDE: decline; degenerate; depreciate; descend; deteriorate; ebb; fade; fail; fall; falter; fizzle; flag; flop; lessen; lower; recidivate; regress; relapse; renege; retrogress; revert; sink; slump; stray; wane; weaken; worsen

BACKWARD: *à reculons*; adverse; anti-(pathic); antipathetical; astern; atypic(al); backwoodsy; barbarian; barbarous; behindhand; caudal; contra(-acting); contrary; counterclockwise; dark; dense; difficult; dull; ignorant; loath; low; opposite; past; posterior; reactionary; rearward; regressive; reluctant; retarded; retrograde; retrorse; reverse(d); shy; slow; sluggish; stupid; tardy; uncivilized; uncultured; unprogressive; unrefined; BACKWARDNESS: barbarianism; barbarism; barbarity; ignorance; regression; retardation; retrocession; retrogression; slowness; stupidity; unprogressiveness; unrefinement

BAD: abased; abhorrent; abominable; abysmal; accursed; acute; adverse; afflicting; afflictive; alarming; amiss; amoral; appalling; apprehensive; arrant; asocial; atrocious; avernal; averse; awesome; awful; baleful; baneful; barbaric; barbarous; base; beastly; blamable; blameworthy; blasphemous; blemished; blighted; botchy; brutal; brutish; calamitous; carious; catastrophic(al); chancy; cheap; chthonian; chthonic; coarse; contaminated; contemptible; corrupt(ed); corruptive; counterfeit; crabbed; cracked; crafty; criminal; critical; cross; crucial; cruel; crying; culpable; cursed; damaged; damaging; damnable; damnatory; damned; dangerous; daring; dark; dastardly; deadly; debased; debauched; decayed; deceitful; decisive; dedecorous; defamatory; defective; deficient; defiled; degenerate(d); degenerating; degraded; degrading; dejected; deleterious; delicate; delinquent; deliquescent; demoniac(al); demonic(al); denigrated; denigrating; denigratory; deplorable; depraved; derogative; derogatory; desolate; desperate; destructful; destructive; detestable; detrimental; devastating; devilish; diabolic (al); difficult; dilapidated; dire (ful); dirty; disabled; disagreeable; disastrous; discredible; diseased; disgraced; disgraceful; disgusting; dishonest; dishonorable; dishonored; dismal; disobedient; disparaging; displeasing; disreputable; dissolute; distasteful; distressing; downcast; dread(ful); drear(y); egregious; erroneous; evil(-hearted); evil-minded; execrable; execratory; exigent; exorbitant; extortionate; extreme; failing; fallacious; false; fatal; fated; fateful; faulty; fearful; fell; felonious; feral; fetid; fiendish; fierce; filthy; flagitious; flagrant; formidable; foul; frightening; frightful; funky; furious; gangrenous; ghastly; ghoulish; gloomy; God-awful; gosh-awful; grievous; grim; grisly; gruesome; guilty; half-baked; handicapped; hard; harmful; hateful; hazardous; heinous; hellish; helpless; hideous; hopeless; horrendous; horrible; horrid; horrific; horrifying; hostile; humiliating; humiliative; hurtful; ignitable; ignoble; ignominious; ill(-boding); illegal; illicit; ill-omened; imminent; immoral; impedimental; imperfect; implacable; imprecatory; improper; impure; inaccurate; inadequate; inauspicious; incomplete; incondite; incorrect; indecent; infamous; infelicitous; inferior; infernal; inglorious; inhuman(e); inimical; iniquitous; injurious; insecure; insufficient; intractable; invalid; irritable; irritating; jeopardous; killing; lacking; lacunal; lacunar; lamentable; lawless; leprous; lethal; lewd; libelous; libertine; loathsome; loose; low (-minded); Luciferian; lurid; lustful; macabre; malefic(ent); maledictory; malevolent; malicious; maliferous; malific(ant); malign (ant); malum; *manqué*; mean; mediocre; menacing; menial; Mephistophelian; mephitic; mildewed; mischievous; miscreant; miserable; monstrous; morbid; morbific; morbose; mortal; mortifying; murderous; musty; nasty; naughty; nefarious; nocent; nocuous; noisome; notorious; noxious; objectionable; obloquial; obnoxious; obscene; odious; odorous; offensive; ominous; opprobrious; outrageous; overpowering; painful; pandemoniac(al); parlous; perfidious; periculous; perilous; pernicious; perverse; perverted; pestiferous; pestilent(ial); poisonous; polluted; poor; portentous; precarious; premeditated; profane; profligate; punk; putrescent; putrid; raging; rakehell(ish); rampant; rank; rascally; rebarbative; redoubtable; regretful; regrettable; relegated; remorseful; repellant; reprehensible; reprehensive; repugnant; repulsive; revolting; risky; rotten;

ruinous; run-down; Satanic(al); saturnine; savage; scandalized; scandalous; scarlet; scatheful; septic; serpentine; severe; shabby; shamed; shameful; shameless; shocking; sick(ly); sinful; sinister; sinistrous; slanderous; soiled; sordid; sorry; sour; spiteful; spoiled; spurious; squalid; stinking; stygian; suboptimal; substandard; sullied; surly; tainted; tartarean; terrible; terrifying; threatening; tragic(al); traumatic; treacherous; troublesome; ugly; ulcerous; unangelic; unauspicious; unbeneficial; unbenevolent; unchaste; uncivil(ized); unclean; underhand(ed); undesirable; unfavorable; unfit; unfortunate; unhealthful; unhealthy; unholy; unlawful; unlucky; unmentionable; unpleasant; unpleasing; unprincipled; unprofitable; unpropitious; unrespectable; unrespected; unrestrained; unsalutary; unsanitary; unsatisfactory; unsavory; unsound; unsterile; unsuccessful; unsuited; unvirtuous; unwholesome; unworthy; urgent; venomous; vicious; vile; villainous; viperish; virtueless; virulent; void; vulgar(ized); wanton; weak; wicked; woeful; worthless; wrathful; wretched; wrong; BADNESS: (**see** "crime") abomination; awfulness; baseness; calamity; corruption; criminality; delinquency; depravity; despicability; diabolism; dilapidation; disaster; disease; disrepute; evil(doing); evil-mindedness; evilness; flagrancy; gangrene; harm; hurt; ignominy; immorality; infamy; iniquitousness; leprosy; malady; malconduct; malefaction; maleficence; malevolence; malignancy; malignity; malum; misfortune; naughtiness; opprobrium; perfidy; rottenness; scourge; sin(fulness); sinisterity; suffering; vice; viciousness; villainy; virulence; wickedness; wrong

BADGE: award; bar; button; characteristic; cognizance; decoration; device; distinction; emblem; ensign; flag; honor; indication; insigne; insignia (pl.); label; odor; palm; pin; mark; medal; note; prize; recognition; reward; ribbon; shield; sign; star; symbol; token

BADGER: (**see** "harass") annoy; bait; bedevil; confuse; pester

BAFFLE: addle; astonish; astound; balk; bemuse; benumb; best; bewilder; block; check(mate); circumvent; confound; confuse; counteract; cozen; cross; dash; daze; deceive; defeat; deflect; defraud; disappoint; disconcert; discourage; distract; dumbfound; dupe; electrify; elude; euchre; evade; faze; flabbergast; foil; fox; frustrate; gull; hamstring; hinder; impede; intrigue; kibosh;

muddle; neutralize; nonplus; nullify; obfuscate; obscure; outfox; outmaneuver; outwit; perplex; pose; prevent; puzzle; rattle; short-circuit; stagger; stick; stop; stultify; stun; tease; thwart; unsettle; upset; wreck; BAFFLING: astonishing; balky; bewildering; confusing; disconcerting; enigmatic(al); inexplicable; intriguing; mysterious; obfuscatory; obscure; odd; perplexed; perplexing; puzzling; BAFFLEMENT: see "confusion" and "perplexity"

BAGGAGE: (see "equipment") apparatus; appurtenances; bags; belongings; clothing; dunnage; equipage; furnishings; gear; impedimenta (pl.); luggage; outfit; paraphernalia (pl.); tackle; traps; trunk(s)

BAILIWICK: (see "field" and "jurisdiction") area; authority; command; office; province; range; sphere; vicinity

BAIT: **v.** (see "harass") afflict; annoy; attack; badger; bedevil; bribe; check; chivy; decoy; entice; exasperate; feed; gall; goad; heckle; hector; hound; lure; nag; persecute; pester; plague; ride; ruffle; seduce; snare; tease; tempt; trap; try; worry; BAIT: **n.** see "allurement"

BALANCE: **v.** accord; adapt; adequate; adjust; agree; alleviate; amend; apportion; arrange; atone; attune; checkmate; classify; combine; compare; compensate; complement; concur; coordinate; correct; correspond; counter(act); counterbalance; counterpoise; countervail; deliberate; equal(ize); equate; equilibrate; equilibrize; equiponderate; erase; even; firm; fit; fluctuate; harmonize; hesitate; indemnify; integrate; jibe; join; level; librate; manage; match; mesh; neutralize; normalize; ration; reciprocate; recompense; recoup; redress; regulate; reimburse; relieve; remunerate; repay; requite; restore; reward; rhythmize; satisfy; set(tle); square; stabilize; syntonize; tally; true; tune; unify; waiver; weigh; BALANCE: **n.** accord; adjustment; agreement; alleviation; apportionment; arrangement; arrear(s); attunement; common sense; composure; control; correspondence; counterbalance; counterpoise; credit; distribution; emolument; equality; equalizaton; equanimity; equilibration; equilibrium; equipoise; equipollence; equiponderance; equiponderation; equitableness; equity; evenness; excess; harmony; homeostasis; libration; match; neutralization; normality; normalizing; osmosis; payment; poise; proportion; recompense; remainder; remnant; remuneration;

reprisal; requital; resistance; restitution; return; reward; sanity; scale(s); serenity; settlement; stability; stabilization; surplus; symmetry; tension; tone; tranquility; unification; weight; BALANCED: (see "equal") Apollonian; calm; compensative; compensatory; corresponding; equable; equalized; equanimous; equipollent; equivalent; even; fair; harmonious; harmonized; identical; impartial; just; level; like; matched; neutral(ized); normal(ized); parallel; proportional; proportionate; rational; restrained; rhythmic(al); same; serene; stabilized; symmetrical; syntonic; tantamount; uniform; unruffled; weighed; BALANCING: compensative; compensatory; equilibrant; equilibratory; equipollent; equiponderant; isonomic; libratory; neutralizing; poised; stabilizing; symmetrical

BALD: alopecic; bare; barren; base; crude; devoid; epilated; glabrate; glabrescent; glabrous; hairless; lacking; meager; mere; naked; nude; outright; palpable; paltry; patent; plain; polled; severe; shaved; sheer; sparse; stark; ugly; unadorned; undisguised; utter; worthless; BALDNESS: acomia; alopecia; atrichia; atrichosis; calvities; phalacrosis

BALDERDASH: (see "nonsense") baloney; bosh; bull; drivel; flubdub; froth; jargon; rot; stuff; trash

BALE: bundle; calamity; disaster; harm; package; parcel; sorrow; suffering; torment; woe; BALEFUL: baneful; calamitous; deadly; disastrous; evil; harmful; maleficent; malevolent; malign(ant); pernicious; suffering

BALK: (see "baffle") beat; block; cease; check; decline; defeat; delay; demur; disappoint; disapprove; dissent; except; falter; foil; frustrate; hesitate; hinder; impede; interpose; lick; object; pause; quibble; rear; rebel; recoil; refuse; scruple; shy; stick; stop; strain; thwart; waver; BALKY: (see "contrary") mulish; recalcitrant; restive; shy; stubborn

BALL: bolus; bullet; conglobation; cotillion; dance; earth; game; globe; globule; mass; orb; party; pellet; pill; marble; responsibility; sphere; spheroid

BALLAST: balance; poise; resistance; roughage; stability; weight

BALM: alleviation; anodyne; aroma; assuagement; balsam; cerate; ceroma; comfort; consolation; ease; exudation; help; inunction; mildness; mitigation; nard; nourishment; odor; ointment; redolence; relaxation; relief; remedy; remission; restorative; salve; solace; spice; succor; sustenance; unguent; warmth; BALMY: anodyne; anodynic; anodynous; aromatic; balsamic; benign; bland; calm; comforting; crazy; dreamy; easy; favonian; fragrant; gentle; golden; halcyon; happy; healing; lenitive; mild; mitigating; peaceful; placid; posh; quiet; redolent; relaxing; serene; soft; soothing; spicy; sunny; sweet; temperate; tranquil; warm

BAMBOOZLE: (see "fool") hoodwink; mislead

BAN: v. (see "banish" and "enjoin") anathematize; bar; block; cancel; condemn; damn; exclude; execrate; exile; expatriate; expel; extradite; forbid; hinder; interdict; outlaw; prevent; prohibit; proscribe; proscript; relegate; remove; restrain; taboo; tabu; BAN: n. (see "banishment") anathema; block; censure; censuring; condemnation; curse; disapproval; edict; enjoinder; exclusion; execration; exile; injunction; interdict(ion); prohibition; proscript(ion); restraint; taboo; tabu; veto; BANNED: banished; barred; blocked; canceled; censured; condemned; damned; disallowed; enjoined; excluded; exiled; expatriated; expelled; extradited; forbidden; interdicted; outlawed; prevented; prohibited; proscribed; rejected; relegated; removed; restrained; unpermitted

BANAL: asinine; average; bourgeois; common(place); corny; daily; derivative; drab; everyday; familiar; fatuous; flat; forced; hackneyed; homely; humdrum; inane; insipid; jejune; low(-class); ordinary; pedestrian; plain; platitudinous; plebeian; prosaic(al); prosy; routine; silly; stale; stereotyped; stereotypical; stock; tedious; trifling; trite; trivial; unimportant; unoriginal; usual; vapid; vulgar; worn-out

BAND: v. see "league;" BAND: n. aggregate; aggregation; army; assemblage; baldric; belt; body; bond; canaille; cest(us); cingle; circle; circuit; circumference; claque; clique; club; cohort; collection; combo; compact; company; connection; cordon; corporation; covey; crowd; district; division; drove; fascia; fascicle; fillet; flock; force; gang; gathering; girdle; group; herd; horde; host; legion; liaison; ligation; liga-

ture; link(age); multitude; musicians; nexus; number; orchestra; people; populace; posse; press; rabble; region; restraint; riffraff; ring; sash; section; sector; set; shackle; streak; strip; stripe; taenia; tape; throng; tie; trait; tribe; union; varletry; zone

BANDAGE: v. (see "bind") connect; cover; dress; fasten; support; swaddle; swathe; tape; BANDAGE: n. binding; cincture; cloth; compress; fillet; ligate; ligature; spica; support; swathing; tape; truss; wrap-(ping)

BANDIT: badman; booter; brigand; burglar; bushwhacker; caco; cateran; corsair; criminal; crook; dacoit; desperado; fleecer; footpad; freebooter; fugitive; gangster; gunman; highwayman; holdup man; hood-(lum); ladrone; looter; marauder; mobster; outlaw; pad; picaroon; pirate; plunderer; ravisher; reaver; robber; thief; thug; whyo; yegg

BANE: anathema(tization); blight; calamity; contamination; curse; death; destruction; evil; execration; harm; malediction; malignancy; malison; nuisance; pain; pest(icide); pestilence; pestilency; poison; rottenness; scourge; taint; toxicity; toxin; trouble; venenation; venom; virulence; virus; woe; BANEFUL: (see "deadly") evil; noxious; pestiferous; pestilential; toxic; toxiferous; vile; virulent

BANISH: abolish; anathematize; ban; bar; blackball; blackmail; block(ade); bolt; boycott; cancel; cast (out); censor; clear; close; condemn; confiscate; count out; curse; damn; debar; deport; depose; deprive; disbar; discharge; disfrock; dislodge; dismiss; disown; dispatch; dispel; disperse; displace; dispose; dispossess; dissipate; disthrone; divest; drive (away or out); drop; drum (out); eject; eliminate; emit; estop; evict; exclude; excommunicate; execrate; exile; expatriate; expel; expropriate; extradite; extrude; fire; forbid; foreclose; interdict; isolate; lock out; ostracize; oust; outlaw; preclude; prevent; prohibit; proscribe; punish; reject; release; relegate; relieve; remove; repel; resolve; sack; scatter; segregate; separate; sequester; shunt; strew; strip; suspend; transport; unfrock; usurp; withdraw; BANISHMENT: anathema(tism); anathematization; bar; cancellation; censorship; censure; condemnation; curse; debarring; deportment; Diaspora; discharge; dismissal; displacement; dispossession; edict; ejection; elimination; eviction; exclusion; excommunication; execration; exile; expatriation; expulsion; extradition; extrusion; fugitivity; interdiction; ostracism; ouster; preclusion; prevention; prohibition; proscription; punishment; rejection; release; relegation; removal; segregation; separation; sequestration; suspension; taboo; tabu; transportation; withdrawal

BANK: **v.** cache; count; depend; deposit; finance; heap; lean; pile; rebound; reckon; rely; save; store; trust; BANK: **n.** bar; brae; brink; cache; coast; cushion; dealer; depository; depot; dune; earth; grade; heap; hill; incline; institution; knoll; mass; mound; pile; protection; ramp; reef; ridge; ripa; safe; sand; shore; slope; stack; storehouse; tier: vault; BANKER: broker; capitalist; dealer; financier; lender

BANKRUPT: **v.** bare; bereave; break; curtail; cut; debilitate; denude; deplete; deprive; despoil; destroy; diminish; dispossess; dissipate; divest; drain; empty; erode; evacuate; exhaust; fail; fold; impoverish; lessen; reduce; rob; ruin; sap; smash; spoil; strip; BANKRUPT: **a.** bare; barren; broke(n); curtailed; denuded; depleted; deprived; destitute; destroyed; dispossessed; divested; dominated; drained; empty; eroded; evacuated; exhausted; folded; impecunious; impoverished; insolvent; moneyless; penniless; poor; ruined; sterile; stripped; BANKRUPTCY: barrenness; debilitation; denudation; depletion; deprivation; despoliation; destitution; destruction; diminishment; dispossession; divestation; exhaustion; failure; foreclosure; impecuniosity; impoverishment; insolvency; ruin; sterility

BANNER: **a.** (**see** "outstanding") distinguished; excellent; signal; BANNER: **n.** award; badge; banderol(e); bunting; burgee; color; device; emblem; ensign; flag; gonfalon; guidon; headline; jack; labarum; legend; motto; oriflamme; pennant; pennon; prize; sign(al); standard; streamer; symbol

BANQUET: **v.** (**see** "feast") dine; eat; feed; regale; sup; wine; BANQUET: **n.** (**see** "feast") feed; food; junket; meal; spread; symposium

BANTER: **v.** belittle; burlesque; chaff; contemn; deride; disdain; fleer; gibe; guy; jeer; jest; jibe; josh; kid; lampoon; laugh; mock; persiflate; quiz; rag; rail; rally; rib; ridicule; scoff; scorn; scout; slight; slur; sneer; taunt; toast; trick; twit; BANTER: **n.** asteism; badinage; belittlement; burlesque;

caricature; chaff; contempt; contumely; denigration; derision; disdain; irony; jeering; jest; joking; lampoonery; mockery; mocking; nonsense; persiflage; playfulness; raillery; ridicule; sarcasm; sardonicism; satire; scorn; scurrility; slight; slur; wit

BAR: **v.** (**see** "banish" and "block") barricade; bolt; cancel; check; choke; circumvent; clog; close; confine; contain; dam; debar; deprive; deter; eject; exclude; fasten; foil; forbid; foreclose; forestall; gag; halt; hamper; hinder; hold; impede; intercept; isolate; latch; lock; obstruct; obviate; oust; override; preclude; prevent; prohibit; proscribe; reject; relegate; remove; repress; restrain; restrict; segregate; separate; shut; siege; stay; stem; stop; stymie; subdue; suppress; thwart; BAR: **n.** (**see** "barricade") banishment; bank; barrier; bench; block(age); bolt; cancellation; clog; deprivation; ejection; estoppal; fence; fid; grating; groggery; hampering; hindrance; impediment; law; obstruction; preclusion; prohibition; proscription; pub; rail(ing); reef; rejection; relegation; removal; repression; restraint; restriction; rod; saloon; segregation; shoal; staff; stop(page); suppression; BARRED: **see** "banned"

BARB: arrow; beard; briar; hook; irritation; jag; nag; prickle; projection; sarcasm; shaft; spear; spike; spine; thorn; trouble; vexation

BARBARIAN: **a.** (**see** "savage") atrocious; backward; barbaresque; barbaric; barbar(i)-ous; brutal; crude; cruel; fell; feral; ferocious; fierce; Gothic; gross; harsh; inhuman(e); philistinic; philistinish; procrustean; rough; rude; tramontane; tyrannical; tyrannous; unchristian; uncivil(ized); uncultured; unrefined; wild; BARBARIAN: **n.** **see** "savage;" BARBARITY or BARBARISM: backwardness; barbarianism; barbariousness; brutality; cannibalism; cannibality; cruelty; degradation; demoralization; ferity; ferocity; inhumanity; philistinism; primitivity; savagism; savageness; savagery; tyranny; unrestraint; wildness

BARE: **v.** advertise; air; clean; decorticate; defoliate; defrock; denude; denudate; depilate; deplume; deprive; devastate; disrobe; divest; erode; expose; hull; open; pare; peel; pluck; plunder; remove; reveal; rob; skin; strake; strip; uncover; undress; unfrock; unrig; unrobe; unveil; weaken; BARE: **a.** arid; austere; bald; barren; blank; bleak; clean; deficient; desolate(d); destitute;

devoid; divested; dry; dull; effete; empty; exhausted; exposed; fallow; flat; free; frugal; fruitless; hairless; hollow; immature; inadequate; inane; infecund; infertile; insufficient; jejune; lacking; manifest; meager; mere; minimum; naked; needy; nude; open; outright; plain; raw; scant(y); scrimpy; severe; sheer; simple; stark; unadorned; unarmed; uncovered; undressed; unimpaired; unimproved; unornamented; unpainted; utter; void; wanting; BARELY: faint; hardly; merely; plainly; scantily; scanty; scarcely

BARGAIN: **v.** (**see** "deal") agree; arrange; barter; buy; cavil; compromise; conduct; confer; consult; contract; dicker; discuss; dispose; hack; haggle; hawk; manage; mediate; negotiate; palter; parley; sell; settle; trade; traffic; transact; treat; truck; BARGAIN: **a. see** "cheap;" BARGAIN: **n.** agreement; buy; compact; contract; deal; pact; steal

BARK: (**see** "howl" and "skin") covering; explosion; hull; rub; scrape; ship; snap; warp(per)

BAROQUE: (**see** "ornate") elaborate; extravagant; flamboyant; gingerbread; grotesque; rococo

BARREL: **see** "cask"

BARREN: (**see** "bare") acarpous; acrid; arid; aseptic; bald; blank; bleak; clean; dead; desolate; devoid; divested; dry; dull; effete; empty; fallow; flat; fruitless; hungry; immature; infecund; infertile; inhospitable; jejune; juvenile; lacking; naked; needy; nude; nonparous; nulliparous; open; plain; poor; scanty; severe; sheer; simple; stark; stereotyped; stereotypical; sterile; stern; stupid; threadbare; trite; unadorned; unarmed; uncovered; uncultivated; uncultured; undressed; unfilled; unfructuous; unfruitful; uninspiring; uninteresting; unoccupied; unornamented; unplowed; unproductive; unresponsive; untilled; vacant; vacuous; void; waste; worthless; BARRENNESS: desert; desolation; destitution; infecundity; infertility; sterility; waste(land)

BARRICADE or BARRIER: abatis; arrest-(ation); bar; block(ade); blockage; bolt; boundary; breastwork; bulwark; ceiling; check; chock; circumscription; clog; confine; cordon; dam; defense; demarcation; divider; division; door; enclosure; estoppel; exclusion; fence; fetter; frame; gate; grating; guard(rail); halter; hampering; hedge;

hindrance; hitch; impalement; impedance; impediment; inhibition; interference; interruption; isolation; law; limit; line; manacle; obstacle; obstruction; occlusion; oppilation; pale; palisade; parapet; pen; preclusion; prevention; prison; prohibition; proscription; protection; rail(ing); rampart; redoubt; repression; resistance; restraint; restriction; retardation; roadblock; screen; segregation; separation; sepiment; septum; shield; snag; stockade; stop(page); stopper; suppression; thwarting; wall

BARTER: **v.** auction; bandy; bargain; buy; commute; compromise; contract; deal; dicker; dispose; exchange; haggle; hawk; interchange; market; mediate; negotiate; palter; parley; permute; reciprocate; rotate; sell; settle; share; shuffle; substitute; swap; trade; traffic; transact; transfer; treat; truck; vend; BARTER: **n.** (**see** "deal") commerce; commutation; deal; exchange; *quid pro quo*; sale; swap; trade; traffic; transaction

BASE: **v.** (**see** "establish") depend; hinge; peg; pin; predicate; rest; BASE: **a.** (**see** "bad" and "coarse") abject; avaricious; brutal; brutish; caitiff; cheap; contemptible; corrupt; counterfeit; covetous; cowardly; dastardly; debased; deceitful; degenerate(d); degraded; degrading; despicable; dirty; disgraceful; dishonest; dishonorable; filthy; foul; grubby; humble; ignoble; impure; infamous; inferior; lewd; low(-minded); mean(-spirited); menial; mercenary; niggardly; obscene; pedestrian; petty; plebeian; poor-spirited; proletarian; rascally; scaly; scurrilous; seamy; seedy; servile; shabby; shameful; shameless; sluttish; snide; sordid; spurious; squalid; substandard; substratal; substrate; substrative; tin; ugly; unworthy; venal; vile; vulgar; wicked; worthless; BASE: **n.** authority; basement; basis; bed(rock); bottom; camp; carrier; contemptibleness; cornerstone; cost; essence; foot(ing); foundation; frame(work); fundament(um); ground(s); groundwork; law; matrix; pattern; pedestal; philosophy; platform; plinth; premise; principium; principle; radical; root; stratum; subject; substrate; substratum; support; theory; thesis; underpinning; understructure; BASENESS: (**see** "coarseness") contemptibility; dastardliness; degeneration; degradation; despicability; disgrace; filth; foundationlessness; impurity; inferiority; knavery; meanness; rascality; servility; shame; sordidity; sordidness; squalidity; turpitude; unrefinement; venality; vulgarity; wickedness

BASELESS: (**see** "false") bottomless; ground-less; idle; reasonless; unfounded; un-grounded; unsupported; untrue

BASHFUL: (**see** "timid") aloof; backward; blushing; charay; coy; Daphnean; decorous; demure; detached; diffident; distant; grave; hesitant; humble; mim; modest; mouselike; nice; prim; prissy; proper; prudish; reluctant; reserved; retiring; sedate; self-conscious; sensitive; shamed; shame-faced; shameful; sheepish; shrinking; shy; skittish; sly; sober; solemn; staid; timorous; uncoquettish; unsociable; verecund; wary; BASHFUL-NESS: backwardness; coyness; demureness; demurity; diffidence; doubt; hesitancy; humility; *mauvais honte*; modesty; prudery; prudishness; reluctance; reserve; sensitivity; shame; sheepishness; shyness; timidity; timidness; timorousness; unsociability; vere-cundity; wariness

BASIC: ABC; abecedarian; abecedary; al-kaline; arch; basal; base; basil(ar); canonical; capital; cardinal; central; chief; classic(al); componental; constitutional; constitutive; critical; crucial; deep-rooted; deep-seated; dominant; earliest; earthly; elemental; elementary; essential; fatal; first-rate; fore-most; foundational; fundamental; general; good; hypostatic(al); important; inborn; inchoate; indispensible; influential; in-grained; inherent; initiatory; innate; integral; intrinsic; introductory; irreducible; lawful; leading; main; major; natural; necessary; needed; needful; nominal; obligated; origi-nal; orthodox; outstanding; overriding; paramount; permanent; plain; positive; premier(e); prescribed; prevailing; primal; primary; prime(val); primitive; primordial; principal; proper; pure; quintessent(ial); ranking; real; requisite; rude; rudimental; rudimentary; ruling; salient; significant; simple; sovereign; standard; staple; sub-stantial; substantive; substrate(d); superior; supreme; true; ultimate; unavoidable; under-lying; ultimate; vital; BASICNESS: basi-cality; essentiality; fundamentality; integrity; intrinsicality; primality; primariness; primi-tivity; quintessence; ultimacies (pl.); ulti-macy; ultimate reality

BASIN: beaker; bowl; chafer; crater; cup; depression; dish; dock; drain; font; hollow; laver; pan; reservoir; sink; stoup; tank; valley; vessel

BASIS: (**see** "base") assumption; authority; axiom; bed(rock); beginning; bottom; cause; condition; cornerstone; cost; criterion; es-sence; floor(ing); foot(ing); foundation; frame; frame of reference; framework; fundament(al); fundamentum; grassroots; ground(s); groundwork; justification; matrix; motive; origin; philosophy; platform; point; *point d'appui*; *pou sto*; premise; presupposition; principium; principle; proof; proposition; radical; rationale; reason; root; rule; stan-dard; stratum; strength; subject; support; theory; thesis; understructure; unit

BASK: apricate; delight; luxuriate; rejoice; revel; sun; wallow; warm

BASKET: box; cabas; cage; container; corb; corf; crate; creel; gabion; goal; hamper; kish; maund; pannier; point; receptacle; vessel

BASTARD: **a.** abnormal; counterfeit; debased; false; fatherless; hybrid; illegal; illegitimate; irregular; lowbred; misbegotten; mongrel; nameless; nonstandard; spurious; unfathered; unnatural; BASTARD: **n.** bantling; by-blow; *filius nullius*; *filius populi*; hybrid; illegiti-mate; love child; mongrel; natural child; whoreson

BAT: aliped; brick; club; flittermouse; hag; mammal; noctule; racket; serotine; spree; stick; vampire

BATH: ablution; balneation; bask; dip; liquid; pool; shower; soaking; spa; swim; tub; washing; water

BATHE: (**see** "clean") absorb; bask; bath; cleanse; cover; enwrap; immerse; lave; moisten; overspread; shower; steep; suffuse; swim; wash; wet

BATTER: (**see** "attack") assail; beat; bom-bard; bray; bruise; contuse; cripple; crush; damage; demolish; dent; destroy; disable; frush; injure; K.O.; maim; mangle; mar; maul; mayhem; paste; pound; ram; smash; strike; traumatize; wound

BATTERY: armament; array; assault; bat-tering; beating; cell(s); emplacement; group; guns; implement; series; set; unit; utensils

BATTLE: **v. see** "fight" and "strive;" BATTLE: **n.** (**see** "attack") action; affair; affray; bout; brush; collision; combat; com-petition; conflict; contest; controversy; encounter; engagement; feud; fray; onset; protest; push; skirmish; strife; struggle; war-(fare)

BAUBLE: (see "trifle") bibelot; doodad; gaud; gewgaw; gimcrack; keepsake; knickknack; plaything; thingumabob; toy; trinket; triviality

BAWL: (see "cry" and "howl") bellow; bleat; proclaim; roar; scold; shout; wail; weep

BAY: color; compartment; cove; creek; division; estuary; fiord; frame; gulf; honor; horse; inlet; laurel; niche; nook; opening; position; recess; renown; section; sinus; sound; voe; water; window

BEACH: (see "shore") sand; strand; waterfront

BEAK: bill; lorum; mouth(piece); neb; nib; nose; point; proboscis; promontory; spout; tip

BEAM: v. see "glow;" BEAM: n. bar; boom; caber; crossbar; flash; glance; gleam; glint; glow; lever; light; mast; pole; rafter; ray; rump; shaft; signal; smile; span; spar; sprit; stud; support; template; templet; timber; width; yard; BEAMING: (see "cheerful") beamy; bright; gay; joyous; lucent; mirthful; radiant; rosy; sparkling

BEAR: (see "endure") abide; accept; adduce; affect; afford; apply; assume; beget; behave; birth; breed; bring; brook; carry; cart; cause; cherish; conduct; contain; continue; convey; create; deduce; deliver; demean; deport; depress; develop; drive; engender; enroll; entertain; escort; exercise; exert; extrude; father; fetch; force; generate; get; give; go; harbor; hatch; have; hold; impart; impel; implicate; impregnate; increase; inseminate; invite; involve; lead; maintain; manage; mother; move; multiply; nurture; originate; permit; pertain; pilot; pipe; portage; postulate; press; proceed; produce; progenerate; propagate; provoke; pullulate; raise; reach; rear; receive; register; render; reproduce; ride; shepherd; shift; ship; sire; spread; stand; steer; submit; succeed; suffer; suggest; support; sustain; sway; take; tender; thrust; tolerate; tote; transfer; transmit; transport; usher; wear; weigh; wield; win; yield; BEARABLE: (see "tolerable") acceptable; supportable

BEARD: v. see "defy" BEARD: n. ane; appendage; arista; avel; awn; barbel; bristle; fringe; goatee; hair; mustache; tuft; Vandyke; whisker(s); BEARDED: aristate; awned; awny; barbate; hairy; hirsute; pogoniate; unshaven; unshorn

BEARING: (see "air") address; aim; application; attention; attitude; azimuth; base; behavior; carriage; conduct; connection; course; drop; *démarche*; demeanor; deportment; direction; environment; front; habit; influence; manner(ism); mask; mien; orientation; poise; port; pose; position; posture; presence; pressure; pretense; purport; relation(ship); seat; significance; situation; stance; stand; support; thrust; trend

BEAST: animal; behemoth; brute; carnivora (pl.); carnivore; creature; mammal; monster; quadrumane; quadruped; BEASTLY: abominable; animal(ic); animalistic; base; bestial; brutal; brutish; carnal; coarse; cruel; disgusting; distasteful; fell; feral; fierce; fleshy; gross; indecent; lewd; lustful; mammalian; savage; sensual; swinish; unpleasant; vile; wild; zoological

BEAT: v. (see "defeat") ache; annihilate; anticipate; assail; avail; baffle; balk; baste; batter; beset; best; bewilder; box; bruise; cane; castigate; cheat; check(mate); circumvent; clout; conquer; crush; cudgel; cuff; curb; dash; daunt; decimate; defraud; dent; destroy; dismay; disorganize; distance; dominate; down; drive; drub; drum; eclipse; elude; excel; exhaust; fatigue; flagellate; flatten; flog; floor; foil; force; forestall; forge; frustrate; fustigate; gain; hammer; hit; impel; kill; knock; K.O.; lace; lambaste; larrup; lash; lick; mar; master; mix; murder; nullify; oppress; outdistance; outdo; outfight; outfox; outlast; outnumber; outrun; outstrip; outwit; overcome; overmaster; overpower; overwhelm; palpitate; paste; pelt; pepper; perplex; poke; pound; prevail; pummel; punish; quell; ram; rebuff; reduce; repress; repulse; reverse; rout; ruin; scour; scourge; scout; search; shape; shellac; sink; skin; slam; slap; slog; slug; smite; spank; strike; subdue; subject; subjugate; subvert; suppress; surmount; surpass; swamp; swat; take; teme; tan; tap; thrash; throb; thump; thwart; tick; top; tread; trim; triumph; upset; vanquish; vitiate; wale; wallop; wap; welt; whack; whip; whop; win; worsen; worst; BEAT: a. (see "fatigued") beaten; conquered; crushed; cuffed; exhausted; flagellated; flogged; hammered; lambasted; licked; mastered; overcome; overpowered; pummeled; punished; rebuffed; reversed; ruined; tired; weak(ened); BEAT: n. accent(uation); arsis; cadence; characteristic; emphasis; ictus; impact; inflection; intonation; mark; measure; palpitation; precinct; pulsation; pulse; range; resort; rhythm; sound; stress; stroke; swing; tap; tempo;

throb; tick; BEATING: (**see** "defeat")
battering; lacing; pummeling; shellacking;
trouncing; vanquishing

BEATIFY: adore; bless; canonize; consecrate;
enchant; extol; glorify; hallow; macarize;
sanctify; transport; worship; BEATITUDE:
benediction; benison; blessing; bliss; ecstasy;
felicity; grace; invocation; joy; prayer; sanctification; transport

BEAU: blade; buck; coxcomb; dandy; dude;
escort; flame; fop; gallant; lover; nob;
steady; swain; sweetheart; swell; toff

BEAUTIFY: (**see** "adorn") adonize; beatify;
enhance; gild the lily; glorify; BEAUTIFUL:
accomplished; adonic; attractive; beauteous;
becoming; bonny; captivating; charming;
choice; comely; cute; dainty; delectable;
delicate; delightful; deluxe; divine; dressy;
elegant; enticing; esthetic(al); excellent;
exquisite; fair; *fait à peindre*; fascinating;
fashionable; fetching; fine; finished; flawless;
good(-looking); gorgeous; graceful; gracile;
handsome; impressive; *joli(e)*; lovely; luxuriant; luxurious; majestic; ornamental;
ornate; outstanding; pearly; perfect(ed);
personable; petite; pleasing; pleasurable;
polished; posh; precious; pretty; pulchritu-
dinous; rare; *recherché*; refined; seemly;
shapely; sleek; smart; *soigné*; *soignée* (fem);
spectacular; splendid; stately; stunning;
stylish; sumptuous; superb; superlative;
supernal; sweet; tempean; transcendent;
winsome; BEAUTY: accomplishment;
adornment; attractiveness; beauteousness;
belle; brilliance; charm; comeliness; daintiness; delicacy; delight; elegance; embellishment; enticement; excellence; exquisiteness;
fascination; felinity; finish; glory; gloss;
gorgeousness; grace; grandeur; grandiloquence; grandiosity; handsomeness; knock-
out; looker; loveliness; luxuriance; luxuriousness; luxury; magnificence; majesty; perfection; polish; prettiness; pulchritude;
radiance; refinement; resplendence; resplendency; splendor; style; symmetry; transcendence; BEAUTIFYING: cosmetic

BECKON: bid; call; challenge; command;
conscript; demand; designate; draft; entice;
evoke; gesture; impel; invite; invoke; muster;
nominate; order; petition; prompt; request;
require; select; signal; summon; utter;
wave; yell

BECLOUD: (**see** "confuse") adumbrate;
bedim; befog; befoul; blear; blur; cloud;
conceal; darken; dim; diminish; dull;

eclipse; fade; fog; hide; mask; muddle;
obfuscate; obnubilate; obscure; obscurify;
perplex; shadow; taint; tarnish

BECOME: accord; accrue; adorn; arise;
arrive; awake(n); beautify; bedeck; befit;
begin; behoove; beseem; burgeon; change;
conform; decorate; emanate; embellish;
emerge; ensue; evolve; fit; flow; gain;
garnish; go; grace; grow; happen; harmonize;
increase; issue; like; loom; manifest; pass;
raise; rear; reconcile; rise; spring; stem;
suit; tally; tower; upswing; wax; BECOM-
ING: (**see** "beautiful") applicable; appropriate; apt; attractive; befitting; beseeming;
comely; decent; fashionable; fit(ting); good;
graceful; harmonizing; meet; neat; pertinent;
proper; seemly; suitable; worthy

BED: bank; base(ment); basis; bedrock;
berth; billet; bottom; cluster; concentration;
cot; couch; cradle; crib; doss; foot(ing);
foundation; frame(work); fundament(um);
ground; lair; layer; litter; lodging; matrix;
stratum; support; surface; underpinning;
understructure

BEDECK: (**see** "adorn") begem; bejewel;
decorate; diamondize; ornament

BEDEVIL: (**see** "annoy") bewitch; corrupt;
harass; pester; puzzle; spoil; vex

BEDLAM: (**see** "hubbub" and "noisy")
insane; lunatic; mad

BEETLE: **v. see** "project;" BEETLE: **n.**
amara; bug; carab; chafer; cockroach;
hispa; insect; meloe; scarab; weevil

BEFALL: accrue; achieve; advance; advene;
appear; approach; arise; arrive; attain;
bechance; become; betide; betoken; chance;
come; emerge; ensue; enter; eventuate;
fall; fare; follow; hap(pen); hazard; issue;
land; occur; originate; reach; relent; result;
rise; risk; spring; stem; supervene; succeed;
venture

BEFIT: (**see** "become" and "appropriate")
befitting; proper; seemly; suitable

BEFORE: aborning; accelerated; advanced;
afore; ahead; already; ante(cedaneous);
antecedent; anterior; anticipatory; avant;
avant-garde; awaiting; betimes; ci-devant;
confronting; *coram*; earlier; early; elementary; embryonic; ere; facing; first;
former(ly); forward; from; front(line);
hasty; heretofore; immature; incipient;

initial; inopportune; leading; nascent; old; onward; original; pioneer; precedent; preceding; precipitate; precipitous; precocious; preliminary; premature(ly); premundane; prevenient; previous(ly); primeval; primitive; primordial; prior; senior; soon(er); timely; unripe; until; untimely

BEFOUL: **see** "contaminate"

BEG: adjure; appeal; ask; beseech; cadge; coax; conjure; crave; cry; decline; demand; entreat; evade; high-pressure; implore; importunate; importune; imprecate; inquire; invoke; maund; pester; petition; plead; pray; press; pry; pump; pursue; question; renege; request; seek; sidestep; solicit; sue; summon; supplicate; tease; trouble; urge; worry; BEGGAR: cadger; clapperdudgeon; fellow; gaberlunzie; idler; lazar; mendicant; pariah; pauper; petitioner; pleader; solicitor; starveling; suppliant; supplicant; BEGGARLY: (**see** "petty") begging; contemptible; despicable; indigent; mean; needy; pleading; sordid; squalid; tatterdemalion

BEGET: (**see** "bear") breed; create; engender; father; generate; get; have; mother; procreate; progenerate; propagate; reproduce; sire; yield; BEGETTER: **see** "parent"

BEGIN: activate; actuate; admit; announce; arise; assay; attempt; auspicate; bloom; blossom; board; broach; bud; build; burgeon; cause; celebrate; command; commence; compel; conceive; concoct; consecrate; constitute; contrive; coronate; create; crown; dawn; dedicate; depart; derive; detonate; develop; devise; effect; effloresce; elicit; emanate; embark; emerge; encroach; endeavor; engage; enlist; enroll; enter; establish; fabricate; fall; file; foment; force; form; found; generate; germinate; go; goad; hire; implant; inaugurate; indoctrinate; induce; induct; infiltrate; ingress; initiate; inspire; institute; instruct; introduce; invent; invest; jump; kindle; lead; leap; let; motivate; necessitate; open; ordain; originate; penetrate; permeate; pierce; plan; pop; precipitate; preface; present; proceed; propound; provoke; raise; roll; sail; seek; settle; sow; spark; spawn; spring; sprout; spur; start; stimulate; strive; teach; tee off; test; trigger; try; undertake; venture; vitalize; yield; BEGINNER: abecedarian; actuator; amateur; apprentice; aspirant; bellwether; boot; candidate; catalyst; catechumen; conscript; convert; dabbler; debutante; detonator; developer; devotee; dilettante; disciple; entrant; founder; freshman; ham; inaugurator; inceptor; *ingénue*; initiate; initiator; inventer; layman; learner; motivator; neophyte; neoteric; novice; novitiate; originator; pathblazer; pathbreaker; pathfinder; pioneer; postulant; postulate; precursor; probationary; proselyte; punk; pupil; recruit; rookie; scholar; settler; starlet; starter; student; trailblazer; trainee; tyro; uninitiate; volunteer; votary; BEGINNING: **a.** *ab initio* (**adv.**); *ab ovo* (**adv.**); A.B.C.; abecedarian; abecedary; aboriginal; aborning; abortive; alpha; basic; catechumenical; causal; commencing; concipient; dawning; elemental; elementary; embryonic; first; fresh; fundamental; genetic; germinal; head; inchoate; inchoative; incipiative; incipient; incomplete; incunabular; inexperienced; *in fieri*; initial (ly); initiatory; introductory; late; nascent; natal; neoteric; new; novel; original; parturient; potential; primary; primitive; primordial; recent; root; rudimental; rudimentary; source; starting; undeveloped; uninitiated; vestigial; virginal; BEGINNING: **n.** (**see** "birth") A.B.C.; accession; action; actuation; aim; alpha; anlage; antecedent; approach; assay; attempt; author; baptism; base; basis; bloom; blossoming; bud; burgeoning; case; cause; ceremony; childhood; commencement; conation; conatus; coronation; crowning; dawn(ing); daybreak; debut; dedication; determinant; determination; detonation; doctrine; door(way); efflorescence; effort; egg; element(al); embryo; endeavor; entrance; etiology; eve; exordium; factor; first base; foundation; fount(ain); front; fundamental; gate; genesis; germ; go; graduation; ground(s); horizon; impulsion; inauguration; inception; incipience; incipiency; incunabula (pl.); incunabulum; indoctrination; induction; infancy; ingestion; initiation; innovation; installation; *in statu nascendi*; institution; introduction; investiture; ism; kickoff; lawsuit; lead; motive; nascency; object; occasion; off; onset; onslaught; opening(wedge); origin(ation); outset; overture; party; preamble; preface; prelude; prelusion; premiere; *premier pas*; presentation; primordium; principium; principle; prologue; prolusion; provenance; provocation; pullulation; purpose; reason; rite; root; rudiment; scratch; seed; send-off; shoot; shot; sill; source; spawning; spirit; spring; sprout; stab; start; subject; suit; test; theory; threshold; trial; try; undertaking; upshot; venture; verge; vestige

BEGONE: **see** "depart" and "departed"

BEGUILE: (**see** "charm" and "cheat") allure;

amuse; attract; bait; befool; betray; blandish; cajole; captivate; capture; circumvent; coax; cozen; deceive; decoy; delude; divert; draw (away); dupe; ensnare; entice; entrap; flatter; fool; gull; hoax; hoodwink; induce; instigate; inveigle; lure; manipulate; persuade; seduce; snare; solicit; tease; tempt; trap; trick; vamp; wheedle; wile; work

BEHALF: (see "support") benefit; benison; favor; interest; profit; side; stead

BEHAVE: accord; acquit; act (up); agree; bear; brook; carry; comport; conduct; conform; demean; deport; direct; function; govern; guard; guide; handle; harmonize; jibe; lead; manage; manipulate; negotiate; operate; oversee; pilot; quit; regulate; render; run; square; steer; suit; supervise; tally; treat; usher; walk; work; BEHAVIOR: (see "air") act(ion); attitude; attitudinization; bearing; breeding; carriage; comportment; conduct; course; culture; deed; demeanor; deportment; discipline; ergasia; ethics; ethos; etiquette; front; function; habit(s); management; manner(s); mien; operation; performance; p's and q's; play; port; posture; pretense; treatment; walk; way

BEHEMOTH: (see "huge") elephantine; monstrous

BEHEST: (see "command") bid(ding); demand; law; mandate; order; request; rule

BEHIND: a. abaft; aft; after; arrear(s); astern; back(ing); backward; behindhand; below; caudal; en arriéré; following; guiding; in arrears; inferior; late; past; posterior; prompting; provoking; pushing; rearward; regulating; remiss; retarded; secondary; slow; supporting; tardy; unadvanced; upholding; BEHIND: n. (see "buttocks") bottom; derriére; gluteus; podex; posterior

BEHOLD: apprehend; attend; descry; detect; determine; discern; discover; distinguish; espy; examine; experience; explore; eye; find; heed; inspect; investigate; look; mark; monitor; note; notice; observe; perceive; recognize; regard; remark; scrutinize; see; view; voilà; watch; witness

BEING(S): (see "men") actuality; animal; beast; bios; creation; creature; devil; earthling; ens; entia (pl.); entity; esse(nce); existence; existent; flesh; human(ity); individual; life; living; man(kind); mortal; ontology; person(ality); reality; wretch

BELDAM(E): see "hag"

BELIEVE: (see "accept") adhere; attest; cherish; conceive; conclude; consider; credit; deem; embrace; esteem; estimate; expect; fancy; feel; gather; hold; imagine; infer; judge; opine; reckon; regard; suppose; surmise; take; think; trow; trust; value; ween; worship; BELIEF(S): acceptance; acceptation; acception; acquiescence; adherence; approval; assent; assurance; cabala; canonicity; certainty; church; concept(ion); conclusion; confessional; confidence; conjecture; consensus; conviction; convincement; credence; credenda (pl.); credendum; credit; credo; creed; cult; dedication; denomination; devotion; diagnosis; doctrine; dogma; doxy; earnestness; estimate; estimation; evaluation; expectation; faith; fancy; feeling; fideism; fidelity; formula; gospel; gullability; gullibility; honesty; idea; idée fixe; imagination; impression; inclination; intention; ism; judgment; leaning; loyalty; maxim; mind; notion; opinion; orthodoxy; persuasion; philosophy; pistology; position; precept; principle; profession; proposition; regard; reliance; religion; resolution; ritual; rule(s); sect; sense; sentiment; sincerity; slant; surmise; symbol; system; teaching; tenet; testament; theory; thinking; thought; tradition; trend; troth; trust; understanding; view(point); weight; Weltanschauung; worship; BELIEVABLE: (see "plausible") credible; creditable; trustworthy; BELIEVER: see "follower;" BELIEVABILITY: see "plausibility"

BELITTLE: (see "degrade") abase; accurse; asperse; bastardize; belie; bemean; blacken; calumniate; censure; chagrin; cheapen; condemn; criticize; darken; debase; decry; deduct; defame; defile; deglamorize; deglorify; demean; demote; denigrate; denounce; deprave; deprecate; depreciate; depress; deride; derogate; desanctify; detract; devalue; diminish; disbelieve; discount; discredit; disesteem; disgrace; dishonor; disparage; dispraise; disvalue; doubt; downgrade; dwarf; fall; humble; humiliate; ignore; impair; impute; injure; lessen; libel; lower; malign; minify; minimize; mispraise; misrepresent; mitigate; mortify; palliate; pejorate; pervert; prostitute; prostrate; reduce; reflect; relegate; relieve; reproach; revile; rust; sap; scandalize; scold; shame; shatter; slander; slight; slur; smear; smirch; smooth; sneer; splatter; spoil; squelch; stain; stigmatize; stoop; subdue; submit; sully; taint; tarnish; traduce; trample (on); underrate; undervalue; vilify;

vilipend; vitiate; vulgarize; weaken; BELIT-TLEMENT: aspersion; cheapening; contempt; decline; defamation; deflation; depreciation; derision; derogation; detraction; disbelief; discredit; disesteem; disestimation; disgrace; dishonor; disparagement; dispraise; disrepute; indignity; lessening; loss; minimization; misprision; pejoration; revile; scandal; shame; smear; sour grapes; stigma(tization); traducement; traduction; vilification

BELL: alarm; buzzer; call; campana; campane; carillon; chime; codon; glockenspiel; gong; knell; ring; sanctus; signal; siren; tintinnabula (pl.); tintinnabulum; tocsin; warning

BELLIGERENT or BELLICOSE: **a.** (see "hostile") aggressive; agonistic; argumentative; armigerous; assertive; bristling; bristly; combative; contentious; disputatious; fireeating; furious; irate; mad; martial; militant; oppugnant; pugilistic; pugnacious; quarrelsome; taurine; truculent; umbrageous; unpacific; unreconciled; unreconstructed; warlike; BELLIGERENT: **n.** aggressor; *bashi-bazouk*; combatant; competitor; warrior; BELLIGERENCE or BELLIGERENCY: (see "hostility") combativeness; militancy; militantness; pugnacity; quarrelsomeness; truculency

BELLOW: (see "cry" and "howl") bawl; roar; weep

BELONG: appertain; apply; bear; conform; fit; go; inhere; own; pertain; relate; BELONGING(S): adjunct(s); application; assets; chattels; clothing; effects; equipment; estate; garb; garments; gear; goods; lands; means; personalia (pl.); property; realty; relatives; trappings; traps

BELOVED: (see "sweetheart") dear; loved

BELOW: adjunct; ancillary; auxiliary; beneath; descending; down(ward); inferior; inside; low(er); lowest; menial; neath; nether(ward); puisne; satellite; satellitic; secondary; servile; *sotto*; subalternate; subjacent; subject; submissive; suboptimal; subordinate; subservient; substrative; under(lying); underneath; vassal

BELT: **v.** see "hit," BELT: **n.** area; baldric; band; cest(us); cingle; circuit; circumference; clime; cordon; district; division; dominion; girdle; latitude; longitude; quarter; region; ring; sash; section; sector; space; strip; trace; waist; zone

BEMOAN: (see "lament") deplore; grieve

BENCH: bar; board; court; desk; exedra; foundation; judge; ledge; pew(age); platform; seat; settee; shelf; stool; stratum; support; table; terrace; throne; tribune; worktable

BEND: **v.** angle; arch; arcuate; bow; buckle; bulge; change; circumflex; constrain; crease; crimp; crook; crouch; crush; curve; decline; deflect; determine; deviate; direct; dispose; diverge; divert; divest; double; flex; fold; force; fork; genuflect; give; guide; incline; incurve; inflex; influence; kink; knell; kowtow; lean; mold; pleat; predispose; press; prize; reflect; resolve; sag; stoop; subdue; submit; turn; twine; twist; vine; warp; wrap; yield; BEND: **n.** angle; arc; arch; arcuation; aspect; bending; bias; bow; buckling; bulge; circumflexion; corner; crease; crook; crouch; curvature; curve; deflection; deviation; divergence; diversion; effect; elbow; flexuosity; flexure; fold; fork; guise; inclination; incurvation; incurvature; inflection; influence; intrigue; kink; kyphosis; phase; pitch; position; quirk; sag; scoliosis; slant; stoop; submission; tortuosity; trend; turn(ing); twist; view; warp(age); wrinkle; yielding

BENEATH: (see "below") lower; under(neath)

BENEDICTION: (see "blessing") dedication; invocation; prayer

BENEFACTOR: advocate; agent; angel; backer; champion; defender; donor; encourager; friend; grantor; guardian; guest; guide; helper; host; Maecenas; patron; philanthropist; Prometheus; promoter; protector; saint; Samaritan; savior; sponsor; supporter; sympathizer; upholder; BENEFACTION: (see "gift") bounty; grant; reward

BENEFICENT: (see "benevolent") mild; unoppressive

BENEFIT: **v.** advance; advantage; aid; assist; avail; behoove; better; boost; boot; favor; further; gain; help; improve; profit; promote; BENEFIT: **n.** (see "patronage") aid; advantage; annuity; assist(ance); avail; backing; behoof; benefaction; benefice; beneficence; benevolence; benison; blessing; boon;

boost; compensation; concession; favor; furtherance; gain; gift; good; grant; help; income; increment; interest; odds; payment; pension; point; privilege; promotion; purpose; sake; BENEFICIAL: **see** "advantageous"

BENEVOLENT: affectionate; altruistic; amiable; benefic(ial); beneficent; benign(ant); bland; bountiful; charitable; compassionate; disposed; eleemosynary; favorable; friendly; generous; genteel; gentle; good; gracious; grandfatherly; helpful; hospitable; humane; humanitarian; kind(ly); largehearted; lenient; liberal; loving; mild; munificent; opportune; philanthropic(al); profitable; salubrious; salutary; sanative; solicitous; sympathetic; temperate; tender(hearted); tolerant; understanding; unmercenary; wholesome; BENEVOLENCE: (**see** "bounty") charity; compassion; humanity; kindliness

BENIGN(ANT): beneficial; bland; bountiful; convivial; fatherly; favorable; friendly; genteel; gentle; good; gracious; grandfatherly; grandpaternal; intimate; jovial; kind(ly); merry; mild; paternal; salutary; solicitous; suave; temperate; tolerant; understanding; wholesome

BENT: **a.** (**see** "crooked") arcate; arched; askew; awry; bias(ed); bowed; circumflex; determined; flexed; flexuous; geniculate; hooked; inclined; incurvate; intent; pronate; resolute; resolved; stooped; swayed; turned; wry; BENT: **n.** (**see** "aptitude" and "bias") affectation; capacity; disposition; field; flair; genius; gift; grass; inclination; intent; interest; knack; leaning; mood; penchant; predilection; resolve; set; squint; talent; taste; tendency; trend; turn

BENUMB: (**see** "deaden") anesthetize; daze; stupefy

BEQUEATH: behest; bequest; bestow; command; devise; endow; entrust; leave; settle; transmit; will; BEQUEST: behest; devise; endowment; gift; heritage; inheritance; legacy; settlement; testament; will

BERATE: (**see** "criticize") abuse; animadvert; attack; blame; calumniate; castigate; censure; charge; chastise; chew (out); chide; condemn; correct; decry; denigrate; denounce; dig; disapprove; discipline; discredit; disparage; excoriate; execrate; flay; flog; frustrate; jaw; lambaste; lash; objurgate; opprobriate; rail; rake; rate;

rebuff; rebuke; reprimand; reproach; reprobate: reprove; revile; scare; scarify; scold; scorch; score; slam; slap; slate; slur; stigmatize; upbraid; vilify; vituperate

BEREFT: (**see** "destitute" and "lost") forlorn; forsaken; left; poor

BERSERK: (**see** "enraged") amok; crazed; frantic; frenzied; mad; wild

BERTH: appointment; base; bed; billet; cot; couch; cradle; crib; destination; dock; job; lair; leeway; litter; lodge; lodging; margin; mattress; nest; office; pad; pallet; pier; place; position; post; room; sack; support; wharf

BESEECH: (**see** "beg") adjure; appeal; ask; conjure; crave; entreat; implore; importune; imprecate; obsecrate; obtest; plead; pray; press; solicit; sue; summon; supplicate; urge; BESEECHING: imploratory; importunate; prayerful; precative; precatory; solicitous; supplicatory

BESET: **v.** (**see** "attack") assail; beat; bedevil; beleaguer; blockade; burden; devil; dog; harass; harry; hound; infest; obsess; occupy; pelt; pester; plague; siege; surround; trouble; worry; BESET: **a. see** "infested"

BESIDE(S): (**see** "but") abreast; abutting; again(st); along(side); anon; aside; near; over; then; too; with ; yet

BESIEGE: (**see** "attack") assail; beleaguer; beset; crowd; grind; hem; importune; pester; plague; press; solicit; storm; surround

BESMEAR or BESMIRCH: (**see** "soil") stain; sully; tar; tarnish

BESPEAK: accost; address; argue; arrange; attest; claim; engage; foretell; hint; hire; imply; indicate; order; portend; request; reveal; show; signify; tell

BEST: **v.** (**see** "beat") conquer; outdo; win; BEST: **a.** (**see** "choice") A-one; aristocratic; capital; chief; cream; clite; excellent; excelling; finest; first(-grade); first-line; first-rate; front; gilt-edge(d); good; grand; headmost; *hors concours*; largest; leading; main; most; *nulli secundus*; optimum; *par excellence*; preeminent; prime; select; superior; superordinary; superordinate; supreme; surpassing; tops; ultimate; BEST: **n.** advantage; choice; chosen; *corps d'elite* (pl.); cream; *crème de la crème*; elite; excellence;

ne plus supra; *ne plus ultra*; optimity; optimum; plum; preeminence; preference; prime; select; supremacy; tops; ultimacy

BESTIAL: (**see** "cruel") animal(ic); animalistic; barbaric; barbarous; brutal; brutish; depraved; savage; wild

BESTOW: (**see** "award") add; aid; apply; bequeath; confer; deposit; devise; devote; divide; donate; give; grant; loan; locate; place; pour; present; put; quarter; rain; render; stow; will; BESTOWAL: (**see** "award") conferment; grant; presentation

BET: **v.** ante; chance; gamble; hazard; hedge; lay; maintain; play; pledge; plunge; risk; speculate; stake; wager; BET: **n.** (**see** "gamble") ante; hazard; risk; speculation; wager

BETIDE: (**see** "befall") betoken; forebode; happen; presage

BETOKEN: (**see** "portend") announce; augur; befall; betide; bode; connote; denominate; denote; designate; divine; evince; forebode; foreshow; hint; imply; import; indicate; intend; mark; mean; name; notify; portend; prefigure; presage; shadow; show; signify; specify

BETRAY: (**see** "fool") abandon; beguile; blab; deceive; delude; desert; disclose; double-cross; dupe; ensnare; entice; entrap; fail; gull; hoax; hoodwink; indicate; inveigle; knife; mislead; peach; persuade; reveal; seduce; sell; share; show; snare; tell; trap; trick; two-time; vamp; wile; BETRAYAL: apostasy; deceit; deception; disclosure; double cross; duplicity; enticement; entrapment; inveiglement; perfidy; prodition; revelation; seduction; snare; treachery; treason; trick; triplicity; BETRAYER: (**see** "traitor") apostate; backslider; defector; deserter; escapee; escaper; expatriate; heretic; Judas; rat; recalcitrant; recreant; renegade; seducer; turncoat; turntail

BETROTH: (**see** "engage") affiance; espouse; pledge; plight; promise; troth

BETTER: **v.** abate; adjust; advance; aid; ameliorate; amend; assuage; atone; bate; cleanse; correct; doctor; ease; emend; exceed; excel; fix; help; improve; increase; lessen; medicate; mend; mollify; optimalize; promote; purify; reform; refurbish; relieve; renew; repair; repristinate; restore; revise;

surpass; BETTER: **a. see** "improved;" BETTERMENT: **see** "improvement"

BETWEEN: among; average; betwixt; connecting; interjacent; intermediary; intermediate; intervenient; intervening; joining; jointly; medial; medium; middle(-of-the-road); middling; moderate; parenthetical; reasonable; separating; shared; so-so; through

BEVERAGE: (**see** "drink") cocktail; coffee; draught; juice; libations; liquid; milk; nectar; negus; potable; potation; tea; water; wine

BEVY: (**see** "group") assemblage; band; bloc; clique; clutch; collection; covey; drove; flight; flock; gaggle; gang; herd; knot; mass; multitude; pack; school; squad; swarm; team

BEWAIL: (**see** "lament") bemoan; complain; cry; deplore; grieve; keen; moan; moon; regret; rue; sorrow; wail; weep; BEWAILMENT: (**see** "lamentation") cry; deploration; grief; moaning; sorrow; weeping

BEWARE: (**see** "avoid") bypass; dodge; elude; eschew; evade; flee; fly; omit; refrain; shun; skip; skirt

BEWILDER: addle; astonish; astound; baffle; balk; bemuse; benumb; block; check(mate); circumvent; confound; confuse; counteract; daze; defeat; disconcert; distract; dumbfound; electrify; elude; evade; faze; flabbergast; foil; frustrate; hinder; impede; intrigue; metagrobolize; muddle; nonplus; obfuscate; obscure; outwit; perplex; post; prevent; puzzle; rattle; stagger; stop; stun; tease; BEWILDERED: addled; amazed; asea; astonished; astounded; baffled; bemused; confused; dazed; *désorienté*; disconcerted; disconnected; disoriented; distraught; dumbfounded; electrified; *éperdu*; fazed; flabbergasted; frustrated; lost; muddled; nonplussed; outwitted; perplexed; puzzled; ratttled; staggered; stunned; thunderstruck; uncertain; BEWILDERMENT: bafflement; confusion; daze; dazzlement; disorientation; distraction; embranglement; obfuscation; perplexity; puzzlement; tangle

BEWITCH: (**see** "charm") allure; attract; beguile; captivate; capture; delight; dominate; enamor; enchant; ensorcel(l); exorcise; fascinate; hex; hoodoo; hoodwink; influence; jinx; jonah; magnetize; mesmerize; seduce; take; thrill; BEWITCHMENT: (**see** ("charm") hex; hoodoo; jinx; jonah; sorcery; spell; voodoo

BEYOND: above; additional; advanced; ahead; apart; away; besides; by; exceeding; excelling; external; farther; further; greater; leading; more; out; over (and beyond); past; superior; surpassing; ultra; yonder

BIAS: (**see** "prejudice") affectation; bent; bigotry; coloring; diagonal; diathesis; disposition; engagement; fanaticism; fascination; flare; illiberality; inclination; incline; insularity; interest; intolerance; knack; leaning; mood; narrow-mindedness; outlook; partiality; *parti pris*; penchant; peninsularity; predilection; predisposition; prepossession; proclivity; provinciality; slant; slope; sway; talent; taste; temperament; tendency; trend; turn; warp; BIASED: affected; affectionate; bent; bigoted; *borné*; colored; denominational; determined; diagonal; fanatic(al); illiberal; insular; insulated; intolerant; isolated; little; loaded; manic; monastic; municipal; narrow(-minded); oblique; opinionated; parochial; partial; partisan; pedantic; peninsular; petty; predisposed; prejudiced; prejudicial; prone; provincial; rabid; sectarian; sectional; shallow; slanted; slanting; sold; strict; subject; susceptible; tendentious; tending; unclinical; undifferent; unobjective; unreasonable; warped; zealous

BIBELOT: (**see** "curio") decoration; keepsake; ornament(ation); trinket

BIBULOUS: (**see** "drunk") absorbent; absorbing; tippling

BICKER: (**see** "argue") debate; differ; object; pettifog; quarrel; spat; war; wrangle

BID: **v.** appeal; ask; beg; beseech; call; charge; cite; command; conjure; cry; declare; demand; direct; enjoin; entreat; give; implore; importune; invite; lend; move; offer; open; order; petition; plead; pray; present; proclaim; proffer; propose; propound; represent; respond; seek; solicit; submit; suggest; supplicate; tempt; tender; undertake; urge; volunteer; BID: **n.** (**see** "supplication") announcement; appeal; attempt; call; charge; citation; command; conjuration; cry; declaration; demand; direction; entreaty; imploration; invitation; move; offer(ing); opening; order; overture; petition; plea; prayer; proclamation; proffer; representation; request; solicitation; submission; suggestion; tender; undertaking; urge; urging

BIDE: abide; await; bear; continue; delay; dwell; endure; exist; face; inhabit; last;

linger; live; lodge; remain; reside; rest; sojourn; stand; stay; stop; submit; suffer; tarry; tolerate; wait; watch; withstand

BIG: (**see** "huge" and "large") chief; considerable; filled; full; high-sounding; imposing; leading; magnitudinous; majestic; notorious; outstanding; powerful; preeminent; pregnant; pretentious; prominent; royal; swelling; teeming

BIGOT: enthusiast; fanatic; fiend; lunatic; maniac; provincial; racist; sectarian; visionary; zealot; BIGOTED: (**see** "biased") blind; fanatical; inegalitarian; intolerant; narrow(-minded); opinionated; prejudiced; prejudicial; provincial; sectarian; stubborn; zealous; BIGOTRY: (**see** "prejudice") fanaticism; insularity; intolerance; narrowmindedness; peninsularity; provincialism; sectarianism; sectionalism

BILATERAL: (**see** "double") binary; bipartisan; doubled; dual(istic); duplicate; reciprocal; synallagmatic; twin; twofold

BILK: (**see** "deceive" and "fool") balk; check; disappoint; frustrate

BILL: act; beak; charge; chart; check; claim; compensation; cost; credit; damage(s); debit; declaration; document; dun; entertainment; expense(s); fee; imposition; indictment; injunction; invoice; law; levy; list; mandate; menu; money; neb; nib; note; obligation; onus; placard; poster; price; program(me); rate; score; statement; statute; supplication; tab; tax; ticket; toll(age)

BILLET: (**see** "berth") appointment; destination; epistle; job; letter; lodge; note; office; place; position; post; spot

BILLINGSGATE: (**see** "abuse") ribaldry; scorn

BILLOW: **v.** bulge; gush; heave; ripple; rise; roll; rush; soar; surge; swell; toss; undulate; wave; BILLOW: **n.** breaker; bulge; gush; heave; ripple; rise; roll(er); rush; swell(ing); undulation

BIN: **see** "compartment"

BINATE: (**see** "double") paired; twin

BIND: apprentice; arrest; article; associate; assure; attach; bandage; bar; block; bond; capture; cement; chain; check; cinch; clamp; cleave; clinch; cling; clog; clutch; coapt;

cohere; colligate; combine; commit; compel; confine; confirm; conform; connect; constipate; constrain; contract; curb; dam; dedicate; delegate; detain; embound; embrace; encircle; engage; entrust; fasten; fetter; fix; gain; get; gird; glue; glutinate; grasp; grip; guarantee; hamper; hamstring; handcuff; hitch; hobble; hog-tie; hold; hug; imprison; indenture; involve; jam; join; keep; knit; ligate; link; maintain; manacle; marry; moor; mortar; mortgage; nail; obligate; paste; pin(ion); pledge; preserve; promise; protect; putty; restrain; restrict; rivet; rope; seal; secure; seize; sentence; settle; shackle; solder; splice; stick; strap; strengthen; support; swathe; tape; tether; tie; tighten; trammel; trust; vow; wed; win; wrap; wreathe; yoke; BINDING: **a.** astrictive; astringent; cohesive; connective; constraining; contracting; faithful; imperative; indissoluble; ligative; loyal; obligatory; severe; shackled; stringent; BINDING: **n.** accord; affinity; agreement; astriction; astrictive; bandage; bond; border; cement; chain; charter; cinch; cincture; cohesion; collateral; colligation; compact; connection; constraint; contract(ion); covenant; debenture; duty; fetter; glue; guarantee; handcuff; hitch; hold; joint; kinship; liaison; ligation; ligature; linchpin; link(age); mortgage; nexus; obligation; pledge; recognizance; restraint; restriction; shackle; stringency; tether; tie; truss; union; yoke

BINGE: (**see** "spree") carousal; orgy; party; rampage; splurge

BIOGRAPHY: anamnesis; autobiography; *curriculum vitae*; history; life; memoir(s); personalia (pl.); profile; prosopography; recount; reminiscence(s); vita

BIRTH: accouchement; actuation; ancestry; beginning; blood; commencement; confinement; creation; dawn; daybreak; debut; delivery; descent; embarcation; emergence; epiphenomenon; etymology; extraction; foundation; genesis; geniture; genealogy; germ; history; impulsion; inauguration; inception; inchoation; incipience; incipiency; incunabula (pl.); incunabulum; initiation; innovation; introduction; line(age); nascence; nascency; nativity; onset; opening; origin(ation); outset; parentage; parturition; pedigree; *premier pas*; primordium; procreation; provenance; rise; root; source; start; stemma

BISECT: cleave; cross; divide; halve; intersect; separate; split

BIT: (**see** "amount") allowance; alms; atom; bite; blob; contribution; crumb; crust; cut; dash; dole; dollop; dose; drain; driblet; drill; drop; eyelash; farthing; fig; fleabite; fragment; glimmer; granule; groat; hair; inconsequence; iota; jot; leaving; lump; micron; milimeter; minim(um); mite; molecule; molehill; nihility; nothing(ness); nugacity; ort; part(icle); penny; piece; piffle; pin; pittance; portion; quanta (pl.); quantity; quantum; quiddling; rag; sample; scintilla; scrap; shard; sip(pet); sketch; sliver; smack; smell; smidgen; snaffle; snap; snip; somewhat; song; sou; soupçon; spark; speck; splinter; spot; straw; swallow; swig taste; tidbit; tinge; tittle; token; tool; touch; trace; trifle; triviality; tuft; whip; whisker; whisper; whit; wisp

BITE: **v.** carp; champ; chaw; chomp; chumble; corrode; crunch; crush; cut; eat; gnaw; gobble; grind; grip; impress; insalivate; manducate; masticate; munch; nibble; nip; pierce; respond; snap; snarl; sting; BITE: **n.** (**see** "bit") chaw; cut; food; nibble; quid; snack; sting; BITING: (**see** "bitter") acid(ulous); acrid; acrimonious; angry; caustic; censorious; cold; corroding; corrosive; chilly; crisp; critical; cutting; discourteous; fierce; fiery; gruff; hard; harsh; hot; incisive; irate; ironic(al); mad; malign(ant); mordacious; mordant; nippy; painful; piercing; piquant; poignant; pungent; racy; rancorous; raw; rigorous; rodent; sarcastic; severe; sharp; shrewd; snappish; snappy; sour; surly; tart; unkind; vinegary; virulent

BITTER: (**see** "biting") acerb(ic); acid; acrid; acrimonious; angered; caustic; crabbed; crabby; cruel; determined; displeased; distasteful; distressing; ferocious; galling; grievous; harsh; hateful; irate; mad; nettled; painful; poignant; relentless; resentful; rigorous; rude; sarcastic; savage; severe; sore; sour; stringent; unpalatable; unsavory; vehement; virulent; BITTERNESS: acerbity; ache; acidity; acor; acrimony; anger; bad blood; bile; causticity; displeasure; distress; distaste(fulness); enmity; gall; grief; harshness; hate(fulness); ire; malice; pain; poignancy; rancor; resentment; rigor; rudeness; rue; sarcasm; savagery; severity; soreness; stringency; venom; virulence; wormwood

BIZARRE: (**see** "odd") antic(al); atypical; baroque; chimerical; curious; daedal(ic); daedalian; droll; eccentric; eerie; esoteric; exotic; extraordinary; extravagant; fanciful; fantastic; freakish; funny; grotesque; ludicrous; mythical; oddish; outlandish; *outré*; peculiar; picturesque; quaint; queer; quixotic; ridiculous; rococo; showy; singular; strange; uncomfortable; uncommon; unconventional; weird; whimsical

BLAB: (**see** "gossip") chatter; gab; reveal; tell

BLACK: angry; atramental; atramentous; atrous; colored; dark; dirty; discreditable; dishonorable; ebon(y); gloomy; hostile; illegal; illicit; inky; jet; murky; nigrescent; nigrine; noir; pitch(y); raven; sable; sad; secret; sooty; stained; sullen; swart; tarred; tarry; villainous; wicked; BLACKEN: (**see** "belittle") besmear; besmirch; char; cloud; darken; defame; denigrate; deprecate; depreciate; dirty; discredit; disparage; ink; japan; nigrify; polish; revile; shine; slander; smear; soil; stain; sully; tarnish; vilify; vilipend; BLACKNESS: inkiness; night; nigrescence; nigritude; pigmentation

BLACKGUARD: **v. see** "slander;" BLACKGUARD: **n.** cad; criminal; culprit; demon; devil; gamin; heel; knave; miscreant; rapscallion; rascal; rat; renegade; reprobate; rogue; rounder; ruffian; scamp; scoundrel; swindler; tough; trickster; varlet; villain; wretch

BLACKMAIL: (**see** "extort") coerce; extract; wrest

BLADE: arm; bit; buck; cutter; dandy; edge; fellow; fop; gallant; knife; leaf; oar; person; propeller; surface; sword(sman)

BLAME: **v.** (**see** "charge") accredit; accuse; allege; animadvert; arraign; arrogate; ascribe; assign; attribute; betray; blast; brand; call; censure; cite; condemn; criminate; criticize; damn; declare; denounce; implicate; impute; incriminate; inculpate; indict; involve; reprehend; reprimand; reproach; reprove; stigmatize; BLAME: **n.** (**see** "charge") accusal; accusation; allegation; animadversion; arraignment; ascription; attribution; calumny; censure; citation; condemnation; contumely; crimination; culpa(bility); declaration; defamation; delation; denouncement; disapproval; disgrace; dishonor; disrespect; fault; guilt; impeachment; imputation; incrimination; inculpation; indictment; obloquy; odium; onus; reflection; reprehension; reproach -(ment); reproof; responsibility; stigma; BLAMABLE or BLAMEWORTHY: (**see** "guilty") accusable; accusatival; accusative; censurable; condemnable; condemnatory;

criminative; culpable; demeritorious; imputational; incriminative; inculpable; inculpatory; peccable; reprehensible; reprovable

BLAMELESS: (**see** "innocent") immaculate; impeccable; impeccant; inculpable; irreproachable; pure; unblamable; unfaulty; unimpeachable; unrebukable; unreprovable

BLANCH: (**see** "bleach") etiolate; pale; whiten

BLAND: affable; amiable; anodyne; anodynic; anodynous; apathetic; balmy; banal; benign-(ant); bored; breezy; calm; casual; cavalier; comfortable; complaisant; courteous; demulcent; dull; easy(going); effortless; emollient; favonian; flat; flavorless; forceless; gentle; glib; gratuitous; halcyon; inane; indifferent; indulgent; informal; ingratiating; insipid; kind(ly); lackluster; lax; lenient; lenitive; lifeless; mild; monotonous; natural; outgiving; outgoing; peaceable; peaceful; placid; pleasant; pliant; pointless; relaxed; savorless; sedate; slow; soft(ening); soothing; suave; supple; tame; tasteless; tractable; tranquil(izing); trite; unagitated; unperturbed; unruffled; unsavory; untroublesome; vapid; weak; wearisome; wishy-washy

BLANDISH: (**see** "allure" and "charm") cajole; coax; flatter; seduce; wheedle

BLANK: **a.** arid; bald; bare; barren; bleak; blind; clean; devoid; divested; empty; open; plain; unadorned; unfilled; unoccupied; vacant; vacuous; void; white; worthless; BLANK: **n.** application; emptiness; form; paper; space; vacancy; vacuum; void

BLANKET: **v. see** "cover;" BLANKET: **n.** afghan; brot; cotter; cover(ing); fabric; layer; manta; pelt; poncho; quilt; serape; sheet; shroud; throw; wool

BLARE: attack; bang; blast; blazon; brilliance; discharge; éclat; explosion; fanfare; fanfaron; flamboyance; gale; glare; gust; peal; pyrotechnics; sensationalism; sound; spotlight; tantara; trumpet; wind

BLASÉ: (**see** "bland") apathetic; bored; disinterested; effete; indifferent; jaded; lackadaisical; nonchalant; pallid; sated; satiated; sophisticated; spent; surfeited; tedious; tired; tuckered; undazzled; unimpressed; uninterested; unraptured; wearied; weary; world-weary; world-wise

BLAST: **v.** (**see** "shoot") attack; blare; blight; blow; burst; clap; curse; damn; detonate; dynamite; fulminate; pop; ruin; shatter; split; BLAST: **n.** activity; attack; bang; blare; blight; blow(out); bomb; burst; clap; curse; detonation; discharge; dynamite; explosion; fiasco; flaw; fulmination; gale; gust; noise; operation; party; pop; pyrotechnics; shot; sound; wind

BLATANT: (**see** "boisterous") brazen; clamorous; coarse; glib; gross; loud; noisy; obtrusive; obvious; offensive; prominent; raucous; silly; strident; vehement; vocal; vociferous; vulgar; BLATANCY: **see** "boisterousness"

BLAZE: **v.** (**see** "burn") deflagrate; disseminate; fire; flame; flare; flash; glare; gleam; glow; ignite; kindle; light; oxidize; proclaim; singe; BLAZE: **n.** brightness; brilliance; burning; conflagration; deflagration; fire; flame; flare; flash; glare; gleam; glow; light; mark; outburst; shot; spot; BLAZING: **see** "fiery"

BLAZON: **see** "display" and "flaunt"

BLEACH: acromatize; albify; blanch; decolorize; dye; etiolate; fade; lighten; pale; purify; whiten; BLEACHED: (**see** "white") achromatized; alabaster; ashen; blanched; blond(e); decolorized; etiolated; lightened; purified; whitened

BLEAK: (**see** "austere") arid; ascetic; bare; barren; cheerless; chilly; cold; cruel; cutting; damp; deficient; depressing; desolate; dismal; distressing; dour; drab; drastic; drear(y); dull; empty; exposed; extreme; fallow; frightful; frigid; frozen; gloomy; grave; harsh; icy; inexorable; joyless; raw; relentless; rigid; rigorous; ruthless; severe; sharp; Spartan(ic); sterile; stern; stiff; stormy; stringent; tough; unbending; uncompromising; uncultivated; unproductive; unrelenting; unsheltered; unyielding; vacant; vacuous; waste; wild; wind-swept; windy; xerotic

BLEED: deplete; diffuse; diminish; discharge; dissipate; drain; draw (off); empty; escape; extort; extract; extravasate; exudate; exude; fleece; flow; leak; mulct; ooze; phlebotomize; remove; sacrifice; sap; seep; shed; spend; sweat; sympathize; venesect; vent; weaken; BLEEDING: **see** "bloody"

BLEMISH: **v.** blot(ch); blur; break; bruise; cloud; crack; cut; damage; deface; defect; deform; dent; destroy; disable; disfashion; disfigure; disgrace; dishonor; distort; harm; hurt; impair; injure; maim; mangle; mar; mark; mayhem; mutilate; pit; rift; rot; rust; scar(ify); scrape; scratch; smear; smirch; soil; speck; split; spoil; spot; stain; stigmatize; sully; taint; tarnish; uglify; warp; BLEMISH: **n.** absence; bang; blob; blot(ch); blur; botch; break; bruise; bug; cleft; cloud; crack; cranny; crevice; cut; damage; defacement; default; defect; deficiency; deficit; deformity; demerit; dent; disability; disadvantage; disfiguration; disfigurement; disgrace; dishonor; distortion; error; failure; fallacy; fault; fissure; flaw; fleck; foible; frailty; handicap; harm; hole; hurt; impairment; impediment; imperfection; inadequacy; injury; irregularity; lack; lacuna; lapse; lesion; loss; macula; maculation; macule; malformation; manque; mar; mark; mayhem; moil; mole; mutation; need; odds; pit; rent; rift; rima; rot; rust; scar(ification); scrape; scratch; shortcoming; slur; smear; smirch; speck; split; spoilage; spot; stain; stigma; sully; tache; taint; tarnish; tear; uglification; unsoundness; vice; want; warp(ing); weakness; wrinkle; BLEMISHED: (**see** "faulty") unsound

BLENCH: (**see** "cower") avoid; cow; cringe; elude; evade; falter; fawn; fear; flinch; pale; quail; recoil; retract; shake; shirk; shrink; start; stoop; submit; swerve; truckle; wince; withdraw; yield

BLEND: **v.** (**see** "combine") absorb; accrete; agree; amalgam(ate); associate; centralize; coalesce; compress; concrete; concretize; condense; confirm; conflate; consolidate; cream; fade; fuse; grade; graduate; harden; harmonize; homogenize; inosculate; integrate; join; knit; league; lithify; melt; merge; mingle; mix; organize; petrify; pool; prepare; reduce; settle; shade; solidify; strengthen; temper; thicken; tinge; tone; unify; unite; BLEND: **n.** (**see** "combination") accretion; amalgam(ation); association; centralization; coalescence; combination; compression; condensation; confirmation; conflation; fusion; gradation; grade; hardening; harmonization; homogenization; inheritance; inosculation; joint; knit; league; merger; mix(ture); montage; organization; petrification; pool; settling; shade; solidification; strengthening; tempering; thickening; tincture; tinge; tone; unification; union; unisonance; unit(ion)

BLESS: adonize; adore; apotheosize; approve; beatify; commend; condemn; consecrate;

curse; damn; dedicate; deify; devote; enchant; encourage; endow; exalt; extol; favor; glamorize; glorify; guard; hallow; idealize; idyl(l)ize; keep; laud; macarize; pedestalize; pray; preserve; protect; revere; sacralize; sanctify; stellify; thank; transport; venerate; BLESSING: (**see** "glorification") approval; beatitude; benediction; benison; boon; encouragement; felicitation; glory; grace; invocation; praise; prayer; sanctification; transport; worship; BLESSED: beatified; blest; consecrated; dedicated; divine; favored; fortunate; hallowed; happy; holy; pleasing; sacred; sanctified; venerated; BLESSEDNESS: **see** "happiness"

BLIGHT **v.** corrupt; debase; decay; decompose; defile; degenerate; deteriorate; disintegrate; freeze; frost; frustrate; impair; infect; mildew; mold(er); poison; pollute; putrefy; putresce; ruin; shrink; spoil; taint; tarnish; undermine; wither; BLIGHT: **n.** blast; corruption; decay; decomposition; degeneration; destruction; deterioration; disease; disintegration; disorder; famine; freeze; frost; impairment; infection; mildew; mold(ering); poison; pollution; putrefaction; rot; ruin; rust; shrinkage; smut; spoilage; taint; tarnish; venom; withering

BLIND: **v.** bedazzle; befool; blindfold; camouflage; cloak; clog; conceal; darken; dazzle; deceive; dull; hide; hood; mask; screen; secrete; seel; shade; shutter; veil; BLIND: **a.** abortive; amaurotic; blank; camouflaged; cloaked; concealed; covered; defective; deficient; dense; dim; drunk(en); dull; eyeless; gazeless; heedless; hidden; hooded; ignorant; ill-defined; incomplete; inobservant; insensible; masked; obtuse; reckless; screened; secreted; shaded; shuttered; sightless; undiscerning; unintelligible; unobjective; unobservant; unseeing; veiled; BLIND: **n.** blindfold; camouflage; covering; decoy; dodge; hood; mask; pretext; ruse; screen; shade; shutter; stall; subterfuge; veil; BLINDNESS: ablepsia; ablepsy; anopsia; cecity; dazzlement; ignorance; obscurity; sightlessness

BLINK: **v.** condone; coruscate; evade; flash; flicker; ignore; neglect; nic(ti)tate; recognize; shun; signal; twinkle; wink; BLINK: **n.** coruscation; flash; flicker; fulguration; gleam; glimmer; instant; moment; nic(ti)tation; signal; trice; twinkle; wink(ing)

BLISS: beatitude; blessedness; content(ment); delight; ecstasy; elysium; enchantment; enjoyment; exaltation; exuberance; exultation; felicity; gaiety; gayness; gladness; glee;

happiness; heaven; heedlessness; joy; paradise; pleasure; rapture; rejoicing; revelry; rhapsody; transport; zest; BLISSFUL: beatific; beatified; blessed; blithe(some); cheerful; contented; delighted; delightful; ecstatic; Edenic; elysian; enchanted; enjoyable; exalted; exuberant; exultant; felicific; felicitous; gay(some); glad; gleeful; halcyon; happy; heavenly; heedless; holy; jolly; jovial; joyful; joyous; merry; paradisiac(al); pleasurable; rapturous; rejoicing; revelrous; rhapsodic; sprightly; transported; zestful

BLISTERING: (**see** "burning") grueling; inexorable; intense; scorching; severe

BLITHE(SOME): (**see** "blissful") airy; casual; cheerful; ecstatic; gay(some); glad; happy; heedless; jolly; jovial; joyful; lighthearted; light-minded; merry; sprightly; zestful

BLOAT: (**see** "swell") bulge; dilate; distend; enlarge; expand; ferment; hypertrophy; increase; inflate; intumesce; protrude; puff; stuff; tauten; tumefy; tumesce; BLOATED: **see** "swollen"

BLOC: agreement; cabal; camarilla; cartel; circle; circuit; clan; claque; clique; combination; combine; conclave; confederacy; conspiracy; control; corner; corps; coterie; coup; exclusiveness; exclusivity; faction; galaxy; gang; group; intrigue; junta; monopoly; pact; paper; party; patent; plot; pool; ring; sect; set; side; splinter group; syndicate; treaty; trust; union

BLOCK: **v.** (**see** "bar") arrest; banish; beset; blockade; bolt; brake; check; choke; close; confine; curb; dam; delay; deprive; deter; drag; eject; end; estop; fail; fasten; foreclose; freeze; halt; impede; inhibit; inter; interfere; isolate; latch; lock; obstruct; occlude; oppilate; oust; plug; preclude; prevent; prohibit; proscribe; ram; reject; remove; restrict; retard; segregate; separate; shore; shut; siege; slow; spike; stay; stop; stymie; support; thwart; BLOCK: **n.** (**see** "barricade") aggregate; area; arrest(ation); blockade; blockage; brake; check; chock; curb; cut; dam; delay; drag; frame; group; hindrance; impediment; inhibition; interference; interruption; land; mass; nog; obstacle; obstruction; occlusion; oppilation; pedestal; platform; plinth; plug; portion; prevention; square; stay; stop; street; stymie; support

BLOCKHEAD: (**see** "fool") Abderite; ass;

bonehead; boob(y); chowderhead; chucklehead; clodpate; clown; crackpot; dolt(head);
dope; doughhead; dumbbell; dumbhead;
dummkopf; dummy; dunce; dunderhead;
dunderpate; dupe; fathead; featherhead;
flathead; gaup; good-for-nothing; goose;
gump; half-wit; hammerhead; harebrain;
idiot; jackass; knothead; knucklehead; kook;
lackwit; loggerhead; loon; lug; lunkhead;
moron; muddlehead; nincompoop; ninny;
nitwit; numbskull; oaf; oddball; rattlebrain;
simp(leton); softhead

BLOOD: (**see** "ancestry") birth; butchery;
consanguinity; cruor; descent; extraction;
fluid; genesis; gore; kin(dred); kinship;
life; line(age); manslaughter; murder;
nativity; passion; people; personnel; plasma;
race; sap; serum; stock; temper; war;
BLOODY: barbaric; barbarous; bleeding;
bloodcurdling; bloodthirsty; butcherly;
cruel; gory; merciless; murderous; sanguinary

BLOOM or BLOSSOM: **v.** appear; arise;
begin; brighten; bud; burgeon; develop;
effloresce; emanate; emerge; flourish; flower;
glow; grow; prosper; ripen; unfold; BLOOM
or BLOSSOM: **n.** beginning; best; bud;
burgeoning; culmination; down; efflorescence; elect; elite; florescence; flower(ing);
flush; furze; fuzz; glow; heyday; incipience;
maturescence; peak; perfection; posy;
prime; prosperity; pullulation; ripening;
spirit; youth; BLOOMING: (**see** "flowery")
abloom; efflorescent; florescent; prosperous;
ripe; youthful

BLOT: **v.** abolish; annul; blob; calumniate;
cancel; clean; cloud; daub; dele(te); destroy;
discolor; effect; eliminate; eradicate; erase;
excise; expunge; extinguish; extirpate; kill;
mottle; murder; nullify; obliterate; omit;
remove; scrub; sponge; spot; stain; stigmatize; strike; BLOT **n.** or BLOTCH: (**see**
"blemish") blain; bleb; blob; bulla; cloud;
daub; defect; deletion; discoloration; disgrace; eradication; erasure; extirpation;
imperfection; macula(tion); nullification;
obliteration; removal; reproach; spot;
stain; stigma

BLOW: **v.** (**see** "boast") bloat; bluster; brag;
buffet; depart; destroy; dilate; disregard;
distend; enlarge; err; escape; expand; flee;
fulminate; gasp; inflate; intumesce; hiss;
leave; misplay; muff(le); pant; puff; rant;
spend; squall; squander; storm; swell; toot;
vaunt; whiffle; whistle; BLOW: **n.** (**see**
"boast") action; assault; attack; binge;

box; calamity; clout; concussion; conk;
coup; cuff; cut: dint; disaster; expansion;
gale; hit; hurt; impact; knock; lash; leak;
loss; misfortune; muff(le); plug; punch;
rap; shake; shock; slap; slug; squall; stratagem; strike; stroke; thump; trauma(tism);
whack; wind(storm); wound

BLUE: **a.** aqua; azure(an); bice; bluish; ceru-
lean; cobalt; dejected; depressed; depressing;
despondent; dismal; eton; extreme; gloomy;
glum; indigo; low; melancholy; off-color;
perse; profane; puritanical; *risqué*; sad;
smalt; teal; turquoise; unpromising; violet;
BLUE(S): **n.** boredom; dejection; despondency; deterioration; doldrum(s); dullness;
dumps; ennui; gloom(iness); horrors; inactivity; listlessness; megrim(s); melancholia;
melancholy; moodiness; navy; nerves; retardation; sadness; slack; slump; song; tedium

BLUEPRINT: (**see** "plan") outline; pattern;
program

BLUFF: **v.** (**see** "feign") act (a part); assume;
boast; deceive; deter; dissuade; frighten;
mislead; sham; BLUFF: **a.** (**see** "blunt" and
"brusque") abrupt; bold; brazen; coarse;
discourteous; explosive; frank; gruff; hearty;
impolite; impulsive; make-believe; outspoken; plain; rough; rude; rugged; short;
steep; uncivil; unmannerly; BLUFF: **n.**
(**see** "boast") artificiality; bank; cliff; deception; insincerity; make-believe; pretense;
pretension; puff; sham; BLUFFER: **see**
"pretender"

BLUNDER: **v.** (**see** "err") botch; bungle;
fail; fault; flounder; flub; fumble; goof;
lapse; lurch; mess; misdo; mismanage;
misstep; mistake; slip; trip; tumble; BLUN-
DER: **n.** (**see** "error") blooper; boner; boo-
boo; botch; breach; break; bull; bungle;
failure; fault; *faux pas*; fiasco; flub; fluff;
gaff(e); goof; impropriety; lapse; mess;
misadventure; misconception; mishap;
mismanagement; misplay; miss; misstep;
mistake; muddle; parapraxia; parapraxis;
slip; solecism; stumble; stupidity; trip;
BLUNDERING: **see** "bungling"

BLUNT: **v.** (**see** "deaden" and "dull") anesthetize; assuage; benumb; daze; deluster;
devitalize; dilute; hebetate; narcotize;
stupefy; weaken; BLUNT: **a.** abrupt; apathetic; benumbed; bluff; bold; bromidic;
brusque; callous; candid; cold; comatose;
common(place); conventionalized; cool;
crass; curt; dead(ened); deadish; deliberate;

dense; devitalized; dim(med); dingy; direct; doltish; drab; dreary; dry; dull(ed); dumb; flat; forthright; frank; gleamless; gloomy; gruff; guileless; harsh; heavy; hebetate; hebetudinous; humdrum; impassive; inactive; inane; inanimate; inconsiderable; inert; insensible; insensitive; insipid; jejune; lackadaisical; lackluster; languid; languorous; leady; lethargic; lifeless; listless; loggy; logy; lumbering; lusterless; matter-of-fact; mirthless; monolithic; monotonous; moronic; oafish; obtund; obtuse; opaque; outspoken; plain; pleasureless; point-blank; pointless; ponderous; prosaic(al); prosy; rough; routine; routinized; rude; sensationless; simple; slack; slow; sluggish; sodden; stagnant; stark; stolid; stuffy; stupefied; stupid; tactless; tedious; tepid; thick; thickheaded; tiresome; trite; unceremonious; undiplomatic; undisguised; unequivocal; unfeeling; unfriendly; unpointed; untactful; vapid; BLUNTNESS: bluffness; brusquerie; candidness; dullness; gruffness; hebetude; inconsideration; insensibility; obtusity; rudeness; tactlessness; vapidity; witlessness

BLUR: **v.** (**see** "blot") blemish; blob; cloud; darken; daub; dim; disappear; dwindle; fade; fog; muffle; obscure; smear; smudge; stain; sully; thicken; veil; BLUR: **n.** (**see** "blot") blemish; blob; cloud; defect; fog; indefiniteness; indistinctness; macula; smear; smudge; spot; stain; stigma; sully; BLURRED: **see** "faint" and "indistinct"

BLURT: (**see** "exclaim") blab; ejaculate

BLUSH: **v.** (**see** "flush") bloom; color; glow; mantle; redden; BLUSH: **n.** (**see** "flush") bloom; color; erubescence; glow; redness; rubedo; rubescence; tinge; BLUSHING: **see** "bashful"

BLUSTER: (**see** "boast") blow; bull; hector; puff; rage; roar; rodomontade; ruffle; storm; swagger; swash(buckle); BLUSTERING: **see** "swaggering"

BOARD: **v.** accost; address; embark; emplane; encroach; enter; feed; house; lodge; mount; BOARD(S): **n.** association; cabinet; council; deal; diet; eats; fare; feed; keeps; league; lumber; meals; panel; plank; stage; table; tray; tribunal

BOAST: **v.** blandish; blow; bluff; bluster; bombast; brag; bull(y); crow; cry; deceive; delight; display; enlarge; exalt; exuberate; exultate; flaunt; flourish; fulminate; gas-

conade; gladden; gloat; glorify; have; hector; inflate; jubilate; leap; lord; possess; preen; proclaim; puff; rage; rant; rave; rejoice; roar; rodomontade; ruffle; self-glorify; sham; storm; swagger; swash(buckle); threaten; toot; triumph; trumpet; vapor; vault; vaunt; whiffle; whistle; BOAST(ING): **n.** blow; bluff; bluster; bombast; brag; bravado; deception; delight; display; ecstasy; elation; exuberance; exultation; fanfaronade; flamboyance; gasconade; glee; glory; jactitation; ostentation; panache; parade; pomp(osity); pride; puff(ery); rodomontade; self-glory; sham; swagger; vainglory; vaunt; verve; BOASTFUL: agog; bluffing; blustering; boasting; bombastic; braggadocian; braggy; declamatory; delighted; ecstatic; elated; euphoric; exultant; flowery; glad; grandiloquent; grandiose; *guindé*; happy; inflated; joyous; jubilant; magniloquent; ostentatious; pompous; pretentious; rodomontade; self-glorifying; sonorous; swaggering; swashbuckling; swollen; thrasonic(al); triumphant; tumescent; tumid; turgescent; turgid; vainglorious; vaporing; vaunting; vocal; windy; wordy; BOASTER: braggadocio; braggart; bravado; cockalorum; deceiver; fanfaron; gasconader; hector; jackanapes; jingo; loudmouth; megalomaniac; puff(er); rodomontade; Scaramouche; sham; show-off; swashbuckler; vaporer

BOB: agitate; blow; clip; cut; dock; duck; jerk; lob; lop; move; nod; prune; rap; tap; truncate

BODE: (**see** "portend") augur; divinate; divine; feel; foretell; indicate; presage

BODY: (**see** "group") agglomeration; aggregate; aggregation; amount; anatomy; army; assemblage; assembly; association; audience; band; bevy; bole; bulk; bunch; cabinet; cadaver; carcass; caucus; chapter; circle; class; clay; club; cluster; clutch; cohort; collection; college; colony; company; conglomeration; congregation; congress; contingent; convention; convocation; corporation; corpse; corpus; coterie; crowd; division; ensemble; extent; figure; flock; force; form-(ation); foundation; frame; gang; gathering; hecatomb; herd; horde; host; hull; human; import; legion; legislature; levee; licham; lodge; mass; meaningfulness; meeting; mess; ministers; mob; multitude; number; organism; organization; parliament; party; passel; people; person(s); physique; posse; post; quanta (pl.); quantum; remains; sect; section; senate; session; set; significance;

society; stem; stiff; stoma; structure; sturdiness; substance; substantiality; sum; swarm; synod; text; throng; torso; total; tribe; troop; trunk; unit; whole; BODILY: **see** "corporeal"

BOG: **v.** immerse; impede; mire; ooze; sink; submerge; BOG: **n.** fen; marsh; moor; morass; quagmire; slough; swamp; syrt; BOGGY: fenny; marshy; miry; quaggy; spongy; swampy; turgid; watery; wet

BOGUS: (**see** "false") artificial; brummagem; counterfeit; factitious; fake(d); fictitious; forged; fraudulent; phony; pretended; pseudo; sham; spurious; substituted; supposititious; synthetic(al); traitorous; treacherous; treasonable

BOIL: **v.** (**see** "agitate" and "rage") bubble; churn; cook; decoct; effervesce; erupt; rush; seethe; steam; stew; storm; BOIL: **n.** anthrax; eruption; furuncle; furunculosis; lesion; pimple; rage; sore; BOILING: **see** "mad"

BOISTEROUS: agitated; big-mouthed; blatant; brawling; brazen; clamorous; coarse; disorderly; excitable; excited; exuberant; furious; gross; high; ill-mannered; loud (-mouthed); noisy; obstreperous; obvious; offensive; raucous; robustious; roisterous; rough; rowdy(dowdy); stormy; strident; termagant; truculent; tumultuous; uninhibited; unrestrained; unruly; vehement; violent; vocal; vociferous; vulgar; BOISTEROUSNESS: blatancy; clamor; disorder; hooliganism; horseplay; rowdiness; rowdyism; unrestraint; unruliness; yahooism

BOLD: adventuresome; adventurous; antagonistic; arresting; arrogant; audacious; aweless; awesome; blunt; boldhearted; brash; brave; brazen; cavalier; challenging; chancy; chivalresque; chivalric; chivalrous; confident; conspicuous; courageous; dangerous; daredevil(ish); daring; dashing; dauntless; defiant; determined; doughty; enterprising; errant; eye-catching; fearless; fierce; fiery; firm; flippant; foolhardy; fortitudinous; forward; free; gallant; gambling; game; gritty; gutty; hardy; hasty; hazardous; heady; Herculean; heroic; high-spirited; Icarian; impavid; impertinent; impudent; incautious; indomitable; insolent; intrepid; lionhearted; magnanimous; malapert; manly; martial; mature; militant; nervy; nippy; perilous; pert; piquant; plucky; plump; precarious; precipitate; presumptuous;

prominent; pugnacious; pungent; quixotic; rash; rebellious; recalcitrant; reckless; redoubtable; refractory; resolute; ripe; risky; rude; Samsonian; *sans peur*; sassy; saucy; self-reliant; severe; shameless; sheer; Spartan(ic); speculative; spirited; spunky; stalwart; sta(u)nch; steep; stern; stout(-hearted); strong; temerarious; tenacious; unafraid; unalarming; unanxious; unblanching; uncalculating; uncautious; unchary; undaunted; undespairing; undeterred; unfearful; unflinching; unquivering; unrestrained; unshrinking; untrammeled; valiant; valorous; venturesome; venturous; wild; BOLDNESS: adventure; arrogance; assumption; assurance; audacity; backbone; brass(iness); bravado; braveness; bravery; brazenness; cheek(iness); chivalry; cojones; confidence; constancy; courage(ousness); crust; daredeviltry; daring; dauntlessness; decision; derring-do; determination; doughtiness; eagerness; effrontery; face; fiber; fidelity; fire; firmness; fortitude; gall; gallantry; gameness; grit; guts; hardihood; heart; heroism; impudence; incautiousness; indomitability; insolence; insolency; integrity; intrepidity; intrepidness; manhood; manliness; mettle; militancy; nerve; offense; offensiveness; perseverance; pertness; pluck; presumption; prowess; pugnaciousness; pugnacity; rashness; rebellion; recklessness; resolution; rudeness; sand; sassiness; sauciness; self-reliance; shamelessness; spirit; spunk; stability; strength; temerity; temper; tenacity; toughness; undauntedness; unrestraint; valiance; valiancy; valor; venture-(someness); wildness; will

BOLSTER: **v.** (**see** "aid") beef(up); cushion; escalate; expand; heighten; increase; intensify; pad; reinforce; repair; stiffen; supplement; support; uphold; BOLSTER: **n.** cushion; pad; pillow; support

BOLT: **v.** (**see** "bar" and "block") blurt; close; dredge; eat; elope; escape; exclude; fasten; flee; gorge; gulp; latch; lock; run; screen; shut; sieve; sift; spring; start; BOLT: **n.** bar; breech; catch; closure; cloth; fastener; latch; lock; patch; pawl; pin(tle); rivet; rod; shutter; toggle

BOMB: atom; grenade; hydrogen; neutron; shell; weapon; BOMBARD: (**see** "attack") shell; strafe; BOMBARDMENT: (**see** "attack") cannonade; rafale; shelling; siege; strafing

BOMBAST: balderdash; bluster; boast; braggadocio; braggart; bravado; claptrap; cockalorum; extravagance; fanfaron; flamboyance; flamboyancy; floweriness; fluency; fustian; gas(conade); gasconader; grandiloquence; grandiosity; hector; inflation; jackanapes; jingo; magniloquence; megalomaniac; ostentation; panache; pomp(osity); pride; rage; rant; rhapsody; rodomontade; Scaramouche; swashbuckler; tumescence; tumidity; tympany; vaporer; verve; BOMBASTIC: bluffing; blustering; boastful; braggadocian; declamatory; flowery; fluent; fustian; grandiloquent; grandiose; *guindé*; highfalutin; high-flown; inflated; magniloquent; orotund; ostentatious; pompous; pretentious; rhapsodic(al); rhetorical; rodomontade; self-glorifying; sonorous; swaggering; swashbuckling; swollen; thrasonic(al); tumid; turgescent; turgid; vainglorious; vocal; windy; wordy

BOND: **v.** (**see** "bind") cement; glue; hold; link; mortgage; shackle; tie; unite; yoke; BOND(S): **n.** accord; affinity; agreement; astriction; bail; bandage; binder; binding; cement; charter; cohesion; collateral; compact; connection; covenant; debenture; duty; glue; hold; kinship; liaison; ligation; ligature; link(age); mortgage; nexus; note; obligation; pledge; recognizance; relation(ship); securities; security; shackle; solder; stocks; tether; trust; union; vow; yoke; BONDAGE: binding; captivity; chains; connection; domination; enslavement; helotry; indenture (ship); liaison; linkage; obligation; oppression; restraint; serfdom; servitude; shackle; slavery; subjugation; thralldom; union; yoke

BONER: (**see** "error") contretemps

BONUS: additament; award; bounty; cumshaw; dividend; extra; gift; gratuity; lagniappe; laurel; medal; meed; pay(ment); premium; prize; profit; redress; remembrance; reward; satisfaction; subsidy; surplus; tip

BONY: angular; barren; gaunt; hard; lank(y); lean; meager; osseous; scant(y); scrawny; skeletal; skinny; slender; slim; spare; sparse; stiff; thin; tough

BOOB: (**see** "blockhead") dope; Philistine; simpleton

BOOK: account; almanac; anthology; autobiography; biography; blotter; brochure; casebook; diary; directory; document(ary); encyclopedia; epistle; exposition; fable; fiction; folio; history; journal; judgment; knowledge; ledger; libretto; literature; log; manual; manuscript; masterpiece; monograph; novel(ette); opinion; opus; pack(et); pamphlet; potboiler; record; register; repertory; romance; saga; standards; story; symposium; text; title; tome; treatise; volume; work; writing; BOOKISH: academic; bibliognostic; erudite; knowing; learning; lettered; pedantic; philomathic(al); scholarly; scholastic; studious; thoughtful

BOOM: **v.** (**see** "flourish") bloom; blossom; boast; bud; burgeon; develop; drum; flood; grow; increase; luxuriate; prosper; push; resound; rise; roar; rumble; soar; BOOM: **n.** (**see** "flourish") efflorescence; explosion; prosperity; resound; roar; success; support

BOOMERANG: backfire; bounce; echo; err; kick; miscalculate; recoil; resile; return; ricochet

BOON: **v.** advance; assist; boost; favor; help; BOON: **a.** beneficial; benign(ant); bountiful; convivial; intimate; jovial; merry; salutary; BOON: **n.** (**see** "patronage") advantage; aid; assist(ance); avail; award; benediction; benefaction; benefit; benevolence; blessing; boost; favor; furtherance; gain; gift; graciousness; grant; gratuity; help; kindliness; profit; sake; solicitude

BOOR: Boeotian; bromide; bucolic; bumpkin; cad; carl(ot); cearl; churl; clod(hopper); clown; cornball; countryman; dolt; drag; drip; dullard; fool; goop; grobian; hick; hind; knave; lout; oaf; peasant; Philistine; pill; rube; rustic; vulgarian; yahoo; yokel; BOORISH: (**see** "rude") artless; awkward; backwoodsy; bromidic; bucolic; churlish; cloddish; clodhopper; clownish; coarse; countrified; crude; curt; disagreeable; dull; gauche; gawky; ill-mannered; loutish; oafish; peasant; philistinic; rough; rugged; rustic; savage; stupid; uncouth; ungracious; ungrateful; unpolished; unsophisticated; vulgar; yokelish; BOORISHNESS: gaucherie; grobianism; rudeness; rusticity; stupidity

BOOST: **v.** (**see** "elevate") abet; aid; assist; augment; back; bolster; champion; coach; exalt; heave; help; hoist; increase; kite; lift; plug; promote; push; raise; rear; recommend; shore; train; tutor; BOOST: **n.** (**see** "help") hand; shot

BOOTY: bride; fleece; gain; gift; graft; haul;

loot; money; pelf; pillage; plunder; purchase; reward; spoil(s); swag

BOOZE: (see "alcohol" and "drink") bout; intoxicant; spree

BORDER: **v.** abut; approach; band; bind; bound; communicate; confine; connect; contact; edge; engage; fringe; hem; impact; join; meet; ornament; rim; ring; skirt; touch; trim; verge; BORDER: **n.** (see "edge") abutment; ambit; band; binding; boundary; bounds; brim; brink; circumference; communication; compass; confine(s); connection; contiguity; design; edging; end; engagement; extremity; flank; fringe; frontier; girth; hem; impact; joint; junction; juncture; liaison; limbus; limit(s); line; marge; margin; mark; meeting; outline; outskirts; perimeter; periphery; precipice; rand; rim; ring; selvage; shore; side; skirt; synchondrosis; syzygy; threshold; taction; tangency; tip; touch(ing); trim; union; verge; wall; BORDERING: **see** "contacting"

BORDERLINE: (**see** "doubtful") circumferential; controversial; debatable; doubtsome; dubious; dubitable; equivocal; intermediate; liminal; limitrophe; marginal; peripheral; problematic(al); questionable; skeptical; suspicious; unsure; vague

BORE: **v.** (**see** "annoy" and "irk") drill; eat; enlarge; grind; grub; labor; move; open; penetrate; perforate; pierce; prick; punch; push; slave; stare; tunnel; BORE: **n.** (**see** "boor") auger; bit; caliber; diameter; drill; eagre; gauge; gimlet; hole; thickness; tide; tool; tunnel; width

BOREDOM: (**see** "dreariness") dismality; dullness; ennui; ennuyé; loneliness; melancholia; melancholy; monotony; tediousness; tedium; tiresomeness; uninterestedness; wearisomeness

BOSH: (**see** "nonsense") silliness

BOSS: **v.** (**see** "lead"); **n.** (**see** "leader") taskmaster

BOTCH: (**see** "bungle") blemish; defect; flaw; hodgepodge; mishmash; patchwork

BOTHER: **v.** (**see** "annoy") ail; anger; disconcert; distress; disturb; excite; faze; fret; harass; harry; intrude; irk; irritate; meddle; molest; mystify; perplex; plague; tamper; tease; torment; trouble; upset;

worry; BOTHER: **n.** (see "annoyance") ado; anxiety; botheration; bustle; concern; discomfort; distress; disturbance; fuss; harassment; intrusion; irritation; molestation; nuisance; perplexity; puzzlement; torment; trouble; vexation; worry; BOTHERSOME: **see** "annoying"

BOTTLE: **v.** (**see** "preserve") check; confine; corner; restrain; BOTTLE: **n.** canteen; carafe; carboy; container; costrel; cruet; cruse; decanter; flagon; flask; liquor; phial; vial

BOTTOM: (**see** "base") basement; basis; bed(rock); buttocks; essence; floor; foot(ing); foundaton; fundament(um); ground(work); lees; nadir; platform; root; rump; sole; source; substance; substrate; substratum; support; underpinning; underside; understructure; BOTTOMLESS: **see** "boundless"

BOUNCE: **v.** (**see** "bound") boomerang; carom; dart; discharge; dismiss; echo; eject; expel; fire; hop; jump; kick; leap; lope; pounce; react; rebound; recoil; recover; reecho; reflect; repercuss; resile; return; reverberate; ricochet; sack; skip; spring; trot; BOUNCE: **n.** bound; buoyancy; carom; echo; elastic(ity); hop; jump; kick; leap; life; liveliness; lope; pounce; reaction; rebound; recoil; recovery; reecho; reflection; repercussion; resilience; resiliency; reverberation; ricochet; skip; spirit; spring; sprint; trot; vault; verve; zest

BOUND: **v.** (**see** "bounce") astrict; border; box; cage; check; circumscribe; confine; constrain; constrict; contain; coop; corner; cramp; crate; crib; curb; dart; define; delimit; delineate; demarcate; embosom; encase; enclose; encompass; fasten; fence; fetter; fix; hedge; hem; hold; hop; house; impale; impound; imprison; incarcerate; intern; jail; jump; leap(frog); limit; locate; lock; lope; mark; pen; pounce; prevent; restrain; restrict; sally; scud; seclude; secure; skim; spring; stint; tap; tape; vault; wall; BOUND(ED); **a.** apprenticed; articled; assured; astricted; bordered; boxed; caged; captive; certain; chained; checked; circumscribed; close-knit; combined; confined; constipated; constrained; contained; contracted; cooped; cornered; costive; cramped; crated; cribbed; curbed; defined; delimited; delineated; demarcated; encased; enclosed; encompassed; fastened; fenced; fettered; finite; firm; fixed; hedged; held; hemmed; housed; impaled; impounded; imprisoned;

incarcerated; indentured; interned; jailed; leaped; limited; located; locked; obliged; penned; pounced; prevented; resolved; restrained; restricted; roped; secluded; secure(d); separated; shut; taped; tied; trapped; vaulted; walled; wrapped

BOUNDS: ambit; area; barrier; boundary; bourn(e); brink; circumference; circumscription; confines; district; edge; end; environs; fence; frontier; haunt; hedge; hem; landmark; limit(s); line(s); locality; mark; measure; milieu; neighborhood; outline; outskirts; perimeter; periphery; precinct; province; purlieu; restraint; rim; term(ination); terminus; territory; verge; wall

BOUNDARY: barrier; border(land); bo nds; bourn(e); circumference; confines; edge; environ(s); extent; fence; frontier; hedge; landmark; limit(s); line; margin; mark; milieu; neighborhood; perimeter; periphery; purlieu; rim; scope; terminal; termination; territory; threshold; verge; wall

BOUNDER: (see "cad") heel; rascal; scoundrel; varlet

BOUNDLESS: (see "eternal") bottomless; excessive; illimitable; immeasurable; immoderate; in(de)terminable; indeterminate; inexhaustible; infinite; limitless; measureless; shoreless; unbounded; uncircumscribed; undiminishable; unfathomable; unfathomed; unmeasureable; unrestrained; vast

BOUNTEOUS or BOUNTIFUL: (see "generous" and "liberal") fertile; fruitful; good; overgenerous; plenteous; prolific

BOUQUET: (see "aroma") aura; compliment; corsage; flowers; fragrance; nosegay; odor; perfume; posy; scent; smell

BOUT: (see "attack") activity; conflict; contest; essay; fight; fray; jab; match; outburst; round; set-to; sickness; siege; spell; trial; turn

BOW: v. (see "defer") arc; arch; bend; cater; condescend; cow; curts(e)y; deign; favor; give; grant; honor; humble; incline; lower; oblige; pander; patronize; sag; salaam; salute; serve; stoop; yield; BOW: n. arc; arch; bend; crescent; curts(e)y; curve; honor; kowtow; prow; reverence; salaam; salute; stoop; yielding; BOWED: arcate; arched; arcuate(d); bent; humbled; inclined; kyphotic; semierect; stooped

BOWL: arena; basin; beaker; crater; cup; depas; dish; mazer; pan; scyphus; stadium; vessel

BOX: v. (see "bound" and "hit") clout; cuff; encase; enclose; fight; spar; stow; BOX: n. arca; ark; barrier; basket; bin; booth; cabinet; case; casket; chest; cist; coffer; coffin; compartment; container; cupboard; crate; fix; kist; limit; locker; loge; package; pew; pickle; receptacle; restraint; safe; seat; stall; till; trunk

BOY: beau; boyfriend; bub; bud; chap; conformist; ephebus; favorite; fellow; juvenile; lad; lover; male; nipper; page; paramour; pupil; servant; shaver; son; spalpeen; stripling; student; sweetheart; tad; teenager; valet; waiter; youth; BOYISH: ephebic; immature; juvenile; puerile; youthful; BOYISHNESS: boyhood; boyism; juvenility; puerility; youth(fulness)

BOYCOTT: (see "avoid") blackball; blacklist; disapprove; ostracize; shun; strike

BRACE: v. (see "support") confront; enliven; fasten; freshen; gird; invest; invigorate; lace; nerve; poise; prepare; prop; refresh; reinforce; shore; spike; steel; stiffen; strengthen; strut; tie; truss; BRACE: n. (see "support") bracket; couple; crutch; fastener; fortification; girder; leg; pair; prop; reinforcement; shore; spike; spur; stay; stiffener; strengthener; suspender; tie; truss; two; yoke; BRACING: brisk; fresh; healthful; invigorating; quick; recreational; refreshing; reinforcing; roborant; salubrious; stimulating; strengthening; tonic; vigorating; vigorous; zestful

BRACKET: (see "category") brace; class(ification); file; genre; group(ing); level; strut; support

BRAG: see "boast;" BRAGGER: (see "boaster") braggadocio; braggart; fanfaron; loudmouth; puffer; rodomontade; swashbuckler

BRAID: v. (see "weave") decorate; embroider; intermingle; mix; ornament; plait; trim; BRAID: n. band; brede; cord; cue; decoration; edging; embroidery; finish; gold; hair; lace(t); ornament; orris; plait; queue; ribbon; scrambled eggs; trim(ming); wreath

BRAIN: Brahmin; cerebrum; cognition; cognoscenti (pl.); encephalon; faculty; genius; illuminato; intellect(ual); intelligentsia (pl.); inwit; leader; mahat; mentality; mind; noesis; nous; penetration; philosopher; psyche; reason; sense; sensorium; thinker; understanding; will; wit(s); BRAINY: (see "intellectual") cerebral; clever; ingenious; intelligent; knowing; learned; smart; sophisticated; witty

BRAKE: **v.** (see "block") check; curb; delay; deter; drag; hinder; retard; slow; stop; BRAKE: **n.** (see "block") copse; fen; thicket; woods

BRANCH: **v.** (see "diverge" and "divide") arborize; bifurcate; decentralize; derive; divagate; divaricate; enlarge; extend; fork; furcate; ramify; spread; subdivide; BRANCH: **n.** arborization; area; arm; bifurcation; bow; chapter; creek; department; divarication; divergence; division; enlargement; extension; facility; fork; leg; limb; member; office; outlet; phylum; rame; rami (pl.); ramification; ramus; section; spread(ing); sprig; spur; stolon; stream; subdivision; tributary; twig; BRANCHING: (see "diverse") arborized; bifurcate(d); biramose; biramous; cladose; divaricate(d); divergent; diverting; radial; radiating; ramifying; ramose; ramous; tangent(ial); tentacular

BRAND: **v.** (see "label") blot; burn; expose; identify; mark; name; sear; signal; stain; stamp; stencil; stigmatize; tag; taint; BRAND: **n.** (see "label") burn; design; flambeau; flaw; hallmark; identification; kind; make; mark; name; pattern; sign-(ature); stain; stamp; stencil; stigma; sword; tag; taint; torch; trademark; type; variety

BRANDISH: (see "flaunt") air; attract; blazon; boast; display; expose; flourish; shake; signal; swing; toss; vaunt; wave

BRASH: (see "brazen" and "hasty") audacious; bold; bumptious; ebullient; foolhardy; forward; fresh; gay; impertinent; impetuous; indecorous; presumptuous; reckless; sassy; saucy; temerarious; untactful; BRASHNESS: see "audacity"

BRASS: (see "audacity") alloy; boldness; bronze; cheek; composition; effrontery; freshness; gall; hubris; impertinence; impudence; insolence; intrepidity; metal; nerve; officer(s); presumption; sand; sassiness; sauciness; shamelessness; temerity; BRASSY: (see "bold" and "brazen") cheap; forward; resolute; shameless; shrill; strident

BRAVADO: (see "bombast") luster; flamboyance; ostentation; panache; pomp-(osity); pride; swagger; verve

BRAVE: **v.** (see "defy") beard; challenge; confront; dare; disobey; face; fight; flout; front; oppose; resist; revolt; rise; scorn; spurn; venture; withstand; BRAVE: **a.** (see "bold") adventurous; audacious; bold-hearted; bright; cavalier; chivalresque; chivalric; chivalrous; colorful; courageous; dashing; dauntless; defiant; doughty; excellent; fearless; firm; fortitudinous; gallant; gritty; heroic; intrepid; lionhearted; manly; martial; militant; nervy; plucky; resolute; Spartan(ic); splendid; stalwart; stout (hearted); unafraid; unblenching; undaunted; unflinching; unquivering; unshaking; unshrinking; valiant; valorous; venturesome; BRAVERY: (see "boldness") audacity; brass; bravado; braveness; chivalry; courage-(ousness); daring; dauntlessness; derring-do; display; doughtiness; fearlessness; fortitude; gallantry; grit; guts; hardihood; heroism; intrepidity; intrepidness; manhood; mettle; militancy; nerve; pluck; prowess; resolution; temerity; valiancy; valor

BRAWL: **v.** see "quarrel;" BRAWL: **n.** (see "fight") ado; affray; altercation; brannigan; broil; brouhaha; commotion; confrontation; contention; controversy; din; discord; disputation; dispute; dissension; disturbance; donnybrook; fracas; fray; melee; muss; noise; quarrel; riot; row; ruckus; rumpus; scrap; shindy; squabble; strife; to-do; tumult; uproar; wrangle

BRAZEN: (see "audacious" and "bold") blatant; bowelless; brash; brassy; brazen-faced; callous; cheap; cheeky; clangorous; crass; daring; defying; dishonest; extreme; forward; gaudy; hard; harsh; hubristic; immodest; impudent; insolent; intense; nervy; pert; presumptuous; rash; resolute; sassy; saucy; shameless; shrill; strident; unabashed; unscrupulous; untactful; BRAZENNESS: see "audacity" and "boldness"

BREACH: (see "break") abruption; abscission; blunder; cleft; contravention; crack; crevasse; crevice; desuetude; difference; disagreement; discord; dissention; encroachment; error; *faux pas*; fissure; fracture; gaffe; gap; hiatus; impropriety; infraction; infringement; interruption; nonfeasance; nonfulfillment; nonobservance; opening; overstepping; quarrel; rent; rupture; schism; scission; separaton; sin; solecism; split;

suspension; tear; transgression; trespass; unfulfillment; violation; wedge

BREADTH: (see "scope" and "width") amplitude; expansiveness; extent; spaciousness

BREAK: v. abscise; accustom; alienate; alter; analyze; bankrupt; beat; bend; blast; breach; burgeon; burst; cashier; cave; change; chip; chop; clash; clear; close; collapse; comminute; corrode; crack; crumble; crush; curb; cut; dash; decay; decompose; decrease; decrypt; defeat; dehisce; demolish; depart; destroy; detach; deteriorate; detonate; devastate; differ; diminish; disagree; disassociate; discipline; disconnect; discontinue; disengage; disestablish; disgregate; disintegrate; disjoin(t); dislocate; dismantle; dismiss; disprove; disregard; disrupt; dissent; dissever; dissociate; distract; disunify; disunite; divaricate; downgrade; eliminate; end; enter; erode; erupt; escape; exhaust; expand; explode; fail; fall; fault; fire; flake; force; fractionate; fracture; fragment(al)ize; fragmentate; give; go; hack; halt; happen; impart; impede; implode; infringe; initiate; interfere; interrupt; inure; invalidate; kill; lacerate; leap; level; liquidate; melt; nick; occur; open; overthrow; overturn; part; penetrate; pierce; pluck; pop; publicize; pulverize; putrefy; putresce; quarrel; race; ravage; raze; reduce; rend; remove; reveal; rip; rot; ruin; rupture; rust; sack; sally; scatter; schismatize; scrap; separate; shatter; shear; shock; smash; snap; soften; solve; speed; splint(er); split; spoil; spring; spurt; start; stop; sunder; suspend; tame; tear; tell; train; transgress; trespass; triturate; undermine; undo; unravel; vary; violate; weary; wrack; wreck; BREAK(ING): n. abruption; abscission; alienation; aperture; armistice; blast; blunder; bore; botch; breach; breakdown; breath; breather; burgeon(ing); burst(ing); c(a)esura; cessation; change; chip; cleft; collapse; commutation; contravention; corrosion; crack(ing); cranny; crash; crevasse; crevice; crumb(ling); dash; debacle; decay; decline; decomposition; deferment; degradation; delay; demoralization; departure; destruction; deviation; difference; disagreement; disassociation; discontinuance; discontinuation; discontinuity; disestablishment; disharmony; disintegration; disjunction; dislocation; disorganization; disruption; disrupture; dissent(ion); dissociation; dissolution; disunification; disunion; disunity; diversion; diversity; division; eruption; failure; fast; faux pas; fissure; flaw; forbear-

ance; fracture; fragmentation; gaffe; gap; halt; hole; impropriety; infraction; infringement; interference; interim; intermission; interregnum; interruption; interstice; interval; lacuna; leap; loophole; lull; opening; overstepping; pause; plunge; pop; postponement; quarrel; race; recess; reduction; rent; reprieve; respite; rest; rift; rima; rot; ruin; run; rupture; rush; sally; salvo; schism; scission; separation; shattering; shift; sin; smash; solecism; space; speed; splinter(ing); split; spoilage; start; stay; stop; suspension; switch; tear; transgression; trespass; truce; variation; violation; wedge; BREAKABLE: brittle; crisp; crumbling; delicate; evanescent; fracturable; fragile; frail; frangible; friable; perishable; short; tenuous; thin; transitory; weak

BREATH: afflatus; anima(tion); aura; breathing; breeze; effluvia (pl.); effluvium; emanation; exhalation; exhalement; exhaust; expiration; flatus; fume; halitus; inhalation; inspiration; life; odor; pause; pneuma; puff; reek; respiration; respite; smell; smoke; sniff; spirit; steam; stop; suggestion; utterance; vapor; vitality; whiff; whisper; wind; BREATHE: abide; aspire; be; blow; continue; emanate; emit; endure; evince; exhale; exhaust; exist; expel; expire; express; gasp; grow; gulp; huff; inhale; inspire; live; maintain; ooze; pant; percolate; reek; remain; respire; show; smell; sniff; speak; subsist; survive; suspire; thrive; utter; wheeze; BREATHER: see "pause"

BREECH: (see "blunder") behind; bore; buttocks; crotch; derrière; doup; gluteus; podex; posterior(ity); pudenda (pl.); pudendum; rear

BREED: v. bear; beget; cause; create; cultivate; develop; engender; farm; father; foster; generate; get; grow; hatch; have; impregnate; increase; inseminate; multiply; nurture; originate; populate; procreate; produce; progenerate; propagate; raise; rear; reproduce; sire; spread; tend; till; train; yield; BREED: n. (see "progeny") class; descendants; family; fruit; group; issue; kin; kind; offshoot; offspring; phylum; product; race; scion; seed; sort; stock; strain; successors; variety; young; BREEDING: see "culture"

BREEZE: (see "air") aura; blast; bluster; breath; cinch; current; disturbance; gale; gust; pirr; quarrel; rumor; stir; tempest; victory; wind; zephyr; BREEZY: see "airy"

BREVIARY: (**see** "digest") abridgement; brief

BREVITY: abridgement; aphorism; brachylogy; breviloquence; briefness; brusquerie; compactness; comprehensiveness; conciseness; concision; condensation; crispness; distillation; economy; ephemerality; fleetness; impermanence; impermanency; laconism; momentariness; monosyllabicity; pith(iness); precision; shortage; shortness; succinctness; terseness; transitoriness; trenchancy; volatility; wit

BREW: **v.** (**see** "prepare") concoct; confect; contrive; cook; decoct; devise; foment; gather; hatch; impend; make; plan; plot; stem; BREW: **n.** (**see** "preparation") ale; batch; beer; concoction; decoction; mixture

BRIBE: **v.** bait; corrupt; lubricate; offer; oil; palm; pervert; pollute; reward; suborn; tempt; tip; undermine; BRIBE(RY): **n.** bait; boodle; corruption; douceur; favor; graft; gratuity; grease; hush money; lubrication; oil; payment; payola; pourboire; price; reward; sop (to Cerberus); subornation; tip; venality

BRIDGE: **v.** (**see** "Link") connect; couple; cross; shunt; span; traverse; BRIDGE: **n.** arch(way); auction; contract; connection; coupling; cross(ing); culvert; framework; gain; game; joint; junction; juncture; nexus; overpass; passage(way); pons; pontoon; span; teeth; tie; transition; union; unit; viaduct; way; yoke

BRIDLE: **v.** (**see** "check") arrest; control; curb; direct; govern; halter; harness; repress; restrain; rule; show; BRIDLE: **n.** (**see** "check") arrest; bit; control; curb; government; guide; halter; harness; moderation; rein; restraint; snaffle

BRIEF: **v.** abbreviate; abridge; abstract; analyze; bobtail; clip; coach; compact; compress; concentrate; condense; contract; curtail; cut; deflate; digest; diminish; distill; dock; epitomize; indoctrinate; inform; lessen; limit; narrow; outline; pare; prune; reduce; retrench; shorten; shrink; shrivel; simplify; squeeze; summarize; synopsize; truncate; BRIEF: **a.** abbreviated; abridged; abstracted; aphoristic; bluff; blunt; breviloquent; brusque; cabalistic; compact; compendious; comprehensive; compressed; concentrated; concise; condensed; consolidated; contracted; crisp; cryptic(al); cursory; curt; curtailed; deciduous; dense; distilled; ellip-

tic(al); ephemeral; ephemerous; epigrammatic(al); episodic(al); evanescent; fast; few; firm; fleeting; fugacious; fugitive; hard; hasty; impermanent; in a nutshell; laconic(al); limited; momentary; monosyllabic; packed; passing; pithy; pointed; precise; pregnant; pressed; preterient; prevalent; quick; rapid; scant; sententious; shifting; short(ened); short-lived; sketchy; slight; snappish; snappy; snippy; snug; solid; speedy; succinct; summary; superficial; swift; Tacitean; telegrammatic; telegrammic; temporal; temporary; terse; thick; tight; topical; transient; transitory; trenchant; trig; vanishing; vaporous; volatile; witty; BRIEF: **n.** abbreviation; abbreviature; abridgment; abstraction; analysis; aperçu; article; breviary; capsule; catalog(ue); compend(ium); condensation; conspectus; curtailment; decrease; digest; diminishment; distillation; epitome; inventory; lexicon; narrowing; narrowness; outline; pandect; plan; précis; prospectus; puckering; reduction; retrenchment; schema; shortening; shrinkage; sketch; statement; study; summarization; summary; summation; survey; syllabus; sylloge; synopsis; system; BRIEFNESS: **see** "brevity"

BRIGAND: (**see** "bandit") plunderer

BRIGHTEN: (**see** "polish") animate; burn; burnish; cheer; clean; clear; effulge; enliven; flame; freshen; furbish; gild; illuminate; increase; neaten; refurbish; scrub; shine; BRIGHT: acute; aglitter; alert; animated; apt; attractive; aureate; auroral; aurorean; auspicious; beaming; beamy; brilliant; brisk; cheerful; cheery; clear; clever; conspicuous; dazzling; effulgent; fiery; fine; flashing; fresh; fulgent; fulgid; gaudy; gay; glad; glaring; glazed; gleaming; glittering; glorious; glossy; glowing; gorgeous; grand; happy; illuminated; illustrious; incandescent; intelligent; iridescent; irradiant; jolly; keen; lambent; light; lucent; lucid; luminescent; luminous; lustrous; magnificent; meteoric; neat; nitid; opalescent; promising; quick; radiant; red(dish); refulgent; refurbished; resplendent; rich; rosy; rutilant; scintillant; scintillating; sharp; shining; shiny; showy; signal; smart; sparkling; spirituel(le); splendid; splendorous; striking; sunny; transparent; undimmed; virtuosic; vivacious; vivid; wise; witty; BRIGHTNESS: acuity; acumen; acuteness; animation; brilliance; brilliancy; éclat; effulgence; élan; fame; flame; flare; florescence; fluorescence; flush; freshness; fulgor; gaiety; glare; glass(iness); glaze; gleam; glory; glow; illumination; incandescence; intelligence; irradiation; lambency;

luminance; luminescence; luminosity; luster; magnificence; nitidity; nitor; opalescence; oriency; orientness; perspicacity; pomp; radiance; radiancy; refulgence; refulgency; resplendence; resplendency; rutilation; scintillation; sheen; shine; sparkle; splendor; sunniness; vivacity

BRILLIANT: (**see** "bright") alert; clever; conspicuous; distinguished; effulgent; eminent; flashing; flashy; gay; glittering; glorious; glowing; good; illustrious; intelligent; iridescent; keen; luminescent; luminous; lustrous; magnificent; merry; meteoric; opalescent; radiant; resourceful; rich; sage; scintillant; scintillating; shining; showy; signal; sparkling; splendid; splendiferous; splendorous; striking; virtuosic; vivid; wise; witty; BRILLIANCE or BRILLIANCY: (**see** "brightness") astuteness; cleverness; éclat; effulgence; effulgency; élan; fame; fire; flame; flash; gaiety; glare; glory; incandescence; intelligence; light; luminance; luminescence; luminosity; luster; lustrousness; magnificence; nitidity; oriency; orientness; pomp; refulgence; refulgency; resplendence; resplendency; scintillation; splendor; virtuosity; vivacity; wit

BRIM: (**see** "brink") border; circumference; edge; rim

BRING: accompany; adduce; advance; attend; attract; bear; beget; birth; carry; cause; chaperon(e); command; conduct; contain; convey; convoy; deliver; distribute; drive; effect; engender; escort; fetch; get; guide; induce; institute; lead; move; overcome; persuade; pilot; produce; recall; rise; shepherd; steer; submit; take; tender; tote; transport; usher

BRINK: (**see** "border") bank; bluff; boundary; bounds; brim; brow; circumference; confine; crest; ditch; edge; edging; end; eve; extremity; foss(e); frontier; junction; juncture; limit; line; lip; marge; margin; mark; onset; periphery; precipice; rand; ridge; rim; sea; shore; threshold; tip; top; verge

BRISK: active; acute; agile; airy; alacritous; alert; alive; allegro; animated; breezy; busy; cheery; cool; dapper; ebullient; effervescent; energetic; enlivened; fast; fleet; fresh; galvanic; hurrying; intense; kedge; keen; live(ly); merry; nimble; nippy; peppery; peppy; perky; pressing; prompt; quick; rapid; rushing; sharp; snappy; spirited; sprightly; spry; stimulating; swift; tangy; trenchant; trotty; vivacious; warm; yare;

zestful; zippy; BRISKNESS: acuteness; agility; alacrity; alertness; animation; ebullience; ebulliency; effervescence; energy; fleetness; freshness; keenness; liveliness; nimbleness; pep(per); perkiness; promptitude; quickness; rapidity; sharpness; shortness; snappiness; spiritedness; sprightliness; spryness; stimulation; swiftness; vivacity; vividity; zest; zip

BRITTLE: (**see** "breakable") calculating; cold; crisp; crumbling; crumbly; delicate; difficult; dry; evanescent; fickle; flaky; fragile; frail; frangible; friable; meager; mealy; mortal; perishable; pulvurulent; sharp; short; tenuous; thin; transitory; weak; BRITTLENESS: delicacy; fragility; frangibility; friability; meagerness; tenuity; tenuousness; thinness; weakness

BROACH: (**see** "announce") air; begin; break; express; introduce; launch; open; publish; utter; vent(ilate); voice

BROAD: (**see** "general") all-inclusive; ample; big; boundless; clear; coarse; colossal; comprehensive; cosmic; deep; distended; expanded; expansive; extended; extensive; extreme; far-flung; far-reaching; full; generalized; global; illimitable; inclusive; indelicate; intensive; large; liberal; magnitudinous; open; patent; plain; *risqué*; roomy; spacious; thick; tolerant; unlimited; unmistakable; untold; vast; wide(spread); worldwide; BROADEN: dilate; educate; ennoble; expand; extend; increase; liberalize; spread; thicken; widen

BROADCAST: (**see** "air") advertise; declare; diffuse; disseminate; express; publicize; publish; radiate; say; scatter; seed; send; simulcast; sow; spread; strew; telecast; televise; tell; transmit; voice

BROGUE: (**see** "dialect") accent; shoe

BROIL: (**see** "brawl") disturbance; quarrel; tumult; turbulence

BROKE: (**see** "penniless") bankrupt

BROKEN: bankrupt; bent; collapsed; contrite; cracked; crushed; cut; dashed; defeated; demolished; destroyed; dilapidated; disconnected; discontinuous; discrete; disengaged; disjoined; disjointed; dislocated; disreputable; disunited; fractional; fractured; fragmental; fragmentary; fragmentized; hopeless; humble; imperfect; infringed; interrupted; irregular; lacerated; pierced; reduced; rent; ripped; rough; ruined;

ruptured; schismatised; separated; shattered; smashed; snaggled; snapped; spasmodic; split; subdued; sundered; tamed; tatterdemalion; torn; trained; unmendable; violated; weakened; zigzag

BROOD: **v.** abrade; chafe; cogitate; dawdle; develop; fret; fuss; gestate; hatch; incubate; moon; mope; nest; originate; plan; plot; ponder; pout; scheme; sit; stew; sulk; vex; weep; worry; BROOD: **n.** (**see** "family") breed; clutch; covey; flock; fruit; fry; hatch; issue; litter; multitude; nest; nid(e); offspring; progeny; yield; young

BROOK: **v.** (**see** "abide") accept; await; bear; dwell; endure; face; live; lodge; reside; sojourn; stand; stomach; suffer; tolerate; withstand; BROOK: **n.** bourn(e); burn; creek; rill(et); rivulet; run(nel); stream(let)

BROTHER: bo; buddy; cadet; chap; chum; companion; comrade; coreligionist; crony; fellow; fra(ter); friar; kin(sman); mate(y); monk; oblate; pal; partner; peer; sib(ling); BROTHERHOOD or BROTHERLINESS: companionship; fellowship; fraternity; group; kindliness; kindness; kinship; partnership; sodality; union; BROTHERLY: affectionate; amiable; amicable; buddy-buddy; cherishing; companionable; fraternal; kind

BROW: (**see** "brink") crest; edge; forehead; frons; front; margin; mien; ridge; rim; superciliary ridge; top

BROWBEAT: (**see** "coerce") bludgeon; bulldoze; bully; cow; dictate; domineer; dragoon; frighten; hector; intimidate; overawe; scare; subdue; swashbuckle

BROWN: bronze; brunescent; brunneous; cordovan; dark; dun; dusky; ecru; gloomy; sienna; sepia; sorrel; tan(ned); unbleached

BROWNIE: dwarf; elf; fairy; fay; gnome; goblin; imp; kobold; nis(se); nix(ie); ouphe; pixie; puck; shee; sprite

BROWSE: consume; eat; feed; forage; graze; hunt; look; nibble; pasture; skim

BRUISE: **v.** abrade; batter; beat; bray; contuse; cripple; crush; damage; dent; disable; humble; hurt; injure; maim; mangle; mar; maul; mayhem; paste; pound; ram; smash; squeeze; traumatize; wound; BRUISE: **n.** abrasion; battery; contusion; damage; dent; ecchymosis; hurt; ictus;

injury; laceration; lividity; mayhem; petechia; shiner; trauma(tism); welt; wound; BRUISED: abraded; battered; beaten; contused; crippled; crushed; dented; disabled; humbled; hurt; injured; lacerated; livid; maimed; mangled; marred; mauled; smashed; traumatized

BRUSH: **v.** (**see** "clean") abrade; affect; dismiss; flick; frisk; graze; nick; ricochet; scrape; scratch; shave; touch; whisk; BRUSH: **n.** abrasion; action; broom; cleaner; contusion; copse; duster; encounter; fight; fray; graze; nick; ricochet; scratch; shave; shrubs; skirmish; thicket; touch; tuft; whiskbroom

BRUSQUE: (**see** "abrupt") bluff; blunt; brisk; curt; discourteous; frank; gruff; hasty; impolite; rude; sharp; short; terse; uncivil; violent: BRUSQUENESS: abruptness; brusquerie; impoliteness; incivility; rudeness;

BRUTAL or BRUTISH: abominable; animal(ic); animalistic; barbaric; barbarous; base; beastish; beastly; bestial; bitter; bloodthirsty; brutalized; brute; caddish; carnal; coarse; cruel; deadly; destructive; devastating; dire; disgusting; distasteful; earthy; extreme; fell; feral; ferine; ferocious; fierce; furious; grim; gross; harsh; indecent; inhuman(e); insensate; low; malign(ant); mammalian; merciless; physical; pitiless; Procrustean; rapacious; ravenous; relentless; rude; ruthless; sanguinary; savage; sensual; severe; sinister; swinish; tartarly; tough; troglodytic; truculent; unbearable; unfeeling; unpleasant; untame(d); vandalic; vandalistic; vehement; vile; vindictive; violent; vulgar; wild; BRUTALITY: acharnement; aggressiveness; animalism; awesomeness; barbarism; barbarity; baseness; beastliness; bestiality; bitterness; brutalization; brutalness; bruteness; brutishness; carnality; coarseness; cruelness; cruelty; destructiveness; devastation; ferity; ferociousness; ferocity; fierceness; furiousness; harshness; hostility; impetuosity; inhumanity; malevolence; mercilessness; rapacity; relentlessness; ruthlessness; savagery; swinishness; truculency; vandalism; vehemence; BRUTE: (**see** "animal") bruiser; Caliban; ruffian; scoundrel

BUBBLE: **v.** (**see** "seethe") boil; churn; effervesce; gurgle; BUBBLE: **n.** air; bead; bleb; blister; delusion; effervescence; foam; glob(ule); promise; trifle; BUBBLING: (**see** "seething") boiling; churning; ebullient; effervescent; gurgling; mad

BUCK: (see "dandy" and "resist") balk; deer; man; stag

BUCKLE: bend; bow; cave; cavitate; collapse; contract; crumble; disintegrate; dissolve; equip; explode; fail; fall; fasten; flop; fold; founder; implode; kink; prepare; sag; shatter; shrink; sink; tie; tumble; twist; warp; weave; wilt; wrench; yield; BUCKLING: see "collapse"

BUCOLIC: a. (see "rural") agrarian; agrestic; Arcadian; campestral; countrified; geoponic; georgic; idyllic; naive; natural; pastoral; provincial; rustic; simple; sylvan; unsophisticated; villatic; BUCOLIC: n. (see "rustic") bumpkin; eclogue; idyl; simpleton

BUD: v. (see "arise" and "bloom") begin; blossom; burgeon; develop; effloresce; emanate; emerge; germinate; graft; pullulate; sprout; BUD: n. (see "beginning" and "bloom") blossom; bulb; burgeoning; child; cion; deb(utante); efflorescence; gemma; germ; graft; incipience; incipiency; knop; pullulation; scion; shoot; spirit; sprout; youth

BUDDY: (see "brother") bo; chum; colleague; companion; compeer; comrade; confederate; confrere; crony; fellow; friend; mate(y); pal; partner; sidekick

BUDGET: v. allocate; allot; allow; apportion; appropriate; assign; authorize; award; bestow; consign; deal; designate; dispense; distribute; divide; dole; earmark; formulate; give; grant; plan; portion; prorate; provide; ration; set; share; slice; split; stock; supply; BUDGET: n. allocation; allotment; allowance; amount; apportionment; appropriation; assignment; authorization; award; bag; batch; bestowal; bunch; bundle; consignment; deal; designation; distribution; division; dole; gift; grant; measure; money; pack(et); parcel; plan; portion; prescription; program; provision; quantity; ration; requirement; roll; share; slice; stock; subscription; supply: wallet

BUFFET: v. (see "beat") baste; batter; box; contend; cuff; drive; force; hit; lambaste; pummel; slap; strike; strive; struggle; thrash; toss; BUFFET: n. bar; counter; credenza; sideboard; stool

BUFFOON: (see "clown" and "fool") actor; antic; comedian; comic; droll; grobian; harlequin; humorist; jape; jester; joker; merry-andrew; mime(r); mimic; stooge; wag; wit; zany; BUFFOONERY: (see "foolishness") clownage; clownishness; humor; jest; loutishness; mimicry; nonsense; zanyism

BUG: v. (see "annoy") wiretap; BUG: n. annoyance; beetle; chinch; cimex; cockroach; craze; defect; dor; elater; fad(dist); hobby(ist); insect; Insectivora (pl.); germ; hemipter; louse; mite; nit; pediculus; problem; roach

BUGABOO or BUGBEAR: alarm; apprehension; *bête noir*; bog(e)y; boogeyman; boogieman; dread; fear; ghost; goblin; gremlin; hobgoblin; *loup-garou*; Mumbo Jumbo; ogre; phantom; problem; scare; specter; terror; threat; wraith

BUILD: v. (see "make") chisel; compile; compose; constitute; construct; contrive; create; develop; enhance; erect; establish; exalt: fabricate; fashion; form(ulate); found; frame; manufacture; organize; produce; raise; rear; structure; unite; BUILD: n. (see "make") arrangement; composition; frame(work); makeup; physique; stature; structure BUILDING: apartment; barracks; cathedral; church; edifice; erection; establishment; fabric(ation); house; pile; structure; tenement; BUILT: see "made"

BULGE: v. bag; beetle; billow; bloat; extend; extrude; jut; obtrude; pop; project; protrude; protuberate; surge; swell; thrust; tumefy; tumesce; BULGE: n. advantage; beetling; billow; bloating; bump; convexity; extension; extrusion; form; gibbosity; hump; increase; jutting; knob; knot; obtrusion; projection; protrusion; protuberance; rise; salient; swelling; BULGING: billowing; convex; full; gibbous; gouty; jutting; obtrusive; overlarge; protrudent; protrusive; protuberant; swollen; thrusting; tumescent

BULK: accretion; accumulation; agglomeration; agglutination; aggregate; aggregation; all; amount; assemblage; body; collection; conglomeration; crowd; corpulence; dimension; extent; figure; flock; force; form; gathering; gross; group; heaviness; horde; intensity; largeness; magnitude; majority; mass; number; organization; pile; pool; quanta (pl.); quantity; quantum; raft; shape; size; sum; swarm; thickness; total; volume; weight; whole; BULKY: clumsy; corpulent; fat; gross; heavy; large; magnitudinous; massive; material; meaty; ponderous; stout; thick; unwieldly; voluminous; weighty; BULKINESS: corpulency; massivity; ponderosity; voluminosity

BULLDOZE: (see "bully") dig; force; ram

BULLETIN: (see "announcement") advertisement; bill; catalog(ue); dodger; flash; memo(randum); newscast; notice; poster; publication; sales pitch; statement

BULLY: v. (see "coerce") bludgeon; browbeat; bulldoze; cow; domineer; dragoon; force; frighten; hector; intimidate; ram; scare; BULLY: a. dashing; excellent; first-rate; gallant; jolly; jovial; BULLY: n. (see "tyrant") bruiser; hector; intimidator; ruffian

BULWARK: bastion; breakwater; castle; citadel; defense; embankment; fort(ification); fortress; parapet; protection; rampart; safeguard; sconce; security; shelter; shield; support; tower; wall

BUMP: v. (see "hit") clash; collide; conflict; contact; contravene; crash; demote; dislodge; dismiss; displace; encounter; encroach; impact; impinge; jolt; jostle; kiss; knock; meet; oppose; strike; touch; BUMP: n. bulge; clash; collision; conflict; contact; contravention; crash; demotion; difficulty; dismissal; encounter; encroachment; hump; impact; impingement; jam; jar; jolt; jostle; kiss; knock; knot; lump; meeting; obstacle; opposition; projection; protuberance; ridge; strike; swelling; touch(ing); welt; wheal

BUMPKIN: (see "rube") boor; bucolic; rustic; yahoo

BUNCH: v. (see "gather" and "group") accumulate; agglutinate; protrude; BUNCH: n. (see "gathering" and "group") accumulation; agglutination; aggregate; aggregation; bale; budget; bundle; cluster; clutch; collection; crowd; fagot; grouping; hand; hump; knot; lot; pack; pad; parcel; protuberance; set; swelling; tuft; wisp

BUNDLE: amount; bale; band; bindle; bolt; bunch; collection; hank; lot; mass; pack (-age); packet; pad; parcel; quanta (pl.); quantity; quantum; roll; sheaf; truss; vinculum; wrap

BUNGLE: v. (see "err") batter; befoul; blemish; botch; break; bruise; butcher; carve; confuse; cripple; crush; cut; dabble; destroy; disfigure; dub; fail; fault; flatten; flounder; flub; fluff; fumble; garble; goof; hack; kill; injure; jumble; lacerate; lapse; lurch; maim; mangle; mar; maul; mess; miscue; misdo: mishandle; mismanage; mis-play; miss; misstep; mistake; mix; muddle; murder; muss; mutilate; rip; ruin; slaughter; slay; slice; slip; spoil; stumble; tear; trip; wound; BUNGLE: n. (see "error") botch; confusion; failure; fiasco; fluff; fumble; garbling; goof; hacking; jumble; killing; mangle; mangling; mess; miscue; misplay; miss; murder; muss; mutilation; slaughter; slaying; slice; spoilage; tear; BUNGLING: amateurish; awkward; blundering; bunglesome; butchering; butterfingered; clumsy; failing; floundering; gauche; inadequate; inapt; inept; inexpert; maladroit; mangling; messing; messy; muddlebrained; muddleheaded; muddy(-minded); murdering; mutilating; slaughtering; slaying; slicing; spoiling; stumbling; tearing; tripping; unskilled; unskillful

BUOY: (see "elate") levitate; lift; lilt; raise; rise; stimulate; support; sustain; BUOYANT: (see "elated") airy; blithe(some); cheerful; corky; elastic; floating; gay; happy; hopeful; light(hearted); lilting; lively; resilient; spirited; sprightly; springy; spriteful; spry; stimulated

BURDEN: v. afflict; beset; charge; check; clog; complicate; crowd; cumber; disable; distress; encumber; freight; hamper; handicap; hinder; impede; lade; lard; load; obstruct; oppress; overburden; labor; plague; press; saddle; tax; tire; trouble; vex; weigh; BURDEN: n. bane; blame; care; cargo; charge; check; claim; clog; complication; cost; cross; debt; difficulty; distress; drag; drain; drawback; duty; embarrassment; encumbrance; expense; fardel; freight; goods; hampering; handicap; hindrance; impediment; imposition; incubus; infliction; labor; lading; lien; load; millstone; mortgage; necessity; obligation; obstacle; obstruction; onus; *onus probandi*; overburdening; perplexity; plague; press; property; responsibility; stigma; strain; task; tax; trouble; weight; BURDENED or BURDENSOME: afflicted; beset; clogged; cumbered; disabled; distressed; encumbered; freighted; hagridden; hampered; handicapped; heavy-laden; impedimental; impedimentary; impeditive; impregnated; labored; larded; loaded; obligated; obstructed; obstructive; oppressed; overdriven; overpowering; overtaxed; plagued; ponderous; pregnant; pressed; pressing; serious; superincumbent; toilsome; troublesome; wearisome

BURLESQUE: v. (see "deride") ape; caricature; chaff; copy; disdain; fleer; imitate; mime; mock; overdo; pasquinade; ridicule;

scorn; scout; taunt; tease; twit; BUR-
LESQUE: **n.** (**see** "derision") caricature;
comedy; exaggeration; farce; fleer; imitation;
parody; pasquinade; revue; ridicule; travesty

BURLY: athletic; brawny; bulky; endo-
morphic; fat; fleshy; heavy; husky; obese;
powerful; pyknic; robust(ious); rough; stout;
strong; sturdy; thick; vigorous; weighty

BURN: **v.** anger; blaze; blister; brand; calcine;
cauterize; cense; char; cheat; consume;
cremate; deaden; deflagrate; destroy; diminish; dissipate; electrocute; exhaust; fire;
flame; flare; flash; glare; gleam; glow; ignite;
incinerate; inflame; kindle; light; lust;
oxidize; raze; roast; scald; scorch; scorify;
sear: singe; sizzle; smart; smolder; spend;
squander; sterilize; sting; tingle; torrify;
waste; yearn; BURN: **n.** anger; blaze;
blister; brand; brook; cauterization; flame;
flare; flash; glare; gleam; rill; singe; stream;
BURNING: **a.** ablaze; afire; alight; angry;
ardent; blazing; blistering; calescent; calid;
candent; caustic; conflagrant; consuming;
disgraceful; eager; fervent; fervid; feverish;
fiery; flaming; fulgent; glowing; grueling;
heated; hot; ignited; incalescent; incandescent; incensed; inflamed; inflaming; intense;
irate; lighted; lit; mad; mordant; passionate;
peppery; red; roasting; scalding; scathing;
scorching; scorifying; searing; severe;
shocking; sizzling; smarting; stinging; sultry;
sweltering; torrid; torrifying; urgent;
vehement; withering; BURNING: **n.** blaze;
cautery; cineration; combustion; conflagration; consuming; cremation; fire; heat;
oxidation; sizzling; ustulation; BURNABLE:
combustible; conflagratory; explosive; flammable; ignescent; inflammable; inflammatory

BURROW: **see** "excavate"

BURST: **v.** (**see** "break") burgeon; cave;
change; collapse; dehisce; detonate; effloresce; erupt; expand; explode; flash; fly;
fulminate; implode; launch; leap; open;
plunge; pop; puff; race; reave; rend; resound; rupture; rush; sally; shatter; speed;
splint(er); split; sprout; spurt; torpedo;
unfold; BURST: **n.** (**see** "break") burgeon
(-ing); change; dash; eruption; explosion;
fit; flash; flaw; implosion; leap; plunge; pop;
race; rupture; rush; sally; salvo; shattering;
spasm; speed; splintering; split; spurt(ing);
unfolding

BURY: (**see** "cover") cache: cloak; conceal;
engross; entomb; hide; inearth; inhume;

inter; plant; secrete; sheathe; shroud; sink;
submerge; veil

BUSINESS: action; activity; adventure; af-
fair(s); agency; art(ifice); artistry; assiduity;
assiduousness; assignment; attention; avocation; barter; berth; billet; buying; calling;
care; career; charge; chore; clientele; commerce; commercialism; communication;
communion; company; concern; concoction;
constancy; control; corporation; course;
craft; creation; curriculum; dealings; device;
diligence; diligency; diligentness; direction;
duty; employment; encumbrance; endeavor;
energy; engagement; enterprise; errand;
essay; establishment; exchange; experience;
exploit; factory; feat; field; firm; fixture;
foundation; function; gadget; gamble; game;
gear; handicraft; heed; industrialism; industry; initiative; installation; institution; intensity; interchange; interest; interrelationship; job; joint; *jus commercii*; keenness;
knowledge; labor; layout; learning; *les
affaires*; life; line; matter; mercantilism;
merchandise; métier; mission; occupation;
office; operosity; organization; outfit; palaver; partnership; patronage; performance;
perseverance; place; plan; ploy; position;
post; practice; procedure; process; profession;
progress; project; province; prudence;
pursuit; quest; race; racket; right; risk;
role; route; schedule; scheme; science;
selling; service; shop; situation; skill;
solicitude; sphere; station; steadfastness;
stint; task; technique; thing; toil; trade;
traffic; transaction; turkey; undertaking;
venture; vigilance; virtuosity; vocation;
walk; way; work(s); workshop; world

BUSTLE: (**see** "action") activity; ado; agitation; buzz; commotion; confusion; disturbance; emergency; flurry; frisk; fuss;
haste; hurry; hustle; motion; movement;
pother; rush; rustle; scuffle; scutter; stir;
struggle; to-do; tournure; tumult; turmoil;
whirl; work

BUSY: (**see** "active") abustle; abuzz; assiduous; attentive; bustling; diligent; employed;
engaged; engrossed; fast; humming; industrious; intent; lively; meddling; occupied; officious; on the jump; operose; running;
sedulous; solicitous; unleisured; working

BUSYBODY: (**see** "meddler") gadfly; intermeddler; omnibus; pryer; quidnunc;
snoop(er); zealot

BUT: also; and; barely; barring; besides;
else; except; excluding; further(more); how-

beit; however; just; merely; moreover; nevertheless; only; provided; save; still; though; too; unless; yet

BUTCHER: (see "bungle") blemish; botch; destroy; hack; kill; mangle; mayhem; murder; mutilate; slash; slaughter; slay; slice; spoil; tear; BUTCHERY: see "carnage"

BUTTOCKS: backside; behind; bottom; breech; bum; clunes(pl); clunis; croup; crupper; cushions; *derrière*; doup; *fesse*; fundament; *glutei maximi* (pl); gluteus; *gluteus maximus*; hams; haunches; hindquarters; hunkers; hunkies; lumbar region; nates; natis; podex; posteriority; pyges; rear; rump; seat; spheromata (pl.); spread; stern; tail

BUTTRESS: (see "support") abutment; counterfront

BUY: accept; acquire; approve; bargain; barter; bribe; employ; expend; gain; get; hire; market; negotiate; obtain; pay; procure; purchase; redeem; secure; shop; vend; BUYER(S): agent; client(age); clientele;

consumer; customer; emptor; patient; patron; purchaser; vassal; vendee

BUZZ: (see "hum") call; confusion; dart; disturbance; ring; rumor; rush; turmoil; whirl; whizz; zoom

BY: abreast; abutting; against; along(side); anon; aside; at; beside; between; close; connecting; contingent; interjacent; intermediary; intermediate; intervenient; joining; near; past; per; through; via; with

BYGONE: (see "ago") antiquated; buried; dead; elapsed; extinct; former; olden; outmoded; out-of-date; passé; past; quondam; yore

BYPASS: (see "avoid") circumnavigate; circumvent; detour; dodge; eschew; evade; ignore; neglect; short-circuit; shunt; sidestep

BYWORD: (see "saying") aphorism; catchword; epithet; maxim; motto; phrase; proverb; saw; saying

C

CABAL: (see "conspiracy") bloc; clique; combination; conclave; confederacy; connivance; conspiracy; coup; faction; gang; group; intrigue; junto; machination; party; plot; ring; set; union

CABIN: berth; caboose; coach; compartment; cote; cottage; dugout; hovel; hut; lodge; nest; nook; refuge; sanctuary; shack; shed; shelter; stateroom

CABINET: advisers; almirah; ambry; board; box; bureau; case; chamber; chest; closet; collection; compartment; console; cupboard; drawers; highboy; hutch; locker; lowboy; ministry; repository; room; space; stall; vault

CACHE: v. (see "conceal" and "hoard") store; thesaurize; treasure; CACHE: n. (see "hoard") collection; concealment; loot; safe; saving(s); store(house); supply; thesaurus; treasure; treasury

CAD: bounder; heel; knave; rascal; rogue; rounder; ruffian; scoundrel

CADENCE: accent; beat; cadency; coordination; harmony; ictus; lilt; measure; melody; meter; modulation; pace; pattern; periodicity; regularity; rhythm; sequence; sound; swing; symmetry; tempo; throb; time; tone

CAGE: v. (see "confine") box; coop; imprison; incarcerate; intern; jail; pen; CAGE: n. (see "jail") area; bars; basket; bin; box; cell; chest; compartment; crate; enclosure; frame(work); hutch; pen; prison; vault; CAG(E)Y: (see "cunning") foxy; hesitant; shrewd; wary

CAJOLE: (see "entice") allure; beg; beguile; blandish; charm; cheat; coax; decoy; flatter; inveigle; lure; manipulate; palaver; palp; seduce; tease; trick; wheedle; work; CAJOLEMENT: (see "allure" and "charm") cajolery

CAKE: v. see "harden;" CAKE: n. baba; bannock; block; bread; bun; cookie; crust; flan; loaf; mass; muffin; tart; torte

CALAMITY: accident; adversity; affliction; Armageddon; atrocity; bale; bankruptcy; battle; blow; cataclysm; catastrophe; clash; combat; conflagration; conflict; death; debacle; deluge; denouement; destruction; difficulty; disaster; dissention; distress; doom; failure; fiasco; fight; flood; grief; hardship; harm; holocaust; hostility; ill(fortune); ill luck; illness; injury; loss; malady; malevolence; misadventure; misery; misfortune; mishap; rebellion; reverse; revolt; ruin; sadness; sickness; smash; sorrow; strife; tragedy; trial; tribulation; trouble; upheaval; violence; war(fare); woe(fulness); wrack; wreck; CALAMITOUS: (see "adverse") afflictive; cataclysmal; cataclysmic(al) catastrophal; catastrophic(al); dangerous; deplorable; desperate; dire(ful); disastrous; distressful; distressing; doomed; dreadful; evil; hapless; harmful; holocaustic; misfortunate; ominous; precipitous; sad; terrible; tragic(al); unfortunate; unlucky; woeful

CALCULATE: (see "contemplate") add; adjudge; adjudicate; adjust; analyze; anticipate; appraise; ascertain; assay; assess; capitalize; cast; comprehend; compute; conjecture; consider; count; deduce; deem; design; determine; develop; diagnose; divine; establish; estimate; evaluate; evalue; examine; expect; feel; figure; forecast; foresee; frame; gather; gauge; guess; imagine; infer; interrupt; intuit; judge; justify; levy; look; measure; opine; perceive; plan; plot; ponder; portend; predict; prepare; presage; prognosticate; project; realize; reason; reckon; score; sense; settle; solve; speculate; study; suppose; surmise; suspect; tally; test; theorize; think; total; value; weigh

CALENDAR: agenda (pl.); agendum; almanac; catalog(ue); category; chart; chronicle; chronology; circuit; diary; docket; ephemeris; journal; list; log; range; record; register; table; tablet; tariff; zodiac

CALIBER: (**see** "capacity") ability; bore; breadth; degree; diameter; gauge; quality; talent

CALL: **v.** address; announce; appeal; appoint; bawl; beckon; bellow; bid; bring; challenge; charge; christen; cite; clamor; clepe; command; conscript; consider; convene; convocate; convoke; cry; deliver; demand; denominate; denote; describe; designate; dial; draft; dub; ejaculate; elicit; entitle; estimate; evocate; exclaim; gesture; guess; halt; impel; indicate; invite; invoke; magnetize; mesmerize; move; muster; name; nominate; ordain; order; page; petition; phone; prompt; pull; request; require; roar; rouse: rule; scream; select; shout; shriek; signal; speak; stop; style; subpoena; summon; suspend; telephone; tell; term; utter; visit; vociferate; wave; yell; CALL: **n.** announcement; appeal; beckon(ing); bellow; bid; citation; command; conscription; convocation; cry; demand; draft; impulse; invitation; invocation; justification; magnetization; muster; necessity; nomination; notice; obligation; occasion; order; petition; prompting; pull; request; requirement; scream; selection; shout; shriek; signal; stop; subpoena; summons; visit; wave; yell

CALLING: (**see** "business") activity; impulse; work

CALLOUS: (**see** "stubborn") adamant(ine); anesthetic; careless; cold(-blooded); coldhearted; confirmed; cruel; dedolent; emotionless; hard(-boiled); hardened; horny; impenitent; impertinent; impiteous; indifferent; indurate(d); indurative; inexorable; inflexible; insensible; insensitive; obdurate; obtuse; pachydermatous; rude; thick(ened); thick-skinned; tough; unaffected; unfeeling; unmoving; unsympathetic; unyielding; willful; CALLOUSNESS: (**see** "stubbornness") hardness; impenitence; impenitency; indifference; induration; inflexibility; insensibility; insensitivity; obduracy; rudeness; toughness

CALLOW: (**see** "green") immature; inexperienced; rude; unfledged; untried; young; youthful

CALM: **v.** (**see** "appease") abate; allay; alleviate; alloy; ameliorate; appease; assuage; bait; comfort; compose; conciliate; condone; console; control; cow; cure; daunt; deaden; defeat; diminish; dose; down; ease; encourage; extenuate; gladden; help; hush; inspire; inspirit; lenify; lessen; limit; lower;

lull; manage; mediate; mitigate; moderate; modify; mollify; pacify; palliate; placate; please; propitiate; qualify; quash; quell; quench; quiesce; quiet(en); reassure; reconcile; reduce; regulate; relieve; remedy; remit; restrain; salve; satisfy; sedate; settle; slake; slow; smooth; sober; soften; solace; soothe; stay; still; subdue; subjugate; subside; suppress; sympathize; tame; temper; tranquilize; vanquish; weaken; CALM; **a.** (**see** "appeased") affable; alleviative; alleviatory; ameliorative; amiable; amicable; apathetic; arrested; assuasive; assured; balmy; benign; bland; bovine; bright; callous; calmative; calming; changeless; clear; clement; cold; collected; comfortable; comforting; complacent; complaisant; compliant; composed; conciliating; conciliative; conciliatory; considerate; contained; content; cool; cooperative; courteous; courtly; dead; decorous; *dégagé*; deliberate; demure; detached; diplomatic; dispassionate; dispassive; docile; domesticated; dormant; dovelike; easy (-going); enduring; enjoyable; equanimous; eudaemonic; expressionless; favonian; felicitous; fixed; forbearing; genial; genteel; gentle; glassy; grateful; grave; halcyon; harmonious; henotic; hermetic(al); humane; humbled; hushed; immobile; immovable; impartial; impassioned; impassive; imperturbable; imperturbed; impervious; inactive; inanimate; indifferent; inert; insensate; insensible; irenic(al); jaunty; judicial; kind; lazy; lenient; lenitive; level; limpid; longanimous; maidenly; matter-of-fact; meek; mellow; mild; milky; mitigating; mitigative; modest; mollifying; monotonous; moribund; motionless; neighborly; nepenthean; nonchalant; oasitic; objective; pacific; palliative; passionate; passive; pastoral; patient; peaceable; peaceful; pellucid; permanent; persuasive; philosophic(al); phlegmatic(al); phlegmatous; placative; placatory; placid; pleasant; pleased; pleasing; pliant; possessed; propitiating; propitiatory; propitious; quiescent; quiet; rational; reconciled; remedial; replete; repose; reserved; resigned; restful; restrained; rigid; *sans souci*; sated; satisfied; sedate; sedentary; self-assured; self-composed; self-possessed; serene; serious; sessile; set(tled); silent; silken; smooth(ed); smug; sober; solemn; soothed; soothing; stable; stagnant; staid; static; stationary; steady; still(ed); stilly; stoic(al); stolid; subdued; submissive; sweet; tame(d); tempean; temperate; tender; tolerant; torpid; torporific; tractable; tranquil(ized); unaggressive; unagitated; unalarmed; unanxious; unastonished; unblinking; unchanging; uncomplaining; undaunted;

undisturbed; unemotional; unexcited; unexciting; unflurried; unflustered; unimpassioned; unmartial; unmilitary; unmoved; unmoving; unobtrusive; unpassioned; unperturbable; unperturbed; unruffled; untroubled; unvexed; unvicious; unwarlike; CALM(NESS); **n.** (**see** "appeasement") accord; agreement; amelioration; amity; apathy; assuagement; ataraxia; ataraxy; atonement; balance; balm; comfort; complacency; composedness; composure; conciliation; concord; condolence; constancy; contentment; control; *détente*; dispassion; ease; easiness; endurance; equability; equalization; equanimity; equation; equilibrium; equipoise; equiponderance; equitableness; eudaemonia; eudaemony; euphoria; evenness; felicity; firmness; forbearance; gravity; harmony; help; homeostasis; hush; impassivity; imperturbability; imperturbation; indifference; indulgence; inspiration; lackadaisy; lassitude; leniency; lenity; limpidity; longanimity; lull; mitigation; moderation; mollification; nepenthe; nirvana; nonchalance; objectivity; order; pacification; passiveness; passivity; patience; peace(fulness); persuasion; philosophy; phlegm; placidity; pleasure; pococurantism; poise; posture; proportion; quiescence; quiet-(ism); quietness; quietude; reason; reconciliation; relief; repose; requiescence; reserve; resignation; rest; restraint; *sangfroid*; sanity; satisfaction; saturation; *savoir faire*; seduction; self-control; self-possession; sereneness; serenity; settlement; silence; sobriety; sop; stability; steadfastness; stillness; submission; sufferance; sympathy; tranquility; tranquilization; unexcitedness; unhurriedness; unperturbability

CALUMNIATE: (**see** "abuse" and "belittle") accuse; asperse; attack; belie; blacken; chagrin; charge; defame; denigrate; detract; impair; impute; injure; libel; malign; misrepresent; scold; slander; slur; traduce; vilify; CALUMNY: abuse; accusation; aspersion; defamation; denigration; detraction; lampoon; libel; misrepresentation; slander; traduction; villainy

CAMOUFLAGE: (**see** "conceal") cover; disguise; hide

CAMPAIGN: **see** "expedition"

CAN: **see** "container" and "preserve"

CANCEL: abolish; abrogate; annul; blot (out); counteract; counterbalance; countermand; deface; dele(te); destroy; drop; efface; eliminate; eradicate; erase; expunge; frustrate; invalidate; negate; neutralize; nullify; obliterate; offset; oppose; postmark; prohibit; quash; recall; relinquish; remit; remove; repeal; repudiate; rescind; retract; revoke; ruin; scratch; scrub; stamp (out); stop; strike; undo; vacate; veto; vitiate; void; withdraw; write off; CANCELLATION: (**see** "elimination") abrogation; annulment; cassation; counteraction; deletion; destruction; disaffirmation; elimination; expunction; forgiveness; invalidation; negation; nullification; obliteration; opposition; prohibition; recall; recession; remission; reversal; revocation; scratch; scrub(bing); stop(page); undoing; veto; vitiation; write-off

CANCER: adenocarcinoma; carcinoma; carcinosarcoma; carcinosis; epithelioma; excrescence; malignity; neoplasm; sarcoma; scirrhus; tumor

CANDID: aboveboard; artless; blunt; *bona fide*; childlike; conscientious; crude; disinterested; earnest; easy; fair; forthright; forward; frank; gauche; genuine; guileless; honest; honorable; ignorant; impartial; implicit; inartistic; incorruptible; ingenuous; innocent; just; naif; naive; natural; nescient; open (-minded); outspoken; plain; pretenseless; pure; real; rude; serious; simple(-minded); sincere; straightforward; straight-from-the-shoulder; true(-blue); truthful; unconcealed; undesigning; undogmatic; unexaggerated; unfeigned; unflattering; unposed; unprejudiced; unreserved; unskillful; unsophisticated; unsubtle; unvarnished; unwary; white; wholehearted; whole-souled; CANDIDNESS: **see** "candor"

CANDIDATE: (**see** "beginner") aspirant; choice; hopeful; nominee; office seeker; seeker; striver; student

CANDOR: (**see** "honesty") artlessness; candidness; fairness; frankness; guilelessness; impartiality; ingenuousness; innocence; naiveté; openheartedness; simplicity; sincerity; unsophistication

CANDY: caramel; comfit; confection; cream; fondant; fudge; kiss(es); lolly(pop); nougat; praline; sugar; sweet(s); sweetment; taffy

CANE: **v.** (**see** "punish") beat; whack; CANE: **n.** bamboo; cylinder; malacca; rattan; rod; sorghum; staff; stem; stick; walking stick

CANNY: (**see** "cautious" and "cunning") careful; clever; frugal; sharp(-witted)

CANON: axiom; book; clergyman; code; command; constitution; criteria (pl.); criterion; convention(ality); custom; decision; decree; determination; dicta (pl.); dictum; discipline; doctrine; example; formula; guide; law; list; maxim; model; norm; order; ordinance; precedent; precept; principle; procedure; pronouncement; regula(tion); ritual; rubric; rule; schedule; song; standard; statute; supremacy; theorem; theorum; tradition; CANONICAL: acceptable; accepted; authoritative; axiomatic; basic; conventional; customary; doctrinaire; legal; legitimate; normal; orthodox; preceptive; procedural; regulatory; sanctioned; standard; statutory; supreme; traditional; CANONIZE: see "deify"

CANT: **v.** bend; bevel; careen; cast; deviate; heel; incline; lean; list; lurch; slant; slope; sway; throw; tilt; tip; toss; CANT: **n.** (**see** "dialect") bias; incline; pretense; slant; slope: sway; tip

CANTANKEROUS: (**see** "perverse" and "stubborn") curmudgeonish; curmudgeonly; rantankerous

CANVAS(S): **v.** (**see** "solicit") circulate; debate; determine; discuss; examine; inquire; investigate; peddle; poll; spread; vote; CANVAS: **n.** cloth; material; painting; picture; poll; sail; tent

CAP: **v.** (**see** "excel") climax; cover; crown; overlay; seal; CAP: **n.** apex; beanie; beret; climax; cloche; coif; cork; coronet; cover-(ing); crown; eton; fez; galerum; galerus; headpiece; helmet; hood; layer; lid; overlay; protection; seal; tam; top; turban

CAPABLE: (**see** "competent") able; accomplished; adequate; apt; consummate; effective; efficient; expert; fit(ted); licensed; possible; potent(ial); powerful; practical; productive; qualified; reliable; resourceful; responsible; sciential; skillful; smart; strong; susceptible; virtuosic; CAPABILITY: (**see** "competency") ability; capableness; capacity; efficiency; expertise; potentiality; power; qualification; resourcefulness; resources; skill; strength; use(fulness)

CAPACITY: (**see** "competency") ability; adeptness; adequacy; adroitness; ambidexterity; amplitude; aptitude; aptness; attainment; bent; bore; brains; breadth; caliber; candlepower; capability; capableness; competence; content; degree; dexterity;

diameter; duty; *dynamis*; dynamism; effectiveness; efficiency; eligibility; endowment; energy; expanse; expertise; extent; facility; faculty; fitness; flair; force; freedom; gauge; genius; gift; horsepower; ingeniosity; ingenuity; instinct; intellect; intelligence; job; knack; knowledge; latitude; leadership; length; limitation; magnitude; measure; might; number; office; panurgy; performance; perspective; place; position; potency; potentiality; power; proficiency; puissance; qualification; quantity; resourcefulness; role; room; situation; size; skill(fulness); space; spread; stature; strength; sufficiency; talent; training; turn; use(fulness); versatility; vigor; virtuosity; volume; width; wisdom; yield; CAPACIOUS: accommodable; ample; baronial; broad; cavernous; copious; expansive; extensive; inclusive; large; limitless; magnitudinous; much; powerful; roomy; spacious; suitable; unlimited; virtuosic; voluminous; wide

CAPER: **v.** (**see** "frisk") bound; cavort; curvet; dance; frolic; gambol; hop; jump; leap; play; prance; romp; skip; spring; tittup; CAPER: **n.** (**see** "whim") activity; antic; bound; capriccio; capriole; caracole; cavort; condiment; curleycue; curvet; dance; dido; frisk; frolic; gambade; gambado; hop; jump; leap; lope; marlock; performance; ploy; prance; prank; pursuit; romp; saltation; tittup; trick; turn

CAPITAL: **a.** (**see** "basic") chief; excellent; extraordinary; extreme; fatal; first-class; good; important; main; major; predominant; primal; prime; principal; prominent; proper; serious; CAPITAL: **n.** (**see** "money" and "wealth") estate; facilities; goods; stock

CAPRICE: (**see** "caper" and "whim") boutade; fad; fancy; freak; humor; idea; impulse; mood; notion; quirk; temper; vagary; whimsey; whimsicality; CAPRICIOUS: (**see** "fickle" and "whimsical") episodic(al); fluky; freakish; irresponsible; skittish

CAPSIZE: (**see** "upset") collapse; fold; overturn

CAPSULE: (**see** "concentration") abbreviation; abridgement; ampule; compilation; compression; conciseness; condensation; consolidation; container; contraction; desication; detonator; distillation; epitome; essence; inspissation; medicine; outline; pericarp; pill; pod; reduction; sheath; shell; shortening; solidification; survey; synopsis; tabloid; theca; wafer

CAPTAIN: (see "leader") chief(tain); commander; head(master); master; officer; skipper

CAPTION: banner; cavil; display; explanation; header; heading; headline; inscription; leader; legend; name; quibble; title

CAPTIOUS: (see "fickle" and "whimsical") capricious; carping; caviling; censorious; critical; cynical; fretful; hypercritical; insidious; irascible; overstrict; perverse; petulant; quibbling; splenetic; testy; touchy; undependable

CAPTIVATE: allure; amuse; attract; bewitch; capture; charm; divert; dominate; elate; enamor; enchant; enrapture; enslave; ensorcel(l); enthrall; entrance; exalt; excite; fascinate; flatter; gladden; gratify; infatuate; influence; ingratiate; jubilate; lure; magnetize; mesmerize; overpower; please; satisfy; seduce; subdue; take; transport; win; woo; CAPTIVATING: (see "alluring" and "attractive") charming; diverting; enchanting; seductive; winning; CAPTIVITY: (see "bondage") binding; chains; domination; oppression; restraint; subjugation

CAPTURE: v. (see "captivate") annex; apprehend; appropriate; arrest; arrogate; bag; carry; catch; clutch; collar; commandeer; confiscate; control; cop; defeat; dominate; entrap; fix; get; grab; grasp; impound; land; latch; lure; nab; net; overpower; possess; preempt; prehend; rob; sack; seize; sequester; snare; snatch; subdue; sweep; tackle; take; trap; usurp; win; yoke; CAPTURE: n. (see "seizure") control; entrapment; possession; usurpation

CARAVAN: campaign; cavalcade; convoy; cruise; crusade; excursion; expedition; escort; fleet; group; jaunt; journey; odyssey; pageant; parade; peregrination; pilgrimage; pilgrims; proceeding; procession; quest; reconnaissance; safari; series; tour; train; travel(ers); trek; trip; van; voyage

CARDINAL: (see "basic") capital; central; chief; critical; essential; extraordinary; important; leading; main; primary; principal; vital

CARE: v. (see "protect") attend; cherish; consider; control; cultivate; develop; educate; encourage; feed; foster; further; heed; keep; maintain; manage; monitor; mother; nourish; nurse; nurture; pamper; proctor; protect; provide; rear; regard; suckle; superintend; tend; wish; CARE: n. advertence; advertency; anxiety; application; apprehension; assiduity; attention; attentiveness; awareness; bother; burden; caution; charge; circumspection; concern; conciseness; conscientiousness; conservation; consideration; control; cultivation; custody; defense; detention; development; diligence; direction; discipline; disquietude; durance; economy; education; efficiency; effort; encouragement; fear; fondness; forethought; frugality; furthering; grief; guardianship; heed; husbandry; intendence; interest; keeping; love; maintenance; management; notice; nourishment; nursing; nurturance; nurture; nurturing; observation; occupation; order; organization; pain(s); pampering; paternalism; patience; patronage; perception; perpetuation; planned management; precaution; preparation; preservation; proctorship; protection; prudence; recognition; regard; reservation; respect; responsibility; safekeeping; scruple; sickness; solicitation; solicitude; sorrow; study; suffering; superintendence; supervision; sustenance; sustentation; sustention; tending; thought; thrift(iness); trouble; trust; tutelage; upkeep; vigil(ance); ward; wariness; watchfulness; weariness; worry; CAREFUL(LY): (see "attentive") accurate; advised; alert; analytical; anxious; apprehensive; arch; artful; astute; calculated; calculating; canny; cautious; chary; choosy; circumspect(ive); clever; close-grain(ed); concerned; conscientious; considerate; conderative; considered; contemplative; cool; crafty; critical; cunning; dainty; decisive; definite; diplomatic; discerning; discreet; discriminating; discriminatory; economical; exact; fair; faithful; foxy; gingerly; guarded; heedful; honest; honorable; judicious; just; keen; knowing; leery; loyal; meditated; meticulous; mindful; nice; observant; observing; overcautious; painstaking; particular; perfect; perspicacious; politic; precise; premeditated; proper; provident; prudent(ial); punctilious; punctual; rational; regardful; rigid; sagacious; sage; scrupulous; serious; shady; sharp; shrewd; slow; sly; smart; sober; solicitous; squeamish; studied; subtle; thorough; thoughtful; thrifty; tricky; unhurried; upright; vigilant; wary; watchful; wise; CAREFULNESS: (see "caution") attentiveness; circumspection; foresight; heed; judiciality; judiciousness; meticulosity; perfection(ism); perfectness; prudence; scrupulosity; solicitude; wisdom; CARELESS and CARELESSNESS: see "below"

CAREEN: cant; heel; incline; lean; list; lurch;

overturn; slant; slope; sway; tilt; tip; toss; upset; weave

CAREER: (see "business") affairs; course; curriculum; direction; experience; field; flight; life; passage; profession; progress; pursuit; race; route; rush; speed; sphere; walk; way; world

CAREFREE: careless; casual; debonair(e); *dégagé*; drifting; easygoing; fickle; frivolous; glib; happy(-go-lucky); imperturbable; improvident; incautious; indifferent; insouciant; irresponsible; jaunty; lighthearted; neglectful; negligent; nonchalant; random; *sans souci*; trifling; uncareful; unconcerned; undemanding; unforethoughtful; unruffled

CAREFUL AND CAREFULNESS: see under "care"

CARELESS: (see "apathetic;) blameworthy; butterfingered; casual; culpable; cursory; *dégagé;* delinquent; derelict; desultory; dilatory; disheveled; dowdy(ish); easy; erratic; frowsy; gay; haphazard; hasty; heedless; improvident; imprudent; inaccurate; inadvertent; inattentive; incautious; incurious; indifferent; indiscreet; indolent; irreparable; languid; lax; lazy; lenient; loose; malfeasant; messy; misfeasant; motiveless; mussy; neglectful; negligent; nonchalant; oblivious; offhand; perfunctory; pococurante; prideless; promiscuous; ragged; rakish; random; rash; raunchy; reckless; remiss; respectless; shabby; shiftless; shoddy; slack; slapdash; slatternly; slippery; slipshod; sloppy; slouchy; sloven (-ly); spontaneous; superficial; thoughtless; unconcerned; unfastidious; unheedful; unkempt; unmethodical; unmindful; unpremeditated; unrestrained; unsolicitous; unstudied; unthorough; untidy; wasteful; wild; CARELESSNESS: (see "apathy") blameworthiness; culpa(bility); culpableness; dishevelment; disinclination; disinterest; dowdiness; heedlessness; improvidence; imprudence; inaccuracy; inattention; incaution; incuriosity; indifference; indiscretion; irresponsibility; laxity; laxness; looseness; messiness; mussiness; neglect; negligence; nonchalance; perfunctoriness; pococurantism; promiscuity; raffishness; recklessness; reluctance; remission; slapdash; sloppiness; superficiality; unconcern(edness); unrestraint; untidiness; wastefulness; wildness

CARESS: baby; bill; cherish; coddle; comfort; console; coo; cosset; court; cuddle; dally; dandle; embrace; encourage; favor; flatter; fondle; gratify; hug; humor; indulge; kiss; love; neck; nuzzle; pamper; pat; pet; spoil; stroke; toy; woo; CARESSIVE: affectionate; amative; amatory; caressing; comforting; dandling; embracing; endearing; fondling; indulgent; loving

CARGO: (see "burden") baggage; commerce; commodities; freight; goods; lading; load; mail; merchandise; property; stock; stores; stuff; trade; wares

CARICATURE: **v.** ape; burlesque; chaff; copy; deride; disdain; distort; exaggerate; fleer; imitate; libel; mime; mimic; mock; persiflate; rag; rail; rally; ridicule; satirize; scorn; scout; slight; slur; sneer; taunt; tease; trick; twit; CARICATURE: **n.** (see "derision") burlesque; cartoon; chaff; disdain; exaggeration; farce; imitation; libel; mimicry; mockery; parody; postiche; ridicule; sardonicism; satire; scorn; scurrility; skit; slight; slur; squib; travesty

CARNAGE: barbarism; barbarity; blood(shed); butchery; decapitation; deracination; destruction; doom; eradication; extermination; extirpation; gore; havoc; holocaust; killing; massacre; mangling; mayhem; murder; mutilation: perdition; pogrom; ruin; slaughter; slaying

CARNAL: animal(ic); animalistic; barbarous; bloody; bodily; corporeal; cruel; earthy; fleshy; gross; lewd; lustful; pornographic; sensual; sexual; swinish; temporal; unspiritual; vulgar; worldly; CARNALITY: see "lewdness"

CAROUSE: **v.** binge; debauch; deprave; dissipate; drink; feast; frolic; jollify; revel; roister; royster; spree; CAROUSE: **n.** bacchanalia; binge; bouse; bout; carnival; carousal; compotation; debauch(ery); dissipation; excess; festival; festivity; frolic; jamboree; jollification; merrymaking; orgy; rampage; revel(ry); roister; royster; saturnalia; spree; wassail; CAROUSING: bacchanal(ian); bacchantic; orgiastic; roystering

CARP: (see "censure") argue; bicker; cavil; complain; criticize; disparage; dissent; drum; haggle; nag; nibble; niggle; pettifog; protest; quibble; shift; shuffle

CARRIAGE: (see "airs") baby buggy; bearing; buggy; bus; conveyance; demeanor; deport(ment); framework; front; gait; manner; mien; motion; passage; perambulation; perambulator; pipe; port; posture; pram;

support; surry; transport(ation); trolley; vehicle; waftage; wagon; wheelchair

CARRY: bear; behave; bring; capture; cart; contain; convey; cover; deduce; deliver; demean; deport; expire; fetch; harbor; have; hold; impart; implicate; involve; keep; maintain; move; portage; prance; print; publish; reach; remove; render; ride; shift; ship; stand; succeed; suffer; support; sustain; sway; take; tender; tolerate; tote; transfer; transmit; transport; weigh; wield; win

CARTEL: (**see** "bloc") agreement; card; corner; letter; monopoly; pact; paper; pool; treaty

CARVE: (**see** "cut") allot; apportion; butcher; castrate; chisel; chop; divide; engrave; expunge; expurgate; fashion; form; hew; incise; lash; make; pare; part; reduce; rip; saw; sculpt(ure); section; serve; sever; shape; shorten; slash; slice; slit; subdivide; tear

CASE: (**see** "cabinet") box; chest; compartment; rack; set

CASH: (**see** "money") bills; change; coin(age); currency; darby; dust; exchange; specie; wampum

CASHIER: **v. see** "dismiss;" CASHIER: **n.** bursar; comptroller; disbursing officer; exchequer; paymaster; purser; teller; treasurer

CASK: bareca; barrel; butt; cade; case; drum; hogshead; keg; pipe; puncheon; tub; tun; vat; vessel

CASKET: acerra; bier; box; case; catafalque; chest; cist; coffin; pall; pix; pyx; reliquary; repository; sarcophagus; tye

CAST: **v.** add; arrange; assign; banish; bear; bounce; calculate; cashier; chuck; contrive; count; create; decide; deposit; devise; direct; disbar; discard; disfigure; fire; flick; fling; flip; form(ulate); heave; hurl; hurtle; impel: jilt; junk; launch; mold; oust; pitch; plan; reckon; remove; rid; rock; sack; send; shape; shed; sling; slough; spew; spit; spout; spurt; sum; throw; toss; turn; twist; unfrock; vomit; warp; yield; CAST: **n.** actors; appearance; arrangement; aspect; assignment; cashier; chance; character; color; complection; complexion; *corps dramatique*; discharge; dismissal; disposition; ejection; eviction; exile; expression; expulsion; fate; feature; firing; fling; form; glance; heave; hue;

hurling; impression; kind; launching; look; matrix; nature; ouster; pitch; removal; riddance; sacking; shade; shedding; spit; spout; spurt; suggestion; throw; tincture; tinge; tint; toss(ing); troupe; turn; twist; type; venture; visage

CASTAWAY: bum; derelict; exile; hull; ne'er-do-well; outcast; pariah; tramp; waif; wreck

CASTE: ancestry; blood; breed; clan; class; clique; consanguinity; degree; descent; development; division; face; family; fraternity; genealogy; genesis; gens; gola; grade; history; kin(dred); kinship; line(age); nativity; nature; order; pariah; paternity; pedigree; prestige; race; rank; set; sorority; status; stemma; stock; strata (pl.); stratification; succession; sutra; tribe; unit; varna

CASTIGATE: (**see** "berate") beat; censure; chastise; chide; correct; criticize; decry; discipline; execrate; fine; flog; fustigate; jaw; lambaste; objurgate; oppugn; punish; rail; rate; rebuff; rebuke; reprehend; reproach; reprove; reverse; revile; rib; scold; score; slate; subdue; upbraid; vituperate

CASTLE: abode; Buckingham; bulwark; chateau; citadel; donjon; fastness; fort(ification); fortress; garrison; home; keep; kremlin; mansion; muniment; refuge; residence; retreat; rook; stronghold; town

CASTRATE: asexualize; change; cut; delete; desexualize; devitalize; emasculate; eunuchize; geld; remove; ruin; spay; weaken; CASTRATION: asexualization; demasculinization; devitalization; emasculation; eunuchism; eviration; gonadectomy; mutilation; orchidectomy; ruination

CASUAL: **a.** accidental; adventitious; by-the-way; careless; chance; chancy; circumstantial; comfortable; contingent; cursory; desultory; digressive; easy; erratic; eventful; external; extrinsic; fitful; fortuitous; free; glib; haphazard; heedless; idle; impromptu; inadvertent; incidental; inconstant; indefinite; indifferent; involuntary; irregular; lax; light; loose; misadventurous; misfortunate; motiveless; natural; nonchalant; nonessential; occasional; odd; offhand; once-over-lightly; precarious; promiscuous; purposeless; rambling; random; ready; seasonal; shifting; simple; slight; stray; superficial; uncertain; undeliberate; undesigned; unexpected; unforced; unforeseen; unfortunate; unimportant; unintended; unintentional; unmethodical; unmethodized; unmotivated; unplanned; unpredictable; unpremeditated; unstudied; unsubstantial; unthinking; untoward; unwitting; wavering; CASUAL: **n.** (**see** "vagabond") accident; drifter; dropout; gaberlunzie; itinerant; vagrant; CASUALTY: **see** "loss"

CAT: **see** "feline"

CATACLYSM: (**see** "calamity") catastrophe; convulsion; deluge; disaster; flood; holocaust; misfortune; upheaval; CATACLYSMIC: **see** "deadly" and "terrible"

CATALOG(UE): **v. see** "arrange;" CATALOG(UE): **n.** (**see** "arrangement") book; canon; compendium; description; enumeration; form(at); index; invoice; list; nomenclature; pamphlet; price; prospectus; record; register; repertorium; repertory; roll; roster; rota; schedule; series; table; tariff

CATASTROPHE: (**see** "calamity") Armageddon; blow; cataclysm; death; denouement; disaster; fiasco; holocaust; misery; misfortune; tragedy; CATASTROPHIC(AL): **see** "deadly"

CATCH: **v.** allure; apprehend; arrest; attain; attract; bag; beguile; bewitch; captivate; capture; check; clasp; collar; contact; contain; contract; control; cop; deceive; decoy; detain; detect; discern; enmesh; ensnare; entangle; entice; entrap; fasten; field; find; fool; gather; get; grab; grapple; grasp; grip; harpoon; hinder; hold; hook; implicate; incur; intercept; interrupt; inveigle; involve; jail; land; latch; lure; mislead; nab; nail; net; nip; notice; outstrip; overreach; overtake; overtop; pass; pinch; reach; receive; restrain; rope; save; secure; seduce; seize; snag; snare; snatch; spear; still; stop; strike; tackle; take; tangle; trap; win; CATCH: **n.** allurement; apprehension; arrest; beguilement; bewitchment; captivation; capture; check; clasp; deception; decoy; detainment; detent; device; ensnarement; enticement; entrapment; fastener; fragment; gimmick; hook; interception; joke; latch; pinching; seizure; snare; snatch; tackle

CATECHUMEN: (**see** "beginner") learner; neophyte; novice; trainee

CATEGORY: (**see** "class") assignment; bracket; calendar; caste; classification; cohort; concept; denomination; division; family; field; generation; genre; genus; grade; group(ing); heading; kind; league; level;

lexicon; nature; number; order; place; range; rank; rubric; species; tribe; way; CATEGORICAL: **see** "chronological"

CATER: bend; bow; concede; condescend; curts(e)y; defer; deign; favor; feed; humble; humor; kowtow; lower; oblige; pander; patronize; purvey; salute; serve; stoop; supply; unbend; yield

CATHOLIC: (**see** "universal") broad; comprehensive; general; inclusive; liberal; papal

CAUCUS: assembly; association; cabal; conference; convention; council; election; group; meeting; pole; primary; senate; vote

CAUSE: **v.** (**see** "begin") command; compel; constitute; create; derive; develop; direct; effect; elicit; foment; force; generate; get; goad; induce; initiate; inspire; lead; let; make; motivate; necessitate; originate; pound; precipitate; spring; spur; start; yield; CAUSE: **n.** (**see** "beginning") action; agent; aim; antecedent; author; basis; case; causa; determinant; doctrine; etiology; factor; fount(ain): fountainhead; genesis; ground(s); interest; ism; key; lawsuit; motive; object; occasion; origin(ation); party; philosophy; provenance; purpose; reason; root; source; spring; subject; suit; theory

CAUSTIC: **a.** (**see** "acid") abrasive; acidulous; acrid; acrimonious; acute; alkaline; backbiting; biting; bitter; burning; cankerous; corrosive; cutting; destructive; erodent; escharotic; etching; ferocious; fierce; gnawing; gruff; ill-humored; incisive; keen; malevolent; malign(ant); mordant; painful; penetrating; pungent; pyrotic; raw; rusting; rusty; salty; sarcastic; satirical; savage; scathing; severe; sharp; snappish; tart; testy; trenchant; virulent; vitriolic; weakening; wearing; witty; CAUSTIC: **n.** alkali; corrosive; lime; lye; phenol

CAUTERIZE: (**see** "burn") brand; char; deaden; scar(ify); sear; singe; sterilize;

CAUTION: **v.** admonish; advise; alert; apprise; arouse; awaken; command; counsel; cry; cry havoc; exhort; flag; forewarn; heed; inform; intimate; notify; previse; protest; sermonize; signal; summon; threaten; warn; CAUTION: **n.** admonishment; admonition; advice; alarm; alert; astucity; astuteness; attention; attentiveness; augury; beacon; bell; blinker; calculation; canniness; care(fulness); cautiousness; caveat; chariness; circumspection; circumspectiveness; cleverness; cohortation; concern; consideration; counsel; craft(iness); cunctation; cunning; diplomacy; discernment; discretion; economy; example; exhortation; fear; flag; foresight; forethought; foretoken; foxiness; guarantee; guard; heed-(-fulness); hint; homily; hortation; instruction; intimidation; judgment; judiciality; judiciousness; keenness; meticulosity; mindfulness; monition; notice; observance; omen; order; penetration; perfection(ism); perfectness; perspicacity; pledge; portent; preachment; precaution; prediction; premonition; presentiment; prevision; prudence; reason; reminder; reservation; reserve; safety; sagacity; sapience; scrupulosity; self-constraint; self-restraint; sermon; signal; siren; slyness; solicitude; strategy; suavity; subtlety; summons; surety; threat; thrift; tocsin; vigilance; wariness; warning; watchfulness; wisdom; CAUTIOUS: (see "attentive" and "careful") active; admonitory; alert; Argus-eyed; calculating; canny; cautionary; chary; circumspect(ive); conservative; deliberate; delicate; discreet; expectant; Fabian; foresighted; guarded; heedful; judicious; knowing; methodical; meticulous; mindful; monitorial; Nestorian; overcareful; provident; prudent(ial); scrupulous; shrewd; shy; squeamish; thrifty; vigilant; wary; watchful; wise

CAVALCADE: (see "caravan") journey; pageant; parade; procession; raid; safari; sequence; series; train

CAVE: v. (see "break") burst; collapse; hollow; implode; submit; undermine; CAVE: n. (see "cavity") antra; antrum; cavern; cell; cellar; chamber; crypt; den; grot(to); hole; hollow; lair; opening; recess; sinus; tunnel

CAVIL: (see "argue" and "carp") criticize; object

CAVITY: antra(pl.); antrum; aula; camera; cave; cavern; cavitation; cell; cellar; chamber; compartment; crater; crypt; den; dent; depression; depth; enclosure; excavation; fissure; gap; geode; grave; grot(to); hole; hollow; lair; lumen; mine; opening; pit; pocket; recess; sinus; tunnel; vacuole; vacuum; vault; vestibule; void; yawn

CAVORT: v. see "caper" and "play;" CAVORT: n. antic; bound; caper; curvet; dance; dido; frisk; frolic; gambade; gambado; gambol; hop; leap; lope; marlock; prance; prank; romp; skip; spring; tittup

CEASE: (see "close" and "abstain") avast; conclude; cut; desist; die; disappear; discontinue; drop; end; expire; fade; fail; finish; forbear; halt; intermit; leave (off); pause; peter (out); quit; refrain; relinquish; resign; retire; stay; stint; stop; succumb; terminate; vanish; withdraw; yield; CEASELESS: (see "constant") continual; continuous; pauseless; stanchless; unending

CEDE: (see "assign") abandon; accord; concede; convey; deliver; devise; give; grant; leave; relinquish; resign; submit; surrender; transfer; waive; will; yield

CELEBRATE: award; cite; commemorate; dedicate; dine; drink; entertain; eulogize; exhilarate; extol; exuberate; fete; glorify; honor; keep; memorialize; observe; panegyrize; regale; remember; revel; signalize; solemnize; wine; CELEBRATION: award; banquet; birthday; blow(out); ceremony; citation; commemoration; commencement; commendation; dedication; dinner; drink; entertainment; eulogy; exhilaration; exuberation; feast; festival; fete; fiesta; frolic; holiday; honor; gaiety; graduation; jubilation; jubilee; medal; memorial(ization); mirth; monument; observance; observation; occasion; ovation; party; picnic; plaque; potlatch; remembrance; revel(ry); rite; service; solemnization; CELEBRATED: (see "eminent") famous; honored; noted; renowned

CELEBRITY: acclaim; acclamation; bigwig; brain; conspicuity; conspicuousness; dignity; distinction; éclat; elevation; eminence; esteem; estimation; exaltation; fame; glory; greatness; height; honor; illustriousness; intellectuality; kudos; laurels; leader; leading light; light; lion; luster; magnificence; magnificent; majesty; name; nobility; noble; notable; notoriety; paramountcy; prestige; prominence; rank; recognition; regard; renown; report; repute; resplendence; resplendency; salience; saliency; star; success; superiority; title; transcendence; transcendency; VIP; wonder

CELERITY: (see "haste") acceleration; alacrity; dispatch; expedition; hurry; promptitude; quickness; rapidity; speed; swiftness; velocity

CELESTIAL: (see "angelic") charismatic; divine; empyrean; ethereal; etheric; heaven-born; heavenly; holy; Olympian; Olympic; otherworldly; spiritual; supernal; supernatural; supreme; transcendental; unearthly; uranic

CELL: bar; bin; box; cage; cavity; compartment; cubicle; cubiculum; cytode; dwelling; egg; enclosure; fiber; germ; grave; group; house; jail; loculus; neuron(e); pen; prison; protoplasm; receptacle; room; vault

CEMENT: **v.** (**see** "adhere" and "bind") cohere; establish; glue; heal; join; knit; mortar; paste; putty; solder; stick; unify; unite; CEMENT: **n.** asphalt; binder; concrete; mortar; pavement; putty; solder; union

CEMETERY: boneyard; burial (*or* burying) grounds; *campo santo*; catacomb; city of the dead; Golgotha; graveyard; necropolis; ossuary; polyandrium

CENOBITE: **see** "monk"

CENSOR: **v.** (**see** "ban") expurgate; CENSOR: **n.** (**see** "critic") Cato; detractor; CENSORIOUS: (**see** "critical") calumnious; captious; castigative; castigatory; censorial; condemnatory; defamatory; excoriative; faultfinding; severe; slanderous; stigmatic(al); stinging; vituperative

CENSURE: **v.** (**see** "criticize") abuse; anathematize; animadvert; attack; ban; belittle; blame; calumniate; carp; castigate; charge; chastise; chew (out); chide; complain; condemn; curse; damn; decry; denigrate; denounce; depreciate; derogate; detract; dig; disapprove; discipline; discredit; disparage; dispraise; doom; excoriate; flay; groan; grumble; hiss; hit; impeach; impugn; judge; lambaste; lash; minify; minimize; nag; nip; objurgate; opprobriate; pettifog; publicize; punish; quibble; rail; rake; rebuke; reflect; reprimand; reproach; reprobate; reprove; revile; scare; scarify; scold; scorch; score; sentence; slam; slap; slate; slur; stigmatize; traduce; vilify; vituperate; CENSURE: **n.** admonition; anathematization; animadversion; ban; blame; calumniation; carping; castigation; catcall; cavil; chastisement; complaint; condemnation; contumely; criticism; critique; curse; damn(ation); denigration; denouement; denunciation; deprecation; depreciation; derision; derogation; detraction; diatribe; dig; disapprobation; disapproval; discouragement; disfavor; dislike; displeasure; doom; dressing down; excommunication; excoriation; fire; going-over; hiss; impeachment; impugnation; interdiction; invective; judgment; minification; minimization; nip; obloquy; odium; opprobrium; pettifoggery; protest; punishment; quibbling; raillery; rebuff; rebuke; reprehension; repri-

mand; reproach; reprobation; reproof; review; riot act; roasting; satire; scarification; scourge; scurrility; sentence; slap; stricture; thunderball; traducement; venom; vilification; vituperation; wrath

CENSUS: canvas(s); computation; count; enumeration; list; number; people; poll; population; table; tabulation; tally; total

CENTER: **v.** adjust; aim; collect; concentrate; converge; fix; focalize; focus; pivot; point; spot; CENTER: **n.** aim; average; axis; axle; bone; bull's-eye; centrum; concentration; convergence; core; cynosure; dot; epicenter; essence; eye; fiber; foci (pl.); focus; ganglion; gaze; gist; group; heart; hearth; home; hub; interior; issue; kernel; knot; limelight; look; mainstream; marrow; Mecca; middle; midmost; midpart; midpoint; midst; midway; nave; navel; nerve; nest; nidus; nub; nucleus; omphalos; origin; pith; pivot; plug; point; scene; seat; sight; source; spindle; spine; spool; stage; staple; stem; target; umbilicus; CENTRAL: average; axial; basic; between; centric(al); concentrated; concentric; decisive; dominant; equidistant; essential; focal; halfway; inner; interior; intermediate; leading; mean; medial; median; medieval; mediocre; mesial; middle(most); middling; midmost; midway; moderate; nuclear; pivotal; polar; principal; prominent; umbilical; CENTRALIZING: amalgamative; centripetal; consolidating; integrative

CEREMONY: (**see** "celebration") commencement; graduation; observances; ovation; parade; procedure; rite; usage(s); wedding

CERTAIN: absolute; accurate; actual; acute; apodictic(al); appointed; arithmetical; assertible; assured; authentic; authoritative; bent; binding; bold; bound(ed); careful; categorical; *che sarà sarà*; circumscribed; clear-cut; cocksure; cogent; complete(d); conclusive; confident; confirmed; constant; consummate; consummative; consummatory; convinced; correct; critical; crucial; decided; decisive; definite; definitive; delineated; dependable; dernier; destined; determinate; determinative; determined; direct; distinct(ive); dogmatic(al); dominated; doomed; do-or-die; doubtless; downright; emphatic; end(ing); enduring; established; eventual; everlasting; evident; exact(ing); exhaustive; explicit; express; extreme; fatal; fated; figured; final; finished; finite; finitive; firm; fixed; flat; foreordained; forthright; frank; genuine; guaranteed; hard; honest;

identifiable; identified; imminent; immovable; immutable; imperative; implacable; inalienable; incontestable; incontrovertible; indisputable; individual; indomitable; indubitable; ineluctable; inescapable; inevitable; inexorable; infallible; inflexible; invincible; irreconcilable; irrefrangible; irrefutable; irresistible; judgmental; last(-ditch); latest; limited; manifest; material; mathematical; necessary; noncontradictory; objective; obvious; official; open; out-and-out; outright; overconfident; particular; peculiar; peremptory; perfect; plain; positive; precise; predestined; preemptory; pure (and simple); real; reliable; required; resolute; resolved; safe; *sans doute*; set(tled); sheer; simple; *sine dubio*; special; specific; stable; stark; steadfast; supreme; sure; sweeping; tangible; tenacious; telling; terminal; terminating; thorough(going); true; ultimate; unalienable; unalterable; unambiguous; unassailable; unavoidable; unchallengeable; unconditional; unconditioned; uncontestable; undeniable; undenied; undeterred; undisguised; undisputed; undoubted; undubitable; unequivocal; unerring; unfailing; unfaltering; unflagging; unhesitant; unhesitating; unmisgiving; unmistakable; unmitigated; unqualified; unquestionable; unreserved; unrestrained; unrestricted; unswerving; unwavering; unyielding; utter; whole(hearted); CERTAINTY: accuracy; actuality; assurance; authenticity; authoritativeness; care(fulness); certainness; certitude; cinch; conclusion; consummation; correctitude; correctness; definiteness; definitiveness; definitude; determinancy; eventuality; exactitude; exactness; fidelity; finality; finitude; flawlessness; incontrovertibility; indisputability; indubitability; inevitability; infallibility; meticulosity; meticulousness; necessity; perfection; positivism; precision; probabilism; punctuality; punctualness; reality; reliability; resolution; right(ness); rigor(ousness); scrupulosity; securement; security; sureness; surety; tangibility; teleology; trustworthiness; truth; ultimacy; ultimateness; unequivocalness

CERTIFICATE: archive; bill; bond; certification; charger; chronicle; commission; contract; credential; deed; degree; diploma; document(ary); draft; guarantee; instrument; lease; letter; license; memo(randum); note; paper; papyri (pl.); papyrus; recommendation; record; script; sheepskin; stock; testimonial; warrant; will; writing; voucher

CERTIFY: (**see** "affirm") approve; assure; attest; aver; avouch; avow; conform; declare; depose; determine; evince; guarantee; license; notarize; qualify; seal; stamp; swear; testify; verify; vouch

CERTITUDE: (**see** "confidence") certainness; certainty; fact; knowledge; truth

CESSATION: (**see** "armistice") abeyance; abeyancy; cloture; death; desition; discontinuance; end; halt; intermission; interval; letup; lull; moratorium; pause; peace; period; quiet(ness); quietude; recess; remission; reprieve; respite; rest; stay; stop

CHAFE: **v.** abrade; abrase; anger; annoy; bark; erase; erode; file; fret; frot; fume; gall; gnaw; grate; graze; grind; harass; heat; incense; irritate; madden; nettle; peeve; rage; rankle; rasp; roughen; rub; ruffle; scrape; scratch; score; vex; wear; CHAFE **n.** *or* CHAFING: (**see** "abrasion") erosion; friction; grind; heat; intertrigo; irritation; nettling; passion; rage; rubbing; scratch; vexation; wear

CHAFF: *blague*; bran; glume(s); hull(s); husk; peel; pods; refuse; rinds; scale; scurf; shucks; skin; straw; trash

CHAGRIN: (**see** "embarrassment") disappointment; discomfiture; discomposure; dismay; disquiet(ude); distress; humiliation; mortification; obloquy; shame; vexation

CHAIN: **v.** (**see** "connect") bond; catenate; concatenate; confine; fasten; fetter; hobble; hold; join; link; manacle; obstruct; repress; restrain; restrict; rope; shackle; tether; unite; CHAIN(S): **n.** (**see** "connection") arrangement; bond(s); cable; captivity; catena(tion); catenary; circuit; combination; concatenation; confines; course; fetter(s); file; group; gyve; hobble; imprisonment; link; manacle; network; obstruction; progression; range; repression; restraint; restriction; row; sequence; series; set; shackle; string; succession; suite; tether; torque; train; vinculum

CHAIR: (**see** "seat") bench; chairman(ship); office; position; profession; rocker; sedan; stool; support; throne

CHALLENGE: **v.** (**see** "face") accuse; arouse; brave; call; cite; claim; dare; defy; demand; examine; excite; impugn; invite; object; protest; provoke; question; require; risk; stimulate; summon; taunt; test; venture; CHALLENGE: **n.** accusation; call; dare; defiance; demand; dispute; exception;

gauntlet; impugnation; invitation; objection; protest; question; requirement; risk; summons; taunt; test; venture

CHAMBER: (**see** "room") apartment; area; bedroom; bin; berth; camera; cavern; cell(ule); compartment; concameration; container; crypt; cubicle; cubiculum; digs; division; flat; hall(way); hollow; kiva; loculus; receptacle; salon; space; stateroom; vault

CHAMPION: **v.** (**see** "aid") advocate; back; boost; challenge; defend; defy; espouse; fight; help; squire; support; uphold; CHAMPION: **n.** (**see** "advocate") ace; aide; angel; backer; combatant; defender; exponent; fighter: helper; hero; knight; medalist; Perseus; protagonist; squire; supporter; victor; warrior; winner; CHAMPIONSHIP: advocacy; espousal; defense; laurels; leadership; superiority; support; supremacy; title; victory; win

CHANCE: **v.** (**see** "befall") adventure; betide; happen; hazard; occur; risk; venture; CHANCE: **a.** (**see** "casual") accidental; contingent; fortuitous; CHANCE: **n.** (**see** "fate") accident(ality); adventure; break; calamity; calculated risk; casualty; *casus fortuitus*; circumstance; contingence; contingency; contretemps; disaster; event; fortuitousness; fortuity; fortune; gamble; hap(penstance); hazard; inadvertence; inadvertency; incident; injury; kismet; lot; luck; misadventure; mischance; misfortune; mishap; misstep; occurrence; odds; opportunity; pass; peradventure; question; random; reversal; reverse; risk; scrape; situation; slip; speculation; tide; time; tychism; venture

CHANGE: **v.** (**see** "advance") adapt; alchemize; alter(ate); alternate; amend; barter; bend; better; break; castrate; commute; convert; convey; decrease; deflect; deliver; detour; develop; deviate; differ; digress; disappear; discard; diverge; diversify; dwindle; emend; evolve; exchange; fade; fix; fluctuate; flutter; improve; increase; interchange; interpolate; jump; maneuver; manipulate; metamorphose; metastasize; modify; mold; move; mutate; oscillate; pass; permutate; permute; promote; qualify; rearrange; rearray; reciprocate; reduce; remove; render; renegotiate; renew; renovate; repair; replace; replenish; repristinate; reverse; revise; revolutionize; shed; shift; shilly-shally; spay; substitute; sway; swerve; swing; switch; tack; totter; trade; transfer;

transfigure; transform; transmit; transmogrify; transmutate; transmute; transplant; transpire; transubstantiate; turn; undulate; vacillate; vary; veer; wave; waver; weave; withdraw; worsen; wrest; CHANGE: **n.** (**see** "advancement") adaptation; alteration; alternance; alternation; amendment; break; coins; commutation; conversion; currency; decrease; detour; development; deviation; difference; disparity; divergence; diversification; evolution; exchange; fluctuation; flux; heterization; improvement; increase; jog; jump; loss; maneuver; manipulation; materialization; metamorphosis; metastasis; modification; modulation; money; move(ment); mutability; mutation; permutation; process; promotion; rearrangement; reciprocation; removal; renewal; renovation; repair; replacement; replenishment; repristination; reversal; reverse; reversion; saltation; substitution; succession; switch; trade; transfer; transfiguration; transformation; transit(ion); transmogrification; transmutation; transplantation; transportation; transposition; transubstantiation; turn(about); turnover; upheaval; variance; variation; variety; waver; withdrawal; worsening; CHANGED: see "varied;" CHANGEABLE: adaptable; adaptational; alterable; alterative; alternative; ambivalent; amenable; amendable; amphibolic; amphibolous; apt; capricious; chameleonic; disciplinable; disciplined; docible; docile; educa(ta) ble; elastic; erratic; evolutionary; excitable; feverish; fickle; fidgety; fitful; fitting; flexible; fluctuating; fluid; giddy; governable; inconsistent; inconstant; influenceable; instructive; iridescent; irresolute; itinerant; kaleidoscopic; labile; malleable; mercurial; metamorphic; metamorphous; manipula(ta)ble; mobile; movable; mutable; nervous; nomadic; notional; plastic; pliant; protean; Proteuslike; quicksilver; quickwitted; restless; shifting; shrewd; sprightly; suitable; teachable; temperamental; tractable; transitional; uncertain; unsettled; unstable; unsteady; vagrant; variable; variant; variational; varying; versatile; vertiginous; volatile; wavering; whimsical; CHANGEABLENESS: adaptability; alterability; ambivalence; capriciousness; fickleness; inconstancy; inequality; iridescence; lability; levity; mutability; variableness; versatility; volatility; volubility

CHANGELESS: (**see** "timeless" and "unending") constant; even; uniform

CHANGELING: **see** "child"

CHANNEL: (**see** "course") agent; aqueduct;

artery; avenue; beam; bed; cable; canal; chain; chute; conduit; direction; ditch; drain; drift; duct; flow; flume; flute; furrow; gat; gate(way); groove; gut; gutter; kennel; line; main; means; media (pl.); medium; mode; mote; opening; orbit; organ; outlet; passage(way); path(way); pipe(line); policy; procedure; proceeding; process(ion); progress(ion); race; rate; river; road(way); route; row; run; rut; schedule; sequence; series; sewer; sinus; sound; stem; step; strait; strategy; stream; street; stria; succession; sweep; swing; system; tack; tactic; thread; topic; track; trade; trajectory; trek; trend; trough; tube; tune; turn; vein; watercourse; water(way); wire

CHANT: (**see** "sing" and "song") cantillation; intonation; litany

CHAOS: (**see** "confusion") abyss; Babel(ism); chasm; discord; gulf; hell; heterogeneity; irrationality; jumble; madness; mess; muss; shambles; snarl; Tophet; unreason; vacuum; void; CHAOTIC: (**see** "confused") disordered; disorganized; hellish; heterogeneous; irrational; jumbled; mad; messy; unorganized

CHAP: **v.** break; burst; crack; fissure; frostbite; mark; rend; rive; roughen; slit; split; CHAP: **n.** (**see** "boy") chink; cleft; crack; fellow; fissure; frostbite; jaw; rent; rift; rive; split; sport; tear

CHAPEL: assembly; association; bethel; chantry; choir; church; gathering; hall; kirk; meeting; oratory; room; sanctuary; service; worship

CHAPERON(E): **v.** (**see** "attend") convoy; escort; guard; monitor; protect; usher; CHAPERON(E): **n.** (**see** "attendant") convoy; duenna; escort; governante; governess; guard(ian); guide; hood; matron; monitor; protector; scout; surveillant; usher

CHAPTER: (**see** "body") assembly; branch; cell; clan; class; contingent; division; lodge; meeting; organization; passage; post; section; unit

CHAR: (**see** "burn") blacken; carbonize; scar; singe

CHARACTER: alphabet; aspect; bent; capacity; card; cast; category; characteristic; cipher; class; clay; cloak; clothes; color; composition; conscience; constitution; development; device; disposition; distinguish-

ment; eccentric; emblem; entry; essence; estimation; ethos; expression; fabric; feather; feature; fiber; figure; form(at); formation; function; genius; habit; heart; humor; ilk; inclination; individual(ization); kidney; kind; letter; life; makeup; man; mark; mettle; mode; naturalness; nature; note; part; pattern; person(age); personality; physique; position; predilection; printing; proclivity; propensity; property; quality; queer; quintessence; rank; reality; rectitude; representation; reputation; role; shape; sign; size; sort; species; spirit; stamina; stamp; standing; state; strain; strength; stripe; structure; stuff; style; substance; symbol; temper(ament); tenor; texture; timber; timbre; trait; trend; type; vigor; virility; writing; zombie

CHARACTERISTIC: **a.** (**see** "distinctive") classificatory; definitive; delineative; descriptive; descriptory; diacritical; distinguishing; emblematic; exemplary; expositive; expository; general; illustrative; indicating; indicative; individual; inherent; model; pathognomonic(al); peculiar; picturesque; quintessential; regular; representative; singular; symbolic(al); symptomatic; typic(al); unique; unusual; CHARACTERISTIC(S): **n.** (**see** "character") accent; accessory; accoutrement; appendage; attitude; attribute; badge; bearing; cachet; cast; color; custom; distinction; eccentricity; endowment; essence; feature; haecceity; hallmark; idiosyncrasy; indication; individuality; landmark; lineament; manner(s); mark; mien; nature; note; oddity; peculiarity; perquisite; power; property; proprium; quality; sign; singularity; style; substance; symbol; symptom; trace; tradition; trick; uniquity; whimsicality

CHARACTERIZE: (**see** "classify") bracket; call; channel; define; delineate; describe; designate; distinguish; draw; equate; indicate; label; mark; paint; portray; represent; separate; ticket

CHARGE: **v.** accredit; accuse; adjure; allege; anathematize; animadvert; arraign; arrogate; ascribe; assail; assault; assess; assign; attack; attribute; berate; betray; bid; bill; blame; blast; burden; call; calumniate; censure; certify; challenge; cite; command; comminate; commission; condemn; credit; criminate; criticize; curse; damn; declare; decry; degrade; delate; denounce; denunciate; depute; detract; direct; disapprove; disclaim; disparage; drive; emphasize; enjoin; entrust; exaggerate; excoriate; execrate; exhort; fill; fulminate; furnish; give; impeach; impose; imprecate; impregnate; impute; incriminate; inculpate; indict; intrust; inveigh; lambaste; lay; levy; license; load; lower; menace; objurgate; oppose; order; present; price; protest; rate; recognize; reform; reprehend; reprimand; reproach; reprove; reveal; revile; rush; sanction; saturate; scathe; scold; stigmatize; sue; tax; threaten; urge; vilify; vouch (for); warrant; CHARGE: **n.** accusal; accusation; allegation; anathema; animadversion; arraignment; ascription; assault; attack; attribution; behest; bill; blame; calumniation; calumny; care; censure; check; citation; claim; command; commination; compensation; concession; condescension; contention; cost; credit; crimination; culpa-(bility); curse; custody; damage(s); debit; declaration; delation; denouement; detraction; diatribe; disapproval; dun; electricity; excoriation; execration; exhortation; expense(s); explosion; fault; fee; guilt; impeachment; imposition; imprecation; imputation; incrimination; inculpation; indictment; injunction; innuendo; instruction; insult; invective; kick; levy; liberty; list; load; lunge; management; mandate; money; note; objurgation; obligation; obloquy; odium; onus; order; payment; plunge; power; price; protest(ation); rate; reflection; reprehension; repression; reproach(ment); reproof; responsibility; revile; rush; scold(ing); score; shot; statement; stigma; supervision; tab; tax; threat; ticket; tithe; vituperation

CHARITY: affection; aid; alms; altruism; assist(ance); benefaction; benefic(ence); benefit; benevolence; benison; bequest; bestowal; blessing; bonus; boon; bounty; care; caritas; concession; condescension; devise; dole; donation; endowment; favor; gain; generosity; gift; grace; grant; gratuity; handsel; help; honorarium; kind(li)ness; lagniappe; largess(e); leniency; lenity; liberality; love; maintenance; mercy; munificence; patronage; philanthropy; pity; prize; protection; provision; ruth; solicitude; sponsorship; support; sympathy; tenderness; tip; windfall; CHARITABLE: (**see** "benevolent") affectionate; altruistic; benefic(ent); benign; bighearted; caritative; condescending; eleemosynary; generous; gracious; helpful; kind(ly); human(e); humanitarian; kind; largehearted; lenient; liberal; merciful; munificent; philanthropic; sympathetic; tender; unmercenary

CHARLATAN: bilker; Cagliostro; cheat(er); deceiver; empiric; fake(r); fraud; humbug;

imposter: knave; mountebank; pretender; quack(salver); rascal; rogue; sharp(st)er; swindler; trickster

CHARM: **v.** allay; allure; amuse; assuage; attract; bait; befool; beguile; beseech; besot; bewitch; blandish; cajole; calm; captivate; capture; check; coax; conjure; contrive; control; decoy; delight; disarm; divert; dominate; draw; elate; enamor; enchant; enrapture; enravish; ensnare; ensorcel(l); entertain; enthral(l); entice; entrap; entreat; exalt; excite; exorcise; fascinate; felicitate; flatter; gladden; gratify; hex; hold; induce; inebriate; infatuate; inflame; influence; ingratiate; instigate; inveigle; invoke; jubilate; juggle; lead; lure; luxuriate; magnetize; motivate; move; oil; persuade; please; ravish; regale; revel; satisfy; seduce; snare; solicit; soothe; spellbind; spur; subdue; summon; sway; take; tantalize; tempt; thrill; translate; transport; trap; vamp; woo; CHARM: **n.** abracadabra; abraxas; allure(ment); amiability; amulet; amusement; anito; appeal; attraction; attractiveness; avatar; bait; beauty; beckon(ing); beguile(ment); bewitchery; bewitchingness; bewitchment; blandishment; bliss; cajole(ment); cajolery; captivation; captivity; comeliness; coquetry; decoy; delectation; delicacy; deliciousness; delight; diversion; ecstasy; elation; elegance; enchantment; encitement; enjoyment; ensorcellment; entertainment; enticement; entrancement; entrapment; entreaty; exaltation; exuberance; fascination; festivity; fetish; fixation; gladness; glamo(u)r; glee; grace; gratification; greegree; grigri; happiness; illusion; imploration; incantation; incitement; inducement; infatuation; influence; instigation; inveiglement; invitation; juju; love; luck; lure; madstone; magic; magnetism; mascot; merriment; mesmeration; mesmerism; mirth; mojo; mystery; obeah; obi; oblectation; ornament; periapt; persuasion; phylactery; pleasure; poise; power; prepossession; provocation; rapture; raptus; ravishment; relic; revel(ry); rite; satisfaction; seducement; seduction; siren; snare; solicitation; song; sorcery; spell; stimulation; symbol; talisman; temptation; token; touchstone; transport; trap; tune; wile; witchery; CHARMING: (**see** "pleasing") artistic; attractive; bewitching; captivating; chic; *chichi*; clever; dapper; delicate; delightful; dexterous; elegant; enchanting; entrancing; exciting; fascinating; fashionable; felicitous; irresistible; jaunty; lively; magnetic; mesmeric; modish; natty; neat; nice; nifty; personable; pert; phylacteric; pleasant; pleasing; posh; resistless;

smart; smooth; *soigné*; *soignée*; (fem.); sophisticated; spruce; stylish; swank; sweet; tempting; trig; trim; winsome; CHARMED: **see** "entranced;" CHARMER: belle; calmer; enchanter; enchantress; exorcist; magician; siren; sorcerer; tempter

CHART: **v.** (**see** "map") arrange; delineate; design; diagram; draft; draw; graph; mark; outline; plan; plot; project; scheme; sketch; survey; CHART: **n.** (**see** "map") arrangement; delineation; design; diagram; draft; drawing; graph; history; outline; plan; plat; plot; project; record(s); schema; scheme; sketch; summary; table

CHARTER: **v.** (**see** "commission") constitute; create; empower; endow; establish; franchise; grant; hire; inaugurate; lease; let; license; rent; CHARTER: **n.** (**see** "commission") canon; constitution; conveyance; decalogue; deed; exception; franchise; grant; guarantee; immunity; instrument; lease; license; magnac(h)arta; permit; power; privilege; warrant(y)

CHASE: course; dispel; dog; drive; ensue; expel; follow; hasten; hound; hunt; maintain; oust; persecute; persist; pursue; quest; remove; ride; run; rush; seek; shadow; shag; stalk; tag; tail; track; trail

CHASM: abysm; abyss; Avernus; blank; breach; break; canyon; cleft; deep; depth; deviation; difference; disagreement; division; fissure; gap; Gehenna; gorge; gulf; gully; hell; hiatus; hole; interval; omission; opening; opposition; pit; profundity; rent; rift; separation; split; valley; void; vorago

CHASTE: (**see** "pure") abstemious; ascetic; austere; clean; continent; decent; decorous; demure; discreet; guileless; immaculate; incorrupt(ed); innocent; modest; moral; plain; proper; refined; severe; simple; stainless; undefiled; unstained; unsullied; vestal; virgin(al); virtuous; CHASTITY: (**see** "purity") abstention; abstinence; ascesis; continence; decency; decorousness; decorum; delicacy; demureness; demurity; honor; innocence; integrity; maidenliness; modesty; pucelage; pudicity; purity; verecundity; virginity; virtue

CHASTEN: (**see** "chastise") abase; afflict; chagrin; correct; degrade; demean; denigrate; disgrace; dishonor; humble; humiliate; lower; minify; moderate; mortify; perfect; punish; purify; reduce; refine; restrain;

shame; smite; soften; squelch; sterilize; strengthen; subdue; tame; temper; try

CHASTISE: (**see** "chasten") afflict; beat; blame; cane; castigate; censure; chide; correct; discipline; flog; humiliate; imprison; lash; punish; rebuke; reprimand; reprove; scold; slap; spank; strap; swingle; switch; taunt; thrash; tongue-lash; trim; whip

CHASTISEMENT: (**see** "discipline") imprisonment; punishment; scolding; tonguing

CHAT(TER): **v.** (**see** "speak") babble; cackle; chin; confab(ulate); converse; coze; debate; din; gab; gossip; hobnob; jaw; parley; prate; prattle; schmooze; talk; visit; CHAT(TER): **n.** (**see** "speech") babble; bavardage; cackle; causerie; colloquy; confabulation; conversazione; debate; dialogue; gab(ble); gibber(ish); gossip; intercourse; interlocution; jabber; palaver; parlance; parley; prate; prattle; prose; speech; talk; tattle; twaddle; visit; yap

CHEAP: abject; bargain (basement); base; bedizened; beggarly; blaring; blatant; brassy; brummagem; cheesy; chintzy; claptrap; coarse; common; contemptible; crummy; cut-rate; depreciated; despicable; disesteemed; flamboyant; flashy; florid; garish; gaudy; gingerbread; glaring; gross; inadequate; inconsequential; inconsiderable; inexpensive; inferior; insignificant; loud; low; meager; mean; measly; meretricious; minor; ostentatious; paltry; petty; picayune; picayunish; piddling; pinchbeck; pitiable; pitiful; poor; popular; puny; reduced; scurvy; second-rate; shabby; shoddy; showy; slight; small; sneaking; sneaky; snide; sordid; sorry; tasteless; tawdry; tin(horn); tinny; tinsel; trashy; trifling; trivial; uncostly; undercharged; underpriced; undersold; unexpensive; ungenerous; unimportant; valueless; vile; vulgar; worthless; CHEAPEN: **see** "lower;" CHEAPNESS: bedizenment; cheesiness; flashiness; flummery; paltriness; showiness; tawdriness; trashiness; undervaluation; worthlessness

CHEAT: **v.** (**see** "fool") bamboozle; befool; beguile; betray; bilk; bunco; burn; chicane; chisel; circumvent; clip; copy; cozen; deceive; defraud; delude; disappoint; dissemble; divert; drib; dupe; elude; entice; entrap; euchre; fabricate; fake; finagle; flam; fleece; flimflam; fob; foil; foist; fraud; fub; gouge; gudgeon; gull; gyp; have; hoax; hocus; honeyfuggle; hoodwink; jockey; juggle; lure; outwit; overcharge; overreach;

ream; renege; rook; seduce; sham; short-change; skin; steal; stick; sting; swindle; take (in); touch; trick; trim; trip; victimize; whipsaw; CHEAT **n.** *or* CHEATER: (**see** "rascal") bilker; Cagliostro; charlatan; deceiver; deception; empiric; fake(r); fraud; humbug; imposter; imposture; knave; mountebank; pretender; quack(salver); rogue; rook; sharp(st)er; swindler; trickster

CHECK: **v.** abate; abort; admonish; affirm; agree; allay; alleviate; amelioriate; annul; appease; arrest; ascertain; assuage; atten-uate; baffle; ban; bar(ricade); block; bob-ble; bolt; bottle(neck); brake; bridle; calm; catch; cease; censure; checkmate; chill; choke; clash; clog; close; comfort; compare; compress; compromise; concur; confine; confirm; constrain; constrict; contain; con-trol; cool; corner; counter(act); counter-balance; counterpoise; cow; crimp; cripple; curb; curtail; cushion; cut; cut back; cut down; dally; dam; dampen; deaden; debar; decline; decrease; defeat; degraduate; degress; delay; depreciate; depress; deprive; detain; deter; determine; detract; diminish; direct; disburden; discipline; discourage; dishearten; dispirit; disrupt; dissuade; drop; dwindle; ease; ebb; embarrass; encumber; end; enfeeble; enjoin; exhaust; extinguish; forbid; freeze; frustrate; gag; glut; govern; grade down; guide; halt; hamper; hinder; hold; ice; impede; imprison; incommode; infrigidate; inhibit; interdict; interfere; intern; interrupt; investigate; jail; jam; keep; kibosh; lease; lessen; let up; lighten; limit; lock; lower; lull; mark; meliorate; mellow; minimize; mitigate; moderate; mollify; monitor; nab; narrow; nip; nullify; observe; obstruct; obtrude; occlude; offset; oppilate; oppose; oppress; pacify; palliate; paralyze; pause; placate; please; plug; plunge; prevent; probe; prohibit; proof-read; proscribe; punish; quake; qualify; quash; quell; quench; quiet(en); rebuff; rebuke; refrain; refrigerate; regulate; rein; relax; relieve; remit; repress; restrain; restrict; retard; retrench; retrogress; reverse; rid; rule; salve; sap; scan; sink; slack(en); slake; slide; slow (up); smoothe; smother; snub; soften; solace; soothe; sta(u)nch; stay; stifle; stop(per); strangle; stunt; stymie; subdue; subside; substantiate; suffocate; suppress; tally; temper; test; thin; throttle; tranquilize; unburden; unload; verify; veto; void; wane; watch; weaken; wear; wedge; wither; withhold; CHECK: **n.** abatement; adjustment; allayment; alleviation; annul-ment; appeasement; arrest; attenuation; ban; bar(ricade); barrier; bit; block; bot-

tleneck; brake; bridle; calmness; checkmate; choke; choking; comfort; comparison; com-press(ion); compromise; confirmation; con-solidation; content(ment); counterbalance; countermove; counterpoise; curb; dam; damper; declination; decline; decrease; decrement; decrescence; decrescendo; degres-sion; demolishment; deprivation; detention; determination; difficulty; diminishment; diminuendo; diminution; disburdenment; discipline; discouragement; disengagement; ebb; embarrassment; embolus; encumbrance; end; exhaustion; extenuation; failure; fall; freeze; frustration; gate; government; gover-nor; halt; hamper(ing); hindrance; hold; impasse; impediment; impedimenta (pl.); inhibition; inspection; interference; investi-gation; jam; lease; lessening; letup; lighten-ing; lock; lowering; mark; melioration; minimization; mitigation; moderation; modi-fication; mollification; narrowing; nullifica-tion; observation; obstacle; obstruction; occlusion; omission; oppilation; opposition; order; pacification; palliation; paralysis; pause; peace; placation; plug; proofread-ing; quiet(ness); quietude; rebate(ment); rebuff; rebuke; reduction; regulator; rein; relaxation; relief; remission; repose; rest; restraint; restriction; retardation; re-trenchment; retrogression; reversal; reverse; run-down; shrinkage; slack(ening); snaffle; snub; solace; stay; stenosis; stop; strangle; strangling; strangulation; stymie; subsidence; substantiation; suppression; tally; test; thin-ning; throttle; tranquility; unconstraint; unrestraint; valve; verification; wane; wan-ing; wedge

CHECKERED: **see** "variegated"

CHECKMATE: (**see** "check") baffle; bottle; catch; checkrein; control; corner; defeat; gain; hem; hold; lick; monopolize; restrain; stymie; thwart; trap; tree; undo

CHEEK: (**see** "audacity") boldness; brass(i-ness); bucca; buttock; chap(s); gall; gena; impudence; jole; jowl; nerve; sass(iness); sauciness; temerity

CHEER: **v.** (**see** "animate") acclaim; aid; allay; alleviate; applaud; assist; assuage; calm; clap; comfort; condole; console; cry; delight; divert; ease; elate; embolden; encourage; energize; enliven; entertain; fortify; gladden; gratify; hail; help; inspire; inspirit; invigorate; laud; lighten; mitigate; nurse; please; praise; protect; pull (for); quiet(en); raise; refresh; rejoice; relieve; root; rouse; salute; satisfy; shout; smooth;

soften; solace; soothe; stimulate; stir; succor; support; tranquilize; CHEER: **n.** acclaim; acclamation; aid; alleviation; animation; applause; bravo; calm; clap; comfort; consolation; contentment; convenience; cordiality; coziness; drink; ease; éclat; elation; encouragement; entertainment; fare; favor; feeling; food; frolic; fun; gaiety; glee; help; hilarity; hope; hurrah; huzza; jollity; laudation; liveliness; mirth; mitigation; ole!; plaudit; pleasantry; praise; rah!; refreshment; rejoicing; relaxation; relief; repast; repose; rest; root; satisfaction; shout; smile; solace(ment); spirit; viva!; warmth; welcome; CHEERFUL *or* CHEERING: (**see** "pleasant") agreeable; animate(d); anticipative; ardent; beamish; blithe(some); bonny; bright; buoyant; certain; chirpy; chirrupy; confident; consolatory; consoling; contented; convenient; cordial; cosh; cosy; cushy; easy; ebullient; elated; encouraged; encouraging; enlivened; enlivening; enthusiastic; eudaemonic; eupeptic; euphoric; exhilarative; expectant; favorable; friendly; gay; genial; glad(some); gleg; good; gracious; gratified; gratifying; happy; heartening; heartwarming; hearty; high; hopeful; inspired; inspirited; inspiriting; jocular; jocund; jolly; joyful; joyous; kind; light-(-hearted); lively; merry; mirthful; nepenthean; optimistic; overoptimistic; oversanguine; overzealous; pert; placid; pleasing; plethoric; posh; pretty; promising; protected; quiet; radiant; riant; roseate; rosy; sanguinary; sanguine; sanguinical; satisfied; smiling; snug; soft; solacing; sparkling; spirited; sprightly; sunny; tranquilizing; vivacious; volatile; unruffled; warm; winsome; CHEERFULNESS: (**see** "animation" and "pleasantry") buoyancy; cordiality; delight; ebullience; ebulliency; eudaemonia; eudaemony; exhilaration; festivity; geniality; gladness; graciousness; happiness; heartiness; jocularity; jocundity; jollity; joviality; joy-(ousness); optimism; merriment; mirth(fulness); sanguinity; solace; spirit; sprightliness; verve; vigor; vivacity; warmth; well-being

CHEERLESS: (**see** "austere") ascetic; bleak; clouded; cloudy; cold; colorless; dark; dejected; disheartening; dismal; dispiriting; drab; drear(y); dull; gloomy; glum; gray; sad(dened); stormy; wintry

CHERISH: (**see** "admire") adore; adulate; aid; apotheosize; appreciate; canonize; care; cheer; comfort; covet; cultivate; dote; embosom; encourage; enjoy; enshrine; entertain; esteem; extol; foster; guard; harbor; hold; honor; hope; hug; idealize;

idolize; indulge; keep; like; love; mother; nourish; nurse; nurture; pet; preserve; prize; protect; revere(nce); save; shelter; spiritualize; support; sustain; tend; treasure; value; venerate; worship; CHERISHED: **see** "precious"

CHEST: arca; ark; basket; box; breast; cabinet; case; casket; cist; coffer; coffin; compartment; container; crate; cupboard; fund; kist; locker; safe; stronghold; thorax; till; treasury; trunk

CHEW: **v.** bite; champ; chavel; chaw; chomp; chumble; consume; crunch; crush; eat; gnaw; grind; insalivate; manducate; masticate; meditate; munch; nibble; nip; reprimand; ruminate; scold; upbraid; CHEW: **n.** bite; chaw; cud; nibble; nip; quid

CHIC: (**see** "charming") alert; artistic; brisk; clever; dapper; dexterous; elegant; fashionable; jaunty; lively; modish; natty; nifty; personable; pert; posh; smart; smooth; *soigné*; *soignée* (fem.); sophisticated; spruce; stylish; swank; trig; trim

CHICANERY: (**see** "trick") artifice; connivance; conniving; deception; duplicity; sophistry; subterfuge

CHIDE: (**see** "admonish") berate; blame; brawl; censure; chasten; chastise; clamor; complain; contend; disapprove; rake; rate; rebuke; reprimand; reproach; reprove; scold; tongue-lash; upbraid; wrangle

CHIEF: **a.** (**see** "basic") arch; capital; cardinal; consequential; controlling; dominant; elder; eminent; essential; first; foremost; grand; great(est); head; highest; important; influential; leading; main; major; outstanding; overriding; paramount; predominant; preeminent; premier(e); prevailing; primal; primary; primate; prime; principal; prominent; ranking; ruling; salient; signal; significant; sovereign; staple; superior; top; vital; CHIEF: **n.** (**see** "leader") captain; chairman; chef; commandant; commander; director; elder; emperor; factotum; general(issimo); head; hierarch; imperator; king; officer; rais; reis; ruler; sachem; sagamore; skipper; superior; supervisor; thane; titan

CHILD: arab; babe; baby; bairn; bantling; bata; brat; changeling; chit; cion; daughter; dependent; descendant; disciple; elf; gamin; infant; issue; juvenile; kid; minor; moppet; offspring; papoose; product; result; scion;

shaver; sibling; son; sprite; sprout; subsidiary; tad; teen; tike; toddler; tot; toto; tyke; whelp; youngster; CHILDISH: asinine; babyish; boyish; credulous; foolish; immature; infantile; infantilistic; infantine; infantlike; juvenile; naive; namby-pamby; pantywaist; petty; puerile; senile; silly; simple; young; CHILDLIKE: bashful; compliant; deferential; dewy-eyed; docile; dutiful; elfin; forbearing; frank; gentle; gullible; humble; ingenuous; innocent; meek; naive; obedient; plastic; pliable; pliant; submissive; tame; teachable; tractable; trusting; yielding; CHILDISHNESS: dotage; feeblemindedness; feebleness; imbecility; immaturity; infancy; infantility; ingenuousness; juvenility; nonage; precocity; puerilism; puerility; rawness; senescence; senility; youth(fulness); CHILDHOOD: see "nonage"

CHILDREN: babes; babies; bantlings; brats; changelings; chits; cions; daughters; dependents; descendants; family; infants; issue; juveniles; kids; minors; moppets; offspring; posterity; progeny; scions; siblings; sons; tads; teens; toddlers; tots; tykes; whelps

CHILL: v. check; cool; dampen; depress; discourage; dishearten; dispirit; freeze; frost; ice; infrigidate; moderate; nip; quake; refresh; refrigerate; shiver; temper; CHILL(Y); a. (see "cold") airish; algid; arctic; breezy; chilled; depressing; discouraging; disheartening; dispiriting; distant; formal; freezing; fresh; frigid; frosty; gelid; glacial; icy; nippy; raw; refrigerated; rigorous; severe; shivering; shivery; stormy; temperate; unfriendly; windy; CHILL: n. ague; frost; gelidity; ice; refrigeration; rigor; severity; unfriendliness

CHIMERICAL: (see "fantastic") fanciful; imaginary; phantasmagoric(al); romantic; unreal(istic); utopian; vain; whimsical; wild

CHINA: ceramic(s); crockery; dish(es); Dresden; plate(s); porcelain; Spode; tableware

CHINK: (see "break") aperture; bore; cleft; crack; cranny; crevasse; crevice; fissure; gap; hole; interspace; interstice; lacuna; loophole; opening; rent; rift; rima; space; split

CHIP: v. (see "break") chop; cut; flake; fracture; fragmentize; hack; nick; splinter; split; CHIP: n. see "break"

CHIPPER: (see "gay") alert; blithe(ful); blithesome; buoyant; cheery; cocky; ebullient; ecstatic; effervescent; ethereal; exuberant; festive; frolicsome; jaunty; larksome; larky; light; lively; merry; perky; playful; roguish; spirited; sportive; sprightly; spry; trig; trim; vigorous; vivacious

CHISEL: (see "cheat") carve; cut; etch; fabricate; form; intrude; sculpt; CHISELER: beggar; cadger; cheat(er); leech; moocher; sponger; stooge

CHIVALROUS: (see "gallant") brave; chivalresque; chivalric; civil; courageous; courteous; courtly; dashing; fair; generous; genteel; heroic; honorable; intrepid; kind; kingly; knightly; noble; polite; valiant; valorous; warlike; CHIVALRY: arete; boldness; bravery; civility; courage(ousness); courteousness; courtesy; courtliness; dash; fearlessness; fortitude; gallantry; generosity; gentility; grit; hardihood; heroicalness; heroism; honor(ableness); integrity; intrepidity; kindness; knight-errantry; knighthood; manliness; nerve; nobility; pluck; politeness; prowess; valiancy; valor; virtue

CHOICE: a. ace; alternative; A-one; appropriate; best; careful; chosen; clubby; cream; dainty; delicate; desirable; discriminating; discriminative; elect(ive); elegant; elite; esoteric; excellent; excelling; exclusive; exquisite; fancy; fastidious; fine(st); first(-grade); first-line; fond; gilt-edge(d); good; judgmental; largest; leading; most; *nulli secundus*; optimum; *par excellence*; picked; plummy; preeminent; premium; prime; rare; *recherché*; right; select(ed); sumptuous; superior; supernacular; supernal; superordinary; superordinate; supreme; surpassing; top(s); ultimate; uncommon; utmost; voluntary; well-chosen; willing; CHOICE: n. (see "best") ace; acme; alternant; alternate; alternative; candidate; chosen; cream; desire; discretion; discrimination; elect(ion); elective; elite; form; freedom; gleaning; harvest; judgment; mind; option; pick; plum; pole; preference; prime; privilege; rarity; referendum; right; seizure; select; selection; superior(ity); top(s); toss-up; vote; will

CHOKE: (see "clog") burke; check; chock; close; compress; constrain; constrict; dam; damp(en); fill; gag; glut; hinder; muffle; muzzle; obstruct; pack; plug; prevent; repress; silence; smother; squeeze; stifle; stop; strangle; suffocate; suppress; throttle

CHOLERIC: (**see** "angry") bilious; cantankerous; crabbed; crabby; cranky; cross; curmudgeonish; curmudgeonly; fiery; furious; hot-tempered; huffy; iracund; irascible; irate; irritable; mad(dened); petulant; raging; splenetic; testy; touchy; waspish; wrathful; CHOLER: (**see** "anger") bile; fury; irascibility; rage; spleen; wrath

CHOOSE: adjudge; adjudicate; adopt; announce; anoint; answer; arbitrate; arrange; call; collect; conclude; control; crown; cull; cut; decide; declare; decree; designate; detach; determine; direct; dispose; doom; elect; embrace; espouse; favor; figure; find; fix; gather; glean; grasp; harvest; judge; measure; name; opt(ate); ordain; order; particularize; pick; please; pluck; prefer; rate; reap; regulate; remove; resolve; rule; screen; seize; select; sentence; separate; settle; solve; take; terminate; umpire; vote; want; will; CHOOSY: **see** "careful;" CHOOSING: alternative; discretional; discretionary; discriminative; eclectic; facultative; optional; preferential; selective; voluntary

CHOP: axe; butcher; chip; cleave; cut; dice; drive; hack; hatchet; hew; lacerate; mangle; mayhem; mince; mutilate; nick; notch; rive; sever; shape; slash; slit; strike

CHORE: (**see** "job") affair; business; chare; duty; employment; function; operation; role; stint; task; work

CHORUS: accord; assonance; choir; company; concert; concord(ance); dancers; harmony; melody; refrain; rhythm; singers; song(s); sounds; unanimity; unit; utterance

CHRONIC(AL): accustomed; addicted; confirmed; constant; continual; continuous; customary; deep; deep-dyed; deep-rooted; deep-seated; established; fixed; general; habitual; hard-bitten; hardened; hard-shell; inborn; indomitable; ingrained; intractable; inured; inveterate; irradicable; lingering; long-lasting; methodical; native; obstinate; periodical; permanent; perpetual; persistent; prevalent; progressive; prolonged; regular; rooted; routine; serious; set(tled); slow; stubborn; systematic; troublesome; uncompromising; unending; unyielding; usual; veteran

CHRONICLE: account; annal(s); answer; chart; diary; epistle; explanation; history; legend; letter; narration; narrative; recital;

recitation; record; register; report; response; statement; story; summary; tale; write-up; writing

CHRONOLOGICAL: **see** "consecutive"

CHUCKLE: (**see** "laugh") exult

CHUM: **see** "buddy"

CHURCH: autem; basilica; bethel; cathedral; chapel; clergy; congregation; denomination; diocese; dome; ebenezer; episcopate; fane; flock; hierarchy; hieron; iglesia; kirk; kovil; masjid; mission; mosque; pagoda; parish; religion; samaj; sect; service(s); sheepfold; spirituality; synagogue; synod; tabernacle; temple; tera; worship

CHURL: (**see** "boor") bondsman; bumpkin; carl; ceorl; clod(hopper); clown; countryman; hind; knave; lout; miser; niggard; oaf; peasant; rustic; serf; vassal; villein; CHURLISH: abrupt; blunt; brief; brusque; crabbed; crabby; crusty; curt; cutting; dour; gruff; pettish; rude; rustic; snappish; snappy; snippy; sordid; sour; sulky; sullen; surly; testy; ungracious

CINCH: **v.** (**see** "bind") assure; fasten; gird; grip; guarantee; secure; tighten; CINCH: **n.** actuality; assurance; breeze; certainty; certitude; cincture; definitude; exactitude; exactness; fidelity; girth; necessity; pipe; reality; snap; victory

CINCTURE: baldric; band; belt; cestus; cinch; compass; enclosure; fillet; girdle

CINDER(S): (**see** "waste") ash(es); clinker(s); coals; dregs; dross; ember(s); refuse; remains; scoria; scum; sediment; slag; sullage; trash

CIPHER: **v.** see "figure;" CIPHER: **n.** code; cryptogram; device; figure; key; monogram; naught; nobody; nonentity; nothing; nullity; number; puzzle; symbol; zero

CIRCLE: **v.** belt; bend; case; circulate; circumnavigate; circumscribe; circumvallate; coil; compass; contort; convolute; coop; corral; crimp; curl; curve; embosom; encase; encircle; enclose; encompass; enfold; envelop; frame; friz(zle); grid(le); gyrate; gyre; hedge; hem; hoop; immure; impale; include; invest; kink; loop; meander; orbit; revolve; ring; roll; rotate; sheathe; span; spin; surround; swirl; turn; twine; twirl; twist; vine; wheel; whirl; wind; wrap;

wreathe; writhe; CIRCLE: **n.** ambage; ambit; area; association; bloc; carol; chapter; circuit; circumference; circumlocution; class; clique; coil; compass; conference; convolution; cordon; coterie; course; cycle; diadem; diameter; disk; district; division; elite; frame; friends; galaxy; girdle; globe; group; gyration; gyre; halo; hoop; influence; lap; league; loop; orb(it); party; period; periplus; realm; region; revolution; rhomb; rigol; ring; roll; rotary; rotation; round; route; scope; set; society; sphere; spiral; swirl; system; tour; twist; vortex; wheel; whirl; zodiac; zone

CIRCUIT: (**see** "circle") ambage; ambit; area; association; calendar; circumference; circumlocution; circumnavigation; compass; conference; coterie; course; cycle; detour; district; group; gyre; hookup; lap; league; loop; orbit; path; periplus; region; revolution; ring; route; scope; system; tour; zodiac; zone; CIRCUITOUS: **see** "winding"

CIRCULAR: **a.** annular; bent; bulbous; circling; circuitous; circumferential; cochleate; coiled; coiling; compass; contorted; convolute(d); corkscrew; crimped; crinkled; crispate; curled; curving; cyclic(al); cycloid-(al); cylindrical; discoid; elliptic(al); globate; globular; helical; helicoid; indirect; kinked; nummiform; nummular; orbed; orbic(ular); oundy; plump; revolving; ringed; rolled; rotating; rotund; round; screwy; spherical; spheriform; spheroid(al); spiral; twisted; volute(d); whorled; winding; CIRCULAR: **n.** (**see** "announcement") advertisement; bill; bulletin; catalog(ue); dodger; leaflet; letter; mail; notice; notification; pamphlet; poster; publication; spread; tract

CIRCULATE: advertise; air; blare; blaze; blazon; broadcast; communicate; diffuse; disseminate; distribute; flow; function; go; mix; move; orbit; pass; peddle; permeate; pervade; proclaim; promulgate; propagandize; propagate; publish; radiate; revolve; rise; rotate; run; scatter; send; shed; sow; spread; strew; teach; transmit; turn

CIRCUMFERENCE: (**see** "circuit") ambit; border; boundary; bounds; compass; confine(s); edge; edging; extent; girth; hem; limit(s); margin; perimeter; periphery; rim; verge

CIRCUMLOCUTION: (**see** "redundance") ambage; evasion; periphrasis; prolixity; redundancy; verbiage; verbosity; winding

CIRCUMSCRIBE: (**see** "bound") constrict; define; limit

CIRCUMSPECT: (**see** "careful") alert; attentive; cautious; considerate; considerative; guarded; heedful; judicious; observant; vigilant; wary

CIRCUMSTANCE(S): accident; accompaniment; account; action; adjunct(s); adventure; antecedent; arrangement(s); atmosphere; attack; background; break; case; casualty; ceremony; chance; circumstantiality; complication; composition; concomitant; condition(s); contingency; crisis; date; decor; description; detail(s); development; digression; distance; education; element(s); enumeration; environment; epic; episode; estate; event(uality); example; exemplification; exigency; experience; fact(s); factor; fate; feature; fix; footing; fortune; goings-on; happening; heredity; history; inadvertency; incident; information; interim; interlude; interval; item; juncture; lay of the land; lineage; matter; meticulosity; milieu; minutia; minutiae (pl.); nature; occasion; occurrence; ornamentation; particular(ity); particulars; past; pedigree; phase; pickle; place; point; position; posture; precedence; precedent; procedure; scene; seizure; sequence; setting; situation; specificality; specification; specifics; state; story; support; surroundings; technicalities; technicality; thing(s); tiding; training; transaction; CIRCUMSTANTIAL: accidental; accompanying; adventitious; contingent; detailed; ephemeral; episodal; inadvertent; incidental; itemized; minute; occasional; particular(ized); pertinent; recurring; supporting; surrounding; temporary; transitory

CIRCUMVENT: (**see** "avoid") baffle; balk; bobble; cheat; check; cozen; dodge; dupe; encircle; encompass; evade; foil; forestall; frustrate; hinder; nullify; outdo; outwit; overcome; prevent; thwart; trick; vitiate

CIRCUS: (**see** "show") carnival; exhibit(ion); hippodrome; spectacle; spectacular; stadium

CITADEL: Alamo; bastion; bulwark; castle; chateau; donjon; fastness; fort(ification); fortress; garrison; keep; muniment; refuge; retreat; rock; stronghold; tower

CITE: (**see** "accuse") adduce; allege; arouse; arraign; call; censure; challenge; command; criminate; evoke; extract; impeach; indict; invite; invoke; know; mention; muster;

name; plead; point; provoke; quote; recall; reproach; summon; tell; warn

CITIZEN(S): aboriginal; aborigine; autochthon; burgher; cit(oyen); civilian; commoner; constituency; constituent; denizen; domestic; dweller; elector; freeman; habitué; indigine; inhabitant; ite; John Q. Public; national; native; oppidan; people(s); primitive; resident; son; subject; townsman; urbanite; voter

CITY: aggregation; cosmopolis; megalopolis; metropolis; municipality; population; urban district

CIVIC: administrative; civil; commercial; communal; governmental; lay; municipal; patriotic; polite; politic(al); public; secular; social; societal; sovereign; urbane

CIVIL: (see "civic") affable; attentive; bland; ceremonial; chivalric; chivalrous; civilized; clement; complacent; considerate; cordial; courteous; courtly; cultured; debonair(e); deferential; discreet; easy(-going); educated; gallant; genteel; gentle; gracious; hend(e); hospitable; human(e); ingratiating; kind; legal; legitimate; mannered; mannerly; nonclerical; obliging; orderly; parliamentary; peaceful; polished; polite; politic(al); presentable; public; quiet; refined; respectful; secular; shipshape; sophistical; suave; tame; urbane; well-bred; well-mannered; CIVILITY or CIVILITIES: (see "courtesy") (the) amenities; conventionalities; cordiality; gentility; polish; (the) proprieties; propriety; (the) urbanities

CIVILIZE: (see "educate") advance; conventionalize; cultivate; debarbarize; instruct; polish; rationalize; refine; socialize; teach; train; unbarbarize; CIVILIZATION: see "refinement"

CLAIM: v. advance; affirm; allege; ask; assert; aver; avouch; avow; challenge; contend; declare; demand; depose; exact; insist; maintain; postulate; pretend; proclaim; profess; protest; reckon; require; say; signify; state; swear; testify; verify; voice; CLAIM: n. appeal; application; assertion; challenge; contention; contract; declaration; demand; deposition; homestead; insistence; lien; mortgage; privilege; request; right; statement; testimony; title

CLAMOR: v. (see "cry") appeal; beseech; bewail; blare; claim; demand; deplore; howl; lament; moan; noise; proclaim; pule; rage;

roar; shout; snivel; sob; squall; threaten; weep; whine; yell; CLAMOR: n. alarm; alarum; alarums and excursions; appeal; bawl; blare; boohoo; brouhaha; clang(or); cry; deploration; din; entreaty; gaff; groan; howl; hubbub; hue; lachrymation; lamentation; noise; outcry; racket; rage; roar; rumpus; shout; snivel; sound; squawk; squeal; threat; tumult; uproar; whimper; whine; CLAMOROUS: beseeching; bewailing; blaring; blatant; boisterous; clangorous; crying; demanding; demonstrative; deploring; effusive; howling; importunate; lamenting; moaning; noisy; pressing; puling; raging; resonant; roaring; shouting; sniveling; sobbing; squawking; squawling; strepitous; threatening; tumultous; urgent; vibrant; vociferant; vociferous; weeping

CLAN: (see "caste") bloc; class; clique; collection; division; family; fraternity; gens; group; name; party; race; rank; sept; set; sib; sorority; status; tartan; tribe; unit; CLANNISH: close; grouped; secret; tribal; united

CLANDESTINE: (see "secret") arcane; cabalistic; closemouthed; concealed; confidential; esoteric; foxy; furtive; illicit; mystic(al); occult; sneaky; stealthy; surreptitious; top-drawer; unavowed; undercover; underhand(ed); veiled

CLANGOR: (see "clamor") clang; din; hubbub; noise; roar; sound; uproar

CLAPTRAP: (see "twaddle") nonsense; trash

CLARIFY: (see "explain") clean; clear(up); defecate; define; depurate; disclose; elucidate; elutriate; enlighten; explicate; expound; free; illume; illuminate; illustrate; interpret; purify; resolve; reveal; settle; simplify; solve; subtilize; unravel; unscramble; CLARIFICATION: (see "clearness") definition; depuration; disclosure; éclaircissement; elucidation; elutriation; enlightenment; exegesis; explanation; explication; illustration; interpretation; purification; revelation; settling; simplification; CLARITY: (see "clearness") directness; orderliness; pellucidness; perspicacity; precision

CLASH: v. (see "bump") brawl; collide; conflict; contravene; crash; differ; disagree; dispute; encroach; fight; hit; impinge; jar; jolt; jostle; knock; oppose; quarrel; shock; skirmish; thwart; wrangle; CLASH: n. (see "bump") brawl; bruit; brunt; collision; conflict; crash; difference; disagreement;

discord; dispute; dissension; fight; impact; impingement; jar; jolt; jostle; knock; noise; opposition; quarrel; shock; skirmish; sound; strife; wrangle

CLASP: brace; buckle; catch; clamp; clinch; cling; clip; clutch; embosom; embrace; encircle; enclose; encompass; enfold; enwrap; fasten; fold; grab; grapple; grasp; grip; hold; hook; hug; latch; lob; lop; pin; possess; retain; seize; surround; take; wrap

CLASS: **v.** see "classify;" CLASS: **n.** (see "classification") bloc; body; bracket; breed; caste; category; circle; clan; clinic; clique; club; collection; company; concept; coterie; cult; degree; denomination; description; distinction; division; domain; estate; family; fraternity; genera (pl.); generation; genre; gens; genus; grade; group; ilk; kind; league; level; mettle; name; order; party; phyla (pl.); phylum; prestige; pupils; race; rank; rate; rating; recitation; rubric; school; sect(ion); seminar; sept; session; set; sorority; sort; species; sphere; standing; status; stripe; students; tartan; tribe; tutorial; type; unit; value; variety

CLASSIC: **n.** (see "standard") book; composition; masterpiece; model; opus; CLASSIC(AL): **a.** (see "standard") appropriate; authoritative; basic; chaste; correct; customary; enduring; first-rate; good; Greek; historical; Latin; masterly; pure; recognized; reliable; Roman; traditional; typical; valuable; vintage

CLASSIFY: (see "arrange") adjudge; alphabetize; assign; associate; assort; bracket; catalog(ue); categorize; characterize; code; codify; collimate; compartmentalize; define; delineate; demarcate; departmentalize; describe; descry; designate; differentiate; digest; discern; discriminate; dispose; distinguish; distribute; divide; file; group; hierarchize; indicate; individualize; label; list; mark; marshal; perceive; pigeonhole; place; plan; portray; rank; rate; reckon; register; represent; segregate; separate; signalize; sort; stamp; subjectify; systematize; ticket; type; typify; CLASSIFICATION: (see "arrangement" and "class") analysis; assignment; assortment; bracket; categorization; category; compartment(alization); department(alization); departmentation; distribution; division; family; file; gens; genus; group(ing); hierarchization; individualization; level; nomenclature; order; plan; position; rating; sequence; sort(ing); species; stratification; subjectification; sub-

ordination; system(atics); systemization; tariff; taxis; taxonomy

CLATTER: (**see** "din") babble; chatter; clamor; clangor; clash; confusion; gossip; noise; pandemonium; prattle; racket; rattle

CLAUSE: (**see** "condition") article; contingency; covenant; detail; item; paragraph; particular(ity); passage; plant; point; provision; proviso; section; segment; sentence; stipulation

CLAW: **v.** burrow; clench; clinch; delve; dig; grab; grasp; grub; handle; hold; hook; hug; jab; lacerate; maul; mutilate; paw; penetrate; poke; probe; punch; scoop; scrape; scratch; shovel; spade; tear; unearth; wound; CLAW: **n.** chela; hand; hook; laceration; nail; paw; poke; punch; scoop; scrape; scratch; talon; tear; unce; uncus; unguis; wound

CLAY: argil; bole; dirt; dust; earth; kaolin(e); loess; man; mire; mud; nature; people; sod; soil

CLEAN(SE): **v.** absolve; absterge; bathe; brush; clarify; clear; correct; defeat; defecate; depurate; deterge; disinfect; dislodge; dress; dust; elutriate; empty; eradicate; exhaust; expiate; expurgate; filter; flush; free; fumigate; gut; lave; mop; mundify; polish; prune; purge; purify; rid; rinse; sanify; scour; scrape; scrub; shower; sponge; sterilize; strip; swab; sweep; wash; wet; wipe; CLEAN: **a.** abstergent; abstrusive; aseptic; bathed; chaste; cleansed; clear; decent; empty; entire; faultless; free; fresh; germless; grimeless; guiltless; healthful; healthy; hygienic; immaculate; impeccable; impeccant; incontestable; indefectible; innocent; kosher; neat; new; outright; perfect; polished; pristine; prophylactic; pure; purified; salubrious; salutary; sanitary; smooth; spick-and-span; sportsmanlike; spotless; stainless; sterile; straight; thoroughgoing; trim; unadulterated; uncontaminated; uncorrupted; undefiled; unmixed; unpolluted; unreserved; unsoiled; unsordid; unspoiled; unstained; unsullied; untarnished; unvitiated; washed; wholesale; wiped; CLEANSING: **a.** abluent; abstergent; abstersive; cathartic; detergent; expiatory; purgatorial; purifying; sanitizing; sterilizing; CLEANSING: **n.** ablution; abstersion; acquittal; balneation; depuration; elutriation; expiation; lavage; lavation; lustration; purgation; purification; sanitation; sterilization; washing; CLEANLINESS: ascesis; chastity;

faultlessness; hygiene; immaculacy; impeccability; indefectibility; purity; sanitation; spick-and-spanness; sterility; sterilization

CLEAR: **v.** (**see** "clean") absolve; acquit; authorize; certify; clarify; cleanse; demonstrate; disappear; discharge; disembarrass; disentangle; ease; edulcorate; empty; enlighten; exhaust; exonerate; explain; explicate; extricate; free; gain; justify; liberate; net; open; pay; redeem; release; relieve; remove; resolve; rid; scour; settle; solve; subtilize; top; unchoke; unclog; vanish; vindicate; CLEAR: **a.** absolute; accessible; accurate; Addisonian; amorphous; apparent; audible; authoritative; authorized; avowed; blaring; blatant; bright; broad; categoric(al); certain; clairvoyant; clarion; clean; clear-cut; cloudless; cogent; cognizable; colorless; compelling; comprehensible; conclusive; conspicuous; convictive; convincing; crystal(line); defined; definite; definitive; delineated; demonstrable; demonstratable; determinate; determinative; determined; diaphanous; direct; discernible; disentangled; distinct(ive); easy; eminent; emphatic; emptied; empty; ethereal; evident; exact; exoteric; explicit; exposed; express; fair; fine; first-hand; fixed; forceful; forcible; forthright; forthwith; frank; full; glaring; glassy; graphic; head-on; honest; incontrovertible; indisputable; indubitable; intelligible; intended; iridescent; likely; limpid; literal; literate; lucent; lucid; luculent; luminous; lustrous; manifest; noncontradictory; noteworthy; noticeable; obvious; open; ostensible; out-and-out; outspoken; overt; palpable; patent; pellucid; perceivable; perceptible; perspicacious; perspicuous; persuasive; phanic; plain(spoken); plausible; point-blank; pointed; polished; positive; potent; precise; premeditated; presumable; presumed; presumptive; *prima facie*; public; pure (and simple); radiant; rational; recognizable; refulgent; sanctioned; sane; satisfactory; seeable; self-evident; sensible; serene; shallow; sharp; sheer; shining; simple; sound; specific; straight(away); straightforward; straight-thinking; striking; suasive; sunny; symptomatic; tangible; telling; thin; translucent; transparent; transpicuous; trenchant; truthful; unambiguous; unblemished; unblurred; unclouded; uncompromising; unconcealed; unconditional; uncrypted; undarkened; understandable; undimmed; undiscolored; undisguised; undistorted; unequivocal; ungarbled; unhampered; unhidden; unhindered; unhooded; unimpeded; unlimited; unmistakable; unobscure(d); unobstructed; unper-

plexed; unqualified; unquestionable; unquestioned; unspoiled; unspotted; unsullied; valid; verbatim; visible; vivid; CLEARNESS: (**see** "clarification") certainty; clairvoyance; clarity; cogency; concentration; conspicuity; conspicuousness; crystallinity; crystallization; definition; diaphaneity; distinctness; evidentness; exactness; explication; explicitness; focus; glaringness; limpidity; limpidness; lucidity; luminosity; manifestness; noticeability; obviousness; patency; pellucidity; perspicacity; perspicuity; precision; prominence; radiance; refulgence; resplendency; sanity; sheerness; sonority; soundness; translucence; translucency; transparency; unambiguity; vividity; vividness

CLEARHEADED: (**see** "perceptive") quick; understanding

CLEAVE: (**see** "adhere" and "separate") bisect; chop; cling; cohere; cut; dispart; dissolve; disunite; divide; hang; hew; hold; join; link; part; penetrate; pierce; rend; rip; rive; sever; slit; split; stick; sunder; tear; unite

CLEFT: **a.** (**see** "separated") cloven; cracked; divided; forked; parted; split; CLEFT: **n.** (**see** "separation") breach; break; chasm; cleavage; commissure; crack; crevasse; crevice; defile; division; fissure; fracture; gap; gash; incision; indentation; interstice; joint; juncture; parting; rift; rima; seam; slit; split

CLEMENT: (**see** "mild") benign; benignant; compassionate; easy(going); forbearing; forgiving; gentle; human(e); indulgent; kind; lenient; merciful; soft; tender; tolerant; CLEMENCY: **see** "mercy"

CLERGY: abbotship; churchmen; clergymen; clerics; cloth; divines; *gens d'église* (pl.); ministers; ministry; parsons; pastors; preachers; prelates; priests; pulpit; pulpitarians; rabbis; rectors; spirituality

CLERGYMAN: abbé; abbot; altarist; canon; chaplain; churchman; cleric(al); clerk; cloth; curate; curé; dean; divine; Dominican; dominie; ecclesiastic; *gens d'église* (pl.); hierophant; homilist; man of the cloth; minister; ordinary; padre; parson; pastor; *père*; preacher; prelate; priest; prior; pulpitarian; rabbi; rector; reverence; reverend; vicar

CLERK: agent; clergyman; cleric; layman;

minister; recorder; register; registrar; saleslady; salesman; salesperson; scholar; scribe; secretary; tradesman; tradesperson

CLEVER: able; adept; adroit; agile; alert; amusing; apt; artful; assured; astucious; astute; bright; cagey; canny; capable; cleverish; competent; cool; crafty; cunning; cute; daedal(ian); daedalic; deft; dexterous; discerning; discriminating; endowed; expert; facile; fit; foxy; funny; gifted; good; habile; handy; happy; heady; imaginative; ingenious; intellectual; intelligent; inventive; keen; knowing; learned; meet; neat; nifty; nimble; oily; original; pat; penetrating; penetrative; perspicacious; proficient; qualified; quick; resourceful; roguish; sagacious; sapient; sharp; shrewd; skilled; skillful; slick; sly; smart; smooth; spiritual; subt(i)le; talented; trained; wary; well-made; wily; wise; witty; CLEVERNESS: ability; acumen; adroitness; agility; alertness; aptitude; artfulness; astucity; astuteness; canniness; capability; craftiness; cunningness; cuteness; deftness; dexterity; discernment; esprit; expertise; foresightedness; foxiness; hability; ingenuity; ingenuosity; intelligence; inventiveness; keenness; learning; nimbleness; originality; penetration; perspicacity; prudence; quickness; resourcefulness; sagacity; shrewdness; skillfulness; slyness; subtlety; wariness; wiliness; wisdom; wit(tiness); wryness

CLEW: **see** "clue"

CLICHÉ: **a.** (**see** "trite") banal; bromidic; commonplace; hackneyed; pedestrian; stereotyped; stereotypical; vapid; CLICHÉ: **n.** banality; bromide; jejunity; pedestrianism; stereotype; tag; triteness; truism; vapidity

CLIENT: buyer; constituent; consumer; customer; dependent; henchman; patient; patron; purchaser; retainer; vassal; vendee

CLIMATE: **see** "environment"

CLIMAX: **v.** ascend; compete; crown; crest; culminate; mount; scale; spike; surmount; top; CLIMAX: **n.** acme; alp; apex; apogee; bloom; cacumen; cap(sheaf); capstone; climacterium; consummation; crest; crisis; crown; culmination; cusp; denouement; flood; floodtide; focus; grand finale; head; height; hill; knob; maximum; meridian; noon(time); orgasm; peak; perfection; perihelion; pinnacle; piton; point; promontory; scale; situation; spike; spire;

sublimity; summit; superlative; tide(mark); top; tor; turning point; ultimate; vertex; zenith

CLIMB: **v.** (**see** "ascend" and "rise") arise; clamber; creep; elevate; escalate; gain; grow; increase; mount; raise; ramp; reach; scale; shin; transcend; twine; vine; CLIMB: **n.** (**see** "rise") ascendence; ascendency; ascent; elevation; escalation; gain; grade; gradient; growth; incline; increase; leadership; mastery; pitch; power; raise; rise; surge; sway; transcendence; upswing; CLIMBER: alpinist; arriviste; *nouveau riche*; opportunist; parvenu; vine

CLINCH: (**see** "bind") capture; clamp; clutch; complete; confirm; embrace; end; fasten; fetter; gain; get; grasp; grip; hitch; hold; hug; indenture; nail; pin(ion); rivet; seal; secure; seize; settle; shackle; snatch; struggle; win; wrest; wrestle

CLING: (**see** "adhere" and "clinch") agglutinate; bank; cleave; cohere; embrace; grasp; hang; hold; hug; linger; persevere; persist; rely; remain; stay; stick; thrust; vine; CLINGING: (**see** "adherent") adamant; adherescent; agglutinant; coherent; persistent; tenacious; viscid; viscous

CLIP: barb; blow; bob; buckle; catch; clamp; clasp; climb; cling; clutch; crop; cut; decrease; diminish; divest; dock; encircle; encompass; fasten; hinder; hold; hook; hug; latch; lessen; lob; lop; mince; pare; peel; pin; prune; rap; reduce; remove; shave; shorten; skin; slice; trim; whack

CLIQUE: (**see** "bloc") cabal; camarilla; charmed circle; circle; club; conclave; conspiracy; *corps d'elite*; coterie; coup; faction; fraternity; gang; group; intrigue; junto; party; plot; ring; set; sodality; sorority; syndicate; trust

CLOAK: **v.** (**see** "blind") camouflage; cloister; clothe; conceal; cover; deceive; disguise; dress; hide; hood; mantle; mask; muffle; mute; robe; screen; secrete; shade; shield; shut(ter); veil; wrap; CLOAK: **n.** (**see** "blind") camouflage; cape; capot(e); character; cover(ing); decoy; disguise; dodge; dolman; dress; garment; grego; hood; mantle; mask; pall; pretense; pretext; robe; role; ruse; sagum; screen; shade; shield; shutter; subterfuge; veil; wrap; CLOAKED: (**see** "secret") arcane; cabalistic; clandestine; disguised; esoteric; furtive;

illicit; larvated; muffled; muted; mystic(al); occult; screened; stealthy; surreptitious; veiled; wrapped

CLOCK: **v.** check; cover; determine; eye; follow; guard; observe; mark; mind; monitor; police; protect; register; see; shield; supervise; survey; tend; time; watch; CLOCK: **n.** bell; chronometer; dial; gong; horologue; hour(glass); meter; monitor; nef; sundial; timepiece; timer; watch

CLOD: (**see** "fool") clay; clown; dirt; dolt; earth; ground; humus; loam; lump; sod; soil; turf; CLODDISH: **see** "stupid"

CLOG: **v.** bar; block; check; chock; choke; close; compress; congest; constrain; curb; dam; damp(en); dance; encumber; fetter; fill; halt; hinder; impede; jam; obstruct; occlude; oppilate; overload; pack; plug; restrain; restrict; retard; screen; shackle; silence; smother; squeeze; stifle; stop; strangle; stuff; suffocate; suppress; walk; CLOG: **n.** bar; blockade; check; chock; compress(ion); congestion; constraint; constriction; curb; damper; dance; encumbrance; fetter; gag; glut; hampering; hindrance; impediment; jam; load; obstruction; oppilation; patten; plug; pressure; prevention; rein; restraint; retardation; shackle; shoe; silence; smothering; stifle; stifling; stoppage; stopper; stuffing; suffocation; suppression; throttle

CLOISTER: **v.** cloak; conceal; immure; isolate; quaratine; seclude; sequester; veil; CLOISTER: **n.** abbey; aisle; arcade; convent; friary; halt; isolation; monastery; nunnery; quarantine; sequestration; veil

CLOSE: **v.** abut; adjourn; bar; bind; block; border; calk; cease; chock; choke; clog; complete; conclude; confine; constrain; cut; dam; debar; deny; desist; die; diminish; disappear; discontinue; drop; enclose; end; estop; exclude; expire; fade; fail; fasten; fill; finish; fold; halt; intermit; join; leave; lock; meet; near; obstruct; obturate; occlude; pause; peter (out); quit; refrain; refuse; resolve; seal; settle; shut; stay; stitch; stop; succumb; suspend; terminate; tighten; unite; vanish; withdraw; yield; CLOSE: **a.** (**see** "near") abutting; adjacent; adjoining; caged; closish; compact; confined; confining; congested; contiguous; dense; exclusive; final; firm; frugal; hot; immediate; imminent; jacent; joining; muggy; near(by); neck and neck; neighboring; niggardly; nigh; nip and tuck; particular;

penned; precise; propinquitous; restraining; restricted; reticent; rigorous; secluded; secret; shut; silent; similar; stale; stingy; strict; stuffy; sultry; taut; thick; tight; CLOSE: **n.** (**see** "conclusion") cessation; closing; cloture; coda; commencement; end; finale; finish outcome; termination; CLOSED: **see** "shut"

CLOSET: **v.** (**see** "conceal") cloister; immure; isolate; seclude; secrete; sequester; shut; CLOSET: **n.** ambry; cabinet; chamber; cupboard; ew(e)ry; locker; press; repository; room; space; stall; vault

CLOT: **v.** (**see** "thicken") agglutinate; clump; cluster; coagulate; congeal; curdle; fix; freeze; gather; gel; harden; ice; immobilize; jell; lump; mass; pectize; preserve; press; set; solidify; stabilize; stick; stiffen; thrombose; CLOT: **n.** agglutination; bunch; clump; cluster; coagulation; coagulum; concrete; congelation; gathering; gelation; group; hardness; jelly; knot; lump; mass; mott; patch; solidification; thrombosis; tuft

CLOTHE: (**see** "dress") accouter; adorn; apparel; array; attire; bedeck; blanket; caparison; cloak; couch; cover; deck; drape; endow; endue; envelop(e); express; garb; habilitate; invest; overspread; portray; represent; robe; swathe; tailor; tog; vest(ure); wrap; CLOTHES *or* CLOTHING: (**see** "dress") accouterments; apparel; array(ment); atmosphere; attire; blankets; costume; cover(ing); dress; duds; equipage; equipment; frippery; frock; garb; garment(s); gear; guise; habiliment(s); harness; investiture; linen; outfit; rags; raiment; regalia; rig; stuff; style; toggery; togs; uniform; vestments; vesture; wardrobe; wear(ables)

CLOUD: **v.** adumbrate; becloud; bedim; befog; befoul; bewilder; blacken; blear; blur; complicate; conceal; confine; confuse; cover; darken; delude; denigrate; depress; dim(inish); disguise; dull; dun; dwindle; eclipse; envelop(e); fade; fail; fog; haze; hide; hood; lower; mask; muddle; obfuscate; obliterate; obnebulate; obnubilate; obscure; obscurify; overcast; overcloud; overshadow; overspread; perplex; reduce; sadden; screen; shade; shadow; shield; stain; stupefy; sully; taint; tarnish; thicken; wane; CLOUD: **n.** blur; cirrus; cumulus; defect; fog; haze; mass; mist; nebula; nimbus; nubia; overshadowing; screen; shade; shadow; shame; stain; stigma; stratus; sully; swarm; taint; tarnish; vapor; CLOUDY *or* CLOUDED: (**see** "obscure") blurred; blurry; cleerless; confused; dark(ened); dim; dismal; dispirited; dreamlike; dreamy; dubious; dull; filmy; foggy; fuliginous; gloomy; hazy; indefinite; indistinct; lowery; misty; murky; nebular; nebulated; nebulose; nebulous; nimbose; nubilous; obscured; ominous; opaque; overcast; roily; shadowy; smoky; turbid; uncertain; unclear; vague; vaporous; wispy; CLOUDINESS: (see "dimness") fuliginosity; gloom(iness); indefiniteness; indistinctness; nebulosity; obnubilation; obscurity; obstruction; tenuosity; turbidity; uncertainty; vagueness

CLOUT: (see "beat") hit; strike

CLOWN: (see "fool") actor; antic; aper; baboon; buff(oon); bumpkin; card; churl; clod(pate); comedian; comic; countryman; cutup; droll; grobian; harlequin; hooligan; humorist; jape; jester; joker; lout; lubber; merry-andrew; mime(r): mimic: oaf; Pierrot; Punch(inello); punster; rube; rustic; Scaramouche; stooge; wag; wit; yokel; zany; CLOWNISH: awkward; baboonish; boorish; buffoonish; coarse; clumsy; droll(ish); green; humorous; loutish; raw; rough; rude; rustic; zany; CLOWNISHNESS: see "buffoonery"

CLOY: (see "glut") clog; fill; flood; gorge; gratify; overfeed; overfill; pall; sate; satiate; saturate; surfeit; weary

CLUB: alliance; association; athen(a)eum; band; bat; billy; body; brotherhood; card; coalition; colony; combination; compact; company; consortium; coterie; cudgel; fraternity; fratority; group; guild; league; lodge; mace; membership; nightstick; order; organization; society; sodality; sorority; staff; stick; team; threat; truncheon; weapon

CLUE: allusion; ball; characteristic; clew; criteria (pl.); criterion; cue; fingerprint; foreboding; forewarning; giveaway; guide; hint; illusion; implication; indication; inference; innuendo; insinuation; insinuendo; intimation; key; landmark; lead; notice; odor; pointer; reference; sign; signal; smell; suggestion; suspicion; symptom; thread; thumbprint; tip(-off); twine; warning; whiff; whisper

CLUMP: v. (see "clot") agglutinate; aggregate; bunch; cluster; group; heap; knot; lump; mass; patch; CLUMP: n. agglutina-tion; aggregation; bunch; cluster; clutch; group; grove; heap; knot; lump; mass; mott; patch; tuft

CLUMSY: awkward; big; bulky; bungling; butchery; butterfingered; callow; clownish; coarse; cumberous; cumbersome; elephantine; fumbling; gauche; gawkish; gawky; graceless; green; heavy; ill-adapted; ill-made; ill-proportioned; inapt; incoherent; incompetent; inconvenient; ineffective; inefficient; inelegant; inept; inexpert; infelicitous; inopportune; jumbo; laborous; left-handed; loutish; lumbering; lumpish; maladroit; ponderous; rigid; rough; rude; rustic; senseless; shy; silly; slow; stiff; stumbling; stupid; tactless; tense; ugly; unapt; uncouth; uneasy; unfit; ungainly; ungraceful; unhandy; unhappy; unskilled; unskillful; unsociable; unwieldly; wooden; CLUMSINESS: (see "awkwardness") crudity; cumbersomeness; fumblingness; gaucheness; gaucherie; ineptness; maladroitness; ponderosity; ungainliness; ungracefulness; unwieldiness

CLUSTER: v. accumulate; agglomerate; agglutinate; aggregate; amass; assemble; associate; bunch; clump; collect; conglomerate; crowd; flock; gather; group; knot; lump; mass; nest; nucleate; pile; unite; CLUSTER: n. accumulation; agglomeration; aggregation; amount; army; assemblage; association; band; clump; clutch; collection; conglomeration; congregation; crowd; cyme; fascicle; flock; gathering; glomerule; group; knot; lump; mass; nest; nucleation; nucleus; number; pile; CLUSTERED: aciniform; agglomerated; aggregatory; assembled; associated; banded; bunched; c(a)espitose; crowded; fascicular; gathered; lumped; massed; nested; nucleated; piled

CLUTCH: v. (see "claw") clench; clinch; cluster; control; crush; grab; grasp; grip; group; hold; hug; nab; retain; seize; snatch; take; CLUTCH: n. brood; bunch; cluster; control; coupling; group; handbag; hatch(ing); lever; nest; power; set; talon

COACH: v. see "teach;" COACH: n. araba; bus; cabin; car(riage); docent; governor; instructor; manager; mentor; pedagog(ue); pilot; stage; teacher; trainer; tutor; vehicle

COAGULATE: see "clot" and "thicken"

COALESCE: (see "combine") absorb; agree; blend; coagulate; concresce; concrete; congeal; embody; fuse; incorporate; integrate; join; league; merge; mix; telescope; unionize; unite; COALITION *or* COALECENCE: (**see** "combine") alliance; blend; combination; compact; confederacy; confederation; congealment; congelation; conspiracy; entente; front; fusion; group; incorporation; league; merger; treaty; understanding; union

COARSE: (**see** "crude") animal(ic); animalistic; artless; barbaric; barbarous; base; bawdy; broad; brutish; callow; careless; clownish; common; crass; crude; cruel; crusty; curt; degenerate; degraded; degrading; despicable; dirty; dull; earthly; elemental; Falstaffian; fat; filthy; foul; gauche; green; gross; grubby; hairy; hard; harsh; heavy; ignoble; ignorant; ill-bred; ill-mannered; immature; impure; inapt; incondite; indelicate; inelegant; inept; inexpert; inferior; inurbane; loose; loutish; low; material; mean(spirited); obscene; obtuse; offensive; ordinary; petty; plain; plebeian; primitive; profane; randy; rascally; raucous; raw; ribald; rough; rowdy; rude; rugged; rustic; scurrilous; shabby; shameful; shameless; sordid; squalid; stark; stupid; thick; tramontane; troglodytic; ugly; uncivilized; uncultivated; unfine; ungainly; ungraceful; unpolished; unrefined; unskilled; vile; vulgar(ian); COARSENESS: (**see** "crudity") artlessness; barbarism; barbarity; buffoonery; contemptibility; crassness; dastardliness; degeneration; degradation; despicability; disgrace; filth; gaucherie; *grossièreté*; grossness; impurity; indelicacy; inelegance; ineptitude; ineptness; inferiority; inurbanity; knavery; meanness; plebeianism; primitivity; rascality; rawness; roughness; rudeness; rusticity; scurrility; servility; shame; sordidness; stupidity; turpitude; unrefinement; unskillfulness; vulgarity; wickedness

COAT: **v.** (**see** "cover") clothe; crust; galvanize; glaze; incrust; invest; overlay; paint; plaster; plate; protect; spread; COAT: **n.** (**see** "cover") bark; blanket; blazer; capote; carapace; covering; crust; cutaway; duster; envelope; galvanization; glaze; husk; incrustation; integument; jacket; jerkin; layer; membrane; paint; patina; plate; plating; protection; rind; shell; skin; toga; tunic; ulster

COAX: (**see** "allure") appeal; beckon; beg; cajole; charm; coddle; enamor; entice; fawn; flatter; influence; inveigle; invite;

lure; manipulate; persuade; seduce; solicit; soothe; tease; tempt; urge; wheedle

COBBLE: (**see** "patch" and "repair") make; mend

COCKY: (**see** "sassy") arrogant; bold; brash; brazen; bumptious; cheeky; chipper; conceited; disdainful; disrespectful; flip(pant); forward; fresh; impertinent; impudent; insolent; jaunty; nervy; pert; proud; rude; saucy; smart(-aleck); smart-alecky

CODDLE: (**see** "baby") caress; cherish; coax; console; cook; fondle; hug; humor; indulge; kiss; love; nurse; pamper; pet; please; satiate; satisfy; spoil

CODE: behavior; canon; cipher; clue; codex; cryptogram; cryptograph(y); digest; dogma; key; law; precept; principle(s); puzzle; regulation(s); rule(s); secret; signal; standard; statutes; symbol; systematization; table; tabulation; CODIFY: classify; digest; file; index; standardize; systematize; tabulate

COERCE: actuate; alarm; bend; blackmail; bleed; bluster; bludgeon; boss; browbeat; bulldoze; bully; cause; check; choke; command(eer); compel; conjure; constrain; control; cow; curb; demand; dictate; direct; discipline; distrain; distress; dominate; domineer; dragoon; draw; drive; educe; elicit; enforce; enjoin; exact; execute; extort; extract; force; frighten; fulminate; goad; govern; hector; hound; impel; impose; impress; imprison; impulse; influence; institute; intimidate; invoke; lash; levy; limit; lord (over); make; manacle; master; menace; milk; necessitate; obligate; oblige; oppress; order; overawe; possess; predominate; press; prevail; prod; push; reinforce; repress; require; restrain; ride; rule; scare; shake down; shove; squeeze; steamroller; stifle; subdue; subject; swashbuckle; sway; take; tax; terrify; terrorize; threat; thrust; torture; tyrannize; urge; wrench; wrest; wring; COERCION; bond(age); blackmail; bludgeon; captivity; coarctation; command; compression; compulsion; compulsoriness; constraint; constriction; contraction; control; demand; dictation; discipline; distraint; distress; domination; durance (vile); duress; enforcement; exaction; extortion; extraction; fetter; force; hampering; heat; hindrance; implementation; imprisonment; impulse; impulsion; inhibition; intimidation; levy; limitation; manacle; necessity; need; obligation; oppression; power; pressure;

requirement; reserve; restraint; restriction; shakedown; squeeze; steamroller; stifle; stifling; strain; strangulation; strap; stricture; stultification; tax; tension; terror; toll; torture; tyranny; urgency; violence; COERCIVE: (see "imperative") compelling; compulsatory; compulsory; obligatory; oppressive

COFFIN: bier; box; case; casket; catafalque; chest; cist; pall; pix; sarcophagus; tye

COGENT: (see "potent") apposite; authoritative; brief; compelling; concise; constraining; convincive; effective; forceful; forcible; good; important; intense; lusty; persuasive; pertinent; powerful; sinewy; sovereign; stalwart; strong; telling; timely; trenchant; urgent; valid; well-founded; witty; COGENCY: see "force" and "potency"

COGITATE: (see "think") lucubrate; plan; plot; ponder

COGNATE: (see "related" and "relative") akin; similar

COGNIZANT: (see "aware") conscious; knowing; COGNIZANCE: (see "awareness") apprehension; attention; badge; cognition; consciousness; control; conviction; discernment; emblem; feeling; heed; intuition; jurisdiction; knowledge; mark; notice; observation; perception; perspicacity; surveillance; vigilance; watchfulness

COGNOMEN: (see "name") surname

COHERE: (see "adhere") agglutinate; agree; cement; cleave; cling; coincide; conglutinate; fit; glue; glutinize; hold; solidify; stick; suit; unify; unite; COHERENCE: see "union"

COIL: v. (see "circle") convolute; curl; encircle; encompass; loop; pool; spiral; twine; twirl; twist; vine; wind; wrap; COIL: n. (see "circle") affairs; ansa; confusion; convolution; curl; difficulty; helix; loop; querl; ringlet; roll; scroll; spiral; trouble(s); tumult; twirl; twist; world

COIN: v. create; fabricate; forge; invent; make; manufacture; mint; produce; shape; stamp; strike; COIN(S): n. (see "money") change

COINCIDE: (see "agree") accede; admit; allow; concur; conform; consent; correspond; fit; harmonize; jibe; match; overlap; overlay;

permit; suit; tally; COINCIDENTAL: see "concurrent"

COLD: airish; algid; aloof; apathetic; arctic; assured; bleak; blunt; boreal; breezy; calculated; certain; cheerless; chilled; chilling; chilly; cold-blooded; cool(ed); dead; defenseless; deliberate; depressing; detached; discouraging; disheartening; dispassionate; dispirited; distant; dull; emotionless; faint; formal; freezing; fresh; frigid; frosty; gelid; glacial; glassy; gloomy; hard; heartless; hyperborean; iced; icy; idle; impersonal; indifferent; inhibited; inhospitable; inhuman(e); insensible; low; marmoreal; matter-of-fact; midwintry; nippy; passionless; polar; raw; refrigerated; reserved; rigorous; severe; shivering; shivery; squeamish; stale; stoical; stony; strange; sure; temperate; unemotional; unenthusiastic; unfeeling; unfriendly; unheated; uninteresting; unpracticed; unprepared; unready; unresponsive; unsociable; unused; unsympathetic; unwarmed; unwarming; unwavering; unyielding; wint(e)ry

COLLAPSE: v. (see "fall") bankrupt; bend; bow; break; buckle; burst; bust; cave; cavitate; contract; cropper; crumble; crumple; degenerate; die; disintegrate; dissolve; drain; drop; empty; exhaust; fail; flatten; flop; flounder; fold; implode; liquefy; liquidate; puncture; ruin; sag; shatter; shrink; sink; topple; tumble; wilt; wreck; yield; COLLAPSE: n. (see "fall") atelectasis; bankruptcy; bend; break(down); buckling; burst; bust; cataclysm; cavitation; crumbling; crumpling; debacle; debasement; degradation; descent; disgrace; disintegration; disorganization; disruption; dissolution; downfall; drop; enervation; enfeeblement; explosion; failure; fall; flop; foundering; *götterdämmerung*; helplessness; holocaust; implosion; labefaction; liquefaction; liquidation; misfortune; overthrow; prostration; reversal; reverse; rout; ruin; shattering; shock; sink(ing); stampede; suppression; termination; thaw; topple; tumble; vanishment; vanquishment; Waterloo; wilting; wrack; wreck; yielding

COLLAR: v. (see "catch") arrest; grab; grasp; nab; steal; tackle; COLLAR: n. band; bertha; cincture; circlet; curb; eton; fichu; gorget; molding; ring; shackle; torque

COLLATE: see "compare"

COLLATERAL: a. (see "allied") ancillary;

associated; concomitant; concurrent; connected; indirect; oblique; parallel; related; secondary; subordinate; subsidiary; tangential; COLLATERAL: **n.** (**see** "money") bond; guarantee; insurance; security

COLLATION: (**see** "refreshment") comparison; conference; description; gathering; luncheon; meal; parallel; reading; repast; tea

COLLEAGUE: (**see** "assistant") associate; confrere; consort; mate

COLLECT: (**see** "accumulate") accrue; acquire; add; agglomerate; agglutinate; aggregate; amass; archive; assemble; attain; attract; bag; band; bank; buy; cache; coacervate; collate; compare; compile; concentrate; conclude; conflate; conglomerate; congregate; control; convene; converge; convoke; cord; crowd; cull; cumulate; deduce; drift; earn; fill; gain; garner; gather; get; glean; group; grow; harvest; heap; herd; hide; hoard; huddle; increase; infer; keep; lay away; lay up; levy; load; marshal (l); mass; mingle; mobilize; muster; obtain; pick; pile; pool; preserve; pyramid; reap; receive; rick; round; save; scavage; scavenge; scrap; sheathe; shock; socialize; stack; store; summon; sweep; tax; thesaurize; treasure; unite; COLLECTION: (**see** "band") accretion; accruement; accumulation; acervation; acquirement; addition; adversaria (pl.); agglomerate; agglomeration; agglutination; aggregate; aggregation; album; amassing; amassment; ana(lect); analecta (pl.); anthology; archive(s); assemblage; bag(ful); bank; battery; boodle; bulk; caboodle; cache; clutch; coacervation; cock; collectanea (pl.); collectivity; colluvies; company; compendium; compilation; composure; conflagration; congeries; conglomeration; congregation; convention; corpus; crestomathy; crop; crowd; cumulation; debris; deposit; depot; dictionary; dividend; drift; exhibit; fardel; fascicle; file; fistful; fortune; fun; gallery; gang; gathering; gobs; grab bag; group; growth; handful; harvest; heap(s); herd; heterogeneity; hoard; increase; increment; incrustation; ingathering; interest; levy; library; list; load(s); lot(s); mass; materials; menagerie; miscellanea (pl.); miscellaneity; miscellany; mob; money; mountains; museum; muster; nest (egg); nucleation; number; omnibus; pack; pile; plate; pool; potpourri; profusion; pyramid; quantity; rack; raft; ragbag; repertory; riches; savings; scrapings; set; shock; slew; stack; stock; supplies; supply; sylloge;

symposium; thesaurus; thrift; treasure; treasury; troop; variety; works; zoo

COLLEGE: academy; assemblage; club; company; coterie; faculty; institute; institution; lycée; multiversity; school; seminary; university

COLLIDE: (**see** "bump") attack; clash; conflict; contact; crash; displace; encounter; encroach; hit; hurtle; impact; impinge; jam; jar; jog; knock; meet; oppose; strike; touch; wreck; COLLISION: attack; bump; clash; compact; concussion; conflict; contact; crash; disagreement; displacement; encounter; encroachment; hit; impact(ion); impingement; infringement; jam; jar; jog; knock; meeting; opposition; renitency; retroaction; shock; smash; touch(ing); war(fare); wreck

COLLOQUY: (**see** "chat") causerie; collocation; confabulation; conference; conversation; debate; dialectics; dialog(ue); discourse; discussion; parley; reading; talk

COLLUDE: (**see** "plot") abet; combine; confederate; connive; conspire; contrive; intrigue; machinate; plan; scheme; COLLUSION: **see** "plot"

COLONIZE: (**see** "base") commence; establish; found; gather; initiate; invent; isolate; organize; originate; set(tle); start; swarm; COLONY: aggregation; base; crowd; foundation; gathering; group; habituation; hive; installation; nest; number; organization; plantation; protectorate; settlement; start; swarm

COLOR: **v.** affect; blacken; blush; condition; disguise; distort; dye; embellish; exaggerate; flush; glow; imbue; influence; infuse; mantle; misrepresent; paint; redden; shade; shape; stain; taint; tincture; tinge; tint; tone; COLOR(S) **n.** *or* COLORING: appearance; aspect; banner; blee; blue; blush; cast; character(istic); chroma(tism); complexion; couleur; disguise; dye; embellishment; ensign; exaggeration; flag; flush; green; guise; hue; jack; kind; look; nature; orange; paint; patina; pennant; pigment(ation); plausibility; pretext; quality; rainbow; red; rubescence; semblance; shade; sort; spectrum; stain; taint; tincture; tinge; tint; tone; variety; vein; violet; vividness; yellow; zest; COLORED *or* COLORFUL: (**see** "biased") adorned; aligned; dazzling; embellished; exaggerated; exotic; feigned; gorgeous; juicy; negro(id); oriented; picturesque;

pretended; rainbow; resplendent; rich; romantic; rubescent; scenic; showy; slanted; splendaceous; splendacious; splendid; vivid; zestful

COLORLESS: (see "pale") achlorophyll-(ace)ous; achromatic; achromatous; achromic; achromous; ashen; banal; blanched; cheerless; clear; crystall(ine); decolorized; diatonic; drab; dull; etiolate(d); hueless; lifeless; mousy; neutral; pale; pallid; plain; transparent; trite; uninteresting; wan; white

COLOSSAL: (see "huge") elephantine; epic; extensive; gigantic; grand; great; mastodonic; powerful; strong; vast; COLOSSUS: (see "giant") monolith; monster; ogre; prodigy; titan

COLUMN: (see "arrangement") alphabetization; array; article; assortment; cylinder; file; formation; line; list; pilaster; pillar; post; prop; row; scheme; shaft; stack; succession; support; system; table; tabulation; upright

COMA: anesthesia; bunch; carus; epilepsy; hypnosis; lethargy; seizure; sleep; stupor; torpidity; torpor; tuft; unconsciousness; COMATOSE: anesthetized; asleep; drowsy; dull; epileptic; heavy; hypnogenic; hypnogogic; hypnotic; inactive; indolent; insensible; latent; lazy; lethargic; motionless; numb; oscitant; out; quiescent; quiet; sleeping; sleepy; sluggish; slumbering; somniferous; somnolent; torpescent; torpid; unawake(ned); unconscious; unwake(ne)d

COMBAT: v. (see "fight") assail; attack; battle; contend; contest; cope; counter-(mine); defy; duel; face; joust; oppose; storm; struggle; wrestle; COMBAT: n. (see "fight") action; attack; battle; belligerence; belligerency; brush; conflict; contact; controversy; duel; engagement; fray; fury; hostility; joust; rencontre; skirmish; storm; strife; struggle; war(fare); COMBATIVE: (see "hostile") aggressive; agonistic; argumentative; armigerous; assertive; bellicose; belligerent; bristly; contentious; disputatious; fire-eating; irate; mad; martial; militant; oppugnant; pugnacious; quarrelsome; taurine; truculent; unpacific; warlike; COMBATANT: see "enemy"

COMBINE: v. absorb; accrete; add; agree; amalgam(ate); amalgamize; annex; associate; blend; coagulate; coalesce; compress; concrete; concretize; conflate; congeal; conjoin; connect; consolidate; cooperate; coordinate; couple; cream; double; dovetail; embody;

federate; fuse; grade; graduate; group; harmonize; homogenize; integrate; interlock; intermarry; join; laminate; league; marry; melt; merge; mesh; mingle; mix; pool; prepare; shade; solidify; splice; syncretize; synthesize; telescope; temper; tinge; tone; unite; wed; weld; COMBINE n. or COMBINATION: accretion; agglutination; aggregate; aggregation; alliance; amalgamation; association; blend; bloc(k); cabal(a); cartel; coalescence; coalition; collection; combinate; compact; complex; compound; confederacy; confederation; conflation; congealment; congelation; conjoinment; conjugation; conjunction; conjuncture; consolidation; conspiracy; coordination; corner; corporation; coterie; entente; faction; federation; fusion; gradation; grade; group; harmonization; homogenation; inosculation; integration; junto; key; lamination; league; machine; marriage; merger; mix(ture); package; party; plot; polysynthesis; pool; ring; sequence; shade; solidification; syncretism; syndicate; synergism; synthesis; tempering; tincture; tinge; tone; treaty; trust; unanimity; understanding; union; unit(ion); COMBINED: coalesced; combinatorial; combinatory; concatenated; conjoint; comparcenary; hand-in-hand; joined; joint; simultaneous; solidified; unanimous; undivided; united

COMBUSTION: blaze; burning; cautery; cineration; conflagration; confusion; cremation; fire; heat; oxidation; sizzling; tumult; ustulation

COME: (see "happen") accrue; achieve; advance; appear; approach; arise; arrive; attain; bechance; become; befall; betide; chance; emanate; emerge; enter; fare; follow; heed; issue; land; near; occur; originate; reach; relent; spring; stem; succede; visit

COMEDIAN: (see "clown)" antic; buff(oon); card; comic; fool; jester; punster; stooge; wag; wit; COMEDY: (see "farce") buffoonery; burlesque; diversion; foolishness; laughter; slapstick; travesty; wit

COMEDOWN: anticlimax; bathos; comeuppance; contretemps; *déclassement*; defeat; dejection; delusion; denigration; despair; disappointment; disenchantment; frustration; humiliation; letdown; mockery; setback

COMELY: (see "beautiful") agreeable; attractive; becoming; bonny; decent; decorous; fair; fitting; graceful; handsome;

lovely; nice; personable; pleasant; pleasing; pretty; seemly; suitable; COMELINESS: (**see** "beauty" and "grace") attractiveness; gracefulness; seemliness

COMESTIBLE: (**see** "food") dish; eatable; eats; edible

COMFORT: **v.** (**see** "aid") alleviate; assist; assuage; calm; cheer; condole; console; delight; divert; ease; encourage; gladden; gratify; help; nurse; nurture; please; protect; quiet(en); relieve; satisfy; solace; soothe; stay; strengthen; succor; support; tranquilize; COMFORT: **n.** (**see** "aid") alleviation; appurtenance; assistance; assuagement; balm; calm; charm; cheer; condolence; consolation; convenience; delectation; delight; diversion; ease; encouragement; enjoyment; gratification; help; homeliness; intimacy; life of Riley; nepenthe; nurture; pleasure; protection; quiet(ude); quilt; relaxation; relief; repose; rest; satisfaction; security; snugness; strength; succor; support; tranquility; COMFORTABLE *or* COMFORTING: (**see** "cheerful") casual; cheering; cheery; commodious; consolatory; consoling; contented; convenient; cosh; cozy; cushy; divertive; easy; encouraging; euphoric; familiar; friendly; *gemütlich*; genial; glad(some); gratifying; homey; intimate; natural; nepenthean; placid; pleasant; pleasing; pleasurable; posh; protected; quiet; relaxed; restful; safe; satisfied; secure; simple; snug; soft; tranquilizing; unruffled; warm

COMIC(AL): **a.** (**see** "funny") amusing; Aristophanic; burlesque; diverting; droll; farcical; harlequin; humorous; laughable; ludicrous; mirthful; opéra-buoffe; risible; witty; COMIC: **n.** (**see** "comedian") comicality; comicalness; comique; droll; *farceur; farceuse* (fem.); harlequin; humorist; merry-andrew; mime; mimic

COMITY: (**see** "courtesy") amenity; association; civility; consideration; exchange; friendliness; reciprocity; suavity; urbanity

COMMAND: **v.** act; adjudge; administer; admonish; appoint; behest; bid; call; charge; choose; compel; control; cover; decide; decree; demand; designate; determine; dictate; direct; dispatch; dominate; doom; elect; enact; enjoin; establish; evoke; exact; force; formulate; govern; guide; head; impel; imperate; impose; influence; instruct; lead; manage; ordain; order; predominate; prescribe; preside; prevail; prompt; pro-

nounce; proscribe; require; rule; send; sentence; set(tle); shout; speak; suggest; summon; sway; tell; warn; will; write; yell; COMMAND: **n.** (**see** "authority") act; adjuration; administration; admonishment; announcement; arret; ban; behest; bid(ding); bull; call; canon; caveat; charge; commandment; commission; compulsion; control; decision; decree; decrement; decretum; demand; determination; dicta (pl.); dictamen; dictate; dictation; dictum; direction; discipline; domination; dominion; doom; edict; enactment; enjoinder; exaction; fiat; force; government; guidance; guide; headquarters; helm; imperative; imposition; influence; injunction; instruction; interdiction; irade; judgment; law; lead(ership); management; mandament; mandate; mandatum; manifesto; mastery; nisi; notice; order; ordinance; organization; power; precept; prescription; predomination; proclamation; pronouncement; pronunciamento; proscription; protocol; regency; regime(n); regnancy; regula(tion); reign; request; requirement; rescript; rubric; rule; ruling; sanction; settlement; shout; sovereignty; statute; summons; supremacy; sway; system; ukase; vocative; warning; will; write; yell; COMMANDING: (**see** "dictatorial") august; authoritative; autocratic; chief; coercive; compelling; confident; exalted; governmental; grand(iose); haughty; imperative; imperial; imperious; imposing; kingly; leading; mandatory; peremptory; predominant; self-assumed; sovereign; COMMANDER: **see** "chief"

COMMANDEER: (**see** "take") coerce; compel; seize

COMMANDMENT: (**see** "command") caveat; fiat; injunction; instruction; law; mandament; mandate; mandatum; order; ordinance; power; precept; rubric; rule; statute

COMMEMORATE: (**see** "celebrate") award; cite; dedicate; eulogize; fete; honor; keep; memorialize; observe; panegyrize; remember; signalize; solemnize; COMMEMORATION: (**see** "celebration") birthday; ceremony; citation; commencement; dedication; drink; eulogy; graduation; honor; medal; memorial(ization); monument; observance; plaque; remembrance; revel(ry); service(s); solemnization; stamp

COMMENCE: **see** "begin;" COMENCEMENT: (**see** "birth" and "start") approach; ceremony; graduation; kickoff; onset; onslaught; overture; source; COMMENCING: **see** "beginning"

COMMEND: (**see** "applaud") approve; bespeak; charge; cite; commit; compliment; congratulate; entrust; extol; felicitate; give; honor; laud; laureate; panegyrize; praise; recommend; COMMENDABLE: (**see** "excellent" and "praiseworthy") acclamatory; admirable; adorable; adulatory; approbatory; archetyp(ic)al; cheering; commendatory; complimentary; congratulatory; credible; creditable; elegiac; encomiastic(al); estimable; eulogistic(al); exemplary; exemplificative; exemplificatory; glorifying; good; honorable; honorific; ideal(istic); idolatric; idolatrous; illustrative; illustrious; laudable; laudative; laudatory; meritorious; panegyric-(al); pious; recommendatory; COMMENDATION: (**see** "applause") accolade; approbation; approval; award; citation; compliment; congratulation; encomium; encore; eulogium; eulogy; felicitation; glorification; greeting; honor; laudation; laureation; medal; panegyric; praise; rave; recommendation; tribute

COMMENSURATE: adequate; appropriate; coequal; coextensive; commensurable; congruent; correspondent; corresponding; enough; equal; equivalent; even; homological; homologous; isonomous; level; parallel; proportionate; relative; relevant; rhythmic; sufficient; suitable; symmetrical

COMMENT: **v.** (**see** "discuss") air; altercate; annotate; argue; confabulate; confer; converse; cover; criticize; debate; deliberate; descant; dilate; discerp; discourse; dispute; elaborate; examine; expand; expatiate; expiate; expostulate; expound; gloss; hash over; instruct; interpret; lecture; negotiate; note; notice; observe; reason; remark; sift; talk; wrangle; COMMENT: **n.** annotation; aside; commentary; criticism; descant; discourse; discussion; examination; exegesis; explanation; exposition; expostulation; implication; instruction; interpretation; item; lecture; negotiation; notes; obiter (dictum); observation; opinion; postil; reasoning; remarks; suggestion; talk; treat-(ment); wrangle; COMMENTARY: account; analogy; analysis; exegesis; explanation; footnote; gloss(ary); interpretation; marginalia (pl.); memoir(s); notes; remarks; treatment; COMMENTATOR: annotator; announcer; critic; exegete; explainer; expositor; expounder; glossator; interpreter; scholiast

COMMERCE: (**see** "business") barter(ing); buying; commercialism; communication; communion; dealings; exchange; industry; interchange; interrelationship; mercantilism; merchandise; merchandising; selling; trade; trading; traffic; transaction; COMERCIAL: industrial; mercantile; mercenary

COMMINGLE: (**see** "mix") combine; mingle

COMMISERATE: (**see** "condole") grieve; lament; pity; sorrow; sympathize; COMMISERATION: (**see** "pity") compassion; condolence; empathy; ruth; sympathy

COMMISSION: **v.** appoint; assign; authorize; commit; constitute; create; crown; declare; delegate; depute; designate; empower; enable; endow; establish; found; franchise; grant; hire; impute; lease; let; license; ordain; order; organize; originate; permit; rent; start; substitute; transfer; COMMISSION: **n.** act; agency; allowance; authority; authorization; bidding; body; brevet; canon; certificate; charge; charter; command; commitment; committal; compensation; constitution; decalogue; decree; deed; delegation; deputation; dictation; diploma; direction; directive; document; edict; errand; establishment; fee; franchise; grant; immunity; inauguration; injunction; installation; instruction; instrument; investment; job; judgment; law; lease; license; mandate; mandatum; magna c(h)arta; obligation; order; ordination; permission; permit; perpetuation; pledge; power; precept; prescript; privilege; proxy; rank; task; transfer; warrant; writ

COMMIT: (**see** "bind") address; allot; allow; arrest; assign; cede; commend; commission; confide; consign; contract; dedicate; delegate; deliver; design; designate; dispense; do; entrust; expose; give; help; imprison; involve; mail; obligate; perform; perpetuate; place; pledge; promise; pull; recommend; refer; relegate; rely; resign; reveal; say; sentence; surrender; transact; transfer; trust; vow; yield; COMMITTED: bound; *engagé*; engaged; entrusted; pledged; promised

COMMITTEE: board; body; commission(ers); executors; guardian(s); organization; representative; surrogate

COMMODIOUS: (**see** "capacious") ample; baronial; broad; cavernous; comfortable; convenient; copious; expansive; extensive;

fit; large; limitless; magnitudinous; roomy; spacious; suitable; unlimited; voluminous; wide

COMMODITY: (**see** "article") goods; item; merchandise; product; staple; stock; stuff; thing(s)

COMMON: accepted; accustomed; adequate; animal; available; average; banal; base; carnal; cheap; chronic; classic(al); coarse; coetaneous; coeval; commonplace; communal; constant; consuetudinary; contemporaneous; contemporary; continuous; conventional; crass; crude; current; customary; deep-seated; democratic; demotic; depraved; *de règle*; *de rigueur*; domestic; dull; earth(l)y; established; everyday; existent; existing; extant; fair; fashionable; fixed; frequent; general; generic; going; gross; habitual; hackneyed; heathenish; household; inferior; informal; ingrained; intractable; inured; joint; known; lewd; low; mean; mediocre; medium; mere; middle (of the road); mutual; popular; prescriptive; present-day; prevailing; prolonged; public; realistic; reciprocal; regular; related; rife; rooted; routine; scurrile; scurrilous; second-rate; settled; shared; substandard; sweaty; tawdry; temporal; topical; traditional; trifling; trite; typical; undisguised; undivided; unenclosed; unfantastic; universal; unnoble; unrefined; unreserved; unspiritual; usual; vernacular; vulgar; COMMONNESS: base(ness); carnality; commonality; generality; indiscriminateness; informality; mutuality; peasantry; permanency; promiscuity; promiscuousness; temporality; typicality; vernacularity; vulgarity

COMMONER(S): bourgeois; hoi polloi; masses; multitude; plebeian; riffraff; roturier

COMMONPLACE: **a.** (**see** "common" and "dull") administrative; asinine; banal; boring; bourgeois; corny; crude; customary; cut-and-dried; daily; diurnal; domestic; down-to-earth; drab; dry; dull; earth(l)y; everyday; familiar; fatuous; flat; formal; functional; habitual; hackneyed; hoary; homely; household; humdrum; inane; incidental; insipid; intimate; jejune; lowclass; matter-of-fact; mechanical; mere; monotonous; natural; normal; old; ordinary; pedestrian; perfunctory; plain; platitudinal; platitudinous; plebeian; pompless; prevalent; prosaic(al); prosy; quotidian; ready-made; regular; rough; routine; rude; shopworn; silly; stale; stereotyped; stereotypical; stock;

tedious; threadbare; tired; tiresome; tiring; trifling; trite; trivial; twice-told; ugly; unadorned; unattractive; uneventful; unexceptional; unexcited; unexciting; unglamorous; unglorified; uniform; unimaginative; unimportant; uninteresting; unnoteworthy; unoriginal; unremarkable; unvarnished; usual; vapid; vulgar; wearisome; weary; workaday; well-worn; worn(-out); COMMONPLACE(NESS): **n.** asininity; banality; bathos; bromide; cliché; dailiness; domesticity; familiarity; formality; habituality; inanity; incidentalness; insipidity; intimacy; jejunity; mechanicality; monotony; peasantry; pedestrianism; perfunctoriness; platitude; platitudinism; prevalence; regularity; staleness; tediousness; tedium; triteness; triviality; truism; vapidity

COMMONWEALTH: commonweal; commune; community; people; public; republic; state; welfare

COMMOTION: ado; afflatus; agitation; babelism; bedlam; blast; blather; blazonry; boom; bother; bouleversement; brouhaha; bustle; buzz; clamor; clangor; clatter; coil; confusion; convulsion; craze; difficulty; din; disorder; display; disturbance; eddy; effort; engagement; excitement; exertion; fanfarade; fanfare; fanfaron(ade); ferment; flare; flourish; flurriment; flurry; fluster; flutter; frenzy; fret; furor(e); fury; fuss; gust; haste; hell; hoopla; hubble-bubble; hubbub; hue and cry; hullabaloo; hurlyburly; hurry; hustle; imbroglio; instigation; insurrection; madness; mania; noise; ostentation; pandemonium; paroxysm; perturbation; pother; racket; rage; rally; restlessness; riot; ruffle (and flourish); rush; shock; show; spasm; squall; stink; stir; storm; tantara; tantivy; tarantara; tear; tempest (in a teapot); to-do: trouble; tumult; turbulence; turmoil; uncertainty; unrest; upheaval; uproar; violence; war(fare); welter; whirl; work

COMMUNE: **v.** advise; argue; chat; communicate; confabulate; confer; consult; converse; debate; dilate; discourse; discuss; divulge; gossip; impart; parley; reveal; share; speak; talk; treat; COMMUNE: **n.** (**see** "area") commonalty; commons; commonwealth; communion; comunity; conversation; district; realm; town(ship); COMMUNION: accord(ance); antiphon; association; bond; church; coaction; coadjuvancy; collaboration; combination; commune; communication; concord(ance); concurrence; contact; cooperation; co-venture; creed; cult; dealings; Eucharist; exchange; faith; fellowship; friendship; harmony; host; impartment; integration; interchange; liaison; mass; meeting; mutualism; mutuality; negotiation; sacrament; sect; solidarity; symbiosis; synergism; synergy; talk; teamwork; togetherness; unanimity; union; unity; viaticum

COMMUNICATE: (**see** "announce") advise; call; confer; connect; consult; contact; converse; convey; debate; deliver; dial; disclose; discuss; disseminate; divulge; impart; join; meet; negativate; negotiate; open; parley; promulgate; publish; reach; reveal; say; send; share; speak; state; talk; telegram; tell; touch; transmit; treat; wire; write: COMMUNICATION: (**see** "communion") call; connection; contact; impartment; intelligence; letter; negotiaton; parley; meeting; talk; telegram; transmission; wire

COMMUNITY: (**see** "area") agreement; body (politic); city; commonweal; commonwealth; commune; communion; concord; congregation; district; environment; environs; family; fellowship; group; kinship; likeness; microcosm; milieu; municipality; participation; partnership; people(s); province; public; region; settlement; society; state; town(ship); village

COMMUTE: (**see** "change") alter; compensate; exchange; interchange; substitute; travel

COMPACT: **a.** (**see** "brief" and "firm") close(-knit); compendious; compressed; concentrated; concrete; condensed; conglomerate; consolidated; contracted; crammed; crowded; dense; filled; firm; full; grouped; hard; heavy; homogenous; intense; massed; packed; piled; pithy; populous; pressed; serried; snug; solid(ified); sound; stocky; strong; stuffed; succinct; tamped; terse; thick; tight; trig; COMPACT: **n.** adjustment; agreement; alliance; bargain; bond; cartel; case; compendium; compromise; confederation; consolidation; contract; covenant; league; pact; transaction; treaty; unit

COMPANION: (**see** "aide" and "assistant") abettor; accessory; accompaniment; accomplice; affiliate; ally; associate; associator; buddy; chaperone; chum; coadjutor; cohort; colleague; comate; compeer; comrade; concomitant; confederate; confrere; consociate; consort; counterpart; crony; deputy; escort; familiar; follower; friend; handmaid(en); helper; mate(y); pal; partner; peer; satellite;

socius; sport; spouse; subsidiary; supporter; traveler; twin; wife; COMPANIONABLE: **see** "agreeable;" COMPANIONSHIP: **see** "fellowship"

COMPANY: actors; aggregate; aggregation; army; assemblage; assembly; associate; association; band; bevy; body; bunch; caucus; circle; clique; cluster; cohorts; collection; companionship; conclave; congregation; convention; convocation; coterie; crew; crowd; ensemble; enterprise; firm; flock; following; gang; gathering; group; guest(s); herd; horde; legion; meeting; mob; multitude; party; people; posse; resort; retainers; retinue; set; society; soldiers; squad; suite; swarm; team; throng; troop; troupe; two; visitor(s)

COMPARE: analyze; assimilate; cf; clarify; collate; confer; contrast; determine; differ; discern; discriminate; dissect; distinguish; equate; estimate; evaluate; even; examine; explore; inquire; inspect; investigate; liken; mark; match; measure; observe; parallel; parse; probe; proofread; pry; relate; sift; test; try; vie; COMPARABLE: (**see** "similar") akin; alike; commensurate; compatible; concordant; congruent; correspondent; equipollent; equiponderant; equivalent; fitting; harmonious; homeopathic; homogeneous; homologous; like; noncontradictory; parallel; proper; proportionate; related; same; similar; suitable; synonymous; uniform; COMPARABILITY: commensurability; commensuration; compatibility; equiponderance; equivalence; homogeneity; proportionality; uniformity; COMPARISON: analogy; antithesis; collation; contrast; correspondence; equating; equivalence; homogeneity; likeness; likening; metaphor; model; parable; parallel(ism); pattern; proofreading; similarity; simile; similitude; simulacra (pl.); standard; COMPARATIVE: (**see** "comparable" above) analogic(al); analogous; approximate; collative; metaphorical; near; parallel; relative; similar

COMPARTMENT: apartment; area; bedroom; berth; bin; booth; box; cabinet; camera; case; cavern; cell(ule); chamber; concameration; container; crypt; cubicle; cubiculum; digs; division; flat; hall(way); hatch; loculus; part; pew; pigeonhole; receptacle; region; room; salon; section; space; stall; stateroom; subdivision; till; vault

COMPASS: **v.** (**see** "achieve") accomplish; attain; circumnavigate; circumscribe; comprehend; conclude; consummate; contain;

contrive; devise; embosom; embrace; encase; encircle; enclose; enfold; enlace; environ; frame; gain; gird(le); hedge; hem; hoop; immure; impale; obtain; plot; reach; skirt; surround; wreathe; zone; COMPASS: **n.** ambit; area; boundary; bounds; capacity; circuit; circumference; circumnavigation; circumscription; curve; degree; divider; division; environs; extent; field; gyro; horizon; limit; orbit; pitch; purview; range; scope; size; sphere; sweep; volume; wreath; zone

COMPASSION: (**see** "mercy") benevolence; charity; clemency; commiseration; conscience; feeling; grace; heart; humanity; kindness; leniency; lenity; pathos; pity; rue; ruth; sensibility; sympathy; tenderness; understanding; yearning; COMPASSIONATE: (**see** "merciful") benevolent; clement; human(e); kind(hearted); lenient; soft(hearted); sympathetic; tenderhearted; understanding

COMPATIBLE: (**see** "harmonious") accordant; agreeable; agreeing; comparable; concordant; congenial; congruent; consentaneous; consonant; fit(ting); homogenous; noncontradictory; proper; suitable; synonymous; uniform; COMPATIBILITY: (**see** "accord") comparability; congruity; consentaneousness; homogeneity; suitability; tolerance; uniformity

COMPEL: (**see** "coerce") actuate; cause; coact; command(eer); constrain; discipline; domineer; dragoon; drive; enforce; enjoin; exact; exert; force; hector; impel; make; move; necessitate; obligate; oblige; order; press; reduce; require; shanghai; shove; thrust; COMPELLING: (**see** "obligatory") coercive; cogent; convincing; demanding; dominative; domineering; driving; impelling; imperious; insistent; moving; potent; powerful; pressing; strong; telling; urgent

COMPEND(IUM): (**see** "brief") abbreviature; abridgement; abstract; aperçu; breviary; catalog(ue); compilation; condensation; digest; distillation; epitome; inventory; lexicon; outline; pandect; précis; sketch; summarization; summary; survey; syllabus; sylloge; synopsis

COMPENSATE: (**see** "balance") adjust; advance; agree; alleviate; amend; ante; atone; correct; counterbalance; counterpoise; countervail; defray; discharge; equal(ize); expend; hire; indemnify; jibe; liquidate; melt; neutralize; offset; pay; recom-

pense; recoup; redress; reimburse; relieve; remit; remunerate; rend; repay; requite; restore; return; reward; satisfy; settle; spend; square; tally; tip; treat; yield; COMPENSATION: (**see** "balance" and "payment") adjustment; advantage; alleviation; amending; balm; benefit; counterbalance; counterpoise; emolument; equalization; gain; hire; honorarium; indemnity; interest; neutralization; pay; perquisite; profit; recompense; remuneration; reprisal; requital; restitution; return; reward; salary; solatium; toll

COMPETE: (**see** "contend") compare; contest; cope; emulate; encounter; face; fight; force; grapple; match; oppose; pit; rival; run; seek; strive; struggle; vie; war; wrestle; COMPETITION: (**see** "contest") comparison; concourse; contention; contestation; dog-eat-dog; fight; game; heat; match; opposition; pace; race; rival(ry); run; strife; struggle; trial; war(fare); COMPETITOR: (**see** "antagonist") adversary; candidate; combatant; corival; enemy; entrant; foe; opponent; protagonist; rival

COMPETENT: able; accomplished; adept; adequate; advantageous; apposite; apt; artistic; attained; authoritative; businesslike; capable; capax; clever; consummate; desirable; dexterous; drilled; educated; effective; effectual; efficacious; efficient; eligible; endowed; enough; entitled; expedient; expeditious; expert; facultative; familiar; finished; fit(ted); good; handy; ingenious; instructed; intelligent; knowing; knowledgeable; licensed; meet; old(er); operant; panurgic; perfect(ed); potent; powerful; practical; practiced; professional; proficient; proper; puissant; purposeful; qualified; ready; resourceful; rightful; salable; salty; sane; satisfactory; satisfying; seasoned; skilled; skillful; smart; sophisticated; strong; successful; sufficient; suitable; systematic; talented; taught; tested; trained; tried; versant; versatile; versed; veteran; weighed; well-handled; wise; worthy; COMPETENCE *or* COMPETENCY: ability; accomplishment; acumen; adeptness; adequacy; admissibility; adroitness; ambidexterity; amplitude; aptitude; aptness; artistry; astucity; astuteness; attainment; authority; background; brains; caliber; capability; capableness; capacity; career; character; consummation; culture; degree; demonstration; dexterity; diameter; discernment; discipline; disposition; economy; education; effectiveness; effectivity; effectuality; efficacy; efficiency; eligibility; endowment; expedition; experience; expertise;

expertness; facility; faculty; familiarity; finesse; finish; fitness; flair; force; function; genius; gift; grasp; handiness; ingeniosity; ingenuity; instinct; intellect; intelligence; knack; knowledge; latitude; leadership; legitimacy; license; magnitude; mastery; means; measure; might; perfection; performance; permit; perspicacity; potency; potentiality; power; practice; prerogative; property; qualification; quality; reason; resourcefulness; resources; right; sense; size; skill(fulness); smartness; sophistication; space; stature; strength; success; sufficiency; suitability; talent; training; turn; validity; versatility; vigor; virtuosity; volume; use(fulness); width; will; wisdom; wit; worthiness

COMPILE: (see "arrange") assemble; collect; compose; edit; enumerate; list; pile; prepare; select; write; COMPILATION: (see "arrangement") accretion; ana; anthology; book; code; collection; digest; document; enumeration; list; selection(s); writing

COMPLACENT: (see "smug") calm; deferential; phlegmatic; placid; pliant; yielding

COMPLAIN: (see "argue") accuse; allege; appeal; aver; beef; bellyache; bemoan; bewail; carp; cavil; charge; claim; creak; croak; cry; demur; deplore; disapprove; dissent; expostulate; fret; fuss; gnar; grieve; gripe; groan; grouse; growl; grumble; grunt; howl; inveigh; keen; kick; lament; moan; mourn; mumble; murmur; mutter; object; oppose; oppugn; protest; question; quibble; rail; rebel; regret; remonstrate; repine; resent; resist; rumble; snarl; squall; squawk; squeal; strike; wail; whimper; whine; yammer; yell; yowl; COMPLAINT: (see "charge") accusation; ailment; allegation; argument; beef; censure; clamor; cri de coeur; cry; declaration; demur; deprecation disapproval; disease; disorder; dissent; expostulation; fuss; grievance; gripe; grouch; growl; grumble; grumbling; howl; jeremiad; keen; kick; lament(ation); murmur; mutter(ing); objection; opposition; protest(ation); quarrel; querimony; querulity; quibble; rebellion; remonstrance; remonstration; resentment; shout; simper; snivel; sob; squawk; squawl; squeal; strike; tirade; wail; weep; whimper; whine; yammer; yell

COMPLAISANT: (see "kind") affable; amiable; amicable; civil; compliant; courteous; eager; gracious; lenient; obliging; pleasing; pliable; pliant; polite; politic(al); ready; smooth; suave; supple; suppliant; willing; yielding

COMPLETE: v. (see "accomplish") achieve; attain; climax; close; conclude; consummate; crown; do; end; execute; exhaust; finalize; finish; fulfill; make; negotiate; perfect; perform; realize; sign; terminate; COMPLETE(D): a. absolute; accomplished; all; altogether; choate; clean; close; concluded; consummate(d); consummative; dead(ly); deep-dyed; developed; done; educated; ended; entire; established; exact; extensive; fair; finalized; finished; fulfilled; full(-dress); full-scale; graduated; gross; implemented; intact; integral; livelong; mature; out-and-out; perfect(ed); plenary; proficient; profound; pukka; pure; rank; realized; regular; replete; ripe; round; saturated; saturative; sole; sound; stark; strict; sweeping; taught; terminated; thorough; total; trained; true; unabridged; unbroken; undamaged; unexpurgated; unharmed; unimpaired; uninjured; unmitigated; unqualified; untouched; uninvioated; utter; whole; wide; COMPLETION or COMPLETENESS: (see "accomplishment") actuality; actualization; closure; completement; consummation; development; entireness; entirety; exhaustion; fait accompli; finality; finish; fulfillment; negotiation; perfection; realization; termination; utterness

COMPLEX: a. abstract; abstruse; acroamatic; chaotic; complicate(d); composite; confused; conglomerate; convoluted; daedal(ian); daedalic; dark; deep; difficult; disordered; entangled; esoteric; Gordian; hard; hermetic(al); heterogeneous; hidden; hodgepodge; hydra-headed; inaccurate; incondite; incorporeal; inexplicable; intricable; intricate; involute(d); involved; knotty; labyrinthian; labyrinthine; manifold; mazy; metaphorical; mingled; mixed; multiform; mystic(al); nebulous; obscure; plexiform; profound; puzzling; rarefied; recondite; remote; sinuous; sophisticated; speculative; subtle; supernatural; tangled; theoretical; transcendental; twisted; COMPLEX(ITY): n. (see "difficulty") abstractum; abstruseness; abstrusity; aggregate; area; attitude; combination; complex(ed)ness; complexus; complicacy; composite(ness); compound; confusion; conglomeration; entanglement; fantasia; group; intricateness; intricacy; involution; involvement; jumble; knot; labyrinth; maelstrom; maze; medley; mixture; network; node; nodus; plexus; plot; puzzle; sinuosity; snag; snare; snarl; system; tangle; technicality; twist; web

COMPLEXION: (see "color") appearance; aspect; blee; cast; disposition; hue; humor;

impression; look; mood; shade; state; temper-(ament); tenor; tinge; tint; vein

COMPLIANT: **see** after "comply"

COMPLICATE: (**see** "confuse") complexify; compound; embarrass; entangle; increase; intort; involve; knot; perplex; snarl; tangle; twist; COMPLICATED: (**see** "complex") abstruse; complicate; dark; deep; difficult; disordered; Gordian; hard; incomprehensible; inextricable; involved; knotty; messy; prolix; recondite; tangled; technical; COMPLICATION: (**see** "complexity") circumstance; complexus; confusion; conjuncture; difficulty; entanglement; intricacy; involution; involvement; maelstrom; maze; node; nodus; plot; sinuosity; snag; snare; snarl; technicality; thing; twist

COMPLIMENT: **v.** (**see** "praise") adulate; commend(ate); congratulate; eulogize; extol; felicitate; flatter; laud; macarize; panegyrize; sympathize; COMPLIMENT: **n.** (**see** "praise") adulation; bouquet; commendation; congratulation; encomium; eulogy; felicitation; flattery; laudation; panegyric; recognition; respect; trade-last; tribute

COMPLY: accede; accept; acknowledge; acquiesce; act; adapt; adhere; admit; adopt; agree; allow; answer; approve; assent; attend; coincide; concur; condescend; conform; defer; do; endorse; endure; espouse; follow; hear; heed; honor; meet; mind; obey; observe; perform; respect; respond; satisfy; serve; submit; surrender; toe (in); undertake; welcome; worship; yield; COMPLIANT: accommodating; acquiescent; amenable; assentatious; assiduous; complaisant; cooperative; disposed; docile; ductile; educa(ta)ble; facile; influenceable; malleable; obsequious; pliable; pliant; ready; sequacious; servile; submissive; subservient; tractable; trainable; yielding; COMPLIANCE: abidance; acceptance; acceptation; acquiescence; admission; approval; assent; assiduity; attention; cession; compliancy; concession; concord; condescendence; condescension; conformation; conformity; continuance; continuation; cooperation; facility; harmony; obsequence; obsequience; obsequity; observance; plasticity; pliancy; sequacity; yielding

COMPONENT(S): aspect; circumstance; constituency; constituent; detail; element; essence; factor; factum; feature; form(at); fraction; gene; germ; hardware; incident; influence; ingredient; integral; integrant;

item; link; makeup; material(s); matter; member; metal; moiety; number; occurrence; part; pattern; phase; piece; principle; property; section; segment; situation; structure; substance; substitute; unit; woof

COMPORT: accord; acquit; act (up); agree; bare; behave; brook; carry; conduct; conform; demean; deport; direct; function; govern; guide; handle; harmonize; hold; jibe; lead; manage; manipulate; negotiate; operate; oversee; pilot; quit; regulate; render; run; square; steer; suit; supervise; tally; test; walk; COMPORTMENT: **see** "behavior"

COMPOSE: (**see** "calm") adjust; arrange; collect; compile; constitute; construct; create; design; dispose; draft; fashion; form(ulate); frame; harmonize; integrate; make; methodize; prepare; produce; redact; repose; set(tle); smooth; tranquilize; write; COMPOSED: (**see** "calm") adjusted; arranged; collected; compiled; constituted; constructed; created; designed; disposed; drafted; fashioned; formulated; framed; integrated; made; methodized; prepared; produced; settled; tranquilized; COMPOSURE: (**see** "calmness") adjustment; aplomb; composedness; composition; countenance; equability; equanimity; harmony; mien; phlegm; placidity; poise; posture; quiet(ude); repose; *sangfroid*; *savoir faire*; self-possession; serenity; sobriety; stability; stillness; temper(ament); temperance; tranquility

COMPOSITION: (**see** "makeup") adjustment; aggregate; agreement; arrangement; arrayment; article; character; chemistry; combination; compensation; compound; compromise; constituency; constituent(s); constitution; construction; essay; etude; fantasia; feature; form(ation); formulation; ingredients; invention; mixture; monopoly; music; nature; opus; organization; pattern; personality; picture; piece; rondo; satisfaction; settlement; setup; shape; sonata; structure; suite; symphony; synthesis; temperament; theme; writing

COMPOSURE: **see** under "compose"

COMPOUND: **v.** (**see** "create") add; adjust; augment; blend; combine; complicate; compose; comprise; conglomerate; form(ulate); join; make; mingle; mix; settle; unite; COMPOUND: **a.** (**see** "complex") complicate(d); composite; conglomerate; hodgepodge; COMPOUND: **n.** area; blend;

chemical; complex; composite; composition; compositum; enclosure; fantasia; formulation; hodgepodge; jumble; medicine; medley; mixture; olio; settlement; substance; union

COMPREHEND: (see "apprehend") anticipate; ascertain; comprise; conceive; constitute; construe; contain; cover; dig; discern; distinguish; embody; embosom; embrace; enclose; encompass; enfold; envelop(e); enwrap; experience; fathom; feel; foresee; foreshadow; gain; get; grab; grasp; hold; imagine; imply; include; incorporate; interpret; intuit; involve; know; learn; note; notice; observe; perceive; pierce; realize; recognize; savvy; see; seize; sense; subsume; swallow; take (in); think; understand; COMPREHENSION: (see "discernment") anticipation; apprehension; ascertainment; cognition; comprehensiveness; connotation; fathom; feeling; gain; grasp; inclusion; interpretation; intuition; involvement; ken; knowledge; largeness; noesis; notice; observation; penetration; perception; perspicacity; profundity; realization; reason-(ing); recognition; scope; sense; understanding; width; COMPREHENSIVE: (see "universal") all-around; all-inclusive; catholic; circumspective; connotated; consolidated; detailed; ecumenical; embodying; embracing; embracive; encircling; enclosing; encompassing; encyclopedic(al); far-reaching; grand; including; inclusive; incorporated; intensive; synoptic; transcendental; unexcluding; unexclusive; wide(-ranging); widespread; wide-spreading; COMPREHENSIBLE: (see "plain") discernible; embraceable; gatherable; gaugeable; inferable; interpretable; learnable; measurable; perceivable; teachable; understandable

COMPRESS: v. (see "abreviate") abridge; bandage; bind; choke; cling; close; concentrate; condense; constrict; constringe; contract; crowd; curtail; deflate; digest; firm; hug; pack; pinch; press; reduce; repress; restrain; shrink; squash; squeeze; strain; strangle; strangulate; tamp; tie; wrap; COMPRESS: n. bandage; gauze; pledget; stupe; wrap(ping); COMPRESSED: (see "abbreviated" and "succinct") choked; close(d); compact; concentrated; condensed; consolidated; contracted; dense; hard; packed; pressed; solid; squashed; squeezed; terse; tight

COMPRISE: (see "comprehend") compose; consist; constitute; contain; cover; embody; embrace; enclose; encompass; hold; include; involve; seize; take (in)

COMPROMISE: v. (see "arrange" and "settle") adjust; arbitrate; average; chagrin; compound; contain; embarrass; embrace; endanger; expose; hold; humiliate; inhere; jeopardize; lie; reside; shame; COMPROMISE: n. (see "arrangement" and "settlement") abatement; adjustment; arbitration; average; chagrin; commitment; committal; concession; conciliation; embarrassment; humiliation; jeopardy; medium; surrender; understanding

COMPULSORY: (see "imperative") corecive; involuntary; necessary; needed; needful; COMPULSION: (see "coercion") command; constraint; duress; force; impulse; impulsion; necessity; need; obligation; power; pressure; requirement; restraint; stranglehold; stress; stringency; urgency; violence

COMPUNCTION: (see "regret") anxiety; compassion; conscience; demur; grief; lamentation; longing; misgiving; penitence; pity; qualm; reluctance; remorse; scruple; sorrow; unease; uneasiness; woe; worry; COMPUNCTIOUS: (see "regretful") anxious; compassionate; grievous; lamentable; penitent(ial); qualmish; regretful; reluctant; remorseful; sorry; uneasy; woeful

COMPUTE: (see "calculate") add; appraise; ascertain; asses; average; capitalize; cast; count; deduce; determine; estimate; evaluate; figure; frame; gauge; guess; infer; interpret; judge; justify; rate; reckon; score; settle; solve; sum; tally; total; COMPUTATION: see "reckoning"

COMRADE: (see "friend") ally; *alter ego*; associate; *bon camarade*; buddy; chum; colleague; companion; compeer; confrere; crony; fellow; frater; mate(y); pal; peer; COMRADESHIP: (see "fellowship") association; camaraderie; companionship; comradeliness; comradery; esprit (de corps); friendliness; friendship

CONCATENATE: (see "connect") chain; join; link; unite; CONCATENATION: (see "connection") chain; linkage; series; union

CONCAVE: arched; curved; depressed; dipped; dished; hollow(ed); vaulted; void; CONCAVITY: bowl; crater; curve; dent; depression; dip; dish; hole; hollow; pit; vault

CONCEAL: (see "cover") avoid; bury; cache;

camouflage; cloak; closet; couch; disguise; dissemble; eclipse; ensconce; hide; hood; huddle; inter; mantle; mask; muffle; mute; obscure; palm; plant; protect; robe; screen; seal; secrete; sequester; sheathe; shield; shroud; sink; skulk; soft-pedal; stifle; submerge; vanish; veil; withdraw; withhold; wrap; CONCEALED: (see "covered") abey; ant; backstage; buried; cached; clandestine; cloaked; covert; delitescent; dormant; hidden; inner; kinetic; larvate(d); latent; mantled; masked; mysterious; planted; potential; quiescent; robed; screened; secreted; shielded; shrouded; soft-pedaled; submerged; sunk; surreptitious; varnished; veiled; withdrawn; withheld; wrapped; CONCEALMENT: (see "cover") clandestinity; covering; cover-up; delitescence; disguise; dissimulation; dormancy; eclipse; hiding; obscuration; occultation; screening; secrecy; secreting; submerging; surreption; withdrawal

CONCEDE: acknowledge; acquiesce; admit; agree; allow; assent; begrudge; capitulate; cede; give; grant; octroy; own (up); permit; surrender; waive; yield; CONCEDED: see "undeniable;" CONCESSION: see "admission"

CONCEIT: admiration; amour-propre; assurance; boastfulness; caprice; concept(ion); ego(centricity); egocentrism; egomania; ego(t)ism; esteem; fancy; flatulence; folly; haughtiness; hauteur; idea; mauvaise honte; narcissism; outrecuidance; pomposity; presumption; pride; self-centeredness; self-esteem; self-importance; selfishness; self-love; solipsism; thought; vagary; vanity; whim; CONCEITED: arrogant; assured; bumptious; dogmatic(al); egomaniac(al); ego-(t)istic(al); haughty; hubristic; opinionated; overweening; pragmatic; presumptive; presumptuous; priggish; self-centered; self-esteemed; self-important; selfish; vain-(glorious)

CONCEIVE: aim; anticipate; apprehend; ascertain; aspire; beget; begin; believe; calculate; chart; comprehend; concoct; consign; contemplate; contrive; couch; create; delineate; design(ate); destine; determine; devise; devote; diagram; discern; distinguish; draft; draw; dream; end; etch; experience; fabricate; fancy; fashion; feel; figure; foresee; foreshadow; form(ulate); frame; gather; grasp; guess; hold; ideate; imagine; include; infer; intend; interpret; intuit; invent; know; learn; long; make; meditate; note; observe; originate; perceive;

phrase; plan; plot; ponder; produce; project; propose; realize; recognize; regard; savvy; scheme; see; sense; sketch; start; study; suppose; swallow; think; understand; visualize; ween; CONCEPT(ION): see below

CONCENTRATE: v. (see "condense") abstract; agglutinate; aim; alembicate; assemble; center; centralize; collect; conglomerate; consolidate; contract; converge; distil; epitomize; exalt; extract; fix; focalize; focus; gather; heap; infuse; intensify; mass; nucleate; pile; polarize; purify; reduce; refine; thicken; trickle; unify; unite; vaporize; CONCENTRATE: n. see "essence" CONCENTRATED: (see "thick") brief; close; concise; hardened; intense; intensive; intent; massed; nucleated; pointed; punctual; refined; searching; strong; undiluted; whole; CONCENTRATION: (see "capsule") agglutination; centering; centralization; cogitation; concentrate; condensation; conglomeration; convergence; density; distillate; distillation; essence; focalization; focus; grouping; increase; inspissation; intensification; mass; meditation; memory; polarization; quintessence; raptness; refinedness; refinement; saturation; strength; thickness; thought; unification

CONCEPT(ION): (see "belief") abstraction; aim; apprehension; ascertainment; assumption; category; comprehension; conceit; construction; contrivance; conviction; design; device; dream; fancy; feeling; framework; grasp; guess; hypothesis; idea(tion); image; imagination; inference; invention; knowledge; learning; notation; notion; observance; observation; perception; philosophy; plan; plot; postulate; postulation; presupposition; principle; prochronism; prolepsis; proposition; realization; recognition; regard; rubric; schematics; scheme; sense; supposition; system; tenet; theory; thought; understanding; universal; view; vision; visualization

CONCERN: v. affect; allude; apply; bear (on); bother; care; distress; disturb; engage; engross; hold; implicate; import; interest; involve; matter; obligate; occupy; pertain; refer; relate; touch; trouble; CONCERN-(MENT): n. affair; altruism; anxiety; apprehension; bother; business; care; caution; company; consequence; consideration; contraption; contrivance; conviction; corporation; distress; engagement; event; factory; fear; firm; gadget; grief; heart; import(ance); institution; interest; matter; moment; occupation; office; preoccupation; proposition; regard; relation; shop; solicitude; thoughtfulness; trouble; uncertainty; uneasiness; worry; CONCERNED: affected; apprehensive; anxious; bothered; careful; conscious; distressed; disturbed; engaged; engrossed; held; implicated; intense; interested; involved; moved; obligated; occupied; rapt; regardful; solicitous; solicitudinous; thoughtful; touched; troubled; uneasy; versant; worried

CONCERT: (**see** "accord") agreement; concord(ance); entertainment; harmony; music; mutuality; orchestration; performance; plan; reciprocity; recital; togetherness; unanimity; union

CONCESSION: acknowledgment; admission; allowance; appeasement; approval; assent; award; boon; capitulation; condescendence; condescension; endorsement; franchise; grant; handshake; indulgence; medal; monopoly; pledge; promise; recognition; reconciliation; reduction; reward; right; sanction; stoop; support; yielding

CONCILIATE: (**see** "calm") adjust; appease; atone; ease; mollify; pacify; placate; propitiate; reconcile; satisfy; tame; tranquilize; win(over); CONCILIATORY: (**see** "calm") alleviative; alleviatory; conciliative; cooperative; diplomatic; forgiving; gentle; harmonious; lenient; lenitive; mild; mollifying; namby-pamby; pacific(atory); palliative; persuasive; placative; placatory; politic(al); propitiating; propitiatory; suave; winning; CONCILIATION: (**see** "calmness") adjustment; appeasement; atonement; cooperation; goodwill: harmony; mediation; mitigation; mollification; pacification; persuasion; propitiation; reconciliation; satisfaction; settlement; symmetry; tranquilization

CONCISE: (**see** "brief") aphoristic; brusque; compact; compendious; comprehensive; condensed; crisp; cryptic(al); curt(ailed); cute; distilled; economical; elliptic(al); epigrammatical; hard; in a nutshell; laconical; pithy; pointed; precise; pregnant; pressed; sententious; short(ened); succinct; summary; Tacitean; telegrammatic; telegraphic; telescoped; terse; trenchant; truncated; CONCISENESS: (**see** "brevity") aphorism; brusquerie; compactness; comprehensiveness; condensation; crispness; distillation; economy; laconism; pith(iness); precision; succinctness; terseness; trenchancy

CONCLUDE: (**see** "close") bind; complete; confine; consider; constrain; decide; deduce; effect; enclose; end; estimate; eventuate; figure; finalize; finish; gather; graduate; guess; infer; judge; oblige; reach; reason; reckon; resolve; rest; settle; speculate; terminate; CONCLUSION: adjournment; block; cessation; close; closure; coda; commencement; completion; confinement; consequence; consequent; constraint; consummation; death; debarring; decision; deduction; denial; desistence; determination; diminishment; disappearance; discontinuance; disposal; drop(ping); education; end; envoi; epilogue; estoppal; exclusion; expiration; extremity; finale; finality; finalization; finding; finishing; folding; followthrough; fruition; graduation; halt; illation; inference; judgment; last; leaving; liquidation; locking; observation; obstruction; obturation; occlusion; opinion; oppilation; outcome; pause; period; prohibition; proof positive; quittance; realization; rear; refusal; remark; resolution; resolve; result; sealing; settlement; shutting; sticking; stitching; stopping; summary; summation; suspension; tail; termination; upshot; view; withdrawal; wrap-up; yielding; CONCLUSIVE: authoritative; certain; cogent; consummative; consummatory; convincing; decisive; decreed; definitive; determinate; documented; enacted; ensconced; established; evident; final; fixed; illative; inaugurated; instituted; inveterate; irrefutable; last; ordained; proved; set(tled); substantiated; sure; telling; terminal; ultimate; unanswerable; unequivocal

CONCOCT: (**see** "arrange") brew; compose; confect; contrive; cook; develop; devise; fabricate; fake; falsify; frame; hatch; invent; lie; make; mix; plan; plot; prepare; process; toss; vamp

CONCORD: (**see** "agreement") accord; amity; compact; concordance; congeniality; consonance; covenant; harmony; pact; peace; rapport; rapprochement; simultaneity; stipulation; synchroneity; terms; treaty; unanimity; unity; CONCORDANT: (**see** "agreeable") agreeing; congruent; consonant; correspondent; corresponding; harmonious; irenic; peaceful; synchronous; unanimous; unisonal; unisonant; unisonous

CONCRETE: actual; compact; compressed; definite; definitive; dense; enduring; established; exact; factual; firm; fixed; hard(ened); immovable; impregnable; inflexible;

iron; material; particular; physical; positive; practical; real; resolute; rigid; solid(ified); sound; specific; tangible; tenacious; united; unswerving; unwavering; usable; well-founded; workable

CONCUR: (see "agree") accord; acquiesce; approve; assent; certify; chime; coincide; combine; conjoin; consent; cooperate; endorse; harmonize; jibe; join; meet; symbolize; synchronize; unite; CONCURRENCE: (see "agreement") accordance; acquiescence; adherence; approval; assent; coincidence; coinstantaneity; combination; concomitance; concourse; conjunction; consent(ation); contemporaneity; contract; cooperation; endorsement; harmony; junction; simultaneity; synchroneity; synchronization; syndrome; unanimity; union; CONCURRENT: (see "contemporary") associated; coeval; coexistent; coincident(al); coinstantaneous; contemporaneous; contemporary; converging; equal; intersecting; joint; meeting; simultaneous; synchronous; unanimous; united

CONCUSS: (see "shake") agitate; clash; coerce; force; jar; jolt; shock; vibrate

CONDEMN: (see "censure") anathematize; ban; blame; confiscate; convict; curse; damn; decry; denounce; disapprove; doom; hiss; judge; reprove; sentence; CONDEMNED: see "doomed;" CONDEMNATION: (see "censure") anathema; conviction; damnation; denunciation; disapproval; doom; obloquy; odium; scorn; wrath

CONDENSE: (see "concentrate") abbreviate; abridge; boil (down); coalesce; combine; compact; compile; compress; consolidate; contract; cram; cut; decoct; deflate; deposit; desiccate; distil; encapsulate; epitomize; harden; inspissate; liquefy; merge; outline; pack; precipitate; reduce; shorten; shrink; solidify; summarize; synopsize; tabulate; telescope; thicken; truncate; CONDENSED: (see "brief" and "concise") concentrated; inspissated; thick; CONDENSATION: (see "capsule") abbreviation; abridgement; compactness; compilation; compression; concentrate; concentration; conciseness; contraction; deposit; epitome; essence; precipitation; rarefaction; shortening; synopsis

CONDESCEND: acquiesce; bend; bow; cater; concede; consent; defer; deign; grant; favor; honor; humble; humiliate; humor; kneel; kowtow; lower; oblige; pander;

patronize; purvey; salute; serve; stoop; supply; unbend; vouchsafe; yield; CONDESCENDING: acquiescent; deferent; haughty; humble; humiliative; obliging; patronizing; supercilious; yielding

CONDIGN: (see "deserved") adequate; ample; appropriate; commensurate; due; earned; enough; equal; equivalent; exemplary; fair; fit(ting); just(ifiable); justified; meet; merited; proper; qualified; right(ful); rigorous; satisfactory; severe; sufficient; suitable; suited; warranted; worthy

CONDITION: v. (see "prepare") adapt; agree; contract; control; covenant; diet; discipline; drill; educate; equip; fatten; fix; instruct; mend; modify; persuade; process; ready; repair; restore; stipulate; teach; train; trim; CONDITION(S): n. accident-(ality); agreement; angle; article; atmosphere; birth; case; casualty; cause; chance; circumstance(s); circumstantiality; circumstantialness; class; clause; contingency; contract; environment; estate; event(uality); facet; feather; fine print; fortuitousness; fortuity; ground(s); if; juncture; mode; mood; nature; niche; obstacle; paragraph; particular(s); passage; peril; phase; place; plank; plight; point; predicament; prerequisite; provision(s); proviso; rank; repute; requisite; reservation; risk; section; segment; sentence; spirit; stage; state; station; status; stipulation; strings; temper(ament); temperature; tentativeness; term(s); (in) trim; CONDITIONAL: (see "contingent") circumstantial; dependent; iffy; limitative; maybe; perhaps; provisional; provisory; reserved; supposed; supposi(ti)tious; tentative; uncertain; CONDITIONALITY: (see "condition(s)") tentativeness

CONDOLE: commiserate; grieve; lament; pity; sorrow; sympathize; CONDOLENCE: (see "pity") commiseration; compassion; empathy; grief; regret(s); rue; ruth; sorrow; sympathy

CONDONE: (see "acquit") abet; absolve; assist; chaperone; countenance; disregard; encourage; favor; forget; forgive; help; ignore; justify; overlook; pardon; remit; sanction; wink

CONDUCT: v. acquit; act (up); administer; bear; begin; behave; chair; chaperone; comport; conform; convey; convoy; deduce; demean; deport; direct; escort; execute; function; govern; guard; guide; hand(le);

lead; manage; manipulate; negotiate; operate; ordain; oversee; pilot; quit; regulate; render; run; safeguard; shepherd; show; squire; steer; supervise; take; transmit; treat; usher; walk; work; CONDUCT: **n.** (see "behavior") acquittal; act(ion); administration; air(s); attitude; bearing; convoy; deed; demeanor; deport(ment); direction; government; guidance; habit; management; manipulation; manner; mien; operation; praxis; regulation; rendition; supervision; treatment; walk; CONDUCTOR: boss; chairman; chaperone; cicerone; conveyor; director; escort; executor; governor; guard; guide; handler; helmsman; leader; maestro; manager; mediator; negotiator; overseer; pastor; pilot; propagator; scout; shepherd; squire; steersman; supervisor; usher

CONDUIT: (see "channel") aqueduct; cable; canal; chute; course; ditch; drain; duct; gully; gut(ter); main; means; medium; opening; passage(way); pipe(line); race; river; route; sewer; sinus; trough; tube; wire

CONFECTION: bonbon; *bonne bouche*; cake; candy; caramel; cate; cimbal; comfit; cream; delicacy; fondant; kiss(es); mixture; nougat; praline; preparation; preserve; sweetmeat; sweets; tidbit

CONFEDERATE: **v.** (see "combine") ally; band; federate; join; league; unionize; unite; CONFEDERATE: **n.** (see "associate") abettor; ally; conspirator; CONFEDERATION: (see "alliance") band; compact; federation; league; union

CONFER: advise; apply; ask; award; bestow; collogue; compare; conclave; confabulate; consider; consult; converse; counsel; deliberate; discourse; discuss; donate; endow; federate; gather; give; grant; group; huddle; meet (with); parley; powwow; present; seek; talk; treat; yield; CONFERENCE: assembly; association; board; body; cabal; cabinet; caucus; chat; circuit; colloquium; colloquy; concilium; conclave; confabulation; congress; consideration; consistory; consultation; conversation; council; debate; deliberation; dialogue; diet; discourse; discussion; federation; gathering; group; huddle; interview; junto; league; meeting; ministry; palaver; parley; powwow; quorum; Sanhedrin; seminar; senate; symposium; synod; talk

CONFESS: (see "admit") accept; acknowledge; affirm; assent; attest; avow; certify; concede; confide; declare; disclose; divulge; grant; impart; manifest; own; profess;

recognize; relieve (oneself); reveal; shrive; tell; testify; trust; unburden; yield; CONFESSION: (see "admission") acknowledgment; affirmation; assent; attestation; avowal; communion; concession; confidence; creed; declaration; disclosure; divulgence; peccavi; profession; revelation; statement; testimony

CONFIDE: (see "admit") assure; bank; believe; commit; confess; consign; count (on); depend; entrust; impart; lean; reckon; rely; share; tell; trust; CONFIDENCE: (see "assurance") aplomb; assuredness; belief; boldness; certainty; certitude; courage; credence; credit; discretion; eagerness; faith; forwardness; hope; impudence; mettle; positivism; presumption; reliance; secrecy; self-assurance; spirit; spunk; stock; surety; trust(fulness); vote; CONFIDENT: assured; bold; brave; certain; commanding; confidential; courageous; dogmatic; eager; expert; forward; hopeful; peremptory; positive; presumptuous; ready; reliant; sanguine; self-assured; self-confident; skilled; sure; trustful undoubtful; unmisgiving; CONFIDENTIAL: (see "discreet") classified; covert; *entre nous*; esoteric; familiar; hidden; hushed; hush-hush; intimate; man-to-man; private; privy; secret; *sub rosa*; top-drawer; top-secret; trustful; trustworthy

CONFIGURATION: see "outline"

CONFINE: **v.** (see "bound") astrict; bind; border; bottle; box; cage; check; circumscribe; coarct; constrict; contain; coop; corner; cramp; crate; crib; curb; dam; demarcate; encase; enclose; encompass; exclude; fasten; fence; fetter; ghettoize; guard; handcuff; hedge; hem; hole; house; immure; impale; impound; imprison; incarcerate; include; intern; jail; latch; limit; lock; narrow; pen; pin; prevent; reduce; restrain; restrict; rope; seclude; secure; segregate; separate; shut; stint; straiten; surround; tether; tie; trammel; trap; wall; CONFINE(S): **n.** (see "boundary") milieu; neighborhood; precinct; purlieu; scope; territory; CONFINED: (see "bound" and "restrained") caged; captive; captured; chained; held; immured; penned; restricted; segregated; shut; trapped; unreleased

CONFIRM: acknowledge; affirm; approve; assent; assert; assure; attest; authenticate; authorize; aver; avouch; consign; consolidate; coronate; corroborate; crown; delegate; deputize; endorse; establish; evince; fix; fortify; franchise; grant; guarantee;

initiate; justify; legalize; legislate; license; maintain; notarize; ordain; patent; permit; prove; ratify; sanction; seal; second; settle; stamp; strengthen; substantiate; support; sustain; tell; thicken; underwrite; validate; verify; vindicate; warrant; CONFIRMED: (see "chronic") affirmed; authenticated; authorized; avouched; corroborated; countersigned; crowned; deputized; endowed; established; evinced; franchized; granted; guaranteed; habitual; hard-bitten; hardshell; indomitable; initiated; invested; inveterate; justified; legalized; legislated; licensed; notarized; ordained; ordered; proved; proven; ratified; sanctioned; sealed; set; substantiated; sustained; unyielding; validated; verified; veteran; vindicated; CONFIRMATION: acknowledgment; affirmance; affirmation; authentication; authorization; coronation; corroboration; guarantee; inauguration; initiation; investiture; ordination; proof; ratification; sanction; stamp; substantiation; truth; validation verification; CONFIRMATORY: see "corroborative"

CONFISCATE: (see "usurp") appropriate; commandeer; forfeit; grab; grasp; seize; sequester; take

CONFLICT: v. (see "clash") bump; collide; differ; disagree; dispute; encroach; impact; impinge; knock; oppose; strike; touch; CONFLICT: n. abrasion; action; anger; antagonism; battle; bout; bump; clash; collision; combat; competition; confliction; contention; contest; crosscurrent; difference; disagreement; discord; disharmony; disputation; dispute; dissention; duel; encroachment; engagement; feud; fight; fray; friction; impact; impingement; indecision; interference; knock; opposition; recklessness; resistance; riot; rub; ruction; strife; strike; struggle; uncertainty; unfriendliness; war-(fare); wrangling; CONFLICTING: (see "antagonistic") abhorrent; antithetical; contending; incompatible; incongruous; inconsistent; inharmonious; irreconcilable; resistent; uncertain; unreconcilable; warring

CONFORM: (see "adapt") bend; bow; cater; coincide; comply; concede; condescend; consent; conventionalize; defer; favor; fit; goose-step; harmonize; hew; humble; humiliate; keep; kneel; kowtow; naturalize; oblige; patronize; regularize; regulate; solicit; square; stoop; stylize; unbend; yield; CONFORMABLE: (see "accepted" and "adaptable") compliant; conventional; correspondent; deferent(ial); ethical; favorable;

harmonious; regular; regulated; submissive; CONFIRMATION: see "accord"

CONFOUND: (see "confuse") abash; addle; amaze; astonish; babelize; baffle; befuddle; bemuse; bewilder; complicate; compound; confuse; corrupt; damn; dash; discomfit; disconcert; dismay; embarrass; faze; flummox; fluster; frustrate; fuddle; mingle; overthrow; perplex; petrify; phase; puzzle; rattle; spoil; stun; stupefy

CONFRONT: (see "face") accost; affront; brave; breast; challenge; compare; dare; defy; encounter; meet; oppose; oppress; resist; stand; threaten

CONFUSE: (see "confound") abash; addle; amaze; astonish; babelize; baffle; bedim; befog; befuddle; bemuse; bewilder; blend; blur; chagrin; complexify; complicate; compound; corrupt; darken; dash; derange; dim; disarrange; discomfit; disconcert; dismay; disorient; distract; disturb; embarrass; embrangle; embroil; entangle; faze; floor; flummox; fluster; flutter; fog; giddify; hoax; intort; involve; knot; jumble; mask; mingle; mix(up); muddle; mysticize; mystify; nonplus; obfuscate; obscure; perplex; perturb; petrify; puzzle; rattle; riddle; snarl; stagger; stick; stop; stump; stun; stupefy; tangle; twist; upset; CONFUSED or CONFUSING: addlebrained; addled; addlepated; anarchic(al); asea; baffled; baffling; befuddled; bemused; bewildered; bewitched; blurred; chagrined; chaotic; cluttered; cockeyed; confounded; confounding; crazy; dazed; deranged; désorienté; disarranged; disconcerted; disheveled; disordered; disorganized; disoriented; distraught; embarrassed; entangled; farraginous; fevered; feverish; flurried; flustered; foggy; fouled-up; frantic; frenetic; frustrated; fuzzy; helter-skelter; heterogeneous; higgledy-piggledy; huggermugger; hurly-burly; immethodic(al); inchoate; inchoative; incoherent; incomprehensible; indiscriminate; inordinate; insane; inverted; irregular; jumbled; lawless; mad; messy; misorderly; mixed(-up); motley; muddled; muzzy; mystified; nebulous; noisy; obfuscated; obfuscatory; obscure; opaque; orderless; pandemoniac(al); perplexed; puzzling; raddled; random; rattled; riotous; slatternly; snafu; snarled; stumped; stunned; tangled; topsy-turvy; tumultuous; turbulent; undirected; unhinged; unorderly; unorganized; unrestrained; unruly; unseemly; unsettled; upset; woolly; CONFUSION: abyss; ado; agitation; alarm; alarums and excursions; anarchism; anarchy; ataxia;

babble; babel(ism); bafflement; bedlam; bewilderedness; bewilderment; brouhaha; bustle; buzz; chaos; chasm; clang; clutter; coil; combustion; commotion; confusia; dazzlement; defect; delirium; derangement; dilemma; din; dirt(iness); disarrangement; disarray(ment); discomfiture; discomposure; discord; dishevelment; dislocation; disorder; disorganization; disorientation; disturbance; dust; embarrassment; embranglement; embroilment; entanglement; fog; havoc; hell; heterogeneity; hodgepodge; hooroosh; hubbub; hugger-mugger; hurly-burly; imbalance; incoherence; irrationality; irregularity; jumble(ment); katzenjammer; lawlessness; litter; madness; maelstrom; mess; mishmash; misorder; mixture; mix-up; moil; muddle; mumbo jumbo; muss; mystification; noise; nonplus; obfuscation; overthrow; pandemonium; perplexity; pi; poser; profusion; quandary; riot; rush; shambles; snafu; snarl; throe; Tophet; trouble; tumble; tumult; turbidity; turbulence; turmoil; unbalance; uncertainty; unreason; unrestraint; unruliness; untidiness; uproar; vacuum; void; welter; whirl(pool); wilderness; witches' brew

CONFUTÉ: (see "disprove") confound; controvert; defeat; deny; expose; falsify; negate; overcome; rebut; refute; silence; squelch; CONFUTATION: see "disproof"

CONGÉ: bow; clearance; curtsy; departing; dismissal; farewell; leave(-taking); passport; permission

CONGEAL: chill; clot; cluster; coagulate; coalesce; concretize; cool; curdle; fix; freeze; gather; gel; glaciate; harden; ice; immobilize; jell; lump; mass; paralyze; pectorize; preserve; press; rigidify; set; solidify; stabilize; stick; stiffen; thicken; thrombose

CONGENER: class; cognate; genus; kind; look-alike; race; relative

CONGENIAL: (see "hospitable") amiable; amicable; approachable; appropriate; attractive; boon; companionable; consonant; convivial; cordial; courteous; friendly; genial; gracious; gregarious; happy; human(e); kind; kindred; neighborly; pleasant; receptive; sociable; social; sympathetic; tender; welcome; CONGENIALITY: see "hospitality"

CONGENITAL: (see "hereditary") ancestral; constitutional; essential; familial; hereditable; inborn; inbred; inherent; inherited; innate; maternal; native; paternal; patrimonial; transmitted; unacquired

CONGLOMERATE: v. (see "accumulate") agglutinate; amass; assemble; cluster; collect; gather; heap; mass; muster; pile; stack; CONGLOMERATE n. or CONGLOMERATION: (see "accumulation") agglutination; assemblage; blob; cluster; collection; heap; imbroglio; mass; muster; pile; stack

CONGRATULATE: (see "praise") commend; compliment; felicitate; laud; macarize; sympathize; CONGRATULATION: see "praise"

CONGREGATE: (see "assemble") amass; collect; concentrate; convene; convocate; convoke; crowd; flock; herd; huddle; mass; meet; muster; pack; press; rally; swarm; teem; throng; troop; troupe; CONGREGATION: (see "assemblage") amassment; assembly; body; brethren; church; collection; community; convention; convocation; denomination; flock; fold; gathering; group; herd; host; huddle; meeting; muster; pack; parish; sect; swarm; troop

CONGRESS: assemblage; assembly; association; conclave; conference; connection; council; intercourse; legislature; meeting; organization; senate; synod

CONGRUENT or CONGRUOUS: (see "harmonious") coinciding; corresponding; fitting

CONJECTURE: v. (see "assume") believe; conceive; divine; fancy; foresee; guess; hypothesize; imagine; infer; opinionate; portend; postulate; presume; presuppose; speculate; suppose; surmise; suspect; theorize; think; CONJECTURE: n. (see "assumption") belief; conception; fancy; guess(work); hypothecation; imagination; inference; opinion; postulation; presumption; presupposition; speculation; supposition; surmise; theorem; theorum; theory; thought; view; CONJECTURAL: (see "assumed") hypothetical; imaginary; speculative; stochastic; suppositional; supposi(ti)tious; theoretical

CONJOIN: (see "connect") adjoin; affix; associate; attach; combine; concatenate; join; unite; CONJUNCTION: (see "connection") and; as; association; but; combination; et; if; joint; junction; nor; or; since; than; tie; union; unition

CONJURE:(**see** "charm") beg; beseech; constrain; contrive; entreat; imagine; implore; invent; invoke; juggle; recall; summon

CONNECT: adjoin; affix; anastomose; articulate; associate; attach; bind; bond; bridge; catenate; cement; chain; cohere; combine; communicate; concatenate; couple; dovetail; engage; fasten; fetter; fix; glue; handcuff; hitch; hold; implicate; imply; indicate; interlink; interlock; involve; join; link; lock; loop; manacle; marry; mesh; relate; shackle; tack; tap; tie; unite; CONNECTED, CONNECTING *or* CONNECTIVE: affined; affixed; anastomotic; articulate(d); associated; attached; binding; bound; bridged; cemented; coadunate; coadunative; combined; conjoined; conjunctive; contiguous; continuous; coupled; hitched; interlinked; interlocked; joined; jointed; ligated; ligative; linked; locked; osculant; pertinent; related; syndetic; tacked; united; CONNECTION: affinity; alliance; and; arrangement; as; association; attachment; bond(s); bridge; but; cable; catena(tion); chain; circuit; clan; colligation; combination; communication; community; concatenation; conjunction; consanguinity; contact; context; contiguity; cord; coupling; crossing; denomination; et; faction; hitch; if; implication; job; joint; junction; juncture; kinship; liaison; ligament; ligature; link(age); lock; manacle; nexus; nor; occasion; or; position; reference; relation(ship); relative; sect; sequence; series; shackle; since; string; succession; symphysis; synapse; synchondrosis; than; tie; train; union; unition; vinculum

CONNIVE: (**see** "plot") abet; blink; cabal; collude; combine; confederate; conspire; contrive; disregard; foment; ignore; incite; intrigue; machinate; overlook; plan; scheme; tolerate; unite; wink; CONNIVANCE: **see** "plot"

CONNUBIAL: (**see** "domestic") conjugal; *en famille*; familial; familiar; homey; household; interior; marital; matrimonial; residential

CONQUER: (**see** "beat") acquire; avail; check(mate); control; crush; curb; daunt; decimate; defeat; deracinate; dismay; disorganize; dominate; domineer; down; gain; lick; master; oppress; overcome; overmaster; overpower; override; overthrow; overwhelm; prevail; quash; quell; reduce; repress; rout; secure; subdue; subject; subjugate; surmount; surpass; take; tame; trample; tread; triumph; uproot; vanquish; win; worst; CONQUER-

ABLE: beatable; crushable; defeatable; disorganized; domitable; expungable; masterable; overpowering; overriding; reducible; repressible; resistless; surmountable; surpassable; vanquishable; vincible; vulnerable; CONQUERABLENESS: controllability; crushability; subjectibility; surmountableness; vincibility; vulnerability; weakness

CONQUEST: (**see** "defeat") acquisition; annihilation; conquering; debacle; decimation; destruction; downfall; lacking; mastery; overcoming; overthrow; reduction; repulse; repulsion; reversal; reverse; rout; shellacking; subduction; subjection; subjugation; triumph; vanquishment; victim; victimization; victory; Waterloo; worsening

CONSANGUINEOUS: (**see** "akin") affiliated; agnate; collateral; congeneric; kindred; related

CONSCIENCE: (**see** "feeling") ardor; awareness; casuistry; character; compassion; compunction; conscientiousness; consciousness; conviction; empathy; fervor; fondness; heart; inwit; love; mind; pity; scruple; sense; sensibility; thought

CONSCIENTIOUS: (**see** "careful") attentive; correct; detailed; exact; fair; faithful; honest; honorable; just; leal; loyal; meticulous; righteous; rigid; scrupulous; strict; upright

CONSCIOUS: (**see** "alive") active; advised; affected; apprehensive; apprised; awake; aware; breathing; certain; cognizant; concerned; conscient; felt; informed; keen; knowing; live; living; mannered; mindful; perceiving; perceptive; perspicacious; rational; reacting; recognizing; responsive; sensible; sentient; sure; visible; CONSCIOUSNESS: (**see** "feeling") awakening; awakenment; awareness; breathing; certainty; cognizance; knowledge; living; percipience; percipiency; perspicacity; rationality; reaction; realization; recognition; responsiveness; sensibility; sentience; sentiency

CONSCRIPT: draft; enlist; enrol(l); muster; recruit

CONSECRATE: anoint; bless; commemorate; commit; confirm; consign; crown; dedicate; deify; destine; devote; enshrine; hallow; honor; inaugurate; inscribe; ordain; present; sacralize; sanctify; seal; vow; CONSECRATION: **see** "deification"

CONSECUTIVE: (**see** "orderly") aligned; alphabetic(al); alphabetized; back to back; calendrical; categorical; chronologic(al); consequential; continuous; *en suite*; following; running; sequacious; sequarious; sequent(ial); serial; seriate; *seriatim*; successional; successive

CONSENT: **v.** (**see** "allow") abide; accede; accept; accord; acknowledge; acquiesce; acquire; admit; agree; approbate; approve; assent; comply; concur; confer; cooperate; corroborate; countenance; endure; give; grant; hear; indulge; loan; permit; recognize; sanction; stomach; suffer; tolerate; yield; CONSENT: **n.** (**see** "allowance") acceptance; accord(ance); acknowledgment; acquiescence; admission; agreement; approbation; approval; assent(ation); compliance; concurrence; cooperation; corroboration; countenance; permission; permit; ratification; recognition; sanction; sufferance; toleration; unanimity

CONSEQUENCE(S): (**see** "end") aftermath; concern; conclusion; consectary; consecution; continuation; contrecoup; corollary; dignity; distinction; effect; emanation; event(uality); execution; fruit(age); import (ance); inference; interest; issue; moment; occasion; offshoot; outcome; outgrowth; proposition; ramification; repute; residual; residuum; result; sequela(e); significance; upshot; value; weight; worth; CONSEQUENT(IAL): accompanying; chronologic(al); consecutive; continuing; corollary; following; important; indirect; principal; residual; resultant; self-important; sequent(ial); serial; seriate; *seriatim;* subsequent(ial); succesional; successive; superimposed

CONSERVE: (**see** "hoard") cache; can; freeze; guard; hide; husband; keep; manage; prepare; preserve; protect; reserve; save; shield; uphold; CONSERVATIVE: **a.** (**see** "conventional") cautious; die-hard; discreet; hidebound; lethargic; moderate; moss-backed; nonprogressive; old-fashioned; Old-Guard; ossified; preservative; protective; reactionary; safe; stable; Tory; traditional(istic); ultraconservative; unenterprising; CONSERVATIVE: **n.** conventionalist; diehard; dodo; fogy; fossil; mossback; nonprogressive; Old Guard; praetorian; preservative; reactionary; standpatter; Tory; CONSERVATION: (**see** "care") economy; husbandry; keeping; perpetuation; planned management; preservation; protection; reservation; sustenance; sustentation; sustention

CONSIDER: accept; cast about; cogitate; conclude; contemplate; contrive; count; deem; deliberate; determine; enter(tain); esteem; examine; excogitate; favor; figure; hash; heed; hesitate; judge; listen; mind; mull (over); muse; pause; perpend; ponder; predict; premeditate; prepend; question; rate; ratiocinate; reason; reckon; reflect; regard; research; respect; review; revolve; roll; see; stop; study; suppose; survey; take under advisement; think; thrash (out); treat; understand; weigh; CONSIDERATE: careful; charitable; circumspect; concerned; courteous; deliberate; delicate; devoted; diplomatic; forbearing; kind; merciful; prudent; reasonable; regardful; respectful; sincere; tactful; tender; thoughtful; understanding; unselfish; well-meaning; CONSIDERABLE: (**see** "much") cognizable; extensive; fair; good; great; healthy; hefty; important; intense; intensive; large; major; many; massive; notable; numerous; perceptible; remarkable; rich; significant; CONSIDERATION: account; advisement; altruism; attention; care; caution; cogitation; cognizance; concern; contemplation; courtesy; deliberation; determination; devotion; dispensation; esteem; estimation; excogitation; favor; forbearance; heed; honorarium; mercy; motive; opinion; payment; perpension; prudence; quarter; *quid pro quo*; quiet; reason; recompense; regard; respect; reward; sanction; sincerity; tact; tenderness; thought(fulness); understanding; unselfishness; worship

CONSIGN: address; allot; assign; cede; commend; commission; commit; confide; confine; confirm; consecrate; contract; dedicate; deliver; design; destine; direct; dispense; entrust; express; give; help; imprison; involve; mail; obligate; place; pledge; promise; recommend; refer; relegate; rely; remand; remit; resign; reveal; say; send; sentence; shift; surrender; transfer; trust; yield

CONSIST: (**see** "contain") comprehend; comprise; embody; embrace; enclose; entail; exist; harbor; hold; house; include; inhere; lie; occupy; reside

CONSISTENT: (**see** "harmonious") commensurate; compatible; comportable; concordant; conforming; congenial; congruent; consentaneous; consonant; constant; continuous; dependable; even; invariable; isogenous; regular; reliable; steady; unchanging; uncontradictory; undeviating; uniform; CONSISTENCY: (**see** "accord") coherence; compatibility; congruence; congruity; consistence; consonance; constancy; correspondence; evenness; firmness; harmony; homogeneity; invariability; isogeny; persistence; persistency; regularity; temperance; temperateness; texture; uniformity

CONSOLE: (see "calm") allay; cheer; comfort; condole; ease; encourage; gladden; help; inspire; inspirit; relieve; solace; soothe; sympathize; CONSOLATION: (see "sympathy") calm(ness); cheer; comfort; condolence; ease; encouragement; help; inspiration; relief; solace; sop; warmth

CONSOLIDATE: (see "blend") centralize; coalesce; combine; compress; concretize; condense; confirm; conflate; desegregate; harden; join; knit; lithify; merge; mix; organize; petrify; pool; reduce; settle; solidify; strengthen; thicken; unify; unite; CONSOLIDATION: see "blend"

CONSONANT: a. (see "agreeable") consistent; resonant; sympathetic; CONSONANT: n. dental; fortis; lenis; spirant; uniform

CONSORT: v. (see "mingle") associate; harmonize; CONSORT: n. (see "associate") husband; mate; spouse; wife

CONSPICUOUS: (see "notable") apparent; blatant; bulging; celebrated; clear; commanding; distinct; distinguished; eminent; excellent; extraordinary; famed; famous; glaring; great; illustrious; important; impressive; loud; majestic; manifest; marked; memorable; noted; noteworthy; noticeable; obvious; open; ostensible; outstanding; patent; plain; projecting; prominent; protrudent; protruding; public; renowned; salient; showy; signal; significant; striking; unique; unusual; visible

CONSPIRE: (see "plot") colleague; collude; confederate; contrive; machinate; plan; scheme; unite; CONSPIRATIVE or CONSPIRATORIAL: cabalistic; Catilinarian; collusive; confederate(d); conniving; conspiring; designing; plotting; CONSPIRACY: (see "plot") association illégale; bloc; cabal; clan; clique; collusion; combination; conclave; confederacy; conjuration; connivance; conspiration; coup; faction; gang; group; intrigue; junto; machination; party; plan; ring; set; underground; union

CONSTANT: abiding; ageless; agelong; around-the-clock; boundless; ceaseless;

changeless; continent; continual; continuing; continuous; durable; endless; enduring; established; eternal; eterne; even; ever-(lasting); faithful; fast; firm; fixed; granitic; immemorial; immortal; immovable; immutable; imperishable; incessant; indestructible; inexhaustible; infinite; interminable; interminate; invariable; invariant; inveterate; lasting; leal; limitless; loyal; many; measureless; numerous; pauseless; perdurant; perennial; permanent; perpetual; persevering; persistent; protracted; regular; remaining; resolute; sempitern(al); settled; stable; staunch; steadfast; steady; still; stout; strong; tight; tough; tried; true; unbounded; unbroken; unceasing; unchangeable; unchanged; unchanging; undecomposable; undeviating; undying; unending; unfading; unfailing; unflagging; uniform; unintermittent; uninterrupted; unlimited; unperishable; unperishing; unremittent; unremitting; unswerving; unvarying; unwaning; CONSTANCY: (see "continuation)" ceaselessness; continuity; continuousness; courage; devotion; endlessness; endurance; eternality; eternalness; everlastingness; fidelity; firmness; fixity; fortitude; indestructibility; infinitude; infinity; permanence; permanency; perpetuality; perpetuity; reliability; reliance; sempiternity; stability; steadfastness; steadiness; strength; tenacity; toughness; uniformity

CONSTERNATION: (see "alarm") affright; amazement; anxiety; apprehension; arousal; awe; dismay; disquiet(ude); distraction; disturbance; dread; exasperation; fear; fright; horror; panic; perturbation; petrification; scare; surprise; terror; trepidation; wonder

CONSTITUENT: (see "component") detail; elector; element; factor; feature; form(at); ingredient; integral; item; makeup; matter; member; part; phase; piece; principal; segment; substance; voter

CONSTITUTE: appoint; cause; compose; comprise; confirm; consist; construct; contain; cover; create; depute; embody; embrace; enact; encompass; erect; establish; fashion; fix; forge; form; found; frame; hold; inaugurate; include; initiate; involve; make

CONSTITUTION: (see "character") capacity; cast; charter; code; composition; decalogue; development; disposition; document; essence; establishment; form(at); formation; habit; health; heart; humor;

law; lustihood; Magna C(h)arta; makeup; mettle; nature; ordinance; organization; personality; physique; proclivity; propensity; spirit; stamina; state; strain; strength; stripe; structure; temper(ament); tenor; texture; tone; trait(s); vigor; virility; vitality

CONSTRAIN: (**see** "coerce") bend; check; choke; compel; conjure; distress; dominate; domineer; force; handcuff; impel; imprison; influence; limit; make; manacle; oblige; oppress; restrain; restrict; squeeze; stifle; tie; withhold; CONSTRAINT: (**see** "coercion") bond(age); captivity; compulsion; constriction; distress; durance (vile); duress; embarrassment; exigency; force; imprisonment; limitation; obligation; oppression; reserve; restriction; squeeze; stifle; stifling

CONSTRICT: (**see** "constrain") astrict; astringe; bind; choke; compress; constringe; contract; cramp; curb; deflate; gag; hamper; hamstring; inhibit; knot; limit; manacle; narrow; press; pucker; restrain; restrict; rope; shrink; squeeze; stiffen; strain; strangle; strangulate; strap; stultify; tie; tighten; CONSTRICTION: (**see** "coercion") astriction; choking; coarctation; compression; constipation; constraint; contraction; fetter; hampering; hindrance; inhibition: knot; limitation; manacle; oppression; restraint; restriction; rope; squeeze; stenosis; strain; strangulation; strap; stricture; stultification; tightening; tourniquet; CONSTRICTED: (see "restrained") constringent

CONSTRUCT: (**see** "make") arrange; assemble; build; compile; complete; compose; concoct; confect; constitute; create; deduce; develop; do; draw; effect; erect; establish; execute; fabricate; fashion; forge; form(ulate); found; frame; improvisate; improvise; invent; manufacture; mint; organize; produce; raise; rear; shape; style; synthesize; write

CONSTRUCTIVE: advantageous; affirmative; architectonic; beneficial; constitutive; cooperative; definitive; encouraging; helpful; inferred; medicinal; positive; rational; remedial; salutary; therapeutic; useful

CONSTRUE: analyze; clarify; clear (up); decipher; decode; define; diagnose; dissect; elucidate; explain; explicate; expound; illuminate; illustrate; infer; interpret; parse; read; render; resolve; solve; translate; understand; unfold; unravel

CONSUETUDE: (**see** "custom") habit; practice; usage; use; wont

CONSULT: (**see** "confer") advise; apply; ask; consider; deliberate; huddle; seek

CONSUME: (**see** "destroy") absorb; assimilate; burn; devour; diminish; dissipate; drink; eat; engage; engross; engulf; expend; finish; fritter; imbibe; monopolize; partake; perish; rust; spend; squander; swallow; toss; use; utilize; waste; wear; CONSUMING: (**see** "destructive") devouring; edacious; voracious; CONSUMPTION: (**see** "destruction") decay; intake; usage; use; utilization; waste; wear

CONSUMMATE: **v.** (**see** "end") complete; finish; perfect; CONSUMMATE: **a.** absolute; accomplished; arrant; capable; competent; complete(d); downright; entire; excellent; expert; extreme; finest; finished; full; highest; ideal; masterful; masterly; perfect; proficient; sheer; skilled; skillful; unmitigated; whole

CONTACT: **v.** see "border"; CONTACT: **n.** abutment; association; boundary; brim; brink; circumference; clash; collision; communication; contiguity; contingence; contingency; edge; edging; encounter; end; engagement; extremity; flank; frontier; hem; impact; joint; junction; juncture; liaison; limbus; limit; line; margin; mark; meeting; overlapping; periphery; rank; relationship; rim; seat; selvage; skirmish; synchondrosis; syzygy; taction; tangency; threshold; tip; touch(ing); union; CONTACTING: abutting; attingent; bordering; communicating; contactual; contiguous; edging; joining; juxtapositional; marginal; meeting; skirmishing; tangential; touching

CONTAGIOUS: catching; communicable; contaminating; contractable; corrupt(ing); corruptive; demoralizing; epidemic; infectious; infective; noxious; pathological; pestilential; poisonous; septic; vitiating; CONTAGION: (**see** "corruption") abscess; contagiosity; contagiousness; contamination; disease; infection; inflammation; influence; miasma; pathology; poison; pollution; pox; purulence; putrescence; septicity; spread; taint; virus

CONTAIN: bear; bind; bound; bring; carry; cart; check; coalesce; comprehend; comprise; concretize; confine; consist; control; convey; coop; corral; embed; embody; embox;

embrace; encase; encircle; enclose; encompass; enfold; entail; envelop(e); enwrap; epitomize; express; halt; harbor; have; hem; hold; house; imply; imprison; incarcerate; incase; include; incorporate; inhere; integrate; involve; jail; keep; lie; occupy; organize; pen; personify; pipe; prevent; reside; restrain; sheathe; shelter; ship; stem; subsume; suppress; surround; tender; transmit; transport; unite; wall (in); withstand; wrap; CONTAINED: (**see** "calm") composed; controlled; supported; sustained; CONTAINER: barrel; basket; bottle; bowl; box; can(ister); carriage; casket; coffin; conveyance; crate; flask; jar; kettle; pack-(age); packet; pot; receptacle; urn; vase; vehicle

CONTAMINATE: (**see** "corrupt") attaint; befoul; blacken; debase; defile; deprave; desecrate; harm; infect; injure; poison; pollute; soil; spoil; stain; sully; taint; tarnish; violate; vitiate; CONTAMINATED: (**see** "contagious") defiled; dirty; filthy; infected; insanitary; polluted; septic; unsterile; vile; CONTAMINATION: (**see** "contagion" and "corruption") debasement; depravity; infection; poison; pollution; putrefaction; putrescence; stain; taint; tarnish; vitiation

CONTEMPLATE: (**see** "anticipate") analyze; appraise; assay; assess; calculate; cogitate; comprehend; compute; conceive; conjecture; consider; deduce; deem; design; determine; develop; diagnose; divine; envisage; envision; establish; estimate; evaluate; evalue; examine; excogitate; expect; face; feel; foresee; foreshadow; frame; gather; gauge; gaze; guess; hypothesize; imagine; infer; intend; interpret; intuit; judge; justify; look; measure; mull (over); muse; observe; opine; perceive; plan; plot; portend; postulate; predict; prepare; presage; presuppose; pretend; prognosticate; propose; purpose; rate; ratiocinate; realize; reason; recall; reckon; regard; ruminate; sense; solve; speculate; study; surmise; survey; test; theorize; think; value; view; weigh; CONTEMPLATION: (**see** "anticipation") cognition; consideration; design; envisagement; excogitation; expectation; meditation; muse; perception; plan; plot; postulation; purpose; reasoning; recollection; reflection; rumination; speculation; study; thought; view

CONTEMPORARY: **a.** advanced; alive; associated; attending; coetaneous; coeternal; coeval; coexistent; coincident(al); coinstantaneous; concomitant; conjugate; contemporanean; contemporaneous; current; equal; existing; extant; isochronous; joint; living; modern; simultaneous; synchronous; united; CONTEMPORARY: **n.** (**see** "associate") coeval; fellow; CONTEMPORARINESS: coetaneity; coincidentality; concomitance; concomitancy; contemporaneity; modernity; simultaneity; symbiosis; synchroneity; synchronicity

CONTEMPT: (**see** "disdain") abuse; arrogance; arrogancy; contemptuousness; contumacy; contumely; defiance; denigration; depreciation; derision; detestation; disesteem; disestimation; disgrace; dislike; disobedience; disparagement; growl; hate; haughtiness; hauteur: hubris; humiliation; indignation; insolence; insult; loathing; misprision; mockery; reproach; sarcasm; sassiness; sauciness; scabbiness; scorn; scurviness; shame; CONTEMPTIBLE: abhorred; abhorrent; abject; base; beggarly; cheap; contemptuous; contumelious; cowardly; degenerated; degraded; denigrating; depraved; derisible; derisive; despicable; dictatorial; dirty; disdainful; disesteemed; disgraceful; dishonorable; disliked; dispiteous; grubby; hateful; haughty; hubristic; humiliating; insolent; insulting; lousy; low; mean; pedicular; pediculous; pitiable; pitiful; poor; sarcastic; sassy; saucy; scabby; scurrilous; scurvy; sneering; sordid; sorry; supercilious; toplofty; trashy; trivial; vile; worthless

CONTEND: antagonize; argue; assert; battle; box; challenge; claim; combat; compare; compete; contest; controvert; cope; debate; dispute; emulate; encounter; exert; face; fight; grapple; maintain; match; measure; meet; oppose; oppugn; pit; press; pull; reason; resist; rival; run; scuffle; seek; strive; struggle; tug; tussle; vie; war; wrestle; CONTENDER: **see** "antagonist"

CONTENT(ED): **a.** (**see** "calm") appeased; *dégagé*; easy; enjoyable; gratified; pleased; replete; *sans souci*; sated; satiated; satisfied; smug; snug; soothed; tranquilized; unperturbed; CONTENT(S): **n.** amount; cubiture; equipment; furniture; satisfaction; substance; volume; CONTENTMENT: (**see** "calmness") complacency; enjoyment; eudaemonia; eudaemony; euphoria; felicity; gratification; pleasure; quiet(ude); repose; satisfaction; saturation; serenity; smugness; tranquility; unperturbedness

CONTENTION: (**see** "contest") altercation; case; charge; claim; competition; conflict;

contestation; controversy; discord; dissidence; donnybrook; effort; exertion; feud; hostility; lawsuit; litigiosity; matter; quarrel; rebellion; riot; rivalry; squabble; strife; struggle; thesis; war(fare); wrangle; CONTENTIOUS: (**see** "argumentative") bellicose; belligerent; contentional; contradictious; disagreeable; disagreeing; disputable; disputatious; dissentious: dissident; factious; fretful; hostile; irritable; litigious; mutinous; oppugnant; perverse; quarrelsome; querulous; recalcitrant; ructious; seditious; unpeaceable; unpeaceful; unruly; warring

CONTEST: **v.** altercate; antagonize; argue; battle; brush; charge; clash; combat; compete; contend; contradict; controvert; cope; debate; defend; deny; discuss; disprove; dissent; emulate; encourage; face; feud; joust; match; measure; meet; moot; push; quarrel; race; rebut; refute; resist; rival; run; skirmish; strive; struggle; sue; vie; war; withstand; wrangle; CONTEST: **n.** action; affair; affray; alarm; altercation; argument; assault; battle; bout; brawl; brouhaha; brush; chessboard; claim; clash; combat; comparison; competition; concourse; conflict; contention; contestation; contradiction; controversy; debate; defense; denial; discord; discussion; disputation; dispute; dissention; dissidence; disturbance; donnybrook; duel; effort; emulation; event; exertion; exhibition; feud; fight; fracas; fray; furōr(e); game; heat; hostility; joust; lawsuit; litigation; litigiosity; marathon; match; matter; meet; melee; opposition; pace; polemics; push; quarrel; race; rebellion; refutation; riot; rivalry; run; scare; scuffle; set-to; show; skirmish; spat; squabble; squabbling; strife; struggle; suit; terror; tournament; tourney; trial; tumult; turmoil; uproar; velitation; war(fare); wrangle; CONTESTANT: (**see** "antagonist") agonist; candidate; contender; disputant; entry; fighter; opponent; opposer; rival; wrangler; wrestler; CONTESTING: agonistic(al); rival(rous); skirmishing; warring

CONTIGUOUS: (**see** "close") abutting; adjacent; adjoining; attached; bordering; coadjacent; contacting; conterminous; continuous; coterminous; juxtaposed; juxtapositional; meeting; near(by); neighboring; next; nigh; touching; unbroken; uninterrupted

CONTINENT: **a.** (**see** "pure") chaste; decent; moderate; modest; possible; restrained; sober; temperate; CONTINENT: **n.** Africa; America; Antarctica; Asia; Atlantis; Australia; Europe; heartland; Lemuria; main(land)

CONTINGENT: accessory; accidental; adjectival; adjective; adjuvant; ancillary; auxiliary; beholden; casual; chance; chancy; circumstantial; collateral; conditional; contributory; dependent; derivative; doubtful; empirical; iffy; inchoate; indebted; intrinsic; liable; likely; limited; maybe; perhaps; possible; provisional; provisory; reliable; reliant; reserved; risky; satellite; satellitic; secondary; servile; subject; subordinate; subservient; subsidiary; succursal; supposed; supposi(ti)tious; tangential; tributary; uncertain; CONTINGENCY: (**see** "condition") accident(ality); case; casualty; chance; circumstantiality; circumstantialness; danger; event(uality); fortuitousness; fortuity; juncture; peril; proviso; risk; subserviency; tentativeness; uncertainty

CONTINUE: abide; advance; be; comply; draw (out); endure; exist; extend; haunt; insist; keep; last; lengthen; linger; live; maintain; perdurate; perdure; perpetrate; perpetuate; perseverate; persevere; persist; postpone; preserve; prevail; proceed; prolong; prorogue; protract; remain; resume; retain; spin; stand; stay; stick; survive; sustain; wait; wear; CONTINUATION: (**see** "endurance") abidance; being; compliance; continuance; continuity; continuousness; continuum; duration; *durée*; endlessness; endurance; eternity; everlastingness; existence; extension; firmness; incessancy; infinitude; infinity; insistence; inveterateness; maintenance; perdurance; perpetuality; perpetuation; perpetuity; perseveration; persistence; persistency; prevalence; prolongation; protraction; reservation; reserve; resumption; sempiternity; sequel; steadiness; survival; tenacity; CONTINUAL *or* CONTINUOUS: (**see** "constant") abiding; around-the-clock; ceaseless; consecutive; consistent; constant(ly); endless; enduring; established; eternal; even; ever(lasting); extending; flowing; haunting; incessant; inveterate; pauseless; perdurant; perpetual; perpetuating; persevering; persistent; prevailing; progressive; prolonged; protracted; recurrent; regular; running; sempiternal; sequential; steady; stretching; successive; unbroken; unceasing; undivided; unending; unintermittent; uninterrupted; unpausing; unremitting

CONTORT: (**see** "distort") bend; coil; curl; deform; gnarl; grimace; pervert; snarl; turn; twist; warp; wreathe; writhe; CON-

TORTED: **see** "distorted"; CONTOR-
TION: **see** "distortion"

CONTOUR: (**see** "outline") appearance;
arena; arrangement; configuration; curve;
feature(s); figure; form(at); formation;
lineament; periphery; physiognomy; posture;
profile; shape; silhouette; sphere; terrain;
topography

CONTRACT: **v.** (**see** "brief") abbreviate;
abridge; affiance; agree; assure; bargain;
bind; catch; compact; compress; condense;
confine; constrict; covenant; curtail; deflate;
diminish; draw; engage; epitomize; flex;
guarantee; incur; knit; lease; lessen; limit;
narrow; pledge; promise; pucker; recede;
reduce; restrict; shorten; shrink; shrivel;
squeeze; stipulate; summarize; take; thicken;
tighten; transact; wrinkle; CONTRACT:
n. (**see** "agreement") accord; arrangement;
assurance; bargain; bond; cartel; clause;
compact; covenant; convention; engagement;
guarantee; lease; liability; mise; negotiation;
tion; pact; pledge; promise; stipulation;
transaction; treaty; CONTRACTION:
(**see** "brief") abbreviation; abridgement;
condensation; constriction; curtailment;
decrease; diminishment; epitome; flexure;
lessening; limitation; narrowing; pang;
puckering; reduction; restriction; shortening;
shrinkage; shrinking; shriveling; spasm;
terms; thickening; tightening; twitch; wrinkle

CONTRADICT: (**see** "deny") belie; cross;
disclaim; disown; disprove; dispute; gainsay;
impugn; negate; oppose; rebut; refute;
resist; CONTRADICTORY: (**see** "incongruent") ambivalent; antonymous; contradictious; contradictive; contrary; equivocal;
incompatible; inconsistent; opposite; paradoxical; repugnant; schizoid; uncertain;
CONTRADICTION: (**see** "denial") ambivalence; anomaly; antilogy; antinomy;
antithesis; contrariety; disclaimer; enigma;
gainsaying; incompatibility; inconsistency;
negation; opposition; paradox; rebuttal;
refutation

CONTRARY: (**see** "stubborn") absonant;
adverse; ambivalent; antagonistic; antipodal; antithetic(al); arrogant; balky; cantankerous; contradictious; contrarient; con-
trarious; contrawise; counter; cross-grained;
diametrical; disgreeable; discrepant; disinclined; disobedient; dissimilar; dissonant;
fractious; froward; hardheaded; hardhearted;
hostile; hotheaded; incompatible; inverse;
irascible; mulish; mutinous; obstinate; opposed; opposite; ornery; perverse; petulant;

prejudicial; recalcitrant; refractory; restive;
self-willed; truculent; unfavorable; unlike;
wayward; CONTRARINESS: **see** "stubbornness"

CONTRAST: **v.** (**see** "compare") oppose;
CONTRAST: **n.** (**see** "difference") comparison; discord; dissimilarity; distinction;
divergence; divergency; diversity; heterogeneity; heterology; incongruity; irregularity; opposition; unlikeness; variance

CONTRAVENE: breach; contradict; deny;
disagree; dispute; disregard; dissent; encroach; hinder; impinge; infract; infringe;
interrupt; intervene; intrude; invade; obstruct; offend; oppose; poach; quarrel;
tamper; thwart; transgress; trespass; violate;
CONTRAVENTION: breach; contradic-
tion; crime; disagreement; dispute; dissention; encroachment; hindrance; impingement; infraction; infringement; interruption; obstruction; offense; opposition; quarrel;
sin; transgression; trespass; vice; violation

CONTRETEMPS: (**see** "embarrassment")
accident; boner; break; disturbance; fracas;
incident; mischance; mishap; mistake;
scrape; slip; syncopation

CONTRIBUTE: (**see** "aid") add; afford;
allocate; ante; assist; bequest; bestow;
cause; come across; concur; conduce; confer;
cooperate; dole; donate; enter; favor; furnish;
further; give; grant; help; introduce; kick
in; lend; loan; present; provide; share;
shell out; subscribe; supply; tend; tip;
tithe; write; CONTRIBUTION: (**see**
"aid") allocation; alms; amount; ante;
article; assignment; benefit; charity; dole;
donation; essay; gift; grant; greeting; import;
largess(e); money; offering; pay(ment);
portion; present; share; sum; tax; tip;
widow's mite; writing; CONTRIBUTORY:
(**see** "aiding") accessorial; accessory; adjectival; adjective; adjuvant; auxiliary;
participating; satellite; satellitic; supplemental

CONTRITE: (**see** "penitent") apologetic;
broken; crushed; humbled; mournful; regretful; remorseful; repentant; rueful; sad;
scrupulous; sorry; worn; CONTRITION:
see "sorrow"

CONTRIVE: (**see** "arrange") afford; brew;
cajole; cast about; cause; conceive; concert;
concoct; confect; conjure; create; design;
devise; dream; effect; engineer; execute;
fabricate; fashion; find; form(ulate); frame;

get; guide; hatch; invent; invoke; lay; make; manage; maneuver; manipulate; move; originate; plan; plot; produce; project; scheme; shape; show; stage; start; succeed; think; weave; work; CONTRIVANCE: (see "apparatus") appliance; arrangement; artifice; cleverness; concern; contraption; design; device; fanglement; gadget; gear; ingenuity; invention; inventiveness; machine; mechanism; plan; plot; project; ruse; scheme; skill; tool; trick

CONTROL: **v.** abate; absorb; administer; arrange; attend; balk; brake; bridle; cage; chain; change; check(rein); choose; coach; coact; coerce; command; conduct; conquer; contain; contrive; cope; copyright; corner; create; cultivate; curb; deal; determine; develop; devise; direct; discipline; dispense; dispose; dominate; drive; educate; effect-(uate); engineer; execute; exercise; fashion; finagle; forge; govern; grasp; guide; handle; have; hierarchize; hinder; hold; humble; husband; influence; jockey; keep; lead; lease; manage; maneuver; manipulate; marshal; master; measure; moderate; mold; monopolize; move; navigate; negotiate; nurse; nurture; occupy; operate; order; overlook; oversee; pen; pilot; plan; plot; ply; police; pool; possess; predominate; preside; prevail; prevent; regulate; reign; rein; repress; restrain; rule; run; scheme; shackle; shift; slacken; steer; strap; strategize; subdue; subjugate; superintend; supervise; survey; sway; swing; syndicate; tame; tend; test; tether; thwart; train; transact; treat; use; verify; wangle; watch; wield; work; CONTROL: **n.** (see "power") absorption; administration; advantage; application; ascendency; authority; bit; bloc; brake; bridle; care; cartel; charge; check-(rein); clutch; coaction; coercion; cognizance; combination; combine; command; conduct(ion); coordination; copyright; corner; cultivation; development; direction; dispensation; disposal; disposition; domination; dominion; education; exclusiveness; exculsivity; generalship; government; governor; grasp; hand; handle; handling; helm; hierarchization; hold; husbandry; influence; jurisdiction; key; law; leadership; leash; management; maneuver; manipulation; mastery; method; negotiation; obedience; occupation; operation; ownership; pact; patent; patronage; pool; possession; predomination; press; prevalence; procedure; regime; regulation; reign; rein; repression; reserve; restraint; rule; sanction; self-government; self-restraint; shackle; sovereignty; strap; string(s); subjugation; superinten-

dence; supervision; survey; sway; sword; syndicate; syndication; technique; test; training; treaty; trust; upper hand; verification; watch; work; CONTROLLER: (see "manager") comptroller; governor; manipulator; regulator; superintendent; supervisor; CONTROLLED: (see "calm" and "steady") caged; held; tame; tethered

CONTROVERSY: (see "argument") altercation; argumentation; brannigan; competition; contention; contest(ation); debate; difficulty; disagreement; discussion; disputation; dispute; dissention; disturbance; fight; furor(e); litigation; opposition; polemics; quarrel; spat; strife; suit; trial; uproar; wrangle; CONTROVERSIAL: (see "argumentative") contentious; debatable; dialectic(al); discursory; disputable; disputed; dissentious; doubtful; dubious; dubitable; equivocal; eristic; factious; moot; polemic-(al); questionable; quodlibetary; quodlibetic(al)

CONTROVERT: (see "contest") argue; contradict; debate; defend; deny; discuss; disprove; dispute; dissent; face; meet; moot; oppose; quarrel; rebut; refute; wrangle

CONTUMELY: (see "disdain") abuse; contempt(uousness); haughtiness; hauteur; hubris; humiliation; insolence; insult; rudeness; sassiness; sauciness; scorn; CONTUMACIOUS: (see "stubborn") contemptious; contumelious; despiteful; disdainful; haughty; humiliating; insolent; insulting; obdurate; obstinate; pert; perverse; rude; sassy; saucy; scornful; willful

CONTUSE: (see "bruise") beat; crush; injure; mayhem; pound; scrape; scratch; squeeze; wound

CONUNDRUM: (see "joke") enigma; mystery; perplexity; poser; puzzle; question; rebus; riddle; tangle

CONVENE: (see "assemble") accumulate; agglutinate; appear; call; collect; congregate; converge; convoke; gather; hold; meet; muster; sit; summon; CONVENTION: see below

CONVENIENT: accessible; accommodating; adapted; advantageous; appropriate; auspicious; becoming; beneficent; beneficial; close; comfortable; desirable; easy; efficient; eligible; expedient; expeditional; favorable; fit(ting); golden; good; handy; helpful; near(by); nigh; opportune; preferable;

preferent(ial); profitable; proper; propitious; ready; remunerative; right; seasonable; serviceable; strategic; strategetic(al); suitable; suited; tactical; useful; CONVENIENCE: accessory; accommodation; advantage; appliance; avail; benefit; comfort; device; ease; edge; efficiency; expedience; expediency; favor(ableness); fitness; foothold; freedom; handicap; handiness; help; improvement; interest; lead; leverage; mastery; odds; opportuneness; opportunity; preference; preferment; privilege; prize; profit; sake; service; suitability; superiority; tool; utility; windfall

CONVENTION: (**see** "assemblage") academicism; agreement; assembly; association; axiom; caucus; conference; congress; contract; covenant; custom; decora (pl.); decorum; encampment; etiquette; form-(ality); gathering; meeting; mode; organization; orthodoxy; pattern; practice; preference; preferment; principle; properties; propriety; protocol; representation; rule; sanction; synod; usage; CONVENTIONAL; abstract; academic; accepted; according to Hoyle; appropriate; artificial; *au fait*; Babbittical; bourgeois; ceremonial; ceremonious; comfortable; common(place); contractual; conventionalized; conventionary; correct; customary; decent; decorous; die-hard; established; factitious; formal; genteel; institutive; lethargic; modest; moralistic; nomic; nonprogressive; old-fashioned; Old-Guard; ordinary; orthodox; orthodoxic -(al); ossified; pedantic; Philistine; Philistinic; prevalent; proper; reactionary; regular; representative; right; safe; sanctioned; stable; stilted; stipulated; stylized; Tory; traditonal(istic); tralatitious; trite; ultra-conservative; unenterprising; usual; Victorian; CONVENTIONALITY: academicism; commonplaceness; conformity; conventionalism; decorum; formalism; formality; orthodoxy; preference; preferment; principles; proprieties; protocol; ritualism; sanctions

CONVERGE: (**see** "meet") disembogue; CONVERGENCE: (**see** "meeting") anastomosis; concurrency; confluence; conflux; convergency; joining; synchondrosis

CONVERSE: **v.** (**see** "commune") advise; argue; chat; colloquialize; confabulate; confer; consult; converse; debate; dilate; discourse; discuss; divulge; gossip; impart; parley; reveal; share; speak; talk; treat; CONVERSE: **a.** (**see** "opposite") contrary; obverse; reverse(d); CONVERSANT: **see**

"informed;" CONVERSATION: (**see** "speech") causerie; chat; colloquy; communion; confabulation; conference; conversazione; debate; dialogue; discourse; discussion; intercourse; interlocution; palaver; parlance; parley; talk

CONVERSION: (**see** "change") changeover

CONVERT: **v.** alter; apply; change; decode; exchange; forge; make; misappropriate; modify; persuade; process; redeem; reduce; reform; remodel; renew; reverse; transform; translate; transmute; transpose; turn; use; win; CONVERT: **n.** disciple; neophyte; novice; proselyte; recruit

CONVEX: (**see** "arched") bowed; bulging; circular; curved; gibbous; rounded; rounding

CONVEY: (**see** "carry") alienate; assign; auction; barter; bear; cadge; cart; change; communicate; deduce; deed; deliver; devise; donate; feed; gesture; give; grant; have; impart; implicate; import; lead; mean; mediate; move; pass; pipe; present; register; remove; sell; send; shift; take; tote; trade; transfer; vend; CONVEYANCE: (**see** "carriage") deed; demise; grant; instrument; machine; passage; pipe; sale; transfer(ence); transmission; transportation; transporting; vehicle; waftage; will; wire

CONVICT: **v.** (**see** "condemn") damn; doom; judge; sentence; CONVICT: **n.** (**see** "criminal") condemned; felon; inmate; lifer; prisoner; termer

CONVICTION: (**see** "belief") awareness; certainty; concept(ion); concern; convincement; credit; credo; creed; dogma; faith; opinion; persuasion; philosophy; religion; satisfaction; sect; sense; sentence; tenet; view(point)

CONVINCE: (**see** "demonstrate" and "prove") brainwash; propagandize; CONVINCING: (**see** "clear") assuring; authoritative; believable; cogent; compelling; conclusive; convictive; demonstrable; evident; lucent; luculent; official; patent; persuasive; plausible; potent; recognizable; sanctioned; satisfactory; satisfying; sound; suasive; telling; valid

CONVIVIAL: (**see** "cordial") amiable; amicable; blithe(some); festal; festive; gay; genial; hospitable; jolly; jovial; joyous; merry; sociable; social; warm; CONVIVIALITY: **see** "cordiality"

CONVOKE: (**see** "meet") assemble; bid; call; cite; collect; convene; convocate; gather; hold; muster; summon; CONVOCA-TION: (**see** "meeting") agglutination; assembly; commencement; congregation; congress; convening; convention; council; gathering; mustering; summons

CONVOY: **v.** (**see** "escort") accompany; attend; chaperone; conduct; guard; guide; lead; man(age); pilot; protect; shepherd; shield; squire; steer; support; tend; usher; watch; CONVOY: **n. see** "caravan" and "escort"

CONVULSE: agitate; confuse; disturb; excite; fracture; laugh; overthrow; rock; shake; stir; writhe; CONVULSION: agitation; agony; anger; attack; cataclasm; catatonia; commotion; confusion; crisis; disorder; earthquake; eclampsia; explosion; fit; furor; fury; grand mal; jactitation; laugh; orgasm; orogeny; outburst; overthrow; paralysis; paroxysm; petit mal; rage; seizure; shaking; shrug; spasm; storm; strain; stress; tantrum; throe; tremor; upheaval; CONVULSIVE: agitative; cataclasmic; catatonic; convulsant; convulsionary; eclamptic; epileptic; explosive; funny; laughable; laughing; orgasmic; paralyzing; paroxysmal; rocking; rollicking; shaking; spasmatic; spasmic; spasmodic(al); spastic; uncontrollable

COOK: **v.** bake; boil; braise; broil; concoct; confect; contrive; develop; devise; doctor; enervate; evolve; fabricate; falsify; fix; frame; fry; grill; happen; hatch; improvise; invent; kill; make; occur; poach; prepare; process; roast; ruin; sauté; seethe; shirr; steam; stew; sun; undo; COOK: **n.** chef; *chef de cuisine*; cuisinier; cuisinière (fem.); culinarian; doctor

COOL: **v.** calm; check; chill; dampen; depress; dishearten; dispute; freeze; frost; ice; infrigidate; nip; refresh; refrigerate; shiver; temper; COOL: **a.** airish; airy; algid; analytic(al); antagonistic; apathetic; arctic; breezy; calm; carefree; cautious; chilled; chilly; clinical; cold(-blooded); collected; competent; deliberate; depressing; detached; discouraging; disheartening; disimpassioned; dispassionate; distant; drafty; formal; freezing; fresh; frigid; frosty; gelid; glacial; icy; impassive; imperturbable; indifferent; judicial; level-headed; nervy; nippy; nonchalant; passive; placid; poised; possessed; raw; refrigerated; resolute; restful; rigorous; serene; shivery; staid; stormy; sure; temperate; unaffected; unconcerned; uncordial;

unemotional; unexcited; unfeeling; unfriendly; unneighorly; unperturbed; unresponsive; unruffled; wintery; COOLNESS: calm(ness); cautiousness; chill(iness); cold-bloodedness; competence; competency; deliberation; detachment; dispossession; equanimity; frigidity; frost(iness); gelidity; iciness; impassivity; imperturbability; indifference; nonchalance; passivity; phlegm; placidity; poise; rawness; refrigeration; resolution; rigor; *sangfroid*; self-possession; serenity; steadiness; temperateness; unconcern; uncordiality; unfriendliness; unneighborliness

COOP: (**see** "pen") enclose; inhibit; obstruct; restrain

COOPERATE: (**see** "aid") agree; ante; assist; associate; coact; coadjute; collaborate; colleague; combine; communicate; concur; conspire; contribute; divide; dole; donate; further; give; grant; help; integrate; join; lend; mingle; partake; participate; plan; play; plot; share; subscribe; unite; CO-OPERATION: (**see** "aid" and "communion") assist; assistance; association; coaction; coadjuvancy; coefficiency; collaboration; combination; commune; concurrence; conspiracy; conspiration; contribution; co-venture; flexibility; help; integration; liaison; mutualism; symbiosis; synergism; synergy; teamwork; unanimity; union; unity; COOPERATIVE: agreeable; associative; coactive; collaborative; coefficient; combined; flexible; joint; ready; social; synergetic(al); synergic; synergistic; tractable; united; willing; yielding

COORDINATE: **v.** (**see** "balance") accord; adapt; adjust; arrange; classify; combine; concur; equal(ize); fit; harmonize; integrate; manage; mesh; organize; rank; rate; rhythmize; syntonize; tune; COORDINATE: **a.** (**see** "balanced") concurrent; equal; rhythmic(al); similar; syntonic

COPE: (**see** "complete" and "contend") arch; band; contest; encounter; grapple; rival; struggle; vie; war; wrestle

COPIOUS: (**see** "abundant") abounding; affluent; ample; bounteous; bountiful; cornucopian; exhaustless; exuberant; full; generous; inexhaustible; lavish; lush; luxuriant; measureless; overflowing; plentiful; plenty; plethoric; profuse; replete; rich; rife; superfluous; teeming; wealthy

COPY: **v.** (**see** "mimic") ape; burlesque;

counterfeit; double; draw; duplicate; echo; estreat; feign; follow; forge; imitate; list; match; mock; parody; parrot; record; repeat; reproduce; sample; simulate; sketch; trace; transcribe; write; COPY: **n.** (**see** "duplicate") apograph; archetype; burlesque; carbon; counterfeit; counterpart; drawing; echo; ectype; effigy; estreat; example; extract; facsimile; forgery; imitation; likeness; manuscript; match; material; mockery; model; picture; prototype; record; reduction; repetition; replica; reproduction; resemblance; sample; similarity; similitude; simulation; sketch; spare; stuff; text; tracing; transcript(ion); twin; version

CORD: bond; cable; chain; filament; leash; line; nerve; rib(bon); rope; sequence; series; stretch; string; succession; tendon; thread; tie; torsade; twine; wire; wood

CORDIAL: amiable; amicable; ardent; blithe -(some); cheerful; convivial; courteous; festal; festive; friendly; gay; genial; gracious; heartfelt; hearty; hospitable; invigorating; jolly; jovial; kind(ly); merry; real; sincere; sociable; social; solicitous; tender; vigorous; vital; warm; CORDIALITY: amicability; ardency; ardor; cheer(fulness); courteousness; courtesy; favor; fervor; festivity; friendliness; friendship; gaiety; gayness; geniality; graciosity; graciousness; heartiness; hospitality; invigoration; jolliness; jollity; joviality; merriment; mirth(fulness); regard; sincerity; sociability; solicitude; tenderness; warmth

CORDON: badge; barrier; braid; circle; coping; cord; enclosure; ensign; lace; line; ribbon; rope; series; star; string

CORE: (**see** "center") axis; axle; bone; centrum; essence; fiber; focus; ganglion; gist; heart; home; hub; interior; kernel; knot; middle; midpoint; nave; nidus; nub; nut; pith; pivot; plug; source; spool; staple

CORK: **v.** ca(u)lk; close; dam; fill; obstruct; occlude; peg; plug; seal; stop; stuff; CORK: **n.** bobber; bung; core; dam; filling; float-(er); obstruction; occlusion; peg; pledget; plug; stopper; stopple; tamp(i)on; wad; wedge

CORNER: **v.** bottle; catch; check(mate); checkrein; control; converge; defeat; force; gain; hem; hold; meet; monopolize; restrain; stymie; thwart; trap; tree; undo; CORNER: **n.** (**see** "angle") bend; cant; coign(e); control; elbow; herne; ingle; intersection;

monopoly; niche; nook; place; position; quoin; recess; secret; trust; viewpoint

COROLLARY: **a.** (**see** "supplementary") associated; auxiliary; complementary; consequential; equivalent; resulting; tangential; COROLLARY: **n.** accompaniment; adjunct; auxiliary; consectary; consequence; contributory; deduction; dogma; equivalent; inference; porism; proposition; result; theorem; theorum; theory; truism

CORONATE: see "crown"

CORPOREAL: (**see** "physical") actual; bodily; carnal; concrete; constitutional; corporal; fleshy; hylic; lusty; material; natural; palpable; real; somatic; substantial; tangible; visible; vital

CORPULENT: (**see** "fat") abdominous; adipose; beefy; bulky; burly; fleshy; heavy; husky; lusty; massive; obese; plump; porky; portly; pudgy; rotund; round; stout; tubby; weighty

CORRECT: **v.** (**see** "adjust") adapt; alter; ameliorate; amend; aright; balance; better; calibrate; castigate; chasten; chastise; check; compensate; counteract; cure; darn; discipline; doctor; edit; emend; enhance; equalize; expiate; fix; heal; help; improve; inform; manipulate; mend; modify; modulate; neutralize; O.K.; okay; patch; punish; purify; readjust; rebuild; rebuke; recognize; rectify; redress; refashion; reform; refurbish; regenerate; regulate; remedy; renew; renovate; repair; reshape; resolve; restore; retouch; retrieve; revamp; revise; reword; rewrite; right; service; set; shape; sharpen; stabilize; standardize; steady; straighten; temper; transform; transmogrify; transmute; true; tune; CORRECT: **a.** (**see** "accurate") acceptable; accepted; according to Hoyle; accurate; actual; adequate; airtight; A-O.K.; appropriate; apropos; apt; *au fait*; authentic; balanced; classic(al); clear; *comme il faut*; conforming; conventional; cricket; decorous; definite; *de rigueur*; dignified; documentary; due; elegant; exact; factual; fit(ting); genuine; honest; inarguable; just; kosher; lawful; legitimate; licit; literal; meticulous; nice; objective; O.K.; okay; orthodox; pertinent; precise; prim; principled; prissy; proper; punctilious; real; rectitudinous; regular; right(ful); sanctioned; scrupulous; sincere; sound; square; stabilized; staid; standard; steadied; straight; strict; suitable; true; truthful; unarguable; undeviating; upright; valid; CORRECTABLE: (**see** "teachable") amenable; amendable; corrective; corrigible; emendatory; fixable; perfectible; tractable; CORRECTION: adjustment; alteration; amendment; chastening; chastenment; chastisement; check; compensation; discipline; emendation; emendment; equalization; punishment; rebuke; rectification; redress; reform(ation); remedy; renovation; repair; resolution; retribution; revision; straightening; tempering; tuning; CORRECTNESS: balance; correctitude; decorousness; decorum; exactitude; exactness; fitness; fittingness; orderliness; orthodoxy; propriety; recognition; right; scrupulosity stability;

CORRELATIVE: a. (see "mutual") corresponding; equal; interrelated; reciprocal; CORRELATIVE: n. either; if; neither; nor; or; then

CORRESPOND: (see "agree") accord; coincide; communicate; compare; complement; conform; connect; correlate; equal; equate; fit; harmonize; jibe; match; parallel; quadrate; reciprocate; register; resemble; square; suit; tally; write; CORRESPONDING: (see "commensurate") accompanying; adequate; appropriate; coextensive; commensurable; congruent; congruous; correspondent; equal; equivalent; even; homological; homologous; isonomous; level; matched; paired; parallel; pertaining; proportionate; relative; relevant; rhythmic; sufficient; suitable; symmetrical; teamed; wedded; yoked; CORRESPONDENCE: accord; agreement; balance; coincidence; commensurability; commensuration; comparability; complement; conformation; congruity; correlation; equality; equiponderance; equivalence; harmonization; harmony; homogeneity; homology; letters; mail; match(ing); reciprocation; resemblance; similarity; symmetry

CORROBORATE: (see "affirm") approve; attest; back; brace; certify; confirm; countersign; endorse; establish; fortify; notarize; prove; ratify; sanction; second; strengthen; substantiate; support; sustain; testify; validate; vindicate; CORROBORATIVE: adminicular; authenticative; confirmatory; corroboratory; justificatory; vindicatory

CORRODE: (see "erode") abrade; burn; canker; consume; decay; destroy; diminish; disintegrate; eat; etch; gnaw; impair; rot; rust; waste; weaken; wear; CORROSIVE: (see "caustic") acid; acrid; biting; corroding; destructive; diminishing; diseased; disintegrating; disintegrative; erodent; mor-

dant; sarcastic; weakening; CORROSION: see "erosion"

CORRUGATED: creased; crimped; crumpled; folded; furrowed; pleated; puckered; rugate; rumpled; seamed; wrinkled

CORRUPT: v. abscess; adulterate; attaint; bait; bastardize; befoul; begrime; besmirch; blackmail; blight; bribe; buy; confound; contaminate; debase; debauch; decay; decline; decompose; defile; degenerate; degrade; demoralize; deprave; deprecate; descend; desecrate; destroy; deteriorate; devitalize; dirty; dishonor; disintegrate; fester; foment; harm; infect; inflame; injure; inquinate; lower; lubricate; maturate; mildew; moil; oil; pervert; poison; pollute; purchase; putrefy; putresce; ravage; retrograde; retrogress; riddle; rot; ruin; sabotage; sap; seduce; sink; soil; spoil; stain; suborn; subvert; sully; suppurate; taint; tarnish; tempt; ulcerate; undermine; violate; vitiate; weaken; worsen; CORRUPT(ED): a. adulterated; Augean; base; bastardized; bestial; bought; bribed; cankerous; contagious; contaminated; contaminating; debased; debauched; decadent; declined; decomposed; defiled; degenerate(d); degraded; demoralized; demoralizing; depraved; deteriorated; devitalized; dirty; dishonorable; disintegrated; dissolute; evil; filthy; immoral; impure; infected; infectious; insanitary; lewd; low; mean; mercenary; Neronian; noxious; outmoded; peccant; perverse; perverted; pestilential; polluted; purchasable; putrescent; putrid; rank; retrograde; retrogressed; rotted; rotten; ruined; salable; sceptic; scrofulous; shameless; spoiled; tainted; tarnished; undermined; unscrupulous; unsterile; venal; vicious; vile; vitiated; vitiating; wayward; weakened; wicked; worsened; CORRUPTION: *abâtardissement*; abscess; abuse; Augean stables; bastardization; bestiality; blight; boodle; bribe(ry); canker; contagion; contamination; crime; debasement; debauchery; debauchment; decay; declination; decline; decomposition; defilement; degeneracy; degenerateness; degeneration; degradation; demoralization; depravation; depravement; depravity; depreciation; desecration; deterioration; devitalization; disease; disgrace; disintegration; evil; fester(ing); flagitiousness; graft; immorality; impurity; infamy; infection; inflammation; iniquity; lewdness; license; maturation; miasma; mildew; miscreancy; outrage; pathology; perversion; poison; pollution; pox; price; profanation; profligacy; purulence; pus(tule); putrefaction; putrescence; putridity; retrogradation; retrogression; rot(tenness); scrofulosis; Sodom; squalor; stain; subornation; suppuration; taint; tarnish; turpitude; ulcer (ation); venality; vice; vileness; vilification; villainy; violation; vitiation; vulgarity; vulgarization; wickedness; worsening

CORSAIR: (see "pirate") privateer

CORTEGE: (see "retainers") convoy; following; parade; procession; retinue; suite; train

CORUSCATE: (see "gleam") diamondize; glitter; shine; sparkle

COSMOS: (see"heavens") (the) all; all creation; allness; being; creation; earth; eternity; existence; expanding universe; firmament; galaxy; globe; harmony; heaven; henad; infinity; macrocosm(os); mappemonde; megacosm; metagalaxy; microcosm(os); microcosmus; monad; multiverse; *mundus*; nature; nebula; nulliverse; olam; omneity; order; plenum; reality; realm; space; system; universe; *via lactea*; (the) void; world; COSMIC(AL): (see "heavenly") catholic; earthly; grand(iose); harmonious; infinite; mundane; orderly; unfathomed; universal; vast

COSSET: (see "caress") baby; cuddle; fondle; pamper; pet

COST (see "expense") amount; charge; deprivation; detriment; expenditure; extravagance; loss; outlay; output; pain; penalty; price (tag); suffering; tab; COSTLY: (see "expensive") dear; detrimental; dispendious; elegant; esteemed; exorbitant; extortionate; extravagant; high; inestimable; invaluable; lavish; posh; precious; priceless; prodigal; rich; sumptuous; uneconomic(al); valuable; wasteful; worthy

COSTUME: (see "dress") ensemble; fashion; style; suit; uniform

COTERIE: (see "bloc") camarilla; circle; circuit; clique; galaxy; group; junto; set; society

COTTAGE: (see "cabin") hut; shack; shelter

COUCH: **v.** bed; conceal; crouch; describe; express; hide; lie; lurk; phrase; recline; settle; skulk; sneak; squat; steal; stoop; style; term; utter; word; write; COUCH: **n.** bed; davenport; den; divan; settee; sofa

COUCHANT: (see "prone") abed; crouching; lying; squatting; supine

COUNCIL: (see "conference") assembly; association; board; body; cabal; cabinet; caucus; concilium; conference; congress; consistory; consultation; diet; federation; group; junto; legislaure; meeting; ministry; powwow; quorum; Sanhedrin; senate; synod

COUNSEL: **v.** (see "advise") admonish; advocate; caution; chide; conduct; consult; deliberate; guide; instruct; proctor; recommend; warn; COUNSEL: **n.** (see "advice") admonishment; admonition; advocacy; advocate; attorney; barrister; caution; consultant; consultation; deliberation; direction; discussion; guidance; guide; instruction; lawyer; opinion; proctor; recommendation; rede; solicitor; warning; COUNSELOR: (see "advocate") guide; lawyer; mentor; proctor; solicitor

COUNT: **v.** (see "add") account; bank; calculate; cast; census; compute; consider; enumerate; esteem; estimate; expect; figure; foot; include; judge; matter; number; predict; reckon; recollect; regard; rely; sanction; score; signify; tabulate; tally; tell; tot(al); COUNT: **n.** (see "census") addition; cadence; calculation; cast; computation; enumeration; estimation; figure; footage; number; prediction; reckoning; score; tabulation; tally; total

COUNTENANCE: **v.** (see "approve") abet; acknowledge; condone; encourage; face; favor; own; sanction; support; COUNTENANCE: **n.** appearance; approval; aspect; color; comportment; composure; encouragement; expression; face; favor; lineament; look; mien; mug; permission; physiognomy; puss; sanction; support; temper(ament); visage

COUNTER: **v.** (see "oppose") attack; check; combat; contend; fight; neutralize; nullify; offset; COUNTER: **n.** asset; base; case; desk; easel; frame; meter; money; platform; score; shelf; stall; stand; station; table; tally

COUNTERACT: (see "oppose") antagonize; balance; check; compensate; contrapose; defeat; destroy; equalize; equate; even; frustrate; hinder; neutrlize; nullify; offset; resist; thwart

COUNTERFEIT: **v.** (see "fake") adulterate; affect; ape; assume; cheat; copy; deceive; defraud; devise; fabricate; feign; forge;

fraud; imitate; mock; pretend; sham; simulate; trick; COUNTERFEIT: **a.** (**see** "false") adulterated; affected; apocryphal; artificial; assumed; base; bogus; Brummagem; colorable; copied; deceitful; deceptive; delusive; dishonest; ersatz; fabricated; factitious; faked; feigned; fictitious; fictive; forged; fraudulent; illusory; imitated; imitation; inauthentic; phony; pinchbeck; pretended; pseudo(logical); queer; sham; simulated; snide; spurious; supposititious; synthetic(al); tin; unauthentic; uncanonical; unreliable; COUNTERFEIT: **n.** adulteration; adulterator; assumption; copy; dishonesty; fabrication; fake; forgery; fraud; hypocrite; imitant; imitation; imitator; imposter; mountebank; pretender; sham; simulation; simulator

COUNTERMAND: **v.** (**see** "cancel") abolish; abrogate; annul; counteract; dele(te); destroy; drop; efface; eliminate; eradicate; erase; expunge; frustrate; invalidate; nullify; obliterate; offset; oppose; prohibit; quash; recall; relinquish; repeal; rescind; revoke; scrub; stop; undo; vacate; void; COUNTERMAND: **n.** (**see** "cancellation") abolishment; abrogation; annulment; counteraction; deletion; destruction; disaffirmance; disaffirmation; elimination; eradication; expunction; invalidation; nullification; obliteration; opposition; prohibition; recall; recision; remission; repeal; rescisson; reversal; revocation; stop(page); vitiation

COUNTERPART: (**see** "duplicate)" complement; copy; double; duel; facsimile; image; imitation; likeness; match; mate; model; obverse; opposite; parallel; replica(tion); shadow; similitude; simulation; twin

COUNTERSIGN: **v.** (**see** "approve") certify; confirm; corroborate; endorse; esteem; license; sanction; seal; sign; COUNTERSIGN: **n.** (**see** "approval") certification; countermark; gesture; license; mark; password; sign(al); signature; watchword

COUNTLESS: (**see** "many") considerable; diverse; gobs; incalculable; infinite; innumerable; legion; lots; manifold; multitudinous; myriad; numerous; plenty; scads; sundry; unnumbered; unnumerable; various

COUNTRY: area; boondocks; borough; citizenry; clime; continent; county; demesne; district; domain; environment; environs; expanse; ground(s); hinterland; home(land); nation; outback; pais; parish; people(s); populace; population; province; realm; re-

gion; seat; shire; sod; soil; sphere; state; sticks; territory; tract; upland; vale; weld

COUP: action; assault; attack; blow; feat; plan; play; ploy; scoop; stratagem; strike; stroke; surprise; takeover

COUPLE: **v.** (**see** "associate") bind; bond; combine; conjugate; connect; copulate; fasten; join; link; marry; match; mate; pair; tie; unite; yoke; COUPLE: **n.** brace; couplet; duo; dyad; gemini; pair; span; twain; twins; two(some); yoke; COUPLED: accompanying; allied; associated; attendant; binary; binate; coadunate; coadunative; combined; concomitant; conjugate; connected; consociate; dual; duple; dyadic; fastened; gemeled; joined; linked; married; matched; mated; paired; tied; united; wedded; yoked; COUPLING: (**see** "link") linchpin

COURAGE: (**see** "boldness") audacity; backbone; bravado; bravery; cojones; confidence; constancy; daring; dauntlessness; derring-do; determination; doughtiness; fiber; fidelity; fire; fortitude; gallantry; grit; guts; hardihood; heart; heroism; integrity; intrepidity; manhood; mettle; nerve; pluck; pot-valiantry; prowess; pugnaciousness; pugnacity; resolution; sand; spirit; spunk; steel; strength; temper; tenacity; toughness; valor; venture; virtue; COURAGEOUS: (**see** "bold") audacious; boldhearted; brave(hearted); chivalrous; confident; determined; fearless; fiery; fortitudinous; gallant; game; gutty; hardy; Herculean; intrepid; lionhearted; magnanimous; nervy; plucky; pugnacious; resolute; Spartan(ic); spirited; spunky; sta(u)nch; stout(hearted); tenacious; undaunted; unflinching; valiant; valorous

COURIER: (**see** "guide") agent; attendant; carrier; cicerone; dragoman; estafette; messenger; orderly; scout

COURSE: **v.** (**see** "drift") beat; careen; circulate; discharge; drain; drive; emit; empty; flood; flow; flush; flux; gallop; glide; go; gush; hunt; issue; move; ooze; originate; parade; pass; pour; proceed; progress; pulsate; pursue; rise; run; schedule; seep; shed; slide; spout; spread; spring; start; stem; surge; tack; teem; thread; tide; transverse; trek; trend; well; COURSE: **n.** (**see** "channel") action; afflux(ion); ambit; aqueduct; artery; attitude; avalanche; behavior; canal; careen; chain; chute; circuit; circulation; conduct; conduit; curriculum; curve; cycle; deluge; *démarche*; diet; direction;

discipline; ditch; drain; drift; duct; efflux-(ion); effusion; emanation; emission; flood-(ing); flow(age); flume; flush; flute; freshet; game; gang(way); groove; gush(ing); gut-(ter); heat; inundation; issuance; issue; journey; lap; layer; line; main; maneuver; march; means; medium; method; mode; move(ment); orbit; outlet; pace; parade; passage(way); path(way); pipe(line); plan; policy; pouring; procedure; proceeding; process(ion); progress(ion); race; rate; regime(n); rise; road(way); rote; route; row; run(ning); rush; schedule; seepage; sense; sequence; series; sewer; spate; spout(ing); spread; spring; step; strait; strategy; stream; street; subject; succession; swing; system; tack; tactic; tenor; thread; tide; topic; tor-rent; track; trade; trajectory; trek; trend; trip; trough; tube; tune; turn; vein; walk; wash; water(course); wave; way; wire

COURT: **v.** (**see** "solicit") allure; attract; bid; curry; favor; induce; inveigle; invite; provoke; seek; serve; spark; sue; treat; woo; COURT: **n.** advisers; area; arena; assembly; attention(s); bar; bench; body; building(s); curia; field; fora (pl.); forum; homage; judge(s); judicature; judiciary; jurisdiction; palace; parvis; patio; quadrangle; retinue; seat; sesson; street; train; tribunal; yard

COURTEOUS: affable; attentive; aulic; bland; ceremonial; chivalric; chivalrous; civil; considerate; cordial; courtly; debonair-(e); deferent(ial); elegant; flattering; gallant; genteel; gracious; hospitable; ingratiating; kingly; mannered; mannerly; obliging; obsequious; parliamentary; polished; polite; princely; queenly; refined; respectful; ritual(istic); royal; stately; suave; unctuous; urbane; wellborn; well-bred; well-mannered; well-spoken; COURTESY: address; adroit-ness; affability *agréments*; (the) amenities; amenity; association; attentiveness; cere-mony; chivalrousness; chivalry; civility; comity; consideration; (the) conventiona-lities; conventionality; cordiality; courteous-ness; courtliness; custom; deference; deferen-tiality; elegance; exchange; flattery; friend-liness; gallantry; gentility; gentleness; gift; grace; graciousness; gratuity; homage; hos-pitableness; hospitality; indulgence; kind-ness; kingliness; manners; obeisance; polish; politeness; (the) proprieties; propriety; pro-tocol; queenliness; reciprocity; refinedness; stateliness; stature; suavity; unctuosity; (the) urbanities; urbanity

COURTLY: (**see** "courteous") aulic; cere-monial; civil; elegant; flattering; hend;

kind; kingly; obsequious; polished; polite; princely; queenly; refined; rich; ritual-(istic); royal; stately; suave; unctuous

COVENANT: (**see** "contract") accord; agree-ment; assurance; bond; cartel; clause; com-pact; guarantee; mise; pact; promise; stipula-tion; transaction; treaty

COVER: **v.** assemble; besmear; blanket; bury; cache; camouflage; cap; change; cloak; closet; clothe; coat; color; command; com-prise; conceal; couch; counterfeit; crust; daub; defend; discuss; disguise; dissemble; dress; eclipse; embrace; enclose; encom-pass; encrust; enfold; ensconce; entomb; envelop(e); face; falsify; film; flood; furl; glaze; gloss (over); hide; hood; huddle; include; incrust; inearth; inhume; insure; inter; invest(igate); lap; mantle; mask; masquerade; misrepresent; muffle; mumm; obliterate; obscure; overlay; overtop; paint; palm; patch; plant; plaster; plate; preserve; pretend; protect; reach; remove; report; robe; roof; screen; seal; secrete; sequester; shade; sham; shelter; shield; shroud; smear; soft-pedal; spread; stifle; submerge; superimpose; surround; swab; swarm; swathe; sweep; top; travel; traverse; varnish; veil; wash; watch; whitewash; withdraw; withhold; wrap; COVER(ING): **n.** apron; ark; asylum; awning; bark; blanket; bonnet; burr; camouflage; canopy; cap(sule); cara-pace; carpet; case; change; clandestinity; cloak; closet; clothing; coat; cocoon; color; command; concealment; container; cosy; counterfeit; coverage; coverture; cover-up; crust; cutaway; deception; delitescence; den; disguise(ment); dissimulation; dorm-ancy; duster; eclipse; enclosure; envelope; film; fleece; flood; glass; glaze; guard; hair hat; hiding; hood; hull; husk; incrustation; insurance; integument; investment; jacket; jerkin; lap; layer; lid; mantle; marquee; mask; membrane; nap; obscuration; occul-tation; operculum; paint; patina; peeling; pelage; plate; plating; pleating; preserve; pretense; pretension; pretext; protection; quilt; refuge; retreat; rind; roof; rug; screen; seal; secrecy; secreting; shade; shawl; sheath-ing; sheet; shell; shelter; shroud(ing); shrub-bery; skin; spread(ing); submerging; superim-position; surreption; swarm; tarp(aulin); tegument; tent; thatch; thicket; tile; toga; top; tunic; ulster; umbrella; varnish; veil; vestment; vesture; whitewash; withdrawal; wool(ens); wrap(per); COVERED: abeyant; armored; backstage; blanketed; buried; cached; camouflaged; clad; clandestine; cloaked; clothed; coated; concealed; counterfeit; covert; delitescent; dormant; dossed; dressed; falsified; feigned; glossed; guarded; hidden; hooded; incognito; inner; insured; interred; larvated; latent; mantled; masked; mysterious; obscured; painted; planted; private; privy; protected; quiescent; robed; roofed; screened; secluded; secrete(d); sham; sheathed; sheltered; shrouded; sly; soft-pedaled; submerged; sunk; surreptitious; thatched; thin; topped; underlying; varnished; veiled; whitewashed; withdrawn; withheld

COVERT: **a.** (**see** "covered") concealed; hidden; latent; masked; private; privy; quiescent; secluded; secret(ed); sheltered; sly; surreptitious; underlying; veiled; COVERT: **n.** (**see** "cover") asylum; copse; den; lair; refuge; shelter; shrubbery; thicket; wood

COVET: begrudge; cherish; crave; desire; envy; grudge; hanker; long; pant; pine; rankle; resent; spite; want; wish; yearn; COVETOUS: acquisitive; *alieni appetens*; avaricious; avid; eager; envious; extortionate; frugal; grasping; greedy; lustful; lusting; mercenary; miserly; parsimonious; penurious; prehensile; rapacious; sordid; COVETOUSNESS: acquisitiveness; avarice; avariciousness; cupidity; desire; envy; greediness; grudge; hanker(ing); jaundice; jealousy; longing; lust; malice; miserliness; opprobrium; parsimony; penury; pining; pleonexia; prejudice; rapacity; resentment; spite; unpopularity; venality; wish(ing); yearning

COW: **v.** (**see** "daunt") awe; browbeat; bulldoze; bully; dastardize; dishearten; dragoon; faze; intimidate; overawe; rattle; threaten; COW(S): **n.** Bos; Bovidae (pl.); bovine; ruminant

COWARD(LY): **a.** afraid; base; caitiff; chickenhearted; chicken-livered; contemptible; cowering; craven(hearted); dastardly; defeated; faint(hearted); fearful; frightened; gutless; irresolute; lily-livered; poltroon(ish); pusillanimous; recreant; reluctant; scared; shy; sneaky; spineless; spiritless; timid; timorous; tremulous; vanquished; vicious; vile; villainous; white-livered; yellow; COWARD: **n.** cad; caitiff; craven; dastard; milksop; poltroon; quitter; rat; recreant; sneak; turncoat; turntail; COWARDICE: cowardliness; cravenness; dastardliness; defeatism; faintheartedness; fear; fright; gutlessness; irresolution; poltroonery; pusillanimity; recreance; recreancy; reluctance; shyness; sneakiness;

spinelessness; spiritlessness; timidity; timorousness; tremulounesss; vileness; villainy

COWER: avoid; bend; blench; cow; crawl; cringe; crouch; curl; elude; evade; falter; fawn; flinch; hesitate; huddle; kowtow; pale; quail; quake; quiver; recoil; retract; retreat; shake; shirk; shrink; slink; sneak; start(le); stoop; submit; swerve; toady; truckle; veer; weaken; wince; withdraw; wither; wonde; yield

COXCOMB: (**see** "dandy") dandiprat; fop; mollycoddler; toff

COY: (**see** "bashful") aloof; arch; artful; attractive; charming; chary; clever; coquettish; cunning; cute; demure; distant; foxy; impish; ingenious; modest; nice; pat; pert; picaresque; playful; pretty; proper; reluctant; reserved; roguish; sassy; saucy; shrinking; shy; skittish; sly; timid; wary; COYNESS: artfulness; bashfulness; cleverness; coquetry; cunning; dalliance; demureness; demurity; impishness; minauderie; modesty; playfulness; reluctance; reserve; roguishness; sassiness; sauciness; shyness; slyness; timidity; wariness

COZEN: (**see** "cheat") beguile; bilk; chisel; deceive; defraud; delude; dupe; fake; gull; gyp; hoax; hoodwink; outwit; sham; skin; sting; swindle; trap; trick; trim; victimize

COZY: **a.** (**see** "comfortable") cautious; comforting; cosh; cushy; easy; familiar; gemütlich; homey; intimate; pleasant; posh; safe; secure; snug; soft; toasty; COZY: **n.** covering; quilt; COZINESS: (**see** "comfort") homeliness; intimacy; intimateness; security; snugness

CRABBED *or* CRABBY: *acariâtre*; acerb(ic); acidulent; acidulous; bilious; bitter; brash; cantankerous; caustic; choleric; churlish; contrary; cranky; cross; crotchety; curmudgeonish; curmudgeonly; difficult; edgy; exasperated; feverish; fretful; furious; grouchy; grumpy; hot; ill-humored; ill-natured; impatient; intractable; intricate; irascible; irritable; irritated; liverish; melancholy; obscure; peevish; peppery; perverse; pettish; petulant; querulous; rebarbative; sharp; snappish; snappy; splenetic; sullen; surly; temperamental; testy; touchy; unpredictable; vinegary; waspish; CRABBEDNESS: acerbity; asperity; bitterness; cantankerousness; choler; churlishness; contrariness; crankiness; melancholy; peevishness;

petulance; spleen; sullenness; surliness; testiness

CRACK: **v.** (**see** "split") break; chap; cleft; cut; damage; destroy; fissure; fracture; mark; pop; rend; roughen; slit; snap; CRACK: **n.** (**see** "blemish") bang; break; chink; cleat; cleft; cranny; crevice; cut; damage; fissure; fracture; furrow; gag; hairline; impairment; jest; joke; mark; niche; noise; opening; pop; quip; recess; rent; rift; rime; rip; slit; split; tear

CRACKPOT: (**see** "blockhead") fool; lunatic

CRADLE: cader; container; crèche; cunabula (pl.); foundation; frame(work); infancy; matrix; origin; rocker; scaffold; slee; support

CRAFT: ability; argosy; art(ifice); artistry; boat; business; finesse; guild; guile; ingeniosity; métier; occupation; power; profession; proficiency; ship; skill(fulness); talent; trade; vessel; vocation; work; CRAFTY: (**see** "cunning") adept; adroit; ambidexterous; arch; artful; astucious; astute; cag(e)y; canny; careful; cautious; designing; dexterous; double-dealing; duplicitous; foxy; ingenious; insinuating; knowing; Machiavellian; politic(al); shrewd; skillful; sly; smart; sophisticated; subtle; tricky; unscrupulous; vulpine; wide-awake; wily; wise; CRAFTINESS: (**see** "cunning") astucity; astuteness; callidity; diablerie; finesse; flyness; ingeniosity; ingenuity; knowledge; skillfulness; sleight (of hand); slyness; trickery; unscrupulosity; wile; wisdom

CRAFTSMAN: (**see** "artisan") artificer; handicrafter

CRAM: (**see** "crowd") bone (up); cloy compress; confine; cramp; drive; feed; fill; force; glut; gorge; grind; jam; learn; overfeed; overload; overstuff; pack; poke; press; push; ram; restrain; sate; satiate; stow; study; stuff; teach; thrust; CRAMMED: (**see** "crowded") cloyed; glutted; overfed; overstuffed; sated; satiated

CRAMPED: (**see** "crowded") compressed; confined; crammed; cribbed; dampened; incapacious; incommodious; narrow; restrained; restricted

CRANK: brace; bracket; crab; crotchet; fanatic; grouch; handle; whim; winch

CRANKY: (**see** "crabby") cantankerous; choleric; crabbed; cross; crotchety; difficult; erratic; grouchy; irascible; irritable; nervous; peevish; perverse; petulant; querulous; sour; splenetic; testy; touchy; unpredictable; vinegary; waspish

CRASH: **v.** (**see** "break") blast; burst; catapult; enter; fail; hurtle; ram; ruin; shatter; shock; smash; splint(er); CRASH: **n.** (**see** "break") blast; breaking; burst(ing); cloth; failure; ruin; smash; sound

CRASS: (**see** "crude") coarse; dense; dull; dumb; gross; raw; rough; rude; stupid; thick; unfeeling; unrefined; vulgar

CRAVE: (**see** "aspire") beg; beseech; care; covet; demand; desiderate; desire; entreat; envy; fancy; hanker; hope; hunger; itch; long; lust; need; pant; pine; pray; require; seek; solicit; thirst; want; will; wish; yearn; yen; CRAVING: **n.** (**see** "appetite") appetence; appetency; appetition; desideration; desideratum; desire; envy; hankering; hope; hunger; itch; longing; lust; need; thirst; voracity; want; yearn(ing); yen; CRAVING: **a. see** "appetizing"

CRAVEN: (**see** "cowardly") afraid; dastardly; defeated; fainthearted; mouselike; mousy; poltroon(ish); scared; timid; timorous; vanquished

CRAWL: (**see** "creep") cringe; drag; fawn; grovel; inch; lag; sidle; slide; slither; snake; swim; trail

CRAZE: **v.** (**see** "derange") confuse; impair; madden; perplex; puzzle; unbalance; CRAZE: **n.** bug; custom; fad; fashion; favor; fever; frenzy; hobby; insanity; intensity; madness; mania; mode; passion; popularity; rage; style; trend; vogue

CRAZY *or* CRAZED: (**see** "insane") amok; askew; balmy; batty; berserk; buggy; crackbrained; cracked; crackpot; crooked; cuckoo; daffy; daft; damaged; delirious; demented; deranged; disordered; distracted; distraught; dizzy; dopey; eccentric; erratic; far-out; feverish; flipped; foolish; frantic; frenetic; frenzied; funny; goofy; hallucinatory; harassed; impractical; infatuated; irrational; jumbled; kooky; loco; lunatic; mad; maniac(al); manic; nutty; obsessed; odd(ball); off; paranoid; peculiar; rabid; ree; screwy; slaphappy; unhinged; unsane; unsound; unusual; upside-down; wacky; wild; CRAZINESS: **see** "insanity"

CREAK: (see "grate") grind; groan; rasp; rub; scrape; scratch; squeak

CREAM: best; butterfat; candy; confection; cosmetic; elite; emulsion; essence; foam; froth; gist; lotion; ointment; sauce

CREASE: (see "crimp") corrugate; fold; furrow; graze; pleat; pucker; rick; rumple; seam; wrinkle; CREASED: see "corrugated"

CREATE: (see "breed") appoint; arrange; begin; blend; build; causate; cause; coin; compose; comprise; conceive; conglomerate; constitute; construct; derive; descend; design; effect; emanate; establish; fabricate; fashion; father; forge; form(ulate); generate; grow; hatch; head; hew; imagine; impose; inaugurate; initiate; institute; invent; make; manufacture; mint; mother; occasion; originate; plan; proceed; procreate; produce; propagate; raise; rear; reproduce; rise; seed; set; shape; sire; spring; start; stem; work; write; CREATIVE: see "inventive;" CREATION: accomplishment; appointment; arrangement; art(icle); beginning; birth; building; composition; cosmos; creatures; design; development; effect; evolution; fabrication; fashion; generation; genesis; growth; invention; manufacture; masterpiece; nascency; origin(ation); poiesis; production; reproduction; universe; work(s); world; CREATIVE: constructive; demiurgic; fecund; fertile; formulative; fructuous; fruit-bearing; fruitful; generative; genetic; imaginative; ingenious; inventive; new; novel; original; poietic; pregnant; productive; profitable; profuse; proliferative; prolific; proligerous; Promethean; reproductive; resourceful; rich; teeming; visionary; yielding; CREATOR: (see "ancestor" and "maker") creativeness; creativity; God; originator; trailblazer; CREATIVITY:(see "fertilization") artistry; inventiveness; originality; productiveness

CREATURE: animal; beast; being; bios; creation; dependent; earthling; ens; entia (pl.); entity; esse(nce); existence; fellow; flesh; human(ity); individual; instrument; life; man(kind); minion; mortal; ontology; person; slave; thing; wretch

CREDIBLE: (see "believable") authentic; authorized; faithful; official

CREDIT: v. (see "acknowledge") ascribe; believe; blame; charge; impute; loan; thank; trust; CREDIT: n. acknowledgement; ascription; assent; asset; award; balance;

belief; blame; charge; concession; confidence; confirmation; credence; credibility; credo; creed; cult; deduction; doctrine; dogma; endorsement; esteem; faith; favor; honor; imputation; influence; ism; loan; merit; obligation; power; rating; recognition; renown; reputation; repute; sanction; sect; standing; support; tenet; thanks; trust-(worthiness); weight; CREDITABLE: allowable; answerable; ascriptive; authentic; authorized; believable; chargeable; deserving; good; honorable; meritable; merited; official; praiseworthy; reputable; respectable; responsible; suitable; trustworthy

CREDULOUS: confident; green; guileless; gullible; imprudent; innocent; naive; simple; trustful; unsuspicious; unwary

CREED: (see "belief") church; confessional; credo; cult; denomination; doctrine; dogma; doxy; faith; formula; ism; philosophy; principle(s); rule(s); sect; symbol; system; tenet; testament

CREEP: crawl; cringe; drag; fawn; glide; grovel; inch; lag; sidle; skulk; slide; sling; slip; slither; snake; sneak; steal; tingle; trail; worm; CREEPING: crawling; cringing; dragging; gliding; groveling; inching; lagging; ophidian; procumbent; prostrate; reptant; reptatorial; reptilian; serpentine; serpiginous; servile; slow; snakelike; snaky; sneaking; subreptary; sycophantic; trailing; worming

CREST: (see "summit") acme; apex; apogee; arête; badge; bearing; cap(stone); climacterium; climax; comb; cop(ple); courage; coxcomb; crisis; crown; culmination; device; edge; emblem; flood(tide); focus; garland; head; peak; perihelion; pinnacle; plume; point; pride; ridge; rim; seal; sublimity; summit; tide; tip; tuft; turning point; vertex; zenith

CREVICE: (see "crack") break; cleft; cranny; crevasse; fissure; niche; opening; recess; rift; rime; slit; split

CREW: (see "assemblage") band; complement; detail; faculty; followers; gang; gobs; group; hands; mariners; mob; oars; party; people; retainers; sailors; servants; set; staff; supporters; tars; team; throng; workers

CRIME: arson; assault; attack; defalcation; delict(um); embezzlement; evil; fault; felony; infraction; iniquity; malfeasance; malum; misdeed; misdemeanor; misfeasance;

moral turpitude; murder; offense; peccadillo; sin; tort; transgression; treason; venality; vice; violation; wrong(doing)

CRIMINAL: **a.** (**see** "bad") blameworthy; culpable; defamatory; delinquent; deplorable; disgraceful; excessive; extortionate; felonious; flagitious; guilty; illegal; illicit; immoral; infamous; iniquitous; malefic; malevolent; malign(ant); nefarious; nocent; reprehensible; reprehensive; unlawful; vicious; vile; violent; wicked; wrong; CRIMINAL: **n.** captive; condemned; convict; crook; culprit; defector; delinquent; felon; gangster; gunman; housebreaker; infractor; inmate; lawbreaker; lifer; malefactor; malfeasant; malfeasor; miscreant; murderer; outlaw; perpetrator; prisoner; racketeer; thief; thug; transgressor; wrongdoer; yegg

CRIMP v. (**see** "crease") bend; convolute; corrugate; cramp; crinkle; crisp; curl; cut; flute; fold; friz(zle); furrow; gash; inhibit; kink; plait; pleat; pucker; ruck; rumple; warp; weave; wrinkle; CRIMP: **n.** bend; convolution; corrugaton; crinkle; curl; flute; fold; frizzle; furrow; gash; kink; notch; pleat; pucker; ruck; rumple; wave; wrinkle

CRINGE: (**see** "cower") bow; crawl; crouch; fawn; quail; quake; quiver; sneak; stoop; submit; truckle; wince; yield;

CRINKLE: **v. see** "crimp;" CRINKLE: **n.** bend; convolution; corrugation; curl; fold; kink; rumple; rustle; winding; wrinkle

CRIPPLE: (**see** "disable") enfeeble; halt; hamper; hamstring; harm; hobble; hurt; impair; injure; lame; main; mar; mayhem; unfit; weaken; CRIPPLED: **see** "disabled"

CRISIS: accident; acid test; acuteness; calumny; catastrophe; Charybdis; climacteric; climacterium; climax; conjuncture; constraint; convulsion; cramp; criticality; cruciality; crux; danger; death; demand; desperation; difficulty; dilemma; disaster; distress; embarrassment; emergency; essential; exigence; exigency; exposure; extremity; fear; fix; flap; hardship; head; immediacy; imminence; imminency; impact; imperilment; jam; jeopardy; juncture; *mauvais pas*; menace; moment of truth; mountain; necessity; need; nip; obstacle; pain; pang; panic; paroxysm; pass; peril(ousness); pickle; pinch; plight; precipice; predicament; pressure; push; quandary; quicksand; requirement; risk; rub; scrape;

shortage; situation; squeeze; state; stint; storm; strain; strait; stress; threat; trap; trial; turning (point); uncertainty; urgency; venture; vertex; vicissitude; vortex; want; zero hour

CRISP: (**see** "fresh") biting; bright; brisk; brittle; clean(-cut); clear; cold; concise; crackling; crunchy; curled; curly; cutting; firm; friable; frigid; frosty; icy; intensive; jaunty; lively; neat; new; pert; sharp; short; smart; snappish; snappy; spalt; sprightly; springy; stiff; terse; trim; vivacious; washed; wavy; well-groomed; wrinkled

CRITERION (CRITERIA *pl.*): ability; axiom; canon; capacity; criterium; degree; evidence; extent; fact; gauge; graduate; ground; index; indication; indicia (pl.); law; mark; measure(ment); meter; metrics; model; norm; principle; proof; rank; rule(r); scale(s); size; standard; test; thermometer; touchstone; trait; trial; type; unit; universal; volume; yardstick

CRITIC: Aristarch; booer; carper; castigator; Cato; cavalier; censor; censurer; cognoscente; complainer; connoisseur; cynic; debunker; denunciator; detractor; exegete; expert; faultfinder; feuilletonist; *frondeur*; iconoclast; judge; malcontent; momus; pundit; repiner; reviewer; slater; Zoilus; CRITICAL: acerb(ic); acute; bad; basic; biting; bold; bordering; calumnious; cancerous; captious; cardinal; careful; carping; castigative; castigatory; caviling; censorial; censorious; chancy; chary; choosy; climacteric(al); climactic(al); close; condemnatory; consequential; crucial; cynical; dainty; dangerous; dapper; deadly; dear; decisive; defamatory; definitive; delicate; demanding; denunciative; derisive; detailed; difficult; dilemmatic; dire; discriminating; distinct(ive); emergency; epochal; epic making; essential; eventful; eventual; exact(ing); exclusive; excoriative; exigent; extreme; fastidious; faultfinding; fearful; feral; fine; finical; finicking; finicky; foolhardy; foppish; formidable; foul; fussy; grave; hazardous; high; hypercritical; ignitable; imminent; imperative; important; incautious; indispensible; injurious; insecure; ironic; jeopardous; memorable; menacing; meticulous; mincing; momentous; murderous; nice; obligatory; overnice; paramount; parlous; particular; perilous; poignant; pointed; precarious; precise; prominent; prudish; querulous; rash; reckless; resolute; risky; sarcastic; scrupulous; searching; sensitive; serious; severe; signal; significant; slanderous; spruce; squeamish; stigmatic(al); telling; threatening; ticklish; touch-and-go; touchy; treacherous; trenchant; trying; uncautious; uncertain; unchary; unhealthful; unhealthy; unparalleled; unreasonable; venturous; vital; vituperative; vulnerable; weighty; wicked; Zoilean; CRITICALITY: **see** "crisis"

CRITICIZE: abuse; afflict; animadvert; assail; attack; begrudge; berate; blame; burn; calumniate; carp; castigate; cavil; censure; chafe; charge; chasten; chastise; chew (out); chide; condemn; correct; debase; decry; denigrate; denounce; depreciate; deride; devastate; dig; disapprove; discipline; discommend; discountenance; discredit; disparage; evaluate; excoriate; execrate; flay; flog; fustigate; groan; grumble; harry; hiss; hit; impeach; impugn; jaw; judge; jump (on); lambaste; lash; lecture; lick; nag; nip; objurgate; opprobriate; paddle; pan; peck; pettifog; punish; quibble; rag; rail; rake; rate; rebuff; rebuke; reflect; reject; reprehend; reprimand; reproach; reprobate; reprove; revile; ridicule; rip; roast; satirize; scar; scarify; scoff; scold; scorch; score; scourge; skin; slam; slap; slate; slur; snipe; spank; stigmatize; swinge; switch; tongue-lash; upbraid; vilify; vituperate; whip; CRITICISM: (**see** "censure") animadversion; attack; castigation; cavilingness; critique; denigration; depreciation; derision; diatribe; disapproval; disparagement; evaluation; excoriation; fire; hiss; impugnation; judgment; lecture; nit-picking; rebuff; reprimand; reproach; reproof; review; ridicule; roasting; satire; scarification; scourge; slam; slap; stigma; stricture; venom; vituperation

CRONE: **see** "hag"

CRONY: (**see** "pal") chum; friend

CROOK: **v.** (**see** "curve") arch; bend; curl; deviate; meander; twist; wind; CROOK: **n.** (**see** "criminal" and "curve") bend; chiseler; curl; deviation; felon; quirk; swindler; thief; twist; CROOKED: (**see** "curved" and "dishonest") agee; akimbo; alop; amiss; angular; arcate; arched; arcuate; askant; askew; atwist; awry; bent; biased; bowed; circuitous; circumflex(ed); corkscrew; corrupt; crafty; curled; curved; deviating; devious; dishonest; dishonorable; distorted; evil; flexuous; fraudulent; geniculate; inclined; incurvate; insidious; meandering; misaligned; oblique; perfidious; pronate; rent; sinuous; sneaky; snide; stealthy;

surreptitious; swayed; tortuous; tricky; twisted; unconscionable; unprincipled; unreliable; unscrupulous; vermiculate; vicious; villainous; winding; wry; zigzag; CROOKEDNSS: **see** "dishonesty"

CROP: **v.** (**see** "clip") bob(tail); cut; trim; CROP(S): **n.** batch; collection; craw; cultivation; farms; fields; food; forage; fruit(s); fruitage; fruition; gatherings; gleaning; grain; growth; harvest; hay; lot; outcome; patch; proceeds; produce; products; profit-(s); quirt; results; returns; rewards; stomach; store(s); throat; tillage; whip; winnings; yield

CROSS: **v.** (**see** "meet") cancel; contradict; crossbreed; cut; decussate; eradicate; go; hybridize; interbreed; intersect; oppose; pass; span; strike; transect; transgress; transverse; traverse; CROSS: **a.** (**see** "peevish") acidulous; bilious; bitter; choleric; contentious; crabbed; crabby; cranky; decussate; fractious; fretful; grouchy; gruff; grumpy; hybrid; ill-natured; irascible; moody; morose; nettled; opposing; opposite; perverse; quarrelsome; querulous; restive; snappish; snappy; surly; touchy; waspish; CROSS: **n.** affliction; anguish; ankh; burden; crucifix(ion); decussation; difficulty; distress; encumbrance; gibbet; illness; impediment; incubus; misfortune; onus; rood; trial; tribulation; triskelion; trouble; weight; CROSSING: **see** "connection"

CROTCHET: (**see** "fad") dodge; peculiarity; trick; whim(sicality)

CROUCH: (**see** "cringe") bend; fawn; squat; stoop

CROW: **v.** (**see** "boast") brag; cry; exalt; exuberate; swagger; vapor; vaunt; CROW: **n.** bird; caw; corbie; Corvus; rook

CROWD: **v.** agglutinate; assemble; circle; cluster; cram; collect; colonize; compress; confine; conquest; cram; cramp; crush; encumber; fill; flock; force; gather; glut; gorge; grind; group; herd; huddle; hurry; impact; jam; mass; mob; move; oppress; overload; pack; pile; press; push; ram; restrain; rout; saturate; serry; slow; squeeze; stuff; swarm; teem; throng; thrust; CROWD: **n.** (**see** "band") agglutination; aggregate; aggregation; army; assemblage; assembly; body; bunch; circle; clique; club; cluster; clutch; cohort; collection; colony; combo; company; concourse; congestion; congregation; convention; crush; drove; flock; force; gang; gathering; group; herd; horde; huddle; instrument; jam; legion; mass; meeting; mob; multitude; myriad; number; pack; posse; press; push; rabble; ring; ruck; set; shoal; squeeze; swarm; throng; tribe; union; CROWDED: chockablock; chockful; chock-full; close; compact(ed); compressed; concentrated; condensed; confined; congested; crammed; cribbed; dense; filled; full; incapacious; incommodious; jammed; multitudinous; narrow; numerous; packed; populous; restrained; restricted; serried; stiff; teeming; thick; thronged

CROWN: **v.** adorn; anoint; cap; choose; climax; complete; coronate; crest; diadem; encircle; encompass; enrich; inaugurate; install; keystone; laureate; surmount; top; CROWN: **n.** (**see** "crest") adornment; apex; arête; aureole; bezel; cap(stone); chaplet; circlet; climax; coin; comb; copestone; corona; coronal; coronet; culmination; diadem; dome; empire; garland; hair; head(dress); honor; keystone; laurel; pate; peak; plume; reward; ridge; scepter; sovereignty; summit; taj; tip; top; trophy; tuft; vertex; wreath; zenith

CRUCIAL: (**see** "acute" and "critical") climacteric(al); climactic(al); dangerous; decisive; definitive; essential; exacting; exigent; extreme; imminent; important; intense; intersecting; poignant; pointed; searching; severe; telling; testing; transverse; trenchant; trying; urgent

CRUDE: (**see** "coarse" and "curt") artless; backward; bald; bare; boorish; callow; coarse-grained; crass; crusty; dense; dull; dumb; elemental; gauche; green; gross; hairy; harsh; ignorant; ill-mannered; immature; inapt; incomplete; inelegant; inept; inexpert; inurbane; low; naked; obvious; offensive; plain; plebeian; primitive; primordial; raffish; raw; rough(-spoken); rude; rugged; rustic; shaky; sheer; simple; squalid; stark; stupid; thick; ugly; uncompleted; uncooked; uncouth; uncultivated; uncultured; undeveloped; unelaborate; unelegant; unfeeling; unfinished; unpolished; unrefined; unrevised; unripe; unskilled; unskillful; untrained; unvarnished; unworked; utter; vulgar; wretched; CRUDENESS or CRUDITY: (**see** "coarseness") artlessness; gaucherie; grobianism; harshness; ignorance; immaturity; imperfection; impoliteness; inaptness; ineptitude; ineptness; plebeianism; primitivity; rawness; roughness; rusticity; unskillfulness; vulgarity

CRUEL: (**see** "savage") animal(ic); barbaric; barbar(i)ous; beastly; bestial; bitter; bloodthirsty; brutal; brutish; butcherly; callous; cannibalic; cannibalistic; cold-blooded; coldhearted; conscienceless; crazed; crude; cutthroat; dangerous; deadly; demoniac-(al); despiteful; destructive; devastating; diabolical; dire; dispiteous; disregardful; distressing; Draconian; enraged; extreme; fell; feral; ferocious; fey; fiendish; fierce; gory; Gothic; grim; gross; hard(ened); hardhearted; harsh; heartless; heathenish; hellish; homicidal; impiteous; implacable; indurate; inelaborate; inexorable; inhuman-(e); malevolent; malicious; marblehearted; merciless; murderous; Neronian; pagan; painful; Philistinic; pitiless; procrustean; punitive; rapacious; ravening; relentless; remorseless; revengeful; rigorous; rough; rude; rugged; ruthless; sadistic; sanguinary; satanic; stern; Tarquinian; tramontane; truculent; turbulent; tyrannic(al); tyrannous; unchristian; uncivil(ized); undomesticated; unelaborate; unfeeling; unkind; unrefined; unrestrained; unsympathetic; vengeful; vicious; violent; wanton; wicked; wild; Yahooish; CRUELTY: (**see** "savageness") barbarism; barbarity; bestiality; bloodthirstiness; brutality; callousness; cannibalism; cannibality; cold-bloodedness; cruelness; despitefulness; devil(t)ry; ferity; ferocity; fiendishness; hardheartedness; harshness; hellishness; implacability; induration; inhumanity; malice; ruthlessness; sadism; savagery; truculence; truculency; tyranny; vengeance; wickedness

CRUMBLE: (**see** "decay") break; collapse; crush; decline; decompose; degenerate; deteriorate; diminsih; disintegrate; dissolve; dwindle; fail; fall; fold (up); macerate; molder; mush; pulverize; putrefy; putresce; rot; ruin; rust; spoil; CRUMBLY: breaking; collapsing; crisp; decomposing; degenerating; deteriorating; diminishing; fragile; frangible; friable; pulverizing; pulverous; pulverulent; rusting; short

CRUSADE: (**see** "expedition") battle; campaign; caravan; drive; excursion; jihad; quest; undertaking; war; CRUSADER: advocate; campaigner; driver; evangelist; Messiah; messiahship; CRUSADING: driving; evangelical; evangelistic; messianic; zealous

CRUSH: **v.** (**see** "annihilate") bray; bruise; burden; comminute; compress; congest; conquer; crowd; crumble; dash; defeat; depress; destroy; extinguish; force; fracture;

grind; hug; humble; jam; mash; mush; oppress; overcome; overpower; overrun; overwhelm; press; pulverize; push; quash; quell; shatter; smash; squash; squeeze; stamp; stave (in); steamroller; stifle; subdue; subjugate; suppress; CRUSH: **n.** annihilation; burden; compression; congestion; crowd; crumbling; defeat; destruction; difficulty; grind(ing); infatuation; jam; mashing; oppression; overpowering; press; pulverization; push; ruin; shattering; smash(ing); squeeze; CRUSHING: **see** "decisive" and "overwhelming"

CRUST: **v.** cake; calcify; coat; concrete; concretize; congeal; cover; encrust; harden; indurate; laminate; overlay; scab; solidify; stratify; CRUST: **n.** cake; caking; calcification; coat(ing); cover(ing); deposit; dirt; film; hardening; hull; incrustation; lamina(tion); layer; paint; patina; ply; rind; scab; scum; shell; stratificaton; stratum; tier; CRUSTY: bluff; blunt; crabbed; crabby; crude; crusted; curt; dirty; filthy; fretful; gruff; pettish; snappy; testy; vile

CRY: **v.** advertise; appeal; bawl; beg; bemoan; beseech; bewail; blare; boohoo; call; claim; complain; demand; deplore; exclaim; fret; grieve; groan; hoot; howl; keen; lament; languish; moan; mourn; peep; proclaim; protest; publicize; pule; rage; repine; roar; rue; shout; sign; snivel; sob; sough; squall; threaten; ululate; wail; weep; whimper; whine; yell; yelp; yowl; CRY: **n.** (see "clamor") appeal; bawl; boohoo; complaint; deploration; entreaty; exclamation; fad; fashion; groan; howl; hue; lachrymation; lament(ation); mode; peep; protest; rage; rumor; shout; sign; slogan; snivel; sough; style; ululation; vogue; wail; whimper; whine; yell; yelp; yowl; CRYING: (see "clamorous") acute; clamant; groaning; growling; heinous; imminent; notorious; pressing; puling; sniveling; sobbing; urgent; weeping; whimpering; whining

CRYPTIC(AL); (see "brief") abbreviated; cabalistic; curt; dark; elliptic(al); enigmatic(al); hidden; obscure; occult; puzzling; secret; vague

CRYSTAL(LINE): (see "clear") amorphous; colorless; diaphanous; glassy; hard; ice; icy; lucid; luculent; pellucid; transparent; unobstructed

CUD: bolus; chew; plug; quid; rumen

CUDDLE: (see "hug") embrace; nestle; snuggle

CUDGEL: (see "club") stick; truncheon; weapon

CUE: (see "hint") allusion; clue; forewarning; gesture; glimpse; illusion; implication; inference; inkling; innuendo; intimation; key; mark; movement; nod; opportunity; pointer; rod; sign(al); suggestion; tail; tip; track; trail; warning; watchword; whisper

CUL-DE-SAC: (see "trap") blind alley; block; deadlock; difficulty; dilemma; diverticulum; impasse; obstruction; predilection; stalemate

CULL: **v.** (see "choose") extirpate; gather; hoe; pick; pile; pluck; select; weed (out); CULL(S): **n.** (see "dupe") seconds; selection

CULMINATION: (see "acme") aftermath; apex; apogee; climacteric; climacterium; climax; completion; consequence; consummation; crown; denouement; end; height; high noon; high tide; meridian; noon; payoff; peak; pinnacle; point; residual; residuum; roof; root; spire; summit; tip; top; vertex; zenith

CULPABLE: (see "guilty") blameworthy; condemnatory

CULT: (see "belief") church; conviction; creed; dedication; denomination; devotion; doctrine; dogma; faith; persuasion; religion; ritual; sect; system; tenet; theory; worship

CULTIVATE: (see "advance") breed; civilize; culture; develop; educate; encourage; farm; foster; further; grow; harrow; hoe; husband; improve; naturalize; nurse; plow; prepare; protect; raise; rear; refine; school; tame; teach; tend; till; train; CULTIVATED: (see "cultured" and "polite") educated; informed; thoroughbred

CULTURE: agar; amenity; art; artistry; behavior; breeding; civility; civilization; conventionality; courtesy; courtliness; cultivation; custom; debarbarization; delicacy; diplomacy; discipline; discrimination; education; elegance; erudition; experience; finesse; gentility; gloss; grace; grooming; improvement; knowledge; learning; luster; manners; medium; opinion; polish; politeness; propriety; refinement; religion; *savoir-faire*; scholarship; smoothness; suavity; taste; tillage; training; traits; urbanity; CULTURED: (see "polite") aesthetic; cavalier; civil(ized); conventional; courteous; couth; cultivated; delicate; diplomatic;

discriminative; educated; elegant; erudite; esthetic; experienced; genteel; instructed; learned; literate; lustrous; mannered; mannerly; nice; polished; politic; refined; scholarly; *soigné*; *soignée*; (fem.); suave; tactful; taught; trained; urbane

CUNNING: **a.** adept; adroit; alert; ambidexterous; arch; artful; artistic; astucious; astute; cag(e)y; calculating; callid; canny; careful; chary; clandestine; clever; covert; crafty; daedal(ian); daedalic; designing; devious; dexterous; diplomatic; discerning; discreet; double-dealing; duplicitious; evasive; expedient; fetching; foxlike; foxy; furtive; guarded; guileful; helpful; hesitant; ingenious; insidious; insinuating; intelligent; judicious; keen; knowing; knowledgeable; Machiavellian; mindful; parlous; penetrating; politic(al); prudent; resourceful; sagacious; scrupulous; secret(ive); sharp; shifty; shrewd; skilled; skillful; skulking; sly; smart; sneaky; sophisticated; stealthy; subtle; surreptitious; thrifty; treacherous; tricky; underhanded; unscrupulous; vigilant; vulpine; wary; watchful; wily; wise; CUNNING: **n.** art-(ifice); astucity; astuteness; caginess; callidity; canniness; caution; chicanery; circumspection; coolness; cooniness; craft-(iness); deceit; dexterity; diablerie; finesse; foxiness; guile; heed; ingenuity; ingenuosity; insidiousness; knowledge; legerdemain; prestidigitation; sagacity; shrewdness; skill-(fulness); sleight (of hand); stratagem; strategy; subtlety; trickery; unscrupulosity; unscrupulousness; wile; wiliness; wisdom

CUPIDITY: (**see** "greediness") avarice; avidity; covetousness; desire; gluttony; greed; intemperance; itch(ing); lust; miserliness; piggishness; plunder; rapacity; selfishness; stinginess; venality; voracity

CURB: **v.** (**see** "control") abate; balk; bridle; chain; check; conquer; conserve; foil; guard; guide; harness; hold; keep; limit; lock; maintain; moderate; pen; preserve; protect; rein; repress; rescue; restrain; rule; shackle; shield; slack(en); spare; strap; subdue; sustain; thwart; CURB: **n.** (**see** "control") bit; bridle; casement; check; edge; harness; limit; pen; repression; restraint; shackle; strap

CURE: **v.** (**see** "preserve") corn; cry; doctor; embalm; fix; free; freeze; heal; rectify; redress; relieve; remedy; restore; salt; save; season; smoke; treat; CURE: **n.** antidote; drug; medicament; medicine; preservation; recovery; regimen; remediation; remedy;

restoration; therapy; tonic; treatment; CURE-ALL: catholicon; elixir; nostrum; panacea; theriac; CURABLE: curative; healing; medicable; preservative; remediable; remedial; restorative; sanable; sanative; sanatory; therapeutic(al); tractable; treatable; vulnerary; CURATIVE: (**see** "healing") medicinal; remedial; restorative; sanatory; therapeutic(al)

CURIO: antique; bibelot; bric-a-brac; curiosa (pl.); curiosity; decoration; keepsake; knickknack; memento; memorial; museum piece; *objet d'art*; relic; remembrance; reminder; souvenir; token; trinket; trophy; virtu

CURIOUS: aggressive; agog; bizarre; disquisitive; eccentric; eerie; extraordinary; fantastic; forward; grotesque; inquiring; inquisitive; inquisitorial; intrusive; meddlesome; meddling; nosy; odd; overcurious; peculiar; peeping; probing; prurient; prying; queer; rare; scrutinizing; searching; singular; snooping; snoopy; strange; suspicious; uncommon; unnatural; unusual; weird; CURIOSITY: (**see** "oddity") aggressiveness; bizarrerie; curio; curiosa (pl.); disquietude; eccentricity; grotesquerie; inquisitiveness; interest; intrusiveness; mystery; nosiness; novelty; piquancy; prurience; pruriency; rarity; scrutiny; singularity; snoopiness; spectacle; suspicion; weirdliness; wonder

CURL: **v.** (**see** "circle") bend; coil; contort; convolute; crimp; friz(zle); kink; ripple; roll; shrink; spiral; twine; twist; wave; weave; wind; writhe; CURL: **n.** bend; berger; coil; contortion; crimp; crispation; eddy; friz; kink; ringlet; ripple; roll; spiral; tress; twist; wave; CURLY: (**see** "circular") coiled; contorted; convolute(d); corrugated; crimped; crinkled; crispate; curled; kinked; ringed; rippled; rolled; snaky; twisted; waved; wavy

CURRENCY: (**see** "money") bills; cash; circulation; coinage; coins; currentness; medium (of exchange); notes; predominance; predomination; prevalence; regnance; regnancy; scrip; specie.

CURRENT: **a.** (**see** "common") accepted; accustomed; coetaneous; coeval; contemporaneous; contemporary; customary; existing; extant; general; genuine; going; habitual; instant; living; modern; passing; popular; present(-day); prevailing; prevalent; rapid; recent; rife; topical; unusual; CURRENT: **n.** (**see** "trend") air; breeze;

course; direction; drift; electricity; flow; gale; gust; line; motion; movement; route; stream; temper; tempest; tendency; tenor; thought; tide; time; tone; vein; vogue; wind; zephyr

CURSE: **v.** (**see** "swear") afflict; anathematize; beshrew; blaspheme; comminate; condemn; damn; denounce; doom; excommunicate; execrate; fulminate; harass; imprecate; invoke; maledict; objurgate; proscribe; punish; rail; rant; threaten; vilify; CURSE: **n.** anathema(tization); ban; bane; blasphemy; calamity; commination; condemnation; contamination; damnation; denunciation; destruction; evil; excommunication; execration; expletive; fulmination; harm; imprecation; malediction; malison; misfortune; proscription; scourge; slander; swearing; tabu; threat; trouble; vilification; woe; wrath; CURSED: (**see** "bad") accursed; anathematic(al); blasted; blighted; comminatory; confounded; damnatory; detestable; execrable; hateful; imprecatory; maledictory; odious; vicious; vile; virulent; wicked

CURSORY: (**see** "brief") careless; desultory; fast; hasty; passing; quick; rapid; scant; short; slight; speedy; superficial; swift; transient

CURT: (**see** "brief") abbreviated; abrupt; bluff; blunt; brusque; churlish; concise; condensed; crabbed; crabby; crude; crusty; cryptic(al); cutting; disagreeable; discourteous; disrespectful; dour; gruff; impertinent; impolite; indecorous; insolent; laconic(al); pettish; precise; rude; sassy; saucy; snappish; snappy; snippy; sour; sulky; sullen; surly; tart; terse; testy; unceremonious; uncivil; uncourtly; uncouth; ungentlemanly; ungracious; ungrateful; unmannerly; unpolished; unpolite; unrefined

CURTAIL: (**see** "abbreviate") abate; abridge; bobtail; brief; clip; cut; decrease; deprive; diminish; dock; economize; elide; eliminate; excise; lessen; limit; lop; omit; pare; reduce; remove; retrench; shorten; slash; stop; trim; truncate

CURVE: **v.** arch; arcuate; bend; bow; circumflex; concave; convex; crook; curl; depress; deviate; dip; dish; divert; hollow; hook; meander; snake; swing; turn; twist; vault; veer; weave; wind; zigzag; CURVE: **n.** ambit; arc; arch; arcuation; bend; bow; bowl; circuit; circumference; concavity; convexity; convolution; course; crater;

crook; curvation; curvature; dent; depression; detour; deviation; dip; dish; ess; flexure; graph; hole; hollow; hook; ogee; parabola; pit; quirk; sinuosity; trend; turn; twist; vault; veer; wave; CURVED *or* CURVING: agee; akimbo; alop; angular; arcate; arched; arciform; arcuate; askant; askew; atwist; awry; bent; bowed; circuitous; circumflex(ed); concave; convex; convolute(d); crescentic; crooked; curvaceous; curvesome; depressed; deviating; devious; dished; distorted; falciform; flexed; flexuous; hollow(ed); hooked; incurvate; involute(d); meandering; oblique; rolled; scrolled; sinuous; snaky; tortuous; twisted; undulating; vaulted; wavy; winding; wry; zigzag; CURVATURE: arc(uation); bend; curl; kyphosis; lordosis; scoliosis; sinuosity

CURVET: (**see** "caper") bound; gyrate; leap; prance

CUSHION: **v.** (**see** "protect") bolster; buffer; defend; guard; minimize; mitigate; muffle; pad; palliate; preserve; save; screen; shelter; shield; support; suppress; CUSHION: **n.** (**see** "protection") bag; bolster; buffer; guard; hassock; mat; pad; pillow; screen; seat; support

CUSP: (**see** "tooth") angle; apex; corner; peak; point

CUSTODY: (**see** "care") charge; control; detainment; detention; durance (vile); guardianship; keeping; maintenance; preservation; proctorship; protection; safekeeping; superintendence; CUSTODIAN: (**see** "protector") caretaker; Cerberus; chaperone; cicerone; claviger; concierge; conductor; custos; guard(ian); guide; jailor; janitor; leader; master; scout; teacher; tutor; warden

CUSTOM(S); addiction; assuetude; behavior; character(istic); conduct; constitution; consuetude; convention; courtesy; culture; demeanor; disposition; duty; ethics; ethos; fashion; folkway(s); form(ality); groove; habit(ude); habituation; habitus; law; manner; method(s); mode; mores; observance; path; patronage; pattern; practice; praxis; precedent; prescription; procedure; protocol; regularity; rite; ritual; rota; rote; routine; rubric; rule; rut; state; style; system; tax; tendency; trade; tradition; tribute; trick; usage; use; way; wont; CUSTOMARY: accepted; accustomed; administrative; available; average; cheap; chronic; classic(al); common(place); communal; constant; consuetudinary; continuous; conventional; (in) course; current; cut-and-dried; *de règle*; *de rigueur*; deepseated; democratic; demotic; domestic; dull; earthly; earthy; epidemic; everyday; familiar; fashionable; fixed; frequent; general; genetic; hackneyed; household; informed; ingrained; intractable; inured; known; mere; middle (of the road); mutual; nomic; obstinate; ordinary; permanent; persistent; plain; plebeian; popular; prescriptive; prevalent; prolonged; public; realistic; regular; rife; rooted; routine; settled; shared; traditional; trite; typical; universal; usual; vernacular; vulgar

CUSTOMER(S): (**see** "buyer") client(age); clientele; patient; patron(age); purchaser; vendee

CUT: **v.** abbreviate; ablate; abscind; abscise; absciss; adulterate; amputate; apportion; bob(tail); bowdlerize; break; butcher; cancel; carve; cease; chip; chisel; chop; cleave; clip; cross; curtail; dele(te); detach; dilute; diminish; disarticulate; disassociate; disconnect; disengage; disjoin(t); disperse; dissociate; dissolve; disunite; divide; divorce; dock; edit; elide; eliminate; emasculate; end; engrave; excide; excise; expunge; expurgate; exscind; extirpate; extract; fashion; fell; form; gash; hack; hew; hurt; incise; interrupt; intersect; isolate; lance; lash; lessen; lob; lop; lower; make; mow; nick; notch; ostracize; pare; part(ition); pierce; prune; reap; reduce; reject; remove; rend; resect; rip; saw; score; sculpt(ure); section; separate; serrate; serve; sever; shape; shear; shorten; slash; slice; slit; snip; snub; split; stop; subdivide; sunder; swerve; syncopate; tear; terminate; trim; uncouple; unhook; veer; weaken; CUT: **n.** abbreviation; abscission; amputation; butchering; cancellation; carving; chopping; cleft; clip; curtailment; deletion; dilution; disconnection; division; elimination; emas-

culation; engraving; excision; expunging; expurgation; extirpation; fraction; gash; incision; lash; lesion; lob; lop; nick; notch; part(ition); piece; portion; pruning; reduction; rejection; resection; rip(ping); scar; scission; score; scoring; section; segment; serration; shaping; share; slab; slash; slice; slit; snip; snub; weakening; wound; CUT: **a. see** "disconnected;" CUTTING: **a.** (**see** "acute") burning; crisp; curt; edged; keen; mordant; painful; piercing; sarcastic; sharp; snappish; trenchant; CUTTING: **n.** curtailment; emasculation; extirpation; incision; scion; scission; severance; shortening; slip; sundering; uncoupling; wounding

CUTE: (**see** "coy") attractive; charming; clever; ingenious; mannered; personable; pretty; sweet

CYCLE: age; bicycle; bike; circle; circuit; course; eon; epoch; era; interval; journey; lap; loop; month; orbit; period; periplus; revolution; ring; round; saros; sequence; series; sphere; surge; turn; upsurge; upturn; vehicle; week; wheel; year; CYCLIC(AL): epochal; periodic(al); recurrent; secular; sequential; weekly; yearly

CYNIC: Antisthenes; curmudgeon; Diogenes; dismal Jimmy; egotist; grouch; melancholiac; misanthropist; misanthropos; pessimist; skeptic; snarler; Timon; CYNICAL: derisive; despairing; disbelieving; distrustful; faultfinding; gloomy; grouchy; ironical; melancholy; misanthropic(al); misogynic; misogynous; morose; pessimistic; sarcastic; sardinian; sardonic; satirical; sneering; CYNICISM: Dadaism; derision; despair; disbelief; gloom; irony; melancholia; miserabilism; pessimism; sarcasm; sardonicism; satire; *weltschmerz*

CYNOSURE: allurement; attraction; charm; enticement; fascination; glamo(u)r; lodestar; lure; polestar

D

DABBLE: (see "meddle") fool; fuss; intervene; intrude; moisten; potter; pry; snoop; splash; splatter; sprinkle; tamper; tinker; trifle; DABBLER: amateur; collector; dilettante; interloper; intermeddler; intervener; intruder; meddler; novice; pryer; quack; sciolist; snoop(er); trifler

DAEDAL(IAN): (see "cunning" and "intricate") artistic; ingenious; skillful

DAFT or DAFTY: (see "crazy") foolish; insane; mad; silly

DAILY: aday; circadian; diurnal; per diem; quotidian

DAINTY: a. (see "delicate") airy; beautiful; birdlike; bonny; careful; choice; decorous; elegant; ethereal; exquisite; fastidious; fine; fussy; gossamer(y); groomed; little; lovely; modish; neat; nice; overnice; palatable; particular; petite; pleasing; pretty; prissy; rare(fied); refined; savory; small; soft; soigné; soignée (fem.); squeamish; sweet; tender; DAINTY: n. (see "delicacy") cate; tidbit; DAINTINESS: (see "delicacy") elegance; ethereality; friandise; frill

DALLY: (see "dawdle") delay; loiter; philander; play; procrastinate; shilly-shally; sport; tarry; toy; trifle; vacillate

DAM: v. bar; block; bolt; choke; clog; close; confine; deprive; deter; exclude; fasten; hamper; hinder; impede; isolate; latch; lock; obstruct; preclude; prevent; prohibit; proscribe; restrain; restrict; shut; stem; stop; suppress; DAM: n. bar(ricade); barrier; block(ade); blockage; bolt; clog; hampering; hindrance; impediment; mother; obstruction; parent; restraint; restriction; stop(page); suppression; weir

DAMAGE: v. (see "injure") bang; break; bruise; bungle; deface; deform; degrade; despoil; destroy; disfigure; distort; disturb; founder; harm; hurt; impair; mar; mark; mayhem; mutilate; prejudice; ruin; scathe; scratch; spoil; twist; warp; weaken; wound; wreck; wrong; DAMAGE: n. (see "injury") bane; bang; break; bruise; charge; cost; crack; decay; defacement; degradation; destruction; deterioration; detriment; disfiguration; distortion; expense; fault; harm; hurt; impairment; injury; insult; loss; mark; mayhem; mutilation; ruin; rust; scratch; sorrow; warp(age); waste; wear; wound; wreck; wrong; DAMAGING: (see "injurious") destructive; detrimental; harmful; hurtful; impairing; inimical; injurious; malign(ant); nocent; nocuous; noxious; prejudicial; ruinous; shocking; traumatic; venomous; wrong

DAMN: (see "swear") ban(ish); condemn; confound; curse; denounce; devote; doom; execrate; punish; ruin; DAMNABLE: see "execrable"

DAMP(EN): v. (see "depress") check; deaden; diminish; discourage; dispirit; extinguish; lessen; moisten; muffle; mute; reduce; restrain; retard; soak; soft-pedal; stifle; wet; DAMP: a. clammy; dank; depressed; dismal; dull; humid; juicy; moist(y); wet

DANCE: (see "cavort" and "gambol") glide; leap; skip; spring; DANCER: alma; ballerina; chorine; danseuse; performer

DANDY(ISH): a. (see "great") coxcombical; fine; first-rate; foppish; vain; DANDY: n. bean; beau; Beau Brummel; blade; blood; buck; coxcomb; dandiprat; dude; exquisite; fop; incroyable; jackanapes; jake; Johnny; macaroni; petit-maître; popinjay; swell; toff

DANGER: (see "crisis") acuteness; adventure; adventurement; adventurism; calumny; chance; Charybdis; criticality; cruciality; desperation; disaster; distress; exigency; exposure; extremity; fear; hazard; imminence; imperilment; insecurity; instability; jeopardy; man-trap; menace; pass; peril(ousness); pitfall; precipice; quicksand; risk; snare; threat; trap; uncertainty; venture; DANGEROUS: (see "desperate") acute; bad; bold; cancerous; chancy; critical; crucial; destructive; devastating; dire;

dread(ful); endangering; exigent; explosive; exposed; extreme; fearful; feral; foolhardy; formidable; foul; grim; harmful; hazardous; hostile; hot; Icarian; ignitable; imminent; injurious; insecure; instable; jeopardous; killing; life-endangering; loaded; malign-(ant); menacing; murderous; ominous; parlous; periculous; perilous; precarious; rash; reckless; rickety; risky; severe; shaky; threatening; thundering; tottery; treacherous; uncertain; unchary; unhealthful; unhealthy; unsafe; venturesome; vulnerable; wicked

DANGLE: (**see** "hang") droop; loll; lop; oscillate; pend(ulate); suspend; sway; swing; wave; DANGLING: **see** "hanging"

DAPPER: (**see** "charming" and "dashing") alert; brisk; chic; debonair(e); elegant; jaunty; lively; natty; neat; nifty; posh; raffish; rakish; smart; *soigné*; *soignée* (fem.); sophisticated; sporty; sprightly; spruce; stylish; swaggering; trig; trim

DAPPLED: (**see** "variegated") dotted; patched; piebald; spotted

DARE: **v.** (**see** "defy") challenge; confront; expect; face; front; goad; invite; presume; provoke; risk; tempt; venture; DARE: **n.** (**see** "challenge") confrontation; risk; venture; DARING: **a.** (**see** "dangerous") adventuresome; adventurous; audacious; bold; brave; brazen; challenging; courageous; fearless; foolhardy; fortitudinous; Icarian; imaginative; impudent; intrepid; new; novel; perilous; picaresque; rash; risky; risqué; stout; striking; tempting; unafraid; unconventional; unsafe; venturesome; venturous; vivacious; DARING: **n.** **see** "boldness"

DARK(ENED): abstruse; adiaphanous; adumbral; ambiguous; atramental; atramentous; backward; benighted; black; bleared; blurred; blurry; brunette; cabalistic; caliginous; cheerless; Cimmerian; clouded; cloudy; concealed; crepuscular; dense; despondent; dim; dismal; dispirited; doubtful; dubious; dull; dun; dusk(y); ebon(y); faint; filmy; foggy; fuliginous; gloomy; hard; hazy; hidden; ignorant; incomprehensible; indistinct; indistinguishable; inexplicable; iniquitous; inky; joyless; lackluster; latent; lightless; low; maniac; miry; misty; murky; mysterious; mystic; nebulated; nebulose; nebulous; obscure; occult; ominous; opaque; overcast; primitive; profound; rayless; retarded; roily; sad; secret(ive);

shadowy; sinister; smoky; somber; stygian; subdued; swart(hy); tenebrious; turbulent; uncertain; unclear; unknown; unlighted; unlikely; unlit; unluminous; unlustrous; unrefined; vague; wan; wicked; DARKEN: (**see** "cloud") adumbrate; becloud; bedim; befoul; conceal; confuse; denigrate; depress; dim; dun; hide; mask; muddle; obfuscate; obscure; perplex; sadden; taint; tarnish; DARKNESS: dark; despondency; distress; fuliginosity; gloom(iness); ignorance; indefiniteness; indistinction; indistinctness; lightlessness; murk; night(fall); obscurity; raylessness; shade; shadow; tenebrosity; twilight; umbra(ge)

DARLING: **a.** (**see** "cute") beautiful; delightful; fair-haired; DARLING: **n.** acushla; baby; beloved; *chéri*; *chérie* (fem.); dear; delight; doll; favorite; love; pet; sweet-(heart)

DART: **v.** (**see** "dash") bound; cast; elance; flit; flutter; fly; hurl; hurry; jump; launch; leap; play; race; rush; scoot; scud; speed; spring; start; streak; throw; DART: **n.** arrow; fléchette; javelin; lance; missile; sumpit

DASH: **v.** (**see** "dart") besmirch; bespeckle; blotch; bounce; break; cast; confound; confuse; crush; depress; flash; flit; fly; hurl; hurry; jump; launch; leap; play; race; rush; smash; splash; splatter; sprint; sully; DASH: **n.** (**see** "bit") animation; ardor; burst; courage; dollop; drive; *éclat*; *élan*; energy; flash; force; hint; obelus; ostentation; power; race; rush; shade; spirit; splash; streak; tantivy; tinge; touch; vein; verve; vigor; vitality; DASHING: alert; brave; bright; brilliant; brisk; bully; chic; clever; dapper; distinguished; doggy; effulgent; elegant; excellent; fashionable; flashing; flashy; gallant; gay; gleaming; glittering; glowing; headlong; illustrious; impetuous; iridescent; jaunty; keen; lively; luminescent; luminous; lustrous; magnificent; merry; meteoric; natty; neat; nifty; opalescent; ostentatious; posh; precipitate; radiant; rakish; reckless; resourceful; rich; scintillant; scintillating; shiny; showy; smart; *soigné*; *soignée* (fem.); sophisticated; spanking; sparkling; spirited; splashing; splendid; splendorous; spruce; striking; stylish; trim; virtuosic; vivid; wise; witty

DASTARD: (**see** "coward") sneak; DASTARDLY: **see** "cowardly"

DATA (DATUM sing.): (**see** "facts") principles

DATE: (see "engagement") appointment; circumstance; day; era; event; fruit; occasion; rendezvous; target; time; tryst

DAUB: (see "smear") swish

DAUNT: affright; agitate; alarm; alert; amate; amaze; appal(l); arouse; astonish; astound; awe; bemuse; benumb; bewilder; browbeat; bulldoze; bully; check; confuse; conquer; cow; dastardize; dazzle; deaden; deject; depress; deter; discourage; dishearten; dismay; disquiet; disturb; dragoon; excite; faze; floor; foil; frighten; horrify; imperil; intimidate; overawe; perplex; perturb(ate); petrify; rattle; scare; shock; startle; strike terror; stun; stupefy; terrify; terrorize; threaten; thwart; torpify; unman; unnerve; upset

DAWDLE: dally; daydream; delay; dillydally; doodle; dream; fiddle(-faddle); hesitate; idle; lag; loiter; moon; mope; play; poke; potter; procrastinate; quiddle; shilly-shally; stay; tarry; toy; trifle; vacillate; wait; waste

DAWN aurora; beginning; cockcrow; daybreak; daylight; dew; genesis; opening; origin; precursor; renaissance; sunrise; sunup; uprise

DAY: age; date; dawn; daylight; epoch; era; lifetime; occasion; sun; time

DAYDREAM(ING): (see "fancy") autism; castle in the air; introspection; introspectiveness; mooning; phantasm; phantasy; reverie; romanticizing; stargazing; woolgathering

DAZE: v. (see "daunt") amaze; anesthetize; astonish; astound; awe; bemuse; benumb; bewilder; blind; confuse; dazzle; deaden; fog; impress; overawe; overpower; paralyze; perplex; petrify; shine; shock; stun; stupefy; surprise; torpify; DAZE: n. amazement; anesthesia; awe; bewilderment; confusion; fog; paralysis; perplexity; petrification; shock; stupefaction; surprise; torpidity; torpor; trance

DAZZLE: (see "daze") amaze; astonish; astound; bewilder; blind; confine; confuse; drown; impress; outshine; overawe; overpower; reflect; shine; stun; surprise; DAZZLING: adazzle; amazing; astonishing; astounding; bewildering; blinding; bright; brilliant; confusing; crystalline; foudroyant; fulgent; fulgid; fulgurant; fulgurating; garish; gleaming; iridescent; meteoric; pris-

matic; pyrotechnic(al); radiant; resplendent; shining; showy; splendorous; stunning; surprising; DAZZLEMENT: (see "astonishment") amazement; bewilderment; blindness; brightness; brilliance; confusion; fulguration; gleam; glitter; iridescence; opalescence; radiance; reflection; resplendence; shine; show; splendor; surprise

DEAD: abrupt; ad patres; alamort; amort; apathetic; asleep; barren; belowground; bloodless; breathless; calm; comatose; complete; deceased; defunct; demised; departed; deserted; done; doomed; dull; elapsed; exact; exanimate; exhausted; expired; extinct; extinguished; fey; flat; gone; idle; inactive; inanimate; indolent; inert; infertile; inorganic; insensate; insensible; insentient; irrevocable; lapsed; late; latent; lazy; lethargic; lifeless; lost; low; lusterless; monotonous; moribund; motionless; muffled; nonexistent; nonliving; nonviable; numb; obsolete; out; passé; powerless; slow; sluggish; sodden; spent; spiritless; stagnant; still; stolid; supine; tired; torpid; total; unalive; unmoving; unproductive; unrecoverable; unresponsive; DEADEN: anesthetize; assuage; benumb; blunt; cauterize; conceal; cover; damp(en); daze; depress; dull; freeze; hebetate; hypnotize; kill; lethargize; muffle; mute; narcotize; numb; obscure; obtund; pad; paralyze; retard; silence; smother; soft-pedal; stifle; stupefy; suppress; weaken; DEADENED: see "numb;" DEADLY: baneful; biocidal; cadaverous; calamitious; catastrophic(al); complete; condemned; dangerous; deathful; deathly; destined; destructive; determined; devastating; dire; disastrous; doomed; extreme; fatal; fateful; fell; feral; fey; harmful; implacable; injurious; internecine; killing; lethal; lethiferous; life-endangering; macabre; malicious; malign(ant); mortal; mortiferous; mortuary; murderous; noxious; ominous; penetrating; pernicious; pestilent(ial); poisonous; portentous; predestined; predetermined; preordained; prophetic; ruinous; stygian; terminal; toxic; toxiferous; truculent; unerring; unfailing; venomous; viperish; vitriolic; vituperative

DEAL: v. administer; agree; allot; apportion; arrange; assign; auction; bargain; barter; bestow; buy; cavil; commute; compromise; contract; deliver; dicker; dispose; distribute; divide; dole; exchange; give; haggle; market; measure; mete; negotiate; palter; parley; portion; ration; reach; sell; share; swap; trade; traffic; transact; treat; truck; DEAL: n. affair; agreement; allotment; apportionment; assignment; buy; commerce; communication; commutation; compact; conspiracy; contract; dealings; distribution; division; dole; gift; interaction; interchange; job; lot; negotiation; pact; play; portion; *quid pro quo*; safe; share; trade; traffic; transaction; DEALER: agent; broker; distributor; factor; manufactor; merchant; middleman; monger; seller; trader; trafficker; vendor

DEAR: **a.** (**see** "affectionate") amorous; beloved; cherished; costly; darling; earnest; extravagant; fond; good; heartfelt; high; invaluable; lavished; loved; loving; precious; priceless; scarce; sumptuous; sweet; tender; valuable; DEAR: **n. see** "darling"

DEARTH: (**see** "deficiency") deficit; famine; inadequacy; lack; need; paucity; scarcity; shortage; want; weakness

DEATH: abolishment; abolition; annihilation; Beyond; cancellation; consummation; *coup de grâce*; curtains; *debitum naturae*; decease; defunction; demise; demolition; departure; destruction; dissolution; doom; doomsday; dormancy; drowning; end(ing); evanishment; exit(us); extermination; extinction; fatality; finis; finish; (the) Four Horsemen: (the) Grim Reaper; hell; Hereafter; homicide; inactivity; insensibility; lifelessness; mort-(ality); murder; nonexistence; (the) Pale Horse; passing; perdition; physical extinction; quenching; quietus; repose; rest; silence; sleep; starvation; suppression; DEATHLY: (**see** "deadly") cachectic; cachexic; cadaverous; destructive; fatal; lethal; mausolean; morbid; murderous; stygian; terminal

DEBAR: (**see** "banish") ban; bar; close; dam; disable; disbar; disenable; disfrock; disqualify; disthrone; estop; exclude; hinder; prevent; prohibit; restrain; retire; shut; unfrock

DEBASE: (**see** "belittle") abase; abuse; adulterate; alloy; bastardize; bemean; coarsen; contaminate; corrupt; defame; defile; deglamorize; degrade; demean; demote; denigrate; deprave; depreciate; deteriorate; dilute; discredit; disgrace; dishonor; downgrade; harm; heathenize; humble; impair; lower; minimize; outrage; paganize; pejorate; pervert; pollute; profane; prostitute; prostrate; reduce; riddle; sap; shame; spoil; stigmatize; stoop; sully; taint; vilify; violate; vitiate; vulgarize; weaken; DEBASED: **see** "wicked"

DEBATE: **v.** altercate; argue; argufy; battle; bicker; brawl; canvass; cavil; clash; complain; contemplate; contend; controvert; converse; deliberate; differ; disagree; discept; discuss; dispute; dissent; examine; fend; fight; fuss; jangle; maintain; plead; quarrel; reason; rebut; reflect; rupture; scrap; spat; squabble; strive; struggle; study; talk; tiff; tussle; wrangle; wrestle; DEBATE: **n.** altercation; argument(ation); battle; brawl; canvass; clash; complaint; colloquy; controversy; conversation; deliberation; dialectic(s); disagreement; discussion; disputation; dispute; dissent(ion); feud; fight; fuss; jangle; quarrel; reflection; row; rupture; talk; tiff; tussle; wrangle; DEBATABLE: argumentative; contentious; controversial; controvertible; dialectic(al); discursory; disputable; disputatious; disputed; doubtful; dubious; dubitable; equivocal; factious; forensic; moot; parliamentary; polemic(al); questionable; quodlibetary; quodlibetic(al)

DEBAUCH: **v.** binge; carouse; contaminate; corrupt; debase; defile; deprave; dissipate; drink; feast; harm; injure; lure; mar; pervert; pollute; roister; royster; seduce; spoil; spree; vitiate; DEBAUCH(ERY): **n.** (**see** "carousal") bout; dissipation; excess; frolic; orgy; revel; spree

DEBILITATE: (**see** "weaken") attenuate; cripple; damage; devitalize; disable; drain; enervate; enfeeble; exhaust; harm; hurt; impair; mar; prostrate; sap; soften; tire; unman; unnerve; DEBILITATED: (**see** "weak") adynamic; asthenic; bedridden; burned-out; burnt-out; cachectic; cachexic; decrepit; deficient; enervated; enfeebled; exhausted; feeble; impaired; impotent; infirm; lame; phthisic(al); puny; sick(ly); tubercular; tuberculous; weakened; worn-(out); DEBILITY: (**see** "weakness") adynamia; asthenia; atony; cachexia; cachexy; debilitation; decrepitude; enervation; enfeeblement; exhaustion; fatigue; feebleness; frailty; impairment; impotence; impotency; infirmity; languor; lassitude; marasmus; puniness; pusillanimity; susceptibility; tenderness; tenuity; underpower; vulnerability

DEBONAIR(E): (**see** "elated") affable; blithe(some); bright; buoyant; carefree; cheery; chipper; cocky; courteous; elegant; gay; genteel; gracious; jaunty; lighthearted; lithe; lively; nonchalant; perky; polite; sprightly; suave; urbane

DEBRIS: (**see** "waste") accumulation; dirt;

driblets; fragments; garbage; lees; oddments; orts; refuse; remains; rubbish; scree;
screenings; sediment; trash; trivia

DEBT: (**see** "liability") arrearage; arrears;
charge; debit; default; deficiency; deficit;
duty; failure; fault; indebtedness; IOU:
lack; lapse; loss; neglect; negligence; obligation; responsibility; sin; trespass; want

DECADENT: (**see** "old-fashioned") antediluvian; archaic; archaistic; decayed; declined;
degenerated; *démodé*; demoded; effete;
fin-de-siècle; moribund; obsolescent; outmoded; out-of-date; overripe; passé; regressive; spent; DECADENCE *or* DECAD-
ENCY: (**see** "decay") archaism; decadent-
(ism); declination; decline; deterioration;
exhaustion; regression

DECAY: **v.** blight; break; collapse; corrupt;
crumble; crush; decline; decompose; defile;
degenerate; degrade; destroy; deteriorate;
dilapidate; diminish; disintegrate; dissipate;
dissolve; dwindle; exhaust; fail; fall; fold-
(up); impair; liquefy; macerate; mildew;
mold(er); pulverize; putrefy; putresce; resolve; rot; ruin; rust; separate; shrink;
sicken; spoil; taint; tarnish; yellow; waste;
wear; wither; wrack; wreck; wrinkle;
DECAY: **n.** archaism; blight; collapse;
corruption; decadence; decadency; decadent-
(ism); declination; decline; decomposition;
decrepitness; decrepitude; defilement; degeneracy; degeneration; *délabrement*; demoralization; deterioration; dilapidation;
diminishment; disintegration; disrepair;
dissipation; dissolution; downfall; failure;
feebleness; havoc; impairment; labefaction;
liquefaction; mildew; mold(ering); mortification; necrosis; neglect; putrefaction;
putrescence; putridity; rot; ruin; rust;
shrinkage; spoilage; squalidity; stubbornness; taint; tarnish; waste; wear; withering;
wreck(age); DECAYING: **see** "rotting;"
DECAYED: **see** "old-fashioned"

DECEASE: **see** "die;" DECEASED: (**see**
"dead") defunct; gone; late; lost

DECEIT: **see** under "deceive"

DECEIVE: (**see** "cheat" and "fool") abuse;
balk; bamboozle; befool; beguile; belie;
betray; bilk; cajole; camouflage; caricature;
check; circumvent; cloak; collude; color;
confuse; counterfeit; cover; cozen; defraud;
delude; disappoint; disguise; dissemble;
dissimulate; distort; double-cross; dupe;
enmesh; ensnare; entangle; entrap; equivo-

cate; euchre; exaggerate; falsify; fast-talk;
feign; finagle; flan; frustrate; garble; gull;
hoax; hocus; honeyfuggle; hoodwink; hide;
humble; illude; inveigle; lie; lure; malign;
mask; misdirect; misguide; mishandle;
misinform; mislabel; mislead; misrepresent;
misstate; mock; outwit; palm off; pretend;
screen; seduce; sile; simulate; snare; snow;
swindle; trap; trick; two-time; veil; victimize;
DECEITFUL *or* DECEPTIVE: (**see** "illusive") alluring; artful; baffling; Barmecidal;
beguiling; cabalistic; clandestine; cunning;
deceptious; delusional; delusive; delusory;
dishonest; disloyal; dissembling; dissimulat-
ing; double-dealing; doublehearted; duplicitous; eely; elusive; ephemeral; equivocal;
evasive; faithless; fallacious; false; fictitious;
fleeting; fraudulent; fugitive; gnathonic;
guileful; hollow; illusional; illusory; impalpable; imposterous; insidious; intangible;
lubric(i)ous; magical; mendacious; misleading; obliquitous; perfidious; phantasma-
goric(al); saponaceous; serpentine; sinuous;
sirenic(al); slick; snaky; specious; spurious;
subtle; surreptitious; treacherous; treasonable; tricky; underhand(ed); unrealistic;
untrustworthy; vague; venal; wily; wrong;
DECEIT: DECEPTION *or* DECEPTIVE-
NESS: (**see** "illusion") affectation; apparition; artifice; bamboozlement; beguilement;
betrayal; bubble; camouflage; caricature;
cheating; chicanery; chimera; circumvention; collusion; concealment; counterfeit;
covin; cozenage; craft(iness); crookedness;
cunning; deceitfulness; defraudation; delusion; despience; disguise; dishonesty; dishonor; disingenuity; disloyalty; dissimulation; distortion; double-dealing; dream;
duplicity; elusiveness; error; evasion; exaggeration; fabrication; faithlessness; fake(ry);
false alarm; false front; falsehood; falseness;
falsification; falsity; fancy; feint; fourberie; fraud(ulence); fugitivity; gambit;
ghost; guile(fulness); hanky-panky; hoax;
hocus(-pocus); humbug; hypocrisy; *ignis
fatuus*; ignominy; illusiveness; imitation;
improbity; indirection; indirectness; infamy;
infidelity; insidiousness; insincerity; intangibility; inveiglement; jape; knavishness;
legerdemain; lie; lubricity; ludification;
lying; Machiavellianism; magic; malconduct;
mauvaise foi; mendacity; mirage; misrepresentation; mockery; obliquity; perfidy;
phantasm(agoria); phantasmata (pl.);
phantom; prestidigitation; pretense; pretension; pretext; prevarication; representation; roguery; roguishness; ruse; sanctimoniousness; sanctimony; sham; simulation;
sinisterity; sinisterness; sinuosity; speciosity;
speciousness; specter; spoof; spook; strata-

gem; subterfuge; subtlety; swindle; Tartuffery; tortuosity; treachery; treason; trick-
(ery); triplicity; underhandedness; unfairness; unfaithfulness; unscrupulosity; untrustworthiness; vile; vision; wile; will-of-
the-wisp; DECEIVER: betrayer; charlatan;
deluder; dissembler; dissimulator; fake(r);
imposter; liar; magician; mountebank; prestidigitator; quack(salver); rogue; sham;
sharp(st)er; swindler; trickster

DECENT: acceptable; adequate; appropriate;
becoming; befitting; calm; chaste; comely;
conventional; correct; decorous; demure;
dignified; dressed; fit; formal; good; honorable; meet; modest; moral; nice; noble;
orderly; polite; prim; proper; pure; satisfactory; sedate; seemly; staid; sufficient;
suitable; unobjectionable; virtuous; DEC-
ENCY: chastity; decora (pl.); decorum;
deportment; dignity; discipline; fitness;
form(ality); grace; manners; modesty;
order(liness); politeness; propriety; pudency;
purity; seemliness; suitability; virtue;
DECENCIES: (the) conventionalities;
conventions; decora (pl.); (the) proprieties

DECEPTIVE, DECEPTION: **see** under
"deceive"

DECIDE: adjudge; adjudicate; announce;
answer; arbitrate; arrange; choose; collect;
conclude; control; cull; declare; decree;
determine; dijudicate; direct; dispose; doom;
elect; embrace; end; espouse; favor; figure;
find; fix; judge; measure; opt(ate); order;
pick; please; prefer; rate; regulate; remove;
resolve; rule; select; sentence; separate; settle;
solve; take; terminate; umpire; vote; want;
DECIDED: clear-cut; determined; promised;
resolved; set(tled); unmistakable; unquestionable; DECISION: adjudication; announcement; answer; aplomb; arbitrament;
arbitration; arret; choice; conclusion; consequence; decree; definitude; determination;
dijudication; disposal; disposition; doom;
fait accompli; finding(s); firmness; issue; judgment; mandate; mandatum; mettle; nerve;
opinion; outcome; policy; rating; report;
res adjudicata; resolution; resolve; result;
rule; ruling; sentence; settlement; termination; upshot; verdict; volition; vote; way;
will

DECIMATE: (**see** "annihilate") abolish;
demolish; deracinate; destroy; slay; subtract;
uproot

DECIPHER: (**see** "understand") decode; interpret; read; solve; translate; unfold; unravel

DECISION: **see** under "decide"

DECISIVE: (**see** "certain") absolute; authoritarian; authoritative; categorical; clear-
cut; conclusive; cool; critical; crucial; crushing; definite; definitive; determinative;
dictatorial; inexorable; judgmental; overwhelming; resolute; ringing; ruling; telling;
thoughtful; unalterable; unequivocal; unmistakable; unquestionable; virile; withering

DECK: **v.** (**see** "array") adorn; apparel;
begem; diamondize; dress; embellish;
DECK: **n.** (**see** "floor") pack; platform;
story

DECLAIM: (**see** "expound") advertise; advocate; affirm; air; analyze; blare; blazon;
comment; declare; defend; discourse; discuss;
elocute; elucidate; explain; exposit; express;
harangue; inform; instruct; mouth; orate;
present; profess; promulgate; rant; recite;
rhetorize; speak; spout; state; teach; utter;
vent; voice; DECLAMATORY: bombastic;
Ciceronian; elocutionary; grandiloquent;
magniloquent; melodramatic; oratorical;
rhetorical; stilted; DECLAMATION: **see**
"oration"

DECLARE: (**see** "say") acknowledge; advertise; affirm; allege; announce; annunciate;
assert; aseverate; aver; avouch; avow;
broadcast; decide; designate; dispose; explain; exposit; expound; maintain; manifest;
meld; name; nuncupate; pledge; predict;
proclaim; promulgate; publish; recite;
show; speak; spread; state; swear; utter;
vote; vow; DECLARATION: (**see** "announcement") acknowledgement; advertisement; affirmation; annunciation; asservera-
tion; avowal; bid; call; complaint; exposition; manifesto; pleading; pledge; proclamation; profession; publication; statement;
utterance; vow; warrant; white paper;
DECLARATORY: (**see** "assertive")
affirmative; assertorial; declarative; enunciative; expository; proclamative; promulgative

DECLINE: **v.** abate; age; avoid; backslide;
balk; bend; blanch; blur; cease; change;
dangle; decay; decrease; degenerate; degrade; delay; demur; depreciate; descend;
deteriorate; deviate; die; dim(inish); dip;
disappear; dismount; droop; drop; dull;
dwindle; ebb; enervate; etiolate; evanesce;
evaporate; exhaust; fade; fail; fall; falter;
fizzle; flag; flop; forbear; incline; inflect;
jade; lag; languish; lapse; leave; lessen; lose;

lower; melt; nod; pale; pass; peter (out); pine; pitch; plunge; precipitate; quit; recede; recidivate; refuse; regress; reject; relapse; renege; retreat; retrogress; sag; sere; set(tle); sicken; sink; slip; slouch; slump; spurn; stoop; stray; subside; tire; toboggan; vanish; wane; waste; wax; weaken; wilt; wither; wrinkle; yellow; DECLINE: **n.** abatement; afternon; attenuation; curtailment; decadence; decay; declination; declivity; decrease; defervescence; degeneration; degenerescence; degradation; *dégringolade*; demotion; depreciation; deterioration; diminishment; diminuendo; diminution; disintegration; downtrend; downturn; dusk; dwindling; eve; evening; eventide; failure; fall; fizzle; flop; inclination; incline; involution; leaning; lessening; loss; recession; refusal; regression; rejection; repudiation; retreat; retrogression; sinking; slip; slump; sunset; toboggan; twilight; wasting; weakening; wrinkling

DECLIVITY: (**see** "incline") cliff; decline; descent; dip; downgrade; drop; fall; grade; gradient; hill; inclination; pitch; ramp; scarp; slant; slope

DECOCTION: (**see** "drink") boiling; extract; infusion; preparation

DECOMPOSE: (**see** "decay") analyze; break (up.); crumble; degenerate; degrade; digest; disintegrate; liquefy; melt; putrefy; putresce; resolve; rot; rust; separate; sour; spoil; DECOMPOSITION: (**see** "decay") degeneration; disintegration; dissociation; liquefaction; putrefaction; putrescence; rot; spoilage

DECOR: (**see** "decoration") atmosphere; background; motif; ornament(ation); scenery; setting

DECORATE: (**see** "adorn") bedeck; border; cite; commendate; deck; do; edge; embellish; emblazon; enrich; festoon; flourish; furbish; garland; garnish; grace; honor; lace; ornament; paint; redo; refurbish; trim; DECORATION: (**see** "adornment") appointment; atmosphere; award; background; badge; braid; campaign ribbon; caparison; citation; cup; decor; edging; embellishment; emblazonment; embroidery; festoon; filigree; flourish; frill; frog; garland; garnishment; garniture; gingerbread; gold; honor; insigne; insignia (pl.); lace; medal; medallion; molding; motif; niello; order; ornament(ation); ribbon; scenery; scrambled eggs; setting; trick; trim; trophy; DECORATIVE: (**see** "attractive") alluring; appealing;

appointed; delightful; fanciful; filagree; gingerbread; ornamental

DECOROUS: (**see** "decent") calm; comely; conventional; correct; dignified; formal; orderly; polite; prim; proper; sedate; staid

DECORUM: (**see** "decency") appropriateness; convention; correctness; decora (pl.); decorousness; dignity; discipline; form(ality); manners; modesty; order(liness); politeness; propriety

DECREASE: **v.** (**see** "check") abate; abbreviate; abridge; adulterate; age; alleviate; ameliorate; assuage; attenuate; cease; curtail; cut (back); cut down; damp(en); decay; deceive; decline; degenerate; degrade; delay; demote; denigrate; depreciate; depress; deteriorate; digress; diminish; dip; discourage; disparage; droop; drop; dwindle; ease; ebb; enfeeble; evaporate; exhaust; extenuate; fade; fail; fall (off); falter; fizzle; flag; flop; free; grade down; hinder; impair; lighten; limit; lose; lower; minify; minimize; mitigate; moderate; modify; mollify; narrow; palliate; pejorate; plunge; recede; recidivate; reduce; relapse; relax; relieve; renege; repress; retrench; retrogress; revert; sag; sap; set(tle); shrink; sicken; sink; slip; slump; soften; soothe; stem; stop; subside; temper; thin; want; wax; weaken; wither; worsen; DECREASE: **n.** (**see** "check") abatement; abbreviation; abridgment; adulteration; alleviation; amelioration; assuagement; attenuation; backslide; belittlement; contraction; curtailment; cutdown; decadence; decay; declination; decline; declivity; decrement; decrescence; decrescendo; defervescence; degeneration; degenerescence; degradation; degression; *dégringolade*; delay; demotion; denigration; depreciation; deterioration; diminishment; diminuendo; diminution; discouragement; disintegration; downbeat; downtrend; drop; dwindling; ebb; exhaustion; extenuation; failure; fall; fizzle; flop; hindrance; impairment; inclination; incline; involution; lessening; limitation; loss; minification; minimization; mitigation; moderation; modification; mollification; narrowing; palliation; pejoration; recession; recidivation; reduction; refusal; regression; relaxation; relief; repression; repudiation; retreat; retrenchment; retrogression; reversion; sagging; shrinkage; sickening; sinking; slip; slump; stop; subsidence; thinning; tide; wane; wasting; weakening; wear; worsening; DECREASING: (**see** "lessening") declinatory; decrescendo; waning; worsening

DECREE: **v.** (**see** "command") act; adjudge; adjudicate; adjust; appoint; choose; decide; determine; dictate; direct; doom; elect; enact; enjoin; establish; judge; ordain; order; prefer; prescribe; pronounce; rule; sentence; set(tle); will; DECREE: **n.** (**see** "command)" act; adjudication; arret; breve; bull; canon; decision; decrement; decretum; determination; direction; doom; edict; enactment; fiat; irade; judgment; law; mandate; mandatum; manifesto; nisi; order; ordinance; prescription; pronouncement; pronunciamento; proscription; rule; ruling; sanction; sentence; settlement; ukase; will; writ

DECREPIT: (**see** "aged") ancient; bedridden; creaky; decayed; dilapidated; enervated; enfeebled; feeble; fragile; frail; infirm; old; senile; superannuated; wasted; weak(ened); worn(-out); DECREPITUDE: (**see** "feebleness") decay; dilapidation; infirmity

DECRY: (**see** "censure") belittle; condemn; criticize; denigrate; denounce; deprecate; depreciate; derogate; detract; discredit; disparage; minimize; traduce

DEDICATE: (**see** "consecrate") bless; commemorate; commit; destine; devote; enshrine; hallow; honor; inscribe; ordain; present; sanctify; vow; DEDICATION: appointment; blessing; commemoration; commission; commitment; confirmation; consecratedness; consecration; deification; devotedness; devotement; devotion; enshrinement; enthusiasm; faithfulness; hallowing; ordination; presentation; sanctification; stick-to-itiveness; vow; zeal(otry)

DEDUCE: believe; collect; conclude; conduct; consider; construct; convey; decide; deduct; deem; derive; estimate; figure; gather; gauge; guess; hariolate; infer; judge; opine; prove; reason; reckon; resolve; speculate; think

DEDUCT: (**see** "diminish") abate; bate; cancel; cut; deduce; dele(te); dock; infer; rebate; reduce; remove; retrench; shave; subtract; take; withdraw; withhold; DEDUCTIVE: deductible; dogmatic; illative; inferential; DEDUCTION: (**see** "diminishment") abatement; conclusion; corollary; deductibility; derivation; diminution; hariolation; inference; inferentialism; opinion; reason; reckoning; reduction; subtraction; thought; withdrawal; write-off

DEED: **v.** charter; convey; sell; transfer;

DEED: **n.** (**see** "act") accomplishment; achievement; action; charter; commission; conveyance; doing; exploit; fact; fait; feat; gest(e); indenture; performance; reality; record; *res gestae* (pl.); transaction; transfer

DEEM: account; believe; cherish; conceive; consider; esteem; estimate; gather; hold; imagine; infer; judge; opine; reckon; regard; suppose; think; value

DEEP: absorbed; abstruse; abysmal; basic; bass; bottomless; cavernous; chronic; complex; comprehensive; cunning; devious; difficult; engrossed; entangled; erudite; exhaustive; extreme; far; fathomless; fundamental; grievous; hard; heavy; hermetic(al); inexplicable; ingrained; intellectual; intense; involved; knowledgeable; learned; low; mysterious; obscure; penetrating; plumbless; profound; recondite; rooted; sagacious; sage; scholarly; serious; subterranean; thick; unalloyed; unfathomed; unmixed; wise DEEPNESS: (**see** "depth") abstrusity; profundity

DEEP-SEATED: (**see** "chronic") deep-dyed; genuine; ingrained; lasting; thorough

DEFACE: (**see** "blemish") blotch; deform; destroy; disfigure; distort; impair; injure; mar; mark; mayhem; mutilate; scar; spoil

DEFAME: (**see** "belittle") abuse; asperse; besmirch; blacken; calumniate; debase; decry; degrade; denigrate; disparage; impair; libel; malign; revile; scandalize; slander; smirch; splatter; sully; traduce; DEFAMATION: aspersion; calumny; denigration; detraction; libel; revile; scandal; slander; traduction; DEFAMATORY: calumnious; denigratory; injurious; invidious; libelous; offensive; scandalous; slanderous

DEFAULT: (**see** "defect") debt; deficit; failure; forfeit(ure); lack; lapse; loss; mora; neglect; negligence; want

DEFEAT: **v.** (**see** "beat") annihilate; avalanche; baffle; balk; beset; bowl over; break; bury; calm; capture; check(mate); circumvent; confound; confuse; confute; conquer; control; cow; crush; curb; decimate; defraud; delude; deluge; demolish; depress; destroy; devastate; discomfort; disenchant; disentrance; dishearten; disillusion; dismay; dominate; down; drown; drub; eat; eclipse; engulf; enslave; finish; flood; foil; frustrate; have; inundate; kill; lace; lick; master; murder; nullify; oppress; outdate; outdo;

outfight; outfox; outlast; outmaneuver; outsmart; outstrip; overcome; overmaster; overpower; override; overrun; overthrow; overturn; overwhelm; pacify; quash; quell; quiet; ravish; rebuff; reduce; repress; repulse; reverse; rout; ruin; shellac; sink; skin; skunk; slay; steamroller; stop; stun; subdue; subject; subjugate; subvert; suppress; surmount; swallow; swamp; take; tame; thwart; trample; trim; triumph; upset; vanquish; whack; win; worsen; DEFEATED: beaten; licked; unconscious; worsened; DEFEAT: **n.** acquisition; annihilation; anticlimax; bathos; battering; beating; black eye; bouleversement; circumvention; comeuppance; contretemps; crush(ing); debacle; decimation; defeasance; deluge; delusion; denigration; despair; destruction; devastation; discomfiture; disillusion(ment); downfall; enslavement; failure; frustration; humiliation; labefaction; lacing; letdown; mastery; mockery; overcoming; overthrow; pummeling; rebuff; reduction; repulse; reversal; reverse; rout; setback; shellacking; subduction; subjection; subjugation; subversion; triumph; trouncing; vanquishment; victim; Waterloo; worsening

DEFECT: (**see** "blemish") absence; botch; bug; crack; default; deficiency; demerit; disability; disadvantage; drawback; error; failure; fallacy; fault; flaw; foible; forfeit(ure); frailty; handicap; hindrance; hole; impediment; imperfection; inadequacy; irregularity; lack; lacuna; lapse; loss; *manque*; need; neglect; negligence; shade; shortcoming; speck; spot; stain; touch; want; weakness; DEFECTIVE: amiss; bad; blameworthy; blemished; botched; botchy; cracked; crippled; deficient; dilapidated; disabled; erroneous; failing; fallacious; faulty; handicapped; ill; impedimental; imperfect; improper; inaccurate; incomplete; incorrect; infelicitous; inferior; insufficient; lacking; lacunal; lacunar; *manqué*; mediocre; reprehensible; shabby; shopworn; short; sick(ly); suboptimal; substandard; unfit; unsound; weak(ened); wrong

DEFEND: (**see** "fight") abet; back; confront; contest; controvert; cope; cover; embrace; encourage; espouse; excuse; expound; face; guard; hold; insure; justify; maintain; oppose; parry; protect; repel; resist; safeguard; save; screen; secure; shelter; shend; shield; stand; support; uphold; vindicate; DEFENSE: abatis; abetment; aegis; alibi; ammunition; apologetics (pl.); apologia; apologiae (pl.); apology; argument; armament; armor; arms; battle; bulwark; confrontation; contention; contest; controversy; cover; encouragement; epaulement; espousal; excuse; exoneration; extenuation; fight; fort-(ification); fortress; fracas; fray; guard-(ianship); guns; immunity; insurance; justification; maintenance; munitions; obstacle; opposition; ordnance; parapet; plea; protection; rampart; resistance; safeguard; sconce; scrap; screen(ing); scuffle; security; set-to; shelter; shield; stand; skirmish; struggle; support; tilt; tower; trial; vindication; wall; DEFENDER: attorney; Paladin; protagonist; protector; DEFENSIVE: counteractive; fighting; martial; phylactic; pugnacious

DEFENSELESS: (**see** "helpless") bare; guardless; indefensible; inexcusable; naked; open; pathetic; silly; unjustifiable; unprotected; unshielded; untenable

DEFER: accede; adjourn; agree; arch; bend; bow; capitulate; comply; concede; continue; court; cow(er); cringe; crouch; curtsy; delay; flatter; forbear; give; grovel; halt; hold; honor; humble; incline; intermit; keep; kneel; kowtow; postpone; procrastinate; prolong; prorogue; protract; remain; remand; remit; restrain; retain; retard; salute; slaver; slow; stay; stoop; stop; submit; supersede; surrender; suspend; table; temporize; toady; wait; woo; yield; DEFERENCE: abjection; abnegation; accession; admiration; adoration; agreement; allegation; allegiance; appreciation; bow; capitulation; compliance; *congé*; consideration; continuance; cringe; crouch; curtsy; deferentiality; deferment; delay; devoir; devotion; dignity; eminence; esteem; estimation; favor; fealty; fidelity; flattery; forbearance; gentility; genuflexion; grovel(ing); homage; honor; humbleness; humility; illustriousness; intermission; kowtow; liege; liking; love; lowliness; loyalty; majesty; mansuetude; meekness; merit; moderation; modesty; obeisance; obsequiousness; obsequity; patience; placidity; postponement; prestige; procrastination; prolongation; prominence; prorogation; protraction; regard; remand; renown; reputation; repute; reserve; respect; restraint; retardation; reverence; sacredness; salaam; salutation; salute; servility; standing; stature; status; stay; submission; submissiveness; surrender; suspension; sycophancy; tameness; toadying; tolerance; toleration; tranquility; tribute; unctuosity; unctuousness; valuation; value; veneration; virtue; wait; worship; worth; yielding; DEFERENTIAL: abject; complacent; considerate; courteous; deferent; dutiful; fawning; gnathonic; humble;

loyal; meek; modest; obeisant; obsequious; oleaginous; parasitical; regardful; respectful; restrained; reverential; servile; submissive; subservient; sycophantic; toadying; unctuous; venerative; worshiping; yielding

DEFIANT: (**see** "bold") antagonistic; audacious; challenging; courageous; fearless; fierce; fiery; impudent; insolent; intrepid; martial; military; nervy; perilous; plucky; rash; rebellious; recalcitrant; refractory; temerarious; unafraid; **DEFIANCE:** antagonism; audacity; challenge; confrontation; contempt; effrontery; hostility; impudence; insolence; opposition; rebellion; recalcitrance; refractoriness; resistance; temerity

DEFICIENT: bobtail; crude; defective; elementary; faulty; fractional; fractionary; fragmental; fragmentary; futile; Icarian; immature; imperfect(ed); impotent; impoverished; inadequate; inchoate; inchoative; incompetent; incomplete; ineffective; inefficacious; inept; infirm; insignificant; insolvent; insufficient; lacking; lesser; lost; *manqué*; mediocre; minus; paltry; partial; poor; puerile; rudimentary; scant(y); scarce; short; shortened; smaller; sparse; sterile; syncategorematic; thin; truncated; underdeveloped; undereducated; understrength; unfinished; unfit; unideal; unlearned; unperfected; unproductive; unqualified; unready; unripe; untaught; untrained; wanting; weak(ened); without; **DEFICIENCY:** dearth; deficit; *faiblesse*; failure; famine; foible; handicap; impediment; imperfection; impotency; inadequacy; insolvency; lack; lacuna; *manque*; need; paucity; scantiness; scarcity; shortage; shortness; sterility; ullage; want; weakness

DEFICIT: (**see** "shortage") deficiency; loss

DEFILE: **v.** (**see** "corrupt") befoul; begrime; belittle; besmirch; contaminate; corrupt; debase; debauch; dirty; dishonor; infect; moil; poison; pollute; ravish; seduce; soil; spoil; stain; sully; taint; tarnish; violate; vitiate; **DEFILED:** see "impure;" **DEFILE:** **n.** abra; gate(way); gorge; pass; **DEFILEMENT:** (**see** "corruption") adulteration; contamination; dirtiness; impurity; indecency; lewdness; licentiousness; pollution; putrescence; taint; tarnish; uncleanliness; unwholesomeness; vitiation

DEFINE: ascertain; assign; bound; characterize; circumscribe; clarify; clear; construe; decipher; decode; delineate; demarcate; describe; determine; diagnose; diagno-

sticate; dissect; distinguish; elucidate; explain; explicate; expound; fix; formulate; identify; illuminate; illustrate; interpret; limit; locate; mark; name; outline; parse; prescribe; reserve; set(tle); solve; specify; translate; unfold; unravel

DEFINITE *or* **DEFINITIVE:** (**see** "certain") actual; approved; arithmetical; binding; bound(ed); careful; circumscribed; clear; cogent; defined; delineated; determinate; determinative; determined; distinct; dogmatic(al); emphatic; established; exact; explicit; firm; fixed; hard; identifiable; identified; incontrovertible; limited; manifest: material; mathematic(al); objective; official; particular; plain; positive; precise; real; set(tled); special; tangible; unambiguous; unqualified; **DEFINITENESS:** (**see** "certainty") definitiveness; definitude; finality; finitude; inevitability; precision; tangibility; unambiguity

DEFLATE: (**see** "collapse") burst; contract; drain; empty; exhaust; flatten; humble; impale; lessen; puncture; reduce; sag; shrink

DEFLECT: (**see** "deviate") avert; bend; change; curve; depart; detour; diverge; divert; move; parry; sway; swerve; turn; twist; veer; ward; wrest

DEFORM (**see** "distort") alter; compress; contort; cripple; deface; disfigure; fracture; gnarl; impair; injure; maim; mangle; mar; mayhem; misshape; spoil; uglify; warp; **DEFORMED:** (**see** "distorted") contorted; defaced; disfigured; gnarled; impaired; injured; maimed; misshaped; warped; **DEFORMITY:** (**see** "distortion") contortion; contracture; corruption; deformation; depravity; disfigurement; flaw; fracture; impairment; impropriety; injury; malformation; mayhem; ugliness

DEFRAUD: (**see** "fool") bamboozle; befool; beguile; bilk; cheat; chouse; cozen; deceive; defeat; delude; dishonor; dupe; fleece; foil; guile; gull; gyp; hoax; hoodwink; prey; rob; stick; swindle; trick; trim; victimize; wrong

DEFRAY: (**see** "compensate") ante; discharge; liquidate; meet; pay; reimburse; requite; satisfy; settle

DEFT: (**see** "clever") adroit; agile; apt; artful; assured; cunning; dexterous; expert; facile; fit; foxy; handy; ingenious; meet; neat;

nimble; pat; quick; skilled; skillful; slick; smooth

DEFY: accuse; arouse; beard; brave; break; call; challenge; cite; claim; combat; confront; contemn; contend; dare; demand; disobey; disregard; excite; face; fight; fling; flout; front; goad; ignore; impugn; infract; infringe; invite; meet; mock; mutiny; neglect; oppose; protect; provoke; question; rebel; reject; repudiate; require; resist; revolt; rise; risk; scorn; slight; spurn; summon; taunt; tempt; test; trespass; unheed; venture; violate; withstand; DEFIANCE: **see** "bravery" and "dare"

DEGENERATE: **v.** bastardize; collapse; corrupt; debase; debauch; decay; decline; decompose; degrade; demean; depreciate; deride; descend; deteriorate; devitalize; disintegrate; dissipate; drop; erode; fall; impair; lessen; lower; melt; perish; pitch; putresce; retrograde; retrogress; rot; rust; set(tle); sicken; sink; slip; sour; stoop; wane; wear; worsen; DEGENERATE(D): **a.** (see "corrupt") debased; debauched; decadent; decayed; degrade; deteriorated; devitalized; effete; lewd; low; outmoded; retrograde; retrogressed; vicious; wicked; worsened; DEGENERATION *or* DEGENERACY: (**see** "corruption") abasement; *abâtardissement*; bastardization; comedown; debasement; debauchery; debauchment; decadence; decay; declension; declination; decline; declivity; defilement; degenerateness; degenerescence; degradation; degradement; degres-

sion; *dégringolade*; *délabrement*; depravation; depravity; deterioration; dip; disintegration; dissipation; devitalization; drop; fall; flagitiousness; graft; immorality; impairment; impurity; infamy; infection; inflammation; labefaction; lessening; lewdness; lowering; miasma; mildew; pathology; perversion; pitch; poison; pollution; pot; profligacy; putrescence; putridity; retrogradation; retrogression; rot(tenness); ruin; rust; scrofulosis; sinking; slant; slip; slope; Sodom; squalor; stoop(ing); taint; tarnish; venality; vice; vileness; virus; vitiation; wallow; worsening

DEGRADE: (**see** "belittle") abase; asperse; bestialize; brand; brutalize; calumniate; censure; cheapen; corrupt; damage; darken; debase; debauch; decompose; defame; defile; defraud; degenerate; dehumanize; demean; demote; denigrate; denounce; depose; deprive; descend; diminish; discredit; disgrace; disgrade; dishonor; fall; humble;

humiliate; imbrute; insult; lower; mortify; pejorate; pervert; rape; reduce; relegate; ruin; scandalize; shame; shend; slander; soil; spot; stain; stigmatize; subtract; sully; taint; tarnish; vilify; violate; weaken; DEGRADED *or* DEGRADING: (**see** "disgraceful") abandoned; abased; bad; base; contaminated; corrupt(ed); damaged; darkened; debased; debauched; degenerate(d); degenerating; dehumanized; denigrated; denigratory; denunciatory; derogative; derogatory; despicable; diminishing; dirty; discreditable; discredited; disgraced; dishonorable; dishonored; disparaging; disreputable; distorted; humbled; humiliated; humiliating; humiliative; ignoble; ignominious; infamous; inglorious; libelous; low-(ered); mean; menial; mortifying; notorious; obnoxious; odious; opprobrious; perverted; relegated; scandalized; scandalous; shamed; shameful; shocking; slanderous; sordid; squalid; terrible; unrespectable; unrespected; vulgar(ized); wicked; DEGRADATION: abasement; abjection; aspersion; blot; brand; calumniation; calumny; censure; contempt; corruption; crime; damage; debasement; decadence; declination; degeneration; degradement; dehumanization; demoralization; demotion; denigration; deposition; depravity; deprecation; depreciation; derision; derogation; descent; diminishing; diminishment; discredit; disesteem; disestimation; disgrace; dishonor; disparagement; disrepute; entropy; humiliation; ignominy; ill repute; improbity; infamy; insult; lowering; minimization; obloquy; odium; opprobrium; pejoration; reduction; reproach; ruin; scandal; shame(fulness); shendfulness; shending; slander; spot; squalidity; squalor; stain; stigma(tization); stigmata (pl.); subtraction; taint; turpitude; vilification; wallow; weakening; weakness

DEGREE: category; class(ification); coefficient; difference; dimension; distance; distinction; division; echelon; elevation; extent; girth; gradation; grade; gradient; honor; intensity; interval; length; level; limit; mark; measure(ment); notch; nuance; order; pitch; point; position; proportion; quality; range; rank; rate; rating; ration; scope; score; shade; size; space; stage; standard; step; standing; station; status; step; term; title

DEHUMANIZE: automate; automatize; barbarize; bestialize; brutalize; imbrute; mechanize; robotize

DEHYDRATE: bake; cake; dehumidify;

desiccate; devitalize; dry; evaporate; exsiccate; parch; scorch; shrivel; weaken

DEIFY: apotheosize; canonize; consecrate;
elevate; ennoble; enshrine; exalt; glorify;
hallow; honor; idolize; pedestal; sacralize;
sanctify; spiritualize; transcend; transfigure;
DEIFICATION: apotheosis; canonization;
consecration; elevation; ennoblement;
enshrinement; exaltation; glorification;
hallowing; idolization; transcension; transfiguration

DEIGN: (see "condescend") bow; concede;
consent; kneel; kowtow; stoop; vouchsafe

DEITY: (see "god") divinity; godhead;
supreme being

DEJECT: (see "discourage") abase; dishearten; dispirit; DEJECTED: (see "gloomy")
abased; à la mort; amort; ashamed; blue;
chapfallen; cheerless; chilly; crestfallen;
depressed; depressing; disconsolate; discouraged; disheartened; dismal; dispirited;
doleful; dolorous; down(cast); downhearted;
down-in-the-mouth; drear(y); droopy;
frustrating; funereal; hangdog; humble;
inconsolate; joyless; lachrymose; low(-spirit-
ed); melancholic; melancholy; mopey;
muddy; pouting; prostrate; sad(dened);
sombre; DEJECTION: (see "depression")
abasement; dejectedness; disconsolateness;
dismality; dispiritedness; downheartedness;
gloominess; low-spiritedness; melancholy;
prostration; sadness

DELAY: v. (see "arrest") abide; adjourn;
apprehend; balk; bide; block; break; bridle;
capture; check; collar; continue; curb;
cut; dally; dawdle; defer; derail; detain;
dillydally; disconnect; discontinue; disrupt;
disturb; divert; drag; flag; forbear; halt;
hamper; hesitate; hinder; hold; idle; impede;
intercept; interfere; intermit; lag; laten;
lessen; linger; loiter; obstruct; pause; postpone; pretermit; prevent; procrastinate;
prolong; prorogue; protract; put off; recess;
remain; remand; restrain; retard; saunter;
shelve; slack(en); slow; sojourn; stall; stay;
stop; suspend; table; tarry; temporize;
thwart; upset; wait; waive; DELAY: n. (see
"arrest") adjournment; apprehension; armistice; arrestation; arrestment; block(age);
breach; break; capture; check; continuance;
cunctation; curb; deferment; derangement;
detention; disruption; forbearance; halt;
hampering; hangfire; hesitation; hiatus;
hindrance; hold; impediment; interference;

intermission; interval; lag; lapse; lessening;
lingering; loitering; moratorium; obstruc-
tion(ism); pause; postponement; procrastination; prolongation; prorogation; protraction; putting off; recess; remand; respite;
retardation; slackening; sojourn; space;
stall; stay; stop(page); suspension; tarriance;
tarry; temporization; wait

DELEGATE: v. (see "commission") appoint;
assign; authorize; commit; declare; depute;
designate; impute; nominate; substitute;
transfer; DELEGATE(S) n. or DELEGA-
TION: (see "committee") agent; assistant;
attorney; authority; authorization; body;
commission(er); congressman; deputy;
envoy; factor; guardian; legate; messenger;
organization; proxy; representative; senator;
sub(stitute); substitution; surrogate; vicar-
(iate); viceroy; DELEGATED: delegatory;
deputed; deputized; substitutionary; vicarial;
vicarious

DELETE: (see "blot" and "omit") blue-
pencil; cancel; dele; destroy; efface; eliminate;
erase; expunge; extinguish; kill; nullify; obliterate; remove; scrub; separate; sponge;
strike; winnow

DELIBERATE: v. (see "contemplate") cogitate; conceive; confer; consider; consult;
council; debate; estimate; excogitate; judge;
measure; meditate; muse; plan; ponder;
prepend; ratiocinate; reason; reflect; ruminate; study; surmise; think; weigh;
DELIBERATE: a. (see "careful") advised;
aforethought; calculated; calculating; canny;
cautious; chary; choosy; cold(-blooded);
considered; contemplate; contemplative; cool;
decisive; designed; impersonal; intended;
intentional; matter-of-fact; meant; meditated; plain; planned; plotted; ponderate;
pondered; ponderous; premeditated; prepense; prudent(ial); rational; slow; steady;
studied; thorough; thoughtful; unhurried;
voluntary; warm; willful; willing; DELI-
BERATION: (see "contemplation") advisement; attention; care; cogitation; conference;
consideration; consultation; counsel; debate;
decision; deliberateness; design; discussion;
envisionment; excogitation; expectation;
judgment; meditation; muse; penetration;
perception; plan; ponderation; postulation;
premeditation; prepense; purpose; reason-
(ing); recollection; reflection; rumination;
speculation; study; survey; thought; view;
weight; willfulness

DELICATE: agreeable; airy; arachnoid;

beautiful; birdlike; bonny; breakable; brittle; careful; cautious; charming; choice; cobwebby; crisp; critical; dainty; dangerous; decorous; delicious; delightful; deteriorable; diaphanous; diplomatic; discriminating; discriminative; effeminate; elegant; emasculate; ephemeral; epicene; ethereal; evanescent; exquisite; fastidious; feeble; filmy; fine; finical; fleeting; flimsy; fragile; frail; frangible; friable; fussy; gentle; girlish; glassy; gossamer(y); hothouse; hypersensitive; infirm; insubstantial; judicious; kidglove(d); lacy; lenient; little; lovely; maiden-(ish); maidenly; mild; milky; miss-nancyish; modish; neat; nebular; nebulous; nice; overnice; palatable; particular; petite; pleasing; precarious; precise; pretty; prissy; rare-(fied); refined; savory; sensitive; shaky; short-lived; sick(ly); silken; silky; sissy; skilled; skillful; slender; slight; small; soft; *soigné; soignée* (fem.); squeamish; superfine; sweet; tactful; tasty; tender; tenuous; thin; ticklish; timorous; touchy; transparent; trivial; uncertain; unmanly; unsubstantial; weak; willowy; womanly; DELICACY: *bonne bouche;* cake; cate; confection; daintiness; dainty; delicateness; delicatesse; diplomacy; discretion; discrimination; effeminacy; elegance; ethereality; exquisiteness; fastidiousness; femineity; femininity; finesse; fragility; frailty; *friandise;* gentleness; girlishness; insubstantiality; kickshaw; lightness; maidenliness; meticulosity; modesty; nicety; piquancy; precariousness; preciosity; precision; refinement; sensibility; sensitivity; squeamishness; subtlety; susceptibility; tact; tenderness; tenuity; tidbit; weakness; womanliness

DELICIOUS: (**see** "appetizing") ambrosiac; ambrosial; appealing; appetible; choice; dainty; delectable; delicate; delightful; enchanting; esculent; exquisite; flavorful; flavorous; gustable; gustatory; luscious; luxurious; nectarean; nectareous; orexigenic; palatable; piquant; pleasing; rare; rich; sapid; savory; spicy; sweet; tangy; tasty; tempting; toothsome

DELICT: (**see** "offense") crime; delinquency; impropriety; malfeasance; misfeasance; sin; tort; transgression; violation; wrong(doing)

DELIGHT: **v.** (**see** "captivate") amuse; bask; charm; divert; elate; enchant; exalt; feast; felicitate; gladden; gratify; jubilate; luxuriate; regale; revel; satiate; satisfy; take; transport; treat; DELIGHT: **n.** (**see** "charm") amusement; bliss; delectation;

delicacy; deliciousness; diversion; dream; ecstasy; elation; enchantment; enjoyment; exaltation; exuberance; exultation; feast; felicity; festivity; gladness; glee; gratification; happiness; *jouissance;* joy(ance); joyancy; joyousness; jubilation; love; merriment; mirth; oblectation; paradise; pleasure; rapture; raptus; ravishment; revel(ry); satisfaction; transport; treat; DELIGHTED *or* DELIGHTFUL: agreeable; amusing; blissful; captivating; charming; congenial; delectable; delicate; delicious; delightsome; diverting; divine; dreamy; Edenic; enchanting; entrancing; felicitious; festive; glad; gratified; gratifying; happy; heavenly; ideal(istic); jolly; joyful; joyous; jubilant; jubilative; lovely; luscious; merry; mirthful; paradisiac(al); pleasant; rapturous; refreshing; satisfying; taking

DELINEATE: (**see** "describe") chart; depict; design; draft; draw; emphasize; evoke; express; figure; illustrate; indicate; limn; map; mark; outline; paint; picture; plan; plot; portray; relate; render; represent; show; sketch; speak; tell; trace; write; DELINEATION: **see** "description"

DELINQUENCY: (**see** "transgression") immorality; moral turpitude; DELINQUENT: (**see** "criminal") defalcator; defaulter; sinner

DELIQUESCE: desiccate; disappear; dissolve; liquefy; melt; rarefy; thaw

DELIRIOUS: (**see** "frantic") agitated; berserk; crazed; crazy; demoniac(al); demonic-(al); deranged; enthusiastic; excited; frenetic(al); frenzied; furious; insane; intoxicated; mad; maniac(al); noisy; phrenetic(al); rabid; raging; raving; wandering; DELIRIUM: (**see** "frenzy") dementia; disorientation; excitement; insanity; lunacy; madness; mania; rabidity; restlessness

DELIVER: bear; beget; bring; carry; cede; commit; communicate; conduct; consign; convey; deal; disburden; discharge; discourse; distribute; emancipate; emit; enunciate; escort; exempt; exonerate; express; extricate; fetch; free; give; grant; lead; liberate; manumit; pronounce; redeem; release; relieve; remove; rescue; resign; rid; save; send; speak; steer; surrender; vent; unburden; unload; utter; vent; yield; DELIVERANCE *or* DELIVERY: (**see** "discharge") atonement; bestowal; disburdenment; disbursement; distribution; emancipation; enunciation; exoneration; extrication;

flow; freedom; liberation; manumission; parturition; presentation; reclamation; redemption; release; removal; rescue; resignation; riddance; salvation; shot; surrender; yielding

DELUDE: (**see** "fool") bamboozle; cheat; circumvent; cozen; deceive; elude; evade; fake; mislead; mock; spoof; trick; victimize; DELUSION: (**see** "deception") apparition; artifice; bubble; chimera; circumvention; cozenage; deceit(fulness); dream; error; fake(ry); fallacy; fancy; fraud(ulence); ghost; hallucination; *ignis fatuus*; illusion; mirage; misconception; mockery; phantasm-(agoria); phantasmata (pl.); phantom; ruse; specter; spoof; spook; trick(ery); vision; wile; will-of-the-wisp; DELUSIVE: (**see** "deceptive") beguiling; delusional; delusory; fallacious; phantasmagoric(al); unrealistic

DELUGE: abundance; avalanche; cataclysm; cataract; cloudburst; downpour; eagre; excess; flood; flow; freshet; inundation; ocean; outpouring; overflow(ing); oversupply; rush; saturation; sea; soak(ing); spate; stream; superabundance; surplus(age); tide; torrent

DELVE: (**see** "dig") dip; explore; grub; investigate; mine; probe; spade; study; till; wade (in)

DEMAND: **v.** adjure; appeal; arraign; ask; beg; behest; beseech; bid; call; challenge; charge; cite; claim; command; commission; crave; cry; decree; destine; dictate; direct; dispute; dun; enjoin; exact; expostulate; force; implore; importune; inquire; insist; instruct; levy; marshal; necessitate; oblige; ordain; order; persist; pray; prepare; prescribe; press; purpose; quest; request; require; rule; scream; seek; send; solicit; stress; summon; supplicate; tax; urge; will; yell; DEMAND: **n.** adjuration; appeal; arraignment; behest; bid; bill; call; caveat; challenge; charge; claim; command; commission; cry; decree; decretal; dictation; directive; dun; duty; edict; eutaxy; execution; exigency; expostulation; fiat; force; imperative; imploration; imposition; injunction; inquiry; insistence; instruction; law; load; mandate; mandatum; monition; need; notice; obligation; order; ordinance; persistence; precept(ion); pressure; prohibition; query; question; regulation; request; requirement; requisition; rule; run; screen; solicitation; stress; summons; supplication; use; will; writ; yell; DEMAND-

ING: (**see** "hard") arduous; binding; challenging; clamorous; difficult; exacting; exigent; fastidious; forceful; imperative; importunate; insistent; insisting; obligatory; onerous; persistent; persisting; pressing; rigorous; solicitous; steep; stiff; strenuous; stressing; supplicative; taxing; trying; urgent; vociferous

DEMEAN: (**see** "degrade") abase; behave; carry; comport; conduct; debase; deport; descend; humble; humiliate; lower; DEMEANOR: (**see** "air") action; appearance; attitude; bearing; behavior; carriage; conduct; deportment; front; manner; mien; posture; stance; stand(ing)

DEMENTED: (**see** "deranged") crazed; crazy; daffy; daft; foolish; frenzied; idiotic; insane; irrational; loony; luny; mad; maniac-(al); manic; nutty; obsessed; rabid; unsound; wild

DEMIGOD: **see** "hero"

DEMOLISH: (**see** "break") destroy; devastate; dismantle; dissever; elide; eliminate; end; kill; level; murder; overthrow; overturn; pluck; ravage; raze; reduce; remove; ruin; sack; scrap; shatter; smash; undo; wrack; wreck

DEMON: (**see** "devil") familiar; fury; genie; genius

DEMONSTRATE: air; argue; arrange; attract; bare; blandish; blazon; boast; brag; brandish; debate; depict; describe; disclose; display; emblazon; establish; evince; exhibit; explain; expose; flare; flash; flaunt; flourish; flout; flutter; gesture; illustrate; manifest; model; obtrude; open; ostentate; pander; pose; present; proclaim; promulgate; prove; reflect; represent; reveal; shake; show; splash; splurge; sport; spread; stage; swing; teach; test; toss; try; uncase; unfold; unfurl; unmask; unveil; verify; DEMONSTRATION: apod(e)ixis; argument; collection; contest; disclosure; display; drama; drawing; drill; effusion; effusiveness; event; evidence; exercise; exhibition; experience; experiment; explanation; exposure; fair; game; gesture; illustration; manifestation; museum; ostentation; pageant(ry); parade; performance; picture; play; presentation; recital; representation; revelation; riot; scene; show-(case); showing; show-off; teaching; test; trial; uncovering; verification; DEMONSTRATIVE: (**see** "unrestrained") absolute; apod(e)ictic(al); deictic; effervescent; effusive; epideictic; exhibitive; exuberant; gushing; immoderate; limitless; overflowing; probative; scaturient; showy; spontaneous; theatrical; unreserved; vehement

DEMORALIZE: (see "corrupt" and "discourage") debauch; destroy; pervert; seduce; undermine; weaken

DEMOTE: (see "belittle") debase; denigrate; depreciate; downgrade; minify; minimize; pejorate; reduce; relegate; DEMOTION: see "degradation"

DEMULCENT: **a.** (see "bland") balmy; emollient; lenitive; sedative; soft(ening); soothing; DEMULCENT: **n.** balm; emollient; lenitive; ointment; salve; sedative

DEMUR: **v.** (see "balk") clash; delay; disagree; disapprove; dispute; dissent; except; hesitate; interpose; object; pause; scruple; shy; stop; strain; waver; DEMUR: **n.** balk; block(age); check; defeat; delay; difference; difficulty; disagreement; disappointment; disapproval; disputation; dispute; dissension; dissidence; dissident; exception; falter; frustration; hesitation; impediment; indecision; interposition; irresolution; nonargument; nonconcurrence; nonconformity; objection; odds; pause; recoil; recusance; recusancy; refusal; scruple; stop; uncertainty; waver

DEMURE: (see "bashful") coy; decorous; diffident; grave; mim; modest; nice; prim; proper; prudish; sedate; seemly; shy; sober; solemn; staid; uncoquettish

DEN: (see "lair") cave(rn); cavea; covert; dive; haunt; hole; home; retreat; room; sink; study; warren

DENIAL: see after "deny"

DENIGRATE: (see "belittle") asperse; darken; defame; deglamorize; deglorify; depreciate; desanctify; devalue; disesteem; disparage; dispraise; downgrade; sully; vilify

DENIZEN: (see "inhabitant") cit(izen); dweller; habitué; native; resident; voter

DENOMINATE: (see "call") christen; denote; designate; dub; entitle; indicate; name; style; term; DENOMINATION: (see "class") category; church; cult; money; name; sect; sort; value

DENOTE: (see "portend") announce; attest; augur; betide; betoken; bode; connote; denominate; describe; designate; evince; forebode; foreshadow; foreshow; hint; imply; import; indicate; intend; mark; mean; name; notify; prefigure; presage; preshadow; show; signify; specify

DENOUNCE: (see "charge") abrade; accuse; anathematize; arraign; assail; bare; berate; blame; censure; comminate; condemn; criticize; curse; damn; debunk; decry; degrade; delate; denudate; denude; denunciate; deny; detract; disclaim; disclose; disinter; disparage; display; endanger; excoriate; execrate; expose; fulminate; imperil; implicate; indict; inveigh; jeopardize; lambaste; lower; menace; objurgate; oppose; present; protest; rail; rate; reprehend; reprimand; reproach; reprove; reveal; revile; scathe; scold; show (up); stigmatize; subject; threaten; uncover; unearth; unhood; unmask; unshroud; unveil; vilify; vituperate; DENUNCIATION: (see "charge") accusation; airing; anathema; arraignment; blame; calumniation; calumny; censure; commination; condemnation; curse; delation; denouncement; detraction; diatribe; disclosure; display; excoriation; execration; fulmination; imprecation; indictment; insult; invective; jeopardy; objurgation; presentation; protest(ation); reprimand; reproach(ment); reproval; revile; scold(ing); threat; vilification; vituperation; DENUNCITORY: accusatory; censorious; comminatory; denunciative; excoriative; fulminous; slanderous; threatening; vituperative

DENSE: close; compact(ed); compendious; compressed; concentrated; condensed; conglomerate(d); consolidated; contracted; crass; crowded; dull; dumb; extreme; filled; firm; full; grouped; hard; heavy; homogeneous; impacted; intensed; massed; nebulous; obscure; obtuse; opaque; packed; piled; populous; pressed; serried; slow-witted; snug; solid; sound; stocky; stolid; strong; stupid; succinct; teeming; terse; thick(headed); tight; turbid; unclear; united; DENSITY: closeness; compactness; concentration; condensation; condensedness; mass; solidity; stupidity; thickness

DENUDE: (see "bare") deprive; divest; erode; expose; strip; undress; unrobe; unveil; weaken

DENY: abjure; abnegate; belie; contradict; controvert; counteract; declaim; denegate; denounce; deplete; disacknowledge; disaffirm; disavow; disclaim; dismiss; disown;

dispel; disprove; dispute; expel; forbid; gainsay; impugn; negate; negative; prohibit; rebut; recant; refuse; refute; reject; renege; renounce; repudiate; resist; restrain; subvert; traverse; withhold; DENIAL: abjurgation; abnegation; contradiction; contrariety; declaimer; *démenti*; denegation; denouncement; disacknowledgment; disaffirmance; disaffirmation; disavowal; disclaimer; disclamation; gainsaying; incompatibility; negation; opposition; paradox; prohibition; rebuttal; recantation; refusal; refutation; rejection; renege; renouncement; renunciation; repudiation; restraint

DEPART: abandon; abscond; absquatulate; blow; bolt; cease; decamp; decease; deliquesce; deplete; desert; deviate; die; digress; diminish; disappear; dissolve; drop; egress; elope; erode; err; escape; evanesce; evanish; evaporate; exit; expire; fade; fall; flee; fly; forsake; fugitate; go; hasten; hide; hie; lam; lapse; leave; lose; melt; move; pass; perish; quit; recede; relinquish; remove; resolve; retire; retreat; run; sail; scamper; scram; skedaddle; skip; steal (away); subside; swerve; terminate; transfer; transplant; vamoose; vanish; vanquish; vaporize; vary; veer; volatize; withdraw; DEPARTED: (**see** "dead") absconded; begone; blown; bygone; ceased; decamped; deceased; deserted; deviated; died; digressed; disappeared; eloped; escaped; fled; flown; gone; lapsed; late; left; moved; offed; passed; perished; quit; removed; retired; retreated; sailed; scrammed; skipped; swerved; vamoosed; vanished; veered; went; withdrew; DEPARTURE: abscondence; adieu adios; death; decease; depletion; desertion; deviation; digression; diminution; disappearance; dissolution; divergence; elopement; emigration; error; escape; evanescence; evanishment; evanition; evaporation; excursion; exit; exodus; lapse; leave(taking); quittance; relinquishment; removal; resolution; retirement; retreat; sailing; subsidence; termination; vanishment; vaporization; withdrawal

DEPARTMENT: area; arrondissement; bailiwick; branch; bureau; camera; canton; class(ification); commandry; compartment; demesne; district; division; domain; environment; environs; field; locale; location; neighborhood; office; pale; precinct; province; purlieu; quarter; realm; region; section; sector; sphere; station; subdivision; territory; tract; unit; ward; zone

DEPEND: (**see** "rely") bank; base; count (on); hang; hinge; lean; lop; pin; ply; predicate;

reckon; rest; stay; trust; turn; DEPENDABLE: (**see** "trustworthy") authentic; authoritative; calculable; esteemed; faithful; firm; inerrable; inerrant; inerratic; infallible; innocent; leal; loyal; official; predictable; regular; reliable; safe; sane; secure; sound; tried (and true); trusted; yeomanly; DEPENDENCE *or* DEPENDENCY: (**see** "reliance") adjunct; appendage; apron string; colony; dominion; fief; guardianship; loyalty; province; servility; trust; tutelage; DEPENDENT: **a.** (**see** "contingent") adjectival; adjective; auxiliary; beholden; circumstantial; collateral; conditional; derivative; feudatory; indebted; liable; open; possible; reliable; reliant; secondary; servile; subject; subordinate; subservient; subsidiary; succursal; vassal; DEPENDENT: **n.** (**see** "subsidiary") auxiliary; child; client; collateral; contingent; derivative; hanger-on; minion; retainer; sponger; subordinate; subservient; vassal

DEPICT: (**see** "delineate") depicture; describe; draw; etch; evoke; express; illustrate; imagine; indicate; limn; paint; picture; portray; relate; render; represent; sketch; speak; tell; write

DEPILATE: dehair; pluck; shave; strip; unhair

DEPLETE: bankrupt; bare; break; clean (out); debilitate; deprive; dig; diminish; discharge; dissipate; divert; drain; dry; dump; empty; erode; evacuate; evaporate; exhaust; fail; impoverish; lessen; reduce; relieve; remove; ruin; sap; smash; spoil; strip; unload; vacate; weaken; wear; DEPLETED: see "empty"

DEPLORE: (**see** "lament") bemoan; bewail; complain; condemn; cry; deprecate; disapprove; envy; fret; grieve; moan; mourn; pity; protest; ravage; regret; resent; rue; sorrow; wail; DEPLORABLE: abominable; accursed; bad; calamitous; contemptible; despicable; disreputable; doleful; execrable; grievous; lachrymose; lamentable; mournful; odious; pitiable; plaintive; plangorous; regretful; regrettable; sad(dened); shocking; sorrowful; tearful; terrible; unfortunate; wretched

DEPONE: affirm; attest; aver; depose; swear; testify

DEPORT: acquit; act; banish; behave; carry; comport; conduct; demean; depose; exile; transport; DEPORTMENT: (**see** "air") action; address; bearing; behavior; carriage;

comportment; conduct; decency; demeanor; exile; manner; mien; posture; propriety; DEPORTATION: **see** "banishment"

DEPOSE: affirm; assert; aver; avouch; banish; degrade; depone; deport; deposit; deprive; destool; dethrone; discrown; disenthrone; displace; disseize; divest; evict; exile; oust; remove; strip; swear; testify; transport; uncrown; unhorse; unseat; upset

DEPOSIT: **v.** accumulate; agglutinate; amass; bank; bury; cache; collect; depose; drift; dump; ensconce; enter; gather; heap; hide; hoard; lay (away); lay up; lodge; park; pawn; pile; place; pledge; put; save; set(tle); store; DEPOSIT: **n.** (**see** "hoard") accumulation; agglutination; bed; cache; cash; deposition; dregs; drift; film; lees; marl; money; ooze; patch; pawn; payment; plaque; pledge; pocket; precipitation; security; sediment; silt; store; DEPOSITORY: (**see** "bank") cache; depot; fund; repository; safe; storehouse; treasury; vault; warehouse

DEPOT: armory; arsenal; cache; collection; gare; magazine; station; stop; store(house); terminal; warehouse

DEPRAVE: (**see** "corrupt") debase; debauch; defile; degenerate; demoralize; depreciate; malign; pervert; pollute; seduce; DEPRAVED: (**see** "corrupt") bestial; corrupted; debased; debauched; degenerate(d); dissolute; evil; immoral; lewd; Neronian; Neronic; perverse; perverted; putrid; shameless; vicious; vile; vitiated; wayward; wicked; DEPRAVITY: (**see** "corruption") bestiality; degeneracy; demoralization; depravement; disgrace; evil; immorality; infamy,; iniquity; lewdness; license; licentiousness; miscreancy; perversion; pollution; putridity; rottenness; turpitude; vice; villainy; wickedness

DEPRECATE: (**see** "deplore") belittle; bewail; condemn; depreciate; diminish; disapprove; insult; protest; ravage; regret; rue; write off

DEPRECIATE: (**see** "belittle") cheapen; debase; debilitate; decline; decry; demote; denigrate; denounce; deprecate; depress; detract; devalue; diminish; disesteem; disestimate; disparage; dispraise; disvalue; fall; lessen; lower; malign; minify; pejorate; revile; rust; slump; traduce; trample (on); underrate; undervalue; vilify; vilipend; wear; write off; DEPRECIATION: (**see** "belittlement") cheapening; decline; denigration; devaluation; disesteem; disestima-

tion; disparagement; dispraise; lessening; loss; minimization; misprision; pejoration; rust; slump; traducement; wear

DEPREDATE: (**see** "pillage") maraud; plunder; prey; ravage; rob; spoil; waste

DEPRESS: abase; abate; ail; burden; calm; check; chill; crush; damp(en); dash; deaden; debase; degrade; deject; dent; depreciate; diminish; dip; discourage; dishearten; disparage; dispirit; enervate; extinguish; extirpate; humble; humiliate; impoverish; lessen; lower; muffle; mute; oppress; overcome; press; quiet(en); reduce; restrain; retard; sadden; sag; sink; stifle; subjugate; sway; trouble; weigh (down); wet-blanket; DEPRESSING *or* DEPRESSIVE: **see** "drear(y);" DEPRESSED: *à la mort*; amort; blue; brokenhearted; burdened; chapfallen; crestfallen; crushed; damp(ened); dejected; diminished; dire; disheartened; dismal; dispirited; downcast; enervated; flat; gloomy; heartsick; heavyhearted; lifeless; lonesome; low(-spirited); melancholic; melancholy; mournful; overcast; pessimistic; restrained; retarded; sad(dened); sick(ly); stifled; stopped; troubled; vaporish; DEPRESSION: abasement; blues; burden; cavity; col; damp; dejectedness; dejection; dent; despair; diminishment; dimple; dip; disconsolateness; discouragement; dismality; disparagement; dispiritedness; doldrums; downheartedness; downswing; dullness; dumps; ennui; fossa; gloominess; heartsickness; humiliation; hypochondria; hypochondriasis; lassitude; low-spiritedness; megrims; melancholia; melancholy; misery; mortification; nadir; oppression; pit; sadness; sag; slump; sorrow; spleen; tristesse; trough; valley; weight

DEPRIVE: bankrupt; bare; bereave; break; curtail; cut; debar; degrade; denudate; denude; deplete; depose; despoil; destroy; dethrone; diminish; disestablish; disinherit; dismantle; disown; dispossess; dissipate; divest; dock; doff; drain; eject; empty; erode; evacuate; exhaust; impoverish; oust; peel; reduce; relieve; remove; rob; ruin; sap; shave; smash; spill; spoil; strip; take; tire; uncloak; unclothe; uncover; undress; weaken; DEPRIVATION: bereavement; cost; curtailment; cut; denudation; depletion; deprival; deprivement; despoliation; destruction; diminishment; dispossession; dissipation; divestation; divestiture; ejection; evacuation; exhaustion; impoverishment; loss; ouster; penalty; poverty; reduction; removal; robbery; suffering

DEPTH: abstrusity; abyss; acumen; acuteness; deepness; depression; drop; extent; gulf; ocean; penetration; perspicacity; pit; profundity; sagacity; sea

DEPUTE: (**see** "appoint") assign; authorize; commission; delegate; deputize; empower; entrust; franchise; institute; name; nominate; send; trust; warrant

DEPUTY: (**see** "delegate") agent; assistant; envoy; factor; posse (pl.); proxy; representative; sub(stitute); substitution; surrogate; vicar; viceroy

DERANGE: confuse; craze; disarrange; discourage; distemper; disturb; impair; interrupt; madden; mess (up); unbalance; upset; DERANGED: confused; crazed; crazy; daffy; daft; demented; *détraqué*; disarranged; disordered; distracted; disturbed; foolish; frenzied; idiotic; impaired; insane; irrational; looney; luny; mad(dened); maniac-(al); manic; messed; messy; nutty; obsessed; psychopathic; rabid; unbalanced; unsound; upset; wild; DERANGEMENT: (**see** "confusion") brainstorm; disarrangement; disease; disorder; distemper; heterogeneity; mess; mixture; muss

DERELICT: **a.** abandoned; alone; barren; bleak; cheerless; dejected; deserted; desolate; devoid; dilapidated; dismal; drear(y); faithless; forgotten; forlorn; forsaken; hopeless; lapsed; left; lifeless; lone(ly); lorn; neglected; neglectful; negligent; remiss; run-down; solitary; unused; wasteful; wild; woebegone; woeful; wrecked; DERELICT: **n.** bum; castaway; exile; hull; ne'er-do-well; outcast; pariah; tramp; waif; wreck

DERIDE: ape; banter; belittle; burlesque; caricature; chaff; contemn; copy; disdain; exaggerate; flaunt; fleer; gibe; grimace; grin; guy; imitate; jeer; jest; jibe; josh; kid; lampoon; laugh; libel; mime; mimic; mock; overdo; pasquinade; rag; rail; rally; rib; ridicule; satirize; scoff; scorn; scout; slight; slur; smirk; sneer; taunt; tease; twit; DERISION: asteism; banter; belittlement; burlesque; caricature; cartoon; chaff; contempt; contumely; denigration; disdain; exaggeration; farce; fleer; irony; irrision; irritation; lampoon(ery); laughingstock; libel; mockery; parody; pasquinade; pastiche; ridicule; sarcasm; sardonicism; satire; scorn; scurrillity; slight; slur; sport; travesty; DERISIVE *or* DERISORY: contemptible; disdainful; exaggerative; farcical; imitative; irrisory; jeering; mocking; ridiculous; sarcastic;

sardonic; satanic; satiric(al); scouting; scurrilous; slurring; sneering; taunting; teasing

DERIVE: accrue; acquire; adapt; appear; arise; arrive; ascend; begin; burgeon; cause; conclude; deduce; deduct; descend; draw; educe; elicit; emanate; emerge; evolve; flow; gain; generate; get; grow; infer; issue; lift; loom; materialize; obtain; originate; proceed; raise; rear; soar; spring; stem; surge; tower; trace; upspring; DERIVATION: (**see** "birth") beginning; deduction; descent; emergence; epiphenomenon; etiology; etymology; extraction; genesis; incipience; incipiency; introduction; lineage; nascence; nascency; onset; opening; origin(ation); parturition; pedigree; procreation; provenance; rise; seed; stemma; DERIVATIVE: (**see** "auxiliary") derivational; epiphenomenal; etiological; secondary; supplementary

DEROGATE: (**see** "belittle") annul; decry; defame; deglamorize; deglorify; degrade; demean; demote; denigrate; detract; devalue; diminish; discredit; disesteem; disestimate; disgrace; dishonor; disparage; dispraise; disvalue; downgrade; dwarf; humble; humiliate; lessen; minify; minimize; reduce; repeal; scandalize; slight; stigmatize; sully; taint; tarnish; DEROGATORY: (**see** "degrading") abased; debased; depreciatory; derogative; detracting; disdainful; disgraced; disparaging; humiliating; snide

DESCANT: **v.** (**see** "comment") dilate; discourse; discuss; enlarge; expiate; note; remark; say; sing; DESCANT: **n. see** "song"

DESCEND: (**see** "degenerate") alight; decline; degrade; demean; derive; dip; dismount; drop; fall; issue; lower; originate; pitch; pounce; precipitate; set(tle); sink; slip; slope; stoop; subside; swoop; worsen; DESCENDANT(S): brood; cion; family; followers; future; futurity; generation; heir(s); issue; lineage; litter; offspring; posterity; progeny; prototype; race; scion; seed; stock; succession; young; DESCENT: (**see** "degeneration") abasement; ancestry; anticlimax; assault; birth; blood(line); comedown; consanguinity; debasement; declension; declination; decline; declivity; degradation; degradement; degression; derivation; descendency; dip; drop; extraction; fall; family; genesis; hill; inheritance; issue; kin(ship); line(age); lowering; lurch; origin(ation); parentage; pedigree; phylum; pitch; race; slant; slip; slope; stemma; stock; stoop(ing); strain; succession; swoop; theogony

DESCRIBE: blazon; blueprint; chart; chronicle; clarify; define; delineate; denote; depict; design; detail; display; draft; draw; emphasize; etch; evoke; explain; explicate; expound; express; figure; illustrate; indicate; interpret; limn; make; mark; narrate; outline; paint; pictorialize; picture; plan; plot; portray; present; recount; relate; render; report; represent; show; signify; sketch; speak; state; tell; trace; write; DESCRIPTION: account; blazoning; blueprint; category; chronicle; clarification; class(ification); definition; delineation; denotation; depiction; design(ation); detail; diction; discourse; display; draft; drawing; etching; explanation; explication; exposition; expression; figure; ilk; illustration; image; indication; interpretation; map; narration; narrative; nature; outline; picture; plan; plot; portrait(ure); portrayal; portrayment; presentation; prospectus; recital; report; representation; sketch; sort; species; survey; tracing; type; version; way; writing; DESCRIPTIVE: (**see** "characteristic") classificatory; definitive; delineative; descriptory; distinguishing; expositive; expository; illuminative; illustrative; picturesque; representative; typical

DESCRY: (**see** "behold") apprehend; attend; detect; determine; discern; discover; distinguish; espy; examine; explore; find; heed; inspect; investigate; look; mark; monitor; note; notice; observe; perceive; recognize; remark; scrutinize; see; sight; spot; spy; view; watch; witness

DESECRATE: (**see** "debase") abase; abuse; coarsen; contaminate; corrupt; defame; defile; deglamorize; degrade; demean; deprave; depress; discredit; disgrace; dishonor; heathenize; humble; lower; mar; mark; outrage; paganize; pervert; pollute; profane; prostitute; stigmatize; sully; taint; trample (on); violate; vulgarize; DESECRATION: (**see** "corruption") abuse; contamination; debasement; defilement; outrage; perversion; pollution; profanation; taint; vilification; violation; vitiation; vulgarization

DESERT: **v.** (**see** "abandon") abdicate; abscond; absent; absquatulate; betray; clear out; decamp; defect; depart; elope; empty; escape; evacuate; forsake; leave; quit; rat; renege; renounce; withdraw; DESERT: **n.** meed; merit; recompense; reward; sand; waste; wild; wilderness; DESERTER: (**see** "traitor") apostate; A.W.O.L.; backslider; betrayer; convert; defector; escapee; escaper; expatriate; fugitive; heretic; Judas; rat;

recreant; renege; seceder; straggler; tergiversator; turncoat; turntail; DESERTION: (**see** "abandonment") abdication; abrogation; abscondence; absentation; absenteeism; absquatulation; aloneness; apostasy; betrayal; defection departure; despoliation; elopement; evacuation; recreancy; renege; renunciation; solitariness; tergiversation; DESERTED: **see** "desolate"

DESERVE: earn; merit; rate; warrant; win; DESERVED: commendable; commendatory; condign; creditable; deserving; due; earned; eminent; estimable; excellent; exemplary; fit(ting); honorable; just(ifiable); meet; merited; meritorious; praiseworthy; prestigious; rated; suitable; valuable; warranted; worthy

DESICCATED: (**see** "dry") anhydrous; arid; parched; seared; sere; siccate; stale; vapid

DESIGN: **v.** (**see** "conceive") aim; aspire; calculate; chart; consign; contemplate; contrive; create; delineate; designate; destine; determine; devise; devote; diagram; draft; draw; end; etch; fashion; figure; form(ulate); include; intend; invent; meditate; plan; plot; produce; project; propose; purpose; scheme; sketch; study; DESIGN: **n.** (**see** "arrangement") aim; aspiration; construction; contrivance; creation; decor(ation); delineation; destination; device; diagram; direction; draft; draught; drawing; end; enterprise; fashion; figure; form; frame(work); goal; ideal: insigne; insignia (pl.); intendment; intention; invention; map; mechanics; method; methodology; model; mold; monogram; motif; motive; object; orderliness; outline; pattern; picture; plan; plot; project(ion); proposal; purport; purpose; regularity; scheme; sketch; stamp; stripe; DESIGNED: **see** "intentional;" DESIGNING: **see** "crafty"

DESIGNATE: (**see** "apportion" and "name") allot; appoint; assign; call; characterize; choose; circumscribe; command; declare; delegate; denominate; denote; design; dictate; distinguish; earmark; elect; entitle; express; finger; give; identify; induct; label; mark; name; nominate; pick; point; prescribe; qualify; schedule; select; set (aside); signify; specify; stigmatize; stipulate; style; tap; term; title; DESIGNATION: allotment; appointment; apportionment; assignation; assignment; award; bestowal; characterization; charge; choice; circumspection; commission; connotation; consultation; date; declaration; delegation; denomination; description; distinction; election; endowment; engagement; entitlement; expression; identification; indication; induction; interview; job; labeling; meeting; name; nomination; order; ordination; portion; position; rendezvous; representation; reservation; schedule; selection; settlement; specification; station; stipulation; style; term; time; title; tryst; turn; warrant

DESIRE: **v.** (**see** "crave") aim; ask; aspire; beg; beseech; care; covet; demand; desiderate; entreat; envy; fancy; hanker; hope; hunger; incline; irritate; itch; long; love; lust; need; pant; pine; pray; prefer; request; require; seek; seethe; solicit; stew; thirst; tingle; want; will; wish; yearn; yen; DESIRE:- **n.** (**see** "appetite") aim; appetency; appetibility; *appétit*; appetition; aspiration; attraction; belly; care; choice; concupiscence; craving; desiderata (pl.); desideratum; emotion; end; envy; Eros; ferment; hankering; heart; hope; hunger(ing); impulse; inclination; intention; irritation; itch(ing); libido; longing(ness); love; lust; mind; need; orexis; passion; petition; pleasure; preference; proclivity; propensity; request; restlessness; stomach; striving; thirst; urge(ncy); voracity; want; will; wish; yearn(ing); zest(fulness); DESIRABLE: (**see** "favorable") acceptable; advantageous; advisable; appetible; appetitious; attractive; beneficial; choice; desiderative; enviable; excellent; expedient; good; healthy; ideal; optive; optimal; orective; pleasing; plummy; proper; rare; satisfactory; suitable; suited; valuable; votive; well; wise; wishful; worthwhile; worthy; DESIROUS: **see** "wild;" DESIRABILITY: **see** "expedience"

DESIST: abstain; avast; cease; conclude; cut; die; disappear; discontinue; drop; ease; end; expire; fade; fail; finish; forbear; halt; intermit; leave (off); pause; peter (out); quit; refrain; relinquish; resign; retire; stay; stint; stop; succumb; terminate; vanish; withdraw; yield

DESOLATE: abandoned; alone; barren; bereaved; bleak; cheerless; companionless; dejected; deserteed; devastate(d); devoid; dilapidated; disconsolate; disheartened; dismal; drear(y); forgotten; forlorn; forsaken; gaunt; hopeless; joyless; lapsed; left; lifeless; lone(ly); lorn; neglected; ruined; run-down; sad(dened); solitary; sorrowful; stark; unused; waste(d); wild; woebegone; woeful; DESOLATION: abandonment; aloneness; barrenness; bleakness; cheerlessness; dejection; depression; desert; desertion; despair;

destitution; disconsolation; dismality; gloom(iness); havoc; joylessness; loneliness; misery; ruin; sadness; solitariness; sorrow(fulness); starkness; waste; wilderness; woe

DESPAIR: (**see** "disconsolation") dejection; depression; despairingness; desperation; despondency; disappointment; discouragement; disheartenment; futility; gloom; grief; hopelessness; joylessness; recklessness; sadness; unhopefulness; urgency; wretchedness; DESPERATE: acute; anxious; appalling; audacious; bad; bold; calumnious; cancerous; chancy; compelling; critical; crucial; dangerous; daring; deadly; decisive; delicate; dilemmatic; dire; disastrous; emergency; excoriative; exigent; extreme; fearful; fierce; foolhardy; forlorn; formidable; foul; frantic; frightful; furious; grim; hazardous; helpless; hopeless; ignitable; imminent; impetuous; indispensible; injurious; insecure; intense; irretrievable; jeopardous; lost; menacing; murderous; needy; ominous; outrageous; overmastering; overpowering; parlous; perilous; precarious; rash; reckless; resolute; rocky; severe; shocking; threatening; ticklish; touch-and-go; touchy; treacherous; uncautious; uncertain; unchary; unhealthful; unhealthy; unsafe; vain; venturous; vulnerable; wicked; wild; wretched; DESPERATION: (**see** "despair") danger; desperateness; extremity; imminency; peril

DESPICABLE: (**see** "base") contemptible; despised; hated; scorned; wicked

DESPISE: (**see** "abhor") abominate; contemn; detest; disdain; disgust; dislike; disprize; disrespect; hate; loathe; reprehend; scorn; scout; spurn; DESPISABLE *or* DESPISED: (**see** "abhorrent") abject; abominable; contemptible; contemptuous; contumelious; despicable; detestable; disdainful; dislikeable; disrespectful; downtrodden; execrable; foul; hateful; loathesome; nauseating; nauseous; odious; repelling; reprehensible; repugnant; scornful; underfoot; vile; villainous

DESPOIL: (**see** "ruin") attack; bereave; decimate; defile; deflower; denudate; denude; deprive; divest; fleece; injure; pillage; plunder; rape; ravage; ravish; reave; rifle; riot; rip; rob; sack; seduce; strip; wreck

DESPONDENT: (**see** "gloomy") abject; apathetic; crushed; crying; dejected; depressed; despairful; despairing; disconsolate; discouraged; disheartened; disheartening; dispirited; downcast; forlorn; funebrial;

funebr(i)ous; funereal; glum; grim; hopeless; hypochondriac(al); inconsolable; inconsolate; lachrymose; low(-spirited); melancholy; sad(dened); weeping; DESPONDENCY: (**see** "gloom") apathy; blues; darkness; dejectedness; dejection; depression; despair; disconsolation; discouragement; disheartenment; dismality; dispiritedness; doldrums; forlornity; gloominess; hopelessness; hypochronoria(sis); inertia; lachrymals; megrims; melancholia; melancholy; morosity; pall; pessimism; sadness; saturninity; woe; wretchedness

DESPOT: anarch; autarch; authoritarian; autocrat(or); Caesar; caudillo; commissar; czar; despot(ist); dictator; disciplinarian; hierarch; king; man on horseback; martinet; mogul; monarch; oligarch; praetor; rigorist; ruler; sadist; satrap; sovereign; totalitarian; tsar; tyrant; DESPOTISM: absolutism; authoritarianism; autocracy; Caesarism; caudillismo; dictature; harshness; magisteriality; monopolization; power; praetorianism; prerogative; sovereignty; totalitarianism; tyranny; DESPOTIC: absolute; absolutistic; anarchistic; apostolic(al); arbitrary; autarchic(al); authoritarian; autocratic; canonical; determinate; dictatorial; dogmatic; domineering; extreme; harsh; hierarchic(al); imperative; imperious; magistratical; majestic(al); Neronian; nondemocratic; oppressive; positive; preemptory; rigoristic; rigorous; totalitarian; tyrannic(al); tyrannous; willful

DESTINATION: (**see** "aim") aspiration; bourne; course; design; direction; doom; end; fate; goal; intendment; intention; hope; lot; mark; object(ive); philosophy; plan; point; port; purpose; termination; terminus; *terminus ad quem*; use; will; wish

DESTINE: (**see** "doom") assign; condemn; consign; curse; damn; dedicate; design(ate); devote; direct; end; intend; judge; mark; ordain; order; predestine; predetermine; preordain; require; sentence; DESTINY: (**see** "doom") chance; decree; end(ing); eure; fate; foreordination; fortune; future; goal; judgment; lot; portion; predestination; sentence; star

DESTITUTE: (**see** "poor") bankrupt; bare; barren; beggarly; bereft; broke; deficient; desolate; devoid; divested; empty; forsaken; impecunious; impoverished; indigent; innocent; insolvent; lacking; lost; needy; penniless; penurious; pinched; void; DESTITUTION: (**see** "poverty") bankruptcy;

deficiency; distress; emptiness; impecuniosity; impecuniousness; impoverishment; indigence; insolvency; lack; mendacity; need; pauperism; penury; pinch; privation; squalor; want

DESTROY: (**see** "kill") abate; abolish; abrogate; absorb; annihilate; assimilate; burn; butcher; cancel; cannibalize; consume; corrode; counteract; crush; decapitate; decimate; defeat; delete; demolish; deprive; deracinate; despoil; devastate; devitalize; devour; dilapidate; diminish; discredit; dismantle; dispatch; dissipate; drink; eat; engulf; eradicate; erase; erode; exhaust; exploit; expunge; exterminate; extinguish; extirpate; finish; fritter; guillotine; harry; immolate; mangle; massacre; mayhem; meat-ax; mortify; murder; mutilate; neutralize; nip; nullify; obliterate; overcome; overpower; overthrow; overwhelm; perish; pillage; plunder; poison; prey; pulverize; punch; puncture; rape; rapine; ravage; remove; rifle; rob; root (out); ruin; sabotage; sack; shatter; slaughter; slay; spend; spoil; strip; subvert; swallow; swamp; sweep; tear; undo; uproot; utilize; vandalize; vanquish; vitiate; waste; weaken; wrack; wreck; DESTROYED: **see** "ruined;" DESTROYER: **see** "tyrant"

DESTRUCTIVE: aneretic; annihilating; annihilative; annihilatory; antibiotic; bad; baneful; biocidal; brutal(ized); cataclysmic; consuming; consumptive; corrosive; deadly; decisive; deleterious; demoralizing; devastating; devastative; devouring; dire; edacious; fatal; ferocious; harmful; inimical; injurious; internecine; lethal; malign(ant); murderous; noxious; pernicious; poison(ous); ruinous; shattering; subversive; suicidal; terrible; voracious; wasteful; wasting; wild; withering; wrackful; DESTRUCTIVENESS: brutality; destructivity; malignancy; sabotage; subversion; DESTRUCTION: abolishment; abolition; annihilation; barbarism; barbarity; blood(shed); butchery; cancellation; cannibalism; cannibalization; carnage; cataclysm; catastrophe; collapse; crash; decapitation; decay; death(blow); decadence; decimation; defeat; deletion; demolishment; demolition; deracination; desolation; despoilage; despoliation; devastation; dilapidation; disintegration; disposal; dissolution; doom; end(ing); eradication; erasure; excision; exploitation; extermination; extinction; extirpation; fall; *götterdämmerung*; havoc; holocaust; immolation; invalidation; killing; loss; mangle; massacre; mortification; murder(ousness); mutilation;

neutralization; nullification; paralysis; perdition; pestilence; pogrom; ruin; sabotage; slaughter; slaying; spoliation; utilization; vandalism; vandalization; waste; wrack

DESULTORY: (**see** "casual") accidental; adventitious; chance; chancy; contingent; cursory; digressive; easy; erratic; eventful; fitful; fortitudinous; haphazard; heedless; idle; impromptu; inadvertent; inconstant; indefinite; irregular; lax; loose; nonchalant; offhand; purposeless; rambling; random; shifting; simple; slight; superficial; unmethodical; unmethodized; unplanned; unsustained; wavering

DETACH: ablate; abscind; abscise; abstract; amputate; bob(tail); cleave; cut; dele(te); disassociate; disconnect; disengage; disentangle; disjoin; dissociate; disunite; divide; dock; draft; eliminate; emasculate; excise; expunge; expurgate; exscind; extirpate; extract; fell; fractionate; fragmentalize; fragmentate; insulate; isolate; lob; lop; mow; part(ition); prescind; prune; pry; remove; resect; saw; segregate; separate; sever; shorten; snip; split; subdivide; sunder; uncleave; uncouple; undo; unfasten; unfix; unhook; untie; wean; withdraw; DETACHED: alone; aloof; analytical; apart; apathetic; away; bashful; calm; cautious; chary; circumspect; clinical; cloistered; cold; cool; coy; cut; demure; disassociated; disconnected; discrete; disengaged; disjoined; dispassionate; dissociated; distant; disunited; egocentric; elusive; enisled; excised; exclusive; fragmented; fragmentized; frosty; gelid; hermetic(al); icy; impersonal; indifferent; insular; insulated; isolated; lofty; modest; moodish; objective; off(ish); only; poker-faced; segregated; separate(d); sequestered; severed; sheltered; shy; silent; stately; stony; taciturn; timid; unaffiliated; unapproachable; unbiased; uncommunicative; unconnected; undemonstrative; unemotional; unfriendly; withdrawn; DETACHMENT: abruption; aloofness; apathy; crew; detail; disassociation; disconnection; discreteness; discretion; disengagement; dissociation; disunion; fragmentation; indifference; insularity; insulation; isolation; item; part; piece; portion; sector; segregation; separateness; separation; severance; squad; unconcern; unfriendliness; unworldliness; withdrawal

DETAIL: **v.** account; arrange; describe; enumerate; itemize; limn; list; name; note; number; particularize; plan; plot; recapitulate; recite; reckon; recount; relate; rehearse;

report; say; specify; tell; total; DETAIL(S); **n.** (**see** "circumstance") account; circumstantiality; crew; description; detachment; enumeration; equipment; furniture; item(s); mechanics; meticulosity; minutia; minutiae (pl.); part(icularity); piece; portion; respect; section; sector; specialty; specification; specifics; squad; technicalities; technicality; DETAILED: (**see** "minute") closeup; comprehensive; concentrated; play-by-play; pointed; punctilious; punctual; word-for-word

DETAIN: (**see** "check") arrest; block; bridle; cage; confine; control; coop; corner; curb; delay; halt; harness; hinder; hold; intern; jail; keep; nab; prevent; repress; restrain; retain; retard; slack(en); slow (up); stay; stop; tether; withhold; DETAINMENT: **see** "custody"

DETECT: (**see** "discover") apprehend; ascertain; bare; capture; catch; descry; determine; discern; disclose; divine; elicit; espy; exhume; experience; expose; find; hear; identify; learn; locate; notice; perceive; recognize; reveal; scent; see; sense; smell; spot; uncover; unmask; DETECTION: apprehension; arrest; ascertainment; capture; discernment; discovery; elicitation; exposure; grasp; identification; intuition; perception; recognition; revelation; DETECTABLE: **see** "comprehensible"

DETENTION: (**see** "custody") delay; hold

DETER: (**see** "discourage") check; disadvise; dissuade; divert; frighten; hinder; inhibit; persuade; prevent; restrain; restrict; scare; stop; terrify; warn

DETERGE: **see** "clean"

DETERIORATE: (**see** "degenerate") bastardize; corrupt; decay; decline; decompose; degrade; depreciate; diminish; disintegrate; dissipate; ebb; erode; impair; lessen; lower; melt; perish; putrefy; putresce; retrogress; rot; ruin; rust; sicken; sink; slip; sour; spoil; tarnish; vitiate; wane; weaken; wear; worsen; DETERIORATING: decadent; decaying; declensional; declinatory; degenerative; deteriorative; ebbing; eroding; falling; lessening; oxidizing; perishing; retrograde; retrogressing; rusting; tarnishing; waning; weakening; wearing; worsening; DETERIORATION: (**see** "degeneration") bastardization; corruption; debasement; debauchery; decadence; declension; declination; decline; degenerescence; degradation;

dégringolade; *délabrement*; disintegration; dissipation; doldrums; fall; impairment; infection; inflammation; labefaction; lessening; mildew; pollution; pot; profligacy; putrescence; putridity; retrocession; retrogression; rot(tenness); ruin; rust; spoilage; tarnish; vileness; vitiation; weakening; wear; worsening

DETERMINE: acquire; add; adjudicate; adjust; appraise; arbitrate; ascertain; bound; calculate; calibrate; certify; compute; conclude; consider; contrive; control; decide; define; delimit(ate); delineate; design; detect; develop; devise; dijudicate; direct; discover; do; dominate; end; estimate; evaluate; examine; figure; find; fit; fix; foreordain; gain; gather; gauge; get; glean; govern; hear; identify; impel; influence; intuit; judge; learn; limit; map; mark; measure; mold; number; ordain; pinpoint; prefigure; prove; read; realize; receive; reckon; regulate; resolve; rule; scrutinize; sentence; set(tle); solve; study; survey; terminate; test; trace; type; weigh; DETERMINED: (**see** "certain") bent; bold; bound(ed); decided; decisive; definite; definitive; do-or-die; dominative; figured; fixed; foreordained; immovable; indomitable; necessary; predestined; preemptory; required; resolute; resolved; set(tled); tenacious; unalterable; undeterred; unwavering; DETERMINATION: adjudication; arbitrament; arbitration; ascertainment; calculation; conclusion; consideration; courage; decision; definition; dijudication; endeavor; ending; examination; finding; fixation; fortitude; gall; grit; guts; impulsion; judgment; mettle; nerve; pluck; purpose; resoluteness; resolution; resolve; ruling; sand; scrutiny; solution; spirit; stamina; survey; DETERMINABLE: **see** "comprehensible"

DETEST: (**see** "hate") abhor; abominate; dislike; execrate; loathe; reject; scorn; spurn; DETESTABLE: (**see** "hateful") abhorrent; abominable; adverse anathematic(al); annoying; bad; despicable; hateable; loathing; loathsome; odious; outrageous; repugnant; unnatural; wretched; DETESTATION: (**see** "hate") abhorrence; abomination; anathema; contempt; despicability; execration; loathing; loathsomeness; odium; repugnance; repugnancy

DETHRONE: depose; destool; discrown; disenthrone; oust; remove; strip; uncrown; unhorse; unseat; upset

DETOUR: **v.** (**see** "avoid") avert; bypass;

deflect; depart; deter; deviate; distract; diverge; divert; dodge; escape; fend; parry; prevent; reroute; shunt; sidestep; sidetrack; skirt; switch; thwart; turn; twist; ward (off); wind; DETOUR: **n.** avoidance; bypass; deflection; departure; deviation; divergence; diversion; dodge; escape; prevention; roundabout; shunt; side step; sidetrack; switch

DETRACT: (**see** "belittle") asperse; calumniate; debase; decry; defame; denigrate; deprecate; depreciate; derogate; diminish; disparage; divert; draw; lessen; libel; malign; minify; minimize; reduce; slander; vilify; DETRACTING: (**see** "degrading") denigratory; derogative; derogatory; diminishing; disparaging; diverting; libelous; slanderous; DETRACTION: (**see** "degradation") backbiting; calumny; censure; defamation; denigration; deprecation; depreciation; derogation; diminishment; disparagement; diversion; minimization; scandal; slander; subtraction; vilification

DETRIMENT: (**see** "harm") bane; cost; damage; evil; hurt; injury; loss; mischief; DETRIMENTAL: (**see** "harmful") adverse; baneful; costly; damaging; deadly; deleterious; destructive; evil; hurtful; inimical; injurious; malefic; malign(ant); mischievous; nocuous; noisome; noxious; offensive; pernicious; poison(ous); prejudicial; toxic; unwholesome

DETRITUS: (**see** "waste") fragments; rubbish

DEVASTATE: (**see** "destroy") demolish; despoil; harry; meat-ax; overcome; overpower; overwhelm; pillage; plunder; rape; ravage; raze; rob; ruin; sack; scorch; spoil; strip; waste; wreck; DEVASTATING: (**see** "destructive") annihilating; wasting; withering; DEVASTATION: (**see** "destruction") demolishment; despoilage; despoliation; havoc; murder(ousness); overthrow; pillage; plunder; rapine; ravage; ruin; spoliation; waste

DEVELOP: (**see** "advance") age; arrange; bud; burgeon; calculate; cause; constitute; create; culminate; cultivate; delineate; determine; differentiate; dilate; disclose; drift; educate; effloresce; elaborate; enlarge; establish; evolve; expand; expound; extend; flourish; flower; form; furnish; gain; generate; germinate; grow; incubate; investigate; make; manifest; materialize; maturate; mature; muster; nourish; nurse; open; orchestrate; organize; outline; plan; plot;

prepare; produce; promote; prosecute; prospect; prove; ripen; search; shape; strengthen; trace; uncover; unfold; unfurl; unroll; work (up); DEVELOPED: adult; advanced; aged; culminant; differentiated; grown; materialized; mature(d); organized; produced; ripened; unprimitive; DEVELOPMENT: (see "advancement") circumstance; consummation; culmination; cultivation; differentiation; drift; education; elaboration; episode; event; evolution; excrescence; florescence; gain; generation; germination; growth; incubation; investigation; manifestation; maturation; maturescence; maturity; morphosis; nature; occurrence; ontogeny; operation; organization; outgrowth; phenomenon; phylogeny; process; production; prosecution; search; situation; state; subdivision; transition; unfolding; upgrowth; work-up

DEVIATE: (see "avoid") avert; bend; bypass; change; curve; decline; deflect; depart; detour; digress; divagate; divaricate; diverge; divert; divide; drift; err; fluctuate; incline; lapse; lean; meander; move; offend; parry; recede; roam; rove; shift; sin; skip; slip; slue; split; squirm; stray; sway; swerve; tack; turn; twist; vary; veer; wander; ward (off); warp; waver; wrest; yaw; DEVIATING: (see "winding") aberrant; anomalous; circuitous; crazy; curved; curving; deviant; deviated; devious; divaricative; divergent; errant; excursional; excursionary; excursive; flexuous; maniac(al); manic; meandering; parenthetic(al); roundabout; serpentine; straying; tortuous; wandering; DEVIATION or DEVIANT: aberrance; aberration; anomaly; circuity; deflection; delusion; departure; detour; deviance; deviate; difference; digression; divarication; divergence; drift(age); eccentricity; error; excursion; fault; flexuosity; hallucination; heresy; homosexual; inclination; insanity; intransigence; lapse; leaning; leeway; license; mania; noncomformity; paramorph; shortcoming; sinuoity; sport; squint; tangency; tortuosity; variant; veering; wandering

DEVICE: (see "apparatus") accessory; accouterment; adjunct; appliance; artifice; badge; business; contraption; contrivance; design; dingus; emblem; figure; fraud; gadget; gear; image; implement; insigne; insignia(pl.); invention; knickknack; machination; machine; mark; motif; notion; plan; procedure; project; rule; ruse; scheme; signal; stratagem; tackle; target; tool; trick; utility; wheeze; wile

DEVIL(S): Apollyon; archfiend; Azazel; Beelzebub; Belial; brat; cacod(a)emon; demon; deuce; Diabolus; dickens; dule; energumen; fanatic; fiend; fury; geni (pl.); genius; goblin; Hugon; imp; incubi; (pl.); incubus; knave; *Le Maudit*; libertine; Lucifer; Mephistopheles; monster; ogre; Old Nick; Old Scratch; reprobate; rip; rogue; roué; sadist; Satan; Satanas; scamp; scoundrel; serpent; succubi(pl.); succubus; swindler; tear; tempter; wretch; DEVILISH: annoying; atrocious; avernal; awful; bad; cruel; damaging; demoniac(al); demonic(al); derisive; detrimental; diabolic(al); difficult; elfish; elvish; evil; excessive; extreme; fiendish; fierce; foxy; frantic; frenzied; frightful; ghoulish; gruesome; harmful; hellish; hideous; hurtful; impious; impish; infernal; ingenious; inhuman(e); injurious; knavish;

Luciferian; maledictory; malevolent; malicious; Mephistophel(i)an; mephitic; misfortunate; monstrous; pert; playful; roguish; sardonic; Satanic(al); saturnine; scampish; spiteful; troublesome; unevangelic; unpleasant; venomous; vicious; wicked; DEVIL(T)RY: annoyance; art; cruelty; damage; demonization; detriment; diablerie; diabolism; disservice; enchantment; evil; fiendishness; ghoulishness; hankypanky; hellishness; hocus-pocus; hurt; inhumanity; injury; magic; malevolence; maliciousness; malignity; mischief; mischievousness; misdeed; misfortune; pain; roguery; roguishness; satanism; satanity; saturninity; sickness; sorrow; trouble; unpleasantry; wickedness; witchcraft; wrack

DEVIOUS: (see "winding") ambagious; ambivalent; anfractuous; astray; backstairs; circuitous; circular; circumferential; circumlocutious; circumlocutory; collateral; contemptible; crafty; crooked; deceitful; deep; deviating; dishonest; errant; erratic; erring; foxy; furtive; indirect; ingenious; insincere; labyrinthian; labyrinthine; louche; low; mazy; mean; misleading; mysterious; oblique; obscure; off course; out-of-the-way; perverse; remote; round(about); roving; serpentine; shifty; sinful; sinister; sinuate; sinuous; sly; snide; stealthy; subtle; tortuous; treacherous; tricky; underhanded; unfair; unscrupulous; wandering; DEVIOUSNESS: (see "winding") aimlessness; ambiguity; ambivalence; anfractuosity; circuity; circumbendibus; circumferential; circumlocution; deceitfulness; deviation; dishonesty; duplicity; errancy; indirection; indirectness; insincerity; sinuosity; tortuosity;

treachery; trickery; underhandedness; unfairness; unscrupulosity

DEVISE: (see "arrange") bequeath; compass; compile; concert; concoct; confect; construct; contrive; cook; counterfeit; demise; design; determine; fabricate; fake; find; frame; invent; leave; lower; ordain; machinate; plan; plot; premeditate; preordain; scheme; shape

DEVITALIZE: (see "weaken") attenuate; cripple; curtail; damage; debilitate; decay; decompose; dehydrate; denervate; desiccate; destroy; disembowel; emasculate; enervate; enfeeble; eviscerate; exenterate; exhaust; fatigue; harm; hurt; impair; lower; prostrate; reduce; refine; retrogress; rot; strain; suck; tire; undermine; unman; unnerve; upset; wane; wear; DEVITALIZATION: see "weakness"

DEVOID: (see "bare") barren; destitute; empty; free; hollow; immature; inadequate; inane; jejune; lacking; naked; needy; nude; scant(y); sheer; stark; unadorned; uncovered; undressed; unimpaired

DEVOIR: (see "duty") respects; task

DEVOTE: (see "apply") addict; adore; allot; apportion; appropriate; assign; concentrate; consign; damn; dedicate; design; destine; direct; doom; give; hallow; honor; provide; revere(nce); strive; study; worship; DEVOTED: (see "devout" and "zealous") ardent; consecrated; earnest; fervent; loving; loyal; pious; religious; reverent; serious; sincere; zealous; DEVOTION: (see "application") addiction; adherence; adoration; allegiance; altruism; ardency; ardentness; ardor; attachment; consignment; constancy; devotedness; earnestness; enthusiasm; faith; fanaticism; fealty; fervency; fervor; fidelity; love; loyalty; novena; piety; regard; religion; religiosity; reverence; truth; worship; zeal(otry)

DEVOTEE: (see "follower") adherent; admirer; aficionada (fem.); aficionado; amateur; angel; apostle; backer; minion; partisan; supporter; votary; zealot

DEVOTION: see under "devote"

DEVOUR: (see "destroy" and "eat") annihilate; appropriate; bolt; consume; corrode; cram; down; engulf; erode; feast; glut; gorge; gormandize; gulp; prey; rust; seize; swallow; waste; wolf; DEVOURING: (see "destructive") annihilative; annihilatory; consuming; corrosive; edacious; gluttonous; voracious; vorant; wasteful

DEVOUT: (see "holy") ardent; blessed; chaste; consecrated; dedicated; devoted; devotional; divine; earnest; fervent; godly; good; hallowed; hearty; immaculate; liege; loyal; pietistic(al); pious; prayerful; pure; religiose; religious; reverent; righteous; sacred; sacrosanct; saintly; serious; sincere; solemn; spiritual; unspotted; unstained; unworldly; worshipful; zealous

DEWY: bedewed; cool; fresh; moist; refreshing; roral; roric; roscid

DEXTERITY: ability; address; adeptness; adroitness; agility; alertness; aptitude; aptness; art(fulness); cleverness; craft(iness); cunning; deftness; dexterousness; diplomacy; ease; expertise; expertness; facility; faculty; finesse; grace; hability; knack; magic; palmistry; practice; prestidigitation; prowess; quickness; readiness; resourcefulness; righthandedness; *savoir faire*; skill(fulness); sleight (of hand); tact; trickery; wittiness; DEXTEROUS: able; adept; agile; alert; artful; clever; crafty; deft; expert; facile; good; graceful; habile; handy; ingenious; keen; neat; nimble; practiced; quick; ready; resourceful; righthanded; shrewd; skilled; skillful; slick; smart; tricky; witty

DIABOLIC(AL): (see "devilish") fiendish; ingenious

DIADEM: (see "crown") empire; sovereignty

DIAGNOSE: (see "analyze") diagnosticate; identify; solve; DIAGNOSTIC: analytic(al); distinctive; pathognomonic(al); prodromal; symptomatic

DIAGRAM: v. (see "map") chart; design; diagrammatize; draft; draw; graph; plan; plot; scheme; sketch; trace; DIAGRAM: n. (see "map") aim; blueprint; chart; conception; design; draft; drawing; elevation; floor plan; gamut; graph; plan; plot; schema; schemata (pl.); scheme; sketch; survey; tracing; view

DIALECT: (see "jargon") argot; cant; colloquialism; drawl; idiom; language; lingo; lingua franca; patois; patter; slang; speech; vernacular(ism); vernacularity; vulgarism

DIALOG(UE): causerie; collocution; colloquy; confabulation; conference; debate; dialectics; discourse; discussion; duologue; interlocution; parley; reading; talk

DIAMETER: bore; breadth; caliber; chord; extent; gauge; module; thickness; width

DIAPHANOUS: (see "clear") crystal(line); delicate; ethereal; fine; insubstantial; lucid; pellucid; sheer; thin; transparent

DIARY: blotter; book; calendar; chart; chronicle; docket; journal; *journal intime*; list; log; names; record; register

DIATRIBE: (see "irony") asteism; derision; lampoon; mockery; philippic; raillery; ridicule; sarcasm; satire; screed; tirade

DICKER: (see "barter") deal; swap; trade

DICTATE: (see "command") control; decree; designate; direct; enjoin; govern; impel; impose; ordain; order; prescribe; prompt; require; rule; speak; suggest; tell; write; DICTATORIAL: arbitrary; arrogant; august; authoritarian; authoritative; autocratic; cavalier; coercive; commanding; compelling; confident; contemptuous; controlling; cruel; czaristic; demanding; despotic; determinative; dictative; dictatory; doctrinaire; doctrinal; dogmatic(al); dominant; dominating; dominative; domineering; governing; grandiose; haughty; hierarchic(al); imperative; imperious; imposing; lordly; magisterial; mandatory; masterful; masterly; narrow; Neronian; Neronic; opinionated; opinionative; oppressive; oracular; overbearing; overpowering; overriding; overwhelming; paramount; peremptory; positive; predominant; preeminent; preemptory; prevailing; prevalent; principal; pronunciative; totalitarian; transcendent; tyrannical; tyrannous; warlike

DICTATOR: (see "despot") anarch; authoritarian; autocrat(or); caudillo; commissar; despotist; man on horseback; oligarch; ruler; tyrant; DICTATORSHIP: (see "despotism") absolutism; authoritarianism; Caesarism; caudillismo; dictature; harshness; monopolization; totalitarianism; tyranny

DICTION: (see "language") description; enunciation; expression; phrase(ology); pronunciation; speech; style; verbiage; vocabulary; wording; words

DICTIONARY: anthology; atlas; calepin; collection; concordance; cyclop(a)edia; delectus; *dictionnaire*; digest; encyclopedia; gazetteer; glossary; gradus; handbook; heptaglot; hexaglot; idioticon; index; language; lexicon; list; nomenclature; onomasticon; pentaglot; polyglot; repository; speech; storehouse; synonymicon; terminology; terms; thesaurus; treasury; vocabulary; wordbook; word finder; word guide; words; word-stock; *Wörterbuch*

DICTUM: apothegm; dicta (pl.); maxim; opinion; principle; pronouncement; saying; statement

DIDACTIC(AL): (see "instructive") erudite; moralistic; pedantic; pompous

DIE: **v.** cease; close; collapse; conclude; decay; decease; decline; depart; deteriorate; disappear; discontinue; drown; elapse; emit; end; exit; expire; fade; fall; go; languish; lapse; melt; mold; pass (away); perish; pop off; recede; rot; shrivel; sleep; slip; smother; starve; stop; subside; suffocate; terminate; waste; wither; DIE: **n.** block; cube; mold; plate; sicca; stamp

DIET: aliment; allotment; allowance; board; course; dish; drink; fare; fast; food; meal; nutriment; nutrition; provender; provisions; ration(s); regime(n); repast; support; sustenance; table; victuals

DIFFER: argue; change; compare; complain; contend; contradict; contrast; debate; deviate; differentiate; disagree; dissent; diverge; misunderstand; quarrel; vary; veer; wrangle; DIFFERENCE: argument; change; cleavage; comparison; complaint; complexity; contention; contrast; controversy; debate; degree; deviation; differentia; differentiae (pl.); disagreement; discord; discrepance; discrepancy; discrimination; disparity; disproportion; dispute; dissent(ion); dissimilarity; dissimilitude; dissonance; distinction; divergence; divergency; diverseness; diversity; excess; gap; gradation; hairline; heterogeneity; heterology; hiatus; incongruity; inequality; irregularity; margin; misunderstanding; nuance; odds; opposition; otherness; quarrel; separation; severance; shade; shadow; spat; unlikeness; variance; variation; variety; wrangle; DIFFERENT: alternate; anomalous; anon; another; antipodal; antithetic(al); atypical; deviating; discordant; disparate; dissimilar; distinct; divergent; diverse; diversified; diversiform; else; heterogeneous; heterologous; heterotypic(al); incongruent; incongruous; ingenious; irregular; manifold; new; odd; opposite; other-(wise); quaint; separate; several; special; sundry; unique; unlike; unsimilar; unusual; various; varying; DIFFERING: antagonistic; different(ial); discordant; discrepant; discriminative; dissenting; dissonant; diverse; heterogeneous; heteromorphic; incongruent; incongruous; inharmonious; opposite; singular; unharmonious; unlike; varying

DIFFERENTIATE: (**see** "compare") determine; differ; discern; discriminate; distinguish; equate; liken; mark; match; parallel; test; vie

DIFFICULT: adamant(ine); arduous; Augean; austere; awkward; bad; brazen; brittle; bruising; calculating; callous; challenging; clamorous; coarse; cold-blooded; complex; confirmed; cool; crushing; dark; deep; demanding; dense; devastating; devious; distressing; disturbing; effortful; exacting; execrable; exhausting; exigent; fiendish; firm; fixed; flinty; forbidden; formidable; frenetic; glassy; grievous; grinding; hairy; hampering; hard(-hearted); harsh; hazardous; heavy; Herculean; hostile; impenetrable; impenitent; importunate; inclement; incorrigible; indurate(d); inexorable; inflexible; insensible; insusceptible; intense; intensive; intractable; inured; involved; irksome; irregular; knotty; labored; laborious; laborsome; murderous; mysterious; nasty; obdurate; obscure; onerous; operose; oppressive; overwhelming; painful; perplexing; persistent; perverse; pitiless; ponderous; pressing; profound; punishing; puzzling; recondite; resistant; rigid; rigorous; rocky; rough; ruthless; scabrous; sclerotic; serious; severe; slavish; steely; steep; stern; stiff; stony; strenuous; stressful; strict; stringent; strong; stubborn; sweaty; taxing; terrible; thorny; tiresome; toilsome; tough(ened); troublesome; trying; turbulent; unaccommodating; unbridled; unmanageable; unpleasant; unruly; unyielding; uphill; urgent; vexatious; vicious; vicissitudinous; vigorous; violent; weighty; worrisome; DIFFICULTY: abstrusity; ache; anguish; arduousness; argument; barrier; bewilderment; bind; bump; cavil; coil; complexity; complexus; complicacy; complication; conglomeration; contention; controversy; crisis; crux; demur; dilemma; disagreement; discrepancy; disorder; dispute; distress; doubt; embarrassment; embroglio; embroilment; entanglement; fix; Gordian knot; hardness; hardship; hazard; hindrance; hot water; humiliation; ill(ness); imbroglio; impediment; intricacy; involvement; irregularity; jam;

jumble; knot; maelstrom; misfortune; misunderstanding; node; nodule; nodus; nonplus; objection; obscurity; obstacle; pain; pang; pass; perplexity; perversity; pickle; pinch; plight; predicament; problem; puzzle-(ment); quagmire; quandary; quarrel; rack; rigor; riptide; roughness; rub; scabrousness; scrape; set-to; snag; snare; snarl; spat; stitch; strait; strenuosity; stress; strife; struggle; suffering; task; thorn; throe; trap; trial; trouble; twist; uncertainty; unkindness; unlikeness; vicissitude; vortex

DIFFIDENT: (**see** "bashful") backhanded; chary; coy; doubtful; hesitant; modest; reluctant; reserved; shrinking; shy; timid; verecund; DIFFIDENCE: (**see** "bashfulness") coyness; doubt; hesitancy; modesty; reluctance; reserve; sheepishness; shyness; timidity; timidness; timorousness; verecundity

DIFFUSE: **v.** air; break up; broadcast; circulate; deplete; destroy; diminish; dismiss; dispatch; dispel; disperse; disseminate; dissipate; dissolve; distribute; divaricate; divide; expand; extend; exude; glow; lavish; melt; mix; move; orbit; pervade; pour; promulgate; propagate; publish; radiate; revolve; rotate; scatter; separate; shatter; shed; sow; spread; squander; suppress; strew; vanish; waste; wear; DIFFUSE: **a.** copious; dispersed; disseminated; expanded; full; lavish; osmotic; pervaded; prolix; scattered; sown; spread; strewn; verbose; widespread; wordy; DIFFUSION: circulation; dispersal; dispersion; dissemination; distribution; expansion; extension; exudation; flow; osmosis; passage; prolixity; promulgation; publication; radiation; scattering; seeding; shedding; spread; strewing

DIG: advance; appreciate; burrow; cavitate; claw; delve; deplete; dip; discern; disentomb; disinter; dredge; drill; drudge; examine; excavate; exhumate; exhume; explore; fathom; grasp; grub; hollow; hook; investigate; jab; lacerate; like; mine; mutilate; paw; penetrate; perforate; plumb; poke; probe; prod; prospect; punch; quarry; reconnoiter; revive; scoop; scrape; scratch; scrutinize; search; seek; shovel; sink; spade; study; survey; tear; thrust; till; uncover; understand; unearth; wound

DIGEST: **v.** (**see** "brief") abridge; absorb; abstract; assimilate; brook; codify; comprehend; consider; curtail; decompose; macerate; master; metabolize; ponder; reduce; shorten; soften; study; summarize; DIGEST:

n. (**see** "brief") abridgement; abstract(ion); aperçu; breviary; capsule; compendium; compilation; conspectus; epitome; glance; insight; outline; pandect; précis; prospectus; sketch; study; summary; summation; synopsis; system; DIGESTION: (**see** "absorption") alimentation; assimilation; eupepsia; eupepsy; metabolism; pepsis

DIGIT: cipher; figure; finger; integer; number; numeral; phalanx; toe; unit

DIGNIFY: (**see** "exalt") aggrandize; ennoble; extol; glorify; honor; nobilitate; pedestal; sanctify; DIGNIFIED: (**see** "exalted") august; correct; courtly; decorous; elegant; elevated; eminent; ennobled; excellent; gracious; grandiose; grave; high; honorable; illustrious; imperial; important; imposing; impressing; impressive; kingly; lofty; lordly; magisterial; majestic; meritorious; noble; poised; pompous; princely; proud; queenly; reserved; respected; sedate; serious; solemn; staid; stately; stern; stiff; sublime; togated; worthy; DIGNITY: amenities; augustness; civilities; consequence; convenances; conventions; courtliness; decency; decora (pl.); decorum; elegance; eminence; ennoblement; esteem; estimation; excellence; face; gentility; glory; grace; grandeur; grandiosity; gravity; honor; importance; lordliness; magisteriality; magnificence; majesty; merit; nobility; office; poise; pomp; position; pride; proprieties; propriety; rank; repute; reserve; seriousness; solemnity; standing; state; stateliness; station; stature; status; virtue; worth(iness)

DIGNITARY: (**see** "official") mogul; panjandrum; sovereign; VIP; wig

DIGRESS: (**see** "avoid") depart; detour; deviate; divagate; divaricate; diverge; meander; parenthesize; swerve; turn; veer; DIGRESSION: aberration; apostrophe; artifice; aside; avoidance; bypass; camouflage; circumlocution; circumvention; deception; departure; detour; deviation; discursion; divagation; divarication; divergence; dodge; duplicity; ecbole; episode; equivocation; escape; escapism; eschewal; evasion; excursion; flight; irrelevancy; maneuver; obliquity; obviation; parenthesis; rejection; renunciation; repudiation; resignation; retraction; revocation; runaround; shift; stratagem; subterfuge; swerve; tangency; tangent; trick; DIGRESSIVE: (**see** "winding") aberrant; apostrophic; circuitous; deceptive; desultory; devious; discursive; disingenuous; dissembling; divergent; duplicitous; elusive;

episodic; equivocal; escapist; excursional; excursionary; excursive; oblique; parenthetic(al); purposeless; rambling; random; serpentine; shifting; shifty; shuffling; sinuous; slippery; sly; snaky; tangential; Thackerayan; tortuous; tricky; vagrant

DILAPIDATE: (**see** "decay") crumble; decline; decompose; degenerate; destroy; fail; putrefy; putresce; rot; ruin; rust; sicken; spoil; taint; tarnish; waste; wrack; wreck; DILAPIDATED: aged; ancient; beggarly; creaky; crumbled; decayed; decaying; declined; decomposed; decrepit; degenerated; desolate; destroyed; disreputable; exhausted; hoary; neglected; misused; putrescent; putrid; ramshackle; retrograde; retrogressed; retrogressive; rickety; rotted; rotten; ruined; run-down; rusted; rusty; seedy; shabby; shaky; squalid; superannuated; tatterdemalion; threadbare; tired; wasted; worn; wrecked; DILAPIDATION: (**see** "decay") crumble; decomposition; decrepitness; decrepitude; degeneration; depreciation; despair; downfall; feebleness; havoc; mortification; necrosis; neglect; putrefaction; putrescence; rot; ruin; rust; spoilage; spoliation; squalidity; tarnish; waste; wreck(age)

DILATE: (**see** "enlarge") amplify; augment; broaden; descant; discourse; discuss; distend; elaborate; enhance; escalate; expand; expatiate; extend; grow; hypertrophy; increase; inflate; intensify; magnify; spread; stretch; swell; talk; tumefy; tumesce; widen; DILATION: (**see** "enlargement") amplification; augmentation; broadening; dilatation; distension; elaboration; enhancement; escalation; expansion; expatiation; extension; growth; hypertrophy; increase; inflation; intensification; magnification; spread; stretch; swell(ing); tumefaction; tumescence; widening; DILATED: **see** "enlarged"

DILATORY: (**see** "slow") creeping; dawdling; delaying; dronish; drowsy; gradual; hasteless; inactive; inching; indolent; inexcitable; lagging; languorous; late; latent; latrede; lax; lingering; procrastinating; remiss; retarded; slack; slow; sluggish; tardy; torpescent; torpid; unenergetic; unhasty; unhurried

DILEMMA: (**see** "difficulty") coil; crisis; cross; crux; distress; embroglio; entanglement; fix; jam; knot; mess; nonplus; obstacle; perplexity; pickle; pinch; plight; predicament; problem; puzzle; quandary; rub; scrape; situation; snare; strait; thorn; trap; trouble; vicissitude

DILETTANTE: amateur; connoisseur; dabbler; devotee; ham; layman; neophyte; nonprofessional; novice; tyro

DILIGENT: active; acute; agile; agog; alert; alive; arrect; assiduous; astir; attentive; avid; awake; aware; brisk; bristling; careful; cautious; cirumspect(ive); conscious; considerate; considerative; eager; earnest; excited; exhilarative; guarded; hard-working; heads-up; heedful; indefatigable; industrious; intelligent; intent; judicious; keen; knowing; laborious; lively; moving; nimble; observant; operose; painful; painstaking; perceptive; percipient; persevering; perspicacious; pert; prepared; prompt; quick(-witted); ready; resourceful; roused; sedulous; sharp; solicitous; steadfast; steady; stirred; stirring; studious; sudden; swift; unwearied; vigilant; wary; watchful; wide-awake; zealous; DILIGENCE: (see "business") activity; agility; alertness; application; assiduity; assiduousness; attention; awareness; briskness; care(fulness); caution; cautiousness; circumspection; consideration; constancy; diligency; diligentness; eagerness; exhilaration; heed; industry; intensity; judiciousness; keenness; labor; liveliness; nimbleness; operosity; perception; percipience; perseverance; perspicacity; promptness; prudence; quickness; quick-wittedness; readiness; resourcefulness; sedulity; solicitation; solicitude; steadfastness; vigilance; watchfulness; zealotry; zealousness

DILUTE: **v.** attenuate; cut; debase; diminish; enfeeble; qualify; rarefy; reduce; temper; thin; water; weaken; DILUTE(D): **a.** attenuated; cut; enfeebled; homeopathic; qualified; rarefied; thin(ned); washed-out; washy; .watered(-down); waterish; watery; weak

DIM: **v.** (see "cloud") becloud; bedim; befog; blear; confuse; darken; diminish; dip; dull; dwindle; eclipse; fade; fail; fog; lower; mask; muddle; obfuscate; obnubilate; obscure; obscurify; perplex; reduce; shadow; taint; tarnish; wane; DIM: **a.** (see "dark") bleared; blurred; blurry; brumous; caliginous; cheerless; cloudy; confused; crepuscular; darkened; darkish; depressing; dismal; dispirited; dubious; dull; dusk(y); faint; fogged; foggy; fuliginous; gloomy; hazy; indistinct; indistinguishable; lackluster; low(ery); misty; muddy; murky; myopic; nebular; nebulated; nebulose; nebulous; nubilous; obscure(d); ominous; opaque; overcast; roily; shadowy; smoky; subdued; tenuous; turbid; uncertain; unclear; unlighted; unlikely; unlit; unluminous; unlustrous; unrefined; vague; vapor-

ous; wan; weak; DIMNESS: cloudiness; crepuscle; diminishment; dwindling; fog; fuliginosity; gloom; mist; nebulosity; obfuscation; obnubilation; obscuration; obscurity; obstruction; opacity; tenuosity; turbidity; uncertainty; unclearness; vaporosity

DIMENSION(S): (see "degree" and "extent") capacity; girth; measurement; proportion; size

DIMINISH: (see "dim") abate; abridge; ameliorate; attenuate; bate; belittle; cancel; check; compress; contract; corrode; curtail; cut; damage; damp(en); debase; decay; decline; decrease; deduce; deduct; degrade; delate; depreciate; depress; deprive; deteriorate; detract; dip; disappear; discount; disparage; dissipate; dissolve; dive; dock; draw; dull; dwindle; ease; eat; ebb; end; erode; evaporate; exceed; extenuate; fail; faint; fall; fritter; impoverish; lessen; let up; lighten; lower; melt; mitigate; moderate; modify; nip; outweigh; overshadow; palliate; peter (out); ploy; plunge; prune; rebate; recede; reduce; regress; relieve; remit; remove; restrain; restrict; retard; retrench; retrograde; sap; shave; shorten; shrink; sicken; sink; slacken; slake; slip; slow (up); subside; subtract; taper; tarnish; wane; weaken; wear; whittle; withdraw; wither; withhold; DIMINISHMENT **or** DIMINUTION: abatement; abridgement; amelioration; attenuation; check; compression; contraction; curtailment; declension; decrease; decrescendo; deductibility; deduction; depreciation; depression; deprivation; diminuendo; discount; dive; dwindling; ebbing; extenuation; imperfection; lessening; letup; lowering; mitigation; moderation; modification; omission; palliation; plunge; rebate(ment); reduction; regression; relief; remission; restraint; restriction; retardation; retrenchment; retrogression; shortage; shrinkage; sinking; slackening; slip; subsidence; subtraction; tapering; waning; wear; withdrawal; withering

DIMINUTIVE: **a.** (see "little") bantam; dwarfish; microscopic; midget; miniscule; minute; peewee; petite; petty; pint-size(d); puny; runty; small; teeny; tiny; wee; DIMINUTIVE: **n. see** "dwarf" and "replica"

DIN: ado; annoyance; babble; babel; bedlam; brouhaha; cacophony; chatter; clamor; clangor; clash; clatter; confusion; crisis; flap; hubbub; hullabaloo; loudness; noise; pandemonium; prattle; racket; rattle; turmoil; uproar

DINE: banquet; eat; fare; feast; feed; regale; sup

DINGY: (**see** "dirty") begrimed; besmirched; blackened; dark; dim; discolored; dismal; disordered; drab; dull; dun; dusky; faded; grim(y); mean; ourie; shabby; smoky; soiled; squalid; stained; tarnished; worn

DINT: attack; blow; dent; force; impression; imprint; nick; notch; power; pressure; stroke

DIP: **v.** (**see** "diminish") bail; dap; decline; delve; depress; dive; dop; douse; drop; duck; dunk; immerse; incline; lade; ladle; lower; pitch; plunge; sag; scoop; sink; slip; slope; sop; souse; swim; tilt; veer; DIP: **n.** (**see** "diminishment") decrease; delve; delving; depression; dive; plunge; sag; slope; swim

DIPLOMA: certificate; certification; charter; commission; degree; document; license; paper; sheepskin

DIPLOMAT: agent; ambassador; ambassadress; attaché; consul; diplomatist; envoy; legate; minister; nuncio; plenipotentiary; representative; DIPLOMATIC: (**see** "adroit") artful; bland; conciliatory; consummate; crafty; delicate; discriminative; finished; foxy; gracious; polished; polite; politic(al); shy; smooth; suave; tactful; urbane; wily; DIPLOMACY: (**see** "adroitness") address; art(fulness); asurance; coolness; equilibrium; graciosity; graciousness; perpendicularity; poise; resolution; selfpossession; stability; suavity; tact(fulness); urbanity

DIRE: (**see** "bad") afflictive; awesome; awful; baneful; calamitous; catastrophic(al); cheerless; deadly; deplorable; desolate; desperate; destructive; devastating; direful; disastrous; dismal; dispirited; dread(ful); drear(y); evil; exigent; extreme; fatal; fearful; fell; funest; grievous; harmful; harrowing; horrendous; horrible; horrid; horrific; implacable; pernicious; malevolent; malign(ant); morbific; mortal; murderous; ominous; overpowering; painful; pernicious; poisonous; ruinous; severe; shocking; terrible; toxic; ugly; urgent; vicious; woeful

DIRECT: **v.** administer; aim; allot; apply; assign; bid; boss; canalize; cause; channel; coach; command; conduct; conn; consign; control; designate; destine; determine; devote; dispatch; dominate; domineer; energize; engineer; extend; focalize; focus; gesture; govern; guide; head; hold; hurl; indicate; influence; inform; inspect; institute; instruct; label; lead; level; mail; manage; maneuver; mark; marshal; mastermind; mediate; move; operate; order; organize; pilot; pitch; place; point; police; post; prescribe; preside; project; push; regularize; regulate; request; rule; send; smooth; steer; superintend; superscribe; supervise; sway; teach; tell; tend; toss; train; usher; wend; DIRECT: **a.** *or adv.* (**see** "clear") absolute; *ad rem*; attentive; blunt; categorical; clearcut; distinct(ive); effective; exact; explicit; express; firsthand; forthright; forthwith; frank; frontal; full; genuine; head-on; homely; honest; immediate; inevitable; instant; level; lineal; natural; near; open; out-and-out; pertinent; plump; positive; primary; prompt; quick; short(est); sincere; speedy; straight(forward); straightaway; straightway; truthful; uncluttered; uncompromising; unconditional; undeviating; unequivocal; unhampered; unqualified; verbatim; DIRECTION: (**see** "aim") address; axis; azimuth; bearing; behest; bend; bid(ding); channel; charge; command; conduct; control; counsel; course; current; design; drift; education; end; explicitness; gesture; goal; guidance; hand; inclination; indication; instruction; label; line; maintenance; management; mandate; mandatum; maneuver; objective; operation; order; orientation; path; plan; prescription; presidence; purpose; quarter; role; rule; schooling; sign(al); sphere; stream; summons; superintendence; superscription; supervision; teaching; tendency; tenor; training; trend; vein; way

DIRECTOR: (**see** "leader") administrant; administrator; boss; chair(man); chief(tain); coach; commander; comptroller; conductor; guide; head(master); impresario; instructor; manager; master; pilot; professor; regisseur; ruler; scout(master); superintendent; supervisor; teacher; DIRECTORSHIP: **see** "leadership"

DIRGE: coronach; elegy; eulogy; hymn; lament; Linos; linus; monody; psalm; requiem; song; threnody; wail

DIRTY: **v.** begrime; blacken; defile; discolor; dull; fade; foul; soil; DIRTY: **a.** abusive; adulterated; Augean; base; bawdy; begrimed; besmirched; blackened; contaminated; contemptible; corrupt; cowardly; crummy; crusted; crusty; dark; defiled; degraded; depraved; despicable; dim; dingy; discolored; diseased; disgusting; dishonorable; disreputable; drab; draggled; dull; dun; dusk(y); excremental; excrement(iti)-ous; faded; fecal; feculent; fetid; filthy; foul; grievous; grim; grimy; grubby; hateful; immoral; immund; impetiginous; impure; indecent; indelicate; infected; insanitary; lewd; licentious; loathsome; lousy; low; mangy; mean; molded; muddy; nasty; noxious; obscene; offensive; old; ordurous; ourie; polluted; putrefactive; putrescent; putrid; recrementitious; repulsive; rusted; rusty; saprogenic; scatologic(al); scaturient; scurrilous; shabby; slimy; smelly; smoky; smutty; soiled; sordid; squalid; stained; stercoraceous; streaked; sullied; tarnished; treacherous; unbathed; unchaste; unclean; underhanded; unkempt; unpure; unpurified; unscrupulous; unsterile; unsterilized; unswept; untidy; unwashed; unwholesome; ustulate; verminous; vile; DIRT: **see** "filth"

DISABLE: cripple; disadvantage; disparage; disqualify; disrupt; encumber; enfeeble; fetter; gruel; halt; hamper; hamstring; handicap; harm; hinder; hobble; hogtie; hurt; impair; impede; incapacitate; injure; lame; maim; mar; mayhem; retard; sap; shackle; unfit; weaken; DISABLED: broken-down; crippled; disadvantaged; disqualified; encumbered; enfeebled; fettered; halt; hampered; hamstrung; handicapped; harmed; hindered; hobbled; hogtied; *hors de combat*; hurt; impaired; impeded; incapacitated; injured; kaput; lame(d); maimed; marred; retarded; unfit; weakened; DISABILITY: amputation; crippling; disablement; disadvantage; discrimination; disqualification; encumbrance; enfeeblement; fetter; hampering; handicap; harm; hindrance; hurt; illness; impairment; impediment; inability; incapacitation; incapacity; incompetence; incompetency; injury; invalidity; lameness; restraint; restriction; retardation; sickness; unfitness; weakness

DISADVANTAGE: **v. see** "disable;" DISADVANTAGE: **n.** (**see** "disability") burden; damage; debit; defect; detriment; disinterest; disqualification; encumbrance; injury; hampering; handicap; hindrance; hurt; impediment; incapacitation; inconvenience; incubus; injury; loss; odds; prejudice; restraint; restriction; weakness; weight; DISADVANTAGEOUS(**see** "unfavorable") damaging; hurtful; incapacitating; prejudicial; unadvantageous; wrong

DISAGREE: (**see** "argue" and "differ") contend; discept; dispute; dissent; quarrel; vary; wrangle; DISAGREEABLE *or* DIS-

AGREEING: (**see** "argumentative") antagonistic; baleful; baneful; boorish; contentious; cross; crude; curt; discomfortable; discordant; disharmonious; dislikeful; displeasing; disputatious; dissentient; dissenting; dissentious; dissentive; dissident; dissonant; distasteful; distressful; divisive; evil; fulsome; ghastly; grating; harmful; harsh; hurtful; incompatible; incongruous; inconsistent; inconstant; inharmonious; jarring; loathsome; obnoxious; odious; offensive; painful; rancid; rank; repugnant; rotten; sour; strident; troublesome; ugly; uncongenial; unfavorable; ungenial; ungenteel; ungracious; ungrateful; unhappy; unharmonious; unlikely; unpalatable; unpleasant; unsavory; unsuitable; untasteful; unthankful; varying; DISAGREEMENT: (**see** "difference") antagonism; breach; cleavage; contravention; *désagrément*; disagreeableness; disamenity; discord(ance); discordancy; disharmony; disparity; disputation; dispute; dissent(ience); dissention; dissidence; dissonance; divergence; division; embroglio; embroilment; entanglement; fissure; hostility; imbroglio; incompatibility; incongruity; inconsonance; odds; quarrel; rift; schism; spat; strife; unpleasantness; variance; wrangle

DISALLOW: **see** "refuse" and "reject;" DISALLOWED: (**see** "banned") disapproved

DISAPPEAR: (**see** "depart") abscond; cease; deliquesce; deplete; die; diminish; dissipate; dissolve; drop; erode; evanesce; evanish; evaporate; exit; expire; fade; fall; lapse; melt; pass; perish; recede; relinquish; resolve; scram; skedaddle; subside; terminate; vamoose; vanish; vaporize; volatilize; volatize; DISAPPEARANCE: (**see** "departure") abscondence; death; depletion; diminution; dissolution; evanescence; evanishment; evanition; evaporation; lapse; resolution; subsidence; termination; vanishment; vaporization; volatilization

DISAPPOINT: (**see** "defeat") balk; delude; disenchant; disentrance; dishearten; disillusion; dismay; foil; fool; frustrate; let down; mock; thwart; DISAPPOINTMENT: (**see** "defeat") anticlimax; bathos; contretemps; delusion; denigration; despair; disaffection; discontent; disenchantment; disillusionment; dislike; frustration; heartbreaker; humiliation; letdown; mockery; setback; DISAPPOINTING *or* DISAPPOINTED: anticlimactic(al); bathetic; defeated; deluded; disenchanted; disillusioned; frustrated; humiliated; let down; suboptimal; substandard; thwarted; unsatisfactory

DISAPPROVE: (see "criticize") assail; balk; begrudge; boo; carp; catcall; cavil; censure; condemn; demur; deprecate; depreciate; deride; disallow; discommend; discountenance; dislike; disparage; dissent; except; expostulate; groan; grumble; hiss; lambaste; mind; object; protest; quibble; rebuke; refuse; reject; remonstrate; reprobate; resist; DISAPPROVAL: (see "censure") admonition; blame; boo; catcall; censorship; condemnation; demur; deprecation; depreciation; disapprobation; discountenance; disfavor; dislike; displeasure; dissent; exception; groan; grumble; hiss; objection; odium; protest(ation); quibble; rebuff; rebuke; remonstrance; remonstration; reproach; reprobation; scruple; taboo; tabu; DISAPPROVING: admonitory; blaming; censorious; condemnatory; critical; deprecative; deprecatory; disapprobative; disapprobatory; disparaging; displeasing

DISARRANGE: see "disturb; DISARRANGED: (see "confusing") undraped

DISARRAY: (see "confusion") agitation; chaos; derangement; disarrangement; disarrayment; discomfiture; discomposure; dishabille; dishevelment; dislocation; disorder; disorganization; disturbance; hodgepodge; hubbub; jumble; litter; mess; mishmash; mixture; muss; pandemonium; tumble; tumult; turbulence; turmoil; unrestraint; unruliness; untidiness

DISASTER: (see "calamity") accident; adversity; atrocity; bale; cataclysm; catastrophe; debacle; destruction; distress; failure; fiasco; fire; harm; holocaust; illness; loss; misadventure; misery; misfortune; mishap; precipice; sickness; smash; DISASTROUS: (see "calamitous") adverse; cataclysmal; cataclysmic(al); catastrophal; catastrophic(al); dangerous; deplorable; desperate; dire(ful); doomed; dreadful; harmful; misfortunate; ominous; precipitous; terrible; tragic(al); unlucky; unpropitious; untoward

DISAVOW: (see "deny") abjure; abnegate; contradict; declaim; denounce; disacknowledge; disaffirm; disclaim; disown; dispute; gainsay; negate; recant; refuse; reject; renounce; repudiate; DISAVOWAL: (see "denial") abnegation; adjuration; contradiction; denouncement; disacknowledgment; disaffirmation; disclaimer; disclamation;

negation; recantation; renunciation; repudiation

DISBELIEF: (see "doubt") denial; dubitancy; incredibility; incredulity; misbelief; miscreance; rejection; skepticism; unbelief; uncertainty; DISBELIEVER: (see "skeptic") agnostic; aporetic; dissenter; dissident; doubter; doubting Thomas; giaour; heretic; infidel; nullifidian; Pyrrhonist; questioner; recusant; theophobist; unbeliever

DISBURDEN: (see "unload") discharge; disencumber; rid

DISBURSE: (see "exhaust") consume; defray; deplete; discharge; drain; dwindle; empty; evacuate; expend; extract; liquidate; pay; purchase; sap; spend; tax; use; waste; weaken

DISCARD: (see "abandon") banish; bench; cast (off); chuck; desert; discharge; dismiss; dispose; divorce; drop; dump; eliminate; emit; erase; expunge; fling; jettison; junk; molt; oust; reject; relieve; remove; repudiate; scrap; scrub; shed; shoot; shuck; slough; toss; unload; DISCARDING: (see "abandonment") banishment; defenestration; desertion; dismissal; divorce(ment); elimination; ouster; rejection; repudiation

DISCERN: (see "observe") analyze; apprehend; behold; demarcate; descry; detect; diagnose; differentiate; discover; discrepate; discriminate; distinguish; divine; espy; experience; find; foresee; guess; ken; learn; look; note; notice; perceive; recognize; remark; secern; see; select; separate; uncover; understand; view; watch; DISCERNING: (see "noticeable") acute; analytical; astucious; astute; clairvoyant; clear-headed; clear-sighted; diagnostic; discreet; discriminating; discriminatory; judicious; keen; knowing; knowledgeable; learned; observant; open-eyed; penetrating; penetrative; perceptive; perspicacious; sagacious; sensible; sensitive; sharp; trenchant; watchful; DISCERNMENT: acumen; apperception; apprehension; ascertainment; astucity; awareness; bias; care; clairvoyance; clear-sightedness; cleverness; cognition; comprehension; cunning; delicacy; detection; differentiation; discrimination; empathy; evaluation; feeling; foresight; grasp; heed; insight; instinct; introspection; intuition; judgment; keenness; ken; knowledge; learning; noesis; observation; penetration; perception; perspicacity; perspicuity; preference; profundity; prudence; realization; reason(ing); recognition; restriction; sagacity; sapiency; scope; selectiveness; selectivity; sense; shrewdness; tact; taste; telegnosis; understanding; wisdom; DISCERNIBLE: **see** "comprehensible"

DISCHARGE: **v.** absolve; acquit; annul; bounce; cancel; cashier; cast; clear; consign; convey; deal; deliver; demit; deprive; detach; disband; disburden; disburse; discard; disembogue; disemploy; disencumber; disengage; disentangle; disgorge; dismiss; disown; dispatch; dispense; disperse; dissolve; distribute; divert; drain; drop; eject; eliminate; emanate; emancipate; emit; empty; end; erupt; evaporate; execute; exempt; exhale; exonerate; expel; express; extricate; exude; fire; fling; fulfill; give; grant; gush; issue; liberate; liquidate; loose(n); ooze; open; oust; outpour; pay; perform; pour; pronounce; quash; redeem; reek; regurgitate; reject; release; relegate; relieve; remand; remove; report; rescue; rid; run; sack; satisfy; save; scout; send; separate; sever; shed; shelve; shoot; speak; spurt; squirt; sunder; surrender; terminate; transmit; trickle; unbind; unburden; unfasten; unload; unmesh; unravel; untie; untwist; utter; vent; voice; vomit; waive; wean; yield; DISCHARGE: **n.** abreaction; absolution; accomplishment; acquittal; acquittance; annulment; atonement; blast; bounce; cancellation; *congé*; *congée* (fem.); delivery; detachment; disbursement; disencumbrance; dismissal; distribution; ejection; elimination; emancipation; emission; exoneration; expulsion; extraction; fire; flow; flux; freedom; fulfillment; issue; liberation; liquidation; manumission; ouster; performance; profluvium; redemption; release; removal; rescue; resignation; riddance; salvation; salvo; separation; shake; shooting; shot; surrender; unloading; vent; volley; waiver; weaning; yielding

DISCIPLE(S): adherent; aficionada (fem.); aficionado; apostle; apprentice; buff; child; devotee; fan; fanatic; follower; harbinger; ist; learner; lover; messenger; preacher; proselyte; pupil; satellite; scholar; school; sectary; sectator; student; supporter; teacher; votary

DISCIPLINE: **v.** admonish; amerce; beat; bridle; cage; cane; castigate; censure; chasten; chastise; check; control; correct; curb; deprive; drill; drub; exercise; fine; flagellate; flog; govern; guide; harness; hierarchize; hit; hurt; imprison; incarcerate; indoctrinate; instruct; inure; jail; lambaste; lash; lead; lick; monitor; mulct; nurture; organize; penalize; police; punish; rebuke;

regiment; regulate; rein; reprimand; reproach; reprove; requite; restrain; restrict; retaliate; revenge; scold; score; scourge; sentence; slap; smite; strike; switch; teach; thump; torture; train; trump; whip; DISCIPLINE: **n.** admonishment; admonition; amercement; approach; ascesis; asceticism; bridle; castigation; chastenment; chastisement; check; control; correction; culture; curb(ing); curriculum; demerit; deprivation; dressing down; drill; education; exercise; expiation; fine; flagellation; flogging; forfeit(ure); going-over; government; handicap; handling; harness; imprisonment; incarceration; instruction; inurement; lambasting; learning; lecture; lesson; method; Nemesis; obedience; order(liness); organization; penalization; penalty; penance; punishment; punition; purgatory; rebuke; regime; regulation; reproof; restraint; restriction; retaliation; retribution; revenge; run; torture; training; treatment; vengeance; vindication; whipping; DISCIPLINARY: ascetic; austere; castigatory; chastening; chastising; correctional; corrective; disciplinal; disciplinatory; expiatory; flagellant; penal; penitentiary; punishing; punitive; punitory; retaliative; retaliatory; retributive; strict; vindicative; vindicatory; DISCIPLINARIAN: discipliner; drillmaster; driver; enforcer; martinet; monitor; muscleman; policeman; precisian; rigorist; sabbatarian; Simon Legree; slave driver; taskmaster; teacher; trainer; tsar; tyrant; whipcracker

DISCLAIM: (**see** "deny") abjure; abnegate; contradict; declaim; denounce; disacknowledge; disaffirm; disavow; disown; dispute; gainsay; negate; recant; refuse; reject; renounce; repudiate

DISCLOSE: (**see** "announce") air; appear; arrive; bare; betray; blab; clarify; confess; declare; demonstrate; develop; disburden; discover; display; divulge; evidence; evince; exhibit; explain; expose; express; impart; indicate; inform; loom; manifest; mark; open; prevail; proclaim; promulgate; publicize; publish; reveal; show; spring; strip; tell; unbosom; unclose; uncover; undress; unfold; unkennel; unmask; unveil; unwrap; utter; DISCLOSURE: (**see** "announcement") airing; apocalypse; arrival; betrayal; clarification; communication; confession; declaration; demonstration; denouncement; denunciation; descrial; development; display; divulgation; divulgence; exhibition; explanation; exposition; exposure; expression; impartment; indication; information; manifestation; presentation;

proclamation; promulgation; pronouncement; publication; publicity; revelation;
uncovering; undressing; unmasking; utterance

DISCOLORED: (**see** "dirty") black; dull(ed);
faded; mildewed; molded; rusty; stained;
streaked; tarnished; tinged; ustulate; yellowed; DISCOLORATION: blackness;
dirtiness; drabness; dullness; dustiness;
ecchymosis; grime; mildew; mold; petechia;
rust; smokiness; stain; streak; tarnish; tinge;
yellowishness

DISCOMFIT: (**see** "embarrass") defeat; disconcert; frustrate; humble; humiliate; perplex; puzzle; rout; thwart

DISCOMFORT: (**see** "ache") affliction;
agony; anguish; anoyance; anxiety; chagrin;
discomfiture; discomposure; disease; dis-
quiet(ude); distress; dolor; dysphoria; embarrassment; excruciation; exhaustion; grief;
heat; humiliation; hurt; inconvenience;
inquietude; malaise; misease; misery; over-
crowding; pain; pang; perturbation; pressure; rack; sorrow; stitch; suffering; throb;
throe; torment; travail; trouble; twinge;
uncomfort(ableness); uneasiness

DISCOMPOSE: (**see** "annoy") agitate; confuse; disarrange; disarray; discomfit; discommode; disconcert; displace; displease;
disquiet; disturb; embarrass; faze; fluster;
inconvenience; jar; perturb; trouble; unnerve; unsettle; upset; DISCOMPOSURE:
see "uneasiness"

DISCONCERT: (**see** "annoy") abash; baffle;
bowl (over); disarray; discomfit; discomfort;
discompose; discountenance; embarrass;
faze; frustrate; humble; humiliate; overwhelm; perplex; puzzle; rattle; ruffle;
squash; thwart; upset; DISCONCERTING:
see "uneasy"

DISCONNECT: **see** "end;" DISCONNECT-
ED: (**see** "distinct") apart; broken; choppy;
cleft; cloven; cut; desultory; detached; discrete; disjoined; disjointed; dissociated; dissolved; disunited; divorced; ended; fractional; interrupted; isolated; open; parted;
rambling; removed; resected; segregated;
separate(d); severed; staccato; sundered;
uncoupled; unhooked; unplugged

DISCONSOLATE: (**see** "desolate" and "sad")
beat; cheerless; downcast

DISCONTENT(ED): **a.** (**see** "dissatisfied")

discomfited; disturbed; dissentious; fractious;
frustrated; insubordinate; malcontent; mutinous; restless; seditious; uncontented; uneasy;
ungratified; unsatisfied; DISCONTENT-
(MENT): **n.** (**see** "dissatisfaction") discomfiture; dysphoria; frustration; inquiet-
(ude); insubordination; malaise; malcon-
tentment; restlessness; sedition; uneasiness

DISCONTINUE: (**see** "end") abandon;
break; cease; disrupt; intermit; interrupt;
pause; sever; stop; surcease; suspend;
terminate; DISCONTINUANCE: (**see**
"end") abandonment; break; cessation;
desistance; discontinuation; intermission;
interruption; phase out; removal; retreat;
severance; shutdown; surcease; suspension;
termination; withdrawal

DISCORD: (**see** "anger") animosity; antagonism; *brouillerie*; cacophony; clash; cleavage;
conflict; contention; contrast; difference;
disagreement; disharmony; disruption; dissension; dissidence; dissonance; disturbance;
disunity; division; enmity; fissure; harshness;
incongruity; inharmony; jangle; noise; opposition; rancor; rupture; scission; strife;
variance; war(fare); DISCORDANT: (**see**
"angry") abhorrent; absonant; ajar; antagonistic; cacophonous; clashing; conflicting;
contentious; contradictory; disagreeable;
disagreeing; disconsonant; discording; disharmonious; disputatious; dissident; dissimilar; dissociable; dissonant; gladiatorial;
harsh; heterogeneous; incongruous; inconsistent; inharmonic; inharmonious; irreconcilable; jarring; noisy; quarrelsome; stubborn; untunable; untuneful

DISCOUNT: **v.** (**see** "belittle") deduct;
diminish; disparage; disregard; ignore;
kick back; lessen; minify; minimize; reduce;
underrate; DISCOUNT: **n.** (**see** "diminishment") allowance; deduction; diminishment;
drawback; hindrance; kick back; rebate;
reduction

DISCOUNTENANCE: (**see** "disfavor")
abash; disconcert; discourage

DISCOURAGE: abash; check; dampen;
dash; daunt; deject; demoralize; depress;
deter; disadvantage; disadvise; disappoint;
discountenance; disenchant; disencourage;
dishearten; disillusion; dismay; disparage;
dispirit; dissuade; divert; frighten; frustrate;
hamper; hinder; hobble; inhibit; intimidate;
lessen; obstruct; oppose; persuade; prevent;
repel; repress; restrain; scare; score; stop;
terrify; wet-blanket; DISCOURAGEMENT:

(see "despondency") check; demoralization; depression; deterrence; deterrent; disappointment; disparagement; dissuasion; hampering; hindrance; hobble; fright; frustration; gloom(iness); intimidation; obstruction; opposition; repression; repulsion; restraint; scare; DISCOURAGING *or* DISCOURAGED: (see "dejected") chilly; depressing; drear(y); formal; frustrating; gloomy; intimidating; repressing; restraining

DISCOURSE: **v.** (see "speak") argue; arguify; colloquialize; confer; converse; debate; deliver; descant; dilate; discuss; dissert; expound; instruct; lecture; parley; prelect; reason; talk; teach; tractate; DISCOURSE: **n.** (see "speech") address; argument; assertion; colloquy; conference; conversation; descant; discussion; disquisition; dissertation; enumeration; explanation; homily; instruction; lecture; message; monograph; narration; oration; parlance; parley; prelection; recital; remarks; screed; sermon; statement; talk; thesis; tract; treatise; treatment; words; writing

DISCOURTEOUS: brusque; contemptible; contemptuous; contumelious; curt; derisive; despicable; discreditable; disrespectful; fresh; ill-mannered; impertinent; impious; impolite; impudent; infamous; insolent; inurbane; irreverent; opprobrious; respectless; rude; sassy; saucy; uncivil; undutiful; ungallant; unmannerly; unrespectful; vulgar; DISCOURTESY: (see "disrespect") brusqueness; *brusquerie*; contempt(uousness); contumely; curtness; derision; despicability; disrespect; humiliation; ill manners; impertinence; impiousness; impoliteness; impudence; incivility; insolence; insuavity; inurbanity; irreverence; opprobrium; pertness; profanation; rudeness; sassiness; sauciness; slight; uncivility; ungallantry; unmannerliness; vulgarity

DISCOVER: apprehend; ascertain; bare; catch; contrive; descry; detect; determine; discern; disclose; disinter; divine; divulge; elicit; espy; exhume; experience; expose; figure; find; hear; hit; identify; impart; invent; learn; locate; notice; observe; originate; perceive; recognize; reveal; see; sense; smell; spot; strike; uncover; unearth; unkennel; unmask; DISCOVERER: creator; detective; informer; inventor; originator; patentee; patentor; pathfinder; scout; spy; trailblazer; DISCOVERY: (see "invention") ascertainment; descrial; detection; determination; discernment; disclosure; experience; find; invention; origination;

revelation; DISCOVERABLE: **see** "perceivable"

DISCREDIT: **v.** (see "belittle") asperse; censure; denigrate; destroy; disbelieve; disgrace; dishonor; disparage; dispute; doubt; explode; impeach; invalidate; question; reflect; reproach; revile; shame; shatter; smear; suspect; weaken; DISCREDIT: **n.** (see "belittlement") aspersion; denigration; disbelief; disesteem; disestimation; dishonor; disparagement; disrepute; doubt; ignominy; impeachment; invalidation; obloquy; odium; reproach; revile(ment); scandal; shame; smear; suspicion

DISCREET: attentive; careful; cautious; circumspect(ive); civil; classified; covert; discerning; discretive; *entre nous*; esoteric; familiar; heedful; hidden; hushed; hush-hush; intelligent; intimate; judicial; judicious; moderate; muted; polite; politic(al); private; privy; prudent; restrained; reticent; sagacious; secret; sensible; Solomonic; *sub rosa*; taciturn; tactful; top-drawer; trustful; trustworthy; unobtrusive; wary; watchful; wise; DISCRETION: (see "assurance") attention; care(fulness); caution; choice; circumspection; confidence; credit; delicacy; diplomacy; discernment; discreetness; faith; finesse foresight; government; heed; hope; intelligence; judgment; liberty; moderation; modesty; permission; politeness; privacy; prudence; reliance; reserve; restraint; reticence; sagaciousness; sagacity; secrecy; sense; surety; taciturnity; tact(fulness); taste; trust(fulness); trustworthiness; wariness; watchfulness; will; wisdom; DISCRETIONAL: **see** "choosing"

DISCRIMINATE: (see "discern") analyze; apprehend; behold; demarcate; differentiate; discrepate; distinguish; extricate; recognize; secern; segregate; select; separate; DISCRIMINATING *or* DISCRIMINATIVE: see "delicate;" DISCRIMINATION: (see "discernment") acumen; bias; care; delicacy; differentiation; doom; evaluation; foresight; heed; insight; judgment; penetration; perception; prudence; restriction; segregation; selectiveness; selectivity; sense; taste; wisdom

DISCUSS: (see "comment") air; altercate; argue; arguify; canvass; confabulate; confer; converse; cover; debate; delate; deliberate; descant; dilate; discept; discourse; dispute; elaborate; examine; expand; explain; expostulate; expound; hash over; huddle; negotiate; reason; sift; talk; treat; wrangle; DISCUSSION: (see "comment") altercation; argument(ation); bull session; colloquium; colloquy; confabulation; conference; conversation; counsel; dialectic; discourse; disputation; dispute; disquisition; dissertation; essay; explanation; exposition; expostulation; huddle; inquiry; narrative; negotiation; palaver; probe; screed; seminar; sermon; speech; study; symposia (pl.); symposium; talk; thesis; tract; treatment

DISDAIN: **v.** abhor; contemn; denigrate; deprecate; depreciate; deride; despise; detest; disesteem; dislike; disparage; flaunt; flout; hate; humble; humiliate; insult; loathe; mock; reproach; scorn; snoot; spurn; underrate; undervalue; DISDAIN: **n. (see** "contempt") abhorrence; abuse; airs; arrogance; contemptuousness; contumacy; contumely; defiance; denigration; deprecation; depreciation; derision; detestation; disesteem; disestimation; disgrace; dislike; disobedience; disparagement; hate; haughtiness; hauteur; hubris; humiliation; indignation; insolence; insult; loathing; misprision; mockery; pride; reproach; rudeness; sarcasm; sass(iness); sauciness; scorn; scurviness; shame; snootiness; DISDAINFUL: **(see** "scornful") contemptible; derisive; detestable; dispiteous; hateful; insulting; loathesome; scornful; snooty

DISEASE: affection; affliction; ailment; blast; blight; cancer; cholera; complaint; contagion; decay; derangement; diseasedness; disorder; distemper; epizootic; evil; fever; illness; indisposition; infection; infirmity; leprosy; malady; malignancy; mange; misery; morbus; nausea; paroxysm; pathology; pathosis; plague; queasiness; seizure; sickness; sore; trouble; vapors; visitation; DISEASED: **(see** "sickly") cancerous; contaminated; disordered; evil; fevered; feverish; ill; indisposed; infirm; leprous; malign(ant); mangy; morbid; morbific(al); morbose; pathologic(al); peccant; queasy; sick; troubled; unhealthful; unhealthy; unsound; unwholesome

DISEMBARK: **(see** "arrive") debark; deplane; detrain; land; leave

DISENCUMBER: **(see** "disengage" and "rid") discharge; extricate; lighten; unburden; unclog; unload

DISENGAGE: **(see** "discharge") clear; detach; disembroil; disencumber; disentangle; disjoin; dissolve; divorce; evolve; extricate; free; liberate; loose(n); part; release; rid; separate; sever; slip; sunder; unbind; un

mesh; unravel; untangle; untwist; wean; withdraw

DISENTANGLE: **(see** "discharge") detach; disembroil; divorce; evolve; extricate; free; liberate; part; release; sever; sleave; sunder; unmesh; unravel; untwist

DISESTEEM: **(see** "belittle") disfavor; dislike; disregard; undervalue

DISFAVOR: **(see** "dislike") detriment; disadvantage; disapproval; discountenance; disesteem; disinvolvement; displeasure; disregard; disrepute; odium; opprobrium; repulsion

DISFIGURE: **(see** "blemish") damage; deface; deform; disfashion; distort; impair; maim; mangle; mar; mark; mayhem; mutilate; scar(ify); spoil; uglify; warp; DISFIGUREMENT: **(see** "blemish") blot; damage; defacement; disfiguration; distortion; mar; mark; mayhem; mole; scar(ification); uglification; warp(age)

DISGORGE: **(see** "emit") discharge; embogue; heave; regurgitate; retch; spit; vomit

DISGRACE: **v. (see** "degrade") abase; asperse; brand; calumniate; debase; defame; discredit; dishonor; embarrass; humble; humiliate; scandalize; shame; slander; soil; spot; stain; stigmatize; sully; taint; DISGRACE: **n. (see** "degradation") abasement; aspersion; blot; brand; calumniation; calumny; contempt; crime; debasement; defamation; depravity; disfavor; dishonor; disrepute; humiliation; ignominy; ill repute; infamy; obloquy; odium; opprobrium; reproach; scandal; shame; shendship; slander; spot; stain; stigma; stigmata (pl.); taint; tarnish; turpitude; DISGRACEFUL: abased; base; burning; corrupt(ed); cowardly; criminal; darkened; debased; defamatory; degenerate(d); dehumanized; denigrated; denigratory; derogative; derogatory; despicable; diminishing; foul; glaring; humble; humiliated; humiliating; humiliative; ignoble; ignominious; indign; infamous; inglorious; libelous; low(ered); menial; mortifying; notorious; obliquitous; odious; opprobrious; outrageous; perverted; relegated; scandalized; scandalous; scurrilous; seamy; shamed; shameful; shocking; slanderous; sordid; squalid; stigmatical; unbecoming; unhonored; vulgarized; yellow

DISGUISE: **v. (see** "cover") affect; assume;

camouflage; change; cloak; color; conceal; counterfeit; dissemble; falsify; feign; hide; mask; masquerade; mumm; obscure; pretend; screen; sham; shroud; travesty; veil; whitewash; DISGUISE: **n.** (**see** "cover") assumption; camouflage; change; cloak; color; counterfeit; cover(ture); deception; disguisement; face; mask; masquerade; misrepresentation; pretense; pretension; screen; shade; sham; shroud; speciosity; speciousness; travesty; veil; whitewash; DISGUISED: (**see** "covered") clandestine; cloaked; colored; concealed; counterfeit; covered; falsified; feigned; incognito; masked; obscure(d); pretended; sham; surreptitious; *travesti*; *travestie* (fem.); veiled; whitewashed

DISGUST: **v.** (**see** "abhor") abominate; cloy; despise; detest; loathe; nauseate; repel; repulse; revolt; shock; sicken; stomach; surfeit; DISGUST: **n.** (**see** "abhorrence") abomination; annoyance; antagonism; antipathy; aversion; detestation; dislike; distaste; enmity; hatred; horror; hostility; loathing; nastiness; nausea; odium; offense; opposition; rancor; repugnance; repulsion; repulsiveness; revolt; shock; squeamishness; trial; unsavoriness; vexation; DISGUSTING: (**see** "abhorrent") abominable; annoying; beastly; disgraceful; disgusted; foul; fulsome; horrible; loathsome; nasty; nauseating; *nauseéux*; nauseous; odious; offensive; rancorous; rank; repellant; repugnant; repulsive; revolting; shocking; sickening; squeamish; unpalatable; unsavory; vile; wicked

DISH(ES): boat; bowl; casserole; ceramics; charger; china(ware); crock(ery); cruse; dishware; food; girl; meal; patera; patina; petri; plate; platter; porcelain; recipe; saucer; trough; tureen; vessel; viand

DISHARMONY: (**see** "disagreement") antagonism; cacophony; discord(ance); disharmonism; dissention; dissidence; dissonance; incongruity; variance; DISHARMONIOUS: (**see** "disagreeable") disputatious; dissident; dissociable; dissonant; divisive; incongruous

DISHEARTEN: (**see** "daunt") amate; cow; deject; depress; deter; discourage; unman; unnerve; DISHEARTENING: **see** "cheerless" and "desolate;" DISHEARTENMENT: **see** "despondency"

DISHEVELED: (**see** "askew") deranged; disordered; frowsy; messy; mussed; ratty;

ruffled; seamy; seedy; shabby; slipshod; tousled; unkempt; untidy

DISHONEST: amiss; artificial; circuitous; corrupt; counterfeit; crafty; crooked; deceitful; deceptive; deviating; devious; dishonorable; disingenuous; disreputable; dissembling; distorted; double-faced; duplicitous; evil; faithless; false; feigned; feigning; flexuous; fraudulent; hypocritical; ignominious; insidious; insincere; irregular; knavish; lying; Machiavellian; meandering; meanspirited; mendacious; meretricious; misleading; oblique; perfidious; phony; roguish; shifty; sinister; sinuate; sinuous; snide; specious; stealthy; surreptitious; tortuous; treacherous; tricky; twisted; two-faced; unconscionable; underhand(ed); unfair; unfaithful; unhonest; unprincipled; unscrupulous; untrue; untrustworthy; untruthful; vicious; villainous; winding; DISHONESTY: (**see** "deceit") crookedness; dishonor; disingenuity; duplicity; faithlessness; falseness; falsity; fraud(ulence); ignominy; improbity; indirection; indirectness; infamy; knavishness; Machiavellianism; malconduct; *mauvaise foi*; perfidy; roguery; roguishness; sinisterity; sinisterness; sinuosity; treachery; trickery; triplicity; unfairness; unfaithfulness; unhonesty; unscrupulosity; villainy

DISHONOR: **v.** (**see** "degrade") brand; debase; debauch; defile; disgrace; humble; humiliate; lower; mortify; pejorate; pervert; rape; ruin; scandalize; seduce; shame; stain; violate; wrong; DISHONOR: **n.** (**see** "degradation") blot; brand; disgrace; disrepute; ignominy; ill repute; improbity; infamy; insult; obloquy; odium; opprobrium; ruin; scandal; shame; stain; stigma; stigmata (pl.); vilification; DISHONORABLE: (**see** "disgraceful") base; cowardly; despicable; disesteemed; disestimable; dishonest; disreputable; foul; ignoble; ignominious; infamous; inglorious; obloquious; opprobrious; scandalous; shameful; slanderous; unhonored; yellow

DISILLUSION: (**see** "discourage") disenchant; disillusionize; waken

DISINCLINED: (**see** "averse") afraid; backward; bashful; chary; coy; demurring; discouraged; disinterested; doubtful; grudging; hesitant; indisposed; inertial; lazy; loath(some); obstinate; opposed; opposing; opposite; passive; recalcitrant; refractory; reluctant; remiss; repellant; repulsive; resisting; shy; slack; slow; tardy; undisposed;

uneager; unenthusiastic; unresponsive; unwilling; unwishful; wary; DISINCLINA-TION: see "disinterest"

DISINGENUOUS: (see "sly") cunning; false; foxy; tricky

DISINHERIT: (see "deprive") disown

DISINTEGRATE: (see "break") corrode; crash; crumble; crush; decay; decentralize; decompose; desegregate; destroy; deteriorate; disorganize; disrupt; dissolve; erode; fragmentize; melt; putrefy; putresce; reduce; rend; rot; rust; scatter; separate; shatter; spoil; DISINTEGRATION: (see "break") breakdown; breakup; collapse; corrosion; crash; crumbling; decay; decentralization; declination; decline; decomposition; degradation; demoralization; destruction; disorganization; disruption; dissolution; fragmentation; melting; putrefaction; putrescence; reduction; rot; rust; separation; shattering; spoilage; waste

DISINTER: delve; dig; disentomb; exhume; expose; unbury; uncover; unearth; untomb

DISINTEREST: (see "carelessness") apathy; disadvantage; disinclination; disinterestedness; hesitation; indisposition; inertia; laziness; objectivity; passivity; reluctance; unconcern(edness); underactivity; DISINTERESTED: (see "averse") apathetic; candid; cool; disinclined; dispassionate; halfhearted; hesitant; impassionate; impersonal; indifferent; indisposed; inertial; lazy; nonpartisan; objective; passive; reluctant; unbiased; underactive; undiscriminating; unenquiring; unenthusiastic; uninfluenced; uninterested; unprejudiced; unprejudicial; unresponsive; unwilling

DISJOIN(T): (see "divide") cut; disarrange; disarticulate; discerp; dislocate; dismember; disunite; divorce; luxate; part(ition); separate; sunder; unjoin(t); DISJUNCTION: (see "separation") discontinuity; disunion; divorce(ment); parting; sundering

DISLIKE: v. (see "abhor") despise; detest; disapprove; discountenance; disesteem; disfavor; disgust; disrelish; grudge; hate; loathe; mind; resent; scorn; DISLIKE: n. (see "abhorrence") alienation; antipathy; aversion; detestation; disaffection; disapprobation; disapproval; discountenance; disenchantment; disesteem; disestimation; disfavor; disgust; disinclination; displeasure; disregard; disrelish; disrespect; disrepute;

distaste; enmity; estrangement; grudge; hate; hostility; loathing; odium; opprobrium; repugnance; repugnancy; resentment; revulsion; DISLIKABLE: (see "abhorrent") antipathetical; averse; detestable; odious; repugnant; repulsive; unbelieved; unenvied; unloved

DISLOCATE: decentralize; disalign; disarrange; disarticulate; discerp; disconnect; disjoin(t); disjunct; dismember; displace; disturb; disunite; divide; divorce; luxate; misalign; part(ition); remove; segregate; separate; shift; slip; splay; sunder; uncouple; unjoin(t); DISLOCATON: decentralization; disalignment; disarrangement; disarticulation; discerption; disconnection; discontinuity; disjunction; dismemberment; disorder; displacement; disruption; disturbance; division; divorce(ment); luxation; malalignment; misalignment; moving; parting; partition; removal; segregation; shift(ing); sundering; uncoupling

DISLODGE: (see "displace") drive (out); eject; evict; expel; move; oust; remove; rid; rock; shake; topple; unhorse; unlodge; unroot; uproot

DISLOYAL: (see "treacherous") disaffected disobedient; faithless; false(hearted); fickle; mutinous; perfidious; recreant; seditious; traitorous; treasonable; treasonous; unfaithful; unreliable; unscrupulous; unstable; untrue; untrustworthy; viperous; DISLOYALTY: betrayal; dastardliness; disaffection; disobedience; duplicity; faithlessness; falsity; *fides Punica*; infidelity; mutiny; perfidy; *Punica fides*; Punic faith; rebellion; recreancy; sabotage; sedition; traitorousness; traitorship; treachery; treason; triplicity; villainy

DISMAL: abandoned; Acheronian; Acherontic; austere; blue; calamitous; cheerless; dark; dejected; depressing; dingy; dire(ful); dispirited; dispiriting; dispiteous; doleful; dolorous; drear(y); dull; funebrial; funebrous; funerary; funereal; gloomy; glum; gray; inept; joyless; lachrymose; lugubrious; melancholic; melancholy; miserable; mournful; murky; ominous; sad(dened); sinister; somber; sombre; sorry; sullen; weak; DISMALITY: (see "austerity") blues; cheerlessness; dismalness; dolor; dreariness; gloom(iness); lugubrosity; melancholia; sadness

DISMANTLE: annul; bulldoze; cannibalize; demolish; deprive; destroy; devastate; dismember; divest; erase; level; mutilate;

obliterate; prostrate; raze; rescind; ruin; strip; subvert; tear (down); unrig; wreck

DISMAY: **v.** (**see** "frighten") abash; alarm; amaze; appal(l); awe; bowl (over); cow; daunt; depress; disconcert; disenchant; dishearten; disillusion; disturb; faze; horrify; horrorize; intimidate; overwhelm; panic; petrify; perturb; rattle; scare; shock; startle; subdue; terrify; terrorize; upset; DISMAY: **n.** (**see** "fright") abashment; alarm; anxiety; awe; consternation; depression; disenchantment; disheartenment; disillusionment; dismayedness; dread; fear; funk; horror; intimidation; panic; perturbation; petrification; scare; shock; terror

DISMEMBER: (**see** "dismantle" and "tear") disarticulate; discerp; disjoin(t); mangle; mutilate; separate; unjoin(t)

DISMISS: (**see** "discharge") amand; bounce; brush off; cashier; cast (off); demit; deprive; disband; discard; disemploy; disown; dispatch; dispense; disperse; divest; drop; eject; expel; fire; manumit; oust; quash; reject; relegate; remand; remove; sack; scout; shed; shelve; waive; DISMISSAL: (**see** "discharge") bounce; brush-off; cashiering; congé; congée (fem.); deprivation; disemployment; divestation; ejection; manumission; ouster; rejection; relegation; removal; sacking; shake; waiver

DISMOUNT: alight; deplane; descend; detrain; disassemble; land; unhorse

DISOBEY: (**see** "defy") break; disregard; ignore; infract; infringe; mutiny; oppose; rebel; resist; revolt; sin; transgress; trespass; violate; DISOBEDIENT: (**see** "insubordinate") defiant; disloyal; disobeying; disregardful; fractious; insubmissive; intractable; mutinous; nonconforming; oppositious; oppositive; perfidious; rebellious; recalcitrant; recusant; refractory; resistant; treacherous; treasonous; unmanageable; unobedient; unruly; DISOBEDIENCE: (**see** "insubordination") contempt; defiance; disloyalty; disregard; ignoration; infraction; infringement; insubjection; insubmission; intractability; intractableness; mutiny; nonconformance; noncooperation; opposition; perfidy; rebellion; recusance; recusancy; refractoriness; resistance; sin; transgression; treachery; treason; trespass; unruliness; violation

DISORDER: (**see** "confusion") ailment; alarums and excursions; anarchism; anarchy;

babel(ism); bedlam; boisterousness; bouleversement; brouhaha; bustle; chaos; clutter; coil; derangement; dirt(iness); disarrangement; disarray; discomposure; disease; dishevelment; disorganization; distemper; disturbance; embroilment; grime; hash; havoc; heterogeneity; illness; indecency; indisposition; infirmity; irregularity; jumble(ment); lawlessness; litter; malady; malignancy; mess; misconduct; misdeed; misdemeanor; misorder; mixture; moil; muddle; pandemonium; pathology; profusion; riot; sickness; snarl; throe(s); trouble; tumult; turbulence; turmoil; unrestraint; unruliness; upheaval; DISORDERED: *or* DISORDERLY: (**see** "confusing") bedraggled; boisterous; chaotic; cluttered; confused; crazy; deranged; disarranged; diseased; disheveled; disorganized; distempered; distraught; farraginous; fevered; forlorn; haphazard; heterogeneous; hurly-burly; ill; immethodic(al); inchoate; inchoative; incoherent; indecent; inordinate; insane; inverted; irregular; jumbled; lawless; mad; messy; misorderly; noisy; orderless; pandemoniac(al); pathologic(al); riotous; scattered; sick(ly); slatternly; topsy-turvy; tumultuous; turbulent; undirected; unhinged; unorderly; unorganized; unregulated; unrestrained; unruly; unseemly; unsettled; unsystematic; untrimmed; uproarious

DISORGANIZED: (**see** "disordered") demoralized; deranged; disarranged; fragmental; fragmentary; fragmentized; helterskelter; heterogeneous; incoherent; indecisive; inveterate; planless; unhinged; unsystematic

DISOWN: (**see** "deny") abjure; disavow; disclaim; dismiss; expel; renounce; repudiate;

DISPARAGE: (**see** "belittle") asperse; decry; defame; denigrate; deprecate; depreciate; derogate; detract; diminish; disable; discredit; dishonor; dispraise; downgrade; lessen; libel; lower; malign; minimize; pejorate; reduce; slur; traduce; underrate; weaken; vilify; DISPARAGING: denigrating; depreciating; depreciative; depreciatory; derogative; low; minimizing; pejorative; unfavorable; DISPARAGEMENT: (**see** "belittlement") aspersion; contempt; defamation; denigration; depreciation; derogation; detraction; discredit; disgrace; dishonor; dispraise; indignity; meiosis; minimization; misprision; pejoration; sour grapes; traducement; traduction; vilification

DISPARATE: different; discrete; dissimilar;

distinct; heterogeneous; separate; unequal; DISPARITY: see "dissimilarity"

DISPATCH: **v.** banish; clear; diffuse; diminish; direct; discharge; disperse; execute; expedite; facilitate; hasten; kill: mail; post; scatter; send; slay; speed; telegraph; wire; DISPATCH: **n.** celerity; diligence; direction; dispersal; expedition; facilitation; facility; haste; killing; letter; mail; message; note; post; riddance; scattering; shipment; speed-(ing); telegram; wire

DISPEL: (**see** "banish") clear; dispatch; disperse; dispose; dissipate; eject; expel; oust; reject; repel; resolve; satisfy; scatter; settle; strew

DISPENSE: (**see** "apportion") absolve; administer; allot; assign; contribute; deal; dismiss; dispose; distribute; divide; doctor; dole; excuse; exempt; forgo; furnish; give; grant; handle; help; lend; parcel; portion; prepare; provide; rate; ration; release; relieve; sell; waive; DISPENSATION: administration; allotment; apportionment; assignment; contribution; deal; dismissal; disposal; distribution; division; dole; economy; excuse; exemption; faculty; favor; furnishing; gift; grant; help; license; loan; management; ordering; parceling; pardon; plan; portion; prerogative; provision; ration; release; relief; scheme; waiver

DISPERSE: (**see** "diffuse") break (up;) broadcast; circulate; dismiss; dispatch; dispel; disseminate; dissipate; dissolve; distribute; divide; expand; extend; melt; part; provide; promulgate; propagate; publish; radiate; scatter; separate; sever; shatter; shed; spread; sow; strew; suppress

DISPIRITED: (**see** "depressive") blue; downcast; flat; lifeless; pessimistic; sad

DISPLACE: (**see** "dismiss") banish; depose; derange; dethrone; devour; dislodge; displant; dispose; disturb; drive (out); eject; evict; expel; fire; lose; misalign; misplace; move; oust; remove; rock; shake; supplant; swallow; topple; unhorse; unlodge; unseat; unsettle; uproot; DISPLACED: banished; *dépaysé*; deranged; dethroned; disarranged; dislodged; dispossessed; disturbed; ectopic; ejected; expelled; homeless; luxated; misaligned; misplaced; ousted; removed; supplanted; uprooted; unsettled

DISPLAY: **v.** (**see** "flaunt") air; arrange; attract; bare; blazon; boast; depict; describe;

disclose; emblazon; evince; exhibit; expand; expose; extend; manifest; model; open; ostentate; parade; pose; proclaim; represent; reveal; shake; show; splash; splurge; sport; spread; stage; swing; toss; uncase; unfold; unfurl; unmask; unveil; vaunt; wave; DISPLAY: **n.** (**see** "arrangement") array; blazonry; bravery; cavalcade; description; disclosure; *éclat*; *étalage*; exhibition; exposition; exposure; fireworks; flash; flourish; galaxy; layout; magnificence; manifestation; ornament(alism); ornamentation; ornateness; ornature; ostentation; pageant(ry); panoply; parade; pomp(osity); presentation; pretense; procession; publicity; pyrotechnics; revelation; scene; sham; show(case); spectacle; spectacular; splash; splendor; splurge; spread

DISPLEASE: (**see** "anger") afflict; annoy; chafe; disgust; dissatisfy; disturb; exasperate; fail; frustrate; irritate; madden; miff; offend; pique; provoke; rile; roil; unfulfill; vex; DISPLEASURE: (**see** "anger") annoyance; aversion; depression; disapproval; discomposure; disgust; dislike; dissatisfaction; exasperation; gloom; ill humor; indignation; irritation; melancholy; offense; pique; umbrage; unsatisfaction; vexation; DISPLEASED: (**see** "dissatisfied") exasperated; frustrated; irritated; maddened; offended; piqued; provoked; riled; roiled; unsatisfied

DISPORT: (**see** "play") amuse; divert; entertain

DISPOSE: (**see** "apportion") abandon; arrange; bestow; decide; discard; dispense; distribute; fix; give; liquidate; place; prepare; propend; scrap; sell; set(tle); tend; vote; DISPOSED: accountable; addicted; agreeable; amenable; answerable; apt; arranged; bent; biddable; coercive; complacent; compliant; conciliable; congenial; controllable; docile; dutiful; faithful; favorable; fit; fixed; inclinable; inclinatory; inclined; liable; loyal; malleable; obedient-(ial); obeisant; obsequious; open; passive; pliable; pliant; predisposed; prone; propending; propense; ready; receptive; reconcilable; resigned; respectful; set(tled); sold; suasive; subject; tending; tractable; truckling; willing; yielding; DISPOSAL: **see** "disposition"

DISPOSITION: administration; agreement; animus; aptitude; arrangement; attitude; bent; bestowal; bias; character; complexion; control; destruction; diathesis; dispensation; disposal; distribution; drive; fate; feeling; grain; heart; humanism; human nature;

idiosyncrasy; inclination; individuality; liquidation; management; metal; mind; mood; morale; nature; outcome; personality; predisposition; proclivity; propensity; sale; settlement; spirit; temerity; temper(ament); tendency; testament; train; will

DISPOSSESS: (see "banish") commandeer; confiscate; deprive; divest; eject; expropriate; evict; oust; sequester; strip; usurp; DISPOSSESSION; (see "banishment") abstraction; confiscation; deprivation; displacement; divestiture; divestment; eviction; expropriation; homelessness; ouster; sequestration; usurpation; DISPOSSESSED: (see "displaced") homeless; lumpen; uprooted

DISPROPORTIONATE: (see "uneven") unrelated; unrelative

DISPROVE: confute; controvert; defeat; deny; invalidate; negate; overcome; rebut; refute; DISPROOF: confutation; defeat; exposure; invalidation; negation; refutation; silence; truth

DISPUTE: v. (see "argue") agitate; altercate; arguify; bicker; brawl; conflict; contend; contest; contravene; controvert; debate; deny; disagree; disclaim; discuss; dissent; feud; fight; haggle; palter; polemize; quarrel; question; scrap; spar; spat; squabble; struggle; tiff; wrangle; DISPUTE: n. agitation; altercation; argument(ation); brawl; broil; conflict; contention; contest; contravention; controversy; debate; disagreement; discussion; disputation; dissent(ion); divergence; feud; fight; forensic; haggle; invective; polemic; quarrel; question; rhubarb; rift; scrap; skirmish; spat; squabble; strife; struggle; tiff; tilt; velitation; wrangle; DISPUTABLE: see "doubtful"

DISQUALIFY: (see "debar") defrock; deprive; disable; disbar; disenable; disfrock; divest; estop; exclude; incapacitate; injure; prevent; prohibit; restrain; superannuate

DISQUIET(UDE): (see "anxiety") agitation; alarm; angst; besetment; brouhaha; chemistry; disquietness; disturbance; dread; dyspathy; dysphoria; embarrassment; excitement; fear; ferment; fever; fright; inquietude; misgiving; nervousness; panic; restlessness; scare; terror; timidity; unease; uneasiness; unrest; wrong; vexation

DISQUISITION: (see "discussion") dissertation; essay; exegesis; inquiry; probe; search; speech; theme; treatise; writing

DISREGARD: v. (see "defy") cancel; disobey; fling; forget; ignore; mock; neglect; omit; overlook; skip; slight; unheed; waive; wink; DISREGARD: n. (see "inattention") defiance; disremembrance; disrespect; irreverence; license; rashness; DISREGARDFUL: (see "cruel" and "inattentive") disobedient; unmindful

DISREPUTE: (see "degradation") discredit; disgrace; dishonor; ignominy; infamy; odium; opprobrium; scandal; shame; squalor; stigma(tization); stigmata (pl.); DISREPUTABLE: (see "degraded") abandoned; bad; base; despicable; dirty; discreditable; discredited; disgraceful; ignoble; ignominious; infamous; inglorious; low; mean; notorious; obnoxious; odious; opprobrious; scandalous; shameful; shocking; sordid; squalid; tattered; terrible; unrespectable; unrespected; vile; vulgar; worn

DISRESPECT: brusqueness; brusquerie; contempt; contumely; derision; discourtesy; discredit; disobedience; humiliation; impertinence; impiety; impoliteness; impudence; incivility; insolence; insuavity; inurbanity; irreverence; misesteem; pertness; profanation; rudeness; slight; undutifulness; ungallantry; unmannerliness; vulgarity; DISRESPECTFUL: (see "discourteous") contemptuous; contumelious; derisive; despicable; discreditable; impertinent; impious; impolite; infamous; insolent; irreverent; opprobrious; pert; respectless; rude; sassy; saucy; scurrilous; uncivil; undutiful; unrespectful

DISRUPT: (see "break") destroy; discontinue; distract; gash; hamper; harass; impede; interfere; interrupt; restrict; rupture; shatter; stop; DISRUPTION: (see "break") bombshell; breakdown; cataclasm; cataclysm; collapse; debacle; destruction; interference; interruption; intrigue; rupture; stampede; stop

DISSATISFY: (see "displease") fail; frustrate; unfulfill; DISSATISFACTION: clamor; disapprobation; discomfiture; discontent; disgruntlement; disorder; displeasure; dissidence; dysphoria; failure; frustration; indignation; inquietude; insubordination; malaise; malcontent; regret; restlessness; sedition; touble; undertone; uneasiness; DISSATISFIED: disaffected; discomfited; discontent(ed); disgruntled; displeased; dissentious; disturbed; fractious; frustrated; insubordinate; insurgent; malcontent; moody; mutinous; rebellious; restless; seditious; uncontented; uneasy; unpleased; unpleasurable; unsatisfied

DISSECT: (see "analyze") anatomize; cut; divide; isolate; part; separate

DISSEMBLE: (see "deceive") act (a part); cloak; conceal; cover; disguise; disseminate; feign; hide; mask; pretend; screen; veil; DISSEMBLING: see "false" and "hypocritical"

DISSEMINATE: (see "circulate") advertise; air; blare; blaze; blazon; broadcast; communicate; publish; radiate; scatter; send; sow; spread; strew; teach; transmit

DISSENT: v. (see "balk") demur; differ; disagree; dispute; except; mutiny; object; riot; vary; DISSENT(ION): n. (see "demur") clash; cleavage; difference; disagreement; disputation; dispute; dissidence; exception; faction; intrigue; jar; nonagreement; nonconcurrence; nonconformity; objection; odds; recusance; recusancy; unpeace; DISSENTIENT: (see "argumentative") disagreeing; dissentious; dissident; factional; factious; heretical; nonconforming; DISSENTER: disputant; dissentient; dissident; heretic; mutineer; nonconformist; recusant; rioter; sectary

DISSERTATION: (see "discussion") dialectic; discourse; disputation; disquisition; essay; exegesis; lecture; narrative; oration; screed; sermon; study; talk; thesis; tract; treatise

DISSERVICE: (see "harm" and "injury") mischief

DISSIDENT: (see "contentious") fractious; refractory; unmanageable; unpeaceable; unpeaceful; unruly

DISSIMILAR: (see "different") anomalistic; anomalous; discordant; disparate; divergent; diverse; heterogeneous; incongruous; odd; unalike; unanalogous; unequal; unlike; unsimilar; DISSIMILARITY: (see "difference") anomalism; anomaly; discord(ance); discordancy; disparity; disproportion; dissimilitude; distinction; divergence; divergency; heterogeneity; incongruity; oddity; unlikeness

DISSIPATE: (see "diffuse") break (up); deplete; destroy; diminish; disappear; dispel; disperse; dissolve; dwindle; fritter; lavish;

loose; scatter; spread; squander; strew; vanish; waste; wear

DISSOLUTE: (see "bad") abandoned; beastly; corrupt; debauched; degenerate(d); degraded; depraved; disreputable; evil; fast; immoral; impure; lawless; lax; lewd; libertine; licentious; loose; low; lustful; profligate; rakehell(y); rakish; shameless; unchaste; unrestrained; wanton; wicked

DISSOLVE: (see "abolish") ablate; abrogate; annihilate; annul; blend; cancel; close; collapse; crumble; cut; decompose; deliquesce; destroy; deteriorate; die; diminish; disappear; disconnect; discontinue; disentangle; disintegrate; disperse; dissipate; disunite; divide; divorce; dwindle; eliminate; end; eradicate; evaporate; expunge; fade; fuse; immerse; kill; liquefy; melt; mollify; perish; reduce; release; render; revoke; run; soften; solve; squander; subdue; suppress; terminate; thaw; undo; unfreeze; untie; vanish; waste; DISSOLUTION: (see "collapse") death; deterioration; diminishment; dispersal; dwindling; end; enfeeblement; excess; extravagance; liquefaction; reduction; revocation; softening; suppression; termination; thaw; vanishment

DISSONANT: (see "discordant") disagreeable; dissident; incongruous

DISSUADE: (see "deter") disadvise; restrain; stop

DISTANCE: v. (see "beat") outstrip; DISTANCE: n. aloofness; coldness; degree; detachment; difference; disparity; expanse; extent; farawayness; farness; gap; interval; latitude; length; limit; march; measure; meridian; mileage; offing; pace; perspective; reach; remoteness; remove; reserve; run; separation; space; span; spread; step; stride; trip; walk; way; DISTANT: abroad; absent; afar; afield; aloof; apart; aside; away; beyond; cold; cool; detached; different; dispassionate; far(-flung); far-off; farthest; forane; foreign; further; future; haughty; indifferent; indirect; indistinct; off; out; overseas; remote; removed; reserved; separate(d); shy; squeamish; strange; thence; tramontane; ulterior; ultramontane; unemotional; unfriendly; unintimate; utmost

DISTASTE: (see "aversion") abhorrence; abomination; antipathy; disinclination; dislike; disrelish; hate; hatred; opprobrium; oppugnance; repugnance; repugnancy; revulsion; unwillingness; DISTASTEFUL:

(see "averse") acid; Augean; beastly; brackish; disagreeable; fastuous; fulsome; greasy; hateful; impalatable; insufferable; loathsome; nauseating; nauseous; noxious; obnoxious; offensive; opprobrious; repellant; repugnant; revulsive; salty; sour; unpalatable; unpleasant; unsweet; unwanted; unwelcome

DISTEND: (see "enlarge") amplify; bloat; dilatate; dilate; elongate; enlarge; expand; extend; grow; hypertrophy; increase; inflate; magnify; puff (up); stretch; swell; widen; DISTENDED: (see "enlarged") amplified; bloated; blown (up); bulgy; dilatative; dilated; elongated; gravid; grown; hypertrophied; increased; inflated; magnified; patulous; stretched; swollen; tumescent; tumid; tympanic; widened; DISTENTION: (see "enlargement") amplification; dilatation; dilation; elongation; enlargement; expansion; hypertrophy; increase; inflation; magnification; stretch; swelling; tumescence; tumidity; turgescence; tympanites; tympany; widening

DISTILL: (see "concentrate") alembicate; condense; drop; extract; infuse; purify; trickle; vaporize

DISTINCT: alone; apart; articulate; asunder; atwain; audible; bisulcate; branched; cleancut; clear(-out); cleft; cloven; cogent; comprehensible; cut; definite; definitive; detached; determinate; different; disassociated; discernible; disconnected; discrete; disjointed; dismembered; dissected; dissociated; distinguished; disunited; divaricate; divergent; divorced; eminent; fair; fractional; free; incisive; isolated; legible; lucid; manifest; notable; obvious; outstanding; palpable; parceled; partite; partitioned; patent; plain; prominent; prorated; quartered; removed; resected; sectional; sectioned; segregated; separate(d); several; severed; sharp; single; sole; special; split; staccato; sundered; trenchant; twain; typical; unattached; unchained; uncoupled; unequivocal; unique; unlike; unmistakable; unquestionable; unusual; visible; DISTINCTIVE: certain; characteristic; clearcut; definite; definitive; diacritic(al); diagnostic; differential; direct; discernible; discriminating; dissimilar; *distingué*; distinguished; distinguishing; evocative; extraordinary; famous; flamboyant; honorific; illustrious; indicating; indicative; individual -(izing); inherent; juicy; majestic; notable; notorious; particular; pathognomonic(al); peculiar; quintessential; rare; redolent;

separate(d); signal; significant; singular; spanking; special; symbolic(al); symptomatic; transcendent(al); typical; unique; unusual; visual; DISTINCTION: acclaim; acuteness; bouquet; cachet; characteristic; class; consequence; contrast; *cum laude*; difference; differentia(tion); discrimination; disparity; dissimilarity; distinctiveness; divergency; division; eminence; favor; finesse; fitness; gradation; grade; hallmark; honor; importance; lineament; manner; mark -(edness); name; nicety; note; nuance; particularity; renown; reputation; repute; severance; shade; significance; specialty; style; subtlety; superiority; timbre; trademark; value; variation; worthiness

DISTINGUISH: (see "classify") analyze; call; characterize; define; delineate; demarcate; describe; descry; designate; differentiate; discern; discrepate; discriminate; divide; indicate; label; mark; perceive; portray; represent; secern; separate; sever -(alize); signalize; singularize; stamp; think; ticket; typify; DISTINGUISHED: (see "eminent") celebrated; conspicuous; distinct; *distingué*; excellent; famous; gentle; glorified; glorious; high; honored; honorific; illustrious; majestic; noble; notable; noted; notorious; preeminent; renowned; signal; significant; splendid; superlative; supreme; towering; transcendent; DISTINGUISHING: (see "distinctive") definitive; diagnostic; differential; signal; DISTINGUISHABLE: (see "distinct") characteristic; designable; designative; differential; identifiable; separable; severable

DISTORT: alter; amplify; bend; coil; color; compress; contort; cripple; curl; deface; deform; disfigure; embellish; falsify; fracture; garble; gnarl; grimace; impair; injure; maim; mangle; mar; mark; misconstrue; misinterpret; misshape; pervert; snarl; spoil; torture; turn; twist; uglify; warp; wreathe; wrench; writhe; wry; zigzag; DISTORTED: (see "crooked") agee; alop; amiss; angular; askew; athwart; awry; bent; bowed; circuitous; cockeyed; contorted; crippled; defaced; deformed; disfigured; falsified; garbled; gnarled; impaired; injured; maimed; marred; meandering; misconstrued; misinterpreted; misshapen; oblique; perverted; proportionless; sinuous; tortuous; twisted; unsymmetrical; warped; wry; zigzag; DISTORTION: alteration; astigmatism; astigmia; bend; contortion; contracture; corruption; deformation; deformity; depravity; disfigurement; falsehood; falsification; flaw; fracture; impairment; impropriety; injury; malformation; misconstruction; misrepresentation; perversion; torsion; turn; twist(ing); ugliness; warp; wryness

DISTRACT: (**see** "confuse") addle; amuse; baffle; balk; befuddle; bemuse; bewilder; confound; daze; dazzle; disconcert; dismay; disrupt; disturb; divert; draw (away); embarrass; embroil; entertain; fluster; harass; madden; mislead; mystify; nonplus; perplex; perturb; puzzle; rattle; stump; stupefy; unnerve; unsettle; upset; DISTRACTED: (**see** "confused") absentminded; acosmic; addled; agitated; aloof; amused; baffled; befuddled; bemused; bewildered; confounded; crazed; crazy; dazed; dazzled; deranged; detached; disconcerted; dismayed; disordered; distracted; distraught; disturbed; diverted; embarrassed; entertained; frantic; harassed; insane; mad-(dened); mystified; nonplussed; obsessed; perplexed; perturbed; preoccupied; puzzled; rattled; raving; stumped; stupefied; unnerved; unsettled; upset; wild; worried; DISTRACTION: (**see** "confusion") agitation; amusement; bafflement; bewilderment; chaos; coil; dazzlement; delirium; disarrangement; disarray(ment); dismay; disorder; disorientation; disruption; dissention; disturbance; diversion; entertainment; escape; jumble; madness; mess; mishmash; mixture; moil; muddle; nonplus; obfuscation; perplexity; perturbation; preoccupation; puzzlement; recreation; relief; snafu; snarl; tumult; turmoil; uncertainty

DISTRAUGHT: (**see** "distracted") agitated; anxious; crazed; crazy; deranged; disordered; frantic; mad; obsessed; stirred (up); upset; wrought (up)

DISTRESS: **v.** (**see** "pain") ache; afflict; agitate; ail; bother; discomfit; discomfort; distrain; disturb; exhaust; grieve; grill; harass; harrow; hurt; incommode; offend; plague; suffer; torment; trouble; try; upset; worry; DISTRESS: **n.** (**see** "pain") ache; adversity; affliction; agitation; agony; ailment; *angoisse*; angst; anguish; bereavement; bother; burden; calamity; consternation; constraint; cruciation; danger; disaster; disturbance; dolor; fantod(s); fear; grief; grievance; harassment; hurt; ill(ness); labor; misery; misfortune; mortification; need; offense; pang; passion; penance; plague; rack; remorse; sorrow; suffering; torment; trial; tribulation; trouble; umbrage; uneasiness; unhappiness; woe; worry; DISTRESSING *or* DISTRESSED: (**see** "painful") afflictive; aggrieved; agonizing; atro-

cious; bitter; burdensome; calamitous; caustic; cruel; damaging; deplorable; dire-(ful); disagreeable; disastrous; distasteful; distressful; dolorous; dreadful; flagrant; forlorn; frightening; galling; grievous; grilled; harassing; hard; harrowing; heinous; hurtful; keen; laborious; macabre; mad; miserable; misfortunate; mortifying; necessitous; offensive; painful; pathetic; perturbed; plaintive; raw; regretful; rigorous; sad(dened); savage; shrewd; sore; sorrowful; sorry; suffering; tiresome; troublesome; uneasy; unhappy; unpleasant; vexatious; virulent; woeful

DISTRIBUTE: admeasure; administer; allocate; allot; allow; appoint; apportion; appropriate; arrange; assign; assort; authorize; award; bestow; branch; budget; choose; classify; consign; contribute; deal; decide; designate; direct; disburse; dispense; dispose; divide; dole; earmark; expend; fractionalize; furnish; give; halve; help; issue; lend; liquidate; measure; mete; number; parcel; partition; place; plan; portion; prescribe; prorate; provide; ramify; rate; ration; regulate; release; rend; rive; scatter; section(alize); segmentalize; segmentize; separate; set(tle); share; slice; sow; spend; split; spread; sunder; supply; tear; unjoin(t); DISTRIBUTION: allocation; allotment; allowance; alms; appointment; apportionment; appropriation; arrangement; array-(ment); assignment; assortment; budget; circulation; class(ification); consignment; contingent; deal; delivery; disbursement; dispensation; dispersal; dispersion; disposal; disposition; divarication; diversification; dividend; division; dole; expenditure; gift; grant; gratuity; group(ing); issuance; measure(ment); number; parcel; part(ition); pattern; percentage; phylum; pittance; plan; portion; proportion; quota; randomization; range; rate; ration; sale; section(alization); separation; share; species; split; spread; stock; supply; system; territory

DISTRICT: area; arrondissement; bailiwick; belt; branch; bureau; camera; canton; circle; circuit; class(ification); commandery; compartment; demesne; department; division; environment; environs; field; locale; locality; neighborhood; parish; precinct; province; purlieu; quarter; realm; region; section; sector; sphere; station; subdivision; suburbs; territory; tract; unit; vicinity; ward; way; wick; zone

DISTRUST: **v.** (**see** "doubt") fear; misdoubt; mistrust; suspect; unbelieve; DISTRUST:

n. (see "doubt") anxiety; apprehension; disfaith; fear; misdoubt; misgiving; skepticism; suspicion; unbelief; uncertainty; untrustfulness; untrustworthiness; wariness; worry; DISTRUSTFUL: see "suspicious"

DISTURB: (see "annoy") affect; agitate; alarm; alter; arouse; beset; confuse; damage; derange; disarrange; disarray; discomfit; discommode; discompose; disconcert; dismay; displace; disquiet; distress; embarrass; excite; faze; fluster; fray; fret; frighten; harass; harry; incommode; inconvenience; interfere; jar; jostle; meddle; molest; move; nag; nettle; overset; perplex; perturb(ate); pester; plague; rattle; rile; rock; roil; rouse; ruffle; scare; shake; shift; shock; stir; terrify; torment; touch; trouble; unbalance; unsettle; upset; worry; DISTURBED: (see "agitated") restless; shocking; terrifying; tormenting; troublesome; untranquil; upsetting; DISTURBANCE: (see "annoyance") ado; agitation; alarm; altercation; besetment; breach; breeze; bristle; brouhaha; buzz; commotion; confusion; contretemps; controversy; derangement; discomfiture; disorder; disquiet(ude); distress; excitement; fracas; frenzy; furor(e); hubbub; hurry; incident; incitement; interruption; jar; kick(up); molestation; muss; nuisance; perturbation; puzzlement; quarrel; rabblement; riot; ripple; rout; rush; scare; shock; trouble; tumult(uation); turmoil; whirl(wind); wind

DISUNITE: (see "break") alienate; disassociate; disjoin(t); dissociate; disunify; divorce; part; separate; DISUNITY: (see "break") alienation; disassociation; disjunction; dissention; dissociation; disunification; disunion; divorce(ment); parting; separation

DISUSE: atrophy; corrosion; decay; degeneration; desuetude; erosion; impairment; obsolescence; oxidation; patina; rust; unmaintenance; verdigris

DITCH: **v.** see "abandon;" DITCH: **n.** acequia; canal; channel; dike; drain; foss(e); gut; moat; relais; rut; sap; sewer; slough; trench; trough; watercourse; waterway; zanja

DITHYRAMBIC: boisterous; elevated; euphoric; frenetic; impassioned; unrestrained; wild

DIVAGATE: (see "diverge") deviate; digress; ramble; stray; wander

DIVE: (see "drop") bar; den; dip; dump; gainer; honky-tonk; joint; plunge; swan

DIVERGE: (see "diversify") alter; bifurcate; branch; deflect; depart; derive; detour; deviate; differ; digress; divagate; divaricate; divide; enlarge; extend; furcate; leave; parenthesize; part; ramble; ramify; rift; separate; spread; stray; subdivide; swerve; turn; twist; vary; veer; wander; DIVERGENCE: alteration; bifurcation; branch(ing); deflection; departure; detour; deviation; difference; digression; disagreement; dispute; dissimilarity; divagation; divarication; division; divorce(ment); gap; obliquity; parenthesis; parting; partition; rambling; rift; spread; straying; swerve; tendency; turn; twist; variation; veer; wandering; DIVERGENT: (see "diverse") centrifugal; departing; deviant; deviating; different; disagreeing; disharmonious; disintegrative; disjunctive; dissentious; dissociable; dissociative; divisory; factional; fissiparous; oblique; parenthetical; partial; remote; schismatic(al); schizoid; separatist; separative; spreading; tangent(ial); tentacular; wandering

DIVERSIFY: alter; arborize; branch; change; dapple; depart; deviate; differ; diverge; dot; intersperse; mix; rotate; spot; sprinkle; variate; variegate; vary; DIVERSE or DIVERSIFIED: (see "mixed") altered; arborized; changed; dappled; departing; deviant; deviating; different; differing; disharmonious; disintegrative; disjunctive; dissentious; dissociable; dissociative; distinct; divaricated; divergent; diversiform; diverting; divisory; factional; fissiparous; heterogeneous; manifold; motley; multifarious; multiform; multiplex; multiplicious; multivarious; nonuniform; oblique; parenthetical; protean; radial; radiating; ramifying; ramose; remote; spreading; tangent(ial); tentacular; unlike; varied; variegated; variform; DIVERSITY: (see "variety") diversification; heterogeneity; multiplicity; nonuniformity; ramification; rotation; variation; variegation

DIVERSION: see under "divert"

DIVERT: alter; amuse; avert; avoid; beguile; bend; change; curve; deceive; deflect; delay; derail; detour; detract; deviate; digress; disport; dissuade; distract; entertain; interrupt; modify; parry; play; please; recreate; regale; shift; shunt; sidetrack; stall; sway; swing; switch; turn; twist; unbend; veer; withdraw; DIVERSION: alteration; amusement; attraction; bend; change; curve; detour; deviation; digression; distraction; entertainment; exhibition; pastime; play;

pleasure; recreation; relaxation; rest; sideshow; sport; switch; turn; twist; variation

DIVEST: (see "deprive") bar; bare; defrock; denudate; denude; depose; dethrone; dismantle; dispossess; disthrone; doff; empty; oust; peel; reduce; remove; shave; strip; tirl; uncloak; unclothe; uncover; undress; unfrock; DIVESTED: see "bare" and "destitute"

DIVIDE: (see "distribute") alienate; allot; apportion; atomize; bifurcate; bisect; branch; classify; cleave; cut; deal; detach; disaffect; disarticulate; disassociate; discerp; disconnect; disengage; disjoin(t); dissect; dissociate; dissolve; distinguish; disunite; divaricate; diverge; divert; divorce; dole; enlarge; extend; fence; fork; fractionalize; fractionate; fragmentalize; fragmentate; furcate; grade; graduate; halve; isolate; lot; luxate; mark; number; parcel; part(ition); portion; prorate; quarter; ramify; ration; rend; rive; section(alize); segmental(ize); segmentize; separate; sever; share; split; spread; subdivide; sunder; tear; trisect; unjoin(t); DIVIDED or DIVIDING: (see "distinct") apart; asunder; atwain; bifurcate(d); bisulcate; branched; cleft; cloven; cut; detached; disassociated; disconnected; discrete; dismembered; dissected; dissociated; disunited; divaricate(d); divergent; fractional; halved; parceled; partite; partitioned; prorated; quartered; sectional; sectioned; separate(d); several; severed; single; sole; special; split; staccato; sundered; twain

DIVIDEND: (see "share") allotment; apportion(ment); bonus; cut; deal; distribution; division; earning; melon; part; portion; quota; quotient; rate; ration; return; reward; slice

DIVINATION: (see "prediction") acumen; augury; chronomancy; crystallomancy; feeling; forecast; foretelling; fortune-telling; insight; intuition; metagnomy; omen; presage; prognosis; prognostication; prophesy; vaticination

DIVINE: v. (see "predict") conjecture; discern; discover; foresee; foretell; guess; infer; locate; perceive; portend; suppose; DIVINE: a. (see "angelic") admirable; ambrosiac; ambrosial; beatific; beautiful; blessed; canonized; celestial; cherubic; deific; deiform; empyrean; ethereal; godlike; godly; good; heaven-born; heavenly; holy; Olympian; otherworldly; pietistic; pious; religious; sacred; saintly; sanctified; seraphic; spiritual;

sublime; superhuman; supermundane; supernal; unearthly; unprofane; DIVINE: n. see "clergyman;" DIVINITY: see "god"

DIVISION: (see "distribution") alienation; apportionment; border; category; chasm; circle; class(ification); cleavage; compartment; country; department; detachment; difference; disagreement; discerption; discord; disjunction; dismemberment; dissolution; distribution; district; disunion; disunity; divarication; divergence; dividend; edge; epic; fence; field; fission; fissure; fraction; fragment; gradation; grade; group(ing); leaf; leg; line; mark; measure; opposition; parcel; part(ition); phylum; piece; polychotomy; portion; quarter; ration; realm; schism; scission; section; segment; separation; share; side; species; stratum; sundering; system; term; territory; unit; variance; wall

DIVISIVE or DIVISIBLE: centrifugal; departing; deviant; deviating; different; disharmonious; disintegrative; disjunctive; dissentious; dissociable; dissociative; divergent; divisory; factional; fissiparous; oblique; parenthetical; partible; schismatic(al); schizoid; separatist; spreading; tangent(ial)

DIVORCE: (see "separate") unjoin

DIVULGE: (see "announce") advertise; air; betray; blab; blurt; broadcast; confide; disclose; evulgate; gossip; impart; promulgate; publicize; publish; relate; repeat; reveal; spill; squeal; tattle; tell

DIZZY: (see "faint" and "giddy") addled; asea; foolish; heedless; inane; silly;

DO: accomplish; achieve; actual(ize); actuate; answer; arouse; arrange; behave; cause; cheat; clean; commit; compass; complete; conclude; conduct; constitute; consummate; contrive; cook; credit; decorate; direct; discharge; effect; enact; end; establish; execute; exercise; exert; fashion; finish; fulfill; gain; guide; happen; implement; impress; induce; issue; make; manage; negotiate; obtain; operate; pay; perform; perpetuate; play; practice; prepare; produce; prosecute; provide; put; reach; realize; render; secure; serve; set(tle); shape; solve; succeed; suffice; suit; swindle; take; transact; undertake; wage; wash; work

DOCILE: (see "teachable") amenable; childlike; compliant; docible; dutiful; gentle; governable; influenceable; innocent; meek:

mild; naive; obedient; plastic; pliable; pliant; soft; submissive; tame; tractable; treatable; trusting; yielding

DOCK: **v. see** "shorten;" DOCK: **n.** basin; harbor; jetty; mooring; peer; wharf

DOCKET: (**see** "calendar") agenda (pl.); agendum; list

DOCTRINE: (**see** "belief) article; cabala; cant; conviction; credence; credenda (pl.); credo; creed; cult; dogma; faith; ism; logic; lore; opinion; maxim; persuasion; philosophy; precept; principle; proposition; religion; ritual; rule(s); sect; sentiment; system; teaching; tenet; theory; view

DOCUMENT: **v. see** "prove;" DOCUMENT: **n.** archive; bill; certificate; certification; chronicle; commission; contract; credential; deed; diploma; documentary; draft; instrument; lease; letter; license; memo(randum); note; paper; papyri (pl.); papyrus; parchment; recommendation; record; scripture; stock; testimonial; voucher; will; writing

DODDERING: aged; anile; decrepit; enervated; feeble; foolish; frail; ill; inane; infirm; sensecent; senile; shaky; sick(ly); superannuated; weak(ened); wobbling; wobbly

DODGE: **v. see** "avoid;" DODGE: **n.** (**see** "artifice") blind; excuse; game; gloss; pretense; pretension; racket; ruse; scheme; shift; stall

DOER: (**see** "worker") actor; agent; director; executor; feasor; maker; operator; performer; perpetrator; toiler

DOG: **v.** catch; follow; hunt; hound; seek; shadow; tag; tail; track; trail; DOG: **n.** canine; cur; fellow; hound; mastiff; mongrel; mutt; pooch; rascal; wretch

DOGGED: (**see** "unyielding") obstinate; stubborn; unremitting; unshakable

DOGMA: (**see** "doctrine") belief; cant; creed; ism; opinion; sect; tenet; view; DOGMATIC(AL): (**see** "dictatorial") arbitrary; arrogant; authoritarian; authoritative; autocratic; biased; cavalier; coercive; commanding; despotic; doctrinaire; doctrinal; dominant; dominating; domineering; grand-(iose); haughty; hierarchic(al); imperative; imperious; imposing; magisterial; narrow; opinionated; oppressive; oracular; over-

bearing; peremptory; positive; pronunciative; rigoristic; sophomoric; totalitarian; tyrannical; tyrannous

DOLDRUM(S); (**see** "blues") boredom; calm; dejection; deterioration; downswing; dullness; dumps; ennui; inactivity; lethargy; listlessness; megrims; retardation; slack; slump; tedium

DOLE: **v. see** "divide;" DOLE: **n.** (**see** "distribution") allotment; alms; apportion-(ment); disposal; distress; gift; gratuity; grief; misery; part; pittance; portion; regret; share; sorrow; trial; woe

DOLEFUL: abject; austere; black; bleak; blue; cheerless; chilly; cold; cruel; cutting; dark; defunctive; dejected; depressing; desolate; dirgeful; disconsolate; disheartening; dismal; dispiriting; distressing; doloroso; dolorous; dour; drab; drear(y); dree; dull; elegaic; empty; frightful; frigid; funerary; funereal; gloomy; glum; grave; gray; grievous; harsh; heavy; icy; joyless; lamentable; lugubrious; melancholy; miserable; moanful; mournful; obsequial; pathetic; piteous; pitiful; plaintive; raw; relentless; rigid; rigorous; rueful; sad(dened); solemn; somber; sorrowful; sorry; stark; strict; stringent; teary; *tristesse*; wistful; woeful

DOLL: dummy; figure; girl; manikin; mannequin; moppet; toy; woman

DOLLAR: bean; bill; buck; coin; money; one-spot; peso; simoleon

DOLT: (**see** "fool" and "blockhead") ass; bumpkin; cabbagehead; chowderhead; chucklehead; clod; dumbbell; dummy; dunce; fathead; idiot; jackass; loon; numbskull; oaf; schnook; simp(leton)

DOMAIN: (**see** "area" and "dominion") arrondissement; baron(r)y; career; class; demesne; department; district; empire; experience; fief; field; function; hierarchy; jurisdiction; life; parish; precinct; principality; property; province; realm; region; responsibility; society; sovereignty; sphere; territory; world; zone

DOMESTIC: **a.** (**see** "native") common; connubial; domesticated; *en famille*; familiar; fireside; home; household; housewifely; housewifish; indigenous; interior; internal; local; marital; matrimonial; residential; tame; DOMESTIC: **n.** homeworker; houseworker; maid; native; servant; DOMES-

TICATED: (see "tame") *dominae naturae*; DOMESTICITY: conjugality; connubiality; familiarity; housekeeping; housewifery

DOMICILE: (see "house") abode; apartment; city; cottage; country; digs; district; dormitory; dwelling; habitation; home(stead); hotel; hovel; inn; jurisdiction; lodge; mansion; palace; quarters; residence; roof; shack; shelter; tavern; tenement; territory; villa

DOMINATE: bully; captivate; capture; charm; command(eer); control; direct; domineer; dragoon; envelope; govern; guide; influence; master; override; oversway; overthrow; possess; predominate; prevail; rule; subject; sway; top; DOMINANT *or* DOMINATING: (see "dictatorial") autocratic; besetting; breathless; central; chief; commanding; controlling; despotic; determinative; domineering; eminent; first; governing; imperious; lordly; outstanding; overbearing; overriding; overshadowing; overwhelming; paramount; predominating; preeminent; prepotent; prevailing; prevalent; principal; ruling; superior; surpassing; transcendent; DOMINATION *or* DOMINANCE: ascendence; ascendency; authority; command; control; dominion; influence; leadership; mastership; mastery; possession; preeminence; preponderance; preponderancy; prevailment; rule; sovereignty; superiority; superordination; sway; transcendency; weight

DOMINEER: (see "coerce") bluster; boss; bully; hector; lord; master; override; ride; tyrannize; DOMINEERING: (see "dictatorial") arbitrary; arrogant; authoritative; autocratic; bossy; commanding; cruel; czaristic; despotic; dominative; haughty; hectoring; imperious; masterful; masterly; oppressive; overbearing; overriding; proud; tyrannical; tyrannous

DOMINION: (see "area" and "domain") ascendency; authority; colony; command; control; country; department; district; dominance; domination; dynasty; empire; estate; fief; government; hierarchy; influence; jurisdiction; kingdom; lordship; ownership; power; property; realm; region; reign; right; rule; seign(i)ority; sovereignty; string; succession; superiority; supremacy; suzerainty; sway; territory; title; transcendency

DONATE: bequest; bestow; confer; contribute; dole; emit; give; grant; loan; present; share; supply; tip; transfer; DONATION: allocation; alms; amount; ante; assessment; assignment; benefit; boon; charity; contribution; dole; gift; grant; gratuity; largess(e); money; offering; payment; portion; present-(ation); share; sum; tip; widow's mite

DONE: accomplished; achieved; ceased; closed; completed; cooked; concluded; consummate(d); dead; decorous; discharged; dissolved; ended; executed; exhausted; *factum est*; finalized; finished; finite; finitive; kaput; over; past; performed; spent; stopped; terminated; through

DOOM: **v.** condemn; curse; damn; destine; devote; end; excommunicate; predestine; sentence; DOOM: **n.** calamity; chance; condemnation; death; decision; decree; destination; destiny; destruction; discrimination; end(ing); cure; extinction; fate; foreordination; fortune; future; goal; judgment; lot; ordinance; penalty; portion; predestination; sentence; star; tragedy; verdict; DOOMED; abandoned; bereft; condemned; damned; destined; fatal; fateful; fey; forlorn; penalized; sentenced

DOOR: (see "opening") access; avenue; chance; egress; entrance(way); gate(way); home; ingress; inlet; means; opportunity; passage(way); path(way); portal; postern; route; threshold; vent

DOPE: (see "fool") nincompoop

DORMANT: abed; abeyant; anesthetized; asleep; comatose; cryptic; dead; drowsy; hibernant; hypnotic; idle; immobile; inactive; inert; insensate; insensible; latent; lethargic(al); moribund; motionless; numb; out; passive; potential; prone; quiescent; quiet; relaxed; resting; sleeping; sluggish; slumbering; slumb(e)rous; somniculous; somnolent; stationary; suspended; torpescent; torpid; unaroused; unawakened; unevoked; unprogressive; unroused; DORMANCY: abeyance; anesthesia; coma; hibernation; idleness; immobility; immobilization; inactivity; latency; neglect; quiescence; relaxation; rest(ing); sleep; sluggishness; somnolence; suspension; torpidity; torpor; unprogressiveness

DOSE: amount; bolus; deal(ing); dosage; draft; dram; draught; drug; formula; measure; medicine; minim; part; pill; portion; potion; powder; prescription; quantity; ration; recipe; remedy; shot; slug; swallow

DOTAGE: (see "senility") age; childishness;

decrepitude; feebleness; fondness; imbecility; senescence

DOTARD: **see** "fool"

DOUBLE: **v.** combine; couple; fold; lap; mate; pair; reinforce; DOUBLE: **a.** bigeminal; bilateral; binary; binate; bipartisan; bipartite; counterpart; coupled; deceitful; dual(istic); dual-purpose; duple(x); duplicate(d); folded; hypocritical; insincere; married; matching; mated; paired; reciprocal; reinforced; synallagmatic; twice; twin; twofold; two-sided; DOUBLE: **n.** *alter ego*; carbon (copy); counterpart; duality; duo; duplex; duplicate; image; semblance; similitude; sub(stitute); twin; two(fold); twoness; understudy; DOUBLENESS: dichotomy; duality; duplicity

DOUBLE-DEALING: (**see** "crafty") ambidextrous; deceptive; duplicitous

DOUBT: **v.** demur; disbelieve; dissent; distrust; fear; hesitate; impugn; misdoubt; misgive; mistrust; pause; question; suspect; unbelieve; waver; DOUBT: **n.** agnosticism; ambiguity; ambivalence; anxiety; apprehension; cold feet; denial; disbelief; disdain; disfaith; dissent; distrust; dubiety; dubiosity; dubiousness; dubitation; fear; hesitancy; hesitation; impugnation; incertitude; incredibility; incredulity; indecision; irresolution; misapprehension; misbelief; miscreance; misdoubt; misgiving; mistrust; negativism; negativity; perplexity; presentiment; problem; Pyrrhonism; query; rejection; reserve; sardonicism; scruple; scrupulosity; skepsis; skepticism; suspense; suspicion; unbelief; uncertainty; waver; DOUBTING: **see** "doubtful;" DOUBTER: **see** "skeptic"

DOUBTFUL: ambivalent; aporetic; apparent; apprehensive; borderline; controversial; controvertible; *cum grano salis*; debatable; dilemmatic; disdainful; disputable; disputatious; dissident; distrustful; distrusting; doubting; doubtsome; dubious; dubitable; dubitant; equivocal; fabular; factious; fearful; hesitant; improbable; inconstant; incredible; incredulous; indeterminate; irresolute; legendary; liminal; limitrophe; marginal; moot; negativistic; negatory; pending; perilous; peripheral; problematic(al); Pyrrhonian; Pyrrhonic; questionable; recusant; sardonic; shaky; skeptical; skittish; suspicious; tottering; unbelieving; uncertain; unclear; undecided; undetermined; unformed; unformulated; unknown; unlikely;

unpredictable; unpromising; unresolved; unsettled; unstable; unsure; vacillating; vacillatory; vague; volatile; wavering; wobbly

DOUBTLESS: **see** "certain"

DOUGHTY: (**see** "bold") able; awesome; brave; courageous; fearless; frightening; heroic; intrepid; redoubtable; severe; stern; strong; valiant

DOUR: (**see** "unyielding") dogged; forbidding; glum; grim; hard; harsh; obstinate; right; severe; sour; stern; sullen; surly; taciturn; DOURNESS: **see** "sourness"

DOVETAIL: **v.** (**see** "fit") agree; combine; connect; insert; interlock; intersect; join; suit; DOVETAIL **n.** fitting; insert; tenon; tongue

DOWDY: (**see** "untidy") old-fashinoed; ragged; seedy; slatternly; slovenly

DOWN: **v.** (**see** "defeat") crush; kill; suppress; swallow; DOWN: **a.** *or* **adv.** abed; alow; asleep; below; beneath; buried; conquered; crushed; descending; flattened; floored; inferior; licked; low; lying; mastered; nether; pronate; prostrate; recumbent; sad(dened); serious; sick; southerly; under; DOWN: **n.** eider; feathers; floccus; floss; fuzz; hair; lanugo; nap; pubescence; wool; DOWNY: floccose; flocculent; flossy; fluffy; furry; fuzzy; lanate; laniferous; lanuginous; pilar; pubescent; soft; soothing; tosy; villous; warm; woolly

DOWNCAST: (**see** "cheerless") blue; dejected; depressed; disheartened; dispirited; low; melancholic; melancholy; sad(dened); sick

DOWNFALL: (**see** "collapse") comeuppance; debasement; defeat; degradation; *dégringolade*; descent; destruction; disgrace; disintegration; drop; failure; finish; labefaction; misfortune; overthrow; punishment; rain; reverse; ruin; topple; trap; victory; Waterloo; wrack; wreck

DOWNGRADE: (**see** "belittle" and "denigrate") lower; reduce

DOWNRIGHT: (**see** "certain") absolute; arrant; blunt; candid; clear; consummate; direct; explicit; extreme; flat; forthright; forthwith; frank; honest; obvious; open; out-and-out; outright; plain; positive; sheer; simple; sincere; stark; undisguised; unmitigated; unreserved; utter; very

DOWNWARD: (see "below") beneath; descending; inferior; low(er); lowest; neath; nether(ward); subordinate; under(lying); underneath

DOZE: see "drowse"

DRAB: (see "austere") cheerless; colorless; common(place); dark; dingy; doleful; dour; dun; everyday; grave; gray; grey; hard; heavy; insipid; lifeless; monotonous; ordinary; plain; pompous; sad; sober; somber; subfusc(ous); unvarnished

DRAFT: v. (see "outline") call; chart; compose; conscript; copy; demand; design; detach; diagram; draw; figure; form(ulate); frame; indicate; levy; limn; map; muster; DRAFT: n. air; breeze; call; chart; check; claim; conscription; current; depth; design; diagram; dose; dram; draught; drawing; drink; gorge; group; gully; intake; levy; load; manuscript; map; money; muster; note; plan; plot; portion; potion; protocol; pull; scheme; selection; shot; sketch; summary; swallow; tracing; traction; writing

DRAG: v. (see "retard") clog; crawl; dawdle; delay; draw; force; hamper; harrow; haul; hinder; impede; inch; leg; lengthen; obstruct; procrastinate; protract; pull; restrain; retard; slow; slump; slur; snig; tow; trail; tug; DRAG: n. clog; crawl; delay; hampering; harrow; hindrance; impediment; lag; obstacle; obstruction; procrastination; restraint; retardation; retardment; slowness; slump

DRAIN: v. bleed; deplete; diminish; discharge; dissipate; ditch; draw; dwindle; empty; escape; exhaust; extort; extract; extravasate; exudate; exude; flow; leak; ooze; sap; seep; shed; spend; vent; weaken; DRAIN: n. bung; burden; channel; conduit; culvert; ditch; hole; outflow; outlet; pipe; sewer; sink; sluice; strain(er); tap; trench; vent

DRAMA: (see "show") art; burletta; catastrophe; climax; comedy; enactment; fantasy; farce; legit; mask; masque; minstrel; movie; opera; play; spectacle; spectacular; stage; theater; tragedy; DRAMATIC(AL): (see "showy") artificial; cloak-and-dagger; compelling; declamatory; elocutionary; histrionic; lyric(al); melodramatic; operatic; ostentatious; rhapsodic; romantic; scenic; stagy; striking; tense; theatric(al); thespian; tragic(al); vivid; DRAMATIST: dramaturge; playwright

DRASTIC: (see "harsh") extreme; final; last-ditch; powerful; Procrustean; purging; radical; rigorious; severe; stern; vigorous; violent

DRAUGHT: see "draft"

DRAW: v. (see "allure") abduct; abstract; adduct; allot; attenuate; attract; breathe; contract; delineate; depict(ure); derive; describe; design; diminish; divert; draft; drag; drain; elicit; engrave; entice; etch; eviscerate; evoke; extract; fascinate; form(-ulate); gain; gather; hail; haul; heave; illustrate; induce; influence; inhale; lead; limn; lure; move; paint; picture; portray; protract; pucker; pull; pump; purse; remove; represent; rouse; seduce; select; siphon; sketch; stalemate; stretch; take; tap; tie; tole; tow; trace; tug; wheedle; win; wrinkle; DRAW: n. (see "allurement") fascination; pull; seduction; standoff; tie; DRAWN: see "taut;" DRAWING: see "picture"

DRAWBACK: (see "defect") disability; disadvantage; fault; flaw; handicap; hindrance; impediment; incapacitation; injury; refund; stultification

DREAD: v. see "fear;" DREAD(FUL): a. (see "bad") abysmal; alarming; apprehensive; awesome; awful; dangerous; dire(ful); dismal; doughty; drear(y); extreme; fearful; formidable; frightening; frightful; horrendous; horrible; horrid; horrific; offensive; perilous; portentous; redoubtable; revolting; shocking; terrible; terrifying; tragic(al); tremendous; wretched; DREAD: n. (see "alarm") angst; anxiety; apprehension; awe; bugaboo; consternation; cowardice; dismay; dreadfulness; fear(fulness); fright; horror; panic; peril; reverence; scare; terror; timidity; trepidation; trepidity

DREAM: v. (see "imagine") conceive; daydream; fancy; fantasize; ideate; long; moon; muse; plan; romance; scheme; yearn; DREAM: n. (see "imagination") aim; apparition; chimera; daydream; deception; delusion; eidolon; fallacy; fancy; fantasia; fantasy; ghost; goal; hallucination; idea(l); illusion; image; muse; phantasma; phantasmata (pl.); phantasy; phantom; purpose; reverie; romance; scheme; specter; spirit; trance; vagary; vision; wraith; DREAMY: (see "fantastic") abstracted; chimerical; delightful; dreamful; dreamlike; fantastical; fantasque; hazy; ideal; idle; impractical; indistinct; langorous; languid; misty-eyed;

moony; nebulous; pleasing; sentimental; shadowy; soothing; utopian; vague; DREAMER: (**see** "visionary") fantasist; idealist; ideologist; ideologue; *luftmensch*; phantast; romancer; romanticist; schemer; utopian

DREAR(Y): alange; annoying; banal; bleak; blue; boring; cheerless; colorless; comfortless; dark; dejected; depressing; desolate; dire; discouraged; disheartening; dismal; dispiriting; drab; dull; gloomy; insular; isolated; joyless; lonely; melancholic; melancholy; monotonous; plain; sad(dened); somber; stereotyped; stereotypical; stupid; tedious; tiresome; unappealing; unattractive; unenjoyable; unenjoyed; uninteresting; wintery; DREARINESS: (**see** "austerity") annoyance; banality; bleakness; boredom; cheerlessness; depression; desolation; dismality; dismalness; dullness; ennui; fatigue; glumness; insularity; isolation; languor; listlessness; loneliness; lornness; melancholia; melancholy; monotony; sadness; surfeit; tediousness; tedium; tiresomeness; uninterestedness; wearisomeness

DREGS: (**see** "waste") debris; draff; dross; exuviae; faex; feculence; grounds; lees; magma; mud; orts; refuse; remainder; remains; residue; residuum; rubbish; scum; sediment; silt; sludge; sordes; sordor; vestige; wash

DRENCH: douse; drown; hose; imbrue; imbue; immerse; overwhelm; permeate; pervade; ret; saturate; soak; sog; sop; souse; steep; submerge; wash; wet

DRESS: **v.** accessorize; accouter; adorn; align; apparel; arrange; array; attire; bandage; bedeck; blanket; caparison; clothe; comb; costume; cover; curry; deck; dight; embellish; equip; furbish; furnish; garb; garnish; gown; groom; habilitate; invest; outfit; portray; preen; prepare; ready; rig; robe; scold; style; swathe; tailor; tog; uniform; vest(ure); DRESS: **n.** accessories; accouterment(s); adornment; apparel; appearance; array(ment); attire; blankets; caparison; cloth(es); clothing; costume; cover(ing); drapery; dressing; duds; equipage; equipment; feathers; finish; form; frippery; frock; garb; garments; garnish(ment); gear; getup; gown; grand; toilette; guise; haberdashery; habiliment; habit; harness; investiture; investments; livery; makeup; panoply; plumage; raiment; regalia; rig; robe; stuff; style; toggery; togs; toilette; trappings; uniform; vestment(s); vesture; wear(ables);

DRESSY: (**see** "elaborate" and "ornate") chic; elegant; sharp; *soigné*; *soignée* (fem.); stylish

DRIED: (**see** "dry") arid; baked; dehydrated; desiccated; sere; withered

DRIFT: **v.** accumulate; deposit; deviate; evolve; float; issue; mass; meander; move; ramble; roam; rove; shift; sinuate; skid; slide; sway; swerve; twist; vary; veer; wander; wind; DRIFT: **n.** accumulation; action; aim; bearing; course; current; cycle; deposit; design; development; deviation; direction; drain(age); effort; end; evolution; flood; flow(age); heap; import; inclination; inference; intent(ion); issuance; issue; leeway; line; maneuver; march; meander; meaning; motive; move(ment); object(ive); pace; pile; procedure; proceeding; progress(ion); purport; purpose; rate; rise route; rush; schedule; scope; series; sideslip; skip; slant; slide; speed; spread; stream; sweep; swing; system; tack; tactic; tendency; tenor; thought; thrust; tide; torrent; trajectory; trend; turn; veer(ing); velocity; volley; wave; DRIFTER(S): (**see** "vagabond") casual; flotsam and jetsam; gaberlunzie; itinerant; temporizer; vagrant; DRIFTING: (**see** "unsettled") anchorless; helmless; rudderless

DRILL: **v.** bore; catechize; discipline; enter; excavate; exercise; instruct; penetrate; perforate; pierce; practice; prepare; probe; puncture; regulate; rehearse; teach; train; DRILL: **n.** auger; bit; bore; catechism; cloth; discipline; exercise; exhibition; gimlet; instruction; practice; preparation; probe; regulation; teaching; tool; training

DRINK: **v.** absorb; down; englut; engulf; gulp; guzzle; imbibe; ingest; ingurgitate; nip; quaff; sip; sup; swallow; swig; swill; swizzle; taste; tipple; toast; tope; DRINK(ING): **n.** (**see** "intoxication") alcoholism; beverage; bibation; bracer; brew; celebration; chaser; cheer; coffee; decoction; dipsomania; draft; dram; draught; drunkenness; ebriety; ebriosity; extract; glass; guzzle; imbibing; imbibition; inebriation; inebriety; infusion; ingurgitation; juice; libation; liquid; liquor; milk; nectar; negus; ocean; pony; potable; potation; potion; potomania; preparation; quaff; refreshment; repast; shot; sip; slug; snifter; snort; swallow; swig; swizzle; tea; tippling; toast; tot; wassail; water; wine(bibbing); DRINKER: (**see** "drunkard") compotator; guzzler; tippler; tipster

DRIP: bleed; dribble; drizzle; escape; exude; fall; leak; mist; ooze; overflow; seep; sile; spill; trickle

DRIVE: **v.** act(ivate); advance; animate; arouse; budge; call; catapult; coact; coerce; compel; constrain; contrive; control; course; dash; depart; direct; dislodge; dispel; drum; effect; egg; encourage; enkindle; enliven; excite; exert; fire; flagellate; force; forge; glide; go; goad; hammer; hurl; hurry; hurtle; hustle; impel; incite; influence; inspire; instigate; kindle; manipulate; march; motivate; navigate; press; probe; produce; progress; project; prompt; propel; provoke; punch; push; race; ram; repel; repulse; ride; rush; shove; spur; stab; start; steer; stimulate; surge; thrust; thump; travel; urge; whip; DRIVE: **n.** (**see** "energy" and "movement") alley; arousal; campaign; cause; coercion; conation; conatus; course; direction; disposition; dynamics; dynamism; élan; encouragement; energy; enthusiasm; exertion; fervor; fever; fire; force; impetus; impulse; impulsion; incitation; incitement; inducement; influence; inspiration; intensity; interest; jasm; lane; longing; momentum; motivation; move; need; press(ure); provocation; punch; push; ride; road; stimulation; stimulus; stir; street; strike; surge; tendency; tension; thrust; tour; trip; urge; urging; vector; vitality; will (to power)

DRIVEL: (**see** "nonsense") claptrap; dishwater; eyewash; humbug; maundering; mush; slaver; tomfoolery

DRIZZLE: (**see** "drip") drop; mist; mizzle; rain; shower; spray; sprinkle; spritz; wet

DROLL: **a.** (**see** "amusing") antic; clownish; comic; diverting; facetious; funny; humorous; jocular; laughable; ludicrous; merry; mirthful; odd; queer; risible; waggish; whimsical; witty; zany; DROLL: **n.** (**see** "fool") buffoon; clown; comic; jester; Punch; wag; wit; zany; DROLLERY: (**see** "foolishness") *drôlerie*; humor; jest; raillery; whim(sey); whimsicality; whimsicalness

DRONE: **v. see** "hum;" DRONE: **n.** (**see** "loafer") bee; bum; idler; parasite; sluggard; sponger

DROOP: (**see** "decline") attenuate; bend; dangle; debilitate; devitalize; drain; drop; enervate; enfeeble; fade; fail; fall; flag; incline; leave; lop; nod; pend; pine; quit; sag; sap; sink; slouch; stoop; tire; unman; wilt; DROOPED *or* DROOPING: alop; attenuated; declined; devitalized; disabled; drained; drooped; droopy; dropped; enfeebled; exhausted; faded; fading; failing; falling; flaccid; flagging; inclined; lackadaisical; languid; languorous; lax; lazy; lethargic; limp; nodding; nutant; sagged; sagging; sapped; shrinking; sinking; slouched; slouching; stooped; tired; unmanned; unnerved; weak(ened); wilted; wilting

DROP: **v.** (**see** "abandon") alight; bounce; break (off); cancel; cease; dangle; decline; decrease; descend; dip; disappear; discard; discontinue; dismiss; drag; drib(ble); drip; drive; droop; dump; fall; fire; flop; incline; jettison; leave; lessen; lower; omit; pend; plop; plummet; plunge; quash; remove; retreat; sack; sag; shed; sink; skid; slide; slouch; spend; stop; swoop; trickle; unload; vacate; vanish; void; wilt; withdraw; DROP: **n.** (**see** "abandonment") bead; bit; blob; decline; depth; descent; discontinuation; dive; dram; drib(ble); driblet; drip; droop; fall; glob(ule); gutta; incline; lull; minim; pendent; plop; relinquishment; sag(ging); shedding; skid; slide; slot; slump; stoop; swoop; trickle; withdrawal

DROSS: (**see** "waste") ash(es); *caput mortua*(pl.); *caput mortuum*; chaff; cinders; clinker(s); coals; dregs; impurity; refuse; remains; scobs; scoria; scum; sediment; slag; sullage; trash

DROUGHT: aridity; dearth; dryness; emptiness; insufficiency; lack; necessity; need; shortage; thirst; want

DROVE: (**see** "group") atajo; bevy; bow; clutch; creaght; crowd; flock; following; gaggle; herd; manada; mulada; multitude; pack; remuda; school; swarm

DROWN: (**see** "drench") dazzle; extinguish; immerse; inundate; overwhelm; stun

DROWSE: doze; nap; nod; sleep; slumber; DROWSY: (**see** "comatose") anesthetic; dormant; heavy; hypnogenic; hypnogenous; hypnogogic; hypnotic; inactive; indolent; lazy; lethargic; oscitant; sleepy; sluggish; somniferous; somnific; somnolent; somnorific; soporific; torpescent; torpid; DROWSINESS: dormancy; dullness; inactivity; indolence; latency; laziness; lethargy; narcosis; oscitancy; oscitation; quiescence; sleepiness; sluggishness; somnolence; sopor; stupor; torpidity; torpor

DRUDGE: (**see** "labor") fag; grind; grub; hack; moil; plod; slave; toil; work

DRUG: dope; dose; elixir; medicine; mixture; narcotic; opiate; pharmaceutic(al); philter; physic; potion; powder; preparation; prescription; purgative; purge; remedy; sedative; simple; specific; sulfa; tonic

DRUM: **v.** (**see** "beat") canvass; carp; drive; expel; force; frap; solicit; strike; tap; DRUM: **n.** barrel; bongo; cask; cylinder; fish; kettle; snare; tabor(et); tambourine; tattoo; timbal; timbrel; tom-tom; traps; tympanum

DRUNK(EN): **a.** alcoholic; bacchanal(ian); bacchantic; bagged; bibacious; bibulous; blind; boozy; cockeyed; crapulent; crapulous; crocked; dipsomaniacal; elated; excited; exhilarated; full; groggy; heady; imperious; inebriated; inebrious; intemperate; intoxicated; jagged; lit; loaded; numb; maudlin; mellow; merry; muddled; oiled; out; pickled; pie-eyed; pixilated; poisoned; polluted; potted; ripe; sloppy; soaked; sodden; soshed; sotted; sottish; soused; stewed; stinking; tight; tipsy; unsteady; wet; wobbly; DRUNK (ARD): **n.** alcoholic; bacchanal; bacchant; bacchante (fem.); bender; bibber; boozer; compotator; debauchee; dipsomaniac; drinker; guzzler; imbiber; inebriate; jag; libertine; lush; oenophilist; rummy; sot; souse; sponge; tippler; tipster; toper; tosspot; winebibber; DRUNKENNESS: (**see** "intoxication;") alcoholism; dipsomania; ebriety; ebriosity; inebriation; inebriety; jag; potomania

DRY: **v.** arefy; bake; blot; burn; cake; char; clean; dehumidify; dehydrate; desiccate; devitalize; empty; evaporate; exsiccate; parch; preserve; roast; scorch; sear; shrivel; solidify; toast; torrify; wipe; wither; DRY: **a.** adust; anhydrous; arenaceous; arid; baked; bare; barren; brittle; brut; caked; cynical; dehydrated; desiccated; desiccative; dried; droughty; dull; empty; impassive; insipid; jejune; juiceless; lean; lifeless; matter-of-fact; monotonous; parched; plain; sandy; sapless; scorched; seared; sec; sere; shriveled; siccate; solidified; stale; sterile; thirsty; torrid; unadorned; unemotional; uninteresting; unmoist(ened); unproductive; unwatered; unwet; vapid; wasted; withered; xerotic; DRYNESS: **see** "drought"

DUAL: (**see** "double") bilateral; bipartisan; coupled; doubled; dualistic; duplex; duplicate(d); gemeled; married; paired; reciprocal; synallagmatic; twin; two(fold); wed(ded)

DUB: (**see** "name") knight

DUBIOUS: (**see** "questionable") ambivalent; controversial; debatable; disputable; doubtful; equivocal; fishy; hesitant; moot; obscure; paradoxical; problematical; provocative; questioning; reluctant; seamy; shadowy; shady; shaky; suspicious; uncertain; unclear; unconvinced; unconvincing; undecided; undetermined; unlikely; unpromising; vague

DUCK: (**see** "avoid") bow; cringe; dip; dive; lower; plunge

DUCT: aorta; canal; channel; chute; conduit; course; ditch; flue: flume; furrow; gat; groove; meatus; opening; outlet; passage-(way); pipe; race; route; run; sinus; tube; vas; vessel

DUCTILE: (**see** "teachable") compliant; docile; dutiful; elastic; facile; flexible; influenceable; malleable; plastic; pliable; pliant; soft; tensile; tractable; trusting; yielding

DUD: botch; deficiency; drag; dummy; error; failure; fizzle; flop; fluff; lemon; misfit; mistake; pain

DUDE: (**see** "dandy") bean; Beau Brummel; blade; buck; coxcomb; dandiprat; fop; jackanapes; Johnny; macaroni; popinjay; swell; tenderfoot; toff

DUDGEON: (**see** "anger") annoyance; antagonism; bitterness; ill humor; indignation; ire; irritation; madness; malice; offense; pique; provocation; resentment; spleen; vexation

DUE: (**see** "adequate") appropriate; ascribable; collectable; coming; condign; enough; fair; fit(ting); in arrears; just(ifiable); justified; lawful; legal; meet; necessary; outstanding; owed; owing; payable; proper; reasonable; regular; requisite; right(ful); scheduled; sufficient; suitable; suited; traceable; uncollected; unpaid; unrecompensed; unremunerated; unrepaid; valid; worthy

DUEL: (**see** "fight") *affaire d'honneur*; box; combat; conflict; monomachy; rencontre; spar; DUELIST: **see** "fencer")

DUET: duo; pair; *pas de deux*; song; two

DULCET: agreeable; ariose; charming; harmonious; honeyed; melleous; melliferous; mellifluent; mellifluous; mellisonant; melodic; melodious; pleasant; pleasing; sirupy; syrupy; soft; sonorous; soothing; sugared; sugary; sweet(ened); tuneful

DULL: **v.** (**see** "blunt") blind; deluster; devitalize; discolor; dispirit; stupefy; DULL: **a.** adenoid(al); anserine; apathetic; asinine; benumbed; bland; blockheaded; blunt(ed); boring; bovine; brainless; bromidic; brutish; callous; claybrained; cloudy; colorless; comatose; common(place); conventional-(ized); crass; damp; dark; dead(ened); deadish; delustered; dense; devitalized; dim(med); dingy; discolored; distinctionless; doltish; drab; drear(y); drowsy; dry; dullard; dumb; dun; dusty; faded; fatiguing; flat; gaumless; gleamless; gloomy; gross; half-hearted; heavy; hebetate; hebetudinous; hopeless; humdrum; hyposensitive; idle; impassive; inactive; inanimate; indistinct; inert; inexcitable; inexpressive; infestive; insensate; insensible; insensitive; insipid; irksome; jejune; lackadaisical; lackluster; languid; languorous; leady; lethargic; lifeless; listless; logy; long(-winded); lumbering; lusterless; matte; mechanical; menial; mirthless; monolithic; monotonous; moronic; muddy; muffled; murky; musty; muted; muzzy; numb(ed); oafish; obtund; obtuse; opaque; oscitant; overcast; pale; palling; pedestrian; phlegmatic(al); pinheaded; plain; pleasureless; pointless; ponderous; prosaic(al); prosy; routine; routinized; sensationless; senseless; sheenless; slack; slow(-moving); sluggish; sodden; soporific; stagnant; stale; stereotyped; stereotypical; still; stodgy; stolid; stupid; stylized; subdued; tame; tedious; tepid; thick(headed); tiresome; trite; twodimensional; unadventurous; unalert; unalive; unamusing; unanimated; unappealable; unappealing; unattractive; unenlivened; unentertained; unentertaining; uneventful; unfeeling; unfunny; uninspired; unintelligent; uninteresting; unlively; unpointed; unresponsive; unsensational; un-showy; unstimulating; unwhetted; unzealous; vacant; vacuous; vapid; vexatious; wearisome; witless; wooden; DULLNESS: apathy; blandness; blues; bluntness; boredom; colorlessness; commonness; crassitude; depression; dimness; dishwater; dispiritedness; doldrums; drabness; dreariness; drowsiness; dumbness; ennui; fatigue; hebetude; idleness; impassivity; inaction; inactivity; inanity; indifference; indolence; inertia; inertness; infestivity; insensitivity; insipidity; jejunity; lackadaisy; lackluster; languor; lassitude; laziness; lethargy; lifelessness; listlessness; melancholia; mental retardation; mirthlessness; monotony; moronity; nonchalance; numbness; obtuseness; obtusity; opacity; oppression; oscitance; oscitancy; phlegm; platitude; ponderosity; prosaism; quiet(ude); retardation; sadness; simplicity; slackness;

sleep(iness); sloth(fulness); sluggishness; stagnancy; stereotypy; stodginess; stolidity; stupidity; supineness; supinity; tediousness; tedium; tepidity; torpidity; torpor; *tristesse*; triteness; vacuity; vapidity; witlessness; yawn

DULLARD: (**see** "boor" and "dunce") Boeotian; moron

DUMB: (**see** "mute" and "stupid") aphonic; crass; doltish; dull; foolish; ignorant; inarticulate; inexpressive; quiet; silent; speechless; taciturn; uncommunicative; unsmart; voiceless

DUMMY: **a. see** "artificial;" DUMMY: **n.** (**see** "fool") decoy; doll; dolt; dumbbell; effigy; figurehead; *homme de paille*; imitation; layout; manikin; mannequin; mannikin; nincompoop; pel; scarecrow; sham; simpleton; straw man

DUMP: (**see** "unload") discharge; drop; fire; jettison; plunge

DUN: **v.** (**see** "demand") ask; bill; darken; implore; importune; press; seek; solicit; urge; DUN: **a.** dark; dingy; drab; dull; gloomy; DUN: **n.** bill; solicitation

DUNCE: (**see** "fool") ass; blockhead; Boeotian; booby; coot; dolt; dope; dullard; dumbbell; dunderhead; dupe; goon; goose; half-wit; idiot; ignoramus; jughead; lout; moron; nincompoop; ninny; numbskull; nut; oaf

DUNG: defecation; dejecta (pl.); droppings; dump; egesta; ejecta(menta); excrement; excreta(pl.); excretion; feces; feculence; manure; ordure; rejectamenta; stool; waste

DUPE: **v.** (**see** "fool") bamboozle; befool; bilk; cheat; chouse; cozen; deceive; defraud; delude; fraud; gull; hoax; hoodwink; sell; take; touch; trick; victimize; DUPE: **n.** (**see** "fool") butt; cat's-paw; cull(y); gudgeon; gull; instrument; laughingstock; mark; monkey; pigeon; slave; tool; touch; victim

DUPLICATE: **v.** (**see** "copy") complement; counterfeit; double; echo; image; imitate; match; mate; mirror; reproduce; trace; DUPLICATE: **a. see** "same;" DUPLICATE: **n.** apograph; bis; burlesque; carbon (copy); copy; counterfeit; counterpart; ditto; double; drawing; dual; dummy; duple(x); echo; ectype; effigiation; effigy; extract; facsimile; figure; forgery; ikon; image;

imitation; likeness; mannequin; match; mate; mirror; mockery; parallel; picture; portrait; record; reduction; repetition; replica(tion); representation; reproduction; resemblance; sample; shadow; sketch; similitude; simulacrum; simulation; spare; statue; tracing; transcript(ion); twin; version

DUPLICITY: (see "trick") art(ifice); chicane(ry); cunning; deceit; deception; doubledealing; doubleness; fraud; guile; Machiavellianism; pretense; pretension; trickery

DURABLE: (see "constant") abiding; ageless; changeless; continuing; endless; enduring; everlasting; firm; incessant; indestructible; infinite; iron; lasting; leathery; permanent; perpetual; remaining; stable; stout; strong; tough; unchangeable; undying; DURABILITY: (see "constancy") agelessness; endlessness; endurance; eternality; eternalness; fixity; indestructibility; permanence; permanency; reliability; reliance; stability; steadfastness; steadiness; strength; tenacity; toughness; uniformity; wear(ability)

DURATION: (see "constancy") continuance; endurance; extent; imprisonment; incarceration; infinitude; infinity; lastingness; length; life; longanimity; period; permanence; permanency; perpetuality; perpetuity; prolongation; protension; quantity; restraint; space; span; standing; strength; term; time

DURESS: (see "coercion") stranglehold

DUSK: candlelight; crepuscle; evening; gloaming; gloom; indefiniteness; indistinctness; nightfall; semidarkness; twilight; DUSKY: (see "dim") cloudy; crepuscular;/ dark(ened); darkish; depressing; dusk; gloomy; indefinite; indistinct; murky; obscure; opaque; shadowy; swart(hy); tawny

DUST: (see "waste") ash(es); briss; confusion; coom(b); dirt; film; humiliation; lint; particles; powder; remains; smut; soot; stive; stour; trash; DUSTY: dirty; powdery; pulverous; pulverulent; sooty

DUTY: accountability; acknowledgment; agreement; amenability; assignment; bond; burden; business; calling; care; cess; char; charge; check; chore; compulsion; constraint; contract; courtesy; cross; debt; deference; deferentiality; demand; devoir; dharma; domain; employment; encumbrance; excise; fealty; feu; function; impost; indebtedness; integrity; IOU: job; jurisdiction; levy;

liability; load; mandate; mission; mortgage; must; necessity; note; oath; obligation; obstruction; office; onus; oughtness; pledge; position; post; pressure; promise; recognition; recognizance; reliability; rent(al); responsibility; right; role; service; sphere; station; stint; supervision; tariff; task; tax(ation); tie; toll; tour; tribute; trust; urgency; vocation; vow; work; DUTIFUL: accountable; childlike; courteous; customary; deferent(ial); devout; docile; duteous; filial; liable; pious; responsible; submissive; trustful

DWARF: v. (see "belittle") stunt; DWARF(ISH): a. (see "small") achondroplastic; diminutive; elfin; homuncular; lilliputian; little; microscopic; nanitic; nanoid; sesquipedalian; DWARF: n. bantam; crile; diminutive; durgan; elf; fairy; fay; gnome; homunculi (pl.); homunculus; lilliputian; manikin; mannequin; midget; miniature; nix; pigmy; pixy; puck; Rumpelstiltskin; runt; sesquipedal; shee; sprite; troll; DWARFISHNESS: achondroplasia; dwarfism; infinitesimality; minitude; nanism

DWELL: (see "abide") await; bide; bunk; consist; continue; delay; harp; house; inhabit; lie; linger; live; lodge; occupy; pause; perch; remain; reside; sojourn; stay; stop; tarry; tenant; DWELLING: (see "house") abode; apartment; bungalow; cabin; casa; castle; cottage; dar; domicile; establishment; eyrie; flat; habitation; home; hut; hutch; igloo; joint; manor; mansion; nest; palace; quarters; residence; teepee; tenement; tent; DWELLER: see "inhabitant"

DWINDLE: (see "abate") abridge; curtail; decline; decrease; degenerate; dim(inish); discolor; drain; drip; ebb; exhaust; fade; fail; fritter; lessen; narrow; peter (out); pine; recede; reduce; shorten; shrink; taper; thin; want; waste; DWINDLING: see "abatement"

DYE: v. (see "color") imbue; infuse; paint; stain; tinge; tint; DYE: n. (see "color") coloring; paint; pigment(ation); stain; tinge; tint

DYING: agonal; ceasing; declining; degenerating; dwindling; ebbing; failing; fey; going; *in articulo mortis*; *in extremis*; moribund; shrinking; wasting

DYNAMIC(AL): (see "energetic") active; advancing; driving; effective; efficient; expanding; forceful; high-powered; kinetic;

live; manly; potent; powerful; strong; vigorous; virile; vital

DYNASTY: authority; control; country; domain; dominance; domination; dominion; empire; estate; fief; government; hierarchy; influence; jurisdiction; kingdom; lordship; power; property; realm; region; reign; rule; seignority; seniority; sovereignty; succession; superiority; supremacy; suzerainty; territory; title; transcendency

E

EAGER: afire; aghast; agitated; agog; animated; anticipative; anxious; apprehensive; ardent; athirst; avaricious; avid; burning; craving; desirous; earnest; ecstatic; energetic; enthusiastic; esurient; excited; fain; fanatical; fearful; fervent; fervid; fiery; fired (up); fond; forward; glowing; gluttonous; greedy; heated; hot; hungry; impassioned; impatient; impetuous; importunate; inflamed; insatiable; intense; intent; keen; longing; passionate; rapturous; ravenous; restive; roused; solicitous; spirited; stirred; strenuous; strong; urgent; vehement; vigorous; vivacious; voracious; warm; willing; yare; yearning; zealous; EAGERNESS: (see "enthusiasm") ardency; ardentness; ardor; avidity; boldness; demonstrativeness; desire; ecstasy; empressement; energy; esurience; excitement; fainness; fanaticism; fervency; fervor; fire; forwardness; glow; greed; heat; intensity; passion; precocity; rapture; rush; solicitation; solicitude; speed; spirit; strength; stress; urgency; vehemence; vigor; vivacity; voracity; warmth; zeal(otry); zest

EAR: attention; audience; auricle; awareness; corn; handle; hearing; heed; knob; lug; pinna; projection; spike

EARLY: (see "before") aborning; ahead; betimes; elementary; embryonic; first; forward; incipient; matinal; matutinal; nascent; old; original; pioneer; precipitate; precipitous; primeval; primitive; primordial; punctual; seasonable; soon; sudden; timely; wee; young

EARN: (see "accomplish") achieve; acquire; attain; deserve; effect(uate); gain; get; make; merit; obtain; perform; procure; reach; realize; receive; secure; win; EARNED: see "condign;" EARNING(S): (see "income") dividends; fee(s); fruits; honorarium; interest; proceeds; produce; products; profits; receipts; rentals; resources; results; returns; revenue; royalty; salary; sales; stipend; taxes; tolls; wage(s)

EARNEST: (see "serious") ardent; busy; decided; determined; devoted; devotional; devout; diligent; eager; fervent; firm; fixed; grave; immovable; importunate; intense; intent; obstinate; prayerful; resolute; sedate; sincere; sober; solemn; staid; steady; studious; thoughtful; urgent; warm; weighty; zealous; EARNESTNESS: adherence; allegiance; ardency; ardor; ascesis; austerity; authoritativeness; criticality; cruciality; danger; determination; devotedness; devotion; diligence; eagerness; enthusiasm; faith(fulness); fealty; fervency; fervor; fidelity; firmness; gravity; heaviness; importance; intenseness; intensity; love; loyalty; resolution; reverence; sedateness; seriosity; seriousness; significance; sincerity; sobriety; solemnity; steadfastness; steadiness; studiouness; thoughtfulness; unction; warmth; weight; zeal(otry)

EARTH: argil; bole; clay; cosmos; country; dirt; erd; globe; ground; kaolin(e); land; loess; mire; mud; orb; people; planet; sod; soil; sphere; terra; *terra firma*; vale; world; EARTHLY: carnal; cosmopolitan; factual; global; material; mortal; mundane; planetary; possible; profane; realistic; secular; sublunary; telluric; temporal; terrene; terrestrial; worldly; EARTHY: (see "vulgar") animal; base; basic; carnal; chthonian; chthonic; clayey; coarse; dirty; elementary; Falstaffian; fleshy; gross; gutty; hedonic; hedonish; Hogarthian; low; material; mortal; mundane; pagan; practical; profane; Rabelaisian; racy; realistic; risqué; salty; sensual; sordid; temporal; terrestrial; unspiritual; visceral; worldly

EASE: v. (see "check") abate; adjust; aid; allay; alleviate; ameliorate; appease; assist; assuage; better; calm; comfort; compromise; conciliate; console; cure; cushion; decrease; defend; desist; dim(inish); disburden; ebb; excuse; expedite; extenuate; facilitate; fall; flatter; free; further; gratify; grease; heal; help; justify; lessen; lighten; loosen; lower; lubricate; mask; meliorate; mellow; mince; mitigate; moderate; modify; mollify; oil; pacify; palliate; placate; please; quicken; quiet(en); recede; reduce; relax; release; relieve; remedy; repose; rest; rid; salve;

screen; set(tle); slack(en); slow; smooth; soften; solace; soothe; stop; subside; thin; tranquilize; treat; unburden; unload; varnish; veil; veneer; vindicate; wane; weaken; EASE: **n.** (**see** "check") abatement; address; adjustment; adroitness; allayment; alleviation; amelioration; appeasement; assuagement; balm; betterment; calmness; comfort; compromise; consolation; content(ment); convalescence; cure; detachment; diminishment; diplomacy; disburdenment; disengagement; easiness; expertise; expertness; extenuation; facility; flattery; freedom; grace; gratification; holiday; idleness; inunction; knack; leisure(liness); lessening; life of Riley; lightening; melioration; mitigation; moderation; mollification; naturalness; oil; otiosity; pacification; palliation; peace; placation; pleasure; poise; primrose path; quiet(ness); quietude; readiness; recreation; reduction; relaxation; relief; remedy; repose; respite; rest; salve; savoir faire; security; smoothness; solace; suavity; suppleness; surcease; tact(fulness;) tranquility; treatment; unconstraint; unction; unguent; unrestraint; urbanity; vacation; EASING: **a.** alleviative; alleviatory; ameliorative; appeasing; assuaging; calming; comforting; consolatory; consoling; diminishing; disburdening; extenuating; gratifying; lenitive; lessening; lightening; meliorative; mitigative; mollifying; nepenthean; pacificatory; palliative; palliatory; placative; pleasing; quieting; relaxing; relieving; resting; slowing; softening; solacing; soothing; tranquilizing; EASING: **n.** (**see** "ease") alleviation; assuagement; *détente*; mitigation; mollification; nepenthe; palliation; tranquilization

EAST: Asia; eastland; estriche; Levant; Orient; sunrise

EASY: (**see** "simple") accessible; amiable; apathetic; artless; assuasive; bland; calm; casual; cavalier; cheap; clear; clever; comfortable; complaisant; conventional; *coulant* courteous; cushy; deft; *dégagé*; dexterous; easygoing; effortless; emollient; expert; extroverted; facile; favonian; flexible; fluent; fluid; free; gentle; glib; gradual; halcyon; hands-down; indifferent; indulgent; informal; ingenious; ingratiating; insipid; jaunty; kind(ly); laborless; lax; laxative; leisurely; lenient; lenitive; light; low-pressure; manageable; mild; mitigating; mitigatory; mollifying; natural; nepenthean; obvious; outgiving; outgoing; pacificatory; painless; palliative; palliatory; peaceable; peaceful; placative; placid; pleasing; plush; quick;

quiet(ing); ready; relaxed; relaxing; relieving; resting; royal; skilled; skillful; slow(ly); slowing; smooth; soft(ening); solacing; soothing; suave; supple; susceptible; tame; tender; tranquil(izing); unagitated; unconcerned; unconstrained; unhasty; unhurried; unrestrained; unruffled; untroublesome; urbane; wishy-washy; yielding

EASYGOING: (**see** "carefree" and "easy") calm; placid

EAT: banquet; board; bolt; bore; canker; consume; corrode; defeat; destroy; devour; digest; dine; dispatch; down; erode; fare; feast; feed; forage; fret; gnaw; gobble; gorge; graze; grub; gulp; ingest; ingurgitate; manducate; nibble; perforate; ravage; rust; sate; sup; swallow; take; taste; tuck (away); use; waste; wear; EATABLE: **a.** (**see** "edible") alimentary; cibarious; comestible; delicious; esculent; sapid; tasteful; tasty; EATABLE: **n.** (**see** "food") comestible; edible; tidbit; EATING: **a.** caustic; consuming; corrosive; devouring; edacious; erosive; fretting; gnawing; ingestible; ingestive; voracious; EATING: **n.** assimilation; consumption; devourment; dining; ingesting; ingurgitation; manducation

EBB: (**see** "abate") decay; deceive; decline; dim(inish); fail; fall; lessen; recede; reflux; regress; retire; retreat; return; revive; sink; taper; wane; waste

EBULLIENT: (**see** "enthusiastic") agitated; boiling; bubbling; dithyrambic; ecstatic; excessive; exuberant; fervent; feverish; glad; joyful; joyous; overflowing; seething; stewing; EBULLIENCE: (**see** "joy") bubble; ecstasy; enthusiasm; exuberance

ECCENTRIC: **a.** (**see** "abnormal") aberrant; anomalous; atypic(al); bizarre; cantankerous; capricious; comical; cranky; crotchety; curious; deviating; dotty; droll; erratic; fantastic; far-out; grotesque; idiosyncratic; irregular; nutty; odd(ball); off-center; *outré*; peculiar; quaint; queer; singular; strange; uncommon; unconventional; unusual; wayward; whimsical; ECCENTRIC: **n.** aberrant; beatnik; Bohemian; comic; crank; deviant; gink; oddball; queer; ECCENTRICITY: (**see** "abnormality") aberration; bizarrerie; brainstorm; caprice; dottiness; fantasticality; fantasticalness; idiosyncrasy; kink; lunacy; nuttiness; oddity; oddness; peculiarity; queerness; quiddity; quirk; singularity; twist; whimsicality

ECCLESIASTIC(AL): **a.** churchly; clerical; religious; sectarian; ECCLESIASTIC: **n.** (**see** "clergyman") abbé; abbot; churchman; cleric(al); curé; divine; minister; padre; pastor; *père*; prelate; priest; prior

ECHO: **v.** (**see** "mimic") answer; ape; copy; duplicate; emulate; imitate; iterate; mirror; mock; parody; parrot; rebound; reduplicate; reflect; repeat; repercuss; reply; resound; respond; reverberate; revoice; ricochet; ridicule; ring; sham; simulate; ECHO: **n.** answer; apism; copy; echoing; emulation; imitation; iteration; mimesis; mimetism; mimic; mockery; parody; parrotry; polyphony; rebound; reflection; repetition; repercussion; reply; response; result; reverberation; ricochet; ridicule; sham; simulation; survival; trace; vestige; ECHOIC: imitative; iterative; onomatopoe(t)ic(al); polyphemic; polyphonous; reduplicative; repercussive; reverberative; reverberatory

ÉCLAT: applause; brilliance; brilliancy; dash; energy; fame; glory; honor; pageantry; pomp(osity); praise; publicity; renown; repute; resplendence; resplendency; splendor

ECLIPSE: (**see** "shadow") beat; cloud; darken; dim(inish); excel; extinguish; hide; obscure; outshine; reduce; shade; shroud; stain; sully; surpass; veil

ECONOMIZE: (**see** "save") eke; husband; manage; pare; patch; reduce; retrench; scrape; scrimp; spare; squeeze; sting; supplement; ECONOMY: (**see** "care") caution; conciseness; efficiency; frugality; husbandry; management; order; organization; parsimony; plan; prudence; reduction; saving; scheme(s); structure; system; thrift; ECONOMIC(AL): careful; cautious; chary; circumspect; frugal; material; particular; planned; profitable; provident; prudent; reserving; saving; sparing; stingy; thrifty; underspending; wary

ECSTASY: (**see** "bliss") animation; blitheness; buoyancy; cheer(fulness); delight; ebullience; emotion; euphrosyne; exaltation; excitement; exhilaration; exuberance; exultation; feeling; festivity; frenzy; fun; gaiety; geniality; gladness; glee; jocularity; jocundity; jollification; joviality; joy(fulness) joyousness; jubilation; larkiness; levity; lightheartedness; madness; merrymaking; mirth; nepenthe; rapture; rejoicing; revelry; rhapsody; sportiveness; sprightliness; trance; transport; vivacity; yeastiness; ECSTATIC: **see** "blissful"

EDACITY: (**see** "appetite") avarice; gluttony; greed; voraciousness; voracity

EDDY: **v.** (**see** "gyrate") circle; reverse; rotate; spin; spiral; swirl; turn; twirl; whirl(pool); EDDY: **n.** agitation; backlash; bore; Charybdis; circle; current; flurry; gyration; spasm; spin; spiral; swirl; turn; twirl; vortex; whirl(pool)

EDGE: **v.** (**see** "border") band; bind; bound; fringe; hem; hone; inch; move; ring; sharpen; sidle; skirt; trim; whet; EDGE: **n.** *or* EDGING: abutment; acrimony; advantage; ambit; arris; band; bank; border; boundary; bounds; braid; brim; brink; circumference; compass; confine; connection; contiguity; crest; decoration; design; division; effectiveness; end; energy; escarpment; fimbriation; flange; flap; force; frill; fringe; front-(ier); gall; girth; hem; intensity; joint; junction; juncture; keenness; labrum; lace; lead; leeway; limbus; limit(s); line; lip; majority; marge; margin(ality); mark; odds; overage; perimeter; periphery; precipice; rand; relish; rim; ring; ruche; savor; selvage; sharpness; shore; side; skirt(ing); spur; stimulus; strip; synchondrosis; syzygy; tangency; tassel; tip; tolerance; trim; union; verge; vigor; wall; zest

EDIBLE: **a.** alimentary; appetiable; cibarious; comestible; eatable; esculent; nonpoisonous; succulent; EDIBLE: **n. see** "food"

EDICT: (**see** "command") act; announcement; arret; ban; behest; bull; decree; fiat; irade; judgment; law; mandate; mandatum; manifesto; notice; order; ordinance; proclamation; pronouncement; pronunciamento; pronunciation; rescript; rule; ukase; writ

EDIFY: **see** "elevate" and "enlighten"

EDIT: adapt; alter; amend; blue-pencil; check; compile; correct; cut; delete; eliminate; emend; issue; omit; prepare; publish; read; redact; refine; revise; verify; EDITION: (**see** "version") form; impression; issue; printing; production; EDITOR: diaskeuast; *rédacteur*; redactor; reviser; scribe; writer

EDUCATE: acculturate; acquaint; admonish; advance; advise; apprise; brainwash; bring (up); civilize; coach; condition; conventionalize; counsel; cultivate; debarbarize; develop; direct; discipline; disclose; divulge; drill; edify; elucidate; enlighten; expand; extend; grow; humanize; illume; illuminate;

impart; inculcate; indoctrinate; inform; instruct; irradiate; notify; nurse; nurture; open; perfect; persuade; polish; prepare; raise; rationalize; rear; refine; school; socialize; strengthen; superintend; supervise; teach; tell; train; tutor; urbanize; EDUCATED: accomplished; advanced; bookish; broadened; certified; civilized; coached; conditioned; conventionalized; cultivated; cultured; debarbarized; degreed; developed; didactic(al); disciplined; donnish; drilled; enlightened; erudite; experienced; expert; graduated; humanized; informed; instructed; knowledgeable; knowledged; learned; lettered; literate; nursed; nurtured; pansophic; pedantic; perfected; persuaded; philomathic (al); polished; polymathic(al); prepared; raised; reared; recondite; refined; scholarly; schooled; skilled; socialized; strengthened; supervised; taught; trained; tutored; versed; EDUCATION: (see "competency") acculturation; advice; background; breeding; competence; conditioning; counsel; cultivation; culture; curriculum; development; direction; discipline; disclosure; divulgence; drilling; éclaircissement; edification; elucidation; endowment; enlightenment; equipment; erudition; humanization; illumination; inculcation; indoctrination; information; instruction; knowledge; learning; luminosity; notification; nurture; pedagogics; pedagogy; preparation; refinement; revelation; satisfaction; scholarliness; scholarship; scholasticism; schooling; skill; strengthening; study; teaching; three R's; training; truth; tuition; wisdom; EDUCATIONAL: academic; collegiate; didactic; disciplinary; doctrinal; edificatory; educative; enlightening; illuminant; illuminating; illuminative; informative; instructional; instructive; pedagogic(al); propaedeutic(al); scholastic(al); supervisory; training; tutorial; EDUCATOR: see "teacher"

EDUCE: arrive (at); call; cause; derive; discover; disengage; drag; draw; elicit(ate); evolve; extort; extract; infer; provoke; pull; pump; stretch; wrest; wring

EERIE: bizarre; curious; eldritch; fantastic; frightening; frightful; ghastly; ghostly; grotesque; haunting; horrible; horrific; jittery; mysterious; nervous; odd; peculiar; phantasmagorical; phantasmal; phantasmic; queer; scary; skittish; spookish; strange; uncanny; weird

EFFACE: (see "erase") annul; blot; cancel; dele(te); destroy; eliminate; eradicate; expunge; kill; nullify; obliterate; overshadow; remove; sponge

EFFECT: v. (see "do") accomplish; achieve; actuate; arouse; cause; compass; conclude; conduct; constitute; consummate; contrive; create; end; establish; execute; exert; fashion; finalize; finish; found; fulfill; gain; guide; impress; induce; issue; make; manipulate; move; negotiate; obtain; operate; perform; produce; reach; realize; secure; shape; succeed; take; transact; work; EFFECT: n. accomplishment; advantage; aftermath; appearance; causation; cause; conclusion; consequence; consummation; development; drift; encroachment; end; essence; event; fact; finish; force; fruit; gist; growth; impact; impingement; import; imprint; influence; infringement; intention; issue; manifestation; mark; outcome; performance; product; purport; purpose; reality; realization; residual; residuum; result; scar; sequel; stamp; upshot; work; EFFECTIVE or EFFECTUAL: (see "great") able; authoritative; capable; cogent; consequential; devastating; direct; dynamic; efficacious; efficient; emphatic; executive; forceful; impactful; impressive; influential; mighty; operant; operative; overwhelming; patent; pleasing; potent; powerful; productive; satisfying; sovereign; strong; substantial; substantious; superior; supreme; telling; valid; vigorous; virtual; weighty; EFFECTIVENESS: (see "greatness") edge; effectivity; efficaciousness; efficacy; energy; force; power; presence; prestige; strength; voltage; wattage; weight

EFFEMINATE: (see "delicate") emasculate; emotional; epicene; fastidious; finical; gentle; girlish; gynecian; gynecic; maiden(ish); maidenly; mild; milky; miss-nancyish; muliebrial; silken; silky; sissy; soft; timorous; unmanly; voluptuous; weak; womanish; womanlike; womanly; EFFEMINACY: (see "delicacy") feminality; femineity; femininity; gentleness; girlishness; maidenhood; maidenliness; muliebriety; weakness; womanity; womanliness

EFFERVESCE: aerate; boil; bubble; churn; cook; ebulliate; ferment; fizz; foam; froth; fume; gurgle; hiss; rage; rave; steam; stew; EFFERVESCENT: aboil; agitated; boiling; bubbling; buoyant; churning; dithyrambic; ebullient; ecstatic; effusive; elastic; exuberant; foaming; foamy; frothy; fuming; gay; gleeful; intense; seething; steaming; violent; volatile; zestful

EFFETE: (see "weak") barren; decadent; degenerate(d); enervated; exhausted; fruitless; idle; old; outmoded; out-of-date; purposeless; soft; spent; tired; unfruitful; unproductive; unprolific; wearied; wearisome; worn(out)

EFFICACY: (see "power") capacity; cogency; competence; competency; dint; effectiveness; efficiency; energy; force; pep; potency; strength; vigor; virtue; vitality

EFFICIENT: (see "competent") able; accomplished; adept; businesslike; capable; clever; dexterous; effective; effectual; efficacious; expedient; expeditious; experienced; expert; ingenious; operant; potent; practical; professional; proficient; purposeful; satisfactory; skilled; skillful; strong; systematic; virtuosic; well-balanced; well-oiled; EFFICIENCY: (see "competence") ability; accomplishment; capability; capacity; competency; consummation; economy; effectiveness; effectivity; effectuality; efficacy; energy; expedition; expertise; finesse; ingenuity; performance; potency; power; productivity; proficiency; skill(fulness); strength; virtuosity

EFFIGY: (see "duplicate") copy; doll; dummy; effigiation; facsimile; figure; icon; image; likeness; manikin; model; picture; portrait; representation; simulacrum; statue

EFFLUVIUM: aura; cachet; discharge; effluvia (pl.); efflux(ion); emanation; exhaust; fetidness; fetidity; fetor; flatus; flux; gas; mephitis; miasma; nidor; odor; outflow; outpouring; perfume; putridity; reek; scent; smell; sniff; stench; stink; vapor; waste

EFFORT: act(ion); activity; advance(ment); animation; application; assiduity; assiduousness; attempt; automation; bustle; care; college try; conatus; conspiration; contention; crusade; drive; dynamism; endeavor; energy; enterprise; essay; evolution; exertion; expenditure; flurry; force; hurry; hustle; impetus; impulse; labor; locomotion; lunge; machination; maneuver; march; might; momentum; motion; movement; nisus; operation; pain(s); perspiration; power; produce; progress(ion); pull; result; rhythm; shift; spadework; speed; spurt; stab; start; stir; strain; stress; stride; strife; stroke; struggle; sweat; sweep; tempo; toil; travel; trend; trial; trouble; try; tug; undertaking; velocity; work

EFFRONTERY: (see "boldness") assurance; audacity; brass; brazenness; cheek(iness); daring; gall; gallantry; guts; immodesty; impudence; insolence; insolency; nerve; offense; offensiveness; presumption; sassiness; sauciness; shamelessness; temerity

EFFULGENCE: (see "brightness") brilliance; éclat; glare; glory; glow; luster; radiance; rutilation; sheen; shine; splendor

EFFUSIVE: (see "unrestrained") clamorous; demonstrative; ebullient; emotional; expressive; extravagant; exuberant; generous; gushing; gushy; immodest; lavish; maudlin; mawkish; outpouring; prodigal; scaturient; sentimental; unreserved; EFFUSIVENESS: ebullience; ebulliency; effusion; emotion; extravagance; exuberance; exuberancy; generosity; immodesty; lavishness; mawkishness; outpouring; prodigality; sentimentality; unreserve; unrestraint

EGG: v. see "urge;" EGG: n. idea; nit; ova (pl.); ovum; seed; spore

EGO: Atman; egoity; egotism; id; jivatma; self(-esteem); selfhood; selfishness; will; EGOISM: (see "conceit") narcissism; solipsism; EGOTISM: (see "conceit") arrogance; assurance; boastfulness; dogmatism; ego(centricity); egocentrism; egomania; esteem; haughtiness; pomp(osity); presumption; pride; self-centeredness; self-importance; selfishness; vanity; EGO(T)ISTIC (AL); (see "conceited") arrogant; boastful; bombastic; dogmatic; egocentric; egomaniac (al); haughty; hubristic; inflated; opinionated; overweening; pompous; pragmatic; presumptive; presumptuous; prideful; priggish; proud; self-centered; self-important; selfish; showy; vain(glorious); EGO(T)IST: dogmatist; egocentric; egomaniac; hedonist; prig

EGREGIOUS: (see "bad") asocial; execrable; extraordinary; extravagant; extreme; flagrant; gross; notorious; shocking; unending; vicious

EGRESS: (see "exit") departure; door(way); egression; emergency; issuance; outlet; postern; vent

EJECT: banish; bounce; cashier; cast; chuck; debar; deprive; disbar; discard; discharge; dislodge; dismiss; dispossess; divorce; drive (out); emit; eruct(ate); evict; exclude; exile; expectorate; expel; fire; fling; force (out); heave; hurl; impel; jilt; junk; molt; oust;

pitch; project; regurgitate; remove; rid; sack; send; shake; shed; sling; slough; spew; spit; spout; spurt; throw (out); toss; unfrock; unhorse; void; vomit; EJECTION: **see** "eviction"

EKE: (**see** "economize") elongate; enlarge; fill; increase; lengthen; magnify; patch; squeeze; stretch; supplement

ELABORATE: **v.** adorn; amplify; array; beautify; bedeck; brighten; color; deck; develop; devise; diamondize; discuss; dress; embellish; emblazon; embroider; enhance; enrich; expand; expatiate; explain; fancify; fashion; garnish; gild; improve; labor; lard; ornament(ate); paint; plan; plot; polish; refine; rouge; trim; unfold; ELABORATE: **a.** adorned; bedecked; complex; complicated; deluxe; detailed; diligent; dressy; embellished; exotic; extravagant; full; gaudy; great; intricate; laborious; large; minute; ornate; ostentatious; painstaking; painted; rococo; showy; spectacular; stupenduous; sumptuous; ELABORATION: (**see** "ornamentation") adornment; atmosphere; detail; development; elegancy; embellishment; enhancement; exegesis; expatiation; explanation; fancification; frill; garnishment; improvement; opulence; ornament(ation); paint; polish; refinement; rouge; show; sumptuosity

ÉLAN: (**see** "zest") ardor; brilliance; dash; eagerness; enthusiasm; spirit; verve; vigor; zeal(otry)

ELAPSE: (**see** "die") end; expire; glide; go; lapse; pass; roll; run; slip; stop; stretch; terminate

ELASTIC: (**see** "flexible") adaptable; amendable; buoyant; changeable; effervescent; expansive; limber; lithe; lively; plastic; pliant; receptive; resilient; rubbery; springy; supple; tolerant; volatile; ELASTICITY: (**see** "flexibility") bounce; buoyancy; effervescence; expansiveness; give; limberness; litheness; plasticity; receptivity; resilience; resiliency; spring(iness); stretch; suppleness; tolerance; volatility

ELATE: animate; buoy; cheer; delight; ecstasize; enliven; enrapture; exalt; excite; exhilarate; exult; fire; flush; inflate; inspire; inspirit; intoxicate; levitate; lift; lilt; please; raise; spur; stimulate; stir; support; sustain; ELATED: affable; airy; animated; blissful; blithe(some); bright; buoyant; carefree; cheerful; cheery; chipper; cocky; courteous;

debonair(e); dithyrambic; ecstatic; enlivened; enraptured; eud(a)emonic(al); euphoric; exalted; excited; exhilarated; exuberant; exultant; fey; fired; floating; flushed; gay; glad; glowing; gracious; happy; heady; high; hopeful; inflated; inspired; inspirited; intoxicated; jaunty; joyful; joyous; levitated; lifted; light(hearted); lilted; lithe; lively; nonchalant; perky; pleased; prideful; rapturous; spirited; sprightly; spriteful; spry; spurred; stimulated; suave; transported; uppish; uppity; urbane; wild; ELATION: airiness; bliss; blitheness; delight; ecstasy; elatement; eud(a)emonia; euphoria; exhilaration; exuberation; exultation; glow; happiness; joy; levitation; lightheartedness; rapture; spirit(edness); sprightliness; transport

ELDER(LY): (**see** "aged") anile; antiquated; *d'un certain âge*; first; former; geriatric; gray; mature; old(er); prior; senile; senior; superannuated; venerable; veteran; ELDERLINESS: (**see** "senility") anility; antiquity; senescence; seniority; superannuation; venerability; ELDEST: (**see** "oldest") earliest; eigne; firstborn

ELDRITCH: eerie; frightful; ghastly; uncanny; weird

ELECT: **v.** (**see** "choose") authorize; call; cull; decide; designate; direct; dispose; fix; judge; name; opt(ate); ordain; order; pick; prefer; resolve; select; settle; take; vote; will; ELECT: **a.** (**see** "elite") choice; chosen; cream; exclusive; selected

ELEEMOSYNARY: **see** "charitable"

ELEGANT: (**see** "beautiful") chic; choice; classical; comely; concinnous; Corinthian; correct; courtly; dainty; dashing; deluxe; dignified; dressy; excellent; exquisite; extra (ordinary); fashionable; fine; genteel; golden; gorgeous; grand; kingly; lofty; luxuriant; luxurious; majestic; modish; neat; noble; ornate; pleasing; plush; polished; polite; posh; precise; prime; queenly; rare; *recherché*; refined; restrained; rich; royal; sharp; sleek; smart; *soigné*; *soignée* (fem); splendid; stately; stylish; sumptuous; superb; super(fine); superior; supernacular; supernal; tasteful; ultra; urbane; well-groomed; ELEGANCE: (**see** "beauty") comeliness; concinnity; courtliness; dignity; ease; excellence; finery; gaiety; gentility; grace; kingliness; luxe; luxuriance; luxuriousness; luxury; neatness; opulence; opulency; polish; precision; queenliness; refinement; restraint;

richness; *savoir faire*; *savoir vivre*; simplicity; sumptuosity; taste; urbanity

ELEGY: dirge; lament(ation); monody; poem; requiem; threnody

ELEMENT(S): atom; component; constituent; detail; essence; factor; feature; germ; ingredient; integral; integrant; item; link; makeup; material; metal; note; origin; part; pattern; phase; piece; principal; property; substance; unit; woof; ELEMENTARY *or* ELEMENTAL: abecedarian; abecedary; basal; base; basic; basilar; canonical; classic(al); componental; crude; earliest; earthy; easy; first; fundamental; hypostatic(al); inchoate; incomplex; ingrained; inherent; initiatory; innate; integral; intrinsic; introductory; irreducible; lawful; natural; nominal; orthodox; plain; prescribed; primal; primary; primeval; primitive; primordial; pure; rude; rudimental; rudimentary; simple; substrate; ultimate; uncombined; unmixed; vital

ELEPHANTINE: (**see** "huge") clumsy; enormous; heavy-footed; immense; massive; pachydermatous; ponderous; thick-skinned

ELEVATE: advance; aggrandize; aggravate; animate; augment; better; boost; buoy; cheer; civilize; climb; develop; dignify; edify; elate; endow; enhance; enlarge; enlighten; enliven; ennoble; enrich; erect; escalate; esteem; exaggerate; exalt; excite; exhilarate; expand; extol; fire; fly; forward; further; gladden; glorify; graduate; heave; heft; heighten; help; hoist; honor; idealize; idyllize; improve; increase; inspire; inspirit; intensify; intoxicate; invigorate; jack; kite; lift; refresh; respect; soar; spiritualize; stimulate; strengthen; sublimate; titillate; tower; transcend; upgrade; worsen; ELEVATED: **see** "dignified" and "exalted;" ELEVATION: advancement; aggrandizement; aggravation; edification; eminence; enhancement; enlargement; enlightenment; ennoblement; enrichment; escalation; esteem; exaggeration; exaltation; exhilaration; expansion; furtherance; glorification; grade; graduation; heave; height(ening); help; highness; hill; mount(ain); ornamentation; plan; position; progression; promotion; push; raise; ridge; rise; stature; sublimation; transcendency; worsening; ELEVATOR: escalator; hoist; lift

ELF: brownie; child; dwarf; fairy; fay; gnome; goblin; imp; kobold; nis(se); nix(ie); ouphe; pixie; puck; shee; sprite

ELICIT: (**see** "educe") call; cause; derive; discover; drag; draw; elicitate; evoke; extort; extract; gain; provoke; pull; pump; stretch; wrest; wring

ELIGIBLE: (**see** "competent") able; advantageous; apt; available; desirable; educated; entitled fit(ted); licensed; meet; prepared; qualified; ready; suitable; trained; worthy; ELIGIBILITY: **see** "fitness"

ELIMINATE: (**see** "abolish") abrogate; annihilate; annul; balance; banish; blot (out); burn; cancel; cast (out); clear; consume; cut; decimate; defecate; dele(te); demolish; deracinate; destroy; detach; devastate; discharge; dislodge; displace; drop; efface; eject; epilate; eradicate; erase; evict; excise; exclude; excrete; expel; expunge; exterminate; extinguish; extirpate; ignore; invalidate; kill; level; neutralize; nullify; obliterate; offset; omit; ooze; oust; overshadow; perspire; prune; purge; quash; raze; reduce; relinquish; remove; rescind; resect; revoke; rid; root (out); run; scratch; screen; scrub; separate; sift; sponge; stamp (out); strike; supplant; suppress; sweat; undo; unroot; uproot; urinate; vacate; vitiate; void; ELIMINATION: (**see** "cancellation") abolishment; abolition; abrogation; banishment; decimation; defecation; deletion; deracination; destruction; detachment; disaffirmance; disaffirmation; discharge; dislodgement; displacement; divestation; eviction; excision; exclusion; excretion; expulsion; expunction; extirpation; invalidation; neutralization; nullification; obliteration; ooze; ouster; perspiration; recision; remission; removal; rescission; reversal; riddance; scratch; scrubbing; separation; supplantation; suppression; sweat; undoing; urination; vitiation; write-off

ELITE: **a.** (**see** "best") choice; cream; *nulli secundus*; select; superior; ELITE: **n.** (**see** "aristocrat") aristocracy; aristoi (pl.); *bas bleu*; best; blueblood; bluestocking; choice; *corps d'elite* (pl.); cream; *crème de la crème*; elect; elitist; flower; *gens de condition* (pl.); gentry; magnifico; *ne plus supra*; *ne plus ultra*; royalty; society; superior; supernaculum

ELIXIR: arcanum; catholicon; cure-all; essence; medicine; panacea; placebo; stimulant; tonic

ELONGATE(D): distended; extended; increased; lengthened; lengthy; prolate; prolonged; protracted; stretched

ELOPE: (see "leave") abscond; absquatulate; depart; escape; flee; quit; ELOPEMENT: (see "leave") abscondence; absquatulation; departure; escape; quittance

ELOQUENT: Ciceronian; Demosthenian; Demosthenic; expressive; facund; flowery; fluent; glib; golden-tongued; grandiloquent; impassioned; magniloquent; oratorial; oratoric(al); powerful; rubescent; silver-tongued; vocal; voluble; ELOQUENCE: eloquentness; expressiveness; expressivity; facundity; grandiloquence; grandiosity; magniloquence; oratory; rubescence; volubility

ELSE: (see "additional") apart; beside(s); different; instead; other(wise)

ELUDE: (see "avoid") baffle; cheat; delude; dodge; escape; evade; fence; flee; fly; foil; frustrate; hide; outfox; outwit; parry; shun; slip; ELUSIVE: (see "deceptive") baffling; cunning; eely; ephemeral; equivocal; evasive; fleeting; foxy; fugitive; illusory; impalpable; insidious; intangible; lubric(i)ous; oily; saponaceous; serpentine; subtle; surreptitious; ELUSIVENESS: (see "deception") evasion; fugitivity; insidiousness; intangibility; lubricity; oiliness; subtlety

EMACIATED: atrophied; attenuated; cachectic; cachexic; cadaveric; cadaverous; enfeebled; fleshless; gaunt; lank; lean; macilent; meager; narrow; poor; skeletal; skinny; tabescent; thin; wasted; EMACIATION: attenuation; cachexia; feebleness; gauntness; lankness; leanness; macies; marasmus; meagerness; poverty; skinniness; tabefaction; tabes; tabescence; waste

EMANATE: (see "arise") derive; emerge; emit; exhale; flow; issue; loom; materialize; originate; proceed; radiate; reek; rise; spread; spring; stem; EMANATION: (see "effluvium") ancestry; aura; cachet; consequence; derivation; discharge; ectoplasm; efflux(ion); effulgence; emergence; emission; flow; flux; gas; halo; issuance; issue; materialization; miasma; nidor; odor; origin(ation); outcome; outflow; perfume; provenance; radiation; rise; spread; spring; vapor

EMANCIPATE: (see "free") acquit; affranchize; clear; deliver; discharge; dislodge; exempt; liberate; loose(n); manumit; pretermit; release; rescue; unfetter; unshackle

EMBARK: (see "begin") board; commence; depart; engage; enlist; invest; sail; start; venture

EMBARRASS: abase; abash; annoy; awe; bother; chagrin; complicate; compromise; confound; confuse; consternate; cow; daunt; dent; discomfit; discomfort; discompose; disconcert; discountenance; dishearten; distress; disturb; entangle; faze; floor; flummox; fluster; frighten; hamper; harass; hinder; humble; humiliate; impair; impede; inconvenience; intimidate; mortify; overawe; perplex; plague; puzzle; rattle; shame; slap; squelch; subdue; torment; trouble; uncomfort; vex; worry; EMBARRASSMENT: abasement; abashment; accident; annoyance; awkwardness; bother; chagrin; compromise; confusion; consternation; constraint; contretemps; difficulty; disagreement; disappointment; discomfiture; discomfort; discomposure; disconcertion; discountenance; dismay; disquiet(ude); distress; disturbance; encumbrance; entanglement; exigency; fracas; fright; frustration; gaucherie; hampering; harassment; hindrance; humiliation; imbroglio; impediment; incident; inconvenience; intimidation; mischance; mishap; mistake; misunderstanding; mortification; obloquy; obstacle; perplexity; perturbation; scrape; shame; slap; slip; squelch; tension; torment; trouble; unease; uneasiness; vexation; EMBARRASSED: abashed; awkward; bothered; chagrined; compromised; confused; cowed; daunted; discomfited; discomposed; disturbed; floored; flurried; flustered; foolish; hampered; hangdog; humbled; humiliated; impeded; mortified; nonplused; perplexed; plagued; puzzled; rattled; shamed; troubled; uneasy; vexed

EMBEDDED: deep-seated; encapsulated; enclosed; ensconced; impacted; nested; nidulate; penetrated

EMBELLISH: (see "elaborate") adorn; amplify; array; beautify; bedeck; brighten; deck; decorate; diamondize; distort; dress; emblazon; embroider; enhance; enrich; garnish; gild; lard; ornament; paint; polish; sequin; rouge; trim; EMBELLISHED: see "ornate;" EMBELLISHMENT: see "ornamentation"

EMBEZZLE: (see "steal") appropriate; defalcate; filch; forge; lift; loot; misappropriate; misuse; peculate; pilfer; purloin; rifle; rob; EMBEZZLER: defalcator; peculator; pilferer; stealer; thief; EMBEZZLEMENT: (see "stealing") abstraction; appropriation; defalcation; forgery; larceny; malversation; misappropriation; misuse; peculation; substraction; theft

EMBITTER: (**see** "anger") acerbate; aggravate; envenom; exacerbate; ire; madden; misuse; poison; sour; EMBITTERMENT: (**see** "anger") aggravation; exacerbation; ire; malignancy; poison(ing); rancor

EMBLEM: attribute; badge; button; cognizance; colophon; cross; decal; design; device; eagle; ensign; favor; figure; flag; idol; image (ry); insigne; insignia (pl.); mark; model; monogram; motif; object; ornament; palm; patch; pennant; prototype; shield; sign; star; statue; symbol; token; totem; type; EMBLEMATIC: (**see** "symbolic") allegorical; figurative; pathognomonic; representative; schematic

EMBODY: (**see** "contain") coalesce; comprehend; comprise; concretize; embrace; encapsulate; epitomize; express; incarnate; include; incorporate; integrate; organize; personify; unite; EMBODIMENT: avatar; comprehension; Epiphany; epitome; essence; genius; image; impersonification; incarnation; inclusion; incorporation; integration; matter; organization; personification; quintessence; union

EMBOLDEN: (**see** "animate") abet; arouse; cheer; drive; encourage; enliven; excite; fire; flush; force; impel; importune; incite; inspire; inspirit; instigate; invigorate; liven motivate; move; press; prompt; push; quicken; rouse; spur; stimulate; stir; urge; vitalize

EMBRACE: **v.** (**see** "accept") adhere; admit; adopt; annex; believe; caress; cherish; choose; circumscribe; clasp; clinch; cling; clutch;' comprehend; comprise; contain; cover; cuddle; defend; embody; embosom; enarm; encircle; enclose; encompass; enfold; espouse; fold; grasp; hold; hug; include; incorporate; join; keep; kiss; love; press; reach; receive; seize; support; take (in.); undertake; welcome; EMBRACE: **n.** acceptance; accolade; caress; clasp; cling; clutch; embracement; encirclement; enclosure; grasp; hug; incorporation; seizure; EMBRACING: (**see** "comprehensive") circumscriptive; clasping; embodying; enclosing; encompassing; hugging; including; inclusive; incorporated; osculant

EMBROIDER: (**see** "embellish") adorn; decorate; elaborate; exaggerate; sew

EMEND: (**see** "alter") amend; correct; criticize; edit; improve; rectify; reform; repair; revise; rewrite

EMERGE: (**see** "appear") accrue; arise; arrive; ascend; awake(n); become; begin; burgeon; debouch; disembogue; effloresce; egress; emanate; evolve; exist; flow; grow; happen; issue; live; loom; manifest; materialize; mount; originate; pass; raise; rear; return; rise; soar; spring; stem; surge; tower; upspring; EMERGENCE: (**see** "appearance") arrival; ascension; awakening; beginning; burgeoning; come-out; debouchment; debut; efflorescence; egress(ion); emanation; evolution; growth; happening; issuance; materialization; origination; rise; spring; surge

EMERGENCY: **a.** see "makeshift;" EMERGENCY: **n.** (**see** "crisis") accident; difficulty; dilemma; distress; exigency; expediency; expedient; immediacy; imminence; imminency; juncture; makeshift; necessity; need; pass; pinch; pressure; resort; state; stopgap; strait; substitute; urgency

EMIGRATE: (**see** "depart") abandon; egress; flee; fly; go; leave; move; quit; transfer; transplant; EMIGRATION: abandonment; departure; egression; exodus; hegira; horde; move(ment); quittance; swarm(ing); transplantation

EMINENT: acclaimed; august; brainy; cardinal; celebrated; celebrious; chief; classic(al); commemorable; commemorative; commemoratory; conspicuous; consummate; dignified; distinct; *distingué*; distinguished; elevated; esteemed; estimable; evident; exalted; excellent; famed; famous; farfamed; formidable; glorified; glorious; great; heroic; honorable; honored; honorific; illustratory; illustrious; immortal: impressive; inimitable; leonine; lionized; lofty; magnific (al); magnificent; magnified; main; majestic; noble; notable; noted; noteworthy; notorious; outstanding; palmary; paramount; peerless; praiseworthy; preeminent; prestigious; projecting; prominent; protruding; ranking; recognized; redoubtable; renowned; reputable; resplendent; salient; shining; signal; significant; sovereign; splendent; splendid; star; successful; superior; superlative; supreme; tall; towering; transcendent(al); unequaled; venerable; well-known; EMINENCE: (**see** "celebrity") acclaim; altitude; cardinal; conspicuity; conspicuousness; dignity; distinction; elevation; esteem; estimation; exaltation; fame; fortune; glory;

height; hill; honor; illustriousness; kudos; laurels; luster; magnificence; magnificent; majesty; nobility; notability; note; notoriety; paramountcy; perch; prestige; pride; projection; prominence; protuberance; rank; recognition; renown; report; reputation; repute; resplendence; rideau; salience; saliency; state; success; superiority; title; tor; transcendence; transcendency

EMISSARY: (see "agent") ambassador; delegate; deputy; envoy; factor; go-between; intermediary; investigator; legate; mediator; messenger; proxy; representative; scout; spy

EMIT: (see "discharge") disembogue; disgorge; eject; emanate; empty; erupt; evaporate; exhale; express; exude; fling; give; gush; issue; loose(n); ooze; open; outpour; publish; reek; regulate; regurgitate; release; report; shed; spurt; squirt; transmit; trickle; utter; vent; voice; vomit; yield

EMOLLIENT: a. (see "soothing") malactic; mollifying; soft(ening); supple; EMOLLIENT: n. anodyne; balm; calmative; demulcent; embrocation; lotion; narcotic; nard; ointment; palliative; salve; tranquilizer

EMOLUMENT: (see "wages") compensation; earnings; fee; gain; hire; honorarium; income; lucre; pay(ment); perquisite; profit; rate; recompense; remuneration; salary; stipend

EMOTION(S): abreaction; affection; affectivity; agitation; anxiety; ardor; attitude; compassion; compunction; conviction; desire; ecstasy; élan; emotionality; emotivism; emotivity; empathy; enthusiasm; exaltation; excitement; fear; feeling; fever; fire; fondness; fume; grief; heart; heat; ire; love; mood; onde; passion; pathos; perception; pity; presentiment; rapture; responsiveness; rhapsody; sensation; sensitivity; sentiment; spleen; sympathy; temerity; temper (ament); tingle; tremor; turmoil; vehemence; EMOTIONAL: abreactive; affected; affectionate; affective; agitated; anxious; aroused; demonstrative; disturbed; dithyrambic; dramatic; ecstatic; effeminate; effusive; excited; exclamatory; feelingful; fevered; feverish; fired; flustered; histrionic; hyperactive; hysteric(al); impassioned; inflamed; loving; melodramatic; mental; nervous; overexcited; overwrought; passionate; perturbed; rapturous; rhapsodic(al); romantic; ruffled; sentimental; shaken; soulful; stressful; tender; theatric(al); unrestrained; unstable; unsteady; upset; vehement

EMOTIONLESS: (see "unfeeling") stony; unmoved

EMPATHY: (see "emotion") compassion; feeling; pity; ruth; sensitivity; sentimentality; sympathy; understanding

EMPEROR: (see "ruler") Atahualpa; autokrator; Caesar; czar; dairi; imperator; Inca; kaiser; king; mikado; monarch; sovereign; tsar

EMPHASIZE: (see "accent") accelerate; accentuate; aggravate; amplify; draw; enhance; exacerbate; exclaim; force; hammer; heighten; highlight; hit; insist; italicize; iterate; maintain; mark; pound; press; reiterate; repeat; stress; swear; underline; underscore; yell; EMPHATIC: clear; coercive; cogent; compelling; conspicuous; definite; delineated; dogmatic; exclamatory; forceful; imperative; insistent; loud; outspoken; pronounced; resounding; striking; vehement; vigorous; EMPHASIS: (see "accent") acceleration; forcefulness; insistence; iteration; play; pressure; prominence; reiteration; repetition; stress; underlineation; underscore; underscoring; vehemence; vigor

EMPIRIC: (see "quack") charlatan; experimenter; faker; imposter; EMPIRICAL: experimental; factual

EMPLOY: (see "use") apply; busy; commission; contract; devote; engage; engross; enlist; govern; hire; invoke; involve; occupy; pick; procure; run; sell; spend; utilize; wear; wield; work; EMPLOYMENT: see "work"

EMPOWER: (see "appoint") allow; authorize; commission; commit; delegate; depute; deputize; enable; endow; establish; franchise; grant; license; name; nominate; ordain; order; permit; sanction; warrant

EMPTY: v. (see "deplete") bare; clean; deprive; discharge; divest; drain; dry; dump; evacuate; exhaust; fire; pour; relieve; remove; unload; use; vacate; EMPTY: a. bankrupt; bare; barren; blank; bleak; clean; clear; depleted; deprived; destitute; devoid; discharged; dissipated; divested; drained; dry; evacuated; exhausted; fat; foolish; frivolous; fustian; hollow; hungry; idle; impoverished; inane; meaningless; mild; naked; pretentious; purposeless; relieved; removed; stark; stripped; unfilled; unfrequented; unfulfilled; uninhabited; unloaded; unoccupied; untenanted; useless; vacant;

vacated; vain; void; EMPTINESS: barrenness; blankness; depletion; divestation; evacuation; exhaustion; form(ality); frivolity; inanition; inanity; lack; leerness; nakedness; need; nihility; nothing(ness); nudity; nullibicity; nullibiety; pretension; purposelessness; removal; senselessness; shallowness; vacuity; vacuum; void

EMPYREAN: (see "heaven") cosmos; ether; firmament; sky; sublimity; EMPYREAL: (see "heavenly") aerial; airy; celestial; empyrean; ethereal; planetary; sublime

EMULATE: (see "mimic") ape; compete; contend; copy; counterfeit; duplicate; equal; imitate; match; rival; strive; vie

ENABLE: (see "appoint") allow; authorize; capacitate; commission; delegate; employ; empower; endow; establish; invest; let; name; nominate; ordain; order; permit; sanction; warrant; ENABLING: delegative; empowering; facultative; permissive; sanctionative

ENACT: (see "authorize") decree; do; enjoin; establish; make; ordain; pass; perform; play; portray; represent; ENACTMENT: (see "law") authorization; bill; canon; code; decree; edict; legislation; mandate; mandatum; ordinance; passing; regulation; representation; rule; statute

ENAMOR: (see "charm") captivate

ENCAMPMENT: abode; bivouac; camp; castrametation; commandery; convention; étape; location; tent

ENCASE: (see "enclose") surround

ENCHAIN: (see "restrain") bind; encircle; enslave; fasten; fetter; handcuff; hold; manacle; pin; rivet; shackle

ENCHANT: (see "allure") attract; bewitch; captivate; capture; charm; delight; enamor; enrapture; ensorcel; enthrall; entice; fascinate; hypnotize; influence; infuse; intoxicate; mesmerize; permeate; please; seduce; thrill; transfix; transport; witch; ENCHANTING: captivating; Circean; delightful; divine; fascinating; heavenly; hypnotic; intoxicating; seductive; sirenic(al); ENCHANTMENT: (see "allure") allurement; bewitchment; captivation; capture; charm; conjuration; ensorcellment; fascination; gramary(e); hypnotism; incantation; influence; intoxication; magic; necromancy;

seduction; sorcery; sortilege; spell; transfixion; witchcraft; witchery; ENCHANTRESS: charmer; *charmeuse*; Circe; *femme fatale*; lamia; seducer; seductress; siren; sorceress; vampire; witch

ENCIRCLE: (see "circle") belt; circumnavigate; circumscribe; circumvallate; clasp; compass; contain; embosom; embrace; encase; enclose; encompass; enfold; enlace; environ; frame; gird(le); hedge; hem; hoop; hug; immure; impale; reach; ring; sheathe; skirt; span; surround; wall; wreathe; zone; ENCIRCLING: circumambient; circumferential; enclosing; encompassing; enfolding; hemmed; hemming; peripheral; skirting; walled; ENCIRCLEMENT: see "compass"

ENCLOSE: (see "encircle") box; cage; case; circumscribe; confine; contain; coop; corral; embar; embed; embosom; embox; embrace; encase; encircle; enclave; enclose; encompass; envelop(e); environ; enwrap; fence; fold; hedge; hem; hold; house; hug; imprison; incarcerate; incase; include; invaginate; jail; mew; pen; pin; pit; ring; sheathe; surround; veil; wall; wrap; ENCLOSURE: cage; case; coop; corral; empalement; enclave; fence; field; jail; mew; patio; pen; prison; ring; room; sep(iment); sept; stockade; sty; territory; wall; yard

ENCOMIUM: (see "commendation") accolade; approbation; approval; compliment; congratulation; encore; eulogium; eulogy; glorification; laudation; panegyric; praise; tribute

ENCOMPASS: (see "encircle" and "enclose") beset; comprehend; envelop(e); enwrap; gird; include; invest; span; surround; veil; wrap; ENCOMPASSING: see "enveloping"

ENCORE: (see "afresh") again; anew; bis; *de novo*; more; over; reappearance; recall; repeat; repetition

ENCOUNTER: v. (see "attack") assault; battle; brush; clash; collide; combat; conflict; contact; contest; debate; dispute; engage; experience; face; fight; find; meet; skirmish; struggle; undergo; ENCOUNTER: n. (see "attack") action; assault; battle; brush; clash; collision; combat; conflict(ion); contact; contest; debate; dispute; engagement; experience; fight; fray; meet(ing); skirmish; struggle; war(fare)

ENCOURAGE: (see "aid") abet; animate; approve; boost; cheer; comfort; countenance; create; cultivate; embolden; enliven; exhilarate; exhort; expostulate; favor; flatter; foment; fortify; foster; further; goad; harden; hearten; help; impel; incite; induce; indulge; inspire; inspirit; instigate; invite; nerve; pamper; praise; produce; promote; protect; raise; rally; reinforce; rouse; sanction; spur; steel; stimulate; stir; strengthen; support; urge; welcome; ENCOURAGING: (see "aiding") approbatory; auspicious; exhortative; exhortatory; helpful; hortative; hortatory; inspirational; inspiring; inspiriting; inviting; persuasive; propitious; protreptic(al); psychagogic; sanctionative; ENCOURAGEMENT: (see "aid") approbation; approval; excitation; exhortation; expostulation; favor; fomentation; fortification; furtherance; help; incentive; inducement; inspiration; instigation; invitation; nerve; patronage; promotion; protreptic; sanction; sponsor(ship); stimulation; support; welcome

ENCROACH: (see "invade") enter; hold; impinge; infract; intrude; occupy; seize; transgress; trespass; usurp; violate

ENCUMBER: (see "burden") check; clog; complicate; crowd; hamper; handicap; hinder; impede; load; obstruct; oppress; overburden; saddle; weigh; ENCUMBRANCE: (see "burden") check; claim; clog; complication; debt; difficulty; drag; drawback; embarrassment; handicap; impediment; incapacitation; incapacity; incubus; interest; lien; loan; mortgage; obstacle; obstruction; overburdening; perplexity; weight

END: **v.** abandon; abolish; abrogate; abscind; abscise; absciss; accomplish; adjourn; annihilate; break; cease; close; complete; conclude; consume; consummate; culminate; cut; deactivate; decease; defeat; desist; destroy; determine; die; disassociate; discharge; discontinue; disrupt; dissociate; dissolve; effect; eventuate; execute; exhaust; expire; extinguish; finalize; finish; fire; fold (up); halt; inactivate; intermit; interrupt; kill; leave; lift; murder; pass; pause; perfect; perform; phase out; process; quench; quit; relinquish; result; sack; settle; sever; spike; stop; surcease; suspend; terminate; upend; win; wind up; wrap up; END: **n.** abandonment; abrogation; accomplishment; achievement; adjournment; aftermath; aim; amen; annihilation; Armageddon; boundary; break; butt; cessation; close; coda; completion; conclusion; consecution; consequence; consummation; *coup de grâce*; death; delimita-

tion; demolition; denouement; design; desistence; destination; destruction; determination; disassociation; discharge; discontinuation; dissociation; dissolution; doom; downfall; effect; emanation; ending; event(uality); execution; exitus; expiration; extremity; fate; finale; finality; finial; finis(h); fragment; fruit; goal; grand finale; halt; intent(ion); intermission; interruption; issue; last; limit (ation); lot; moment; object(ive); occasion; offshoot; omega; outcome; outgrowth; perfection; period; phase out; point; polish; purpose; ramification; refinement; relinquishment remainder; remnant; removal; residual; residuum; result; retreat; rump; sake; scope; sequel; sequela(e); settlement; severance; showdown; shutdown; significance; stop; stub; suffix; surcease; suspension; tail; term (inal); termination; terminus; thirty; threshold; time; tip; toe; upshot; value; weight; win; windup; withdrawal; worth; wrap-up; ENDING *or* ENDED: **a.** (see "done") consummative; desinent(ial); desitive; finitive; terminable; terminal; terminative; terminatory; ENDING: **n.** (see "end") coda; conclusion; death; desinence; destruction; determination; disintegration; dissolution; epilogue; finale; finality; finis(h); liquidation; settlement; termination; windup

ENDANGER: chance; compromise; dare; expose; hazard; imperil; jeopardize; menace; peril; risk; stake; threaten; venture; vie; ENDANGERED: exposed; fraught; imperiled; jeopardized; periled; risked; threatened

ENDEARING: see "lovable"

ENDEAVOR: **v.** (see "intend") aim; aspire; attempt; contend; emulate; essay; exert; seek; speculate; strive; struggle; try; undertake; venture; vie; ENDEAVOR: **n.** (see "intent") aim; aspiration; attempt; business; conatus; determination; effort; emulation; essay; experiment; exertion; nisus; occupation; pursuit; speculation; struggle; study; trial; try; undertaking; venture

ENDLESS: (see "constant") ageless; boundless; ceaseless; continuous; enduring; eternal; eterne; ever(lasting); illimitable; immortal; imperishable; incessant; infinite; interminable; interminate; lasting; limitless; many; measureless; numerous; permanent; perpetual; protracted; sempitern(al); unbounded; unceasing; undying; unending; unlimited; ENDLESSNESS: (see "continuation") continuity; endurance; eternal(ity); everlastingness; infinitude; infinity; perpetuity; sempiternity

ENDORSE: (see "approve") abet; accept; acknowledge; advertise; advocate; attest; back; certify; commend; confirm; corroborate; countersign; drum; guarantee; inscribe; notarize; O.K.; pass; pledge; praise; ratify; recommend; register; sanction; seal; second; sign; superscribe; support; thump; undertake; underwrite; uphold; verify; vouch; warrant; ENDORSEMENT: (see "approval") signature; testimonial

ENDOW: (see "grant") award; bestow; clothe; commission; empower; endue; enrich; furnish; invest; warrant; ENDOWMENT: (see "grant") accomplishment; ap(p)anage; benefaction; benefit; bequest; boon; bounty; capacity; commission; donation; dower; education; equipment; fund; gift; gratuity; investment; largess(e); perquisite; power; present(ation); qualification; talent; warrant

ENDUE: (see "grant") clothe; credit; digest; dower; endow; enhance; furnish; heighten; invest; supply; vest

ENDURE: (see "last") abide; accept; affect; afford; allow; assume; bear; bide; brook; carry; comply; continue; convey; countenance; dress; drive; exert; exist; experience; feel; force; give; go; harbor; have; hold; impel; live; manage; perdure; permit; persist; press; proceed; provoke; receive; remain; retain; spend; stand; submit; suffer; support; survive; sustain; swallow; take; tolerate; undergo; wear; weather; withstand; ENDURING; (see "lasting") abiding; ceaseless; chronic; classic(al); constant; continual; diuturnal; durable; endless; established; everlasting; immarcescible; imperishable; iron; leathery; long-suffering; meek; monotonous; monumental; patient; perdurable; perennial; permanent; perpetual; perseverant; persistent; prolonged; protensive; sempiternal; standing; strong; stubborn; sturdy; unfailing; wearing; ENDURANCE: (see "continuation") abidance; compliance; constancy; continuance; continuity; diuturnity; durability; duration; fortitude; good; limit; longanimity; longevity; marathon; monumentality; perdurability; perdurance; permanence; perseverance; perseveration; propensity; sempiternity; stamina; strength; sufferance; suffering; sustenance; tolerance; toleration; trial; use; wear

ENEMY: (see "antagonist") adversary; aggressor; attacker; combatant; competitor; foe; gladiator; harm; Nemesis; opponent; rival; unfriend

ENERGIZE: (see "animate") arouse; brace; fortify; hearten; inspire; inspirit; instil; rouse; stimulate; stir; strengthen

ENERGY: activity; arm; athleticism; bent; bounce; capacity; conation; conatus; constitution; dash; direction; drive; dynamics; dynamism; éclat; edge; efficiency; élan; energetics; enterprise; enthusiasm; exertion; fervor; fire; force; go-ahead; gusto; guts; heat; impetus; impulse; impulsion; intensity; jasm; mettle; might; momentum; motivation; nerve; output; passion; pep; potency; power; press (ure); puissance; punch; push; spirit; start; steam; sthenia; strength; strenuosity; tension; thrust; thunder; verve; vigor(ousness); vim; violence; virtue; vitality; vivacity; will; work; zeal(otry); zip; ENERGETIC: (see "active") advancing; aggressive; athletic; bold; brawny; brisk; charged; con brio; driving; dynamic(al); effective; efficient; enterprising; forceful; hard-hitting; hard-spirited; high-powered; hustling; impetuous; industrious; kinetic; lusty; masculine; masterful; muscular; peppy; potent; powerful; puissant; pushful; pushy; resolute; robust (ious); sthenic; stout; strenuous; strong; supercharged; vigorous; violent; viral; vital; vivacious; vivid; zealous

ENERVATE: (see "debilitate") attenuate; devitalize; disable; drain; enfeeble; exhaust; impair; sap; soften; tire; unman; unnerve; weaken; ENERVATED: (see "weak") decrepit; disabled; enfeebled; feeble; old; shaky; worn-out; ENERVATION: see "debility"

ENFOLD: see "enclose"

ENFORCE: (see "coerce") compel; constrain; dragoon; drive; exact; execute; force; goad; hector; impel; implement; impose; invoke; lash; oblige; operate; press; reinforce; require; tax; urge; ENFORCED: coercive; compelled; compelling; compulsory; disciplinary; driving; exacting; forced; impelling; mandatory; obligatory; peremptory; pressing; required; tyrannical; tyrannous; ENFORCEMENT: (see "coercion") compulsion; compulsoriness; discipline; drive; duress; exaction; extortion; fulfillment; implementation; obligation; operation; oppression; tyranny

ENFRANCHISE: (see "free") deliver; emancipate; liberate; manumit; naturalize; release

ENGAGE: affiance; allure; amuse; appoint; arrange; assume; attack; attract; authorize;

battle; betroth; bind; busy; captivate; capture; commission; concern; contain; contract; defend; delegate; depute; divert; embrace; employ; engross; enlist; enter(tain); espouse; fight; fill; further; gain; guarantee; hire; hold; interlink; interlock; intertwine; invite; maintain; marry; mesh; obligate; occupy; participate; pledge; plight; promise; require; reserve; retain; secure; take; troth; use; wed; work; ENGAGED: (**see** "busy") affianced; espoused; meshed; ENGAGE-MENT: affair; affiance; appointment; assignation; assignment; attachment; attack; attraction; betrothal; betrothment; bias; commission; commitment; concern; contract; date; day; dispute; employment; enlistment; entrance; espousal; event; fight; invitation; involvement; meeting; obligation; occasion; pledge; plight; prepossession; promise; proposition; rendezvous; skirmish; target; time; tryst

ENGENDER: (**see** "breed") bear; beget; cause; create; cultivate; father; foster; generate; get; nurture; originate; populate; procreate; produce; propagate; sire

ENGINE: (**see** "apparatus") contrivance; device; diesel; donkey; instrument; invention; jet; locomotive; machine(ry); means; mogul; motor; turbine

ENGINEER: (**see** "direct") contrive; manage; maneuver; supervise

ENGRAVE: carve; chisel; corrode; cut; delineate; design; draw; erode; etch; furrow; impress; imprint; incise; infix; inscribe; mark; outline; print; rist; ENGRAVING: carving; design; etching; picture; print; xylograph

ENGROSS: (**see** "absorb") allure; apply; attract; bewitch; busy; captivate; capture; charm; consume; copy; engage; enhance; fascinate; fill; hold; influence; monopolize; occupy; use; write; ENGROSSED: (**see** "absorbed") busy; captivated; captured; charmed; deep; employed; entangled; fascinated; intent; involved; monopolized; occupied; pensive; preoccupied; rapt; studious

ENGULF: (**see** "absorb") bury; deluge; devour; eat; entomb; fill; flood; gobble; gulp; imbibe; inundate; invade; overflow; overpower; overwhelm; plunge; sink; submerge; swallow; swamp; whelm

ENHANCE: (**see** "elevate") adorn; advance; aggravate; augment; beautify; better; endow; enlarge; enrich; escalate; exacerbate; exaggerate; exalt; extol; heighten; improve; increase; intensify; lift; ornament; raise; wax

ENIGMA: (**see** "puzzle") ambiguity; ambivalence; complexity; conundrum; mystery; problem; question; rebus; riddle; secret; ENIGMATIC(AL): (**see** "puzzling") ambiguous; ambivalent; complex; cryptic(al); elliptic(al); equivocal; inexplicable; mysterious; mystic(al); obscure; occult; perplexing; problematic(al); recondite; vague

ENISLED: (**see** "isolated") alone; apart; marooned; moored; quarantined; separated; solitary

ENJOIN: admonish; advise; ban; bar; bid; block; command; condemn; counsel; damn; debar; decree; direct; disallow; enforce; exact; exalt; exclude; execrate; expel; forbid; force; halt; hinder; inhibit; interdict; interfere; ordain; order; outlaw; preclude; prevent; prohibit; proscribe; regulate; relegate; require; restrain; stop; warn

ENJOY: (**see** "like") admire; appreciate; approbate; bask; cherish; delight; dig; entertain; esteem; experience; fancy; gratify; have; hold; like; love; occupy; own; possess; prize; relish; respect; savor; take; treasure; undergo; use; value; ENJOYMENT: (**see** "pleasure") appreciation; approbation; charm; comfort; delectation; delight; ecstasy; entertainment; exultation; fancy; felicity; festivity; flavor; fruition; fun; gladness; gratification; gust(o); happiness; indulgence; jocularity; joy; liking; love; merriment; mirth; occupation; ownership; pleasure; possession; rapture; relish; satisfaction; sensuality; tang; use; zest(fulness); ENJOYABLE: (**see** "pleasurable") delectable; entertaining; fine; nice; pleasing; satisfying; zestful

ENLARGE: accumulate; add; advance; aggrandize; amass; amplify; augment; balloon; bloat; bore; broaden; color; descant; dilate; discourse; discuss; distend; elaborate; elongate; embellish; embroider; enhance; escalate; exacerbate; exalt; exceed; expand; expatiate; extend; fatten; greaten; grow; heighten; hypertrophy; improve; increase; inflate; intensify; intumesce; invent; lengthen; magnify; omnify; overact; overdo; overemphasize; overstate; pad; pontificate; protuberate; puff; pyramid; ream; romance; snowball; spread; stretch; surpass; swell; talk; thrive; tumefy; tumesce; widen;

ENLARGED: ampliate; amplicative; am-plificatory; amplified; augmented; bloated; blown(-up); broadened; built(-up); bulbous; bulgy; colored; dilatated; dilated; distended; elaborated; elongated; embellished; embroid-ered; enhanced; escalated; exacerbated; exalted; exceptional; exfoliated; expanded; explicated; extended; extravagant; fabulous; fat; fustian; gravid; greater; grown; heightened; hyperbolic(al); hypertrophic; hypertrophied; increased; incredible; inflated; intensified; intumescent; larger; lengthened; magnified; mythomaniac(al); obese; overdone; overdrawn; overweening; padded; prolonged; protracted; pyrami-dal; spread; stretched; swollen; thickened; tumefactive; tumescent; tumid; turgescent; turgid; tympanic; weighty; widened; ENLARGEMENT: accession; accumula-tion; adornment; advancement; aggrandize-ment; aggravation; amassment; amplifi-cation; augmentation; delation; dilation; distension; elaboration; elongation; embel-lishment; enhancement; escalation; excess; excrescence; expansion; expatiation; exten-sion; extravagance; growth; hypertrophy; improvement; increase; intensification; intumescence; largeness; liberation; magnifi-cation; majoration; megalomania; Mun-chausenism; mythomania; obesity; out-growth; overacting; overemphasis; overstate-ment; padding; prolongation; protraction; stretch; swelling; tumefaction; tumescence; turgescence; widening

ENLIGHTEN: (see "educate") acquaint; admonish; advise; apprise; civilize; counsel; direct; disclose; divulge; edify; elucidate; illume; illuminate; impart; inculcate; in-doctrinate; inform; instruct; irradiate; notify; open; school; teach; tell; train; ENLIGHT-ENMENT: (see "education") advice; counsel; direction; disclosure; divulgence; *éclaircissement*; edification; education; elucida-tion; illumination; incandescence; inculca-tion; indoctrination; information; instruc-tion; luminosity; notification; satisfaction; schooling; teaching; training; truth

ENLIST: (see "enter") attract; embody; engage; enroll; get; hire; incorporate; in-duce; muster; obtain; participate; register; retain; utilize

ENLIVEN: (see "animate") actuate; amuse; awake(n); brighten; charm; cheer; delight; divert; elate; encourage; enthuse; evoke; exhilarate; fire; gladden; gratify; incite; inspire; inspirit; invigorate; percolate; please; quicken; refresh; reinvigorate; rouse; satisfy; smarten; spur; stimulate; stir; varie-gate; vivify; wake(n)

ENMESH: (see "ensnare") catch; engage; entangle

ENMITY: (see "hate") acrimony; animosity; animus; antagonism; antipathy; aversion; bitterness; disgust; dislike; grudge; hatred; hostility; ill will; malevolence; malice; malignity; opposition; pique; rancor; resent-ment; spite; unfriendliness; unfriendship

ENNUI: (see "dreariness") blues; boredom; fatigue; languor; listlessness; surfeit; tedium; vapors

ENORMOUS: (see "huge") abnormal; co-lossal; cyclopean; cyclopic; elephantine; extreme; gargantuan; gigantic; great; im-mense; inordinate; large; magnitudinous; mammoth; monstrous; monumental; pon-derous; prodigious; stupendous; titanic; vast; ENORMITY: (see "hugeness") am-plitude; collosality; immensity; magnitude; monstrosity; vastitude; vastity; vastness

ENOUGH: (see "adequate") abundant; am-ple; bas(ta); bus; competent; complete; copious; enow; full(y); plenteous; plenty; *quantum sufficit* (abb; q.s.); quite; sufficient; when

ENRAGE: agitate; anger; annoy; chafe; craze; exasperate; excite; goad; incense; incite; inflame; infuriate; ire; irk; irritate; madden; nettle; pique; provoke; roil; ENRAGED: (see "angry") agitated; angered; annoyed; berserk; crazed; exasperated; excited; frenzied; furious; incensed; inflamed; in-furiated; irate; ired; irked; irritated; mad (dened); maniac(al); manic; nettled; pas-sionate; piqued; provoked; roiled; savage; ENRAGEMENT: see "furor"

ENRAPTURE: (see "charm") allure; be-witch; captivate; capture; delight; ecstasize; enamor; enchant; enravish; ensorcel(l); enthral(l); enthuse; entice; fascinate; inflame; gratify; please; ravish; translate; transport

ENRICH: (see "adorn" and "fertilize") add; deck; diamondize; endow; expand; fatten; fortify; garnish; gild; improve; increase; lard; ornament; pinguefy; prosper; salt; strengthen; thrive

ENROLL: (see "list") enfold; engross; enlist; enter; impanel; inscribe; insert; matriculate;

muster; record; recruit; register; serve; subscribe

ENSCONCE: (see "cover") conceal; embed; establish; hide; settle

ENSEMBLE: (see "aggregate") aggregation; collection; combination; group; pair; suite; unification

ENSNARE: (see "entangle") benet; catch; circumvent; cop; deceive; decoy; enmesh; entice; entrap; inveigle; lure; mousetrap; nab; net; noose; seduce; sniggle; tempt; trap; trick

ENSORCEL(L): (see "charm") bewitch; delight; enchant; enrapture; fascinate; transport

ENSUE: (see "follow") arise; derive; happen; issue; pursue; result; stem; strive; succeed

ENTANGLE: (see "ensnare") bewilder; capture; catch; circumvent; complicate; confuse; embroil; enmesh; ensnarl; entice; entrap; embroil; intertwine; interweave; intrigue; inveigle; involve; knot; lure; mat; mire; net; noose; perplex; ravel; scheme; snare; snarl; tangle; trap; trick; twist; weave; wind; ENTANGLEMENT: brouhaha; chaos; coil; complexity; complication; confusion; discord; embarrassment; embranglement; embroilment; ensnarement; hitch; illaqueation; imbroglio; impediment; intricacy; involution; involvement; knot; labyrinth; lure; maelstrom; maze; morass; net; perplexity; scheme; snare; snarl; tangle; tela; trap; trick; war; web

ENTENTE: (see "alliance") accord; agreement; agrément; coalition; pact; treaty; understanding; undertaking

ENTER: (see "begin") admit; advance; attract; board; bore; come; consider; contribute; deposit; embark; embody; encroach; engage; enroll; examine; file; get; hire; incorporate; induce; infiltrate; ingress; initiate; inscribe; insert; interject; intrude; invade; join; list; mix; muster; obtain; open; participate; pass; penetrate; permeate; pierce; poach; probe; record; register; retain; spread; start; trespass; understand; utilize; ENTERING or ENTRY: incursion; infiltration; ingress(ion); insertion; interjection; intrusion; invasion; penetration; trespass; ENTRANCE: see "passage"

ENTERPRISE: (see "business") action; activity; adventure; company; design; emprise; endeavor; energy; engagement; enthusiasm; essay; exploit; feat; force; go-ahead; gumption; hazard; industry; initiative; partnership; performance; plan; project; push; quest; risk; scheme; spirit; undertaking; venture; war; work; zeal(otry); zealousness; zest; ENTERPRISING: (see "energetic") promising; up-and-coming

ENTERTAIN: amuse; beguile; board; charm; cheer; cherish; consider; delight; disport; distract; divert; enjoy; enliven; enthuse; exhilarate; feed; fete; gratify; honor; house; inspirit; interest; lodge; occupy; please; receive; recreate; regale; shelter; solace; tittivate; treat; welcome; ENTERTAINING: (see "amusing") diversional; diverting; divertive; festive; interesting; recreational; recreative; sportful; ENTERTAINMENT: amusement; banquet; beguilement; board; charm cheer; concert; dance; dancing; delight; distraction; diversion; divertissement; enjoyment; exhilaration; fare; feast; feed; festival; festivity; fete; fiesta; frolic; fun; gaiety; game; gratification; hobby; hospitality; lodging; merriment; merrymaking; passetemps; pastime; performance; picnic; play; pleasantry; pleasure; program; reception; recreation; repast; revel(ry); shelter; show; social; solace; sport; tittivation; treat

ENTHUSIASM: ardentness; ardor; dash; dedication; devotement; devotion; eagerness; earnestness; ebullience; ebulliency; ecstasy; élan; emotion; euphoria; excitement; exhilaration; exuberance; fanaticism; fascination; feeling; fervency; fervor; fever; fire; frenzy; furor; fury; gaiety; heart; hilarity; impetuosity; insanity; inspiration; intensity; interest; intoxication; joy(fulness); joyousness; love; lust(iness); madness; mania; merriment; mirth; nourishment; passion; rabidity; rapture; raptus; spirit; transport; vehemence; verve; vigor(ousness); warmth; zeal(otry); zealousness; zest; ENTHUSIASTIC: active; afire; ardent; avid; boiling; bubbling; contagious; delirious; devoted; dithyrambic; ebullient; ecstatic; euphoric; excessive; excited; exhilarated; exuberant; fervent; fervid; feverish; fired; flamboyant; frantic; frenzied; gaga; glad; glowing; *gung ho*; happy; hearty; impassioned; insane; intense; intoxicated; joyful; joyous; keen; lusty; lyrical; mad (dened); maniac(al); missionary; obsessed; overflowing; passionate; perfervid; phrenetic(al;) rabid; rapturous; raving; rhapsodic(al); seething; stewing; unrestrained; vehement; vigorous; warm; wholehearted;

wild; zealous; zestful; ENTHUSIAST:
bigot; buff; bug; devotee; energumen;
exalté; fan(atic); zealot

ENTICE: allure; attract; bait; beguile; blandish; cajole; captivate; capture; charm;
cheat; coax; decoy; delight; draw; ensnare;
entertain; entrap; flatter; impel; incite;
induce; instigate; inveigle; lead (on); manipulate; motivate; outpower; persuade; seduce; snare; solicit; spur; steal; tease; tempt;
tole; trap; trick; urge; vamp; wheedle;
work; ENTICING: alluring; attractive;
beguiling; bewitching; captivating; Circean;
engaging; exotic; glamorous; orphic; picturesque; prepossessing; seducible; seductive; sirenic(al); ENTICEMENT: (see
"charm") allure(ment); attraction; bait;
beguile(ment); cajolement; cajolery; decoy;
entrapment; flattery; inducement; instigation; inveiglement; lure; seducement; seduction; temptation; trap; wile

ENTIRE: (see "full") all; complete; comprehensive; continuous; exclusive; gross;
homogenous; intact; integral; livelong; perfect; plenary; pure; *pur et simple*; sheer;
solid; thorough; throughout; total; unabridged; uncut; undifferentiated; undiluted;
undiminished; undivided; unexpurgated;
whole(hog); ENTIRETY: aggregate; amplitude; completeness; completion; complexity; integrality; integrity; perfection;
repletion; satiation; satiety; sum; surfeit;
total(ity); whole (hog)

ENTITLE: (see "name") appoint; call; christen; commission; designate; dub; elect;
enable; establish; merit; nominate; ordain;
qualify; style; ENTITLED: see "eligible"

ENTITY: (see "unit") being; component;
ens; essence; existence; existent; individual;
monad; nature; object; one; organism; self-
containment; soul; substance; substantive;
thing

ENTOURAGE: (see "followers") following;
parade; procession; retinue; surroundings;
train

ENTRANCE: v. (see "entice") delight;
enrapture; entertain; overpower; EN-
TRANCE: n. access(ion); adit(us); admission; admittance; aisle; anteroom; appearance; approach; atrium; avenue; commencement; credit; debit; debut; door(way);
entree; entry; foyer; gate(way); hall(way);
incursion; ingress(ion); initiation; inlet;
introduction; introitus; intrusion; invasion;

lane; lobby; mouth; opening; os; pass(age);
passageway; penetration; postern; probe;
record; road(way); stile; trespass; vestibule;
walk(way); way

ENTRANCED *or* ENTRANCING: attracted;
bewitched; captivated; captured; charmed;
delighted; delightful; enchanted; enraptured;
entertained; entertaining; enticing; fascinated; fascinating; mesmerized; musical;
Orphean; orphic(al); overpleasing; overpowering; pleasing; rapt; sonorous; sweet;
tempting; transported; winsome

ENTRAP: (see "catch") allure; attract;
beguile; bewitch; captivate; capture; deceive;
decoy; ensnare; entangle; entice; fool; hold;
hook; implicate; inveigle; involve; lure;
mislead; seduce; snare; sniggle; tangle

ENTREAT: (see "beg") adjure; appeal; ask;
beseech; coax; conjure; crave; cry; halse;
implore; importunate; invoke; petition;
please; pray; request; solicit; sue; summon;
supplicate; urge; ENTREATY: adjuration;
appeal; cry; imploration; imprecation;
obsecration; petition; plead(ing); prayer;
request; solicitation; supplication; urge;
urging

ENTREE: (see "entrance") admission; dish;
entresse; entry; ingress(ion)

ENTRUST: (see "commit") allow; bank;
confide; consign; count; obligate; permit;
recommend; rely; surrender; trust

ENTRY: (see "entrance") access; admission;
avenue; credit; debit; entree; gate; incursion; ingress(ion); interruption; intrusion;
invasion; item; minute; note; opening;
passage(way); penetration; probe; record;
trespass

ENTWINE: (see "wind") attach; embosom;
embrace; encircle; enclave; entangle; fold;
intertangle; interweave; involve; join;
loop; mingle; tangle; twist; vine; weave;
wind; wreathe

ENUMERATE: (see "detail") add; arrange;
ascertain; catalog(ue); compile; compute;
count; figure; list; name; number; recapitulate; recite; reckon; recount; rehearse;
relate; score; sum; tally; tell; total; ENU-
MERATION: (see "arrangement") cata-
log(ue); census; citation; compilation; count;
figure; list; recapitulation; reckoning; score;
sum; tale; tally; total

ENUNCIATE: (see "announce") advertise; articulate; blare; claim; declaim; delare; enounce; expound; express; foretell; formulate; inform; proclaim; pronounce; speak; state; talk; tell; utter; voice; ENUNCIATION: see "announcement"

ENVELOP(E): **v.** (see "cover") attach; circumfuse; coat; conceal; dominate; enclose; encompass; enfold; entwine; fold; hide; obscure; pervade; possess; roll; shroud; surround; swathe; wrap; ENVELOP(E): **n.** (see "covering") burr; cap(sule); case; container; cover; integument; investment; jacket; pocket; receptacle; shroud; vesture; wrap(per); ENVELOPING: ambient; circumferential; encircling; enclosing; encompassing; enwrapped; invested; pervading; pervasive; surrounded; surrounding; veiled

ENVIRON: **v.** (see "encircle") enclose; encompass; envelop(e); enwrap; gird(le); hem; pervade; surround; ENVIRON(S): **n.** (see "area") ambience; ambiente; atmosphere; background; community; compass; conditions; district; entourage; habitat; hem; influence; locale; milieu; *mise-en-scène*; neighborhood; outskirts; precinct; purlieu; realm; region; suburbia; suburbs; surroundings; vicinage; vicinity; zone; ENVIRONMENT: (see "area" and "habitat") ambience; ambient(e); climate; climature; clime; condition; context; medium; milieu; place; setting; surroundings; vicinity; zone

ENVOY: ablegate; agent; ambassador; ambassadress; commissioner; consul; deputy; diplomat; legate; messenger; minister; nuncio; plenipotentiary; representative; senator

ENVY: **v.** (see "covet") begrudge; deplore; desire; grudge; hanker; long; pant; pine; rankle; resent; spite; wish; yearn; ENVY: **n.** (see "covetousness") desire; grudge; hanker(ing); jaundice; jealousy; longing; malice; opprobrium; pining; prejudice; resentment; spite; unpopularity; wish; yearning; ENVIOUS: see "covetous"

EPHEMERAL: (see "brief") episodic(al); fleeting; fugitive; immaterial; intangible; momentary; short(ened); short-lived; temporary; topical; transient; transitory; vanishing; vaporous

EPIC: (see "heroic") Homerian; Homeric; huge; legendary; narrative; poetic(al); significant; traditional

EPICUREAN: **a.** Apician; gastronomical; gluttonish; go(u)rmand; hedonistic; luxurious; sensual; sensuous; sybaritic; voluptuous; EPICURE(AN): **n.** *bon vivant*; connoisseur; friand; gastronome(r); glutton; go(u)rmand; gourmet; hedonist; sybarite; trencherman

EPIDEMIC: **a.** (see "general") common; contagious; epidemial; epidemiologic(al); generalized; pandemic; prevailing; prevalent; spread; wide(spread); EPIDEMIC: **n.** attack; contagion; disease; outbreak; pest; plague; spread

EPIDERMIS: see "skin"

EPIGRAM: (see "witticism") adage; aphorism; apothegm; epigrammation; maxim; mot(to); poem; quip; saw; saying; EPIGRAMMATIC(AL): (see "witty") compact; concise; pithy; sage; terse

EPISODE: (see "circumstance") action; adventure; attack; break; contingency; development; digression; drama; epic; event; fact; fit; goings-on; happening; incident; interim; interlude; interval; occasion; occurrence; scene; seizure; sequence; situation; story; tiding; EPISODIC(AL): (see "circumstantial") capricious; ephemeral; episodal; incidental; occasional; recurring; temporary; transitory

EPISTLE: (see "letter") billet(-doux); communication; composition; lesson; mail; message; missive; note; reply; report; rescript; writing

EPITHET: (see "name") agnomen; appellation; byname; byword; curse; designation; epitheton; label; name-calling; pejorative; phrase; tag; title; word

EPITOME: (see "abridgement") abstract; breviary; brief; compend(ium); condensation; contraction; curtailment; digest; embodiment; essence; outline; preçis; synopsis

EPOCH: (see "age") division; eon; episode; era; event; period; time; turning point

EQUABLE: adequate; calm; coequal; commensurate; constant; corresponding; equal (ized); equanimous; equivalent; even; fair; identical; impartial; just; level; like; matched; parallel; proportional; regular; same; serene; steady; still; tantamount; tranquil; uniform; unruffled; unvarying

EQUAL: **v.** (see "balance") compare; coordinate; correspond; emulate; equalize; equate; even; pair; parallel; make; match; meet; tie; EQUAL: **a.** adequative; alike; analogous; balanced; coequal; commensurable; commensurate; companion; compensative; compensatory; concentric; concurrent; coordinate; correlative; corresponding; egalitarian; equable; equalized; equanimous; equational; equidistant; equipollent; equiponderant; equipotential; equitable; equivalent; even; fair; flat; flush; harmonious; harmonized; honest; identical; impartial; isometric; isonomic; isonomous; just; legal level; like; matched; matching; mated; meet; mutual; neutralized; normal; objective; paradromic; parallel(ed); planate; proportional; proportionate; reasonable; reciprocal; regular; serene; similar; smooth; stabilized; stable; steady; suitable; symmetrical; synallagmatic; tantamount; tied; tranquil: true; unbiased; uniform; unprejudiced; unvarying; valid; weighted; EQUAL: **n.** balance; coequality; coetaneity; coeval; compeer; contemporaneity; coordinate; equability; equanimity; equivalent; evenness; exactness; fairness; identical(ity); impartiality; match; par; peer; placidity; quits; regularity; same; serenity; smoothness; uniformity; EQUALITY: (see "equalization)" adequation; analogy; commensurability; equiponderance; equivalence; evenness; identicality; identity; isonomy; justice; levelness; par(ity); resemblance; sameness; tie; uniformity

EQUALIZE: (see "balance" and "equal") adequate; adjust; compensate; coordinate; correct; dole; emulate; equate; equiponderate; even; liberate; librate; match; meet; neutralize; osmose; pair; ration; reciprocate; stabilize; tie; unify; EQUALIZATION: (see "equality") adequation; adjustment; balance; equability; equableness; equalitarianism; equanimity; equatability; equilibrium; equipoise; equiponderance; equiponderation; isonomy; osmosis; proportionality; ration; reciprocation; stabilization; unification; EQUALIZING: egalitarian; isonomous; osmotic; unifying

EQUANIMITY: (see "calm") balance; calmness; composure; control; equalization; equation; equipoise; equiponderance; equitableness; evenness; imperturbability; phlegm; poise; *sangfroid*; *savoir faire*; self-control; serenity; temper(ament)

EQUILIBRIUM: (see "calm") balance;

calmness; composure; constancy; control; equanimity; equipoise; firmness; homeostasis; objectivity; poise; reason; sanity; serenity; stability; steadfastness

EQUIP: accouter; arm; buckle; capacitate; caparison; clothe; dress; educate; endow; fit (out); furnish; garb; gird; habilitate; outfit; prepare; provide; qualify; ready; ring; stock; supply; train; EQUIPMENT: accouterment(s); apparatus; appliance; appointment(s); appurtenance(s); armamentaria (pl.); armamentarium; arms; array; assets; baggage; bags; belongings; caparison; clothing; decor; dunnage; education; endowment; equipage; finery; fitment (s); fittings; fixtures; furnishing(s); garb; garments; gear; habiliment(s); impedimenta (pl.); impediments; instrumentaria (pl.); instrumentarium; instruments; luggage; machinery; material; matériel; moveables; oufit; panoply; paraphernalia; preparation; property; regalia; resources; services; set; stock; stuff; supplies; supply; tackle; tools; trappings; traps; trunks; wearables

EQUIPOISE: (see "calm") balance; calmness; counterbalance; equanimity; equilibrium; evenness; perpendicularity; poise; posture

EQUITABLE: (see "equal") equiponderant; even; fair; honest; impartial; just; legal; objective; reasonable; unbiased; unprejudiced; upright; valid

EQUIVALENT: adequative; alike; analogical; analogous; coimplicant; commensurate; compensative; congruent; convertible; corollary; corresponding; counterpart; duplicate; equal; equipollent; equiponderant; homogeneous; homologous; identic(al); isonomous; like; same; similar; synonymous; tantamount; tit for tat; twin; uniform; unisonant; unisonous; EQUIVALENCE: (see "equality") alikeness; correspondence; equability; exchangeability; homogeneity; uniformity

EQUIVOCAL: (see "ambiguous") ambivalent; amphibolic(al); cryptic(al); double-edged; doubtful; dubious; enigmatic(al); evasive; hazy; inconclusive; indefinite; indeterminate; indistinct; inscrutable; involved; multivocal; mysterious; obscure; perplexing; problematic(al); questionable; suspicious; uncertain; undecided; vague

EQUIVOCATE: (see "avoid") deceive; dodge; escape; evade; fence; fib; hedge;

lie; mislead; palter; question; quibble; shuffle; tergiversate; weasel

ERA: (**see** "age") cycle; date; eon; epoch; event; period; stage; time

ERADICATE: (**see** "eliminate") abolish; annihilate; annul; blot (out); burn; consume; decimate; dele(te); deracinate; destroy; devastate; efface; eradicate; erase; expunge; exterminate; extinguish; kill; level; raze; remove; root (out); slay; smother; stamp (out); unroot; uproot

ERASE: (**see** "eliminate") abolish; annihilate; annul; balance; blot; cancel; dele(te); destroy; efface; eradicate; excise; expunge; extinguish; kill; neutralize; nullify; obliterate; offset; overshadow; remove; sponge; ERASURE: (**see** "elimination") annihilation; cancellation; deletion; eradication; excision; expunction; extirpation; neutralization; nullification; obliteration; removal

ERE: before; prior; rather

ERECT: **v.** (**see** "build") constitute; construct; create; develop; elevate; establish; exalt; hoist; magnify; make; raise; rear; ERECT: **a.** (**see** "upright") noble; orthograde; orthostatic; perpendicular; right; standing; straight; vertical

EREWHILE: ago; formerly; heretofore; once; onetime; quondam; sometime

ERODE: ablate; abrade; burn; canker; cavitate; consume; corrode; decay; denude; deplete; destroy; deteriorate; diminish; disappear; disintegrate; eat; etch; frit; gnaw; impair; oxidize; putrefy; putresce; rot; rub; rust; slough (off); ulcerate; undermine; wash; waste; weaken; wear; EROSION: ablation; abrasion; canker; cavitation; corrosion; decay; denudation; gnawing; oxidation putrefaction; putrescence; rot; rub; rust(ing); ulceration; wash; weakening; wear(ing)

EROTIC: (**see** "lewd") amative; amatory; amorous; ardent; arousing; carnal; concupiscent; erogenous; lustful; passionate; provocative; sensual; sensuous; sexual; voluptuous

ERR: backfire; blunder; bobble; boomerang; botch; bungle; deviate; encroach; fail; fall; fault; flounder; flub; fluff; garble; goof; lapse; lurch; mess; miscalculate; miscarry;

mischoose; miscue; misdirect; misdo; misestimate; misfield; mishandle; misinterpret; misjudge; mismanage; misplay; misquote; miss; mistake; mistranslate; muddle; offend; sin; slip; spoil; stray; stumble; trespass; trip; tumble; violate; wander; ERRATIC *or* ERRING: aberrant; blundering; bungling; capricious; changeable; circuitous; crackbrained; crackpot; desultory; deviating; devious; eccentric; errant; erroneous; fallible; fickle; floundering; fluctuating; fumbling; hallucinatory; improper; insane; irregular; manic; mistaken; nomadic; odd; quaint; queer; sinful; strange; stumbling; tangent(ial); transgressing; uncertain; uneven; unpredictable; unreliable; unsound; unstable; vagarious; vagrant; variational; wandering; wayward; wild; ERRANT: (**see** "deviating" and "devious") erring; failing; fallible

ERRONEOUS: (**see** "incorrect") apocryphal; deviating; devious; erring; fallacious; imprecise; inaccurate; inexact; mistaken

ERROR: aberrancy; aberration; barbarism; blemish; blooper; blunder; boner; boo-boo; botch; break; bull; bungle; carelessness; clinker; corrigendum; corruption; defect; delinquency; demerit; dereliction; detriment; deviation; discrepancy; drawback; errata (pl.); erraticism; failing; failure; fall(acy); falsehood; fault; *faux pas*; fiasco; flaw; flub; fluff; foible; frailty; gaff(e); goof; *grivoiserie*; hole; illusion; imperfection; imprecision; impropriety; inaccuracy; inadequacy; inadvertence; inattention; indiscretion; inexactitude; lapse; *lapsus linguae*; mess; misadventure; miscalculation; mischoice; misconception; miscue; misdeed; misdemeanor; misdirection; misestimation; mishap; misinterpretation; mismanagement; misnomer; misplay; misprint; miss; misstep; mistake; misstatement; mistranslation; muddle; neglect; negligence; offense; omission; oversight; parapraxia; parapraxis; peccadillo; pitfall; shortcoming; sin; slip; solecism; spoilage; stumble; stupidity; transgression; trip; veniality; vice; violation; weakness; wrinkle; wrong(doing)

ERUDITE: (**see** "learned") bookish; cultured; didactic(al); donnish; moralistic; pedantic; pompous; recondite; scholarly; wise; ERUDITION: (**see** "learning") culture; knowledge; learnedness; letters; lore; scholarship; science; wisdom

ERUPT: (**see** "explode") burst; eject; expel; gush; release

ESCAPADE: (see "adventure") antic; dare; dido; experience; frolic; gambit; gest(e); harlequinade; indiscretion; lark; peccadillo; ploy; prank; vagary

ESCAPE: v. abscond; avoid; blow; bolt; break; decamp; defect; depart; desert; disappear; drip; elope; elude; eschew; evade; flee; fly; go; hide; hie; issue; jump; lam; leak; leave; ooze; quit; run; rush; scat; scram; seep; shun; vamoose; ESCAPE: n. abscondence; absence; avoidance; bolt; break; circumvention; decampment; departure; desertion; disappearance; distraction; drip; elopement; evasion; getaway; hideaway; leak(age); ooze; opening; quittance; relief; run; rush; seep(age); slit; vent

ESCHEW: (see "avoid") abstain; escape; evade; fear; forbear; forgo; shun; shunt

ESCORT: v. accompany; attend; chaperone; collaborate; conduct; convoy; guard; guide; lead; man; manage; pilot; protect; see; shepherd; shield; show; squire; steer; support; take; tend; usher; watch; ESCORT: n. attendant; beau; cavalier; chaperone; cicerone; collaborator; convoy; entourage; gallant; guard(s); guidance; guide; leader; protector; retinue; shepherd; shield; squire; sweetheart; usher; vis-à-vis

ESOTERIC: (see "mysterious") abstract; abstruse; acroamatic; arcanal; arcane; cabalic; cabalistic; confidential; Eleusinian; freemasonic(al); Gnostic(al); hieratic; inaccessible; inner; Masonic; metaphysical; metempiric(al); mystic(al); occult; private; rare(fied); recondite; Rosicrucian; secret; sphingal; sphinxine; subtle; transcendent(al); unusual; veiled

ESPOUSE: (see "engage") abet; adopt; affiance; assume; back; betroth; defend; embrace; further; guarantee; maintain; marry; pledge; plight; promise; support; take; troth; wed

ESPRIT: (see "spirit") cleverness; intelligence; liveliness; morale; spiritedness; vigor; vivacity; wit(tiness) zeal(otry); zealousness; zest (fulness)

ESPY: (see "find") behold; descry; discern; discover; note; notice; observe; perceive; recognize; see; spot; spy; view

ESSAY: v. (see "begin") attempt; dare; endeavor; strive; test; try; venture; work; ESSAY: n. (see "beginning") article; attempt; composition; discourse; disquisition; dissertation; editorial; effort; endeavor; exegesis; narrative; paper; result; screed; story; test; theme; thesis; tract(ate); trial; venture

ESSENCE: abstract; aspect; attar; attribute; aura; basis; being; blood; cachet; cell; center; character(istic); cloth; clyssus; component; concentrate; concentration; concoction; condensation; constituent; consubstantiation; contexture; copy; core; courage; crux; decoction; decoctum; durability; effect; element; elicitation; elixir; embodiment; ens; epitome; essential(ity); estreat; excerpt; existence; extract(ion); extractum; fabric; fiber; filament; flavor (ing); fluid; focus; form; fortitude; frame (work); fundament(ality); genealogy; gist; good; ground; heart; hub; indispensability; integrality; interior; inwardness; juice; keest; kernel; kind; knot; marrow; material; matter; meaning; meat; medulla; middle; midpoint; muscle; nature; necessity; need; nerve; nourishment; nub; nucleus; odor; outline; part and parcel; pattern; pep; perfume; perquisite; pith; plan; point; principle; property; quality; quintessence; quotation; reality; requirement; root; sap; scent; selection; sense; shred; significance; sinew; soul; spirit; stamina; strength; structure; stuff; style; substance; sum and substance; synopsis; texture; thread; tissue; truth; upshot; vigor; vim; virtuality; virtue; vitality; warp; weave; woof

ESSENTIAL: a. (see "basic") basal; cardinal; characteristic; chief; componental; constitutional; constitutive; critical; crucial; dominant; elemental; elementary; foremost; formal; fundamental; general; good; hypostatic(al); idiopathic; important; inchoate; indispensable; influential; ingrained; inherent; initiatory; innate; integral; intrinsic; main; necessary; needed; needful; obligate (d); primary; quintessential; requisite; significant; substantial; substantive; true; unavoidable; vital; ESSENTIAL: n. (see "essence") characteristic; component; constituent; desiderata (pl.); desideratum; element; essentiality; indispensability; necessity; need; part and parcel; perquisite; requirement; sine qua non; substance; tissue

ESTABLISH: (see "commission") appoint; authenticate; authorize; base; build; calculate; cement; check; circumstantiate; colonize; confirm; constitute; construct; convince; coronate; corroborate; create; crown; decree; demonstrate; determine; develop; effect; empower; enact; endow;

ensconce; entitle; erect; evince; fasten; fix; found; guarantee; identify; implant; induct; initiate; install: instate; institute; introduce; invest; justify; lay out; lodge; make; manifest; open; ordain; organize; originate; persuade; pin; place; plant; prove; provide; raise; root; sear; seat; secure; set(tle); show; solve; start; structure; substantiate; sustain; verify; vindicate; vouch; ESTABLISHED: (see "conclusive") authenticated; authoritative; checked; chronic; constructed; convinced; deep-rooted; deteriorated; determinative; determined; documented; enacted; endowed; ensconced; enshrined; erected; evidenced; evinced; fixed; guaranteed; inaugurated; ingrained; instituted; institutive; inveterate; justified; lodged; manifest(ed); ordained; proved; set(tled); solved; substantiated; sure; vouchsafed; ESTABLISHMENT: (see "business") agency; college; colony; constitution; corporation; dwelling; factory; faculty; fixture; foundation; government; house(hold); installation; institution; joint; layout; menage; office; residence; school; settlement; shop; station; university; workshop

ESTATE: acres; allod(ium); ap(p)anage; appurtenances; assets; belongings; buildings; chattels; circumstances; class; condition; constitution; decree; demesne; effects; fief; form; fortune; freehold; goods; hereditament(s); holdings; interest(s); land(s); manor; money; ownership; patrimony; personalia (pl.); plantation; position; possession(s); principality; property; rank; resources; riches; rights; s(e)ign(i)ory; situation; standing; state; status; substance; tenure; wealth

ESTEEM: **v.** admire; adore; appraise; appreciate; believe; bow; capitulate; cherish; comply; deem; defer; devote; dote; exalt; favor; hold; honor; judge; like; love; merit; pedestalize; prize; raise; regard; repute; respect; revere(nce); think; treasure; venerate; worship; ESTEEM: **n.** (see "deference") account; admiration; adoration; appreciation; approbation; approval; awe; consideration; deferentiality; devoir; devotion; dignity; distinction; eminence; estimableness; estimation; favor; fealty; homage; honor; illustriousness; liking; love; loyalty; majesty; merit; notability; obeisance; obsequiousness; popularity; praise; prestige; pride; prominence; regard; renown; reputation; repute; respect; reverence; standing; stature; status; use; valuation; value; veneration; virtue; worship; worth; ESTEEMED: ace-high; admired; adored; A-one; appre-

ciated; celebrated; cherished; commendatory; costly; eminent; estimable; exalted; favored; honored; illustrious; liked; loved; majestic; meritorious; notable; praised; praiseworthy; precious; prestigious; prominent; regarded; renowned; reputed; respected; revered; reverenced; treasured; valuable; valued; venerated; virtuous; worshiped; worthy; ESTIMABLE: **see** "worthy"

ESTIMATE: **v.** adjudge; adjudicate; aim; appraise; ascertain; assay; assess; audit; budget; calculate; capitalize; compute; conclude; count; esteem; evaluate; figure; fix; gauge; guess; judge; judicate; measure; mete; number; place; predict; prize; project; rank; rate; reason; reckon; set; think; valuate; value; weigh; ESTIMATE: **n.** or ESTIMATION: (see "esteem") appraisal; appreciation; assessment; assignment; calculation; capitalization; comprehension; computation; evaluation; figure; forecast; guess; honor; idea; judgment; opinion; prediction; projection; rating; reckoning; valuation; weight

ESTRANGE: (see "divide") alienate; detach; disaffect; disunite; divert; divorce; draw; part; separate; sever; sunder; wean; withdraw

ESURIENT: (see "greedy") avid; hungry; voracious

ETCH: (see "engrave") bite; chisel; corrode; cut; delineate; design; draw; erode; furrow; impress; imprint; incise; inscribe; mark; outline

ETERNAL: abiding; absolute; ageless; amaranthine; bottomless; boundless; ceaseless; changeless; chronic; constant; continual; continuous; cosmic; deathless; diuturnal; durable; endless; enduring; ever(lasting); excessive; fadeless; fixed; granitic; illimitable; immarcescible; immeasurable; immortal; immutable: impenetrable; imperishable; incessant; inconceivable; indefaceable; indefectible; indefinite; indelible; indestructible; indeterminable; indissoluble; ineffaceable; ineradicable; inerasable; inextirpable; infinite; interminable; irradicable; irremovable; irreversible; irrevocable; lasting; limitless; measureless; nonperishable; perdurable; perdurant; permanent; perpetual; persistent; self-existent; sempiternal; solid; stable; steadfast; supertemporal; timeless; unalterable; unbegotten; unbounded; unceasing; unchangeable; unchanging; uncircumscribed; uncreated; undiminishable; undying; unending; uneradicable; unerasable; unfailing; unfathomable; unfathomed; universal; unlimited; unmeasureable; unrestrained; vast; ETERNALITY: see "permanence;" ETERNITY: (see "age") aeon; diuturnity; eon; eternality; everlastingness; eviternity; Ewigkeit; glory; immortability; immortality; indefinitude; infinitude; infinity; olam; perpetuality; perpetuity; sempiternity; tenuity; time(lessness)

ETHER: (see "air") amyl; anesthetic; atmosphere; drug; empyrean; ester; heaven(s); ozone; sky; space

ETHEREAL: (see "airy") aerial; aery; celestial; dainty; delicate; diaphanous; disembodied; empyreal; empyrean; exquisite; fairy; fine; fragile; heavenly; immaterial; incorporeal; insubstantial; light; rare; refined; spiritual; supernal; tenuous; thin; unembodied; ETHEREALITY: (see "airiness") diaphaneity; etherealness; insubstantiality

ETHICAL: (see "moral") accepted; conformable; correct; decent; good; honest; noble; right(eous); virtuous; ETHICS: (see "morals") correctness; customs; decency; honesty; morality; principles; propriety; virtue

ETIOLATE: blanch; bleach; fade; pale; weaken; whiten

ETIQUETTE: (see "manners") action(s); behavior; ceremony; conduct; convention (ality); conventions; custom; decora (pl.); decorum; deportment; form(ality); mien; politeness; (the) proprieties; propriety; protocol; rules; urbanity

EULOGIZE: (see "applaud") boost; commend; exalt; extol; glorify; laud; magnify; panegyrize; pedestal; praise; EULOGY: (see "applause") commendation; eloge; encomium; eulogium; exaltation; glorification; laudation; paean; panegyric; praise; tribute; EULOGISTIC: (see "commendable") acclamatory; approbatory; cheering; commendatory; complimentary; congratulatory; elegiac; encomiastic; eulogistical; glorifying; laudatory; panegyric(al); praiseworthy; recommendatory

EUPHONY: (see "accord") concord(ance); harmony; lilt; melody; meter; rhythm; symphony

EVACUATE: (see "abandon") clear (out); defecate; deprive; desert; eject; emit; empty; expel; flee; fly; forsake; leave; move; purge; quit; remove; siphon; urinate; vacate; void; withdraw

EVADE: (see "avoid") baffle; bilk; camouflage; cavil; circumvent; cloak; cover; deceive; dissemble; dodge; duck; elope; elude; equivocate; escape; finesse; flee; fly; foil; leapfrog; lie; maneuver; palter; parry; prevaricate; quibble; screen; shift; shun; shunt; shy; slip; tergiversate; thwart; trick; veil; EVASION: (see "digression") artifice; avoidance; camouflage; circumlocution; circumvention; deception; dodge; duplicity; equivocation; escape; escapism; flight; maneuver; obliquity; runaround; shift; stratagem; subterfuge; tergiversation; trick; EVASIVE: (see "digressive") cunning; deceptive; disingenuous; dissembling; duplicitous; eely; elusive; equivocal; escapist; evanescent; foxy; nebulous; oblique; opportunistic; shifty; shuffling; shy; slippery; tricky

EVALUATE: adjudicate; appraise; ascertain; assay; assess; calculate; charge; consider; count; discriminate; estimate; examine; figure; gather; judge; measure; number; ponder; rate; regard; tax; test; think; trace; value; vote; weigh

EVAPORATE: (see "vanish") atomize; decline; depart; desiccate; diminish; disappear; dissolve; distil(l); dry; emit; evanesce; exhale; expel; lose; melt; shrink; steam; vaporize; volatize; weaken

EVEN: v. (see "balance") equal(ize); level; match; plane; regulate; rival; set(tle); smooth; square; stabilize; tie; true; EVEN: a. (see "equal") balanced; calm; clear; constant; continuous; direct; equable; equanimous; equitable; exact; fair; fifty-fifty; flat; flush; glabrous; horizontal; impartial; just; level; matched; moderate; open; parallel(ed); placid; plain; plane; pure; quiet; regular; same; *semper eadem*; serene; smooth; square; steady; straight; sweet; thorough; tied; true; unbroken; uniform; unruffled; unshaken; EVENNESS: (see "equality") balance; calm; consistency; continuity; directness; equability; equanimity; exactness; fairness; flatness; impartiality; justice; justness; levelness; parallel; placidity; regularity; serenity; smoothness; uniformity

EVENING: (see "decline") afternoon; crepuscle; dusk; eve; eventide; P.M.; soiree; sunset; twilight

EVENT: (see "party") accident; activity; adventure; affair; breakthrough; calamity; case; casus; chance; circumstance; circumstantiality; condition; consequence; contest; contingency; date; deed; disaster; doing(s); effect; episode; eventuality; experience; exploit; fact(um); feat; happening; incident; issue; landmark; occasion; occurrence; outcome; phenomenon; process; result; sequel; tiding; time; tournament; upshot

EVENTUAL: (see "ultimate") final

EVENTUATE: (see "result") close; conclude; end; finalize; happen; occur

EVER: (see "always") aye; constantly; continually; e'er; eternal(ly); everlasting; evermore; extremely; forever; immensely; invariably; perpetually

EVERLASTING: abiding; adamantine; aeonian; ageless; agelong; amaranthine; changeless; constant; continual; continuing; dateless; diuturnal; durable; endless; enduring; eonian; eternal; eterne; forever; granitic; hourless; immarcescible; immarcescible; immemorial; immortal; imperishable; incessant; indefectible; indefinite; indelible; indestructible; inexhaustible; infrangible; in perpetuity; in saecula saeculorum; intemporal; interminable; inviolable; lasting; perpetual; sempiternal; tedious; timeless; unceasing; unchangeable; unchanging; undying; unending; unfading; unperishable; unrestricted; wearisome; EVERLASTINGNESS: (see "eternity") diuturnity; eviternity; immortability; immortality; imperishability; imperishableness; indefinitude; infinity; perpetuality; perpetuity; sempiternity; time (lessness); unendingness

EVERYWHERE: (see "universal") altogether; boundless; common; endemic;epidemic; far and near; far and wide; infinite; omnipresent; pandemic; peregrine; prevalent; thoroughly; ubiquitous; wherever; worldwide

EVICT: (see "eject") banish; cashier; debar; deprive; disbar; discard; discharge; dispossess; exclude; expel; fire; force (out); oust; recover; remove; sack; unfrock; EVICTION: banishment; deprivement; discharge; dispossession; ejection; exclusion; exile; expulsion; ouster; removal

EVIDENT: (see "clear") apparent; broad; certain; cognizable; conclusive; conspicuous; convincing; demonstra(ta)ble; discernible; distinct(ive); eminent; glaring; incontrovertible; indisputable; indubitable; lucent; luculent; manifest; noteworthy; noticeable; obvious; open; overt; palpable; patent; perceivable; perceptible; plain; ponderable; public; rampant; recognizable; sensible; symptomatic; tactile; tangible; transparent; unmistakable; visible

EVIDENCE: v. (see "testify") affirm; attest; confirm; deduce; demonstrate; depone; derive; develop; display; establish; evince; exhibit; express; indicate; manifest; occasion; probate; prove; provoke; reveal; show; speak; test; trace; verify; EVIDENCE: n. (see "facts") attestation; clew; criteria (pl.); criterion; data (pl.); datum; demonstration; grounds; indication; manifestation; mark; proof; sign; symptom; testament; testimony; token; trace; track; voucher; witness

EVIL: a. (see "bad") accursed; angry; baleful; baneful; base; corrupt(ed); depraved; demoniac(al); devilish; diabolic(al); disagreeable; foul; gangrenous; guileful; harmful; ill(-doing); immoral; inauspicious; infernal; iniquitous; lewd; low; Luciferian; malefic(ent); malevolent; malicious; malign (ant); malum; mean; miscreant; miserable; nefarious; noxious; offensive; pernicious; pestiferous; pestilent(ial); Satanic(al); serpentine; sinful; sinister; sinistrous; slanderous; unblessed; undesirable; unfortunate; unholy; unlucky; unpleasant; vicious; virulent; wicked; wrathful; wretched; wrong; EVIL: n. (see "badness") abomination; baseness; calamity; corruption; depravity; diabolism; disaster; disease; gangrene; harm; hurt; infamy; iniquitousness; iniquity; malefaction; maleficence; malevolence; malignancy; malum; misfortune; scourge; sin(fulness); sinisterity; suffering; vice; viciousness; virulence; wickedness; wrong

EVINCE: (see "evidence") attest; confirm; demonstrate; disclose; display; exhibit; indicate; manifest; occasion; prove; provoke; reveal; show

EVOKE: (see "arouse") awake(n); call; cite; depict; educe; elicit; enliven; exact; excite; invoke; live; provoke; recreate; rouse; stimulate; stir; suggest; summon; wake(n)

EVOLUTE: (see "advance") accumulate; develop; drift; evolve; expand; grow; mass; materialize; metamorphose; transform;

unfold; unroll; wax; EVOLUTION: accumulation; advancement; change; development; drift; expansion; genesis; growth; maneuver; materialization; metamorphosis; movement; ontogeny; outgrowth; phylogeny; process; progress(ion); transformation; transition; unfolding; unfoldment

EVOLVE: (see "advance") accumulate; deduce; derive; develop; disengage; disentangle; drift; educe; effloresce; emit; evaluate; exhibit; germinate; grow; unfold; unfurl; unroll; wax

EXACERBATE: (see "aggravate") deepen; embitter; enrage; exasperate; excite; expand; increase; infuriate; intensify; irk; irritate; provoke; tease; worsen

EXACT: v. (see "coerce") ask: claim; compel; demand; dragoon; extort; extract; force; hector; impose; levy; require; take; tax; wrest; wring; EXACT(ING): a. (see "rigid") accurate; arduous; arithmetical; careful; ceremonious; complete; conscientious; correct; deadly; definite; definitive; demanding; determinate; difficult; direct; due; even; exigent; faithful; fastidious; flat; formal; ideal; just; literal; literatim; lucid; mathematical; meet; meticulous; minute; nice; onerous; particular; perfect; pointed; precise; prompt; proper; punctilious; punctual; refined; reliable; right; rigoristic; rigorous; scrupulous; severe; sheer; slavish; specific; stern; stiff; strenuous; strict; thorough; tight; timely; true; unambiguous; undeviating; unequivocal; unerring; utter; verbatim; word-for-word; EXACTNESS: (see "certainty") accuracy; correctitude; correctness; definitude; determinacy; exactitude; fidelity; meticulosity; precision; punctuality; punctualness; scrupulosity; truth; EXACTION: see "coercion"

EXAGGERATE: (see "enlarge") amplify; color; embellish; embroider; enhance; expand; heighten; increase; invent; magnify; overact; overdo; overemphasize; overstate; pad; pontificate; romance; stretch; EXAGGERATED: (see "enlarged") abnormal; amplificatory; amplified; bizarre; colored; eccentric; embellished;embroidered; exceptional; extravagant; fabulous; fustian; heightened; hyperbolic(al); incredible; magnified; mythomanic; outré; overdone; overdrawn; overweening; padded; stretched; wild; EXAGGERATION: (see "enlargement") adornment; amplification; burlesque; embellishment; enhancement; expansion; extravagance; hyperbole; increase; inven-

tion; largeness; magnification; megalomania; Munchausenism; mythomania; ornamentation; overacting; overemphasis; overstatement; padding; phantasm(ata); stretch; wildness

EXALT: aggrandize; apotheosize; applaud; canonize; consecrate; deify; dignify; elate; elevate; enhance; ennoble; enshrine; eternalize; etherealize; extol; glorify; heighten; heroize; honor; increase; intensify; laud; magnify; nobilitate; pedestal; praise; promote; raise; refine; respect; revere(nce); sanctify; spiritualize; stellify; subtilize; transcend; transfigure; venerate; EXALTED: aggrandized; apotheosized; august; baronial; canonized; courtly; deified; dignified; elated; elegant; elevated; eminent; enhanced; ennobled; enshrined; esteemed; estimable; eulogistic(al); extolled; formal; grand(iose); high; honorable; honorific; illustrious; imperial; imposing; impressive; inspiring; Junoesque; kingly; leonine; lofty; lordly; magisterial; magnific(al); magnificent; magnified; majestic; marvelous; meritorious; nobilitated; noble; opulent; palatial; pedestalized; praiseworthy; Praxitelean; preeminent; princely; proud; queenly; redoubtable; regal; respected; royal; sculpturesque; sedate; serene; serious; solemn; splendid; splendiferous; splendorous; staid; stately; statuesque; stellified; sublime; togated; transcendent; transfigured; venerable; worthy; EXALTATION: aggrandizement; apotheosis; augustness; canonization; consecration; courtliness; deification; dignification; dignity; divinization; ecstasy; elevation; eminence; enhancement; ennoblement; enshrinement; esteem; estimation; ethereality; etherification; euphoria; excitement; extolment; frenzy; glorification; gloriousness; grandeur; greatness; honor; intensification; kingliness; kingship; lordship; lustrousness; magisteriality; magnificence; majesty; merit; nobilitation; nobility; opulence; praise; preeminence; princeliness; regality; repute; respect; reverence; seriousness; solemnity; spiritualization; state; stateliness; stellification; sublimity; sumptuousness; transcendence; transfiguration; veneration; virtue; worth(iness)

EXAMINE: analyze; anatomize; appose; ascertain; ask; assay; audit; break (down); canvas(s); catechize; check; clarify; collate; comb; consider; debate; delve; determine; dig; discuss; dissect; divide; enter; evaluate; excogitate; explore; eye; fathom; feel; finger; handle; hear; inquire; inspect; interrogate; investigate; look; manipulate; measure;

notice; observe; oversee; palpate; parse; part; penetrate; perceive; perlustrate; peruse; pick; pioneer; plumb; poll; pore; probe; prospect; pry; pump; pursue; question; quiz; rake; ramble; range; read; reconnoiter; rummage; scan; scout; scrutinize; search; see; seek; separate; sift; solicit; solve; sound; spade; spy; study; survey; test; titrate; trace; try; verify; weigh; EXAMINATION: analysis; anatomy; assay; audit; breakdown; catechism; check(up); clarification; critique; determination; dissection; dissolution; division; evaluation; exploration; going-over; inquest; inquiry; inquisition; inspection; interrogation; investigation; manipulation; measurement; notice; oral; perlustration; perscrutation; perusal; poll; probe; prospection; pursuit; quest; quiz; reconnaissance; reconnoiter; request; research; resolution; review; safari; scrutiny; search; separation; solution; speculation; study; survey; test; titration; trial; verification; weight; EXAMINER: anatomist; inspector; teacher

EXAMPLE: archetype; case; copy; design; drawing; exemplar; exemplification; exemplum; ideal; illustration; instance; item; lead; model; paradigm; paragon; parallel; pattern; piece; precedent; precept; problem; prototype; representation; rule; sample; specimen; standard; swatch; type; typification; unit; universal; warning

EXASPERATE: (**see** "anger") acerbate; annoy; blood; chafe; enrage; exacerbate; excite; gall; incense; inflame; infuriate; ire; irk; irritate; nettle; peeve; pique; provoke; roil; vex; EXASPERATION: (**see** "anger" and "consternation") testiness

EXCAVATE: (**see** "dig") burrow; cavitate; delve; drill; exhume; expose; grub; hollow; penetrate; perforate; scoop; shovel; sink; spade; EXCAVATION: (**see** "hole") cavitation; cavity; hollow; mine; pit; shaft; trench; well

EXCEED: (**see** "surpass") beat; cap; diminish; eclipse; enlarge; exaggerate; excel; extinguish; outdo; outnumber; outpace; outreach; outrival; outrun; outscore; outshine; outstrip; outvie; outweigh; overdo; overpass; overreach; overshadow; overtax; overtop; overwhelm; pass; precel; predominate; shine; star; top; transcend; win; EXCEEDING (LY): excessive; extremely; inordinate; notably; profound; superfluous; superlative(ly); surpassing; transcendent; vast(ly); very

EXCEL: (**see** "exceed") eclipse; extinguish; precel; shine; star; surpass; top; transcend; EXCELLING: preeminent; supereminent; surpassing; transcendent; transcending

EXCELLENT: acclamatory; admirable; adorable; adulatory; A-one; approbatory; attractive; banner; best; blue-ribbon; bravo; bully; capital; cheering; choice; class A; classy; commendable; commendative; commendatory; complimentary; congratulatory; consummate; corking; crackerjack; credi(ta)ble; dashing; desirable; distinguished; divine; elegant; elegiac; eminent; encomiastic(al); estimable; euge; eulogistic(al); exceptional; excessive; exemplary; expert; exquisite; extraordinary; extravagant; famous; fanciful; fancy; fine(st); first-class; first-line; first-rate; gallant; glorifying; glorious; good; high(-class); honest; ideal(istic); idolatric; idolatrous; immense; incomparable; inexplicable; laudable; laudative; laudatory; magnificent; marvelous; meritorious; mirific; *ne plus supra*; *ne plus ultra*; nonpareil; notable; noteworthy; novel; *nulli secundus*; outstanding; panegyric(al); paramount; perfect; pious; pleasing; praisable; praise-worthy; preeminent; premium; preternatural; prime; prominent; proper; pure; rare; *recherché*; recommendatory; remarkable; rich; royal; screaming; select(ed); signal; significant; singular; solid; sovereign; splendid; splendiferous; splendorous; sterling; supereminent; superior; superlative; supernal; superordinary; supreme; surpassing; tiptop; top(s); uncommon; undeniable; unexampled; unique; unparalleled; unprecedented; unsurpassed; unusual; valiant; valuable; whizbang; wondrous; worthy; EXCELLENCE: arete; consequence; craftsmanship; dignity; divineness; divinity; eminence; excellentness; fame; grace; ideal; magnificence; markmanship; merit; paramountcy; perfection; praise; preeminence; probity; prominence; prowess; purity; quality; selectivity; splendor; standing; stature; status; superiority; transcendence; valor; value; virtue; worth(iness)

EXCEPT: **v.** (**see** "exclude") bar; exempt; object; omit; qualify; reject; release; EXCEPT: **conj.** besides; but; unless; EXCEPTION: affront; complaint; demur; deviation; doubt; exclusion; exemption; objection; offense; omission; qualification; reserve; restriction; EXCEPTIONAL: (**see** "excellent") aberrant; aberrative; abnormal; choice; extraordinary; incomparable; inexplicable; nonpareil; novel; outstanding; preeminent; preternatural; *recherché*; remarkable; scarce; signal; singular; superior; supernal: supernatural; superordinary; uncommon; unexampled; unique; unparalleled; unprecedented; unusual

EXCERPT: **v. see** "select;" EXCERPT(S): **n.** abstract; analecta (pl.); analects; choice; chrestomathy; cital; citation; collectanea (pl.); *disjecta membra* (pl.); essence; extract (ion); fragment; miscellanea (pl.); *morceaux choisis*; motto; paraphrase; passage; quotation; quote; reference; report; sample; scrapiana (pl.); selection; verse

EXCESS: (**see** "abundance" and "superfluity") copiosity; copiousness; debauch(ery); difference; dissipation; excessiveness; exorbitance; exorbitancy; extravagance; flood; furbelow; gingerbread; glut; gobs; gravy; immoderation; inordinateness; intemperance; interest; lavishness; lots; luxuriance; luxus; margin; nimiety; odds; overabundance; overflow; overplus; plenty; plenum; plethora; prodigality; profit; profusion; prolixity; redundance; redundancy; remainder; repletion; sate; satiety; *satis superque*; superabundance; superabundancy; supererogation; superflux; surfeit; surplus(age); wastefulness; EXCESSIVE: (**see** "extreme") abundant; *à gogo*; all-fired; bountiful; copious; *de trop*; devilish; elevated; exceeding; exorbitant; extortionate; extra(vagant); exuberant; fabulous; fancy; ferocious; flooded; flooding; galore; generous; gingerbread; great(er); hog-wild; immoderate; inconsolable; inexhaustible; inordinate; intemperate; intolerable; large; lavish; liberal; lush; luxuriant; luxurious; needless; nimious; nonessential; numerous; ornamentative; over(abundant); overboard; overflowing; overfull; overloaded; overmuch; plentiful; pleonastic; plethoric; prodigal; profligate; profuse; rampant; rank; reckless; recrementitious; redundant; replete; sheer; spare; steep; superabundant; supererogatory; superfluous; superlative; supernatural; surpassing; surplus; thick; towering; ultra; unconscionable; undue; unlimited; unmerciful; unnecessary; unreasonable; unrestrained; unrestricted; unstinted; utter; wasteful

EXCHANGE: **v.** (**see** "barter") alternate; commute; convert; counterchange; interchange; pass; reciprocate; replace; rotate; sell; shuffle; sub(stitute); swap; trade; transfer; transpose; EXCHANGE: **n.** alternation; bank; barter; bourse; center; communion; commutation; deal; give-and-take; interchange; market; pit; *quid pro quo*; reciprocity; redemption; replacement; rotation; sale;

shift; shop; store; substitute; substitution; swap; trade; traffic; transaction; transfer; transposition

EXCHEQUER: bank; bourse; exchange; finances; fisc; purse; treasury

EXCISE: **v.** (**see** "cut") collect; detach; erase; exact; expunge; extirpate; fine; impose; levy; rate; remove; resect; retrench; tax; EXCISE: **n.** assessment; cess; collection; customs; duty; estreat; extraction; fee; fine; impost; levy; rate; revenue; seizure; tax; tithe; toll; tribute

EXCITE: (**see** "aggravate") activate; affect; agitate; anger; annoy; arouse; augment; awaken; bestir; chafe; commove; elate; electrify; elevate; enrage; exacerbate; exasperate; fillip; fire; flush; galvanize; goad; heat; hurry; impassion; incense; incite; increase; induce; inflame; infuriate; inspire; inspirit; intoxicate; irritate; kindle; lash; madden; move; pique; precipitate; provoke; raise; rally; rankle; roil; rouse; shiver; shock; startle; stimulate; sting; stir; suscitate; taunt; tease; thrill; tingle; weaken; whet; work; worry; EXCITED: (**see** "enthusiastic") activated; afire; agasp; aggravated; agitated; agitato; agog; angered; animated; aroused; astir; atingle; avid; awakened; breezy; chafed; delirious; elated; emotional; enraged; exacerbated; exasperated; febrile; feverish; fired; frenetic; frenzied; gay; goaded; hectic; incensed; increased; induced; inflamed; infuriated; inspired; inspirited; intoxicated; irritated; kindled; mad(dened); moved; overheated; overwrought; passionate; piqued; provoked; raised; roiled; roused; stimulated; stirred; violent; warm; worked (up); EXCITING *or* EXCITATORY: alarmable; alarmist; breathless; breathtaking; captivating; excitable; excitative; high (-strung); hyperactive; hysteric(al); ignitable; incitative; incitory; intense; intriguing; precipitating; provocative; riotous; stimulating; stimulatory; stirring; temperamental; thrilling; EXCITEMENT: ado; agitation; alarm; alarums and excursions; anger; annoyance; augmentation; bustle; commotion; concitation; ecstasy; emotion; enragement; exaltation; fanteeg; fantigue; feeling; ferment; fever; fever pitch; fomentation; frenzy; fume; furor(e); fury; gaiety; heat; hoopla; hurry; hyperactivity; hysteria; incitation; instigation; intoxication; irritation; madness; mania; merriment; orgasm; passion; precipitation; racket(ry); raptus; sensation; state; stimulation; stimulus; stir;

tension; thrill; tingle; to-do; transport; uproar; violence; worry

EXCLAIM: bawl; blurt; call; clamor; command; cry; ejaculate; noise; outcry; proclaim; rejoice; roar; scream; shout; tell; utter; vociferate; yell; EXCLAMATION: call; clamor; command; conclamation; cry; ecphonesis; ejaculation; expletive; hallelujah; interjection; outcry; proclamation; protest; roar; scream; shout; vociferation; yell; yoo-hoo; EXCLAMATORY: ejaculatory; emotional; emphatic; expletive; expletory; proclamatory; vociferant; vociferous

EXCLUDE: (see "banish") bar; blackball; block; boycott; count out; debar; defrock; deport; dethrone; disbar; discharge; drop; eject; eliminate; except; excommunicate; excuse; exempt; exile; exonerate; expel; expunge; fence; free; ghettoize; limit; object; omit; ostracize; oust; preclude; prevent; prohibit; purge; qualify; refuse; reject; release; relieve; remove; restrain; seclude; segregate; separate; suspend; unfrock; unhorse; EXCLUSION: (see "banishment"); censorship; debarring; ejection; elimination; exception; excommunication; exile; expulsion; fence; omission; ostracism; ouster; preclusion; prevention; rejection; segregation; separation; sequestration; suspension

EXCLUSIVE: (see "alone") aristocratic; clannish; cliqu(e)ish; cliqu(e)y; elect; enisled; entire; expensive; fashionable; limited; limiting; narrow; only; particular; peculiar (some); posh; private; restricted; restrictive; select; single; snobbish; sole; solitary; special; stylish; undivided; whole; EXCLUSIVENESS: clannishness; cliqueism; exclusivity; narrowness; particularism; particularity; restrictiveness; segregation; selectivity; separateness; separatism; snobbishness; solitariness

EXCOGITATE: (see "think") consider; contrive; devise; dream; examine; invent; muse

EXCOMMUNICATE: (see "banish") anathematize; bar; defrock; exclude; interdict; ostracize; unfrock; EXCOMMUNICATION: (see "banishment") anathema(tism); anathematization; censure; interdiction; ostracism

EXCORIATE: (see "abrade") blister; burn; censure; chafe; curse; excrecate; flay; gall; gouge; lash; mark; peel; revile; scar(ify); score; scorch; skin; slash; upbraid

EXCREMENT: (see "dung") defecation; dejecta (pl.); droppings; ejecta (pl..); excreta (pl.); excretion; feces; feculence; manure; ordure; stercory; stercus; stool; waste

EXCRESCENCE: (see "growth") development; enlargement; fungus; knob; lump; outgrowth; protrusion; superfluity; wart

EXCRETE: (see "eliminate") discharge; ooze; perspire; separate; sweat

EXCULPATE: (see "acquit") absolve; clear

EXCURSION: caravan; circuit; cruise; depature; deviation; digression; drive; enterprise; excursus; expedition; exploration; hike; jaunt; journey; movement; outing; paseo; peregrination; promenade; quest; raid; ramble; reconnaissance; ride; safari; sally; sortie; tour; travel; trek; trip; undertaking; voyage; walk

EXCUSE: **v.** (see "acquit") absolve; conciliate; condone; defend; disregard; exculpate; exempt; exonerate; explain; extenuate; forget; forgive; forgo; free; gloss; ignore; intellectualize; justify; liberate; overlook; palliate; pardon; pass; pretermit; rationalize; release; remit; reprieve; spare; tolerate; vindicate; waive; wink; EXCUSE: **n.** (see "acquittal") absolution; acquittance; alibi; amnesty; apology; come-off; conciliation; condonation; defense; dispensation; dodge; exculpation; exemption; exoneration; explanation; extenuation; forgiveness; freedom; gloss; grace; indulgence; intellectualization; justification; mercy; out; palliation; pardon; plea; pretense; pretext; provocation; rationalization; reason; release; remission; show; vindication; waiver; EXCUSABLE: apologetic; condonable; defensible; dispensable; forgivable; justifiable; pardonable; venial

EXECRATE: (see "abhor") abominate; anathematize; berate; condemn; contemn; curse; damn; denounce; detest; hate; imprecate; objurgate; rate; reprehend; revile; EXECRABLE: (see "bad") abominable; awful; base; cursed; damnable; damned; despicable; detestable; horrifying; lamentable; low; odious; offensive; poor; reprehensible; repulsive; revolting; vile; wretched

EXECUTE: (see "accomplish") achieve; act(ualize); administer; attain; close; complete; conduct; consummate; discharge; dispatch; do; effect(uate); enforce; finalize; finish; force; fulfill; gain; give; govern; hand; kill; make; obtain; perpetrate; play;

reach; realize; rule; seal; sign; speed; use; EXECUTION: (**see** "accomplishment") electrocution

EXECUTIVE: (**see** "leader") administrator; boss; brass(hat); chairman; director; foreman; judge; magistrate; officer; president; secretary

EXEMPLARY: (**see** "commendable") archetyp(ic)al; classic(al); exemplificative; exemplificatory; ideal(istic); illustrative; model; monitory; paradigmatic(al); prototyp(ic)al; standard; EXEMPLAR: (**see** "example") archetype; copy; exemplum; ideal; model; pattern; prototype; sample; specimen; standard; universal

EXEMPT: **v.** (**see** "exclude") deliver; discharge; except; excuse; exonerate; forgive; free; indemnify; release; relieve; remove; save; EXEMPT(ED): **a.** apart; excepted; excluded; excused; exonerated; forgiven; free(d); immune; relieved; removed; untouchable; EXEMPTION: discharge; dispensation; essoin; exception; exoneration; franchise; freedom; immunity; impunity; indemnification; indulgence; liberation; privilege; release; relief; removal; safety;

EXERCISE: **v.** (**see** "act") apply; discipline; do; drill; effect(uate); employ; exert; gymnasticize; harass; operate; perform; ply; practice; school; study; tax; train; use; vex; wield; EXERCISE: **n.** (**see** "action") activity; application; composition; discipline; drill; employment; execution; exertion; exhibit; gymnastics; harassment; lesson; maneuver; nisus; operation; performance; practice; praxis; study; task; test; theme; training; use; work

EXERT: (**see** "act") contend; direct; do; drive; effect(uate); endeavor; exercise; force; grind; impose; impress; labor; operate; perform; ply; press; pull; push; rival; spurt; stir; strain; stretch; struggle; tax; thrust; toil; try; tug; work; EXERTION: (**see** "action") bout; contention; dint; direction; drive; effort; endeavor; exercise; force; grind; labor; pains; power; press; pull; push; spurt; stir; strain; stretch; struggle; thrust; toil; trouble; tug; vigor; wield; work

EXFOLIATE: **see** "scale"

EXHALE: aspire; blow; breathe; emanate; emit; evince; exhaust; expel; expire; express; gasp; gulp; huff; inspire; ooze; pant; percolate; reek; smell; sniff; suspire; wheeze;

EXHALATION: (**see** "breath") air; aura; effluvia (pl.); effluvium; emanation; evaporation; exhalement; exhaust; expiration; flatus; fume; odor; reek; smoke; steam; vapor

EXHAUST: **v.** consume; decay; deplete; deprive; destroy; deteriorate; devitalize; diminish; disburse; discharge; discomfort; distress; distribute; drain; dwindle; eject; emit; empty; evacuate; evaporate; expend; extract; fag; fatigue; finish; flog; gratify; indulge; jade; liquidate; overdo; overspend; overstrain; overtax; pay; pour; purchase; sap; shoot; spend; squander; suck; tax; tire; use; waste; weaken; wear; weary; wreck; EXHAUST: **n.** (**see** "exhalation") effluvia (pl.); effluvium; suction; EXHAUSTED: (**see** "fatigued") beat; blown; bushed; careworn; consumed; dead; debilitated; depleted; deprived; destroyed; devitalized; dilapidated; dissipated; done; drawn; effete; empty; fagged; fretted; gaunt; gone; haggard; harrowed; impoverished; jaded; lean; limp; meager; overdone; overdriven; overtaxed; petered; scrawny; spare; spent; thin; tired; wan; washed-out; wasted; weak(ened); wearied; weary; worn(-down); worn-out; wrinkled; EXHAUSTION: (**see** "fatigue") decadence; depletion; devitalization; emptiness; enervation; overstrain; sellout; weakness; weariness

EXHIBIT: **v.** (**see** "air") advertise; array; demonstrate; disclose; display; dramatize; drill; evince; explain; expose; express; flaunt; flourish; grandstand; have; hold forth; illustrate; manifest; march; marshal; mount; offer; parade; picture; present; promenade; represent; reveal; show; stage; state; uncover; unmesh; unveil; vent; wear; EXHIBIT(ION): **n.** (**see** "demonstration") array(ment); attraction; ceremony; collection; contest; disclosure; display; diversion; drama; drawing; drill; event; evincing; exercise; exposure; fair; flourish; game; manifestation; march; museum; ostent (ation); pageant(ry); performance; picture; play; pomp(osity); presentation; procession; promenade; recital; representation; revelation; show(case); showing; show-off; sideshow; spectacle; spectacular; splendor; uncovering

EXHILARATE: (**see** "elevate") animate; boost; buoy; cheer; elate; elevate; enliven; fire; gladden; inspire; inspirit; intoxicate; invigorate; please; refresh; stimulate; stir; titillate; EXHILARATED: (**see** "animated") buoyant; cheerful; ebullient; ecstatic; elated; enlivened; enthused; enthusiastic; euphoric; exhilarant; exhilarative; heady; impassioned; inspired; inspirited; intoxicated; invigorated; rapturous; titillated; zealous; zestful; EXHILARATION: (see "animation") buoyancy; cheer; ebulliency; ecstasy; elation; enlivenment; euphoria; fire; gaiety; glee(fulness); headiness; hilarity; intoxication; invigoration; joy(ousness); refreshment; stimulation; stir; titillation; zeal(otry); zest(fulness)

EXHORT: (see "caution") advise; encourage; incite; persuade; preach; prophesy; sermonize; urge; warn; EXHORTATION: (see "caution") advice; cautiousness; cohortation; counsel; encouragement; incitation; persuasion; preachment; sermon; warning

EXHUME: (see "dig") delve; disentomb; disinter; excavate; exhumate; expose; grub; revive; spade; uncover; unearth

EXIGENCY: (see "crisis") constraint; demand; difficulty; distress; embarrassment; emergency; essential; exigence; fix; juncture; necessity; need; pass; pinch; plight; pressure; requirement; strain; strait; urgency; want; EXIGENT: see "dire" and "urgent"

EXIGUOUS: (see "meager") attenuated; diminutive; fine; narrow; scant(y); slender; small; spare; sparse; tiny; wee

EXILE: v. (see "banish") deport; drive; eject; expatriate; expel; extradite; ostracize; relegate; separate; EXILE: n. (see "banishment") absence; deportation; Diaspora; ejection; expatriate; expatriation; extradition; fugitive; fugitivity; ostracism; relegation; separation; transportation

EXIST: (see "breathe") abide; be; continue; endure; grow; live; maintain; remain; subsist; survive; thrive; EXISTENCE: (see "actuality") animation; being(ness); continuity; corporality; corporeity; duration; ens; entity; esse(nce); existent; life; maintenance; materiality; reality; state; status; substantiality; substantivity; survival; way

EXIT: v. depart; die; egress; elope; emigrate; escape; flee; go; issue; withdraw; EXIT: n. aisle; death; demise; departure; door(way); egress(ion); elopement; emigration; end; escape (route); exitus; exodus; flight; going; hegira; issuance; outlet; postern; road; route; vent; way; withdrawal

EXODUS: (see "exit") departure; egress;

emigration; escape; flight; fugitivity; going; hegira; withdrawal

EXONERATE: (see "acquit") absolve; clear; exculpate; excuse; exempt; forgive; free; pardon; release; relieve; remit; vindicate; EXONERATION: (see "acquittal") absolution; clearance; exculpation; exemption; freedom; pardon; release; relief; remission; vindication

EXORBITANT: (see "expensive") costly; dear; exceeding; excessive; extravagant; extreme; greedy; *hors de prix*; inordinate; sky-high; steep; unjust; unreasonable

EXORCISM: charm; exorcization; expulsion; formula; incantation; rite; sorcery; spell; witchery

EXORDIUM: beginning; foreword; introduction; opening; overture; preamble; preface; prelude; proem; prologue

EXOTERIC: a. comprehensible; exterior; external; known; open; outside; plain; popular; public; EXOTERIC: n. alien; outsider

EXOTIC: (see "showy") alien; elaborate; extraneous; foreign; glamorous; mysterious; *outré*; peregrine; picturesque; *recherché*; rich; romantic; strange; EXOTICISM: see "unusualness"

EXPAND: (see "add") accelerate; amplify; augment; delate; develop; dilate; distend; educate; elaborate; enhance; enlarge; enrich; escalate; evolve; exaggerate; expatiate; explain; explode; extend; flan; foam; grain; grow; increase; inflate; intumesce; lengthen; luxuriate; magnify; multiply; mushroom; open; pass; proliferate; splay; spread; sprout; stretch; stuff; swell; tumefy; tumesce; unfold; widen; EXPANDED: see "spread;"

EXPANSIVE: (see "wide") dilatable; dila(ta)tive; elastic; expandable; generous; genial; lithe; resilient; rubbery; springy; supple; EXPANSION: (see "addition") amplification; augmentation; development; diastole; dila(ta)tion; enlargement; evolution; exacerbation; exaggeration; expansiveness; extension; growth; hypertrophy; increase; mushrooming; proliferation; prolongation; rise; spread; sprouting; stretch; tumescence; tumidity; tympany; widening; EXPANSIVENESS: see "spaciousness"

EXPANSE: (see "area") acre(s); acreage;

breadth; broadness; distance; extension; extent; field; firmament; length; limit; mass; ocean; orbit; range; reach; scope; sea; sphere; spread; stretch; sweep; tract; waste (ness); width; wildness

EXPATIATE: (see "add") amplify; descant; dilate; discourse; elaborate; enlarge; expand; rant; speak; spread; tell; wander

EXPATRIATE: (see "banish") deport; exile; expel; proscribe; ostracize; withdraw

EXPECT: (see "anticipate") await; bank; believe; contemplate; dare; deem; dream; foresee; hope; look; presume; presuppose; rely; suppose; think; trust; wait; wish; EXPECTED or EXPECTANT: (see "anticipatory") anticipant; anticipated; anticipative; awaited; contemplated; contingent; deemed; foreseen; hoped; inchoate; inchoative; incipient; obligated; possible; potential; pregnant; prospective; unsurprised; wished; EXPECTATION: (see "anticipation") assumption; belief; contemplation; expectancy; future; hope; presumption; prospect; supposition; thought; trust; waiting; wish

EXPECTORATE: eject; emit; spatter; spew; spit

EXPEDIENT: a. (see "favorable") advantageous; advisable; astucious; astute; auspicious; desirable; efficient; expediential; fit (ting); opportune; opportunistic; politic(al); practical; proper; propitious; suitable; useful; EXPEDIENT: n. (see "fitness") advisability; advisableness; contrivance; desirability; device; dodge; expedience; expediency; makeshift; means; resort; resource(s); self-interest; stopgap; suitability; temporization

EXPEDITE: (see "hasten") accelerate; advance; bribe; dispatch; ease; expediate; extricate; facilitate; grease; hie; high; hurry; issue; oil; quicken; run; rush; speed; EXPEDITION: (see "caravan") acceleration; campaign; celerity; cruise; crusade; drive; enterprise; entrada; excursion; excursus; exploration; haste; hike; hurry; jaunt; journey; outing; peregrination; promenade; promptness; quest; raid; ramble; reconnaissance; ride; safari; sally; sortie; speed; tour; travel; trek; trip; undertaking; voyage; walk; EXPEDITIOUS: see "fast"

EXPEL: (see "banish") cast; disbar; discharge; dislodge; dismiss; disown; displace; dispossess; drive (out); drum; egest; eject; eliminate; emit; evaporate; evict; exclude;

execrate; exile; expatriate; expectorate; extrude; free; oust; proscribe; relegate; remove; sack; spit; vent; EXPULSION: (see "banishment") discharge; dismissal; displacement; dispossession; ejection; elimination; eviction; exclusion; exile; expatriation; extrusion; ouster; proscription; relegation; removal

EXPEND: (see "exhaust") disburse; distribute; gratify; indulge; pay; pour; purchase; spend; tire; wreak; EXPENDITURE: (see "expense") disbursement; effort; indulgence; outlay; output; payment; purchase

EXPENSE(S): amount; burden; charge; cost; deprivation; detriment; disbursement; effort; expenditure; indulgence; loss; money; outgo; outlay; pain; payment; price (tag); purchase; stipend; suffering; sum; tab; tag; tax; upkeep; EXPENSIVE: confiscatory; costly; dear; detrimental; dispendious; elegant; esteemed; exceeding; excessive; exclusive; exorbitant; extravagant; extreme; greedy; high; *hors de prix*; inestimable; inordinate; lavish; plush; posh; precious; priceless; prodigal; rare; rich; sky-high; steep; stiff; sumptuous; uneconomic(al); unjust; unreasonable; valuable; wasteful; worthy

EXPERIENCE: v. (see "suffer") accomplish; brave; discover; do; encounter; enjoy; feel; find; hold; know; learn; live; meet; permit; realize; sample; see; subject; sustain; test; try; undergo; use; EXPERIENCE: n. (see "competency") acquaintance(ship); adeptness; affairs; background; capability; capacity; career; competency; culture; demonstration; discipline; education; episode; escapade; event; experiment; facility; familiarity; happening; knowledge; life; observation; ordeal; participation; practice; result; skill; sophistication; suffering; test; training; trial; tribulation; use; versatility; wisdom; work; world; EXPERIENCED: (see "competent") able; accomplished; adept; capable; consummate; expedient; expert; familiar; finished; knowing; knowledge(e)able; old(er); practiced; salty; seasoned; skilled; skillful; sophisticated; tested; trained; tried; versant; versatile; versed; veteran; weighed; wise

EXPERIMENT: v. (see "research") assay; attempt; demonstrate; endeavor; examine; exercise; experience; feel; investigate; practice; tamper; test; try; EXPERIMENT: n. (see "research") assay; attempt; demonstration; endeavor; examination; exercise; experimentation; investigation; ordeal; practice; proof; test; trial; undertaking; EXPERIMENTAL: contingent; developmental; empirical; experimentative; factual; intentional: investigative; tentative; trial-and-error

EXPERT: **a.** (**see** "able") ace; adapted; adept; adroit; ambidextrous; A-one; apt; *au fait*; capable; clever; competent; consummate; crack; deft; dexterous; educated; excellent; experienced; facile; knowing; knowledgeable; licensed; notable; outstanding; practiced; professional; proficient; qualified; skilled; skillful; tested; trained; versatile; versed; virtuosic; whiz-bang; EXPERT: **n.** ace; adept; arcanist; artist(e); authority; cognoscente; connoisseur; consultant; doyen; doyenne (fem.); esthete; illuminato; journeyman; licensee; master; past master; past mistress; pro(fessional); seer; shark; specialist; virtuoso; whiz(bang); wizard; EXPERTNESS: adeptness; adroitness; ambidexterity; expertise; expertism; hability; know-how; proficiency; skill(fulness); versatility; virtuosity

EXPIATE: accord; adapt; adjust; agree; appease; atone; avert; conciliate; condone; medicate; mollify; pacify; placate; propitiate; purge; quiet(en); reconcile; rectify; restore; settle; shrive; soothe; square; EXPIATION: accord; amends; appeasement; cross; hair shirt; penance; propitiation; recompense; reconciliation; redemption; reparation; satisfaction; trial

EXPIRE: (**see** "die") cease; close; conclude; discontinue; elapse; emit; end; exhale; lapse; pass; perish; slip; terminate

EXPLAIN: account (for); annotate; answer; clarify; clear (up); construe; decipher; define; demonstrate; depurate; disclose; elaborate; elucidate; elutriate; enlighten; exhibit; expand; expatiate; explicate; exposit; expound; illume; illuminate; illustrate; interpret; justify; manifest; prove; rationalize; resolve; reveal; riddle; settle; simplify; solve; speed; teach; translate; unfold; unravel; unscramble; EXPLANATORY: analytical; discursive; epexegetic(al); essayistic; exegetic-(al); explanative; explicative; explicatory; expositive; expository; hermeneutic; interpretative; paraphrastic(al); resolutive; resolutory; EXPLANATION: alibi; annotation; answer; clarification; commentary; construction; demonstration; description; disclosure; disquisition; *éclaircissement*; elaboration; elucidation; elutriation; enlightenment; excuse; exegesis; explication; exposition; gloss(ary); illumination; illustration; interpretation; justification; key; legend; manifestation;

meaning; proof; rationale; rationality; reconciliation; revelation; significance; simplification; solution; translation; understanding; EXPLAINER: (**see** "expounder") cicerone; elucidator; explanator; exponent; interpretator; interpreter; professor; teacher

EXPLICIT: (**see** "clear") absolute; categoric (al); certain; clean-cut; clear-cut; definite; definitive; determinate; distinct(ive); exact; expressed; fixed; full; intelligible; lucid; manifest; obvious; open; outspoken; plain; pointed; positive; precise; specific; unambiguous; unequivocal; unmistakable; unqualified; unquestionable

EXPLODE: (**see** "break") burst; cave; collapse; detonate; discharge; discredit; erupt; expand; fire; flash; fulminate; implode; mushroom; pop; puff; rend; resound; run; rupture; shatter; splinter; split; torpedo; EXPLOSIVE: **a.** combustible; dangerous; detonative; dynamitic; effusive; flammable; fulminative; fulminous; noisy; pyrotechnic (al); resounding; shattering; volatile; volcanic; EXPLOSIVE **n.** *or* EXPLOSION: blast; blowup; bumb; break; burst; clap; collapse; deflagration; detonation; discharge; dynamite; eruption; fiasco; flash; fulmination; gust; implosion; noise; outbreak; outburst; pop; rejection; rupture; sound; splintering; split; upheaval

EXPLOIT: **v.** (**see** "fool") advertise; bilk; bleed; clip; cultivate; manipulate; milk; play; publicize; use; utilize; work; EXPLOIT: **n.** (**see** "action") achievement; act; deed; fame; feat; gest(e); heroism; quest; work; EXPLOITING: destructive; exploitive; managing; manipulative; predaceous; predacious; predatory; wasteful; EXPLOITATION: (**see** "manipulation") advertising; destruction; predacity; publicity; utilization; waste

EXPLORE: (**see** "dig") delve; examine; fathom; feel; investigate; palpate; penetrate; pioneer; plumb; probe; prospect; ramble; range; reconnoiter; scout; scrutinize; seek; spade; spy; survey; test; wander; EXPLORATION: (**see** "examination") inquest; inquiry; investigation; probe; prospection; reconnaissance; reconnoiter; safari; scrutiny; search; survey; test

EXPLOSIVE: **see** under "explode"

EXPONENT: (**see** "backer") advocate; example; explainer; expounder; illustration; index; indication; ite; supporter; symbol; symptom

EXPOSE: (see "denounce") abandon; advertise; air; bare; debunk; denudate; denude; denunciate; desert; dig; disclose; discover; disinter; display; endanger; excavate; exhibit; exhume; gamble; give; hazard; husk; imperil; jeopardize; open; parade; peel; present; reveal; risk; show; shuck; skin; strip; subject; uncover; unearth; unhood; unhusk; unmask; unscreen; unshadow; unshroud; unveil; venture; voice; weather; EXPOSURE: (see "disclosure") airing; aspect; denouncement; denunciation; display; exhibition; exposition; hazard; jeopardy; peril; presentation; risk; unmasking; unveiling; ventilation; venture; vulnerability; weather

EXPOSTULATE: see "demand" and "protest"

EXPOUND: advertise; advocate; air; analyze; argue; blazon; comment; construe; declaim; defend; define; discourse; discuss; dissect; elocute; elucidate; explain; exposit; express; gloss; harangue; inform; instruct; interpret; mouth; orate; present; promulgate; rant; recite; rhetorize; speak; sport; state; teach; treat; utter; vent; voice; EXPOUNDER: exegete; exegetist; exponent; expositor

EXPRESS: **v.** abreact; air; assert; call; communicate; couch; declare; define; delineate; denote; depict; describe; designate; despatch; do; embody; emit; enunciate; evince; explain; forward; indicate; intone; mail; mean; portray; press; reflect; render; say; send; ship; show; signify; sketch; speak; state; symbolize; tell; trace; utter; vent(ilate); voice; write; EXPRESS: **a.** (see "certain") accurate; clear(-cut); definite; determinate; determinative; determined; distinct(ive); exact; explicit; fast; intelligible; lucid; manifest; obvious; open; plain; positive; possible; precise; specific; unmistakable; unquestionable

EXPRESSION: (see "aspect") appearance; attitude; composure; countenance; declaration; depiction; diction; direction; effusion; expressivity; facies; grimace; idiom; issue; locution; manifestation; mien; opinion; phrase(ology); posture; remark; saying; sign; statement; style; term; token; utterance; visage; word

EXPRESSIVE: (see "eloquent") articulate; emphatic; fluent; forceful; indicative; meaningful; oratoric(al); pointed; pregnant; revealing; rhetorical; sententious; significant; suggestive; telling; voluble; EXPRESSIVE-

NESS: (see "eloquence") articulateness; expressivity; oratory; plangency; rhetoric; significance; tone

EXPULSION: see "eviction"

EXPUNGE: (see "annihilate") cancel; dele-(te); destroy; discard; drop; efface; eradicate; erase; exclude; expurgate; obliterate; omit; remove; scrape; slash; strike

EXPURGATE: (see "censor") bathe; bowdlerize; castrate; cleanse; emasculate; expunge; exscind; purge; purify

EXQUISITE: (see "beautiful") accomplished; choice; dainty; delicate; discriminative; exact; excellent; finished; flawless; ingenious; perfect(ed); precious; rare; *recherché*; sensitive; *soigné*; *soignée* (fem.); superlative; transcendent

EXSCIND: (see "cut") excise; expurgate; extirpate; remove; resect

EXSICCATE: (see "dry") bake; dehydrate; desiccate; evaporate; parch; shrivel

EXTANT: see "contemporary"

EXTEMPORARY *or* EXTEMPORANEOUS: (see "impromptu") autoschediastic; extempore; improvised; improviso; makeshift; offhand(ed); spontaneous; sudden; uncalculated; unexpected; unpremeditated; EXTEMPORIZATION: autoschediasm; extemporaneity; improvisation; improvision; spontaneity; spontaneousness; unpremeditation

EXTEND: (see "add") advance; amplify; augment; beetle; broadcast; broaden; continue; develop; diffuse; dilate; direct; distend; eke; elongate; enlarge; expand; further; increase; jut; lengthen; lie; offer; overexert; proffer; project; prolong; promulgate; propagate; protract; protrude; ramify; reach; renew; roll; scatter; shoot; span; spin; spread; spring; straighten; stretch; surpass; sweep; swell; thrust; unbend; widen; EXTENSION: (see "addition") augmentation; broadening; compass; development; elongation; enlargement; expansion; furthering; increase; lengthening; prolongation; protraction; spread; EXTENT: (see "area") ambit; amplitude; caliber; circumference; compass; comprehension; comprehensiveness; course; degree; diameter; dimension; distance; gauge; height; intensity; length; level; limit; magnitude; measure; pitch;

prolongation; proportion; quota; ramification; range; reach; scope; size; space; span; sweep; thickness; tune; EXTENSIVE: complete; comprehensive; considerable; cyclopedic(al); extensional; extraordinary; far-flung; far-reaching; illimitable; indiscriminate; large; latitudinal; latitudinous; legion; lengthy; magnitudinous; many; massive; measureless; numberless; numerous; panoramic; sweeping; thorough; wholesale; wide; widened; widespread

EXTENUATE: (**see** "ease") diminish; lessen; mince; moderate; palliate; thin; weaken

EXTERIOR: **see** "external"

EXTERMINATE: (**see** "annihilate") abolish; decimate; demolish; deracinate; destroy; eradicate; execute; extinguish; extirpate; kill; murder; slaughter; slay; uproot; EXTERMINATION: (**see** "annihilation") abolishment; death; decimation; destruction; eradication; extinction; extirpation; murder; slaughter

EXTERNAL *or* EXTERIOR: **a.** accidental; adventitious; alien; apart; beyond; bodily; circumferential; cortical; ectal; exogenous; exoteric; extraneous; extrinsic(al); foreign; out(er); outside; outward; peripheral; physical; public; superficial; surface; ulterior; visible; EXTERNAL *or* EXTERIOR: **n.** boundary; externality; extraneity; outside; outwardness; peel; periphery; rind; shell; skin; surface

EXTINCTION: (**see** "death") abolishment; abolition; annihilation; cancellation; extermination; quenching; quietus; suppression

EXTINGUISH: (**see** "abolish") abate; annihilate; block; check; choke; crush; damp; deracinate; destroy; douse; drown; eclipse; end; eradicate; erase; excel; expel; exterminate; extirpate; kill; murder; nullify; obscure; out; overthrow; quash; quell; quench; remove; repress; slaughter; slay; smother; snuff; stamp (out); starve; stifle; suppress; uproot

EXTIRPATE: (**see** "abolish") annihilate; dele(te); deracinate; destroy; eradicate; erase; excise; exterminate; kill; murder; remove; root (out); slaughter; slay; stamp (out); uproot

EXTOL: (**see** "applaud") approbate; canonize; celebrate; commend; deify; emblazon; enhance; enshrine; eulogize; fetishize; glorify; laud; magnify; panegyrize; praise; proclaim; sanctify; spiritualize; worship

EXTORT: (**see** "coerce") bilk; blackmail; bleed; draw; educe; elicit; exact; extract; force; intimidate; milk; squeeze; wrench; wrest; wring; EXTORTION: (**see** "coercion") exaction; force; shakedown; squeeze

EXTRA: **a.** (**see** "extraordinary") accessory; added; additional; adjunct(ive); bonus; *de trop*; excessive; more(over); over; plus; redundant; spare; special; superfine; superfluous; superior; supernumerary; surplus; ultra; EXTRA: **n.** accessory; additional; bonus; more; redundance; redundancy; superabundance; supererogation; superfluity; supernumerary

EXTRACT: **v.** (**see** "abstract") cite; cut; deplete; derive; detach; **dig**; distil(l); draw; educe; elicit; estreat; evoke; evulse; exact; excerpt; extirpate; extort; extricate; grub; leach; mine; obtain; pry; pull; remove; render; select; separate; withdraw; EXTRACT: **n.** (**see** "essence") abstract; concentrate; concentration; concoction; condensation; copy; decoction; elicitation; estreat; excerpt; extraction; flavoring; genealogy; juice; pith; quintessence; quotation; sap; selection; synopsis

EXTRACTION: (**see** "birth") descent; elicitation; genealogy; line(age); origin(ation); parentage; separation

EXTRANEOUS: (**see** "remote") accidental; alien; exoteric; exotic; extrinsic; foreign; irrelevant; outer; outside; spurious; superfluous; ulterior; unessential; unrelated

EXTRAORDINARY: abnormal; adept; amazing; arresting; big; bizarre; celebrated; clever; conspicuous; curious; dignified; distinctive; distingished; egregious; eminent; eventful; exalted; exceptional; extensive; *extraordinaire*; fabulous; famous; gigantic; great; heroic; honored; huge; illustrious; impressive; inordinate; king-sized; marvelous; melodramatic; memorable; monstrous; notable; notorious; odd; outrageous; outstanding; particular; phenomenal; powerful; prodigious; prominent; raging; rare; *recherché*; remarkable; renowned; sensational; signal; significant; singular; skillful; special; stately; striking; superfine; superhuman; superlative; tremendous; uncommon; unordinary; unprecedented; unusual; whopping; wonderful; worthy

EXTRAVAGANT: (**see** "superfluous") absurd; abundant; affluent; Babylonian; Babylonic; bountiful; copious; costly; dear; dispendious; egregious; elaborate; exaggerated; excessive; exorbitant; extreme; exuberant; fanatic(al); fancy; fantastic(al); farcical; flighty; flush(ed); foolish; galore; gaudy; gothic; immoderate; important; improvident; incredible; inordinate; intemperate; irrational; lavish; liberal; Lucullan; lurid; lush; luxuriant; luxurious; magnificent; melodramatic; nimious; openhanded; opulent; plenteous; prodigal; profligate; profuse; profusive; prominent; rampant; rash; raving; reckless; redundant; replete; showy; shrill; sumptuous; superabundant; superfluous; thick; thriftless; ultra; uncommon; unending; unfrugal; unreal; unreasonable; unreasoning; unrestrained; unstinted; vivid; wanton; wasteful; wild; wonderful; EXTRAVAGANCE: (**see** "superfluity") abundance; bombast; bountifulness; bounty; *E la*; enthusiasm; exaggeration; excessiveness; exorbitance; extravagancy; extravaganza; fanaticism; grandiosity; immoderation; improvidence; insanity; intemperance; lavishness; lunacy; lusciousness; luxuriance; magnificence; nimiety; opulence; prodigality; profligacy; profusion; rampancy; redundance; redundancy; rhapsody; superabundance; superfluity; superflux; unreason(ableness); unrestraint; unthrift(iness); wantonness; wastefulness

EXTREME: abundant; acute; all-fired; almighty; arrant; bitter; bizarre; brutal; brutish; complete; conclusive; consummate; copious; cruel; dangerous; deadly; deep; demoniac(al); dense; desperate; despotic; *de trop*; devilish; dire; drastic; dreadful; eccentric; egregious; end; enormous; exceeding; excessive; exigent; exorbitant; extortionate; extra; extravagant; exuberant; fanatical; fancy; fantastic(al); far(-out); farthest; fearful; ferocious; final; flooded; flooding; forward; frantic; frightful; gingerbread; great(er); greatest; grim; harsh; hellish; high(est); immoderate; impiteous; inconsolable; incredible; inexhaustible; inexorable; inhuman(e); inordinate; intemperate; intense; intensive; intolerable; intransigent; large; last; lavish; left; liberal; lush; luxuriant; malicious; maximum; merciless; needless; nimious; nonessential; notorious; numerous; odd; ornamental; outermost; outrageous; *outré*; over(abundant); overboard; overflowing; overful; overloaded; overmuch; overweening; pitiless; pleon-

astic; plethoric; prodigal; prodigious; profligate; profuse; rabid; radical; rank; rare; reckless; recrementitious; redundant; relentless; remote; replete; rigorous; ruthless; sadistic; satanic(al); severe; shocking; spare; stark; steep; stern; strong; super(abundant); supererogatory; superfluous; superlative; supernatural; surplus; terminal; terrible; thick; towering; tyrannical; tyrannous; ultimate; ultra; unco; uncompromising; unconservative; unconventional; undue; unmerciful; unnecessary; unreasonable; urgent; utmost; utter(most); vast; vengeful; vindicative; wasteful; way-out; wicked; EXTREMIST: (**see** "radical") *avant-garde*; ultraconservative; ultraist

EXTREMITY: apex; arm; border; bound(s); brink; climax; conclusion; crisis; danger; death; desperation; edge; end; foot; hand; height; leg; limb; limit; pole; rear; shift; tail; term(inal); termination; tip; toe; urgency; verge

EXTRICATE: (**see** "free") clear; deliver; differentiate; discriminate; disembarass; disembroil; disencumber; disengage; disentangle; disentwine; expedite; extract; help; liberate; loose(n); release; relieve; rescue; save; squirm (out); untangle; untie; untwine;

EXTRINSIC: (**see** "outer") accessory; accidental; adventitious; alien; contingent; external; foreign

EXUBERANT: (**see** "extravagant" and "unrestrained") demonstrative; dithyrambic; ecstatic; effervescent; effusive; elated; euphoric; giddy; gleeful; glowing; gushing; heady; hearty; impulsive; irreverent; joyous; laughing; overflowing; pert; proud; spontaneous; unreserved; vehement

EXUDE: (**see** "ooze") bleed; diffuse; discharge; emanate; emit; exhale; flow; issue; leak; osmose; percolate; perspire; reek; secrete; seep; spew; strain; stream; sweat; transude; trickle; EXUDATION: aura; discharge; emanation; emission; excretion; extravasation; exudate; gum; ooze; orgasm; osmosis; perspiration; pitch; resin; sap; sudor; sweat; tar; transudate; transudation; trickle; weeping

EYE: (**see** "see") center; glance; judgment; look; nucleus; orb; photoreceptor; scrutiny; sight; view; vision

F

FABLE: allegory; apologue; canard; concoction; deceit; fableau; fabliau; fabliaux (pl.); fabrication; fabulosity; falsehood; falsity; fantasy; fib; fiction; figment; flam; forgery; fraud; guile; hypothecation; imagination; inaccuracy; invention; inveracity; legend; lie; mendacity; misrepresentation; misstatement; Munchausenism; narration; novel; parable; perjury; pretense; prevarication; pseudology; romance; roorback; scheme; sham; simulation; slander; story; supposition; tale; talk; tarradiddle; untruism; untruth; web; yarn; FABULAR: (see "fabulous" and "fictional") allegoric(al); apocryphal; fictitious; historical; legendary; mythical; mythologic(al); parabolical; prevaricative; Scheherazadian; storied; unreal; FABLER: allegorist; fableist; fabricator; fabulist; improvisatore; improvisatrice (fem.); improvisor; mythmaker; mythologist; Scheherazade; storyteller

FABRIC: (see "essence") canvas; character; cloth; constitution; contexture; erection; factory; fleece; frame(work); gauge; linen; material; plan; quality; structure; style; substance; textile; texture; tissue; warp; weave; web; woof; wool

FABRICATE: (see "make") arrange; build; coin; compile; compose; concoct; confect; construct; create; devise; erect; fabulize; falsify; fashion; feign; forge; form(ulate); frame; improvisate; improvise; invent; manufacture; mint; mysticize; prepare; produce; scheme; shape; tailor; trump up; vamp; weave; FABRICATION: (see "fable") art; compilation; concoction; confection; construction; craft; creation; deceit; falsehood; fiction; figment; forgery; guile; impromptu; improvisation; invention; lie; myth; novel; opus; preparation; production; romance; scheme; web; FABRICATOR: (see "maker") compiler; composer; creator; fabulist; forger; inventor; liar; parabolist; producer

FABULOUS: (see "fabular") absurd; amazing; apocryphal; exaggerated; extraordinary; fabricated; false; fictitious; imaginary; incredible; legendary; marvelous; mythical; mythologic(al); outstanding; remarkable; ridiculous; romantic; storied; unreal; untrue

FACADE: (see "front") angle; appearance; cover-up; face; facet; form; pane; rear; side; window dressing

FACE: v. accost; accuse; affront; answer; arouse; beard; breast; browbeat; bully; call; challenge; cite; claim; combat; compare; confront; contemn; contemplate; contend; controvert; dare; defy; demand; disobey; disregard; encounter; fight; fling; flout; front; goad; head; invite; look; maintain; meet; mock; oppose; oppress; protect; provoke; question; rebel; recognize; resist; respect; revolt; rise; risk; scorn; slight; spurn; stand; taunt; tempt; threaten; venture; withstand; FACE: n. (see "aspect") angle; appearance; assurance; audacity; boldness; cheek; confidence; countenance; dial; dignity; disguise; effrontery; exterior; facade; facet; feature; front; grimace; impertinence; impudence; map; mask; moue; mug; nerve; obverse; outside; pan; phase; phiz; physiognomy; prestige; pretense; pretension; puss; semblance; side; snoot; surface; visage

FACET: (see "aspect") angle; bezel; cutlet; face; fillet; phase; side; surface

FACETIOUS: (see "funny") comic(al); droll; humorous; jesting; jocose; jocular; laughable; merry; pleasant; sportive; sprightly; waggish; witty

FACILE: (see "easy") able; adroit; apt; artful; assured; clever; compliant; deft; dexterous; docile; expert; flexible; fluent; free; glib; ingenious; light; pliable; pliant; poised; proficient; quick; ready; resourceful; skilled; skillful; smooth; specious; superficial; tactful; unrestrained; yielding

FACILITATE: (see "ease") aid; assist; bribe; expedite; frank; free; further; grease; help; lubricate; oil; quicken; smooth

FACILITY: (see "ability") adroitness; agency;

art(fulness); cleverness; compliance; dexterity; easiness; efficiency; establishment; expertise; expertness; facet; facilitation; freedom; knack; means; office; outlet; pliancy; poise; proficiency; quickness; readiness; skill(fulness); tact (fulness)

FACSIMILE: (**see** "copy") archetype; duplicate; example; imitation; likeness; match; model; prototype; replica; reproduction; resemblance; similarity; similitude; simulation; twin

FACT(S): (**see** "actuality") certainty; certitude; circumstance; clincher; criteria (pl.); criterion; data (pl.); datum; deed; *donnée*; effect; event; evidence; facta (pl.); facticity; factuality; factum; fait; *fait accompli*; fate; feat; grounds; happening; knowledge; manifestation; occurrence; particular(ity); phenomenon; proof; reality; score; statistics; testament; truth

FACTION: (**see** "bloc") cabal; circle; clamor; clan; clique; combination; combine; corps; coterie; discord; dissention; division; group; intrigue; junto; party; ring; sect; set; side; splinter (group); split; tumult

FACTIOUS: (**see** "argumentative") angry; contentious; demagogic; dissident; divisive; factional; insubordinate; rebellious; recalcitrant; refractory; seditious; turbulent; tyrannical; tyrannous; warring

FACTITIOUS: (**see** "artificial") bogus; conventional; counterfeit; ersatz; fabricated; factitial; false; phony; sham; simulated; spurious; synthetic; unnatural

FACTOR: (**see** "component") agent; bailiff; banker; broker; circumstance; consignee; constituent; delegate; doer; element; factum; gene; incident; influence; ingredient; manager; number; occurrence; part; proxy; reeve; situation; steward; substance; vicar

FACTORY: business; establishment; fabric; mill; plant; shop; works; workshop

FACTOTUM: agent; handyman; jack-of-all-trades; servant; valet

FACTUAL: (**see** "actual") correct; documentary; earthy; empirical; exact(ing); experimental; genuine; literal; objective; prosaic(al); real; true; valid

FACULTY: ability; agency; aptitude; authority; bent; brain(s); branch; capability; capacity; cognition; competence; crew; dexterity; dispensation; endowment; flair; force; function; gift; ingenuity; instinct; intellect; knack; license; means; mind; permit; power; prerogative; profession; professoriat(e); property; reason; resources; right; sense; skill; staff; talent; teachers; turn; will; wit

FAD: (**see** "fashion") bug; caprice; craze; cry; *dernier cri*; fancy; foible; hobby; ism; mania; megrim; mode; monomania; rage; style; vagary; vogue; whim(sicality)

FADE: (**see** "decline") blanch; blend; blur; cease; change; decrease; die; dim; disappear; droop; drudge; dull; dwindle; enervate; etiolate; evanesce; exhaust; fag; languish; lapse; leave; lose; melt; pale; pass; peter (out); pine; recede; retreat; sink; slave; tire; toil; vanish; want; waste; weary; wilt; wither; worry; FADED: bedraggled; decreased; dim(med); dingy; dull; faint; jaded; languid; lapsed; lost; pale; passé; seedy; shopworn; soiled; wilted; withered; worn

FADELESS: (**see** "permanent") amaranthine; immarcescible; indelible

FAG: (**see** "fade") droop; drudge; exhaust; flag; jade; sink; slave; tire; toil; weary; worry

FAIL: abandon; abort; bungle; cease; collapse; decline; decrease; default; desert; deteriorate; dim(inish); disappoint; droop; drop; dwindle; enfeeble; err; fall; falter; fizzle; flag; flop; fluff; flunk; forgo; founder; lack; languish; lapse; lose; miscarry; miss; neglect; omit; plunge; quit; refuse; retrogress; stop; trip; weaken; wither; worsen; FAILURE: absence; absentation; also-ran; bankruptcy; botch; bungle; breakdown; *brutum fulmen*; bust; catastrophe; clinker; collapse; cropper; *culbute*; defalcation; default; defection; deficiency; delinquence; dereliction; deterioration; disappointment; disaster; dud; error; fiasco; fizzle; flop; fluff; goose; egg; inexecution; insolvency; laches; lack; lapse; lemon; loss; miscarriage; misfeasance; misfit; mistake; neglect; negligence; noncompliance; nonexistence; nonfeasance; nonperformance; omission; plunge; pretermission; refusal; ruin; shipwreck; smash; stop; trip; turkey; washout; weakening; FAILING: (**see** "failure") blot; defect; deficiency; error; fault; foible; frailty; illness; lack; want

FAINEANT: (**see** "idle") inactive; indolent;

ineffectual; inert; lazy; otiose; FAINEANCE
or FAINEANCY: **see** "laziness"

FAINT: **v.** choke; dim(inish); fade; fail;
falter; keel; languish; suffocate; swelter;
swoon; FAINT: **a.** amorphous; blurred;
blurry; caliginous; cloudy; confused; dark-
(ened); dim(med); dizzy; dreary; dull;
ethereal; exhausted; faltering; fatigued;
feeble; foggy; giddy; hazy; halfhearted;
hesitant; inconspicuous; indefinite; indifferent; indiscernible; indistinct; indistinguishable; ineffectual; insubstantial; irresolute;
languid; light; listless; misty; muddy;
nebular; nebulous; obliterate; obscurant;
obscure; oppressive; pusillanimous; queasy;
queer; shadowy; smudged; soft; spineless;
spiritless; suffocating; timid; uncertain;
undefined; undistinct; vague; vaporous;
wan; weak; wearied; weary; woolly; FAINT:
n. choking; suffocation; swoon; syncope

FAIR: **a.** absolute; adequate; affable; agreeable; attractive; auspicious; beautiful;
blond(e); candid; civil; clear; cloudless;
comely; common(place); complete; considerable; considerate; continent; decent;
dispassionate; distinct; dry; due; equable;
equitable; even; evenhanded; feminine; fine;
frank; full; gracious; handsome; honest;
honorable; impartial; impersonal; indifferent; inexpensive; judicial; judicious; just-
(ified); la-la; legible; light; likely; limited;
mean; medial; median; mediocre; medium;
middle (of the road); middling; mitigatory;
moderate; modest; normal; objective; open;
ordinary; passable; pleasant; pleasing; prevalent; promising; prudent; pure; real;
reasonable; regulated; restrained; rich;
satisfactory; sober; so-so; sparing; standard;
stark; steady; sufficient; sunny; temperate;
tolerable; typical; unbiased; unbigoted;
uncolored; unprejudiced; upright; usual;
utter; valid; vernacular; vulgar; worth(y);
FAIR: **n.** bazaar; carnival; exhibit(ion);
gala; kermis; picnic; show; FAIRNESS:
beauty; candidness; candor; disinterestedness; dispassion; equableness; equity; evenhandedness; frankness; honesty; honor;
impartiality; integrity; judiciality; justness;
moderation; reasonableness; rightness;
straightforwardness; unprejudice; uprightness

FAIRY: banshee; brownie; dwarf; elf; fay;
genius; goblin; gremlin; hob; imp; jinnee;
kelpie; kelpy; leprechaun; nix(ie); nymph;
peri; pix(ie); puck; shee; spirit; sprite;
sylph; undine

FAITH: (**see** "belief") assent; assurance;

confidence; conviction; credence; credit;
credo; cult; doctrine; dogma; earnestness;
fideism; fidelity; gospel; honesty; loyalty;
opinion; persuasion; pistology; reliance;
religion; sincerity; stock; tenet; troth; trust;
view(point); weltanschauung

FAITHFUL: (**see** "careful") accurate; attached; attentive; binding; conscientious;
constant; credible; dependable; devoted;
exact; fair; fast; firm; honest; honorable;
incorruptible; just; leal; liege; loving; loyal;
meticulous; obedient; perfect; pure; reliable;
resolute; rigid; scrupulous; sincere; sta(u)nch;
steadfast; straight; strict; sure; tight; tried;
true(hearted); trustworthy; trusty; undistorted; unswerving; unvarying; unwavering;
upright; worthy; FAITHFULNESS: accuracy; allegiance; ardentness; attention;
carefulness; conscientiousness; constancy;
credibility; dependability; devotion; exactitude; exactness; fairness; fealty; fidelity;
honesty; honor(ableness); justice; loyalty;
meticulosity; obedience; perfection; purity;
reliability; resoluteness; scrupulosity; sincerity; steadfastness; truth(fulness); trust-
(worthiness); veracity; verity; worthiness;
zeal

FAITHLESS: (**see** "dishonest" and "false")
disloyal; fickle; inconstant; perfidious; rebellious; treacherous; treasonable; trothless;
tyrannous; unstable

FAKE: **v.** (**see** "counterfeit") adulterate;
belie; cheat; color; concoct; confute; deceive;
defraud; deviate; devise; distort; doctor;
fabricate; falsify; forge; fraud; garble; imitate; lie; mislabel; mislead; misrepresent;
mistake; mock; pretend; sham simulate;
trick; FAKE(D): **a.** (**see** "false") colored;
concocted; counterfeit; deceitful; deceptive;
devised; doctored; fabricated; falsified;
forged; fraudulent; imitation; imitative;
mock; pretended; sham; simulated; spurious;
tricky; FAKE(R): **n.** Cagliostro; charlatan;
cheat(er); counterfeit(er); deceit; deceiver;
deception; epigone; empiric; fabrication;
fakement; feint; fraud; hoax; humbug;
hypocrite; imitation; imposter; impostor;
imposture; mountebank; Pharisee; phony;
pretender; quack(salver); ringer; sham;
swindler; Tartuffe; trick(er); trickster;
FAKERY: **see** "imposture"

FALL: **v.** abate; begin; bow; break; buckle;
burst; cascade; cavitate; collapse; come;
cropper; crumble; decline; decrease; degenerate; descend; die; diminish; disappear;
disintegrate; dissolve; divide; droop; drop;

empty; exhaust; err; expire; fail; flatten; flop; fold; founder; go; happen; impinge; issue; lapse; lessen; light(en); liquidate; lower; occur; pass; perish; plop; plummet; plunge; precipitate; puncture; recede; relapse; roll; ruin; sag; separate; set(tle); shatter; shed; sin; sink; slip; slump; spill; stray; strike; stumble; subside; topple; toss; totter; tumble; weaken; wilt; wreck; FALL: **n.** anticlimax; autumn; bankruptcy; break(down); buckling; capitulation; cascade; cataclysm; cataract; cavitation; collapse; crumbling; debacle; decline; declivity; decrease; degradation; descent; diminishment; disgrace; disintegration; disorganization; disruption; dissolution; downfall; droop; drop(ping); error; failure; flop; foundering; *Götterdämmerung*; header; holocaust; inclination; lapse; misfortune; overflow; pitch; plop; plunge; prostration; relapse; reverse; rout; ruin; sag; season; shattering; shedding; sin; sink(ing); slip; slope; spill; surrender; tide; topple; tumble; vanishment; Waterloo; wilting; wrack; wreck

FALLACY: (**see** "falseness") aberration; casuistry; deception; delusion; equivocation; erroneousness; error; evasion; fallaciousness; falsity; idolum; illogicality; illusion; lie; misconception; mistake; paradox(icality); phantasy; pseudodoxy; sophism; sophistry; subterfuge; untruism; FALLACIOUS: (**see** "false") apocryphal; deceptive; erroneous; evasive; illogical; paralogistic; pseudo(logical); pseudodox; sophistical

FALLIBLE: errant; erratic; human; inaccurate

FALSE: (**see** "fake") *ab absurdo*; affected; apocryphal; apostate; apostatic; arrant; artificial; assumed; Barmecidal; base(less); bogus; bottomless; brummagem; colorable; compromising; contrived; copied; counterfeit; crocodilian; crooked; deceitful; deceptive; delusive; dishonest; dishonorable; disloyal; dissembling; dissimulative; doublecrossing; double-dealing; dramatic; duplicitous; erroneous; ersatz; evasive; fabricated; factitious; faithless; faked; feigned; fictitious; fictive; forged; fraudulent; groundless; histrionic; hydra-headed; hypocritical; idle; ignominious; illogical; illusional; illusive; illusory; imaginary; imaginative; imitated; imitation; imitative; imprudent; inaccurate; inauthentic; incorrect; infamous; insincere; lying; Machiavellian; melodramatic; mendacious; meretricious; *papier-mâché*; paralogistic; phony; pinchbeck; postiche; pretended; pseudo(logical); pseudodox; quasi; queer;

renegade; shadowy; shallow; sham; simulated; snide; sophisticated; specious; spectral; spurious; stagy; substituted; supposititious; synthetic(al); theatric(al); tin; traitorous; treacherous; treasonable; truthless; two-faced; unauthentic; uncanonical; unconvincing; unfaithful; ungenuine; ungrounded; unnatural; unreal; unreliable; untrue; untrustful; untrustworthy; unveracious; unwise; wrong; FALSENESS *or* FALSITY: aberration; artificiality; casuistry; deceitfulness; deception; delusion; dissimulation; duplicity; equivocation; erroneousness; error; evasion; fable; faithlessness; falselessness; hypocrisy; idolum; illogicality; illusion; inaccuracy; insincerity; inveracity; lie; mendacity; misconception; misrepresentation; mistake; paradox(icality); perfidy; phantasy; pretension; pseudology; pseudodoxy; sham; simulation; sophism; sophistry; speciosity; subterfuge; treachery; triplicity; unfaithfulness; untruism; untrustfulness; untrustworthiness; untruth

FALSEHOOD: (**see** "fable") canard; deceit; deception; duplicity; error; fabrication; fallacy; falsity; fib; fiction; flam; fraud; invention; inveracity; lie; lying; mendacity; misrepresentation; misstatement; Munchausenism; perjury; pretense; prevarication; pseudology; roorback; slander; story; tale; tarradiddle; treachery; untruth

FALSIFY: (**see** "fake") adulterate; belie; confute; counterfeit; deceive; deviate; disappoint; distort; forge; frustrate; garble; lie; mislabel; mislead; misrepresent; misstate; warp

FALSITY: **see** "falsehood"

FALTER: (**see** "hesitate") decline; demur; dodder; doubt; fail; flinch; fluctuate; hobble; limp; misstep; pause; quail; quaver; recoil; reel; shrink; sidestep; slip; stagger; stammer; stumble; stutter; totter; tremble; vacillate; waver; weaken

FAME: (**see** "celebrity") acclaim; character; credit; cry; distinction; *éclat*; elevation; eminence; esteem; estimation; exaltation; fortune; glory; honor; illustriousness; kudos; laurels; luster; nobility; note; notoriety; notoriousness; popularity; prestige; price; pride; publicity; recognition; regard; renown; report; reputation; repute; rumor; star; success; vogue; FAMED: (**see** "eminent") acclaimed; celebrated; conspicuous; distinguished; esteemed; estimable; exalted; glorious; great; heroic; honorable; illustrious;

notable; noted; notorious; prestigious; recognized; renowned; storied; successful

FAMILIARIZE: (see "accustom") acclimate; acclimatize; acquaint; habituate; indoctrinate; instruct; orient(ate); popularize; teach; FAMILIAR: accepted; acquainted; approved; *au fait*; brotherly; casual; chummy; close; common; confidential; conversant; cozy; customary; domestic; easy; familial; forward; fraternal; free (and easy); frequent; friendly; habitual; household; informal; insolent; intimate; intrusive; inward; known; natural; offhand; old; ordinary; practiced; presumptuous; proverbial; sisterly; skilled; snug; standard; thick; unceremonious; unconstrained; unconventional; unformal; unorthodox; unreserved; unrestrained; used; usual; versant; versed; welcome; well-established; well-known; widespread; FAMILIARITY: acquaintance(ship); chumminess; confidentiality; friendliness; habit; impropriety; informality; insolence; intimacy; inwardness; knowledge; liberty; usage

FAMILY: aggregation; ancestry; breed; brood; children; clan; clutch; community; covey; descendant(s); dynasty; fellowship; flock; fruit; genealogy; genera (pl.); gens; group; hatch; hearth; house(hold); ilk; issue; kin; line(age); litter; menage; multitude; name; nest; offspring; paternity; pedigree; posterity; progeniture; progeny; race; retinue; (s)cion; sept; set; staff; stirps; stock; tribe; yield; young

FAMINE: (see "need") barrenness; dearth; exigency; (the) Four Horsemen; hunger; lack; necessity; poverty; scarcity; shortage; starvation; wolf

FAMISHED: see "hungry"

FAMOUS: (see "eminent") celebrated; celebrious; classic; commemorable; commemorative; commemoratory; *distingué*; excellent; far-famed; first-rate; honored; illustratory; illustrious; leonine; notable; renowned; reputable; successful; venerable; well-known

FAN: v. cool; flutter; foment; stimulate; stir; strike; winnow; FAN(S): n. acolyte; addict; adherent; admirer; aficionada (fem.); aficionado; apostle; buff; circulator; devotee; enthusiast; fiend; flabellum; follower; following; rooter; votary

FANATIC(AL): a. (see "biased") bigoted; extravagant; frenzied; illiberal; partial;

mad; manic; phrenetic; rabid; ultra; unreasonable; visionary; wild; FANATIC: n. (see "bigot") energumen; enthusiast; fiend; lunatic; maniac; visionary; zealot

FANCIFUL: (see "imaginary") absurd; bizarre; capricious; chimerical; dreamy; ethereal excellent; fantastic(al); fickle; fine; fitful; grotesque; illusory; imaginative; inconstant; odd; poetic(al); queer; quixotic; romantic; subjective; unreal; unrestrained; vaporous; whimsical

FANCY: v. (see "imagine") believe; daydream; desire; dream; enjoy; like; love; relish; romanticize; visualize; FANCY: a. (see "excellent") excessive; extravagant; fanciful; fine; gingerbread; ideal; irregular; ornate; premium; rococo; select(ed); sequined; top; whimsical; FANCY: n. antic; capriccio; caprice; chimera; conceit; concept(ion); daydream(ing); desire; dream; fad; fantasia; fantasy; fondness; *fata morgana*; humor; idea(l); illusion; image; imagination; inclination; introspection; liking; love; megrim; mode; mooning; notion; phantasm; phantasmata (pl.); phantasy; predilection; preference; relish; reverie; romanticizing; stargazing; supposition; taste; vagary; vaporosity; vision; whim(sey); whimsicality; woolgathering

FANFARE: (see "commotion") ado; blazonry; boom; display; fanfarade; fanfaron-(ade); fireworks; flourish; ostentation; pyrotechnics; ruffle and flourish; show; tant(a)-tara

FANFARON: boaster; braggart; bully; fanfare; hector; swaggerer

FANG: see "tooth"

FANTASTIC(AL): abstracted; absurd; aerial; airy(-fairy); antic; baroque; bizarre; capricious; chimerical; comic(al); delightful; delusional; delusive; dreamful; dreamlike; dreamy; eccentric; erratic; exaggerated; extraordinary; extravagant; extreme; fanciful; fantasque; farfetched; fey; foolish; gothic; grotesque; ideal(istic); illusional; illusionary; ivory-tower; Laputan; mythical; nebulous; nonrealistic; notional; odd; *outré*; particular; pleasing; poetic(al); preposterous; preternatural; quaint; queer; quixotic(al); romantic; sentimental; shadowy; singular; soothing; startling; strange; supernatural; theoretical; translunary; unbelievable; uncommon; unearthly; unreal(istic); unrestrained; unsubstantial; unsuitable; Utopian; vague;

vain; visionary; whimsical; wild-eyed; wonderful

FANTASY: (see "imagination") apparition; autism; conceit; concept(ion); daydream; desire; dream; ethereality; fancy; fantasia; fantasticality; freak; hallucination; idea; ideality; image; inclination; notion; phantasm; phantasmata (pl.); phantasy; reverie; thought; unreality; vagary; vision; whim(sey); whimsicality

FANTOD: distress; fidget; fit; fuss; hysteria; irritability; irritation; megrim; outburst; pet; sulk; tension; worry

FAR: (see "advanced") abroad; afar; away; beyond; deep; distant; far-flung; far-out; farthest; forane; furthest; long; modern; much; off; overseas; progressed; remote; removed; tramontane; ultramontane; wide(ly); FARTHEST: farthermost; furthermost; latest; outer(most); remotest; ultimate; FARTHER: see "beyond"

FARCE: buffoonery; burlesque; caricature; comedy; comicality; drollery; exode; extravaganza; forcemeat; harlequinade; humor; lampoon(ery); mockery; opéra bouffe; opera buffa; parody; pasquinade; ridiculosity; sham; show; slapstick; stuffing; travesty; FARCICAL: (see "funny") absurd; amusing; Atellan; burlesque; comic(al); droll; extravagant; laughable; ludicrous; ribald; ridiculous; risible; showy

FARE: v. diet; dine; eat; go; journey; progress; prosper; succeed; travel; FARE: n. (see "diet") aliment; allowance; board; charge; cost; course; dish; drink; entertainment; fee; food; meal; nutriment; nutrition; passenger; pay; provisions; rate; station; regime(n); repast; support; sustenance; table; ticket; token; victuals

FAREWELL: a. departing; final; good-bye; parting; valedictory; FAREWELL: n. (see "good-bye") adieu; adios; aftertaste; ave; bye-bye; chant du cygne; congé; departure; envoi; furlough; leave(taking); parting; utimum vale; vale(diction)

FARFETCHED: (see "ridiculous") catachrestic; forced; laborious; outré; preposterous; recherché; strained

FARMER: agriculturist; agronomist; cotter; cropper; granger; husbandman; planter; producer; ruralist; ryot; sower; tenant

FARSIGHTED: (see "prophetical") far-reaching; farseeing; hyperopic; presbyopic; presbytic; prescient; sagacious; telepathic; telescopic; wise

FASCICLE: bunch; bundle; cluster; collection; glomerule; group; sheaf

FASCINATE: (see "attract") allure; bait; beguile; bewitch; call; captivate; capture; charm; court; delight; draw; enamor; enchant; enrapture; ensorcel(l); enthral(l); entice; entrance; flaunt; guile; hold; influence; interest; invite; lure; magnetize; mesmerize; overpower; pull; rapture; ravish; seduce; solicit; spellbind; summon; take; tempt; transfix; transport; woo; FASCINATED or FASCINATING: (see "attractive") absorbing; alluring; appealing; beguiling; captivating; charming; Circean; delightful; enchanting; engrossing; enthralling; enticing; entrancing; interesting; inviting; irresistible; mesmeric; piquant; rapturous; ravishing; seductive; sirenic(al); spellbound; strange; taking; transfixed; FASCINATION: (see "attraction") absorption; appeal; astonishment; beguilement; bewitchery; bewitchment; captivation; charm; delight; enchantment; engrossment; ensorcellment; enticement; guile; influence; interest; invitation; lure; magnetism; mesmerism; piquancy; pull; rapture; raptus; ravishment; seduction; spell; surprise; transport; wonder

FASHION: v. (see "make") accommodate; adapt; adjust; alter; build; compile; compose; constitute; construct; contrive; control; create; design; devise; effect; elaborate; erect; fabricate; fit; forge; form(ulate); frame; guide; invent; manipulate; manufacture; model; modify; mold; pattern; picture; plan; plot; represent; shape; style; suit; tailor; transform; FASHION: n. appearance; arrangement; attitude; breeding; bug; caprice; convention; course; custom; decor(ation); decorum; dernier (cri); design; drift; etiquette; fad; fancy; figure; flair; foible; form; habit; hobby; ism; le bon ton; mania; manner; megrim; method; mode; mood; monomania; motif; nature; order; pattern; picture; plan; practice; precedent; prevalence; procedure; rage; rule; scheme; shape; state; style; taste; tenor; timber; ton; tone; trade; trend; usage; vagary; vogue; way; wear; whim(sicality); wont; FASHIONABLE: à la mode; chic; dapper; elegant; genteel; jaunty; lace-curtain; modish; mondain(e); natty; new; nifty; popular; posh; recherché; sleek; smart; soigné; soignée; (fem.) sophisticated; spruce; stylish; swagger; tonish

FAST: **v.** (**see** "fasten") diet; FAST(ENED); **a.** abrupt; accelerated; *à corps perdu*; active; agile; alert; apace; brisk; busy; celeritous; dissipated; dissolute; double(-quick); engaged; expeditious; expeditive; explosive; express; fixed; flashy; fleet; Gadarine; gay; hasty; high-stepping; immovable; intemperate; irremovable; lively; locked; loose; meteoric; nimble; precipitate; precipitous; prompt; quick; rapid(-fire); reckless; shut; sporty; stable; staunch; steadfast; stuck; sure; swift; tenacious; tied; unchangeable; velocious; wild

FASTEN: add; affix; anchor; associate; attach; belay; bind; bolt; bond; catch; cement; chain; cling; clip; close; combine; connect; couple; establish; fix; glue; graft; hang; hitch; impale; join; lace; link; lock; moor; nail; peg; pin; restrain; rivet; rope; seal; secure; sew; splice; stake; stamp; staple; stitch; strap; subjoin; tack; tape; tether; tie; transfix; trap; unite; wire; yoke; FASTENER: bolt; button; catch; clamp; clasp; cleat; clevis; cotter; device; halter; hasp; lock; nail; peg; pin; rope; snap; snib; staple; string; tack; wire; zipper

FASTIDIOUS: (**see** "particular") chary; choosy; clean; critical; dainty; delicate; demanding; difficult; effeminate; exact(ing); fine; finical; finicky; fussy; immaculate; meticulous; nice; overnice; per(s)nickety; precise; prissy; prudent; prudish; scrupulous; sensitive; squeamish; stylish

FAT: **a.** abdominous; abundant; adipose; beefy; bulbous; burly; chubby; coarse; corpulent; fertile; filled; fleshy; foolish; fruitful; greasy; gross; heavy; impressive; juicy; large; lucrative; lusty; luxuriant; massive; obese; oily; oleaginous; pinguid; plump; portly; productive; profitable; prosperous; pudgy; pursy; pyknic; rich; roly-poly; rotund; stocky; stout; substantial; swollen; thick; tubby; wealthy; weighty; FAT: **n.** adeps; adiposity; avoirdupois; butter; cholesterol; corpulence; ester; fatness; flesh; grease; lard; lipa; lipids; obesity; oil; oleo (margarine); pinguidity; richness; rotundity; suet; unction; FATTEN: (**see** "enrich") add; batten; expand; fertilize; pinguify; prosper; thrive; FATTENING: enriched; lipogenous; pinguescent; rich; steatogenous; FATTY: adipose; cohesive; corpulent; greasy; oily; oleaginous; sticky; unctious; unctuose; unctuous

FATAL: (**see** "deadly") baneful; calamitous; condemned; destructive; dire; disastrous;

doomed; fateful; feral; lethal; lethiferous; malicious; malign(ant); mortal; mortiferous; murderous; pernicious; pestilent(ial); poisonous; prophetic; ruinous; toxic; FATALITY: **see** "death"

FATALISM: determinism; foreordination; necessarianism; passivity; predestination; predetermination; predeterminism; submissiveness

FATE: accident(ality); break; calamity; casualty; *casus fortuitus*; chance; circumstance(s); contingence; contingency; contretemps; cross; death; destiny; destruction; determination; disaster; disposition; doom; end; fatality; finish; foreordination; fortuitiveness; fortuity; fortune; gamble; goal; grace; hap(penstance); hazard; inadvertence; inadvertency; incident; injury; issue; kismet; lot; luck; manifest destiny; misadventure; mischance; misfortune; mishap; misstep; moira; moirai (pl.); necessity; Nona; odds; opportunity; outcome; peradventure; portion; predestination; predetermination; providence; random; result; reversal; reverse; risk; ruin; slip; speculation; stars; tide; time; tychism; ultimacy; upshot; venture; will of the gods; FATED *or* FATEFUL: (**see** "deadly") appointed; catastrophic(al); condemned; destined; determined; doomed; doomful; doomlike; fatal; fey; obliged; ominous; portentous; predestined; predetermined; preordained; prophetic

FATHER: **v.** (**see** "breed") author; beget; create; found; originate; produce; sire; FATHER: **n.** abba; Adam; ama; ancestor; author; begetter; cause; confessor; creator; dad; Deity; forefather; founder; genitor; God; old man; origin(ator); pa; papa; parent; pater; patriarch; paw; pere; pop; precursor; predecessor; priest; producer; progenitor; prototype; sire; source; FATHERLY: benign; kind; parental; paternal; patriarchal; solicitous; FATHERHOOD: fathership; paternality; paternity

FATHOM: **v.** (**see** "ascertain") comprehend; delve; dig; divine; find; investigate; measure; plumb; plummet; probe; seek; sound; test; try; understand; FATHOM: **n.** comprehension; depth; grasp; measure(ment); penetration; profundity; understanding

FATIGUE: **v.** (**see** "tire") bore; debilitate; deplete; drain; enervate; exhaust; fag; jade; overdo; sap; tucker; weaken; weary; FATIGUE: **n.** (**see** "weakness") adynamia; boredom; debilitation; decadence; depletion; devitalization; dreariness; dullness; dyspnea; enervation; ennui; exhaustion; faintness; feebleness; hypokinesia; hypokinesis; impuissance; inanition; irritation; labor; lackadaisy; languor; lassitude; lethargy; listlessness; monotony; overstrain; tedium; tiredness; tiresomeness; toil; weariness; wearisomeness; work; FATIGUED: (**see** "exhausted") adynamic; beat; blown; bushed; consumed; dead; debilitated; depleted; deprived; destroyed; devitalized; dilapidated; done; down; drained; dyspneic; effete; empty; enervated; fagged; feckless; feeble; footloose; gone; hackneyed; helpless; impoverished; jaded; languescent; languorous; lassitudinous; lethargic; limp; listless; overdone; overweary; overworked; rundown; spiritless; tired; unrefreshed; unrelaxed; unrested; weak(ened); wearied; weary; worn(-down); worn-out

FATUOUS: (**see** "absurd") asinine; foolish; idiotic; inane; silly; simple; stupid; unintelligent; vacant; vacuous; witless

FAULT: **v.** (**see** "err") blunder; bungle; fail; FAULT: **n.** (**see** "error") blame; blemish; break; crime; culpa(bility); damage; default; defect; delinquency; demerit; dereliction; detriment; drawback; eccentricity; failing; failure; flaw; fluff; foible; frailty; guilt; hole; imperfection; inadequacy; infirmity; lapse; misdeed; misdemeanor; mistake; neglect; negligence; omission; peccadillo; shortcoming; sin; slip; spot; transgression; venality; vice; weakness; wrinkle; wrong(doing)

FAULTFINDING: **a.** (**see** "critical") captious; carping; censorial; censorious; condemnatory; cynical; hypercritical; querulous; scrupulous; unreasonable; FAULTFINDING: **n.** captiousness; criticality; cynicism; querulousness; scrupulosity; FAULTFINDER: (**see** "critic") carper; caviler; censor; censurer; complainer; cynic; *frondeur*; malcontent; momus; repiner

FAULTLESS: (**see** "clean") clear; correct; free; guiltless; ideal; immaculate; impeccable; impeccant; indefectible; infallible; innocent; irreproachable; perfect; purified; spotless; undeviating; unerring; FAULTLESSNESS: cleanliness; immaculacy; impeccability; indefectibility; purity; spick-and-spanness

FAULTY: (**see** "defective") amiss; bad; blamable; blameworthy; blemished; deficient; dilapidated; erroneous; imperfect; improper;

inaccurate; incorrect; lacking; reprehensible; sick(ly); suboptimal; substandard; unfit; unsound; unwanted; wrong

FAUX PAS: (**see** "blunder") boner; bull; error; flub; fluff; gaff(e); lapse; misstep; mistake; slip; solecism

FAVOR: **v.** (**see** "aid") abet; accommodate; assist; attend; bless; choose; condone; consider; countenance; ease; encourage; esteem; facilitate; help; like; oblige; patronize; prefer; regard; resemble; spare; support; sustain; FAVOR: **n.** (**see** "aid") accommodation; advantage; approbation; approval; assist-(ance); attention; badge; behalf; benefit; bias; boon; condescension; consideration; dispensation; emblem; encouragement; esteem; gift; goodwill; grace; indulgence; interest; kindness; largesse; letter; odds; partiality; partisanship; patronage; pledge; popularity; preference; privilege; regard(s); right; sponsorship; support; token; FAVORED: (**see** "esteemed") blue-eyed; preferred

FAVORABLE: acceptable; advantageous; advisable; affirmative; agreeable; appetible; appetitious; approbative; approbatory; appropriate; approving; apropos; apt; astucious; astute; attractive; auspicious; beneficial; beneficent; benign(ant); blessed; bright; choice; commendatory; condescending; convenient; desiderative; desirable; dexter; disposed; efficient; eligible; encouraging; enviable; excellent; expedient(ial); favored; favoring; fit(ting); fortunate; friendly; genial; golden; good; gracious; happy; healthy; helpful; hopeful; ideal; inclinable; inclined; ingratiating; likely; lucky; meet; merciful; mild; miraculous; opportune; opportunistic; optative; optimal; optimistic; optimum; orective; partial; pat; pertinent; pleasant; pleasing; plummy; politic(al); practical; precipitous; preferent(ial); profitable; promiseful; promising; proper; propitious; prosperous; providential; rare; ready; reassuring; remunerative; right; ripe; roseate; rosy; salutary; satisfactory; seasonal; serendipitous; strategetic; strategic(al); successful; suitable; suited; sympathetic; tactful; tempestive; tendentious; timely; useful; valuable; votive; warm; well; wise; wishful; worthy

FAVORITE: (**see** "idol") beloved; cosset; darling; dear; hero; loved; *mignon*; minion; partisan; *persona grata*; pet; standby; toady; FAVORITISM: bias; cordiality; encouragement; esteem; idolatry; heroism; nepotism; partiality; patronage; predilection; sanction; veneration; worship

FAWN: **v.** (**see** "defer") bow; court; cower; cringe; crouch; ecstasize; flatter; grovel; humble; kowtow; slaver; toady; woo; FAWN(ING): **n.** (**see** "deference") bow; cringe; crouch; deer; flattery; grovel(ing); kowtow; obsequiousness; obsequity; servility; sycophancy; toadying; unctuosity; unctuousness; FAWNING: **a.** (**see** "deferential") abject; gnathonic; obsequious; oily; oleaginous; parasitical; servile; subservient; sycophantic; toadying; unctuous

FAZE: (**see** "embarrass") abash; bother; daunt; dent; disconcert; disturb; rattle; worry

FEALTY: (**see** "allegiance") constancy; duty; faith(fulness); fidelity; homage; honor; humility; loyalty; oath; obligation; respect

FEAR: **v.** apprehend; awe; cower; daunt; doubt; dread; eschew; frighten; hesitate; misdoubt; panic; suspect; terrify; FEAR: **n.** (**see** "anxiety") affright; agitation; alarm; apprehension; awe; caution; concern; consternation; dismay; disquiet(ude); distress; doubt; dread; eeriness; emotion; feeling; fright; funk; horripilation; horror; hysteria; intimidation; misdoubt; misgiving; nervousness; panic; phobia; reverence; scare; solicitude; terror; thing; timidity; trembling; tremor; trepidation; trepidity; worry

FEARFUL: (**see** "anxious") afraid; alarming; appalling; apprehensive; awed; awesome; awful; calamitous; cowardly; craven; dangerous; difficult; dire; dismayful; doubting; doughty; dreadful; effeminate; extreme; faltering; fearsome; feckless; formidable; frightening; frightful; ghastly; grim; grisly; gruesome; horrendous; horrible; horrific; hysterical; intimidating; large; nervous; numerous; ominous; panicky; pavid; redoubtable; scared; shaky; shuddering; shy; skittish; spiritless; terrible; terrific; terrifying; timid; timorous; trembling; trepid; undaring; wavering; weak; FEARFULNESS: (**see** "timidity") panickiness; terror; trepidity

FEARLESS: (**see** "bold") audacious; aweless; brave; chivalrous; courageous; daring; dauntless; firm; fortitudinous; gallant; gutty; hardy; heroic; impavid; indomitable; intrepid; resolute; *sans peur*; spirited; temerarious; unafraid; unalarming; unanxious; undaunted; undespairing; unfearful; unfearing; unflinching; unfrightened; unquailing; unwincing; valiant; valorous; FEARLESSNESS: (**see** "boldness") audacity; bravery; chivalry; courage(ousness); daring; fortitude;

gall(antry); guts; indomitability; intrepidity; resolution; valor

FEASIBLE: (**see** "possible") capable; likely; potential; practicable; reasonable; suitable

FEAST: banquet; carouse; delight; dine; eat; entertain; feed; fete; gratify; regale; revel; sup; treat; wine; FEAST: **n.** banquet; barbecue; carousal; carouse; convivium; dinner; entertainment; epulation; feasting; feed; festival; festivity; fete; fiesta; food; junket; meal; picnic; repast; revel; spread; symposium; treat

FEAT: (**see** "accomplishment") achievement; act(ion); attainment; deed; effort; exercise; exertion; exploit; gest(e); gymnastic(s); gyration; maneuver; performance; prestidigitation; quest; stunt; *tour de force*; trick; victory

FEATHER(S): condition; down; flag; kind; mood; nature; penna; pinna; plumage; plume; quill; species; spirits; trim; tuft; wing

FEATURE(S): (**see** "appearance") article; aspect; attraction; cachet; cast; character(istic); constituent; countenance; eccentricity; element; face; facies; factor; favor; film; form; habitus; hallmark; item; landmark; lineament; look; makeup; mark; mien; motif; note; oddity; part; peculiarity; physiognomy; physique; picture; shape; singularity; story; structure; token; topography; trait; visage; way

FECES: **see** "dung"

FECKLESS: (**see** "helpless") awkward; fatigued; impractical; incompetent; indifferent; ineffective; inefficient; irresponsible; lazy; meaningless; purposeless; shiftless; spiritless; unreliable; unskilled; unthinking; weak; worthless

FECULENT: (**see** "filthy") fecal; foul; muddy; roily; turbid

FEDERATION: affinity; alliance; association; axis; band; body; bund; coalition; compact; company; confederacy; confederation; consociation; consortion; contract; fusion; group; league; monopolization; monopoly; partnership; party; society; union

FEE: (**see** "charge") amount; appraisement; benefice; bill; bribe; compensation; consideration; cost; customs; dues; duty; emolument; estate; evaluation; excise; expenditure; expense; fare; fief; figure; gratuity; honorarium; money; outlay; pay(ment); price; rate; recompense; remuneration; retainer; reward; sacrifice; sum; tab; tariff; tax; tip; toll; valuation; value; wage

FEEBLE: adynamic; anemic; asthenic; dead; debilitated; decrepit; deficient; delicate; depleted; dilapidated; dim(med); doddering; done (in); dotty; drained; dyspneic; effete; emaciated; empty; enervated; enfeebled; exhausted; fagged; faint; fatigued; feckless; flabby; flaccid; flickering; forceless; fragile; frail; gone; helpless; impaired; impotent; impuissant; inadequate; indistinct; ineffective; ineffectual; inferior; infirm; insipid; insubstantial; lame; languid; languorous; lassitudinous; lethargic; limp; listless; namby-pamby; nerveless; phthisic(al); pluckless; pointless; poor; powerless; puny; run-down; shaky; sick(ly); soft; spiritless; tired; tottering; tubercular; uncertain; unsubstantial; wan; weak(ened); worn(-down); worn-out; FEEBLENESS: adynamia; anemia; asthenia; debilitation; debility; decay; decrepitness; decrepitude; deficiency; depletion; delicacy; dilapidation; dotage; dyspnea; emaciation; emptiness; enervation; exhaustion; faintness; fatigue; fragility; helplessness; impotence; impotency; impuissance; inadequacy; infirmity; lassitude; lethargy; listlessness; poverty; senility; tenuity; weakness

FEEBLEMINDED: see "foolish;" FEEBLE-MINDEDNESS: hypophrenia; mental deficiency; moronity

FEED: v. (see "feast") aggravate; augment; convey; cram; dine; eat; fatten; fill; foster; fuel; furnish; give; glut; gratify; graze; grub; maintain; nourish; nurse; nurture; pasture; prey; provide; push; satisfy; stoke; strengthen; subsist; suckle; supply; support; sustain; table; FEED: n. (see "food") crops; fodder; meal; repast

FEEL: v. affect; ail; appreciate; believe; claw; contact; emote; endure; examine; experience; experiment; explore; find; finger; fish; fumble; grope; handle; hold; hurt; intuit; know; palp(ate); paw; perceive; pity; react; savor; search; sense; suffer; taste; think; tingle; touch; undergo; understand; FEEL: n. esthesia; experience; feeling; palpation; quality; sensation; sentience; sentiency; tone; touch; FEELING: (see "emotion") accord; affectation; affection; appreciation; ardor; atmosphere; attitude; awareness; belief; character; cognizance; compassion; compunction; conception; conscience; conscien-

tiousness; consciousness; conviction; disposition; ecstasy; empathy; enthusiasm; exaltation; excitement; fear; fervor; fondness; heart; hurt; impression; insight; intuition; love; mind; mood; nature; opinion; passion; perception; percipience; pity; precognition; prescience; presentiment; reaction; responsiveness; scruple; sensation; sense; sensibility; sensitivity; sentience; sentiency; sentiment; sympathy; temper-(ament); tenderness; thought; tingle; touch(ing)

FEIGN: (see "pretend") act (a part); affect; allege; assume; attitudinize; bluff; color; deceive; disguise; dissemble; distort; fabricate; falsify; forge; garble; invent; lie; mask; mislead; posture; sham; simulate; weave; FEIGNED: (see "artificial" and "counterfeit") Barmecidal; illusory; insincere; make-believe; unreal

FEINT: (see "artifice") blind; expedient; pretense; ruse; stratagem; trick; wile

FELICITATE: (see "praise") bless; compliment; congratulate; greet; macarize

FELICITY: (see "happiness") aptness; bliss; ease; ecstasy; fortune; grace; happiness; heaven; joy; paradise; success; FELICITOUS: (see "happy") appropriate; apt; charming; delightful; easy; felicific; heavenly; opportune; paradisiac(al); pat; pleasant

FELINE: a. catty; Felid; feliform; graceful; sly; stealthy; treacherous; FELINE: n. cat; felid; *Felidae* (pl.); felinity; *Felis*; *Felis domestica*; leopard; lion; panther; puma; tiger

FELL: v. beat; cut; down; hew; kill; knock down; K.O.; slaughter; FELL: a. (see "ferocious") awesome; barbarous; beastly; brutal; cruel; deadly; dire; feral; fierce; grim; inhuman(e); malevolent; murderous; relentless; savage; sinister

FELLOW: beggar; blade; bloke; boy; bozo; chap; companion; comrade; confrere; contemporary; creature; cuss; dick; dog; don; egg; equal; gallant; galoot; guy; joker; lad; man; mate; pal; peer; pup; sport; sweetheart; thing; younker

FELLOWSHIP: (see "friendliness" and "friendship") alliance; association; *bon camaraderie*; bonhom(m)ie; brotherhood; brotherliness; camaraderie; comity; communion; companionship; company; comradeliness; comradery; comradeship; consociation; conviviality; corporation; esprit; *esprit de corps*; family; foundation; fraternity; freemasonry; geniality; intimacy; mutuality; partnership; sociality; society; sodality; union

FELON: (**see** "criminal") convict; crook; culprit; housebreaker; malefactor; misfeasor; outlaw; paronychia; thief; whitlow; FELON-IOUS: (**see** "bad") base; criminal; evil; illegal; malign(ant); premeditated; unlawful; vile; villainous; FELONY: **see** "crime"

FEMALE: **n.** (**see** "woman") dam; dame; feminie (pl.); femme; girl; gorgon; lady; mother; sister; womankind; FEMALE **a.** *or* FEMININE: delicate; distaff; effeminate; fair; feminal; girlish; gynecian; gynecic; ladylike; maidenish; maidenly; maternal; muliebral; passive; soft; tender; unmanful; unmanlike; unmanly; unmasculine; woman-(ish); womanlike; womanly; FEMININITY: effeminacy; femaleness; feminality; femineity; feminineness; feminity; muliebrity

FENCE: **v.** (**see** "confine") barricade; circumscribe; dodge; duel; enclose; encompass; equivocate; evade; exclude; guard; hedge; impale; parry; protect; repel; restrain; restrict; separate; shield; shuffle; surround; tilt; ward (off); FENCE: **n.** (**see** "barricade") barrier; boundary; bulwark; circumscription; enclosure; exclusion; guard; hedge; impalement; palisade; protection; rail(ing); restraint; restriction; separation; sepiment; septum; shield; stockade; wall

FENCER: duelist; foilsman; sabreur; swordsman

FEND: (**see** "avoid") avert; defend; parry; protect; provide; repel; shift; shove; ward (off)

FERAL: (**see** "brutal") animal(istic); barbaric; barbarous; beastly; deadly; fell; ferine; ferocious; fierce; malign(ant); rapacious; savage; untamed; wild

FERMENT: **v.** (**see** "agitate") boil; brew; change; churn; effervesce; excite; foam; foment; fret; instigate; seethe; simmer; stew; work; FERMENT: **n.** (**see** "agitation") barm; brew; change; disorder; effervescence; enzyme; excitement; fever; foam; foment-(ation); instigation; leaven; stew; tumult; uproar; yeast

FEROCIOUS: (**see** "brutal") aggressive; animal(istic); awesome; barbaric; barbarous;

beastly; bitter; bloodthirsty; brutish; cruel; deadly; destructive; devastating; dire; excessive; extreme; fell; feral; ferine; fierce; frightful; furious; grim; inhuman(e); malevolent; malign(ant); merciless; murderous; pitiless; rapacious; ravenous; relentless; ruthless; sanguinary; sanguine; savage; sinister; tartarly; truculent; untamed; vandalic; vandalistic; vehement; violent; wild; FEROCITY: (**see** "brutality") acharnement; aggressiveness; destructiveness; devastation; ferity; ferociousness; fierceness; furiousness; hostility; impetuosity; inhumanity; malevolence; rapacity; relentlessness; ruthlessness; savagery; truculency; vandalism; vehemence

FERTILIZE: enrich; fatten; fecundate; fecundify; fortify; fructify; generate; impregnate; improve; pollinate; proliferate; spermatize; stimulate; strengthen; supply; FERTILE: (**see** "creative") abounding; abundant; ample; copious; exuberant; fat; fecund; fructuous; fruit-bearing; fruitful; generative; generous; green; inventive; lush; luxuriant; original; plentiful; plentitudinous; pregnant; productive; profitable; profuse; proliferative; proliferous; prolific; proligerous; propagative; rank; reproductive; rich; teeming; uberous; yielding; FERTILIZATION: enrichment; fecundation; impregnation; indoctrination; infusion; insemination; permeation; pervasion; pollination; proliferation; spermatization; FERTILITY: birthrate; creativeness; creativity; fecundity; fertileness; fructuousness; fruitfulness; lust; performance; pregnancy; productivity; prolificity

FERVOR: (**see** "ardor") animation; devotedness; devotion; earnestness; *élan*; enthusiasm; fanaticism; feeling; fervency; ferventness; fever; heat; intensity; interest; love; passion; religiosity; warmth; zeal(otry); zealousness; FERVENT *or* FERVID: (**see** "ardent") afire; agog; animated; avid; burning; devout; eager; earnest; ebullient; ecstatic; enthusiastic; evangelistic; excited; febrile; feverish; fiery; glowing; hot(-blooded); impassioned; intense; passionate; pious; religious; romantic; sincere; tender; vehement; warm; zealous

FESTER: **v.** (**see** "corrupt") abscess; foment; inflame; maturate; putrefy; putresce; rankle; rot; suppurate; ulcerate; FESTER: **n.** (**see** "corruption") abscess; lesion; maturation; pus(tule); putrefaction; putrescence; suppuration; ulcer(ation)

FESTIVE: (**see** "joyous") carnivalesque;

celebrious; convivial; delightful; festivous; gay; jolly; joyful; pleasurable; revelrous; sportive; FESTIVAL *or* FESTIVITY: (**see** "joy") ale; banquet; bee; carnival; celebration; cheer(fulness); conviviality; delight; ecstasy; elation; enjoyment; epulation; exaltation; exuberance; fair; feast; feis; felicity; fete; fiesta; gaiety; gala; gladness; glee; gratification; happiness; hilarity; holiday; jamboree; jocundity; jollification; jolliness; jollity; *jouissance*; joviality; joy(ousness); jubilation; jubilee; kermis; Mardi Gras; merriment; merrymaking; mirth; picnic; pleasure; rapture; raptus; rejoicing; revelry; symposium; transport

FESTOON: bucranium; decoration; garland; laurels; swag; wreath

FETE: **v.** (**see** "celebrate") commemorate; dine; entertain; extol; honor; regale; wine; FETE: **n.** (**see** "celebration") banquet; commemoration; dinner; entertainment; feast; festival; fiesta; holiday; picnic; FETED: dined; entertained; honored; wined

FETID: (**see** "stinking") foul; fusty; malodorous; mephitic; musty; nasty; noisome; offensive; olid; putrid; rancid; rank; repulsive; smelly

FETISH: (**see** "charm") amulet; anito; avatar; fixation; incantation; juju; mascot; mojo; obeah; obi; periapt; phylactery; prepossession; rite; talisman; voodoo

FETTER: **v.** (**see** "bind") bar; block; bond; chain; check; clog; constrain; curb; dam; detain; hamper; hamstring; handcuff; hobble; hogtie; manacle; restrain; shackle; tie; trammel; truss; yoke; FETTER(S): **n.** bar; basil; binder; binding; block(age); bond(age); chain; check; clog; constraint; curb; custody; dam; detention; durance; duress; gyve; hampering; handcuffs; hitch; hobble; irons; linkage; manacle; restraint; restriction; shackle; slavery; tether; tie; trammel; truss; yoke

FEUD: **v.** (**see** "fight") altercate; argue; battle; bicker; brawl; broil; contend; contest; disagree; dispute; fuss; quarrel; riot; spat; war; wrangle; FEUD: **n.** (**see** "fight") affray; altercation; animosity; antagonism; argument; battle; bickering; bitterness; brawl; broil; conflict; contention; contest; controversy; disagreement; dispute; dissention; enmity; fracas; fray; fuss; hostility; quarrel; riot; spat; strife; vendetta; war; wrangle

FEVER: (**see** "agitation") anxiety; ardor; calenture; cauma; craze; delirium; desire; disease; emotion; enthusiasm; excitement; febricity; ferment; fervor; fire; flush; frenzy; haste; heat; hyperpyrexia; impetuosity; intensity; passion; pyrexia; warmth; FEVERISH: (**see** "agitated") afire; anxious; ardent; delirious; emotional; enthusiastic; excited; febrile; fey; fired (up); flushed; flustered; fretful; hasty; hectic; hot; impassioned; inflammatory; intense; jumpy; mad; nervous; passionate; pyretic; pyrexial; pyrexic; sultry; unstable; warm

FEW: bunch; handful; less; little; minority; rare; scant; scarce; small; some; sparcity; (*or* sparsity); sparse; FEWNESS: (**see** "scarcity") dearth; exigency; exiguity; paucity; scantiness; sparsity; undercrowding

FEY: clairvoyant; dead; dying; elated; elfin; gay; irresponsible; mad; otherworldly; touched; visionary; wild

FIAT: (**see** "command") act; commission; decision; decree; edict; endorsement; order; permission; pronouncement; pronunciation; sanction; writ

FIB: (**see** "lie") *blague*; falsehood; prevarication; tar(r)adiddle; white lie

FIBER: (**see** "essence") abaca; ambary; cell; character; chingma; coir; cordage; core; courage; da; datil; durability; feru; fibril; filament; fortitude; hair; hemp; imbe; jute; material; muscle; pattern; pita; raffia; rhea; rope; shag; shred; sinew; sisal; stamina; staple; strand; strength; structure; textile; texture; thread

FICKLE: (**see** "frivolous") capricious; carping; caviling; censorious; chameleonic; changeable; changeful; critical; crotchety; cynical; erratic; faithless; fanciful; fitful; fleeting; flighty; giddy; harebrained; helter-skelter; hypercritical; illogical; inconsistent; inconstant; irresolute; light; mercurial; mutable; overstrict; perverse; petulant; purposeless; quibbling; quicksilver; quixotic; shifting; spasmodic; splenetic; temperamental; testy; touchy; uncertain; unfixed; unpredictable; unreliable; unsettled; unstable; unsteady; vacillating; variable; variegated; varying; vertiginous; volatile; voluble; wavering; whimsical

FICTILE: (**see** "plastic") molded; pliable

FICTION: (**see** "fable") allegory; apologue;

assumption; fabrication; falsehood; fancy; fantasy; figment; forgery; hypothecation; imagination; invention; legend; lie; makeup; myth; novel; pretense; romance; story; supposition; tale; untruth; yarn; FICTIONAL, FICTITIOUS *or* FICTIVE: allegoric(al); apocryphal; artificial; assumed; Barmecidal; bogus; counterfeit; deceptive; erroneous; fabricated; fabular; fabulous; fallacious; false; fanciful; feigned; fraudulent; hypothetical; illusory; imaginary; imaginative; invented; legendary; lying; mendacious; mythical; mythologic(al); parabolic(al); pretended; prevaricative; Scheherazadian; sham; simulated; spurious; storied; unreal; untrue; untruthful

FIDELITY: accuracy; adherence; allegiance; ardor; attachment; conscientiousness; constancy; constantness; devotedness; devotion; duty; earnestness; exactitude; exactness; faith(fulness); fealty; hold; homage; honor; humility; integrity; lealty; love; loyalness; loyalty; oath; obedience; obligation; piety; resolution; respect; sincerity; sta(u)nchness; steadfastness; support; tenacity; troth; trueness; trustworthiness; truth

FIDGET: **v.** (**see** "fret") agitate; chafe; fuss; jitter; stew; tinker; toss; trifle; twitch; worry; FIDGET: **n.** agitation; anxiousness; dysphoria; fantod; fret; fuss; impatience; jitter; nervousness; restlessness; stew; twitch; uneasiness; worry; FIDGETY: (**see** "fretful") agitated; anxious; disturbed; hectic; impatient; nervous; restive; restless; uneasy; unrestful

FIELD: (**see** "area") acre; activity; arena; bounds; business; category; clearing; division; domain; enclosure; expanse; glebe; grid; ground; group; jurisdiction; land; lea; limits; lot; meadow; métier; milieu; occupation; pasture; place; province; pursuit; range; region; scope; space; specialism; specialty; sphere; terrain; territory; trade; venue; vocation; walk

FIEND: (**see** "devil") addict; bug; demon; energumen; fanatic; imp; monster; sadist; Satan; FIENDISH: (**see** "devilish") atrocious; avernal; bad; cruel; demoniac(al); demonic(al); diabolic(al); difficult; fierce; frantic; frenzied; frightful; gruesome; hellish; hideous; infernal; inhuman(e); malevolent; malicious; malign(ant); Mephistophelian; monstrous; sadistic; sardonic; satanic(al); saturnine; sinister; unpleasant

FIERCE: (**see** "savage") angry; barbaric;

barbar(i)ous; cruel; crushing; enraged; fell; feral; ferine; ferocious; fiendish; fiery; furious; grim; heated; hostile; immoderate; impetuous; inhuman(e); leonine; lupine; merciless; outrageous; passionate; pugnacious; raging; rampant; taurine; tigerish; truculent; uncultivated; uncultured; unrestrained; untrained; violent; wild; zealous

FIERY: (**see** "angry") afire; animated; ardent; blazing; burning; choleric; combustible; evangelical; evangelistic; fervent; fervid; feverish; fierce; fired; flaming; flammable; flammatory; flashing; flashy; furious; glowing; hot; igneous; impassioned; impetuous; inflamed; intense; irascible; irritable; nettlesome; passionate; rash; red(-hot); spirited; vehement; vivacious

FIESTA: **see** "fete"

FIGHT: **v.** abet; altercate; argue; assail; attack; back; battle; bicker; box; brawl; broil; combat; conflict; confront; contend; contest; controvert; cope; counter; defend; defy; disagree; disobey; dispute; dissent; disturb; duel; engage; face; fend; feud; fuss; guard; hold; impugn; joust; justify; maintain; militate; oppose; parry; protest; quarrel; rebel; repel; resist; riot; row; safeguard; save; scrap; scuffle; secure; shield; skirmish; slug; spar; spat; stand; storm; strive; struggle; support; test; tilt; uphold; vindicate; wage; war; wrangle; wrestle; FIGHT: **n.** ado; affray; altercation; animosity; antagonism; argument; attack; barney; battle; belligerency; bickering; bout; brannigan; brawl; broil; brouhaha; brush; clash; combat; commotion; conflict; confrontation; contention; contest; controversy; din; disagreement; discord; disobedience; disputation; dispute; dissention; disturbance; donnybrook; duel; encounter; engagement; enmity; essay; feud; fracas; fray; free-for-all; fuss; hostility; jab; match; melee; muss; opposition; outburst; pugnacity; quarrel; rebellion; resistance; riot; round; row; rumpus; scrap; scrape; scuffle; set-to; shindy; siege; skirmish; spar; squabble; strife; struggle; test; tilt; trial; tumult; uproar; vendetta; war; wrangle; FIGHTER: boxer; combatant; gladiator; pugilist; prizefighter; soldier; warrior; FIGHTING: (**see** "hostile") agonistic; antagonistic; bellicose; belligerent; disputatious; militant; oppugnant; pugnacious; taurine; truculent

FIGMENT: (**see** "image") apparition; fabrication; fiction; phantasm(agoria); phantom; specter; wraith

FIGURATIVE: allegorical; allusive; anagogical; inventive; metaphoric(al); parabolic-(al); poetic(al); symbolic(al); synecdochic-(al); tralatitious; tropological; visionary

FIGURE: **v.** (**see** "think") add; assume; calculate; cast; cipher; compute; conclude; consider; count; decide; design; foot; outline; plan; portray; reckon; regard; represent; solve; sum; total; FIGURE: **n.** (**see** "image") allegory; amount; appearance; body; character; confirmation; construction; design; device; diagram; digit; doll; effigy; emblem; figurine; form(ation); grandeur; illustration; insigne; insignia (pl.); likeness; manikin; mark; motif; number; numeral; outline; pattern; personage; phantasm; photo(graph); picture; price; puppet; rank; representation; riches; shape; silhouette; solid; statue; substance; sum; symbol; type; wealth; worth

FILAMENT: dowl; fiber; fibril; hair; harl; line; strand; tendril; textile; thread; vein

FILCH: **see** "steal"

FILE: **v.** arrange; begin; commence; deposit; enter; grind; pigeonhole; line; list; lodge; polish; record; refine; rub; sharpen; smooth; store; FILE: **n.** cabinet; carlet; chart; dossier; drawer; following; line; quannet; rank; rasp; record; row; tier; tool; train

FILIGREE: **a.** decorative; fanciful; gingerbread; ornamental; unsubstantial; FILIGREE: **n.** decoration; design; gingerbread; lace; openwork; ornament

FILL: block; caulk; choke; complete; cram; distend; eke; execute; feed; flood; fulfill; involve; jam; line; load; meet; obstruct; occupy; overburden; pack; pad; permeate; pervade; prime; provide; plug; pour; put; sate; satiate; satisfy; saturate; stock; store; stuff; suffuse; supply; surfeit; swell; FILLED: complete(d); crammed; distended; fat; flooded; full; glutted; gorged; gravid; jammed; lined; loaded; occupied; overburdened; packed; padded; permeated; pervaded; preoccupied; replete; sated; satiated; satisfied; saturated; stocked; stuffed; suffused; supplied; surfeited; swollen

FILLIP: **v.** excite; snap; stimulate; tonic; urge; FILLIP: **n.** excitement; stimulation; stimulus; tonic

FILM: blur; cloud; coating; covering; deposit; haze; lamina; layer; membrane; mist; movie; nebula; negative; patina; pellicle; picture; plaque; plate; reel; scum; skin; X-ray; FILMY: clouded; cloudy; diaphanous; dim-(med); dreamy; ethereal; fine; gauzy; glassy; glazed; hazy; indefinite; indistinct; insubstantial; membranous; misty; nebular; nebulose; obscure; pellicular; pelliculate; pellucid; shadowy; tenuous; vague; vaporous; volatile

FILTER: **v.** clean; drain; infiltrate; ooze; osmose; percolate; purify; refine; screen; seep; separate; sieve; sift; strain; FILTER: **n.** cleaner; colander; colature; drain; ooze; osmosis; percolator; screen; seepage; sieve; strainer

FILTH(INESS): contamination; corruption; defilement; dirt(iness); dregs; dung; excrement; excreta (pl.); feces; fecula; feculence; immundity; impurity; lees; manginess; muck; mud; nastiness; obscenity; offal; ordure; pollution; putrefaction; putrescence; putridity; recrement; refuse; sediment; smut; soil; sordes; sordidness; squalidity; squalor; uncleanliness; FILTHY: (**see** "dirty") Augean; contaminated; corrupted; crummy; crusty; defiled; degraded; dingy; excremental; excrementitious; fecal; feculent; foul; immund; impetiginous; impure; lousy; mangy; muddy; nasty; noxious; obscene; pedicular; polluted; putrefactive; putrescent; putrid; recrementitious; scabrous; scatologic(al); soiled; sordid; squalid; stercoraceous; unclean(ly); underhanded; unhealthy; unwholesome; verminous; vile

FINAGLE: (**see** "cheat") calculate; contrive; design; euchre; figure; foist; manage; maneuver; plan; plot; scheme; swindle; wangle

FINAL: (**see** "certain") complete(d); conclusive; consummate; consummative; consummatory; decisive; definite; definitive; dernier; end(ing); eventual; finitive; last (-ditch); latest; perfect; supreme; telic; telling; terminal; terminating; terminative; ultimate; unalterable; vital; FINALITY: (**see** "certainty") conclusion; consummation; *coup de grâce*; death; definitude; end(ing); eventuality; finish; finitude; inevitability; perfection; teleology; termination; ultimacy; ultimateness

FINALE: (**see** "finality") coda; completion; conclusion; death; end(ing); finis

FINANCIAL: fiscal; monetary; pecuniary; sumptuary; FINANCES: (**see** "money")

accounts; estate; exchequer; funds; gold; income; purse; resources; revenue; wealth

FIND: **v.** ascertain; attain; behold; catch; chance; confront; contrive; decide; declare; descry; detect; determine; devise; discern; discover; encounter; espy; estimate; evaluate; evalue; examine; experience; feel; ferret out; figure; glean; hold; hunt; invent; learn; locate; measure; meet; note; notice; observe; perceive; procure; provide; reach; recognize; recover; regard; scrounge; see; spot; spy; supply; surprise; survey; trace; uncover; unearth; view; weigh; FIND: **n.** *ben trovato*; bonanza; *découverte*; discovery; El Dorado; serendipity; treasure (trove)

FINE: **v.** amerce; charge; forfeit; mulct; penalize; punish; sconce; tax; FINE: **a.** (see "excellent") acute; admirable; arachnoid; attenuated; beautified; bright; capillary; choice; clarified; clear; comminuted; dainty; delicate; diaphanous; ducky; elegant; ethereal; exact; exquisite; fair; fastidious; filmy; fragile; good; gossamer(y); hair-splitting; handsome; homeopathic; hunky-dory; impalpable; insubstantial; intangible; jim-dandy; keen; magnificent; minute; nice; noble; notable; pleasing; precise; pure; purified; rare; refined; sensitive; sharp; skilled; skillful; slender; slight; small; splendid; subt(i)le; subtilized; sunny; superior; sweet; tenuous; thin; tiny; wonderful; FINE: **n.** amercement; forfeit(ure); levy; loss; penalty; punishment; sconce; scot; tax

FINERY: adornment; array; caparison; decoration; elegance; frippery; gaiety; gewgaws; gilt; gold; jewelry; jewels; ornamentation; regalia; togs; trappings; trimmings

FINGER: **v.** designate; feel; handle; identify; indicate; meddle; palp(ate); pilfer; purloin; touch; FINGER: **n.** concern; dactyl(us); digit(al); index; interest; part; pinkie; pointer; share

FINICAL *or* FINICKY: (see "critical") dainty; dapper; fastidious; finicking; foppish; fussy; meticulous; mincing; nice; overnice; particular; prudish; scrupulous; spruce; squeamish

FINIS: (see "finality") conclusion; *coup de grâce*; death; end(ing); finish; termination

FINISH: **v.** (see "end") accomplish; arrive; close; complete; conclude; consume; consummate; defeat; do; dress; effect; execute;

exhaust; kill; mill; murder; perfect; perform; point (up); polish; process; refine; result; sandpaper; smooth; terminate; win; FINISH: **n.** (see "end") accomplishment; close; coda; completion; conclusion; consummation; downfall; edging; effect; execution; finis; perfection; polish; refinement; sheen; shine; surface; termination; terminus; veneer; win; windup; FINISHED: able; accomplished; adept; *au fait*; closed; completed; concluded; consumed; consummate (d); culminated; done; educated; ended; executed; exhausted; expired; exquisite; kaput; over; perfect(ed); performed; polished; processed; proficient; refined; skilled; smooth; *soigné*; *soignée* (fem.); spent; suave; terminated

FIRE: **v.** animate; arouse; axe; blaze; burn; can; char; conflagrate; detonate; discharge; dismiss; drop; eject; excite; expel; flame; glow; heat; hurl; ignite; illuminate; inflame; inspire; kindle; light; oust; purge; redden; sack; scorch; sear; shoot; stimulate; stir; FIRE: **n.** (see "fervor") animation; ardor; blaze; brilliancy; burning; combustion; conflagration; courage; criticism; drive; eagerness; embers; enthusiasm; fever; flame; genius; glow; heat; holocaust; ignis; ignition; inferno; inspiration; light; luminosity; passion; sparks; stimulation; vivacity; warmth; wildfire

FIREARM: arm(s); Colt; derringer; gat; gun; mortar; musket; pistol; revolver; rifle; weapon

FIREBRAND: (see "incendiary") agitator; conflagrationist; hothead; troublemaker

FIREBUG: arsonist; conflagrationist; conflagrator; firebrand; incendiary; kindler; pyromaniac; pyrophile; torch

FIREWORKS: display; *feu d'artifice*; fizgig; fun; girandole; petard; pyrotechnic(s); salute; trouble

FIRM: **v.** concretize; crystallize; establish; fix; gel; harden; jel; solidify; stabilize; straighten; FIRM: **a.** adamantine; assured; bound; certain; close(-knit); compact; compressed; concrete; constant; convinced; definite; dense; dependable; determined; devoted; dogged; dyed-in-the-wool; enduring; established; exact; fast; fixed; grounded; hard; healthy; immovable; impregnable; indissoluble; ineradicable; inexpugnable; inexpungeable; inflexible; iron; loyal; material; moored; particular; peremptory;

persevering; persistent; pertinacious; physical; preemptory; real; resolute; rigid; rigorous; robust; rockbound; rooted; rugged; secured; set(tled); severe; single(-minded); solid(ified); sound; specific; stable; sta(u)nch; stark; steadfast; steady; stiff; stocky; stout; strict; strong; substantial; sure(footed); sustained; tangible; taut; tenacious; thick; thorough; tight; true; unassailable; unbendable; unbending; uncompromising; unconquerable; unfaltering; unflinching; uninfluenced; united; unshakable: unshaken; unswayed; unswerving; unwavering; unyielding; well-founded; FIRM: **n.** business; company; concern; corporation; enterprise; industry; partnership; FIRMNESS: adhesiveness; consistency; constancy; decision; determination; doggedness; endurability; hardness; inclemency; indissolubility; permanence; permanency; persistency; pertinacity; resolution; rigor; security; solidarity; solidity; soundness; stability; steadfastness; stiffness; tenacity; thickness; unshakableness; vertebration

FIRMAMENT: ether; expanse; heavens; sky; sphere; vault; welkin

FIRST: **a.** aboriginal; ace; ahead; alpha; antecedent; A-one; beginning; best; capital; cardinal; chief; earliest; eldest; elementary; embryonic; foremost; former; front; highest; inaugural; inceptive; inchoate; inchoative; indigenous; initial; initiatory; introductory; leading; maiden; main; nascent; new; oldest; original; outstanding; pathbreaking; preceding; preeminent; premier(e); primary; prime(val); primitive; primogenital; primordial; primus; principal; pristine; rudimental; rudimentary; senior; signal; star; stellar; superior; supreme; trailblazing; FIRST: **n.** aboriginal; aborigine; alpha; beginning; commencement; onset; preeminence; princeps; FIRST-CLASS: **see** "superior"

FISH: angle; cast; feel; hunt; poke; probe; search; seek; troll; FISHER(MAN): angler; piscator; Waltonian; FISHING: piscation

FISSURE: blemish; breach; break; chasm; chink; cleavage; cleft; crack; cranny; crevice; disagreement; discord; division; flaw; fracture; gap; groove; interstice; leak; opening; rent; rift; rima; rime; seam; slit; split; sulci (pl.); sulcus

FIT: **v.** accommodate; accustom; adapt; adjust; agree; align; attune; befit; belong; clothe; coapt; coincide; collimate; combine;

condition; conform; connect; engage; equalize; equip; fare; fashion; frame; gear; gee; go; harmonize; insert; interlock; intersect; join; match; mate; measure; meet; mesh; modulate; mold; prepare; provide; ready; rig; seat; set; shape; stabilize; suit; tailor; teach; train; true; tuck; tune; FIT(TING): **a.** able; adapted; adequate; adjusted; applicable; apposite; appropriate; apropos; apt; becoming; calculated; capable; *comme il faut*; competent; condign; conditioned; congruent; congruous; consonant; convenient; correct; decent; decorous; deserved; disposed; due; duly; eligible; expedient; fair; felicitous; fitted; germane; hale; happy; healthy; ideal; idoneous; just; kosher; legitimate; licensed; likely; measured; meet; necessary; pat; pertinent; prepared; proper; prudent; qualified; ready; reasonable; relevant; right(ful); seemly; suitable; suited; timely; trained; warranted; worthy; FIT: **n.** accession; agreement; attack; click; fancy; fury; humor; mood; outbreak; outburst; paroxysm; pet; seizure; spasm; spell; start; stroke; tantrum; tiff; whim(sey); FITNESS: adaptability; adaptitude; advisability; advisableness; applicability; applicableness; appropriateness; aptitude; capability; capacity; coaptation; competency; condition; correctitude; correctness; decora (pl.); decorum; distinction; eligibility; expedience; expediency; fettle; form; idoneity; preparation; preparedness; propriety; qualification; rightness; seemliness; soundness; suitability; truth; worthiness

FITFUL: (**see** "nervous") ambivalent; capricious; changeable; convulsive; desultory; fickle; flickering; impulsive; intermittent; irregular; random; spasmodic; uncertain; unstable; variable; whimsical

FIVE: cinque; pentad

FIX: **v.** adjust; affix; agree; amend; apply; appoint; arrange; assign; attach; bind; capture; concentrate; consolidate; cook; crystallize; cure; decide; define; delimit(ate); determine; doctor; embed; establish; fasten; firm; fixate; focus; freeze; gaze; harden; imbed; implant; inculcate; insert; install; instill; institute; join; limit; locate; lock; make; mark; measure; mend; moor; nail; necessitate; peg; pin(point); place; plant; prepare; preserve; punish; qualify; radicate; repair; restore; rivet; root; secure; set(tle); solidify; stabilize; stare; station; stay; tie; unite; FIX: **n.** box; cruciality; difficulty; dilemma; hole; how-do-you-do; implantation; jam; pickle; plight; predicament;

scrape; spot; FIXATION: concentration; crystallization; fetish; freeze; habit; idea; implantation; solidification; stabilization; tic; FIXED: abiding; absolute; anchored; constant; deep-rooted; deep-seated; defined; determined; durable; enduring; established; fast(ened); firm; flat; focused; frozen; imbedded; immobile; immotile; immovable; immutable; implanted; inadaptable; inalterable; incessant; incommutable; inerratic; inflexible; installed; instituted; intent; inveterate; irremovable; irrevocable; lasting; mended; moored; motionless; moveless; permanent; placed; prepared; provided; repaired; rigid; sedentary; sessile; set(tled); stabile; stabilized; stable; staid; static; stationary; steadfast; steady; still; strict; stubborn; tied; tight; unchanging; unremoved; unswerving; unwandering; unyielding;

FLABBY: (see "slack") ductile; feeble; flaccid; ineffective; infirm; languid; limber; plastic; supple; unfirm; weak

FLACCID: (see "slack") drooping; flabby; hanging; ineffective; lax; limber; limp; loose; pendant; pending; soft; weak; yielding

FLAG: v. (see "decline") delay; droop; fail; faint; fall; lag; languish; procrastinate; sag; sign; signal; sink; tire; wane; wilt; FLAG: n. banderole; banner; bougee; bunting; burgee; colors; ensign; fane; fanion; feather; gonfalon; guidon; iris; jack; marker; nationality; pennant; penon; sign; signal; standard; streamer; trophy

FLAGELLATE: (see "beat") castigate; club; cudgel; drive; flog; lash; punish; scourge; stigmatize; thrash; whip

FLAGITIOUS: (see "bad") atrocious; corrupt; criminal; disgraceful; flagrant; heinous; infamous; nefarious; scandalous; shameful; vicious; villainous; wicked

FLAGRANT: (see "bad") ardent; atrocious; burning; egregious; evil; execrable; flagitious; glaring; glowing; gross; heinous; infamous; malicious; monstrous; nefarious; notorious; odious; outrageous; raging; rampant; rank; scandalous; scarlet; vicious; wanton; wicked

FLAIR: (see "aptitude") ability; bent; brains; capacity; discernment; discrimination; learning; liking; nose; predilection; scent; talent; taste; tendency; wits

FLAKE: v. chip; chisel; desquamate; exfoliate;

laminate; peel; scale; strip; FLAKE: n. chip; desquamation; exfoliation; lamina; layer; scale; scute; shard; shred; squama; FLAKY: desquamative; desquamatory; exfoliative; friable; lamellar; lamelliform; laminar; scabrous; scaly; scurfy; scutate; squamaceous; squamate; squamous

FLAMBOYANT: (see "showy") dazzling; florid; flowery; frilly; garish; gaudy; gingerbread; gorgeous; ornate; ostentatious; overdecorated; resplendent; rococo; splendacious; splendid; unrestrained

FLAME: v. beam; blaze; brighten; burn; enkindle; fire; flare; glaze; glow; ignite; kindle; light; shine; FLAME: n. ardor; beam; blaze; brilliance; burning; enthusiasm; fervor; fire; glaze; glow; heat; light; luminescence; sweetheart; torch; warmth; zeal(ousness)

FLANEUR: bon viveur; flaneuse (fem); idler; loiterer; man-about-town; stroller; trifler

FLANK v. see "border;" FLANK: n. border; loin; side; thigh; wing

FLAP: v. beat; clap; dangle; fling; flop; fluctuate; flutter; fly; hang; pulsate; sway; vibrate; wave; FLAP: n. bangle; crisis; edge; fold; hullabaloo; lappet; projection; tab; tag

FLARE: v. balloon; blaze; burn; dart; dazzle; display; flame; flash; fleck; flicker; glare; gleam; glitter; glow; open; rage; rise; shine; shoot; signal; splay; spread; spring; waver; widen; FLARE: n. anger; blaze; display; flame; flash; flick(er); fusee; glare; gleam; glitter; glow; light; pyrotechnic; rage; torch; FLARING: belling; bouffant(e); dazzling; évasé; flaming; gaping; open; patulous; shiny; showy; spread(ing)

FLASH: v. blaze; blink; burn; burst; coruscate; dash; emit; flame; flare; flicker; fulgurate; glance; glare; glaze; gleam; glint; glisten; glitter; glow; lancinate; light; rush; scintillate; shimmer; shine; shoot; show; signal; spark(le); splash; twinkle; FLASH: n. blaze; blink; brilliance; burst; coruscation; dash; display; flame; flare; flicker; fulguration; glance; glare; glaze; gleam; glimpse; glint; glisten(ing); glitter; glow; instant; light; look; pyrotechnic; rush; scintillation; shimmer; shine; shoot; shot; show; signal; smile; spark(le); splash; twinkle; twinkling; FLASHY: (see "showy") brilliant; cheap; fast; fiery; flamboyant;

flashing; flaunting; garish; gaudy; glaring; glittering; glittery; impetuous; jazzy; loud; meretricious; ostentatious; pretentious; smart; snazzy; sporty; tawdry; tinsel; FLASHING: fulgurating; meteoric; pyrotechnic(al); slashing; sparkling; twinkling

FLASK: betty; bottle; canteen; carafe; container; cruse; ewer; flagon; olpe; vial

FLAT: absolute; banal; bland; broadened; broke; dead; deflated; dejected; depressed; destroyed; dispirited; down(right); dull; even; exact; fallen; fixed; flavorless; flush; horizontal; immature; inactive; inane; insipid; jejune; juvenile; level; lifeless; moneyless; monotonous; planar; planate; plane; pointless; positive; precise; prone; prostrate; ruined; sick; simple; smooth; spiritless; stale; stupid; tabular; tasteless; trite; unclear; uninteresting; vapid; waterish; FLATNESS: banality; deflation; dejection; depression; dullness; horizontality; insipidity; jejunity; lifelessness; monotony; prostration; FLATTENED: applanate; evened; leveled; oblate; planate; planed

FLATTER: adulate; assuage; beguile; blandish; blarney; cajole; coax; compliment; encourage; entice; exalt; extol; fawn; gratify; humor; ingratiate; inveigle; laud; oil; palp; panegyrize; pedestalize; placate; please; praise; soften; soothe; stellify; swage; sway; sycophantize; toady; wheedle; worship; FLATTERY: adulation; allurement; applesauce; assuagement; baloney; beguilement; blandishment; blarney; bosh; cajolement; cajolery; homage; incense; ingratiation; inveiglement; laudation; mush; obsequiousness; oil; palaver; panegyric(s); praise; puffery; servility; self-deception; snow; soap; sugarplum; sycophancy; taffy; unction; unctuosity; FLATTERER: *adulateur*; *adulatrice* (fem.); adulator; eulogist; panegyrist; proneur; sycophant; toady; FLATTERING: (**see** "courtly") ingratiating; obsequious; unctuous

FLAUNT: (**see** "demonstrate") attract; blandish; blazon; boast; brag; brandish; display; exhibit; expose; flash; flourish; flout; flutter; obtrude; parade; shake; swing; toss; traipse; vaunt; wave

FLAVOR: (**see** "appetite") anise; aroma; essence; fragrance; gust(o); odor; piquancy; race; relish; repute; sapor; sauce; savor; season(ing); smack; tack; tang; taste; tincture; tinge; zest; FLAVORFUL: **see** "appetizing" and "palatable;" FLAVOR-LESS: **see** "flat"

FLAW: (**see** "blemish") blast; botch; breach; break; bug; crack; defect; deformity; dent; disfigurement; fault; fissure; fleck; gale; gap; gust; hole; impairment; imperfection; lesion; malformation; mar; mark; rent; rift; rip; rub; scratch; speck; spot; tear; FLAWLESS: (**see** "perfect") exquisite; fleckless; immaculate; impeccant; indefectible; irreproachable; unflawed; FLAW-LESSNESS: (**see** "perfection") immaculacy; impeccability; indefectibility

FLAY: abrade; chafe; censure; criticize; excoriate; flail; flog; grill; pare; peel; probe; punish; rack; reprove; scar(ify); skin; strip; torture

FLEE: (**see** "depart") abscond; absquatulate; avoid; blow; bolt; decamp; desert; elope; elude; escape; fly; forsake; fugitate; go; hasten; hurry; lam; leave; move; quit; retreat; run; scamper; scram; shun; skedaddle; vanish

FLEECE: v. (**see** "cheat") bleed; clip; despoil; mulct; overcharge; plunder; rifle; rob; shear; skin; strip; sweat; take; torture; FLEECE: n. booty; cloth; cover(ing); fabric; hair; nap; pile; skin; wool; FLEECY: lanate; laniferous; woolly

FLEER: (**see** "deride") flaunt; gibe; grimace; grin; jeer; laugh; mock; scoff; scorn; smirk; sneer

FLEET: a. (**see** "hasty") agile; brief; evanescent; fast; fleeting; harefooted; infrequent; nimble; light; occasional; quick; rapid; short(-lived); speedy; swift; transitory; volatile; FLEET: n. argosy; armada; boats; escadrille; flotilla; group; navy; ships; squadron; warships; FLEETING: (**see** "hasty") brief; casual; cursory; deciduous; diaphanous; elusive; ephemeral; ephemerous; etherial; evanescent; fast; fickle; fleet; flighty; fly-by-night; flying; fugacious; fugitive; gossamer(y); impermanent; instantaneous; momentary; moving; passing; perishable; preterient; semelfactive; shadowy; speedy; superficial; swift; temporal; temporary; transient; transitory; unenduring; vanishing; vaporous; volage; volatile; unsubstantial

FLESH: beings; corporeality; family; fat; food; human(ity); kin; life; mankind; meat;

muscle; race; sensitivity; stock; tendon; tissue; viands; weakness; FLESHY: (see "obese") adipose; bodily; burly; carnal; carnose; corporeal; earthy; fat; lascivious; lecherous; libidinous; lustful; meaty; plump; sensual; soft; stout; worldly; FLESHINESS: (see "obesity") adiposity; avoirdupois; corpulence; plumpness; stoutness

FLEX: (see "bend") bow; curve; falsify; fold; genu(flect); kowtow; turn; warp; yield; FLEXURE: (see "bend") arc; crook; curvature; curve; fold; genu; kyphosis; scoliosis; turn(ing)

FLEXIBLE: adaptable; buoyant; changeable; compliant; cooperative; docile; ductile; effervescent; elastic; expansive; fingent; flaccid; limber; limp; lissom(e); lithe(some); lively; manageable; mobile; plastic; pliable; pliant; ready; receptive; resilient; rubbery; springy; subrigid; supple; tolerant; tractable; unfirm; variable; volatile; weak; willing; willowy; yielding; FLEXIBILITY: amenability; bounce; buoyancy; cooperation; docility; ductility; ease; effervescence; elasticity; expansiveness; flaccidity; flexibleness; fluidity; give; limberness; lissomeness; litheness; lithesomeness; maneuverability; mobility; plasticity; pliancy; reciprocity; resilience; resiliency; spring(iness); stretch; suppleness; temper; tolerance; tone; tractability; volatility; weakness; yield

FLICKER: blaze; blink; fail; flair; flame; flit; fluctuate; flunk; flutter; gleam; glint; hover; oscillate; quiver; shimmer; undulate; wave(r); wink; FLICKERING: aflicker; blazing; blinking; feeble; fickle; fluctuating; fluttering; fulgurating; lambent; lancinating; meteoric; oscillating; shimmering; uncertain; undecided; undulating; vacillating; wavering; winking;

FLIGHT: bevy; covey; drove; elopement; escape; evasion; exodus; flock; fugitation; gaggle; group; hegira; herd; hop; journey; migration; mounting; pack; panic; range; rise; rout; soaring; stairs; stampede; trip; volitation; volley; voyage; wing; FLIGHTY: (see "fickle") anile; balmy; barmy; birdwitted; capricious; fleeting; foolish; frivolous; giddy; harebrained; helter-skelter; hoity-toity; imaginative; mad; mercurial; pompous; quicksilver; quixotic; scatterbrained; skittish; swift; transient; unserious; utopian; volatile

FLIMSY: cheap; cobwebby; delicate; diaphanous; enfeebled; ethereal; feeble; fragile; frail; frangible; frivolous; gauzy; gimcrack; gossamer(y); haywire; implausible; inane; ineffective; insignificant; insubstantial; jerry-built; minor; misty; nebulous; pasteboard; poor; puerile; puny; ramshackle; rattletrap; reedy; rickety; shaky; shallow; sickly; slender; sleazy; slight; slim(sy); small; substandard; superficial; tenuous; thin; transparent; trashy; trifling; trivial; undurable; unendurable; unfirm; unsound; unsubstantial; weak; FLIMSINESS: diaphaneity; ethereality; frailty; frivolity; gauziness; insubstantiality; rudeness; shakiness; shallowness; tenuity; tenuousness; unsubstantiality; weakness

FLINCH: (see "cower") avoid; blench; cow; crawl; cringe; crouch; elude; evade; falter; fawn; fear; jerk; pale; quail; recoil; retract; retreat; shake; shirk; shrink; shy; start(le); stoop; submit; swerve; veer; wince; withdraw; wonde

FLING: (see "cast") chuck; discard; disregard; emit; flick; flip; flirt; flounce; heave; hurl; hurtle; launch; pitch; sling; throw; toss

FLINTY: cruel; granitic; hard; obdurate; rigorous; steely; stern

FLIPPANT: (see "fresh") airy; bold; brassy; brazen; chatty; flip; fluent; forward; frivolous; glib; pat; pert; sassy; saucy; smart (-alecky); trifling; voluble; FLIPPANCY: boldness; brassiness; brazenness; flipness; frivolity; persiflage; pertness; sass(iness); sauciness; spontaneity; vivacity

FLIRT: **v.** coquet(te); dally; fling; ogle; philander; play; toy; trifle; FLIRT: **n.** amourette; *amoureuse*; coquet(te); intrigante; Jill; ogler; philanderer; trifler; FLIRTATIOUS: amorous; arch; coquettish; coy; vampirish; FLIRTATION: coquetry; courtship; dalliance; passade; philandering; toying

FLIT: dart; fleet; flicker; flutter; fly; gad; hover; move; pass; scud; skate; skim

FLOAT: **v.** buoy; drift; flood; fly; glide; hover; negotiate; ride; roam; sail; sell; shift; skim; soar; waft; wander; watch; FLOAT: **n.** bob; buoy; cork; raft; FLOATING: (see "aimless") adrift; afloat; awash; buoyed; drifting; flooded; movable; natant; shifting; suspended; wandering; waterborne

FLOCK: **v. see** "congregate;" FLOCK: **n.** (**see** "group") aggregation; army; assemblage; bevy; brood; church; clutch; collection; company; congregation; covey; crowd; drove; fold; gaggle; gang; gathering; hatch; herd; hirsel; hive; horde; litter; lot; mob; multitude; pack; pod; press; raft; school; set; skein; swarm; team; throng; troop; troupe

FLOG: beat; cane; cat; chastise; club; criticize; cudgel; drub; exhaust; flagellate; lambaste; larrup; lash; punish; scourge; strike; tan; thrash; wale; welt; whip

FLOOD: **v.** avalanche; cover; deluge; engulf; fill; flow; glut; inundate; irrigate; overflow; oversupply; overwhelm; stream; swamp; water; FLOOD: **n.** (**see** "deluge") avalanche; cataclysm; cataract; eagre; excess; freshet; inundation; ocean; outpour(ing); overflow(ing); oversupply; rush; sea; spare; stream; superabundance; surplus(age); tide; torrent; FLOODED *or* FLOODING: cataclysmic(al); deluginous; diluvial; inundant; inundated; inundatory; overflowing; superabundant; waterborne

FLOOR: **v.** (**see** "beat") defeat; discomfit; down; embarrass; flatten; foil; K.O.; pave; FLOOR: **n.** audience; base; basis; bottom; carpet; deck; ground; level; parquet; pavement; platform; story; tier

FLOP: **v.** collapse; drop; fail; fall; fizzle; slump; tumble; FLOP: **n.** about-face; collapse; decline; dud; failure; fall; fiasco; fizzle; lemon; slump; tumble; washout

FLORID: embellished; enriched; erubescent; figurative; flourishing; flowery; flushed; gaudy; healthy; luscious; melismatic; ornate; red; rhetorical; rococo; rubescent; rubicund; ruddy; rufous; showy; sunburned; vigorous

FLOUNDER: blunder; dab; grovel; labor; muddle; roll; sink; strive; struggle; thrash; toil; wallow; welter

FLOURISH: **v.** accentuate; accumulate; adorn; advance; bloom; blossom; boast; boom; brag; brandish; burgeon; conquer; decorate; develop; display; effloresce; fatten; flaunt; gain; grow; increase; luxuriate; ornament; parade; ply; prevail; prosper; push; resound; rise; roar; rumble; shake; soar; succeed; swing; thrash; thrive; triumph; twirl; vaunt; wave; wax; wield; win; zoom; FLOURISH: **n.** adornment; advance(ment); boom; curlicue; decoration; display; drive;

explosion; fanfare; flood; ornament(ation); ostentation; parade; paraph; resound; roar; roulade; showiness; zoom; FLOURISHING: affluent; booming; efflorescent; florid; flowering; healthy; in flower; lusty; palmy; posh; prospering; prosperous; rampant; rich; robust; showy; sleek

FLOUT: contemn; deride; despise; disdain; fleer; flount; gibe; insult; jeer; jibe; mock; scoff; scorn; sneer; spurn; taunt

FLOW: **v.** (**see** "course") abound; arise; circulate; derive; discharge; drain; drift; emanate; emit; empty; float; flood; flush; flux; glide; go; gush; inundate; issue; move; ooze; originate; pass; pour; proceed; progress; rise; run; seep; shed; slide; spout; spread; spring; start; stem; stream; teem; tide; wave; well; FLOW: **n.** (**see** "course") afflux(ion); circulation; current; decurrence; drift; effusion; emanation; emission; flood(ing); flowage; flush; flux; gush(ing); inundation; issuance; issue; move(ment); ooze; outpouring; overflowing; passage; pouring; procedure; procession; progress; rise; run(ning); seep(age); spouting; spread; spring; start; stream; succession; tide; trend; wash; wave; well(ing); FLOWING: abundant; affluent; aflow; agush; canorous; cantable; confluent; cursive; derivative; deriving; effluent; emanating; fluent; fluid; flux; liquid; mellifluent; mellifluous; mellisonant; mobile; movable; moving; perfluent; profluent; rising; running; runny; shifting; smooth; sonorous

FLOWER: **v.** (**see** "bloom") blossom; bud; burgeon; develop; effloresce; grow; unfold; FLOWER(S): **n.** best; bloom; blossom; bouquet; bud; elect; elite; posy; spray; FLOWERY: abloom; blooming; bloomy; blossoming; bombastic; efflorescent; embellished; euphuistic; florescent; florid; floriferous; florulent; grandiloquent; inflated; ornate; ostentatious; prosperous; rhapsodic; rubescent

FLUCTUATE: (**see** "change") alter; bellwaver; deflect; deviate; digress; hesitate; oscillate; ramble; shift; sway; swerve; swing; undulate; vacillate; vary; veer; vibrate; wander; wave(r); FLUCTUATION: alteration; ambivalence; change; deflection; deviation; digression; fickleness; hesitation; irresolution; oscillation; shift; sway; swerve; swing; undulation; unsteadiness; vacillation; variation; vibration

FLUENT: apt; changeable; changing; copious;

easy; expert; facile; facund; flowing; fluid; free; glib; gliding; liquid; moving; ready; running; smooth; talkative; unembarrassed; vocal; voluble; wordy; FLUENCY: abundance; *copia verborum*; eloquence; expertise; facility; facundity; glibness; grandiloquence; liquidity; loquaciousness; loquacity; mellifluence; pace; readiness; skill; smoothness; verbosity; volubility; wordiness

FLUFF: **v.** bungle; err; fail; miscue; misplay; miss; FLUFF: **n.** blunder; boner; down; error; fault; floss; lint; miscue; misplay; nap; puff; triviality; wool; FLUFFY: airy; downy; ethereal; flocculent; flossy; light; puffed; puffy; soft; trivial; wooly

FLUID: **a.** (**see** "flowing") changeable; easy; floating; fluent; flux; gaseous; liquid; mobile; movable; moving; nonsolid; oily; running; runny; shifting; smooth; watery; FLUID: **n.** blood; essence; flux; gas; juice; liquid; milk; oil; plasma; sap; serum; steam; vapor; water; FLUIDITY: liquidity; liquidness; mobility

FLUNK: back (out); fail; flinch; miss; retreat; shirk; slip

FLUORESCENCE: brightness; diaphaneity; effulgence; incandescence; luminescence; luminosity; phosphorescence; translumination

FLURRY: (**see** "commotion") ado; agitation; blast; brouhaha; bustle; confusion; disturbance; eddy; excitement; flurriment; fluster; flutter; fret; fuss; gust; haste; hubbub; hurry; pother; shower; spasm; speed; squall; stir; tear; to-do

FLUSH: **v.** animate; bloom; blush; color; empurple; excite; flow; glow; increase; inflame; jump; mantle; raise; redden; rinse; rouse; rush; start(le); suffuse; thrill; FLUSH: **a.** abundant; affluent; even; flat; lavish; level; overflowing; plane; prodigal; prosperous; rich; smooth; FLUSH: **n.** bloom; blush; color; erubescence; fever; glow; growth; reddening; redness; rosiness; rubedo; rubescence; rush; suffusion; thrill; tinge; FLUSHED: aglow; blooming; blushing; colored; erubescent; fevered; feverish; florid; glowing; hectic; lavish; prodigal; prosperous; red-(dened); rich; rosy; rubescent; ruby; scarlet; tinged; vigorous; wealthy

FLUSTER: **v.** addle; agitate; befuddle; confound; confuse; discomfit; discomfort; discompose; disconcert; dismay; disturb; embarrass; excite; faze; flurry; move; muddle; perturb; pother; rattle; ruffle; upset; FLUSTER: **n. see** "commotion"

FLUTTER: agitate; beat; bustle; confuse; fan; flap; flicker; flirt; flit; fluctuate; fly; hover; palpitate; quake; quiver; scurry; shake; throb; tremble; twitter; undulate; vacillate; vibrate; volitate; wave

FLUX: current; diarrhea; discharge; dysentery; flood; flow(ing); outflow; purge; rush; stream; tide; torrent; uncertainty

FLY: **v.** abscond; ascend; aviate; avoid; burst; dart; decamp; elapse; elope; escape; flap; flee; flit; float; flutter; glide; hover; lap; mount; panic; pass; rise; stampede; sun; rush; sail; scud; shoot; shun; skim; soar; tower; vanish; whir; wing; FLY: **n.** carriage; covering; dipteron; insect; opening; pest; tent; FLYING: brief; episodic; evanescent; fast; fleeting; passing; swift; temporary; transient; transitorious; transitory; volant; volitant

FOAM: **v.** anger; boil; bubble; effervesce; expand; foment; froth; fume; lather; rage; spew; spray; spume; whip; FOAM: **n.** barm; beads; beer; bubbles; cream; effervescence; ferment(ation); froth; head; lather; scum; spray; spume; suds; yeast

FOCAL: axial; important

FOCUS: **v.** adjust; aim; center; collect; concentrate; converge; fix; focalize; pivot; point; spot; FOCUS: **n.** (**see** "center") adjustment; centration; centrum; clearness; concentration; core; cynosure; epicenter; heart; hearth; home; hub; issue; kernel; middle; navel; nidus; nucleus; omphalos; origin; point; umbilicus

FODDER: (**see** "food") ammunition; corn; ensilage; feed; forage; hay; oats; provender; provisions; stover; straw

FOE: (**see** "antagonist") adversary; archenemy; attacker; combatant; competitor; enemy; opponent; rival

FOG: **v.** bedim; bewilder; blur; cloud; confuse; haze; obfuscate; obscure; perplex; vaporize; FOG: **n.** aerosol; bewilderment; brume; cloud; confusion; haze; mist; murk; obscurity; perplexity; smog; smoke; spray; stupor; uncertainty; vapor; FOGGY: (**see** "dim") bewildered; brumous; caliginous; cloudy; confused; fogged; groggy; hazy;

indistinct; misty; muddled; murky; nubilous; obscure; tenuous; thick; vague; vaporous

FOIBLE: (**see** "fault") eccentricity; failing; peculiarity; weakness; whimsicality

FOIL: **v.** (**see** "baffle") balk; bar; cheat; check(mate); circumvent; defeat; disappoint; faze; frustrate; defeat; outwit; prevent; repulse; thwart; FOIL: **n.** deuteragonist; épée; leaf; metal; sword; stooge

FOIST: befool; fob; fool; force; impose; interpolate; palm (off); pass (off); thrust

FOLD: **v.** (**see** "bend") clasp; close; crease crimp; double; drape; embosom; end; entwine; envelop(e); hug; incorporate; intertwine; pleat; plicate; reef; replicate; wrap; FOLD: **n.** bend; congregation; convolution; crease; crimp; drape; envelopment; flap; flock; hug; lap; pen; pleat; plica (tion); plicature; ply; reflection; religion; ruga; seam; volution

FOLIAGE: boscage; bouquet; branches; flowers; frondage; frondescence; greenery; leafage; leafiness; leaves; shade; spray; umbrage; verdure

FOLK: congregation; crowd; family; gentry; group; kin(dred); laity; mankind; nation; people(s); persons; race; relatives; society; species; FOLKLORE: belief(s); customs; ethos; history; legends; mythology; sayings; superstitions; traditions

FOLLOW: accept; accompany; ape; attend; chase; conform; copy; dog; ensue; go; happen; hear; heed; heel; hound; imitate; mock; obey; observe; ply; practice; pursue; replace; respond; result; seek; shadow; stalk; stem; strive; succeed; sue; supersede; supervene; tag; tail; trace; track; trail; travel; tread; understand; use; watch; yield; FOLLOWER(S): abettor; acolyte; addict; adherent; admirer; aficionada (fem.); aficionado; amateur; angel; aper; apostle; appreciator; apprentice; assistant; associate; attendant; audience; backer; beau; believer; bigot; buff; captive; claque; clientage; clientele; clique; cohort; companion; copier; courtier; descendants; devotee; disciple; enthusiast; entourage; escort; fan(atic); fiend; following; habitué; habituation; henchman; hound; imitator; ist; ite; liege-(man); lover; mimic; minion; page; parade; partisan; procession; progeny; proponent; protege; pupil; pursuer; retainer; retinue; satellite; school; sectary; sectator; servant;

soldier; squire; successor; supporter; surroundings; train; user; votary; worker; zealot; FOLLOWING: **a.** (**see** "consecutive" and "consequential") ensuant; ensuing; next; sequent(ial); since; succeeding; successive; FOLLOWING: **n.** (**see** "followers") admirers; clientele; cult; drove; fans; followership; patronage; patrons; practice; profession; public; pursuit; retinue; sect; supporters; trade; train; vocation; work

FOLLY: (**see** "absurdity") asininity; ate; *bêtise*; brainlessness; desipience; fatuity; foolery; foolishness; idiocy; idiotcy; imbecility; imprudence; impuissance; inanity; indiscretion; indulgence; levity; lunacy; madness; nonsense; thoughtlessness; unwisdom; weak-mindedness; weakness; whim-(sicality)

FOMENT: **v.** (**see** "incite") abet; arouse; begin; brew; cause; encourage; excite; fester; fire; heat; inflame; initiate; inspire; instigate; intensify; promote; provoke; rouse; sow; stimulate; stir; FOMENT: **n.** compress; ferment; fomentation; stupe

FOND: (**see** "affectionate")" amatory; amorous; ardent; attached; devoted; doting;enamored; foolish; indulgent; infatuated; kind; loving; overindulgent; parental; sentimental; silly; solicitous;tender;vain;zealous;FONDNESS: ardor; affection; appetite; attachment; concern; dearness; desire; devotedness; devotion; diathesis; dotage; inclination; indulgence; liking; love; partiality; penchant; predilection; propensity; regard; relish; solicitude; taste; tendency; tenderness; zeal

FONDLE: (**see** "caress") blandish; coddle; cosset; cuddle; dally; dandle; hug; indulge; pamper; pat; pet; stroke; toy

FONDNESS: **see** under "fond"

FONT: basin; fountain; laver; origin; source; spring; stoup

FOOD(S): aliment; banquet; beef; board; bread; carbohydrates; cates; cheer; chow; chuck (wagon); collation; comestible(s); cooking; cuisine; diet(ary); dietetics; dinner; dish; eatables; eats; edible(s); esculent; fare; farina; fats; feast; feed(bag); flesh; flour; fodder; forage; grain; grist; groceries; grub; gruel; *haute cuisine*; hospitality; ingesta; keep; lunch; manna; meal(s); meat; menu; mess; milk; mush; nourishment; nutrient; nutriment; nutrition; nutritive; pabulum; pap; pastry; piquancy; plate; poi; pork;

porridge; portion; protein; provender; provisions; ration(s); refreshment(s); regimen; repast; salt; snack; subsistence; supply; sustenance; sustentation; table; tea; tiffin; treat; viands; victuals

FOOL: **v.** amble; balk; bamboozle; befool; beguile; betray; bilk; bunco; burn; cheat; check; chicane; chisel; chouse; circumvent; clip; clown; copy; cozen; dally; deceive; defeat; defraud; delude; desert; disappoint; dishonor; dissemble; divert; double-cross; dupe; elude; ensnare; entice; entrap; evade; exploit; fail; fake; finagle; flam; fleece; flimflam; fob; foil; fraud; frustrate; fub; goof; gouge; gudgeon; guile; gull; gyp; have; hoax; hocus; honeyfuggle; hoodwink; hornswaggle; idle; inveigle; jockey; joke; juggle; knife; loiter; lure; manipulate; meddle; milk; mislead; mock; outwit; overreach; peach; persuade; philander; potter; prey; ream; renege; rob; seduce; sell; sham; short-change; skin; skylark; snare; spoof; steal; stick; sting; swindle; take (in); touch; toy; trap; trick; trifle; trim; use; utilize; vamp; victimize; wile; wrong; FOOL: **n.** (**see** "blockhead") Abderite; antic; ass; Boeotian; boob(y); buffoon; butt; cat's-paw; changeling; chub; clod(pate); clown; comedian; comic; coot; cully; dimwit; dolt; dope; dupe; dotard; doughhead; droll; dullard; dumbbell; dunce; dunderhead; dupe; goof; goon; goose; grobian; gull; half-wit; hammerhead; harebrain; harlequin; humorist; idiot; idler; ignoramus; imbecile; jape; jerk; jester; joker; jughead; loon; lout; lackwit; lumpkin; lunkhead; madling; mark; merry-andrew; mime(r); mimic; monkey; morosoph; muttonhead; natural; nincompoop; ninny; nitwit; noddy; numbskull; oaf; Punch; raca; sap; schnook; sham; simp(leton); slave; stooge; tool; touch; underwit; victim; wag; wit; zany; FOOLISH: abashed; Abderian; absurd; anile; asinine; brainless; buffoonish; cock-brained; comic; crazy; daft; desipient; dizzy; donkeyish; dopey; dumb; empty(-headed); fantastic-(al); fat; fat(headed); fatuitous; fatuous; featherbrained; featherheaded; feebleminded; flighty; foolhardy; frivolous; gaga; garish; giddy; goofy; goonish; half-cocked; half-witted; harebrained; headless; heedless; idiotic; idle; ignorant; ill-advised; imbecile; imbecilic; imprudent; inadequate; inane; inept; infatuated; insignificant; irrational; loony; ludicrous; mad; meaningless; nonsensical; nonplussed; paltry; partial; pointless; preposterous; puerile; quarter-witted; ridiculous; scatterbrained; senseless; shallow; silly; simple; soft; stupid; trifling; unintelli-

gent; unserious; unwise; vacuous; witless; zany; FOOLISHNESS: asininity; bosh; brainlessness; brashness; clownage; clownishness; desipience; *drôlerie*; drollery; fatuity; fatuousness; humor; idiocy; ignorance; imprudence; inanity; ineptitude; insipidity; irrationality; jest; loutishness; mimicry; moronity; *niaiserie*; nincompoopery; nonsense; partiality; poppycock; puerility; raillery; recklessness; ridiculosity; rot; senselessness; silliness; stupidity; unseriousness; unwisdom; whim(sey); whimsicality; witlessness

FOOLHARDY: (**see** "reckless") adventurous; bold; brash; daring; desperate; foolish; headlong; heedless; Icarian; impetuous; impulsive; incautious; precipitate; rash; temerarious; thoughtless; venturesome; venturous; wild

FOOT: **v.** add; calculate; case; dance; discharge; estimate; figure; hoof; pay; run; settle; sum; total; walk; FOOT: **n.** base; bottom; dog; hoof; measure(ment); pad; paw; pedal(extremity); pedes (pl.); pedestal; pes; sole; speed; step; swiftness; tail; tread; FOOTING: base; basis; condition; foothold; foundation; groundwork; position; relationship; standing; status; support; term(s); total

FOOTPRINT: mark; pad; pug; spoor; trace; track; tread; vestige; vestigia (pl.)

FOP: adon; Beau Brummel; buck; coxcomb; dandiprat; dandy; dude; incroyable; jacka-dandy; jackanapes; macaroni; nob; *petit-maître*; popinjay; puppy; swell; toff; FOPPISH: (**see** "dandyish") and "vain") coxcombical; coxcombry

FORAGE: **v.** (**see** "attack") foray; pillage; plunder; raid; ravage; rummage; scour; scrounge; search; FORAGE: **n. see** "fodder"

FORAY: attack; forage; incursion; inroad; invasion; pillage; raid; sally; sortie

FORBEAR: abstain; avoid; bear; cease; decline; defer; delay; deny; desist; disuse; drop; endure; eschew; fast; for(e)go; keep; omit; oppose; pause; refrain; refuse; reject; resist; restrain; shun; spare; spurn; stay; stop; suffer; supersede; tolerate; wait; waive; withhold; withstand; FORBEARING: clement; compassionate; forgiving; gentle; indulgent; kind; lenient; longanimous; merciful; mild; patient; piteous; soft(hearted); sympathetic; tender(hearted); tolerant; unvindictive; warm(hearted); FORBEAR-

ANCE: abstinence; avoidance; clemency; compassion; delay; fortitude; grace; graciosity; leniency; longanimity; long-suffering; mercy; mildness; patience; pity; quarter; resignation; stay; sympathy; tenderheartedness; toleration; wait

FORBID: ban; bar; debar; deny; deprive; disallow; enjoin; exclude; hinder; inhibit; interdict; preclude; prevent; prohibit; proscribe; repel; taboo; tabu; veto; FORBIDDING: (see "dangerous") disagreeable; dour; formidable; glassy; grim; hard; harsh; hazardous; hostile; inhibitory; menacing; odious; offensive; repellant; severe; stern; ugly; unfriendly; unpleasant; FORBIDDEN: bluebeard; classified; contraband; debarred; *défendu*; enjoined; inhibitory; prohibited; proscribed; taboo; tabu; verboten

FORCE: **v.** actuate; advance; break; cause; coact; coerce; compel; constrain; crowd; dominate; drag; dragoon; drive; drum; elbow; exact; exert; foist; forge; hammer; hasten; hurry; impel; impose; incite; increase; instigate; intensify; jam; labor; make; manipulate; move; necessitate; oblige; oppress; order; pound; predominate; press; push; ram (through); rush; squeeze; storm; strain; strike; sway; thrust; thump; urge; wrench; wrest; FORCE: **n.** (see "power") activism; agency; agent; aggression; animus; army; brawn; brunt; capacity; coaction; coercion; cogency; compulsion; constraint; crew; demiurge; dint; domination; drive; duress; dynamics; dynamism; edge; effect-(iveness); effort; emphasis; employees; energy; exertion; faculty; gang; greatness; impact; impetus; import; impulse; impulsion; influence; juggernaut; labor; liveliness; might; momentum; muscle; nature; navy; number; numen; opinion; oppression; point; posse; potency; predomination; pressure; puissance; pull; punch; push; restraint; sinew; staff; stimulus; strain; stranglehold; strength; stress; sway; sword; thunder; troops; urge; validity; verge; vigor; vim; violence; vis; vitality; weight; work(men); FORCED: (see "obliged") compelled; constrained; obligated; obliged; pressed; pushed; strained; FORCEFUL *or* FORCIBLE: amain; athletic; cogent; compulsive; dynamic; effective; emphatic; expressive; great; hammer and tongs; impactful; impellant; impelling; insistent; intrusive; lusty; mighty; moving; muscular; perforce; potent; powerful; resounding; stiff; unabated; unequivocal; vigorous; violent; vital; weighty

FORCELESS: **see** "weak"

FOREBODE: adumbrate; augur; betide; betoken; divine; feel; forecast; foretell; portend; predict; preindicate; presage; surmise; FOREBODING: **a.** (see "dangerous") apocalyptic(al); apprehensive; dire; foretelling; frightening; menacing; oracular; orphic; portentous; predictive; premonitory; prognostic; prophetic; FOREBODING: **n.** (see "forecast") augury; feeling; omen; portent; prediction; premonition; presage; presentiment; prognostication

FORECAST: **v.** (see "foresee") anticipate; augur; betoken; bode; calculate; conjecture; contrive; divine; estimate; expect; forebode; foreshadow; foretell; plan; portend; predict; prefigure; presage; prognosticate; prophesy; scheme; soothsay; FORECAST: **n.** augury; conjecture; divination; estimate; foretelling; prediction; prefiguration; prognosis; prognostication; prophecy; FORECASTER: Nostradamus; prognosticator; prophet; seer; soothsayer

FOREFATHER(S): Adam; ancestor; antecedent; ascendant; breed; creator; elder; family; forebear; forerunner; genealogy; house(hold); line; precursor; primogenitor; procreator; progenitor; progenitress (fem.); progenitrix (fem.); prototype; sire; stock

FOREFRONT: *avant-garde*; beachhead; firing line; van(guard)

FOREGO: (see "renounce") eschew; neglect; pass; precede; relinquish; sacrifice; FOREGOING: above; antecedent; anterior; before; former; introductory; past; preceding; prefixal; preliminary; previous; prior

FOREHEAD: brow; forepart; frons; front; metopion; sinciput

FOREIGN: (see "alien") abroad; adventitious; different; distant; ecdemic; epicene; exotic; external; extraneous; extrinsic; far; forane; heathen; heterochthnous; heterogeneous; inappropriate; irregular; irrelevant; nonnative; outer; outside; peregrinate; peregrine; Philistine; remote; removed; repugnant; strange; tramontane; ultramontane; unfamiliar; unknown; FOREIGNER: alien; auslander; emigre; exoteric; gringo; heathen; invader; nonnative; nonresident; outlander; outsider; peregrine; Philistine; stranger; tramontane; ultramontane; FOREIGNNESS: extraneity; heterogeneity; irrelevancy; strangeness

FOREKNOWLEDGE: intuition; precognition; praecognitum; preknowledge; premonition; prenotion; prescience; prevision

FOREMOST: (**see** "best") capital; chief; first; front; grand; headmost; leading; main; preeminent; vanward

FOREORDINATION: **see** "fate"

FORERUN: announce; antecede; anticipate; forestall; foretell; herald; introduce; precede; prelude; scout; usher; FORERUNNER: ancestor; antecedent; antecessor; *avant-coureur*; *avant-garde*; forebear; harbinger; herald; omen; pioneer; precursor; predecessor; premonitor; scout; sign; symptom; trailblazer; vanguard; warning

FORESEE *or* FORESHADOW: adumbrate; anticipate; apprehend; augur; betoken; bode; calculate; conjecture; contrive; divine; envisage; envision; estimate; expect; figure; forebode; foreknow; foretell; herald; hint; indicate; plan; portend; predict; prefigure; presage; previse; prognosticate; prophesy; read; scheme; soothsay; suggest; FORESEEN: (**see** "expected") contemplated; unsurprised

FORESIGHT: divination; foreknowledge; forethought; intuition; precaution; precognition; prescience; prognostication; prophesy; prospection; *prospicience*; prudence

FOREST: boscage; foliage; grove; silva; sylva; timber; trees; wood(s); woodland

FORETELL adumbrate; anticipate; augur; auspicate; bespeak; betoken; bode; calculate; conjecture; contrive; divine; estimate; expect; figure; forebode; forecast; foreshadow; guess; imagine; plan; portend; predict; prefigure; presage; presignify; prognosticate; prophesy; read; scheme; soothsay; vaticinate; FORETELLING: **a.** adumbrated; apocalyptic(al); Delphian; Delphic; divinatory; fatidic; foreboding; oracular; presageful; prophetic(al); pythonic; FORETELLING: **n.** adumbration; augury; auspication; divination; foreboding; foreshadowing; guess; imagination; prediction; prognostication; prophecy; soothsaying

FORETHOUGHT: consideration; foreknowledge; planning; premeditation; prudence

FORETOKEN: (**see** "foretelling") augur(y); omen; portent; premonition; sign; symptom; warning

FOREVER: (**see** "always") *ab aeterno*; *ad infinitum*; aye; ceaseless(ly); constant(ly); continual(ly); endless; eternal(ly); ever; everlasting(ly); *in adfinitum*; *in aeternum*; incessant(ly); in perpetuity; *in perpetuum*; *in saecula saeculorum*; lasting; perpetual(ly)

FOREWARNING: advice; caution; foretoken; notice; omen; portent; sign(al); symptom

FORFEIT: **v.** alienate; amerce; confiscate; fine; lose; mulct; penalize; surrender

FORFEIT(URE): **n.** alienation; amercement; confiscation; debit; fine; loss; penalty; surrender

FORGE: advance; beat; coin; contrive; copy; counterfeit; create; design; devise; drive; duplicate; effect; fabricate; falsify; fashion; feign; form; frame; guide; hammer; imitate; impel; invent; make; manipulate; mint; move; produce; progress; shape; trace; FORGED: coined; copied; counterfeit; derivative; fabricated; falsified; fashioned; formed; imitated; invented; produced; spurious; supposititious; FORGERY: copy; counterfeit(ing) fabrication; feigning; fiction; imitation; invention; pseudograph; supposition

FORGET: disregard; disremember; forgive; ignore; lose; neglect; obliviate; omit; overlook; slight; unlearn; FORGETFUL: abstracted; careless; disregardful; negligent; oblivious; unaware; unconscious; unmindful; FORGETFULNESS: carelessness; lethe; negligence; nepenthe; oblivion; obliviscence

FORGIVE: absolve; acquit; cancel; clear; except; exculpate; excuse; exonerate; forget; free; overlook; pardon; release; relent; remit; FORGIVING *or* FORGIVABLE: absolutory; clement; compassionate; conciliatory; condonable; indulgent; placable; magnanimous; merciful; unvindicative; venial; FORGIVENESS: absolution; acquittal; amnesty; cancellation; clearance; conciliation; condonance; condonation; exculpation; excusing; exoneration; indulgence; pardon; release; remission

FORGO: **see** "forego"

FORGOTTEN: disremembered; forlorn; lost; neglected; overlooked; unremembered

FORK: **v.** bifurcate; bisect; branch; dichotomize; divaricate; diverge; furcate; FORK: **n.** alternative; bifurcation; branch; choice;

crotch; dichotomization; dichotomy; divarication; forking; furcation; graip; prong; spear; tine; wye; FORKED: bidigitate(d); bifid; bifurcate(d); dichotomous; divaricated; forcipate; forficulate; furcate; furciform; horned; pronged

FORLORN: (**see** "abandoned") abject; alone; bedraggled; bereft; comfortless; depressed; deprived; derelict; deserted; desolate; despondent; destitute; disconsolate; disordered; distressed; doomed; forgotten; forsaken; friendless; helpless; hopeless; lone(ly);lonesome; miserable; pitiable; pitiful; rejected; ruined; solitary; sorrowful; woebegone; wretched; vain

FORM: **v.** adjust; arrange; build; cast; compose; conceive; concretize; confect; constitute; construct; contrive; create; crystallize; cut; design; develop; devise; draft; draw; erect; fabricate; fashion; figure; forge; formulate; frame; imagine; invent; make; materialize; model; mold; outline; pattern; plan; plot; prepare; produce; scheme; shape; sketch; spin; state; synthesize; tailor; write; FORM: **n.** appearance; arrangement;blank; body; build; cast; ceremony; character; class; condition; configuration;conformation; contour; convenance(s); convention(ality); cut; design; dress; edition; entity; essence; fashion; figure; figurine; fitness; formality; formation; formula; formulation; foundation; frame; garb; genre; *gestalt*; guide; guise; idea; image; kind; likeness; liturgy; make-(up); manifestation; manner; mode; model; mold; nature; observance; order; outline; pattern; perspective; physique; plan; prescription; procedure; recipe; representation; rite; ritual; rubric; schema; scheme; shape; silhouette; sketch; stamp; state; structure; style; substance; type; vehicle; usage; way; work

FORMAL: abstract; academic; ceremonial; ceremonious; chill(y); constitutive; conventional; courtly; decorous; distant; dogmatic; dressy; essential; exact; formalistic; functional; ideal; liturgical; logical; mechanical; methodical; ministerial; nominal; orderly; ostensible; pedantic; pharisaic(al); pompous; precise; prim; professorial; punctilious; regular; rigid; ritualistic; scholastic(al); schoolteachery; social; solemn; stately; stiff; stilted; stylized; superficial; syntactical; systematic; trig; FORMALITY: academicism; appearance; ceremonial(ism); ceremony; conventionality; form(alism); formalness;liturgy; pedantry; punctilio; regularity; ritual(ism); rituality; solemnity; stiffness

FORMAT: (**see** "form") arrangement; design; getup; outfit; pattern; plan; proportion; rig; scheme; shape; size; sketch; style

FORMATION: (**see** "creation")construction; development; erection; form; growth; line; order; parade; structure

FORMATIVE: (**see** "plastic") constructive; creative; demiurgic; developmental; fictile; impressionable; nascent

FORMER(LY): ago; ancient; antecedent; anterior; anticipatory; anticus; before; bygone; ci-devant; earlier; elapsed; erewhile; erstwhile; ex; first; foregoing; heretofore; late; once; onetime; past; preceding; presumptive; previous; prior; quondam; sometime; whilom; yesteryear

FORMIDABLE: (**see** "awful") dangerous; difficult; dread(ful); fearful; impregnable; indomitable; invincible; large; outstanding; redoubtable; serious; superior; terrible; unconquerable

FORMLESS: airy; amorphous; anidian; arupa; chaotic; crude; deformed; fluid; heterogeneous; immaterial; inchoate; incorporeal; irregular; liquid; nebulous; raw; rough; rude; shapeless; spiritual; unclassified; uncrystallized; unshaped; vague; FORMLESSNESS: heterogeneity; immateriality; incorporeality; incorporeity; nebulosity; shapelessness

FORMULA: convention; creed; doctrine; form; law; method; mixture; model; philosophy; plan; prescription; principle; proportions; proposition; recipe; rite; ritual; rubric; rule; tenet; theory

FORMULATE: (**see** "form")conclude; concretize; confect; define; draw; enunciate; fabricate; fix; forge; materialize; outline; plan; proclaim; reason; scheme; shape; spin; synthesize

FORSAKE: abandon; abdicate; abjure; adjure; desert; disclaim; disdain; disown; drop; evacuate; fail; flee; forego; forswear; leave; quit; relinquish; renounce; resign; surrender; withdraw; FORSAKEN: (**see** "forlorn") abandoned; deserted; rejected FORSWEAR: **see** "forsake"

FORT(RESS): abatis; alcazar; bastille; bastion; breastwork; bulwark; camp; castle; citadel; defense; donjon; dun; escarp(ment); fastness; fortification; garrison; keep; post;

rampart; ravelin; redan; redoubt; salient; stockade; stronghold; tower

FORTIFY: (see "strengthen") arm; brace; confirm; corroborate; embattle; encourage; enrich; gird; help; invigorate; lace; man; munify; prepare; refresh; reinforce; tighten; FORTIFICATION: (see "fort") brace; corroboration; defense; enrichment; help; strengthening

FORTITUDE: see "courage"

FORTUITOUS: (see "accidental") adventitious; casual; causeless; chance; fortunate; hap(py); haphazard; odd; incidental; random; undesigned

FORTUNE: accident; break; chance; destiny; doom; end; estate; fame; fate; possessions; prosperity; riches; star; success; thrift; wealth; welfare; well-being; FORTUNATE: auspicious; beneficial; benign(ant); blessed; blest; dexter; favorable; favored; faust; fortuitous; gratified; happy; healthful; healthy; lucky; meet; miraculous; opportune; propitious; prosperous; providential; reasonable; serendipitous; successful; timely; well

FORTUNE-TELLER: diviner; necromancer; Nostradamus; prognosticator; physiognomist; soothsayer; FORTUNE-TELLING: see "divination"

FORWARD: v. (see "aid") abet; advance; assist; encourage; expedite; foster; further; hasten; help; mail; nurse; promote; send; ship; speed; support; transmit; FORWARD: a. or adv. active; advanced; advancing; afore; ahead; anxious; before; bold(-faced); brash; brassy; brazen; confident; eager; early; en avant; extreme; familiar; flip; fore; forth; free; fresh; gay; impertinent; indecorous; leading; onward; pert; precocious; progressive; prompt; radical; ready; ultra; vain; vanward

FOSSIL: amber; balanite; fogy; petrification; relic; remains; stone; trace

FOSTER: (see "aid") breed; cherish; coddle; comfort; cosset; cultivate; encourage; father; favor; feed; fondle; further; gratify; harbor; house; humor; indulge; lodge; love; mother; nourish; nurse; nurture; oblige; pamper; please; rear; support; tend; warm

FOUL: (see "bad") abusive; carious; coarse; corrupt; dangerous; deadly; defiled; despicable; detestable; dirty; disagreeable; diseased; dishonorable; entangled; evil; execrable; fecal; feculent; fetid; filthy; funky; gross; impure; indecent; leprous; loathsome; low; mephitic; morbid; morbific; nasty; noisome; noxious; obscene; odious; odorous; offensive; pernicious; pestilent(ial); poisonous; polluted; profane; putrescent; putrid; rank; rotten; soiled; squalid; stinking; sullied; tainted; treacherous; unclean; unfavorable; vile; vulgar; wicked

FOUND: base; begin; build; commence; construct; endow; erect; establish; fix; gather; initiate; invent; isolate; lay; organize; originate; raise; set(tle); start

FOUNDATION: base; basis; bed(rock); body; bottom; chassis; core; cornerstone; cradle; endowment; establishment; foot(ing); form; frame(work); fundament; grass roots; ground(work); institution; layer; mount; origin; point d'appui; principium; radical; rock (bottom); root; rudiment(s); settlement; subsoil; substratum; substructure; underpinning; understanding; understructure; warp; warrant

FOUNDER: v. astonish; break (down); collapse; crash; damage; dismay; fail; fall; miscarry; sink; stick; stumble; swamp; welter; wreck; FOUNDER: n. author; builder; creator; originator

FOUNTAIN: aqua; head; fons; font; jet; origin; reservoir; source; spray; spring; upwelling; well

FOXY: (see "cunning") acute; alopecoid; artful; astute; careful; chary; clandestine; clever; crafty; designing; discerning; experienced; foxlike; guileful; insidious; knowing; penetrating; sagacious; secretive; shifty; shrewd; skillful; sly; subtle; tricky; vulpine; wary; wily

FRACAS: (see "brawl") altercation; brouhaha; flap; fraction; ruction; shindy; uproar

FRACTION: (see "fragment") breaking; bit; component; cut; detail; dividend; division; fracas; group; half; modicum; moiety; molecule; parcel; part; piece; portion; quanta (pl.); quantum; quarter; ruction; scrap; section; sector; segment; share; FRACTIONAL: aliquot; fractionary; fragmental; fragmentary; gradual; inconsiderable; insignificant; par pièces; part; partial; piecemeal; sectional; segmental; small

FRACTIOUS: see "stubborn" and "unruly"

FRACTURE: **v.** (**see** "break") comminute; crack; crush; fractionate; lacerate; rend; rupture; separate; shatter; split; tear; violate; FRACTURE: **n.** breach; break(ing); cleft; crack; comminution; contrecoup; crack; fissure; rent; rift; rupture; split; tear; violation; FRACTURED: **see** "broken"

FRAGILE: (**see** "delicate") arachnoid; breakable; brittle; cobwebby; crisp; crumbly; dainty; deteriorable; diaphanous; ephemeral; ethereal; evanescent; feeble; filmy; fine; fleeting; forceless; frail; frangible; friable; frothy; frough; glassy; infirm; nebulous; shaky; short-lived; soft; tender; tenuous; thin; transparent; undurable; unendurable; unsubstantial; weak; FRAGILITY: delicacy; delicateness; diaphaneity; ephemerality; ethereality; evanescence; filminess; frailty; frothiness; insubstantiality; nebulosity; precariousness; tenuity; undurability; unsubstantiality

FRAGMENT(S): amount; analecta (pl.); atom; bit; chip; collectanea ((pl.); component; crumb; cut; detail; detritus; *disjecta membra* (pl.); drop; excerpt; faction; fig; fleck; fraction; grain; granule; iota; jet; loose; end; mite; modicum; molecule; morceau; morsel; odds and ends; oddment; ort; parcel; part(icle); piece(meal); portion; rag; remainder; remnant; residue; rump; sample; scintilla; scrap(s); scrapiana (pl.); section; sector; segment; selection; shard; share; shaving; shred; sliver; snatch; snip; spark; speck; splinter; split; string; strip; swatch; tag; tittle; trace; unit; whisp; wisp

FRAGMENTARY: (**see** "disorganized" and "fractional") unsystematic

FRAGRANT: ambrosiac; ambrosial; aromal; aromatic; balmy; nectarous; olent; perfumed; redolent; refreshing; savory; scented; spicy; sweet; FRAGRANCE: aroma(ticity); attar; bouquet; effluvium; emanation; incense; odor; perfume; pleasantness; redolence; savor; scent; smell; spice; suavity; sweetness

FRAIL: (**see** "flimsy") brittle; delicate; feeble; fragile; frangible; infirm; nebulous; puny; reedy; seedy; sick(ly); slender; slight; slim; small; tender; tenuous; thin; undurable; valetudinarian; weak; wispy; FRAILTY: Adam; blemish; defect; delicacy; failing; fault; feet of clay; flaw; foible; frailness; imperfection; infirmity; insubstantiality; susceptibility; tenuity; tenuousness; vice; weakness

FRAME: **v.** (**see** "arrange") adjust; articulate; build; compose; conceive; construct; fit; imagine; mount; railroad; redact; regulate; utter; FRAME: **n.** armature; arrangement; basis; bin; body; border; build; building; cadre; carcass; casing; chassis; cradle; figure; form; framework; humor; mood; mounting; pattern; plan; rack; shape; skeleton; slate; stand; structure; support; system

FRAMEWORK: (**see** "frame") anatomy; bones; cadre; carcass; conception; cradle; design; fabric; husk; limits; outline; parenchyma; plan; scheme; shell; silhouette; skeleton; sketch; structure; superstructure; support; system; torso; trestle; truss

FRANCHISE: asylum; ballot; charter; choice; coverage; exemption; freedom; grant; immunity; liability; liberty; membership; privilege; right; suffrage; territory; voice; vote

FRANGIBLE: **see** "fragile"

FRANK: **v.** exempt; facilitate; free; help; mail; mark; sign; FRANK: **a.** aboveboard; artless; blunt; candid; childlike; communicable; communicative; demonstrative; direct; disingenuous; downright; easy; familiar; forward; free; genuine; guileless; honest; *ingénu*; *ingénue* (fem.); ingenuous; innocent; luxuriant; manifest; man-to-man; naif; naive; natural; obvious; open(hearted); plain; rank; simple; sincere; straight (forward); talkative; transparent; unabashed; undisguised; unexaggerated; uninhibited; unmistakable; unmistrusting; unreserved; unrestrained; unsophisticated; unvarnished; unwary; vigorous; FRANKNESS: **see** "openness"

FRANTIC: active; agitated; angry; anxious; avid; berserk; corybantic; crazed; crazy; delirious; demoniac(al); deranged; distracted; ecstatic; enraged; enthused; excited; extreme; frenetic(al); frenzied; furibund; furious; hectic; insane; intense; intoxicated; mad; maniac(al); manic; noisy; obsessed; orgasmic; orgiastic; overwhelmed; phrenetic(al); rabid; raging; rapturous; raving; transported; violent; wandering; wild; zealous

FRATERNIZE: **see** "associate"

FRAUD: adventurer; artifice; bunco; charlatan; cheat(er); cheating; chicanery; circumvention; conjurer; covin; cozenage; deceit; deception; delusion; dishonesty; dissimulation; dodge; duplicity; embezzlement; empiric; fake(r); fakery; finagler; fraudulence; guile; hoax; humbug; hypocrite; imposition; imposter; imposture; knave; misrepresentation; mountebank; prestidigitator; pretender; quack(salver); rogue; sham; shark; sharpster; shift; stratagem; subreption; swindle(r); swindling; Tartuffe; thief; treachery; treason; trick(ery); trickster; FRAUDULENT: clandestine; collusive; collusory; counterfeit; deceitful; delusive; dishonest; duplicitous; fake; hypocritical; impostrous; perfidious; sinister; surreptitious; swindling; treacherous; tricky

FRAUGHT: accompanied; attended; burdened; charged; endangered; filled; freighted; full; laden; larded; loaded; threatened

FRAY: **v.** disturb; frazzle; fret; macerate; ravel; rub; strain; tiffle; wear; FRAY: **n.** (**see** "fight") brush; commotion; contest; debate; dispute; hassle; melee; quarrel; riot rub; ruction; skirmish; tumult

FREAK: **n.** abnormality; abortion; antic; caper; capriccio; caprice; capriciousness; crotchet; fancy; flam; humor; idea; lusus; malformation; monstrosity; mutation; notion; oddity; prank; queer; quirk; sport; temperament; vagary; whim(sey); whimsicality; FREAK(ISH): **a.** abnormal; bizarre; capricious; crotchety; eccentric; fanciful; grotesque; malformed; monstrous; notional; odd(ish); queer; uncertain; vagarious; whimsical

FRECKLE(S): ephelides (pl.); ephelis; lentigo spot; tache

FREE: **v.** absolve; acquit; affranchise; allow; clean; clear; commute; deliver; detach; disburden; discharge; disembarrass; disencumber; disengage; disentangle; disentwine; disenthrall; dislodge; dismiss; emancipate; enfranchise! exempt; exonerate; expedite; extract; extricate; facilitate; forgive; frank; help; immunize; lessen; liberate; loose(n); manumit; mitigate; naturalize; pardon; pluck; purify; ransom; redeem; release; relieve; reprieve; rescue; rid; save; unbind; unbridle; unchain; unclog; uncloister; undo; unencumber; unfetter; ungird(le); unhinder; unlock; unmanacle; unshackle; untangle; untie; untwine; unyoke; FREE: **a.** artless; autonomic; autonomous; available; boundless; candid; careless; casteless; clear; complimentary; devoid; disengaged; disentangled; distinct; easy; emancipated; exempt(ed); facile; familiar;

faultless; fetterless; fluid; forward; frank; generous; glib; gratis; gratuitous; immoderate; immune; independent; inexact; ingenuous; irresponsible; lacking; lavish; lax; leisurable; leisurely; liberal; liberated; licentious; loose; magnanimous; native; natural; neutral; open(ed); openhanded; out(spoken); permissible; prodigal; released; relieved; scatheless; secure; self-determining; self-reliant; separate; sovereign; spare; spontaneous; unattached; unbossed; unbound; unbridled; unburdened; unbuttoned; uncaught; unchained; uncombined; uncommitted; uncompensated; unconfined; unconquered; unconstrained; undone; unencumbered; unengaged; unenslaved; unenthralled; unextorted; unfastened; unfettered; ungyved; unhampered; unharmed; unhindered; unimpeded; unimprisoned; unlimited; unlocked; unobstructed; unpaying; unpinned; unprejudiced; unprescribed; unreserved; unrestrained; unrestricted; unstinting; untainted; untangled; untied; untouched; untrammeled; voluntary

FREEDOM: absolution; atonement; authority; autonomy; boldness; *carte blanche*; commutation; deliverance; disengagement; disentanglement; dispensation; ease; elbowroom; emancipation; enfranchisement; exemption; extrication; facility; franchise; freeness; furlough; generosity; immunity; impunity; independence; intimacy; largeness; largess(e); leave; Lebensraum; liberation; liberty; license; magnanimity; manumission; nonrestriction; option; pardon; peace; permission; permit; power; prerogative; privilege; range; ransom; redemption; regeneration; release; reprieve; respite; rest; right; safety; salvation; security; self-determination; self-realization; sovereignty; spontaneity; unrestraint; unrestrictedness

FREETHINKER: agnostic; aporetic; atheist; *esprit fort*; latitudinarian; libertine; nullifidian; skeptic

FREEZE: (**see** "congeal") alienate; anesthetize; benumb; chill; cool; fix; glaciate; harden; ice; immobilize; jell; kill; numb; preserve; rigidify; set; snub; solidify; stabilize; stiffen; stop

FREIGHT: burden; cargo; charge; lading; load(ing); traffic; train; transportation

FRENZY: aberration; afflatus; agitation; anger; anxiety; craziness; deliration; delirium; dementia; derangement; disorientation;

disturbance; ecstasy; enragement; exaltation; excitement; fanaticism; fury; insanity;
intensity; intoxication; lunacy; madness;
mania; obsession; orgasm; paroxysm; rabidity; rage; rapture; raptus; restlessness;
stew; swivet; transport; violence; FREN-
ZIED: (**see** "frantic") berserk; corybantic;
ecstatic; enraged; furibund; furious; hectic;
intoxicated; orgasmic; orgiastic; raging;
rapturous; transported; violent

FREQUENT: **v.** affect; go; habituate; haunt;
iterate; resort; FREQUENT: **a.** common;
current; familiar; habitual; numerous; oft-
(en); ofttimes; periodic(al); persistent; prevalent; recurrent; regular; repeated; thick;
usual; FREQUENCY: commonality; gradation; modulation; perpetuality; oftenness;
prevalence; recurrency; regularity; repetition

FRESH: active; additional; alive; another;
blooming; bold; brassy; brazen; bright;
brisk; brittle; clean(-cut); cold; concise;
cool; crackling; crisp; curled; curly; cutting;
dewy; diligent; firm; flip(pant); freshened;
frosty; green; hardy; healthy; hot; imaginative; impertinent; impudent; incisive; inexperienced; invigorating; juicy; keen; lively;
mint; modern; natural; neoteric; new;
novel; original; perky; pert; pristine; pure;
raw; recent; refreshed; renewed; revised;
revived; rude; sassy; saucy; sharp; smart-
(-alecky); snappish; snappy; spruce; succulent; sweet; terse; unblighted; unhackneyed;
unjaded; unspoiled; untainted; untrained;
unused; unwearied; unwilted; unwithered;
unworn; vernal; vigorous; violent; virgin(al);
vital; vivacious; vivid; youthful; young;
FRESHEN: brighten; cheer; clean(se);
improve; modernize; refresh; refurbish;
reinvigorate; renew; renovate; restore; revive; sponge; vernalize; FRESHNESS: cri-
spiness; dewiness; flippancy; impertinence;
impudence; innovation; invigoration; modernity; refurbishment; renovation; rudeness;
sassiness; sauciness; spontaneity; succulency;
vernalization; vivacity; youthfulness

FRET: abrade; agitate; anger; annoy; bother;
brood; chafe; corrode; dawdle; disturb;
fidget; fray; fume; fuss; gall; gnaw; grate;
harass; irk; jitter; moon; nag; nettle; peeve;
plague; ponder; pout; provoke; repine; rub;
scruple; sit; stew; strain; sulk; swelter; torment; toss; trifle; twitch; wear; weep; worry;
vex; FRETFUL: agitated; angry; annoyed;
anxious; chafed; choleric; disturbed; fidgety;
fractious; fussbudgety; fussy; gusty; harassed;
hectic; hot(-tempered); ill-humored; im-

patient; irascible; irate; irritable; nervous;
peevish; pettish; petulant; querulous; restive;
restless; troubled; uneasy; unrestful; waspish;
wrathful

FRIABLE: (**see** "brittle") crisp; crumbling;
crumbly; dusty; flaky; fragile; frail; mealy;
pulverous; pulverulent; short

FRICTION: (**see** "conflict") abrasion; attrition; clash(ing); contention; disagreement;
dissention; erosion; gall; grating; resistance;
rub; ruction; wear; wrangling

FRIEND(S): acquaintance; adherent; advocate; ally; *alter ego*; ami; amie (fem);
amigo; associate; benefactor; *bon ami*; *bon
camarade*; brother; buddy; cater-cousin;
cher ami; chum; colleague; compadre; companion; compeer; confidant; confidante
(fem.); confrere; crony; Damon and Pythias;
devotee; familiar; fellow; *fidus Achates*; follower; frater; intimate; lover; mate; *mon
vieux*; pal; partisan; partner; patron; peer;
protégé; Quaker; sectary; sweetheart

FRIENDLESS: (**see** "lonely") companionless;
outcast; rejected; unfriended

FRIENDLY: accessible; affable; affectionate;
agreeable; allied; amiable; amicable; amical;
approachable; benevolent; bonhomous;
brotherly; cheerful; chummy; close; comfortable; comforting; companionable; compatible; complaisant; conciliatory; congenial;
convivial; cordial; courteous; familiar; favorable; fond; forthcoming; fraternal; genial;
glowing; good(-natured); good-neighborly;
gracious; gregarious; hearty; helpful; hospitable; intimate; kind(ly); neighborly; pleasant; propitious; saccharine; sisterly; smooth;
sociable; social; sympathetic; tender; unalienated; warm; FRIENDLINESS: (**see**
"friendship") affability; affection; affinity;
amiability; amicability; benevolence; bon-
hom(m)ie; camaraderie; cheer(fulness); cheeriness; companionableness; companionship;
compatibility; complaisance; comradeliness;
comradery; congeniality; conviviality; cordiality; courteousness; courtesy; courtliness; *esprit
de corps*; familiarity; fellowship; fraternity;
geniality; good-naturedness; goodwill; graciosity; graciousness; gregariousness; heartiness;
helpfulness; hospitality; intimacy; joviality;
kindliness; kindness; sociability; warmth

FRIENDSHIP: (**see** "friendliness") accord;
affection; affinity; allegiance; alliance; amicability; amity; association; attachment; *bon
camaraderie*; bonhom(m)ie; brotherhood;

camaraderie; comity; communion; companionship; comradeness; comradery; comradeship; consociation; conviviality; devotion; esprit; *esprit de corps*; esteem; family; favor; fellowship; fondness; foundation; fraternity; freemasonry; friendliness; geniality; good-fellowship; good-neighborliness; intimacy; kindness; love; mutuality; partisanry; partisanship; regard; sociality; society; sodality; sorority; union

FRIGHTEN: affright; alarm; amaze; appall; astonish; astound; awe; benumb; browbeat; cow; daunt; daze; depress; disconcert; disenchant; dishearten; disillusion; dismay; disturb; dumbfound; faze; freeze; horrify; horrorize; intimidate; overwhelm; panic; paralyze; petrify; perturb; rattle; rigidify; scare; shock; startle; stun; stupefy; subdue; terrify; terrorize; upset; FRIGHT: abashment; anxiety; alarm; awe; consternation; depression; disenchantment; disheartenment; disillusionment; dismay(edness); dread; fear; funk; horror; intimidation; ogre; panic; perturbation; scare; startle; terror; FRIGHTFUL *or* FRIGHTENING: alarming; appalling; awesome; awful; bad; desperate; dire(ful); dismay(ful); dread(ful); eerie; egregious; extreme; fearful; fiendish; formidable; ghastly; grotesque; gruesome; hideous; horrendous; horrible; horrific; intimidating; monstrous; objectionable; paralyzing; perilous; petrifying; portentous; prodigious; redoubtable; revolting; scary; shocking; startling; terrible; terrifying; terrorizing; ugly; weird; FRIGHTENED: see "timid"

FRIGID: (see "frozen") arctic; boreal; chilling; chilly; cold; cool; dull; formal; frosty; gelid; glacial; hoary; hyperborean; ice-cold; icy; impassive; indifferent; insipid; lifeless; passionless; plodding; pointless; rigid; senseless; stiff; unfriendly; unsociable

FRILL: (see "air") affectation; bauble; bubble; dainty; delicacy; edging; elaboration; extravagance; furbelow; gingerbread; jabot; ornament(ation); ruche; ruffle; superfluity; FRILLY: see "showy"

FRINGE: **v.** border; bound; edge; trim; FRINGE: **n.** (see "edge") border; boundary; bounds; brink; ciliation; circumference; edging; fimbriation; loma; margin; periphery; peristome; rim; tassel; thrum; trim; verge; zizith; FRINGED: bordered; circumferential; edged; laced; laciniate; laciniose; marginal; trimmed

FRISK (see "frolic") bound; brush; caper; cavort; dance; flick; gambol; hop; jump; leap; play; prance; romp; search; skip; sport; spring; tittup; whisk; FRISKY: (see "lively") chipper; pert; playful

FRITTER: **v.** consume; dally; dawdle; diminish; disperse; dissipate; dwindle; idle; scatter; waste; FRITTER: **n.** bangle; cake; fragment; shred

FRIVOLOUS: (see "fickle") childish; featherbrained; flimsy; foolish; frolicsome; futile; gay; giddy; gimcrack; hoity-toity; idle; inane; inconsequential; insignificant; irrelevant; light(-headed); light-minded; paltry; petty; playful; puerile; shallow; sham; silly; slight; superficial; trifling; trivial; unimportant; unsubstantial; vain; yeasty; FRIVOLITY: absurdity; asininity; emptiness; folly; flummery; frivolousness; fun; gimcrack; gimcrackery; irrationality; jest; *légèreté*; levity; light-mindedness; nugacity; play; purposelessness; sport; superficiality; triflingness; yeastiness

FROCK: attire; coat; dress; garment; gown; habit; kirtle; mantle; robe; shirt; soutane; tunic

FROG: amphibian; anuran; braid; hoarseness; polliwog; toad

FROLIC: **v.** (see "frisk") antic; caper; disport; gambol; jest; lark; play; prank; revel; romp; skylark; sport; FROLIC: **n.** amusement; antic; bee; boutade; caper; caprice; caracole; carousal; dance; dido; diversion; escapade; *espièglerie*; festivity; *fredaine*; frisk; fun; gaiety; gambol; jest; lark; marlock; merriment; mirth; party; picnic; play; ploy; powwow; prank; roguery; romp; sport; spree; vagary; FROLICSOME: (see "lively") antic; chipper; *espiègle*; *folâtre*; gamesome; gay; impish; larkish; larksome; merry; mirthful; pert; playful; prankish; roguish; sportful; sportive; sporty

FRONT: airs; angle; anterior; anticus; appearance; *avant-coureur*; *avant-garde*; bearing; beginning; behavior; brass; brow; coalition; countenance; cover-up; demeanor; dial; effrontery; façade; face; figurehead; fore(head); forepart; impudence; manner; margin; mien; obverse; outlook; physiognomy; posture; van(guard); window dressing

FRONTIER: backwoods; border(land); boundary; bounds; hinterland; interior; line; margin

FROST: failure; fiasco; frigidity; frostiness; hoar; ice; rime; unfriendliness; unsociability; FROSTED *or* FROSTY: (**see** "frigid") arrogant; boreal; chilly; cold; cool; freezing; gelid; hoary; icy; pruinous; rimy; severe; stuck-up; unfriendly; unsociable

FROTH: barm; bosh; despumation; effervescence; confetti; foam; lather; levity; nonsense; scum; spume; suds; triviality; yeast; FROTHY: barmy; effervescent; empty; foamy; frivolous; insubstantial; light; shallow; spumescent; spumous; spumy; trivial; unsubstantial; vain; yeasty

FROWN: disagree; disapprove; glare; glower; lower; pucker; rebuke; scowl; sulk

FROWZY *or* FROWSY: disheveled; mean; musty; scabrous; seedy; shabby; slatternly; squalid; stale; unkempt

FROZEN: benumbed; chilled; chilly; cold; congealed; fixed; frappe; frigid; gelid; hyperborean; iced; icy; immobile; mechanical; petrified; refrigerated; rigid; solidified; stiff; unfriendly; unsympathetic; unthawed

FRUGAL: careful; chary; close; economical; mean; *ménager*; moderate; parsimonious; penurious; plain; provident; prudent; saving; scanty; spare; sparing; Spartan; stingy; stinting; temperate; thrifty; tight; ungiving; unwasteful; FRUGALITY: caution; chariness; closeness; economy; exiguity; moderation; parcity; parsimony; paucity; scantiness; sparingness; thrift(iness)

FRUIT: accomplishment; crop; dividend; effect; fruitage; fruition; grain; issue; offspring; outcome; produce; product(s); profit; progeny; realization; result(s); seed; yield; young; FRUITFUL: abounding; abundant; ample; bountiful; copious; exuberant; fat; fecund; feracious; fertile; fructiferous; fructificative; fructuous; fruitive; generative; gravid; luxuriant; plenteous; procreant; productive; profitable; proliferous; prolific; proligerous; resultful; rich; teemful; teeming; uberous; FRUITFULNESS: copiosity; exuberance; fecundity; fertility; fructuousness; gravidity; pregnancy; productiveness; prolificacy

FRUITLESS: (**see** "futile") abortive; arid; bare; barren; brithless; dead; empty; hollow; idle; incomplete; ineffective; ineffectual; infecund; infertile; irresolute; miscarrying; resultless; sterile; unavailing; unfertile; unfruitful; unproductive; unprofitable; unprolific; unsatisfactory; unsatisfying; unsuccessful; useless; vacuous; vain; worthless

FRUSTRATE: (**see** "baffle") balk; bar; block; bottleneck; check; circumvent; confound; counteract; countermine; cross; dash; defeat; disappoint; disconcert; discourage; foil; hamstring; hinder; impede; kibosh; lame; mar; neutralize; nullify; outwit; prevent; shortcircuit; stop; stultify; thwart; unsettle; upset; wreck; FRUSTRATION: bottleneck; circumvention; defeat; disappointment; discouragement; impediment; short circuit; stultification

FUEL: aliment; coal; coke; combustibles; food; gas(oline); logs; peat; material; reinforcement; wood

FUGITIVE: **a.** (**see** "fleeting") absent; A.W.O.L.; elusive; ephemeral; fleet; infrequent; occasional; volatile; wandering; FUGITIVE: **n.** A.W.O.L.; deserter; *émigré*; escapee; exile; gypsy; outcast; refugee; runaway; vagabond; wanderer

FULCRUM: lever; prop; shore; stay; support; thole

FULFILL: (**see** "accomplish") achieve; answer; attain; complete; consummate; discharge; do; effect(uate); end; enforce; execute; finish; fructify; implement; integrate; meet; obey; observe; perform; reach; realize; satisfy; supply; terminate; FULFILLMENT: accomplishment; consummation; enforcement; execution; fruition; function; implementation; performance; realization; satisfaction; termination

FULGENT: (**see** "radiant") bright; burning; dazzling; scintillating; shining

FULIGINOUS: (**see** "dim") clouded; dark(ened); dusky; murky; obscure; opaque; smoky; sooty

FULL: abounding; abrim; abundant; adult; all; ample; awash; brimming; chock-a-block; cloyed; compact; complete; comprehensive; copious; crammed; crowded; diffuse; direct; drunk(en); engrossed; entire; exact; exhaustive; explicit; fair; glutted; good; gorged; gross; headlong; intact; integral; intoxicated; liberal; lined; loaded; mature; maximum; occupied; orotund; overflowing; oversize(d); packed; perfect; plenary; plentitudinous; plethoric; plump; precipitous; projecting; regular; replete; rotund; rounded; sated; satiate(d); satisfied; stuffed; surfeited; swollen; teeming; thorough; throughout;

tight; torrential; total; tumescent; unabated; unabbreviated; unabridged; uncut; undiluted; undiminished; undivided; unexpurgated; unimpaired; unqualified; whole (hog); FULNESS: abundance; aggregate; amplitude; completion; copiosity; copiousness; entirety; perfection; plen(t)itude; plenum; plethora; plumpness; repletion; richness; satiation; satiety; sum; surfeit; totality; whole (hog)

FULSOME: abhorrent; coarse; detestable; disgusting; foul; gross; loathsome; nauseating; nauseous; odious; odorous; offensive; rank; repulsive; satiating; sickening; smelly; stinking

FUMBLE: **v.** (**see** "err") blunder; botch; bungle; feel; flub; grope; misfield; mismanage; misplay; miss; muff; mumble; paw; search; stammer; stumble; FUMBLE: **n. see** "error"

FUME: **v.** (**see** "anger") bluster; fret; rage; rave; reek; smell; smoke; smolder; storm; FUME: **n.** anger; emotion; excitement; exhalation; gas; odor; passion; reek; smell; smoke; steam; vapor

FUN: amusement; buffoonery; burlesque; caricature; cheer; comedy; comic spirit; diversion; enjoyment; entertainment; farce; festivity; fireworks; foolery; forcemeat; frolic; game; gaiety; gladness; glee; harlequinade; hilarity; humor; jest; jocularity; joke; jollity; joy(fulness); lampoonery; lark; levity; merriment; mirth(fulness); mockery; opera bouffe; parody; pasquinade; play(fulness); pleasantry; pleasure; pranks; recreation; rejoicing; ridicule; ridiculosity; slapstick; sport; FUNNY: absurd; amusing; Aristophanic; Atellan; bizarre; burlesque; clever; comedial; comedic; comic(al); crazy; curious; diverting; droll; enjoyable; entertaining; extravagant; facetious; farcical; fishy; gelastic; gelogenic; gleeful; good; harlequin; humorous; intoxicated; jesting; jocose; jocular; jolly; killing; laughable; ludicrous; merry; mirthful; odd; *opéra-bouffe*; pleasant; queer; rejoicing; ribald; ridiculous; risible; roguish; showy; spurious; strange; trifling; underhanded; uproarious; waggish; witty

FUNCTION: **v.** act; fare; go; operate; perform; play; ply; run; serve; work; FUNCTION: **n.** (**see** "action") act(ivity); affair; attribute; attribution; behavior; capacity; do; domain; duty; end; faculty; fulfillment; goal; job; mechanics; mechanism; nature;

object; occupation; office; operation; part; party; performance; perquisite; power; process; province; quality; rite; role; task; trait; use; work; FUNCTIONAL: occupational; parenchymal; physiological; psychogen(et)ic; psychological; psychosomatic; useful; utilitarian

FUND(S): appropriation; assets; bank; capital; cash; chest; coffer; deposit; endowment; exchequer; hoard; investment; means; money; monies; pool; purse; reserve; resources; securities; stock; store; supply; treasury; wealth

FUNDAMENT: (**see** "base") anus; buttocks; foundation; podex

FUNDAMENTAL: **a.** (**see** "basic") ABC; actual; basal; basilar; capital; chief; constitutional; deep-rooted; deep-seated; elemental; elementary; essential; formative; foundational; indispensible; inherent; intrinsic; irreducible; original; primal; primary; prime; primitive; primordial; principal; pure; quintessential; radical; real; rudimentary; simple; substratal; substrate; substrative; ultimate; underlying; vital; FUNDAMENTAL: **n.** basis; primordial; principle; simplicity; ultimacy; FUNDAMENTALITY: essentiality; integrity; intrinsicality; primality; primariness; primativity; quintessence; reality; ultimacies (pl.); ultimacy; ultimate

FUNERAL: burial; exequies; inhumation; interment; lookout; mass; obsequies; obsequy; observances; requiem; rites; sepulcher; sepulture; service(s); solemnities; wake

FUNEREAL: black; dark; defunctive; dirgeful; doleful; elegiac; exequial; funeral; funerary; gloomy; lugubrious; mournful; obsequial; pathetic; plaintive; sad; solemn; somber; sorrowful; woeful

FUNEST: dire; doleful; fatal

FUNK: coward(liness); fear; fright; panic; paralysis; scare; terror

FUNNY: **see** under "fun"

FUR(S): coat; ermine; hair; hide; pelage; pelt(ry); skin(s)

FURBELOW: falbala; finery; flounce; frill; gingerbread; ornament; ruche; ruffle; superfluity

FURBISH: buff; burnish; clean; polish; renew; renovate; revive; scour; scrub; shine

FURIOUS: (**see** "angry") boisterous; burning; crazy; delirious; desperate; energetic; fanatical; ferocious; fierce; fiery; frantic; frenzied; furibund; giddy; impetuous; inflamed; insane; intense; mad(dened); maniac(al); merciless; outraged; rabid; raging; red(-hot); savage; sharp; stormy; turbulent; vehement; violent; wild

FURL: bundle; cover; curl; fold; hide; roll; stow; wrap; wrinkle

FURNACE: etna; forge; heater; kiln; oven; smelter; stove

FURNISH: accouter; afford; appoint; arm; bestow; capacitate; caparison; cater; clothe; contribute; develop; donate; dress; endow; endue; equip; feed; fit (out); gird; give; grant; habilitate; lend; outfit; prepare; present; provide; qualify; ready; relieve; rig; serve; stock; store; supply; train; yield; FURNISHINGS: (**see** "equipment") accouterment(s); appliances; decor; finery; fitness; fittings; fixtures; gear; mode; movables; regalia; tackle; tools; trappings

FURNITURE: accessories; apparatus; appendages; appointments; contents; details; equipment; fittings; fixtures; furnishings; goods; graith; hardware; movables; stock; supplies

FUROR: (**see** "ado") afflatus; craze; enragement; excitement; flurry; frenzy; furore; fury; hoopla; hubbub; madness; mania; rage; style; tumult; vogue

FURROW: chamfer; channel; corrugation; flute; fluting; gap; groove; rut; seam; sulcus; track; trench; wrinkle

FURTHER: **v.** (**see** "aid") abet; adopt; advance; advantage; assist; back; benefit; cultivate; encourage; espouse; extend; forward; foster; hasten; help; maintain; profit; promote; quicken; raise; speed; strengthen; support; train; FURTHER: **a.** *or* **adv.** (**see** "beyond") additional; advanced; besides; farther; more(over); ulterior; yet; FURTHERMORE: **see** "also"; FURTHERANCE: **see** "help"

FURTIVE: (**see** "cunning") arch; back-alley; backstage; clandestine; covert; crafty; devious; evasive; foxy; secret(ive); secretly; skulking; sly; sneaky; stealthy; stolen; surreptitious; underhanded; wary; wily

FURY: (**see** "anger") acharnement; afflatus; agitation; Erinys; ferocity; fit; frenzy; impetuosity; ire; madness; passion; rage; savagery; truculence; truculency; turbulence; vehemence; violence; wrath

FUSE: (**see** "join" and "unite") ally; amalgamate; ankylose; anneal; assimilate; blend; coalesce; combine; concrete; concretize; conflate; cross; dissolve; hybridize; integrate; interbreed; league; liquefy; marry; melt; merge; mix; run; smelt; solder; solidify; synchronize; syncretize; unify; wed; weld; FUSION: (**see** "union") alliance; amalgamation; ankylosis; assimilation; blend; coalescence; coalition; combination; commixture; conflation; connation; hybridism; integration; liquefaction; league; melting; merger; synchronism; syncretism; synthesis

FUSS: **v.** agitate; annoy; argue; bustle; complain; dispute; disturb; fidget; fight; fluster; fret; fume; hassle; hurry; nag; niggle; preen; protest; putter; worry; FUSS: **n.** (**see** "commotion") ado; agitation; brouhaha; bustle; complaint; dispute; disturbance; fight; flurry; haste; hubbub; hurry; objection; pother; protest; quarrel; row; stir; storm; to-do; worry; FUSSY: bustling; exact; fastidious; finical; finicky; fretful; grandmotherly; irritable; meticulous; overnice; particular; precise; prissy; scrupulous; squeamish

FUSTIAN: bombastic; exaggerated; inflated; good-for-nothing; pompous; trite; tumid; worthless

FUSTIGATE: (**see** "beat") castigate; cudgel; lash; strike; whip

FUSTY: antiquated; fetid; foul; malodorous; mo(u)ldy; musty; putrescent; putrid; rancid; rank; stale; stuffy

FUTILE: abortive; barren; empty; frivolous; fruitless; futilitarian; futureless; gainless; helpless; hollow; idle; inadequate; ineffective; ineffectual; infertile; irresolute; miscarrying; otiose; petty; powerless; profitless; resultless; sterile; toothless; trifling; trivial; unavailing; unrewarding; unsuccessful; useless; vacuous; vain; worthless; FUTILITY: emptiness; frivolity; fruitlessness; inadequacy; ineffectuality; otioseness; otiosity; uselessness; worthlessness

FUTURE: aftertime; anon; becomingness; coming; destiny; downstream; expectation; fate; fortune; futurity; hereafter; offing; posterity; prospect

FUZZ: down; fibers; fluff; fur; lint

G

GAB: **see** "chatter"

GAD: (**see** "roam") idle; gallivant; goad; meander; prowl; ramble; range; rove; saunter; stray; stroll; traipse; trifle; wander

GADFLY: busybody; insect; pest; runabout; stimulator

GADGET(S): business; contrivance; device; dingus; doodad; doohickey; gadgetry; gimcrack; gismo; hickey; hootenanny; invention; jigger; machine; rigamajig; thing(umabob); tool

GAG: **v.** choke; clog; heave; muffle; muzzle; obstruct; prevent; retch; silence; stifle; throttle; GAG: **n.** anecdote; choking; cloture; crack; hoax; jest; muffler; muzzle; obstruction; quip; story; stunt; trick; wheeze; witticism

GAIETY: (**see** "ecstasy") animation; buoyancy; ebullience; elegance; entertainment; Euphrosyne; exhilaration; exuberance; festival; festivity; finery; fun; *gaieté de coeur*; gala; gayness; geniality; jocularity; jocundity; jollification; jollity; joviality; jubilation; larkiness; levity; lightheartedness; merriment; merrymaking; nepenthe; nonchalance; revelry; sportiveness; sprightliness; vivacity; yeastiness

GAIN: **v.** (**see** "advance") accomplish; achieve; acquire; approach; arouse; attain; augment; benefit; clear; consummate; derive; develop; earn; effect; engage; expand; fatten; get; grow; have; improve; increase; net; obtain; persuade; procure; profit; reach; realize; reap; receive; score; secure; steal a march; suffer; wax; win; GAIN: **n.** (**see** "advancement") accomplishment; accretion; achievement; acquirement; acquisition; advance; advantage; aggrandizement; augmentation; benefit; booty; compensation; consummation; development; earnings; enhancement; emolument; improvement; increase; increment; interest; lucre; net; plus; prize; profit; purchase; rate; realization; rent; resources; stealing a march; surplus; windfall; winning(s); GAINFUL: compensatory; profitable; remunerative; remuneratory

GAINSAY: (**see** "deny") contradict; controvert; counteract; disprove; dispute; forbid; impugn; oppose; refute; resist; subvert

GAIT: advance(ment); amble; canter; gallop; gang; lope; pace; progress; rack; rate; run; shamble; speed; step; stride; trot; walk

GALA: **a.** festal; festival; festive; gay; merry; GALA. **n.** banquet; dance; festival; festivity; fete; fiesta; frolic; gaiety; merrymaking; parade; party; picnic; pomp

GALE: air; blast; blow; breeze; outburst; outpouring; storm; tempest; wind

GALL: **v.** (**see** "chafe") abrade; annoy; fret; harass; irritate; madden; peeve; spite; vex; wear; GALL: **n.** (**see** "bitterness") acerbity; anger; assurance; audacity; bile; brass; brazenness; cheek; daring; effrontery; friction; guts; impertinence; impudence; malice; nerve; presumption; rancor; soreness; spite; temerity; GALLING: **see** "bitter"

GALLANT: **a.** admirable; attentive; bold; brave; bully; cavalier; chivalresque; chivalric; chivalrous; civil; courageous; courteous; daring; dashing; dauntless; fair; fearless; fortitudinous; gay; generous; genteel; heroic; high-spirited; honorable; intrepid; kind; kingly; knightly; magnanimous; manly; noble; polite; puissant; resolute; splendid; stalwart; stately; stout(hearted) urbane; valiant; valorous; warlike; GALLANT: **n.** beau; blood; cavalier; *cavalier servente*; chevalier; cicisbeo; date; escort; gentleman; hero; lover; sport; suitor; wooer; GALLANTRY: **see** "chivalry" and "valor"

GALLOP: **v.** careen; hurry; pace; run; rush; scamper; speed; GALLOP: **n.** gait; hurry; pace; run; rush; scamper; speed; tantivy

GALORE: (**see** "abundant") *à gogo*; copious;

de trop; excess; gobs; lots; much; plentiful; profuse

GAMBLE: **v.** ante; bet; chance; expose; hazard; hedge; lay; play; plunge; put (up); risk; speculate: stake; wager; GAMBLE: **n.** ante; bet; chance; hazard; plunge; risk; speculation; stake; uncertainty; wager

GAMBOL: **v.** (**see** "frisk" and "frolic") bound; caper; cavort; curvet; dance; gyrate; leap; play; prance; romp; skip; sport; GAMBOL: **n.** antic; caper; curvet; gyration; leap; prance; romp

GAME: **a.** brave; courageous; daring; disabled; lame; resolute; unyielding; valiant; willing; GAME: **n.** amusement; competition; contest; course; diversion; dodge; entertainment; exhibition; festivity; foolery; frolic; fun; lark; line; match; merriment; occupation; pastime; plan; play; ploy; prank; profession; quarry; racket; recreation; scheme; sport; strategy; tactic; trick; venison; work

GAMIN: **see** "urchin"

GAMINE: **see** "tomboy"

GAMUT: (**see** "range") compass; continuum; diapason; extent; ken; notes; orbit; purview; rainbow; reach; repertoire; scale; scope; series; span; sweep;

GANG: (**see** "group") band; bevy; body; camorra; canaille; Carbonari; clan; clique; club; company; course; crew; crowd; flock; herd; horde; journey; mob; number; outfit; passage; posse; school; sect; set; society; team; tong; tribe; troop

GANGSTER: (**see** "bandit") apache; criminal; gunman; hood(lum); punk; racketeer; robber; ruffian; thug: whyo; yegg

GANGWAY: aisle; passage(way); plank; ramp; walk; way

GAP: aperture; breach; caesura; cavity; chasm; chink; cleft; col; crack; cranny; crevice; difference; discontinuity; distance; fissure; furrow; gape; gulf; hiatus; hole; hollow; inlet; interim; intermission; interregnum; interruption; interspace; interstice; interval; lacuna; notch; opening; orifice; parenthesis; pass(age); ravine; rent; rift; separation; slit; space; span; split; spread; vacuity; vulnerability

GAPE: **v.** dehisce; gap; gaze; glare; gloat;

open; oscitate; peer; spread; stare; yaw; yawn; GAPE: **n.** dehiscence; gap; gaze; glare; opening; oscitance; oscitation; rent; spread(ing); yawn; GAPING: cavernous; open; oscitant; patulous

GARB: **v.** apparel; attire; clothe; costume; custom; dress; invest; GARB: **n.** apparel; attire; clothes; clothing; costume; covering; custom; dress; form; frock; garment(s); habit(s); investiture; investment(s); raiment; style; vestments; vesture; wrap(s)

GARBAGE: (**see** "waste") offal; recrement; refuse; rubbish; scrap(s); sewage; sordes; trash

GARBLE: color; disarrange; distort; falsify; jumble; mess; misquote; misrepresent; misspell; mix; mutilate; pervert; pi; refine

GARGANTUAN: (**see** "huge") colossal; elephantine; gigantic; Homeric; monstrous

GARISH: blaring; blatant; bright; brummagem; cheap; criant; dazzling; flamboyant; flashy; gaudy; giddy; glaring; loud; ostentatious; overdecorated; overdone; revolting; showy; tasteless; tawdry; tinny; vivid; vulgar

GARLAND: **v.** array; crown; decorate; dress; festoon; garnish; honor; trim; wreathe; GARLAND: **n.** accolade; anadem; anthology; array; chaplet; coronet; crown; festoon; fillet; headband; lei; rosary; tiara; trophy; wreath

GARMENT(S): a(b)ba; alb; caftan; cloak; clothing; coat; cotte; dress; equipment; garb; gear; gown; habiliment; mantle; sheath; vestment(s); wrap(per);

GARNER: **see** "accumulate"

GARNISH: **v.** (**see** "adorn") array; beautify; bedeck; diamondize; decorate; deck; embellish; furbish; grace; lard; ornament; strew; trim; GARNISH(MENT): **n.** adornment; array; beautification; decor(ation); embellishment; ornamentation; ostentation; panoply; stoppage; trim

GARRULOUS: (**see** "talkative") vocative; vociferous; voluble; wordy

GAS: accelerator; argon; butane; damp; ether; fuel; fume(s); gossip; helium; neon; petrol; radon; reek; vapor; wind; GASEOUS: aeriform; ethereal; light; reeky; tenuous; thin; vaporous

GASCONADE: **v.** blow; bluster; boast; brag; crow; vaunt; GASCONADE(R): **n.** boast-(er); boasting; bluster(er); braggart; bravado; show-off

GASH: cut; depress; disrupt; incise; score; slash; slit; wound

GASP: blow; breathe; choke; exclaim; exhale; expire; pant; puff

GATE(WAY): arch(way); bar; barrier; channel; dam; defile; door(way); egress; entrance; entry; ingress; intake; opening; port; portal; postern; receipts; sluice; sprue; stairs; stairway; start; stile; toran; torii

GATHER: (**see** "collect") accumulate; acquire; agglomerate; agglutinate; aggregate; amass; assemble; attract; band; catch; clutch; coagulate; collate; compile; conceive; concentrate; conclude; congest; conglomerate; congregate; converge; convoke; crowd; cull; deduce; derive; draw; extract; fold; full; garner; glean; group; guess; harvest; heap; herd; hoard; huddle; infer; judge; marshall; mass; meet; mingle; mobilize; muster; pick; pile; plait; pluck; press; pucker; rally; reap; recollect; reflect; scrape; sheave; shirr; socialize; summon; GATHERING: abscess; accumulation; agglomeration; agglutination; aggregation; assemblage; assembly; at home; band; board; cluster; clutch; collation; collection; colluvies; conference; congestion; convention; convergence; company; compilation; concourse; congregation; congress; convocation; coterie; crowd; harvest; heap; herd; horde; huddle; meeting; minglement; mob; muster; parliament; party; press; rally; reception; rendezvous; rout; society; soiree; store; sum; symposium; throng; turnout

GAUCHE: (**see** "clumsy") awkward; bungling; clownish; inept; left-handed; skew; stiff; twisted; uncouth; ungraceful; unpolished; unrefined

GAUD: **see** "trifle"

GAUDY: (**see** "showy") baronial; baroque; bedizened; bespangled; blatant; brummagem; cheap; chintzy; coarse; dazzling; extravagant; flamboyant; flashy; florid; frilly; garish; gay; gingerbread; glaring; glittering; gross; grotesque; hollow; lurid; meretricious; ornamented; ornate; ostentatious; rococo; scintillating; spangled; sparkling; tawdry; tin(ny); tinsel; vulgar; GAUDINESS: (**see** "showiness") bedizenment; blare; blatancy; flamboyance; frilliness; garishness; ostentation; panoply; tawdriness

GAUGE: **v.** appraise; determine; estimate; evaluate; judge; measure; rate; value; GAUGE: **n.** appraisal; dimensions; extent; measure(ment); meter; model; norm; pointer; rule(r); size; standard; system; type

GAUNT: atrophied; attenuated; barren; bony; cadaveric; cadaverous; desolate; emaciated; grim; haggard; lank(y); lean; meager; scraggy; scrawny; shrunk(en); skeletal; skeletonic; skinny; slender; slim; thin; withered; wizened; wretched

GAUZE: barege; cloth; crepe; fabric; haze; leno; lisse; marli; tulle

GAWK: **v.** fool; gape; gaze; look; ogle; stare; GAWK: **n.** (**see** "fool") booby; boor; bumpkin; cuckoo; lout; simpleton

GAY: Anacreontic; affable; agreeable; airy; alert; amiable; blithe(ful); blithesome; brash; bright; brilliant; buoyant; carnivalesque; cavalier; cheerful; cheery; chipper; cocky; comical; convivial; debonair(e); ebullient; ecstatic; festive; fey; forward; fresh; frivolous; frolic(some); frothy; gamesome; genial; glad(some); happy; high; hilarious; hoity-toity; humorous; impertinent; jaunty; jocose; jocular; jocund; jolly; joyous; jubilant; keen; larksome; larky; laughing; licentious; light; lively; loose; merry; mirthful; nonchalant; perky; phrenetic; playful; Pythian; revelrous; rhapsodic-(al); riant; roguish; *sans souci*; scintillating; showy; spirited; sportive; sprightly; spry; trig; trim; vigorous; vivacious; volatile; waggish; winsome; witty; yeasty; GAYNESS: **see** "gaiety"

GAZE: con; contemplate; eye; fix; gape; gawk; glance; gloat; look; observe; ogle; peer; pore; regard; scan; see; stare; study; view; vigil; watch

GEAR: (**see** "apparatus") accessories; accouterments; apparel; appliances; appointments; armor; baggage; belongings; cam; clothing; cog; equipment; garb; garments; harness; outfit; paraphernalia; rig(ging); tackle; toggery; tools; trappings

GELID: chilly; cold; cool; frosty; frozen; icy; reserved; wint(e)ry

GEM: agate; beryl; cabochon; cake; cameo; diamond; ice; jade; jewel; ligure; muffin;

onyx; opal; ornament; pearl; prize; rock; ruby; sard; spinel; stone; topaz; treasure

GENDER: **v.** beget; breed; copulate; generate; GENDER: **n.** female; male; neuter; sex

GENEALOGY: ancestry; background; birth; blood; derivation; descent; family; heredity; history; kinship; line(age); paternity; pedigree; provenance; stock; strain; succession

GENERAL: (**see** "broad") abstract; all-purpose; approximate; by and large; catholic; common(place); comprehensive; contagious; conventional; cosmic; cosmopolitan; customary; diffuse(d); diversified; ecumenical; encyclic(al); encyclopedic(al); epidemial; epidemic; epidemiologic(al); everyday; everywhere; extensive; familiar; frequent; generalized; generic; gross; habitual; horizontal; inclusive; indefinite; nonproprietary; normal; noted; notorious; ordinary; overall; pandemic; popular; prevailing; prevalent; proverbial; public; rank; regular; rife; spread; total; universal; unlimited; unrestrained; unrestricted; unspecialized; unspecific; unspecified; usual; vague; well-known; whole; widespread

GENERATE: (**see** "bear") arise; beget; breed; cause; copulate; create; effect; engender; form; furnish; gender; impose; make; originate; procreate; produce; propagate; sire; span; spawn; yield

GENERATION: age; breed; category; class; creation; development; era; formation; genesis; gestation; kind; lifetime; period; posterity; procreation; production; race; span; stock; succession; time

GENERIC: (**see** "general") genetic; nonproprietary; universal

GENEROUS: (**see** "abundant") almsgiving; altruistic; ample; beneficent; benevolent; bounteous; bountiful; charitable; chivalrous; copious; expansive; extravagant; fertile; forgiving; free(handed); full; good(-hearted); greathearted; hefty; heroic; hospitable; indulgent; insordid; kind(ly); large; lavish; lenient; liveral; lofty; lush; magnanimous; magnificent; munificent; noble(-minded); open(handed); overgenerous; overindulgent; philanthropic(al); plentiful; powerful; princely; prodigal; profuse; progressive; sizable; sublime; unenvious; unenvying; ungrudging; unrestrained; unrestricted; unselfish; wholehearted; GENEROSITY: abundance; amplitude; beneficence; benevol-

ence; chivalry; copiosity; copiousness; freedom; grace; greatheartedness; largeness; largess(e); latitudinarian; liberality; magnanimity; munificence; openhandedness; philanthropy; plentifulness; plentitude; plenty; prodigality; unselfishness

GENESIS: (**see** "creation") beginning; birth; development; evolution; generation; germination; growth; inchoation; nascency; origin(ation); production

GENIAL: affable; agreeable; amiable; amicable; benign(ant); blithe(ful); blithesome; bonhomous; buoyant; charming; cheerful; cheery; civil; congenial; conversable; convivial; cordial; courteous; debonair(e); easy; expansive; favorable; friendly; gallant; genteel; gracious; hearty; hospitable; ingratiating; jolly; jovial; kind(ly); likable; merry; mild; mirthful; nice; nonchalant; open; pleasant; pleasing; polite; smooth; sociable; spirited; sprightly; suave; sunny; sympathetic; urbane; warm; GENIALITY: affability; amiability; amicability; *bon camaraderie*; bonhom(m)ie; cheerfulness; comradery; congeniality; conviviality; esprit; *esprit de corps*; gentility; glow; graciosity; graciousness; joviality; joyousness; kindness; mirth(fulness); nonchalance; sympathy; warmth

GENIUS: ability; acumen; adeptness; aptitude; astucity; astuteness; bent; brains; capacity; character; deity; demon; discernment; disposition; embodiment; faculty; fire; flair; genie; genre; gift; grasp; inclination; ingenuity; intellect; knack; leaning; mastery; mind; nature; penchant; perspicacity; propensity; quality; skill; spirit; talent; taste; tendency; turn; wisdom; wit; wizard

GENRE: category; class(ification); form; genius; genus; kind; sort; species; style; type

GENTEEL: (**see** "courteous") appropriate; conventional; courtly; elegant; fashionable; gentle; graceful; kingly; polished; polite; puritanical; refined; stylish; Victorian; GENTILITY: **see** "politeness"

GENTLE: (**see** "calm") amiable; amicable; aristocratic; balmy; benign; bland; chivalresque; chivalric; chivalrous; clement; compliant; conciliatory; considered; courteous; courtly; delicate; distinguished; docile; domesticated; dovelike; effeminate; estimable; favonian; genteel; honorable; human(e); humble; hushed; kind; lenient; light; low; maidenly; meek; mellow; mild; milky;

moderate; noble; pacific; peaceful; placid; pleasant; pleasing; pliant; saccharine; serene; silken; soft; soothing; sweet; tame; tender; tractable; tranquil; unvicious; worthy; yielding; GENTLENESS: amiability; amicability; benignancy; chivalry; clemency; consideration; docility; gentility; kindness; leniency; lenity; mansuetude; placidity; refinement; serenity; tenderness

GENTLEMAN: aristocrat; *galantuomo*; gallant; *gentilhomme*; knight; mynheer; opponent; seigneur; seignior; sir; squire; yeoman; GENTLEMANLY: (**see** "courteous") gentlemanlike; seigneurial

GENUINE: (**see** "ACTUAL") apostolic(al); artless; assured; authentic; authoritative; bona fide; canonical; certain; certified; direct; documented; established; exact; factual; firm; frank; full-blooded; full-fledged; honest; incorrupt(ible); ingenuous; kosher; legitimate; natural; official; orthodox; proven; pukka; pure; real; unadulterated; unaffected; unalloyed; uncorrupt-(ed); undisputed; undissembled; undoubted; unfeigned; unmixed; unpresuming; unpresumptuous; unpretended; unpretentious; unquestionable; valid; veritable; warm; GENUINENESS: actuality; apostolicity; authenticity; canonicity; fidelity; ingenuousness; legitimacy; legitimateness; (the) real McCoy; sincerity; truth; validity; veritability

GENUS: (**see** "class") category; genre; order; sort; type

GERM: bacillus; bacteria (pl.); bacterium; beginning; bud; bug; egg; embryo; fount; microbe; microorganism; origin; ova (pl.); ovule; ovum; pathogen; principle; root; rudiment; seed; source; spawn; sperm; spore; sprig; spring; sprout; virus

GERMANE: (**see** "apt") akin; allied; appropriate; apropos; cognate; fit(ting); pertinent; related; relative; relevant; suitable

GERMINATE: (**see** "begin") develop; effloresce; evolve; grow; sprout

GEST(E): action; adventure; deed; exploit; romance; tale

GESTURE: **v.** direct; gesticulate; indicate; mime; mimic; motion; move; nod; shrug; signal; wave; GESTURE: **n.** action; attitude; bearing; behavior; carriage; conduct; demeanor; deportment; direction; gesticulation; indication; manner; mime; mimicry;

motion; movement; nod; pass; pose; posture; proposal; shrug; sign(al); symbol; token; wave

GET: accomplish; achieve; acquire; arrive; ascertain; beget; borrow; breed; buy; catch; cause; choose; collect; compass; comprehend; contrive; cull; derive; earn; effect; find; gain; gather; generate; grab; hire; hit; induce; irritate; kill; learn; lease; manage; move; nail; obtain; persuade; prepare; pick; prevail; procreate; procure; propagate; purchase; puzzle; reach; realize; receive; rent; secure; seize; sire; succeed; take; touch; understand; win

GHASTLY: ashen; awesome; awful; cadaverous; corpselike; deathlike; disagreeable; dismal; dread(ful); fearful; frightening; frightful; ghostlike; ghostly; great; grim; grisly; gruesome; hideous; horrible; horrid; horrific; livid; lurid; macabre; morbid; objectionable; pale; pallid; repellent; repulsive; revolting; shocking; spectral; terrible; terrifying; uncanny; unnatural; unpleasant; wan; weird; GHASTLINESS: grisliness; gruesomeness; hideosity; hideousness; lividity; morbidity; repulsiveness

GHOST: animus; apparition; appearance; bogey; chimera; daemon; *deceptio visus*; delusion; demon; dream; eidolon; elemental; fallacy; fetch; ghoul; ha(u)nt; hallucination; *ignis fatuus*; illusion; image; iota; juba; Ker; larva; manes (pl.); mirage; misconception; particle; phantasm(ata); phantom; phenomena (pl.); phenomenon; poltergeist; reflection; remains; revenant; shade; shadow; soul; specter; spectre; spectrum; spirit; spook; sprite; trace; vision; visitant; will-of-the-wisp; wraith; GHOSTLY: chimerical; chthonian; chthonic; delusional; delusive; dreamy; illusory; phenomenal; scary; shadowy; spectral; spiritual; spooky; supermundane; supernatural

GHOUL: blackmailer; demon; fiend; ghost; graverobber; ogre; vampire

GIANT: **n.** Anak; Balor; Bana; behemoth; Brobdingnagian; colossi (pl.); colossus; Cyclops; Ephialtes; eten; Gargantua; Goliath; Gyges; gyre; Hercules; Hymer; Hymir; jumbo; Loki; mammoth; mastodon; monolith; monster; ogre; Otus; Paul Bunyan; Pantagruel; Polyphemus; prodigy; thurse; titan; Ymir; GIANT **a.** *or* GIGANTIC: (**see** "huge") behemothian; Brobdingnagian; Bunyanesque; colossal; Cyclopean; Cyclopic; elephantime; enormous; gargantuan; giant-esque; gigantean; gigantesque; Herculean; immense; jumbo; large; mammoth; mastodon; mountainous; polyphemian; polyphemic; polyphemous; powerful; prodigious; super(human); tall; titanic; towering; vast; GIANTISM: acromegaly; gigantism; macrosomia

GIBBERISH: (see "jargon") drivel; Greek; jabberwocky

GIBBOUS: bulging; convex; curved; humpbacked; humped; kyphotic; protuberant; rounded

GIBE: v. agree; annoy; ape; chafe; deride; flaunt; fleer; flout; goad; harass; heckle; jeer; mimic; mock; needle; plague; quip; ridicule; scoff; sneer; taunt; twit; vex; GIBE: n. annoyance; derision; harassment; heckle; jeer; mock(ery); quip; ridicule; sarcasm; sneer

GIDDY: capricious; changeable; dizzy; doddering; exuberant; fickle; flighty; foolish; frivolous; furious; garish; gyratory; harebrained; heady; heedless; impulsive; inconstant; intoxicated; light(-headed); light-hearted; shaky; showy; thoughtless; unsteady; vertiginous; volatile; wild

GIFT: (see "charity") alms; aptitude; benefaction; benefice(nce); benefit; benevolence; bent; bequest; bestowal; bonus; boon; bounty; capacity; devise; dole; donation; endowment; faculty; favor; flair; genius; grace; grant; gratuity; handsel; honorarium; kindness; knack; lagniappe; largess(e); legacy; liberality; maintenance; munificence; present(ation); prize; provision; support; talent; tip; turn

GIGANTIC: see under "giant"

GILD: adorn; aureate; brighten; diamondize; embellish; enrich; ornament; overlay; GILDED: (see "ornate") adorned; aureate; aurelian; aurulent; diamondized; embellished; enriched; festooned; luxurious; meretricious; ostentatious; prosperous; tasselled; tessellated; tawdry

GIMCRACK: see "bauble"

GIMMICK: angle; catch; contrivance; device; gadget; gimcrack; gismo; joker; machination; trick; twist

GINGER: dash; *éclat*; energy; fire; go; initiative; liveliness; mettle; pep(per); pluck; spice; spirit; spunk; vigor; vim; voltage; zest; GINGERLY: careful(ly); cautious(ly); daintily; timid(ly)

GINGERBREAD: a. (see "showy") gawdy; ornamented; superfluous; tawdry; GINGERBREAD: n. cake; furbelow; money; ornament; show; superfluity; trim(ming)

GIRD(LE): v. belt; bind; brace; cincture; encircle; enclose; encompass; equip; invest; prepare; provide; strap; strengthen; support; surround; GIRDLE: n. band; belt; binder; cestus; cincture; cord; environ; girth; hoop; obi; ring; sash; strap; support(er)

GIRL: babe; belle; chick; chit; coed; colleen; damosel; damsel; daughter; demoiselle; dish; doll; figure; *fille*; filly; floozy; fräulein; gamine; hoyden; ingenue; *jeune fille*; junior miss; lass(ie); mademoiselle; maid(en); minx; miss; number; nymph(et); pigeon; prostitute; senorita; servant; sis(ter); *soror*; soubrette; sweetheart; tomboy; trick; GIRLISH: see "maidenly"

GIRTH: (see "girdle") band; belt; boundary; cinch; circumference; dimensions; measure(ment); outline; size

GIST: (see "essence") basis; center; core; crux; ground; heart; kernel; marrow; meaning; nub; nucleus; outcome; outline; pith; point; quintessence; sense; significance; substance; sum and substance; tenor; upshot

GIVE: accord; administer; allot; ascribe; assume; attribute; award; bear; bend; bequeath; bestow; bid; bow; break; cede; collapse; commit; communicate; concede; confer; consign; contribute; convey; deal; deliver; designate; devise; devote; dole; donate; emit; endow; execute; expose; feed; fetch; furnish; grant; hand; happen; impart; impute; make; occur; offer; pass; pay; permit; portray; present; produce; proffer; provide; reciprocate; recompense; render; repay; represent; respond; sacrifice; sag; serve; spring; supply; sway; talk; tender; transfer; transmit; utter; voice; waive; will; yield; GIVER: benefactor; bestower; conferrer; donor; eleemosynar; grantor; philanthropist; testator

GLABROUS: bald; even; glassy; hairless; slick; smooth

GLACIAL: arctic; boreal; chilling; cold; congealed; cool; freezing; frigid; frosty; frozen; gelid; hostile; icy; unfriendly

GLAD: blithe(some); bright; cheerful; cheering; cheery; content(ed); delighted; ecstatic; elated; fair; gay; gleeful; gratified; happy; jolly; joyful; joyous; lighthearted; merry; mirthful; pleasant; pleased; radiant; satisfied; thankful; GLADDEN: bless; cheer; comfort; delight; elate; exhilarate; gratify; lighten; please; thank; tickle; GLADNESS: see "glee"

GLADIATOR: athlete; boxer; combatant; controversialist; disputant; fencer; fighter; prizefighter; swordsman

GLAMO(U)R: (see "charm") allure(ment); attraction; attractiveness; aura; bewitchment; cachet; captivation; enchantment; fascination; illusion; magic; mystery; mystique; oomp; poise; spell; window dressing; witchery; GLAMOROUS: (see "showy") alluring; attractive; bewitching; captivating; charming; enchanting; exotic; fascinating; lustrous; mysterious

GLANCE: v. allude; beam; coruscate; dart; effleurer; eye; flash; flit; gaze; gleam; glide; glimpse; glint; graze; hint; look; ogle; peek; peep; rake; rebound; reflect; regard; ricochet; scintillate; scrape; scratch; shine; sight; skim; skip; sparkle; strike; view; wink; GLANCE: n. allusion; *clin d'oeil*; coruscation; *coup d'oeil*; dart; eye; flash; gander; gaze; gleam; glimpse; glint; hit; look; *oeillade*; ogle; peek; peep; rake; rebound; regard; ricochet; scintillation; scrape; scratch; sight; sparkle; strike; view; wink

GLARE: v. blaze; coruscate; dazzle; flame; flare; flash; frown; gaze; gleam; glisten; glitter; glow; glower; reflect; scintillate; scowl; sheen; shimmer; shine; sparkle; stare; GLARE: n. blaze; brilliance; coruscation; dazzlement; flame; flare; flash; frown; garishness; gaze; gleam; glistening; glitter; gloss; glow; glower; reflection; scintillation; scowl; sheen; shimmer; shine; sparkle; GLARING: (see "showy") aglare; audacious; bright; brilliant; conspicuous; flagrant; garish; gaudy; flowering; notorious; obvious; ostentatious; plain; scintillating; scintillescent; scowling; sheer; sparkling; utter

GLASS: n. binoculars; crystal; drink; goblet; lens; mirror; monocle; pane; telescope; tumbler; GLASS(Y): a. apathetic; bright; brilliant; calm; cold; crystal(line); fishy; forbidding; fragile; glabrous; glossy; hard; hyaline; lackluster; lustrous; polished; sanidinic; shiny; silken; silky; sleek; slick; slippery; smooth; translucent; transparent; unsympathetic; unwavering; unyielding; vitreous; vitric

GLAZE: v. burnish; coat; cover; enamel; gloss; ice; incrust; overlay; polish; shine; varnish; veneer; vitrify; GLAZE: n. burnish; coat(ing); enamel; glare; gloss; glow; icing; incrustation; luster; overlay; polish; sheen; shine; translucence; varnish; veneer; vitrification

GLEAM: v. beam; coruscate; dazzle; flash; fulgurate; glaze; glimmer; glint; glisten; glitter; glow; light; phosphoresce; radiate; reflect; scintillate; shimmer; shine; spark(le); GLEAM: n. beam; brightness; coruscance; coruscation; dazzle(ment); flash; fluorescence; fulguration; glance; glint; glitter; glow; luster; phosphorescence; ray; shimmer; shine; spark(le); splendor; trace; GLEAMING: adazzle; agleam; aglisten; aglitter; chatoyant; clinquant; coruscant; coruscating; dazzling; fulgent; fulgid; glossy; lambent; luminous; lustrous; phosphorescent; resplendent; rutilant; shimmering; shimmery; shining; sparkling

GLEAN: acquire; ascertain; collect; cull; find; gather; harvest; learn; pick; reap; strip

GLEE: (see "ecstasy") blitheness; blithesomeness; cheer(fulness); cheeriness; delight; exuberance; exultation; festivity; frolic; fun; gaiety; gladness; hilarity; jollity; joviality; joy(fulness); liveliness; merriment; mirth; rapture; rejoicing; transport

GLIB: (see "talkative") bland; casual; easy; facile; flippant; fluent; free; impromptu; nonchalant; offhand; oily; pat; ready; shallow; slick; smooth; superficial; unforced; unreflecting; unstudied; unthinking; vocal; voluble

GLIDE: coast; creep; elapse; float; flow; fly; glance; glissade; go; lapse; merge; pass; sail; scud; skate; ski; skid; skim; skip; slide; soar; steal; swim

GLIMMER: (see "gleam") waver

GLIMPSE: (see "glance") adumbration; aperçu; flash; foretaste; inkling; once-over; preview; survey

GLINT: see "gleam"

GLISTEN: see "gleam"

GLITTER: see "gleam"

GLOAT: admire; boast; brag; crow; gape; gaze; exult; preen; rejoice; revel; stare

GLOBE: ball; earth; moon; orb; planet; sphere; world

GLOBULE: ball; bead; drop; minim; pill; sphere; spherule; tear

GLOOM(INESS): abasement; apathy; blues; cloud; darkness; dejectedness; dejection; depression; despair; despondency; dimness; disconsolateness; disconsolation; discouragement; disheartenment; dismality; dismalness; dismay; dispiritedness; doldrums; downheartedness; dumps; duskiness; forlornity; heaviness; hopelessness; humiliation; hypochrondria(sis); inertia; lachrymals; lowspiritedness; megrims; melancholia; melancholy; misery; moroseness; morosity; murk(iness); obscurity; pall; pessimism; sableness; sadness; shadow(iness); unsociability; vapors; woe; wretchedness; GLOOMY: abased; Acheronian; Acherontic(al); adusk; *à la mort*; apathetic; blue; brooding; chapfallen; cheerless; chilly; Cimmerian; clouded; crestfallen; crying; dark(some); dejected; depressed; depressing; despairing; despondent; dim; disconsolate; discouraged; disheartened; disheartening; dismal; dispirited; displeased; doleful; dolesome; dolorous; dour; down(cast); downhearted; down-in-the-mouth; drear(y); droopy; dull; dusty; dyspeptic; forbidding; forlorn; frustrating; funebrial; funebr(i)ous; funereal; glum; hangdog; harsh; heavy; hopeless; humble; hypochondriacal; ill-humored; inconsolable; inconsolate; joyless; lachrymal; lachrymose; low(-spirited); melancholic; melancholy; miserable; moody; mopy; morose; muddy; murky; obscure; overcast; peevish; pessimistic; plutonian; plutonic; pouting; prostrate; raptureless; sad(dened); saturnine; sepulchral; somber; sorry; sour; splenetic; stern; stygian; sulky; sullen; surly; tenebrific; tenebrous; uncheerful; unhappy; wan; weeping; wretched

GLORIFY: adonize; adore; apotheosize; beatify; bless; commend; consecrate; deify; divinize; doxologize; enlarge; exalt; extol; favor; glamorize; hallow; honor; idealize; idyl(l)ize; laud; macarize; magnify; pedestalize; praise; proclaim; revere; romanticize; sanctify; stellify; transport; uplift; venerate; worship; GLORIFICATION *or* GLORY: admiration; apotheosis; aura; aureola; beatification; beatitude; beauty; benison; blessedness; blessing; bliss; brightness; brilliance; canonization; consecration; dazzle-

ment; deification; divinization; *éclat*; effugence; eminence; eternality; exaltation; exultation; fame; favor; felicitation; glamorization; grace; grandeur; grandlioquence; grandiosity; halo; honor; idealization; illustriousness; kudos; laudation; luminosity; luster; magnification; magnificence; nimbus; praise; prayer; radiance; renown; repute; resplendence; resplendency; reverence; sanctification; splendor; stellification; suflimity; transport; worship,

GLORIOUS: (**see** "good") brilliant; celebrated; distinguished; ecstatic; elated; eminent; exalted; excellent; famed; famous; illustrious; lofty; magnificent; marvelous; noble; praiseworthy; proud; renowned; resplendent; royal; splendid; splendiferous; splendorous; stately; sublime; superb; wonderful; wondrous

GLOSS: **v.** annotate; blink; cloak; excuse; explain; expound; extenuate; instruct; interpret; japan; mask; minimize; note; palliate; polish; remark; varnish; veneer; whitewash; wink; GLOSS: **n.** brightness; commentary; dodge; enamel; excuse; explanation; glare; glaze; luster; polish; pretense; protection; semblance; sheen; shine; show; sleekness; surface; translation; varnish; veneer; GLOSSY: bright; glacé; glassy; lustrous; nitid; polished; satiny; shiny; silky; sleek; slick; smooth; specious; velvety; GLOSSINESS: (**see** "sheen") brightness; luster; nitidity; silkiness; smoothness; velvet

GLOW: **v.** beam; blaze; blush; brighten; burn; color; effulge; flame; flare; flash; flush; glare; glaze; gleam; glisten; radiate; shine; smile; tingle; GLOW: **n.** ardor; beam; blaze; blush; burning; cheerfulness; effulgence; enthusiasm; fervor; fire; flame; flare; flash; flush; geniality; glare; glaze; gleam(ing); glint; glistening; incandescence; kindle; light; radiation; sheen; shine; smile; tingle; warmth; GLOWING: aglow; alive; ardent; ashine; brilliant; candent; candescent; elated; enthusiastic; excited; exuberant; fervent; fervid; flushed; impassioned; incandescent; intense; joyous; lambent; lively; oriental; perfervid; phosphorescent; phosphoric; radiant; red(dish); refulgent; ruddy; vibrant; vivid; warm

GLUE: **v.** affix; cement; fasten; fix; paste; solder; stick; GLUE: **n.** adhesive; cement; gluten; mucilage; paste; solder; GLUEY: (**see** "glutinous") adhesive; gummy; mucilaginous; sticky; tenacious; viscous

GLUM: (see "gloomy") blue; brooding; dejected; depressed; dismal; displeased; dour; drear(y); ill-humored; low; melancholy; moody; morose; sour; sulky; sullen; surly; GLUMNESS: see "dreariness"

GLUT: v. clog; cloy; cram; feed; fill; flood; gobble; gorge; gratify; overeat; overfeed; oversupply; pall; sate; satiate; saturate; stuff; surfeit; weary; wolf; GLUT: n. cloy; cram(ming); flood(ing); gorge; gorging; oversupply; pall; paunch; satiation; saturation; surfeit; weariness

GLUTINOUS: adhesive; gluey; gummy; mucilaginous; ropy; sizy; slimy; sticky; tenacious; viscid; viscous

GLUTTON: chowhound; cormorant; epicure; gormand(izer); gourmand; gourmet; helluo; hog; pig; wolf; GLUTTONOUS: Apician; avaricious; bulimic; cormorant; crapulent; crapulous; craving; devouring; edacious; epicurean; grasping; greedy; insatiable; lupine; overstuffed; polyphagous; prehensile; preying; rapacious; ravenous; sated; satiate(d); unfilled; unsated; unsatiable; unsatiated; ventripotent; voracious; wolfish; GLUTTONY: avarice; bulimia; crapulence; edacity; gorge; greed; gulosity; hoggishness; orgy; overeating; overindulgence; piggishness; rapacity; satiation; satiety; unsatiability; voracity; wolfishness

GNAW: (see "chew") annoy; bite; champ; chomp; chumble; consume; corrode; crunch; eat; erode; harass; nibble; niggle; plague; rust; waste; wear; worry; vex

GNOME: aphorism; bogey; dwarf; fairy; goblin; gremlin; imp; maxim; nix; saw

GO: abscond; advance; attain; become; begin; belong; betake; break; circulate; decamp; deflect; depart; desert; die; diminish; disappear; egress; elapse; escape; exit; extend; fall; fare; fit; flee; flow; follow; function; glide; happen; harmonize; hie; inch; journey; lead; leave; mosey; move; occur; operate; pass; proceed; quit; reach; recede; repair; retire; retreat; run; sally; sashay; scram; sound; stab; step; stir; succeed; tolerate; travel; traverse; trek; turn; try; vamoose; walk; wane; wend; withdraw; work

GOAD: v. (see "provoke") annoy; badger; dare; defy; dig; drive; egg; gad; gibe; impel; incite; insist; instigate; jab; jog; jostle; lash; needle; nudge; poke; prick; prompt; punish; push; remind; rouse; spur; stick; stimulate; stir; tease; urge; whip; GOAD: n. see "prod"

GOAL: (see "aim") ambition; basket; bourn(e); cage; design; destination; distinction; dream; end; fame; fate; fortune; home; hope; horizon; ideal; intellect; intent(ion); mark; Mecca; meta; mission; object; point; port; post; prospect; purpose; score; star; tally; terminal; termination; terminus; touchdown; will; wish

GOAT: billy; cad; caprid; kid; lecher; libertine; nanny; ruminant; victim; GOATISH: caprine; coarse; hircine; lascivious; lecherous; lewd; lustful; salacious

GO-BETWEEN: agent; broker; emissary; fence; hustler; intermediary; translator

GOBLIN: (see "bugaboo") bhut; bogey(man); elf; fairy; gnome; gremlin; leprechaun; ouphe; pook; puck; sprite; troll

GOD: (the) Almighty; author; creator; deity; divinity; Father; godhead; godhood; Heaven; idol; Jehovah; lord; (the) Most High; Omnipotence; Pantocrator; power; Providence; ruler; GODLY: devout; divine; godlike; holy; pious; religious; reverent; righteous; virtuous; GODLINESS: devotion; divinity; holiness; pietas; piety; reverence; righteousness; spirituality; virtue; GODLESS: (see "unholy") unspiritual

GO-GETTER: see "hustler"

GOING: actions; behavior; current; departure; egress; exit; moving; obtainable; progress; running; way; working

GOLD: Au; aurum; element; gilding; gilt; money; oro; riches; treasure; wealth; GOLDEN: advantageous; aureate; aurelian; aureous; auric; auriferous; aurulent; bright; favorable; flourishing; gala; halcyon; opportune; Pactolian; precious; profitable; radiant; shining; superb; vigorous; yellow

GONE: absconded; absorbed; advanced; ago; broken; dead; departed; empty; exhausted; fatigued; infatuated; involved; kaput; left; lost; out; passé; passed; past; pregnant; ruined; running; spent; unhalted; wasted

GOOD: a. able; adequate; admirable; adroit; advantageous; agreeable; amiable; ample; amusing; appropriate; apt; attractive; auspicious; beatific; beautiful; becoming; beneficial; benevolent; best; blissful; bon(a);

bountiful; bully; bumper; cardinal; chaste; cheerful; choice; classic(al); clever; cogent; comely; commendable; competent; complete; conscientious; considerable; crackerjack; creditable; dear; decorous; delicious; deserving; desirable; discriminating; divine; edible; entirely; estimable; excellent; expert; fair; favorable; fertile; fine; fit; flavorable; friendly; full; funny; genuine; glorious; gracious; guileless; gustatory; healthful; healthy; holy; honest; honorable; honored; immense; incorrupt; innocent; just; kind; loyal; lucrative; magnificent; marvelous; moral; noble; nutritious; palatable; perfect; pious; pleasant; praiseworthy; prime; profitable; proper; propitious; prosperous; pure; real; recognized; reliable; religious; reputable; respectable; responsible; right(eous); ripe; saintly; salubrious; salutary; satisfactory; satisfying; seraphic; serviceable; sincere; sinless; skilled; skillful; smiling; solvent; sound; splendid; splendiferous; splendorous; stainless; strong; sublime; sufficient; suitable; sunny; superb; superior; superlative; thorough(ly); true; unspoiled; untainted; upright; usable; useful; valid; valuable; venerable; virtuous; welcome; well-founded; whole(some); wonderful; wondrous; worthy; GOOD: **n.** advantage; benefit; ethics; happiness; point; prosperity; purpose; success; welfare; GOODNESS: (**see** "virtue") perfection

GOOD-BYE: *à bientôt*; adieu; *adios*; aloha; *à tout à l'heure*; *au revoir a riverderchi*; *auf Wiedersehen*; ave; *bene vale*; *bon voyage*; bye-bye; *chant du cygne*; *congé*; departure; envoi; farewell; leave(taking); parting; riddance; *a riverderchi*; ta-ta; ultimatum; vale(diction)

GOODS: bona; chattels; cloth; commodities; crops; draperies; effects; emblements; estate; fee; freight; implements; lares and penates; material; merchandise; movables; plunder; possessions; property; stock; things; wares; wrack

GOOF: (**see** "blunder") shirk

GOOSE: barnacle; brant; dupe; fowl; gannet; graylag; greylag; iron; ninny; simpleton; solan

GORGE: **v.** bolt; cloy; cram; devour; fill; glut; gormandize; overeat; overfeed; overindulge; pall; sate; satiate; stuff; surfeit; GORGE: **n.** belly; canyon; chasm; couloir; defile; flume; gluttony; gullet; gully; mass; maw; meal; pass; notch; ravine; satiation; satiety; stomach; throat

GORGEOUS: (**see** "showy") colorful; dazzling; dressy; flamboyant; golden; good; grand; magnificent; ornate; resplendent; splendaceous; splendid; superb; terrific

GORY: (**see** "bloody") bloodcurdling; murderous; sanguinary; sensational

GOSPEL: Bible; creed; doctrine; evangel; faith; news; principle; tidings; truth; word

GOSSAMER: airy; cobwebby; delicate; diaphanous; ethereal; flimsy; gauzy; gossamery; light; sheer; tenuous; thin

GOSSIP: **v.** babble; blab; cat; chat(ter); chin; chitchat; claver; norate; prate; reveal; talk; tattle; GOSSIP: **n.** blatherskite; busybody; *caqueterie*; carrytale; clishmaclaver; companion; crony; dirt; hearsay; magpie; *on-dit*; quidnunc; rumor(monger); scuttlebutt; talebearer; tattle(r); GOSSIPY: **see** "talkative"

GOURMET: (**see** "glutton") *bon vivant*; epicure; gastronome(r); gourmand(iser); trencherman

GOVERN: adjust; administer; boss; bridle; check; coach; command; conduct; control; curb; deal; determine; dictate; direct; discipline; dispose; dominate; employ; execute; guide; handle; influence; lead; manage; manipulate; master; measure; minister; moderate; mold; order; oversee; pilot; police; regulate; reign; rein; render; require; restrain; rule; run; superintend; supervise; sway; teach; train; wield

GOVERNMENT(S): (**see** "state") administration; aristocracy; authority; autonomy; bureaucracy; city; command; commonalty; commonweal; commonwealth; control; democracy; dictatorship; direction; discipline; discretion; disposition; domination; dominion; empire; establishment; *état*; executive; guidance; king(craft); kingdom; law; management; manipulation; mastery; method; ministration; monarchy; municipality; nation; order; policy; polity; power; realm; regime(n); regulation; reign; restraint; rule; sovereignty; state; superintendence; supervision; sway; system; town; training; GOVERNMENTAL: **see** "civic"

GOVERNOR: administrator; commandant; comptroller; director; dynast; ethnarch; executive; gubernator; head; magistrate; master; pilot; regent; regulator; satrap; superintendent; viceroy

GRAB: **v.** appropriate; arrest; arrogate; capture; claw; clutch; confiscate; cop; grasp; kidnap; nab; overreach; paw; pounce; restrain; seize; sequester; snap; snatch; steal; swoop; take; GRAB: **n.** appropriation; arrest; arrogation; capture; clutch; confiscation; grasp; kidnapping; seizure; sequestration; snatch; steal

GRACE: **v. see** "adorn;" GRACE: **n.** attractiveness; beauty; benefaction; beneficence; charm; clemency; compassion; considerateness; consideration; decency; dexterity; dignity; dispensation; ease; elegance; este; excellence; fate; favor: felicity; generosity; gift; honor; kindness; lenity; lot; luck; manner; mercy; pardon; piety; polish; prayer; privilege; propriety; refinement; religion; reprieve; seemliness; skill; symmetry; tact; thoughtfulness; title; virtue; GRACEFUL: airy; appropriate; beautiful; becoming; charming; comely; dexterous; easy; elegant; feline; fit(ting); gainly; genteel; gracile; gracious; light(some); lissome; lithe(some); natural; neat; nimble; nymphean; nymphlike; pretty; refined; seemly; skillful; slender; *soigné; soignée* (fem.); sylphic; sylphlike; symmetrical; trim; GRACELESS: **(see** "unrefined") awkward; unelegant; ungraced; ungraceful

GRACILE: graceful; slender; slight; slim; sylphic; sylphlike; thin

GRACIOUS: affable; amiable; artistic; auspicious; beneficent; benevolent; benign(ant); bland; cheerful; cheery; civil; compassionate; condescending; congenial; cordial; courteous; fair; favorable; friendly; generous; genial; gentle; graceful; kind(ly); merciful; mild; nice; pleasing; polite; sociable; sweet; tender; urbane; GRACIOUSNESS: **(see** "grace") benignity; comeliness; condescension; graciosity; lenity; mercifulness

GRADATION: advance(ment); calibration; degree; difference; frequency; graduation; measure(ment); nuance; progress(ion); range; rate; scale; series; stage(s); step(s)

GRADE: **v.** blend; categorize; class(ify); correct; divide; elevate; gradate; graduate; indicate; level; limit; lower; mark; measure; order; position; range; rank; rate; scale; score; size; slope; smooth; sort; standardize; GRADE: **n. (see** "degree") category; class(ification); distinction; division; echelon; elevation; gradation; gradient; hill; incline; level; mark; order; position; quality; range;

rank; rate; rating; scale; score; size; slant; slope; stage; standard; standing; station; step

GRADUAL: continual; continuous; crawling; creeping; fractional; fragmentary; imperceptible; inching; incremental; piecemeal; progressive; regular; slow; step-by-step; subtle; uninterrupted

GRADUATE: **v.** advance; divide; end; finish; grade; mark; measure; pass; qualify; GRADUATE: **n.** alumni (pl.); alumnus; laureate; GRADUATION: **(see** "gradation") advance(ment); calibration; ceremony; commencement; end; finish; measurement; qualification

GRAFT: **v.** bud; fasten; implant; join; slip; splice; sprout; unite; GRAFT: **n.** booty; bribe; bud; cion; gain; gift; haul; loot; money; pelf; pillage; plunder; prey; prize; reward; scion; shoot; spoil(s); sprout; swag

GRAIN: atom; bit; cereal; crystal; fiber; fruit; granule; inclination; iota; jot; kernel; mite; ovule; particle; portion; roughness; sand; scrap; seed; speck; temper; tittle; weight; whit

GRAMMARIAN: lexicographer; philologist; syntactician

GRAND: **(see** "great") admirable; artistic; august; baronial; beautiful; brilliant; chief; commanding; comprehensive; cosmic; definitive; delightful; dignified; elegant; elevated; eminent; epic; exalted; fine; flamboyant; flashing; flashy; foremost; garish; gaudy; glorious; gorgeous; grandiloquent; grandiose; grandioso; Homeric; illustrious; imperial; imperious; imposing; impressive; inclusive; incontrovertible; infinite; kingly; large; lavish; lofty; lordly; lovely; lush; luxuriant; magisterial; magna(nimous); magnificent; magniloquent; main; majestic; noble; opulent; ornate; ostentatious; plush-(y); posh; preeminent; princely; principal; profuse; prominent; radiant; regal; rich; rococo; royal; showy; sovereign; spectacular; splendid; stately; sublime; sumptuous; superb; supercilious; supreme; surpassing; swank(y); swell; transcendent; vast; wonderful

GRANDEUR: **(see** "beauty") brilliance; dignity; elegance; exaltation; figure; flamboyancy; glory; grandiloquence; grandioseness; grandiosity; grandity; greatness; illustriousness; impressiveness; kindliness; luxuriousness; luxury; magnificence; magniloquence; majesty; nobility; opulence; opulency; pomp(osity);preeminence;princeliness;rank; regality; splendor; stateliness; sublimity; sumptuosity; sumptuousness; supremacy; vastity; vastness

GRANDIOSE: (see "grand") apocalyptic(al); bombastic; cosmic; flowery; grandiloquent; Homeric; impressive; magniloquent; majestic; rubescent; stately; turgid

GRANT: v. accede; accord; acknowledge; admit; agree; allot; allow; assume; authorize; award; bequeath; bestow; cede; comply; concede; confer; consent; convey; credit; donate; endow; endue; enrich; furnish; give; heighten; impart; indulge; invest; lend; let; license; loan; octroy; permit; present; reward; subsidize; supply; transfer; vest; vouchsafe; yield; GRANT: n. accession; accord; admission; aggreement; allotment; allowance; ap(p)anage; assignment; award; benefaction; benefit; bequest; bestowal; boon; bounty; cession; compliance; concession; conferment; consent; conveyance; credit; donation; dower; education; enam; enhancement; franchise; fund; gift; gratuity; investment; largess(e); license; loan; permission; permit; perquisite; power; power of attorney; present(ation); privilege; qualification; reward; stipend(ium); subsidy; supply; talent; transfer; warrant

GRAPH: chart; design; diagram; locus; map; plan; scheme; sketch; GRAPHIC: (see "clear") definite; descriptive; diagrammatic; distinct; explicit; expressive; forceful; forcible; illustrative; intelligible; lively; lucid; pictorial; picturesque; precise; sharp; striking; telling; unequivocal; vivid

GRAPPLE: (see "attack") bind; clinch; clutch; come to grips; contend; cope; fasten; grasp; grip; grope; hold; hook; join; lock; oppose; seize; struggle; wrestle

GRASP: v. apprehend; appropriate; capture; catch; clasp; clinch; cling; clutch; comprehend; conceive; deduce; disarm; embrace; encircle; enclose; enfold; enwrap; fasten; fold; grab; grapple; grasp; grip; hold; hook; hug; latch; perceive; pin; possess; realize; retain; seize; sense; shake; snatch; swallow; take; understand; visualize; wrap; GRASP n. apprehension; appropriation; clasp; clinch: clutch; comprehension; control; deduction embrace; grab; grip; hold(ing); insight; perception; possession; reach; realization; retention; seizure; tenure; understanding; GRASPING: acquisitive; *alieni appetens*;

avaricious; avid; close; covetous; greedy; miserly; prehensile; prehensive; rapacious; selfish; tenacious

GRASS: herbage; green(ery); lawn; retirement; sod; turf

GRATE: v. abrade; annoy; chark; distress; fret; gnash; grind; groan; irritate; jar; offend; perturb; rankle; rasp; rub; scrape; scratch; squeak; GRATE: n. basket; fire-(bed); fireplace; grid(dle); hearth; stove; GRATING: a. (see "annoying") displeasing; harsh; hoarse; irritating; raspy; GRATING: n. grid; grill(e); lattice; partition

GRATIFY: (see "please") adorn; amuse; arride; captivate; capture; charm; cheer; comfort; comply; console; content; cuddle; delectate; delight; ease; elate; enravish; enthral(l); enthuse; expend; favor; feed; fondle; gladden; grace; grant; humor; indulge; oblige; pamper; pet; placate; puff; regale; sate; satiate; satisfy; serve; tickle; transport; treat; welcome; wreak; yield; GRATIFYING: see "pleasurable;" GRATIFICATION: (see "pleasure") adornment; captivation; capture; comfort; compensation; contentment; delectation; delight; ease; elation; fondness; grace; gratulation; indulgence; oblectation; placation; realization; recompense; relish; reward; satiation; satiety; self-indulgence; transport; unrestraint; welcome

GRATITUDE: see "thankfulness"

GRATUITY: alms; benefaction; benefice; beneficence; benefit; benevolence; boon; bounty; bribe; charity; courtesy; dole; donation; douceur; favor; fee; gift; honorarium; lagniappe; largess(e); perquisite; pilon; pourboire; present; tip; vail; GRATUITOUS: free; gratis; groundless; needless; spontaneous; unasked; uncalled-for; unfounded; unnecessary; unpremeditated; unprovoked; unsolicited; voluntary; wanton; willing

GRAVE: a. (see "serious") all-important; authoritative; climactic(al); consequential; critical; dangerous; dignified; drab; earnest; funereal; heavy; high; important; intense; melancholy; momentous; monumental; mortuary; quiet; risky; sad; saturnine; sedate; sepulchral; slow; sober; solemn; somber; sombrous; staid; stern; suant; thoughtful; tumultuary; unaccented; weighty; GRAVE: n. catacomb; cell; crypt; fosse; hole; mausoleum; ossuary; pit; repository; sarcophagus; sepulcher; terminus; tomb; vault

GRAVEYARD: **see** "cemetery"

GRAVITATE: attract; decline; drop; fall; incline; seep; settle; sink; tend

GRAY: aged; ashen; cloudy; dismal; drab; dull; dun; elderly; grizzled; hoary; intermediate; leaden; livid; mature; miserable; old; slate

GRAZE: abrade; browse; brush; consume; eat; feed; forage; hunt; nibble; nick; nourish; pasture; ricochet; rub; scratch; shave; skim; touch

GREASE: **v.** (**see** "oil") bribe; expedite; facilitate; GREASE: **n.** fat(ness); lard; lubrication; mort; oil; suet; wax; GREASY: adipose; butyraceous; distasteful; fatty; lardaceous; oily; oleaginous; pinguid; porky; repulsive; saponaceous; sebaceous; shifty; slippery; smooth; unctuous; unreliable; GREASINESS: lubricity; pinguidity; unctuosity; unctuousness

GREAT: **a.** (**see** "huge") able; admirable; all-important; almighty; ample; august; authoritative; bulky; capable; cogent; colossal; consequential; considerable; conspicuous; critical; crucial; dandy; devastating; distinguished; dynamic; effective; effectual; efficacious; efficient; elaborate; eminent; emphatic; enlarged; enormous; epic(al); estimable; excessive; executive; extraordinary; extreme; famous; far-reaching; forceful; gargantuan; ghastly; grand(iose); grave; heavy; Herculean; heroic; Homeric; illustrious; immense; impactful; important; impressive; incalculable; incomputable; influential; intense; keen; large(-scale); limitless; magisterial; *magna*; magnanimous; magnificent; main; majestic; marked; measureless; memorable; mighty; momentous; monumental; noble; notable; noted; notorious; numerous; outstanding; overruling; overwhelming; peachy; potent; powerful; predominant; preeminent; principal; productive; prominent; red-letter; remarkable; renowned; satisfying; signal; significant; sovereign; staggering; strong; sublime; super(abundant); supercolossal; superior; supreme; telling; terrible; terrific; thumping; titanic; uncommon; unforgettable; untold; vast; vigorous; vivid; GREAT: **n.** star; titan; V.I.P.; GREATER: **see** "beyond;"

GREATEST: maximal; maximum; *ne plus*

supra; *ne plus ultra*; optimal; optimum; paramount; preeminent; sovereign; stupendous; utmost; GREATNESS: almightiness; amplitude; comprehension; effectiveness; effectivity; efficaciousness; efficacy; eminence; energy; enormity; estimableness; fame; force; grandeur; grandiosity; immensity; importance; largeness; magnanimity; magnitude; majesty; maximum; might; momentousness; monumentality; nobility; nobleness; power; predominance; predomination; preeminence; presence; prominence; range; renown; scope; size; strength; stupendousness; sublimity; superiority; transcendence; vastity; vastness; volume; width

GREED(INESS): acquisitiveness; avarice; avariciousness; avidity; covetousness; cupidity; desire; eagerness; edacity; gluttony; intemperance; itch(ing); longing; lust; miserliness; parsimony; piggishness; plunder; rapacity; selfishness; stinginess; venality; voracity; GREEDY: acquisitive; avaricious; avid; bourgeois; close; covetous; devouring; eager; edacious; esurient; extortionate; gluttonous; grasping; gripping; hungry; insatiable; keen; mercenary; miserly; omnivorous; parasitic(al); parsimonious; penny-pinching; piggish; pinchbeck; predatory; prehensile; prehensive; rapacious; ravenous; selfish; stingy; tight; venal; voracious; vulpine; widemouthed; wolfish

GREEN: **a.** alive; callow; crude; emerald; fertile; fresh; gullible; immature; inexperienced; leafy; lush; mossy; new; naive; olive; pleasant; raw; rude; temperate; tender; ultramarine; unfledged; unhealed; unripe; unseasoned; unskilled; untried; untrained; verdant; verdured; verdurous; virescent; viridescent; vivid; young; youthful; GREEN: **n.** color; grass; jade; lawn; verd(ure); virility; GREENISH: aeruginous; verdant; verdigrisy; verdured; verdurous; virescent

GREENHORN: (**see** "newcomer") novice; tyro

GREET: accost; address; compliment; hail; halse; meet; receive; salaam; salute; speak (to); welcome; GREETING(S): *accueil*; address; ave; devior; hello; hi; how; kiss; reception; regard(s); salaam; salutation; salute; toast; welcome

GREGARIOUS: (**see** "hospitable") amicable; companionable; convivial; friendly; sociable; social

GRIEF: **see** under "grieve"

GRIEVE: ache; agonize; bemoan; bewail; complain; cry; deplore; distress; droop; fade; flag; fret; lament; languish; long; moan; mope; mourn; pain; pine; rue; sorrow; suffer; sulk; waste; weep; wither; wound; yearn; GRIEF: accident; adversity; affliction; agony; anguish; annoyance; anxiety; bereavement; breakage; calamity; catastrophe; compunction; contrition; desolation; difficulty; disaster; distress; dole; dolor; emotion; evil; failure; grievance; hardship; heartache; heartbreak; lamentation; melancholy; misadventure; misery; misfortune; mishap; mortification; mourning; pain; penitence; regret; remorse; sadness; sorriness; sorrow; torment; trial; tribulation; *tristesse*; trouble; unhappiness; vexation; woe; worry; GRIEVANCE: anger; annoyance; burden; complaint; displeasure; distress; gravamen; grief; gripe; hardship; injury; lament(ation); oppression; suffering; tort; wrong; GRIEVOUS: (**see** "sad") afflicting; afflictive; atrocious; bad; baleful; bitter; burdensome; calamitous; deep; deplorable; desolate; dire; dirty; disconsolate; distressful; distressing; doleful; dolorific; dolorous; evil; grieved; heartbreaking; heartrending; heartsick; heinous; inconsolate; injurious; intense; lamentable; lamented; melancholy; onerous; oppressive; painful; serious; severe; sore; sorrowful; unhappy; woeful

GRILL: afflict; broil; catechize; cook; distress; grate; probe; question; quize; rack; torment; try; vex

GRIM: (**see** "sad") austere; crabbed; cranky; cross; cruel; desperate; dire; fell; ferocious; fierce; forbidding; frightening; frightful; funerary; funereal; ghastly; gloomy; glum; gruesome; grumpy; harsh; horrible; inexorable; macabre; merciless; morbid; moribund; obdurate; pitiless; plutonian; plutonic; relentless; repellant; resolute; rigorous; ruthless; savage; serious; severe; shocking; sinister; sour; stern; sullen; threatening; unamused; unamusing; uncompromising; unsmiling; unyielding

GRIMACE: affectation; contortion; distortion; fleer; frown; grin; leer; mop; moue; pretense; scowl; sham; *simagrée*; smirk; sneer; snoot; squint; wink

GRIME: (**see** "filth") dirt(iness); disorder; smut; soil; soot; sordidness; squalidity; squalor; uncleanliness; GRIMY: dirty; filthy; fouled; scabrous; soiled; squalid; sullied; unclean

GRIN: (**see** "smile") smirk

GRIND: **v.** abrade; afflict; annoy; bray; chew; comminute; coerce; crank; crush; dominate; domineer; drudge; file; gnash; grate; grit; harass; hone; labor; masticate; mill; mull; oppress; plug; polish; powder; pulverize; rasp; rub; sharpen; slave; smooth; tire; toil; trample; triturate; tyrannize; wear; whet; work; worry; GRIND: **n.** annoyance; crush; drudgery; labor; oppression; rut; slavery; task; toil; work

GRIP: **v.** attach; catch; clasp; clutch; control; dominate; domineer; embrace; fasten; grab; grasp; hold; hug; rivet; seize; take; GRIP: **n.** bag; case; clasp; clutch; control; domination; dominion; embrace; grab; grasp; handle; hold; hug; mastery; power; satchel; seizure; spasm; GRIPPING: **see** "intense"

GRISLY: **see** "horrible"

GRIT: bran; brass(iness); courage; decision; determination; dirt; fortitude; gall; gravel; guts; mettle; nerve; pep; pluck; resolution; sand; spirit; stamina; GRITTY: arenaceous; brassy; courageous; fortitudinous; gutty; nervy; plucky; resolute; sabulous; spirited; staminal

GROAN: complain; creak; cry; disapprove; grate; growl; grumble; lament; moan; rasp; sigh; sob; wail; whine

GROOM: **v.** adorn; attend; brush; clean; comb; curry; deck; dress; embellish; festoon; freshen; garnish; maintain; polish; prepare; prime; ready; refine; spruce; tend; tidy; GROOM: **n.** bridegroom; equerry; hostler; manservant; ostler; page; servant; squire; valet

GROOVE: channel; custom; fissure; flute; furrow; habit; hollow; indent(ation); mortise; practice; rabbet; rote; routing; rut; score; scratch; seam; sulci (pl.); sulcus; trench; GROOVED: caniculate; cannellated; chamfered; channeled; furrowed; indented; scored; scratched; scrobiculate; sulcate; trenched

GROPE: *aller à tâtons*; explore; feel; finger; fumble; hesitate; hunt; palpate; probe; question; quiz; reach; search

GROSS: **a.** absolute; aggregate; all; animal(istic); barbaric; barbarous; big; bulky; burly; carnal; cheap; cloddish; coarse;

common; complete; corpulent; corrupt; crass; crude; culpable; dense; dull; earthy; entire; flagrant; flat; fleshy; general(ized); glaring; great; heavy; ignorant; indelicate; inferior; large; lewd; low; macroscopic; manifest; noticeable; oafish; obese; obscene; out-and-out; overall; primitive; rank; repulsive; rough; rude; sensual; shameful; sheer; stocky; stupid; thick; unbecoming; uncultured; unrefined; unwieldly; vulgar; whole; GROSS: **n.** aggregate; bulk; sum; total; whole(sale); GROSSNESS: barbarity; corpulence; crassitude; crassness; crudity; indecency; indelicacy; scurrility; stupidity; vulgarity

GROTESQUE: (**see** "absurd") antic; atypical; baroque; bizarre; clownish; comic(al); distorted; droll; eccentric; eerie; fanciful; fantastic(al); freak(ish); incongruous; misshapen; nonsensical; odd; preposterous; ridiculous; strange; ugly; uncanny; uncouth; unique; unnatural; wild; GROTESQUENESS: absurdity; bizarrerie; clownishness; fantasticality; freakishness; grotesquerie; incongruity; oddity; ridiculosity; uniquity

GROUCH: complaint; crab; crank; grudge; grumbler; GROUCHY: **see** "irritable"

GROUND: **a.** mashed; masticated; milled; powdered; pulverized; triturated; GROUND: **n.** (**see** "grounds") area; base; basis; cause; clay; clod; dirt; earth; estate; floor; foundation; grit; justification; land; lawn; loam; lot; origin; property; ratio; reason; region; scope; sod; soil; subject; support; surface; sward; title; topic; GROUNDED: **see** "firm"

GROUNDLESS: baseless; bottomless; false; idle; reasonless; unfounded; unsupported; untrue

GROUNDS: (**see** "ground") base; basis; campus; cause; condition; criterion; dregs; essence; estate; floor(ing); footing; foundation; gist; justification; lawns; lees; motive; origin; platform; point; premise; principle; proof; quadrangle; rationale; reason; residue; rule; sediment; settlings; sward(s); terrain; yard

GROUP: **v.** accumulate; agglutinate; aggregate; amass; arrange; assemble; associate; belong; bracket; bunch; catalogue; categorize; class(ify); cluster; coagulate; collate; collect; colligate; colonize; combine; conglomerate; congregate; crowd; departmentalize; divide; file; gather; harmonize; mass; muster; pool; unionize; GROUP: **n.** accumulation; agglomeration; agglutination; aggregate; aggregation; amount; army; arrangement; assemblage; assembly; association; atajo; audience; band; battalion; battery; bee; bevy; bloc; block; body; bracket; brigade; brood; bulk; bunch; cadre; camarilla; camorra; canaille; caravan; category; caucus; cavalcade; cell; chain; chapter; church; circle; circuit; clan; class(ification); clique; club; clump; cluster; clutch; cohort; collection; collective; college; colony; combination; community; company; complex; conference; conglomeration; congregation; congress; constellation; convention; convocation; corporation; corpus; coterie; covey; crew; crowd; demos; department; detail; division; draft; drove; elite; ensemble; ethnos; extent; faction; field; file; fleet; flight; flock; fold; following; force; form(ation); fraternity; gaggle; galaxy; gang; gathering; genre; genus; guild; hatch; hecatomb; herd; hierarchy; horde; huddle; junto; kingdom; kist; knot; legion; legislature; levy; litter; lot; machine; mass; meeting; mess; mob; multitude; nest; network; number; octet; order; organization; outfit; pack; parliament; party; passel; people; phylum; pod; pool; populace; posse; press; quanta (pl.); quantum; quartet; raft; realm; ream; regiment; ruck; school; sect; section; senate; sept; series; session; set; sextet; shoal; side; sitting; slate; society; sorority; species; squad; stratum; suite; sum; swarm; synod; system; team; throng; tong; tribe; trio; troop; troupe; trust; union; unit; volley; whole; world

GROVEL: beg; beseech; bow; cower; crawl; creep; cringe; fawn; implore; kneel; kowtow; pray; prostrate; quail; quaver; sneak; stoop; toady; truckle; wallow; welter; GROVELING: **see** "creeping"

GROW: accrete; accrue; adolesce; advance; amplify; arise; augment; become; bloom; boom; bud; burgeon; come; cultivate; develop; dilate; educate; effloresce; enhance; enlarge; evolve; exist; expand; extend; flower; gain; gemmate; germinate; improve; increase; intumesce; luxuriate; maturate; mature; originate; produce; puff; raise; result; ripen; rise; root; spread; sprout; stretch; swell; thicken; thrive; tumefy; turgesce; wax; widen; GROWN: adult; developed; grown-up; mature(d); nubile; ripe(ned); seeded; GROWTH: accretion; accrual; adulthood; augmentation; bloom;

boom; cast; clavus; concrescence; corn; cultivation; development; differentiation; effect; emergence; enhancement; enlargement; evolution; excrescence; excrescency; expansion; extension; fungus; genesis; hair; improvement; increase; knob; knot; lump; maturation; maturescence; maturity; neoplasm; offshoot; origin; outgrowth; pace; plant; polyp; product(ion); proliferation; protrusion; ramification; rise; shoot; size; spread; stand; state; stature; stubble; thicket; thrift; tumor; vegetation; wart; weed; wen

GROWL: (**see** "complain") bemoan; bewail; girn; gnar; groan; grumble; howl; moan; mumble; murmur; mutter; rumble; snarl; yar(l)

GRUB: **v.** delve; dig; drudge; eat; extract; feed; moil; root (out); rummage; search; slave; toil; GRUB: **n.** board; caterpillar; chow; drudge; eats; food; groceries; larva; maggot; victuals

GRUDGE: **v.** begrudge; covet; dislike; hate; GRUDGE: **n.** anger; animosity; animus; antipathy; aversion; complaint; dislike; enmity; envy; grouch; hate; hatred; ill will; jealousy; malevolence; malice; malignity; peeve; pique; rancor; resentment; score; spite(fulness)

GRUESOME: (**see** "bad") appalling; cadaverous; fearful; frightening; frightful; ghastly; gloomy; grim; grisly; hideous; horrible; horrific; horrifying; lurid; macabre; morbid; morbific; morbose; sinister; ugly

GRUFF: (**see** "rude") abrupt; angry; austere; bearish; bluff; blunt; brusque; churlish; crabbed; cross; curt; discourteous; dour; grumpy; harsh; rough; rugged; severe; short; snappish; snarling; sour; stern; surly; unceremonious; uncivil; ungracious

GRUMBLE: (**see** "growl") complain; croak; disapprove; fret; groan; maunder; murmur; mutter; repine; snarl

GUARANTEE: **v.** assure; attest; certify; cover; guard; indemnify; insure; pledge; protect; secure; shield; undertake; underwrite; vouch; warrant; GUARANTEE: **n.** assurance; attestation; bail; bond; certification; collateral; cover; gage; guaranty; indemnification; insurance; mortgage; pawn; pledge; protection; seal; security; shield; surety; token; umbrella; warranty; GUARANTOR: angel; backer; ensurer; insurer;

patron; protector; sponsor; surety; underwriter; voucher; warrantor

GUARD: **v.** (**see** "guide") attend; bridle; chaperone; cloak; convoy; cover; curb; defend; direct; escort; fence; hedge; immunize; keep; mind; patrol; pilot; police; preserve; protect; restrain; safeguard; save; screen; secure; shelter; shield; steer; superintend; tend; usher; watch; GUARD: **n.** (**see** "guardian") attendant; baffle; banister; bulwark; chaperone; cloak; convoy; cover; custodian; custos; defender; defense; director; dog; escort; fence; fender; gateman; guide; hood; keeper; pad; patrol; picket; pilot; police(man); protection; protector; rail(ing); restraint; screen; security; sentinel; sentry; shelter; shield; superintendent; teacher; troops; tutor; usher; ward(en); watch(dog); watchman

GUARDIAN: (**see** "guard") angel; Argus; Cerberus; chaperone; committee; curator; custodian; guide; keeper; leader; patron; protector; sentry; teacher; trustee; tutor; warden; GUARDIANSHIP: **see** "protection"

GUESS: **v.** adjudge; anticipate; appraise; assume; average; believe; calculate; cast; compute; conceive; conjecture; consider; deduce; deem; design; determine; diagnose; divine; estimate; evaluate; extrapolate; fancy; figure; frame; gather; hariolate; hypothesize; imagine; infer; interpret; judge; opine; plan; ponder; postulate; prepare; presage; presume; prognosticate; rate; reason; reckon; scent; smell; speculate; study; suppose; surmise; suspect; theorize; think; value; weigh; GUESS: **n.** adjudgement; anticipation; appraisal; assumption; augury; average; belief; calculation; computation; conception; conjecture; consideration; deduction; design; determination; diagnosis; divination; estimation; evaluation; fancy; figure; hariolation; hypothesis; imagination; inference; interpertation; judgment; opinion; plan; postulation; preparation; prognosis; prognostication; prophesy; rating; speculation; study; supposition; surmise; theory; thought

GUESSWORK: (**see** "guess") conjecture; divination; hariolation; haruspication; hypothesis; postulation; prophesy; speculation; supposition

GUEST: boarder; caller; friend; lodger; patron; rider; visitor

GUIDE: **v.** (**see** "guard") advise; arrange; beacon; chart; conduct; control; contrive; convey; convoy; counsel; create; direct; dominate; effect; engineer; escort; fashion; forge; govern; hand; influence; inspire; instruct; lead; manage; manipulate; map; moderate; move; pilot; protect; regulate; rule; shape; steer; succeed; supervise; teach; usher; work; GUIDE: **n.** (**see** "guard") agent; attendant; beacon; bearer; book; carrier; chart; cicerone; clue; conductor; control(ler); convoy; courier; cynosure; director; dragoman; engineer; escort; estafette; govenor; guardian; index; inspiration; instructor; introduction; key; landmark; leader; lodestar; manager; manipulator; map; mark; marker; measure; mentor; messenger; motto; oracle; orderly; pilot; polestar; protection; protector; rule(r); scout; sign(al); signpost; star; supervisor; teacher; usher; GUIDANCE: chaperonage; ciceronage; direction; guardianship; lead; light; maternalism; paternalism; supervision; torch

GUILD: association; club; fraternity; society; sorority; union

GUILE: (**see** "artifice") craft(iness); cunning; deceit; dishonesty; dissimulation; double-dealing; duplicity; foxiness; fraud; knavery; knavishness; rascality; slyness; stratagem; subtlety; treachery; trick(ery); wile(s); wiliness; GUILEFUL: crafty; cunning; deceitful; dishonest; duplicitous; foxy; knavish; rascally; serpentine; sly; treacherous; tricky; wily; GUILELESS: artless; candid; credulous; frank; gullible; ingenuous; innocent; naive; rude; simple; sincere; undisguised; unsophisticated; unwily

GUILT: blame; compunction; conscience; contrition; crime; criminality; culpa(bility); delinquency; demerit; dereliction; error; fault; grief; iniquity; lamentation; liability; offense; penitence; qualm; regret; remorse; repentance; repining; reprehensibility; reprehension; rue; scruple; self-accusation; self-reproach; sin; wickedness; worry; GUILTY: blameful; blameworthy; censorable; chargeable; contrite; corrupt; criminal; culpable; delinquent; demeritorious; derelict; immoral; indictable; liable; nocent; penitent; reprehensible; reprehensive; sinful; wicked; wrong

GUISE: appearance; arrangement; aspect; cloak; clothes; color; costume; disguise; dress; fashion; form; garb; getup; manifestation; manner; mien; pretense; pretext; semblance; shape; way

GULCH: (**see** "gully") arroyo; cleft; gorge; gut; hollow; ravine; rut

GULF: abysm; abyss; basin; bay; bight; chasm; distance; eddy; gap; interval; pit; pool; rift; space; whirlpool

GULL: **see** "cheat" and "fool"

GULLIBLE: (**see** "naive") credulous; green; guileless; imprudent; innocent; simple; trustful; unsuspicious; unwary; GULLIBILITY: belief; confidence; credence; credulity; cullability; imprudence; naïveté; simplicity; trustfulness; unsuspiciousness; unwariness

GULLY: arroyo; couloir; ditch; donga; gorge; gulch; gullet; gut; gutter; hollow; ravine; wadi

GUM: amra(d); chicle; conima; gingiva; latex; resin; tar; ula (pl.); wax; xylan; GUMMY: (**see** "sticky") glutinous; resinous; unpleasant; viscous; waxy

GUN: **v.** accelerate; hum; rev; shoot; speed; GUN: **n.** arm; armor; cannon; carbine; firearm; gat; hunter; iron; mortar; ordnance; piece; pistol; rifle; rod; sten; weapon

GUSH: burst; disgorge; emit; flow; issue; jet; overflow; pour; rain; rave; regurgitate; sentimentalize; slop; spew; spout; spurt; vomit; GUSHING: (**see** "demonstrative") scaturient; sloppy

GUSTO: appetite; appreciation; ardor; enjoyment; enthusiasm; fire; keenness; liking; palate; pleasure; relish; taste; zeal; zest-(fulness); zip

GUTTER: channel; conduit; cullis; ditch; groove; gully; mire; mud; pipe; spout; trench

GYPSY: caló; czigany; gitano; nomad; rom; Romany; wanderer; Zigeuner; Zincalo

GYRATE: circle; convolute; curve; eddy; reverse; revolve; rotate; spin; spiral; swirl; turn; twirl; vertiginate; whirl(pool); GYRATION: **see** "eddy"

H

HABILE: (see "clever") able; adept; adroit; apt; dext(e)rous; fit; skillful

HABILIMENT(S): apparel; clothes; costume; dress; garb; garment(s); habit; uniform; vestment

HABIT(S): (see "custom") accustomedness; addiction; assuetude; bearing; behavior; character; clothes; conduct; constitution; consuetude; costume; demeanor; disposition; dress; familiarity; fashion; folkways; form; frock; groove; habituation; habitude; habitus; manner; method; mode; mores; order-(liness); path; pattern; physique; practice; praxis; procedure; raiment; regularity; rota; rote; routine; rule; rut; state; style; system; tendency; trade; tradition; usage; use; way; wont

HABITAT: abode; area; ece; element; environment; environs; haunt; home; house; locality; place; purlieu; range; region; residence; site; station; vicinity

HABITATION: abode; apartment; colony; domicile; dwelling; habitat; home; house; inurement; occupancy; residence; residency; settlement; tabernacle; tent; tenancy

HABITUAL: (see "chronic") accustomed; adamant; common; confirmed; consuetudinal; customary; established; familiar; formal; general; hectic; inborn; inveterate; methodical; native; natural; normal; orderly; ordinary; periodical; perpetual; persistent; regular; routine; systematic; usual; wonted

HABITUATE: (see "accustom") acclimatize; addict; drill; enure; familiarize; frequent; gather; hang out; harden; haunt; inure; practice; school; season; teach; toughen; train; use

HACK: v. axe; break; carve; chip; chop; clear; cleave; cough; cut; dice; drudge; hackle; haggle; hatchet; hew; lacerate; mangle; mince; mutilate; nick; notch; rive; sever; shape; slash; slave; slit; strike; toil;

trim; HACK: n. amateur; attempt; blow; bungle(r); cab; chop; cut; hackney; hew-(ing); hireling; horse; mercenary; strike; taxi; try; vehicle; whack; writer

HACKNEYED: (see "commonplace") banal; dull; flat; hoary; inane; jejune; old; ordinary; practiced; shopworn; stale; stereotyped; stereotypic(al); threadbare; tired; trite; twice-told; used; vapid; worn

HADES: see "hell"

HAG: (see "shrew") banshee; bat; beldam(e); crone; Erinys; fury; harpy; harridan; jezebel; termagant; Tisiphone; virago; vixen; witch; Xantippe

HAGGARD: (see "exhausted") anxious; cadaveric; cadaverous; careworn; debilitated; dilapidated; dissipated; drawn; emaciated; fretted; gaunt; harassed; harrowed; lean; meager; pallid; pinched; scrawny; skinny; spare; thin; tired; unruly; untamed; wan; wasted; weak; weary; wild; wild-eyed; worn; wrinkled

HAGGLE: bargain; cavil; chaffer; deal; dicker; fight; hack; higgle; mangle; negotiate; palter; stickle; wrangle

HAIL: acclaim; accost; address; ahoy; applaud; approach; call; greet; herald; honor; salute; signal; speak; stop; storm; summon; welcome

HAIR: braid(s); bristle; capillus; chevelure; crine; crinis; curl(s); down; filament; fur; fuzz; hide; mane; mop; nap; nicety; lock(s); pelt; pigtail(s); pile; pilus; plait; queue; ringlet(s); thatch; tress(es); trifle; HAIRY: barbate; bearded; bristly; ciliate; comate; comose; comous; crinate(d); criniferous; crinitory; crude; hirsutal; hirsute; hispid; lanate; laniferous; lanuginose; nappy; pilar; piliferous; pilose; pilous; polytrichous; pubescent; rough; rugged; shaggy; stubbly; unpleasant; unshorn; velutinous; villoid; villous; HAIRINESS: crinosity; hirsutism; pilosism; pilosity; shagginess

HAIRBREADTH: (**see** "trace") whisker; whisper

HAIRLESS: bald; bare; depilated; depilous; glabrate; glabrescent; glabrous; pelon; shaved; shaven; slick; smooth

HALCYON: (**see** "balmy") affluent; calm; carefree; golden; happy; peaceful; placid; prosperous; quiet; serene; still; tranquil; unruffled

HALE: athletic; brave; brawny; chipper; healthy; hearty; lusty; robust(ious); sound; stout; strong; vigorous; well

HALF: **a.** imperfect; part(ial); semi; HALF: **n.** demi; moiety; recess; rest; semester; term; HALVE: **see** "bisect;" HALVED: bifid; bipartite; bisected; cloven; dichotomous; dimidiate; separated; split

HALFHEARTED: (**see** "dull") lifeless; tepid; unenthusiastic

HALL: atrium; auditorium; aula; building; castle; coliseum; corridor; dorm(itory); entrance(way); entry; foyer; house; lobby; lyceum; manor; odeon; passage(way); residence; room; sala; vestibule

HALLOW: bless; consecrate; dedicate; deify; devote; honor; macarize; revere; sacralize; sanctify; venerate; HALLOWED: blessed; blest; consecrate(d); dedicated; devoted; holy; honored; revered; sacred; sanctified; venerated

HALLUCINATION: aberration; chimera; delusion; error; fallacy; fancy; fantasy; illusion; mirage; phantasm(agoria); phantom; psychosis

HALO: anthelion; aura; aureola; aureole; brough; circle(t); crown; diadem; glory; light; nimbus; ring

HALT: **v.** (**see** "arrest") cease; check; contain; cripple; defer; demur; desist; detain; discontinue; end; hesitate; hold; intermit; linger; pause; rest; stammer; stand; stop; stutter; suspend; terminate; wait; HALT: **a.** crippled; lame; maimed; HALT: **n.** (**see** "arrest") arrestation; cessation; check; cripple; detention; discontinuance; end; hesitation; hold; intermission; pausation; pause; position; rest; stand(ing); station; stop; suspension; termination; wait

HALTER: **v.** (**see** "hamper") bridle; fetter; handcuff; restrain; restrict; secure; HALTER: **n.** bridle; noose; restraint; rope

HALVE: **see** "bisect"

HAMLET: aldea; burg; dorp; dump; grouper; mir; thorp; town; village

HAMMER: **v.** adjust; beat; belabor; drive; drum; emphasize; force; forge; hit; labor; malleate; maul; pound; ram; reiterate; repeat; shape; strike; thump; toil; work; HAMMER: **n.** beetle; gavel; kevel; mallet; martel; maul; ram; sledge

HAMPER: **v.** (**see** "disable") annoy; bar; block; check; clog; confuse; cripple; delay; disconcert; disrupt; embarrass; embroil; encumber; entangle; fetter; foil; halt; halter; hamstring; handcuff; hinder; hobble; hogtie; impede; interfere; manacle; obstruct; oppilate; perplex; prevent; repress; restrain; restrict; retard; shackle; thwart; trammel; HAMPER: **n.** basket; crate; disruption; hanaper; hobble; manacle; obstruction; restriction; *seron*; shackle

HAND: **v.** assist; conduct; deal; furl; give; guide; lead; pass; HAND(S): **n.** ability; agency; applause; assistance; bunch; clap; claw(s); clutches; concern; control; crew; direction; employee; fist; help(er); indicator; interest; laborer; man; management; manus; part; participation; paw(s); pointer; script; signature; skill; staff; supervision; talent; worker; writing

HANDBOOK: Baedeker; cookbook; enchiridion; manual; promptuary; *vade mecum*; HANDFUL(L): bunch; few; grip; some

HANDICAP: **v.** (**see** "disable") burden; disadvantage; encumber; equalize; halt; hamper; hinder; impede; injure; retard; HANDICAP: **n.** (**see** "disadvantage") advantage; bet; burden; disability; encumbrance; hampering; hindrance; impediment; incubus; injury; lisp; odds; race; weight

HANDLE: **v.** (**see** "control") aim; conduct; cope; deal; direct; dispense; dispose; drive; examine; feel; finger; govern; manage; manipulate; maul; negotiate; operate; oversee; palpate; perform; pilot; ply; run; sell; supervise; swing; touch; trade; train; treat; use; wield; HANDLE: **n.** ansa; bail; crank; ear; finger; grip; haft; hank; helve; hilt; knob; lever; lift; lug; name; paw; pommel; stem; stock; throttle; thumb; title

HANDSEL: augury; earnest; favor; foretaste; gift; honorarium; luck; money; present; test; token

HANDSOME: (**see** "beautiful") accomplished; adonic; adroit; agreeable; ample; apt; attractive; bonny; comely; elegant; fair; *fait à peindre*; fine; generous; good-looking; graceful; gracious; imposing; large; liberal; lovely; magnanimous; noticeable; personable; pleasing; pretty; quaint; shapely; sizable; stately; stunning; well-favored; well-proportioned; well-turned

HANDWRITING: autograph; cacography; chirography; fist; griffonage; hand; hieroglyphics; manuscript(ion); penmanship; scrawl; script(ion);

HANDY: (**see** "available") able; accessible; adroit; advantageous; appropriate; apt; around; clever; close; comfortable; convenient; deft; dext(e)rous; easy; expedient; expert; facile; fitting; habile; helpful; hep; ingenious; inventive; multiskilled; near(by); ready; resourceful; seasonable; skilled; skillful; suitable; useful; versatile; HANDINESS: accessibility; adeptness; availability; cleverness; closeness; convenience; dexterity; easiness; expertise; facility; hability; helpfulness; nearness; readiness; resourcefulness; skillfulness; suitability; usefulness; versatility; virtuosity

HANG: **v.** append; attach; cleave; cling; dangle; decline; depend; drape; droop; execute; fasten; hover; idle; impend; incline; lean; loiter; loll; lop; neglect; oscillate; pend(ulate); rely; stick; suspend; sway; swing; wave; HANG: **n.** danglement; drape; droop(ing); knack; pause; slackening; stooping; suspension; swing; HANGING: abeyant; appendicular; dangling; draped; drooping; impending; pendent; pending; pendulant; pendular; pendulous; pensile; poised; sessile; suspended; swinging

HANGER-ON: **see** "minion"

HANKER: covet; crave; desire; hunger; long; pant; pine; starve; thirst; want; wish; yearn; yen

HAP: (**see** "accident") chance; fate; fortune; luck

HAPHAZARD: (**see** "accidental") aimless; bizarre; careless; casual; chance; chancy; disorderly; fortuitous; heterogeneous; hit-or-miss; incidental; indiscriminate; indiscri-minating; irregular; jumbled; mixed; motley; promiscuous; random; risky; slapdash; slipshod; sloppy; sudden; tumultuary; undirected; undisciplined; whimsical

HAPLESS: (**see** "unlucky") chanceless

HAPPEN: accrue; achieve; advance; advene; appear; approach; arise; arrive; attain; bechance; become; befall; betide; chance; come; emerge; ensue; enter; eventuate; exist; fall; fare; follow; give; go; hap; heed; issue; land; light; occur; originate; pass; reach; relent; result; rise; spring; stem; succeed; supervene; transpire; turn (up); visit; HAPPENING(S): (**see** "episode") contingency; event; fact; goings-on; incident; occurrence; tiding

HAPPY: appropriate; apt; auspicious; blest; blissful; blithe(ful); blithesome; buoyant; carnivalesque; charming; cheerful; cheery; congenial; content(ed); cosh; delighted; delightful; easy; ecstatic; Edenic; elated; elysian; enthusiastic; eud(a)emonic(al); euphoric; exuberant; faust; favorable; felicific; felicitous; festive; fitting; fortunate; free; gay; gelastic; glad(some); gratified; halcyon; harmonious; hilarious; jocund; jolly; jovial; joyful; joyous; jubilant; lucky; memorable; merry; mirthful; neat; obsessed; opportune; paradisaic(al); pat; pertinent; pleasant; pleased; proper; propitious; prosperous; rapturous; red-letter; rejoiceful; rejoicing; revelrous; sanguine; *sans-souci*; satisfied; spirited; sprightly; sunny; undepressed; HAPPINESS: aptness; beatitude; blessedness; bliss; celebration; cheer(fulness); contentment; delight; ease; ecstasy; eud(a)emonia; eud(a)emonism; euphoria; euphrosyne; exuberation; exultation; felicity; festivity; fortune; gaiety; glee(fulness); glory; grace; health; hilarity; jollity; joviality; joy(fulness); joyousness; jubilation; merriment; mirth(fulness); paradise; pleasure; prosperity; rapture; raptus; rejoicing; revelry; seventh heaven; success; transport; weal; welfare; well-being

HARANGUE: **v.** declaim; orate; plead; rant; rave; scold; tongue-lash; HARANGUE: **n.** declamation; diatribe; lecture; oration; scolding; screed; sermon; talk; tirade; tongue-lashing

HARASS: afflict; agitate; anger; annoy; assail; attack; badger; bait; bedevil; beg; beset; bother; chafe; confound; curse; discommode; discompose; distract; distress; disturb; dragoon; embarrass; enrage; entice; exacerbate; exasperate; exercise; excite; exhaust; fag; fatigue; flout; fret; gall; gnaw; goad; grill; harry; haze; heckle; hector; hound; impede; importune; incense; inflame; irritate; jade; lure; mock; molest; nag; persecute; pester; plague; press; provoke; raid; rant; ride; ridicule; rouse; ruffle; snare; tantalize; taunt; tease; tempt; tire; torment; trap; trouble; try; weary; worry; vex

HARBINGER: apostle; forerunner; herald; indication; informer; omen; portent; precursor; robin; sign; trailblazer; usher

HARBOR: **v.** accommodate; board; cherish; contain; entertain; feed; foster; hide; hold; host; house; keep; live; nurture; protect; receive; secrete; shelter; shield; HARBOR: **n.** abode; anchorage; asylum; bay; cothon; harborage; haven; home; host; house; inlet; lair; lodge; port; refuge; resting-place; retreat; road(stead); sanctuary; seaport; shelter; shield

HARDEN: (**see** "crust" and "steel") acclimate; acclimatize; calcify; concrete; concretize; congeal; drill; exercise; indurate; inure; jell; set; solidify; toughen; train; HARD-(ENED): acclimated; adamant(ine); arduous; austere; bad; binding; brazen; callous; challenging; clamourous; close; coarse; cold-blooded; compact; concentrated; concrete; concretive; concretized; confirmed; congealed; cruel; dark; deep; definite; demanding; dense; difficult; distressing; emotionless; exacting; exigent; fastidious; fibrous; firm; fixed; flinty; forbidding; glassy; granitic; grievous; habituated; hairy; hardhearted; hardy; harsh; hostile; ill; impenetrable; impenitent; imperative; importunate; inclement; incorrigible; indurate(d); inexorable; inflexible; insensate; insusceptible; intense; intensive; intoxicating; intractable; intricate; inured; inveterate; involved; jelled; jellied; knotty; laborious; laborsome; lost; marble; marmoraceous; marmoreal; near; obdurate; obligatory; obscure; onerous; oppressive; ossified; perplexing; persistent; perverse; petrous; practical; profound; punishing; puzzling; realistic; resentful; resistant; rigid; rigorous; rocky; rough; ruthless; scleroid; sclerotic; searching; set; severe; shameless; sinister; solid(ified); sound; stable; steely; steep; stern; stiff; stony; stout; strenuous; strict; strident; stringent; strong; stubborn; supplicative; taxing; tempered; thick; thorny; tiresome; toilsome; tough-(ened); trained; troublesome; trying; unaffected; unemotional; unfeeling; unjust; unmoving; unpleasant; unrelenting; unre-

mitting; unrepentant; unsparing; unsympathetic; unwavering; unwedgeable; unyielding; urgent; vigorous; violent; vociferous; HARDNESS: acclimation; acclimatization; callousness; concreteness; difficulty; firmness; hardship; harshness; impenitence; inclemency; induration; ossification; petrification; resiliency; resistance; rigidity; sclerosis; severity; solidity; steel; stiffness; stoniness; strenuosity; stubbornness; temper; toughness; troublesomeness

HARDHEARTED: see "stubborn"

HARDIHOOD: (**see** "courage") audacity; fortitude; insolence; resoluteness; robustness; strength; temerity; temper; vigor; will

HARDSHIP: (**see** "adversity") affliction; burden; calamity; catastrophe; cross; difficulty; disaster; distress; drudgery; fatigue; grief; harm; injury; injustice; misadventure; misery; misfortune; oppression; peril; privation; rigor; risk; sadness; severity; slavery; sorrow; suffering; toil; trial; tribulation; trouble; want

HARDY: audacious; bold; brave; brazen; courageous; daring; disciplined; durable; enduring; fearless; firm; flinty; hale; hard; healthy; intrepid; inured; lusty; resistant; resolute; rigid; robust(ious); set; solid; sound; Spartan; stout; strong; sturdy; substantial; tough; vigorous

HARE: bunny; coney; lagomorph; pike; rabbit; rodent; scut; topic

HARK: (**see** "heed") attend; hear; list(en); obey

HARLEQUIN: **a.** buffoonish; clownish; droll; fantastic; odd; zany; HARLEQUIN: **n.** buffoon; clown; jester; Punch; Scaramouche; simpleton; zany

HARM: **v.** abuse; attack; bruise; corrupt; crush; cut; damage; destroy; deteriorate; disserve; hurt; ill-treat; impair; injure; kill; lacerate; maim; maltreat; mar; maul; mistreat; molest; murder; offend; oppress; penalize; prejudice; poison; punish; rupture; scathe; smite; spoil; tear; vitiate; weaken; wound; wrong; HARM: **n.** abuse; bale; corruption; cost; damage; deprivation; destruction; deterioration; detriment; disservice; enemy; evil; hurt; impairment; injury; loss; mischief; misfortune; mistreatment; molestation; poison(ing); sorrow; spoilage; spoliation; wickedness; wrong;

HARMFUL: (see "bad") adverse; antagonistic; atrocious; baleful; baneful; contrary; costly; damaging; dangerous; deadly; deleterious; destructful; destructive; detrimental; evil; fatal; flagrant; grievous; heinous; hostile; hurtful; ill; inimical; injurious; killing; maledictory; malefic(ent); malevolent; malicious; malign(ant); mischievous; murderous; nocent; nocuous; noisome; noxious; offensive; painful; pernicious; pestilent(ial); poisonous; prejudicial; scatheful; sinister; traumatic; troublesome; unbeneficial; unbenevolent; unhealthful; unhealthy; unsalutary; unsanitary; unwholesome; venomous; virulent; wrong; HARMFULNESS: deleteriousness; maleficence; malevolence; malignancy; poison; sinisterity; toxicity

HARMLESS: artless; beneficent; beneficial; benign(ant); blameless; dovish; guiltless; healthy; hurtless; impotent; innocent; innocuous; innoxious; inoffensive; insignificant; insipid; nonpoisonous; nontoxic; pallid; pure; safe; salutary; sanitary; simple; unhurt; unobnoxious; unoffensive; wholesome

HARMONIZE: accord; adapt; adjust; agree; attune; blend; chime; concord; conform; consort; coordinate; correlate; correspond; go; group; jibe; match; mediate; mingle; orchestrate; reconcile; sing; square; symbolize; sympathize; symphonize; synchronize; syncretize; tally; tranquilize; tune; unify; unite; HARMONIOUS: accordant; adapted; adjusted; affable; agreeable; agreeing; alike; Apollonian; Apollonic; Apollonistic; assonant; attuned; balanced; blended; canorous; coincident; coinciding; commensurate; companionable; comparable; compatible; comportable; conciliatory; concinnous; concordant; conforming; congenial; congruent; congruous; consentaneous; consistent; consonant; constant; cordial; corresponding; dependable; dulcet; en rapport; equivalent; euphonic(al); euphonious; eurhythmic; even; fit(ing); friendly; homogeneous; invariable; isogenous; like; ordered; matched; mellifluent; mellifluous; mellisonant; melodic; melodious; musical; noncontradictory; orchestral; orchestrated; proper; rational; reasonable; reconciliatory; regular; reliable; restrained; rhythmic(al); silken; similar; sociable; sonorous; spheral; steady; suitable; sweet; symmetric(al); symphonic; symphonious; synchronic(al); synchronous; syncretic; syncretistic; tuneful; unanimous; unchanging; uncontradictory; undeviating; uniform; unisonant; HARMONY: (see "accord") attunement; compatibility; compatibleness; concinnity; conformance; conformity; congruity; consonance; consonancy; honeymoon; orchestration; rhythm; sonority; symmetry; symphony; tune; unanimity; uniformity; unison; unisonance

HARNESS: v. array; bridle; discipline; equip; hitch; prepare; tame; train; use; utilize; yoke; HARNESS: n. armor; clothing; equipment; gear; graith; leather; routine; tackle; yoke

HARP: dwell; iterate; repeat

HARPOON: v. catch; kill; spear; strike; HARPOON: n. gig; javelin; spear

HARRIDAN: (see "shrew") crone; hag; Jezebel; strumpet; virago; vixen

HARROW: agonize; break; chip; cultivate; dig; disk; distress; drag; fight; lacerate; scrape; scratch; tear; till; torment

HARRY: (see "harass") annoy; assault; attack; devastate; ravage; torment

HARSH: (see "hard") acerb(ate); acerbic; acid(ulous); acrid; annoying; antagonistic; asperous; astringent; austere; biting; bluff; blunt; bristly; brutal; cacophonous; caustic; coarse; crude; cruel; cutting; despotic; disagreeable; discordant; disharmonious; dissonant; dour; Draconian; drastic; dure; exacting; extreme; forbidding; grating; grim; gross; gruff; hardened; inclement; inexorable; inflexible; iron; irritating; jagged; jarring; keen; malign(ant); merciless; militant; pitiless; powerful; Procrustean; radical; ragged; raspy; raucous; raw; relentless; rigid; rigorous; rough; rude; rugged; ruthless; severe; shaggy; sharp; soulless; sour; stark; steely; stern; stiff; still; stony; strict; strident; stringent; tough; truculent; tyrannical; tyrannous; unadorned; uncharitable; uncivil; uneven; unfeeling; ungentle; unharmonious; unkind; unmusical; unpolished; unrelenting; unsmooth(ed); virulent; HARSHNESS: acerbity; asperity; churlishness; despotism; discordance; discordancy; hardness; inclemency; mordacity; raucity; rigidity; rigor; severity; stiffness; stridor; truculence; truculency; tyranny

HARVEST: v. accumulate; collect; cull; forage; gain; garner; get; glean; produce; reap; win; HARVEST: n. accumulation; achievement; amount; batch; collection; crops; food; forage; fruitage; fruits; gain; gathering; gleaning; grain; growth; hay;

increase; increment; ingathering; intake, issue; outcome; proceeds; produce; product(s); profit; result(s); return(s); reward; store; tillage; winning; yield

HAS-BEEN: see "heretofore"

HASH: v. chop; consider; dice; jumble; mince; mix; muddle; review; HASH: n. gallimaufry; goulash; haricot; heterogeneity; hodgepodge; jumble; medley; mess; mince; mixture; muddle; olio; olla podrida; potpourri; ragout; ramekin; *réchauffé*; salmagundi; slumgullion

HASSLE: (see "argument") brawl; brouhaha; coil; contention; controversy; debate; disagreement; dispute; donnybrook; fight; fray; melee; muddle; quarrel; rhubarb; scrap; scrape; spat; struggle; turmoil; wrangle

HASTE: abruptness; acceleration; ado; agitation; alacrity; briskness; bustle; carelessness; celerity; commotion; cursoriness; dash; dispatch; eagerness; *empressement*; excitement; expediency; expedition; expeditiousness; facility; festination; fleetness; flurry; hastiness; heedlessness; hurry; impatience; impetuosity; impetuousness; impulsiveness; impulsivity; indiscretion; irritability; nimbleness; overeagerness; precipitance; precipitancy; precipitateness; precipitation; press; promptitude; promptness; quickness; rapidity; rapidness; rashness; recklessness; rush; speed; suddenness; superficiality; swiftness; tear; thoughtlessness; trot; tumult; velocity; HASTEN: accelerate; advance; agitate; bustle; chase; crowd; dart; dash; dispatch; drive; ease; excite; expedite; facilitate; flee; flurry; flutter; fly; force; forward; grease; hie; hightail; hotfoot; hurry; hustle; impel; intensify; issue; move; oil; press; prod; promote; provoke; push; quicken; race; rouse; run; rush; scamper; scour; scud; scurry; scuttle; skelter; skip; speed; spring; spur; spurt; tear; urge; whisk; HASTY: abrupt; accelerated; *à corps perdu*; active; adventurous; agile; alert; anxious; apace; brief; brisk; busy; careless; celeritous; crazed; cursory; desultory; double(-quick); eager; evanescent; expeditious; expeditive; express; fast; festinate; feverish; fleet(ing); foolhardy; Gadarine; harefooted; headlong; heedless; highstepping; hurried; ill-advised; ill-considered; impatient; impetuous; incautious; indiscreet; irritable; last-minute; lively; meteoric; nimble; overeager; precipitant; precipitate; precipitous; premature; previous; prompt; quick; rapid(-fire); rash; reckless; rushing;

short(-lived); slight; speedy; subitaneous; sudden; superficial; swift; thoughtless; transitory; velocious; wild; winged

HAT: almuce; beanie; beret; boater; bonnet; bowler; busby; cap; caubeen; chapeau; covering; derby; dicer; fedora; felt; fez; headdress; helmet; hood; lid; miter; panama; petasos; sailor; stetson; straw; tam; tile; topi; topper; toque; turban

HATCH: v. breed; brood; concoct; contrive; devise; engrave; fabricate; incubate; invent; originate; plan; plot; produce; scheme; HATCH: n. barrier; brood; compartment; counter; door; floodgate; gate; lid; opening; skylight; wicket

HATE: v. abhor; abominate; anathematize; despise; detest; disdain; dislike; execrate; loathe; reject; resent; scorn; spurn; unlove; HATE: n. *or* HATRED: abhorrence; abomination; acerbation; acrimony; anathema; anger; animosity; animus; antagonism; antipathy; aversion; bitterness; contempt; despicability; despitefulness; detestation; disdain; disgust; dislike; distaste; emotion; enmity; execration; gall; grudge; hostility; ill will; ire; loathing; loathsomeness; malevolence; malice; malignance; malignancy; odium; opposition; pique; rancor; recrimination; repugnance; repugnancy; resentment; retaliation; revenge; scorn; spite; spleen; umbrage; vengeance; vengefulness; venom; wrath; HATEFUL *or* HATED: abhorrent; abominable; anathematic(al); annoying; averse; bad; contemptible; crabbed; crabby; cursed; damnable; defamatory; despicable; detestable; disagreeable; disgusting; dislikable; displeasing; disreputable; distasteful; execrable; execratory; fastuous; foul; grievous; harmful; hateable; heinous; hideous; horrible; horrid; horrific; imprecatory; infamous; invidious; loathing; loathsome; malevolent; malicious; malign(ant); nauseating; nauseous; objectionable; obnoxious; odious; offensive; opprobrious; outrageous; rebarbative; repellant; reprehensible; repugnant; repulsive; revolting; rotten; shocking; spiteful; terrible; uncongenial; unlik(e)able; unloved; unloving; unnatural; vile; wicked; wretched; HATER: abominator; detester

HAUGHTY: (see "arrogant") affected; aloof; assuming; bombastic; cavalier; commanding; confident; contemptuous; contumelious; despiteful; disdainful; distant; factuous; egotistic(al); hoity-toity; glorious; grandiose; hubristic; huffy; imperial; imperious; imposing; imprecatory; insolent; lofty; lordly; majestic; offish; ostentatious; overbearing; patronizing; peremptory; petulant; pompous; pontifical; portentous; preemptory; presumptious; pretentious; prideful; prim; proud(hearted); queenly; scornful; snobbish; snooty; stiff; supercilious; swaggering; toploftical; toplofty; unapproachable; uppish; uppity; vain; HAUGHTINESS: arrogance; contempt; contumacy; contumely; despicability; despicableness; disdain; egotism; fastuosity; hauteur; impudence; insolence; insolency; lordliness; morgue; presumption; pretention; scorn; snobbery; vainglory; vanity

HAUL: **v.** bouse; cart; drag; draw; dray; heave; lade; lug; move; pull; shift; taxi; tug; HAUL: **n.** booty; influence; journey; load; pull; swag; take; trip

HAUNT: **v.** beset; dog; follow; frequent; infest; inhabit; linger; molest; obsess; persecute; persevere; persist; pursue; recur; shadow; stalk; trouble; visit; HAUNT: **n.** abode; den; environ(s); environment; ghost; habitat; host; lair; milieu; nest; purlieu; rendezvous; resort; shade; spirit; visitant; walk; HAUNTING: besetting; disquieting; disturbing

HAUTEUR: (**see** "disdain") arrogance; contempt; contumely; haughtiness; hubris; loftiness; lordliness; pride; scorn; snootiness; superiority; toploftiness

HAVE: accept; achieve; acquire; allow; bamboozle; bear; beget; bribe; carry; categorize; cheat; cherish; contain; control; convey; deceive; defeat; dominate; enjoy; execute; exercise; exhibit; fool; gain; get; hire; hold; include; keep; know; lead; maintain; manifest; obtain; occupy; outmaneuver; outplay; outwit; own; partake; perform; possess; preserve; receive; retain; show; suffer; support; swindle; take; trick; understand; use; wear; win

HAVEN: asylum; bay; cove; harbor; heaven; hithe; home; inlet; lair; port; refuge; rest; shelter

HAVOC: (**see** "confusion") desolation; destruction; devastation; disorder; hell; mess; ravage; ruin; turmoil; waste

HAZARD: **v.** (**see** "endanger") ante; bet; chance; dare; expose; gamble; imperil; risk; stake; try; venture; vie; wager; HAZARD: **n.** accident; calculated; risk;

casualty; chance; contingency; danger; dare; difficulty; fortuity; fortune; gamble; jeopardy; peril; probability; risk; stake; uncertainty; venture; wager; HAZARDOUS: (**see** "dangerous") chancily; chancy; difficult; exposed; nasty; perilous; precarious; risky; shaky; threatening; trying; uncertain; unsafe; unstable; unsteady; venturesome

HAZE: **v.** harass; initiate; punish; HAZE *or* HAZINESS: **n.** brume; cloud(iness); dimness; drizzle; ethereality; film; fog(giness); gloom; grogginess; miasma; mist(iness); nebula; nebulosity; obscurity; pall; smog; smoke; tenuosity; vagueness; vapor(osity); HAZY: (**see** "filmy") clouded; cloudy; dim(med); dreary; ethereal; indefinite; indistinct; misty; nebular; nebulose; nebulous; obscure; shadowy; tenuous; vague; vaporous; weak

HEAD: **v.** (**see** "lead") command; control; direct; guide; mastermind; originate; point; rule; surpass; HEAD: **a.** chief; first; leading; principal; HEAD: **n.** (**see** "leader") aptitude; bean; beginning; belfry; block; boss; brain; cabezza; cap(itulum); capitulum; captain; caption; caput; chairman; chief; climax; coco; command(er); control; cranium; cream; crest; crisis; crown; culmination; direction; director; dome; first; foam; foreman; foremost; fount(ain); front; froth; helm; governor; guide; individual; intellect; intelligence; issue; lead; leadership; master; mastermind; mind; nob; noggin; noodle; nut; origin; pate; peak; person; pinnacle; poise; pole; pressure; principal; regent; rise; ruler; skull; source; spring; summit; supervision; supervisor; talent; *tête*; tip; title; top; understanding; van; warden

HEADACHE: amphicrania; annoyance; bicrania; cephalalgia; cephalodynia; cranialgia; hemicrania; *mal de tête*; megrim; migraine; problem; trouble

HEADDRESS: (**see** "hat") almuce; capeline; coiffure; coronet; crown; hood; miter; pinner; ribbon; tiara; topi; turban; wig

HEADING: **see** "headline"

HEADLAND: bluff; cape; cliff; escarpment; ness; promontory; ras

HEADLESS: acephalic; acephalous; beheaded; foolish; leaderless; rash; senseless; stupid; undirected

HEADLINE: (**see** "caption") banner; display;

head(ing); inscription; leader; screamer; subtopic; title

HEADLONG: *à corps perdu*; breakneck; full; hasty; Gadarene; headfirst; heedless(ly); impetuous; pell-mell; precipitant; precipitate; precipitous; rash; reckless(ly); steep; sudden; *tête baissée*; unswerving(ly)

HEADQUARTERS: administration; base; capitol; center; command; control; office(s); operations; seat

HEADSTRONG: (**see** "heedless") bullheaded; dogged; forward; froward; heady; intractable; obdurate; obstinate; persistent; perverse; rash; stubborn; ungovernable; unruly; violent; wayward; willful

HEADY: clever; exhilarated; giddy; impetuous; intoxicating; rash; reckless; shrewd; smart; violent; willful

HEAL: amend; cement; cure; doctor; fix; knit; mend; pacify; preserve; reconcile; recuperate; remedy; repair; restore; salve; save; soothe; HEALING: assuasive; balsamic; comforting; curative; lenitive; medicamental; medicamentous; medicative; medicinable; medicinal; recuperative; remedial; reparative; resolute; restorative; salubrious; salutary; salutiferous; sanative; soothing; therapeutic(al); vulnerary

HEALTH: condition; fettle; healthiness; pep; prosperity; robusticity; sap; soundness; tone; tonicity; trim; vigor; vim; vitality; weal; well-being; HEALTHY: able-bodied; beneficial; blooming; bracing; considerable; corn-fed; desirable; firm; fit; florid; flourishing; hale; hardy; healing; healthful; hearty; hygeian; hygienic; invigorating; lively; lusty; massive; pert; positive; prosperous; recuperative; restorative; robust(ious); rosy; rugged; salubrious; salutary; sleek; solid; sound; stout; strong; sturdy; tonic; tough; valid; viable; vigorous; viral; vital; well; wholesome

HEALTHFUL: (**see** "healthy") beneficial; curative; good; healthsome; hygienic; invigorating; remedial; restorative; salubrious; salutary; salutiferous; sanitary; sanitive; whole(some); HEALTHFULNESS: eucrasia; healthiness; salubrity; salutariness; wholesomeness

HEAP: **v.** (**see** "collect") accumulate; aggregate; amass; bank; culminate; cumulate; gather; herd; hoard; lavish; load; mass; pile; pyramid; round; stack; HEAP(S): **n.**

abundance; accumulation; acervation; agglomerate; agglomeration; aggregate; aggregation; bank; cob; collection; congeries; cumulus; fistful; gathering; gobs; handful; herd; hoard; load(s); lot(s); lump; mass; number; pack; pile; plenty; profusion; pyramid; raft; shock; stack; total; whole

HEAR: apprehend; attend; audit; consent; hark(en); heed; judge; learn; list(en); perceive; permit; receive; regard; understand; yield; HEARING: airing; arraignment; attention; audience; audition; conference; earshot; examination; investigation; probe; oyer; trial

HEARSAY: bruit; dirt; fame; gossip; notoriety; *on-dit*; *ouï-dire*; report; rumor; scuttlebutt; talk

HEART: (**see** "essence") affection; ardor; attitude; bosom; breast; center; character; chromosome; compassion; concern; conscience; cor; core; courage; disposition; emotion; enthusiasm; feeling; focus; fortitude; gist; goodwill; hub; interior; kernel; knot; liking; love; memory; middle; midpoint; mood; nerve; nub; nucleus; opinion; person(ality); pith; pump; root; rote; sensibility; sincerity; soul; spirit; stamina; strength; taste; temperament; ticker; willingness; zeal

HEARTEN: (**see** "cheer") animate; comfort; embolden; encourage; energize; enliven; fortify; inspire; inspirit; rouse; solace; stimulate; stir; uplift

HEARTH: brazier; fire(place); fireside; grate; home; house

HEARTLESS: (**see** "cruel") barbaric; barbarous; brutal; cold; despairing; despondent; dispiteous; hard; harsh; hopeless; merciless; pitiless; unfeeling; unsympathetic

HEARTY: abundant; ample; animated; approving; ardent; brawny; cheerful; cheery; cordial; deep; devout; earnest; enthusiastic; exuberant; fervent; friendly; full-bodied; gay; genial; glowing; hale; healthy; heartful; invigorating; jolly; jovial; lusty; nourishing; profound; robust(ious); sincere; sound; stout; strong; substantial; thoroughgoing; unfeigned; unreserved; vehement; vigorous; vivacious; warm; well; wholehearted; zealous; zestful

HEAT: **v.** cook; excite; fire; foment; inflame; intensify; roast; steam; warm; HEAT: **n.**

activity; agitation; anger; animation; ardor; blaze; calefaction; calescence; calidity; calor; candescence; cauma; coercion; course; effort; estrus; exasperation; excitement; ferment; fervor; fever; fire; flame; flush; hotness; intensification; intensity; lap; passion; pressure; spark; strain; stress; sultriness; temperature; tension; trial; warmth; zeal

HEATHEN(ISH): **a.** ethnic; foreign; gentile; godless; idolatrous; infidel; irreligious; pagan(ish); strange; unbaptized; uncircumcised; unconverted; unenlightened; unfamiliar; HEATHEN: **n.** ethnic; foreigner; gentile; hedonist; idolator; infidel; pagan; paynim

HEAVE: boost; cast; draw; elevate; fling; gap; haul; hoist; hurl; kick; labor; lift; pant; pull; raise; rear; retch; rise; send; struggle; surge; swell; throw; toss; vomit

HEAVEN(S): above; Abraham's bosom; Beyond; bliss; celestial abode; celestial sphere; cosmos; delight; dome; ecstasy; Eden; Elysian fields; Elysium; empyrean; ether; felicity; firmament; God; happiness; happy hunting grounds; harmony; Hereafter; Nirvana; oblivion; order; paradise; pleasantry; pleasure; realm; skies; sky; sphere; sublimity; system; universe; Utopia; Valhalla; vault(s); welkin; zenith; Zion; HEAVENLY: aerial; airy; angelic; archangelic; beatific; blessed; blissful; celestial; delightful; divine; Edenic; elysian; empyreal; empyrean; enchanting; ethereal; etheric; felicific; felicitous; firmamental; happy; harmonious; heavenlike; nirvanic; Olympian; paradisiac(al); paradisian; paradisic; planetary; pleasurable; rapturous; sacred; seraphic; sublime; supercelestial; supernal; universal; Uranian; Utopian

HEAVY: afflictive; beefy; burdened; burdensome; cloddish; coarse; consequential; corpulent; cumbersome; cumbrous; deep; dense; difficult; doleful; drab; drowsy; dull; elephantine; encumbered; fat; firm; hard; hefty; gloomy; grave; inactive; inert; intense; laborious; large; leaden; massive; massy; onerous; oppressive; ponderous; pregnant; profound; sad; saturnine; serious; sleepy; slow; sluggish; sodden; solid; stout; stupid; substantial; substantious; thick(set); weighty; HEAVINESS: (**see** "weight") avoirdupois; ponderosity; ponderousness

HECKLE: badger; bait; flout; harass; hector; hound; jeer; jibe; molest; pester; pursue; taunt; tease

HECTIC: (**see** "feverish") constitutional; flushed; habitual; persistent; red; restless; septic

HECTOR: browbeat; bully; dragoon; harass; intimidate; scold; swagger; tease; threaten; torment; worry

HEDGE: **v.** bound; circumscribe; dodge; encircle; enclose; equivocate; evade; fence; guard; haw; hem; hinder; limit; modify; obstruct; protect; surround; temporize; HEDGE: **n.** barrier; boundary; defense; enclosure; fence; limit; obstruction; protection; row; septum; weir

HEED: **v.** apprehend; attend; care; consider; hark; hear; list(en); mark; mind; note; notice; obey; observe; perceive; reck; regard; tend; watch; HEED: **n.** advertency; apprehension; attention; attentiveness; care; circumspection; cognizance; consideration; ear; heedfulness; note; notice; observance; observation; perception; regard; watchfulness; HEEDFUL: advertent; attentive; calculating; careful; cautious; circumspect; considerate; listening; mindful; observant; perceptive; reckoning; regardful; vigilant; wary; watchful; HEEDFULNESS: alertness; attentiveness; carefulness; caution; chariness; vigilance; watchfulness; HEEDLESS: abstracted; blithe(some); careless; deaf; foolish; freewheeling; headlong; headstrong; heady; Icarian; imprudent; impulsive; inattentive; incautious; incogitable; incogitant; inconsiderate; independent; indifferent; injudicious; inobservant; intractable; lax; light (-headed); lightminded; listless; mad; merry; neglectful; negligent; oblivious; persistent; precipitate; precipitous; preoccupied; rash; reckless; remiss; slack; thoughtless; trifling; unalert; uncaring; unguarded; unmindful; unobservant; unprotected; unreckoning; unruly; unwary; wild; willful; HEEDLESSness: abstraction; carelessness; *étourderie*; imprudence; inattention; incaution; independence; indiscretion; inobservance; listlessness; neglect; negligence; oblivion; persistence; preoccupation; thoughtlessness; unruliness; unwariness; willfulness

HEEL: **v.** cant; careen; follow; incline; lean; list; obey; overturn; tilt; tip; HEEL: **n.** bounder; cad; calx; crust; dog; knob; louse; rascal; remnant; residue; scoundrel; spur; swine; wretch

HEFT: **v.** handle; heave; hoist; lift; weigh; HEFT: **n.** bulk; heaviness; weight; HEFTY: (**see** "heavy") abundant; big; generous;

imposing; mighty; ponderous; powerful; rugged; weighty

HEGIRA: departure; emigration; exodus; flight; journey; trip

HEIGHT(S): acme; acropolis; altitude; apex; climax; culmination; elevation; eminence; extent; extremity; hill; intensity; loftiness; mountain; pinnacle; pitch; prominence; rank; size; standing; stature; sum(mit); top; zenith; HEIGHTEN: accent; aggravate; amplify; augment; bolster; deepen; elevate; emphasize; endow; enhance; enrich; exacerbate; exaggerate; exalt; highlight; increase; intensify; magnify; sharpen; strengthen; underline

HEINOUS: (see "bad") abominable; atrocious; execrable; hateful; outrageous; shocking

HEIR: atheling; crown prince; daughter; dauphin; heiress; heritor; inheritor; legatee; parcener; scion; son; successor

HELD: see "controlled"

HELL: Abaddon; abyss; Acheron; Aralu; Avernus; barathrum; death; fire and brimstone; Gehenna; Hades; Hail Columbia; havoc; inferno; limbo; Naraka; netherworld; Orcus; Pandemonium; perdition; pit; purgatory; shades; Sheol; Tartarus; Tophet; underworld; HELLISH: Acheronian; Acherontic(al); chthonian; chthonic; demoniac(al); devilish; infernal; pandemoniac-(al); sheolic; stygian; sulphurous

HELM: control; head; lead(er); rein(s); rudder; rule; tiller; wheel; HELMSMAN: leader; master; pilot; quartermaster; steersman; tiller

HELMET: armet; basinet; burgonet; cabasset; casque; galea; galerum; hat; headgear; headpiece; hood; mask; morion; sallet; set; testiere; topi

HELOT: bondsman; esne; serf; slave; Spartan; thrall; vassal

HELP: v. (see "aid") abet; advance; advise; alleviate; appropriate; assist; attend; avail; back; befriend; benefit; better; bolster; collaborate; cooperate; counsel; countenance; cure; dispense; doctor; encourage; extricate; facilitate; favor; fix; fortify; foster; frank; improve; incite; instigate; invigorate; maintain; mend; nourish; nurse; nurture;

participate; prevent; prompt; prop; relieve; remedy; salve; save; second; serve; succor; support; sustain; tend; unhold; HELP: n. (see "aid") abetment; adjuvancy; adminicle; administration; advice; assistanceship; assistantship; attention; benefit; benison; blessing; coadjuvancy; cooperation; counsel; countenance; crew; employee(s); encouragement; faculty; favor; gift; grant; hand; labor; nourishment; profit; prop; refuge; relief; servant(s); staff; succor; HELPER: (see "aide" and "assistant") abettor; accessory; adjunct; adjutant; adjuvant; adminicle; agent; aide-de-camp; ancilla(ry); auxiliary; avail; benefactor; coadjutant; coadjutor; coadjutress (fem.) coagent; collaborator; collaborateur; colleague; confederate; confrere; employee; hand; husband; labor(er); nursemaid; participant; participator; servant; spouse; substitute; teammate; understudy; wife; worker; HELPFUL: (see "beneficial") accessory; accommodating; accommodative; advantageous; affirmative; alleviatory; assistant; assistive; auspicious; auxiliary; constructive; convenient; cooperative; curative; definitive; encouraging; obliging; opportune; pliant; productive; propitious; remedial; salutary; serviceable; subsidiary; therapeutic; useful

HELPLESS: afflicted; aidless; awkward; bedfast; bewildered; defenseless; dependent; disabled; disqualified; exposed; fatigued; feckless; feeble; futile; guardless; impossible; impotent; impractical; impuissant; incapable; incapacitated; incompetent; indefensible; indifferent; ineffective; inefficient; inexcusable; infirm; insane; involuntary; irresponsible; limp; lost; nugatory; pathetic; powerless; purposeless; spineless; sterile; stricken; unable; unjustifiable; unprotected; unqualified; unreliable; unshielded; unskilled; untenable; unuseful; useless; vulnerable; weak; worthless; HELPLESSNESS: (see "incapacity") *brutum fulmen;* fecklessness; impotence; impotency; impuissance; inability; incapability; incompetency; inefficiency; powerlessness; unusefulness; uselessness; worthlessness

HEM: v. border; confine; edge; encircle; enclose; envelop; environ; fence; fold; haw; hedge; hesitate; hinder; limit; restrain; sew; skirt; surround; HEM: n. border; circumference; confines; edge; fence; limit; margin; rim; seam

HENCHMAN: (see "follower") adherent; assistant; attendant; disciple; groom; hatchet man; helper; mercenary; minion; page;

particeps criminis; participant; retainer; satrap; servant; *socius criminis*; squire; supporter; worker

HERALD: **v.** advertise; announce; blazon; foreshadow; foretell; hail; introduce; notify; precede; proclaim; publicize; signal; usher; HERALD: **n.** announcer; *avant-courier; avant-garde*; crier; forerunner; harbinger; messenger; page; precursor; spokesman; usher

HERB(AGE): annual; flora; foliage; grass; greens; leaves; pasturage; pasture; plant; shrub; turf; vegetation; weeds

HERD: **v.** assemble; associate; corral; drive; gather; group; lead; muster; tend; HERD: **n.** assemblage; assembly; bevy; clutch; covey; crowd; drove; flight; flock; gaggle; gang; gathering; group; mob; multitude; pack; people; public; rabble; school; shoal; swarm; troop

HEREDITARY: ancestral; cognate; congenital; connate; connatural; constitutional; derivative; endogamous; endogenous; essential; familial; hereditable; hidden; idiopathic; implanted; inborn; inbred; incestuous; ingenital; ingrown; inherent; inherited; innate; inner; instinctive; institutional; internal; intrinsic; intuitive; lineal; linear; maternal; native; natural; paternal; patriarchal; patrimonial; transmitted; unacquired; HEREDITY: atavism; inheritance; tradition

HERETIC(AL) **a.** agnostic; apostate; Arian; dissentient; heterodox; misbelieving; nonconformist; radical; recusant; renegade; schismatic; skeptical; unorthodox; HERETIC: **n.** agnostic; apostate; Arian; deviationist; dissenter; heresiarch; infidel; innovator; misbeliever; miscreant; nonconformist; recusant; renegade; schismatic; skeptic; traitor; unbeliever

HERETOFORE: ci-devant; emeritus; erenow; erstwhile; former; hitherto; once; onetime; previous; quondam

HERITAGE: birthright; estate; hereditament; inheritance; legacy; lot; patrimony; portion; property; share; tradition

HERMIT: anchorite; ascetic; cave dweller; cenobite; eremite; friar; isolate; monk; nun; pillarist; recluse; solitudinarian; stylite; troglodyte

HERO: Argonaut; demigod; idol; knight; lion; protagonist; star; superman; V.I.P.; warrior; HEROIC: (**see** "bold") brave; chivalrous; courageous; daring; dauntless; epic(al); extreme; fearless; firm; gallant; generous; great; hardy; Homerian; Homeric; Hudibrastic; huge; illustrious; intrepid; large; noble; plucky; powerful; radical; resolute; Samsonian; self-sacrificing; spirited; undaunted; valiant; valorous; Viking

HESITATE: avoid; balk; boggle; dawdle; decline; defer; delay; demur; dodder; doubt; err; fail; falter; fear; flinch; fluctuate; grope; hang; haw; hem; hobble; limp; linger; misstep; pause; ponder; quail; quaver; question; recoil; reel; scruple; shilly-shally; shirk; shrink; shy; sidestep; slip; stagger; stammer; stick(le); stop; stumble; stutter; think; totter; tremble; vacillate; wait; waver; weaken; HESITANT: afraid; averse; backward; balky; cowardly; diffident; disinclined; doubtful; dubious; dubitant; dubitative; faint; faltering; frightened; half-hearted; indecisive; indisposed; loath; reluctant; shilly-shally; shy; spineless; spiritless; tentative; timid; uncertain; vacillatory; weak; HESITATION: balk; demur; doubt; dubiosity; dubitation; hang; indecision; indisposition; pausation; pause; stammering; timidity; vacillation

HETEROGENEOUS: assorted; confused; conglomerate; different; differing; discordant; disparate; dissimilar; diverse; diversified; foreign; haphazard; hodgepodge; incongruous; indiscriminate; messy; mingled; miscellaneous; mixed; motley; nonclassified; nondescript; nonuniform; promiscuous; varied; various

HEW: adhere; axe; chip; chop; cleave; conform; create; cut; dress; fashion; fell; form; hack; hatchet; lop; rive; sculpt(ure); shape; slash; slice; split; stick; trim

HEYDAY: acme; ardor; bloom; blossom; flush; height; joy; prime; spirits; vigor; zenith

HIATUS: aperture; armistice; breach; break; chasm; col; fissure; gap; interruption; interval; lacuna; lapse; opening; passage; pause; recess; rift; space; stoppage

HIDE: **v.** (**see** "hoard") abscond; avoid; blind; bury; cache; camouflage; cloak; closet; coat; conceal; couch; cover; darken; deceive; disguise; dissemble; elude; ensconce; escape; hood; mask; obfuscate; obscure; protect; screen; secrete; sequester; shade; shelter; shield; shutter; stash; suppress; veil; HIDE:

319

n. abscondence; coat; fur; kip; leather; life; obscuration; pelt; sequestration; skin; HIDDEN: abeyant; abstruse; arcane; baffling; cabalistic; cached; clandestine; cloaked; concealed; covered; covert; cryptic(al); cryptogenic; dark; deep; delitescent; dormant; endogenous; enigmatic(al); ensconsed; esoteric; furtive; imperceptible; inapparent; incomprehensible; inexplorable; inherent; innate; inner; inscrutable; invisible; larvate(d); latent; mysterious; obfuscated; obscure; obstruse; occult; potential; profound; quiescent; recondite; remote; screened; secluded; secret(ed); shy; sly; surreptitious; ulterior; unapparent; unbeheld; undercurrent; undescried; undetected; undiscerned; undisclosed; undiscoverable; undiscovered; unexplained; unexposed; uneyed; unforeknowledgable; unobvious; unpredictable; unsearchable; unseeable; unseen; vague; veiled

HIDEAWAY: cache; cave; den; escape; harbor; hermitage; lair; nest; nidus; pad; redoubt; refuge; retreat

HIDEOUS: (**see** "ghastly") appalling; discordant; dismaying; dreadful; embarrassing; fiendish; frightful; gruesome; hateful; horrible; horrid; ludicrous; lurid; offensive; revolting; shocking; ugly

HIE: **go**; hasten; hurry; incite; run; rush; speed; urge

HIGH: abstruse; advanced; aloft; alt(itudinous); ambitious; aristocratic; arrogant; boisterous; bright; cheerful; climactic; critical; dear; distinguished; drunk; edifying; elated; elevated; eminent; exalted; excellent; exciting; extravagant; extreme; first; florid; gay; grave; great; haughty; imperious; important; intense; intensive; lofty; loud; luxurious; malodorous; meritorious; mighty; monumental; mountainous; noble; Olympian; overbearing; paramount; powerful; preeminent; pretentious; principal; prominent; proud; raised; sharp; shrill; soaring; stratospheric(al); steep; stinking; strong; sublime; superior; supernal; supreme; tall; top-bracket; top-echelon; towering; wrathful; HIGHEST: best; classic; loftiest; meridional; paramount; preeminent; supereminent; supernal; supreme; tallest; topmost; vehement; violent

HIGH-CLASS: **see** "superior"

HIGHWAY: artery; avenue; boulevard; *camino real*; course; drive; iter; parkway; pike; road(way); route; street; thoroughfare; throughway; trafficway; turnpike; way

HILARITY: cheer(fulness); Euphrosyne; gaiety; glee(fulness); hijinks; hilariousness; horseplay; jollity; joviality; joy(ousness); laughter; merriment; mirth; revelry; HILARIOUS: (**see** "gay") gleeful; jovial; joyous; laughable; ludicrous; merry; mirthful; noisy; revelrous; rip-roaring

HILL: acclivity; ascent; brae; cop(ple); dene; dune; elevation; grade; heap; height; hillock; hummock; knoll; loma; lomita; mamelon; mesa; monticule; monticulus; morro; mound; mount(ain); rise; slope

HILLOCK: heap; hummock; knoll; monticle; monticulus; morro; mound; rise; tump; tumulus

HINDER: arrest; baffle; balk; bar; block; check; clog; close; counteract; cramp; curb; dam; debar; defer; delay; embar; embarrass; encircle; enclose; encumber; fence; fetter; forbid; forestall; frustrate; hamper; hamstring; handcuff; hedge; hobble; impede; inhibit; interfere; interrupt; intervene; manacle; obstruct; oppose; postpone; prevent; prolong; repress; resist; restrain; retard; stay; stop; strangle; thwart; trammel; HINDRANCE: arrest(ment); bafflement; barnacle(s); bar(rier); block(ade); blockage; check; clog; counteraction; cramp; crimp; dam; delay; disability; drawback; embarrassment; encumbrance; frustration; hampering; hamstring; handicap; impediment; incapacitation; incapacity; inhibition; interruption; manacle; obstacle; obstruction; oppilation; perplexity; resistance; restraint; retardation; roadblock; rub; stay; stop(page); stultification; thwarting

HINGE: **v.** balance; center; depend; hang; pivot; rely; rotate; swing; HINGE: **n.** axis; basis; center; fulcrum; joint; pivot; turning point

HINT: **v.** advise; allude; connote; cue; denote; foreshadow; forewarn; illude; imply; indicate; infer; inkle; insinuate; intimate; mean; mention; nod; notify; point; presage; purport; refer; sign(al); signify; suggest; tell; tip; warn; whisper; wink; HINT: **n.** adumbration; advice; allusion; clew; clue; criterion; cue; dash; forewarning; giveaway; glance; glimmer; glimpse; guide; idea; illusion; implication; indication; inference; inkle; inkling; innuendo; insinuation; insinuendo; intimation; key; landmark; mention; nod; notice; nuance; odor; opportunity; overtone; point(er); reference; sign(al); smell; sniff; suggestion; suspicion; symptom; tendency; thread; tip(-off); trace; trend; umbrage; undertone; warning; watchword; whiff; whisper; wind; wink; wrinkle

HIRE: **v.** bribe; buy; charter; employ; engage; get; grant; have; lease; let; pay; recruit; rent; HIRE: **n.** employment; fee; pay; recruitment; remuneration; salary; stipend; wage(s); HIRED: bought; bribed; chartered; commercial; corrupt; engaged; leased; mercantile; mercenary; rented; venal

HIRELING: (**see** "mercenary") myrmidon; pensionary

HISS: **v.** assibilate; boo; censure; condemn; criticize; denounce; disapprove; fizz; honk; hoot; jeer; knock; razz; scoff; shish; sibilate; siffle; sizzle; spit; twit; HISS: **n.** boo; catcall; censure; condemnation; criticism; denouncement; disapproval; honk; hoot; jeer; knock; razz; scoff; shish; sibilance; sibilant; sibilation; sizzle

HISTORIAN: analyst; annalist; Bede; chronicler; Herodotus; historiographer; Livy; Plutarch; Polybius; Sallust

HISTORY: account; ancestry; annals; archives; autobiography; biography; case; chart; chronicle; drama; events; facts; file; historiography; legend; log; lore; memoirs; narration; narrative; past; recital; recollection(s); record(s); register; story; tale; treatise

HIT: **v.** (**see** "beat") achieve; affect; agree; arrive; attack; attain; bat(ter); bean; beat; belt; bop; box; buffet; bunt; censure; clout; collide; contact; criticize; cuff; discover; emphasize; find; flick; get; hammer; impact; kick; knock; lam; maul; poke; pop; punch; rap; reach; slap; slog; slug; smash; smite; sock; spar; stab; stress; strike; succeed; swat; tap; thrash; thump; wallop; whack; whip; HIT: **n.** blow; bunt; collision; favorite; homer; impact; impression; punch; score; single; slap; stroke; success; thump(ing); wallop; whack

HITCH: **v.** (**see** "fasten") attach; catch; connect; hobble; jerk; knot; marry; pin; tie; unite; yoke; HITCH: **n.** accident; catch; contretemps; entanglement; hobble; impediment; jerk; knot; limp; misadventure; mishap; obstacle; obstruction; pause; snag; stoppage; twitch

HIT-OR-MISS: aimless; *à tort et à travers*; casual; chancy; desultory; haphazard; indiscriminate; random

HOARD: **v.** accumulate; agglutinate; amass; bank; bury; cache; can; coffer; collect; conceal; conserve; couch; deposit; ensconce; garner; gather; guard; heap; hide; husband; keep; lay away; lay up; manage; mass; obscure; pile; preserve; protect; reserve; save; screen; secrete; sequester; shelter; shield; stack; stash; store; supply; thesaurize; treasure; uphold; veil; HOARD: **n.** accumulation; agglutination; amassment; bank; cache; cash; collection; concealment; deposit(ion); depository; depot; fund; heap; hive; loot; mass; money; pile; repository; savings; stack; stock; store(house); supply; thesaurus; treasure; treasury

HOARSE: croaking; grating; guttural; harsh; husky; rasping; raspy; raucous; rough; rusty; strident; stridulent; stridulous; thick; HOARSENESS: huskiness; phonasthenia; rasping; raucity; roughness; stridence; stridency; stridulation; stridulence

HOARY: aged; ancient; candescent; gray; hackneyed; old; mo(u)ldy; musty; remote; stale; trite; venerable; white

HOAX: **v.** see "fool;" HOAX: **n.** artifice; *blague*; canard; cheat; deception; delusion; fake(r); fakery; feint; fraud; gag; humbug; impostor; imposture; joke; mare's nest; ruse; sell; sham; spoof; trick(ery)

HOBBLE: cripple; fasten; fetter; hamper; hitch; hold; manacle; obstruct; shackle; struggle; waver; HOBBLED: fettered; halt; hampered; held; lame; manacled; obstructed; pasterned; shackled; spanceled

HOBBY: amusement; avocation; diversion; enjoyment; fad; game; interest; pastime; pursuit; recreation; sport; whim

HOBGOBLIN: *bête noir*; bogey(man); bugaboo; bugbear; demon; elf; gremlin; imp; ogre; puck; pug; sprite

HOBO: beggar; bum; clochard; gaberlunzie; itinerant; tramp; vagabond; vagrant

HOCUS-POCUS: abracadabra; deceit; fraud; legerdemain; necromancy; nonsense; prestidigitation; sham; thaumaturgy; wizardry

HODGEPODGE: **a.** see "miscellaneous;" HODGEPODGE: **n.** botch; bric-a-brac;

cento; collectanea (pl.); collection; colluvies; farrago; gallimaufry; hash; heterogeneity; jumble; *macédoine*; medley; melange; mess; miscellanea (pl.); miscellaneity; miscellany; mismash; mix(ture); olio; *olla podrida*; *omnium-gatherum*; pasticcio; pastiche; porridge; potpourri; ragout; rumble-bumble; salmagundi; series; smorgasbord; stew; varia (pl.); variety

HOG: barrow; beast; boar; glutton; pig; porker; sow; suid

HOIST: **v.** (**see** "elevate") boost; heave; heft; jack; lift; raise; rear; steal; HOIST: **n.** boost; capstan; crane; derrick; elevator; heave; jack; lift; raise; steal; tackle; theft

HOITY-TOITY: arrogant; fickle; flighty; gay; giddy; irresponsible; pompous; snooty; thoughtless

HOLD: **v.** absorb; accept; accommodate; affirm; aim; apply; arrest; attract; believe; carry; catch; charm; check; clasp; clinch; cling; clutch; comport; comprehend; conceive; confine; consider; constrain; contain; continue; control; convene; convoke; coop; dam; defend; defer; delay; detain; direct; embosom; embrace; enclose; encroach; engage; entrap; esteem; experience; fascinate; fence; fill; fix; grasp; grip; guard; hang; harbor; hatch; have; hinder; house; hug; imprison; judge; keep; last; lock; lodge; maintain; manage; occupy; own; pause; peg; pen; pin; point; possess; predominate; preserve; regard; remain; reserve; resist; restrain; retain; save; stay; stick; stop; store; subsist; support; suspend; sustain; think; transfix; trap; usurp; value; wait; wear; HOLD: **n. see** "control;" HOLDING: abeyance; attachment; attraction; belief; connection; estate; interest; land; occupation; opinion; settlement; tenancy; tenantry; tenantship; tenet; tenure; usurpation

HOLE: aperture; bore; breach; burrow; cave; cavitation; cavity; chasm; concavity; cup; defect; den; dent; dilemma; drain; excavation; eye; fault; fenestra; fistula; fix; flaw; foramen; foramina (pl.); gap; gulf; hollow; lacuna; leak; loss; meatus; mine; opening; orifice; os; perforation; pit; pocket; pore; punctulum; puncture; recess; score; shaft; slot; trench; void; weakening; well; window

HOLIDAY: celebration; feria; ferie; festival; festivity; fete; fiesta; furlough; leave; picnic; playtime; recreation; season; tide; vacation

HOLIER-THAN-THOU: Pecksniffian; religiose; sacrosanct; sanctimonious

HOLINESS: **see** under "holy"

HOLLOW: **a.** apparitional; capsular; cavernous; complete; concave; deceitful; depressed; devoid; empty; false; flimsy; frail; garish; gaudy; idle; imaginary; incomplete; infirm; inflated; insincere; insubstantial; lacking; lacunal; lacunar; showy; sunken; treacherous; unfilled; unsound; unsubstantial; vacant; vacuous; vain; void; weak; HOLLOW: **n.** abyss; basin; bowl; cave; cavern; cavity; channel; chasm; concavity; crater; dell; dent; depression; dimple; dingle; fossa; fovea; gulf; hole; notch; pit; pocket; ravine; scoop; sinus; socket; valley

HOLY: blessed; chaste; consecrated; dedicated; deified; devoted; devotional; devout; divine; earnest; fervent; godly; good; hallow(ed); hearty; immaculate; inviolable; inviolate; pietistic(al); pious; powerful; prayerful; pure; religiose; religious; revered; reverent(ial); righteous; sacramental; sacramentary; sacred; sacrosanct; sainted; saintly; sanctified; sanctimonious; serious; sincere; sinless; solemn; spiritual; undefiled; unprofane; unspotted; unstained; unworldly; venerated; vestal; zealous; HOLINESS: beatification; consecration; deification; devotion; divinity; godliness; grace; hallowedness; immaculacy; inviolability; piety; purity; reverence; sacramentality; sacredness; sacrosanctity; saintliness; sanctification; sanctitude; sanctity; sinlessness; spiritual(i)ty

HOMAGE: (**see** "deference") adoration; allegiance; deferentiality; devotion; fealty; fidelity; flattery; honor; incense; liege; loyalty; obeisance; regard; respect; reverence; sacredness; tribute; veneration; worship

HOME: abode; apartment; asylum; bastion; bungalow; castle; city; cottage; country; den; digs; domicile; door; dwelling; environment; estate; farm(house); fatherland; fireside; flat; focus; goal; God's country; habitat; habitation; haunt; haven; headquarters; hearth(stone); heaven; house; hut; ingle(side); lair; *lares et penates*; location; manor; mother country; motherland; nest; quarters; residence; residency; rest; roof(tree); roost; sanctuary; seat; shelter; tenement; villa

HOMELY: awkward; blunt; coarse; common(place); crude; direct; domestic; familiar; homelike; inelegant; intimate; kindly; natural; plain; rough; rude; simple; thick; ugly; unadorned; unaffected; unappealable; unappealing; unattractive; uncouth; ungainly; unhandsome; unprepossessing; vulgar

HOMERIC: (**see** "great") epic(al); gargantuan; grand(iose); heroic

HOMESICKNESS: *mal du pays*; nostalgia

HOMILY: address; admonition; discourse; exhortation; lecture; oration; sermon; speech; talk

HOMOGENEOUS: (**see** "harmonious") agreeable; alike; blended; comparable; compatible; congruent; congruous; consistent; consonant; entire; equivalent; identical; matched; same; similar; undivided; uniform; whole

HONE: **v.** grind; grumble; pine; sharpen; smooth; strop; whet; HONE: **n.** emery; grindstone; oilstone; strop; whetstone

HONEST: aboveboard; bona fide; candid; conscientious; creditable; direct; equitable; estimable; fair(-minded); faithful; forthright; foursquare; frank; genuine; good; guileless; honorable; humble; impartial; incorrupt-(ible;) ingenuous; innocent; judicial; just; legitimate; meticulous; open; plain; praiseworthy; rectitudinous; reliable; reputable; righteous; right-minded; sacrosanct; scrupulous; simple; sincere; straight(forward); true; trusted; trustworthy; truthful; unassailable; unbribable; uncorrupt(ed); untouched; up-and-up; upright; veracious; worthy; HONESTY: *bona fides*; *bonne foi*; candidness; candor; conscience; constancy; courage; dependability; fairness; faith(fulness); fealty; feeling; fidelity; fortitude; genuineness; good faith; honor; humility; incorruption; innocence; integrity; judiciality; justice; loyalty; merit; naturalness; nobility; principle; probity; propriety; pureness; purity; rectitude; reliability; righteousness; right-mindedness; rightness; scrupulosity; simplicity; sincerity; straightforwardness; truth-(fulness); uprightness; veracity; virtue; worth(iness)

HONEYED: (**see** "dulcet") charming; harmonious; melleous; melliferous; mellifluent; mellisonant; melodic; melodious; sirupy; sugared; sugary; sweet(ened); syrupy

HONOR: **v.** accept; admire; adore; adorn; adulate; belaurel; bow; canonize; cite; commemorate; commend; crown; decorate; deify; dignify; elevate; enhalo; ennoble; esteem; eulogize; exalt; fete; garland; glorify; laud; laureate; nobilitate; panegyrize; pedestalize; praise; raise; recognize; regard; respect; revere(nce); salute; serenade; stellify; trust; venerate; worship; HONOR: **n.** acclaim; accolade; admiration; adoration; adulation; approbation; asset; award; badge; canonization; chastity; citation; commendation; confidence; credit; crown; decoration; deference; deferentiality; deification; dignity; distinction; *éclat*; elevation; eminence; ennoblement; esteem; estimation; eulogy; exaltation; faith; fame; fealty; fete; fullness; garland; glorification; glory; grandeur; homage; integrity; izzat; knighthood; laudation; majesty; medal; name; nobility; notice; obeisance; observance; parole; praise; prerogative; prestige; probity; privilege; purity; recognition; regard; reliance; renown; reputation; repute; respect; reverence; rite; salutation; salute; standing; stellification; title; trust(worthiness); truth(fulness); uprightness; veneration; virginity; virtue; worship

HONORABLE *or* HONORED: (**see** "honest") admirable; belaureled; chivalric; chivalrous; constant; decent; dignified; dutiful; estimable; ethical; exemplary; faithful; good; honorary; illustrious; incorrupt; laureated; noble(-minded); prestigious; pure; reliable; reputable; respectable; respected; revered; righteous; scrupulous; sta(u)nch; straightforward; true; trustworthy; uncorrupt; upright; venerable; venerated; virtuous; worthy

HONORS: civilities; commendations; courtesies; dignities; distinctions; flourishes; prerogatives; privileges; rights; ruffles (and flourishes); salute; titles

HOOD: **v.** blind; cap; cloak; conceal; cover; hide; mantle; mask; obscure; protect; screen; seel; shield; HOOD: **n.** bandit; blind(er); bonnet; canopy; cap(uche); cloak; coif; cover(ing); cowl; gangster; hat; lid; mantle; mask; protecter; protection; screen; shade; sheath; shelter; shield; HOODED: covered; cowled; crested; cucullate; hidden; masked; screened; sheltered; shielded

HOODOO: **v.** (**see** "bewitch") hex; jinx; Jonah; HOODOO: **n.** bewitchment; hex; jinx; Jonah; sorcery; spell; voodoo

HOODWINK: (**see** "cheat" and "fool") blindfold; circumvent; cozen; dupe; seel

HOOK: **v.** bend; catch; clasp; clip; crook; curve; decoy; entrap; fasten; gore; pilfer; snare; snatch; steal; trap; HOOK: **n.** anchor; barb; bend; catch; clasp; crook; curve; fastener; gaff; hamulus; hamus; reaper; sickle; sythe; HOOKED: aduncous; bent; curved; falcanate(d); fastened; hamate; uncinate(d)

HOOP: **v.** clasp; embrace; encircle; enclose; ring; surround; HOOP: **n.** bail; band; belt; circlet; circumference; crinoline; encirclement; ring

HOOT: (**see** "hiss") boo; criticize; cry; denounce; fleer; gibe; honk; jeer; razz; scoff; twit

HOP: **v.** bounce; bound; caper; curvet; dance; frisk; gambol; go; halt; hobble; jump; leap; limp; rebound; scram; spring; HOP: **n.** bounce; bound; caper; circlet; dance; flight; frisk; gambol; journey; jump; leap; prom; rebound; spring; trip

HOPE: **v.** aim; anticipate; aspire; assay; await; bank; believe; bide; calculate; cherish; cogitate; conjecture; consider; contemplate; count; covet; crave; design; desire; dream; emulate; endeavor; envisage; essay; expect; feel; figure; forecast; foresee; guess; hunger; imagine; intend; long; pant; pine; plan; ponder; predict; prepare; propose; purpose; rely; ruminate; seek; sense; soar; speculate; strive; think; thirst; trust; want; wish; yearn; HOPE: **n.** (**see** "anticipation") aim; aspiration; belief; calculation; cogitation; confidence; conjecture; contemplation; design; desire; dream; enthusiasm; expectancy; expectation; faith; feeling; goal; guess; hungering; intention; optimism; plan; prediction; preparation; promise; prospect; reliance; *spes*; thirst; yearning; want; wish; HOPEFUL: auspicious; buoyant; confident; enthusiastic; euphoric; expectant; optimistic; promising; sanguine; utopian; HOPEFULNESS: buoyancy; confidence; enthusiasm; euphoria; expectancy; optimism; sanguinity; trust

HOPELESS: (**see** "despondent") abandoned; abject; crushed; despairful; despairing; desperate; despondent; dejected; downcast; dull; forlorn; futile; gloomy; glum; horizonless; immitigable; impossible; inconsolate; incorrigible; incurable; insoluble; irreclaimable; irretrievable; irrevocable; listless; lost; reckless; remediless; ruined; sad; sardonic; undone; vain; HOPELESSNESS: see "despair"

HORDE: **see** "crowd"

HORIZON: bound; compass; expanse; future; goal; limit; prospect; purview; radius; range; reach; scope; sweep; verge

HORIZONTAL: abed; aclinal; across; couchant; decubital; decumbent; even; flat; flush; general; level; linear; parallel; planate; plane; procumbent; prone; prostrate; recumbent; straight; supine

HORN: antler; beaker; bugle; casque; cornu-(copia); cusp; excrescence; glory; power; pride; prong; spike; spur; tine; trumpet; HORNLESS: acerous; dehorned; mul(l)ey; polled

HORRIFY: **see** "appall;" HORRIBLE *or* HORRID: abhorrent; abominable; alarming; appalling; awful; detestable; dire; disgusting; dread(ful); excruciating; execrable; fearful; formidible; frightful; ghastly; grim; grisly; gruesome; hateful; hideous; horrendous; horrific; loathsome; macabre; nameless; nasty; offensive; repugnant; repulsive; shocking; terrible; ugly; unpleasant; HORROR: abomination; alarm; aversion; awe; consternation; disgust; dismay; dread; fear; fright; grisliness; loathing; repugnance; repugnancy; shock; stupefaction; terror

HORSE: Arab; bay; beast; bidet; charger; cob; colt; courser; dobbin; equine; filly; foal; frame; gee-gee; gelding; hayburner; mare; mount; nag; pacer; palfrey; pinto; plug; pony; roan; stallion; stand; steed; support; trestle; trotter; HORSEMAN: cavalier; cavalryman; centaur; chevalier; dragoon; equestrian; equestrienne (fem.); jockey; rider; HORSEMANSHIP: equestrianism; equitation; *haut école*; manege

HOSPICE: asylum; hotel; imaret; inn; lodge; lodging;

HOSPITAL: clinic; lazarette; *maison de santé*; *maison-dieu*; sanitorium; workshop

HOSPITALITY: amicability; bonhommie; camaraderie; charm; cheer(fulness); congeniality; conviviality; cordiality; courtliness; courtesy; entertainment; favor; feast; festivity; food; friendliness; friendship; geniality; graciosity; graciousness; greeting; heartiness; hospitableness; kindness; lodging; neighborliness; receptivity; repast; salt; salutation; shelter; sociability; tenderness; treatment; warmth; welcome (mat); welcomeness; xenodochy; HOSPITABLE: amicable; attractive; bonhomous; cheerful; companionable; compassionate; compatible; congenial; consonant; convivial; cordial; courteous; festal; festive; friendly; gay; genial; gentle; gracious; gregarious; happy; heartfelt; hearty; invigorating; jolly; jovial; kind(ly); kindred; merry; neighborly; real; receptive; sociable; social; tender; vigorous; vital; warm; welcome

HOST: Amphitryon; army; boniface; crowd; entertainer; horde; innkeeper; landlord; legion; multitude; publican; sacrifice; server; treater; wafer

HOSTILE: adverse; aggressive; agonistic; antagonistic; antipathetic; argumentative; armigerous; assertive; averse; barbaric; barbarous; bellicose; belligerent; bristling; combative; contentious; contrary; disaffected; discontent(ed); discordant; disobedient; disputatious; feral; fierce; fireeating; forbidding; frigid; glacial; gladiatorial; hard; icy; ill(-mannered); inimicable; inimical; insubordinate; irate; irreconcilable; mad; malevolent; malign(ant); martial; militant; military; mutinous; opposing; oppositious; oppugnant; provocative; pugilistic; pugnacious; quarrelsome; rancorous; rebellious; repugnant; resentful; resistant; savage; scrappy; taurine; truculent; umbrageous; unassuageable; unfavoring; unfriendly; unpacific; unpleasant; vehement; virulent; warlike; HOSTILITY: action; affray; animosity; animus; antagonism; antipathy; attack; barbarism; barney; battle; bellicosity; belligerence; belligerency; bout; broil; brush; clash; cleavage; combat(iveness); combativity; conflict; contact; contest; contention; contrariness; controversy; disaffection; discontent; discord(ance); disobedience; dispute; duel; encounter; engagement; enmity; ferity; ferocity; feud; fight; fierceness; fracas; fray; free-for-all; friction; fury; hate; hatred; hostileness; ice; ill will; inimicalness; insubordination; irreconcilability; joust; melee; militancy; militantness; muss; opposition; pique; pugnacity; quarrel; rancor; rebellion; rencontre; resistance; riot; row; schism; scrap; scuffle; set-to; skirmish; strife; storm; struggle; test; tilt; truculency; umbrage; unfriendliness; vehemence; venom; virulence; war(fare)

HOT: (see "burning") ablaze; afire; angry; ardent; biting; blazing; burning; calescent; calid; candent; choleric; close; contraband; eager; excellent; excitable; excited; fervent; feverish; fierce; fiery; fired; flaming; fresh; glowing; good; hasty; heated; impetuous;

incalescent; incandescent; lecherous; lustful; passionate; peppery; popular; pungent; raging; red; sizzling; steamy; sultry; sweltering; thermal; thermic; torrid; tropical; unsafe; urgent; vehement; violent

HOTEL: caravansary; fonda; hospice; hostel(ry); imaret; inn; tavern; xenodochium

HOTHEAD: see "firebrand;" HOTHEADED: see "hasty" and "rash"

HOUND: v. afflict; annoy; badger; bait; bedog; chase; dog; drive; harass; harry; heckle; hector; persecute; pursue; ride; tail; track; trail; worry; HOUND: n. addict; basset; beagle; Cerberus; dog; wolf

HOUSE: v. (see "abide") board; chamber; confine; contain; cover; dwell; encase; enclose; harbor; hold; lodge; provide; secure; shelter; store; stow; HOUSE: n. abode; aerie; apartment; audience; billet; building; bungalow; business; cabin; casa; casino; castle; chalet; chateau; church; cote; cottage; dar; digs; domicile; dormitory; dwelling; establishment; eyrie; family; firm; flat; grange; habitation; hall; hogan; home(stead); hotel; housing; hovel; hut; hutch; igloo; inhabitance; inhabitancy; inhabitation; inn; joint; lineage; lodge; lodging; *maison*; mansion; nest; palace; partnership; quarters; residence; residency; roof; seat; shack; shelter; synagogue; tavern; teepee; temple; tenement; tent; theater; villa

HOUSEHOLD: family; house; menage

HOVEL: cabin; cottage; den; dugout; hut; hutch; lean-to; shack; shanty; shed; shelter; stack; tabernacle

HOVER: cower; crowd; flit; flutter; fly; hang; librate; linger; lurk; poise; suspend; swarm; wait; waver

HOWL: v. bark; bawl; bay; bellow; bellyache; complain; cry; lament; roar; shriek; ululate; wail; whimper; whine; yap; yell; yip; yowl; HOWL: n. complaint; cry; bellow(ing); bellyache; complaint; cry; lament; outcry; roar; shriek; ululation; wail; whimper; whine; yell; yip; yowl

HUB: (see "essence") axis; center; core; eye; focal point; focus; gist; heart; kernel; middle; nave; pith; pivot; spool

HUBBUB: (see "commotion") ado; agitation; Babelism; bedlam; brouhaha; chatter;

clamor; coil; confusion; din; flap; hubble-bubble; hue (and cry); hullabaloo; noise; outcry; tumult; turmoil; uproar

HUDDLE: **v.** assemble; bunch; collect; conceal; confer; cover; crouch; crowd; discuss; gather; group; hurry; jam; jumble; lump; press; HUDDLE: **n.** (**see** "group") bunch; clutch; collection; conference; confusion; crowd; disarray; discussion; disorder; gathering; jumble; lump; meeting; press

HUE: alarm; aspect; cast; clamor; color; complexion; cry; hubbub; outcry; shape; shout(ing); tincture; tinge; tint; tone

HUG: adhere; cherish; clasp; cling; clutch; congratulate; crush; cuddle; embosom; embrace; felicitate; hold; keep; mold; press; vine

HUGE: abnormal; ample; amplitudinous; astronomical; banging; behemothian; boundless; Brobdi(n)gnagian; bulky; Bunyanesque; colossal; cyclopean; cyclopic; dinosauric; elephantine; enorm(ous); epic; expansive; extensive; extreme; galactic; gargantuan; giant(esque); gigantic; great; Herculean; heroic(al); Homeric; immeasurable; immense; imposing; inordinate; Jovian; king-size(d); large; leviathan; limitless; macroscopic; magnitudinous; mammoth; massive; mastodonic; monstrous; monumental; mountainous; oceanic; Olympian; phenomenal; polyphemian; polyphemic; polyphemous; ponderous; prodigious; pyramidal; pythonic; stratospheric(al); stupendous; titanic; tremendous; unbounded; unlimited; vast; whopping; HUGENESS: amplitude; colossality; enormity; giganticness; gigantism; immensity; indefinitude; magnitude; massiveness; massivity; monstrosity; prodigality; vastity

HULLABALOO: **see** "din"

HUM: **v.** bombinate; buzz; croon; drone; murmur; purr; ring; rush; sing; speed; susurrate; whir; whirl; whiz; zoom; HUM: **n.** bombination; buzz; confusion; dart; din; disturbance; drone; murmur; noise; ring; rumor; rush; speed; susurration; tune; turmoil; whirl; whir(r); whiz; zoom; HUMMING: active; agitated; booming; brisk; busy; buzzing; crooning; droning; extraordinary; murmuring; purring; ringing; rushing; seething; singing; speeding; speedy; spirited; strong; teeming; whirling; whirring; whizzing; working; zooming

HUMAN: **a.** (**see** "humane") anthropoid(al);

anthropomorphic; anthropopathic; compassionate; earthborn; enigmatic(al); erratic; fallible; finite; kind; merciful; mortal; mundane; sociable; social; sympathetic; tender; unangelic; worldly; HUMAN: **n.** Adamite; anthropoid; being; biped; boy; child; creature; earthling; girl; hominid; Hominidae (pl.); Homo; *Homo sapiens*; individual; man(kind); mortal; person; soul; woman

HUMANE: benevolent; benign(ant); charitable; clement; compassionate; considerate; cultural; forgiving; gentle; gracious; human(istic); humanitarian; humble; indulgent; kind(hearted); merciful; mild; lenient; philanthropic; pitying; polite; sociable; sympathetic; tender; tolerant; understanding; warm(hearted)

HUMANITARIAN: **see** "benevolent" and "philanthropist"

HUMANITY: (**see** "man" and "mankind") anthropopathy; benevolence; compassion; flesh; kindness; life; multitude; people(s); race; society; species; world

HUMANIZE: anthropomorphize; civilize; educate; incarnate; personify; refine; soften; HUMANIZATION: anthropomorphism; civilization; education; embodiment; incarnation; personification; refinement

HUMBLE: **v.** (**see** "belittle") abase; bow; chagrin; chasten; correct; debase; degrade; demean; demit; denigrate; depress; disgrace; dishonor; embarrass; humiliate; hurt; kowtow; lower; minify; mortify; punish; reduce; restrain; shame; snub; squelch; stoop; subdue; submit; tame; temper; HUMBLE(D): **a.** abased; abject; base; bashful; bowed; bruised; chagrined; chastened; chastised; corrected; coy; debased; degraded; demeaned; denigrated; disgraced; dishonored; docile; embarrassed; forbearing; gentle; genuflectory; honest; human; humiliated; hurt; inferior; insignificant; low(ly); mean; meek; mild; modest; mortified; obscured; penitent; poor; punished; reduced; repentant; reserved; restrained; retiring; reverent; self-effacing; self-possessing; shamed; shrinking; shy; simple; small; sober; squelched; subdued; submissive; tame(d); timid; unassuming; unennobled; unostentatious; unpretentious; unyielding

HUMBUG: **v. see** "cheat;" HUMBUG: **n.** *blague*; bosh; chicanery; deception; drivel; flummery; fraud; hoax; hypocrisy; hypocrite;

impostor; imposture; nonsense; pettifoggery; pretense; pretension; quack(ery); sham

HUMDRUM: boring; common(place); daily; dull; everyday; irksome; listless; monotonous; prosaic(al); prosy; routine; tedious; tiring; trifling; uninteresting; wearisome; weary; workaday

HUMID: damp; dank; hot; moist; soggy; sweltering; vaporous; warm; wet

HUMILIATE: (see "humble") abash; insult; lower; mortify; reduce; scalp; shame; slap; snub; squelch; HUMILIATING: degrading; humbling; humiliative; ignominious; infamous; mortifying; scandalous; shameful; vile; HUMILIATION: abasement; abjection; chagrin; chastenment; chastisement; debasement; degradation; dejection; discourtesy; dust; embarrassment; humble pie; ignominy; indignity; infamy; insult; mortification; outrage; scandal; shame; slap; slight; snub; HUMILITY: (see "deference") abjection; abnegation; humbleness; lowliness; loyalty; meekness; modesty; restraint; self-denial; submission; submissiveness; surrender

HUMOR: **v.** baby; banter; caress; cater; coddle; delight; favor; fondle; gratify; indulge; jest; joke; pamper; pet; placate; please; quip; satiate; satisfy; soothe; spoil; tickle; HUMOR: **n.** badinage; banter; blood; caprice; chaff; comedy; comicality; comicalness; cruor; delight; disposition; drollery; drollness; fancy; farce; farcicality; fluid(s); freak; fun; inclination; jest(ing); jocosity; jocularity; joke; joviality; merriment; mood; piquancy; pleasantry; pungency; quip; quirk; raillery; salt(iness); sap; satire; slap stick; temper(ament); vagary; waggery; whim(sicality); wit; HUMORIST: card; clown; comic; comique; *farceur*; *farceuse* (fem.); joker; jokester; prank(ster); raconteur; raconteuse (fem.); wag; HUMOROUS: Aristophanic; comic(al); droll; dry; facetious; Falstaffian; farcical; funny; humoristic; jocose; jocular; jovial; laughable; ludicrous; mirthful; Pantagruelian; Pantagruelic; piquant; playful; puckish; pungent; Rabelaisian; risible; salty; satirical; sportive; waggish; whimsical; witty; wry; HUMOROUSNESS: *espièglerie*; fun; jocularity; joviality; ludicrousness; mirth; satire; waggishness; whimsicality; wit; HUMORLESS: (see "sad" and "serious") unmirthful

HUNCH: **see** "premonition"

HUNGER: **v.** covet; crave; famish; greed; hanker; long; pine; starve; thirst; yearn; HUNGER: **n.** acoria; appetite; bulimia; covetousness; craving; desire; edacity; esurience; famine; greed; gulosity; hankering; hyperorexia; lack; longing; need; thirst; voracity; yearning; HUNGRY: avid; barren; covetous; craving; eager; edacious; esurient; famished; gluttonous; greedy; insatiable; poor; rapacious; ravening; ravenous; starved; unfed; voracious

HUNT: **v.** chase; dig; dog; drive; ferret; find; follow; harry; hound; inquire; investigate; persecute; poach; probe; pry; pursue; research; scavenge; scour; scout; scrounge; search; seek; shoot; shop; stalk; track; trail; trap; uncover; HUNT: **n.** (the) chase; hunting; inquiry; investigation; persecution; probe; pursuit; quest; research; search; venation; HUNTER: Actaeon; chasseur; dog; gun; hound; huntsman; ja(e)ger; Nimrod; Orion; scavenger; searcher

HURL: cast; catapult; drive; fire; fling; hurtle; impel; launch; pelt; pitch; precipitate; rush; sling; throw; thrust; toss; whirl

HURRY: **v.** (see "hasten") accelerate; agitate; chase; crowd; dash; dispatch; drive; excite; expedite; flee; force; hie; hotfoot; hustle; impel; move; peg; pelt; post; press; quicken; race; run; rush; scurry; speed; spur; stave; tear; HURRY: **n.** (see "haste") acceleration; ado; agitation; celerity; commotion; disturbance; excitement; jump; precipitance; press; quickness; rush; tear; trot; tumult

HURT: **v.** (see "harm") abuse; ache; afflict; bruise; crush; cut; damage; deteriorate; distress; grieve; humble; ill-treat; impair; injure; lacerate; maim; maltreat; mar; maul; offend; oppress; pain; penalize; prejudice; punish; rupture; smite; spoil; suffer; tear; weaken; wound; wrong; HURT: **a.** bruised; contused; damaged; disabled; distressed; grieved; harmed; humbled; impaired; injured; lacerated; maimed; marred; mauled; offended; oppressed; pained; ruptured; smitten; spoiled; torn; weakened; wounded; wronged; HURT: **n.** abuse; accident; ache; affliction; bane; blow; bruise; crush; cut; damage; deterioration; detriment; disadvantage; dolor; grief; harm; ill-treatment; impairment; injury; laceration; lesion; maltreatment; offense; oppression; pain; pang; resentment; rupture; sore; stroke; suffering; tear; wound; wrong; HURTFUL: (see "harmful") atrocious; baleful; baneful; damaging; deleterious; destructive; detrimental; flagrant; grievous; heinous; inimical;

injurious; killing; malevolent; malign(ant); nocent; nocuous; noisome; noxious; painful; pernicious; poisonous; toxic; traumatic; unhealthful; unhealthy; venomous

HUSBAND: **v.** conserve; cultivate; economize; hoard; manage; save; store; HUSBAND: **n.** consort; hoarder; man; mate; partner; *père*; spouse; HUSBANDRY: agriculture; cultivation; culture; farming; frugality; geoponics; management; thrift

HUSH: allay; appease; calm; console; ease; lull; mollify; pacify; quell; quiet(en); repress; settle; sh(ush); silence; soothe; still; suppress; tranquilize; HUSHED: calm; confidential; discreet; gentle; hidden; low; secret; soothing; still; suppressed

HUSK: **v.** bark; harvest; hull; peel; scale; shell; shuck; skin; strip; HUSK: **n.** bark; bract; bran; chaff; cover(ing); envelope; framework; glume(s); hull(s); leam; peel; pod; rind; scale; scurf; shell; shuck; skin; strippings

HUSKY: athletic; brawny; bulky; burly; dry; fat; fleshy; guttural; hardy; harsh; heavy; hoarse; muscular; obese; raucous; robust(ious); rough; stout; strong; sturdy; tall; thick; vigorous; weighty

HUSSY: bag(gage); doxy; jade; Jezebel; minx; quean; slut; trollop; wench

HUSTLE: **see** "hurry;" HUSTLER: ball of fire; fireball; go-getter; hotshot; live wire; prostitute; pusher

HYGIENE: cleanliness; health(iness); prophylaxis; salubrity; sanitation; sterility; HYGIENIC(AL): (**see** "clean") healthful; healthy; prophylactic; salubrious; sanitary; salutary; sterile; therapeutic(al);

HYMN: anthem; canon; canticle; doxology; lyric; ode; magnificat; paean; psalm; song; *Te Deum*; theody

HYPNOTIZE: allure; attract; charm; deaden; entice; entrance; mesmerize; seduce; HYPNOTIC: (**see** "enticing") cataleptic; comatose; lethargic; mesmeric; sleepy; somniferous; soporific

HYPOCRISY: (**see** "deceit") affectation; cant; deception; dissimulation; duplicity; falseness; falsity; guile; imitation; Pharisaism; pietism; piosity; pretense; pretension; religiosity; sanctimoniousness; sanctimony; self-righteousness; sham; simulation; speciosity; Tartuffery; HYPOCRITE: cheat(er); deceiver; dissembler; dissimulator; impostor; Pecksniff; pretender; Tartuffe; HYPOCRITICAL: canting; dishonest; dissembling; dissimulative; false; Pecksniffian; pretentious; religiose; sanctimonious; specious; Tartuffian

HYPOTHECATE: hypothesize; mortgage; pawn; pledge

HYPOTHESIS: assumption; conception; conjecture; divination; guess; if; inference; postulate; postulation; proposal; proposition; scheme; supposition; surmise; system; theorem; theorum; theory; thesis; HYPOTHETICAL: (**see** "theoretical") assume conditional; conjectural; contingent; hypothesized; ideal; imaginary; impracticable; impractical; inferred; postulative; putative; suppositional; supposititious

HYSTERIA: anxiety; delirium; fear; frenzy; mania; nerves; nervousness; neurosis; phobia; vapors; HYSTERICAL: convulsive; emotional; fearful; fitful; maniac(al); nervous; neurotic; rabid; spasmodic; unrestrained; wild

I

ICARIAN: (see "daring") foolhardy; foolish; idiotic; inadequate; rash; unsafe

ICE: crystal; diamonds; floe; frost; gem; glacier; hostility; jewelry; reserve; rime; sherbert; ICY: see "frigid"

ICTUS: accent; attack; beat; blow; bruise; contusion; pulsation; pulse; rhythm; stress; stroke

IDEA: abstraction; aim; belief; conceit; concept(ion); design; *donnée*; egg; fancy; fantasy; fixation; form; ideal: image; imagination; impression; inkling; intent(ion); invention; model; motif; notation; notion; opinion; pattern; percept(ion); philosophy; phrase; plan; point; project; proposal; proposition; purpose; reflection; scheme; standard; statement; supposition; tenet; theme; theorem; theory; thought; vapor; view; wrinkle

IDEAL: **a.** abstract; archetypal; celestial; complete; conceptual; consummate; delightful; dreamy; excellent; exemplary; faultless; fitting; heavenly; hypothetical; ideational; imaginary; immaculate; impractical; intellectual; mental; model; original; perfect; pleasing; prototypal; quadrate; real; standard; supreme; true; unearthly; utopian; visionary; IDEAL: **n.** aim; archetype; beauty; dream; excellence; exemplar; goal; hero; idea; idol; masterpiece; model; nonesuch; nonpareil; norm; original; paladin; paragon; pattern; perfection; phoenix; principle; prototype; purpose; standard; type; IDEALISTIC: aerial; altitudinarian; chimerical; doctrinaire; messianic; paradisiac(al); paradisic(al); Platonic; Platonistic; poetic(al); quixotic(al); romantic; sentimental; unattainable; utopian; visionary; IDEALIST: altitudinarian; avant-gardist(e); Don Quixote; dreamer; romanticist; sentimentalist; utopian; visionary; IDEALIZATION: apotheosis; canonization; deification; spiritualization; IDEALIZE: (see "idolize") apotheosize; canonize; deify; pedestal; spiritualize; worship

IDEATE: (see "think") conceive; dream; invent; preconceive; prefigure

IDENTIC(AL): alike; coincident; concomitant; congruent; equal; equivalent; indistinguishable; isonomous; like; same; selfsame; synonymous; tantamount; twin; uniform; IDENTITY *or* IDENTICALITY: continuum; equivalence; identicalness; selfsameness; synonymity

IDENTIFY: (see "recognize") associate; brand; classify; describe; determine; diagnosticate; discover; distinguish; establish; finger; join; label; mark; nail; name; peg; perceive; place; prove; recognize; see; show; spot; symbolize; tag; IDENTIFICATION: brand; fingerprint; label; mark; photo(graph); recognition; signature; tag; trademark

IDEOLOGY: ism; philosophy; sensationalism; speculation; tenet; theorizing; theory; *Weltanschauung*

IDIOCY: (see "imbecility") amentia; anoesia; derangement; fatuity; folly; foolishness; idiotry; insanity; irrationality; lunacy; mania; mongolism; moronity; senselessness; stupidity

IDIOM: argot; cant; colloquialism; construction; dialect; language; parlance; patois; phrase; speech; style; tongue; vernacular

IDIOSYNCRASY: (see "eccentricity") oddity; way; whim(sicality)

IDIOT: ament; blockhead; booby; cretin; dotard; dunce; fool; imbecile; jester; moron; simpleton; IDIOTIC: cretinous; foolish; Icarian; imbecilic; *impos animi*; lunatic(al); mad; moronic; senseless; simple; stupid

IDLE: **v.** dawdle; drone; fool; gammer; goof; lag; laze; loaf; loiter; moon; sleep; slumber; squander; trifle; waste; IDLE: **a.** aimless; arrested; barren; calm; casual; comatose; dead; defunct; delinquent; *désoeuvré*; dormant; dreamy; empty; *fainéant*; fallow;

fruitless; futile; groundless; hollow; inactive; inanimate; indolent; ineffectual; inert; inoperative; jobless; laborless; lackadaisical; lazy; *le bras croisés*; lethargic; lifeless; light; listless; nonfunctioning; obsolete; off; otiant; otiose; out-of-work; petty; quiescent; quiet; resting; retired; sedentary; shiftless; silent; slothful; sluggish; sorning; stagnant; standing; still; superficial; superfluous; supine; torpid; trifling; trivial; truant; unbusy; unemployed; unoccupied; unplowed; unproductive; unprofitable; unresponsive; untilled; unused; unworking; useless; vacant; vacuous; vain; void; wasted; withdrawn; worthless; IDLENESS **or** IDLING: aimlessness; disoccupation; *flânerie*; folly; idlesse; ignavia; inaction; inactivity; indolence; leisure; otiosity; rust; sedentation; sloth; triviality; unemployment; vanity; IDLER: (**see** "loafer") *badaud*; dawdler; drone; *fainéant*; *flâneur*; *flâneuse* (fem.); fool; laggard; loiterer; lounger; sluggard; trifler; unemployed; vagrant

IDOL: adonis; beloved; cosset; darling; dear; deity; demigod(dess); effigy; emblem; fallacy; favorite; fetish; god(dess); hero; icon; image(ry); lion; loved; *mignon*; minion; partisan; *persona grata*; pet; phantom; standby; star; statue; symbol; teraph; toady; IDOLATER: admirer; adorer; Baalite; heathen; pagan; worshiper; IDOLIZE: admire; adore; apotheosize; canonize; cherish; deify; esteem; honor; idolatrize; love; pedestal; prize; revere; spiritualize; stellify; venerate; worship

IDYL(L): bucolic; eclogue; Eden; georgic; pastoral; poem

IGNOBLE: (**see** "bad") abject; atrocious; base; coarse; contemptible; cowardly; debased; despicable; dishonorable; execrable; flagrant; heinous; humble; immodest; impolite; indecent; infamous; low; mean; petty; plebeian; servile; shameful; sordid; unworthy; vile; vulgar; wicked

IGNITE: (**see** "kindle") detonate

IGNOMINY: (**see** "dishonor") disgrace; infamy; obloquy; odium; scandal; shame; IGNOMINIOUS: (**see** "bad" and "ignoble") atrocious; coarse; contemptible; cowardly; degraded; degrading; depraved; despicable; disgraceful; dishonorable; execrable; flagrant; heinous; humiliating; immodest; indecent; infamous; scandalous; shameful; vulgar; wicked

IGNORAMUS: dolt; duffer; dunce; idiot; moron; nincompoop; nitwit; numbskull; sciolist

IGNORANT: agnostic; analphabetic; artless; backward; barbaric; barbarous; benighted; callow; cloddish; crude; dense; green; gross; guileless; illiterate; immature; incognoscible; incompetent; inerudite; inexperienced; inexpert; innocent; inscient; lacking; lowbrow; nescient; primitive; raw; rude; simple; stupid; thick; unacquainted; unaware; unbookish; uncultured; unedified; uneducated; unenlightened; unfledged; ungrounded; uninformed; uninitiated; uninstructed; unintellectual; unintelligent; unlearned; unlettered; unliterate; unschooled; unseasoned; unskilled; unsmart; unsophisticated; untaught; untrained; untried; untutored; unversed; unwise; IGNORANCE: agnosticism; backwardness; barbarism; barbarity; benightedness; *bêtise*; blindness; crassitude; crudity; ignorantism; ignorasion; illiteracy; innocence; inscience; nescience; obscurantism; primitivity; rusticity; sciolism; simplicity; stolidity; stupidity; unacquaintance; unculture; unintelligence; unwisdom

IGNORE: boycott; cut; disobey; disregard; elide; eliminate; evade; forget; miss; neglect; omit; overlook; reject; slight; snoot; snub; unheed; wink

ILK: breed; character; class; family; genus; kidney; kind; nature; sort; stripe; type

ILL: abed; adverse; aeger; ailing; *à la mort*; amort; bad; boorish; cachectic; cachexic; cantankerous; complaining; crude; cruel; defective; diseased; diseaseful; disordered; distempered; evil; failing; faulty; feeble; fevered; feverish; grumpy; hard; harmful; harsh; hostile; hurtful; impaired; improper; inauspicious; inconvenient; indisposed; inferior; infirm; inimicable; irritable; leprous; maladive; morbid; morbific(al); morbose; nauseated; pale; pallid; pernicious; phthisic; pointless; poor(ly); puny; sallow; sick(ly); suffering; surly; troublesome; tubercular; unfavorable; unfortunate; unfriendly; unhealthful; unhealthy; unlucky; unpolished; unpropitious; unsound; untoward; unwell; unwholesome; upset; valetudinarian; wan; weak; wicked; wrong; ILLNESS: (**see** "disease") disability; hurt; impairment; indisposition; malady; sickness; suffering

ILLEGAL: adulterine; contraband; criminal; crooked; illegitimate; illicit; irregular; misbegotten; nonlegal; nugatory; prohibited; unauthorized; unconstitutional; unlawful; unlegal; unlicensed; unsound; ILLEGITIMATE: bastard; counterfeit; debased; erratic; false; fatherless; illegal; illogical; irregular; misbegotten; mongrel; spurious; supposititious; under-the-counter; unfathered; unlawful; unnatural; unwarranted; wildcat

ILLEGIBLE: undecipherable; unreadable

ILL-HUMORED: cantankerous; captious; caustic; churlish; contentious; crabby; cranky; cross; curmudgeonish; curmudgeonly; displeased; disputatious; gloomy; glum; ill-tempered; irascible; irritable; melancholic; melancholy; nasty; peeved; pettish; petulant; piqued; pugnacious; querulous; ratty; sad; shrewish; splenetic; sullen; surly; temperamental; testy; unsociable; waspish; ILL HUMOR: anger; animus; bile; enmity; illwill; irascibility; ire; irritability; malice; melancholia; melancholy; pettiness; petulance; rancor; sadness; spite; spleen

ILLIBERAL: avaricious; close; greedy; grudging; ignoble; insular; intolerant; limited; myopic; narrow(-minded); parsimonious; petty; prehensile; prejudiced; restricted; stingy; ungenerous; ungiving

ILLICIT: (see "clandestine" and "illegal") under-the-counter; unlawful

ILLITERATE: a. (see "ignorant") analphabetic; inerudite; nescient; uncultured; uneducated; unlearned; unlettered; untaught; ILLITERATE: n. analphabet(ic); ignoramus; nescient; nincompoop; sciolist

ILL-MANNERED: (see "uncivil") coarse; ill-bred

ILLNESS: see under "ill"

ILLOGICAL: acategorical; ambivalent; crazy; demented; equivocal; fallacious; incoherent; incongruent; incongruous; inconsequent; inconsistent; mad; nonlogical; parabolical; paralogical; paralogistic; rambling; specious; spurious; unlogical; unreasonable; unsound; ILLOGICALITY: illogic; incoherence; incoherency; inconsequence; irrelevance; irrelevancy; paralogism; unreasonableness; unsoundness

ILL-TEMPERED: see "ill-humored"

ILLUMINATE: brighten; clarify; decorate; elucidate; emblaze; emblazon; enlighten; explain; fire; highlight; illume; illustrate; instruct; kindle; light(en); ILLUMINATING: bright; clarifying; clear; enlightening; explanatory; fluorescent; incandescent; informative; instructive; light; luminescent; luminiferous; luminous; ILLUMINATION: (see "brightness") enlightenment

ILLUSION: anamorphosis; apparition; chimera; deception; delusion; dream; error; fallacy; fancy; fantasy; *fata morgana*; ghost; hallucination; hallucinosis; *ignis fatuus*; mirage; misapprehension; misconception; mistake; mockery; phantasmata; phantasy; phantom; prestidigitation; rainbow; revenant; sham; specter; spectrum; spirit; vision; ILLUSIVE *or* ILLUSORY: apparent; apparitional; Barmecidal; chimerical; deceptive; diaphanous; dreamy; elusory; ethereal; fanciful; fatuitous; fictitious; foggy; ghostly; illusional; illusionary; illusionistic; imaginary; phantasmagoric(al); phantasmal; phantasmic; phantom; prestidigitatorial; prestidigitatory; spectral; subjective; unreal; visionary

ILLUSTRATE: (see "explain") adorn; arrange; beautify; clarify; delineate; demonstrate; depict; design; display; elucidate; exemplify; exhibit; fashion; imitate; limn; mirror; model; picture; pose; represent; shape; show; sketch; typify; ILLUSTRATION: archetype; arrangement; beau ideal; blueprint; case; clarification; comparison; copy; counterpart; criterion; cut; delineation; demonstration; depiction; depictment; design; diagram; display; drawing; ectype; engraving; example; exemplar; exemplum; explanation; facsimile; figure; form; gauge; ideal; instance; likeness; mannikin; microcosm; mirror; mold; monument; norm; original; outline; paradigm; paragon; pattern; photo(graph); picture; print; sample; simile; sketch; source; specimen; standard; swatch; type; ILLUTRATIVE: *or* ILLUSTRATIONAL: delineative; demonstrative; descriptive; descriptory; exemplary; explanatory; pictorial; picturesque; representative; typical

ILLUSTRIOUS: (see "eminent") august; brilliant; celebrated; conspicuous; dignified; distinguished; exalted; famed; famous; far-famed; formidable; glorified; glorious; great; honored; honorific; immortal; lucent; lustrous; magnific(al); magnificent; majestic; noble; notable; noted; outstanding; prestigious; redoubtable; regal; renowned; respected; resplendent; signal; splendent; splendid; star; superior; superlative; transcendent

IMAGE: (see "figure") alter ego; apparition; appearance; concept(ion); copy; counterpart; depiction; depictment; description; device; drawing; dream; effigy; eidolon; emblem; facsimile; fancy; figment; form; icon; ideal; idol; imagery; imago; impression; incarnation; likeness; metaphor; mold; notion; orant; pattern; perception; phantasm(agoria); phantom; photo(graph); picture; portrait; replica; representation; resemblance; sculpture; semblance; shadow; shape; silhouette; simile; similitude; simulacrum; specter; statue; tableau; teraph; trope

IMAGINE: apprehend; assume; believe; conceive; conjecture; conjure; create; daydream; deem; depict; depicture; desire; dream; fabricate; fancy; fantasize; fictionalize; foretell; form(alize); formulate; guess; hallucinate; ideate; invent; long; meditate; moon; muse; mythologize; opine; picture; plan; presume; prophesy; romance; romanticize; scheme; suppose; surmise; suspect; think; visualize; ween; yearn; IMAGINATION: aim; apparition; assumption; belief; chimera; concept(ion); daydream; deception; delusion; desire; dream; fallacy; fancy; fantasia; fantasticality; fantasy; fiction; genius; goal; hallucination; idea(l); ideality; illusion; image; impression; ingenuity; muse; notion; phantasm; phantasmata (pl.); phantasy; plan; plot; purpose; resourcefulness; revery; romance; scheme; suspicion; thought; trance; unreality; vagary; vision; whim(sey); whimsicality; wit; IMAGINATIVE: (see "creative") allegorical; allusive; anagogical; daring; dreamy; false; fantastic; figurative; fresh; hallucinatory; ideal; ingenuous; inventive; metaphoric(al); new; novel; original; poetic(al); resourceful; unreal; visionary; vivid; witty; wool-gathering; IMAGINARY: absurd; apocryphal; apparitional; bizarre; capricious; chimerical; cloud-built; dreamy; ethereal; false; fancied; fanciful; fantastic(al); fictitious; fictive; grotesque; hallucinative; hallucinatory; hypothetical; ideal(istic); ideational; illusive; illusory; imaginative; in nubilus; insubstantial; legendary; mythical; odd; poetic(al); queer; quixotic(al); romantic; simulated; supposititious; unreal(istic); unsubstantial; utopian; vaporous; veritable; visionary; whimsical

IMBALANCE: see "unbalance"

IMBECILE a. or IMBECILIC: childish; cretinoid; cretinous; demented; deranged; fatuous; foolish; idiotic; impos animi; inane; moronic; nonsensical; senile; silly; stupid; witless; IMBECILE: n. (see "idiot") cretin; dotard; fool; moron; IMBECILITY: amentia; anoesia; cretinism; dementia; derangement; dullness; fatuity; foolishness; hebetude; idiocy; idiotry; inability; ineptitude; insanity; irrationality; lunacy; mania; mongolism; moronity; senility; senselessness; stupidity; weakness; witlessness

IMBIBE: absorb; assimilate; consume; drink; imbue; inhale; osmose; receive; retain; soak; sop; steep

IMBROGLIO: (see "difficulty") brouhaha; cabal; complication; conglomeration; controversy; embarrassment; embroilment; entanglement; flap; intrigue; misunderstanding; plot; set-to; strife; tangle

IMBRUE: defile; drench; implicate; macerate; moisten; soak; sop; stain; steep; wet

IMBUE: animate; color; dye; fire; impregnate; infuse; ingrain; inspire; penetrate; permeate; pervade; saturate; stain; steep; suffuse; tincture; tinge; tint

IMITATE: act; adopt; answer; ape; assume; burlesque; caricature; classicalize; clown; compete; contend; copy; counterfeit; deceive; delude; echo; emulate; exemplify; fake; fashion; feign; fleer; flout; follow; forge; gibe; impersonate; iterate; jape; jeer; jest; lampoon; match; mime; mimic; mock; model; parody; parrot; pattern; personate; personify; play; pose; pretend; quote; reflect; repeat; repercuss; replicate; reply; reproduce; resemble; resound; respond; ridicule; satirize; scoff; scorn; scout; sham; simulate; sneer; spoof; sport; taunt; travesty; vie; IMITATION: apism; artificiality; asteism; badinage; banter; bogus; burlesque; caricature; chaff (ing); contempt; copy(cat); counterfeit; deception; delusion; derision; disregard; duplicate; duplication; echo(ism); emulation; fake(ry); farce; forgery; futility; imitant; imposter; imposture; irony; jeer; jest; lampoon; mimesis; mimicry; mockery; model; parody; pattern; persiflage; postiche; pretense; raillery; repetition; replica; reproduction; sarcasm; satire; scorn; servility; sham; simulacrum; simulation; skit; spoor; sport; travesty; IMITATIVE: (see "mock") counterfeit; derivative; echoic; emulatory; emulous; epigonic; epigonous; false; feigned; imitation(al); incestuous; mimetic; monkey see, monkey do; onomatopoe(t)ic; pretended; pseudo; quasi; sequacious; servile; sham; simulated; slavish; spurious; IMITATOR: (see "imposter") copier; copycat; copyist; emulator; epigone; impressionist; mimic; mocker; monkey; plagiarist; pretender; pseudo; sham; simulator

IMMACULATE: (see "clean") blotless; grimeless; impeccable; pure; sinless; snow-white; spotless; stainless; undefiled; unsinful; unsullied

IMMANENT: dangerous; indwelling; inherent; internal; intrinsic; living; pending; subjective

IMMATERIAL: airy; apparitional; asomatous; celestial; diaphanous; disembodied; ephemeral; ethereal; etheric; extraneous; extrinsic; foreign; gossamer(y); heterogeneous; illusionary; impertinent; inapplicable; inappropriate; incompetent; inconsequent(ial); incorporeal; indifferent; insubstantial; irrelevant; matterless; mental; spiritual; substanceless; tangential; transcendent; transient; unessential; unimportant; unrelated; IMMATERIALITY: diaphaneity; ephemerality; ethereality; incorporeality; incorporeity; indifference; insubstantiality; irrelevancy; unimportance

IMMATURE: amorphous; babyish; boyish; callow; childish; credulous; crude; feeble; fledgling; foolish; green; imperfect; impubic; inadequate; inchoate; incomplete; inexperienced; infantile; infantilistic; infantine; jejune; juvenile; naive; namby-pamby; nouveau; pantywaist; petty; precocious; raw; silly; simple; small; tender; trivial; undeveloped; unfinished; unformed; unformulated; unripe; unseasoned; young; youthful; IMMATURITY: callousness; callowness; childhood; childishness; crudeness; crudity; imperfection; incunabulum; infancy; infantility; juniority; juvenility; nonage; precosity; puerilism; puerility; rawness; unripeness verdancy; youth(fulness)

IMMEASURABLE: abysmal; bottomless; illimitable; immensurable; incommensurable; infinite; unfathomable; vast

IMMEDIATE(LY): abrupt(ly); close; direct(ly); first; forthwith; instant(ly); instantaneous(ly); instanter; near(est); next; now;

posthaste; present(ly); presto; prompt(ly); proximate(ly); speedily; speedy; straightway; sudden(ly); *tout de suite*; undelayed; IMMEDIACY: close quarters; contiguity; directness; instantaneity; proximity

IMMEMORIAL: (see "ancient") dateless; hoary; immemorable; old; primeval; timeless

IMMENSE: (see "huge") astronomical; big; boundless; colossal; elephantine; enorm(ous); excellent; fat; fine; giant; gigantic; good; great; inconceivable; infinite; large; magnitudinous; mammoth; mastodonic; measureless; monstrous; prodigious; stupendous; titanic; tremendous; vast; wide; IMMENSITY: colossality; enormity; greatness; hugeness; immeasurability; immenseness; indefinitude; magnitude; vastitude; vastity; vastness

IMMERSE: absorb; baptize; bathe; bury; cover; dip; dissolve; dive; douse; drench; drown; duck; dunk; embed; engage; engross; engulf; include; infuse; involve; overwhelm; plunge; sink; soak; souse; submerge

IMMINENT: (see "impending" and "ominous") proximate

IMMOBILE: attached; dormant; fast(ened); firm; fixed; frozen; hardened; immobilized; immovable; impassive; implanted; inflexible; motionless; moveless; permanent; relaxed; rigid; rooted; sessile; set; solid; stabilized; stable; stationary; steadfast; stolid; unalterable; unchanging; unmoving; unshiftable; unyielding; IMMOBILIZE: see "stiffen"

IMMODERATE: biased; bigoted; bizarre; boundless; copious; dissipated; doctrinaire; drunk(en); eccentric; exaggerated; excessive; exorbitant; extravagant; extreme; fierce; free; gluttonous; incontinent; inordinate; intemperate; intensive; *outré*; overweening; severe; uncontrollable; unmeasurable; unreasonable; violent; IMMODERATION: copiosity; copiousness; drunkenness; eccentricity; excess(iveness); extravagance; ferocity; gluttony; gulosity; immoderateness; inclemency; incontinency; inordinacy; insobriety; intemperance; severity; unrestraint

IMMODEST: bold; brassy; brazen; coarse; forward; *grivois*; immoral; impudent; indecent; indecorous; indelicate; licentious; nervy; offensive; presumptuous; sassy; saucy; shameless; unabashed; unbashful; uninhibited; unmodest; unrefined; unreserved; unrestrained; unseemly; unshy; IMMODESTY: audacity; boldness; brass(iness); brazenness; cheek; coarseness; daring; effrontery; forwardness; gall; guts; impropriety; impudence; impudicity; indecency; indecorum; indelicacy; nerve; offense; offensiveness; presumption; sassiness; sauciness; shamelessness; temerity; unchastity; unmodesty; unreserve; unrestraint; unseemliness; unshyness

IMMORAL: adulterous; amoral; bad; carnal; corrupt; depraved; dissolute; evil; fleshy; impure; indecent; lecherous; leprous; lewd; libidinous; licentious; loose; lustful; nonmoral; nonprincipled; obscene; pornographic; profligate; salacious; sensual; sinful; slippery; unchaste; unedifying; unmoral; unprincipled; unsavory; unvirtuous; vile; virtueless; wanton; wicked; wrong; IMMORALITY: (see "evil" and "vice") adultery; corruption; depravity; impurity; indecency; lewdness; licentiousness; lust; obscenity; pornography

IMMORTAL: abiding; ambrosial; celebrated; constant; divine; endless; enduring; eternal; forever; imperishable; infinite; lasting; perpetual; undecomposable; undying; unfading; unperishable; unperishing; IMMORTALITY: athanasia; constancy; divinity; endlessness; eternality; eternity; fame; imperishability; infinitude; perpetuality; perpetuity

IMMOVABLE: (see "immobile") adamant(ine); changeless; fast(ened); firm; fixed; immotive; implanted; inexorable; obdurate; obstinate; relentless; rooted; sessile; solid stationary; steadfast; stiff; stubborn; unalterable; unassailable; unshiftable; unyielding

IMMUNIZE: exempt; free; protect; save; sterilize; vaccinate; IMMUNE: exempt; free; guarded; impregnable; invincible; invulnerable; protected; refractory; resistant; safe; IMMUNITY: clearance; dispensation; exemption; exoneration; franchise; freedom; immunization; license; neutrality; prerogative; privilege; prophylactic; prophylaxis; protection; refractoriness; resistance; respite; sanctuary; vaccination

IMMURE: bar; cloister; closet; confine; enisle; entomb; imprison; incarcerate; intern; isolate; jail; limit; seclude; segregate; wall

IMMUTABLE: changeless; constant; divine; eternal; firm; fixed; invariable; permanent;

stable; unalterable; unchangeable; unchanging

IMP: brat; demon; devil; elf; fairy; fay; gamin; gremlin; hobgoblin; peri; pixie; sprite; urchin

IMPACT: blow; brunt; bump; clash; collision; contact; cram; effect; force; impetus; impingement; implication; impression; impulse; jar; jolt; meaning; onset; outcome; percussion; reaction; result; shock; slam; strike; stroke; trauma; wallop

IMPAIR: (see "injure") adulterate; afflict; alloy; blemish; corrupt; cripple; damage; deaden; debase; decrease; deface; defile; deform; degrade; diminish; embarrass; enervate; enfeeble; hamper; harm; hinder; hurt; impede; incapacitate; lame; lessen; maim; mayhem; prejudice; rot; sour; vitiate; warp; weaken; worsen; IMPAIRMENT: (see "flaw") affliction; incapacitation

IMPALE: crucify; deflate; enclose; fence; fix; gig; gore; pierce; spear; spike; spit; stick; surround; torture; transfix

IMPALPABLE: (see "airy") attenuated; delicate; fine; imperceptible; intangible; rare; refined; secret; shadowy; slight; tenuous; undetected; unpalpable; unreal; vague

IMPART: (see "announce" and "communicate") add; bestow; confer; convey; disclose; divide; divulge; enlighten; give; grant; impute; influence; inform; instill; instruct; lend; mention; notify; perfume; purport; reveal; send; share; shed; speak; specify; teach; tell; transmit

IMPARTIAL: candid; cool; disinterested; dispassionate; equal; equ(it)able; even(handed); fair; free; good; honorable; impassionate; impersonal; indifferent; judicial; judicious; just; neuter; neutral; noncombatant; nonpartisan; objective; right; square; unallied; unbiased; unbigoted; undistinctive; uninfluenced; uninvolved; unprejudiced; IMPARTIALITY: detachment; disinterestedness; dispassion; equality; equitableness; equity; evenhandedness; fairness; indifference; judiciality; justness; neutrality; nonpartisanship; objectivity; unprejudice

IMPASSABLE: impenetrable; imperforate; impermeable; impervious; insurmountable; unconquerable; unpassable

IMPASSE: blind alley; block(age); crisis;

cul-de-sac; deadlock; difficulty; dilemma; draw; fix; hitch; horns of a dilemma; obstruction; pickle; predicament; stalemate; tie

IMPASSIONED: afire; animated; ardent; delirious; dithyrambic; enraptured; enthusiastic; evangelistic; excited; exciting; exhilarated; fanatical; fervent; fervid; fevered; feverish; fiery; frantic; frenetic; fuming; furious; hot; hysterical; impetuous; inflamed; intense; maniac(al); passionate; perfervid; raging; rapturous; romantic; stirring; thrilling; transported; vehement; warm; wild; zealous; IMPASSIONATE: see "impartial"

IMPASSIVE: (see "calm") apathetic; callous; cold; comatose; dispassionate; dry; expressionless; hard; hermetic(al); ice-cold; icy; inanimate; indifferent; insensate; insensible; insensitive; insentient; inveterate; invulnerable; matter-of-fact; motionless; nonchalant; objective; passive; pathetic; phlegmatic(al); placid; reluctant; serene; spineless; stoic(al); stolid; torpid; torporific; uneager; unemotional; unimpressionable; unperturbable; unperturbed

IMPATIENT: (see "anxious") afire; agitated; apprehensive; choleric; disturbed; eager; fatigued; fevered; feverish; fidgety; flurried; fretful; fussy; hasty; hurried; ill-humored; impetuous; intolerant; irascible; irritable; irritated; itching; keen; mercurial; nervous; pettish; petulant; precipitate; premature; previous; quicksilver; restive; restless; temperamental; testy; tired; turbulent; uneasy; unpatient; unquiet; unsettled; waspish; wearied; wearisome; worried

IMPAVID: anxious; bold; brave; calm; fearless; intrepid

IMPEACH: accuse; arraign; asperse; blame; censure; challenge; charge; cite; criminate; discredit; dismiss; incriminate; indict

IMPECCABLE: (see "clean" and "precise") flawless; immaculate; irreproachable

IMPEDE: arrest; bar(ricade); block; bridle; check; clog; contravene; cordon; counteract; cross; dam; debar; delay; embarrass; encumber; entangle; estop; fence; fetter; frustrate; halter; hamper; hamstring; handcuff; harass; hedge; hinder; imprison; inhibit; interfere; isolate; jam; kill; limit; manacle; neutralize; obstruct; occlude; oppilate; oppose; pen; preclude; prevent;

prison; prohibit; proscribe; resist; restrain; retard; segregate; separate; shield; short-circuit; smother; stop; strangle; suffocate; suppress; thwart; IMPEDIMENT: (see "barricade") arrest(ment); bar(rier); block-(age); check; clog; cul-de-sac; dam; delay; difficulty; disability; embarrassment; encumbrance; entanglement; fetter; frustration; halter; hampering; hamstring; hindrance; hitch; impedance; impedimenta(pl.); inhibition; limp; lisp; manacle; neutralization; obstacle; obstruction; oppilation; opposition; prohibition; resistance; restraint; restriction; retardation; short circuit; snag; stop(page); stammer; stricture; stutter; suffocation; thwarting; undergrowth

IMPEDIMENTA: (see "equipment") baggage; bags; gear; luggage; movables; personalia; supplies

IMPEL: (see "coerce") actuate; animate; compel; constrain; drive; fire; force; goad; hurl; incite; induce; inspire; inspirit; instigate; motivate; move; operate; press; prick; prod; propel; pull; push; run; start; stimulate; stir; thrust; urge

IMPEND: approach; brew; dangle; hang (fire); loom; menace; threaten; IMPENDING: abeyant; approaching; close; emergent; hanging; imminent; impendent; in abeyance; incumbent; inevitable; likely; menacing; near; nigh; ominous; pressing; threatening

IMPENETRABLE: airtight; bulletproof; impervious; inscrutable; invulnerable; unconquerable; unfathomable; unimpressible; unpenetrable

IMPENITENT: (see "hard") unsympathetic

IMPERATIVE: a. absolute; authoritative; binding; coercive; cogent; commanding; compelling; compulsatory; compulsive; compulsory; convincing; demanding; de rigueur; de règle; despotic; dictatorial; dominant; domineering; driving; enforced; essential; exigent; impelling; impending; incumbent; indispensible; inexorable; insistent; mandatory; masterful; necessary; needful; obligatory; peremptory; preceptive; prerequisite; pressing; required; requisite; strong; telling; urgent; IMPERATIVE: n. command; essential; guide; injunction; mandate; mandatum; necessity; need; obligation; obligement; obligedness; order; prerequisite; rule

IMPERCEPTIBLE: gradual; hidden; impalpable; imperceptive; indiscernible; insensible; invisible; secret; slight; subliminal; subtle; unnoticed; unobservable; unobserved; unperceivable; unperceiving; unseen

IMPERFECT: atelic; bad; blemished; contingent; declinous; defeasible; defective; dilapidated; diminished; erratic; fallible; faulty; frail; imperfective; inadequate; inchoate; inchoative; incipient; incomplete; irregular; lacking; marred; mismade; mismatched; potential; rough; rude; rudimentary; short; suboptimal; substandard; undeveloped; unperfect; unripe(ned); unskilled; wanting; IMPERFECTION: (see "blemish" and "defect") crudeness; crudity; fault; incompleteness; kink; pit

IMPERIAL: (see "grand") august; commanding; demanding; exalted; haughty; imperious; kingly; majestic; noble; purple; regal; royal; self-aggrandizing; sovereign; stately; supreme

IMPERIL: (see "endanger") expose; jeopardize; risk; threaten; uncover

IMPERIOUS: (see "haughty") arrogant; august; authoritative; commanding; compelling; compulsive; dictatorial; dominant; domineering; exalted; high(-and-mighty); impenetrable; imperative; imperial; inscrutable; kingly; lordly; majestic; masterful; overbearing; overruling; proud; regal; royal; sovereign; stately; supreme; urgent

IMPERISHABLE: (see "everlasting") abiding; enduring; eternal; forever; immarcescible; immarcessible; immortal; indestructible; lasting; permanent; perpetual; unperishable; IMPERISHABLENESS: (see "everlastingness") eternality; imperishability; perpetuality; perpetuity; subtility

IMPERMANENT: see "perishable"

IMPERSONAL: cool; deadpan; dehumanized; detached; disinterested; fair; general; impartial; indefinite; infrahuman; inhuman; judicious; just; mechanical; objective; poker-faced; universal

IMPERSONATE: (see "imitate") act; ape; assume; copy; embody; exemplify; feign; mimic; mock; personate; personify; pose; pretend

IMPERTINENT: (see "audacious") brash; brazen; forward; fresh; gay; impish; impudent; inapplicable; inappropriate; incivil;

insolent; insulting; intrusive; irrelevant; irreverent; meddlesome; nosy; obstructive; offensive; officious; presumptuous; rude; sassy; saucy; superfluous; uncivil; unfit; IMPERTINENCE or INPERTINENCY: (see "pertness") arrogance; audacity; boldness; brashness; brass(iness); brazenness; daring; disdain; effrontery; forwardness; gall; guts; impudence; inappropriateness; incivility; insolence; irrelevancy; irreverence; nerve; presumption; rashness; rudeness; sand; sass(iness); sauciness; unfitness

IMPERTURBABLE: (see "calm") assured; cool; dispassionate; impassive; indifferent; jaunty; nonchalant; phlegmatic(al); placid; self-assured; serene; smug; steady; stolid; tranquil; unflappable; unmoved; unruffled

IMPETUOUS: abrupt; à corps perdu; afire; ardent; bold; brash; brazen; burning; eager; energetic; fervent; fervid; fevered; feverish; fierce; fiery; flashy; foolhardy; furious; hasty; headlong; headstrong; heady; heedless; hot; impassioned; impulsive; intractable; obstinate; passionate; perfervid; precipitate; quick; rash; restive; restless; rushing; sharp; sudden; swift; temperamental; ungovernable; unruly; vehement; violent; warlike

IMPETUS: (see "force") ambition; drive; impulse; incentive; stimulus

IMPIETY: blasphemy; disrespect; impiousness; irreverence; profanity; sacrilege; sin; undutifulness; ungodliness; wickedness; IMPIOUS: blasphemous; disrespectful; godless; hypocritical; indevout; irreligious; irreverent; profane; sacrilegious; sinful; undutiful; ungodly; unholy; wicked

IMPINGE: (see "infringe") choke; contact; dash; encroach; pinch; press; sequeeze; touch

IMPISH: cute; elvish; espiègle; frolicsome; kittenish; malignant; mischievous; pert; pesterous; pestiferous; playful; puckish; roguish; sassy; saucy; sly; tricky; whimsical

IMPLACABLE: (see "inflexible") inexorable; unappeasable; unsatisfiable

IMPLANT: base; brainwash; engraft; enroot; establish; fix; graft; imbue; impress; inculcate; infix; infuse; inset; instill; introduce; join; plant; root; seed; set; teach

IMPLAUSIBLE: see "unbelievable"

IMPLEMENT: v. (see "accomplish") achieve; arm; compel; drive; effect(uate); enforce; equip; execute; expedite; fulfill; guide; invoke; operate; perform; realize; supplement; IMPLEMENT: n. (see "equipment") appliance; arm; article; device; engine; gear; gismo; instrument; kit; machine(ry); material; plow; tackle; tool; utensil; utility

IMPLICATE: accuse; attack; blame; compromise; connect; couple; entangle; entwine; imbrue; imply; impute; include; incriminate; inculpate; indict; infer; insinuate; interweave; involve; join; link; relate; tangle; IMPLICATION: allusion; blame; compromise; connection; connotation; deduction; entanglement; hint; imputation; inclusion; incrimination; inculpation; indictment; inference; insinuation; insinuendo; involvement; link; overtone; relation(ship); significance; suggestion; undermeaning

IMPLICIT: implied; inferred; potential; presumed; presupposed; tacit; trusting; unapparent; underlying; understood; unquestioning; wholehearted

IMPLORE: (see "beg") adjure; appeal; ask; beseech; conjure; entreat; importune; invoke; petition; plead; pray; solicit; sue; supplicate; urge

IMPLY: allude; comprehend; comprise; connect; connotate; denote; hint; implicate; include; indicate; induce; infer; infold; insinuate; intimate; involve; mean; predicate; presume; presuppose; purport; signify; suggest; suppose; IMPLIED: connotated; hinted; implicit; indicated; inferred; insinuated; intimated; oral; signified; tacit; unwritten; IMPLICATION: see "allusion" and "innuendo"

IMPOLITE: bluff; blunt; crude; curt; dedecorous; discourteous; disrespectful; ignoble; ill-bred; impertinent; indecorous; inelegant; insolent; inurbane; pert; rude; sassy; saucy; surly; uncivil; uncourtly; uncouth; ungenteel; ungentlemanlike; ungentlemanly; ungracious; unmannerly; unpolished; unpolite; unrefined; IMPOLITENESS: (see "discourtesy") crudeness; crudity; curtness; disrespect; impertinence; incivility; insolence; inurbanity; pertness; rudeness; sassiness; sauciness; ungentlemanliness; unrefinement

IMPORT: v. carry; concern; convey; denote; indicate; introduce; matter; mean; signify; IMPORT: n. concern; connotation; con-

sequence; denotation; drift; duty; impost; indication; intent; matter; meaning; message; purport; sense; significance; signification; substance; trend; value; weight; worth

IMPORTANT: (see "acute") aristocratic; authoritative; basic(al); basilic; capital; cardinal; central; chief; cogent; consequential; critical; crucial; deceptive; definitive; determinative; earthshaking; essential; eventful; front-page; fundamental; grave; great; high; historical; impactful; impactive; influential; large; leading; main; material; momentous; monumental; notable; outstanding; paramount; pivotal; powerful; predominant; prestigious; primary; prime; principal; prominent; real; salient; serious; signal; significant; solemn; strategetic; strategic; substantial; superior; supreme; telling; true; urgent; valuable; vital; weighty; world-shaking; worthy; IMPORTANCE: authoritativeness; concern(ment); consequence; cruciality; dignity; distinction; eminence; essence; gravity; mark; monument; odds; pith; place; prestige; seriousness; signality; significance; solemnity; soundness; strength; stress; urgency; value; weight; worthiness

IMPORTUNE: (see "beg") annoy; appeal; flagitate; high-pressure; implore; pester; press; solicit; tease; trouble; urge; woo; worry; IMPORTUNATE: annoying; begging; burdensome; demanding; insistent; instant; pressing; solicitous; troublesome; urgent

IMPOSE: afflict; burden; coerce; command; create; decree; dictate; enforec; enjoin; entail; foist; force; generate; impress; impute; inflict; insist; intrude; lay; levy; obligate; obtrude; order; press; prevail; require; stamp; subject; suffer; tax; visit; IMPOSITION: see "burden"

IMPOSING: (see "grand") august; commanding; exalted; grandiose; handsome; haughty; hefty; high(-sounding); imperial; impressive; kingly; magisterial; magnific(al); magnificent; majestic; noble; pompous; regal; royal; stately; striking; sublime; superlative; supreme; tall; terrible; towering

IMPOSSIBLE: chimerical; fantastic; hopeless; impotent; impracticable; incapable; insoluble; insuperable; insurmountable; invincible; unacceptable; unpossible; unrealistic; unscalable; unsurpassable; IMPOSSIBILITY: hopelessness; impracticability; incapability;

insolubility; insuperability; invincibility; unconquerability; unpossibility

IMPOST: (see "tax") customs; duty; import; revenue; task; tithe; toll; tribute; weight

IMPOSTER or INPOSTOR: (see "faker") Cagliostro; charlatan; cheat(er); deceiver; epigone; fake; fraud; humbug; hypocrite; mountebank; Pharisee; pretender; quack-(salver); ringer; sham; swindler; IMPOS-TURE: charlatanry; cheating; counterfeit; deceit; deception; duplicity; fake(ment); fakery; fraud; hoax; hocus-pocus; humbug(gery); imitation; mountebankery; pretense; ruse; sham; simulacrum; simulation; swindle

IMPOTENT: (see "weak") deficient; helpless; incapable; insufficient; powerless; sterile; unable; unfit; unqualified; IMPOTENCE or IMPOTENCY: anaphrodisia; deficiency; fecklessness; feebleness; helplessness; impotentness; incapacity; insufficiency; paralysis; sterility; unfitness; weakness

IMPRACTICABLE: impossible; impractical; imprudent; infeasible; insuperable; unpracticable; unpractical; unrealistic; unwise

IMPRACTICAL: academic; chimerical; crackpot; crazy; doctrinaire; dogmatic(al); erratic; escapist; feckless; hypothetical; ideal-(istic); implausible; impracticable; inefficient; inexecutable; insane; irresponsible; ivory-tower(ed); ivory-towerish; Laputan; nonrealistic; pedantic; poetic(al); quixotic-(al); romantic; softheaded; speculative; theoretic(al); unfeasible; unfunctional; unpractical; unwise; unworkable; useless; utopian; visionary

IMPRECATION: abuse; anathema; blame; curse; cursing; execration; indictment; malediction; malison; oath; objurgation; plea; profanity; supplication; vituperation

IMPRECISE: (see "incorrect") unprecise

IMPREGNABLE: (see "secure") formidable; invulnerable; stout; strong; unassailable; unconquerable

IMPREGNATE: brainwash; charge; enter; fecundate; fertilize; imbue; implant; inculcate; indoctrinate; infiltrate; influence; infuse; inject; inoculate; inseminate; instill; interpenetrate; mix; penetrate; perforate; permeate; pervade; pierce; pregnate; soak; steep; tinct; tinge; IMPREGNATION: (see

"fertilization") brainwash; entrance; fecundation; fertilization; inculcation; indoctrination; infiltration; injection; inoculation; insemination; interpenetration; penetration; perforation; permeation; pervasion; pregnancy

IMPRESS: affect; amaze; arouse; astound; awe; coerce; daguerreotype; dent; effect; engrave; enstamp; exert; force; hit; implant; impose; imprint; inculcate; indent; infix; influence; levy; mark; print; register; seal; seize; stamp; strike; surprise; sway; touch; IMPRESSED or IMPRESSING: see "surprised" and "urgent;" IMPRESSION: belief; dent; dint; effect; fancy; feeling; hit; hollow; idea; image; impact; imprint; indentation; influence; inkling; mark; mold; notion; opinion; perception; phenomenon; print; recollection; seal; sensation; stamp; stir; thought; tract; type; IMPRESSIVE: arresting; astounding; deep; dignified; distinguished; eminent; epic(al); exciting; extraordinary; fat; grand; great; heroic; impactful; imposing; memorable; moving; notable; outstanding; pathetic; penetrative; poignant; profound; signal; solemn; solid; stately; stirring; striking; stunning; telling; touching; IMPRESSIVENESS: grandeur; grandiloquence; grandiosity; imposingness; impressivity; magnificence; opulency; penetrativity; solemnity; solidarity; solidity; stateliness

IMPRESSIONABLE: easy; emotionable; emotional; malleable; plastic; pliable; pliant; responsive; senistive; soft; suggestible; susceptible; teachable; tender

IMPRISON: cage; circumscribe; confine; constrain; coop; curb; encase; enclose; enisle; fence; hold; immure; impound; incarcerate; keep; jail; limit; pen; punish; restrain; shut; surround; wall; IMPRISONMENT: circumscription; confinement; durance; durance vile; immuration; immurement; incarceration; jail; limbo; prisonment; punishment; restraint

IMPROBABLE: (see "uncertain") incredible; tall; unbelievable; unlikely; unprobable

IMPROMPTU: abrupt; accidental; ad-lib; ad-libbed; ad libitum; automatic; autonomic; autoschediastic; breezy; brevi manu; brusque; by-the-way; careless; casual(ly); curt; extemporaneous; extemporary; extempore; free; glib; hasty; impetuous; improvisatorial; improvisatory; improvised; improviso; impulsive; indeterminate; indigenous; informal;

instinctive; involuntary; makeshift; mechanical; offhand; prompt; readily; reflex; self-acting; spontaneous; sudden(ly); thoughtless; unavoidable; unbidden; unceremonial; unceremonious; uncontrollable; uncontrolled; unconventional; unexpected; unforced; unplanned; unpremeditated; unprompted; unreflecting; unrehearsed; unstudied; untaught; unthinking; voluntary

IMPROPER: abnormal; amiss; à propos de rien; bad; disgraceful; errant; evil; forbidding; illicit; immoderate; immodest; immoral; impertinent; inaccurate; inappropriate; inapt; incongruous; incorrect; indecent; indecorous; indelicate; inept; inexpedient; inopportune; insubordinate; insurgent; irregular; irrelevant; malodorous; objectionable; perverse; poor; rebellious; risqué; scabrous; scandalous; shocking; solecistic; unacceptable; unapt; unbecoming; uncomely; uncouth; undesirable; undue; unethical; unfit(ting); unjust(ifiable); unladylike; unmeek; unseasonable; unseemly; unsuitable; unsuited; untoward; unwise; vulgar; wicked; wrong; IMPROPRIETY: barbarism; delict; familiarity; faux pas; gaffe; grivoiserie; immorality; indecency; malfeasance; solecism; transgression; violation; wrong(doing)

IMPROVE: adjust; advance; alembicate; ameliorate; amend; augment; benefit; better; brighten; correct; cultivate; develop; edit; educate; elevate; emend; enhance; enlarge; ennoble; exalt; fix; freshen; gain; grow; help; increase; intensify; mend; meliorate; perfect; polish; promote; purify; rectify; refine; reform; refresh; regulate; revise; rise; strengthen; teach; thrive; tighten; train; tune; upgrade; IMPROVEMENT: advancement; amelioration; betterment; correction; education; emendation; enhancement; growth; help; increase; melioration; perfectionment; reclamation; redemption; refinement; reform(ation); revision; rise

IMPROVIDENT: (see "wasteful") carefree; careless; negligent; prodigal; thoughtless; thriftless; unforethoughtful

IMPROVISE: ad-lib; compose; concoct; confect; contrive; devise; extemporize; fabricate; improvisate; invent; vamp; IMPROVISED: see "impromptu;" IMPROVISATION: ad lib; ad libitum; autoschediasm; extemporization; fabrication; impromptu; invention

IMPRUDENT: (see "indiscreet") audacious; careless; foolish; ill-advised; impolite; im-

practicable; impractical; injudicious; negligent; pound-foolish; procacious; prodigal; rash; silly; unwise

IMPUDENT: (see "arrogant") arrant; audacious; blustering; bold(-faced); brash; brassy; brazen(faced); bumptious; cheeky; cocky; contemptuous; contumelious; defiant; disrespectful; domineering; flippant; forward; fresh; haughty; impetuous; incivil; insolent; insulting; intrusive; malapert; offensive; officious; overbearing; overbold; pert; presumptive; presumptuous; proud; rude; sassy; saucy; shameless; supercilious; swaggering; toplofty; uncivil; unmannerly; IMPUDENCE: (see "arrogance") audacity; bluster; boldness; braggadocio; brashness; brass(iness); bumptiousness; cheek(iness); cockiness; contempt; contumacy; contumely; defiance; disdain; disrespect; effrontery; familiarity; flippancy; folly; forwardness; gall; guts; haughtiness; hubris; impertinence; impetuosity; impudency; incivility; insolence; insolency; insult; intrusiveness; lip; mouth; nerve; nerviness; offense; officiousness; overconfidence; pertness; presumption; pride; procacity; protervity; rudeness; sass(iness); sauciness; scorn; shamelessness; swagger

IMPUGN: (see "blame") asperse; assail; attack; challenge; contradict; deny; gainsay; oppose; question

IMPULSE: afflatus; ate; calling; drive; effort; force; impetus; impulsion; incentive; incitement; inclination; insistence; inspiration; instigation; instinct; momentum; motion; motivation; motive; movement; nisus; power; pressure; propension; propensity; push; reflex; signal; spirit; spontaneity; spur; tendency; thrust; trend; urge(ncy); IMPULSIVE: ballistic; capricious; careless; clamorous; compulsive; emotional; excitable; fiery; forceful; giddy; hasty; headlong; heedless; impatient; impellent; impetuous; imprudent; incautious; indiscreet; instinctive; intemperate; passionate; rash; reckless; reflex; spontaneous; thoughtless; unpremediated; vehement; violent; wild; IMPULSIVENESS: impetuosity; impetuousness; impulsivity; rashness; spontaneity; thoughtlessness

IMPUNITY: exemption; freedom; immunity; license; safety

IMPURE: (see "dirty") adulterated; bastard; corrupt; defiled; diseased; filthy; heterozygous; foul; immoral; indecent; infected;

lewd; licentious; macular; mixed; obscene; smutty; sullied; unchaste; unclean; unhallowed; unholy; unpure; unrectified; unsanitary; unsterile; unwholesome; wicked; IMPURITY: adulteration; contamination; corruption; defilement; dirt(iness); disease; dross; immorality; indecency; lewdness; licentiousness; obscenity; pollution; putrescence; rot; scum; uncleanliness; unwholesomeness; waste

IMPUTE: (**see** "blame") accuse; arraign; ascribe; assign; attribute; brand; call; charge; credit; delegate; impart; implicate; inculpate; indict; stigmatize

INABILITY: (**see** "helplesseness" and "weakness") disability; impotence; impotency; incapacitation; incapacity; powerlessness

INACCESSIBLE: (**see** "unattainable") ungettable

INACCURATE: (**see** "incorrect") apocryphal; careless; deceiving; deceptive; defective; discrepant; erroneous; fallacious; fallible; faulty; inexact; misleading; slipshod; sloppy; unliteral; INACCURACY: carelessness; discrepancy; errata (pl.); erratum; fallacy; imprecision; inexactitude; inexactness; misconception; mistake

INACTIVE: (**see** "idle") anergic; calm; comatose; dead; deliquescent; dormant; drowsy; dull; faineant; feckless; flat; idle; inanimate; indolent; inert; inoperative; latent; lazy; lethargic; lifeless; listless; nonfunctional; nonfunctioning; obsolete; otiose; passive; peaceful; quiescent; quiet; retired; sedentary; semiconscious; silent; slothful; sluggish; standing; still; sullen; supine; torpid; unemployed; unreactive; unresponsive; withdrawn; INACTION *or* INACTIVITY: acedia; delay; deliquescence; doldrums; dormancy; drowsiness; ennui; faineance; faineancy; *fainéantise*; fecklessness; idleness; indolence; inertia; inertness; lassitude; laziness; lethargy; otiosity; passivity; procrastination; quiescence; quietude; sedentation; sloth(fulness); slump; stagnation; status; *status quo*; stillness; supinity; torpidity; torpor

INADEQUATE: (**see** "deficient") bungling; clumsy; crippled; destitute; disabled; disproportionate; feeble; foolish; futile; Icarian; immature; impotent; inane; incomplete; ineffective; inefficacious; inept; infirm; insignificant; insufficient; irregular; jejune; lacking; maladaptive; maladjustive; mala-

droit; paltry; perfunctory; poor; puerile; scanty; short; thin; underpaid; underrepresented; unfit; unlearned; unprepared; unqualified; untaught; untrained; wanting; weak(ened); INADEQUACY: dearth; defect; deficiency; famine; fault; incapacitation; incapacity; inefficacy; inefficiency; infirmity; insufficiency; lack; need; nonability; paucity; scarcity; underpayment; undersupply; unfitness; weakness

INADVERTENT: (**see** "accidental") careless; heedless; inattentive; negligent; unintentional; unpremeditated; INADVERTENCY: accidentality; carelessness; heedlessness; inadvertence; inattention; negligence; unpremeditation

INADVISABLE: (**see** "inappropriate") contraindicated; contraindicative; disadvantageous; impolitic; impracticable; inexpedient; inopportune; unadvisable

INANE: (**see** "foolish") absurd; asinine; banal; empty; fatuitous; fatuous; feckless; flat; frivolous; idiotic; idle; imbecile; imbecilic; insignificant; insipid; insubstantial; jejune; meaningless; paltry; pointless; puerile; shallow; silly; stratospheric(al); stupid; trifling; trivial; unsubstantial; vacant; vacuous; vain; vapid; void; INANITY: emptiness; hollowness; inanition; ineptness; insubstantiality; jejunity; lethargy; marasmus; pointlessness; puerility; shallowness; stupidity; vacancy; vacuity; vanity; vapidity

INAPPLICABLE: (**see** "impertinent") unapplicable; unsuitable; unsuited

INAPPROPRIATE: alien; amiss; contraindicated; contraindicative; disadvantageous; discordant; fantastic(al); foreign; impertinent; impolitic; impracticable; improper; inapplicable; inapposite; inapt; incongruous; inept; inexpedient; infelicitous; inopportune; irrelevant; malapropos; tasteless; unadvisable; unapt; unattractive; unbecoming; undue; unfit(ting); unsuitable; unsuited

INAPT: (**see** "clumsy") awkward; crippled; gauche; inadequate; inept; slow; stupid; unapt; unfit; unqualified; unskilled; unskillfull; unsuitable; untaught; untrained

INARTICULATE(D): aphonic; dumb; indistinct; mute; silent; unarticulate(d); unexpressed; unintelligible; unjointed; unspoken; unvocal

INATTENTIVE: absent(minded); absorbed;

abstracted; apathetic; bemused; careless; cruel; disobedient; disregardful; disrespectful; distant; distrait; distraught; dreaming; dreamy; engrossed; forgetful; harum-scarum; heedless; incogitable; incogitant; incurious; lost; musing; neglectful; negligent; oblivious; occupied; oscitant; preoccupied; rapt; remiss; slack; unattentive; unaware; uninquiring; uninterested; unmindful; unnoticed; unobservant; unobserving; unvigilant; unwary; unwatchful; INATTENTION: absentmindedness; abstraction; apathy; carelessness; defiance; disobedience; disregard; disremembrance; disrespect; dreaminess; forgetfulness; heedlessness; ignoration; inadvertency; incogitancy; incuriosity; indifference; irreverence; misfeasance; mockery; mooniness; neglect; negligence; omission; oscitancy; oscitation; preoccupation; rashness; remission; slight; uninterestedness

INAUGURATE: (**see** "begin") auspicate; celebrate; commence; consecrate; coronate; crown; dedicate; enstool; found; induct; install; instill; institute; introduce; invest; open; originate; start; INAUGURATION: (**see** "beginning") accession; commencement; consecration; coronation; dedication; inception; induction; initiation; installation; institution; introduction; investiture; investment; opening; origin(ation); start

INAUSPICIOUS: (**see** "bad") adverse; evil; hostile; ill-boding; ill-omened; malign(ant); ominous; sinister; unauspicious; unfavorable; unlucky; unpropitious

INBORN: (**see** "hereditary") cognate; congenital; connate; connatural; constitutional; derivative; endogamous; endogenous; familial; habitual; idiopathic; implanted; inbred; incestuous; indigenous; ingrained; ingrown; inherent; inherited; innate; instinctive; institutional; intrinsic; intuitive; native; natural

INCANTATION: (**see** "exorcism") charm; enchantment; fetish; hex; obfuscation; rite; sorcery; spell; witchery

INCAPABLE *or* INCAPACITATED: (**see** "helpless") afflicted; disabled; disqualified; feckless; impossible; impotent; inadaptive; incompetent; insane; insufficient; insusceptible; nonadaptive; nonadjustable; powerless; sterile; stricken; unable; unfit; unqualified; worthless; INCAPACITY: (**see** "helplessness") affliction; disability; disablement; disqualification; impotency; impuissance; incapacitation; infliction; invalidism; in-

validity; nonability; powerlessness; superannuation

INCARNATION: avatar; embodiment; genius; image; impersonation; materialization; personification

INCAUTIOUS: (**see** "heedless") careless; imprudent; impulsive; injudicious; rash; stupid; unalert; unguarded; unprotected; unwise

INCENDIARY: **a.** ignitable; inflammatory; seditious; INCENDIARY: **n.** agitator; arsonist; bomb; conflagrationist; exciter; firebrand; firebug

INCENSE: **v.** anger; arouse; burn; enrage; exasperate; excite; inflame; irk; irritate; madden; nettle; perfume; provoke; roil; INCENSE: **n.** anger; burning; exasperation; fragrance; homage; ire; irritation; myrrh; odor; perfume; scent; smoke; wrath; INCENSED: angry; enraged; fired; irate; ired; ireful; mad; nettled; stung; wrathful

INCENTIVE: (**see** "attraction") allure(ment); bait; bribe; catalyst; charm; encouragement; enticement; fillip; goad; ground; impulse; incitation; incitement; inducement; instigation; invitation; lure; motivation; motive; offer; provocation; raise; reason; spell; spur; stimulant; stimulation; stimulus; temptation; urge; whip

INCEPTION: (**see** "beginning" and "origin") inauguraton; ingestion; initiation; principium

INCESSANT: **see** "unending"

INCHOATE: (**see** "beginning") contingent; disordered; expectant; imperfect; inchoative; incipient; incoherent; incomplete; part(ly); potential; recent; rudimentary; unfinished; unorganized; INCHOATION: (**see** "beginning") onset

INCIDENT: **a.** chance; external; liable; prone; subject; INCIDENT: **n.** accident; action; case; chance; circumstance; circumstantiality; concomitant; contingency; contretemps; disturbance; episode; event; factor; fracas; happening; occasion; occurrence; phenomenon; situation; INCIDENTAL: accessory; accidental; accompanying; adventitious; associated; attendant; casual; chance; chancy; circumstantial; collateral; concomitant; concurrent; contingent; dependent; digressive; ejaculatory; episodic(al);

extra; extraneous; fortuitous; interjaculatory; interjectural: interlocutory; intervenient; liable; minor; nonessential; occasional; odd; parenthetic(al); prone; secondary; stray; subject; subordinate; tangential; unwanted

INCIPIENT: (see "inchoate") beginning; commencing; germinal; incipiative; initial

INCISION: acuteness; cicatrix; cleft; cut; gash; penetration; scar; score; slit; wound

INCISIVE: biting; clear-cut; crisp; cutting; distinct; mordant; penetrating; piercing; poignant; trenchant

INCITE: abet; actuate; agitate; animate; arouse; brew; cause; coax; coerce; commove; egg; encourage; excite; exhort; fester; fire; flagellate; foment; goad; heat; impassion; impel; inflame; influence; inspire; inspirit; instigate; intensify; motivate; move; persuade; prick; prod; promote; provoke; raise; rouse; sic; solicit; spark; spur; stimulate; stir; summon; suscitate; sway; taunt; urge; INCITEMENT: abetment; concitation; ferment; fomentation; incentive; incitation; instigation; motive; prod; provocation; solicitation; INCITIVE: animating; animative; catalytic; encouraging; fomentive; hortative; hortatory; incitive; incitory; moving; prodding; provocative; provoking; rousing; spurring; stimulating; stimulatory; stirring; urging

INCLINE: v. bend; bevel; bias; bow; cant; deviate; lean; nod; pitch; slant; slope; stoop; tend; tilt; trend; turn; urge; INCLINE: n. acclivity; bias; clift; decline; declivity; descent; drop; fall; grade; gradient; hill; inclination; ramp; rise; scarp; slant; slope; trend; INCLINATION: acclivity; addiction; affectation; angle; animus; appetite; aptness; attachment; attitude; attraction; bend; bent; bias; bow; coloration; declination; declivity; desire; deviation; diathesis; direction; disposition; drift; fall; fancy; fantasy; fondness; genius; grade; gradient; impulse; incline; intention; knack; leaning; liking; mood; movement; nisus; nod; partiality; penchant; persuasion; pitch; predilection; predisposition; preference; prejudice; proclivity; propensity; slant; slope; spirit; stomach; taste; tendency; thought; trait; trend; versant; wish; INCLINABLE or INCLINED: addicted; addictive; angled; apt; bent; biased; disposed; favorable; leaned; leaning; partial; predisposed; prone; propense; suasible; tendentious; tending

INCLOSE: see "enclose"

INCLUDE: (see "comprehend") admit; bound; comprise; confine; connect; consist; contain; count; cover; design; embody; embosom; embrace; enclose; encompass; enfold; envelop; enwrap; have; hold; immerse; implicate; imply; incorporate; involve; muster; subsume; INCLUSIVE: all-around; broad; capacious; composing; comprehensive; cyclopedic; embracive; enclosing; encompassing; encyclopedic(al); omnibus; portmanteau; scopious; universal

INCOGNITO: alias; anonymous; assumed; authorless; blank; disguised; feigned; hidden; masked; nameless; secret; unidentified; unknown; unsolicited; unsought; veiled

INCOHERENT: clumsy; enigmatic(al); fumbling; illogical; inchoate; incongruous; inconsistent; irrational; jumbled; loose; raving; unclear; vague; wild

INCOME: annuity; benefit; dividends; emolument; fee(s); fruits; gain(s); honorarium; increment; interest; pension; proceeds; produce; profits; receipts; rent(s); rentals; rente; resource; results; return(s); revenue; royalty; salary; sales; stipend; taxes; tolls; usance; wage(s); wealth; windfall

INCOMMODE: (see "annoy") block; bother; discommode; distress; disturb; harass; harry; hinder; impede; inconvenience; molest; plague; trouble; vex

INCOMPARABLE: (see "supreme") unequalable; unmatchable; unmatched; unparallelable; unsurpassable

INCOMPATIBLE: (see "antagonistic") conflicting; disagreeing; discordant; immiscible; incongruent; incongruous; inconsistent; inharmonious; irreconcilable; repugnant; uncongenial; unsuitable

INCOMPETENT: disabled; feckless; helpless; impertinent; inadmissible; inapt; incapable; incapacitated; ineffective; inefficient; inept; insane; irresponsible; lacking; noncompetent; *non compos (mentis)*; unfit; unqualified; untaught; untrained; unworkmanlike; wasteful; weak; INCOMPETENCE: inadequacy; inaptitude; incapability; incapacitation; incapacity; incompetency; ineptitude; insanity; insufficiency; lack; wastefulness; weakness; worthlessness

INCOMPLETE: (see "deficient") contingent;

crude; defective; deficient; elementary; fractional; fractionary; fragmental; fragmentary; half-baked; immature; imperfect(ed); inchoate; inchoative; incipient; incondite; lacking; part(ial); potential; rudimentary; syncategorematic; truncated; unaccomplished; uncomplete(d); undone; unfinished; unperfected

INCOMPREHENSIBLE: ambiguous; enigmatic(al); graspless; impenetrable; indefinite; nebulous; numinous; uncomprehensible; uncomprehensive; undecipherable; unfathomable; ungraspable; unimaginable; unimagined; unintelligible; unrealizable; unthinkable;   INCOMPREHENSIBILITY: ambiguity; enigma; indefinitude; nebulosity

INCONCEIVABLE: see "incredible"

INCONCLUSIVE: see "equivocal" and "uncertain"

INCONDITE: see "incomplete"

INCONGRUENT or INCONGRUOUS: absurd; antonymous; conflicting; contradictious; contradictive; contradictory; contrary; different; disagreeable; discordant; disparate; equivocal; inapposite; inappropriate; incoherent; incompatible; incomplete; inconsistent; inharmonious; mismatched; mismated; odd; opposite; paradoxical; quaint; repugnant; schizoid; uncertain; unsuitable; unsuited

INCONSEQUENTIAL: (see "insignificant") unconsequential; unvital

INCONSISTENT: ambivalent; antagonistic; changeable; contradictious; contradictive; contradictory; contrary; discordant; discrepant; fickle; illogical; immiscible; incoherent; incompatible; incongruent; incongruous; inconstant; inharmonious; irreconcilable; irregular; paradoxical; repugnant; two-minded; uncertain; uneven; unsteady; vacillating; varying; INCONSISTENCY: changeableness; contrarieties (pl.); contrariety; incoherence; incompatibility; incongruence; incongruity; irregularity; misalliance; non sequitur (abb. non seq.); paradox(icality); repugnance; repugnancy; roughness; unevenness

INCONSPICUOUS: (see "obscure") unconspicuous; unemphatic

INCONSTANT: (see "fickle") alternating; ambivalent; capricious; chameleonic; change-

able; changing; desultory; digressive; erratic; faithless; fluctuating; inconsistent; indefinite; mercurial; mutable; perfidious; quicksilver; rambling; random; spasmodic; unsettled; unstable,   untrustworthy;   vacillating; vagrant; variable; vertiginous

INCONTROVERTIBLE: (see "certain") immutable; incontestable; indisputable; irrecusable; irrefrangable; irrefutable; sans doute; sine dubio; unmistakable; unquestionable; unrefutable

INCONVENIENCE: v. (see "annoy") disadvantage; discomfit; discommode; discompose; embarrass; handicap; incommode; trouble; INCONVENIENCE: n. disadvantage; discomfiture; discomfort; embarrassment; handicap; impediment; inconveniency; INCONVENIENT: disadvantageous; discomfortable; embarrassing; ill; inappropriate; incommodious; inexpedient; inopportune; unadapted; unhandy; unseasonable; unsuitable; unsuited; unwieldly

INCORPORATE: amalgamate; assimilate; associate; blend; combine; consolidate; embody; embrace; enfold; envelop(e); fold; fuse; include; introject; join; merge; mix; unite; INCORPORATION: amalgamation; assimilation; association; combination; consolidation; embodiment; fusion; incarnation; inclusion; merger; synthesis; union

INCORRIGIBLE: (see "refractory") unchangeable; unreformable

INCORRECT: apocryphal; base; careless; deceiving; deceptive; deviating; devious; discrepant; erroneous; erring; fallacious; fallible; faulty; imprecise; improper; inaccurate; inexact; misleading; mistaken; perverse; slipshod; sloppy; solecistic; unbecoming; ungrammatical; unliteral; unprecise; unseemly; unsound; untrue; wrong; INCORRECTNESS: see "error"

INCORRUPT(IBLE): (see "honest") inviolable; pure; sacrosanct; unassailable; unbribable; uncorrupt(ible); untouchable

INCREASE: v. accrue; add; advance; aggrandize; aggravate; amass; amplify; augment; beef up; boom; broaden; burgeon; complicate; compound; deepen; develop; dignify; dilate; distend; double; eke; elevate; elongate; enhance; enlarge; escalate; exacerbate; exaggerate; excel; excite; expand; expatiate; extend; fatten; force; fructify; gain; greaten; grow; heap; heighten; hire;

hypertrophy; inflate; intensify; jump; leap; lengthen; magnify; maximalize; mount; multiply; pad; parlay; pile; produce; profit; promote; propagate; pullulate; push; pyramid; raise; recruit; rise; sharpen; snowball; soar; spike; spread; steepen; step up; strengthen; supplement; support; sweeten; swell; thicken; thrive; triple; tumesce; unfold; up; upgrade; wax; whet; widen; INCREASE: **n.** (**see** "advancement") access(ion); accrescence; accretion; accrual; accruement; accumulation; additament; addition; advance; agglutination; aggrandizement; amplification; augmentation; buildup; bulge; burgeoning; concrescence; deepening; development; dilation; elevation; enhancement; enlargement; escalation; exacerbation; exacerbescence; exaggeration; exaltation; expansion; extension; gain; growth; hypertrophy; increment; inflation; intensification; jump; leap; lengthening; magnification; majoration; multiplication; overflow; produce; profit; progress(ion); promotion; raise; return; rise; spread; step-up; supplement(ation); support; surge; swell(ing); thickening; tide; tumescence; upgrade; upsweep; uptrend; wave; widening; INCREASING: accelerating; accelerative; acceleratory; accumulative; advancing; augmentative; booming; crescent; crescive; cumulative; escalating; exacerbative; growing; incremental; multiplicative; overflowing; pyramiding; spreading; supplementing; swelling; tumescent; widening

INCREDIBLE: (**see** "exaggerated" and "unbelievable") improbable; incredulous; steep; unconceivable; unlikely; unthinkable; INCREDULITY: disbelief; doubt; dubiety; mistrust; skepticism; unbelief; INCREDULOUS: **see** "skeptical"

INCRIMINATE: (**see** "blame") accuse; charge; frame; impeach; inculcate; involve

INCUBATE: (**see** "brood") develop; gestate; hatch; originate; plan; plot; scheme; sit

INCUBUS: burden; clog; demon; encumbrance; hindrance; impediment; load; nightmare; onus; spirit

INCULCATE: brainwash; fix; imbue; impart; implant; impress; indoctrinate; inject; instill; propagate; teach; urge

INCUMBENT: (**see** "necessary" and "occupant") overlying; superimposed

INCUR: acquire; bring; contract; gain; meet; obtain; promise; risk; run

INCURABLE: chronic; immedicable; incorrigible; insanable; intractable; irremediable; irreparable; lasting; uncorrectible; uncurable

INCURSION: attack; entering; foray; impingement; influx; infringement; inroad; invasion; irruption; raid; trespass; violation

INDEBTEDNESS: **see** "obligation"

INDECENT: (**see** "lewd") bawdy; coarse; defiled; dirty; feculent; filthy; foul; goatish; *grivois*; gross; immodest; immoral; improper; impure; indecorous; indelicate; low; nasty; obscene; offensive; outrageous; pornographic; randy; ribald; risqué; salty; scurrile; scurrilous; smutty; unbecoming; unchaste; unclean; undecorous; unfit; ungodly; unrespectable; unseemly; unsuitable; vulgar; INDECENCY: (**see** "lewdness") bawdiness; coarseness; feculence; filth(iness); grossness; immodesty; immorality; impropriety; impudicity; impurity; indelicacy; obscenity; pornography; ribaldry; scurrility; unseemliness; vulgarity

INDECISION: ambivalence; anxiety; demur; fluctuation; incertitude; indecisiveness; irresolution; shilly-shally; suspense; uncertainty; vacillation; wavering; INDECISIVE: (**see** "vague") ambivalent; anxious; capricious; doubtful; faltering; halting; hesitant; heterogeneous; imprecise; inconclusive; indefinite; indeterminable; indeterminate; indistinct; ineffective; invertebrate; irresolute; nervous; seesawing; suspenseful; teetery; tottering; uncertain; undecisive; unfixed; unsettled; vacillating; vague; wavering

INDEED: actually; admittedly; aru; assuredly; certainly; honestly; positively; really; truly; undeniably; verily; veritably

INDEFATIGABLE: active; assiduous; busy; diligent; dogged; persevering; persistent; pertinacious; sedulous; strong; tireless; unflagging; unremitting; untiring; unwearable; unwearying; vigorous

INDEFINITE: (**see** "ambiguous") ambivalent; aoristic; blurred; confused; desultory; doubtful; dubious; durable; equivocal; erratic; everlasting; general; hesitant; heterogeneous; impersonal; imprecise; inconclusive; inconstant; indefinitive; indeterminable; indeterminate; indistinct; inexact; infinite; lax; loose; nebulous; obscure; purposeless; rambling; random; shifting; *sine die*; smudged; uncertain; unclear; undecided;

undefined; undeterminable; undetermined; unformalized; universal; unknown; unlimited; unmathematical; unsettled; vague; wavering; INDEFINITENESS: (see "uncertainty") ambiguity; dubiosity; dubiousness; indefinitude; indistinction; inexactitude; inexactness; nebulosity; obscurity; twilight

INDELIBLE: (see "permanent") ineradicable; uneradicable; unerasable

INDELICATE: (see "indecent") coarse; gross; immodest; improper; lewd; nasty; obscene; raw; risqué; rough; rude; salacious; scabrous; tactless; uncouth; unrefined; vulgar; INDELICACY: (see "indecency") impudicity; nastiness; rawness; salaciousness; salacity; scabrousness; vulgarity

INDEMNIFY: bond; compensate; exempt; guarantee; insure; pay; recompense; reimburse; repay; satisfy; secure

INDENT: dent; groove; hollow; impress; jag; join; paragraph; pink; notch; scallop; space; tooth; INDENTATION: crena; crenelet; cut; dent; depression; dinge; dint; groove; hollow; impression; nick; notch; recess; serration; space; INDENTED: crenate; depressed; erose; grooved; paragraphed; notched; serrate(d)

INDEPENDENT: alone; autonomic; autonomous; emancipated; free(wheeling); heedless; isolative; objective; outside; primary; self-existing; self-governing; separate(d); sovereign; strong-minded; unaided; unbiased; unbound; uncommitted; unconstrained; undoctrinaire; unencumbered; unregimented; unrestricted; INDEPENDENCE: autarchy; autarky; autonomy; control; emancipation; freedom; homo sui juris; liberty; objectification; self-existence; self-government; self-sufficiency; sovereignty; unconstraint

INDESCRIBABLE: (see "awful") ineffable; inenarrable; undescribable; unspeakable; untellable; unutterable; vague

INDESTRUCTIBLE: (see "everlasting") adamantine; immarcescible; infrangible; inviolable; unconquerable; undestroyable; undestructible; INDESTRUCTIBILITY: see "everlastingness"

INDETERMINATE: (see "indefinite") aoristic; capricious; doubtful; dubious; equivocal; imprecise; indefinitive; indeterminable;

indistinct; irresolute; spontaneous; uncertain; unclear; undecided; undeterminable; unfixable; unfixed; unknown; unstable; vague

INDEX: concordance; contents; direction; director; exponent; file; finger; fist; forefinger; gnomon; hand; indication; indicator; list; mark; measure; needle; pointer; preface; prologue; ratio; repertory; rule(r); sign; table; token; yardstick

INDIAN: brave; Geronimo; Hindu; redman; squaw; Tonto

INDICATE: adumbrate; allude; argue; attest; augur; bespeak; betoken; call; connote; define; demonstrate; denote; depict; designate; deviate; direct; disclose; evidence; evince; exhibit; express; finger; gesture; grade; imply; infer; intimate; manifest; mark; measure; name; note; notify; outline; point; presage; read; refer; register; reveal; show; signify; speak; specify; suggest; tell; token; INDICATION: adumbration; augur (y); cachet; clew; color; connection; connotation; criterion; depiction; direction; evidence; expression; forewarning; gesticulation; gesture; grade; hallmark; harbinger; hint; index; indication; inference; insignia (pl.); insigne; manifestation; mark; measure; note; notification; odor; omen; pointer; portent; presage; proof; revelation; sample; shadow; show; sign(al); smell; stink; suggestion; symbol; symptom; token; trace; umbrage; INDICATIVE: emblematic(al); pathognomic(al); prodromal; significant; significative; significatory; suggestive; symbolic(al); symptomatic; INDICATOR: (see "index") arrow; clock; dial; finger; fist; ga(u)ge; hand; line; mark; measure; odor; omen; pointer; register; revelation; sign(al); smell; symptom; token; tracer

INDICT: accuse; arraign; attack; blame; censure; charge; cite; denounce; impeach; implicate; prosecute; sue; summon; try

INDIFFERENT: aloof; anapodictic; apathetic; average; blasé; careless; cold; cool; cursory; desensitized; detached; disinterested; fair; feckless; formal; frigid; glib; halfhearted; haughty; heedless; immaterial; impassive; imperturbable; inconsequential; inconsiderate; incurious; insensible; insipid; insouciant; insusceptible; invertebrate; jaunty; judicial; lackadaisical; languid; languorous; Laodicean; lethargic; listless; lukewarm; mechanical; mediocre; medium; middling; moderate; negligent; neutral; nonchalant; numb; passable; passive; perfunctory; phlegmatic; pococurante; poor; purposeless; remiss; shiftless; so-so; spiritless; stiff; stoic(al); stolid; superior; supine; tepid; thoughtless; tolerable; trifling; unaffected; unbiased; uncaring; uncommitted; unconcerned; undeflected; undifferentiated; undistracted; undisturbed; undiverted; unenthusiastic; unfeeling; unimportant; unimpressive; unmoved; unprejudiced; untroubled; worthless;   INDIFFERENCE: acedia; apathy; ascesis; callousness; carelessness; casualness; coldness; detachment; frigidity; hebetude; iciness; impartiality; impassivity; inappetency; inattention; indifferency; inertia; insouciance; lackadaisicalness; lackadaisy; languor; lassitude; laxity; listlessness; minauderie; negligence; neutrality; nonchalance; numbness; perfunctoriness; phlegm; pococurantism; sangfroid; stoicism; stolidity; supineness; supinity; unconcern(edness); unconcernment

INDIGENOUS: aboriginal; domestic; edaphic; endemic; inborn; inherent; innate; internal; native; natural; original

INDIGENT: bankrupt; destitute; down-and-out; down-at-heels; hungry; impecunious; impoverished; insolvent; lacking; moneyless; needy; penniless; penurious; poor; squalid; void; wanting; INDIGENCE: dearth; destitution; distress; famine; hunger; mendacity; need; pauperism; pennilessness; penury; poverty; privation; squalidity; starvation; sting; straits; tenuity; want

INDIGNANT: (see "angry") aroused; hot; incensed; irate; ireful; mad; provoked; resentful; roused; INDIGNATION: (see "anger") acrimony; animosity; annoyance; choler; contempt; disdain; displeasure; dudgeon; exasperation; fury; huff; indignity; irascibility; ire; passion; pique; rage; resentment; scorn; spleen; temper; umbrage; virulence; wrath;   INDIGNITY: abuse; affront; contempt; contumely; discourtesy; disdain; dishonor; disrespect; humiliation; ignominy; impertinence; impudence; incivility; infamy; injury; insolence; insult; lèse-majesté; obloquy; offense; opprobrium; outrage; reproach; scorn; scurrility; slight; unpleasantness; wrong

INDIRECT: (see "devious") ambagious; ambivalent; circuitous; circular; circumferential; circumlocutious; circumlocutory; circumstantial; collateral; consequential; crooked; deceitful; deviating; dishonest; inferential; inferred; mediate; misleading; oblique; roundabout; serpentine; tangential;

INDIRECTION: (see "deviousness") aimlessness; ambiguity; ambivalence; circuity; circumbendibus; circumlocution; circumstantiality; deceitfulness; detour; deviation; dishonesty; duplicity; indirectness; inference; obliquity; sinuosity; tortuosity

INDISCERNIBLE: see "imperceptible"

INDISCREET: audacious; brash; careless; foolish; heedless; ill-advised; impolite; imprudent; incautious; inconsiderate; injudicious; loose-tongued; negligent; pound-foolish; procacious; prodigal; rash; silly; unjudicious; unrestricted; untactful; unwary; unwise; INDISCRETION: audacity; brashness; carelessness; foolishness; heedlessness; imprudence; incaution; inconsiderateness; injudiciousness; negligence; procacity; prodigality; rashness; untactfulness; unwariness; unwisdom

INDISCRIMINATE: (see "haphazard") confused; extensive; heterogeneous; hit-or-miss; indiscriminating; indistinguishable; jumbled; loose; mixed; motley; promiscuous; random; sweeping; undistinguishing; unrestrained; wholesale; INDISCRIMINATION: confusion; heterogeneity; promiscuity; unrestraint; INDISPENSABLE: (see "critical") basal; basic; crucial; de rigueur; essential; expedient; fundamental; necessary; needful; obligatory; prerequisite; required; requisite; sine qua non; vital

INDISPOSED: (see "sick") abed; adverse; aeger; averse; backward; bashful; disinclined; hesitant; indolent; loath; reluctant; shy; unfriendly; unwell; unwilling

INDISPUTABLE: (see "certain") actual; apodictic(al); assured; certain; existing; evident; incontestable; incontrovertible; indubitable; infallible; irrefragable; irrefutable; manifest; obvious; positive; real; sure; unassailable; uncontestable; undebatable; undeniable; undoubtable; undoubted; undubitable; unequivocal; unmistakable; unquestionable

INDISTINCT: (see "faint") ambiguous; amorphous; black; blurred; clouded; cloudy; confused; dark(ened); dim(med); dreary; dull; ethereal; foggy; hazy; indefinite; indiscernible; indistinguishable; insubstantial; light; misty; muddy; myopic; nebular; nebulous; obliterate(d); obscurant; obscure; shadowy; smudged; uncertain; undefined; undistinct; vague; vaporous; woolly; INDISTINCTION: see "obscurity"

INDISTINGUISHABLE: see "unclear"

INDITE: compose; dictate; inscribe; pen; write

INDIVIDUAL: **a.** alone; certain; characteristic; custom-made; distinct(ive); each; idiomatic(al); idiosyncratic; indivisible; inseparable; one; ontogenetic; particular; peculiar; *per capita*; personal; private; separate; single; singular; sole; solo; special; specific; striking; tailor-made; uncommon; unconventional; unique; INDIVIDUAL: **n.** (see "person") member; particularity; party; product; specimen; stag; thing; INDIVIDUALITY see "mannerism"

INDOCTRINATE: (see "teach") brainwash; coach; discipline; edify; familiarize; imbue; impregnate; influence; initiate; inject; instruct; propagandize

INDOLENT: see "lazy"; INDOLENCE: (see "laziness") apathy; faineance; faineancy; idleness; inactivity; indisposition; indolency; inertia; lackadaisy; lethargy; otiosity; sloth(fulness); slowness; sluggardness; sluggishness; tardiness; tranquility

INDOMITABLE: see "intractable"

INDORSE: see "endorse"

INDUBITABLE: (see "certain") evident; indisputable; ineluctable; manifest; open; real; sure; undeniable; undubitable; unquestionable

INDUCE: abet; actuate; allure; arouse; cause; court; drive; effect; encourage; entice; favor; get; impel; incite; influence; inspire; instigate; lead; motivate; move; persuade; prevail; procure; prod; provoke; seduce; seek; spur; tempt; urge; wheedle; INDUCEMENT: drive; encouragement; enticement; favor; incitation; incitement; inspiration; instigation; motivation; persuasion; prod; provocation; raise; seduction; spur; stick; urge

INDULGE: allow; baby; cherish; cocker; coddle; cosset; encourage; expend; favor; fondle; foster; grant; gratify; hug; humor; love; mollycoddle; overeat; pamper; pet; placate; please; sate; satiate; satisfy; spoil; undertake; wet-nurse; wreak; yield; INDULGENCE: compassion; easiness; favor; fondness; grace; gratification; kindness; leniency; lenity; liberality; liking; love; mercy; pleasure; privilege; remission; satisfaction; self-gratification; self-indulgence; tenderness

INDURATE: (see "stubborn") callous; cold-blooded; hard(ened); inconsiderate; inured; obdurate; premeditated; unfeeling

INDUSTRIOUS: (see "active") ambitious; assiduous; attentive; busy; constant; diligent; energetic; engaged; hardworking; indefatigable; intent; laborious; live(ly); occupied; operose; painstaking; persevering; sedulous; steadfast; vigorous; working; zealous; INDUSTRY: (see "activity") ambition; application; enterprise; exertion; industriousness; intentness; labor(iousness); manufacturing; market; operosity; pains; patience; perseverance; persistency; pursuit; sedulity; sedulousness; skill; steadfastness; task; toil; trade; traffic; undertaking; vigor; work; zeal

INEBRIATE: **v.** excite; exhilarate; infatuate; intoxicate; INEBRIATE(D): **a.** (see "drunk") drunken; exhilarated; intoxicated; sloppy; stupefied; tight; tipsy; INEBRIATE: **n.** (see "drunkard") sot; toper

INEFFECTUAL *or* INEFFECTIVE: (see "inefficient") abortive; canceled; clumsy; deleted; dragging; empty; faltering; feckless; feeble; flabby; flaccid; fruitless; fumbling; futile; halting; hollow; idle; impossible; impotent; inadequate; inapt; incapable; inconsequential; inefficacious; inept; infirm; lacking; noneffective; resultless; toothless; unavailing; uncertain; uneffectual; unfruitful; unprevailing; useless; vain; vetoed; void; wasteful; wavering; weak

INEFFICIENT: (see "ineffectual") clumsy; feckless; fumbling; gauche; handless; impractical; inapt; incapable; indisposed; inefficacious; inept; inexpert; irresponsible; lackadaisical; lazy; poor; shiftless; unfunctional; unworkmanlike; wasteful; weak

INELEGANT: (see "crude" and "ugly") awkward; clumsy; discourteous; gauche; graceless; impolite; ungenial; ungenteel; ungraceful; unhandsome

INELUCTABLE: (see "certain") doomed; fated; indubitable; inescapable; inevitable; irresistible

INEPT: (see "clumsy") absurd; asinine; awkward; bungling; foolish; footless; gauche; impotent; inadequate; inappropriate; inapt; lacking; maladroit; pointless; preposterous; senseless; silly; stupid; unapt; unbecoming;

unfit; unfortunate; unhandy; unsuitable; unsuited

INEQUALITY: anomalism; anomaly; changeableness; dichotomy; difference; disparity; disproportion; dissimilarity; divergence; diversity; imparity; inegalitarianism; inequity; injustice; irregularity; roughness; unequality; unequalness; unevenness

INERT: (see "dead") amort; apathetic; asleep; cloddish; comatose; dull; idle; inactive; inanimate; indolent; latent; lazy; lethargic; lifeless; neutral; passive; potential; powerless; quiescent; quiet; slow; sluggish; sodden; still; stolid; supine; torpid; INERTIA: indisposition; inertness; potentiality; quiescence; sluggishness; stillness; stolidity; supinity; torpidity; vis inertiae

INESCAPABLE: certain; *che sarà sarà*; destined; direct; doomed; fated; fateful; imminent; indubitable; ineluctable; ineludible; inevitable; inexorable; irresistible; necessary; needful; sure; unavoidable; unescapable; unevitable

INESTIMABLE: (see "valuable") unestimable

INEVITABLE: see "inescapable"

INEXACT: (see "vague") acategorical; ambivalent; desultory; equivocal; erroneous; false; loose; uncertain; unclear; undetermined; unexact; unstated; INEXACTITUDE: (see "error") equivocality; imponderability; imprecision; inexactness; uncertainty

INEXCUSABLE: excuseless; inexpiable; irremissible; unforgivable; unjustifiable; unpardonable; unprovoked; unwarrantable

INEXHAUSTIBLE: (see "boundless") drainless; unexhaustible

INEXISTENCE: nihilism; nonentity; nonexistence; nullibicity; nullity

INEXORABLE: (see "certain") firm; grim; imminent; immovable; implacable; inescapable; inflexible; obdurate; pitiless; relentless; resolute; severe; unyielding

INEXPEDIENT: (see "inopportune") unexpedient

INEXPENSIVE: (see "cheap") popular; uncostly; unexpensive

INEXPERIENCED: (see "ignorant") amateur(ish); beardless; callow; fledgling; green; immature; incompetent; inconversant; inexpert; maladroit; prentice; raw; rude; unexperienced; unfledged; uninitiated; universal; unpracticed; unproved; unseasoned; unskilled; untaught; untrained; untried; verdant; youthful

INEXPERT: (see "crude" and "inexperienced") handless; illiterate; inefficient; unpracticed; unskilled; untrained

INEXPLICABLE: causeless; enigmatic(al); mysterious; preternatural; strange; supermundane; supernatural; unaccountable

INEXPRESSIBLE: see "untellable"

INFALLIBLE: (see "perfect") certain; divine; indubitable; inerrant; inexhaustable; sure; unerring; unexhaustible; unflagging

INFAMOUS: (see "bad") abhorrent; arrant; atrocious; criminal; dedecorous; despicable; detestable; discreditable; disgraceful; dishonorable; disreputable; evil; heinous; ignominious; inglorious; nefarious; notorious; obloquial; odious; opprobrious; outrageous; scandalous; shameful; vicious; villainous; wicked; INFAMY: abasement; atrocity; criminality; discredit; disgrace; dishonor; disrepute; evil; ignominy; notoriety; obloquy; odium; opprobrium; outrage; scandal; shame; viciousness; villainy; wickedness

INFANT: babe; baby; bairn; child; chile; chit; infans; minor; nursling; papoose; tot; INFANCY: babyhood; *bas âge*; beginning; childhood; cradle; incunabula (pl.); incunabulum; minority; nonage

INFATUATE: (see "charm") befool; besot; captivate; capture; enamor; INFATUATION: attachment; *béguin*; folly; fondness; foolishness; love; madness; passion

INFECT: see "contaminate;" INFECTED: abscessed; contaminated; corrupt; defiled; diseased; impure; poisoned; polluted; purulent; pustular; pustulated; putrescent; septic; spoiled; tainted; toxic; INFECTION: (see "contagion") abscess; contagiosity; contagiousness; contamination; corruption; disease; inflammation; pathology; poison; pollution; purulence; pustulation; putrescence; septicity; sore; INFECTUOUS *or* INFECTIVE: catching; communicable; contagious; contaminating; corrupting; corruptive; demoralizing; pathological; poisonous; septic; sympathetic; vitiating

INFER: (see "assume") collect; conclude; conjecture; consider; deduce; deduct; derive; divine; draw; educe; gather; guess; hint; imply; indicate; judge; portend; presume; reason; regard; suppose; surmise; think; understand; INFERENCE: assumption; conclusion; conjecture; corollary; deduction; education; guess; hint; hypothesis; illation; implication; indication; judgment; presumption; sequitur; supposition; surmise; understanding; INFERENTIAL: conjectural; deductive; denotative; hypothesized; illative; implicative; inferred; presumptuous; putative; supposititious; tacit; understood

INFERIOR: cheap(ened); cheaper; coarse; déclassé; defective; feeble; gross; humble; ill; inadequate; indifferent; infirm; insignificant; junk(y); less(er); low(-class); lower; low-grade; low-level; meager; mediocre; nether; offgrade; paltry; petty; plain; poor(er); punk; puny; sad; scabby; scaly; second(ary); second-class; second-drawer; second-rate; shabby; shoddy; shopworn; slim; subaltern-(ate); subnormal; suboptimal; subordinate; substandard; substitute; threadbare; trifling; undergrade; unimportant; vile; worthless; INFERIORITY: dearth; feebleness; inadequacy; infirmity; lessness; mediocrity; pettiness; poorness; poverty; subnormality; subordination; worthlessness

INFERNAL: (see "bad") all-fired; atrocious; avernal; awful; chthonian; chthonic; cursed; damnable; damned; demoniac(al); devilish; diabolic(al); evil; fiendish; fire-and-brimstone; flagitious; flagrant; hateful; hell(fire); hellish; horrible; horrific; malevolent; malicious; malign(ant); Mephistophelean; Mephistophelian; pandemoniac(al); Satanic; Stygian; Tartarean; vicious; wicked

INFERNO: abyss; Avernus; conflagration; fire (and brimstone); Gehenna; Hades; hell(fire); holocaust; pit; Sheol

INFERTILE: (see "fruitless") abortive; arid; barren; dead; futile; infecund; sterile; unfertile; unproductive; unprolific; INFERTILITY: aridity; barrenness; fruitlessness; futility; infertility; sterility; unfruitfulness; unproductiveness

INFESTED: beset; contaminated; engulfed; harassed; haunted; infected; infiltrated; invaded; overrun; plagued; teeming; tormented; vexed

INFIDEL: agnostic; atheist; disbeliever; heathen; heretic; Kaffir; pagan; Saracen; skeptic; unbeliever

INFILTRATE: see "subvert"

INFINITE: (see "eternal") absolute; boundless; cosmic; divine; endless; illimitable; immeasurable; immense; inconceivable; indefinite; inexhaustible; limitless; unconditioned; unfathomable; unfathomed; universal; unknowable; unlimited; vast; INFINITY: boundlessness; cosmos; endlessness; eternality; eternity; immensity; infiniteness; infinitude; olam; perpetuity; universality; vastitude; vastness; world

INFIRM: (see "sick") adynamic; ailing; anemic; anile; asthenic; broken-down; dangerous; debilitated; decrepit; disabled; doddered; doddering; enervated; enfeebled; exhausted; faltering; feeble; flimsy; fragile; frail; gray; incapacitated; insecure; insincere; invalid; irresolute; lame; languid; loose; paralyzed; precarious; sapless; senile; shaky; sickly; spent; tenuous; tottering; unestablished; unsound; unstable; unsteady; vacillating; wasted; weak(ened); worn

INFLAME: anger; animate; annoy; arouse; awaken; burn; corrupt; enkindle; enrage; enrapture; exasperate; excite; fan; fester; fire; flush; foment; heat; ignite; incense; incite; inspirit; intensify; irritate; kindle; light; pique; prod; provoke; rage; rankle; rekindle; relight; relume; rile; rot; rouse; stimulate; stir; transport; INFLAMMATION: abscess; boil; carbuncle; congestion; contagion; fester; fever; heat; incandescence; infection; phlegmasia; phlogosis; pustule; sore; suppuration; INFLAMMABLE or INFLAMMATORY: accendible; ardent; burnable; burning; carbuncular; combustible; conflagratory; excitable; flammable; hot; ignescent; ignitable; incendiary; irascible; phlogenic; phlogistic; phlogogenetic; piceous; provocative; purulent; red; seditious; suppurative

INFLATE: (see "exaggerate" and "swell") distend; elate; expand; intumesce; tumefy; tumesce; INFLATED: bladdery; bloated; blown; bombastic; dilated; distended; dropsical; exaggerated; expanded; extended; flatulent; hypertrophic; hypertrophied; incrassate; magniloquent; overblown; over-extended; pompous; portentous; showy; swollen; tumescent; tumid; turgent; turgescent; turgid; tympanic; tympanitic; INFLATION: dilatation; dilation; distention; flatulence; hypertrophy; intumescence; pomposity; tumescence; tumidity; turgescence; turgidity; turgor; tympanites; tympany

INFLECTION: accent; angle; bend; crook; curvature; curve; flexure; modulation; pitch; speech; tenor; tone; turn(ing); variation

INFLEXIBLE: (see "rigid") adamant(ine); austere; dogged; firm; fixed; granitic; grim; hard(headed); hidebound; immutable; implacable; implastic; impliable; indocile; inductible; indurate; indurative; inexorable; intractable; intransigent; iron(clad); ironhanded; irreconcilable; obdurate; obstinate; parochial; persistent; puritanical; refractory; relentless; resolute; restive; retractable; rigorous; rockbound; rugged; ruthless; solid; stark; stern; stiff; stony; stout; strict; strong; stubborn; tenacious; tense; unalterable; unbending; uncompliant; uncompromising; unflexible; ungiving; unmodifiable; unrelenting; unyielding; wooden; INFLEXIBILITY: immutability; immutableness; implacability; implacableness; implasticity; indocility; induration; inexorability; intransigence; obstinacy; persistence; persistency; refractoriness; relentlessness; rigidification; rigidity; sternness; unalterability; unmodifiability; unyieldingness

INFLICT: afflict; deal; foist; impose; lay; perpetrate; press; restrain; trouble; wreak; INFLICTION: affliction; cross; crown of thorns; imposition; restraint; trouble

INFLUENCE: v. actuate; affect; alter; arouse; attract; bend; captivate; capture; charm; coerce; command; compel; constrain; control; determine; dominate; domineer; drag; draw; drive; effect; enchant; entice; excite; guide; impart; impel; impregnate; incite; indoctrinate; induce; infuse; inspire; instigate; lead; master; modify; mold; move; persuade; predominate; prejudice; prompt; reason; regulate; restrain; ride; rouse; rule; sell; stir; sway; take; tinge; touch; weigh; win; INFLUENCE: n. area; ascendency; authority; bias; charm; coercion; command; contagion; control; credit; dominance; domination; dominion; drag; duress; effect; emanation; enchantment; favor; force; gravity; guide; hierarchy; import(ance); impulsion; indoctrination; inspiration; jurisdiction; latitude; leadership; lever; mastery; medicine; miasma; motif; motive; patronage; power; predominance; predomination; preponderance; prestige; prominence; puissance; pull; reputation; rule; sanction;

spell; sphere; stranglehold; strength; superiority; supremacy; sway; wire-pulling; INFLUENTIAL: ascendant; authoritative; coercive; commanding; determinative; dominating; domineering; effective; hierarchic(al); important; masterful; potent; powerful; prestigious; principal; prominent; superior; supreme; weighty

INFLUX: accession; epidemic; illapse; immigration; influxion; inpour(ing); inrush; onrush; scourge; spate; tide

INFORM: (see "educate") acquaint; advertise; advise; air; animate; apprise; brief; delate; enlighten; fink; infuse; inspire; instruct; notify; post; rat; show; signal; sing; snitch; squeal; tattle; teach; tell; train; warn; INFORMED: (see "up-to-date") au courant; au fait; cognizant; conversant; enlightened; instructed; intelligent; notified; posted; taught; trained; warned; INFORMATION: advice(s); briefing; comment; data (pl.); datum; detail(s); dope; edge; education; erudition; facts; figures; instruction; intelligence; item; knowledge; learning; lore; lowdown; message; news; notice; remark; sign(al); teaching; tip; training; wisdom; writing; INFORMATIVE: didactic; educational; enlightening; illuminating; informatory; informing; instructive; propaedeutic(al); revealing; telltale

INFORMAL: (see "familiar") breezy; casual; colloquial; easy(going); en famille; extemporaneous; free (and easy); irregular; natural; offhand; ordinary; relaxed; sans façon; sans souci; shirt-sleeve; simple; unceremonious(ly); unconventional; unformal; unofficial; unorthodox

INFORMER: betrayer; delator; fink; nark; quidnunc; rat; revealer; stool (pigeon); tattler; tattletale; telltale

INFREQUENT: (see "irregular") broken; fugitive; intermittent; isolated; occasional; odd; periodic(al); random; rare; scarce; scattered; seldom; separate; sparse; sporadic; strange; uncommon; unfrequent; unique; unusual; INFREQUENCY: intermittency; irregularity; occasionality; rareness; rarity; scarcity; seldomness; sparcity; sporadicity; uniquity; unusuality

INFRINGE: break; contradict; contravene; dispute; disregard; encroach; hinder; impinge; infract; intervene; intrude; invade; obstruct; oppose; poach; tamper; thwart; touch; transgress; trespass; violate; IN-

FRINGEMENT: break; broach; contravention; encroachment; impingement; infraction; intrusion; nonfulfillment; piracy; plagiarism; transgression; trespass; violation

INFURIATE: see "anger" and "madden"

INFUSE: animate; drench; enchant; enthuse; fill; fire; imbue; immix; implant; impregnate; inculcate; influence; ingrain; inject; inoculate; inspire; inseminate; insinuate; instill; introduce; leaven; macerate; mix; permeate; pervade; shed; soak; steep; transfuse; INFUSION: admixture; affusion; decoction; extract; implantation; impregnation; inculcation; injection; inoculation; inpouring; inspiration; installation; instillation; instillment; mixture; permeation; tea; tincture; transfusion

INGENIOUS: (see "clever") adept; adroit; apt; artful; cunning; daedal(ic); deft; expert; exquisite; fine; gifted; handy; inventive; neat; original; prodigal; resourceful; skillful; witty

INGENUE: (see "beginner") debutante; starlet

INGENUITY: (see "intelligence") art; cleverness; adroitness; aptness; expertise; expertness; finesse; skillfulness; stratagem; trick; virtuosity; wit

INGENUOUS: (see "frank") artless; candid; childlike; forward; guileless; honest; innocent; naif; naive; natural; open; quaint; simple; sincere; straight(forward); trusting; unaware; undisguised; unmistrusting; unsophisticated; unwary

INGEST: see "consume" and "eat"

INGRAINED: see "chronic" and "deep"

INGRATIATE: (see "charm") attract; blandish; cajole; captivate; capture; disarm; flatter; oil; seduce; INGRATIATING: (see "slick") oleaginous; unctuous

INGRATITUDE: see "ungratefulness"

INGREDIENT: (see "element") component; constituent; detail; essence; factor; item; part; substance

INGRESS: (see "entrance") access; adit; door; entranceway; entree; entry; foyer; gate; hall; opening; portal

INHABIT: (see "dwell") indwell; occupy; populate; INHABITANT(S): boarder; cit(izen); denizen; domicile; dweller; habitué; inmate; lodger; occupant; people; populace; resident; tenant; voter; INHABITING: domiciliary; indwelling; residentiary

INHALE: breathe; consume; inspire; respire; smell; sniff; swallow; INHALATION: see "breath"

INHARMONIOUS: (see "unharmonious") cacophonous; conflicting; disagreeing; discordant; grating; incompatible; inharmonic; jarring; raspy; unattuned; uncongenial; unmusical; untoned; untuned

INHERE: abide; belong; cleave; dwell; indwell; inhabit; lodge; occupy; reside; stick; INHERENT: (see "hereditary") abiding; basic; characteristic; congenital; connatal; connate; connatural; dwelling; elemental; essential; immanent; inalienable; inborn; inbred; indwelling; infixed; ingenital; ingrained; innate; inseparable; internal; intrinsic; latent; native; natural; potential; radical; subjective; unborrowed

INHERITANCE: benefaction; bequest; entail; estate; gift; hereditament(s); heredity; heritage; legacy; patrimony; succession; INHERITOR: donee; heir; legatee; parcener; INHERITABLE: descendible; hereditable; hereditary; transmissible; INHERITED: ancestral; congenital; descended; hereditary; inborn; innate; transmitted

INHIBIT: (see "check") arrest; ban; bar; bind; choke; constrain; constrict; crimp; curb; deter; diminish; discourage; dissuade; enjoin; forbid; hamper; hinder; imprison; interdict; interfere; limit; obstruct; obtrude; oppress; overcome; prevent; prohibit; proscribe; quench; repress; restrain; retard; snub; stifle; stop; suppress; veto; withhold; INHIBITED: see "restrained"

INHOSPITABLE: (see "unfriendly") inhuman; ungentle; unhuman

INHUMAN(E): (see "savage") barbaric; barbarous; bestial; brutal; brutish; butcherly; cold; cruel; devilish; diabolical; dispiteous; disregardful; Draconian; fell; ferocious; fiendish; fierce; grim; ignoble; impersonal; impiteous; infernal; infrahuman; malevolent; malign(ant); mechanical; merciless; Neronian; nonhuman; pitiless; rancorous; relentless; remorseless; rough; rude; ruffianly; ruthless; Satanic(al); savage; sub-human; superhuman; truculent; unfeeling; ungentle; unhuman; unkind; unmerciful; wanton; wicked

INIMICAL: (see "harmful") adverse; antagonistic; averse; contrary; dangerous; hostile; hurtful; unfavorable; unfriendly

INIQUITY: (see "evil") abomination; crime; hurt; injustice; misdeed; sin; sinfulness; vice; wickedness; wrong; INIQUITOUS: see "evil" and "wicked"

INITIAL(LY) *ab initio;* aboriginal; aborigine; *ab ovo;* beginning; first; head; inchoative; incipient; initiatory; original; rudimental; rudimentary; start(ing); virginal

INITIATE: (see "begin") accelerate; actuate; admit; baptise; build; commence; enter; establish; found; inaugurate; indoctrinate; induct; install; instate; instigate; instruct; introduce; invent; invest; join; lead; open; ordain; originate; propound; receive; release; set(tle); spark; start; stimulate; teach; trigger; INITIATION: (see "beginning") acceleration; actuation; baptism; ceremony; commencement; inauguration; indoctrination; induction; installation; introduction; ordeal; rite; start; INITIATOR: (see "beginner") actuator; bellweather; catalyst; detonator; developer; founder; inceptor; inventor; originator; settler

INITIATIVE: (see "aptitude" and "energy") acceleration; drive; gumption; lead(ership); overture

INJECT: immit; inoculate; insert; interrupt; introduce; intromit; intrude; offer; propose; INJECTION: clyster; congestion; enema; hint; inoculation; intromission; intrusion

INJUDICIOUS: (see "indiscreet") prodigal; unjudicious

INJUNCTION: admonition; ban; command; fiat; interdiction; mandate; mandatum; order; precept; prohibition; taboo; tabu; writ

INJURE: abuse; affront; assault; bang; batter; blemish; break; bruise; bungle; burn; corrupt; cripple; damage; damnify; debase; deface; defile; deform; degrade; despoil; destroy; disable; disfigure; disserve; distort; disturb; exacerbate; founder; fracture; grieve; hamper; harm; hurt; impair; insult; lame; libel; maim; maltreat; mangle; mar(k);

mayhem; militate; offend; prejudice; ruin; scar; scathe; scratch; shock; slander; spoil; sprain; strain; sully; tarnish; traumatize; twist; vitiate; warp; weaken; worsen; wound; wreck; wrench; INJURY: assault; bane; bang; battery; blemish; bruise; damage; damnification; decay; defacement; degradation; destruction; detriment; disservice; distortion; expense; evil; harm; hurt; ill; impairment; iniquity; injustice; insult; lesion; loss; mayhem; mischief; mutilation; offense; outrage; prejudice; ruin; scar; scratch; sorrow; trauma(tism); violence; warp; waste; wear; wound; wreck; wrong; INJURIOUS: abusive; bad; baneful; contagious; damaging; deadly; defamatory; degrading; deleterious; destructive; detrimental; harmful; hurtful; impairing; inimical; iniquitous; invidious; malevolent; malign(ant); mischievous; nocent; nocuous; noisome; noxious; pernicious; poisonous; prejudicial; ruinous; shocking; slanderous; toxic; traumatic; unhealthful; unhealthy; unjust; venomous; wrackful; wrong

INJUSTICE: (see "partiality" and "wrong") inequality; iniquity; unfairness

INKLING: adumbration; clew; clue; glimmer; hint; intimation; notion; odor; overtone; rumor; smell; suggestion; suspicion; trace; undertone; whisper

INKY: (see "black") atramental; atramentous; colored; dark; marked; murky; stained

INLET: arm, bay; bight; cove; creek; door; entrance; fiord; firth; orifice; ria; strait; voe

INN: abode; auberge; caravansary; fonda; hospice; hostel(ry); hotel; lodge; posada; roadhouse; stop; tavern; xenodochium

INNATE: (see "hereditary") congenital; constitutional; endogenous; essential; hidden; idiopathic; inborn; inbred; indigenous; ingenital; ingrained; inherent; inherited; innative; inner; instinctive; internal; intrinsic; intuitive; native; natural; unacquired

INNER: (see "internal") deep; emotional; endogenous; indistinct; inherent; inmost; innate; innermost; inside; interior; intestinal; intestine; inward; mental; middle; nervous; obscure; psychogenic

INNOCENT: Arcadian; artless; blameless; candid; chaste; cherubic; childlike; clean; clear; destitute; direct; distrustless; exemplary; faultless; good; guileless; guiltless;

gullible; harmless; holy; honest; ignorant; immaculate; impeccable; impeccant; inculpable; innocuous; inobnoxious; inoffensive; irreproachable; lily-white; naive; nonpoisonous; offenseless; pastoral; peaceful; permitted; pristine; pure; right(eous); schemeless; seraphic; simple(minded); sinless; snow-white; spotless; undeflowered; undisguised; undissembled; unfallen; unfaulty; unguilty; unimpeachable; unobnoxious; unoffending; unoffensive; unrebukable; unremorseful; unreprovable; unsophisticated; unstained; unsullied; unsuspecting; untainted; untouched; upright; virgin; virtuous; INNOCENCE: artlessness; blamelessness; chastity; holiness; honesty; ignorance; immaculacy; impeccability; impeccancy; inculpability; ingenuousness; innocuousness; naiveté; noninvolvement; purity; righteousness; simplicity; sinlessness; spotlessness; verdancy; virtue

INNOCUOUS: (**see** "harmless") inoffensive; insignificant; insipid; pallid

INNOVATION: beginning; change; first; introduction; invention; novation; novelty

INNUENDO: accusation; allusion; aspersion; connotation; double entendre; hint; implication; insinuation; intimation; odor; slur; smell; *sous-entendu;* suggestion

INNUMERABLE: see "many"

INOFFENSIVE: (**see** "peaceful") harmless; innocent; innocuous; inobnoxious; offenseless; peaceable; unobnoxious; unoffending; unoffensive

INOPPORTUNE: (**see** "untimely") impracticable; improper; inappropriate; inconvenient; inexpedient; intempestive; malapropos; undue; unexpedient; unseasonable; unsuitable; unsuited

INORDINATE: (**see** "excessive") copious; disorderly; extraordinary; extravagant; fabulous; hog-wild; immoderate; irregular; large; over (filled); overflowing; replete; superfluous; undue; unique; unlimited; unrestrained; unrestricted

INQUEST: assize; autopsy; finding; hearing; inquiry; inquisition; investigation; jury; postmortem; probe; question(ing); quiz; search

INQUIRE: **see** "ask" and "examine"; INQUIRY: (**see** "examination") analysis;

catechism; disquisition; explanation; inquest; inquisition; inspection; interrogation; investigation; probe; pursuit; query; quest; question(ing); quiz; reconnaissance; request; research; scouting; scrutiny; search; survey; test; trial

INQUISITIVE: (**see** "curious") aggressive; disquisitive; forward; inquiring; inquisitorial; intrusive; meddlesome; meddling; nosy; overcurious; peeping; probing; prying; scrutinizing; searching; snooping; snoopy; suspicious

INSANE: addled; addlepated; amok; askew; balmy; batty; berserk; buggy; chaotic; compulsive; coo-coo; crackbrained; cracked; crackpot; crazy; cuckoo; daffy; daft; delirious; demented; deranged; disordered; distraught; disturbed; dithyrambic; dizzy; dopey; eccentric; erratic; extravagant; feverish; foolish; frantic; frenetic; frenzied; goofy; hallucinatory; harassed; impractical; incompetent; infatuated; irrational; jumbled; loco; lunatic; mad; maniac(al); manic; morbid; *non compos* (*mentis*); nutty; obsessed; odd; off; paranoid; possessed; psychopathic; psychotic; rabid; ree; ridiculous; schizophrenic; screwy; slaphappy; *tête exalté; tête exaltée* (fem.); unhinged; unreasonable; unsane; unsound; unusual; upside-down; visionary; wacky; wild; witless; wrong; INSANITY: aberration; alienation; amentia; crazedness; craziness; delirium; dementia (praecox); depression; derangement; distraction; dizziness; dopiness; dottiness; egomania; feeblemindedness; *folie;* folly; frenzy; goofiness; idiocy; incompetence; incompetency; lunacy; madness; mania; nuttiness; obsession; paranoia; psychosis; rabidness; schizophrenia; screwiness; unreasonableness; unsoundness (of mind); vesania; wackiness

INSANITARY: contaminated; dirty; feculent; filthy; septic; squalid; unhealthy; unhygienic; unsterilized; unwashed; vile

INSATIABLE: (**see** "gluttonous") unfulfillable; unsatisfiable

INSCRIBE: address; autograph; dedicate; engrave; enroll; enter; etch; impress; legend; mark; print; record; sign; stamp; write; INSCRIPTION: autograph; colophon; description; engraving; enrollment; epigraph; etching; heading; instruction; label; legend; mark; name; printing; record; signature; tablet; title; titulus; writing

INSCRUTABLE: (**see** "hidden") abstruse;

arcane; baffling; cabalistic; dark; deep; enigmatic(al); incomprehensible; inexplainable; inexplorable; inner; mysterious; profound; puzzling; secret; undecipherable; unfathomed; vague

INSECT: **see** "bug"

INSECURE: (**see** "shaky") asea; claptrap; dangerous; dubious; flimsy; hazardous; infirm; instable; loose; perilous; precarious; reeling; rickety; risky; tottering; tottery; uncertain; unfirm; unguarded; unprotected; unreliable; unsafe; unstable; unsteady; unsure; weak(ened); wobbly; INSECURITY: anxiety; apprehension; apprehensiveness; danger; hazard; incertitude; instability; jeopardy; looseness; peril; risk; shakiness; uncertainty; unreliability; unsafety; unsteadiness; weakness

INSEMINATE: fecundate; fertilize; implant; impregnate; inject; inoculate; instill; pregnate; promulgate; seed; sow; spermatize; spread

INSENSIBLE *or* INSENSITIVE: analgesic; anesthetic; apathetic; callous; color-blind; comatose; dull; hardened; impassive; imperceptible; inanimate; indifferent; insensate; insentient; lethargic; lost; meaningless; narcotic; numb; oblivious; obtuse; opiate; pachydermatous; Philistine; Philistinic; rocky; soporific; stolid; stupid; stuporous; surd; thick-skinned; thickskulled; torpid; unaware; unconscious; unfeeling; unimpressionable; unsensitive; INSENSIBILITY *or* INSENSITIVITY: analgesia; anesthesia; apathy; carus; coma; indifference; insentience; lethargy; narcosis; obtuseness; obtusity; sopor; stupidity; stupor; torpidity; torpor; trance; unconsciousness; unfeeling; unimpressionability; unsensitivity

INSERT: **v.** attach; cram; enclose; enroll; fix; immit; implant; infix; ingraft; inject; inlay; inoculate; inset; instill; intercalate; interlard; interpolate; interpose; introduce; intromit; place; plant; probe; shoot; shove; stick; stuff; INSERT(ION): **n.** enclosure; *entredeux;* gore; implantation; injection; inlay; inoculation; inset; installation; intercalation; interlardation; interplantation; interpolation; panel

INSIDE: **see** "interior"

INSIDIOUS: (**see** "sly") arch; cancerous; cankerous; crafty; creeping; cunning; dangerous; deceitful; deceptive; designing; elu-

sive; foxy; guileful; illusory; inching; intriguing; oily; oleaginous; sinuous; slick; slow; snaky; sneaky; snide; subt(i)le; treacherous; tricky; untrustworthy; wily

INSIGHT: (**see** "discernment") acumen; apperception; apprehension; awareness; clairvoyance; cleverness; comprehension; cunning; discrimination; empathy; instinct; introspection; intuition; judgment; keenness; learning; mentality; penetration; perception; perspicacity; perspicuity; shrewdness; understanding; wisdom

INSIGNIA: (**see** "badge") bars; buttons; decorations; emblems; insigne (sing.); marks; medals; regalia; ribbons; stars

INSIGNIFICANT: commonplace; contemptible; diminutive; flimsy; foolish; humble; immaterial; inadequate; inane; inconsequential; inferior; infinitesimal; irrelevant; jerkwater; lacking; lightweight; low; mean -(ingless); microscopic; miniscule; minor; nominal; nonsignificant; paltry; petit; petty; picayune; picayunish; puisne; puny; slight; small; tenuous; trifling; trivial; unconsequential; undistinguished; unimportant; unimposing; unnoticeable; unsignificant; unsubstantial; weak; INSIGNIFICANCE: bauble; contemptibility; immateriality; infinitesimality; insignificancy; insubstantiality; irrelevancy; minitude; trifle; triviality; unimportance; unsubstantiality

INSINCERE: (**see** "dishonest") artificial; counterfeit; crocodilian; deceitful; deceptive; disingenuous; double(-faced); duplicitous; faithless; false; feigned; fulsome; hydraheaded; hypocritical; make-believe; meretricious; phony; specious; theatrical; tongue in cheek; two-faced; untrue; INSINCERITY: applesauce; artificiality; bathos; deceitfulness; dishonesty; disingenuity; dissimulation; duplicity; falseness; hypocrisy; sentimentalism; sentimentality; theatricality

INSINUATE: (**see** "hint") allude; connote; denote; imply; infuse; ingratiate; instill; intimate; mean; mention; penetrate; purport; signify; suggest; whisper; wind; INSINUATION: **see** "hint"

INSIPID: (**see** "bland") banal; barren; cloying; common(place); dead; dry; dull; flat; flavorless; forceless; frigid; frothy; heavy; inane; inanimate; jejune; lackadaisical; lackluster; lifeless; mawkish; monotonous; namby-pamby; palling; plodding; pointless; prosaic(al); prosy; savorless; sirupy;

slow; stale; sugary; sweet; syrupy; tasteless; tepid; treacly; trite; unimpressive; uninspired; uninteresting; unsavory; vapid; watery; weak; wearisome; wishy-washy

INSIST: argue; ask; demand; emphasize; force; importune; maintain; persevere; persist; press; prod; provoke; stress; urge; INSISTENT: compelling; conspicuous; demanding; determined; emphatic; exigent; importunate; impulsive; loud; overdetermined; persevering; persistent; pressing; prominent; urging; vehement

INSOLENT: (see "impudent") arrant; audacious; cheeky; cocky; contemptuous; contumelious; disrespectful; familiar; haughty; hubristic; impertinent; impudent; insulting; offensive; overbearing; pert; presumptuous; proud; sassy; saucy; shameless; snooty; INSOLENCE: (see "impudence") arrogance; audacity; cheek(iness); contempt(uousness); contumacy; contumely; disdain; disrespect; effrontery; familiarity; flippancy; haughtiness; hubris; impertinence; insolency; lip; presumption; pride; protervity; sass(iness); sauciness; scorn; shamelessness; swagger

INSOLVENT: (see "bankrupt") deficient; fortuneless; impecunious; impoverished; indebted; moneyless; penniless; poor; reduced; ruined; straitened

INSOUCIANT: calm; carefree; dreamy; fickle; flighty; giddy; indifferent; lackadaisical; lighthearted; nonchalant; thoughtless; unbothered; unconcerned

INSPECT: audit; check; examine; investigate; look; observe; oversee; probe; prospect; prove; pry; scan; scrutinize; search; see; superintend; supervise; view; INSPECTION: check-over; checkup; examination; inquest; inquiry; investigation; look; overseeing; probe; proof; prospection; reconnaissance; scrutiny; search; study; superintendence; supervision; surveillance; survey; verification; view

INSPIRE: affect; animate; arouse; beacon; breathe; buoy; cause; cheer; elate; encourage; energize; enliven; enrapture; exalt; excite; exhilarate; fire; flush; foment; hearten; imbue; impel; incite; induce; inflate; influence; infuse; inhale; inspirit; intoxicate; motivate; move; occasion; persuade; produce; promote; prompt; provoke; quicken; raise; rouse; spur; stimulate; stir; INSPIRING: animating; awesome; encouraging;

exhilarating; grand(iloquent); heartening; inciting; infusive; inspirational; inspiriting; instigative; luminous; magnificent; moving; quickening; rousing; stimulating; stimulatory; stirring; uplifting; INSPIRATION: afflation; afflatus; brainstorm; breathing; enthusiasm; evocativeness; fury; genius; hint; idea; influence; inhalation; insight; luminosity; promotion; provocation; spur; stimulant; stimulation; stimulus; suggestion; suggestiveness; vision

INSPISSATE: condense; desiccate; dry; evaporate; intensify; thicken

INSTABLE: see "shaky;" INSTABILITY: apprehensiveness; imbalance; incertitude; inconstancy; nervousness; shakiness; unbalance; unfixedness; unstability; unstableness

INSTALL: (see "establish") coronate; crown; fix; inaugurate; induct; initiate; instate; introduce; invest; open; ordain; place; seat; set(tle)

INSTANCE: (see "circumstance") antecedent; case; detail; elucidation; example; exception; exemplification; ground; illustration; impulse; instigation; item; lesson; motive; object; occasion; occurrence; pattern; point; precedent; proof; request; sample; situation; specimen; suggestion; suit; type

INSTANT(ANEOUS): a. current; direct; hair-trigger; immediate(ly); importunate; insisting; momentary; present; pressing; prompt; responsive; semelfactive; simultaneous; urgent; INSTANT: n. blink; *clin d'oeil*; flash; instantaneity; jiff(y); minute; moment; nonce; sec(ond); shake; simultaneity; time; trice; twinkle; twinkling; whiff; wink

INSTIGATE: (see "arouse") abet; actuate; animate; back; dispose; drive; egg; employ; encourage; entice; exhort; ferment; foment; force; goad; impel; incite; induce; influence; infuse; insist; inspire; inspirit; invoke; move; persuade; plan; plot; predispose; press; prevail; prompt; provoke; push; rouse; scheme; shove; spur; start; stimulate; suborn; sway; tempt; urge

INSTIL(L): (see "impregnate") deposit; impart; implant; inculcate; indoctrinate; infiltrate; infuse; inject; inoculate; insinuate; introduce; teach; train

INSTINCT: appetency; appetite; aptitude; bent; capacity; craving; faculty; feeling;

impulse; insight; intuition; propensity; reflex; tendency; wisdom; wish

INSTITUTE: (see "begin" and "direct") advance; establish; offer; promote; raise; INSTITUTION(S): college; establishment; fixture; foundation; government; school; tradition; university

INSTRUCT: apprise; bid; brief; charge; coach; command; direct; discipline; drill; edify; educate; enjoin; enlighten; guide; impart; inculcate; indoctrinate; inform; order; prime; school; show; steer; teach; train; tutor; INSTRUCTIVE: didactic(al); edificatory; educational; expository; informative; moralistic; preceptive; INSTRUCTION: briefing; coaching; didactics; direction; discipline; dosage; education; enlightenment; formula; guardianship; guidance; indoctrination; information; knowledge; lesson; method; order(s); pedagogy; precept; prescription; propaedeutics; protection; recipe; teaching; tuition; tutelage; tutorship; INSTRUCTOR: coach; disciplinarian; docent; doctor; don; educator; guide; informer; lector; lecturer; master; preceptor; prof(essor); regent; teacher; tutor

INSTRUMENT: agency; agent; appliance; armamentaria (pl.); armamentarium; bond; channel; contract; contrivance; creature; deed; device; document; dupe; equipment; gadget; implement; indenture; instrumentaria (pl.); lease; machine(ry); means; medium; organ; paper; person; tool; utensil; vehicle; will; INSTRUMENTALITY: (see "tool") agency; aid; intermediary; means; media (pl.); medium; organ; vehicle; INSTRUMENTAL: accessory; aiding; auxiliary; causal; conducive; contributory; helpful; helping; orchestral; potent; promoting

INSUBORDINATE: contumacious; defiant; disloyal; disobedient; disobeying; disregardful; disrespectful; factious; fractious; insubmissive; insurgent; mutinous; rebellious; recalcitrant; recusant; refractory; resistant; riotous; seditious; unmanageable; unobedient; unruly; INSUBORDINATION: anarchy; contempt; contumacy; defiance; disobedience; disregard; ignoration; impertinence; infraction; infringement; insubjection; insurrection; intractability; intractableness; mutiny; nonconformance; noncooperation; opposition; rebellion; rebelliousness; recusance; recusancy; refractoriness; resistance; revolt; riot(ousness); sedition; sin; transgression; treachery; unruliness; violation; violence

INSUBSTANTIAL: (see "airy") apparitional; arachnoid; delicate; diaphanous; ethereal; feeble; fine; flimsy; foamy; fragile; frail; frothy; gauzy; ghostly; gossamer(y); groundless; imaginary; incorporeal; infinitesimal; insecure; insignificant; insufficient; lacy; loose; misty; precarious; rarefied; shadowy; shaky; shallow; slender; slim; substanceless; superfine; tenuous; trifling; uncertain; unessential; unfixed; unfounded; unreal; unstable; unsteady; vacuous; void; weak

INSUFFERABLE: (see "painful") agonizing; appalling; boring; dire; dreadful; excruciating; grievous; heartrending; intolerable; lengthy; long; painful; pompous; protracted; self-assured; shocking; unbearable; unendurable; uninteresting; unsufferable

INSUFFICIENT: (see "deficient") ill-constructed; ill-made; inadequate; incompetent; incomplete; insubstantial; lacking; lame; scant(y); sparse; understaffed; unfit; unpaid; wretched; INSUFFICIENCY: dearth; deficiency; impotence; impotency; inability; inadequacy; incompetence; incompetency; incompleteness; insufficience; lack; need; paucity; underutilization; unfitness; wretchedness

INSULAR: aloof; ascetic; biased; circumscribed; cloistered; contracted; detached; enisled; eremitic; fenced; illiberal; insulated; isled; isolated; limited; monkish; narrow(ed); narrow-minded; nesiote; parochial; petty; prejudiced; provincial; remote; restricted; solitary; walled

INSULATE: (see "isolate") circumscribe; cover; detach; disconnect; guard; line; protect; restrict; segregate; separate; shield; sterilize; wrap

INSULT: v. (see "offend") abase; abuse; assault; attack; cheapen; debase; degrade; deprecate; dishonor; fig; flout; ignore; injure; knock; outrage; ruffle; slap; slur; snoot; stab; INSULT: n. (see "offense") abuse; affront; assault; attack; cheek; contumely; damage; deprecation; dishonor; incivility; indignity; injury; insolence; invective; knock; offensiveness; outrage; rudeness; slap; slur; stab; INSULTING: see "offensive"

INSUPERABLE: (see "unconquerable") insurmountable; unsurmountable

INSURE: (see "guarantee") assure; back; guard; indemnify; protect; secure; shield; underwrite

INSURGENT: **a.** insubordinate; mutinous; rebellious; riotous; seditious; INSURGENT: **n.** insubordinate; mutineer; rebel; revolter; revolutionist; rioter; INSURGENCE: (see "mutiny") insubordination; insurgency; insurrection; rebellion; riot; sedition; uprising; INSURRECTION: see "mutiny"

INTACT: (see "complete") all; entire; full; integral; perfect; sound; standing; unbroken; uncastrated; undamaged; undeflowered; unharmed; unimpaired; uninjured; untouched; unviolated; whole

INTANGIBLE: (see "airy") aeriform; amorphous; arachnoid; diaphanous; elusive; ephemeral; immaterial; impalpable; imperceptible; incorporeal; insubstantial; invisible; nebular; nebulous; temporary; touchless; transient; transitory; vague; vaporous; INTANGIBLENESS: aeriality; airiness; diaphaneity; incorporeality; insubstantiality; intangibility; nebulosity; transitoriness; vagueness; vaporosity

INTEGRAL: (see "complete") all; centralized; componental; composite; constituent; entire; total; undetached; unified; whole

INTEGRATE: (see "blend" and "combine") modernize; streamline; INTEGRATIVE: centralizing; centripetal; combining; integrable; unifying; INTEGRATION: adjustment; amalgamation; arrangement; blend(ing); combination; consolidation; cooperation; coordination; fusion; joining; merger; mingling; organization; unification; union

INTEGRITY: (see "honesty") candor; completeness; constancy; courage; entireness; entirety; fidelity; fortitude; honor; loyalty; merit; nobility; probity; pureness; purity; rectitude; righteousness; rightness; scrupulosity; scrupulousness; sincerity; soundness; strength; trustworthiness; uprightness; virtue

INTEGUMENT: aril; coat(ing); cover(ing); derm; envelope; feathers; fur; hide; hull; husk; investment; pelt; rind; shell; skin

INTELLECT: (see "intelligence") academe; academist; *bel-esprit;* Brahmin; brain(s); cerebrum; cognition; cognoscente; cognoscenti (pl.); doctor; egghead; encephalon; erudite; faculty; genius; highbrow; illumi-

nato; illuminati (pl.); ingenuity; intellectual; intelligentsia (pl.); inwit; leader; literati (pl.); literato; literatus; longhair; luminary; mahat; mahatma; mentality; mind; noesis; nous; pedant; penetration; percipience; percipiency; perspicacity; professor; psyche; reason; sagacity; sage; savant; sense; sensorium; sophist(ry); sophisticate; student; understanding; will; wit; INTELLECTUAL: **a.** acute; apperceptive; appercipient; brainy; cerebral; clever; cognitive; cultured; epistemic; epistemological; gnostic; highbrow; high-browed; ingenious; intellective; intelligent; keen; learned; literate; meditative; mental; noetic; penetrative; percipient; perspicacious; psychic; psychological; rational; reasonable; reflective; sagacious; sage; sharp; smart; sophic(al); sophistic(al); sophisticated; studious; sublime; theoretic(al); thinking; thoughtful; witty; INTELLECTUAL: **n.** see "intellect" above; INTELLECTUALITY: (see "intellect" above) braininess; brilliance; erudition; ingeniosity; ingenuity; intellectualness; intelligence; mentality; smartness; sophistication; wit(tiness)

INTELLIGENT: acute; alert; apt; artful; astucious; astute; brainy; bright; brilliant; calculating; cerebral; clever; crafty; cunning; dexterous; discerning; expert; foxy; heedful; ingenious; intellectual; intelligible; keen; knowing; knowledgeable; learned; luminous; penetrating; perceptive; percipient; perspicacious; quick-witted; rational; resourceful; sagacious; sage; sapient; sensible; sharp(-witted); shrewd; skillful; smart; subtle; wily; wise; witty; INTELLIGENCE: (see "intellect") acquaintance; acumen; acuteness; address; advice; alertness; aptitude; aptness; brain(s); braininess; brainpower; brilliance; brilliancy; brilliantness; capacity; cleverness; cogito; cognition; communication; comprehension; craft(iness); discernment; expertise; expertness; finesse; grasp; gumption; heed; information; ingeniosity; ingenuity; insight; intellect(uality); judgment; keenness; knowledge; luminosity; mentality; message; mind; news; notice; penetration; perception; perspicacity; perspicuity; rationality; reason; resourcefulness; sagacity; sageness; sapience; shrewdness; skill(fulness); stratagem; subtlety; tiding(s); understanding; virtuosity; wiliness; wisdom; wit(tiness)

INTELLIGIBLE: (see "plain") apprehensible; clear; conceptual; diaphanous; lucid; pellucid; perspicacious; readable; supersensible; suprasensuous; unambiguous; understandable

INTEMERATE: chaste; inviolate; pure; undefiled

INTEMPERATE: (see "immoderate") dissipated; drunk(en); excessive; extravagant; extreme; inclement; incontinent; inordinate; severe; shrill; unequal; violent; wild; IN-TEMPERANCE: (see "immoderation") acrasia; acrasy; drunkenness; excess(iveness); inclemency; incontinence; insobriety; severity; violence

INTEND: (see "aim") aspire; attempt; choose; conceive; contemplate; contend; decide; decree; design; destine; direct; emulate; essay; exert; extend; mean; meditate; ordain; order; plan; plot; propose; purpose; resolve; scheme; seek; speculate; stretch; strive; struggle; suppose; try; undertake; venture; vie; will; INTENT: a. ambitious; aspiring; attentive; bent; busy; concentrated; contemplative; designing; determined; eager; earnest; engrossed; fixed; intense; occupied; preoccupied; rapt; resolved; sedulous; set; zealous; INTENT-(ION): n. (see "aim") ambition; animus; aspiration; attempt; contemplation; decision; design(edness); desire; determination; drift; effort; emulation; end; essay; exertion; experiment; goal; import; intendment; intentionality; malice; meaning; motive; object; plan; premeditation; prepense; pretension; provocation; purport; purpose; reason; resolve; sense; significance; speculation; struggle; trial; try; undertaking; venture; volition; will(fulness); wish; zeal; INTENTIONAL: aimed; calculated; contemplated; decided; deliberate; designed; designful; experimental; intended; meant; meditated; permissive; premeditated; provocative; provoked; purposed; purposeful; reasoned; resolved; studied; thoughtful; thought-out; voluntary; willing

INTENSIFY: accentuate; augment; boil; bolster; deepen; embitter; emphasize; enhance; enlarge; enthuse; escalate; exacerbate; exaggerate; exalt; excite; expand; fire; foment; force; greaten; heat; heighten; hotten; increase; inflame; inspire; inspirit; inspissate; kindle; magnify; mount; redouble; reinforce; repair; rise; sharpen; stiffen; strengthen; supplement; support; swell; thicken; underline; vilify; INTENSE or INTENSIVE: active; afire; ardent; blistering; boiling; breathless; breathtaking; bulging; burning; bursting; comprehensive; concentrated; considerable; consuming; consummatory; enthusiastic; exacerbative; exaggerated; exaggerative; exciting; extreme;

fierce; fiery; forceful; frantic; fulminating; fulmineous; furious; great; gripping; hard; heavy; high; immoderate; inspiring; inspissate(d); intent; kindled; marked; merry; mounting; profound; pronounced; rising; seething; severe; smart; spirited; swelling; terrible; thrilling; thumping; thundering; vehement; vicious; violent; zealous; INTENSITY: (see "force") concentration; efficacy; emphasis; fire; furiousness; fury; heat; immoderation; inflammation; intent; level; pitch; power; saturation; severity; spirit; stress; vehemence; viciousness; vigor(ousness); vivacity; vividness; volume; warmth; zeal(ousness)

INTENTLESS: see "purposeless"

INTER: bury; entomb; inhume; inurn

INTERCALATE: (see "insert") insinuate; interpolate; interpose; interstratify

INTERCEPT: arrest; block; capture; catch; grab; grasp; hinder; interrupt; nab; obstruct; prevent; receive; seize; stop; waylay

INTERCHANGE: (see "exchange") alternate; counterchange; reciprocate; replace; shift; substitute; trade; transpose; INTER-CHANGE: n. (see "exchange") alternation; intercourse; mutuality; quid pro quo; reciprocation; reciprocity; replacement; shift; substitution; trade; transposition; INTER-CHANGEABLE: alternating; commutable; fungible; mutual; reciprocal; reciprocative; replaceable; same; substitutionary

INTERCONNECTING: anastomotic; intercommunicating; interrelated; intimate; syndetic

INTERCOURSE: coitus; commerce; communication; communion; companionship; connection; copulation; dealings; exchange; familiarity; fellowship; fraternity; interchange; intercommunication; interposition; intervention; intimacy; pareunia; venery

INTERDICT(ION): ban(ishment); censure; decree; enjoinder; fiat; injunction; order; prohibition; restraint; suppression; taboo; tabu; veto; writ

INTEREST: v. absorb; affect; amuse; arouse; attract; benefit; cheer; concern; delight; divert; engage; engross; enliven; entertain; gratify; hold; motivate; persuade; please; savor; INTEREST: n. accord; advantage; amusement; attention; attraction; avocation; behalf; benefit; business; cause; claim; concern; consciousness; curiosity; delight; discount; diversion; dividend; drive; entertainment; enthusiasm; estate; excess; excitement; favor; fervor; fever; finger; fire; fortune; gain; good; gratification; hand; hobby; inquisitiveness; intent; loyalty; motivation; part(icipation); party; passion; pleasure; portion; premium; profit; pursuit; readiness; regard; revenue; right(s); share; stake; sympathy; title; usury; weald; zeal; zest; INTERESTING: absorbing; arresting; arrestive; attractive; captivating; charming; curious; divertive; engaging; engrossing; fascinating; gripping; intriguing; piquant; provocative; readable; scintillating; sparkling; striking; succulent; zestful; INTERESTED: (see "concerned") attentive; curious; inquisitive; intent; involved; rapt; versant

INTERFERE: ban; block; check; choke; clash; collide; conflict; delay; disrupt; disturb; fool; fuss; hinder; hold; impede; impose; inhibit; intercede; interlope; intermeddle; intermediate; interpose; interrupt; intervene; jam; meddle; mess; mix (in); molest; obstruct; obtrude; oppose; peep; press; pry; push; restrict; snoop; strangle; supervene; tamper; thrust; tinker; trespass; trifle; INTERFERENCE: ban; block(age); check; delay; hampering; hindrance; impediment; ingerence; inhibition; interception; intercession; intermeddling; interposition; interruption; intervention; intrusion; meddling; mediation; molestation; obtrusion; opposition; restraint; restriction; strangulation; supervention; tampering; trespass; INTERFERING: (see "meddlesome") adventitious; meddling; oppositious; supervenient

INTERIM: a. ad hoc; provisional; temporary; INTERIM: n. (see "interlude") armistice; break; diastem; entr'acte; hiatus; interruption; interval; lapse; meantime; meanwhile; phase

INTERIOR: a. (see "inner") central; domestic; inland; inside; internal; intestinal; remote; wild; INTERIOR: n. belly; bushland; center; core; gut(s); hinterland; inland; inside; intestines; marrow; medulla; middle; pith; upland

INTERLACE: alternate; complicate; disperse; diversify; interlock; interspace; intertwine; interweave; knit; link; lock; mat; mix; plait; twine; twist; unite; vine; weave

INTERLOCK: (see "interlace") engage; interdigitate; interlink; interrelate; intertwine; interweave; mortise

INTERLUDE: armistice; break; cessation; delay; diastem; entr'acte; episode; farce; gap; hiatus; hold; interim; intermezz; intermission; interregnum; interruption; interval; lapse; lull; parenthesis; pause; phase; play; recess; respite; rest; space; stasimon; stop; stretch; suspension; wait

INTERMEDIARY: see "intermediate" and "instrumentality"

INTERMEDIATE: average; between; center; central; equidistant; gray; half(way); in-between; interconnecting; interjacent; intermediary; interposed; intervening; mean; medial; median; mediocre; medium; mesne; mesothetic; middle; middling; midway; neutral; second-rate; so-so

INTERMINABLE: see "endless"

INTERMISSION: (see "interlude") armistice; break; cessation; delay; entr'acte; hiatus; hold; interim; interruption; interval; lull; pause; recess; respite; rest; stop; stretch; suspension; wait

INTERMITTENT: alternating; fitful; fluctuating; fluttering; hesitant; infrequent; interrupted; occasional; periodic(al); recurrent; spasmodic

INTERNAL: domestic; emotional; enclosed; endogenous; inherent; inland; inmost; innate; inner(most); inside; interior; intermural; internecine; intestinal; intestine; intraneous; intrinsic; inward; mental; middle; municipal; nervous; private; psychic; psychogenic; psychologic(al); spiritual; subjective

INTERPOLATE: add; alter; change; corrupt; extrapolate; foist; fold; insert; intercalate; interpose; introduce

INTERPOSE: alter; arbitrate; help; insert; intercede; intercept; interfere; interject; interpolate; interrupt; intervene; intrude; meddle; mediate; mediatize; negotiate; obtrude; sandwich; INTERPOSITION: arbitrament; intercession; interpolation; intervention; intrusion; meddling; mediation; negotiation; obtrusion

INTERPRET: (see "understand") clarify; clear; comprehend; construe; decide; decipher; decode; define; delineate; demarcate; describe; determine; diagnose; diagnosticate; dissect; distinguish; elucidate; explain; explicate; expound; fix; formulate; identify; illuminate; illustrate; infer; limit; mark; name; open; outline; parse; prescribe; read; render; resolve; riddle; scan; set(tle); solve; specify; translate; unfold; unravel; INTERPRETATIVE: constructive; divinatory; exegetic(al); explanatory; expository; hermeneutic; interpretative; prophetic(al); revelatory; significative; INTERPRETATION: construction; definition; diagnosis; elucidation; exegesis; explanation; explication; exposition; illumination; illustration; intendment; intent; meaning; pony; representation; signification; solution; translation; understanding; INTERPRETER: annotator; dragoman; exegete; exponent; expositor; expounder; hierophant; Latiner; scholiast; translator

INTERROGATE: see "question;" INTERROGATION: catechism; examination; inquest; inquiry; inquisition; interpellation; probe; pump; query; quest(ion); quiz; test; INTERROGATOR: catechist; examiner; inquirer; inquisitor; prober; pumper; questioner; tester

INTERRUPT: (see "delay") arrest; break; check; cut; derail; derange; disconnect; discontinue; disrupt; disturb; divert; divide; hinder; intercept; interfere; intermit; prevent; restrain; stop; thwart; upset INTERRUPTION: (see "delay") armistice; arrest; breach; break; derangement; disruption; hiatus; infringement; interference; interim; interlocution; intermission; interpolation; interval; lapse; pause; pretermission; prevention; space; stop; suspension; violation

INTERSECT: anastomose; bisect; break; collide; crisscross; cross; cut; decussate; divide; halve; intertwine; interweave; meet; overlap; transect; INTERSECTION: anastomosis; chiasma; collision; corner; cross-(ing); decussation; division; meeting; overlapping; transection

INTERSTICE: areola; chink; cleft; crack; crevice; gap; interval; orifice; pore; rima; space

INTERVAL: armistice; break; c(a)esura; cycle; delay; distance; episode; gap; hiatus; hold; hole; interim; interlude; intermission; interruption; interstice; lapse; parenthesis; pause; period; phase; pitch; recess; rest; rift; rupture; space; state; stretch; time; wait

INTERVENE: (see "mediate") arbitrate; help; hinder; interfere; interject; interpolate; interpose; mediate; snoop; trespass; INTERVENING: interfering; interjacent; interjaculatory; interjectional; intermediary; intermediate; interpolated; intervenient; mediatorial; mediatory; mesne; middle; parenthetical; pending; INTERVENTION: arbitration; help; hindrance; intercession; interference; intermediation; interposal; interposition; intervenience; mediation; trespass

INTERVIEW: audience; conference; confrontation; consultation; conversation; inquiry; meeting

INTERWEAVE: (see "mingle") blend; intermingle; intertwine

INTIMATE: v. (see "hint") announce; caution; impart; insinuate; warn; whisper; INTIMATE: a. à deux; affectionate; buddy-buddy; chummy; close; confidential; contubernal; dear; en famille; essential; familiar; friendly; homelike; homey; informal; inmost; inner(most); interconnected; internal; interrelated; interwoven; inward; marital; near; palsy-walsy; personal; private; privy; secret; sexual; small; snug; special; tête-à-tête; understanding; unreserved; warm; INTIMATE: n. amie; buddy; chum; colleague; comrade; confidant; confidante (fem.); confrere; crony; dear; fellow; friend; mate; pal; partner; sib; INTIMACY: chumminess; closeness; confidentiality; coziness; familiarity; friendliness; friendship; homeliness; inwardness; liberty; nearness; INTIMATION: (see "hint") adumbration; allusion; announcement; clew; clue; cue; glimmer; idea; inkling; innuendo; notice; notification; odor; smell; suspicion; tendency; trend; whiff; whisper; wind

INTIMIDATE: (see "coerce") abash; abuse; accuse; alarm; bait; browbeat; bulldoze; bully; cow; curse; dastardize; daunt; denounce; dishearten; dragoon; extort; frighten; fulminate; hector; hound; overawe; ride; scare; terrify; terrorize

INTOLERABLE: agonizing; appalling; awful; dire; excessive; extreme; harrowing; horrible; horrific; horrifying; insufferable; insupportable; painful; shocking; terrible; unbearable; unendurable; unsufferable; unsupportable

INTOLERANCE: (see "prejudice") bias; bigotry; dogmatism; illiberality; impatience;

intoleration; narrow-mindedness; narrowness; predilection

INTONE: chant; croon; express; hum; intonate: recite; sing; speak; utter; INTONATION: cadence; chant; expression; hum; modulation; pitch; recitation; resonance; singing; sonance; song; speech; tone; undertone; utterance

INTORTED: (see "twisted") complicated; crooked; curled; deformed; interlaced; intertwined; interwoven; tangled; vined; wound; wreathed

INTOXICATE: alcoholize; befuddle; elate; excite; exhilarate; fuddle; inebriate; madden; muddle; poison; INTOXICATED: (see "drunk") boozy; drunken; elated; excited; exhilarated; funny; heady; inebriated; lit; maudlin; oiled; poisoned; ripe; soshed; sotted; stewed; tight; tipsy; INTOXICANT: alcohol; gin; grog; negus; nepenthe; rum; soma; whiskey; wine; INTOXICATION: alcoholism; bibacity; booziness; crapulence; dipsomania; drunkenness; ebriety; ebriosity; enthusiasm; excitement; exhilaration; frenzy; headiness; inebriation; inebriety; jag; madness; potomania; stupor; winebibbing

INTRACTABLE: balky; cantankerous; contrary; disobedient; dogged; headstrong; incurable; indocile; indomitable; intransigent; irreconcilable; mulish; never-say-die; obstinate; ornery; perverse; riotous; stubborn; sullen; surly; unchangeable; uncontrollable; undisciplinable; unmanageable; unrelievable; unruly; unteachable; untreatable; wild

INTRANSIGENT: disobedient; extreme; intractable; irreconcilable; radical; recalcitrant; uncompromising; uncontrollable; wild; willful

INTREPID: (see "brave") daring; fearless; resolute; INTREPIDITY: (see "bravery") boldness; brass; chivalry; courage; daring; fearlessness; gallantry; guts; heroism; nerve; prowess; valor

INTRICATE: (see "complex") abstruse; chaotic; complicated; confused; convoluted; daedalian; daedal(ic); difficult; disordered; entangled; Gordian; inexplicable; inextricable; involuted; involved; knotted; knotty; labyrinthian; labyrinthine; mazy; obscure; sinuous; tangled; INTRICACY: (see "complexity") abstrusity; complication; confusion; disorder; entanglement; intricate-

ness; involution; knot; labyrinth; maze; tangle

INTRIGUE: v. (see "charm") allure; baffle; beguile; captivate; capture; collude; connive; conspire; design; entangle; excite; finagle; interest; lure; perplex; plan; plot; puzzle; scheme; seduce; INTRIGUE: n. affair; *affaire*; allure(ment); amour; artifice; brigue; cabal; chicanery; collusion; connivance; conspiracy; contrivance; coup; craft(iness); design; dodge; duplicity; entanglement; faction; interest; liaison; lure; machination; maneuver; plan; plot; rendezvous; ruse; scheme; secrecy; secret; seduction; strategy; subtlety; trick(ery); tryst; wile; INTRIGUING: (see "exciting") beguiling; captivating; charming; cloak-and-dagger; conniving; conspiring; designing; fascinating; interesting; puzzling; INTRIGUER: Circe; *femme fatale*; intrigant; intrigante (fem.); siren

INTRINSIC: actual; essential; fundamental; genuine; honest; immanent; inborn; inbred; indwelling; ingrained; inherent; inherited; inner; real; subjective; true

INTRODUCE: (see "begin") admit; adopt; announce; broach; commence; conduct; contribute; debut; dedicate; establish; exhibit; immit; implant; import; inaugurate; inculcate; induct; infuse; initiate; inject; insert; install; instill; institute; intromit; invest; lead; meet; name; open; place; preface; present; raise; start; steer; unmask; unveil; usher; INTRODUCTORY: antecedent; beginning; elementary; inductive; initiative; initiatory; innovatory; isagogic-(al); liminary; manuductive; manuductory; nascent; precursory; prefatorial; prefatory; preliminary; preludial; preludious; prelusive; premonitory; presaging; prolegomenous; prolusory; propaedeutic(al); rudimentary; INTRODUCTION: (see "beginning") commencement; debut; debutant(e); dedication; exordium; explanation; foreword; inauguration; inception; innovation; institution; intromission; investiture; lead; manuduction; meeting; opening; overture; preamble; preface; preliminary; prelude; prelusion; preparation; presentation; primer; proem; prolegomenon; prologue; prolusion; propaedeutic; start; unveiling; ushering

INTROMIT: admit; cram; insert; introduce; pierce; stick

INTROSPECTIVE: autistic; INTROSPECTION: autism; introspectiveness; introspectivism; meditation; recollection; reflection; reverie; self-examination

INTRUDE: barge; chisel; encroach; force; impinge; impose; infringe; interfere; interlope; interpose; invade; meddle; nose (in); obtrude; push; snoop; thrust; trespass; INTRUSIVE: aggressive; encroaching; forceful; impertinent; imposing; interfering; meddlesome; meddling; nosy; officious; pushing; pushy; snooping; snoopy; thrusting; INTRUDER: (**see** "stranger") interloper; invader; meddler; poacher; snooper; trespasser

INTUIT: (**see** "feel") apprehend; know; sense; INTUITION: (**see** "feeling") Anschauung; apprehension; clairvoyance; cognizance; conception; conviction; divination; eidos; foreknowledge; insight; knowledge; noumenon; percipience; percipiency; precognition; prescience; presage; sixth sense; thought; INTUITIVE: clairvoyant; immediate; inborn; instinctive; knowing; natural; noetic; perceiving; perceptive; percipient; prescient; seeing; sensing

INUNDATE: deluge; drench; drown; flood; flow; glut; overflow; overwhelm; submerge; swamp

INURE: acclimatize; accrue; accustom; adapt; benefit; discipline; drill; fall; familiarize; habituate; harden; result; school; season; steel; toughen; train; use

INVADE: attack; encroach; engulf; enter; impinge; infest; infract; infringe; intrude; occupy; overrun; penetrate; permeate; probe; raid; ravish; seize; storm; transgress; trespass; usurp; violate; INVADER: attacker; encroacher; incursionist; intruder; ravisher; trespasser; violator; INVASION: aggression; assault; attack; breach; encroachment; engulfment; entrance; epidemic; foray; fray; impingement; incursion; infestation; ingress; inroad; interruption; intrusion; irruption; push; raid; storm; transgression; trespass; violation

INVALID: **a.** baseless; bedfast; crippled; disabled; feeble; frail; ill; incapacitated; infirm; nugatory; null; null and void; sick-(ly); unlawful; unsound; vain; void; weak; INVALID: **n.** cripple; shut-in; valetudinarian; INVALIDATE: abrogate; annul; cancel; destroy; disable; discredit; eliminate; negate; nullify; overthrow; overturn; quash; repeal; stultify; veto; vitiate; void; weaken

INVECTIVE: abuse; blasphemy; censure; contumely; curse; denunciation; diatribe; fulmination; insult; oath; railing; reproach; smear; vituperation

INVEIGH: (**see** "denounce") assail; blame; censure; chide; complain; condemn; damn; fulminate; protest; rail; reproach; vituperate

INVEIGLE: (**see** "coax") cajole; charm; decoy; entice; entrap; flatter; lure; rope; seduce; snare; swindle; tempt; wheedle; win

INVENT: coin; conceive; concoct; confect; conjure; contrive; create; deceive; design; devise; discover; draft; equivocate; exaggerate; excogitate; fabricate; falsify; fashion; feign; find; forge; form; frame; imagine; lie; machinate; make; misrepresent; misstate; originate; outline; plan; plot; produce; project; romance; scheme; simulate; sketch; trump up; vamp; INVENTION: ascertainment; coinage; concept(ion); concoction; contrivance; creation; deception; decrial; detection; determination; device; discernment; discovery; equivocation; exaggeration; fabrication; fiction; figment; forgery; formulation; gadget; idea; ingenuity; inventiveness; lie; machination; misrepresentation; misstatement; origination; patent; process; project; revelation; simulation; INVENTIVE: (**see** "resourceful") creative; fertile; ingenious; innovational; mechanical; pregnant; INVENTIVENESS: creativity; ingeniosity; ingenuity; invention; wit; INVENTOR: **see** "discoverer"

INVENTORY: account; agenda (pl.); agendum; catalog(ue); compendium; list; record; register; reserve; roll; schedule; stock; store; study; summary; supply; survey; syllabus; tariff; test

INVERT: **see** "reverse"

INVEST: adorn; array; clothe; coat; cover; crown; dress; endow; endue; enrich; envelop; establish; garb; gird; inaugurate; install; instill; ordain; prepare; prove; robe; sift; spend; surround; trust; wash; INVESTMENT: blockage; bond(s); capital; clothing; coat(ing); cover(ing); dress; endowment; envelope; garment; habiliments; inauguration; installation; investiture; layer; robe; siege; stock; wraps

INVESTIGATE: ascertain; audit; cover; delve; dig; divine; examine; explore; fathom; find; fish; indagate; inquire; inquisit; inspect;

interrogate; measure; observe; plumb; plummet; probe; prosecute; prospect; pursue; research; review; scrutinize; search; seek; sift; sound; spy; study; survey; test; trace; try; understand; verify; watch; INVESTIGATION: audit; catechesis; catechism; check(-over); checkup; comprehension; disquisition; examination; exploration; fathom; hearing; indagation; inquest; inquiry; inquisition; inspection; interrogation; look-see; measurement; penetration; perscrutation; probe; prosecution; pursuit; quest; question(ing); reconnaissance; research; review; run-down; scrutiny; search; speculation; study; survey; test; trial; verification; witch-hunt; INVESTIGATIVE: disquisitive; exploratory; interrogative; investigational; investigatory; probative; researching; zetetic; INVESTIGATOR: detective; examiner; researcher; spy; student

INVETERATE: (see "chronic") adamant; addicted; confirmed; continuous; deep-rooted; deep-seated; established; fixed; habitual; hard-bitten; hardened; indomitable; ingrained; inured; long-lasting; obstinate; persistent; recurrent; set(tled); unyielding

INVIDIOUS: annoying; defamatory; envious; galling; hateful; inimical; injurious; irksome; irritating; jealous; malign(ant); obnoxious; odious; provoking; vexatious

INVIGORATE: (see "refresh") animate; brace; embolden; encourage; energize; enliven; exhilarate; fortify; harden; liven; renew; renovate; spur; stimulate; strengthen; vitalize; vivify; INVIGORATING: (see "refreshing") animating; bracing; cordial; crisp; encouraging; energizing; enlivening; exhilarative; hearty; life-giving; nourishing; roborant; spurring; stimulating; stimulatory; strengthening; tonic; zestful; INVIGORATION: animation; encouragement; exhilaration; reanimation; recreation; refreshment; renovation; restoration; revivification; stimulation; tone; vigor; vitality; zest

INVINCIBLE: (see "unconquerable") absolute; Achillean; formidable; impregnable; indomitable; insuperable; resistless; unavoidable; unbeatable; unswerving

INVISIBLE: (see "hidden") imperceptible; inconspicuous; intangible; microscopic; secret; sightless; unseeable; unseen

INVITE: (see "ask") allure; attract; beckon; beg; bid; call; challenge; court; dare;

encourage; entice; lure; offer; open; order; propose; request; seduce; solicit; sue; suggest; summon; tempt; try; urge; welcome; woo; INVITATION: attraction; bid; call; challenge; dare; incentive; invite; lure; offer; proposal; provocation; request(ing); solicitation; suggestion; summons; temptation; urge; welcome

INVOKE: (see "beg") adjure; appeal; beseech; call; conjure; employ; enforce; entreat; implement; implore; instigate; muster; petition; plead; pray; summon; supplicate; INVOCATION: *absit omen*; adjuration; appeal; bismillah; call; conjuration; enforcement; entreaty; incantation; litany; petition; plea; prayer; summons; supplication

INVOLUNTARY: accidental; automatic; automatous; autonomic; coercive; compulsory; inexorable; instinctive; irreparable; mechanical; reflex; self-acting; self-regulating; spontaneous; uncontrollable; unintentional; unmotivated; unpremeditated; unthinking; unwilled; unwilling; will-less

INVOLUTE(D): abstruse; coiled; convolute; curled; intricate; involved; obscure; revolute; rolled; spiraled

INVOLVE: absorb; affect; betoken; coil; commit; complicate; comprise; concern; conclude; connect; contain; denote; embarrass; embrace; embroil; employ; engage; enmesh; ensnare; entail; entangle; entwine; envelop; fill; implicate; imply; include; infold; interest; interpenetrate; link; mean; overwhelm; permeate; ravel; require; shroud; signify; snare; tangle; trap; weave; wind; wrap; INVOLVED: abstruse; affected; committed; complex; complicated; concerned; confused; deep; detailed; embroiled; engaged; engrossed; entangled; entwined; enveloped; gone; hard; implicated; inextricable; infatuated; interested; intricate; involute(d); knotty; labyrinthian; labyrinthine; linked; permeated; snared; snarled; tangled; twisted; wrapped; INVOLVEMENT: coil; complexity; confusion; embroilment; entanglement; implication; involution; mess; snare; tangle; trap

INVULNERABLE: immune; impassive; impregnable; invincible; irresistible; unassailable; unbeatable; unconquerable

INWARD: centripetal; domestic; endogenous; entad; familiar; immanent; ingoing; inner; inside; internal; intestinal; intestine; intimate;

into; intrinsic; mental; muffled; psychic; psychogenic; spiritual; toward; INWARD-NESS: immanence; intrinsicality; intrinsicalness

IOTA: (see "whit") ace; atom; bit; breath; ghost; hair; jot; mite; particle; scruple; splinter; tittle; whisker; whisper

IRASCIBLE: (see "crabby") brash; choleric; cranky; cross; edgy; furious; grumpy; hasty; hot; irritable; peevish; peppery; sharp; snappish; snappy; splenetic; surly; temperamental; testy; vinegary; waspish; IRASCIBILITY: choler; haste; irascibleness; ire; irritability; irritableness; peevishness; pique; rage; wrath

IRE: see "anger" and "resentment;" IRATE: (see "angered") angry; cross; enraged; hot; incensed; infuriated; ired; irked; irritated; mad; nettled; piqued; provoked; wrathful; wroth

IRIDESCENT: brilliant; changeable; flashing; glistening; kaleidoscopic; lustrous; margaritaceous; nacreous; opalescent; pavonine; pearly; pellucid

IRK: (see "annoy") bore; bother; chafe; discompose; disgust; fret; ire; irritate; itch; madden; nettle; pain; perturb; pique; provoke; trouble; upset; vex; weary; worry; IRKSOME: (see "annoying") boring; chafing; disgusting; irritating; painful; provoking; tedious; troublesome; vexing; wearying; IRKED: see "irate"

IRON: v. fetter; flatten; handcuff; press; smooth; IRON: a. enduring; ferric; ferriferous; ferruginous; hard; harsh; inflexible; robust; rude; severe; strong; unrelenting; IRON(S): n. element; fetters; handcuffs; mangle; metal; shackle(s); weapon

IRONY: acerbity; asteism; buffoonery; burlesque; censure; contempt; criticism; derision; diatribe; disapprobation; dissimulation; humor; lampoon; mockery; Pantagruelism; philippic; raillery; ridicule; sarcasm; satire; screed; tirade; wit; IRONIC(AL): acerb(ic); biting; critical; Hudibrastic; Pantagruelian; sarcastic; satirical; witty

IRRATIONAL: aberrant; absurd; addlebrained; addlepated; alogical; asinine; batty; brutish; crazed; crazy; daft; demented; Dionysian; eccentric; erratic; fatuous; feebleminded; fickle; flighty; foolish; grotesque; half-cocked; idiotic; illogical; imbecile;

imbecilic; incoherent; insane; irrationalistic; irresponsible; jumbled; lawless; loony; maniac(al); moronic; nonrational; nutty; odd; preposterous; psychotic; queer; rattlebrained; raving; ridiculous; scatterbrained; silly; strange; stupid; surd; uncertain; unfounded; unreasonable; unsound; unwise; wacky; wild; IRRATIONALITY: absurdity; chaos; confusion; deliration; delirium; fatuity; foolishness; illogicality; imbecility; incoherence; insanity; madness; mania; psychosis; stupidity; unreason(ableness); unsoundness

IRREFUTABLE: see "incontrovertible"

IRREGULAR: (see "unorthodox") aberrant; aimless; amorphous; anomalous; arrhythmic; astrophic; asymmetric(al); atypic(al); bumpy; cabalistic; chaotic; clandestine; crooked; devious; dishonest; disordered; disorderly; distorted; diverse; eccentric; erose; erratic; fluctuating; formless; haphazard; heteroclite; heterogeneous; heteromorphic; illegal; illegitimate; imperfect; improper; inadequate; infrequent; inordinate; intermittent; isolated; jagged; malformed; misaligned; mixed; nonstandard; notched; occasional; odd; periodic(al); promiscuous; queer; ragged; rare; rough; rugged; scarce; scattered; seldom; serrate(d); sparse; spotty; strange; tumultuary; uncharted; unclassifiable; uncommon; undisciplined; unequable; unequal; unfrequent; unlawful; unnatural; unstable; unsteady; unusual; vagabond; vague; whimsical; zygomorphic; IRREGULARITY: aberration; abnormality; anomaly; arrhythmia; asymmetry; bumpiness; caprice; defect; delinquency; deviation; disorder; eccentricity; error; fluctuation; heterogeneity; illegality; illegitimacy; imperfection; impropriety; inadequacy; inequality; infrequency; jagginess; jog; malformation; misalignment; occasionality; oddity; periodicity; promiscuity; rarity; shortage; shortcoming; sporadicity; uncertainty; unevenness; variation; whimsicality

IRRELEVANT: (see "immaterial") à propos de bottes; à propos de rien; extraneous; extrinsic; foreign; heterogeneous; impertinent; inapplicable; inapposite; inappropriate; inconsequent(ial); nihil ad rem; tangential; unessential; unrelated; IRRELEVANCE or IRRELEVANCY: extraneity; foreignness; heterogeneity; impertinence; inapplicability; inappositeness; inappropriateness; inconsequence; inconsequentiality; tangency

IRRELIGIOUS: (see "ungodly") agnostic; atheistic; nonreligious; profane; undevout; unholy; unreligious; unsaintly; unsanctimonious

IRREPARABLE: intractable; irremediable; irreplaceable; irretrievable; irreversible; unbridgeable; unfixable; unreplaceable

IRREPRESSIBLE: disobedient; excitable; free; rash; unconfined; unconstrained; uncontainable; uncontrollable; wild

IRRESISTIBLE: (see "alluring" and "charming") invulnerable; mesmeric; resistless; unresistible

IRRESOLUTE: (see "undecided") faintheart-(ed); fluctuating; pusillanimous; uncertain; vacillating; weak(-kneed); wobbly; IRRE-SOLUTION: see "indecision"

IRRESPONSIBLE: arbitrary; capricious; contrary; feckless; fey; foolish; free; harum-scarum; impracticable; inefficient; irrational; lazy; mad; maniac(al); neutral; scatterbrained; skittish; thoughtless; trigger-happy; unambitious; unconscientious; unreliable; unresponsible; unstable; visionary; wavering; weak; wild; wishy-washy; wobbly

IRREVERENT: agnostic; atheistic; aweless; blasphemous; disrespectful; exuberant; heathenish; impious; indevout; irreligious; irreverential; nonreligious; pert; profane; sacrilegious; undevout; undutiful; ungodly; unholy; unreverent; unsaintly; unsanctimonious; worldly; IRREVERENCE: agnosticism; atheism; blasphemy; disregard; disrespect; heathenism; impiety; irreligiosity; lèse-majesté; profanation; profanity; sacrilege; undutifulness; ungodliness; unholiness; unsanctification; unsanctimoniousness; worldliness

IRREVERSIBLE: see "irrevocable"

IRREVOCABLE: absolute; final; firm; fixed; immutable; intractable; irremediable; irreparable; irretrievable; irreversible; stable; unalterable; unrepealable

IRRITATE: abrade; acerbate; aggravate; agitate; anger; annoy; chafe; disturb; egg; embitter; enrage; exacerbate; exasperate; excite; fluster; foment; fret; gall; get; grate; harass; incense; inflame; intensify; ire; irk; itch; madden; nettle; peeve; perplex; pique; provoke; rankle; rasp; rile; roil; rub; ruffle; stimulate; sting; tease; vex; worry; IRRI-TATED: acerbate(d); angered; angry;

annoyed; congested; cross; exasperated; inflamed; injected; ired; irked; mad(dened); peeved; piqued; provoked; rankled; raw; red(dened); roiled; rough(ened); sore; IR-RITABLE: acrimonious; agitable; agitative; angry; annoying; bilious; cankered; cantankerous; captious; caustic; choleric; churlish; crabbed; crabby; cranky; cross; crotchety; edgy; excitable; fidgety; fiery; fractious; fretful; fussy; grouchy; growly; hasty; huffish; huffy; ill-humored; impatient; iracund; irascible; peevish; perverse; pettish; petulant; puckish; querulous; restless; sensitive; snappish; snappy; spleeny; splenetic-(al); surly; susceptible; temperamental; testy; touchy; vinegary; waspish; IRRITA-BILITY or IRRITATION: acrimony; anger; animosity; bile; biliousness; cantankerousness; congestion; crustiness; fantod(s); fractiousness; fretfulness; hastiness; injection; intertrigo; iracundity; irascibility; ire; peevishness; perversity; pettishness; petulance; querulousness; sulkiness; surliness; tension; touchiness; waspishness; IRRI-TANT: abradant; allergy; nettle; provocation; thorn

IRRUPTION: break; burst(ing); eruption; foray; incursion; inroad; invasion; raid; rushing

ISM: belief; cause; cult; doctrine; dogma; philosophy; practice; sect; system; tenet; theory

ISOLATE: block(ade); circumscribe; cloister; colonize; cover; cut; detach; disassociate; disconnect; dissociate; enisle; exclude; ghettoize; guard; hide; immure; incarcerate; insulate; maroon; pinpoint; protect; quarantine; scatter; screen; seclude; segregate; separate; sequester; shield; shut; ISO-LATED: alone; aloof; apart; ascetic; blockaded; blocked; circumscribed; cloist(e)ral; cloistered; detached; discreet; enisled; excluded; exclusive; hermitic; hidden; immured; incarcerated; insular; insulated; ivory-towered; limited; lone(ly); lonesome; parochial; petty; provincial; quarantined; remote; restricted; scattered; screened; segmental; segmentary; segregated; separated; sequestered; set off; sheltered; shielded; shut(tered); solitary; sporadic; stranded; unaided; unbacked; unfrequented; unique; ISOLATION: aloofness; apartness; ascesis; blockade; blockage; circumscription; decentralization; exclusion; immurement; incarceration; insularity; insulation; quarantine; sanction; segregation; separation; separatism; sequestration; solitariness; solitude

ISSUE: **v.** accrue; arise; authorize; circulate; come; debouch; deliver; descend; discharge; disembogue; distribute; egress; emanate; emerge; emit; ensue; escape; evacuate; eventuate; exit; expedite; express; extravasate; exude; flow; ooze; originate; osmose; print; proceed; promulgate; publicize; publish; result; rise; seep; spew; spout; spread; spring; sprout; start; stem; utter; vent; ISSUE: **n.** aftermath; child; cion; circulation; climax; consequence; copy; crisis; debouchment; denouement; discharge; edition; effect; egress(ion); emanation; emergence; end; evacuation; event(uality); exit; expression; extravasation; focus; fruit; head; incident; issuance; kernel; matter; offspring; outcome; outflow; outgoing; outgrowth; outlet; paper; point; produce; progeny; promulgation; publication; question; result; scion; subject; term; topic; upshot; vent; yield

ITCH: **v.** (**see** "desire") hanker; irk; irritate; long; pine; seethe; stew; tingle; vex; yearn; ITCH: **n.** (**see** "desire") agitation; eczema; ferment; hankering; intertrigo; irritation;

longing; prurience; pruritus; psoriasis; restlessness; scabies; tingle; yearning

ITEM: agendum; article; asset; bit; clause; comment; commodity; component; constituent; detail; element; entry; factor; feature; information; job; line; listing; mark; matter; news; number; object; observation; paragraph; part; particular; piece; product; remark; scrap; specimen; subject; thing; topic; trait; unit; writing; ITEMIZE: analyze; arrange; categorize; detail; list; note

ITERATE: echo; emphasize; reiterate; repeat; resay; restate; retell; reutter; rewrite

ITINERANT: **a.** ambulatory; perambulant; perambulatory; peripatetic; roving; sporadic; traveling; vagabond; walking; ITINERANT: **n.** beggar; bum; drifter; errant; gaberlunzie; gypsy; hobo; nomad; peripatetic; straggler; tramp; traveler; vagabond; vagrant

ITINERARY: circuit; course; eyre; guidebook; journey; maps; plan; record; roadbook; route; tour; trek; trip

J

JACKANAPES: ape; beau; coxcomb; dandy; fop; monkey

JACKET: acton; blazer; blouse; bolero; coat(ing); cover(ing); doublet; envelope; eton; fur; garment; hide; hull; jerkin; jumper; peel(ing); reefer; rind; skin; tunic; vest; wool; wrapper

JACK-OF-ALL-TRADES: factotum; handyman; *homme à tout faire*; pantologist; Proteus

JADED: blasé; dull(ed); frayed; satiated; seedy; shopworn; tired; wearied; weary; worn(-out)

JAGGED: erose; harsh; irregular; lancinate; notched; pointed; ragged; rough; rugged; saw-toothed; serrate(d); sharp; toothed; uneven

JAIL: **v.** bar; box; cage; confine; coop; imprison; incarcerate; intern; pen; JAIL: **n.** bars; Bastille; Bridewell; brig; cage; calaboose; cell; clink; cooler; coop; gaol; guardhouse; hoosegow; jug; keep; limbo; lockup; pen(itentiary); pokey; prison; stir; stronghold; vault

JAM: **v.** block; bruise; cram; crowd; crush; fill; fix; force; impede; interfere; obstruct; pack; press; squeeze; stick; tamp; throng; wedge; JAM: **n.** congestion; crush; difficulty; dilemma; fix; jelly; mess; predicament; pickle; plight; scrape; squeeze; stoppage; wedge

JAR: **v.** bounce; bump; clash; clatter; grate; jangle; jerk; jog(gle); jolt; jounce; preserve; quake; rattle; save; shake; shock; unsettle; vibrate; JAR: **n.** clash; container; dissention; ewer; jug; olla; shake; shock; urn; vibration

JARGON: abracadabra; argot; balderdash; baragouin; *bêche-de-mer*; cant; Chinook; Choctaw; colloquialism; dialect; doubletalk; drawl; drivel; gibberish; Greek; idiom; jabberwocky; jive; language; lingo; lingua franca; mumbo jumbo; mummery; non-

sense; patois; patter; pidgin; rigmarole; slang; vernacular(ism); vernacularity; vulgate

JAUNDICE: bias; envy; hepatitis; icterus; jealousy; prejudice

JAUNT: (**see** "trip") excursion; hike; journey; perambulation; peregrination; ramble; sally; shake; walk

JAUNTY: (**see** "dapper") affable; affected; airy; careless; chic; cocky; debonair(e); easy; fashionable; fine; finical; gay; genial; indifferent; joyful; lighthearted; nonchalant; perky; pert; playful; raffish; rakish; sassy; saucy; showy; smart; *soigné*; *soignée* (fem.); sporty; sprightly; stylish; swaggering; trim; unconcerned

JAW: **v.** berate; chat; gossip; scold; talk; vituperate; JAW: **n.** button; chap; chin; fauces; lips; mandible; maw; maxilla; vise

JEALOUS: covetous; distrustful; doubting; dubious; envious; green-eyed; intolerant; invidious; jaundiced; resentful; solicitous; suspicious; vigilant; zealous

JEER: chafe; deride; gibe; hoot; jape; joke; mock; ridicule; scoff; taunt; tease

JEJUNE: arid; banal; bare; barren; devoid; dry; dull; empty; flat; immature; inadequate; inane; insipid; juvenile; meager; puerile; stale; sterile; uninteresting; vapid

JEOPARDY: (**see** "danger") hazard; peril; risk; venture; JEOPARDIZE: **see** "endanger"

JEREMIAD: complaint; lament(ation); tale; tirade; wail

JERK: **v.** bounce; grab; hitch; lunge; lurch; snap; throw; twitch; yank; JERK: **n.** bounce; cad; hitch; person; snap; tic; twitch; yank; JERKY: bouncy; choppy; disconnected; interrupted; palmodic; spasmodic; twitching

JEST: **v.** banter; clown; fool; gag; gibe; humor; jeer; jibe; joke; laugh; mime; mock; play; quip; quiz; ridicule; sport; taunt; tease; trifle; wisecrack; JEST: **n.** (see "joke") banter; *drôlerie*; drollery; fun; gag; gibe; humor; jocosity; mimic(ry); *mot pour rire*; *plaisanterie*; pleasantness; pleasantry; prank; taunt; tease; wisecrack; witticism; JESTER: (see "fool") clown; droll; *farceur*; *farceuse* (fem.); Goliard; idiot; merry-andrew; railleur; wag

JEWEL: bijou; bijouterie (pl.); brilliant; darling; diadem; diamond; gem; ice; joy; loupe; opal; ornament; prize; stone; treasure; JEWELRY: bangles; beads; bijouterie; gems; ornaments; trinkets

JIBE: (see "jest") agree; dovetail; fit; gee; gibe; harmonize; march; shift; tack; tally

JIFFY: flash; instant; minute; moment; nonce; sec(ond); shake; trice; twinkle; twinkling; wink

JITTERY: ajitter; edgy; fidgety; hectic; jumpy; nervous; restless; rickety; shaky; skittish; spooky; tense; uncertain; undetermined; uneasy

JOB: **v.** buy; sell; speculate; trade; JOB: **n.** achievement; act(ivity); affair; berth; business; chare; chore; connection; craft; deal; duty; employment; enterprise; function; item; office; operation; performance; position; post; product; role; shift; situation; stint; task; trade; undertaking; work

JOCKEY: **v.** cheat; gull; maneuver; outwit; scheme; shift; trick; vie; JOCKEY: **n.** driver; knave; operator; rider; rogue; sharp-(st)er; swindler; vagabond

JOCOSE: animated; buoyant; cheerful; comic-(al); droll; dry; enlivened; facetious; frolicsome; funny; gay; genial; happy; hilarious; humorous; jesting; jocular; jolly; jovial; joyous; lepid; lively; merry; riant; risible; sparkling; sportive; sprightly; vivacious; waggish; witty; JOCUNDITY: **see** "merriment"

JOCULAR: (**see** "jocose") blithe(some); convivial; debonair(e); festive; gay; genial; jesting; playful; merry; rollicking; sportful; sportive; vivacious; waggish; witty; JOCULARITY: **see** "merriment"

JOG: **v.** jag; jolt; jostle; lope; move; notify; nudge; plod; poke; push; remind; stir; trot; trudge; warn; JOG: **n.** change; deviation; jag; jolt; push; turn

JOIN: (**see** "fuse") abut; add; adjoin; affiliate; agglutinate; ally; amalgamate; annex; append; articulate; associate; attach; bind; cement; chain; coagment; coalesce; colleague; colligate; combine; communicate; concatenate; conjoin; conjugate; connect; consolidate; conspire; contact; converge; copulate; couple; dovetail; embrace; enlist; enroll; enter; fasten; glue; graft; harness; identify; implant; incorporate; indent; interconnect; interlock; knit; knot; link; lock; marry; match; mate; matriculate; meet; merge; mesh; miter; mortise; pair; pin; pool; rally; relate; splice; stitch; suture; team; tie; unify; unite; wed; yoke; JOINED: adjoined; affiliated; affined; allied; amalgamated; annexed; appendant; appended; articulated; associated; attached; bound; cemented; chained; coalesced; combined; concatenate(d); conjunct; connected; connecting; contiguous; coupled; dovetailed; embraced; entered; fastened; fused; glued; grafted; harnessed; incorporated; intercatenated; interconnected; interconnecting; linked; locked; married; matched; mated; merged; met; mitered; mortised; paired; pinned; spliced; teamed; tied; unified; united; wed(ded); yoked

JOINT: **a.** see "combined;" JOINT: **n.** articulation; chain; cleft; commissure; connection; contact; couplement; den; dive; dwelling; establishment; flange; fusion; hangout; hinge; internode; junction; juncture; linchpin; link; meeting; miter; mortise; place; pub; resort; seam; suture; synapse; synchondrosis; tenon; union

JOKE: **v.** banter; clown; fool; gag; gibe; humor; jape; jeer; jest; jibe; josh; kid; laugh; mime; mimic; play; pun; quip; rag; rib; ridicule; sport; taunt; tease; toy; trifle; wisecrack; witticize; JOKE(S): **n.** anecdote; banter; *blague*; *drôlerie*; drollery; enigma; facetiosity; farcicality; fun; gag; gibe; hoax; humor; japery; jest; jocosity; jocularity; kidding; laughingstock; laughter; leg-pull(ing); mimicry; *mot pour rire*; mystery; *plaisanterie*; pleasantness; pleasantry; poser; prank; pun; puzzle; quip; raillery; riddle; sally; taunt; tease; trick; wheeze; wisecrack; witticism; JOKING: (**see** "jolly") facetious; jocose; jocular; jocund; jovial; JOKER: bloke; buffoon; card; clown; comedian; *farceur*; *farceuse* (fem.); fellow; fool; funster; gagster; gimmick; guy; humorist; jester; prankster; railleur; trickster; wag; wit

JOLLY: (**see** "jocose" and "jocular") blithe-
(some); bright; bully; buxom; cheerful;
convivial; delightful; festive; frolicsome; gay;
genial; jovial; joyous; merry; mirthful;
playful; splendid; sportive; waggish; witty

JOLT: **v. see** "jar;" JOLT: **n.** blow; bounce;
bump; impact; jounce; reverse; setback;
shock

JOSH: **see** "joke"

JOSTLE: (**see** "jar") agitate; bump; clash;
collide; crowd; disturb; elbow; hustle; jog;
prod; push; rush; shake; shock; shoulder;
shove; struggle; vie

JOT: ace; bit; drop; grain; hair; iota; item;
mark; minim; mite; note; particle; point;
scintilla; scrap; scruple; splinter; tittle;
whisker; whisper; whit

JOURNAL: blotter; book; chart; daybook;
diary; gazette; log; magazine; newspaper;
periodical; publication; record; register

JOURNEY: **v.** cross; go; hike; hop; itinerate;
jaunt; jump; junket; passage; perambulate;
peregrinate; ramble; ride; roam; rove; run;
safari; tour; travel; traverse; trek; trip;
voyage; wander; JOURNEY: **n.** cavalcade;
course; crossing; cycle; entrada; excursion;
expedition; fare; flight; foray; gang; hadj;
hegira; hike; hop; itinerary; itineration;
jaunt; junket; odyssey; passage; perambulation; peregrination; pilgrimage; ramble;
ride; roving; run; safari; tour; travel;
trek; trip; voyage; wandering

JOUST: bout; combat; debate; duel; spar;
tilt; tournament

JOVIAL: (**see** "jocose" and "jocular") blith-
(some); boon; gay; genial; jolly; joyful;
merry; JOVIALITY: conviviality; gaiety;
glee; jocosity; jocularity; jocundity; jovial-
ness; joy(ousness); merriment

JOY: (**see** "festivity") *allégresse*; beatitude;
bliss; blithe(fulness); blitheness; blithesomeness; buoyancy; cheer(fulness); delight;
ecstasy; elation; enjoyment; exuberance;
exultation; felicity; gaiety; gladness; glee;
gratification; happiness; hilarity; jocundity;
jouissance; joviality; joyance; joyancy; joyfulness; jubilation; love; merriment; mirth;
pleasure; rapture; raptus; rejoicing; transport; JOYFUL *or* JOYOUS: (**see** "jocose"
and "jocular") blithe(ful); blithesome; buoyant; carnivalesque; celebrating; celebrious;

cheerful; convivial; delighted; delightful;
ecstatic; elated; enjoyable; exuberant;
exultant; festive; festivous; gay; glad; glowing; gratulant; happy; high-spirited; jocund;
jolly; jovial; jubilant; jubilean; merry;
mirthful; pleasurable; radiant; rapturous;
rejoiceful; rejoicing; revelrous; rollicking;
spirited; sportive; triumphant; zestful;
JOYFULNESS: (**see** "ecstasy") blitheness;
blithesomeness; exuberance; exultation;
glee; joviality; joy(ousness); jubilance; jubilation; jubilee; merriment; rapture; transport

JOYLESS: (**see** "desolate") delightless; drear-
(y); funereal; sad; unenjoyable; unenjoyed

JUBILANT: (**see** "joyous") exultant; glad;
gleeful

JUDGE: **v.** adjudicate; analyze; arbitrate;
conclude; condemn; consider; criticize;
decide; decree; deem; determine; discriminate; doom; esteem; estimate; evaluate;
evalue; gather; hear; infer; measure; opine;
ponder; pronounce; rate; read; reckon;
referee; rule; see; settle; think; try; umpire;
value; weigh; JUDGE: **n.** adjudicator;
arbiter; arbitrator; bench(er); cadi; connoisseur; court; critic; edile; judex; judicature; judiciary; justice; keeper; magistrate;
moderator; referee; umpire; JUDGMENT:
acumen; arret; award; belief; censure;
circumspection; concept(ion); conclusion;
condemnation; criticism; decision; decree;
determination; discernment; discretion; discrimination; doom; estimate; estimation;
evaluation; eye; fiat; foresight; insight;
intellectuality; intelligence; intuition; judiciality; judicium; mandate; mandatum;
mentality; opinion; order; penetration;
prudence; rationality; reason(ing); rule;
sagacity; sense; sentence; sight; tact; taste;
understanding; valuation; verdict; view;
wisdom; wit; writ

JUDICIAL *or* JUDICIOUS: careful; cautious; circumspect; cool; critical; diplomatic;
discerning; discreet; discriminating; equable;
equitable; fair(-minded); intuitive; judg-
matic(al); just; magisterial; politic(al); prudent; rational; reasonable; sagacious; sage;
sane; sensible; sentient; shrewd; sound;
tactful; thoughtful; wary; wise

JUICE: blood; cider; electricity; essence;
exudate; fluid; liquid; milk; plasma; resin;
sap; serum; vitality; water; JUICY: colorful;
damp; distinctive; fat; liquid; moist; piquant;
racy; rainy; rich; succulent; vigorous;
watery

JUMBLE: **v.** blend; botch; confuse; disarrange; distort; garble; hash; mess; mingle; mix; muddle; scramble; shuffle; snarl; tangle; JUMBLE: **n.** botch; capharnaum; chaos; colluvies; confusion; crazy quilt; disarrangement; disorder; farrago; *fatras*; gallimaufry; hash; heterogeneity; hodgepodge; mare's nest; medley; mess; mixture; muddle; olio; olla podrida; patchwork; pi; potpourri; rumble-bumble; salmagundi; scramble; snarl; tangle; JUMBLED: confused; disarranged; farraginous; hashed; hugger-mugger; incoherent; indiscriminate; macaronic; messed; mixed; muddled; pell-mell; pied; scrambled; snarled; tangled

JUMP: **v.** advance; anticipate; begin; bounce; bound; bypass; caper; catapult; change; criticize; dart; escape; evade; flee; flush; hop; hurry; hustle; increase; jerk; leap(frog); leave; pole-vault; pounce; raise; rear; recoil; saltate; shift; skip; spring; start; twitch; vault; JUMP: **n.** advancement; advantage; bounce; bound; caper; change; distance; evasion; hop; increase; jerk; leap; move; recoil; saltation; skip; spring; start; tic; trip; twitch; vault

JUNCTION *or* JUNCTURE: articulation; attachment; combination; connection; contingency; coupling; crisis; crossing; demand; depot; difficulty; exigency; fusion; joint(ure); link(age); linking; meeting; merger; need; nexus; pass; pinch; plight; point; scar; seam; spot; state; station; status; strait(s); suture; synapse; synchondrosis; union; urgency

JUNIOR: **a.** adolescent; below; diminished; juvenile; lower; puisne; smaller; subaltern(ate); subordinate; young(er); youthful; JUNIOR: **n.** bud; cadet; fils; juvenile; miss; namesake; puisne; pupil; son; student; subaltern(ate); subordinate; youngster; youth

JUNK: (**see** "waste") bunk; discard; hokum; narcotic; nonsense; plunder; refuse; scrap; trash

JUNKET: banquet; delicacy; dish; entertainment; excursion; journey; outing; picnic; safari; tour; trip

JUNTA: bloc; cabal; clique; combination; confederacy; coterie; council; faction; gang; league; meeting; party; ring; set

JURISDICTION: area; authority; bailiffry; bailiwick; bounds; circuit; cognizance; compass; constablewick; control; domain; duty; field; freedom; function; gamut; judicature; leeway; limits; obedience; pale; parish; power; province; range; reach; responsibility; right; rule; scope; see; soc; soke; sovereignty; sphere; sway; territory; venue

JURY: array; committee; judges; panel; peers; twelve; veniremen

JUST: **a. or adv.** about; absolutely; accurate(ly); almost; approximate(ly); barely; conscientious; correct(ly); deserved; direct(ly); due; equable; equitable; ethical; even; exact(ly); fair(-minded); fitting; good; honest; honorable; immediate(ly); impartial; incorruptible; judgematic(al); judicial; justifiable; justified; lawful; legal; legitimate; merciful; mere(ly); merited; moral; near(ly); noble; only; precise(ly); proper; quite; real(ly); reasonable; rectitudinous; right(eous); rightful; simply; square; true; unbiased; uncorrupt; upright; very; virtuous; well-founded; worthy

JUSTICE: desserts; dharma; doom; due; equitableness; equity; fairness; honesty; honor; impartiality; integrity; judge; justness; lawfulness; legality; legitimacy; magistrate; merit; Nemesis; penalty; propriety; reason(ableness); rectitude; reward; right(eousness); rightfulness; truth; uprightness; validity; virtue

JUSTIFY: absolve; acquit; adjust; approve; back; clear; confirm; defend; exculpate; excuse; exonerate; explain; maintain; notarize; prove; qualify; redeem; right; sanction; seal; show; stamp; support; uphold; verify; vindicate; warrant; JUSTIFIABLE *or* JUSTIFIED: (**see** "just") confirmed; defensible; excusable; fair; justificative; justificatory; legal; legitimate; orthodox; proved; proven; reasonable; sanctioned; valid; vindicatory; warrantable; warranted; JUSTIFICATION: acknowledgment; alibi; amends; apologetic; apologia; apology; atonement; confirmation; defense; deprecation; excuse; exoneration; explanation; extenuation; pardon; plea; pretext; proof; rationale; reason; regrets; righteousness; title; vindication; warrant

JUVENILE: **a.** adolescent; babyish; beardless; boyish; callow; childish; ephebic; green; growing; immature; inadequate; infantile; jejune; junior; juvenescent; minor; puerile; puisne; schoolgirlish; sophomoric; tender; underage; undeveloped; young; youthful; JUVENILE: **n.** adolescent; baby; boy;

child; ephebus; girl; infant; juniority; juvenility; minor; puisne; teen; youngster; youth

JUXTAPOSITION: abutment; adjacency; contact; contiguity; nearness; proximity; touching

K

KEEN: **v.** bewail; complain; cry; lament; mourn; wail; weep; KEEN: **a.** acrid; acrimonious; acute; agog; alert; appercipient; ardent; argus-eyed; astucious; astute; avid; biting; bitter; brainy; caustic; clever; cute; cutting; discerning; distressing; eager; eagle-eyed; earnest; energetic; enthusiastic; fervent; fine; fresh; gare; gay; great; incisive; intelligent; intense; knowing; lively; mordacious; mordant; nifty; observant; penetrating; perceptive; perspicacious; piercing; piquant; poignant; pointed; precise; pungent; quick; razor-sharp; sagacious; sensitive; sharp-(sighted); shrewd; shrill; stinging; tart; trenchant; unblunted; unhackneyed; unjaded; vehement; vivid; witty; zealous; KEENNESS: acidity; acuity; acumen; acuteness; apperception; ardor; asperity; astucity; braininess; brains; cleverness; discernment; edge; gusto; incisiveness; intelligence; perspicacity; piquancy; poignancy; pungency; rigor; sagacity; sharpness; zest

KEEP: **v.** abstain; adhere; board; celebrate; collect; conceal; conduct; confine; conform; conserve; continue; control; defend; detail; feed; fulfil(l); guard; hold; jail; observe; perform; persevere; persist; possess; practice; preserve; prevent; protect; refrain; remain; reserve; restrain; retain; save; secure; shelter; stock; store; support; sustain; tend; treasure; wait; ward; withhold; KEEP: **n.** board; castle; food; fortress; hospitality; jail; living; maintenance; prison; salt; stronghold; sustenance; KEEPER: **see** "custodian"

KEEPSAKE: (**see** "curio") bibelot; curiosity; emblem; gift; knickknack; memento; memorial; *objet d'art*; relic; reminder; souvenir; token; trophy; virtu

KEN: cognizance; compass; comprehension; domain; field; insight; jurisdiction; knowledge; lore; neighborhood; parish; perception; precinct; prescience; purview; range; reach; recognition; scope; sight; sphere; understanding; view; vision; wisdom

KERNEL: basis; cell; center; chromosome; core; crux; egg; embodiment; essence; extract; focus; germ; gist; grain; heart; hub; interior; issue; marrow; mass; meat; medulla; middle; nest; niblet; nidus; nub; nucleus; nut; pit; pith; point; pulp; quintessence; root; sap; seed; substance; vigor

KEY: answer; bolt; cay; clamp; clavis; clew; clue; code; combination; control; cotter; crib; digital; explanation; guide; island; isle(t); lever; manual; opener; operator; *passe partout*; pin; pitch; pony; principle; reef; solution; spanner; tone; tune; wedge

KEYSTONE: apex; basis; capstone; crown; keynote; principle; sagitta; support; vertex; voussoir; wedge

KICK: **v.** boost; boot; complain; cry; dismiss; drive; funk; gripe; hit; impel; kevel; object; oppose; protest; punt; raise; rebel; rebound; recoil; reject; resist; strike; thrust; KICK: **n.** boot; charge; complaint; cry; gripe; hit; impulse; jerk; jog; jolt; objection; opposition; protest; punt; raise; recoil; resistance; stroke; thrill; thrust; twist; zest

KICKSHAW: bauble; delicacy; food; gadget; gewgaw; tidbit; toy; trifle

KID: (**see** "banter") deceive; fool; horseplay; jest; joke; play

KIDNEY: **see** "kind"

KILL: (**see** "destroy") annihilate; asphyxiate; assassinate; bag; behead; blast; break; burke; butcher; cancel; choke; crucify; deaden; decapitate; de-energize; defeat; delete; deracinate; dispatch; dissolve; down; drown; electrocute; eliminate; end; eradicate; erase; execute; exterminate; extinguish; finish; flee; garrote; gas; get; guillotine; hang; immolate; impede; impress (favorably); jugulate; lapidate; lessen; liquidate; lynch; martyr; massacre; murder; nail; neutralize; numb; obliterate; overcome; repress; rid; ruin; shatter; shoot; sink; slaughter; slay; smash; smite; smother; spoil; stall; stifle; stop; strangle; suffocate;

suppress; terminate; undo; veto; KILLER: **see** "murderer;" KILLING: **a.** amusing; attractive; deadly; deleterious; fatal; hurtful; painful; poisonous; toxic; KILLING: **n.** annihilation; assassination; butchery; capital punishment; carnage; cleanup; deracination; dispatch; eradication; erasure; execution; extermination; extirpation; homicide; manslaughter; murder; obliteration; profit; slaughter; slaying; success

KIN: **see** "kindred"

KIND: **a.** *or* KINDLY: **adv.** accommodating; affable; affectionate; agreeable; amiable; amicable; auspicious; beneficent; benevolent; benign(ant); brotherly; charitable; civil; clement; compassionate; complaisant; compliant; congenial; considerate; cordial; courteous; fatherly; favorable; forbearing; friendly; generous; genial; gentle; goodnatured; gracious; grandfatherly; grateful; human(e); indulgent; lenient; loving; mellow; merciful; mild; motherly; obliging; paternal; philanthropic(al); pitiful; pleasant; pleasing; pliable; pliant; polite; politic; propitious; Samaritan; sincere; sisterly; smooth; soft; suave; supple; suppliant; sympathetic; tender; tolerant; understanding; well-meaning; yielding; KIND: **n.** amount; brand; breed; cast; category; class; color; commodities; description; division; equivalent; essence; family; feather; form; genre; genus; goods; group; ilk; kidney; lot; nature; quality; race; rate; same; sincerity; sort; species; stamp; strain; stripe; tribe; type; variety; way; KINDNESS: affection; amiability; amicability; benefaction; benevolence; benignacy; benignity; charity; clemency; compassion; complaisance; congeniality; consideration; cordiality; easiness; favor; friendliness; friendship; generosity; geniality; genialness; goodness; grace; graciousness; humanity; indulgence; leniency; lenity; love; mercy; philanthropy; pity; *prévenance*; sympathy; tenderness; tolerance; understanding

KINDLE: (**see** "inflame") arouse; burn; detonate; fire; foment; glow; ignite; illuminate; inspire; inspirit; institute; intensify; light; mount; prod; provoke; start

KINDRED: **a.** akin; alike; allied; cognate; congeneric; congenerous; congenital; connected; consanguineous; germane; like; related; sympathetic; KINDRED: **n.** affinity; alliance; birth; blood; clan; connection(s); consanguinity; descent; family; flesh (and blood); folks; genus; kin; kind; kindred-

ness; kindredship; kinfolk; kinship; kith; progeny; race; relation(s); relationship; relatives; sib(ling(s)); species; stock; tie; tribe; variety

KING: chief; dynast; emperor; imperator; leader; lord; master; monarch; potentate; regulus; rex; rey; ruler; sovereign; throne; KINGLY: august; basilic(al); imperial; leonine; lordly; majestic; monarchical; noble; palatine; princely; regal; regnant; royal; sovereign

KINK: **v.** bend; cramp; crease; crick; crochet; curl; entangle; fold; knot; loop; snarl; twist; wind; KINK: **n.** bend; cramp; crease; crick; curl; difficulty; eccentricity; entanglement; fold; imperfection; knot; loop; quirk; snarl; spasm; twist; whim; whirl; wind

KINSHIP: (**see** "kindred") affinity; agnation; community; congener; connection; consanguinity; propinquity; relationship

KISS: **v.** buss; caress; osculate; peck; rebound; ricochet; salute; smack; touch; KISS: **n.** buss; caress; osculation; peck; rebound; ricochet; salute; smack; touching

KIT: bag; box; collection; container; equipment; knapsack; lot; outfit; pack; set; supplies

KNACK: ability; adeptness; adroitness; aptitude; art(fulness); capacity; contrivance; dexterity; ease; expertise; expertness; facility; faculty; feat; feel; genius; gift; hang; inclination; know-how; knowledge; readiness; scheme; skill(fulness); stratagem; swing; talent; tendency; toy; trait; trick; trinket; turn

KNAVE: betrayer; blackguard; cheat; churl; deceiver; deserter; fraud; hypocrite; imposter; informer; jack; lorel; losel; miscreant; rascal; rat; rogue; scamp; Scapin; scoundrel; servant; sharp(st)er; sneak; swindler; traitor; trickster; villain; KNAVISH: churlish; deceitful; dishonest; fraudulent; frolicsome; rascally; roguish; sneaky; traitorous; tricky; underhanded; unscrupulous; villainous; KNAVISHNESS: churlishness; dishonesty; fraud; hypocrisy; knavery; miscreance; rascality; roguery; roguishness; unscrupulosity

KNEEL: **v.** geniculate; genuflex; kowtow; KNEEL(ING): **n.** genuflection; genuflexion; kowtow

KNICKKNACK: bauble; bibelot; curio; gaud; gewgaw; gimcrack; kickshaw; *objet d'art*; plaything; souvenir; toy; trifle; trinket; vanity

KNIFE: **v.** cut; slice; stab; undermine; wound; KNIFE: **n.** barlow; bayonet; blade; bolo; dagger; dirk; lance; machete; parer; scalpel; switchblade; sword; utensil; weapon

KNIGHT: attendant; baronet; Bors; champion; chevalier; esquire; Galahad; gallant; Gareth; horseman; lover; paladin; protagonist; Templar

KNIT: bind; braid; cement; conjoin; connect; consolidate; contract; couple; fasten; heal; interlace; interlock; intertwine; interweave; join; link; marry; plait; tie; unite; weave

KNOB: (**see** "knot") boss; bump; bunch; globule; gnarl; handle; head; hill; hilt; hump; knoll; knop; knurl; lump; node; nurl; peak; pommel; projection; protuberance; stud; swelling; tubercle; umbo

KNOCK: beat; blame; box; buffet; bump; bustle; clash; collide; criticize; cuff; dawdle; decry; discredit; hit; loiter; pound; rap; roam; rove; slam; slander; slap; strike; tap; touch; wander

KNOT: **v.** accumulate; agglutinate; bind; bunch; bundle; clump; cluster; collect; connect; constrict; entangle; fasten; gather; gnarl; group; mass; meet; snarl; tangle; tie; twist; unite; KNOT: **n.** accumulation; agglutination; bond; bump; bunch; bundle; burl; center; clump; cluster; clutch; collection; complication; connection; constriction; core; difficulty; entanglement; excrescence; exostosis; gathering; gibbosity; group; heart; hitch; joint; knag; knurl; lump; mass; meeting; node; nodule; nodus; nub; perplexity; problem; protuberance; puzzle; snag; snarl; swelling; tangle; tuft; union; KNOTTY: bumpy; bunched; clumped; clustered; complex; complicated; difficult; entangled; gathered; gnarled; grouped; hard; intricate; involved; knobby; knotted; nodal; nodose; nodous; nodulated; perplexing; problematical; puzzling; rugged; snagged; snarled; tangled; tough; wiry

KNOW: (**see** "apprehend") ascertain; believe; cognize; comprehend; conceive; credit; discern; distinguish; experience; have; intuit; ken; learn; perceive; possess; profess; realize; recognize; regard; reveal; see; test; think; try; understand; wist; wot; KNOWING *or* KNOWABLE: acute; alert; apprehensive; artful; ascertainable; astute; aware; bright; clever; cognitional; cognitive; cognizable; cognizant; cognoscible; cognoscitive; comprehendible; comprehensible; conceivable; conscious; conversant; cunning; discerning; epistemonic(al); experienced; gnostic; hep; informed; intellectual; intelligenced; intelligent; intelligible; keen; knowledg(e)able; omniscient; pansophic(al); penetrating; perceivable; perceptive; percipient; perspicacious; ratiocinative; rational; sagacious; sapient; scient(al); sharp; shrewd; smart; sophisticated; stylish; wide-awake; wise; KNOWN: couth; eminent; famed; familiar; learned; noted; notorious

KNOW-IT-ALL: smart-alec; wiseacre; wisecracker; wise guy

KNOWLEDGE: acquaintance(ship); apperception; apprehension; art; ascertainment; awareness; certitude; cognition; cognizance; comprehension; consciousness; corpus; cunning; discovery; enlightenment; episteme; erudition; experience; expertise; fact; familiarity; gnosis; information; intelligence; intuition; ken; knack; know-how; learning; light; lore; ology; perception; percipience; realization; recognition; sagacity; sapiency; scholarship; science; scientia; skill(fulness); sophistication; teaching(s); theory; thinking; thought; truth; understanding; wisdom

KNOWLEDGEABLE: **see** "wise"

KOSHER: accepted; clean; genuine; legitimate

L

LABEL: **v.** band; brand; call; classify; describe; design(ate); direct; identify; mark; name; sear; stain; stamp; stencil; stigmatize; tab; tag; taint; ticket; LABEL: **n.** band; brand; burn; card; classification; description; design; direction; epithet; fillet; flambeau; flap; identification; infula; inscription; kind; lappet; make; mark; name; pattern; slip; stain; stamp; stencil; sticker; stigma; tab; tag; taint; tassel; ticket; title; trademark; variety

LABOR: **v.** achieve; burden; contend; distress; drudge; elaborate; endure; fag; grind; grub; hack; hammer; heave; lift; moil; plod; pull; slave; strive; struggle; suffer; sweat; tire; toil; tug; work; LABOR: **n.** achievement; activity; chore; diligence; drudge(ry); effort; elbow grease; employment; exertion; fatigue; force; grind; industry; manpower; men; moil; operation; pains; service; slavery; stress; struggle; sweat; task; toil; transaction; travail; trouble; undertaking; work; LABORER(S): coolie; craftsman; fellah; hand; help; man; manpower; mechanic; navvy; operative; operator; peon; toter; workingman; workman; LABORIOUS: (**see** "difficult") arduous; crushing; diligent; effortful; grinding; hard(working); heavy; Herculean; industrious; irksome; labored; laborsome; onerous; operose; oppressive; ponderous; pressing; slavish; slow; stiff; sweaty; terrible; toilsome; tough; uphill; wearisome; yeoman

LABYRINTH: (**see** "maze") complexity; intricacy; perplexity; puzzle

LACE: **v.** adorn; beat; best; compress; defeat; embroider; fasten; fortify; intertwine; lash; liven; mix; snarl; spike; thrash; thread; tie; trim; LACE: **n.** Alençon; braid; Cluny; cord; edging; embroidery; fillet; net; picot; trim

LACERATE: (**see** "cut") afflict; claw; fracture; harrow; hurt; incise; lancinate; laniate; mangle; pierce; rend; rip; sever; slit; tear; torment; wound

LACK: **v.** (**see** "need") desiderate; fail; miss; omit; owe; require; want; LACK: **n.** (**see** "need") absence; dearth; defect; deficiency; deprivation; desideratum; desideria (pl.); desiderium; destitution; distress; drought; emptiness; exigency; exiguity; failure; famine; fewness; hunger; inadequacy; insufficiency; necessity; paucity; poverty; privation; requirement; scantiness; scarcity; shortage; void; want; LACKING: (**see** "deficient") bare; barren; defective; desiderative; destitute; devoid; divested; empty; exiguous; faulty; hollow; imperfect; incomplete; ineffective; ineffectual; inefficient; inept; insignificant; insufficient; meager; minus; needed; poor; sans; scant(y); short; shy; useless; valueless; void; wanting; worthless

LACKADAISICAL: (**see** "lazy") idle; languid; spiritless; supine; vacuous

LACKEY: flunkey; follower; footman; hanger-on; hireling; mercenary; messenger; minion; orderly; page; servant; toady; valet

LACKLUSTER: distinctless; dull; glassy; insipid; lackadaisical; spiritless; uninspired; vacuous

LACONIC: (**see** "brief") compact; concise; curt; epigrammatic; pithy; pointed; sententious; short; succinct; terse; undemonstrative; witty

LAD: boy; chap; fellow; lover; mate(y); sapling; shaveling; stripling; sweetheart; tad; youngster; younker; youth

LADEN: **see** "fraught"

LADDER: escalator; run; rungs; scale; stee; stepping-stone; steps; sty

LADY: baroness; *belle dame*; burd; chatelaine; countess; dame; domina; donna; female; frau; gentlewoman; grande dame; madam; marchioness; matriarch; matron; mesdames; mistress; queen; sweetheart; viscountess; wife; woman

LAG: dally; delay; drag; flag; hobble; idle; linger; loiter; plod; procrastinate; retard; saunter; shamble; slacken; stave; stay; tarry; trudge; wait

LAGNIAPPE: **see** "tip"

LAIR: asylum; bed; burrow; cave; cavea; cavern; couch; covert; den; dive; harbor; haunt; hideaway; hole; home; hospice; lay; refuge; retreat; room; shelter; study; trap

LAMBENT: beaming; bright; brilliant; flaming; flickering; gleaming; glistening; glowing; lucent; luminous; lustrous; radiant; shimmering; shining; wavering

LAME: **v.** cripple; deform; disable; frustrate; hamstring; hurt; incapacitate; maim; mayhem; nullify; undercut; LAME: **a.** blind; claudicant; crippled; defective; deficient; deformed; disabled; faltering; feeble; gimpy; halt(ing); hobbling; hurt; imperfect; impotent; inarticulate; ineffective; ineffectual; infirm; insufficient; limping; maimed; paralyzed; poor; spavined; unsatisfactory; weak; LAMENESS: crippledom; cripplement; infirmity; limp

LAMENT: **v.** anguish; bemoan; bewail; complain; cry; deplore; deprecate; elegize; envy; fret; gammer; grieve; hone; keen; moan; moon; mourn; pine; pity; regret; repine; resent; rue; snivel; sob; sorrow; ululate; wail; weep; yammer; LAMENT-(ATION): **n.** anguish; complaint; cry; deploration; deprecation; dirge; elegiac; elegy; epicede; epicedium; grief; jeremiad; languishment; moan(ing); mooning; mourning; plangor; regret; repining; sigh; sob; sorrow(ing); threnode; threnody; ululation; wail(ing); weeping; wellaway; LAMENTABLE: (**see** "deplorable") despicable; doleful; execrable; grievous; lachrymose; mournful; plaintive; plangorous; sad(dened); sorrowful; tearful

LAMPOON: **v.** abuse; burlesque; caricature; censure; denunciate; disparage; insinuate; libel; pasquinade; reproach; ridicule; roast; satirize; LAMPOON: **n.** abuse; burlesque; caricature; censure; contumely; denunciation; diatribe; disparagement; farce; iambic; innuendo; insinuation; invective; libel; obloquy; pasquinade; reprehension; reproach; ridicule; roasting; satire; skit; tirade

LANCE: **v.** cut; fling; hurl; lancinate; launch; open; pierce; LANCE: **n.** blade; dart; javelin; spear; weapon

LANCINATE: lacerate; lance; pierce; rend; stab; tear

LAND: **v.** alight; arrive; capture; catch; debark; disembark; gain; light; perch; reach; roost; secure; win; LAND: **n.** acre(age); assart; continent; country; dirt; district; domain; dominion; earth; estate; farm; field; heath; glebe; ground(s); kingdom; lot; meadow; nation; pasturage; pasture; patch; people; property; quarter; realm; realty; region; section; sod; soil; terrain; territory; tract; turf; weald; wold

LANDLORD: boniface; host; innkeeper; lessor; owner; padrone; proprietor

LANDMARK: achievement; bench(mark); boundary; cairn; characteristic; copa; event; guide; object; precedent; precept; principle; señal; stone

LANDSLIDE: avalanche; éboulement; victory; win

LANGUAGE: argot; brogue; colloquialism; description; dialect(alism); diction; enunciation; Esperanto; expression; glottology; idiom; Latin; lingo; *lingua franca*; linguistics; lip; literature; nation; nomenclature; parlance; patois; people; phrase(ology); profanity; pronunciation; slang; speech; style; talk; terminology; terms; tongue; utterance; verbiage; vernacular; vocabulary; wording; words

LANGUID: (**see** "lazy") apathetic; dronish; drooping; droopy; drowsy; dull; enervated; faded; faint; feeble; flagging; heartless; idle; inactive; indifferent; indolent; inert; lackadaisical; languorous; lax; lethargic; listless; otiose; phlegmatic; remiss; sick(ly); slack; slow; sluggish; spiritless; supine; torpid; unindustrious; vacuous; weak; weary

LANGUISH: ail; decline; die; droop; fade; fail; faint; flag; mope; pine; sicken; sink; wallow; wane; waste; weary; welter; wither

LANGUOR: (**see** "apathy") blues; debility; dreaminess; droop; drowsiness; dullness; dumps; enervation; ennui; exhaustion; faintness; fatigue; feebleness; indolence; inertia; kef; keef; kief; lackadaisy; lassitude; laxity; laziness; lethargy; listlessness; phlegm; prostration; sloth(fulness); sluggishness;

stagnation; stupor; supineness; supinity; torpidity; torpidness; torpor; weakness; weariness

LANK(Y): (see "gaunt") gangling; gangly; lean; leggy; meager; scant(y); weedy

LAPEL(S): facing; flap; fold; lappet; revere; revers

LAPSE: **v.** backslide; blunder; bobble; decay; decline; depart; deviate; disappear; dwindle; end; err; escheat; expire; face; fail; fall; fluff; misstep; nullify; pass; recede; relapse; resolve; sin; slip; stop; subside; terminate; LAPSE: **n.** apostasy; backslide; blunder; bobble; boner; bull; crime; declination; decline; departure; deviation; disappearance; ending; error; escheat; expiration; failure; fall; fault; fluff; hiatus; indiscretion; misdemeanor; misstep; mistake; nullification; pass; relapse; shortcoming; sin; slip; stop; termination

LARCENY: (see "theft") abstraction; burglary; embezzlement; pilfering; pillage; purloining; thievery

LARD: **v.** bedeck; decorate; enarm; enrich; garnish; strew; LARD: **n.** axunge; fat; grease; oil; suet; tallow

LARDER: bank; buttery; hoard; pantry; provisions; spence; stock(room); store(house); storeroom

LARGE: (see "huge") abundant; ample; augmentive; baronial; big; broad; bulky; Bunyanesque; capacious; coarse; colossal; commodious; compendious; comprehensive; considerable; copious; corpulent; diffuse; enorm(ous); excessive; extensive; fat; fearful; formidable; generous; giant; giant-size(d); gigantic; grand(iose); grand-scale; great; gross; heavy; heroic; immeasurable; immense; important; imposing; large-scale; lavish; leading; liberal; long; lusty; magnanimous; magnificent; magnitudinous; majestic; massive; mighty; monstrous; notorious; numerous; obese; outsize(d); outstanding; palatial; plenteous; plentiful; populous; portentous; powerful; preeminent; pregnant; pretentious; prodigal; prominent; rambling; significant; spacious; sprawling; staggering; swelling; tall; teeming; thumping; tidy; towering; uncommon; vast; whacking; whole(sale); whopping; wide; LARGE-NESS: bigness; breadth; bulk(iness); capaciousness; colossality; comprehensiveness;

copiosity; copiousness; enormity; enormousness; extensiveness; formidability; freedom; generosity; giantism; grandiosity; immensity; liberality; magnitude; massivity; monumentality; vastity; voluminosity; width; LARGEST: see "utmost"

LARK: adventure; binge; bird; foolery; frolic; fun; game; merriment; prank; romp; sport; spree; trick

LASCIVIOUS: (see "immoral") carnal; fleshy; lewd; libidinous; lustful; salacious; sensual

LASH: **v.** assail; beat; berate; bind; castigate; censure; chasten; chastise; criticize; dash; drive; excite; fasten; flagellate; fling; flog; fly; rate; rush; scold; scourge; secure; slash; smite; strike; stripe; switch; tie; whip; LASH: **n.** blow; censure; criticism; onslaught; punishment; quirk; slash; stroke; switch; thong; whip

LASSITUDE: (see "apathy" and "fatigue") adynamia; enervation; ennui; hypokinesia; indifference; lackadaisy; languor; lethargy; listlessness; weariness

LAST: **v.** abide; bear; bide; brook; continue; countenance; end; endure; exist; experience; extend; harbor; have; hold; perdure; persist; reach; remain; retain; serve; stand; stay; stick; submit; suffer; survive; sustain; tolerate; wear; weather; withhold; withstand; LAST: **a.** closing; concluding; conclusive; definitive; dernier; end; eventful; extreme; final; hindmost; latest; latter; least; lowest; meanest; newest; supreme; terminal; ultimate; utmost; worst; LAST: **n.** closing; coda; conclusion; end; finality; finis; finitude; omega; pattern; remainder; remaining; supreme; utmost; LASTING: abiding; boundless; ceaseless; chronic; classic(al); constant; continual; continuing; continuous; diuturnal; durable; endless; enduring; established; eternal; everlasting; final; fixed; immarcescible; immortal; imperishable; indefaceable; indelible; indissoluble; ineradicable; inerasable; interminable; lifelong; long-suffering; monstrous; monumental; patient; perdurable; perennial; permanent; perpetual; perseverant; protracted; sempiternal; stable; steadfast; strong; stubborn; sturdy; unceasing; unfailing; unremitting; wearing; weathering

LATCH: see "lock"

LATE: advanced; autumnal; behind(hand); bygone; ci-devant; dead; deceased; defunct; delayed; demised; departed; detained; dilatory; elapsed; extinct; former; gone; indolent; lagging; lapsed; lethargic; neoteric; new; overdue; past; procrastinative; procrastinatory; recent(ly); remiss; ripe; slow; sluggish; tardy; LATEST: see "new" and "novel"

LATENT: abeyant; concealed; cryptic; delitescent; dormant; hidden; imperceptible; implicit; implied; inactive; inchoate; inherent; invisible; occult; possible; potential; promising; quiescent; recondite; repressed; secret; sessile; suppressed; undeveloped; unexplained; unknown; unperceived; unrevealed; unseen; veiled; LATENCY: delitescence; dormancy; imperceptibility; incubation; possibility; potentiality; quiescence; quietude; repression; suppression

LATITUDE: (see "range") authority; breadth; compass; distance; extent; freedom; gamut; jurisdiction; length; locality; reach; region; room; rope; scope; space; tolerance; toleration; variance; variation; width

LATTER: (see "last") final; late(r); latest; modern; past; recent; second

LAUD: (see "applaud") acclaim; approbate; celebrate; commend; congratulate; deify; exalt; extol; felicitate; glorify; macarize; magnify; panegyrize; pedestal; praise; sing; stellify; LAUDATION: (see "applause") approbation; clap; commendation; congratulation; deification; encomium; encore; eulogy; extolment; hymn; magnificat(ion); panegyric; praise; psalm; rave; stellification; LAUDABLE or LAUDATORY: acclamatory; admirable; angelic; approbatory; commemorative; commemoratory; commendable; commendatory; deserving; encomiastic; eulogistic; excellent; glorifying; good; grand; honest; honorable; innocent; loving; loyal; magnific(ent); magnifying; noble; panegyrical; praiseworthy; pure; righteous; saintly; true; virtuous; worthy

LAUGH: v. cachinnate; cackle; chortle; deride; faw; fleer; giggle; guffaw; ha-ha; haw-haw; jeer; ridicule; roar; scoff; snicker; snigger; snort; titter; LAUGH: n. advantage; cachinnation; cackle; chortle; chuckle; giggle; guffaw; hee-haw; hilarity; jeer; joke; snort; titter; LAUGHABLE: bizarre; cachinnatory; comic(al); droll(ish); eccentric; farcical; funny; jocose; jocular; ludicrous; merry; mirthful; *pour rire*; quaint;

riant; ridiculous; risible; waggish; whimsical; LAUGHING: blithe(some); gay; gleeful; joyful; joyous; merry; mirthful; riant; LAUGHTER: amusement; cachinnation; exuberance; guffaw; risibility

LAUNCH: (see "introduce") cast; dart; fling; hurl; institute; lash; leap; mount; plunge; promote; shoot; throw

LAURELS: championship; cup; distinction; fame; honor; medal; reputation; ribbon(s); trophy

LAVISH: v. bestow; deplete; dissipate; dote; expend; flood; give; glut; heap; overdo; squander; waste; LAVISH: a. (see "extravagant") abundant; affluent; Babylonian; Babylonic; baronial; bountiful; copious; costly; dear; excessive; exorbitant; exuberant; flush(ed); free; improvident; inordinate; liberal; Lucullan; lush; luxurious; magnificent; openhanded; opulent; overdone; prodigal; profuse; profusive; replete; sumptuous; superabundant; thriftless; unfrugal; unstinted; wasteful; wild; LAVISHNESS: abundance; affluence; affluency; copiosity; copiousness; extravagance; exuberance; improvidence; liberality; luxury; magnificence; opulence; opulency; prodigality; profusion; sumptuosity; waste

LAW(S): act; authority; authorization; axiom; behest; bench; bid(ding); bill; canon; code; command(ment); constitution; control; court; covenant; custom; decree; demand; droit; economy; edict; enactment; equity; ethics; ethos; formula; judge; jurisprudence; jus; legislation; lex; litigation; Magna C(h)arta; manciple; mandate; mandatum; mores (pl.); order; ordinance; passing; policeman; practice; precedent; precept; principle; procedure; regulation; remedy; representation; request; rescript; rubric; rule; ruling; statute; tradition; usage

LAWBREAKER: see "criminal"

LAWFUL: admitted; allowable; authorized; canonical; competent; constitutional; *de jure*; due; equitable; ethical; judicial; juridical; juristic; just; law-abiding; legal; legislative; legitimate; licit; moral; official; ordained; permissible; permissive; permitted; recognized; regular; right(eous); right(ful); statutory; traditional; valid; warrantable; warranted

LAWLESS: (see "criminal") anarchic(al); anomalous; contumacious; defiant; Dionysian; disobedient; disorderly; dissolute; illegal; immoral; infringing; insubordinate; insurgent; lax; mutinous; noncompliant; nonconforming; nonobservant; piratical; rebellious; recalcitrant; recusant; refractory; revolutionary; riotous; ruleless; seditious; subordinate; transgressive; unauthorized; unbounded; unconformable; uncontrolled; undutiful; ungovernable; ungoverned; unlicensed; unobservant; unprincipled; unrestrained; unruly; LAWLESSNESS: anarchy; anomie; defiance; disobedience; disorderliness; illegality; insubordination; insurgency; license; mutiny; nonconformance; rebellion; recalcitrance; recusancy; refractoriness; revolution; riot(ousness); sedition; transgression; unruliness; vice

LAWSUIT: action; case; cause; controversy; litigation; proceeding; prosecution; suit

LAWYER: abogado; advocate; attorney; barrister; counsel(or); jurist; legist; Portia (fem.); solicitor

LAX: careless; dissolute; easygoing; flabby; flaccid; immoral; lackadaisical; lawless; lethargic; licentious; limp; loose; negligent; open; permissive; relaxed; remiss; scattered; slack; soft; undutiful; unobservant; unprincipled; weak

LAY: **v.** aim; allege; alleviate; allay; apply; ascribe; assert; bet; bury; calm; charge; coat; contrive; cover; deposit; found; heap; impose; impute; inflict; inter; pave; place; plant; put; rest; smooth; spread; state; store; LAY: **a.** amateur; nonprofessional; popular; profane; secular; untechnical; LAY: **n.** ballad; ditty; lyric; melody; plan; poem; song; tack; tune

LAYER: (**see** "crust") bed; cake; coat(ing); course; cover(ing); crust; film; fold; hierarchization; lamina; patina; ply; provine; rind; row; scab; scum; sheet; skin; slab; slice; stratification; stratum; thickness; tier; LAYERED: laminated; stratified; superimposed

LAYMAN: amateur; exoteric; laic; laity (pl.)

LAZY: ambitionless; comatose; deliberate(ly); dilatory; dopey; dormant; dozy; dronish; drooping; drowsy; faineant; hebetudinous; hypnotic; idle; inactive; indisposed; indolent; inert(ial); lackadaisical; laggard; languid; languorous; lax; lethargic; leisurely; listless; oscitant; otiose; passive; quiescent; remiss; slack; slothful; slow(ly); sluggard; sluggish;

somniferous; soporiferous; soporific; spiritless; supine; torpescent; torpid; tranquil; unambitious; unenterprising; unindustrious; unzealous; vacuous; LAZINESS: apathy; dilatoriness; faineance; faineancy; *fainéantise*; idleness; impassivity; inactivity; inanition; indisposition; indolence; indolency; inertia; lackadaisy; lassitude; laxity; lethargy; oscitancy; otiosity; passivity; quiescence; remission; sloth(fulness); slowness; sluggardness; sluggishness; spiritlessness; supineness; supinity; tardiness; torpidity; tranquility; vacuousness

LEAD: **v.** allure; antecede; antedate; begin; boss; cause; command; commence; conduct; control; convey; counsel; direct; drag; entice; escort; eventuate; excel; fix; forerun; front; manage; mastermind; open; order; originate; outrank; outstrip; pace; pass; persuade; pilot; precede; preface; proceed; regulate; rule; serve; set; show; spearhead; start; steer; superintend; supervise; surpass; take; top; transcend; LEAD: **n.** advantage; anglesite; antecedence; beginning; cerussite; clue; command; commencement; control; direction; edge; escort; example; front; graphite; guide; head; helm; initiative; leadership; management; margin; metal; pilot; plumbum; precedence; precedent; solder; spearhead; star; superintendent; superior(ity); supervisor; tip; top; van

LEADER(S): administrant; administrator; adviser; advocate; article; baron; bellwether; boss; brain; brass (hat); captain; chairman; champion; chaperone; chefe; chief(tain); coach; command(ant); commander; comptroller; conductor; crown; director; duce; dux; editorial; elder; emperor; ethnarch; example; executive; factotum; flugelman; foreman; front; fugleman; general(issimo); governor(-general); guardian; guide; head(master); heavyweight; helmsman; herder; herdsman; hierarch(y); hierophant; higher-up; honcho; imperator; impresario; instructor; judge; king; leading light; lord; maestro; magistrate; master(mind); mogul; monitor; officer; pacemaker; pacesetter; primate; principal; proctor; protagonist; rais; reis; ringleader; ruler; sachem; sagamore; scout(master); secretary; senior; shepherd; sinew; skipper; soldier; source; speaker; spokesman; star; steward; superintendent; superior; supervisor; teacher; tendon; thane; titan; torchbearer; torchlight; top; tycoon; vanguard; viceroy; victor; warden; wheel; LEADERSHIP: (**see** "lead") aegis; antecedence; ascendence; ascendency; authority; *avant-garde*; capacity; captaincy; captainship;

chiefdom; chieftaincy; chieftainship; command; directorship; dominion; enlightenment; generalship; initiative; management; preeminence; statesmanship; stewardship; superiority; LEADING: advanced; ahead; A-one; *avant-garde*; capital; cardinal; celebrated; chief; conspicuous; directing; distinguished; eminent; enlightened; first; foremost; front; grand; great; guiding; high; important; main; major; manuductive; marked; mighty; *ne plus supra*; *ne plus ultra*; notable; noticeable; notorious; obvious; outstanding; paramount; pathbreaking; popular; preceding; preeminent; premier; primary; prime; principal; prominent; ranking; renowned; salient; signal; sovereign; star; stellar; striking; trailblazing; vanward; well-known

LEADERLESS: headless; unguarded; unguided; unled; unpiloted; unprotected

LEAF: blade; division; foliage; frond; lamina; page; part; petal; sheet; side

LEAFLET: **see** "pamphlet"

LEAGUE: **v.** agree; ally; amalgamate; associate; band; bunch; coalesce; cohere; combine; confederate; fuse; join; unite; LEAGUE: **n.** agreement; alliance; amalgamation; association; band; bloc; bund; cabal; category; coalescence; combination; compact; confederacy; confederation; conference; covenant; fusion; group; hanse; pact; union

LEAK: **v.** (**see** "drip") dribble; drizzle; escape; ooze; osmose; overflow; seep; spill; trickle; LEAK: **n.** chink; crack; crevice; dribble; drip; escape; fissure; hold; loss; ooze; opening; osmosis; seep; spill; trickle

LEAL: (**see** "trustworthy") faithful; loyal; sta(u)nch; true; trusted

LEAN: **v.** bear; bend; bevel; cant; careen; cast; confide; depend; deviate; heel; incline; list; lurch; rest; sag; slant; slope; tend; throw; tilt; tip; toss; trust; LEAN: **a.** angular; attenuated; bare; barren; deficient; emaciated; fatless; gaunt; infertile; lank(y); macilent; meager; poor; rawboned; scant(y); scrawny; skinny; slender; slim; spare; tabescent; thin; unproductive; unremunerative; LEANNESS: angularity; emaciation; gauntness; lankiness; macilency; slenderness; tabescence; thinness; LEANING: **a.** accumbent; bent; biased; inclined; listing; lurching;

predisposed; prejudiced; slanting; susceptible; tendentious; tending; LEANING: **n.** (**see** "prejudice") bent; bias; conatus; declination; disposition; faculty; flair; gift; inclination; opinion; partiality; penchant; predilection; predisposition; proclivity; propensity; slant; slope; susceptibility; tendency; trend; turn

LEAP: **v.** bound; caper; catapult; dance; dive; frisk; gambado; gambol; hop; increase; jump; lunge; plunge; rebound; rise; romp; rush; saltate; skip; spring; vault; LEAP: **n.** antic; bound; caper; capriole; catapult; curvet; dance; dive; entrechat; frisk; frolic; gambade; gambado; gambol; hop; increase; jump; lunge; plunge; romp; sally; saltation; salto; skip; spring; vault; LEAPING: bouncing; capering; frisking; gamboling; playful; plunging; rebounding; romping; saltant; saltatorial; saltatorian; saltatory; sportive; subsultive; subsultory; vaulting

LEARN: (**see** "determine") acquire; apperceive; ascertain; calculate; discover; estimate; evaluate; examine; experience; figure; find; gain; gather; get; glean; hear; imbibe; intuit; measure; memorize; number; perceive; read; realize; receive; study; survey; trace; weigh; LEARNED: (**see** "educated") academic; accomplished; Aristotelian; bookish; cerebral; cultured; didactic(al); donnish; enlightened; erudite; experienced; expert; informed; knowledgeable; knowledged; lettered; literary; literate; moralistic; omniscient; pansophic; pedantic; perceptive; philomathic(al); polymathic(al); pompous; profound; recondite; scholarly; versed; LEARNER: abecedarian; acolyte; alphabetarian; amateur; apprentice; beginner; catechumen; helper; inceptor; novice; novitiate; probationer; pupil; satellite; scholar; student; trainee; understudy; LEARNING: apperception; apprehension; apprenticeship; art; comprehension; culture; discipline; education; enlightenment; erudition; experience; humanism; humanities; information; insight; ken; knowledge; learnedness; letters; lore; maturation; omniscience; pedantry; philology; philosophy; profundity; sagacity; sapience; scholarship; schoolcraft; schooling; science; skill; study; training; understanding; wisdom; wit; LEARNABLE: **see** "comprehensible"

LEASE: charter; contract; convey; grant; hire; let; rent

LEASH: **v.** bind; control; curb; hold; restrain;

rope; secure; tie; LEASH: **n.** binding; check; control; cord; jess; line; restraint; rope; strap; string; thong; tie; tierce

LEAST: **see** "minimum"

LEATHER: calfskin; cowhide; deerskin; kid; morocco; rawhide; roan; suede; vellum; LEATHERY: coriaceous; tough

LEAVE: **v.** abandon; abscond; absquatulate; allow; bequeath; bolt; cease; commit; defect; demise; depart; desert; desist; devise; disembark; diverge; drop; elope; embark; escape; evacuate; exit; fade; flee; fly; forsake; go; jump; let; melt; migrate; move; neglect; omit; part; pass; permit; pull (up) stakes; quit; refer; refrain; relinquish; renounce; resign; retire; retreat; scoot; scram; separate; shove; stop; strand; suffer; transfer; vacate; waive; will; withdraw; yield; LEAVE: **n.** abandonment; abscondence; absence; absquatulation; adieu; alienation; allowance; congé; consent; demise; departure; elopement; escape; evacuation; exit; farewell; furlough; holiday; liberty; license; migration; permission; permit; quittance; relinquishment; renouncement; renunciation; resignation; separation; severance; sufferance; transfer; vacation; waiver; withdrawal; yielding

LEAVEN: **v.** activate; enthuse; ferment; imbue; impregnate; infuse; lift; lighten; permeate; raise; taint; temper; LEAVEN: **n.** activator; alloy; barm; enzyme; ferment; yeast; zyme

LEAVING(S): (**see** "waste") ash(es); bones; culls; dregs; dross; dust; fragments; grounds; hash; leftovers; orts; overs; pieces; refuse; relics; remains; remnants; residue; residuum; rest; scraps; sediment; trash

LECHERY: **see** "lust;" LECHEROUS: (**see** "lustful") goatish; luxurious; provocative; randy; sexy; suggestive

LECTURE: **v.** address; admonish; call down; castigate; discuss; harangue; orate; rate; rebuke; reprimand; reprove; scold; sermonize; speak (to); talk (to); LECTURE: **n.** address; admonition; castigation; class; colloquium; colloquy; discourse; discussion; disquisition; dissertation; dressing down; excursus; harangue; homily; lesson; oration; prelection; rebuke; reprimand; reproof; riot act; scolding; sermon; speech; sympo-

sium; talk; talking-to; teach-in; travelog-(ue); treatise

LEDGE: apron; bar; berm; cay; cleat; coaming; frame; lode; platform; projection; reef; ridge; shelf; sill; vein

LEECH: annelid; gill; parasite; sponge(r); toady; worm

LEER: eye; fleer; look; ogle; scoff; smirk; sneer; stare

LEES: (**see** "waste") draff; dregs; dross; grounds; leavings; offscourings; refuse; remains; sediment; settlings

LEEWAY: (**see** "space") angle; berth; clearance; deviation; drift; freedom; give; grace; jurisdiction; liberty; margin; play; range; room; scope; shortcoming; tolerance; toleration; variation

LEFT: (**see** "departed") communistic; extreme; far-out; gauche; larboard; liberal; port; radical; red; sinister; sinistrad; sinistral; sinistromanual; unconsumed; unexpended; unspent

LEFTOVER(S): (**see** "waste") analecta (pl.); analects; collectanea (pl.); fragments; gleanings; hash; offscourings; overs; *réchauffé*; residue; residuum; surplus(age); vestige

LEG(S): appendage; branch; circuit; course; crus; division; extremity; gam(b); game; lap; limb; link; part; pin(s); portion; prop-(s); shore; stage; support

LEGAL: (**see** "lawful") allowable; authorized; canonical; competent; constitutional; *de jure*; equitable; juridical; juristic; just-(ifiable); leal; legitimate; licit; official; permissive; permitted; sanctioned; sound; square; statutory; titular; valid; warrantable; LEGALITY: constitutionality; lawfulness; legitimacy; validity

LEGATE: ambassador; consul; delegate; deputy; emissary; envoy; governor; nuncio; plenipotentiary; viceroy

LEGEND: account; anecdote; caption; directions; Edda; epic; explanation; fable; fiction; history; inscription; label; lectionary; motto; myth; narrative; old wives' tale; passional; saga; story; tale; title; tradition; wording; LEGENDARY: apocryphal; epic(al); fabulous; fictional; fictitious; mythical; mythological; proverbial; traditional; trailblazing; tralatitious; tribal; unwritten

LEGIBLE: clear; comprehensible; decipherable; diaphanous; distinct; fair; plain; readable; recognizable; scrutable; translatable; transparent; understandable; well-written

LEGISLATOR: assemblyman; congressman; delegate; lawgiver; lawmaker; representative; senator; solon; LEGISLATURE: assembly; boule; congress; Dail; diet; Folketing; Knesset; parliament; Reichstag; senate; Storting

LEGITIMATE: (see "legal") authorized; genuine; law-abiding; lawful; licensed; licit; natural; official; reasonable; recognized; right(ful); sound; square; valid; warranted

LEISURE: convalescence; ease; freedom; holiday; idleness; leisureliness; opportunity; otiosity; *otium*; procrastination; relaxation; repose; rest; time; toom; unemployment; vacation; LEISURELY: (see "lazy") deliberate(ly); easy; free; gradual; procrastinative; slow(ly); unhasty; unhurried

LEND: accommodate; add; afford; furnish; give; grant; help; imbue; impart; lease; let; loan; offer; permit; provide; supply; support

LENGTH: authority; breadth; degree; distance; duration; expanse; extent; extreme; interval; limit; measure; period; prolixity; quantity; range; reach; scope; segment; span; stretch; tautology; time; width; wordiness; LENGTHEN: continue; drag; eke; elongate; expand; extend; increase; pad; prolong; protract; stretch; LENGTHY: (see "prolix") copious; extended; lengthened; long (-winded); prolonged; protracted; tall; tautological; tedious; tiresome; verbose; wordy

LENIENT: (see "easy") assuaging; assuasive; balmy; bland; clement; compassionate; emollient; forbearing; gentle; indulgent; kind; lax; lenitive; merciful; mild; mitigating; moderate; permissive; reasonable; relaxing; remiss; soft(hearted); softening; soothing; tender; tolerant

LENITIVE: (see "easy") anodynic; assuasive; balmy; balsamic; emollient; favonian; gentle; lax(ative); mild; mitigating; palliative; relaxing; soft(ening); soothing; tender

LESION: cut; damage; flaw; gash; hurt; impairment; injury; sore; wound

LESS: fewer; inferior; lesser; lowlier; minor; minus; secondary; slighter; smaller; suboptimal; under

LESSEN: (see "decrease") abate; abbreviate; abridge; adulterate; alleviate; ameliorate; assuage; attenuate; belittle; calm; check; contract; curtail; cut; damp(en); decay; decrease; degrade; delay; demote; denigrate; depreciate; depress; diminish; discourage; drop; dwindle; ease; exhaust; extenuate; fade; free; hinder; impair; liberalize; lighten; limit; lower; minify; minimize; mitigate; moderate; modify; mollify; muffle; mute; narrow; palliate; pass; pejorate; reduce; relax; relieve; repress; shorten; shrink; soften; soothe; stem; stop; temper; thin; wane; weaken; wear; worsen; LESSENING: a. ablatitious; alleviatory; declinatory; decreasing; decrescendo; decrescent; degressive; diminishing; extenuative; narrowing; palliative; palliatory; reductionistic; reductive; relaxing; subtractive; waning; LESSENING: n. (see "decrease") abatement; abbreviation; abridgement; amelioration; attenuation; curtailment; decay; decrescence; degradation; demotion; depreciation; diminishment; diminuendo; diminution; disparagement; exhaustion; extenuation; lightening; lowering; minification; mitigation; moderation; mollification; narrowing; palliation; reduction; repression; shrinkage; weakening; wear

LESSON: censure; class; example; exercise; experience; instruction; lecture; precept; punishment; rebuff; rebuke; reprimand; scolding; study; task; teaching; warning

LET: accord; admit; allow; assign; authorize; award; bear; cause; charter; commission; concede; dismiss; empower; franchise; grant; hire; lease; leave; lend; license; make; permit; release; relinquish; rend; sanction; suffer; unhand; untie; vouchsafe

LETHAL: (see "deadly") cancerous; destructive; devastating; dire; fatal; malign(ant); mortal; poisonous; toxic; toxiferous

LETHARGIC: (see "slow") apathetic; comatose; drowsy; dull; indifferent; inert; inexcitable; lackadaisical; languorous; lazy; listless; passive; patient; semicomatose; sleepy; slow-moving; sluggish; soporific; stuporous; torpid; LETHARGY: apathy; coma; drowsiness; indifference; inertia;

lackadaisy; languor; lassitude; laziness; listlessness; passiveness; passivity; sleep; slumber; stupor; torpidity; torpor; uninterest

LETHE: death; forgetfulness; nepenthe; Nirvana; oblivion

LETTER(S): billet(-doux); character; communication; composition; document; epistle; favor; initial; learning; line; literature; mail; memo(randum); message; missive; note; reply; report; rescript; symbol; type; writing

LEVEE: assembly; bank; dance; dike; durbar; embankment; gathering; party; pier; quay; reception; wharf

LEVEL: **v.** aim; balance; destroy; direct; equal(ize); even; flat(ten); floor; grade; lay; plane; point; raze; smooth; stabilize; train; true; LEVEL: **a.** balanced; bona fide; calm; commensurate; equal(ized); equiponderant; equipotential; even; flat; floored; flush; horizontal; impartial; just; legitimate; matched; penetrating; planate; planed; quiet; regular; smooth(ed); stable; steady; true; unexcited; unflinching; uniform; unwavering; LEVEL: **n.** (**see** "category") degree; echelon; equilibrium; floor; grade; horizontality; intensity; order; plane; plateau; position; rank(ing); rate; terrace; tier; uniformity

LEVER: (**see** "fulcrum") influence

LEVIATHAN: (**see** "huge") crocodile; dragon; monster; serpent; ship; titan; whale

LEVITATE: float; hang; hover; lift; rise; suspend

LEVITY: (**see** "liveliness") buoyancy; changeableness; fickleness; frivolity; fun; gaiety; inconstancy; jocularity; lightheartedness; lightness; merriment; triflingness; volubility

LEVY: **v.** assess; collect; conscript; enlist; estreat; evaluate; exact; fine; impose; muster; rate; require; seize; tax; LEVY: **n.** assessment; cess; collection; customs; duty; estreat; exaction; fee; fine; impost; muster; rate; revenue; seizure; tax; tithe; toll; tribute

LEWD: amative; amatory; amorous; Anacreontic; aphrodisiac; arousing; bawdy; carnal; concupiscent; concupiscible; Cyprian; debauched; defiled; depraved; dirty; dissolute; erogenous; erotic; feculent; filthy; foul; *grivois*; immodest; immoral; improper; impure; indecent; indecorous; indelicate; ithyphallic; lascive; lascivious; lecherous; libertine; libidinous; licentious; low; lubricious; lustful; nasty; obliquitous; obscene; offensive; passionate; pornographic; profligate; provocative; prurient; randy; ribald; risqué; salacious; satyric; scrofulous; scurrile; scurrilous; sensual; sensuous; sexual; sexy; smutty; unchaste; unclean; unrespectable; unsuitable; venereal; voluptuous; vulgar; wanton; LEWDNESS: amorosity; carnality; concupiscence; debauchery; depravity; dirtiness; feculence; filth(iness); immorality; impudicity; impurity; indecency; indelicacy; lasciviency; lasciviousness; lubricity; obliquity; obscenity; passion; pornography; profligacy; pruriency; salacity; scurrility; sensuality; sensuousness; sexuality; voluptuousness; vulgarity; wantonness

LIABLE: accountable; amenable; answerable; apt; assailable; assaultable; attackable; bound; chargeable; exposed; guilty; likely; obligated; obliged; open; prone; responsible; sensitive; subject; susceptible; susceptive; vulnerable; LIABILITY: arrear(s); arrearage; charge; debit; debt; drawback; duty; fault; franchise; guilt; indebtedness; I.O.U.; likelihood; neglect; obligation; obnoxiety; responsibility; sensitivity; sin; susceptibility; trespass; vulnerability

LIAR: Ananias; cheat; deceiver; exaggerator; fabricator; fabulist; faker; falsifier; fibber; hypocrite; knave; Munchausen; pretender; prevaricator; pseudologist; pseudologue; tergiversator; wernard

LIBEL: **v.** abuse; asperse; defame; degrade; denigrate; lampoon; malign; slander; smear; vilify; LIBEL: **n.** abuse; aspersion; calumny; defamation; degradation; denigration; lampoon; satire; skit; slander; smear; squib; vilification; LIBELOUS: abusive; calumnious; defamatory; degradative; denigratory; offensive; salacious; scandalous; slanderous

LIBERAL: **a.** (**see** "generous") abundant; advanced; ample; bounteous; bountiful; broad-minded; catholic; copious; eclectic; extravagant; frank; free(handed); full; handsome; hospitable; knowledg(e)able; large(-minded); latitudinarian; lavish; left; lenient; magnanimous; munificent; open(handed); open-minded; philanthropic(al); princely; prodigal; profuse; progressive; radical; tolerant; unrestrained; unrestricted; LIBERAL: **n.** humanitarian; philanthropist; prodigal; progressive; radical; Young Turk;

LIBERALITY: bounteousness; bountifulness; broad-mindedness; copiosity; generosity; generousness; hospitality; largeness; largess(e); munificence; openhandedness; philanthropy; tolerance; toleration; width; LIBERALIZE: **see** "lessen"

LIBERATE: (**see** "free") absolve; acquit; clear; deliver; detach; discharge; disengage; dismiss; emancipate; extricate; loose(n); manumit; pardon; ransom; redeem; release; reprieve; rescue; save; unchain; unfetter; unpin; unshackle; untie; LIBERATOR: emancipator; manumitter; Messiah; redeemer; redemptor; redemptrix (fem.); LIBERATION: (**see** "salvation") delivery; disengagement; emancipation; enlargement; extrication; freedom; freeing; liberty; manumission; pardon; redemption; release; reprieve; rescue

LIBERTINE: cad; cyprian; debauchee; freethinker; goat; lecher; *paillard*; profligate; rakehell; rip; rounder; satyr; sensualist; thelemite; voluptuary

LIBERTY: (**see** "freedom") absolution; acquaintance; disengagement; emancipation; enfranchisement; exemption; extrication; familiarity; franchise; furlough; immunity; independence; intimacy; leave; liberation; license; magnanimity; manumission; pardon; permission; power; privilege; redemption; release; reprieve; rescue; right; scope

LIBRARY: agency; athen(a)eum; bibliotheca; *bibliothèque*; books; collection; den; gallery; museum; LIBRARIAN: *bibliothécaire*; bibliothecarian

LICE: **see** "louse"

LICENSE: **v.** allow; approbate; approve; authorize; commission; consent; franchise; grant; let; patent; permit; warrant; LICENSE: **n.** (**see** "freedom") abandon(ment); abuse; allowance; authority; authorization; certificate; commission; consent; deviation; disregard; faculty; franchise; grant; laxity; leave; liberty; licentiousness; patent; permission; permit; prerogative; privilege; rein; right; scope; swing; ticket; unrestraint; warrant

LICENTIOUS: (**see** "lewd") free; immoderate; libertine; profligate; rakish; wanton

LICIT: **see** "lawful"

LICK: (**see** "beat") conquer; defeat; flog; lap; moisten; overcome; subdue; thrash; tongue; whip

LID: cap; check; cover(ing); curb; hat; repression; roof; top

LIE: **v.** abide; cavil; couch; deceive; deviate; devise; dissemble; dodge; dwell; equivocate; evade; exaggerate; exist; fabricate; fabulate; fabulize; falsify; feign; fib; invent; linger; lodge; misrepresent; misstate; mythologize; palter; pretend; prevaricate; quibble; recline; repose; reside; rest; sleep; stretch; subsist; tergiversate; LIE: **n.** *blague*; canard; deceit; deception; deviation; equivocation; evasion; exaggeration; fabrication; fabulation; falsehood; falsification; fib; fiction; hyperbole; inexactitude; invention; inveracity; makeup; mendacity; misrepresentation; misstatement; Munchausenism; myth; palter; prevarication; pseudology; roorback; story; tarradiddle; tergiversation; untruth; white lie

LIEU: instead; place; proxy; room; stead; substitute; vice

LIFE: activities; activity; affairs; afflatus; anima(tion); being; biography; bios; blood; breath(ing); career; course; days; duration; endurance; energy; entity; essence; exhalation; existence; experience; flatus; halitus; hide; hours; humanity; inhalation; inspiration; juice; liveliness; livingness; mankind; memoirs; nature; people; period; person; pneuma; respiration; responsiveness; sap; society; source; spirit; vigor; vim; vita; vitality; vivaciousness; vivacity; way; wind; world; zest

LIFELESS: abiotic; adenoidal; amort; anemic; apathetic; azoic; barren; bloodless; colorless; comatose; dead; defunct; depressed; desolate; dispirited; dormant; dull; empty; exanimate; extinct; feeble; flat; gripless; halfhearted; heavy; inactive; inanimate; inert; insensible; insentient; insipid; juiceless; latent; lazy; lethargic; listless; low; passive; quiescent; rigid; sapless; slow; sluggish; spiritless; stagnant; stiff; tame; tepid; torpid; unconscious; unliving; unresponsive; vapid; weak; wooden; LIFELESSNESS: anemia; apathy; bloodlessness; coma; death; defunction; dormancy; dullness; emptiness; immobility; inaction; inactivity; inanimation; inertia; inertness; insensitivity; insentience; insentiency; insipidity; latency; laziness; lethargy; listlessness; passivity; quiescence; quietude; torpidity; vapidity; weakness

LIFETIME: age; being; days; existence; forever; life-span; world

LIFT: **v.** aid; boost; cop; elevate; end; escalate; exalt; filch; heave; heft; heighten; help; hoist; hove; intensify; levitate; plagiarize; project; raise; rear; remove; rescind; soar; steal; surge; swipe; transport; upheave; LIFT: **n.** aid; boost; boot; crane; elevator; escalator; exaltation; handle; heft; heightening; help; hilt; intensification; jack; raise; ride; rise; surge

LIGAMENT: band(age); bond; connection; leader; tendon; tie; tissue; union

LIGATURE: band(age); bond; connection; ligament; rope; suture; taenia; thread; tie; union

LIGHT: **v.** beacon; beam; blaze; dismount; fall; fire; flame; flare; flash; flicker; glare; gleam; glimmer; glitter; glow; ignite; illume; illuminate; kindle; land; perch; roost; settle; shine; sparkle; twinkle; LIGHT: **a. (see** "airy") amusing; blazing; bright; buoyant; carefree; casual; changeable; cheerful; clear; coruscating; diaphanous; easy; effulgent; entertaining; ethereal; facile; faint; fickle; fine; fleet; fluffy; free; frivolous; frothy; gay; gentle; giddy; gleaming; glinting; glittering; glowing; idle; illuminating; imponderable; imponderous; incandescent; inconsiderable; indistinct; leger; lissome; loose; luminary; luminiferous; luminous; lustrous; nimble; porous; portable; quick; scanty; shining; simple; sleazy; slight; small; superficial; trifling; trivial; twinkling; unserious; weak(ened); weightless; LIGHT: **n.** arc; beacon; beam; blaze; brightness; brilliance; bulb; candle; coruscation; cresset; dawn; day(break); effulgence; enlightenment; fire; flame; flare; flash; flicker; fluorescence; glare; gleam; glimmer; glint; glitter; guidance; illumination; incandescence; kleig; knowledge; lamp; lantern; lumen; luminary; lumination; luminescence; luminosity; luster; match; moon; neon; phosphorescence; radiance; reasoning; scintillation; shine; signal; spark; splendor; star; sun-(rise); taper; torch; twinkle; understanding; wattage; window

LIGHTEN: **(see** "ease") alleviate; cheer; diminish; gladden; leaven; levitate; mitigate; moderate; qualify; release; relieve; soften; soothe; temper

LIGHTHEARTED: **see** "carefree" and "debonaire;" LIGHTHEARTEDNESS: blithe-

ness; blithesomeness; buoyance; buoyancy; buoyantness; cheerfulness; ebullience; euphoria; Euphrosyne; gaiety; gladness; jauntiness; nonchalance; sprightliness

LIKE: **v.** admire; adore; appreciate; approbate; bask; become; cherish; choose; delight; dig; dote; elect; enjoy; esteem; fancy; favor; gratify; have; hold; incline; love; occupy; own; parallel; possess; prefer; prize; regard; relish; resemble; respect; savor; suit; value; want; LIKE: **a.** akin; alike; allied; analogous; as; cognate; comparable; congruent; corresponding; equal; equivalent; germane; identical; interchangeable; kin; kind; parallel; related; resembling; same; similar; sympathetic; synonymic; synonymous; uniform; LIKABLE: agreeable; appealing; attractive; comely; contentable; personable; simpatico; sympathetic; LIKELY: advantageous; agreeable; apparent; apt; auspicious; calculated; comely; conceivable; conjectural; contingent; credible; fair; liable; logical; ostensible; plausible; possible; potential; practicable; presumable; presumed; presumptive; *prima facie*; probable; promising; prone; qualified; rational; reasonable; seemly; specious; suitable; supposed; verisimilar; *vraisemblable*; LIKELIHOOD: advantage; chance; credibility; expectation; favor; hope; liability; likeliness; odds; presumption; probability; prospect; supposition; vantage; verisimilitude; verisimility; *vraisemblance*

LIKEN: **see** "compare"

LIKELY: **see** under "like"

LIKENESS: **(see** "resemblance") analogy; appearance; assonance; caricature; copy; counterpart; doll; effigy; equivalence; facsimile; form; guise; icon; image; manikin; painting; parity; photo(graph); picture; portrait; representation; reproduction; semblance; shape; similarity; similitude; statue; synonymity; verisimilitude

LIKEWISE: also; besides; ditto; furthermore; moreover; similar(ly); too

LIKING: **(see** "prejudice") bias; diathesis; esteem; fancy; favor; gusto; heart; inclination; palate; partiality; passion; penchant; predilection; preference; propensity; relish; shine; taste; tooth; use; will

LILLIPUTIAN: **(see** "small") diminutive; dwarf; midget; petty; small-minded

LILT: see "swing"

LIMB: appendage; arm; bough; branch; extremity; fin; leg; manus; member; scion; shoot; wing

LIMBER: acrobatic; agile; elastic; flaccid; flexible; gracile; limp; lissom(e); lithe-(some); loose; nimble; plastic; pliable; pliant; rubbery; supple; untrustworthy

LIMBO: hell; jail; limbus; middle ground; neglect; oblivion; prison

LIMIT: **v.** allocate; allot; assign; astrict; bound; circumscribe; confine; conscribe; constrain; contract; curtail; define; delineate; demarcate; discriminate; encircle; enclose; end; fence; fix; handicap; hedge; hinder; license; mark; number; particularize; prescribe; prevent; qualify; reduce; regulate; restrain; restrict; retard; stifle; stint; withhold; LIMIT(S): **n.** ambit; barrier; border-(land); boundary; bounds; bourn(e); brim; brink; ceiling; circumference; circumscription; condition(s); confines; deadline; definition; delineation; demarcation; duration; edge; end; endurance; extent; extreme; framework; frontier; handicap; hindrance; jurisdiction; last straw; line; margin; mark; maximum; minimum; outside; pale; perimeter; point; prescription; purlieu(s); qualification; radius; range; regulation; resistance; restraint(s); restriction; rim; rule(s); saturation; solstice; space; term(ination); terminus; trial; LIMITATION: boundary; capacity; circumscription; confinement; constraint; constriction; delimitation; duration; endurance; extent; finitude; modification; particularization; qualification; resistance; restraint; restriction; self-denial; sum; time; utmost; LIMITED *or* LIMITING: adjectival; adjective; *borné*; circumscribed; cloist-(e)ral; cloistered; conditional; conditioned; confined; confining; definite; demarcative; denominational; few; finite; impermanent; isolated; little; local; moderate; modest; narrow; parochial; particularized; prescribed; provincial; qualificatory; regional; restrained; restricted; restrictive; retarded; scant; sectarian; segregated; sheltered; short; small; special; temporary; topical; unimaginative

LIMITLESS: (see "vast") boundless; great; huge; illimited; inexhaustible; numerous; unbounded; uncircumscribed; unmeasured; unrestrained; untold

LIMN: decorate; delineate; depict; describe; detail; draw; illume; illuminate; outline; paint; portray; represent

LIMP: **v.** falter; hobble; stumble; LIMP: **a.** crippled; drooping; exhausted; flabby; flaccid; flexible; flimsy; lame; limber; loose; relaxed; rubbery; slack; soft; spiritless; supple; wilted; LIMP: **n.** claudication; faltering; flaccidity; gimp; halt; hitch; hobble

LIMPID: clear; cloudless; crystal(line); diaphanous; lucid; pellucid; pure; serene; sheer; simple; translucent; transparent; untroubled

LINE: **v.** draw; fill; fortify; mark; pack; supply; LINE: **n.** ancestry; border; boundary; business; cable; chain; channel; collineation; contour; cord; course; crease; demarcation; descent; direction; division; echelon; edge; equator; field; file; formation; frontier; furrow; interest; job; kinship; lead; leash; limit(ation); lineage; lineament; mark; métier; note; occupation; profession; race; railroad; range; rank; restriction; ridge; rope; route; row; seam; sequence; stitch; stock; streak; stream; string; stripe; stroke; stuff; succession; suture; tape; thread; trace; trade; trail; train; trend; wad; wire; work; wrinkle

LINEAGE: (see "ancestry") background; birth; blood; derivation; descent; family; genealogy; heredity; kin(dred); kinship; line; origin; pedigree; progeny; provenance; race; sib; source; stemma; stock; strain; succession; tradition; tree

LINGER: (see "abide") continue; creep; dally; dawdle; delay; drag; dwell; falter; haunt; hesitate; hover; inch; lag; lie; live; loiter; lurk; plod; procrastinate; remain; saunter; stay; tarry; totter; traipse; trudge; wait

LINGO: argot; cant; chatter; dialect; drawl; jargon; language; patois; patter; slang; speech; talk

LINGUIST: classicist; glottologist; linguistician; pantoglot; philologist; polyglot; LINGUISTIC: glottologic; philologic(al)

LINIMENT: arnica; counterirritant; embrocation; linimentum; lotion

LINK: **v.** (see "implicate") bind; bridge; catenate; chain; concatenate; connect; couple; cross; drain; enchain; fasten; hitch; interlock; involve; join; loop; marry; pair;

shunt; span; tack; tie; transverse; traverse; unite; yoke; LINK(AGE): **n.** arch; association; chain; concatenation; connection; copula; couple; coupler; coupling; cross(ing); division; element; enchainment; fastener; hitch; joint; junction; juncture; leg; liaison; linchpin; lock; loop; nexus; overpass; passage(way); pons; pontoon; ring; section; segment; span; suture; tie; transition; viaduct; vinculum; union; way; yoke

LINT: down; fiber(s); flax; fluff; fuzz; nap; ravelings; tilmus

LION: cat; celebrity; Felis; hero; Leo; star; V.I.P.

LIP: backtalk; border; edge; flange; fold; impudence; insolence; labellum; labia (pl.); labium; margin; rim; sass; sauciness; speech; spout; words

LIQUEFY: deliquesce; dissolve; fuse; liquesce; melt; run; soften; thaw

LIQUID: **a.** aqueous; clear; deliquescent; dissolved; dulcet; flowing; fluid; juicy; limpid; mellifluous; melted; musical; runny; sappy; serous; smooth; softened; thawed; unconstrained; watery; wet; LIQUID: **n.** (**see** "liquor") blood; fluid; juice; sap; serum; water

LIQUIDATE: (**see** "resolve") adjust; amortize; clear; discharge; dispose; kill; pay; rid; sell; settle

LIQUOR: alcohol; ale; arrak; bath; beer; beverage; bock; brandy; broth; drink; elixir; fluid; gin; gravy; grog; juice; lager; liquid; mead; porter; rum; rye; sake; scotch; soup; spirits; stock; stout; vodka; water; whiskey; wine

LISSOM(E): agile; athletic; flexible; graceful; gracile; light; limber; lithe(some); nimble; pliant; quick; slender; supple; svelte

LIST: **v.** arrange; attend; cant; careen; chronicle; classify; detail; docket; engross; enrol(l); enter; enumerate; file; give; hark; heel; impanel; index; inscribe; insert; itemize; matriculate; muster; name; note; place; recite; record; register; roll; score; show; slant; slope; subscribe; tip; LIST: **n.** account; agenda; agendum; arrangement; array; calendar; canon; cant; careen; catalog(ue); classification; collection; detail; dictionary; docket; enumeration; file; heel; index; inscription; inventory; itemization;

lineup; name; nomenclature; note; record; register; registry; repertory; roll; roster; rota; schedule; slate; subscription; table; tariff; tilt(ing)

LISTEN: (**see** "heed") attend; audit; bug; consider; ear; eavesdrop; hark; h(e)arken; hear; list; obey; receive; tend

LISTLESS: adiaphorous; ambitionless; apathetic; careless; comatose; cool; *dégagé*; dilatory; dispirited; drowsy; dull(ing); enervated; fatigued; forgetful; glassy; hebetudinous; heedless; immobile; impassive; imperturbable; impervious; inactive; inattentive; indifferent; indolent; inert; insipid; lackadaisical; lackluster; languid; languorous; Laodicean; lassitudinous; lazy; leaden; lethargic; listless; lukewarm; mechanical; nonchalant; otiose; pachydermatous; perfunctory; phlegmatic; pococurante; quiet; slack; sleepy; sluggish; spiritless; stoic(al); stupefying; supine; torpescent; torpid; torporific; unconcerned; unenergetic; unenervated; unenthusiastic; unfeeling; unimpressed; uninterested; unmoved; unresponsive; vacuous; LISTLESSNESS: (**see** "apathy") abiotrophy; acedia; dispiritedness; drowsiness; dullness; enervation; immobility; indolence; inertia; insipidity; lackadaisy; languidness; languor; lassitude; laziness; lethargy; melancholia; otiosity; perfunctoriness; sleepiness; sluggishness; spiritlessness; supinity; torpidity; torpidness; torpor; vegetation

LITANY: chant; ectene; ektene; invocation; orison; prayer; recital; rite; rogation; rote; service; supplication

LITERAL: accurate; actual; categorical; conformable; exact; letter-for-letter; letter-perfect; literatim; obvious; plain; precise; prosaic; regular; textual; true; unadorned; undeviating; unembellished; unerring; unimaginative; unsparing; unvarnished; veracious; verbal; verbatim; veritable; word-for-word; LITERALITY: exactitude; grammatolatry; literalness; prosaism; veracity

LITERARY: anecdotal; bookish; cerebral; donnish; editorial; educated; erudite; learned; lettered; literate; scholarly; versed; well-read

LITERATE: cultured; educated; instructed; learned; lettered; literary; lucid; polished; taught; tutored

LITERATURE: (**see** "writing") advertising matter; *belles-lettres*; books; catalog(ue);

compilations; compositions; culture; letters; pamphlets; plays; poetry; publicity; reading; texts; tracts; treatises

LITHE: (**see** "lissome") agile; silken; supple; svelte

LITIGATE: **see** "sue;" LITIGATION: bill; case; declaration; lawsuit; prosecution; suit

LITTER: **v.** jumble; mess; mulch; scatter; strew; LITTER: **n.** bed(ding); bier; brood; coffin; couch; disorder; family; jumble; mess; mulch; offspring; palanquin; refuse; rubbish; sedan; stretcher; trash; untidiness

LITTLE: bantam; brief; contemptible; diminutive; dwarfish; exiguous; feeble; few; illiberal; inappreciable; inconsiderable; inconsiderate; insignificant; light; lilliputian; limited; low; meager; mean; microscopic; midget; miniature; miniscule; minute; narrow; paltry; peewee; petite; petty; pint-size(d); puny; runted; runty; scant(y); selfish; short; slight; small(-minded); stingy; thin; tiny; trifling; trivial; ultramicroscopic; unimportant; weak; wee

LITTORAL: bank; beach; coast; coastal region; ripa; tidewater

LITURGY: ceremony; form(ality); litany; observance; procedure; rite; ritual; service

LIVE: **v.** abide; act; be; bide; board; breathe; cohabit; continue; do; domicile; domiciliate; dwell; endure; exist; experience; feed; flourish; habituate; inhabit; inhere; last; lodge; occupy; outlast; perform; practice; prevail; remain; reside; room; roost; settle; sojourn; stay; stop; subsist; survive; tenant; LIVE: **a.** (**see** "lively") active; afire; alert; alive; animated; breathing; burning; conscious; contemporary; enduring; energetic; existing; extant; functioning; glowing; growing; living; lusty; organic; quick; resilient; sentient; sprightly; surviving; unclosed; unexploded; vigorous; vital; vivid; LIV(E)ABLE: **see** "tolerable"

LIVELIHOOD: (**see** "support") affluence; bread; capital; fortune; income; job; living; means; métier; money; profession; property; resources; riches; subsistence; support; wealth; work

LIVELY: acrobatic; active; agile; airy; alacritous; alert; animated; blithe(some); boisterous; booming; bouncing; bouncy; brilliant; brisk; buoyant; cheerful; chipper;

chirrupy; corky; ebullient; effervescent; elastic; elated; energetic; enlivening; exciting; exhilarated; exhilarative; exuberant; fervent; fervid; feverish; fresh; frisky; frolicsome; gay; graphic; impassioned; impish; intense; jaunty; jolly; keen; larkish; larksome; larky; light-hearted; limber; merry; mirthful; mirthsome; nimble; perk(y); pert; piquant; playful; pointed; prankish; quick; resilient; roguish; ruddy; skittish; sparkling; spirited; spiritous; sportful; sportive; sporty; sprightly; springy; spry; striking; tangy; trotty; unpedantic; vehement; vigorous; vital; vivacious; vivid; volatile; yare; yeasty; zestful; LIVELINESS: acrobatics; acrobatism; agility; alacrity; animation; blithesomeness; bounce; briskness; buoyancy; ebullience; effervescence; élan; elation; energy; esprit; excitement; exhilaration; exuberance; fervency; fervor; fever; force; friskiness; frivolity; frolicsomeness; fun; gaiety; geniality; glee; grig; hilarity; impishness; intensity; intoxication; invigoration; jocularity; jollity; joviality; keenness; levity; life; lilt; merriment; mirth(fulness); nimbleness; pep(per); piquancy; quickness; rapidity; resiliency; roguery; roguishness; sparkle; spirit(edness); sprightliness; spring(iness); spryness; swagger; verve; vim; vigor(ousness); vitality; vivacity; zest

LIVID: anemic; ashen; black-and-blue; bruised; cadaverous; discolored; ecchymotic; ghastly; gray; lurid; pale; pallid; wan; white; whitish

LIVING: **a.** (**see** "live") active; agile; alive; animate(d); breathing; contemporary; effective; enduring; existing; extant; feeling; flowing; functioning; organic; productive; quick; subsisting; surviving; unperished; unquenched; vigorous; vital; vivid; zetetic; LIVING: **n. see** "livelihood"

LOAD: **v.** bias; burden; charge; clog; cram; cumber; encumber; fill; freight; heap; jag; lade(n); lard; onerate; oppress; overburden; pack; stuff; tax; weigh; LOAD(S): **n.** burden; bushel; cargo; charge; collection; demand; encumbrance; freight; impediment; incubus; jag; lading; lot(s); mass; onus; oppression; pack; ponderosity; quantity; resistance; responsibility; stress; tax; weight

LOAFER: *badaud*; beachcomber; bum; chairwarmer; dawdler; derelict; drifter; drone; *flâneur*; *flâneuse* (fem.); flotsam and jetsam (pl.); gaberlunzie; idler; laggard; loiterer; lounger; parasite; shoe; slouch; sponge(r);

sluggard; trifler; unemployed; vagabond; vagrant

LOATH: adverse; averse; backward; bashful; disinclined; indisposed; recalcitrant; reluctant; shy; unwilling

LOATHE: abhor; abominate; anathematize; avoid; despise; detest; dislike; execrate; hate; scorn; LOATHSOME: abhorrent; abominable; anathematic(al); cloying; despicable; detestable; disgusting; dislikable; dispiteous; execrable; foul; hateful; monstrous; nauseating; nauseous; obnoxious; odious; offensive; repugnant; repulsive; revolting; undesirable; unprincipled; unwholesome; vile; LOATHSOMENESS: abhorrence; abomination; antipathy; aversion; despicability; detestation; execration; nausea; *nausée*; odium; qualmishness; repugnance; repugnancy; repulsiveness

LOBBY: **v.** advance; influence; persuade; petition; plead; promote; solicit; LOBBY: **n.** anteroom; corridor; entry; foyer; hall; lounge; vestibule

LOCAL: autochthonous; confined; edaphic; indigenous; insular; limited; narrow; native; parochial; peninsular; provincial; regional; restricted; rural; sectional; topical; vicinal; villagy; LOCALE *or* LOCALITY: (**see** "location") area; arena; authority; belt; district; environ(s); jurisdiction; loci (pl.); locus; milieu; neighborhood; place; position; precinct; purlieu; region; scene; section; sector; site; situation; spot; subdivision; venue; vicinage; vicinity; way; zone

LOCATE: bound; define; discover; divine; establish; find; land; mark; perceive; pinpoint; place; see; set(tle); sight; sit(uate); spot; LOCATION: (**see** "locality") anchorage; area; emplacement; establishment; headquarters; job; land; locale; lot; neighborhood; place; point; position; post; region; seat; site; situation; spot; standing; station; tract

LOCK: **v.** bar(ricade); bind; bolt; button; cage; catch; clasp; confine; detent; embrace; fasten; fix; grapple; hide; hook; hug; imprison; interlace; interlock; jail; jam; join; latch; secure; shut; unite; zip; LOCK: **n.** bar(ricade); bolt; button; catch; clasp; cotter; curl; fastener; fastening; grapple; hair; hasp; hook; latch; ringlet; tress; tuft; zipper

LODGE: **v.** abide; accommodate; billet; board; camp; deliver; deposit; dwell; encamp; entertain; establish; file; harbor; house; incarcerate; live; nest(le); place; provide; quarter; remain; reside; room; roost; settle; shelter; sleep; sojourn; stay; stick; stop; stow; vest; LODGE **n.** *or* LODGING: abode; accommodation(s); barracks; billet; board; cabin; camp; cavern; club(house); cottage; den; dorm(itory); dwelling; encampment; habitation; harbor; hotel; house; housing; hut; inn; lair; nest; quarterage; quarters; residence; resort; room(s); settlement; shelter; sleeper; society; sojourn; union

LOFTY: airy; Alpine; altitudinous; Andean; arrogant; celestial; dignified; distant; divine; elegant; elevated; eminent; esoteric; ethereal; exalted; formal; generous; grand(iloquent); great; haughty; heavenly; high(est); high-minded; imposing; magnanimous; magniloquent; majestic; noble; Olympian; pompous; precipitous; proud; snooty; soaring; stately; steep; stiff; stilted; sublime; supercilious; supernal; supreme; tall; towering; vain

LOG: book; diary; journal; record; timber; wood

LOGIC: *ars artium*; deduction; induction; method; rationale; reason(ing); syntactics; thought; LOGICAL: Aristotelian; Cartesian; clear; cogent; coherent; consistent; dialectical; dianoetic; formal; likely; lucid; methodical; probable; rational; reasonable; sane; sound; valid

LOGION: doctrine; maxim; saying; truth

LOITER: dally; dawdle; delay; dillydally; fritter; idle; interrupt; lag; linger; loaf; poke; ponder; saunter; stall; tarry; wait; LOITERER: beachcomber; bum; dawdler; drone; *flâneur*; *flâneuse* (fem.) idler; loafer; trifler; vagabond; vagrant

LONE(LY) *or* LONESOME: (**see** "alone") companionless; depressed; deserted; desolate; drear(y); enisled; eremitic; forgotten; forlorn; forsaken; friendless; hermitical; infrequent; isolated; lorn; monkish; rejected; secluded; separated; troglodytic; unfrequented; unfriended; LONELINESS: (**see** "desolation") isolation; lonelihood; loneness; lonesomeness

LONG: **v.** ache; aspire; covet; desiderate; desire; dream; hanker; hone; hunger; itch; languish; pant; pine; regret; thirst; tire; want; wish; worry; yearn; yen; LONG: **a.**

diuturnal; elongated; eternal; extended; garrulous; lengthened; lengthy; outstretched; prolix; prolonged; protracted; remote; repetitious; sempiternal; seven-league; slow; stretched; tall; tedious; time-consuming; time-taking; verbose; wordy; LONGING: **a.** aching; appetent; appetitious; covetous; craving; desiderative; desirous; hankering; hungering; itching; languishing; panting; regretting; thirsting; wishing; yearning; LONGING: **n.** appetency; appetite; appetition; craving; desideration; desire; drive; hankering; itch(ing); languishment; longingness; regret; urge; wish; yearn(ing); yen

LOOK: **v.** (**see** "see") anticipate; appear; attend; await; behold; bode; contemplate; descry; discover; examine; expect; eye; face; flash; gaze; glance; glimpse; hope; inspect; ken; leer; observe; ogle; peep; peer; perceive; peruse; pore; pry; regard; respect; scan; scrutinize; search; seek; seem; spy; stare; survey; tend; view; watch; LOOK: **n.** air; appearance; aspect; attention; bearing; behavior; carriage; cast; condition; conduct; contemplation; countenance; discovery; examination; expectation; expression; eyeful; features; flash; gander; gaze; glance; glimpse; hope; inspection; ken; leer; manner; marlock; mien; observance; observation; *oeillade*; ogle; patina; peering; perception; physiognomy; pose; prying; regard; scan; scrutiny; search; seeking; semblance; spying; stare; survey; view; visage; watch

LOOKOUT: belvedere; conner; crow's-nest; cupola; guard; observation; prospect; scout; sentinel; spy; tower; turret; view; watchman; widow's walk

LOOM: (**see** "appear") develop; emerge; materialize; objectify; seem; shape; weave

LOOP: **v.** bend; circle; coil; connect; crook; fall; knot; link; spiral; stitch; turn; LOOP: **n.** ambit; ansa; bend; circle; circuit; coil; crook; curve; curvet; eye; fold; knot; link; noose; ring; rope; spiral; staple; tab; turn; whorl

LOOPHOLE: alibi; aperture; chink; crevice; escape; excuse; loop; opening; out(let); plea; pretext; slit; slot

LOOSE(N): **v.** absolve; detach; discharge; disconnect; disengage; ease; emit; free; liberate; manumit; open; pardon; relax; release; relieve; slacken; slip; spread; unbind; unbuckle; unbutton; unchain; unclamp; unconnect; undo; unfasten; unfurl; ungird(le); unlace; unlash; unlatch; unleash; unlock; unpin; unscrew; unstrap; untie; unzip; LOOSE: **a.** at large; baggy; careless; desultory; detached; diffuse; discharged; disconnected; disengaged; dissolute; distinct; easy; elastic; escaped; fast; flabby; flowing; free; immoral; incoherent; indefinite; inexact; insecure; lax(ative); leaky; lewd; liberated; licentious; limber; limp; messy; negligent; open; out; pardoned; rampant; relaxed; released; remiss; slack(ened); sloppy; sporty; spread; unattached; unbounded; unbuckled; unbuttoned; unchained; unchaste; unclamped; unconfined; unconnected; unconsolidated; undone; unfastened; unfettered; unfirm; unfurled; ungirdled; unlaced; unlashed; unlatched; unleashed; unlocked; unpinned; unrestrained; unscrewed; unserried; unsteady; unstrapped; untethered; untied; untight; vague; wanton; wild

LOOT: **v.** despoil; pillage; plunder; raid; ransack; ravage; rifle; rob; rummage; sack; seize; spoil; steal; strip; LOOT: **n.** booty; haul; money; pelf; pillage; plunder; prize; spoil(s); swag

LOP: crop; curtail; cut; detach; dock; droop; hang; obtruncate; prune; remove; snip; trim; truncate

LOPSIDED: alop; asymmetric(al); disproportionate; unbalanced; uneven; unsymmetrical

LOQUACIOUS: (**see** "wordy") babbling; chattering; fluent; garrulous; glib; noisy; prolix; talkative; verbose; vocal; voluble; LOQUACITY: (**see** "wordiness") babble; fluency; garrulity; glibness; loquaciousness; prolixity; talkativeness; verbosity; volubility

LORD: **v.** boast; brag; domineer; strut; LORD: **n.** baron; Christ; count; earl; God; governor; leader; Kyrios; liege; marquis; noble(man); peer; ruler; viscount; LORDLY: archidiaconal; arrogant; boastful; despotic; dignified; grand(iloquent); grandiose; haughty; honorable; honored; imperial; imperious; kingly; lofty; magnificent; majestic; noble; overbearing; princely; proud; stately; uppish; LORDSHIP: domain; dominion; seigneury; seign(i)ory; sovereignty

LORE: (**see** "tradition") education; erudition; ethos; folkways; hearsay; history; information; knowledge; learning; science; wisdom

LOSE: botch; cede; decline; degenerate; destroy; disappear; drip; drop; escape; estrange; evaporate; fail; falter; forfeit; lag; leak; leave; miscarry; mislay; mislocate; misplace; miss; ooze; osmose; outstrip; rid; ruin; spill; squander; vaporize; volatize; wander; waste; weaken; wither; yield; LOSS: attenuation; bereavement; casualty; damage; death; declination; decline; defeat; degeneration; depreciation; deprivation; destruction; detriment; diminution; disaster; disintegration; divestation; elimination; eradication; evaporation; failure; forfeiture; hold; impairment; injury; leak(age); misfortune; mishap; perdition; privation; riddance; ruin; trouble; waste; weakening; LOST: abandoned; asea; astray; bereft; bewildered; corrupt; damned; denied; departed; desolate; destroyed; disappeared; dissipated; escaped; evaporated; forfeited; forlorn; forsaken; gone; hardened; helpless; insensible; irreclaimable; irrecoverable; irretrievable; lorn; mislaid; misplaced; missed; missing; overwhelmed; perplexed; rapt; reprobate; ruined; spilled; squandered; strayed; subverted; uncertain; unfindable; wasted; LOSER: see "victim"

LOT(S): aggregation; allotment; amount; award; batch; bundle; bushel; caboodle; chance; choice; crew; crowd; destiny; doom; fate; forest; fortune; gob(s); *gogo*; grace; great deal; ground; hap; hatful; hazard; heap(s); heritage; jugful; kind; land; load(s); luck; mass; million(s); mountain; much; number; ocean(s); parcel; part; peck; pile(s); plot; portion; raft; rash; reams; roll; scad(s); sea; set; share; site; slew; sort-(ilege); sum; volumes

LOTION: ablution; astringent; cleanser; cosmetic; embrocation; emollient; liniment; soother

LOTTERY: bingo; chance; contest; gamble; lotto; price; raffle; random; risk; scheme; selection

LOUD: blatant; boisterous; clamorous; clangorous; criant; earsplitting; emphatic; flashy; forte; fortissimo; high; hoarse; insistent; loudmouthed; lusty; mighty; multivocal; noisy; obnoxious; obtrusive; offensive; ostentatious; raised; raucous; roaring; rowdy; sharp; shrill; stentorian; stentorious; strenuous; strident; stridulent; tumultuous; unmodulated; uproarious; vehement; vociferous; voiceful; widemouthed; LOUDNESS: amplification; amplitude; boisterousness; magnitude; volume

LOUNGE: **v.** bask; dawdle; idle; laze; lie; loaf; loll; recline; rest; saunter; sit; LOUNGE: **n.** divan; lobby; parlor; room; settee; sofa

LOUSY: abominable; buggy; filthy; pedicular; pediculous; replete; repulsive; verminous; vile; wormy

LOUT: boor; bumpkin; churl; clodhopper; clown; dumbbell; grobian; lubber; lummox; oaf; simpleton; yokel

LOVE: **v.** admire; adore; appreciate; attach; attract; caress; cherish; desire; devote; dote; emote; enamor; endear; enjoy; fancy; feel; fondle; foster; kiss; like; neck; nuzzle; pat; pedestal; prefer; regard; stellify; stroke; woo; worship; LOVE: **n.** admiration; adoration; *affaire d'amour*; *affaire de coeur*; affection; amor(osity); amorousness; amour; appreciation; ardor; attachment; attraction; benevolence; charity; charm; comfort; Cupid; darling; dear; delectation; delight; desire; devotedness; devotion; ecstasy; emotion; enamor(ment); endearment; enjoyment; entertainment; enthusiasm; Eros; exultation; fancy; feeling; felicity; fervor; flame; flavor; fondness; friendship; fun; gladness; gratification; gust(o); happiness; indulgence; jocularity; joy; *la belle passion*; *la grande passion*; liking; merriment; passion; piety; pleasure; preference; rapture; raptus; regard; relish; satisfaction; sensuality; sentiment; stellification; sweetheart; tang; tenderness; transport; worship; zeal; zest; LOVABLE: (**see** "likable") affectionate; cuddlesome; cuddly; dear; endearing; tender; LOVING: (**see** "affectionate") amative; amatory; amorous; Anacreontic; ardent; brotherly; doting; enamored; endearing; erotic; fervent; fervid; fond; impassioned; indulgent; kind(ly); leal; motherly; over-indulgent; painstaking; passionate; sisterly; tender; true; worshipful; LOVELY: (**see** "beautiful") delightful; desirable; graceful; grand; gratifying; lovable; nice; pleasant; pleasing; satisfying

LOVER: admirer; amour; amo(u)rist; beau; beaux (pl.); beloved; boyfriend; Casanova; cavalier (servente); devoted; dove; flame; gallant; inamorata (fem.); inamorato; leman; Lochinvar; Lothario; minion; paramour; Romeo; squire; swain; sweetheart

LOW: abandoned; abased; abject; backward; bad; base; below; blue; cheap; coarse; common; contemptible; crude; dark; dead; debased; degraded; degrading; dejected;

depleted; depressed; despicable; despondent; dimmed; disgraceful; dishonorable; disparaging; disreputable; dissolute; feeble; foul; funereal; gentle; gross; groveling; Hogarthian; humble(d); hushed; ignoble; ignominious; ill; inexpensive; inferior; leprous; lifeless; little; mean; menial; morose; mourning; muffled; offensive; ordinary; orra; plebeian; poor; prostrate; reptilian; sad(dened); servile; shameless; short; sick; slow; snaky; sneaky; snide; soft; soothing; sunken; unbecoming; under; unfavorable; vile; vulgar(ian); weak; whispered; whispering; worthless

LOWER: **v.** abase; alloy; animalize; bastardize; bemean; cheapen; debase; debauch; decrease; degenerate; deglamorize; degrade; dehumanize; demean; demit; demote; denigrate; depress; derogate; descend; devalorize; devaluate; devalue; dim(inish); dip; disgrace; drop; frown; glower; humble; humiliate; impair; insult; lessen; mark down; minify; minimize; pejorate; reduce; resign; settle; shade; sink; subside; traduce; underestimate; underrate; undersell; undervalue; vilify; weaken; worsen; LOWER: **a.** (see "degenerated") below; beneath; cheaper; inferior; junior; later; nether; smaller; subnormal; substandard; under(neath); underpriced; undervalued; LOWEST: bathetic; bottommost; deepest; nethermost; undermost

LOWLY: (**see** "humble") meek; unennobled

LOYAL: abiding; adhering; allegiant; chauvinistic; constant; dependable; devoted; devout; faithful; fast; firm; *gung ho*; honest; leal; liege; obedient; patriotic(al); pious; sta(u)nch; steadfast; steady; stout; tenacious; tried; true(-blue); truehearted; trustworthy; unswerving; worthy; yeomanly; zealous; LOYALTY: allegiance; chauvinism; constancy; constantness; dependability; devotion; duty; *esprit de corps*; faith(fulness); fealty; fidelity; *gung ho*; homage; honor; loyalness; obedience; patriotism; piety; staunchness; steadfastness; tenacity; troth; trustworthiness; worthiness; zeal(otry); zealousness

LUBRICATE: see "oil"

LUCID: (**see** "clear") bright; clairvoyant; diaphanous; distinct; evident; exact; explicit; intelligible; limpid; literate; lucent; luminous; oriented; pellucid; plain; polished; radiant; rational; refulgent; resplendent; sane; shining; sound; translucent; transparent; unambiguous; understandable; vivid; LUCIDITY: (**see** "clearness") clairvoyance; clarity; diaphaneity; distinctness; exactness; limpidity; luminosity; perspicacity; radiance; refulgence; resplendency; sanity; soundness; transparency; vividness

LUCK: accident; break; chance; charm; destiny; fate; fluke; fortuitism; fortuity; fortune; godsend; grace; handsel; hap(penstance); hazard; lot; propitiousness; prosperity; success; LUCKY: auspicious; benign(ant); blessed; canny; favorable; fortunate; happy; meet; miraculous; mirific; opportune; propitious; prosperous; providential; serendipitous; successful

LUCRATIVE: (**see** "profitable") fat; fruitful; gainful; good; moneymaking; paying; productive; prolific; remunerative

LUCRE: emolument; gain; greed; money; pay; pelf; profit; reward; riches; wealth

LUDICROUS: absurd; amusing; bizarre; burlesque; comic(al); droll(ish); farcical; foolish; funny; hideous; jesting; laughable; odd; quaint; queer; ridiculous; risible; silly; waggish; whimsical

LUG: **v.** carry; drag; hale; haul; pull; tote; tug; LUG: **n.** blockhead; ear; handle; loop; lout; nut; projection; worm

LUGGAGE: baggage; bags; gear; grips; impedimenta (pl.); implement(s); suitcases; traps; trunks; valise(s)

LUGUBRIOUS: (**see** "sad") cheerless; disconsolate; dismal; doleful; funereal; mournful; saddened; sorrowful; *triste*

LUKEWARM: (**see** "indifferent") cool; half-baked; halfhearted; Laodecean; so-so; tepid; uncommitted; unconcerned; unenthusiastic

LULL: **v.** abate; allay; appease; assuage; becalm; calm; cease; compose; ease; hush; mitigate; mollify; pacify; quiet(en); relax; rock; smooth; soothe; still; subside; tranquilize; LULL: **n.** abatement; appeasement; assuagement; calmness; cessation; composure; drop; hush; interval; mitigation; mollification; pacification; quiet(ness); quietude; recess; relaxation; serenity; smoothness; stillness; subsidence; tranquility

LUMBER: **v.** encumber; lade; load; plod; rumble; trudge; LUMBER: **n.** boards;

logs; rubbish; scaffolding; timber; trash; trees; wood

LUMINARY: (see "celebrity") illuminati (pl.); illumination; illuminato; intellectual; leading light; lion; moon; planet; star; sun; V.I.P.

LUMINOUS: bright; clear; diaphanous; edifying; effulgent; enlightened; glowing; illuminated; incandescent; inspiring; intelligent; intelligible; lighted; lit; phosphorescent; radiant; shining; translucent

LUMP: bump; chunk; clod; clump; egg; growth; hunk; knot; majority; mass; node; nodule; nub; protuberance; swelling; tubercle; tumor; wad; wen; LUMPISH: awkward; bulky; clumsy; dull; gross; heavy; inactive; inert; sluggish; stolid; stupid

LUNACY: absurdity; brainstorm; craziness; cretinism; delirium; delusion; dementia; derangement; extravagance; folly; foolishness; furor; greediness; hallucination; insanity; madness; mania; psychosis; stupidity; LUNATIC: **a.** absurd; batty; crazy; delirous; delusive; deranged; foolish; giddy; insane; mad; manic; psychiatric; psychotic; stupid; LUNATIC: **n.** bat; crackpot; crank; eccentric; fool; madman; mani(a)c; nut; oddball; psychotic; screwball

LURCH: blunder; cant; careen; deceive; disappoint; jerk; jolt; lunge; pitch; plunge; roll; shift; stagger; stumble; sway; swing; tip; wallow

LURE: **v.** (see "charm") allure; attract; bait; bewitch; coax; deceive; decoy; delude; draw; ensnare; entice; entrap; fascinate; flatter; inveigle; invite; lead; magnetize; mesmerize; persuade; pull; seduce; snare; tempt; toll; trap; trick; vamp; wile; LURE: **n.** (see "charm") allurement; attraction; bait; bewitchment; cynosure; deception; decoy; delusion; draw; enticement; entrapment; fascination; inveiglement; invitation; lurement; persuasion; provocation; pull; seduction; smile; snare; temptation; toll; trap; trick; wile

LURID: ashen; crimson; dark; dismal; extravagant; gaudy; ghastly; gloomy; grim; grisly; gruesome; hideous; immoral; lewd; livid; melodramatic; morbid; pale; red(dish); risqué; sallow; sensational; sexy; shocking; startling; tabloid; terrible; vivid; vulgar; wan

LURK: couch; hide; linger; prowl; remain; skulk; sneak; steal; sulk

LUSCIOUS: (see "sapid") alluring; attractive; charming; delightful; florid; lush; red; ripe; seductive; voluptuous; willowy

LUSH: abundant; drunk; exuberant; fertile; generous; green; juicy; lavish; luscious; lusty; luxuriant; luxurious; opulent; ornate; plentiful; plush; posh; profitable; profuse; prosperous; rich; sensuous; succulent; sumptuous; thriving; vigorous; voluptuous; wealthy

LUST: avarice; carnality; concupiscence; craving; cupidity; desire; eagerness; enthusiasm; fertility; lasciviousness; lechery; lewdness; lubricity; lustiness; passion; salacity; vigor; wantonness; yen; LUSTFUL: (see "lewd") lecherous; libidinous; lusty; paphian; randy; sexy; wanton

LUSTER: beauty; brightness; brilliance; brilliancy; distinction; effulgence; fame; fulgence; glare; glass; glaze; glitter; glory; gloss(iness); glow; grandeur; honor; iridescence; lucidity; luminosity; nitidity; opalescence; polish; radiance; renown; repute; resplendence; sheen; shine; splendor; LUSTROUS: bright; brilliant; glamorous; gleaming; glossy; illustrious; luminous; naif; nitid; opalescent; radiant; rich; resplendent; satiny; sheer; shining; silken; silky; silvery; LUSTERLESS: ashen; colorless; dim; drab; dull; lifeless; mat; mousy; neutral; pale; pallid; plain; sick(ly); wan; watery

LUSTY: athletic; brawny; corpulent; exuberant; flourishing; forceful; hale; healthful; healthy; hearty; large; loud; lush; lustful; masculine; massive; mighty; muscular; powerful; puissant; robust(ious); sound; stout; strenuous; sturdy; vigorous

LUXURIATE: bask; delight; expand; flourish; glory; grow; indulge; loll; proliferate; revel; thrive; wallow; LUXURIANT: abundant; affluent; baronial; bountiful; copious; dense; elegant; exuberant; fertile; florid; flourishing; frank; fruitful; gross; inventive; lavish; lush; luxurious; opulent; ornate; plenteous; plentiful; princely; prodigal; productive; profuse; proliferous; prolific; rank; rich; sumptuous; superabundant; teeming; uberous; vigorous; voluptuous; LUXURIOUS: Babylonian; baronial; deluxe; elegant; expensive; high; lavish; lecherous; Lucull-(i)an; lush; luxuriant; Lydian; magnificent; opulent; ornate; palatial; plentiful; plush; posh; rich; sensual; silken; sumptuous; sybaritic; *voluptuaire*; voluptuary; voluptuous; LUXURY *or* LUXURIOUSNESS:

affluence; delight; ease; elegance; extravagance; frill; gratification; joy; lavishness; luxe; magnificence; opulence; opulency; ornamentation; princeliness; prolificity; richness; sensuality; silk; splendor; sumptuosity; voluptuosity; voluptuousness

LYDIAN: effeminate; gentle; sensual; soft; voluptuous

LYING: abed; couchant; deceitful; decubital;

decumbent; dishonest; encumbent; equivocating; false; fraudulent; mendacious; misleading; prevaricative; procumbent; prone; prostrate; reclining; recumbent; supine; tergiversatory; untrue; untruthful

LYRIC: canorous; coloratura; dramatic; emotional; melic; melodious; musical; operatic; poetic(al); rhapsodic; sonorous; tuneful; unrestrained

M

MACABRE: appalling; cadaverous; deadly; distressing; fearful; ghastly; ghostly; grim; grisly; gruesome; horrible; lurid; morbid; repulsive; sick(ly); unpleasant

MACERATE: crush; fray; grind; mortify; oppress; ret; soak; soften; steep; torment; vex; waste; wear

MACHIAVELLIAN: crafty; cunning; deceitful; deceptive; dishonest; duplicitous; foxy; guileful; insidious; intriguing; invidious; political; subtle; treacherous; tricky; unscrupulous; wily

MACHINATE: cabal; conspire; contrive; design; devise; intrigue; maneuver; plan; plot; scheme; trick; MACHINATION: artifice; cabal; conspiracy; contrivance; coup; design; device; dodge; intrigue; junta; maneuver; plan; plot; purpose; ruse; scheme; stratagem

MACHINE: apparatus; appliance; auto-(mobile); bloc; cabal; car; combination; contrivance; conveyance; device; engine; force; gadget; group; instrument; mechanism; mill; motor; organization; party; system; tool; vehicle; works; MACHINERY: (see "equipment") enginery; mechanism; parts; stock; system; works

MACILENT: emaciated; lean; marasmic; thin

MAD: *acharné*; acrimonious; aggrieved; *aliéné*; angry; bedlam; berserk; boiling; bubbling; burning; chafed; choleric; crazed; crazy; cross; demented; deranged; disordered; displeased; distracted; distraught; distressed; doting; eager; enraged; enthusiastic; exasperated; excited; exercised; extreme; fanatical; feverish; fey; fierce; fiery; foolish; frantic; frenzied; furious; gay; heated; hilarious; hot; huffy; illogical; impetuous; incensed; indignant; infatuated; inflamed; infuriated; insane; intoxicated; iracund; irascible; irate; ired; ireful; irked; irresponsible; irritated; lunatic; maniac(al); manic; overzealous; piqued; provoked; psychotic;

rabid; radical; raged; raging; rampant; rancorous; rash; raving; red-hot; roiled; roily; schizophrenic; seething; senseless; sore; testy; touched; unreasonable; unrestrained; unwise; violent; virulent; wild; wrathful; wroth; zealous; MADNESS: aberration; acharnement; agitation; anger; bedlam; chaos; confusion; craze; craziness; deliration; delirium; dementia; derangement; desperation; disorder; distraction; distress; disturbance; eagerness; ecstasy; enragement; enthusiasm; exasperation; excitement; extravagance; fad; fanaticism; fever; *folie*; folly; foolishness; frenzy; furor; fury; hallucination; huffiness; impetuosity; infatuation; insanity; intoxication; ire; irresponsibility; irritability; irritation; lunacy; mania; pique; psychosis; rabidness; rabies; rage; rancor; rapture; rashness; schizophrenia; senselessness; unreason; violence; virulence; wildness; wrath; MADDEN: (see "anger") craze; enrage; exasperate; excite; incense; infatuate; infuriate; pique; provoke; vex

MADAM(E): chatelaine; dame; don(n)a; frau; frow; lady; ma'am; mistress; señora; wife; woman

MADCAP: **a.** adventurous; hotspur; impulsive; mad; manic; rash; reckless; wild; MADCAP: **n.** hotspur; maniac

MADE: assembled; built; compiled; composed; constructed; contrived; created; erected; established; fabricated; fashioned; formed; formulated; manufactured; organized; produced; raised; reared; sewn; shaped; styled; tailored; wrought

MAELSTROM: complication; current; eddy; maze; swirl; turmoil; war; whirlpool

MAGAZINE: armory; arsenal; book; chamber; depot; journal; munitions; periodical; publication; repository; storehouse; tabloid; warehouse

MAGIC(AL): **a.** alchemic(al); alchemistic(al); bewitching; cabalistic; charming; goetic;

hermetic(al); incantatory; mystic(al); necromantic; numinous; occult; phylacteric; prestidigitatory; recondite; sorcerous; supernatural; talismanic(al); MAGIC: **n.** abracadabra; alchemy; art; charm; conjuration; conjuring; conjury; diablerie; divination; enchantment; glamo(u)r; gramary(e); incantation; jugglery; legerdemain; necromancy; occultism; prestidigitation; rune; show; skill; sorcery; spell; thaumaturgy; theurgy; voodoo; witchcraft; witchery; wizardry; MAGICIAN: conjurer; Druid; enchanter; legerdemainist; magi (pl.); magus (*or* mage); Mandrake; Merlin; necromancer; prestidigitator; shaman; soothsayer; sorcerer; thaumaturge; thaumaturgist; theurgist; warlock; witch; wizard

MAGISTRATE: (**see** "judge") administrator; alcalde; archon; bailiff; chief; consul; doge; edile; ephor; governor; justice; mayor; official; pr(a)etor; prefect; president; syndic; MAGISTERIAL: (**see** "authoritative") dictatorial; doctrinaire

MAGNANIMOUS: (**see** "generous") abundant; chivalric; chivalrous; courageous; easy; exalted; forgiving; free; handsome; heroic; honorable; liberal; lofty; noble(-minded); philanthropic(al); sizable; sublime; unselfish; MAGNANIMITY: (**see** "generosity") abundance; chivalry; exaltedness; honor; liberality; loftiness; nobility; nobleness; philanthropy; sublimity; unselfishness

MAGNATE: baron; bigwig; grandee; industrialist; lord; mogul; noble(man); peer; shogun; titan; tycoon

MAGNET: attraction; charmer; cynosure; lodestone; polestar

MAGNIFICENT: (**see** "exalted") baronial; brilliant; dignified; elegant; eulogistic(al); extravagant; fine; generous; glorious; grand(iose); great; honorific; illustrious; imperial; imposing; inspiring; kingly; leonine; lordly; lustrious; luxurious; magnific(al); majestic; marvelous; munificent; noble; opulent; palatial; pompous; praiseworthy; princely; proud; regal; spectacular; splendid; splendiferous; splendorous; stately; sublime; sumptuous; terrific; vast; MAGNIFICENCE: (**see** "ostentation") eminence; gloriousness; luxury; princeliness; splendor; state

MAGNIFY: aggrandize; aggravate; amplify; augment; dilate; distend; enhance; enlarge; exacerbate; exaggerate; expand; extend;

extol; glorify; heighten; increase; intensify; laud; lengthen; overstate; panegyrize; praise; stretch; swell; widen

MAGNITUDE: (**see** "size") bigness; breadth; enormity; extent; greatness; importance; length; number; order; power; proportion; quantity; size; wattage; weight; width

MAID(EN): Abigail; bonnie; burd; damsel; gal; girl; lass(ie); miss; servant; soubrette; MAIDENISH *or* MAIDENLY: Daphnean; first; fresh; gentle; girlish; inexperienced; initial; intact; modest; new; timid; unexperienced; untried; unused; vestal; virgin(al); youthful

MAIL: **v.** consign; post; protect; send; MAIL: **n.** armor; carapace; dak; dawn; letters; papers; post; protection

MAIM: (**see** "mutilate") batter; cripple; damage; deform; disable; disfigure; exacerbate; hurt; impair; injure; lame; mangle; mar; mayhem; spoil; wound; wreck; MAIMED: battered; crippled; damaged; disabled; disfigured; hurt; impaired; injured; lamed; mangled; marred; mutilated; truncated; wounded

MAIN: **a.** (**see** "leading") central; chief; foremost; grand; great; major; mighty; necessary; potent; preeminent; primary; prime; principal; sheer; utter; vital; MAIN: **n.** body; conduit; duct; force; ocean; pipe; power; sea; strength

MAINTAIN: advance; affirm; aid; allege; asseverate; assure; attest; aver; avow; be; bear; board; carry; claim; clean; confirm; contend; continue; declare; defend; depone; depose; dominate; emphasize; establish; exist; face; furnish; groom; guard; have; hold; justify; keep; plead; possess; preserve; profess; protect; prove; repair; sanction; secure; stabilize; stress; subsist; support; sustain; swear; testify; unrelinquish; uphold; vindicate; MAINTENANCE: aid; alimony; bearing; behavior; being; board; care; contention; defense; existence; keep; livelihood; preservation; provisions; subsistence; supplies; support; sustenance; sustentation; upkeep; vindication

MAJESTIC: (**see** "exalted") dignified; grand(iose); imperial; kingly; princely; queenly; regal; royal; stately; statuesque; sublime; MAJESTY: (**see** "exaltation") authority; dignity; grandeur; greatness; kingship; lordliness; nobility; power; royalty; sovereignty; splendor; stateliness; sublimity

MAJOR: (see "leading") considerable; greater; main; principal; serious; MAJORITY: adulthood; age; bulk; edge; excess; lump; margin; mass; maturity; most; plurality; predominance; predominancy; predomination; preponderance; seniority; substance; superiority

MAKE: v. accomplish; achieve; appoint; arrange; arrive; assemble; attain; begin; build; carve; catch; cause; chisel; coin; come; compel; complete; compose; concoct; confect; constitute; construct; continue; contrive; cook; create; crochet; deduce; design; develop; devise; do; draw; effect; elaborate; equal; erect; establish; execute; fabricate; fashion; fix; force; forge; form(ulate); found; frame; fulfill; gain; generate; get; give; improvisate; improvise; induce; invent; knit; let; manufacture; mine; model; mo(u)ld; name; ordain; organize; originate; perfect; perform; plan; plot; prepare; proceed; produce; raise; reach; rear; reduce; render; scheme; sculpt(ure); set; sew; shape; start; structure; style; sustain; synthesize; tailor; transform; vamp; weave; whittle; win; write; MAKE: n. arrangement; brand; constitution; construction; form; frame; kind; makeup; manufacture; output; structure; style; type; yield

MAKE-BELIEVE: (see "counterfeit") feigning; feint; fiction; magic; pretender; pretense; pretension; pretext; sham

MAKER: artificer; author; builder; composer; concoctor; constructor; craftsman; creator; designer; deviser; draftsman; fabricator; fabulist; forger; formulator; improvisor; inventer; manufacturer; originator; producer

MAKESHIFT: a. accidental; emergency; expedient; extemporaneous; extemporary; immediate; impromptu; improvisatorial; improvised; rough-and-ready; shifty; stopgap; substitute; sudden; temporary; unexpected; MAKESHIFT: n. (see "emergency") apology; expediency; expedient; impromptu; improvisation; pis aller; resort; stopgap; substitute

MAKEUP: (see "composition") aggregate; arrangement; arrayment; build; character; chemistry; compensation; constituency; constituent(s); constitution; cosmetics; disposition; dress; feature; fiction; form(ulation); ingredients; lie; maquillage; mockery; morphology; paint; personality; replacement; rouge; setup; shape; structure; temper(ament); travesty

MALADROIT: (see "clumsy") awkward; bungling; gauche; inept; tactless; unhandy; unskilled; unskillful

MALADY: (see "disease") ailment; complaint; disorder; distemper; evil; illness; indisposition; infirmity; sickness

MALAPERT: (see "bold") flippant; forward; impertinent; impudent; insolent; pert; rude; sassy; saucy

MALCONTENT(ED): a. (see "dissatisfied") disaffected; discontent(ed); insurgent; moody; rebellious; restless; uneasy; MALCONTENT: n. agitator; Fenian; insurgent; reb(el); troublemaker

MALE: a. (see "masculine") andric; manful; manlike; manly; mannish; potent; staminal; staminated; strong; vigorous; virile; MALE: n. (see "man") boy; father; hand; he; he-man; sir

MALEDICTION: (see "curse") anathema; ban; commination; condemnation; damnation; denunciation; execration; fulmination; imprecation; ire; malison; proscription; slander; taboo; tabu; threat; vilification; wrath

MALEFACTOR: (see "villain") badman; convict; criminal; culprit; delinquent; evildoer; felon; offender; outlaw; rascal; rogue; rounder; ruffian; scamp; scapegrace; scoundrel; sinner; transgressor; vagabond; witch; wretch; wrongdoer

MALEVOLENT: (see "bad") awesome; baleful; bitter; caustic; envenomed; envious; evil; fell; harmful; hating; hostile; hurtful; ill; injurious; malicious; malign(ant); rancorous; sinister; spiteful; treacherous; vicious; wicked; MALEVOLENCE: (see "hatred") envy; evil; grudge; hostility; ill (will); malice; maliciousness; malignity; rancor; sinisterity; spite; spleen; wickedness

MALICE: (see "hatred") abhorrence; animosity; antipathy; bitterness; despitefulness; detestation; enmity; evil; grudge; ill (will); ire; malevolence; malignance; malignancy; pique; rancor; revenge; spite; spleen; umbrage; venom; MALICIOUS: (see "evil") deadly; despiteful; dispiteous; evil-minded; harmful; hurtful; injurious; lethal; snide; spiteful; vicious; wicked

MALIGN: v. (see "asperse") belittle; besmirch; blacken; blaspheme; calumniate;

censure; defame; denigrate; depreciate; detract; dishonor; harm; hurt; libel; misrepresent; revile; scandalize; slander; traduce; vilify; wrong; MALIGN(ANT): **a.** bad; baleful; baneful; blackhearted; cancerous; dangerous; evil; harmful; harsh; heinous; hurtful; ill; inimical; injurious; lethal; malefic; malevolent; malicious; mean; pernicious; poisonous; rancorous; reptile; sinister; strong; unbenignant; vicious; virulent; wicked; MALIGNITY: aspersion; cancer; deadliness; evil; fatality; grudge; malice; malignancy; spleen; traduction; venom; violence; virulence; wickedness; wrong

MALINGER: (**see** "feign") dodge; fake; goldbrick; pretend; sham; soldier

MALISON: (**see** "curse") execration; malediction; torment

MALLEABLE: (**see** "plastic") adaptable; amenable; compressible; ductile; impressionable; pliable; pliant; soft; susceptible; teachable; yielding

MALNUTRITION: cachexia; cacotrophy; malnourishment; marasmus; skinniness; tabescence; thinness

MALODOROUS: (**see** "stinking") bad; fetid; foul; fusty; ill-smelling; improper; mephitic; musty; noisome; noxious; obnoxious; olid; putrescent; putrid; rancid; rank; repulsive; rotten; scandalous; smelly

MALTREAT: (**see** "abuse") beat; castigate; damage; harm; ill-treat; ill-use; injure; maul; mishandle; mistreat; misuse; oppress; persecute; punish; scathe; tyrannize; victimize

MAMMAL: (**see** "animal") ape; bat; bear; cat; deer; dog; hare; Mammalia (pl.); man; primate; quadruped; ruminant; Vertebrata (pl.); vertebrate; whale

MAMMOTH: (**see** "huge") elephantine; gigantic; monstrous; ponderous; weighty

MAN: **v.** brace; control; escort; fortify; manage; master; reinforce; run; staff; strengthen; work; MAN: **n.** anthropoid; ape; being; biped; bird; bozo; chap; Chordata (pl.); creature; earthling; employee; fellow; flesh; gentleman; guy; hand; he; help(er); hombre; hominid; Hominidae (pl.); hominoid; Homo; *Homo sapiens*; human(ity); husband;

individual; jack; laborer; lover; male; mammal; mankind; mate; monsieur; mortal; person(age); personality; player; race; sailor; servant; sir; soldier; somebody; suitor; sweetheart; valet; vassal

MANAGE: (**see** "control") accomplish; administer; administrate; attend; care (for); coach; conduct; contrive; cope (with); cultivate; develop; direct; do; dominate; educate; execute; fend; finagle; get; govern; guide; handle; husband; influence; lead; man; maneuver; manipulate; moderate; negotiate; nurse; nurture; operate; ordain; order; oversee; pilot; prevail; regulate; rule; run; shift; show; steer; superintend; supervise; sway; swing; tend; train; treat; use; wangle; watch; wield; work; MANAGEABLE: administrable; compliant; controllable; docile; governable; plastic; pliable; pliant; tamable; teachable; tractable; yare; MANAGEABILITY: controllability; docility; manipulability; teachability; tractability; MANAGEMENT: (**see** "control") administration; care; charge; conduct(ion); coordination; cultivation; development; direction; dispensation; disposal; disposition; economy; education; generalship; government; handling; husbandry; leadership; maneuver; manipulation; method; negotiation; office; operation; organization; policy; procedure; superintendence; supervision; work; MANAGER: administrant; administrator; agent; arranger; boss; chief; coach; comptroller; conductor; curator; director; economist; executive; executor; gerent; governor; guardian; head; headmaster; impresario; manipulator; master; operator; overseer; pilot; principal; schemer; steward; superintendent; supervisor; trainer

MANDATE: (**see** "commission") authority; authorization; bidding; breve; charge; coercion; colony; command; compulsoriness; decree; dictation; dictatorship; direction; edict; exigency; imperative; injunction; instruction; judgment; law; mandatum; order; precept; prescript; requirement; warrant; writ; MANDATORY: (**see** "imperative") coercive; compelling; compulsory; enforced; exigent; impelling; necessary; obligatory; preceptive; prerequisite; prescriptive

MANEUVER: **v.** (**see** "control") battle; charge; contrive; dance; deceive; devise; direct; drill; engineer; exercise; feint; finagle; guide; jockey; manage; march; marshal; mold; move; parade; pilot; plan;

plot; resort; scheme; shift; steer; strategize; swindle; trick; wangle; MANEUVER: **n.** acrobatic(s); action; artifice; battle; change; dance; deed; device; direction; evolution; exercise; feint; intrigue; management; manipulation; march; method; move(ment); operation; parade; plan; plot; ploy; procedure; resort; ruse; scheme; shift; stratagem; swindle; tactic; trick; variation; wile

MANGLE: **v.** (**see** "bungle") batter; botch; break; bruise; butcher; carve; cripple; crush; cut; destroy; disfigure; flatten; garble; hack; injure; iron; lacerate; maim; mar; maul; mayhem; murder; mutilate; press; rip; ruin; smooth; spoil; tear; wound; MANGLE: **n.** calender; ironer; presser

MANHOOD: adulthood; *âge viril*; bravery; brawn; courage; majority; manliness; masculinity; maturity; muscularity; potency; resolution; virility

MANIA: cacoëthes; craze; craziness; deliration; delirium; desire; excitement; fear; frenzy; hyperactivity; hysteria; infatuation; insanity; lunacy; madness; obsession; passion; psychosis; rabidity; rabidness; MANIAC(AL): **a.** batty; crazed; crazy; delirious; demented; demoniac(al); deranged; excited; frantic; frenzied; hyperactive; hysterical; insane; mad; obsessed; passionate; psychotic; rabid; raving; violent; MANIAC: **n.** bat; crank; lunatic; madman; nut; psychopath; psychotic; screwball

MANICURE: care; clip; cut; pare; polish; trim

MANIFEST: **v.** (**see** "disclose") appear; arrive; bare; declare; develop; display; divulge; evidence; evince; exhibit; have; loom; mark; open; prevail; proclaim; promulgate; publish; reveal; show; tell; uncover; undress; unfold; unmask; unveil; MANIFEST: **a.** apparent; bare; clear; declared; disclosed; displayed; divulged; evident; evinced; exhibited; gross; indubitable; large; macroscopic; obvious; open; overt; palpable; patent; plain; proclaimed; promulgated; public; published; revealed; shown; uncovered; undressed; unfolded; unmasked; unmistakable; unobscured; unveiled; visible; MANIFEST: **n.** display; expression; invoice; list; waybill; MANIFESTATION: (**see** "disclosure" and "embodiment") appearance; display; expression; form; guise; manifesto; materialization; phenomenon; revelation

MANIFESTO: declaration; edict; manifestation; order; ostent; proclamation; rescript; statement; writ

MANIFOLD: (**see** "many") abundant; complex; diverse; moderate; much; multifarious; multitudinous; numerous; replicate; several; sundry; varied; various

MANIKIN: android; automaton; doll; dwarf; figure; golem; mannequin; midget; model; phantom; pygmy; robot; runt

MANIPULATE: (**see** "control") alter; arrange; change; contrive; correct; create; determine; direct; doctor; effect; exploit; fashion; force; forge; guide; govern; handle; juggle; manage; move; operate; play; ply; progress; rig; scheme; shape; shuffle; succeed; swing; treat; trick; use; utilize; wield; work; MANIPULATION: (**see** "control") adjustment; advertising; change; destruction; direction; examination; exploration; force; government; handling; magic; management; operation; *passe-passe*; predacity; prestidigitation; publicity; scheming; *tour de force*; use; utilization

MANKIND: Adam; Anthropoidea (pl.); folk; Hominidae (pl.); *Homo sapiens*; humanity; humans; men; microcosm; mortality; peoples; race; universe

MANLY: **see** "brave" and "masculine;" MANLINESS: arete; boldness; bravery; chivalry; dignity; gallantry; heroism; intrepidity; manfulness; manlikeness; masculinity; nobleness; potency; puissance; resolution; virility

MANNA: (**see** "food") windfall

MANNEQUIN: **see** "manikin"

MANNER(S): (**see** "air") action; address; affectation; airs; appearance; approach; aspect; bearing; behavior; breeding; carriage; ceremony; character; conduct; convention(ality); conventions; courtesy; custom(s); decency; decorum; deportment; description; distinction; ethics; etiquette; expression; fashion; form(ality); front; grace; habit; kind; look; mannerism; means; method; mien; mode; modus; morale; morality; mores (pl.); ostent; poise; politeness; posture; practice; procedure; proprieties; propriety; protocol; *quomodo*; refinement; routine; rules; *savoir faire*; sort; stamp; style; suavity; tact; taste; treatment; urbanity; usage(s); use; vanity; vein; vogue; way; wont; work; world; MANNERISM: affectation; air; artificiality; bearing; characteristic; eccentricity; foible; idiosyncrasy; individuality; peculiarity; preciosity; quirk; singularity; style; whimsicality; MANNERLY: see "polite"

MANNISH: see "masculine"

MANSION: abode; dwelling; house; palace; residence; villa

MANTLE: v. blush; cloak; color; conceal; disguise; hood; mask; screen; shelter; spread; MANTLE: n. blanket; cap; cape; casing; cloak; coat; cover(ing); disguise; envelope; filament; form; frock; garment; hood; pall(ium); robe; screen; sheath; shelter; spread; toga

MANUAL: book; consuetudinary; dial; ench(e)iridion; guide(book); handbook; keyboard; reference (book); reference work; text; *vade mecum*

MANUFACTURE: see "make;" MANUFACTURED: see "made"

MANUMIT: (see "free") deliver; liberate; release; rescue

MANURE: dejecta; dung; ejecta; excrement(s); excreta; feces; feculence; fertilizer; ordure

MANUSCRIPT: article; codex; composition; copy; document; draft; folio; MS; ms; text; vellum; writing

MANY: a. abundant; complex; considerable; copious; countless; crowded; divers(e); excessive; galore; gobs; incalculable; infinite; innumerable; innumerous; legion; limitless; lots; manifold; much; multifarious; multifold; multiple; multiplex; multiplicious; multiplied; multitudinous; myriad-(fold); numberless; numerous; omnibus; plenteous; plentiful; plenty; plural; populous; profuse; rank; replete; scads; several; sundry; teeming; thronged; uncountable; uncounted; unlimited; unnumbered; unnumerable; untold; varied; various; vast; MANY: n. army; company; host; majority; masses; multitude; plenty; plurality; retinue; sundries; variety

MAP: v. arrange; blueprint; chart; conceive; delineate; describe; design; diagram(matize); draft; draw; graph; outline; plan;

plot; project; scheme; sketch; survey; trace; MAP: n. agenda (pl.); agendum; aim; arrangement; blueprint; cartograph; chart; concept(ion); delineation; design; diagram; draft; drawing; elevation; face; floor plan; gamut; graph; itinerary; outline; plan; plat; plate; plot; program; project; representation; schedule; schema; schemata (pl.); scheme; sketch; survey; tracing

MAR: v. (see "bungle") besplatter; blemish; botch; damage; deface; disable; disfigure; impair; impede; injure; harm; hurt; obstruct; ruin; scar; scrape; scratch; spoil; warp; MAR: n. (see "blemish") botch; damage; defacement; disability; disfigurement; impairment; impediment; injury; harm; hurt; obstruction; ruin; scar; scrape; scratch; spoilage; warp(ing)

MARAUD: v. attack; foray; invade; loot; pillage; plunder; raid; ravage; rob; sack; sneak; steal; MARAUD: n. see "raid;" MARAUDER: attacker; brigand; buccaneer; bummer; cateran; invader; looter; pillager; pirate; plunderer; raider; ravager; robber; sacker

MARBLE: a. (see "hard") cold; granitic; inflexible; marmoraceous; marmoreal; rigid; smooth; unfeeling; MARBLE: n. agate; basalt; dolomite; granite; limestone; marl; marmor; mib; sculpture; taw

MARCH: v. advance; border; drill; file; go; hike; jibe; journey; move; pace; parade; patrol; perambulate; proceed; progress; promenade; ramble; step; stroll; strut; tour; tramp; travel; traverse; tread; trek; trudge; walk; MARCH: n. advance(ment); course; distance; drill; expedition; file; hike; journey; move; music; pace; parade; patrol; perambulation; process; progress; promenade; ramble; safari; step; stride; stroll; tour; travel; tramp; trek; trudge; tune; walk

MARGIN: (see "edge") allowance; area; bank; berth; border; brim; brink; brow; circumference; clearance; confine; deviation; difference; eaves; edging; end; equity; excess; flange; fringe; front(ier); lead; leeway; limit; line; lip; majority; marginality; maximum; minimum; overage; periphery; profit; range; rim; room; scope; shore; side; skirt(ing); strand; term; tolerance; verge; MARGINAL: borderline; circumferential; fringed; limited; limitrophe; maximum; minimum; peripheral; questionable

MARINE a. *or* **MARITIME:** admiralty; aquatic; hydrographic; natatorial; nautical; naval; neritic; oceanic; pelagic; seafaring; **MARINE: n.** devil-dog; leatherneck; sailor; sea dog; seafarer; shipping; ships

MARK: v. assign; attend; blemish; blot; bound; brand; characterize; chart; deface; define; delineate; demarcate; denote; dent; design(ate); destine; determine; direct; disfigure; distinguish; divide; dot; dye; engrave; enter; express; grade; graduate; heed; identify; impress; imprint; indicate; jot; label; letter; limit; line; locate; manifest; mar; measure; name; notate; notch; note; notice; number; observe; outline; plot; print; record; register; resemble; scar; scarify; score; scratch; separate; show; signalize; spot; stain; stake (out); stamp; stigmatize; stroke; symbolize; tag; tally; tattoo; ticket; trace; typify; watch; write; **MARK: n.** accent; aim; attention; aura; badge; blemish; blot; boundary; brand; character(istic); cognizance; coin; colophon; criterion; defacement; delineation; dent; die; disfigurement; distinction; division; dot; drawing; earmark; emblem; end; evidence; figure; goal; grade; graffiti (pl.); hallmark; identification; importance; impression; imprimatur; imprint; indication; jot; label; letter; level; limit; line; marker; measure; mole; norm; notation; notch; notice; number; object; observation; point; position; print; proof; rank; rating; record; scar(ification); score; scratch; seal; sign; signature; spoor; spot; stain; stake; stamp; standard; stigma; stigmata (pl.); stob; stone; stroke; symbol; tag; tally; target; tattoo; token; touch; trace; tracing; track; trait; type; vestige; victim; **MARKED:** see "great" and "severe"

MARKER: (see "mark") benchmark; bookmark; cairn; colophon; counter; flag; guide; guidon; monitor; notch; pole; post; scorer; sign(al); stake; standard; stela; stele; stob; stone; tablet; tag

MARKET: v. (see "trade") barter; buy; deal; exchange; sell; traffic; **MARKET: n.** agora; bazaar; bourse; business; emporium; exchange; fair; forum; marketplace; mart; rialto; sale; shop; store; trading post

MAROON: (see "abandon") desert; enisle; isolate; leave; segregate; shipwreck; strand

MARROW: (see "essence") cord; core; interior; keest; medulla; middle; pith; sap; substance; suet; vitality

MARRY: combine; conjugate; consort; couple; elope; espouse; fit; hitch; join; knot; match; mate; pair; team; tie; unite; wed; weld; wive; yoke; **MARRIAGE:** combination; conjugality; connubiality; espousal; knot; match; matrimony; nuptials; tie; union; vow; wedding; wedlock

MARSH: bog; fen; Lerna; liman; mire; morass; quag(mire); slough; slue; swale; swamp; **MARSHY:** boggy; fenny; paludal; paludine; paludous; soggy; spongy; swampy; uliginose; wet

MARSHAL: v. align; arrange; array; assemble; collect; direct; dispose; gather; guide; lead; manage; mobilize; order; parade; rally; range; rank; systematize; usher; **MARSHAL: n.** commander; general; guide; leader; manager; officer; official; policeman; sheriff

MARTIAL: (see "warlike") bellicose; belligerent; military; soldierly

MARTYR: v. afflict; agonize; inflict; kill; persecute; sacrifice; torment; torture; victimize; **MARTYR: n.** sacrifice; saint; sufferer; victim

MARVEL: (see "admire") admiration; amazement; astonishment; freak; *mirabilia* (pl.); miracle; phenomena (pl.); phenomenon; prodigy; sensation; surprise; wonder; **MARVELOUS:** admirable; amazing; astonishing; astounding; excellent; fabulous; magnificent; *magnifique*; meritorious; miraculous; mirific; outstanding; phenomenal; prodigious; remarkable; stupendous; surprising; terrific; transcendent; wonderful; wondrous

MASCULINE: andric; android; bold; brave; daring; dashing; male; manful; manlike; manly; mannish; potent; powerful; puissant; robust(ious); staminal; strong; unfeminine; unwomanly; vigorous; virile(scent); **MASCULINITY:** see "manliness"

MASK *or* **MASQUERADE: v.** befog; blind; block; camouflage; cloak; conceal; cover; curtain; disguise; dissemble; evade; flavor; hide; hush; muffle; obscure; pretend; protect; screen; secrete; shade; shield; shroud; slur; smother; stifle; suppress; veil; **MASK** *or* **MASQUERADE: n.** alias; bearing; blind; camouflage; cloak; concealment; cover(ing); curtain; dance; disguise; dissemblance; domino; evasion; face; hush; image; masker; masque; muffling; pose; pretense; pretension; pretext; protection;

pseudonym; screen; secreting; shade; shield; shroud; smothering; stifling; subterfuge; suppression; veil; visor; MASKED: cabalistic; concealed; covered; cryptic; disguised; hidden; incognita (fem.); incognito; larvate(d); latent; obscure(d); screened; shielded; shrouded; suppressed; veiled

MASS: **v.** accumulate; agglomerate; agglutinate; aggregate; assemble; blend; cake; clot; collect; concentrate; conglomerate; consolidate; deposit; drift; fuse; gather; heap; knot; merge; muster; pile; press; unify; MASS: **n.** accumulation; agglomerate; agglomeration; agglutinate; agglutination; aggregate; aggregation; amount; amplitude; assemblage; body; bolus; bulk; collection; concentration; concretion; congeries; conglomeration; density; deposit; dimension; drift; expanse; gathering; generality; gob; gorge; heap; horde; knot; liturgy; lots; lump; magnitude; majority; massiveness; matter; node; pack; pile; ponderosity; pressure; proletariat; proportion(s); pulp; quantity; raft; rite; sacrament; service; size; solid(ification); solidity; spissitude; substance; sum; thickness; total(ity); tumor; unit; viscosity; volume; wad; weight; whole

MASSACRE: **v.** butcher; decimate; kill; mangle; murder; mutilate; slaughter; slay; MASSACRE: **n.** bloodshed; butchery; decimation; destruction; havoc; mangling; murder; pogrom; slaughter

MASSAGE: effleurage; knead(ing); petrissage; pound(ing); rub(down); stroke; stroking

MASSIVE: (**see** "huge") bulky; dense; elephantine; extensive; heavy; imposing; lusty; notable; mastodonic; monumental; ponderable; ponderous; solid; strong; substantial; voluminous; weighty; wholesale

MASTER: **v.** (**see** "control") break; boss; bridle; command; conquer; defeat; direct; discipline; dominate; domineer; govern; guide; harness; learn; manage; overawe; overcome; overpower; oversee; own; possess; regulate; rule; subdue; subjugate; tame; tyrannize; vanquish; MASTER: **n.** arbiter; artist; authority; boss; boy; captain; chief(tain); commandant; commander; comptroller; conqueror; controller; director; dominator; employer; expert; governor; guide; head; instructor; judge; king(fish); kingpin; leader; lord; magister; man; mentor; overseer; owner; preceptor; principal; proprietor; pundit; rabbi; ruler; sahib; savant; sire;

subduer; subjugator; superintendent; superior; supervisor; teacher; tutor; vanquisher; victor; virtuoso; wizard; MASTERY: (**see** "control") ability; advantage; ascendency; cleverness; command; conquest; dexterity; discipline; dominance; domination; dominion; grasp; grip; influence; leadership; masterdom; power; proficiency; repression; rule; skill; subjection; subjugation; superiority; supremacy; sway; triumph; upper hand; victory; yoke

MASTERFUL: (**see** "skillful") arrogant; authoritative; commanding; consummate; dictatorial; domineering; energetic; imperative; imperious; masterly; overbearing; peremptory; potent; proficient; skilled; sovereign; supreme; vigorous; virtuosic

MASTICATE: chew; crush; cut; grind; knead; manducate; triturate

MAT: **v.** entangle; interweave; interwind; knot; plait; protect; snarl; stick; tangle; twist; MAT: **n.** bolster; border; cloth; cushion; doily; fabric; matrix; mattress; pad; rug; webbing

MATCH: **v.** (**see** "correspond") accord; adapt; agree; approach; befit; cap; combat; compare; compete; contest; copy; couple; duplicate; equal; even; example; fit; fuse; harmonize; marry; mate; pace; pair; paragon; parallel; resemble; rival; sample; square; suit; tally; touch; unite; wed; yoke; MATCH: **n.** accord; agreement; bout; companion; comparison; competition; contest; copy; correspondence; counterpart; duplicate; duplication; equal; fit; fuse(e); fusion; game; harmony; locofoco; lucifer; marriage; mate; pair; parallel; peer; race; resemblance; rival; symmetry; trial; twin; union; vesta; wedding; MATCHED: commensurate; congruent; engaged; equal; equivalent; even; homologous; level; paired; parallel; proportionate; tallied; teamed; twin; wedded; yoked

MATCHLESS: (**see** "perfect") alone; consummate; eminent; faultless; incommensurable; incomparable; inimitable; mated; *ne plus supra*; *ne plus ultra*; peerless; supereminent; superior; superlative; supreme; transcendent; unequaled; unpaired; unparalleled; unrivaled; unsurpassed; unsurpassing

MATE: **v.** (**see** "marry") consort; copulate; couple; fit; hitch; join; match; pair; wed; yoke; MATE: **n.** aide; ally; assistant; associate; brother; buddy; chum; companion; compeer; comrade; confrere; consort; couple; equal; fellow; fere; friend; husband; mariner; match; officer; pal; paragon; partner; sister; spouse; twin; wife

MATERIAL: **a.** bodily; bourgeois; bulky; coarse; corpor(e)al; correspondent; earthy; economic(al); equipotent; essential; hylic; important; massive; meaty; mechanical; momentous; moneymaking; necessary; objective; outward; palpable; pertinent; phenomenal; physical; ponderable; practical; public; real(istic); relevant; sensible; sensual; sensuous; solid; somatic; substantial; tangible; temporal; utilitarian; venal; vital; weighty; MATERIAL(S): **n.** accumulation; armamentaria (pl.); armamentarium; armaments; cloth; components; constituents; corporeality; corporeity; corpulence; data (pl.); datum; earth; element; equipment; fabric; facts; fiber; food; gear; hardware; instrumentaria (pl.); instruments; materiality; materiel; matter; metal; outfit; paste; physicality; provision(s); riches; staple(s); stuff; substance; substantiality; supplies; swatch; tangibility; tangibles; tissue; wealth; woof; work

MATERIALISM: barbarism; Darwinism; evolution(ism); heterodoxy; Philistinism; physicism; pragmatism; utilitarianism; MATERIALIST: corporealist; Darwinist; evolutionist; heterodox; physicist; pragmatist; Sadducee; utilitarian; MATERIALISTIC: (**see** "material") banausic; bourgeois; Democritean; Faustian; moneymaking; Philistine; Philistinic; physicalistic; pragmatic; utilitarian

MATERIALIZE: (**see** "appear") come; develop; emanate; emerge; energize; hypostatize; loom; objectify; reify; shape

MATRICULATE: admit; adopt; enrol(l); enter; register; sign

MATRIMONY: **see** "marriage"

MATRIX: bed; cast; cradle; die; fork; foundation; gangue; mat; mold; pattern; shape; shell; womb

MATTER: **v.** (**see** "concern") count; import; signify; value; MATTER: **n.** (**see** "material") affair; amount; article; atom(s); body; cause; circumstance; concern; condition; constituent(s); content; copy; corpor(e)ality; corporeity; difficulty; element(s); essence; event; fundamentals; gear; ground-

(s); import(ance); issue; item; mail; mass; materiality; meat; object; pith; point; portion; print(ing); problem; pus; quantity; question; reading; sense; significance; stuff; subject; subsequence; substance; substantiality; text; theme; thing; topic; trouble

MATURE: **v.** advance; age; complete; develop; finish; grow (up); harden; inure; maturate; mellow; perfect; prepare; ripen; season; set(tle); MATURE(D): **a.** adult; advanced; aged; complete; developed; due; elderly; finished; fit; full-blown; full-grown; gray; grown (up); hardened; inured; lush; manlike; mannish; maturated; mellow(ed); nubile; payable; perfect(ed); postpubertal; prepared; prime; ready; ripe(ned); seasoned; set(tled); virile; womanish; MATURITY: adulthood; adultness; age; development; education; finish; growth; maturation; maturement; maturescence; ripeness

MAUDLIN: beery; drunk(en); effusive; emotional; fuddled; mawkish; moist; mushy; sentimental; sick(ly); silly; sloppy; slushy; soppy; tipsy; vapid

MAUL: **v.** (**see** "beat") abuse; bruise; club; damage; deform; hit; hurt; injure; mangle; thump; MAUL: **n.** club; gavel; hammer; mace; mallet; shillelagh; stick; truncheon

MAVERICK: **a.** disobedient; recalcitrant; stray; stubborn; unbranded; unmarked; MAVERICK: **n.** calf; dogie; madcap; recalcitrant; stray; yearling

MAWKISH: (**see** "maudlin") effusive; mushy; passionate; sentimental; sick(ly); stale; vapid

MAXIM: adage; ana; aphorism; apothegm; axiom; banality; bijouterie; *bon mot*; bromide; byword; catchword; cliché; conventionality; dicta (pl.); dictum; dit; epigram; gnome; law; logion; motto; pearl of wisdom; platitude; postulate; precept; principle; proverb; rede; rule; saw; saying; sententia; shibboleth; slogan; theorem; theorum; truism; truth; wisecrack; witticism

MAXIMUM: all; full; greatest; highest; limit; margin; most; outside; peak (load); spike; toleration; utmost

MAYBE: **see** "perhaps"

MAZE: bewilderment; coil; complexity; complication; confusion; conglomeration; convolution; difficulty; enigma; entanglement; intricacy; labyrinth; maelstrom; muddle;

perplexity; puzzle; riddle; sinuosity; tangle; twist; web; MAZED: bewildered; lost; perplexed; snarled; stupefied; tangled; twisted

MEADOW: field; grassland; lea; mead; pasturage; pasture; vega

MEAGER: (see "bare") arid; attenuated; barren; deficient; destitute; diminutive; dry; emaciated; exiguous; fine; frugal; gaunt; immaterial; inadequate; inferior; infinitesimal; insufficient; jejune; lacking; lank; lean; lenten; maigre; mere; naked; narrow; parsimonious; poor; sad; scant(y); scratchy; scrawny; scrimpy; skimpy; skinny; slender; slight; slim; small; spare; sparing; sparse; starved; sterile; stinted; tenuous; thin; tiny; wanting; wretched; MEAGERNESS: aridity; barrenness; dearth; deficiency; destitution; exiguity; famine; immateriality; inadequacy; insufficiency; parcity; paucity; poverty; scantiness; sparcity; squalor; stringency; tenuity; want

MEAL: (see "food") bever; breakfast; collation; dinner; eats; fare; farina; feast; feed; flour; gorge; grain; grout; grub; lunch; mess; mush; pinole; refection; repast; snack; table; tea; tiffin; MEALY: blanched; coarse; dry; farinaceous; farinose; floury; friable; pale; pallid; soft; spotty; uneven

MEAN: v. connote; contemplate; convey; decide; denote; design; determine; express; imply; indicate; intend; propose; purport; purpose; signify; spell; undertake; MEAN: a. abject; average; bad; base; beggarly; caitiff; cheap; *chétif*; *chétive* (fem.); contemptible; degraded; despicable; dingy; frowzy; frugal; grubby; humble; ignoble; inferior; intermediary; intermediate; little; low; malicious; malignant; measly; medial; mediocre; medium; middling; miserly; paltry; pernicious; pitiful; poor; reptile; scabby; scanty; scurrilous; seedy; selfish; shabby; shameful; small; snide; sorry; squalid; stingy; vicious; vile; vulgar; wicked; MEAN: n. (see "means") average; center; intermediary; norm; par; rule

MEANDER: deviate; drift; perambulate; peregrinate; ramble; roam; rove; shift; sinuate; skid; slide; stray; swerve; turn; twist; vary; veer; wander; wind

MEANING(S): acceptation; aim; connotation; denotation; design; desire; drift; explanation; gist; idea; impact; import; intend-ment; intent(ion); interpretation; message; object(ive); pattern; pith; power; purport; purpose; semantics; sense; significance; signification; spirit; tenor; translation; understanding; wish; MEANINGFUL: expressive; important; knowledg(e)able; pointed; pointful; pregnant; relevant; sententious; signal; significant; MEANINGLESS: aimless; banal; empty; feckless; foolish; insensible; insignificant; negative; pointless; purposeless; senseless; stupid

MEANNESS: baseness; *chétiveté*; despicability; duplicity; knavery; parvanimity; pettiness; rascality; spite; ungenerosity; wickedness

MEANS: agent; apparatus; assets; avenue; brains; channel; door(way); education; engine; entrance(way); equipment; estate; expedient; faculty; function; gear; go-between; income; instrument(ality); instrumentation; intent; intermediary; living; machine(ry); material; measure; mechanics; medium; might; mode; module; *modus operandi*; money; norm; operator; opportunity; organ; par; performer; pocket; power; process(es); property; purpose; *quomodo*; resource(s); riches; rigging; rule; sense; significance; support; sustenance; system; tackle; technique; vehicle; way; wealth; wherewithal; works

MEANTIME *or* MEANWHILE: *ad hoc*; *ad interim*; interim; temporary

MEASURE: v. allot; apportion; appraise; ascertain; calculate; calibrate; choose; classify; compute; contend; contest; control; deal; deliberate; distribute; draft; estimate; examine; fit; fix; gauge; govern; gradate; grade; graduate; indicate; judge; limit; mark; mete; meter; plan; project; propose; qualify; rate; regulate; rule; scale; separate; standardize; suggest; test; weigh; MEASURE: n. (see "criterion") ability; amount; amplitude; area; bar(ometer); beat; bill; bounds; cadence; caliber; capacity; class; coefficient; computation; criteria (pl.); dance; degree; denominator; dimension(s); distance; division; dose; draft; examination; extent; gauge; grade; graduate; hair; index; indication; law; length; limit; liter; magnitude; mark; measurement; melody; meter; moderation; pitch; plan; project; proposal; proportion; proposition; quanta (pl.); quantity; quota; range; rank; rate; reach; regimen; rotl; rule(r); scale; scope; size; standard; step; suggestion; temperature; test; thermometer; time; touchstone; tune; unit;

volume; weight; yardstick; MEASURED: calculated; classified; computed; deliberate; gauged; graded; graduated; limited; rhythmical; ruled; standardized; weighed; MEASUREMENT: (**see** "measure") amount; area; breadth; bulk; circumference; computation; depth; dimension; distance; examination; height; length; mensuration; meterage; size; test; volume; voluminosity; width; MEASURABLE: (**see** "appreciable" and "comprehensible") calculable; computable; determinable; gaugable; gradable; ratable; regulatory

MEASURELESS: (**see** "boundless" and "eternal") immeasurable; limitless

MEAT: (**see** "food") aliment; beef; carnage; chop; core; essence; flesh; fundamentals; gist; lamb; loin; matter; morsel; mutton; nutriment; pith; pork; steak; substance; sustenance; veal; victuals

MECHANIC: **n.** artificer; artisan; craftsman; hand; machinist; mechanician; operative; operator; worker; workman; MECHANIC-(AL): **a.** administrative; automatic; automatous; autonomic; cold; dehumanized; frozen; impulsive; inhuman; instinctive; inventive; involuntary; perfunctorious; perfunctory; physical; reflective; reflex; robotized; stereotyped; stiff; unfriendly; uninspired

MECHANISM: (**see** "means") action; apparatus; engine; enginery; function; gear; guts; inside(s); machine(ry); mechanics; *modus operandi*; motor; operation; process(es); rigging; system; tackle; technique; works

MECHANIZE: (**see** "dehumanize") robotize

MEDAL: (**see** "award") badge; coin; commendation; decoration; medallion; plaque; prize; reward

MEDDLE: (**see** "interfere") butt in; finger; fool; fuss; handle; interlope; intermeddle; intermediate; interpose; interrupt; intervene; intrude; mediate; mix; obtrude; peep; potter; pry; snoop; tamper; tinker; touch; trespass; trifle; MEDDLER: busybody; buttinsky; interloper; intermeddler; intervenient; Meddlesome Mattie; pryer; quidnunc; snoop(er); tattletale; trifler; zealot; MEDDLESOME *or* MEDDLING: aggressive; curious; fussy; impertinent; impulsive; interfering; interrupting; intervening; intrusive; nosy; obtrusive; officious; peeping;

polypragmatic(al); pragmatical; prying; pushing; pushy; snoopy; MEDDLESOMENESS: impertinence; impudicity; intrusiveness; polypragmatism

MEDIAL *or* MEDIAN: (**see** "average") between; intermediate; mean; mesne; middle; so-so

MEDIATE: arbitrate; conciliate; convey; halve; harmonize; help; intend; intercede; interfere; interject; interpose; intervene; judge; meddle; negotiate; opine; plan; propose; referee; settle; umpire; MEDIATOR: advocate; agent; arbitrator; chairman; go-between; interagent; intercessor; intermediary; intermediate; intervenient; judge; moderator; placator; referee; umpire

MEDICAL: Aesculapian; curative; healing; iatric(al); medicinal; therapeutic; MEDICATE: cure; doctor; dose; drug; heal; treat; MEDICINE(S): alterative; ampule; anesthetic; anodyne; balm (of Gilead); capsule; compound; cordial; cure; dose; drug; elixir; embrocation; influence; laxative; liniment; lotion; *materia medica*; medicament; medicant; medication; mixture; pharmaceutical; pharmacopeia; pharmacy; physianthropy; physics; pill; potion; poultice; powder; preparation; prescription; remedy; salve; simple; specific; stimulant; tablet; therapeusis; therapeutant; therapeutic(s); tincture; tonic; treatment; MEDICINAL: curative; medicative; medicinable; pharmaceutic(al); salutary; salutiferous; sanative; therapeutic(al); theriac(al)

MEDIOCRE: (**see** "average") inferior; second-class; second-drawer; second-rate; so-so

MEDITATE: (**see** "think") cerebrate; chew over; cogitate; concoct; consider; contemplate; contrive; deliberate; design; dwell (on); excogitate; intend; lucubrate; mull; muse; plan; ponder; pore; project; purpose; reason; reflect; remember; revolve; ruminate; speculate; study; weigh; MEDITATIVE: (**see** "thoughtful") Apollonian; Apollonic; Apollonistic; cogitable; cogitabund; cogitative; contemplative; deliberative; nomothetic; pensive; purposeful; reflective; MEDITATION: (**see** "thought") cerebration; cogitation; contemplation; discourse; lucubration; musing; reflection; rumination; study

MEDIUM: **a.** (**see** "average") between; commonplace; fair; intermediate; mean; medial;

median; mediocre; middle; middling; moderate; normal; ordinary; par; representative; so-so; MEDIUM: **n.** (**see** "means") agency; agent; average; channel; compromise; condition; culture; environment; go-between; instrument(ality); intermediary; method; métier; occupation; oracle; organ; prophet; psychic; representative; seer; sibyl; soothsayer; system; vehicle

MEDLEY: admixture; air; blend; brouhaha; charivari; confusion; diversity; fantasia; farrago; *fatras*; gallimaufry; heterogeneity; hodgepodge; jumble; *macédoine*; melange; melee; mingling; miscellany; mix(ture); montage; olio; olla podrida; omnium-gatherum; pasticcio; pastiche; potpourri; salmagundi; song; *tripotage*; tune; variance; variety

MEDULLA: (**see** "essence") cord; interior; marrow; pith; spine; tissue

MEEK: (**see** "childlike" and "modest") bashful; calm; compliant; deferential; dutiful; enduring; forbearing; gentle; humble; humiliating; invertebrate; long-suffering; mild; moderate; patient; phlegmatic; placid; quiet; reserved; serene; sheepish; soft; subdued; submissive; tame; tolerant; tranquil; unpretentious; unproud; unprovocative; unprovoking; weak; yielding; MEEKNESS: (**see** "deference") abnegation; compliance; forbearance; gentility; gentleness; humbleness; humility; mansuetude; moderation; patience; phlegm; placidity; reserve; serenity; submission; submissiveness; tameness; tolerance; toleration; tranquility

MEET: **v.** abut; accost; adapt; agglomerate; agglutinate; aggregate; approach; arrange; assemble; band; battle; bid; bunch; call; categorize; caucus; cite; club; cluster; collect; collide; combat; communicate; concentrate; confer; conform; confront; conglomerate; congregate; congress; conjoin; consolidate; contact; contend; convene; convocate; convoke; cross; crowd; decussate; encounter; equal; face; fill; find; fit; flock; front; fulfill; gather; greet; group; herd; hold; huddle; incur; intersect; join; lap; mass; match; muster; negotiate; occur; oppose; overlap; pack; pay; press; rally; rendezvous; satisfy; see; settle; sit; span; summon; synthesize; swarm; teem; throng; touch; transact; transect; troop; unite; MEET: **a.** adapted; adequate; appropriate; equal; fit(ting); good; proper; right; seemly; suitable; MEET(ING): **n.** agglomeration; agglutination; aggregate; aggregation; agora;

amalgamation; approach(ment); army; arrangement; assemblage; assembly; assignation; audience; band; battle; bevy; body; bunch; caucus; clambake; club; cluster; clutch; collection; college; collision; collocation; combat; commencement; communication; company; concentration; conclave; concourse; concurrency; concursion; conference; confluence; conflux; confrontation; confrontment; conglomeration; congregation; congress; consolidation; constellation; consultation; contest; convening; convention; convergence; convergency; conversation; conversazione; convocation; coterie; council; cross(ing); crowd; decussation; diet; duel; encounter; ensemble; exercises; farrago; flock; gathering; greeting; group; herd; hookup; host; huddle; hunt; intersection; interview; joining; joint; junction; juncture; lapping; legion; legislature; levee; mass; match; melee; moot; multitude; muster(ing); negotiation; overlapping; pack; parliament; parley; party; people; posse; powwow; rally; rencontre; rendezvous; resort; salon; seam; senate; session; society; summons; suture; swarm; symposium; synchondrosis; synod; throng; touching; tourney; transaction; troop; tryst; union

MEGRIM(S): blues; caprice; cephalalgia; despondency; dizziness; dullness; fad; fancy; fit; headache; hypochondria(sis); melancholia; melancholy; migraine; vertigo; whim(sicality)

MELANCHOLY **a.** *or* MELANCHOLIC: (**see** "sad") atrabilarious; atrabiliar; atrabilious; bilious; blue; crabbed; dejected; depressed; despondent; disconsolate; dismal; dispirited; doleful; downcast; drear(y); gloomy; heavyhearted; hypochondriacal; hysterical; lachrymal; lachrymose; liverish; low; lugubrious; mournful; pensive; serious; somber; sorrowful; tearful; tristful; unhappy; wistful; MELANCHOLY **n.** *or* MELANCHOLIA: (**see** "sadness") apanthropia; apanthropy; atrabile; blues; dejection; depression; despondency; doldrums; dumps; ennui; gloom(iness); hypochondria(sis); hysteria; lachrymals; lugubriosity; megrims; misery; sorrow; vapors

MELEE: (**see** "quarrel") affray; brawl; broil; brouhaha; combat; contest; dogfight; fight; fray; medley; *mélange*; riot; row; scrap; scrape; scuffle; set-to; skirmish; struggle; tourney

MELLIFLUOUS: (**see** "melodious") dulcet; flowing; honeyed; mellowed; musical;

smooth; sonorous; sugary; sweet(ened); syrupy; treacly

MELLOW: **v.** age; mature; ripen; season; MELLOW(ED): **a.** adult; aged; amiable; bland; classic(al); dulcet; gay; genial; gentle; intoxicated; jolly; jovial; kind; malm; mature(d); mellifluous; mild; old; orotund; perfected; perfumed; refined; resonant; rich; ripe(ned); seasoned; smooth; soft; sonorous; sweet(ened); tender; vintage; warm

MELODRAMATIC(AL): declamatory; emotional; extravagant; florid; flowery; gaudy; grand(iose); lurid; oratorical; ornate; passionate; rhetorical; sensational; showy; theatrical

MELODY: agreement; air; aria; chime; concord; descant; diapason; ditty; euphony; harmonization; harmony; lyric; measure; melisma; motif; music; orchestration; refrain; rhythm; song; sonority; strain; symphony; syncopation; theme; tone; tune(fulness); unison; MELODIOUS: agreeable; ariose; assonant; canorous; cantabile; clear; dulcet; euphonic; euphonious; flowing; happy; harmonious; honeyed; lyric(al); mellifluous; mellowed; melodic; musical; pleasant; pleasing; orphic; rotund; silvery; sirenic(al); smooth; soft; sonorous; sweet; symphonizing; symphonous; toned; tuned; tuneful; unisonant

MELT: (**see** "dissolve") ablate; blend; decrease; deliquesce; deteriorate; die; diminish; disappear; disintegrate; dissipate; disperse; dwindle; fade; flow; frit; fuse; liquefy; mollify; perish; reduce; render; run; soften; squander; subdue; thaw; unfreeze; vanish; waste

MEMBER: adherent; affiliate; arm; associate; branch; brother; claw; component; constituent; district; element; enrollee; individual; leg; limb; organ; parcel; part; person; piece; portion; rank-and-filer; section sector; segment; unit; MEMBERSHIP: body; franchise; members; rank and file; seat

MEMBRANE: film; fold; layer; membrana; pia; sheet; skin; tela; vellum; web

MEMENTO: (**see** "memorial") bibelot; bric-a-brac; curio; keepsake; knickknack; lagniappe; memorandum; memory; prayer; relic

MEMORABLE: conspicuous; critical; crucial;

distinguished; extraordinary; famous; great; happy; illustrious; important; impressive; long-remembered; marked; momentous; notable; noted; outstanding; prominent; rare; red-letter; signal; significant; uncommon; unforgettable; vivid

MEMORANDUM: abstract; *aide-mémoire*; *aides-mémoire* (pl.); brief; chit; I.O.U.; letter; memento; memoir; memoranda (pl.); memorial; minute; note; record; reminder; report; statement

MEMORIAL: archive; cenotaph; citation; column; commemoration; commendation; cup; decoration; factum; inscription; keepsake; medal; memento; memoir; memorandum; monument; needle; note; pillar; plaque; plate; pleading; record; relic; ribbon; services; shaft; shrine; slab; souvenir; statue; tablet; trace; trophy; vestige; window

MEMORY: afterthought; concentration; heart; memento; mind; mnenonics; recall; recollection; reflection; regret; remembrance; reminder; reminiscence; retention; retrospection; rote; souvenir; wit

MEN: (**see** "man") blokes; crew; force(s); gentlemen; hands; hombres; *hommes*; mankind; mates; menfolks; players; sailors; sirs; soldiers; sons; troops

MENACE: **v.** coerce; cow; dragoon; endanger; frighten; imperil; intimidate; jeopardize; scare; terrify; threaten; warn; MENACE: **n.** anathema; Charybdis; coercion; commination; danger; evil; fear; intimidation; jeopardy; minacity; revenge; Sword of Damocles; terror; threat; vengeance; war; warning; MENACING: (**see** "dangerous") coercive; frightening; imminent; minacious; minatorial; ominous; terrifying; tough; warlike

MEND: (**see** "correct") adjust; ameliorate; amend; better; bolster; calibrate; cobble; cure; darn; doctor; edit; emend; enhance; fix; heal; help; improve; patch; quicken; readjust; rebuild; rectify; reform; refurbish; regenerate; remedy; renew; repair; restore; retouch; revise; set; sew; strengthen; tune

MENDACITY: (**see** "falsehood") deceit; deception; duplicity; fib; lie; lying; prevarication; untruth

MENDICANT: beggar; fakir; friar; gaberlunzie; panhandler

MENIAL: (see "low") dull; household; sordid

MENSTRUATION: catamenia; (the) courses; (the) curse; emmenia; emmenorrhea; eumenorrhea; emmenorrhea; menacme; menarche; menophania; menorrhea; menses; menstrua; menstrual period; (the) monthlies; monthly period; period; sickness

MENTAL: appercipient; cerebral; conceptionistic; conceptive; concipient; emotional; ideal; ideological; immaterial; inner; intellectual; inward; metaphysical; noological; phrenic; psychic(al); psychologic(al); spiritual; subjective; unphysical; MENTALITY: (see "mind") brain(s); braininess; brainpower; intellect(uality); intelligence; sanity; senses; wits

MENTION: v. allude; broach; cite; discuss; hint; intimate; mind; name; note; notice; refer (to); remember; speak; suggest; tell; touch (upon); MENTION: n. allusion; citation; hint; intimation; notation; notice; reference; specification; suggestion; touch

MENTOR: cicerone; coach; counsel(or); guide; preceptor; professor; teacher; tutor

MENU: bill of fare; card; carte; *carte du jour*; cuisine; diet(ary); dishes; fare; food; list; program; regime(n)

MEPHITIC: (see "foul") deadly; mortal; noxious; obnoxious; offensive; pernicious; pestilential; poisonous; profane

MERCENARY: a. abject; avaricious; commercial; greedy; hired; mean; mercantile; selfish; sordid; venal; worldly; MERCENARY: n. extortioner; hack; Hessian; hireling; janissary; moneygrubber; pensionary; vampire

MERCHANDISE: v. see "trade;" MERCHANDISE: n. articles; commerce; commodities; freight; goods; lading; produce; property; stock; stores; stuff; trade; wares; MERCHANT: agent; broker; *commerçant*; coster; dealer; draper; factor; jobber; monger; purveyor; seller; shopkeeper; specialist; storekeeper; taipan; trader; tradesman; trafficker; vendor; vintner

MERCILESS: see under "mercy"

MERCURIAL: (see "changeable") capricious; clever; elegant; erratic; excitable; feverish; fickle; fidgety; fluctuating; inconstant; irresolute; quicksilver; quick-witted; restless; shrewd; sprightly; temperamental; thievish; unstable; unsteady; variable; volatile; wavering

MERCY: benevolence; benignancy; benignity; blessing; blithe; charity; clemency; commiseration; compassion; conscience; consideration; favor; feeling; forbearance; forgiveness; fortune; gentleness; grace; heart; humanity; indulgence; kindness; leniency; lenity; mollification; palliation; pardon; pathos; pity; placidity; pleasantness; quarter; rue; ruth; sensibility; softheartedness; softness; sympathy; tenderness; tepidity; tolerance; toleration; tranquility; understanding; urbanity; yearning; MERCIFUL: (see "mild") benign; charitable; chickenhearted; clement; compassionate; conscientious; considerate; forbearing; forgiving; gentle; gracious; heartfelt; indulgent; kind; lenient; piteous; sensible; soft(hearted); sympathetic; tender(hearted); tolerant; unvindictive; warm(hearted); MERCILESS: (see "austere") barbaric; barbarous; cruel; disputatious; disregardful; fell; feral; furious; hard; harsh; imperative; implacable; inclement; inexorable; inhuman(e); inquisitorial; intolerant; Neronian; obdurate; pitiless; relentless; remorseness; ruthless; *sans merci*; savage; severe; sharp; unfeeling; unsparing; unsympathetic; wanton; wild

MERE(LY) absolute(ly); bare(ly); few; only; pure(ly); sheer; simple; simply; single; small; sole(ly); undiluted; utter(ly)

MERETRICIOUS: (see "cheap") brummagem; counterfeit; deceptive; false; flimsy; gaudy; gauzy; insincere; misleading; pretentious; sham; showy; spurious; tawdry; tinny; tinsel

MERGE: absorb; accord; amalgamate; blend; coalesce; combine; connect; engage; enmesh; entangle; fit; fuse; gear; glide; harmonize; immerse; incorporate; integrate; interlock; join; lock; marry; mesh; mingle; mix; sink; unify; unite; wed; MERGER: absorption; accord; alliance; amalgamation; blend; coadunation; coalescence; coalition; combination; combine; concursion; confluence; connection; engagement; entanglement; fusion; harmonization; harmony; incorporation; interlocking; marriage; mergence; osmosis; trust; union; MERGING: absorptive; amalgamative; coadunative; coalescent; confluent; harmonizing; mingling; osmotic; unifying

MERIDIAN: acme; apex; apogee; climax; culmination; midday; noon; peak; summit; zenith

MERIT: **v.** deserve; earn; rate; reward; warrant; win; MERIT: **n.** badge; commendation; desert; due; eminence; esteem; excellence; exemplarity; honor; justice; mark; meed; prestige; reputation; reward; value; virtue; worth(iness); MERITED *or* MERITORIOUS: commendable; commendatory; condign; creditable; deserved; deserving; due; earned; eminent; estimable; excellent; exemplary; fit(ting); honorable; just(ifiable); meet; meritable; praiseworthy; prestigious; rewarding; rightful; suitable; valuable; venerable; warranted; worthy

MERRY: (**see** "humorous") blithe(ful); blithesome; brisk; carnivalesque; cheerful; debonair(e); exuberant; exultant; festive; frolicsome; gamesome; gay; genial; glad; gleeful; happy; hilarious; intense; jaunty; jocose; jocund; jolly; jovial; joyous; laughing; mirthful; optimistic; playful; sharp; sporting; sportive; sprightly; sunny; MERRIMENT: cheerfulness; conviviality; enjoyment; entertainment; exhilaration; exultation; festivity; frolic; fun; gaiety; geniality; glee; happiness; hilarity; humor; jocularity; jocundity; jocundness; jollity; joviality; joy(ousness); jubilation; lark; laughter; levity; merriness; merrymaking; mirth(fulness); optimism; play; sport(iveness); sunniness

MESH: **v.** (**see** "merge") accord; combine; connect; coordinate; engage; enmesh; entangle; fit; gear; harmonize; interlock; lock; marry; net; snare; trap; unite; MESH: **n.** fabric; gear; net(work); screen; tissue; web; wire

MESS: **v.** (**see** "bungle") befoul; botch; confuse; dabble; damage; derange; disarrange; interfere; jumble; litter; meddle; mix; muddle; muss; play; putter; MESS: **n.** (**see** "bungle") botch; capharnaum; catch; confusion; conglomeration; derangement; difficulty; disarrangement; disorder; feed; heterogeneity; hodgepodge; jumble; kettle of fish; litter; mass; meal; mélange; mixture; muss; potpourri; predicament; quantity; shambles; MESSY: (**see** "slovenly") chaotic; disarranged; disordered; littered; jumbled; mixed; muddled; mussed; unordered; unorderly; unorganized; unpresentable

MESSAGE: bode; cable(gram); call; card; code; communication; discourse; dispatch; epistle; evangel; import; information; intelligence; letter; meaning; memo(randum); mission; missive; note; pitch; report; sermon; significance; statement; teaching; telegram; theme; thought; tidings; transmission; wire; word; writ

MESSENGER: apostle; carrier; courier; delegate; dispatcher; emissary; envoy; forerunner; harbinger; herald; internuncio; Mercury; minister; nuncio; orderly; page; pigeon; prophet; representative; runner

METAL: armament; brass; bronze; courage; iron; material; niello; ore; stamina; steel; strength; sword; tin

METAMORPHOSIS: (**see** "change") alteration; evolution; mutation; transfiguration; transformation; transmogrification; transmutation

METAPHOR: allegory; anagoge; analogy; comparison; metonymy; simile; synecdoche; tralatition; trophe; METAPHORIC(AL): allegorical; analogous; figurative; symbolic(al); synecdochic(al); tralatitious

METAPHYSICAL: (**see** "supernatural") clairvoyant; extraphysical; mental; preternatural; stratospheric(al); subconscious; superphysical; telepathic; transcendent(al)

METER: beat; cadence; dial; euphony; gauge; lilt; measure; pulsation; pulse; regularity; rhyme; rhythm(icity); time; tread; verse

METHOD(S): action; approach; arrangement; command; control; course; creed; custom; design; device; discipline; doctrine; dodge; fashion; form(ula); hint; instruction(s); law; liturgy; logic; management; maneuver; manner; means; mechanics; medium; methodology; métier; mode; modus; *modus operandi*; operation; order(liness); path; pattern; plan; policy; practice; prescription; procedure; proceeding; process; program; protocol; recipe; regularity; rite; ritual; role; rote; routing; rule; schedule; science; skill; standard; step; stratagem; strategy; suggestion; system; tack; tactics; technique; tenet; track; tradition; train; usage; use; way; wrinkle; METHODICAL: arranged; disciplined; drilled; exact; filed; formal; habitual; logical; orderly; patterned; planned; precise; premeditated; regular; standard(ized); systematic

METICULOUS: (see "precise") microscopic; niggling; particular; petty; rabbinic(al); scrupulous

MÉTIER: see "work"

METTLE: (see "spirit") courage; guts; iron; nerve; stamina; strength; temper; vigor; vim; vitality

MIASMA: air; atmosphere; contagion; emanation; gas; influence; malaria; smog; smoke; toxin; vapor

MICROBE: agent; bacilli (pl.); bacillus; bacteria (pl.); bacterium; germ; microorganism; organism; protozoan; virus

MICROCOSM: community; institution; man; miniature; universe; village; world

MICROSCOPIC: accurate; fine; infinitesimal; invisible; meticulous; miniature; minimal; miniscule; minute; small; tiny; ultramicroscopic; unseeable; unseen; wee

MIDDLE: a. (see "central") average; between; halfway; intermediate; internal; intervening; mean; medial; median; medieval; mediocre; mesial; middling; midmost; midway; so-so; MIDDLE: n. (see "center") average; belly; core; essence; foci (pl.); focus; heart; hub; interior; marrow; midmost; midpart; midpoint; midst; midstream; midway; navel; norm; waist

MIDDLING: (see "average") intermediate; medial; mediocre; middle-class; midway; neutral; second-rate; so-so

MIEN: (see "air") action(s); appearance; aspect; bearing; behavior; carriage; condition; demeanor; deportment; expression; feature; front; guise; look; manner; ostent; outline; physiognomy; poise; port; posture; visage

MIGHT: (see "authority") ability; ammunition; arm(ament); capacity; efficacy; energy; force; guns; intensity; main; means; potency; power; puissance; resources; strength; supremacy; (the) sword; vigor; virtue; MIGHTY: (see "powerful") able; athletic; authoritative; bold; efficacious; efficient; enormous; extensive; extraordinary; favorable; great; hefty; Herculean; high; important; imposing; influential; invincible; momentous; notable; omnipotent; potent; puissant; remarkable; robust(ious); Samsonian; strenuous; strong; sturdy; supreme;

valiant; vast; very; vigorous; violent; wonderful

MIGRAINE: see "headache"

MIGRATE: change; leave; move; rove; shift; stroll; transfer; wander; MIGRATION: diaspora; exodus; hegira; move; removal; shift; transfer; trek; MIGRATORY: casual; moving; nomadic; rolling; roving; strolling; transient; unsettled; vagrant; wandering

MILD: amiable; assuasive; balmy; beneficent; benign(ant); bland; calm; clement; compassionate; complaisant; considerate; courteous; easy; effeminate; favonian; forbearing; forgiving; genial; gentle; heartfelt; human(e); indulgent; kind; lenient; lenitive; meek; merciful; milky; mitigative; moderate; mollifying; nonviolent; pacific(atory); palliative; patient; peaceful; piteous; placative; placatory; placid; pleasant; pleasing; quiet; savory; serene; smooth; soft; soothing; suave; subdued; sweet; sympathetic; tame; temperate; tender; tepid; tolerant; tranquil; unoppressive; untroubled; unvindictive; unviolent; velvety; warm(hearted); MILDNESS: amiability; balm; beneficence; benignity; courtesy; geniality; gentility; gentleness; humanity; indulgence; kindness; leniency; lenity; meekness; mercy; moderation; palliation; patience; peacefulness; placidity; pleasantness; pleasantry; serenity; suavity; tepidity; tolerance; tranquility; urbanity; warmheartedness

MILDEW: blight; fungus; fust; mo(u)ld; must; mustiness; rot

MILESTONE: accomplishment; achievement; advance(ment); echelon; mark(er); millennarium; milepost; plateau; point; stele; step

MILIEU: environment; environs; orientation; setting; situation; surroundings

MILITANT: (see "quarrelsome") adamant; bellicose; combatant; combative; fighting; fire-eating; military; tough; warlike

MILITARY: a. combatant; martial; militant; soldierly; warlike; MILITARY: n. army; forces; militia; soldiery; troops

MILITATE: (see "contend" and "fight") count; weigh

MILK: v. bleed; drain; elicit; exhaust; exploit; extract; mulct; sap; squeeze; MILK:

n. extract; fluid; juice; lac(tation); latex; sap; secretion; MILKY: effeminate; gentle; lacteous; lactescent; mild; opalescent; pearly; spiritless; tame; timorous; MILKINESS: lactescence; opalescence

MILL: **v.** comminute; crush; finish; grind; knurl; make; press; pulverize; shape; MILL: **n.** factory; grinder; machine; plant; press; quern; roller; shop

MIME *or* MIMIC: **v.** (**see** "imitate") act; answer; ape; burlesque; clown; compete; contend; copy; counterfeit; echo; emulate; equal; feign; follow; forge; gesture; impersonate; iterate; match; mirror; mock; parody; parrot; portray; rebound; reflect; repeat; repercuss; replicate; reply; reproduce; resound; respond; reverberate; revoice; ricochet; ridicule; ring; rival; sham; simulate; strive; vie; MIME *or* MIMIC: **n.** actor; aper; buffoon; clown; copier; copy(cat); counterfeit; emulator; imitator; impressionist; jester; mocker; sham; simulator; MIMICRY: apism; burlesque; camouflage; caricature; copy; counterfeit; echo(ing); gesture; imitation; impersonation; mimesis; mimetism; mockery; parody; parrotry; representation; ridicule; simulation

MINCE: chop; clip; cut; dice; euphemize; extenuate; hash; minimize; moderate; restrain; slash; walk

MIND: **v.** attend; care; consider; dislike; guard; heed; note; notice; nurse; obey; observe; oversee; perceive; reck(on); regard; remember; see; tend; watch; worry; MIND-(S): **n.** brain(s); brainpower; cerebrum; choice; conscience; consciousness; desire; disposition; faculty; inclination; instinct(ion); intellect(uality); intelligence; judgment; liking; memory; mentality; mood; nous; object; opinion; philosopher; psyche; purpose; rationality; reason; recollection; regard; remembrance; sanity; sense; sensorium; sentiment; skull; soul; spirit; thinker; thought; understanding; view; will; wish; wit(s)

MINDFUL: (**see** "attentive") aware; careful; considerate; hep

MINE: **v.** burrow; deplete; dig; excavate; extract; find; sap; MINE: **n.** bomb; bonanza; cavity; colliery; deposit; El Dorado; excavation; explosive; find; Golconda; lode; pit; quarry; shaft; store; source; vein; wealth

MINERAL: calcite; coal; compound; copper; element; gold; iron; lead; ore; phosphate; quartz; rock; silver; spalt; spar; stone; substance; talc; uranite; uranium

MINGLE: (**see** "associate") admix; amalgamate; blend; coalesce; combine; commix; compound; concoct; confound; confuse; conglomerate; consolidate; entwine; fuse; infiltrate; integrate; interlard; intermix; interpolate; intertwine; interweave; join; meld; melt; merge; mix; troop; unite; weave

MINIATURE: **a.** diminutive; lilliputian; little; microcosmic; microscopic; midget; miniscule; minor; minute; small; wee; MINIATURE: **n.** copy; diminutive; doll; epitome; lilliputian; microcosm; midget; minuscule; model; reduction; representation

MINIM: drop; gutta; iota; jot; tittle; whit; MINIMUM *or* MINIMAL: bare; critical; least; limit; lowest; marginal; minima (pl.); minority; minuscule; separate; smallest; MINIMIZE: (**see** "belittle") censure; condemn; criticize; cushion; decry; degrade; denigrate; denounce; depreciate; derogate; detract; discount; discredit; disparage; gloss; mitigate; palliate; reduce; relieve; smooth; traduce; whitewash

MINION: agent; creature; dependent; deputy; fan; favorite; follower; hanger-on; idol; mercenary; parasite; satellite; subordinate

MINISTER: **v.** administer; aid; assist; attend; dose; furnish; help; lend; nourish; nurse; nurture; officiate; relieve; rescue; serve; shepherd; succor; support; sustain; tend; treat; uphold; visit; MINISTER: **n.** (**see** "clergyman") agent; aide; ambassador; assistant; curate; deacon; domine; ecclesiastic; envoy; hierophant; legate; nuncio; officer; parson; pastor; plenipotentiary; preacher; premier; priest; representative; shepherd

MINOR: **a.** (**see** "small") inferior; lesser; lower; microscopic; miniature; minor-league; minuscule; petit; petty; secondary; shoestring; smaller; subsidiary; underage; unimportant; MINOR: **n.** baby; boy; child; friar; girl; infant; minorite; youth; MINORITY: few; infancy; minimum; nonage; pupilage; teens

MINSTREL: bard; entertainer; François Villon; gleeman; harpist; jongleur; musician; player; poet; rhymer; scald; scop; show; singer; skald; troubadour

MINT: **v.** coin; confect; create; fabricate; forge; invent; make; manufacture; produce; MINT: **n.** herb; hyssop; money; sage; stamp; storehouse; sum

MINUS: (**see** "deficient") lacking; less(er); lost; negative; smaller; wanting; without

MINUSCULE *or* MINISCULE: (**see** "small") diminutive; insignificant; microcosmic; microscopic; miniature; minimal; minor; minute; petite; petty; tiny; unimportant; wee

MINUTE: **a.** (**see** "small") atomic; capillary; careful; closeup; comprehensive; concentrated; critical; detailed; diminutive; elaborate; exact; fine; full; infinitesimal; insignificant; instant; little; meticulous; microscopic; miniature; minimal; minor; minuscule; particular; petite; petty; play-by-play; pointed; precise; short; tiny; trifling; wee; withdrawn; MINUTE: **n.** acta (pl.); detail; entry; flash; instant; item; memo(randum); meticulosity; minutiae (pl.); moment; note; record; second; trice

MINX: colleen; coquette; doll; filly; flirt; girl; hussy; jade; miss; quean

MIRACLE: anomy; marvel; mirabilia (pl.); prodigy; wonder; MIRACULOUS: (**see** "supernatural") marvelous; providential; superb; thaumaturgic(al); wonderful; wondrous

MIRAGE: corposant; *deceptio visus*; deception; dream; *fata morgana*; hallucination; *ignis fatuus*; illusion; phenomenon; St. Elmo's fire; serab; vision

MIRE: **v.** addle; bog; entangle; involve; ooze; stick; MIRE: **n.** bog; fen; glar; marsh; moil; mush; mud; slue; slush; swamp; MIR(E)Y: boggy; dirty; entangled; filthy; involved; lutose; muddy; oozy; slimy; slushy; swampy; uliginous

MIRROR: **v.** imitate; model; reflect; represent; MIRROR: **n.** catopter; crystal; exemplar; glass; ideal; image; model; pattern; reflector; representation; speculum

MIRTH: (**see** "fun") cheer; comic spirit; festivity; gaiety; gladness; glee; hilarity; jollity; joy(ousness); merriment; mirth-(fulness); pleasantry; pleasure; rejoicing; sport; MIRTHFUL: cheery; comical; droll; festive; gay; glad; gleeful; hilarious; jolly; jovial; joyous; merry; pleasurable; rejoiceful; rejoicing; riant; whimsical

MIRTHLESS: (**see** "dull" and "sad") drear-(y); grim; laughterless; serious; sour; vinegary

MISANTHROPE: crab; curmudgeon; cynic; grouch; hater; miser; pessimist; Timon

MISAPPLY: defalcate; embezzle; misappropriate; misuse; steal; MISAPPLICATION: defalcation; embezzlement; infringement; malfeasance; misfeasance; misuse; peculation; substraction; theft; trespass

MISBEHAVIOR: (**see** "misconduct") delinquency; disorderliness; ill conduct; malbehavior; malconduct; mutiny; wrongdoing

MISBELIEF: agnosticism; disbelief; heresy; miscreance; skepticism; unorthodoxy

MISCALCULATE: **see** "misinterpret"

MISCARRY: backfire; boomerang; err; miscalculate; misinterpret

MISCELLANEOUS: assorted; disunited; diverse; haphazard; heterogeneous; indiscriminate; manifold; many; mingled; mixed; odd; pied; promiscuous; random; scattered; several; sundry; varied; various; MISCELLANY: bric-a-brac; collectanea (pl.); heterogeneity; hodgepodge; medley; miscellanea (pl.); miscellaneity; olio; olla podrida; omnium-gatherum; varia (pl.); variety; whatnot

MISCHANCE: (**see** "accident") calamity; catastrophe; contretemps; misadventure; miscalculation; misfortune; mishap

MISCHIEF: (**see** "deviltry") annoyance; damage; detriment; diablerie; disservice; evil; hanky-panky; harassment; hocus-pocus; hurt; ill; impishness; injury; mischievousness; misdeed; misfortune; pain; roguery; roguishness; sickness; sorrow; trouble; wrack; MISCHIEVOUS: (**see** "devilish") annoying; damaging; detrimental; elfish; elvish; evil; foxy; harrasing; harmful; hurtful; impish; injurious; malevolent; misfortunate; pert; playful; prankful; prankish; puckish; roguish; spiteful; troublesome; venomous; wicked

MISCONCEPTION: (**see** "delusion") hallucination; illusion; misapprehension; miscalculation; miscomprehension; misinterpretation; mistake; misunderstanding

MISCONDUCT: beastliness; bestiality; defalcation; delinquency; disorderliness; felony; malbehavior; malconduct; malfeasance; mischief; misdeed; misdemeanor; misfeasance; mismanagement; offense; sin; sociopathy; transgression; wickedness; wrongdoing

MISCREANT: (**see** "rascal" and "villain") criminal; delinquent; felon; heretic; infidel; malfeasant; malfeasor; sinner; transgressor

MISDEED: (**see** "misconduct") crime; defaction; defalcation; delinquency; felony; malfeasance; mischief; misdemeanor; misfeasance; offense; sin; transgression; wickedness

MISDEMEANOR: champerty; crime; delinquency; *délit*; fault; misdeed; offense; sin; tort; transgression; venality

MISDIRECT: **see** "mislead"

MISDO: **see** "misplay"

MISER: churl; curmudgeon; hoarder; money-grubber; nabal; niggard; skinflint; MISERLY: acquisitive; avaricious; avid; churlish; close; covetous; extortionate; frugal; grasping; greedy; gripping; ironfisted; mean; near; niggardly; parsimonious; penny-pinching; penurious; rapacious; sordid; stingy; thrifty; tight; venal; MISERLINESS: **see** "greed"

MISERY: (**see** "agony") ache; affliction; anguish; calamity; cross; desolation; distress; dolor; excruciation; grief; heartache; misfortune; pain; Pandora; penury; privation; purgatory; squalor; suffering; torment; trial; tribulation; unhappiness; woe; MISERABLE: (**see** "painful") abject; aching; afflicted; afflictive; ailing; awful; bad; contemptible; crummy; crushed; despicable; disconsolate; discreditable; dismal; distressed; evil; excruciating; forlorn; friendless; gray; heartbroken; illiberal; impoverished; insufficient; meager; mean; offensive; pitiable; poor; sad; scant(y); shameful; sick(ly); small; sorrowful; stingy; suffering; unhappy; unpleasant; valueless; woebegone; worried; worthless; wretched

MISFORTUNE: (**see** "accident") abomination; adversity; affliction; agony; *angoisse*; bereavement; blow; calamity; catastrophe; cross; curse; depression; desolation; despair; despondency; disaster; distress; evil; failure; hardship; harm; hell; holocaust; hopelessness; ill(ness); infliction; injury; misadventure; mischance; misery; mishap; ordeal;

reverse; ruin; scourge; sorrow; trial; tribulation; trouble; unluck(iness); MISFORTUNATE: **see** "unlucky"

MISGIVING: (**see** "uneasiness") alarm; anxiety; apprehension; cold feet; distrust; doubt; dread; fear; fright; hesitation; premonition; qualm; shyness; suspicion

MISGOVERN: **see** "mismanage"

MISHANDLE: **see** "maltreat" and "mismanage"

MISHAP: (**see** "accident") blunder; bobble; contretemps; error; misadventure; misfortune; misperformance; slip

MISHMASH: (**see** "hodgepodge") hash; heterogeneity; jumble; medley; olio

MISINTERPRET: distort; falsify; miscalculate; misconceive; misread; misreckon; mistake; misunderstand; pervert

MISJUDGE: (**see** "mistake") miscalculate; misconceive; misconstrue; misestimate; mismanage

MISLAY: lose; misplace

MISLEAD: (**see** "deceive") bamboozle; confuse; defraud; delude; dupe; equivocate; gull; hoodwink; lie; lull; lure; misdirect; misguide; mishandle; misinform; mislabel; pervert; seduce; victimize; MISLEADING: (**see** "deceptive") acategorical; ambiguous; ambivalent; confusing; deceiving; delusional; delusionary; delusive; equivocal; factitious; false; illusive; inaccurate; lying; mislabeled; untrue

MISMANAGE: blunk; botch; bungle; distort; err; fumble; miscalculate; misconceive; misconduct; misestimate; misinterpret; misjudge; misreckon; misrule; mistake; misunderstand; MISMANAGEMENT: **see** "misconduct"

MISPLACE: **see** "lose"

MISPLAY: (**see** "bungle") bobble; err; fluff; fumble; grope; miscue; misperform; muff; renege; renig

MISPRISION: contempt; depreciation; disparagement; scorn

MISPRONUNCIATION: cacology; malapropism

MISREPRESENT: (see "deceive") belie; caricature; color; counterfeit; disguise; dissemble; distort; exaggerate; falsify; feign; garble; lie; malign; mislead; misstate; simulate; MISREPRESENTATION: (see "deception") caricature; chicanery; counterfeit; deceit; distortion; exaggeration; falsehood; falseness; falsification; fraud; pretense; simulation; trick(ery)

MISRULE: see "mismanage"

MISS: v. avoid; elude; escape; fail; forego; ignore; lack; lose; miscarry; misfire; muff; need; neglect; omit; overlook; require; skip; underlook; want; MISS: n. damsel; failure; girl; go-by; lass; maiden; oversight; spinster; MISSING: absent; A.W.O.L.; escaped; gone; lacking; lost; mislaid; neglected; omitted; overlooked; skipped; wanting

MISSHAPEN: see "deformed"

MISSILE: arrow; Atlas; bolo; bomb; bullet; dart; grenade; I.C.B.M.; Jupiter; lance; letter; Minuteman; missive; Nike; Polaris; Poseidon; projectile; rock; rocket; sidewinder; spear; Thor; Titan; torpedo; Zeus

MISSION: assignment; embassy; goal; job; legation; lifework; ministry; responsibility; sortie; task; vocation; wish; work

MISSIVE: communication; epistle; letter; line; memo(randum); message; missile; note; report; statement

MISSPEND: frit; lose; misappropriate; squander; waste

MISSTATEMENT: see "falsehood"

MIST: v. becloud; cloud; dim; fog; haze; vaporize; MIST: n. bewilderment; brume; cloud; dimness; drizzle; film; fog; haze; nebula; obscurity; serein; smog; steam; vapor; MISTY: bleary; blurry; brumous; cloudy; caliginous; confused; crepuscular; dim; drizzly; foggy; gauzy; hazy; indistinct; murky; nebular; nebulous; obscure; shadowy; vague; vaporific; vaporous; volatile

MISTAKE: v. blunder; bobble; confuse; err; misapprehend; miscalculate; miscomprehend; misconceive; misconstrue; miscue; misguide; mishear; misinterpret; misque; misquote; misunderstand; slip; MISTAKE: n. barney; blunder; bobble; boner; bull; clinker; delusion; disagreement; embarrassment; errata (pl.); erratum; error; failure;

fallacy; fault; fluff; illusion; imbroglio; inadvertence; inadvertency; lapse; misapprehension; miscalculation; miscomprehension; misconception; miscue; misguidance; misintelligence; misinterpretation; misknowledge; misperception; misplay; misprision; misunderstanding; omission; oversight; slip(up); worry

MISTER: don; husband; monsieur; señor; sir; title

MISTREAT: (see "abuse") disserve; illtreat; ill-use; injure; maltreat; mishandle; misuse; oppress; outrage; punish; thrash; whip; wrong

MISTRESS: amour; chatelaine; concubine; inamorata; maid; materfamilias; matriarch; matron; paramour; woman

MISTRUST: (see "doubt") apprehension; distrust; dubiety; dubiosity; fear; misdoubt; misgiving; presentiment; skepticism; suspision; uncertainty

MISTY: see under "mist"

MISUNDERSTAND: (see "mistake") miscomprehend; misconceive; misconstrue; misinterpret; MISUNDERSTANDING: (see "mistake") brouillerie; disagreement; dissention; embarrassment; error; imbroglio; malentendu; misapprehension; miscomprehension; misconception; misintelligence; misinterpretation; misknowledge; misperception; misprision; quarrel; spat; MISUNDERSTOOD: malentendu; misapprehended; miscomprehended; misinterpreted; misperceived; mistaken; uncomprehended

MISUSE: v. (see "abuse") defalcate; dilapidate; disserve; embezzle; misapply; misappropriate; mistreat; neglect; MISUSE: n. defalcation; embezzlement; maltreatment; misapplication; misappropriation; mistreatment; neglect; negligence; omission

MITE: (see "bit") acarid; arachnid; atom; dash; insect; iota; jot; louse; molecule; monad; mote; particle; sliver; smidgen; speck; sou; tittle; whit

MITER: belt; cap; cidaris; cowl; diadem; dress; fillet; girdle; gusset; hat; headband; headdress; junction

MITIGATE: (see "check") abate; allay; alleviate; appease; assuage; cushion; deaden;

decrease; diminish; ease; lessen; lull; moderate; mollify; pacify; palliate; qualify; quell; relax; relieve; salve; smooth; soften; soothe; subdue; temper; tranquilize; weaken

MIX: **v.** (**see** "associate") alloy; amalgamate; beat; blend; coalesce; combine; commingle; compound; confound; confuse; conglomerate; consort; cross(breed); disarrange; enter; fight; fuse; incorporate; infiltrate; integrate; interfuse; interlace; interlard; intermingle; intertwine; involve; join; jumble; knead; meddle; merge; mess; mingle; muddle; shake; shuffle; stir; toss; triturate; unite; MIX(TURE): **n.** alloy; amalgam-(ation); assemblage; assembly; assortment; batch; blend; brew; caldron; combination; commingling; compost; compound; concoction; confection; confusion; conglomeration; decoction; disarrangement; disorder; dough; farrago; formula; gallimaufry; gumbo; hash; heterogeneity; hodgepodge; hyphenation; jumble; medicine; medley; melange; mess; miscellanea (pl.); miscellaneity; miscellany; mix-up; olio; paste; pastiche; potion; potpourri; preparation; prescription; ratio; salad; salmagundi; smorgasbord; stew; substance; tagraggery; variety; MIXED: amalgamated; amalgamative; associated; coalesced; combined; commingled; confused; conglomerated; crossed; farraginous; fused; heterogeneous; hodgepodge; hyphenated; incorporated; indiscriminate; infiltrated; integrated; interfused; interlarded; intermingled; irregular; joint; macaronic; miscellaneous; nonclassified; nondescript; nonuniform; piebald; potpourri; shuffled; unassorted; unclassified; ungraded; unsorted; varied

MIX-UP: (**see** "mixture") affray; confusion; difficulty; entanglement; fight; melee; snafu; tangle

MOAN: (**see** "cry") bemoan; bewail; complain; deplore; groan; lament; sigh; sob; sough; wail

MOAT: canal; channel; ditch; fosse; graff; protection; trench

MOB: (**see** "band") army; canaille; claque; clique; collection; crowd; drove; flock; gang; gathering; group; herd; horde; host; legion; mass(es); multitude; people; populace; press; proletariat; rabble; riffraff; ring; set; throng; varletry

MOBILIZE: (**see** "organize") arrange; gather; group; marshal; muster; rally; MOBILE:

adaptable; changeable; flexible; flowing; fluid; free; loose; movable; moving; plastic; shifting; unrestricted; unstable

MOCK: **v.** (**see** "imitate") ape; burlesque; caricature; copy; counterfeit; deceive; defy; delude; deride; disregard; echo; feign; fleer; flout; gibe; jape; jeer; jest; jibe; mimic; mirror; pretend; quiz; reproduce; ridicule; satirize; scoff; scorn; scout; simulate; sneer; sport; taunt; MOCK: **a.** counterfeit; false; feigned; imitation; pretended; pseudo; quasi; sham; simulated; spurious; MOCKERY: (**see** "imitation") asteism; badinage; banter; burlesque; caricature; chaff(ing); contempt; counterfeit; deception; delusion; derision; disregard; farce; futility; irony; jeer; jest; makeup; mimesis; mimicry; mockage; parody; persiflage; raillery; reproduction; ridicule; ruse; sarcasm; satire; scorn; sham; sport; travesty

MODE: (**see** "fashion") arrangement; attitude; breeding; condition; convention; course; craze; cry; custom; decor(ation); decorum; drift; etiquette; fad; fashion; flair; form; habit; manner; method; mien; mood; nature; order; pattern; plan; practice; precedent; prevalence; procedure; rage; rule; scheme; state; style; taste; tenor; tone; trade; trend; usage; vogue; way; wont

MODEL: **v.** (**see** "illustrate") arrange; delineate; depict; design; display; exemplify; fashion; imitate; mirror; pose; represent; shape; sit; sketch; MODEL: **a.** archetypal; archetypical; ectypal; exemplary; paradigmatic; prototypal; prototypic; prototypical; typical; MODEL: **n.** (**see** "illustration") anthropomorph; arch(e)type; arrangement; *beau ideal*; blueprint; canon; copy; counterpart; criterion; delineation; depictment; design; drawing; duplicate; ectype; example; exemplar; exemplum; facsimile; figure; form; homunculus; gauge; ideal; image; imitation; likeness; mannequin; man(n)-ikin; matrix; microcosm; miniature; mirror; mold; monument; norm; original; outline; paradigm; paragon; pattern; poser; praxis; principal; prototype; replica; representation; sample; shape; sitter; sketch; source; standard; toy; type

MODERATE: **v.** (**see** "calm") abate; allay; alleviate; alloy; appease; assuage; attempt; bate; control; cushion; deaden; decrease; diminish; direct; ease; extenuate; lessen; limit; lower; lull; manage; mediate; mince; mitigate; modify; mollify; pacify; palliate; preside; qualify; quell; reduce; regulate;

relieve; remit; restrain; rule; salve; slake; slow; smooth; soften; soothe; subdue; temper; tranquilize; weaken; MODERATE: **a.** (**see** "fair") abstemious; abstentious; abstinent; average; bland; calm; central; clement; continent; cool; even; frugal; gentle; indifferent; inexpensive; judicious; limited; mediocre; medium; meek; middle-of-the-road; mild; mitigatory; modest; ordinary; prudent; reasonable; regulated; restrained; slow; sober; soft; so-so; sparing; steady; sweet; temperate; tolerable; two-star; MODERATE: **n.** centrist; MODERATION: (**see** "restraint") abstention; abstinence; continence; discretion; extenuation; golden mean; measure; moderateness; prudence; restraint; soberness; temperance

MODERN: (**see** "new") abreast; advanced; *au courant*; contemporary; current; *fin-de-siècle*; fresh; late(st); moderne; modernistic; neoteric; new; novel; present(-day); progressive; recent; timely; topical; up-to-date; MODERNIZE: refurbish; renew; reorganize; streamline; update

MODEST: bashful; becoming; chaste; civil; compliant; continent; conventional; coy; decent; decorous; deferential; demure; diffident; discreet; dutiful; forbearing; gentle; humble; humiliating; inconsiderable; innocent; insignificant; limited; lowly; maidenly; meek; mild; mim; minute; moderate; moral; patient; phlegmatic; placid; proper; pure; quiet; reasonable; refined; reserved; retiring; self-effacing; serene; shameful; sheepish; sheeplike; shy; simple; small; soft; squeamish; subdued; submissive; tame; timid; timorous; tolerant; tranquil; unassertive; unassuming; unboastful; uncoquettish; undefiled; unobtrusive; unostentatious; unpresuming; unpresumptious; unpresumptive; unpretentious; unproud; unprovocative; unprovoking; verecund; virgin(al); virtuous; yielding; MODESTY: bashfulness; chastity; constraint; coyness; decency; decentness; decorum; delicacy; demureness; demurity; diffidence; diffidency; diffidentness; innocence; maidenliness; pudency; *pudeur*; pudibundity; pudicity; reserve; restraint; shame-(fulness); shyness; timidity; unobtrusiveness; verecundity; virtue

MODIFY: (**see** "alter") abrogate; adapt; add; adjust; affect; amend; change; color; condition; convert; decrease; deflect; diversify; divert; edit; fashion; hedge; improve; increase; influence; lessen; limit; lower; master; moderate; modulate; qualify; recondition; redact; redo; reduce; renew; renovate;

reshape; restrict; revise; shape; soften; subtract; temper; tinge; transform; trim; turn; vary

MODULATE: (**see** "calm") adapt; adjust; attune; change; harmonize; inflect; intone; modify; regulate; sing; soften; temper; tone; tune; vary

MOGUL: (**see** "leader") aristocrat; autocrat; leading light; lord; magnate; Mongolian; nabob; personage; titan; V.I.P.

MOHAMMEDAN: Berber; Islam(ite); Moor; Moslem; Muslem; Mussulman; Saracen

MOIETY: component; fraction; half; part; portion; quarter; share

MOIL: **v.** besplatter; daub; defile; drudge; labor; meddle; soil; spot; stain; toil; trudge; wallow; wet; wrangle; MOIL: **n.** coil; confusion; drudgery; labor; meddling; spot; taint; toil; turbulence; turmoil; uproar; vexation; work; wrangle

MOISTEN: (**see** "wet") anoint; bedew; dampen; humidify; saturate; soak; water; MOIST: aqueous; clammy; damp; dank; dewy; humid(ified); hydrogenous; liquid; marshy; maudlin; muggy; saturated; soaked; sodden; soggy; soppy; soupy; swampy; tearful; watery; wet; MOISTURE *or* MOISTNESS: aquosity; dampness; dankness; dew; humectation; humidity; liquid-(ity); mugginess; precipitation; rain; saturation; swampiness; tearfulness; water; wateriness; wetness

MOLD: **v.** adapt; cast; confect; create; determine; fabricate; fit; form(alize); formulate; hug; influence; knead; make; mix; model; pattern; plasticize; shape; MOLD: **n.** âme; body; cast; design; die; form; frame; fungus; humus; impression; kind; matrix; model; nature; pattern; plasm; prototype; shape; stamp; type; MOLDY: decaying; earthy; fusty; mildewed; musty; old; stale

MOLDING: astragal; cable; cavetto; chain; congé; cyma; decoration; fillet; lozenge; ogee; ovolo; reeding; reglet; rose; scotia; scroll; splay; strip; torus

MOLE: fault; imperfection; jetty; mammal; mark; mound; nevus; pier; quay; spot; starnose; talpa; tape; taupe

MOLECULE: atom; fraction; fragment; ion; mite; monad; particle; unit; whit

MOLEST: (**see** "annoy") abuse; afflict; damage; disturb; harass; haunt; heckle; hurt; ill-treat; ill-use; injure; interfere; maltreat; meddle; misuse; persecute; raid; tamper; torment; trespass; wrong

MOLLIFY: (**see** "soften") abate; allay; ameliorate; appease; assuage; bate; calm; comfort; compose; conciliate; console; ease; flatter; forgive; gratify; hush; lessen; mitigate; moderate; pacify; placate; please; quiet(en); relax; relent; relieve; restrain; satisfy; smooth; soften; soothe; still; temper; tranquilize

MOLLUSK: bivalve; chiton; clam; conch; cuttlefish; murex; mussel; limpet; octopus; ormer; oyster; scallop; shellfish; slug; snail; whelk

MOLT: **v.** cast; change; deplume; discard; exfoliate; exuviate; shed; slough; MOLT-(ING): **n.** deplumation; ecdysis; exfoliation; exuviation; shedding

MOMENT: (**see** "instant") blink; consequence; consideration; element; flash; gravity; import(ance); jiff(y); minute; phase; point; present; sec(ond); shake; significance; stage; time; trice; twinkle; twinkling; value; weight; wink; MOMENTARY: brief; ephemeral; evanescent; flashing; fleeting; instant-(aneous); momentaneous; semelfactive; transient; transitory; MOMENTARINESS: brevity; ephemerality; instantaneity; transience; MOMENTOUS: (**see** "critical") consequential; crucial; epochal; epoch-making; eventful; important; memorable; paramount; prominent; serious; signal; significant; unparalleled; weighty

MONAD: animalcule; atom; entity; molecule; particle; protozoan; unit; univalent

MONARCH: autocrat; butterfly; chief; czar; despot; dictator; dynast; emperor; kaiser; king; potentate; queen; ruler; shah; sovereign; sultan; tsar; tzar

MONASTERY: abbey; cloister; convent; friary; hospice; lamasery; nunnery; priory; MONASTIC: **a.** ascetic; cenobian; cenobitic; conventual; monkish; oblate; reclusive; secluded; solitary; MONASTIC: **n. see** "monk"

MONEY: accounts; assets; bacon; bankroll; bills; bonds; bread; budget; bullion; cabbage; capital; cash; change; check; coin(age); coin of the realm; collateral; currency; cush; deposit; dinero; do-re-mi; dough; dust; duty; estate; exchange; exchequer; finance(s); funds; gelt; gold; greenback(s); grig; income; jack; kale; king's ransom; legal tender; lettuce; loot; lucre; mazuma; means; medium of exchange; mina; mint; moola; notes; paper; pay; pay dirt; payroll; peag(e); pocketbook; pool; possessions; pot; price; property; purse; reserve; resources; revenue; riches; roll; rouleau; script; silver; specie; spondulix; stuff; subsidy; sum; tariff; tax; tender; trash; treasure; tribute; wad; wampum; wealth; wherewithal; windfall; MONETARY: bursal; financial; numismatic(al); nummary; pecuniary; quaestuary; stipendiary; sumptuary

MONEYLESS: **see** "penniless"

MONGER: dealer; draper; mercer; merchant; seller; trader; trafficker; vender

MONGOL: Asian; Buriat; Eleut; Hu; Kalmuk; Khalkha; Shan; Sharra; Tartar; Tatar; Tungus

MONGREL: admixture; cross(breed); cur; hybrid; mixture; mulatto; mutt

MONITION: (**see** "caution") admonition; advice; counsel; hint; indication; information; instruction; intimidation; notice; order; reminder; sermon; summons; warning

MONITOR: **v.** (**see** "caution") advise; check; counsel; guard; instruct; observe; regulate; test; ward; watch; MONITOR: **n.** admonisher; adviser; bell; buzzer; counsel(or); guard; instructor; light; mentor; observer; overseer; pr(a)epositor; reminder; scout; sentinel; signal; siren; teacher; warship; watch(man)

MONK: abbé; abbot; anchoret; anchorite; ascetic; Capuchin; cenobite; dervish; eremite; fakir; Fra; friar; hermit; lama; monastic; padre; prior; recluse; solitudinarian; MONKISH: (**see** "monastic") ascetic; cenobitic

MONKEY: **v.** ape; bother; fool; meddle; mess; mimic; tamper; tinker; trifle; MONKEY: **n.** anthropoid; ape; araba; ateles; capuchin; Cebus; colobus; douc; dupe; fool; grivet; guenon; guereza; kaha; langur; macaque; machin; maha; marmoset; mona; nisnas; patas; primate; quadrumane; rhesus; saguin; sai; saimiri; sajou; saki; sapajou; simian; titi; toque; tota; vervet; vitoe; wanderoo; zati

MONOGRAM: character(s); cipher; design; identification; initials; letters; symbol

MONOLITH: colossus; column; menhir; monument; mountain; needle; obelisk; pillar; shaft; statue; stone

MONOPOLIZE: (**see** "control") absorb; combine; consume; copyright; corner; engross; franchise; incorporate; hold; own; patent; pool; possess; syndicate; MONOPOLY: (**see** "bloc") agreement; cartel; combination; combine; control; copyright; corner; exclusiveness; exclusivity; franchise; incorporation; pact; partnership; patent; pool; possession; syndicate; treaty; trust

MONOTONOUS: (**see** "dull") boresome; boring; calm; changeless; depressive; drab; drear(y); dry; flat; heavy; humdrum; irksome; jejune; long; monotone; monotonic; prosy; protracted; same; slow; stereotyped; stereotypical; sterile; tedious; tiresome; trite; undiversified; uniform; uninteresting; unrelieved; unvaried; unvarying; vacuous; wearing; wearisome; MONOTONY: aridity; barrenness; changelessness; dingdong; dryness; dullness; jejunity; sameness; sterility; tedium; uniformity; vacuity; wearisomeness

MONSTER: Argus; behemoth; brute; Caliban; Cerberus; chimera; demon; enormity; fiend; Frankenstein; ghoul; giant; Gorgon; griffin; harpy; leviathan; monstrosity; ogre; phoenix; sphinx; MONSTROUS: (**see** "huge") abnormal; absurd; atrocious; awful; colossal; deformed; dreadful; enorm(ous); flagrant; frightful; gigantic; grotesque; hateful; heinous; hideous; horrible; horrific; incredible; leviathan; loathsome; malformed; mammoth; monumental; overwhelming; prodigious; shocking; stupendous; terrible; terrifying; titanic; tremendous; uncanny; unnatural; unspeakable; vast; vile; MONSTROSITY: abortion; freak; deviation; malformation

MONTICULE: cone; hill(ock); knob; knoll; mount

MONUMENT: arch; building; cenotaph; column; dolmen; gravestone; mark(er); mausoleum; memento; memorial; menhir; model; monolith; needle; obelisk; pillar; plaque; production; pyramid; record; register; relic; reminder; scroll; shaft; shrine; slab; statue; stone; structure; tablet; testimonial; tomb; tower; work

MOOD: (**see** "air") aspect; atmosphere; attitude; aura; character; condition; conduct; constitution; degree; disposition; feather; feeling; fit; habit; humor; inclination; manner; mien; mode; note; peeve; proclivity; propensity; quality; soul; spirit; state; style; susceptibility; temper(ament); tendency; tone; vein; whim; MOODY: ambivalent; blue; broody; choleric; gloomy; hypochondriacal; malcontent; melancholy; morose; peevish; sullen; temperamental; MOODINESS: blues; choler; doldrums; dumps; gloom; hypochondriasis; malcontent; megrims; melancholia; melancholy; sullenness

MOON: **v.** dawdle; daydream; dream; fret; fuss; idle; gape; gaze; mope; ponder; roam; stare; stew; wonder; worry; MOON: **n.** crescent; Cynthia; Diana; Luna; month; Phoebe; planet; satellite

MOOR: **v.** affix; anchor; attach; berth; bind; dock; fasten; fix; lock; rivet; root; secure; tie; MOOR: **n.** Arab; anchor; Berber; berth; dock; fen; heath; Islam; march; Mohammedan; Muslim; plain; Saracen; waste

MOP: **v.** clean(se); polish; sponge; swab; trounce; wipe; MOP: **n.** dauber; grimace; hair; pout; sponge; swab; tuft

MOPE: abrade; brood; chafe; cogitate; dawdle; fret; fuss; moon; ponder; pout; sit; stew; sulk; weep; worry; vex

MORAL: **a.** accepted; allegorical; catechetic(al); categorical; chaste; conformable; correct; decent; didactic; ethical; faithful; good; high-minded; honest; honorable; imperative; intellectual; just; mental; noble; pious; principled; proper; psychological; pure; rectitudinous; religious; right(eous); tropological; true; upright; virtuous; MORAL(S): **n.** allegory; apologue; chastity; correctness; decency; epimyth; ethics; goodness; habits; honesty; honor; justice; lesson; manners; maxim; (the) moralities; morality; mores (pl.); nobility; obligation; piety; principle(s); probity; propriety; purity; rectitude; religion; righteousness; scrupulosity; standards; truth; uprightness; virtue; MORALISTIC: admonishing; catachistic(al); conventional; didactic(al); erudite; pompous; puritanical; rectitudinous; religious; sabbatarian; scrupulous; sententious; sermonic; MORALITY: **see** "morals"

MORASS: bayou; bog; difficulty; entanglement; fen; marsh; mess; mire; moor; quag(mire); slough; swamp; tangle; thicket

MORBID: (see "morose") abnormal; cachetic; cadaverous; dark; deadly; diseased; gloomy; grisly; gruesome; horrible; horrific; maladive; morbose; pathological; scrofulous; sick(ly); unhealthy; unwholesome; MORBIDITY: cachexia; disease; gloominess; gruesomeness; morbidness; nosiness; unhealthiness; unwholesomeness

MORDANT: acid; acrid; biting; burning; caustic; corrosive; crabby; cross; cutting; erosive; grouchy; gruff; incisive; keen; peevish; perverse; pungent; sarcastic; satirical; scathing; sharp; snappy; snippish; trenchant; uncivil; unsociable;

MORE: additional; again; also; anew; besides; bis; boot; else; encore; extra; further; greater; larger; older; other; plus; too

MORIBUND: cachectic; cachexic; cadaverous; comatose; dormant; dying; fey; ill; sick; unconscious

MORN(ING): A.M.; *ante meridiem*; Aurora; dawn; daybreak; east; Eos; forenoon; matin; sunrise

MORON: (see "fool") boob; dullard; dunce; half-wit; idiot; imbecile; nut; simpleton; MORONIC: brutish; dull; foolish; idiotic; imbecilic; nutty; retarded; simple; stupid

MOROSE: (see "morbid") cantankerous; churlish; crabby; cross; crusty; depressed; despairing; despondent; diseased; dour; funebrious; funereal; gloomy; glum; grouchy; gruff; grum; low; moody; mournful; peevish; perverse; pessimistic; pettish; petulant; saturnine; sick; snappish; snappy; sour; spleenful; spleeny; splenetic; sulky; sullen; surly; testy; uncivil; unsociable

MORSEL: (see "bit") bite; delicacy; fragment; nibble; ort; scrap; snack; snap; sop; taste; teaser; tidbit

MORTAL: a. awful; deadly; destructive; dire; earthly; extreme; fatal; grievous; human; implacable; lethal; overpowering; perishable; poison(ous); serious; severe; tedious; temporal; terrene; toxic; unforgivable; worldly; MORTAL: n. (see "man") being; earthling; human; individual; person

MORTAR: bowl; cannon; cap; cement; compo; grout; gun; mud; plaster; vessel

MORTGAGE: v. hypothecate; impignorate; pledge; MORTGAGE: n. deed of trust; hypothecation; lien; loan; obligation; pledge; trust

MORTIFY: (see "embarrass") abase; abash; deaden; decay; deny; destroy; humble; humiliate; macerate; oppress; punish; subdue; torment; vex; MORTIFICATION: abstinence; chagrin; death; decay; destruction; embarrassment; gangrene; humiliation; necrosis; oppression; penance; putrefaction; putrescence; putridity; torment; vexation

MORTISE: v. fasten; join; MORTISE: n. cavity; groove; hole; joint; notch; slot; tenon

MORTUARY: cemetery; charnel; cinerarium; graveyard; morgue; necropolis; ossarium

MOSAIC: (see "variegate" and "variegation") chimera; design; tiles

MOSS: bog; fungus; lichen; Musci; peat; seaweed; usnea

MOSSBACK: (see "conservative") dodo; fogy; reactionary; rustic

MOTH(S): egger; Heterocera; insect; Io; lepidopter; Lepidoptera; miller; muga; sphinx; tinean; tussah; yucca

MOTHER: v. care; cherish; feed; foster; house; nurse; nurture; protect; suckle; tend; wetnurse; MOTHER: n. abbess; amma; ancestress; dam; genetrices (pl.); genetrix; mamma; mater; narive; nurturer; prototype; original; parent; source; vernacular; MOTHERLY: maternal(istic); matronly; MOTHERLESS: orphaned; unmothered

MOTIF: (see "design") arrangement; idea; influence; motive; note; stimulus; theme

MOTION: act(ion); activity; aestus; agitation; application; carriage; change; clip; course; current; drift; estus; flux; gait; gesture; greeting; impetus; mechanism; motility; move(ment); operation; oscillation; pace; passage; procedure; process; progress; proposal; rate; request; shake; shaking; signal; speed; step; stimulus; stream; stride; suggestion; sway; tempo; tendency; tide; transit(ion); trend; velocity; volitation; wave

MOTIONLESS: (see "calm") dead; dormant; fixed; immobile; impassive; inert; moribund; quiescent; quiet; serene; sessile; stagnant; stale; standing; stationary; still; torpid; unmoving

MOTIVATE: (see "move") actuate; arouse; catalyze; cause; drive; force; goad; impel; incite; induce; influence; inspire; interest; necessitate; orchestrate; prompt; provoke; start; stimulate; stir; urge; MOTIVATION: (see "drive") actuation; arousal; cause; force; impulse; incitation; incitement; inducement; influence; inspiration; provocation; stimulation; stimulus; stir; urge; urging

MOTIVE: (see "aim") ambition; cause; consideration; design; desire; determinant; determination; directive; end; fillip; force; goad; ground; idea; impetus; impulse; incentive; incitement; inducement; influence; instigation; intendment; intention; motif; motivation; mover; necessity; need; object-(ive); pretext; principle; provocation; purpose; reason; regard; spring; spur; stimulation; stimulus; subject; theme; wish

MOTLEY: (see "assorted") diverse; heterogeneous; parti-colored; piebald; variegated

MOTTLED: blotched; dappled; diverse; harlequin; marbled; motley; parti-colored; piebald; pied; pinto; speckled; spotted; variegated

MOTTO: adage; aphorism; apothegm; axiom; *bon mot*; epigram; epigraph; gnome; maxim; mot; proverb; reason; saw; saying; slogan; suggestion; thought; truism; witticism

MOULD: see "mold"

MOULT: see "molt"

MOUND: bank; barrow; bulwark; cumulus; defense; dune; earthwork; elevation; embankment; eminence; fortification; heap; hill(ock); hummock; hump; knob; knoll; mole; monticle; morro; parapet; pile; rampart; rise; scarp; step; tee; tump; tumulus

MOUNT: v. advance; arrange; ascend; augment; bestride; climb; elevate; exhibit; fasten; fix; frame; grow; increase; intensify; kindle; launch; pace; place; position; rise; rouse; scale; set; soar; straddle; stuff; surge; swell; total; tower; MOUNT: n. (see "mound" and "mountain") alp; carriage; chassis; foundation; frame(work); hill; horse; peak; rise; seat; steed; support; undercarriage

MOUNTAIN: alp; butte; crisis; elevation; Everest; heap; heights; hill; hunk; lots; mass; massif; mesa; monolith; mount; obstacle; peak; pile; quantity; slew; summit; tor; MOUNTAINOUS: (see "huge") alpestrine; gigantic; hilly; mountainy; rocky

MOUNTEBANK: (see "faker") charlatan; cheat(er); empiric; entertainer; fraud; hawker; imposter; pitchman; pretender; quack-(salver); rascal; rogue; swindler; trickster

MOURN: (see "cry") bemoan; bewail; complain; deplore; fret; grieve; groan; keen; lament; languish; moan; protest; regret; repine; rue; sigh; sorrow; wail; weep; MOURNFUL: (see "sad") deplorable; depressed; depressing; dire(ful); dismal; dispirited; distressing; doleful; funereal; lamentable; luctiferous; lugubrious; melancholy; moanful; penitent; pensive; pitiful; plaintive; regretful; regrettable; saddened; sorrowful; sorry; threnodic; wistful; woeful; yearnful; MOURNFULNESS: (see "sadness") depression; lamentation; lugubriosity; sorrow; woe

MOUSE: bruise; ecchymosis; mur; Mus; rodent; swelling; vole; weight; MOUSE-LIKE: bashful; mousy; murine; retiring; shy

MOUTH: v. declaim; grimace; mumble; promote; promulgate; pronounce; rail; recite; speak; talk; tell; utter; verbalize; voice; MOUTH: n. bucca; buccal cavity; cavity; conversation; entrance; grimace; hatch; impudence; inlet; lip; mun; muzzle; opening; ora (pl.); orifice; os; rictus; speech; stoma; trap; voice; volubility

MOVE: v. (see "drive") abandon; act(ivate); actuate; advance; affect; agitate; animate; arouse; arrange; bridge; budge; bustle; carry; cause; change; compel; contrive; control; create; dart; depart; direct; dislodge; draw; drift; edge; effect; egg; emigrate; engulf; enkindle; enliven; excite; fashion; fire; flit; flurry; force; forge; glide; go; goad; guide; hop; hurry; hustle; impel; impress; inch; incite; induce; influence; inspire; inspirit; instigate; jump; kindle; leave; lodge; lunge; manipulate; march; migrate; motivate; navigate; operate; pace; penetrate; persuade; play; plod; plow; proceed; progress; prompt; propel; propose; provoke; quiver; recede; relocate; rouse; run; shake; shape; sharpen; shift; ship; speed; spur; stimulate; stir; stray; succeed; transfer; travel; traverse; undertake; urge; walk; wander; whip; withdraw; work; wrest; MOVE: n. (see "movement") abandonment; act(uation); action; advance-(ment); agitation; animation; bustle; carry-

(ing); change; charge; *démarche*; departure; drive; emigration; enlivenment; flit(ter); flurry; glide; goad; going; hop; inducement; instigation; jump; lunge; maneuver; migration; motion; motivation; navigation; operation; pace; persuasion; play; proceeding; proposal; relocation; run; shift; spur; step; stimulation; stir; transplantation; turn; walk; MOVING: actuating; affecting; astir; exciting; forceful; impellent; impelling; impressive; influencing; mobile; motile; nomadic; passionate; pathetic; persuading; pitiful; poignant; rousing; sad; stirring; tender; touching; MOVABILITY: flexibility; maneuverability; mobility; plasticity; MOVABLE: floating; flowing; fluid; inconstant; maneuverable; mobile; motile; shifting; unstable; unsteady; MOVER: accelerator; activator; actuator; catalyst; gadfly; stimulant

MOVEMENT: (see "drive") act(ion); activity; advance(ment); agitation; animation; application; arousal; automation; bandwagon; bustle; change; clearance; crusade; dart(ing); *démarche*; drive; dynamism; effect; emigration; enterprise; evolution; flit(ter); flittering; flow; flurry; ground swell; hurry; hustle; hustling; impetus; impulse; inclination; instigation; locomotion; lunge; maneuver; march; migration; momentum; motion; navigation; operation; parade; passage; play; proceeding; procession; progress(ion); proposal; rhythm; shift; side; speed; start; step; stimulation; stir; stride; stroke; sweep; tempo; tendency; theme; time; transit(ion); travel; trend; undertaking; velocity; wave; way; work

MUCH: (see "abundant") abundance; almost; considerable; gob(s); good; great; heap(s); lot(s); many; plenty; quantity

MUD: depth; dirt; dregs; libel; mire; mush; ooze; silt; slander; slime; sludge; sullage; MUDDY: besmeared; cloudy; confused; dark; dejected; dirty; dull; foul; gloomy; indistinct; miry; moist; muddled; murky; obscure; oozy; slaky; slimy; soiled; turbid; unclean; vague

MUDDLE: v. addle; becloud; befog; befuddle; bemuse; blunder; botch; bungle; cloud; confound; confuse; derange; disarrange; discompose; distort; faze; ferment; flounder; fluster; fog; foul; fuddle; intoxicate; jumble; mess; mix; muddy; mull; mumble; muss; puzzle; roil; squander; stir; stupefy; tangle; upset; waste; MUDDLE: n. botch; chaos; cloud; complexity; confusion; derangement;

dilemma; disarrangement; disturbance; ferment; fog; hodgepodge; jumble; maze; mess; mistake; mix(-up); muss; snafu; soss; stir; tangle; turmoil; uncleanliness; vacuity

MUFFLE: blindfold; conceal; cover; cushion; deaden; disguise; drape; dull; envelope; mute; pad; protect; shroud; silence; soft-pedal; stifle; suppress

MUG: blockhead; container; cup; face; fool; grimace; nog(gin); photo(graph); pot; puss; stein; toby; visage

MUHAMMADAN: see "Mohammedan"

MULCH: cover(ing); litter; manure; protection; sawdust; straw

MULCT: (see "cheat") amerce; bleed; fine; forfeit; milk; punish; steal; swindle

MULL: v. (see "think") bustle; cogitate; crumble; dawdle; err; grind; meditate; mess; moon; mope; muddle; ponder; pulverize; stew; stir; sweeten; worry; MULL: n. cloth; fabric; humus; muslin; spice; steatin

MULTIPLICITY: (see "variety") manyness; manysidedness; multeity

MULTIPLY: amplify; augment; breed; burgeon; enhance; escalate; expand; increase; manifold; proliferate; propagate; pullulate; reproduce; spread; snowball

MULTITUDE: (see "group") agglomeration; agglutination; army; array; assemblage; assembly; collection; concourse; congregation; crowd; galaxy; gathering; herd; horde; host; humanity; kingdom; legion; life; manifold; mankind; mass; mob; multeity; multiplicity; myriad; number; numerousness; pack; people; populace; population; press; proletariat; public; rabble; rout; ruck; shoal; society; swarm; throng; tumult; world

MUMBO JUMBO: bugaboo; confusion; demon; fetish; gibberish; idol; incantation; jargon; mummery

MUNDANE: (see "worldly") carnal; cosmic; earthly; human; laic; mortal; secular; temporal; terrene; terrestrial

MUNICIPAL: city; civic; civil; internal; local; narrow; parochial; political; town; villagic

MUNIFICENT: see "lavish"

MUNIMENT(S): archive; arms; deed; defense; matériel; munitions; record; support; weapon(ry)

MURDER: **v.** (**see** "kill") assassinate; butcher; destroy; execute; finish; harass; mangle; mar; massacre; ruin; slaughter; slay; spoil; tease; torment; MURDER: **n.** assassination; burke; butchery; destruction; execution; homicide; killing; massacre; slaughter; MURDEROUS: (**see** "cruel") bloodthirsty; brutal; cutthroat; dangerous; deadly; destructive; devastating; difficult; dire; fell; fey; gory; homicidal; malefic; malevolent; sanguinary; savage

MURK(INESS): cloudiness; darkness; dismality; dusk; fogginess; fuliginosity; gloom; lowering; obscurity; overcast; turbidity; MURKY: clouded; cloudy; dark; dismal; dull; dusky; foggy; fuliginous; gloomy; misty; obscure(d); overcast; turbid

MURMUR: **v.** (**see** "complain") coo; cry; fret; groan; grumble; hum; lament; mumble; mutter; protest; purr; repine; susurrate; whimper; MURMUR: **n.** (**see** "complaint") cry; groan; grumble; grumbling; hum; lamentation; mumble; muttering; protest-(ation); purr; rumor; susurration; susurrus; undertone; whimper; whisper; MURMURING: low; mormorando; murmurous; purling; purring; susurrant; susurrous

MUSCLE: biceps; brawn; flesh; force; huskiness; musculature; necessity; power; sinew-(s); strength; thew(s); MUSCULAR: (**see** "strong") athletic; brawny; burly; fleshy; forceful; hale; hardy; hearty; Herculean; husky; lusty; mighty; powerful; sinewy; sound; stalwart; stout; strenuous; thewy; vigorous

MUSE: (**see** "think") cogitate; consider; contemplate; deliberate; dream; lucubrate; meditate; moon; mope; mull; ponder; reason; reflect; ruminate; speculate; study; weigh

MUSHROOM: **v.** boom; expand; explode; grow; inflate; multiply; spread; spring (up); MUSHROOM: **n.** agaric; boletus; boom; cepe; champignon; fungus; misy; morel; parvenu; toadstool; umbrella; upstart

MUSH: **v.** crumble; crush; journey; march; travel; trek; walk; MUSH: **n.** atole; drivel; flattery; journey; march; meal; pap; por-

ridge; pudding; sagamité; sentimentality; supawn; MUSHY: gooey; maudlin; mawkish; sentimental; sluggish; soft; soggy; spongy; thick; yielding

MUSIC: agreement; air; aria; art; assonance; concert; concord; euphony; harmonization; harmony; lilt; madrigal; march; melisma; melody; minstrelsy; motet; orchestra(tion); resonance; rhythm; scherzo; score; sonance; song; sonority; sonorization; symphony; syncopation; syntonization; theme; timbre; tones; tune; MUSICAL: aeolian; assonant; canorous; dulcet; euphonic; euphonious; harmonious; lyric(al); melic; melodic; melodious; orchestral; orotund; pleasing; resonant; sonoriferous; sonorous; sweet; symphonic; symphonious; tonal; tuneful; unisonant

MUSS: **v.** confuse; disarrange; dishevel; disorder; litter; rumple; wrinkle; MUSS: **n.** brawl; chaos; commotion; confusion; disarrangement; dishevelment; disorder; disturbance; fight; litter; mess; mix-up; muddle; row; squabble; wrinkle

MUST: **a.** or **adv.** essential; obliged; ought; necessary; required; shall; should; MUST: **n.** essential; fustiness; mildew; mold; necessity; need; obligation; prerequisite; requirement; requisite; sapa; stum; wine

MUSTER: accumulate; array; assemble; collect; comprise; congregate; convene; develop; display; enlist; enroll; exhibit; find; for(e)gather; gather; include; invoke; levy; marshal; number; order; rally; show; summon

MUSTY: antiquated; apathetic; bad; dull; fetid; foggish; foul; frowsy; fusty; hackneyed; hoary; listless; mildewed; mo(u)ldy; old; rancid; spiritless; spoiled; stale; superannuated

MUTATE: alter; change; modify; vary; MUTABLE: (**see** "plastic") alterable; ambivalent; changeable; erratic; fickle; fitful; inconstant; mercurial; quicksilver; unsettled; unstable; unsteady; vacillating; variable; MUTATION: albino; alteration; change; freak; modification; mutant; sport; umlaut

MUTE: **v.** cushion; deaden; muffle; pad; reduce; shroud; silence; subdue; MUTE: **a.** aphonic; calm; deadened; dull; dumb; inarticulate; lene; mum; muted; noiseless; quiet; silent; sourdine; speechless; still; taciturn; uncommunicative; unexpressed;

unpronounced; unspoken; unvocal; voiceless; wordless; MUTENESS: inarticulateness; obmutescence; silence; voicelessness; wordlessness

MUTILATE: alter; batter; cripple; cut; damage; deface; deform; delete; destroy; disable; disfigure; dismember; expunge; garble; geld; hack; hamstring; harm; hurt; impair; injure; lame; maim; mangle; mar; massacre; mayhem; scar; tear; wound; wreck; MUTILATION: alteration; damage; defacement; deformity; destruction; freak; harm; hurt; injury; mayhem; scar; tear; wound; wreck

MUTINY: coup; insubordination; insurgence; insurgency; insurrection; lawlessness; mutinousness; nonconformance; noncooperation; putsch; rebellion; revolt; riot; sedition; strife; treason; tumult; uprising; MUTINOUS: see "lawless" and "riotous"

MUTTER: (see "complain") growl; grumble; moan; mumble; murmur; whimper; whisper

MUTUAL: alternate; alternating; analogous; coincident(al); common; complementary; convertible; cooperating; correlative; corresponding; equal; equivalent; even; homogenous; identical; interchangeable; interdependent; interrelated; joint; like; reciprocal; reciprocative; reciprocatory; same; shared; similar; sinalagmatic; synallagmatic; synchronous; unanimous; unisonant

MUZZLE: v. (see "restrain") censure; check; choke; circumscribe; confine; cope; gag; maul; nuzzle; prevent; repress; restrict; silence; trammel; MUZZLE: n. (see "restraint") censure; check; choking; circumscription; clevis; gag; nose; repression; restriction; silence; snout

MUZZY: (see "confused") befuddled; blurred; dazed; depressing; dull; fuzzy; muddled; stupid; tipsy

MYOPIC: blurred; dim; faint; illiberal; nearsighted; purblind; shortsighted

MYRIAD: a. or n. (see "many") innumerable; legion; lots; multitude; multitudinous

MYSTERY: arcanum; charm; conundrum; craft; curiosity; doctrine; enigma; esotery; glamo(u)r; incomprehensibility; novel; oracularity; paradoxicality; perplexity; play; problem; puzzle; riddle; rite; romance; rune; secret; story; weirdness; MYSTERIOUS *or* MYSTIC(AL): abstruse; anagogical; arcane; ascetic; baffling; cabalistic; clandestine; confidential; cryptic(al); concealed; covert; dark; deep; devious; eerie; eery; elliptic(al); enigmatic(al); epoptic; esoteric; exotic; extraphysical; glamorous; hermetic(al); hidden; impenetrable; inaccessible; incomprehensible; incredible; inexplicable; inscrutable; latent; magical; mysterial; obscure; occult; oracular; Orphean; orphic; paradoxic(al); picturesque; preternatural; private; profound; puzzling; rare; recondite; romantic; runic; secret; sibylline; spiritual; strange; stratospheric(al); supernatural; surreptitious; symbolic(al); telestic; tenebrific; tenebrious; unaccountable; unanalyzable; uncanny; unfathomable; unfathomed; unintelligible; unknown; unrevealed; unsearchable; unsolvable; unusual; vague; weird; MYSTERIOUSNESS: incomprehensibility; inscrutability; mysticality

MYSTIFY: (see "confuse") baffle; befog; bewilder; faze; hoax; mysticize; obfuscate; perplex; puzzle; rattle; riddle; upset

MYTH: allegory; anecdote; fable; fabulosity; fiction; folklore; folktale; imagination; invention; legend; mythology; parable; saga; story; tradition; MYTHICAL: allegorical; anecdotal; apocryphal; arcane; bizarre; fabricated; fabular; fabulous; fantastic; fictional; fictitious; imaginary; imagined; invented; legendary; parabolical; traditional; tralatitious; visionary

N

NAB: (see "catch") apprehend; cop; nail

NABOB: Brahmin; Croesus; deputy; Dives; doyen; governor; *homme de fortune*; Midas; mogul; plutocrat; tycoon; viceroy

NAG: **v.** (see "annoy") badger; bug; disturb; harass; hector; henpeck; oppress; plague; remind; ride; scold; taunt; tease; torment; twit; urge; NAG: **n.** garran; garron; horse; plug; pony; rosinante

NAIL: **v.** (see "catch") arrest; attach; clench; clinch; cop; drive; fasten; fix; get; identify; kill; nab; peg; secure; seize; snatch; steal; trap; unite; NAIL: **n.** boss; brad; claw; hoof; pin; plate; scale; spad; spike; stud; tack; talon; ungual; unguis

NAÏVE: artless; candid; childlike; credulous; dewy-eyed; frank; fresh; green; guileless; gullible; imprudent; inexperienced; ingenuous; innocent; meek; natural; open; plain; quaint; simple; spontaneous; trustful; unaffected; unfeigned; unphilosophic; unsophisticated; unsubtle; unsuspecting; unsuspicious; unwary; NAÏVETÉ: artlessness; credulity; gullibility; inexperience; ingenuosity; ingenuousness; naïveness; naïvety; simplicity; spontaneity; unsophistication

NAKED: (see "undressed") *a nu*; *au naturel*; bald; bare; barren; blate; clear; crude; defenseless; denudate(d); denuded; deprived; *déshabillé*; destitute; divested; *en déshabillé*; evident; exact; exposed; in nature's garb; in one's morocco; *in puris naturalibus*; literal; manifest; meager; mere; nude; obvious; open; plain; raw; *sans vêtements*; scanty; simple; sheer; sky-clad; stark; stripped; *tout nu*; unappareled; unarmed; unattired; unclad; unclothed; unconcealed; uncovered; undiluted; undraped; underclothed; underdressed; undisguised; unembellished; ungarmented; unprotected; NAKEDNESS: Adamitism; deshabille; dishabille; nudism; nudity; undress

NAMBY-PAMBY: childlike; childish; coddled; conciliatory; feeble; inane; insipid; pantywaist; sentimental; silly; soft; trifling; vapid; weak

NAME: **v.** announce; appoint; assign; baptise; brand; call; characterize; choose; christen; cite; clepe; command; declare; define; delegate; denominate; denote; describe; design(ate); dictate; dub; earmark; elect; entitle; enumerate; establish; express; fix; identify; indicate; induct; inform; introduce; label; mark; mention; nominate; ordain; pick; quote; reveal; schedule; select; set; signify; specify; state; stipulate; style; suggest; tap; term; title; y-clept; NAME: **n.** agnomen; alias; allonym; antonomasia; appellation; appellative; autograph; brand; byname; byword; caconym; character; citation; clan; cognomen; cognomination; cryptonym; curse; definition; denomination; denotation; description; designation; distinction; entitlement; enumeration; epithet; eponym; fame; family; handle; honor-(ific); hypocorism; hypocoristic; identification; incognito; indication; label; mark; matronym(ic); metonymy; metronymic; moniker; *nom*; *nom de guerre*; *nom de plume*; nomen(clature); nomination; noun; onym; patronym(ic); praenomen; pseudonym; race; reputation; repute; rubric; sign(ature); sobriquet; specification; style; surname; synecdoche; tag; term; title; word; NAMELESS: alias; anonymous; bastard; horrible; incognita (fem.); incognito; indescribable; ineffable; inexpressible; innominate; obscure; pseudo; repulsive; unacknowledged; unknown; unmentionable; unnameable; unnamed; unspeakable; NAMELESSNESS: anonymity; obscurity

NAMELY: *c'est-à-dire*; i.e.; particularly; scilicet (*abb.* scil.); videlicet (*abb.* viz.)

NAP: **v.** doze; drowse; nod; rest; sleep; NAP: **n.** cover; doze; drowse; fuzz; pile; *ras*; rest; siesta; sleep; slumber; snooze; wink

NAPE: mane; neck; niddick; nucha; scruff; scrag; turnip

NAPKIN: cloth; compress; diaper; doily; serviette; towel

NARCOTIC: **a.** anesthetic; anodynic; comatose; hypnotic; insensible; narcoleptic; nepenthean; sleepy; somniferous; soothing; soporiferous; stupefactive; stuporous; torporific; unconscious; NARCOTIC: **n.** anesthetic; anodyne; bhang; codeine; dope; drug; ether; hemp; heroin; hop; hypnotic; junk; marihuana; morphine; nepenthe; opiate; opium; reefer; sedative; somnifacient; soporific; stupefacient; tea; NARCOSIS: anesthesia; coma; hypnosis; insensibility; narcolepsy; sleep; stupefaction; stupor; torpor; unconsciousness

NARK: **v.** annoy; inform; irritate; note; observe; tease; NARK: **n.** informer; spoilsport; spy; stool pigeon

NARRATE: bruit; chronicle; depict; describe; detail; disclose; enunciate; paint; picture; portray; proclaim; recite; recount; rehearse; relate; reveal; say; tell; unfold; NARRATIVE *or* NARRATION: (**see** "story") account; chronicle; conte; description; fable; history; iliad; novel; odyssey; recital; report; saga; statement; tale; talk; treatise

NARROW: **v.** choke; circumscribe; compress; confine; constrict; contract; decrease; eliminate; lessen; limit; prejudice; reduce; restrict; shrink; NARROW: **a.** biased; bigoted; circumscribed; close; compressed; compressive; condensed; confined; confining; constricted; contracted; decreased; denominational; dogmatic; emaciated; exiguous; hidebound; illiberal; incapacious; incommodious; insular; insulated; isolated; lean; limited; lineal; little; local; meager; municipal; parochial; pedantic; peninsular; petty; prejudiced; provincial; regional; religiose; restricted; right; sanctimonious; scant(y); sectarian; sharp; shrunk(en); small; stenotic; straight; strict; vicinal

NARROW-MINDED: (**see** "narrow") biased; bigoted; *borné*; denominational; dogmatic; illiberal; insular; isolated; little; municipal; parochial; pedantic; peninsular; petty; prejudiced; provincial; sectarian; shallow; strict

NASCENT: (**see** "beginning") aborning; forming; new(born); NASCENCY: (**see** "beginning") birth; genesis; origin(ation)

NASTY: (**see** "dirty") dangerous; defiled; difficult; disgusting; disturbing; excremental; excrement(iti)ous; fecal; feculent; fetid; filthy; foul; grimy; gross; harmful; hazardous; ill-bred; ill-tempered; impetiginous; indecent; indelicate; loathsome; lousy; malicious; mean; mephitic; nauseous; oafish; obscene; odious; offensive; ordurous; polluted; putrescent; putrid; ratty; reptilian; repulsive; ribald; saprogenic; slimy; sluttish; smutty; snide; squalid; stercoraceous; threatening; troublesome; unclean; uncomfortable; unpleasant; vexatious; vile

NATION: commonwealth; country; democracy; empire; government; kingdom; people(s); populace; population; power; public; race; realm; republic; society; state(hood); tribe; NATIONAL: **see** "public" and "citizen;" NATIONALITY: (**see** "race") flag; independence; nationalism; peoples

NATIVE: **a.** aboriginal; autochthonal; autochthonic; autochthonous; born; demotic; domestic; edaphic; enchorial; endemial; endemic(al); free; habitual; inborn; inbred; indigene; indigenous; inherent; inherited; innate; inner; local; natal; natural; normal; original; primeval; primitive; pristine; simple; spontaneous; unadorned; unaffected; unborrowed; wild; NATIVE: **n.** (**see** "citizen") aboriginal; aborigine; autochthonon; daughter; denizen; domestic; indigene; inhabitant; ite; *les aborigènes*; national; primitive; savage; son

NATTY: (**see** "neat") chic; dapper; foppish; jaunty; nifty; posh; smart; *soigné*; *soignée* (fem.); spruce; tidy; trig; trim

NATURAL: actual; artless; candid; casual; comfortable; congenital; direct; easy; elemental; endogenous; essential; fundamental; genetic; genuine; God-given; hereditary; homely; implanted; inartificial; inborn; indigenous; ingenuous; ingrained; inherent; inherited; innate; innative; inner; instinctive; intrinsic; legitimate; lifelike; naïve; native; normal; physical; plain; primitive; probable; raw; real(istic); regular; simple; sincere; spontaneous; straightforward; true; unaffected; unartificial; unborrowed; uncultivated; unfeigned; unlearned; unposed; unpremeditated; unregenerate; unretouched; unsophisticated; unstudied; untaught; untouched; warm; wild; NATURALNESS: (**see** "sincerity") ease; geniality; genuineness; humility; nativeness; nativity; naturality; nature; spontaneity; unsophistication; warmth

NATURALIZE: acclimate; acclimatize; accustom; adapt; adopt; conform; cultivate; domesticate; domesticize; familiarize; habituate; inure; receive; tame; NATURALIZED: acclimated; accustomed; adapted; adopted; domesticated; familiarized; habituated; heterochthonous; inured; tamed

NATURE: (see "character") aspect; bent; cast; characteristic; clay; color; constitution; development; disposition; entity; essence; fabric; feather; feeling; figure; force; form; function; *gestalt*; honor; humor; ilk; inclination; kidney; kind; life; mode; mood; naturalness; outdoors; pattern; physics; predilection; proclivity; propensity; property; quality; quintessence; ratio; reality; science; shape; sort; species; stamp; state; stripe; substance; temper(ament); tenor; texture; type; universe; world

NAUSEA: disgust; dizziness; illness; loathing; paleness; pall; qualm; queasiness; revulsion; sickness; vertigo; vomiting; NAUSEOUS *or* NAUSEATING: abominable; bilious; disgusting; dizzy; fulsome; loathsome; *nauséeux*; offensive; qualmish; repugnant; repulsive; revolting; sickening; squeamish; vertiginous; vestibular; vomiting

NAUTICAL *or* NAVAL: aquatic; marine; maritime; navigational; oceanic; seafaring; seagoing

NAVE: center; core; hub

NAVEL: center; middle; omphalos; omphalus; umbilicus

NAVIGATE: aviate; conduct; contrive; control; course; cruise; direct; go; govern; guide; journey; keel; manage; move; operate; perambulate; pilot; sail; steer; traverse; voyage; walk

NEAR: **v.** approach; approximate; match; touch; NEAR(LY): **a.** or **adv.** about; abutting; adjacent; adjoining; akin; almost; anent; approaching; approximate; at; beside; bordering; by; caged; close; close-at-hand; closefisted; close on; closish; coming; communicating; compact; confined; confining; congested; contiguous; dear; dense; direct; handy; immediate; imminent; impending; intimate; jacent; joining; kin; matching; narrow; near-at-hand; nearish; nearmost; neck-and-neck; neighboring; next; nigh; nip and tuck; parsimonious; penned; propinquant; propinquitous; proximate; recent; resembling; restricted; secluded; short;

stingy; stuffy; sultry; thereabouts; thick; tight; touching; within; NEARNESS: adjacency; appropinquity; approximation; closeness; communion; contiguity; frugality; immediacy; intimacy; kinship; nighness; propinquity; shouting distance; togetherness

NEAT: adroit; bright; chic; chipper; clean; clever; concinnate; concinnous; correct; dainty; dapper; elegant; exact; fastidious; free; groomed; immaculate; ingenious; jaunty; modish; natty; nice; nifty; orderly; plain; posh; precise; prim; proper; proportional; regular; shapely; shining; shipshape; smart; snug; *soigné*; *soignée* (fem.); spic-and-span; spotless; spruce; suitable; systematic; tidy; tosh; trig; trim; uncluttered; undiluted; uniform; well-groomed; NEATNESS: concinnity; elegance; fastidiousness; precision; simplicity; uniformity

NEBULOUS: (see "cloudy") diaphanous; dreamlike; dreamy; foggy; frail; fuliginous; hazy; indefinite; indistinct; misty; nebular; obscure; shadowy; turbid; uncertain; unclear; vague; vaporous; volatile; wispy

NECESSARY: behooving; binding; cardinal; coercing; coercive; compelled; compelling; compulsory; constrained; determined; due; entailed; essential; eventual; evident; exigent; expedient; fixed; forced; impelled; impellent; impelling; imperative; incumbent; indispensable; inescapable; inevitable; inexorable; infallible; mandatory; needed; needful; obligated; obligatory; obliged; peremptory; perquisite; pressing; required; requisite; significant; unavoidable; undeniable; unpreventable; urgent; vital; NECESSITATE: behoove; bind; cause; coerce; compel; constrain; dragoon; entail; force; impel; involve; need; oblige; preempt; require; NECESSITY: coercion; compulsion; condition precedent; constraint; desideration; desideratum; destiny; distress; emergency; essential(ity); exigency; expediency; extremity; fate; force; foreordination; hunger; imperative; indigency; indispensability; inevitableness; mandate; muscle; must; need(fulness); obligation; onus; penury; poverty; preliminary; prerequisite; privation; requirement; requisite; *sine qua non*; starvation; unavoidability; urgency; want; NECESSARILY: eventually; inevitably; perforce; unavoidably

NECK: cervix; collar; collet; collum; isthmus; nape; nucha; scruff; strait; swire

NECKLACE: baldric; beads; chain; choker;

collar; hiaqua; lavalier(e); pearls; rivière; rope; rosary; torque

NECKTIE: ascot; bandana; bow; four-in-hand; scarf; tie

NECROMANCY: conjuration; diablerie; goety; magic; sorcery; thaumaturgy; witchcraft; witchery; NECROMANCER: conjurer; diviner; enchanter; exorcist; magician; soothsayer; sorcerer; thaumaturge; warlock; witch; wizard

NECTAR: ambrosia; amrita; drink; elixir; honey; manna; wine; NECTAR(E)OUS: (**see** "delicious") ambrosial; fragrant; honeyed; savory; sweet

NEED: **v.** crave; desire; lack; necessitate; require; want; wish; NEED(S): **n.** (**see** "necessity") compulsion; craving; dearth; defect; deficiency; demand; deprivation; desiderata (pl.); desideria (pl.); desiderium; destitution; distress; drive; drought; emergency; emptiness; essential(s); essentiality; exigency; extremity; famine; hunger; imperative; inadequacy; indigence; indigency; indispensability; insufficiency; lack; *manque*; misery; must; necessity; obligation; occasion; paucity; penury; pinch; poverty; prerequisite; pressure; privation; requirement; requisite; scarcity; shortage; starvation; strait(s); urgency; vaccuum; void; want; wish; NEEDY: desiderative; desperate; destitute; indigent; insolvent; lacking; necessitous; penurious; pinched; poor; pressing; urgent; wanting

NEEDLE: **v.** embroider; gibe; goad; heckle; hound; incite; irritate; pierce; puncture; ride; sew; spike; strengthen; vex; NEEDLE: **n.** acus; bodkin; eyelet; hand; indicator; obelisk; pointer

NEEDLESS: elective; gratuitous; optional; superfluous; unessential; unnecessary; unobligated; unobliged

NEEDY: **see** under "need"

NEFARIOUS: (**see** "immoral" and "wicked") detestable; evil; iniquitous; vicious

NEGATE: abrogate; annul; avow; cancel; contradict; controvert; deny; disavow; disprove; negative; neutralize; nullify; recant; refute; reject; revoke; veto; NEGATION: abrogation; annihilation; cancellation; contraindication; denial; denigration; disclaimer; negative; never; no; nonentity; nonexistence;

nullification; nullity; *nyet;* obliteration; recantation; refutation; rejection; revocation; veto

NEGATIVE: **v.** (**see** "negate") NEGATIVE: **a.** blank; negatory; neutral; privative; NEGATIVE: **n.** blank; contraindication; denial; film; nae; nay; neutral; nope; nor; not; nullification; privative; refusal; X-ray

NEGLECT: **v.** default; defer; despise; disregard; disrespect; evade; fail; forbear; forget; hang; ignore; leave; misprize; omit; overlook; pigeonhole; pretermit; procrastinate; scorn; shirk; slight; spurn; unfulfill; NEGLECT: **n.** (**see** "negligence") abandonment; absorption; abstraction; carelessness; debt; default; delinquency; dereliction; disregard; disrespect; dormancy; evasion; failure; heedlessness; ignoration; inadvertence; inattention; indifference; indolence; laches; laxity; limbo; malfeasance; misfeasance; miss; noninterference; nonobservance; nonperformance; oblivion; omission; oversight; preoccupation; pretermission; procrastination; remission; remissness; scorn; slackness; slight; thoughtlessness; unfulfillment; NEGLECTED: (**see** "dilapidated") bypassed; unheeded; NEGLECTFUL: (**see** "careless") carefree; *dégagé*; derelict; disused; heedless; inattentive; incautious; jaunty; lax; neglected; negligent; obsolete; reckless; remiss; slack; thoughtless; unattended; untended; unvisited; unwatched

NEGLIGENT: (**see** "careless") delinquent; discinct; forgetful; heedless; improvident; imprudent; inadvertent; inattentive; indifferent; irreparable; lax; loose; neglectful; nonchalant; oblivial; oblivious; offhand; reckless; remiss; slack; thoughtless; uncaring; unheedful; unmindful; unnoticed; unstudied; NEGLIGENCE: (**see** "neglect") default; delinquency; disregard; ignoration; improvidence; imprudence; inadvertency; inattention; indifference; laches; laxity; malfeasance; nonchalance; nonobservance; omission; remission; thoughtlessness

NEGOTIATE: (**see** "bargain" and "deal") accomplish; advise; arrange; assign; barter; communicate; compromise; conclude; conduct; confer; consult; contract; dicker; direct; discuss; float; handle; manage; mediate; meet; parley; practice; sell; settle; trade; traffic; transact; transfer; treat

NEIGHBORHOOD: (**see** "area") alentours; association; community; confines; district; environment; environ(s); fief; habitat;

haunt; locale; locality; milieu; parish; precinct; propinquity; proximity; purlieu(s); region; section; suburb(s); venue; vicinage; vicinity; way; NEIGHBORING: accolent; adjacent; attingent; bordering; contiguous; limitrophe; nearby; propinquant; tangent-(ial); vicinal; NEIGHBORLY: (**see** "friendly") amicable; gregarious

NEMESIS: agent; avenger; comeuppance; fate; inevitability; justice; opponent; penalty; retaliation; retribution; rival

NEOPHYTE: (**see** "beginner") catechumen; conscript; convert; cub; neoteric; novice; proselyte; pup; recruit; student; trainee; tyro

NEOTERIC: (**see** "beginner") fresh; late; modern; new; novel; recent

NERVE: (**see** "boldness") audacity; brass-(iness); center; cheek(iness) coolness; courage(ousness); crust; daring; effrontery; endurance; energy; face; fortitude; gall; grit; gut(s); hardihood; heart; impudence; intrepidity; mainspring; pluck; power; pretense; sand; sciatic; sinew; source; stamina; steel; strength; temerity; tendon; vagus; valor; vigor; wherewithal; NERVOUS: afraid; aghast; agitated; alarmed; anxious; apprehensive; critical; difficult; edgy; excitable; fearful; feverish; fidgety; fitful; forcible; high-strung; hysterical; irritable; jerky; jittery; jumpy; neurotic; on edge; on pins and needles; queasy; quivering; restive; restless; sensitive; shaking; shaky; shy; skittish; spirited; spookish; tense; timid; timorous; touchy; trembling; uneasy; unsteady; volatile; NERVOUSNESS: (**see** "anxiety") agitation; edginess; excitation; fantods; fidgetiness; fidgets; hysteria; irritability; itchiness; jitteriness; jumpiness; jumps; nervosity; neurosis; neuroticism; psychoneurosis; psychosis; quakiness; queasiness; vapors; willies

NEST: abode; accumulation; aerie; aggregation; bed; brood; cave; center; collection; colony; core; den; family; group; hangout; habitat; haunt; hive; home; house; lair; lodge; nid(e); nidus; origin; repository; resort; retreat; shelter; source; swarm

NESTLE: cherish; cuddle; embed; fit; house; lie; lodge; nest; nuzzle; press; settle; shelter; snuggle; spoon

NET: **v.** (**see** "catch") captivate; capture; charm; clean up; clear; cop; entangle; en-

trap; gain; nab; snare; tangle; trap; NET: **n.** fabric; fyke; gain; mesh; netting; profit; scoop; seine; snare; snood; trap; web; weir; wire

NETHER: below; beneath; down; inferior; lower; subaltern(ate); subterranean; under-(ground)

NETTLE: **v.** (**see** "annoy") arouse; fret; irk; irritate; offend; pique; provoke; ruffle; sting; tease; trouble; vex; NETTLE: **n.** plant; rash; urticaria

NETWORK: chain; circuitry; combination; complex; fabric; grid; group; labyrinth; maze; mesh; plexus; *réseau*; *réseaux* (pl.); rete; reticulation; reticulum; scheme; system; tissue; web

NEUTRAL: (**see** "impartial") adiaphorous; balanced; central; colorless; disinterested; fair; free; hueless; impersonal; indefinite; independent; indifferent; inert; intermediate; irresponsible; middle-of-the-road; middling; neuter; nonaligned; noncombatant; nonpartisan; objective; unallied; unbiased; uninvolved; unprejudiced; NEUTRALITY: adiaphoria; detachment; fairness; immunity; impartiality; independence; indifference; irresponsibility; middle-of-the-roadism; nonalignment; nonpartisanship; objectivity

NEVERTHELESS: but; however; nonetheless; notwithstanding; still; *tout de même*; yet

NEW: abreast; advanced; another; *au courant*; beginning; brand-new; clean; contemporary; current; daring; *fin-de-siècle*; fresh; green; immature; inexperienced; juvenile; late(ly); latest; modern(istic); moderne; nascent; neoteric; newborn; newfangled; newfashioned; nouveau; novel; original; pathbreaking; present(-day); progressive; raw; recent; recreated; regenerated; renovated; spanking; strange; timely; topical; trailblazing; unaccustomed; unexampled; unfamiliar; unheard-of; unprecedented; untried; unused; up-to-date; up-to-the-minute; virgin(al); young; youthful; NEWNESS: **see** "freshness"

NEWCOMER: greenhorn; immigrant; Johnny-come-lately; latecomer; mushroom; new-rich; *nouveau riche*; novice; parvenu; upstart

NEWS: advice; bulletin; cable; copy; dope; evangel; flash; gospel; information; intelligence; item; latest; message; notice; report; story; telegram; tidings; word

NEWSPAPER: daily; gazette; journal; newsprint; periodical; press; publication; rag; sheet; weekly

NEXT: abutting; adjacent; adjoining; after; approximal; beside; closest; communicating; contiguous; following; immediate; imminent; intimate; jacent; joining; juxtapositional; juxtapositive; later; nearest; preceding; prochein; proximal; proximate; sequacious; shortest; then; wise

NEXUS: bond; chain; connection; interconnection; joint; junction; link; pin; tie; union

NIBBLE: attack; bite; browse; carp; champ; chew; chomp; cut; experiment; gnaw; nip; peck; pilfer; trifle; try

NICE: accurate; acute; affable; agreeable; appropriate; apt; attractive; benign; careful; charming; chaste; clement; comely; complacent; considerate; critical; cultured; dainty; decorous; delicate; delightful; demure; discerning; discriminating; elegant; enjoyable; exact; excellent; exquisite; fastidious; fine; finical; fit(ting); fussy; good; kind; meticulous; mild; minute; modest; neat; niceish; nifty; outstanding; particular; pernickety; personable; pleasant; pleasing; precise; proper; prudish; queasy; refined; reserved; scrupulous; squeamish; subtile; subtle; suitable; sweet; thoughtful; virtuous; winning; winsome; NICETY *or* NICENESS: accuracy; daintiness; decorum; delicacy; discrimination; distinction; elegance; exactitude; exactness; excellence; fastidiousness; finesse; nuance; preciosity; precision; propriety; prudishness; refinement; reserve; scrupulosity; subtlety

NICHE: alcove; apse; bay; condition; covert; cubicle; employment; job; nook; place; position; recess; retreat; shelter; space

NICK: (**see** "cut") chip; clip; dent; dint; gouge; jag; mar; notch; score; scratch

NICKNAME: agname; agnomen; alias; cognomen; description; epipthet; hypocorism; hypocoristic; moni(c)ker; *petit nom*; pseudonym; sobriquet

NICTITATE: blink; nictate; twink(le); wink

NIDOR: (**see** "odor") aroma; effluvium; reek; savor; scent; smell; stink

NIDUS: (**see** "nest") core; origin; repository; source

NIFTY: (**see** "nice") adept; attractive; chic; clever; enjoyable; excellent; fine; handy; posh; smart; *soigné*; *soignée* (fem.); splendid; stylish

NIGGARD: **a.** (**see** "stingy") avaricious; close; covetous; miserly; scanty; tight; NIGGARD: **n.** miser; piker; stinter; tightwad

NIGH: adjacent; adjoining; almost; anear; at; close; communicating; contiguous; near(by); nearly; neighboring

NIGHT: bedtime; dark(ness); death; eve-(ntide); nightfall; nocturnality; obscurity; P.M.; sleep; NIGHTMARE: alp; anxiety; apprehension; *cauchemar*; dream; fancy; fiend; illusion; incubus; mess; oneirodynia; *pavor nocturnus*; phantasy; succubus; terror; vexation; vision; *Walpurgisnacht*; Walpurgis Night; worry

NIMBLE: (**see** "agile") active; alert; alive; athletic; brisk; bustling; clever; deft; dexterous; elastic; expeditious; expert; fast; gleg; graceful; gracile; light(some); limber; lish; lissom(e); live(ly); plastic; prompt; ready; responsive; sensitive; speedy; spright-(ly); spry; supple; swift; volant; NIMBLENESS: (**see** "agility") cleverness; dexterity; elasticity; expedition; flexibility; gracefulness; gracility; legerity; lightness; lissomeness; suppleness

NIMBUS: air; atmosphere; aura; aureola; cachet; cloud; gloria; glory; halo; odor; vapor

NIMIETY: (**see** "abundance") excess; redundancy; repletion; superabundance

NINCOMPOOP: (**see** "fool") ass; blockhead; dolt; dope; dummy; dunce; goose; idiot; lout; ninny; nitwit; simpleton; witling; zombie

NINETIETH: nonagesimal

NINNY: **see** "nincompoop"

NIP: **v.** bite; blight; catch; censure; check; chill; chip; claim; compress; cut; destroy; diminish; drink; frostbite; pinch; secure; sip; snatch; steal; stop; swallow; vellicate; vex; wither; NIP: **n.** bite; blast; blight; censure; drink; sip; squeeze; swallow; tang

NIPPER(S): biter; boy; chela; claw; costermonger; crab; forceps; hand; incisor; lad; pincers; pliers; teeth; tongs

NISUS: conation; effort; endeavor; impulse; inclination; power; striving; tendency

NITID: (see "shining") bright; gay; glossy; lustrous; resplendent; spruce

NITWIT: (see "blockhead" and "ninny") boob(y); dope; dunce; fool; nincompoop; simpleton; zombie

NOB: (see "fob") blow; handle; head; knave; swell; toff

NOBLE: **a.** aristocratic; august; broad; constant; courtly; dignified; distinguished; elevated; eminent; epic; erect; exalted; excellent; faithful; famous; fine; fortitudinous; generous; good; gracious; grand(iose); high(born); honorable; illustrious; imperial; imposing; impressive; just; liberal; lofty; lordly; magnanimous; magnificent; majestic; moral; notable; outstanding; patrician; prominent; princely; pure; renowned; respectable; sincere; splendid; stately; sublime; superb; superior; supreme; titled; trustworthy; upright; worthy; NOBLE(MAN): **n.** aristocrat; aristoi (pl.); baron; count; duke; earl; grandee; grandioso; lord; magnifico; marquis; patrician; peer; thane; NOBILITY: aristocracy; aristoi (pl.); baronage; blue blood; chivalry; elite; eminence; fortitude; generosity; gentility; gentry; grace; grandeur; integrity; knight; largesse; magnanimity; noblesse; patriciate; peerage; preeminence; rank; station; sublimity; superiority

NOBODY: cipher; *homme de rien*; jackstraw; *nemo*; nonentity; *pessoribus orti*; scarecrow; scrub; straw man

NOCENT: guilty; harmful; hurtful

NOD: **v.** beck; beckon; bow; doze; err; gesture; salute; signal; sway; wink; NOD: **n.** bow; gesture; nutation; salutation; sign; signal; wink

NODE *or* NODULE: bump; complication; difficulty; entanglement; granule; growth; knob; knot; joint; junction; lump; mass; nodus; plot; point; predicament; protuberance; swelling; tubercule; tumor; wen

NOISE: **v.** air; bruit; clang; cry; gossip; rumor; say; shout; sound; spread; talk; tell; NOISE: **n.** acoustics; ado; alarm; Babel; bang; bedlam; blare; blast; blatancy; boisterousness; brouhaha; bruit; cacophony; charivari; clamor; clang(or); clatter; con-

fusion; cry; detonation; din; explosion; fanfare; gossip; hubbub; loquacity; outcry; pandemonium; phonics; pop; racket; report; roar; rumor; scandal; shout; sound; stridor; talk; tintinnabulation; tintamar(re); tumult; uproar; NOISY: agitated; aroar; bedlam; blaring; blatant; boisterous; cacophonous; clamorous; clangorous; creaky; deafening; demonstrative; disquiet; earsplitting; effusive; frantic; hilarious; loquacious; loud; noiseful; obstreperous; pandemoniac(al); piercing; raucous; riotous; rip-roaring; roisterous; rowdy; shrill; slambang; sonorous; strepitant; strepitous; strident; stridulous; termagant; thunderous; tumultuary; tumultuous; turbulent; undisciplined; unquiet; uproarious; vociferous; vulgar; NOISELESS: (see "silent") aphonic; catfooted; deadened; quiescent; stealthy

NOISOME: bad; destructive; disgusting; distasteful; fetid; foul; fusty; harmful; malodorous; mephitic; musty; nasty; noxious; offensive; pernicious; putrid; rancid; rank; rotten; stinking; unwholesome

NOMAD: Arab; gaberlunzie; Gypsy; hobo; itinerant; loner; migrant; peripatetic; roamer; rover; Saracen; Semite; vagabond; vagrant; wanderer; NOMADIC: footloose; itinerant; migrant; migratory; peripatetic; roaming; roving; vagabondish; vagrant; wandering

NOMENCLATURE: appellation; catalog(ue); designation; dictionary; list; name(s); onym; register; term(s); terminology; vocabulary

NOMINAL: approximate; basic; cheap; formal; inconsiderable; inexpensive; insignificant; low; mere; negligible; nuncupative; ostensible; par; pretended; professed; reduced; sheer; simple; slight; small; substantival; supposititious; titular; trifling; trivial; unimportant

NOMINATE: (see "name") appoint; call; denominate; designate; elect; offer; present; propose; select; suggest

NONAGE: childhood; immaturity; infancy; juvenility; minority; pupilage; youth

NONCE: minute; moment; occasion; present; purpose

NONCHALANT: (see "carefree") aloof; careless; casual; debonair(e); *dégagé*; frivolous; glib; happy; imperturbable; incautious; indifferent; insouciant; irresponsible; jaunty;

lighthearted; neglectful; negligent; *sans souci*; scampish; supine; trifling; unconcerned; undemanding; unruffled; NONCHALANCE: (**see** "indifference") casualness; insouciance

NONCONFORMISM *or* NONCOMFORMITY: *avant-gardism*; deviation; disagreement; disbelief; dissent(ion); dissidence; heresy; individuality; neglect; noninterference; nonintervention; recusance; recusancy; refusal; ultraconservatism; NONCONFORMIST: (**see** "disbeliever") *avant-garde*; beatnik; Bohemian; deviationist; deviator; dissenter; dissident; heresiarch; heretic; mossback; oddball; rebel; recusant; renegade; schismatic; schismatist; sectary; standpatter; unconformist; ultraconservative

NONENTITY: cipher; insignificance; naught; nihility; nobody; nonessential; nonexistence; nothingness; nullity; zero

NONESSENTIAL: accidental; adventitious; dispensable; extraneous; gratuitous; incidental; luxury; needless; sumptuous; supererogant; supererogative; supererogatory; unessential; unnecessary; unneeded

NONESUCH: **a.** matchless; model; nonpareil; peerless; supreme; unequaled; unparalleled; unrivaled; NONESUCH: **n.** model; nonpareil; paragon; pattern

NONEXISTENT: (**see** "dead") nonextant; NONEXISTENCE: absence; death; failure; inexistence; negation; no-being; nonbeing; nonentity; unexistence; unreality

NONINTERFERENCE: *caveat emptor*; laissez-faire; laissez-faireism; neglect; nonconformity; nonintervention; nonobservance

NONOBSERVANCE: (**see** "neglect") absorption; abstraction; dereliction; inadvertence; inattention; laxity; omission; negligence; noninterference; preoccupation; slight

NONPAREIL: **see** "nonesuch"

NONPLUS: **v.** (**see** "confuse") baffle; disconcert; faze; floor; mystify; perplex; puzzle; rattle; stagger; stick; stop; stump; NONPLUS: **n.** (**see** "confusion") dilemma; mystification; perplexity; poser; puzzle(r); quandary

NONPROFESSIONAL: **a.** amateur(ish); dilettantish; lay; untrained; NONPROFESSIONAL(S): **n.** amateur; dilettante; laity

NONRELIGIOUS: **see** "secular"

NONSENSE: abracadabra; absurdity; amphigory; applesauce; balderdash; bilge; blah; blarney; blather(skite); bosh; buncombe; bunk(um); chaff; claptrap; drivel; eyewash; fandangle; fandango; fatuity; fiddle-faddle; flamdoodle; flapdoodle; flattery; flimflam; flubdub; flummadiddle; flummery; folderol; folly; foolishness; frills; frivolity; gibberish; hocus-pocus; hokum; hooey; horsefeathers; humbug; imbecility; jabberwocky; jargon; junk; malarkey; monkeyshine; moonshine; muck; *niaiserie*; nugacity; *nugae canorae*; pish(-posh); poppycock; posh; pretense; punk; rigmarole; rot; rubbish; silliness; simplemindedness; stuff; stultiloquence; stultiloquy; taffy; tarradiddle; tomfoolery; tosh; trash; trifles; trivia(lity); trumpery; twaddle; NONSENSICAL: absurd; amphigoric; capricious; foolish; idiotic; imbecilic; fanciful; ludicrous; macaronic; nonsense; notional; paradoxical; preposterous; ridiculous; senseless; silly; simpleminded; stupid; unmeaning; whimsical

NOODLE(S): blockhead; farfel; head; ninny; pasta; simpleton

NOOK: alcove; bay; cant; corner; cove; herne; niche; recess; retreat; shelter

NOON: apex; culmination; meridian; midday; noontide; noontime; twelve

NOOSE: catch; ensnarement; hitch; lariat; lasso; loop; rope; snare; tie; trap

NORM: average; gauge; ideal; mark; maxim; mean; median; model; normal; par; pattern; principle; rule; standard; type

NORMAL: **a.** (**see** "average") analogical; balanced; common; conventional; correct; customary; just; logical; methodical; natural; orderly; ordinary; par; perpendicular; physiological; rational; reasonable; regular; right; sane; sound; standard; typical; uniform; usual; NORMAL: **n.** (**see** "norm") school

NORTH: arctic; northerliness; pole; NORTHERN: arctic; boreal; hyperborean; northward; polar; septentrional

NOSE: **v.** detect; find; nuzzle; pry; scent; smell; sniff; NOSE: **n.** aroma; beak; flair; front (end); muzzle; nares (pl.); nasus; neb; nostrils; nozzle; olfaction; proboscis; prow; schnozzle; snout

NOSEGAY: bouquet; corsage; flowers; odor; perfume; posy; scent

NOSTALGIA: homesickness; longing; melancholia; wish; yearn(ing)

NOSY: (**see** "curious") inquiring; inquisitive; intrusive; meddlesome; meddling; prying; snooping; snoopy; suspicious

NOT: hardly; nary; nay; negation; never; *non*; nought; nowise; otherwise

NOTABLE **a.** or NOTED: apparent; celebrated; clear; commanding; conspicuous; distinct; distinguished; eminent; excellent; expert; extraordinary; famed; famous; glaring; great; illustrious; important; impressive; majestic; manifest; marked; memorable; memorious; mighty; noble; noteworthy; noticeable; notorious; observable; obvious; open; outstanding; patent; plain; powerful; prominent; public; remarkable; renowned; salient; signal; significant; striking; strong; sublime; supereminent; unique; unusual; visible; whiz-bang; worthy; NOTABLE: **n.** **see** "celebrity"

NOTCH: **v.** cut; dent; groove; indent; jab; mark; nick; score; scratch; serrate; undercut; NOTCH: **n.** cleft; crena; cut; defile; degree; dent(iculation); gap; groove; hollow; indentation; indenture; mark(er); nick; peg; score; scratch; serration; space; step; NOTCHED: crenate(d); dentate; denticulate(d); dentiform; erose; serrate(d); serrulate

NOTE: **v.** (**see** "observe") annotate; attend; espy; hear; heed; indicate; mark; perceive; recognize; record; remark; see; show; view; NOTE(S): **n.** adversaria (pl.); annotation(s); billet; call; character(istic); check; chit; cry; dispatch; distinction; element; fame; feature; heed; importance; I.O.U.; jotting; letter; line; loan; melody; memo(randum); minute; mood; motif; notice; observation; record; remark; renown; report; reputation; repute; scrap; scrapiana (pl.); sign; song; sound; strain; tenor; theme; token; tone; tune

NOTEBOOK: adversaria (pl.); cahier; diary; *index rerum*; journal; log; memoranda (pl.); record; register

NOTED: **see** "notable"

NOTEWORTHY: (**see** "eminent" and "notable") conspicuous; marked; markworthy;

noticeable; observable; prominent; remarkable; special

NOTHING: bagatelle; blank; cipher; naught; nihil(ity); nil; nix; nobody; nonentity; nonexistence; not; nothingness; null(ity); oblivion; *rien*; scratch; trifle; vacuity; zero; NOTHINGNESS: annihilation; bagatelle; cipher; death; emptiness; goose egg; meaninglessness; naught; negativity; nihility; nonentity; nonexistence; nullity; oblivion; trifle; trivia (pl.); triviality; vacuity; vacuum; void; wind; zero

NOTICE: **v.** (**see** "observe") acknowledge; allude; attend; comment; discern; distinguish; espy; eye; greet; hail; heed; mark; mention; note; ogle; perceive; recognize; regard; remark; respect; review; see; sense; smell; speak; spot; spy; NOTICE: **n.** advertence; ad(vertisement); advice; announcement; apprehension; attention; awareness; bill; bulletin; civility; cognizance; conspicuity; conspicuousness; demand; edict; evaluation; examination; favor; forewarning; heed; information; intelligence; intention; intimation; knowledge; news; note; observation; order; placard; poster; proclamation; prominence; promulgation; pronouncement; remark; respect; review; spotlight; warning; NOTICEABLE: (**see** "discerning") arresting; clinical; conspicuous; detectable; discernible; extraordinary; glaring; gross; manifest; noteworthy; objective; observable; obvious; outstanding; palpable; perceptible; prominent; remarkable; salient; signal; striking; tangible; verifiable

NOTIFY: (**see** "advertise") acquaint; advise; announce; apprise; approve; blazon; circulate; communicate; convey; declare; denote; diffuse; disclose; disseminate; divulge; emblazon; herald; indicate; inform; proclaim; promulgate; publicize; publish; report; reveal; specify; spread; tell; vent; NOTIFICATION: **see** "report"

NOTION: (**see** "belief") apprehension; bee; bibelot; conceit; concept(ion); device; *donnée*; fancy; gadget; idea; image; imagination; impression; inclination; inkling; intention; knickknack; knowledge; omen; opinion; sentiment; theory; thought; understanding; vagary; vapor; view; whim(sicality); NOTIONAL: abstractive; ambivalent; crotchety; fickle; imaginary; inclined; mercurial; quicksilver; speculative; theoretical; unreal; visionary; whimsical

NOTORIETY: (**see** "fame") *éclat*; glory;

honor; notoriousness; publicity; renown; repute; NOTORIOUS: arrant; bad; base; celebrated; crying; debased; depraved; despicable; discredited; disgraceful; dishonorable; disreputable; egregious; flagrant; infamous; ignoble; ignominious; notable; opprobrious; outrageous; renowned; reprehensible; scandalous; shameful; unmitigated; vile; villainous; well-known

NOTWITHSTANDING: although; aside; but; despite; even; howbeit; however; *malgré*; mauger; maugre; nevertheless; nonetheless; *non obstante*; *quand même*; still; though; *tout de même*; yet

NOURISH: administer; aid; attend; bottle-feed; cherish; develop; educate; feed; foster; maintain; minister; nurse; nurture; pasture; promote; provide; raise; rear; serve; stimulate; strengthen; succor; suckle; support; sustain; tend; train; wet-nurse; NOURISHING: alible; alimental; alimentative; dietary; healthful; hearty; invigorating; nutritious; nutritive; nutritory; restorative; rich; strengthening; wholesome; NOURISHMENT: (see "food") aliment(ation); alms; board; collation; diet; enthusiasm; fare; feed; forage; groceries; keep; living; maintenance; means; nutriment; nutrition; pabulum; provisions; repast; supply; support; sustenance; upkeep

NOUS: alertness; brains; intellect; mind; reason(ing); understanding

NOVEL: **a.** daring; fresh; imaginative; inventive; modern; neoteric; new(fangled); odd; original; rare; recent; strange; striking; uncommon; untried; unusual; up-to-the-minute; wonderful; NOVEL: **n.** book; *Entwicklungsroman*; epic; fiction; narrative; penny dreadful; prose; romance; saga; story; tale; NOVELTY: change; fad; freshness; innovation; inventiveness; neoterism; newness; originality; strangeness; unfamiliarity

NOVICE: abecedarian; acousmatic; amateur; apprentice; beginner; boot; cadet; disciple; ham; initiate; layman; learner; neophyte; neoteric; nonprofessional; novitiate; plebe; postulant; probationer; punk; pupil; recruit; scholar; student; trainee; tyro; younker

NOW: current; existing; extant; forthwith; here; immediately; *in praesente*; instant; nonce; present(ly); since; sometimes; today; yet

NOXIOUS: bad; baneful; contaminated; corrupting; deadly; deleterious; destructive; distasteful; evil; feculent; fetid; foul; harmful; hateful; hurtful; inimical; injurious; insalubrious; malarial; malodorous; mephitic; miasmic; nocent; noisome; obnoxious; offensive; pernicious; pestilent(ial); putrescent; putrid; rank; septic; toxic; unhealthy; unwholesome; venomous; virulent

NOZZLE: (see "nose") beak; channel; outlet; snout; spout; vent

NUANCE: (see "distinction") finesse; gradation; hint; intimation; nicety; midge; shade; subtlety; variation

NUB: (see "kernel") center; core; crux; ear; gist; heart; hub; jab; key; knob; lump; meat; nucleus; pith; point; protuberance; snag; stump

NUBILOUS: (see "cloudy") foggy; indefinite; indistinct; misty; obscure; vague

NUCLEUS: (see "kernel") basis; cadre; cell; center; chromosome; core; egg; focus; germ; heart; hum; mass; middle; midst; nest; nidus; nub; point; root; seed

NUDE: (see "naked") altogether; bare; defoliated; deplumate; exposed; mother-naked; raw; undraped; undressed; ungarmented; unsupported; NUDISM: Adamitism; gymnosophy; naturalism

NUDGE: (see "goad") assist; knob; jog; jostle; poke; prod; punch; push; remind; stir; urge

NUGATORY: (see "worthless") empty; futile; hollow; idle; ineffective; ineffectual; inoperative; insignificant; invalid; sterile; trifling; trivial; unclear; unenforceable; useless; vacuous; vain; vetoed; void

NUGGET: gold; lump; mass; slug; valuable

NUISANCE: (see "annoyance") abomination; bane; boor; evil; harassment; inconvenience; nudnick; offense; pain; pest; pill; plague; sting; vexation

NULLIFY: (see "cancel") abolish; abrogate; annul; counter(act); countermand; dele(te); destroy; efface; erase; expunge; invalidate; lame; lapse; negate; negative; neutralize; obliterate; offset; override; quash; repeal; rescind; revoke; stultify; undo; veto; void; NULL: bare; empty; futile; hollow; idle; ineffective; ineffectual; inoperative; insignificant; invalid; nil; nonexistent; nugatory; *nullis juris*; unclear; unenforceable; useless; vacuous; void; worthless; NULLITY: (**see** "nothing") annulment; invalidity; nihility; nonentity; nothingness; vacuity; NULLI-FICATION: annulment; cancellation; destruction; erasure; invalidation; lapse; negation; nihility; obliteration; recision; rescission; stultification; veto; vitiation; voidance

NUMB: **v.** (**see** "deaden") anesthetize; blunt; daze; dull; narcotize; opiate; NUMB: **a.** anesthetic; anesthetized; benumbed; blunted; clumsy; dampened; dazed; dead(ened); desensitized; drunk; dull; frozen; hebetate; helpless; hypnotized; indifferent; insensate; insensible; insensitive; insentient; lethargic; lifeless; muffled; mute; narcotized; obtund; opiate; paralyzed; rigescent; rigid; sleepy; smothering; somniferous; stifled; stupefied; stupid; torpid; NUMBNESS: see "stupor"

NUMBER: **v.** apportion; ascertain; calculate; compute; count; divide; enumerate; estimate; figure; include; limit; muster; numerate; reckon; restrict; total; NUMBER(S): **n.** aggregate; aggregation; amount; arithmetic; category; census; cluster; collection; colony; company; complement; copy; count; digit; enormity; figure; girl; group; heap; hecatomb; horde; integer; issue; item; legion; lot(s); magnitude; manifold; many; multeity; multifariousness; multiplicity; multitude; myriad; numeral; percentage; per centum; person; position; quantity; score; several; sum; surd; swarm; tally; total; troop; unit; volume; whole

NUMBERLESS: (**see** "many") big; innumerable; innumerous; legion; numerous; unlimited

NUMERAL: (**see** "number") character; figure

NUMEROUS: (**see** "many") abundant; big; considerable; copious; crowded; divers; endless; excessive; extensive; fertile; galore; great; large; legion; limitless; lots; manifold; multifarious; multifold; multiple; multiplex; multitudinous; myriad; plenteous; plentiful; populous; profuse; rank; rife; several; strong; sundry; teeming; thick; thronged; untold; varied; various; vast

NUMBSKULL: (**see** "fool") blockhead; bone-head; dolt; dunce; idiot; lackwit; logger-head; muddlehead; nincompoop; nitwit

NUN: abbess; cenobite; cloisteress; pigeon; priestess; recluse; religious; sanctimonial; sister; votaress

NUNCIO: **see** "ambassador"

NUNCUPATIVE: designative; oral; spoken; unwritten

NUPTIAL: **a.** bridal; hymeneal; marital; matrimonial; NUPTIAL(S): **n.** espousal; marriage; vows; wedding; wedlock

NURSE: **v.** (**see** "care") attend; bottle-feed; cherish; cultivate; develop; educate; encourage; feed; foster; manage; mother; nourish; nurture; pamper; promote; rear; suckle; tend; NURSE: **n.** amah; ayah; bonne; mother; nanny; promoter; sister; sitter

NURTURE: (**see** "nourish" and "nurse") care; cherish; discipline; feed; keep; maintain; mother; raise; rear; support; tend; train; uphold

NUT: (**see** "fool") acorn; almond; betel; core; dolt; eccentric; fruit; head; kernel; mast; pecan; pith; problem; seed

NUTRIMENT: (**see** "food") aliment; diet-(etics); keep; nourishment; nurture; nutrition; pabulum; provender; provisions; subsistence; support; sustenance; viands; victuals; NUTRITIVE *or* NUTRITIOUS: alible; digestive; nourishing; nutrimental; rich; strengthening; wholesome; NUTRITION: (**see** "food" and "nourishment") dietetics

NUTTY: amorous; crackbrained; crackpot; crazy; demented; eccentric; enthusiastic; flavorful; foolish; gaga; loving; piquant; queer; racy; spicy; stimulating; zany; zestful

NUZZLE: (**see** "nudge") burrow; caress; dig; fondle; love; nestle; nose; pet; root

NYMPH: butterfly; Circe; damsel; dryad; Echo; hamadryad; houri; kelpie; larva; maenad; Maia; maiden; muse; naiad; Nereid; nixie; Oceanid; oread; pixie; pupa; sprite; sylph; undine

O

OAF: (see "fool") blockhead; bonehead; boor; changeling; chucklehead; dolt; dullard; dumbbell; dunce; halfwit; idiot; lout; lummox; moron; muddlehead; nincompoop; nitwit; numbskull; simpleton; OAFISH: (see "stupid") ill-bred; ill-mannered; loutish; nasty

OAR: **v.** paddle; ply; pole; row; propel; scull; sweep; OAR: **n.** blade; paddle; pole; propeller; rower; scull; spoon

OASIS: bar; Eden; garden; Merv; refreshment; refuge; relief; spa; spring; wadi

OATH: adjuration; affirmation; anathema; attestation; ban; blasphemy; bond; curse; cursing; declaration; denunciation; execration; expletive; fealty; imprecation; irreverence; malediction; obligation; pledge; profanity; promise; vow; word

OBDURATE: (see "stubborn") adamant(ine); balky; calculated; callous; dogged; firm; hard(ened); harsh; impassive; inert; inflexible; intractable; mulish; obstinate; perverse; recalcitrant; refractory; rough; rugged; severe; stony; sullen; unyielding

OBEDIENT: accountable; acquiescent; amenable; amiable; answerable; biddable; coercible; complacent; compliant; conciliable; controllable; conformable; deferential; devoted; docile; dutiful; faithful; liable; loyal; malleable; obediential; obeisant; obsequious; passive; pliable; pliant; receptive; reconcilable; resigned; respectful; subject(ive); submissive; subservient; tame; tractable; truckling; willing; yielding; OBEDIENCE: acquiescence; allegiance; amenability; compliance; conformity; control; deference; deferentiality; devotion; discipline; docility; duty; fealty; jurisdiction; loyalty; obeisancy; obeyance; obsequiousness; obsequity; receptivity; resignation; respect; rule; subjection; submission; subservience; tractability; yielding

OBEISANCE: (see "deference") allegiance; bow; congé; curtesy; fealty; genuflexion; homage; honor; kneel; kowtow; respect; reverence; salaam; salutation; salute

OBELISK: column; dagger; guglia; mark; monument; needle; obelus; pillar; pylon; shaft

OBESE: adipose; bloated; corpulent; fat; fleshy; liparous; orbicular; plump; ponderous; portly; pudgy; puffy; pursy; pyknic; rotund; rounded; stout; turgid; weighty; OBESITY: adiposis; adiposity; avoirdupois; corpulence; embonpoint; fat; pinguidity; plumpness; portliness; pursiness; rotundity; steatosis; stoutness; turgidity; weight

OBEY: (see "comply") accede; act; answer; assent; concur; conform; defer; do; ear; follow; hear; heed; kneel (to); kowtow; mind; observe; respect; respond; serve; submit; surrender; toe; worship; yield

OBFUSCATE: (see "cloud") bedim; bewilder; confuse; darken; dim; fog; muddle; obscure; perplex; puzzle; rattle; stupefy

OBIT(UARY): death; decease; elegy; mass; monody; necrology; notice; obsequies; release; services; threnody

OBJECT: **v.** (see "disapprove") argue; balk; care; carp; cavil; censor; demur; detest; discard; dislike; dissent; expostulate; hesitate; kick; mind; oppose; protest; quibble; reclaim; reject; remonstrate; repugn; resist; OBJECT: **n.** advantage; aim; article; body; cause; concept(ion); design; end; entity; goal; idea; intent(ion); item; landmark; mark; materiality; matter; meaning; mind; motive; objective; part(icular); person; phenomenon; point; purpose; reality; scope; score; sight; spectacle; target; thing; use; view; vision; OBJECTION: argument; bar; cavil; censorship; complaint; condemnation; demur; disapprobation; disapproval; dislike; displeasure; dispute; dissent; exception; fuss; grumble; opposition; protest(ation); quarrel; question; quibble; remonstrance;

remonstration; scruple; OBJECTIONABLE: (see "offensive") censorable; condemnatory; disagreeable; disputable; distasteful; exceptionable; frightful; ghastly; ill-favored; inappropriate; inexpedient; loathsome; nauseous; noisome; obnoxious; questionable; reprehensible; repugnant; repulsive; revolting; undesirable; unpleasant; unpleasing; unpleasurable; unutterable; unwanted

OBJECTIVE: **a.** actual; clinical; detached; disinterested; dispassionate; documentary; external; factual; fair; impartial; impersonal; indifferent; material; middling; natural; neutral; noncombative; nonpartisan; observable; outer; perceptible; phenomenal; positive; real; unallied; unbiased; uncolored; unemotional; uninvolved; unprejudiced; valid; verifiable; OBJECTIVE: **n.** (see "intent" and "object") aspiration; goal; intention; occupation; opportunity; pursuit; *quaesitum*; reality; target; task; way

OBJURGATE: (see "ban") banish; berate; castigate; chide; curse; damn; decry; execrate; jaw; rebuff; rebuke; reprehend; reproach; reprove; vituperate; OBJURGATION: abuse; castigation; condemnation; criticism; execration; rebuff; rebuke; reproach; reproof; vituperation

OBLIGATE: (see "impose" and "oblige") coerce; compel; constrain; discipline; domineer; dragoon; drive; enforce; enjoin; exact; exert; force; impel; make; necessitate; oblige; order; press; require; shove; thrust; OBLIGATION: (see "duty") acknowledgment; agreement; bond; burden; care; check; chore; compulsion; constraint; contract; custody; debt; encumbrance; fealty; indebtedness; I.O.U.; liability; load; mandate; mortgage; must; necessity; note; oath; obstriction; onus; oughtness; pledge; pressure; promise; recognizance; responsibility; tie; trust; urgency; vow; OBLIGATORY: (see "imperative") binding; coercive; cogent; commanding; compelling; compulsory; compulsive; convincing; demanding; *de rigueur*; domineering; driving; impelling; imperious; incumbent; indispensible; insistent; mandatory; moving; potent; powerful; prerequisite; pressing; required; requisite; strong; telling; urgent

OBLIGE: accommodate; aid; bind; coerce; compel; constrain; drive; favor; force; gratify; help; necessitate; obligate; please; perform; restrain; OBLIGED: beholden; bound; constrained; fated; favored; forced; grateful; gratified; obligated; pleased;

pledged; sure; OBLIGING: accommodating; accommodative; amiable; cooperative; favorable; friendly; grateful; helpful; kind; pliant; OBLIGATION: **see** "engagement;" OBLIGATORY: **see** "mandatory"

OBLIQUE: askance; askant; askew; aslant; awry; beveled; cater-cornered; collateral; crabwise; crooked; devious; diagonal; diverging; duplicitous; elliptical; evasive; inclined; indirect; louche; obscure; off; perverse; sidelong; sideways; sidewise; sinister; slanted; slanting; sloped; sloping; tangential; tilted; underhand

OBLITERATE: (see "cancel") abolish; annihilate; annul; blot; cover; dele(te); destroy; efface; erase; expunge; extirpate; kill; nullify; obscure; paint over; raze; remove; rub (out); sponge; wash (away)

OBLIVIOUS: (see "unaware") forgetful; forgotten; heedless; inattentive; Lethean; neglectful; negligent; nirvanic; oblivial; thoughtless; uncaring; unmindful; unnoticed; OBLIVION: amnesty; disremembrance; forgetfulness; lethe; limbo; neglect; Nirvana; oblivescence; obliviousness; pardon; silence

OBLOQUY: (see "blame") amnesty; calumny; censure; condemnation; contumely; defamation; denigration; disgrace; dishonor; disrespect; odium; reproach; scandal; shame; stigma

OBNOXIOUS: (see "hateful") blameworthy; despicable; detestable; disreputable; faulty; harmful; irritating; loud; noisome; objectionable; odious; offensive; rancid; reprehensible; repugnant; repulsive; septic; shocking; terrible; vile

OBSCENE: (see "lewd") bawdy; dirty; disgusting; filthy; foulmouthed; indecent; ithyphallic; lascivious; pornographic; profane; randy; repugnant; repulsive; risqué; rocky; sexy; shocking; OBSCENITY: coprolalia; coprology; lasciviousness; pornography; satyrism; scatology; vulgarism; vulgarity

OBSCURE: **v.** (see "cloud") adumbrate; becloud; bedim; complicate; conceal; confuse; cover; darken; delude; dim; disguise; eclipse; enclose; envelope; fog; hide; hood; mask; obfuscate; obliterate; obnebulate; obnubilate; overcast; overcloud; overshadow; screen; shade, shadow; shield; slur; thicken; veil; withhold; wrap; OBSCURE(D): **a.**

abstruse; ambiguous; ambivalent; cabalistic; caligious; clouded; cloudy; complicated; concealed; confused; covered; crepuscular; cryptic(al); dark; deep; Delphian; Delphic; difficult; dim; disguised; doubtful; dubious; dull; dusky; eclipsed; elliptic(al); enigmatic(al); equivocal; faint; fameless; hidden; inconspicuous; indecisive; indefinite; indistinct; inscrutable; involved; lowly; murky; mystic(al); nameless; nebulous; obfuscatory; obliterate(d); occult; opaque; oracular; overcast; overclouded; overshadowed; rayless; recondite; remote; retired; secret; shadowed; shadowy; shady; transcendent; turbid; uncelebrated; uncertain; unconspicuous; undetermined; undistinguished; unfathomable; unintelligible; unknown; unseen; vague; veiled; withdrawn; withheld; OBSCURITY: ambiguity; ambivalence; cloud; confusion; darkness; fog; fuliginosity; gloom; haze; inconspicuousness; indefiniteness; indistinction; obfuscation; oblivion; obscuration; opacity; privacy; profundity; seclusion; secrecy; shade; shadow; silence; turbidity; twilight

OBSEQUIES: (see "funeral") mass; obit-(uary); rites; service(s); wake

OBSEQUIOUS: compliant; courtly; cringing; dutiful; fawning; flattering; ingratiating; menial; oily; oleaginous; servile; slavish; slick; subservient; sycophantic; toadying; unctuous

OBSERVE: abide; acknowledge; adhere; allude; apprehend; attend; behold; celebrate; check; comment; contemplate; descry; detect; discern; discover; distinguish; espy; examine; explore; express; eye; follow; gaze; glim; greet; hail; heed; inspect; investigate; keep; look; mark; mention; monitor; nota bene; note; notice; obey; ogle; perceive; recognize; reflect; regard; remark; respect; review; say; scan; scout; scrutinize; see; select; sense; smell; solemnize; speak; spot; spy; stare; study; test; use; utter; view; watch; witness; OBSERVABLE: (see "noticeable") clinical; detectable; discernible; noteworthy; objective; palpable; perceivable; recognizable; verifiable; OBSERVANT: (see "keen") alert; attentive; heedful; mindful; on the qui vive; perceptive; percipient; perspicacious; regardful; sharp-eyed; sharpwitted; OBSERVATION: assertion; attention; comment; conclusion; descant; espial; experience; heed; idea; item; note; notice; observance; opinion; perception; perspicacity; recognition; reflection; regard; remark; speculation; statement; utterance; view; vigil; watch; OBSERVER;

beholder; discoverer; examiner; inspector; investigator; monitor; reviewer; scout; scrutator; scrutinizer; viewer; watchman; witness

OBSESS: beset; crave; dominate; harass; haunt; preoccupy; ride; trouble; OBSESSION: compulsion; craving; craze; domination; fear; fixation; *idée fixe;* impulse; intrusion; mania; phobia; preoccupation; psychosis; thing; tie; OBSESSIVE: (see "dominant") besetting; harassing; haunting; intrusive; troublesome; OBSESSED: beset; harassed; haunted; hipped; preoccupied; troubled

OBSOLETE: ancient; antediluvian; antiquated; antique; archaic; bygone; dead; defunct; discarded; disused; moribund; neglected; obsolescent; old; outmoded; passé; past; rare; rudimentary; shelfworn; timeworn; vestigial; worn(-out)

OBSTACLE: abatis; bar(rier); bulwark; check; complication; crisis; dam; detour; difficulty; drawback; entanglement; hampering; hang-up; hindrance; impediment; involvement; knot; mountain; obstruction; roadblock; snag; stop; stymie; trap

OBSTINATE: (see "stubborn") bigoted; bullheaded; closed-minded; difficult; dogged; dogmatic; dour; *entêté;* firm; fixed; fractious; headstrong; inflexible; intractable; intransigent; irascible; mulish; obdurate; obstreperous; opinionated; pedantic; peremptory; pertinacious; perverse; pervicacious; pigheaded; recalcitrant; refractory; reluctant; renitent; resistant; resolute; self-willed; set; stiff(-necked); sulky; sullen; tenacious; unchangeable; uncooperative; ungovernable; unpliable; unrepentant; unruly; untoward; unwilling; unyielding; willful; OBSTINACY: (see "stubbornness") adamancy; asininity; bullheadedness; contumely; dogmatism; headstrongness; inveteracy; persistence; persistency; pertinacity; pervicaciousness; pervicacity; self-will; tenacity; willfulness

OBSTRUCT: (see "check") arrest; bar(ricade); block; bolt; bottleneck; choke; clog; close; counteract; cripple; dam; debar; disrupt; embarrass; encumber; fill; frustrate; hamper; hinder; impede; incommode; inhibit; interfere; interrupt; jam; lock; occlude; oppilate; oppose; paralyze; plug; prevent; retard; stay; stop; strangle; wedge; OBSTRUCTIVE: arresting; crippling; disrupting; frustrating; hampering; hindering;

impedimental; impedimentary; impeditive; inhibiting; interfering; interrupting; obstruent; occlusive; oppilative; stenotic; strangling; OBSTRUCTION: (**see** "check" and "impasse") arrest(ation); bar(ricade); barrier; bottleneck; bulwark; dam; difficulty; embarrassment; embolus; encumbrance; frustration; hamper(ing); hindrance; impediment; impedimenta (pl); interference; jam; lock; obstacle; oppilation; opposition; paralysis; plug; restraint; restriction; retardation; spoke; stay; stenosis; stoppage; stopper; underbrush; wedge

OBTAIN: (**see** "get") accomplish; achieve; acquire; arrive; buy; collect; compass; derive; earn; effect; exist; gain; gather; get; prevail; procure; purchase; reach; receive; secure; subsist; win

OBTRUDE: (**see** "interfere") attract; eject; flaunt; impose; intermeddle; intrude; meddle; push; thrust; OBTRUSIVE: bumptious; curious; forward; impertinent; imposing; interfering; intermeddling; intruding; intrusive; loud; meddlesome; meddling; offensive; officious; protruding; pushing

OBTRUNCATE: behead; cut; decapitate; hew; lop; retrench; shorten

OBTUND: anesthetized; blunt; deadened; dull; insensitive; obtuse; quelled; reduced

OBTUSE: (**see** "stupid") blunt; dense; dull; insensitive; insentient; obtund

OBVERSE: converse; counterpart; face; front; opposite

OBVIATE: (**see** "avoid") dodge; prevent

OBVIOUS: (**see** "clear") apparent; blatant; blazing; clearcut; comprehensible; conspicuous; definite; definitive; distinct; easy; evident; exposed; frank; glaring; gross; liable; literal; lucid; manifest; noticeable; open(-and-shut); palpable; patent; plain; pointed; positive; prominent; ready; shallow; signal; simple; slick; unambiguous; undisguised; unequivocal; visible; vivid; OBVIOUSNESS: (**see** "clearness") conspicuity; conspicuousness; distinctness; glaringness; lucidity; manifestness; noticeability; patency; prominence; vividity

OCCASION: appointment; break; cause; celebration; ceremony; chance; circumstance; condition; date; drama; engagement; episode; event; exigency; function; ground;

happening; incident; juncture; necessity; need; nonce; occurrence; opening; opportunity; period; reason; rendezvous; requirement; room; scene; season; situation; state; tide; time; tryst; OCCASIONAL: accidental; casual; doubtful; dubious; episodic(al); frequent; fugitive; incidental; indefinite; infrequent; irregular; odd; old; provisional; scarce; sporadic; temporary; transitive; transitory; uncertain

OCCULT: (**see** "abstruse") acroamatic; arcane; concealed; covert; cryptic(al); dark-(ened); esoteric; hidden; inscrutable; latent; mysterious; mystic(al); recondite; secret; stratospheric(al); supernatural; surreptitious; undercover; underground; undetected; undisclosed; unknown; unrevealed; OCCULTATION *or* OCCULTISM: abstrusity; cabala; concealment; eclipse; magic; mystery; obscurity; profundity; secrecy

OCCUPANT: dweller; holder; incumbent; inhabitant; inmate; occupier; possessor; renter; resident; resider; tenant; user; OCCUPANCY: habitation; incumbency; inhabitation; occupation; possession; rental; residency; tenancy; tenure; use

OCCUPATION: (**see** "business") activity; berth; calling; care; career; charge; concern; control; craft; duty; employment; engagement; enterprise; field; function; game; handicraft; holding; incumbency; interest; job; line; medium; métier; mission; occupancy; place; position; possession; profession; province; pursuit; racket; seizure; service; settlement; situation; sphere; station; task; tenancy; tenure; terrain; trade; undertaking; use; vocation; work; OCCUPATIONAL: career; craft; employmental; habitudinal; industrial; professional; situational; vocational

OCCUPY: (**see** "engage") amuse; busy; capture; contain; control; divert; employ; engross; enjoy; entertain; fill; garrison; get; have; hold; inhabit; interest; keep; perch; pervade; populate; possess; reside; seize; settle; take; tenant; use; usurp; OCCUPIED: absorbed; abstracted; active; amused; busy; captivated; captured; complete; employed; engaged; engrossed; filled; inhabited; intent; kept; pensive; rapt; taken; took

OCCUR: (**see** "happen") appear; arise; befall; betide; chance; come; concur; ensure; eventuate; exist; give; go; hap; meet; pass; rise; suggest; transpire; OCCURRENCE: (**see** "circumstance") accident; act(ion);

adventure; appearance; casualty; crisis; episode; event(uality); exigency; experience; happening; incident; item; juncture; occasion; passage; presence; situation; transaction

OCEAN: brine; deep; drink; expanse; main; pond; sea; water; OCEANIC: marine; maritime; nautical; naval; oceangoing; pelagic; seafaring; seagoing; thalassic

OCULAR: ophthalmic; optical; orbital; visible; visual

ODD: abnormal; absurd; additional; alone; anonymous; atypical; azygous; baffling; baroque; bizarre; capricious; casual; chimerical; comical; curious; daedal(ian); daedalic; different; dippy; droll; eccentric; eerie; erratic; esoteric; exceptional; exoteric; extra; extraordinary; extreme; fanatical; fantastic(al); fortuitous; freakish; funny; grotesque; haphazard; idiosyncratic; incidental; individual; inexplicable; irregular; isolated; left; ludicrous; miscellaneous; mysterious; mystifying; nondescript; occasional; occult; oddball; oddish; off; outlandish; outré; over; particular; peculiar; picturesque; quaint; queer; quixotic; random; rare; remaining; remarkable; remote; ridiculous; rococo; scattered; secluded; single; singular; strange; stray; striking; unbalanced; uncharacteristic; uncommon; unconformable; unconventional; uneven; unharmonious; unique; unmatched; unmated; unpaired; unrealistic; unseemly; untypical; unusual; vagarious; weird; whimsical; ODDITY: bizarrerie; caprice; curiosity; eccentricity; fantasticality; grotesquerie; haecceity; idiosyncrasy; oddball; particularity; peculiarity; queerness; quiddity; singularity; strangeness; tic; unique; uniquity; unusuality; vagary; weirdity; whim(sicality)

ODDS: (see "advantage") benefit; chance(s); defect; difference; disadvantage; disagreement; discord; disparity; dissention; edge; excess; favor; handicap; importance; inequality; likelihood; partiality; percentage; probability; ration; use; variance

ODE: canticle; lyric; melody; Pindaric; poem; rhyme; song

ODEUM or ODEON: gallery; hall; theater

ODIOUS: (see "hateful") abhorrent; coarse; despicable; detestable; disagreeable; disgraceful; disgusting; displeasing; disreputable; distasteful; execrable; forbidding;

hideous; horrible; horrid; horrific; immoral; impure; infamous; invidious; loathsome; nasty; nauseating; nauseous; noisome; objectionable; obnoxious; offensive; purulent; putrescent; putrid; repellant; reprehensible; repugnant; repulsive; revolting; rotten; shocking; terrible; ugly; unclean; vile; vulgar; ODIUM or ODIOUSNESS: abhorrence; antipathy; aversion; condemnation; detestation; disgrace; dishonor; dislike; displeasure; disrepute; distaste; hate(fulness); hatred; infamy; invidiousness; loathing; nausea; obloquy; offense; opprobrium; putrescence; reproach; repugnance; repugnancy; repulsiveness; repulsivity; stigma; turpitude

ODOR: aroma(ticity); brume; cachet; effluvia (pl.); effluvium; emanation; estimation; fetidity; fetidness; fetor; flavor; fragrance; fume; gust; mephitis; musk; must; nidor; nimbus; perfume; putridity; redolence; reputation; repute; rot(tenness); savor; scent; smell; stench; stink; waft; ODOROUS: aromatic; balmy; effluvial; fetid; fragrant; ill-smelling; malodorous; mephitic; musky; musty; nidorous; noisome; odorant; odoriferous; offensive; olent; perfumed; putrescent; putrid; redolent; rotten; scented; smelly; stinking

ODORLESS: inodorous; neutral; perfumeless; scentless

OFF: abnormal; abroad; afar; afield; agee; apart; aside; away; crazy; distant; divergent; diverging; eccentric; erroneous; far; from; inaccurate; insane; irregular; oblique; odd; opposite; out; remote; removed; short; slack; slanting; tainted; tramontane; ultramontane; wrong

OFF-COLOR: dingy; dirty; dubious; indelicate; obscene; pornographic; risqué

OFFEND: abase; abuse; affront; anger; annoy; assail; assault; attack; chafe; deprecate; desecrate; discredit; disgrace; dishonor; disoblige; displease; enrage; err; flout; gall; grate; harm; hurt; incommode; injure; insult; irritate; knock; miff; mortify; nettle; profane; outrage; pique; provoke; rage; rasp; shock; sin; slap; slur; stab; transgress; trespass; vex; vilify; violate; OFFENSE: (see "crime") abuse; affront; aggression; annoyance; assault; atrocity; attack; breach; corruption; damage; delict(um); delinquency; deprecation; dishonor; displeasure; dudgeon; effrontery; error; evil; fault; felony; grief; harm; huff; hurt; impropriety;

incivility; indignity; injury; insolence; insult; invective; irritation; knock; malefaction; malfeasance; malum; misconduct; misdeed; misdemeanor; misfeasance; nuisance; onset; onslaught; outrage; peccadillo; pet; pique; resentment; rudeness; scandal; sin; slap; slur; stab; sulk; tort; transgression; trespass; umbrage; veniality; vice; violation; wrong- (doing); OFFENSIVE: **a.** abusive; affronting; aggressive; arrogant; audacious; bad; blameworthy; blatant; coarse; criminal; culpable; defamatory; delinquent; deplorable; disgraceful; disgusting; displeasing; distasteful; dreadful; evil; excessive; execrable; extortionate; felonious; fetid; flagitious; flagrant; foul; gross; guilty; harmful; hideous; horrible; horrid; horrific; illegal; illicit; immoral; impertinent; indecent; infamous; inimical; iniquitous; injurious; insulting; invidious; libelous; loathsome; loud; low; malefic; malevolent; malign(ant); mephitic; nauseous; nefarious; nocent; noisome; noxious; objectionable; obnoxious; obtrusive; odious; odorous; opprobrious; outrageous; pestilential; pushy; putrescent; putrid; rank; rebarbative; reprehensible; reprehensive; repugnant; repulsive; revolting; ribald(rous); ridiculous; rotten; rough; rude; scandalous; scurrilous; shocking; slimy; stinking; unlawful; unpalatable; unrefined; unpleasant; unsavory; unwholesome; verminous; vicious; vile; vulgar; wicked; wrong; OFFENSIVE: **n.** see "attack;" OFFENSIVENESS: arrogance; audacity; blatancy; culpability; delinquency; disgust; distaste; effrontery; evil; indecency; iniquity; insult; loathsomeness; malevolence; malignancy; objectionability; odium; opprobrium; putridity; reprehension; reprehensiveness; repugnance; repugnancy; repulsiveness; rottenness; rudeness; scurrility; temerity; unsavoriness; wickedness

OFFER: **v.** (**see** "bid)" advance; afford; attempt; exhibit; give; hand; hold forth; invite; lend; move; pose; present; pretend; proffer; propose; propound; represent; sacrifice; show; submit; suggest; supply; tempt; tender; treat; undertake; utter; volunteer; OFFER: **n.** (**see** bid") advancement; ante; attempt; exhibit; invitation; move; overture; present; proffer; promise; proposal; reward; temptation; tender; threat; try; undertaking; OFFERING: bid; bribe; contribution; donation; gift; oblation; offer(-tory); opening; opportunity; piacula (pl.); piaculum; present(ation); proffer(ing); proposal; sacrifice; suggestion; tender; tribute

OFFHAND: (**see** "impromptu") abrupt; ad lib(itum); autoschediastic; breezy; *brevi manu*; brusque; by-the-way; careless; casual- (ly); *currente calamo*; curt; extemporaneous; extemporary; extempore; free; glib; hasty; impetuous; improvisatorial; improvisatory; improvised; improviso; impulsive; informal; prompt; readily; spontaneous; thoughtless; unceremonious; unconventional; unpremeditated; unreflecting; unstudied; unthinking

OFFICE: (**see** "business") agency; appointment; authority; bureau; calling; capacity; chair; charge; craft; department; dignity; duty; employment; establishment; function; headquarters; job; métier; mission; part; place; position; post; profession; rank; residence; responsibility; rite; role; room; service; shop; situation; station; stint; task; trade; trust; work

OFFICER(S): adjutant; administrator; agent; bailiff; chief; constable; cop; deputy; director; executive; functionary; master; mate; minister; official; policeman; sheriff; staff

OFFICIAL: **a.** (**see** "authoritative") accredited; administerial; administrative; approved; authorized; cathedral; ceremonious; certain; formal; genuine; governmental; hierarchic(al); ministerial; prescribed; sanctioned; true; OFFICIAL: **n.** (**see** "officer") authority; bashaw; bureaucrat; chief; dignitary; functionaire; functionary; incumbency; incumbent; judge; king; magistrate; mandarin; officialdom; officiality; officiary; panjandrum; pedantocrat; prince; regent; ruler; sovereign; viceroy; V.I.P.

OFFICIOUS: (**see** "meddlesome") aggressive; impertinent; interfering; intrusive; meddling; nosy; obtrusive; pushing; pushy; prying; snooping; snoopy; unofficial

OFFSET: (**see** "balance") checkmate; compensate; counter(act); counterbalance; counterpoise; countervail; neutralize; nullify; reimburse

OFFSHOOT: adjunct; branch; cion; consequence; descendant; digression; expansion; growth; increase; issue; limb; member; offspring; outgrowth; ramification; ramus; rod; scion; shoot; sideline; son; sprig; spring; sprout; spur; subsidiary; tangent

OFFSPRING: (**see** "family") child; cion; descendant(s); fruit; issue; litter; offshoot;

posterity; product; progeniture; progeny; scion; yield; young

OFTEN: (**see** "frequent") frequently; ofttimes; recurrent; repeatedly; repetitive

OGLE: **v.** (**see** "look") eye; glance; leer; OGLE: **n.** (**see** "look") eye; glance; leer; marlock; oeillade

OGRE: *bête noir*; brute; bugbear; demon; giant; Hugon; monster; nightmare; orc; problem

OIL: **v.** anoint; bribe; flatter; grease; lube; lubricate; smear; smooth; tip; OIL: **n.** bribe(ry); cream; fat; flattery; grease; lard; lubrication; oleum; painting; petroleum; sebum; wax; OILY: bland; deceitful; elusive; evasive; fat(ty); fawning; flannelmouthed; flattering; glib; greasy; ingratiating; lardaceous; lubric(i)ous; oleaginous; oleous; pinguid; plausible; polished; sanctimonious; saponaceous; sebaceous; servile; slippery; smeary; smooth(-spoken); suave; unctuous; unguinous; OILINESS: lubricity; pinguidity; plasticity; saponaceousness; servility; unctuosity

OINTMENT: (**see** "balm") balsam; cerate; ceroma; grease; inunction; inunctum; nard; pomade; remedy; salve; unguent

OLD(EN): (**see** "ancient") *ab antiquo;* aboriginal; advanced; ageable; aged; agelong; anile; antediluvial; antediluvian; antemundane; antiquated; antique; archaic; archaistic; bewhiskered; bygone; centuried; chronic; crusted; dated; decrepit; deep-rooted; discarded; elder(ly); experienced; familiar; feeble; former; fusty; grandfatherly; gray; hoary; honored; immemorial; inveterate; long-standing; mature; medieval; mossy; musty; obsolete; Ogygian; Paleolithic; Paleozoic; passé; past; patriarchal; preadamite; prehistoric; prelapsarian; primeval; primitive; protohistoric; quaint; quondam; remote; seared; secular; senescent; senile; shabby; stale; supermundane; time-honored; time-worn; venerable; veteran; weak; worn(-out); wrinkled; yellowed; OLDER *or* OLDEST: elder; eldest; first-born; puisne; senior; staler

OLD AGE: autumn of life; caducity; decrepitude; dotage; evening of life; golden age; maturity; senectitude; senescence; senility

OLD-FASHIONED: ancient; antebellum;

antediluvian; antiquated; archaic; archaistic; classical; conservative; corny; crinoline; dated; decadent; decayed; declined; degenerated; *démodé*; demoded; effete; *fin-de-siècle;* feudal; fogram; fuddy-duddy; fusty; horse-and-buggy; moribund; mossback; Neanderthal; nonprogressive; nostalgic; obsolescent; obsolete; old hat; ossified; outdated; outmoded; out-of-date; overripe; passé; quaint; reactionary; regressive; spent; traditional; troglodytic; ultraconservative; unmodern; unstylish; *vieux jeu;* vintage

OLD PERSON: antediluvian; antiquarian; ci-devant; dotard; fogram; fogrum; fuddy-duddy; graybeard; Methuselah; mossback; patriarch; preadamite; stick-in-the-mud; troglodyte; ultraconservative; veteran

OLEAGINOUS: (**see** "oily") fawning; oleose; oleous; sanctimonious; unctuous

OMEN: augury; auspication; auspice; badge; bodement; boding; divination; foreboding; forecast(ing); foreknowledge; foreshadowing; foretelling; foretoken; handsel; handwriting on the wall; harbinger; haruspication; indication; intuition; mark; ostent; portent; precursor; prediction; premonition; presage; prescience; presentiment; prognosis; prognostication; prophecy; sign; sortilege; symptom; threat; token; warning; OMINOUS: augural; augurous; bad; bodeful; calamitous; dire; doomful; doomlike; fatal; fateful; fearful; foreboding; foreshadowing; foretelling; grave; gravid; imminent; inauspicious; menacing; portentous; premonitory; prophetic; sinister; suggestive; threatening; unpropitious; vatic(al); vaticinal; watchful

OMIT: bar; blue-pencil; cancel; default; delay; dele(te); destroy; disregard; drop; efface; elide; eliminate; erase; evade; except; exclude; expunge; extinguish; fail; forbear; ignore; kill; leave; let; miss; neglect; nullify; obliterate; overlook; pass; preclude; pretermit; refrain; reject; remove; retrench; scrub; separate; skip; slight; slip; spare; sponge; strike; underlook; unmention; OMISSION: cut; default; delinquency; elision; ellipsis; error; exclusion; failure; guilt; misfeasance; neglect; oversight; preterition; pretermission; silence; slight; OMITTED: evaded; excluded; ignored; neglected; precluded; skipped; slighted; unmentioned; untalked-of

ONCE: bygone; elapsed; emeritus; erewhile; erst(while); ever; former(ly); has-been; just;

merely; only; quondam; retired; someday; sometime; whilom

ONE: ace; alone; an; certain; common; equal; identical; individual; merged; only; person; same; single; sole; stag; undivided; unified; unit; united; unity; *uno*; wholeness

ONENESS: accord; harmony; identity; integrity; omneity; sameness; singleness; totality; unanimity; unicity; uniquity; unity; wholeness

ONEROUS: (**see** "burdensome") exacting; oppressive

ONE-SIDED: *ex parte*; partial; unfair; unilateral; unjust

ONLOOKER: (**see** "witness") bystander; spectator

ONLY: alone; barely; best; but; exclusive(ly); extremely; finest; isolated; just; lone(ly); mere(ly); particular; peerless; save; simply; single; singly; sole(ly); solitary; specific; unique

ONOMASTICON: dictionary; glossary; lexicon; list; nomenclature; vocabulary; wordbook

ONSET *or* ONSLAUGHT: affray; assault; attack; beginning; brunt; charge; commencement; impact; onrush; storm

ONUS: blame; burden; charge; debt; duty; incubus; load; necessity; obligation; responsibility; stigma; task; weight

ONWARD: (**see** "ahead") advancing; along; forth; forward; on; progressing

OOZE: **v.** diffuse; discharge; drip; emanate; emit; escape; excrete; exhale; extravasate; exude; filter; flow; issue; leak; osmose; percolate; perspire; reek; secrete; seep; soak; spew; steam; strain; sweat; transudate; transude; trickle; weep; OOZE: **n.** bog; deposit; diffusion; discharge; drip; emanation; emission; escape; excretion; exhalation; extravasation; exudate; exudation; filtration; flow; issue; leak; marsh; mire; mud; osmosis; percolation; perspiration; seep(age); silt; slime; spew; steam; sweat; transudation; trickle; weeping

OPAQUE: abstruse; adiaphorous; clouded; cloudy; dark(ened); dense; dim; dull; fuliginous; impervious; muddy; nubiferous;

obscure; obtuse; shadowy; shady; stupid; thick; turbulent; unclear; unintelligible; vague

OPEN: **v.** accommodate; admit; air; announce; begin; bid; bore; breach; break; broach; burst; clear; commence; communicate; cope; crack; cut; demonstrate; develop; disclose; disconnect; display; emit; enlarge; enlighten; enter; establish; exfoliate; exhibit; expand; explicate; expose; extend; flare; free; gape; inaugurate; initiate; install; instill; interpret; introduce; invite; lead; liberalize; liberate; loose(n); manifest; offer; ope; originate; part; pass; pierce; preface; pry; puff; relax; release; relieve; rend; reveal; rip; rupture; separate; show; space; splay; split; spread; start; tap; tear; unbar; unbind; unblock; unbolt; unbound; uncase; unchoke; unclamp; unclasp; unclog; unclose; unconceal; uncover; undisguise; undo; unfasten; unfeign; unfold; unfurl; unlock; unloose(n); unmask; unobstruct; unprotect; unrestrict; unrip; unroll; unseal; unsheathe; unshut(ter); unstop(per); untie; unveil; unzip; vent; widen; yawn; OPEN: **a.** *or* OPENLY: **adv.** abeyant; aboveboard; accessible; active; affable; agape; ajar; apart; apparent; artless; assailable; assaultable; attackable; available; bold; bare(faced); barren; blank; broad; broken; candid; certain; clear; communicable; communicative; communicatory; conspicuous; cooperative; defenseless; disconnected; disguiseless; disposed; downright; enlarged; enlightened; enterable; even; evident; exoteric; expanded; explicit; exposed; extended; fair; flaring; frank; free(hearted); fresh; gaping; generous; guileless; honest; inaugurated; indubitable; ingenuous; innocent; installed; introduced; known; lax; liable; liberal; limitless; loose; manifest; naïve; naked; notorious; obedient; observable; obvious; operative; originated; out; out-and-out; overt; part(ed); patent; patulous; pierced; plain; plenary; prone; public; rangy; relaxed; relieved; resonant; responsive; ripped; rude; scattered; separated; shelterless; simple; sincere(ly); single; sparse; spread; straightforward; subject; suitable; susceptible; talkative; tolerant; transparent; unabashed; anappropriated; unassuming; unbarred; unblockaded; unblocked; unbolted; unbound; uncaged; unclamped; unclasped; unclogged; unclosed; unconcealed; unconcerned; uncontrollable; uncovered; undecided; undefended; undefined; undisguised; undone; undrawn; unenclosed; unfastened; unfeigned; unflattering; unfolded; unfurled; unguarded; unhampered; unhidden; unimpeded; unlatched; unlocked; unloosened; unmasked; unobscured; unobstructed; unoccupied; unprotected; unraveled; unrepossessed; unreserved; unrestrained; unrestricted; unripped; unsealed; unsettled; unsheltered; unshut; unsophisticated; unstopped; unstoppered; unsupported; unsuppressed; untaken; untied; unveiled; unzipped; unzippered; usable; vacant; visible; vulnerable; wide(ned); yawning; OPENNESS; (**see** "candor") frankness; unreserve

OPEN-AIR: alfresco; *à la belle étoile*; extraforaneous; hypaethral; outdoors; out of doors; *sub Jove*; upaithric

OPENING: access; adit(us); aperture; avenue; bay; beginning; bid; birth; breach; break; canal; cave; cavity; chance; channel; chasm; chimney; cleft; commencement; commencing; commissure; crack; cranny; crater; crevice; dawn; *débouché*; debouchment; debouchure; debut; dehiscence; door(way); egress; entrance(way); entry; escape; excavation; exit; eye(let); fenestra(tion); first; fissure; fistula; flaw; flue; fly; foramen; gambit; gap; gape; gate(way); gulf; gullet; hatch; hiatus; hole; inauguration; ingress; initiation; inlet; installation; interstice; interval; introduction; introitus; invitation; job; keyhole; kickoff; loop(hole); maw; means; meatus; mouth; muzzle; nozzle; occasion; offer(ing); onset; opportunity; oriel; orifice; os; oscitancy; ostiole; outlet; pass; passage(way); peephole; perforation; pinhole; pipe; pore; port; portal; porthole; postern; preamble; preface; prelude; proem; recess; rent; rift; rima; route; sale; separation; shaft; sinus; slit; slot; sluice; socket; space; span; spread(ing); start(ing); stoma; tear; threshold; vacancy; vent; way; window; yawn(ing)

OPERATE: (**see** "control") act; conduct; direct; drive; effect(uate); execute; function; go; guide; labor; lead; man; manage; manipulate; mechanize; perform; pilot; play; push; run; serve; speculate; steer; trade; transact; work; OPERATION: (**see** "action") business; management; manipulation; performance; OPERATING *or* OPERATIVE: effective; efficacious; engaged; functional; manipulable; manipulative; mechanized; mobile; open; operational; physiologic(al); running; trading; transacting; valid; working; OPERATOR: actor; agent; broker; dealer; dentist; doctor; doer; driver; jockey; maker; manager; manipulator; operative; performer; pilot; player; speculator; surgeon; trader; worker

OPERCULUM: cover; flap; lid; opercule; plate

OPHIDIAN: conger; eel; Ophidia (pl.); reptile; serpent; snake

OPIATE: anesthetic; anodyne; dope; drug; hemp; marihuana; morphine; narcotic; opium; sedative; soporific; tranquilizer

OPINE: (**see** "think") believe; cogitate; deem; estimate; gather; judge; mull; state; suppose; surmise; wish

OPINION: academy; appraisal; approval; attitude; belief; concept; conception; conclusion; conscience; consensus; consideration; conviction; counsel; creed; culture; diagnosis; doctrine; dogma; esteem; estimate; estimation; evaluation; expression; force; heart; idea; impression; judgment; leaning; mind; notion; orthodoxy; persuasion; posture; principle; pull; pulsebeat; recommendation; regard; religion; resolution; sentiment; sight; slant; surmise; tenet; thinking; thought; trend; two cents worth; view-(point); weight

OPINIONATED: autotheistic; biased; bigoted; cavalier; conceited; doctrinaire; doctrinal; dogmatic; fanatical; officious; *opiniâtre;* opinioned; philodoxical; pontifical; pragmatic(al); prejudiced; sophomoric; stubborn; unteachable; vainglorious

OPPONENT: (**see** "antagonist") adversary; anti; assailant; attacker; challenger; combatant; competitor; contender; contestant; defendant; disputant; emulator; enemy; foe; gentleman; invader; nemesis; opportunist; rival; warrior

OPPORTUNE: (**see** "favorable") advantageous; appropriate; apropros; apt; auspicious; bright; convenient; expedient; fit(ting); fortunate; golden; happy; lucky; miraculous; pat; pertinent; precipitous; prepared; profitable; propitious; providential; ready; ripe; seasonable; suitable; tempestive; timely; OPPORTUNITY: advantage; break; chance; conjuncture; contingency; elbowroom; experiment; field day; go; hint; juncture; leisure; means; medium; objective; occasion; offering; opening; opportuneness; possibility; room; season; shot; situation; test; tide; time(liness); trial; way

OPPOSE: antagonize; attack; battle; breast; check; clash; collide; combat; compete; conflict; confront; contend; contest; contrast; contravene; cope; counter(act); counterbalance; countermine; countervail; cross; defeat; defy; deny; destroy; disobey; dispute; face; fight; force; frustrate; gainsay; grapple; hinder; impede; impugn; interfere; meet; militate; mutiny; neutralize; nullify; object; obstruct; offset; oppugn; rebel; rebuff; refuse; remonstrate; repel; repugn; repulse; resent; resist; restrain; retaliate; revolt; snub; strive; struggle; thwart; vie; wage; war; withstand; wrestle; OPPOSED *or* OPPOSING: (**see** "antagonistic") adversative; alien (to); contralateral; contrariant; contrary; coped; faced; fronted; hindering; hostile; impeding; inimical; interfering; met; militant; opposite; oppositional; oppositious; oppositive; oppugnant; pitted; pugnacious; repugnant; resistful; resisting; OPPOSITION: anger; antagonism; antipathy; *au contraire;* breach; break; chasm; competition; conflict; confrontation; contrariety; contrariness; contrast; contravention; difference; disaffinity; discord; dissonance; division; enmity; facing; friction; fronting; hate; hostility; interference; militancy; objection; obstacle; oppugnation; perverseness; perversity; recalcitration; refractoriness; remonstrance; remonstration; repugnance; repugnancy; resentment; resistance; revolt; revolution; rivalry; separation; unfriendliness; war(fare)

OPPOSITE: **a.** adversative; adverse; ambivalent; antagonistic; anti; antipathetic(al); antipathic; antipodal; antipodean; antipodic; antithetic(al); antitypical; antonymic; antonymous; contra(dictory); contrary; contrawise; converse; counter(part); diametrical; disparate; diverse; double-dealing; duplicitous; facing; hostile; incompatible; inverse; Janus-faced; Januslike; obverse; opposing; other; over; polar; reciprocal; repugnant; reverse(d); unequal; unlike; unmatched; *vis-à-vis;* OPPOSITE: **n.** antipode; antipodes (pl.); antithesis; antonym; complement; contraposition; contrariety; counterpart; counterpole; double; duplicate; mate; polarity; polarization; replica; spouse; twin

OPPRESS: abuse; afflict; aggrieve; annoy; bait; beset; burden; constrain; crowd; crush; depress; distress; dragoon; extinguish; harass; harry; hound; hunt; load; maltreat; molest; mortify; overburden; overcome; overload; overpower; overwhelm; persecute; pester; press; pursue; rack; rag; ride; squelch; subdue; subjugate; suppress; thrash; torment; trample; trouble; tyrannize; victimize; weigh; whip; worry; wrong; OPPRESSIVE *or* OPPRESSED: absolute;

afflictive; besetting; burdened; burdensome; close; crushing; dictatorial; distressing; domineering; exacting; grievous; harassing; hard; heavy(-handed); hot; humid; onerous; overburdened; overwhelmed; pressed; rigoristic; rigorous; subjugated; sultry; Tarquinian; torrid; trampled; tyrannic(al); tyrannized; tyrannous; unjust; victimized; OPPRESSION: abuse; affliction; aggression; annoyance; burden(someness); constraint; constriction; cross; depression; destruction; dullness; exaction; harassment; lassitude; maltreatment; mastery; molestation; mortification; oppressiveness; persecution; prosecution; rack; repression; subjection; subjugation; suppression; torment; tyranny; vexation; wrong; yoke; OPPRESSOR: see "tyrant"

OPPROBRIOUS: **see** "hateful"; OPPROBRIUM: abuse; contempt; disdain; disgradation; dishonor; disrepute; disrespect; distaste; envy; hate; ignominy; infamy; odium; reproach; shame; unpopularity

OPPUGN: assail; attack; combat; contend; contravert; criticize; dispute; oppose; question; resist; thwart; OPPUGNANT: (**see** "unfriendly") antagonistic; combative; disputatious; opposing; oppositious; resistant; unfavorable; unpropitious

OPT: choose; cull; decide; elect; pick; select; wish; vote

OPTIC(AL): **see** "ocular"

OPTICAL ILLUSION: *deceptio visus; fata morgana; ignis fatuus;* mirage; phantasmagoria; phantasmagory; prestidigitation

OPTIMISTIC(AL): (**see** "cheerful") affirmative; agreeable; arousing; beamish; bullish; cheering; confident; elated; encouraging; enthusiastic; eupeptic; euphoric; expectant; favorable; glad; happy; heartening; hopeful; inspiring; joyous; merry; Micawberish; optimum; overoptimistic; oversanguine; overzealous; Pollyann(a)ish; promising; roseate; rosy; rousing; sanguine; sanguineous; sunny; zealous; OPTIMISM: (**see** "hopefulness") cheer(fulness); elation; enthusiasm; eupepsia; euphoria; hope; inspiration; joy; merriment; Micawberism; overoptimism; Pollyann(a)ism; promise; sanguineness; sanguinity; zealousness

OPTION: (**see** "choice") alternative; decision; discretion; election; elective; freedom; future; pick; preference; privilege; right;

selection; vote; OPTIONAL: alternating; choosing; discretional; discretionary; discriminative; eclectic; elective; facultative; preferential; selective; voluntary

OPULENT: (see "grand") abundant; affluent; baronial; flush; gaudy; golden; grandiose; lavish; lush; luxuriant; magnificent; moneyed; plentiful; plush(y); profuse; replete; rich; ritzy; rococo; showy; sumptuous; wealthy

OPUS: book; composition; etude; labor; manuscript; number; study; work

ORACLE: augur; guide; medium; mentor; prophet; revelation; sage; seer; sibyl; soothsayer; ORACULAR: ambiguous; Delphian; Delphic; divining; esoteric; forecasting; mysterious; mystical; portentous; predictive; presageful; prophetic; pythonic; sage; sapient; vatic(inal); wise

ORAL: aloud; buccal; mouthed; nuncupative; parol(e); phonetic; said; spoken; tacit; told; unwritten; verbal; *viva voce*; vocal; voiced; word-of-mouth

ORATE: (see "declaim") harangue; rhetorize; sermonize; ORATION: (see "speech") declamation; discourse; eloge; encomium; eulogy; harangue; sermon; ORATOR: advocate; declaimer; Demosthenes; oratrix (fem.); perorator; rhetor(ician); speaker; spellbinder; spokesman; ORATORICAL: (see "declamatory") bombastic; Ciceronian; Demosthenean; Demosthenic; elocutionary; eloquent; grandiloquent; melodramatic; rhetorical; ORATORY: bethel; bombast; chapel; declamation; elocution; eloquence; melodramatics; rhetoric

ORBED: circular; globate; lunar; orbic(ular); round; spherical

ORBIT: (see "sphere") ambit; ball; circuit; ellipse; eye; jurisdiction; ken; orb; path; purview; radius; range; region; rounds; scope; sweep; track

ORDAIN: (see "appoint") arrange; assign; authorize; call; choose; command; commission; conduct; consecrate; constitute; crown; decree; delegate; destine; determine; dictate; direct; elect; empower; enact; establish; fate; foreordain; franchise; frock; impose; inaugurate; induct; install; institute; invest; legalize; manage; order; predestine; prepare; prescribe; regulate; send; set(tle); warrant; will; ORDAINED: appointed;

arranged; assigned; authorized; commissioned; consecrated; constituted; crowned; decreed; destined; due; enacted; established; fated; foreordained; franchised; inaugurated; installed; invested; legal(ized); ordered; predestined; prescribed; sent; warranted

ORDEAL: (see "trial") calvary; cross; crucible; endurance; excruciation; experience; gaff; hardship; judgment; rack; strain; suffering; test; tribulation

ORDER: **v.** adjure; align; arrange; array; ask; assign; authorize; beg; beseech; bespeak; bid; bill; call; challenge; charge; choose; cite; claim; command; commission; decree; demand; destine; dictate; direct; dispose; dun; empower; enjoin; enact; exact; expostulate; implore; importune; impose; instruct; levy; line; manage; marshal; necessitate; oblige; ordain; organize; plan; pray; prepare; prescribe; press; prohibit; purpose; regulate; repress; request; require; rule; seek; send; solicit; sort; state; summon; supplicate; systematize; tell; urge; will; ORDER: **n.** adjuration; agreement; alignment; arrangement; array(ment); attention; authority; authorization; behest; bid(ding); bill; brotherhood; call; calm(ness); category; caveat; challenge; charge; claim; class; classification; club; command; commission; concinnity; cosmos; cry; curriculum; decoration; decorum; decree; decretal; degree; demand; design; dictation; direction; directive; discipline; disposition; dun; economy; edict; eutaxy; exaction; expostulation; fiat; file; form(ation); formulation; fraternity; genre; grade; group(ing); harmonization; harmony; husbandry; imperative; imploration; imposition; injunction; instruction; kilter; kind; law; level; line; list; lodge; magnitude; management; mandate; mandatum; method; mode; monition; nature; ordinance; organization; pattern; peace; plan; position; precedence; precept(-ion); procedure; program; prohibition; protocol; quiet(ness); quietude; rank(ing); regularity; regulation; request; requirement; requisition; roster; rota; rule; sequence; serenity; serving; society; solicitation; sort; sphere; state(ment); succession; summary; summons; supplication; syntax; system; tranquility; trend; type; uniformity; union; urgency; will; writ

ORDERLY: **a.** adjusted; aligned; alphabetic(al); alphabetized; appropriate; arranged; arrayed; bandbox; calendrical; calm; categorical; chronologic(al); classified; compact; compatible; congruent; congruous; consecutive; consonant; correct; disposed; *en règle; en* *suite*; exact; harmonious; lined; managed; methodic(al); methodological; neat(ly); parliamentary; peaceable; peaceful; planned; pragmatic; programmatic; proper(ly); quiet; rational; regimental; regimented; regular; regulated; ruled; sedate; sequacious; sequential; serene; seriatim; shipshape; snug; sound; successional; successive; symmetric(al); systematic(al); tidy; trig; trim; unconfused; ORDERLY: **n.** aide; messenger; runner; servant; valet

ORDINANCE: assize; canon; ceremony; control; decree; decretal; direction; disposition; edict; enactment; law; order; precept; prescript; regulation; rite; rule; statute; writ

ORDINARY: **a.** (**see** "average") administrative; banal; common(place); conformable; conventional; current; customary; drab; everyday; familiar; formal; habitual; indifferent; inexpert; inferior; informal; lala; low; mediocre; mere; middling; ministerial; nomic; nominal; noncosmic; normal; plain; poor; prevalent; prosaic; prosy; regular; routine; second-rate; simple; stereotyped; stereotypical; trite; typical; ugly; unadorned; uneventful; unexceptional; unmiraculous; unvarnished; usual; vulgar; vulgate; wonted; workaday; ORDINARY: **n.** book; clergyman; judge; prelate; tavern; ORDINARINESS: averageness; commonplaceness; habituality; informality; mediocrity; simplicity; typicality; usuality; usualness

ORDNANCE: ammunition; armament(s); armor; arms; artillery; cannon; firearms; guns; matériel; mortar(s); weaponry; weapons

ORE: bonanza; coal; coin; hematite; iron; metal; mineral; nickel; rock; source; tin

ORGAN: agency; agent; ear; eye; heart; instrument(ality); journal; kidney; liver; magazine; mean(s); medium; member; newspaper; part; periodical; publication; structure; vehicle; voice

ORGANIC: alive; animate; constitutional; functional; fundamental; inherent; live; living; natural; organismic; organizational; organized; physiological; structural; systemic; vital

ORGANISM: amoeba; animal(cule); animalculum; being; body; entity; individual; monad; monas; organization; person; plant; system; thing

ORGANIZE: (**see** "begin") adjust; arrange; build; cause; classify; commission; constitute; construct; coordinate; design; develop; direct; dispose; energize; establish; fashion; form; found; frame; institute; integrate; manage; mobilize; modernize; orchestrate; order; plan; prepare; produce; ready; settle; shape; start; streamline; structure; systematize; unify; unionize; ORGANIZATION: administration; army; arrangement; association; body; bureau; business; cadre; church; club; command; commission; company; composition; conference; constitution; convention; cosmos; crew; discipline; economy; establishment; firm; frame(work); government; harmonization; harmonizing; harmony; hierarchization; hierarchy; husbandry; institution; integration; league; management; mobilization; organism; outfit; party; personnel; regiment(ation); setup; skeleton; society; staff; stratification; structure; system(atics); systemization; unification; union; unit; whole

ORGY: bacchanal(ia); binge; bout; carousal; carouse; debauch(ery); party; revel(ry); rite; saturnalia (pl.)

ORIENTAL: Asian; Asiatic; bright; Byzantine; Chinese; Eastern; glowing; Japanese; Levantine; ortive; precious

ORIFICE: (**see** "opening") aperture; inlet; outlet; vent

ORIGIN(ATION): (**see** "beginning") author(ship); bed; bibliography; birth; bud; causation; cause; commencement; cradle; creation; dawn; derivation; emanation; etiology; father; focus; foundation; *fons et origo*; font; fount(ain); fountainhead; genesis; germ; growth; head; inauguration; inception; inchoation; incipience; initiation; instigation; lineage; mainspring; matrix; model; nascence; nascency; nature; nest; nidus; occasion; outset; parent(age); primordia (pl.); primordium; provenance; provenience; rise; root; rudiment(s); seed; source; spring; start; stock; substance; supplier; supply; spawning; text; well(spring)

ORIGINAL: aboriginal; alpha; authentic; beginning; birth; causative; chief; creative; elemental; elementary; etiological; first; fontal; formative; fresh; generative; genetic; germinal; germinative; imaginative; inceptive; independent; ingenious; initial; inventive; mint; mother; naissant; nascent; native; neoteric; new; novel; originative; pioneer;

pivotal; primary; prime(val); primitive; primogenial; primogenital; primordial; principal; pristine; protogenic; prototypical; resourceful; rudimentary; seminal; spermatic(al); strange; striking; ultimate; underivative; unhackneyed; unique; unworn; ORIGINALITY: freshness; ingenuity; ingenuosity; inventiveness; newness; novelty; resourcefulness

ORIGINATE: (**see** "create") arise; begin; breed; build; causate; cause; coin; compose; conceive; confect; construct; derive; descend; emanate; engender; fashion; father; flow; form(ulate); grow; hatch; head; inaugurate; initiate; institute; invent; make; manufacture; plan; plot; proceed; procreate; produce; propagate; rise; seed; set; sire; spring; start; stem; spawn; write; ORIGINATOR: (**see** "beginner") father; initiator; inventer; mother; pathblazer; pathbreaker; pathfinder; pioneer; trailblazer

ORNAMENT: **v.** (**see** "adorn") beautify; bedeck; bedizen; begem; deck; decorate; diamondize; edge; embellish; emblazon; emboss; enhance; enrich; festoon; flourish; garnish; gild; paint; polish; spangle; tassel; trim; ORNAMENT: **n.** adornment; amulet; bauble; bead(s); beautification; bedizenment; bracelet; brooch; decor(ation); embellishment; exornation; filigree; frill; garnish(ment); garniture; gem; grace; jewel(ry); ornamentation; ring; scroll; sequin; spangle; tassel; trick; ORNAMENTATION: (**see** "adornment") atmosphere; beautification; decor(ation); development; elegancy; embellishment; enhancement; enrichment; exegesis; expatiation; explanation; fancification; frill; fripperies; frippery; garnish(ment); gaudery; gild; gingerbread; gold; improvement; mounting; opulence; ostentation; paint; polish; refinement; rouge; show; ORNAMENTAL *or* ORNATE: (**see** "showy") adorned; arabesque; attractive; aureate; aurelian; aurulent; baronial; baroque; bombastic; clinquant; colorful; Corinthian; decorated; decorative; dressy; elaborate; elegant; embellished; extravagant; fancy; festooned; flamboyant; florid; flowery; garish; gaudy; gay; gingerbread; gold; grand(iloquent); lush; magnificent; magniloquent; opulent; ornamented; orotund; ostentatious; plush(y); pretentious; resplendent; rich; ritzy; rococo; sequined; spangled; splendid; sumptuous; swank(y); tasseled; tessellated

ORNERY: (**see** "contrary" and "stubborn")

base; cantankerous; common; crabbed; insignificant; lazy; low; mean; ordinary; shiftless; undependable; unmanageable; unreliable

ORT: bit; end; crumb; crust; heel; leaving; leftover; morsel; refuse; remnant; scrap; trifle

ORTHODOX: **see** "sanctioned"

OSCILLATE: (**see** "change") fluctuate; rock; shilly-shally; sway; swing; totter; undulate; vary; vibrate; wag; wave; waver; weave

OSTENSIBLE: (**see** "apparent") clear; conspicuous; likely; obvious; presentable; pretended; probable; semblable; verisimilar

OSTENTATION: (**see** "show") array(ment); boast(ing); bravado; ceremony; dash; display; éclat; elaboration; exhibit(ion); flair; flare; floridity; flourish; frippery; gaudery; glitter; magnificence; magniloquence; ornament(ation); pageant(ry); parade; pomp(osity); pretense; pretentiousness; ritziness; showiness; spectacle; splash; splurge; vainglory; vanity; vaunt(ing); OSTENTATIOUS: (**see** "showy") conspicuous; elaborate; flaring; florid; garish; gaudy; orchidaceous; ornamental; plush(y); ritzy; swank(y); ultrafashionable

OSTIOLE: aperture; opening; orifice; os; pore; stoma

OSTRACIZE: (**see** "banish") abolish; ban; bar; blackmail; cast (out); censure; cut; deport; exclude; exile; oust; punish; scrub; snub

OTHER: (**see** "different") additional; alter(nate); distinct; else; former; further; left; more; otherwise; remaining; second; OTHERNESS: alterity; difference; diversity; OTHERWISE: alias; different(ly); else; or

OTIOSE: empty; functionless; futile; hollow; idle; inactive; indolent; ineffective; ineffectual; lazy; retired; sterile; superfluous; unemployed; useless; vain

OUGHT: **v.** befit; behoove; must; should; OUGHT: **n.** anything; cipher; duty; must; naught; obligation

OUST: (**see** "banish") bar; bounce; cashier; depose; deprive; discard; discharge; dislodge; dismiss; dispossess; disseize; eject; evict;

expel; fire; ostracize; remove; sack; uncrown; unhorse; unpedestal

OUT: **v.** and **a.** abroad; aloud; astray; away; begone; dead; disabled; disclosed; end; ex; exhausted; external(ly); extinguished; far; forth; free; from; *hors de combat*; nonexistent; outlying; public; resigned; retired; revealed; scat!; scram!; unconscious; unfurled; useless

OUT-AND-OUT: (**see** "absolute") arrant; certain; clear; complete(ly); confirmed; consummate; direct; downright; errant; genuine; gross; incontestable; notorious; outright; shameless; sheer; thoroughgoing; unmitigated; unqualified; unreserved; utter; very; wholly

OUTBREAK: brawl; break; bursting; conflict; disturbance; ebullition; epidemic; eruption; explosion; infestation; insurrection; mutiny; outburst; quarrel; rash; rebellion; revolt; revolution; riot; row; rumpus; sally; uprising; violence

OUTBURST: accession; bellow; blaze; blow-up; boutade; clamor; complaint; conclamation; crop; cry; ebullition; eruption; exclamation; explosion; fanfare; fantod; fit; flare(-up); fusillade; gale; gust; howl; noise; objection; outbreak; outcrop; outcry; outflow; outflowing; paroxysm; protest; revolt; roar; sally; scream; screech; shout; spate; spell; start; storm; surge; tantrum; temper; tiff; torrent; tumult; violence

OUTCAST: **a.** abject; degraded; despised; discarded; expatriate; friendless; Ishmaelitish; leprous; rejected; reprobative; vagrant; OUTCAST: **n.** abject; bum; castaway; exile; expatriate; gaberlunzie; hobo; Ishmael; leper; loner; offscouring; pariah; reject; reprobate; vagabond; vagrant

OUTCOME: aftermath; conclusion; consequence; consequent; consummation; cry; denouement; effect; emanation; end; event; exitus; fate; impact; issue; lot; offspring; outgrowth; outlet; produce; progeny; reaction; residual; residuum; result; sequel(a); sequence; termination; upshot; wake

OUTCRY: **v.** bellow; clamor; complain; object; protest; roar; scream; screech; shout; vociferate; yell; yowl; OUTCRY: **n.** (**see** "outburst") auction; bellow; bruit; clamor; complaint; conclamant; conclamation; exclamation; gaff; howl; hue and cry; noise; objection; protest; roar; scream; screech;

shout; tumult; uproar; vociferation; wail; yell; yowl

OUTDATED: **see** "old-fashioned"

OUTDO: (**see** "surpass") beat; best; cap; conquer; defeat; eclipse; exceed; excel; outdazzle; outpace; outshine; outstrip; overcome; overshine; overthrow; pass; top; trump; win; worst

OUTDOORS: (**see** "open-air") alfresco; extraforaneous; hypaethral; upaithric

OUTER: adventitious; alien; ectal; exterior; external; foreign; objective; outside; outward; utter

OUTFIT: **v.** accouter; accoutre; apparel; caparison; clothe; dress; endow; equip; fashion; furnish; garb; organize; rig; suit; supply; tailor; OUTFIT: **n.** accoutrement(s); apparel; armamentaria (pl.); armamentarium; business; caparison; clothes; clothing; dress; endowments; equipage; equipment; flock; frock; format; furnishings; gang; garb; gear; getup; group; herd; instruments; kit; material; office; organization; paraphernalia (pl.); ranch; regalia (pl.); requirements; rig; suit; tackle; team; tools; trappings; troop; unit

OUTFLOW: (**see** "effluvium") overflow; spate; spill

OUTGROWTH: (**see** "consequence") exostosis; offshoot; outcome; ramification; result

OUTLANDISH: (**see** "odd") alien; barbarous; bizarre; cosmic; exotic; fantastic; foreign; freakish; funny; grotesque; indecorous; inelegant; irregular; ludicrous; oddish; *outré*; peculiar; queer; remote; ribald; ridiculous; strange; uncanny; unco; uncouth; unseemly; vulgar

OUTLAST: **see** "survive"

OUTLAW: **v.** ban(ish); bar; disbar; illegalize; prohibit; proscribe; taboo; tabu; unfrock; OUTLAW: **n.** (**see** "bandit") badman; criminal; desperado

OUTLET: aperture; bung; channel; door(way); drain; egress; escape(way); exit(us); faucet; gate(way); hole; issue; lip; loophole; market; meatus; opening; orifice; os; outcome; passage(way); pipe; pocket; port; release; sewer; sink; socket; spout; stream; tap; terminal; vehicle; vent

OUTLINE: **v.** abridge; adumbrate; block; bound; chart; condense; contour; define; delineate; design; diagram; draft; draw; etch; figure; form(ulate); indicate; limit; limn; map; mark; plan; plot; scheme; shape; sketch; summarize; trace; OUTLINE: **n.** abridgement; abstract; adumbration; aperçu; appearance; arrangement; boundary; brief; cadre; capsule; chart; circumference; compendium; condensation; configuration; conformation; conspectus; contour; definition; delineation; demarcation; design; diagram; draft; drawing; epitome; feature(s); figure; form(at); formation; frame(work); limits; lineament; map; perimeter; periphery; physicality; physiognomy; plan; plot; profile; prospectus; prototype; schema; scheme; semblance; shape; sphere; silhouette; sketch; skyline; summary; survey; synopsis; terrain; topography; trace; tracing

OUTLIVE: **see** "survive"

OUTLOOK: anticipation; chances; configuration; expectation; front(age); lookout; mentality; panorama; perspective; perspectivity; policy; position; probability; prognosis; prognostication; prospect; scope; tower; view(point); vista; watch

OUTMODED: antediluvian; antiquated; archaic; archaistic; belated; dated; dead; decadent; *démodé*; demoded; dismoded; effete; *fin-de-siècle*; fogyish; hoary; horse-and-buggy; moribund; mossy; neolithic; obsolete; old (-fashioned); old hat; out-of-date; passé; rusty; troglodytic; unfashionable; unreconstructed; unstylish; used; *vieux jeu*

OUT-OF-DATE: **see** "outmoded"

OUTPOURING: (**see** "outburst") debouchment; *épanchement*; flood; outflow; procession; stream; succession; torrent

OUTPUT: crop; energy; grist; harvest; outflow; power; produce; product(s); production; response; throughput; turnout; yield

OUTRAGE: (**see** "offend") abuse; anger; assault; atrocity; desecration; dishonor; enormity; fury; indecency; indignity; infamy; injury; insult; lese majesty; offense; pillage; profanation; resentment; vilification; violence; ungodliness; wickedness; wrong; OUTRAGEOUS: abhorrent; abusive; arrant; atrocious; disgraceful; extraordinary; extravagant; fantastic; flagrant; heinous; indecent; infamous; injurious; insulting;

monstrous; offensive; shocking; terrible; troublesome; unconscionable; ungodly; unrestrained; violent; whooping; wicked; wrong

OUTRÉ: (**see** "odd") bizarre; eerie; extravagant; strange

OUTRIGHT: (**see** "absolute") arrant; complete(ly); downright; entire; instantaneous-(ly); out-and-out; unreserved(ly)

OUTSET: (**see** "beginning") threshold

OUTSIDE: **a.** advantitious; alien; exogenous; exterior; external; extraneous; extrinsic; foreign; independent; maximum; outer; outward; remote; surface; OUTSIDE: **n.** exterior(ity); external(ity); extraneity; invection; limit; outdoors; utmost; OUTSIDER: auslander; exoteric; foreigner; Ishmael; layman; stranger; tramontane

OUTSPOKEN: articulate; artless; blunt; bold; candid; emphatic; frank; free; plain; unmistakable; unreserved; vocal

OUTSTANDING: A-one; all-star; banner; blue-ribbon; brilliant; conspicuous; continuing; distinct; distinguished; dominant; dominating; due; eminent; excellent; excelling; exceptional; extraordinary; fabulous; first(-grade); first-rate; formidable; illustrious; mandatory; notable; noticeable; noted; owing; paramount; pending; premier(e); projecting; prominent; remaining; remarkable; salient; signal; significant; significative; slambang; star; stellar; striking; sublime; superb; supereminent; supreme; uncollected; unfulfilled; unpaid; unresolved; unsettled

OUTSTRIP: (**see** "surpass") best; cap; defeat; exceed; excel; lead; outdo; outrun; outvie; outweigh; overtake; pass; transcend; win

OUTWARD: apparent; away; ecdemic; ectad; exterior; external; extraneous; extrinsic; foreign; formal; material; outer; outside; superficial; surface

OUTWEIGH: (**see** "surpass") exceed; outdo; outstrip; overshadow; preponderate

OUTWIT: (**see** "baffle") balk; best; cheat; circumvent; cozen; deceive; defeat; defraud; dupe; euchre; foil; fox; frustrate; have; hoodwink; gull; jockey; kill; outdo; outfox; outmaneuver; outplay; overreach; stifle; swindle; take; trick; victimize

OVAL: curvilinear; elliptic(al); nummiform;

nummular; oblong; ovate; ovoid; spherical; spheroidal

OVER: **a.** and **n.** above; across; again; also; aside; athwart; atop; away; beyond; by; dead; done; encore; ended; excess(ive); finished; gone; inordinate(ly); odd; on; opposite; passé; passed; past; preeminent; settled; stopped; superior; surplus; thorough-(ly); through; too; undone; upon

OVERACT: emote; exaggerate; outdo; over-do; OVERACTING *or* OVERACTED: acrobatics; exaggeration; histrionics; theatrics; OVERACTIVE: exaggerative; hyperactive; hyperkinetic; superactive; supererogatory

OVERAWE: abash; browbeat; bully; cow; daunt; dominate; domineer; frighten; hector; intimidate; subdue; sway

OVERBEARING: aggressive; arbitrary; arrogant; authoritative; autocratic; blustering; brazen; cavalier; compelling; crushing; despotic; dictatorial; dogmatic; domineering; dominant; dominative; haughty; hectoring; imperative; imperious; insolent; insupportable; intimidating; lordly; magisterial; masterful; oppressive; overpowering; overwhelming; powerful; preponderating; pressing; proud; supercilious; toplofty; tyrannical; tyrannous; vainglorious

OVERBURDENED: **see** "overloaded"

OVERCAST: (**see** "cloudy") dark; depressed; depressing; gloomy

OVERCOME: (**see** "subdue") awe; beat; best; catch; confute; conquer; crush; defeat; demolish; depress; destroy; devastate; discomfit; dominate; domineer; exceed; get; hurdle; inhibit; kill; lick; master; oppress; outdo; overpower; overrule; overwhelm; prevail; prostrate; quell; quench; restrain; route; rule; smother; still; subjugate; suppress; surmount; throw; upset; vanquish; win

OVERCONFIDENT: certain; cocksure; hubristic; overweening; presumptuous; proud; self-possessed

OVERDO: cloy; exaggerate; exhaust; expend; fatigue; overact; overplay; overreach; overspend; overstress; overtax; satiate; supererogate; tax

OVERDUE: arrear(s); belated; delayed; excessive; late; tardy; unpaid; unsettled

OVEREAT: (**see** "gorge") cloy; glut; gormandize; indulge; overindulge; satiate; wolf

OVERFLOW: **v.** abound; avalanche; deluge; engulf; flood; glut; inundate; overrun; overspread; overwhelm; spate; spill; superabound; swarm; teem; vent; OVERFLOW: **n.** abundance; avalanche; copiosity; cornucopia; deluge; ebullience; enjambment; *épanchement*; excess; flood; glut; inundation; outlet; plethora; profusion; redundance; redundancy; repletion; rest; spate; superabundance; superfluity; surplus; swarm; synaphea; teeming; tide; torrent; vent; OVERFLOWING: abundant; affluent; awash; copious; cornucopian; ebullient; exuberant; flush; full; inundatory; plethoric; profuse; redounding; redundant; replete; scaturient; spating; superabundant; superfluous; surplus; swarming; torrential

OVERHANGING: abeyant; beetling; imminent; impending; jutting; pending; projecting; suspended; threatening

OVERHEAD: **adv.** above; aloft; over; OVERHEAD: **n.** ceiling; charges; cost; expenses; maintenance; sky; upkeep

OVERINDULGENCE: (**see** "gluttony") orgy; overeating; satiation; satiety; wolfishness

OVERJOYED: (**see** "pleased") delighted; elated; enraptured; joyous; jubilant; rejoicing; transported

OVERLAY: ceil; coat; cover; gild; hide; lap; obscure; oppress; overlap; overlie; paint; pave; smother; spread; superimpose

OVERLOADED: burdened; overburdened; overladen; plethoric; sated; surcharged

OVERLOOK: (**see** "excuse") condone; disregard; forget; forgive; ignore; inspect; manage; miss; neglect; omit; oversee; overtop; pardon; pass; pretermit; skip; slight; spare; superintend; supervise; survey; wink

OVERNICE: (**see** "particular") euphemistic; fastidious; meticulous; nice-Nelly; per(s)-nickety; prudish; scrupulous; squeamish; OVERNICETY: correctitude; fastidiousness; per(s)nicketiness; scrupulosity; squeamishness

OVERPOWER: (**see** "defeat") awe; beat; conquer; coerce; crush; deluge; devastate; engulf; entrance; hector; master; override; overrun; overthrow; overwhelm; stun; sub-

due; subjugate; swamp; vanquish; win;
OVERPOWERING: (see "overwhelming")
copious; crushing; masterful; mortal; pressing; shattering; terrific; torrential

OVERREACH: cheat; circumvent; cozen;
deceive; defraud; dupe; exaggerate; exceed;
extend; outwit; overdo; overextend; overtake; overtop; pass; strain; stretch; tax

OVERREFINEMENT: alembication; nicety;
preciosity

OVERRIDE: abrogate; annul; conquer; defeat; dominate; harass; nullify; oppress;
outride; overlap; overpower; overthrow;
overtop; pass; supersede; suppress; trample;
vanquish; veto

OVERRUN: (see "defeat") beset; crush;
despoil; devastate; exceed; harass; infect;
infest; invade; outrun; overpower; overwhelm; ravage; spread; storm; swarm; teem

OVERSEE: (see "control") command; conduct; direct; examine; guide; handle;
inspect; manage; overlook; regulate; scout;
spy; superintend; supervise; survey; watch;
OVERSEER: agent; boss; chief; commandant; commander; curator; director; foreman; guardian; inspector; master; principal;
sentry; superintendent; superior; supervisor;
taskmaster; watch(man)

OVERSHADOW: (see "cloud") adumbrate;
darken; dim(inish); dominate; eclipse;
efface; exceed; obscure; outweigh; shade;
shelter; tower

OVERSIGHT: (see "error") blunder; care;
charge; command; control; direction; failure;
fault; flaw; gaffe; guidance; inadvertence;
inattention; inspection; lapse; management;
mistake; omission; regulation; slip; superintendence; supervision; surveillance; watchfulness

OVERSPREAD: (see "cover") fog; overflow;
paint; pall; scatter; strew; wash

OVERSTATEMENT: (see "exaggeration")
embellishment; hyperbole; ornamentation

OVERT: (see "open") apparent; evident;
manifest; obvious; plain; public; undisguised

OVERTAKE: (see "catch") attain; involve;
outstrip; overreach; overtop; pass; reach;
rejoin; seize; win

OVERTHROW: v. capsize; collapse; confound; confuse; conquer; debar; defeat;
demolish; derange; destroy; dethrone; devastate; dislodge; disorganize; disrupt; disthrone; exterminate; level; overcome; overpower; override; overturn; overwhelm;
reverse; revolt; rout; ruin; subdue; subjugate; subvert; surmount; topple; tumble;
uncrown; unhorse; upend; upset; vanquish;
worst; wreck; OVERTHROW: n. bouleversement; collapse; *coup d'état*; debacle;
defeasance; defeat; destruction; disorganization; disruption; extermination; labefaction;
reverse; revolution; rout; ruin; topple;
tumble; vanquishment; wreck

OVERTOP: (see "defeat") cover; dwarf;
eclipse; exceed; excel; obscure; override;
surpass; tower; transcend

OVERTURE: approach; beginning; bid;
commencement; initiative; music; offer;
opening; prelude; proem; proposal; proposition; request; tender

OVERTURN: (see "overthrow") capsize;
invalidate; keel; pancake; spill; subvert;
tilt; tip; unhorse; upend; upset

OVERWHELM: (see "defeat") avalanche;
bear down; beat; bowl (over); bury; confound; conquer; crush; deluge; demolish;
destroy; devastate; dismay; drown; engulf;
flood; inundate; oppress; overcome; overpower; override; overrun; overthrow; quell;
quiet; ravish; rout; ruin; sate; satiate; sink;
slay; steamroller; storm; stun; subdue;
subjugate; submerge; suppress; surprise;
swallow; swamp; take (by storm); triumph;
upset; vanquish; OVERWHELMED *or*
OVERWHELMING: cataclysmal; cataclysmic; copious; crushing; decisive; deluginous; devastating; frantic; ineffable;
inundatory; knee-deep; murderous; overpowering; shattering; stunning; terrible;
terrific; torrential; withering

OVERWORK: see "tire"

OVERWROUGHT: (see "emotional")
affected; agitated; disturbed; excited;
flustered; high-strung; hysteric(al); impassioned; inflamed; infuriated; nervous; overdone; overexcited; perturbed; ruffled;
shaken; tired; upset

OWING: (in) arrear; ascribable; attributable;
belated; due; indebted; obligated; obliged;
overdue; owed; payable; unpaid; unsettled

OWN: acknowledge; admit; allow; assent; avow; concede; confess; control; countenance; disclose; divulge; have; hold; master; monopolize; possess; recognize; retain; reveal; OWNERSHIP: deed; dominion; mastery; monopoly; possession; proprietorship; right; title

P

PABULUM: (see "food") aliment; fodder; fuel; grist; hay; manna; nourishment; nutrient; nutriment; support; sustenance

PACE: **v.** advance; amble; gallop; lead; lope; match; measure; move; precede; proceed; regulate; run; speed; step; stride; trot; walk; PACE: **n.** advancement; canter; clip; competition; course; distance; example; exhibit; fluency; footstep; gait; gallop; growth; impetus; lope; measure; nave; passageway; rack; rapidity; rate; routine; run; space; speed; step; stride; tempo; timing; trace; tread; trot; velocity; walk

PACIFIC: (see "peaceful") irenic(al); pacifist-(ic); tranquil

PACIFY: (see "calm") abate; allay; alleviate; ameliorate; appease; assuage; compose; conciliate; ease; lull; mitigate; moderate; mollify; placate; quiet(en); reconcile; relieve; settle; soften; soothe; stay; subdue; temper; tranquilize; PACIFICATION: abatement; alleviation; amelioration; appeasement; conciliation; mitigation; moderation; mollification; propitiation; reconciliation; subdual; tranquilization; PACIFICATORY: (see "peaceful") alleviatory; conciliatory; irenic-(al); mollifying; pacifistic; placative; propitiative; tranquilizing

PACK: **v.** arrange; assemble; bale; bundle; burden; carry; caulk; collect; compress; congregate; cram; crowd; depart; fill; finish; go; jam; load; package; possess; prepare; press; push; ram; send; squeeze; stop; stow; stuff; tamp; tote; wad; PACK: **n.** amount; bale; boodle; bundle; burden; carton; collection; container; crowd; deck; drove; flock; gang; group; heap; herd; knapsack; load; mass; multitude; package; pile; set; shock; truss; wad

PACKAGE: **v.** (see "pack") encase; enclose; wrap; PACKAGE: **n.** (see "pack") bale; barrel; box; bundle; carton; case; combination; composite; container; crate; packet; parcel; wrapper

PACT: agreement; bargain; cartel; compact; contract; covenant; pactum; treaty; understanding

PAD: **v.** (see "pack") add; amble; bolster; cram; cushion; exaggerate; expand; increase; lengthen; muffle; mute; stuff; tamp; thicken; tramp(le); trudge; truss; PAD: **n.** bed; bolster; bunch; bundle; compress; cot; cover; cushion; footfall; guard; horse; mat; leaf; pillion; pillow; protection; quilt; road; route; table; tampon; truss; wad

PADDLE: **v.** dabble; punish; spank; thrash; whip; PADDLE: **n.** blade; flipper; oar; scoop; scull; spoon

PADDOCK: enclosure; field; frog; lot; park; pasture; toad; yard

PAGAN: **a.** atheistic; gentile; heathen(ish); idolatrous; irreligious; skeptical; ungodly; PAGAN: **n.** atheist; ethnic; gentile; heathen; hedonist; idolater; paynim; savage; skeptic; unbeliever

PAGE: **v.** (see "call") attend; serve; summon; wait; PAGE: **n.** assistant; attendant; boy; child; leaf; messenger; orderly; record; servant; writing

PAGEANT(RY): (see "display") cavalcade; éclat; exhibition; magnificence; ostentation; parade; pomp(osity); pretense; procession; publicity; sham; show; sideshow; spectacle; spectacular; splendor

PAIN: **v.** ache; afflict; agonize; ail; bother; cramp; discomfit; discomfort; distress; disturb; draw; exhaust; grieve; grill; harass; harrow; hurt; irk; offend; pant; pierce; plague; provoke; rankle; smart; stab; sting; suffer; throb; torment; trouble; try; twinge; upset; worry; PAIN: **n.** ache; affliction; agitation; agony; ailment; *angoisse*; angst; anguish; anxiety; bale; bereavement; bother; burden; calamity; care; catch; consternation; constraint; cramp; cruciation; discomfort; distress; disturbance; dolor; effort;

excruciation; fantod(s); grief; grievance; harassment; headache; hurt; hyperalgesia; illness; laceration; lancination; malady; martyrdom; migraine; misery; misfortune; mortification; offense; pang; paroxysm; penalty; penance; plague; punishment; rack; regret; remorse; smart(ing); soreness; sorrow; stab; sting; stitch; suffering; throb; throe; torment; torture; travail; trial; tribulation; trouble; twinge; umbrage; unease; uneasiness; unhappiness; woe; worry; PAINFUL: abject; aching; afflicted; afflicting; afflictive; aggrieved; agonal; agonizing; ailing; annoying; atrocious; bad; bitter; burdensome; calamitous; caustic; cruel; cutting; damaging; deplorable; dire; disagreeable; disastrous; distasteful; distressful; distressing; dolorific; dolorous; excruciating; galling; grievous; grilling; harassing; hard; harrowing; heinous; hurtful; hyperalgesic; insufferable; intolerable; irksome; killing; lancinating; miserable; offensive; pathetic; perturbed; piercing; plaintive; raw; regretful; rigorous; sad; savage; sore; sorrowful; sorry; stabbing; suffering; tender; throbbing; tiresome; torminous; tortuous; torturesome; troublesome; unbearable; uneasy; unendurable; unpleasant; upsetting; vexatious; virulent; woeful; worrying; wrenchful; wrenching

PAINS: (see "trouble") care; caution; effort; exertion; labor; punishment; toil; trouble; work; worry

PAINT: **v.** adorn; beautify; brush; color; cosmeticize; cover; decorate; delineate; depict; describe; draw; enamel; gloss; limn; picture; portray; represent; rouge; sketch; smear; spread; stain; swab; taint; tinge; variegate; varnish; veneer; PAINT: **n.** color; cosmetic; cover; decoration; enamel; gloss; lipstick; makeup; maquillage; pigment; rouge; spread; stain; varnish; veneer

PAIR: **v.** agree; associate; brace; conjugate; couple; join; marry; match; mate; team; yoke; PAIR: **n.** brace; conjugation; counterpart(s); couple; duality; duo; dyad; ensemble; match; mates; opener; partnership; set; span; team; twain; twins; two(some); yoke; PAIRED: bigeminal; binary; duplex; dyadic; gemel; jumelle; matched; mated; teamed; wed(ded)

PAL: (see "buddy") accomplice; ally; chum; companion; comrade; confederate; confrere; crony; fellow; friend; mate(y); partner; sidekick

PALACE: building; house; mansion; praetorium

PALATABLE: (see "appetizing") acceptable; agreeable; delicious; flavorable; flavorful; flavorous; flavorsome; gustable; luscious; pleasant; reliable; relishing; sapid; saporous; savory; spicy; tasteful; tasty; toothsome

PALATE: relish; taste; uvula; velum

PALAVER: **v.** argue; chat; confer; converse; debate; discourse; discuss; parley; powwow; speak; talk; treat; utter; wheedle; PALAVER: **n.** (see "conference") affair; balderdash; business; cajolery; chat(ter); colloquy; conversation; debate; discussion; flattery; flummery; parley; powwow; rigmarole; talk; twaddle

PALE: **a.** achrom(at)ic; achromatous; achromous; anemic; ashen; ashy; blanched; bleached; bloodless; cadaverous; cheerless; cinerous; clear; colorless; crystal(line); decolorized; diatonic; dim; drab; drawn; dull; etiolate(d); faded; faint; feeble; ghastly; ghostly; gray; grim; haggard; hueless; ischemic; leukemic; lifeless; livid; mealy; mousy; neutral; pallescent; pallid; pastel; pasty; peaked; plain; sallow; sickly; tired; transparent; wan; waxen; waxy; white; whitish; PALE: **n.** area; barrier; enclosure; fence; jurisdiction; limit; picket; region; stake; PALENESS: achromia; etiolation; ghastliness; ghostliness; ischemia; lividity; pallidity; pallor; pastiness

PALISADE: cliff; defense; enclosure; fence; fort(ification); paling; stake; stockade

PALL: **v.** cloak; cloud; cloy; deaden; deject; dishearten; dispirit; drape; dull; fail; glut; gorge; jade; sate; satiate; shroud; sicken; smoke; surfeit; tire; PALL: **n.** cloak; cloth; cloud; coffin; covering; dejection; failure; fog; glut; mantle; satiation; satiety; shroud; smoke; surfeit

PALLET: bed; blanket; cushion; mattress; pad(dle); paillasse; pawl; quilt(s)

PALLIATE: (see "ease") abate; alleviate; cloak; conceal; conciliate; cover; cushion; defend; diminish; disguise; excuse; extenuate; hide; justify; lessen; lighten; mask; mitigate; moderate; reduce; relieve; screen; soften; varnish; veil; veneer; vindicate; whiten; PALLIATIVE: **see** "sedative"

PALLID: (**see** "pale") leukemic; thin; watery; whitish

PALM: **v.** bribe; conceal; foist; handle; hide; impose; manipulate; obtrude; steal; tip; touch; PALM: **n.** decoration; prize; symbol; tree; triumph; trophy

PALMIST: chirognomist; chiromancer; PALMISTRY: chirognomy; chiromancy; dexterity; trickery

PALMY: **see** "prosperous" and "serene"

PALPATE: examine; explore; feel; pat; touch; PALPABLE: apparent; clear; discernible; distinct; manifest; noticeable; obvious; patent; perceivable; plain; tactile; tangible

PALTER: bargain; chaffer; dodge; elude; equivocate; fib; haggle; gratify; lie; parley; quibble; shift; traffic; trifle; truckle

PALTRY: (**see** "cheap") base; beggarly; *chétif; chétive* (fem.); childish; contemptible; despicable; foolish; inadequate; inconsequential; inferior; insignificant; lacking; low; mean; measly; petty; picayune; picayunish; pitiable; pitiful; puny; slight; small; sneaking; sneaky; sorry; tinny; trashy; trifling; trivial; unimportant; vile; worthless

PAMPER: (**see** "caress") baby; cherish; cocker; coddle; comfort; console; cosset; encourage; fondle; gratify; hug; humor; indulge; kiss; mollycoddle; nurse; pet; please; satiate; satisfy; spoil

PAMPHLET: booklet; brochure; cahier; essay; leaflet; manual; monograph; tract; treatise

PAN: **v.** boil; cook; criticize; fry; ridicule; PAN: **n.** basin; container; dish; face; kettle; lappet; pot; tab; utensil; vessel

PANACEA: catholicon; cure-all; elixir; nepenthe; placebo; remedy; solace

PANDEMONIUM: (**see** "commotion") ado; bedlam; brouhaha; clamor; clangor; clatter; coil; confusion; din; disorder; hell; hubbub; hullabaloo; noise; racket; tumult; uproar

PANDER: bawd; cater; cringe; fawn; gratify; pimp; procure; subserve; toady; truckle

PANEGYRIC: encomium; eulogy; laudation; praise; tribute

PANEL: board; cushion; group; hurdle; insert; jury; label; list; names; pad; partition; saddle; section; series; slate; survey; tablet

PANG: (**see** "pain") ache; agony; anguish; distress; rack; sorrow; spasm; stab; stitch; throe; twang; want

PANORAMA: (**see** "range") cyclorama; jurisdiction; painting; scene; sweep; view; vista

PANT: aspire; blow; desire; gasp; heave; hyperventilate; huff; long; palpitate; pine; puff; pulsate; respire; sigh; throb; yearn; PANTING: anhelation; dyspnea; hyperpnea; hyperventilation; palpitation

PANTRY: ambry; buttery; closet; cupboard; larder; spence

PAPER: bond; certificate; composition; deed; diploma; document; essay; instrument; money; monograph; notes; papyri (pl.); papyrus; parchment; publication; rag; sheepskin; sheet; study; theme; thesis; tract; vellum; writing

PAR: (**see** "average") balance; equality; level; mean; median; norm(ality); parity; standard; sterling; value

PARABLE: (**see** "allegory") apologue; comparison; fable; moral; similtude; story; tale

PARACLETE: advocate; aider; comforter; consoler; intercessor; pleader

PARADE: **v.** (**see** "exhibit") air; array; display; expose; file; flaunt; flourish; maneuver; march; marshal; masquerade; process; promenade; review; show; strut; vent; walk; PARADE: **n.** (**see** "exhibition") array(ment); cavalcade; ceremony; display; exposition; file; flourish; formation; listing; maneuver; march; masquerade; movement; ostentation; pageant(ry); pomp(osity); pretention; procession; promenade; recital; review; show; spectacle; splendor; succession

PARADIGM: **see** "model"

PARADISE: (**see** "heaven") Abraham's bosom; bliss; delight; Eden; Elysian fields; Elysium; felicity; garden; happiness; happy hunting grounds; Nirvana; oblivion; pleasure; Utopia; PARADISIAC(AL): (**see** "heavenly") delightful; Edenic; elysian; felicific; felicitous; happy; nirvanic; pleasurable; utopian

PARADOX: absurdity; ambivalence; anomaly; antilogy; antinomy; antithesis; contradiction; contrariety; enigma; incompatibility; inconsistency; mystery; negation; opposition; rebuttal; refutation

PARAGON: (**see** "ideal") criterion; diamond; equal; masterpiece; match; mate; model; nonesuch; nonpareil; paladin; paradigm; pattern; phoenix; rival; standard; type

PARAGRAPH: article; clause; composition; indentation; item; notice; passage; plank; section; subdivision; theme; verse

PARALLEL: **v.** (**see** "equal") compare; correspond; match; PARALLEL: **a.** (**see** "equal") alike; analogous; companion; concentric; concurrent; congruent; congruous; correlative; correspondent; corresponding; equalized; equidistant; interdependent; isometric; like; matching; paradromic; same; similar; twin; uniform; PARALLEL: **n.** *alter ego*; analogue; analogy; companion; congruency; correlative; correspondent; counterpart; equality; example; likeness; match; resemblance; similarity; twin; uniformity

PARALYZE: bottleneck; congeal; cripple; daze; deaden; destroy; numb; obstruct; prevent; rigidify; scare; shock; stupefy; throttle; torpify; unnerve; PARALYSIS: cowardliness; funk; hemiplegia; impotence; inaction; palsy; paraplegia; paresis; shock; stagnation; stroke; stupor; terror; torpidity; torpor

PARAMOUNT: (**see** "eminent" and "foremost") above; chief; dominant; dominating; high(est); leading; predominating; sovereign; superior; supreme; transcendent; unique

PARAMOUR: cicisbeo; concubine; leman; lover; mistress

PARAPET: breastwork; earthwork; protection; rampart; wall

PARAPHERNALIA: (**see** "equipment") apparatus; appurtenances; gear; luggage; tackle; tools; trumpery; trunks

PARAPHRASE: amplification; condensation; *oratio obliqua*; recapitulation; restatement; synopsis

PARASITE: autophyte; bootlick(er); bug; bur(r); drone; favorite; fawner; flatterer; flea; flunky; freeloader; fungus; germ; hanger-on; leech; lickspit; lickspittle; louse; rust; saprophyte; smut; sponge(r); sycophant; tick; toady; virus; PARASITIC(AL): fawning; freeloading; saprophytic; sycophantic(al); toadying

PARCEL: **v.** allot; apportion; award; bundle; collect; deal; distribute; divide; dole; grant; mete; ration; wrap; PARCEL: **n.** allotment; award; bale; batch; box; bundle; carton; collection; deal; distribution; division; dole; fragment; group; land; lot; pack(age); packet; part; piece; plot; portion; ration; section; tract

PARCH: (**see** "dry") bake; burn; char; desiccate; roast; scorch; sear; shrivel; toast; torrify; wither; PARCHED: (**see** "dry") adust; anhydrous; arid; bare; barren; desiccated; seared; shriveled; sterile; thirsty; torrid; unproductive; withered

PARCHMENT: bond; deed; diploma; document; forel; paper; sheepskin; skin; vellum; writing

PARDON: **v.** (**see** "excuse") absolve; acquit; condone; emancipate; exonerate; forego; forget; forgive; free; overlook; pass; release; remit; reprieve; spare; tolerate; waive; PARDON: **n.** (**see** "excuse") absolution; acquittal; amnesty; condonation; emancipation; exoneration; forgiveness; freedom; grace; indulgence; mercy; oblivion; release

PARE: (**see** "clip") cut; decrease; diminish; divest; flay; lessen; peel; reduce; remove; resect; shave; shorten; skin; slice; trim

PARENT: ancestor; author; begettor; cause; dad; dam; father; genetrix (fem.); genitor; mamma; mater; mom; mother; origin(ator); papa; pater; producer; progenitor; sire; source; PARENTAL: (**see** "fatherly") motherly

PARENTHETIC(AL): (**see** "incidental") digressive; ejaculatory; episodic(al); interjaculatory; interjectional; interjectural; interlocutory; *par parenthèse*; tangential

PARITY: (**see** "equality") analogy; equivalence; evenness; levelness; likeness; par; resemblance; sameness

PARK: **v.** assemble; deposit; establish; leave; place; set(tle); sit; store; PARK: **n.** arboretum; area; basin; campus; claire; commons; green; grounds; grove; hall; promenade; reserve; valley; zoo

PARLEY: **v.** (**see** "palaver") argue; chat; confer; converse; debate; discourse; discuss; speak; talk; treat; utter; PARLEY: **n.** (**see** "conference") address; argument; chat; conference; conversation; debate; discourse; discussion; talk

PARLIAMENT: assemblage; assembly; conference; congress; council; Dail; diet; gathering; legislature

PARODY: **v.** (**see** "imitate") ape; burlesque; caricature; copy; mimic; mirror; lampoon; satirize; spoof; PARODY: **n.** (**see** "imitation") bit; burlesque; caricature; copy; lampoon; satire; skit; spoof; travesty,

PAROL: nuncupative; oral; pleading; unwritten; verbal

PAROXYSM: (**see** "convulsion") agitation; agony; anger; attack; crisis; emotion; exacerbation; explosion; fit; furor; fury; jac(ti)tation; orgasm; outburst; rage; seizure; spasm; storm; tantrum; throe; tremor

PARROT: **v.** (**see** "imitate") echo; mimic; mock; parody; repeat; PARROT: **n.** ara-(ra); bird; cockatoo; corella; kaka; kea; lory; poll(y); repeater

PARRY: **v.** (**see** "avoid") avert; defend; deflect; dodge; elude; evade; fence; fend; prevent; repartee; retort; shift; sidestep; step; ward; PARRY: **n.** (**see** "avoidance") defense; deflection; evasion; fence; prevention; repartee; retort; shift; sidestep; step

PARSIMONIOUS: (**see** "stingy") meager; poor; retentive

PARSON: **see** "clergyman"

PARSONAGE: benefice; manse; rectory

PART: **v.** (**see** "divide") allot; apportion; break; depart; detach; die; disjoin(t); disunite; diverge; fork; fragmentize; leave; open; partition; quit; rend; relinquish; segregate; separate; sever; spread; sunder; tear; widen; PART: **n.** aliquot; allotment; award; bit; chip; chunk; component; concern; constituent; crumb; cut; detail; district; division; duty; element; faction; feature; finger; fraction; fragment; function; half; ingredient; integral; integrant; interest; item; leaf; lot; lump; member; moiety; office; organ; parcel; particle; particular(ity); piece; place; portion; position; quanta (pl.); quantum; quarter; region; remnant; role; section;

sector; scrap; share; side; slice; some; spot; stage; stretch; structure; submultiple; substance; tittle; token; tract; twin; unit; PARTED: (**see** "apart" and "disconnected") bifid; bifurcated; cleft; cloven; deceased; dichotomous; estranged; open; partite; segregated; separated

PARTAKE: bear; consume; cooperate; drink; eat; experience; have; participate; receive; share; suffer; taste; try; use

PARTIAL: biased; *ex parte*; favorable; favored; foolish; fractionary; fragmental; fragmentary; half(way); inclined; incomplete; one-sided; particular; partisan; predisposed; prejudiced; segmented; some; unilateral; unjust; PARTIALITY: bias; favor(itism); fondness; foolishness; friendship; inclination; injustice; interest; liking; nepotism; odds; partisanry; partisanship; predilection; taste; zealotry

PARTICIPATE: (**see** "cooperate") act; aid; ante; assist; associate; bestow; coact; collaborate; colleague; communicate; concur; conspire; contribute; divide; dole; donate; enlist; further; give; grant; help; join; lend; mingle; partake; plan; play; plot; shape; subscribe; supply; unite; use; PARTICIPATION: (**see** "cooperation") act; assistance; contribution; experience; hand; share; use; PARTICIPANT(S): antagonist; combatant; doer; *dramatis personae* (pl.); entrant; entry; partaker; participator; partner; party; sharer

PARTICLE: (**see** "fragment") ace; amount; atom; bit; crumb; drop; element; fig; fleck; ghost; grain; granule; iota; jot; mite; molecule; morsel; mote; part; piece; portion; ray; scintilla; scrap; scruple; shred; spark; speck; spot; thread; tittle; trace; unit; whit

PARTICULAR: **a.** (**see** "critical") accurate; actual; alone; captious; careful; characteristic; chary; choosy; circumstantial; clean; clerkish; close; dainty; delicate; demanding; detailed; difficult; distinct(ive); especial; exact(ing); exclusive; extraordinary; fastidious; fine; finical; finicky; fussy; immaculate; individual; intimate; lone; meticulous; minute; nice; odd; overnice; overprecise; peculiar; per(s)nickety; personal; precise; prissy; private; prudent; prudish; rabbinic-(al); respective; scrupulous; sensitive; separate; singular; sole; special; specific; squeamish; strict; stylish; unique; PARTICULAR: **n.** article; characteristic; circumstance; clause; commodity; detail; fact; feature; finicalness; finickiness; instance;

item; paragraph; part(icularity); plank; point; proposition; regard; respect; stipulation; thing

PARTING: cleavage; disassociation; disjunction; dismemberment; dissociation; dissolution; disunion; division; estrangement; joint; leave-taking; separation; sundering

PARTISAN: **a.** (**see** "partial") biased; dogmatic; factionary; unneutral; PARTISAN: **n.** adherent; advocate; aficionada (fem.); aficionado; ally; backer; champion; disciple; factionary; factioneer; flag-waver; follower; friend; guerilla; halberd; henchman; ite; nonneutral; partialist; sectarian; supporter; sympathizer; zealot; PARTISANSHIP: bias; championship; favor(itism); fondness; friendship; nepotism; partiality; partisanry; predilection; taste; team; unneutrality; zealotry

PARTITION: **v.** (**see** "divide") allot; apportion; bar; deal; distribute; dole; fence; part; screen; separate; sever; wall; PARTITION: **n.** allotment; analysis; apportionment; barrier; distribution; divider; division; fence; hedge; line; part; scantle; screen; separation; sept; severance; wall

PARTNER: accomplice; ally; associate; auxiliary; chum; coadjutor; colleague; companion; confederate; confrere; consort; coparcener; husband; mate(y); pal; pard; partaker; participant; sharer; spouse; teammate; wife; PARTNERSHIP: accomplicity; alliance; association; business; cahoot(s) comates; company; connection; fellowship; firm; interest; marriage; mutuality; participation; union

PARTY: assemblage; assembly; at home; bacchanal; bash; bee; bender; binge; blast; bloc; blow(out); brannigan; cabal; carousal; cause; celebration; circle; clique; clutch; company; conclave; confederacy; conspiracy; coterie; dance; detachment; drunk; event; faction; fellowship; following; frolic; gala; gang; gathering; group; high jinks; individual; interest; intrigue; jag; junto; lark; league; levy; litigant; organization; orgy; participant; partisanship; picnic; potlach; powwow; reception; ring; sect; set; shindig; shindy; side; social; society; soiree; splurge; spree; squad; symposium; tea; troop; troupe; wassail; whoop-de-do

PARVENU: arriviste; Johnny-come-lately; mushroom; newcomer; *nouveau riche*; snob; upstart

PASQUINADE: burlesque; farce; lampoon; parody; pasquil; satire; squib

PASS: **v.** achieve; adjudicate; admit; advance; approve; attain; authorize; blow over; bygo; circulate; confirm; convey; cross; deport; develop; devolve; die; discharge; distribute; elapse; elide; endorse; exceed; exchange; expire; fade; fall; flit; give; glide; go; graduate; hand; happen; intromit; judge; lapse; leave; lessen; manipulate; move; neglect; occur; omit; open; osmose; outstrip; overlook; override; overstep; overtake; penetrate; permeate; permit; proceed; prolong; promote; pronounce; protract; relay; roll; skip; slip; spend; spin; stretch; subside; succeed; surpass; terminate; throw; toss; transact; transcend; transfer; transmit; transport; travel; traverse; utter; vanish; wear; while; PASS: **n.** avenue; col; crisis; defile; difficulty; gap; gesture; ghat; intromission; juncture; lapse; license; manipulation; notch; opening; order; passage; permission; permit; pinch; plight; predicament; road; route; situation; state; stew; strait; ticket; way

PASSABLE: (**see** "average") acceptable; adequate; admissible; current; fair; mediocre; middling; moderate; ordinary; permissible; presentable; satisfactory; small; so-so; sufficient; tolerable; trafficable; traversable

PASSAGE(WAY): access; accommodation; act; adit; aditus; aisle; alley; atrium; avenue; channel; clause; conveyance; corridor; course; defile; door(way); duct; enactment; fare; flight; gang(way); gap; gate(way); hall(way); hiatus; introitus; journey; lobby; migration; movement; opening; os; paragraph; part; pass; path; porch; pore; progress; ramp; road; route; run(way); sanction; section; shaft; sidewalk; slip; strait; text; thoroughfare; ticket; toll; tour; traffic; transaction; transference; transit(ion); transmission; travel; trip; voyage; walk(way); way

PASSÉ: aged; antiquated; bygone; decadent; faded; *fin-de-siècle*; obsolescent; obsolete; out(moded); superannuated; worn(-out)

PASSENGER: fare; itinerant; pilgrim; rider; tourist; traveler; voyager; wayfarer

PASSING: (**see** "fleeting") casual; cursory; ephemeral; evanescent; exceedingly; fly-by-night; momentary; moving; superficial; temporary; transient; transitory; very

PASSION: affection; agitation; agony; anger; ardor; blood; craving; craze; cross; desire; devotion; distress; eagerness; ecstasy; emotion; enthusiasm; evangelism; excitement; feeling; fervor; fever; fire; flame; frenzy; heartthrob; heat; impulse; infatuation; intensity; ire; joy; liking; love; lust; martyrdom; pain; rapture; raptus; spleen; suffering; temper; throe; torridity; transport; trial; urge; vehemence; will; yen; zeal; PASSIONATE: angry; ardent; bacchanalian; bacchic; burning; Dionysian; eager; ebullient; enraged; enthusiastic; evangelistic; excited; Faustian; feverish; fiery; highspirited; hot(-blooded); impassioned; impetuous; intemperate; intense; irascible; orgiastic; precipitate; quick-tempered; sensual; sultry; torrid; unrestrained; vehement; violent; voluptuous; warm; wild

PASSIVE: (see "apathetic") dormant; feminine; idle; inactive; indifferent; inert; inexcitable; invertebrate; latent; lethargic; lifeless; negative; obedient; pathic; patient; pliable; pliant; quiescent; quiet; receptive; reluctant; stoic(al); submissive; supine; uneager; unresisting; unresistive; unresponsive; yielding; PASSIVENESS: (see "apathy") inactivity; lifelessness; passivity; stoicism; submission

PASSPORT: congé; identification; license; pass; permission; permit; safe-conduct; ticket; voucher

PASSWORD: countersign; *mot de passe*; *mot d'ordre*; *mot du guet*; *passe parole*; sesame; shibboleth; token; watchword

PAST: (see "ago") accomplished; after; agone; ancient; antiquated; beyond; by(gone); dead; distant; elapsed; eld; ended; former; gone; historical; obsolete; old; over; passé; quondam; remote; since; spent; then; through; up; yesteryear; yore

PASTE: v. adhere; cement; glue; patch; repair; spread; stick; PASTE: n. adhesive; cement; dough; glue; gum; imitation; material; mixture; pap; pastry; strass; stuff

PASTIME: (see "entertainment") amusement; diversion; game; hobby; passetemps; play; recreation; sport

PASTOR: see "clergyman"

PASTORAL: a. Arcadian; bucolic; country; geoponic; georgic; idyllic; innocent; picturesque; poetic(al); rural; rustic; shep-

herdly; simple; spiritual; Theocritean; PASTORAL: n. idyl; poem; song

PASTRY: cake; eclair; flan; food; paste; pie; puff; tarts; strudel; sweets

PASTURE: v. agist; feed; graze; nourish; range; PASTURE: n. agistment; feeding ground; grass(land); grazing; herbage; lea; meadow; pasturage; range; retirement

PASTY: anemic; ashen; ashy; doughy; magmatic; pale; pallid; sickly; soft; sticky; wan; white

PAT: v. caress; dab; hug; stroke; tap; PAT: a. appropriate; apt; fit(ting); fixed; happy; immovable; opportune; pertinent; suitable; timely; PAT: n. blow; butter; caress; dab; lump; stroke; tap

PATCH: v. cover; darn; eke; fix; glue; mend; paste; renovate; repair; squeeze; PATCH: n. bit; blemish; clout; emblem; field; ornament; overlay; parcel; piece; plaque; plot; remnant; scrap; tract; vamp

PATCHWORK: cento; heterogeneity; hodgepodge; jumble; medley; mixture; potpourri; variegation

PATENT: a. (see "clear") apparent; conspicuous; evident; expanded; glaring; manifest; notorious; obvious; open; patented; plain; right; salient; unconcealed; unobstructed; PATENT: n. copyright; grant; invention; license; monopoly; privilege; right

PATERNAL: see "fatherly"

PATH: access; berm; byway; circuit; course; direction; footway; groove; lane; line; method; niche; orbit; passage(way); pathway; road(way); route; run(way); trace; track; trail; walk(way); way

PATHETIC: (see "pitiful") affecting; defenseless; emotional; melancholy; moving; pitiable; plaintive; poignant; sad; silly; stirring; teary; touching; weeping

PATHFINDER: see "pioneer"

PATHOS: see "compassion" and "sympathy"

PATIENT: (see "calm") bovine; charitable; composed; cool; dispassionate; enduring; forbearing; gentle; impertubable; longanimous; long-suffering; meek; passive; peaceful; philosophic(al); placid; quiet; resigned;

restrained; sedate; serene; steadfast; stoic-(al); submissive; temperate; tolerant; uncomplaining; undaunted; unimpassioned; unruffled; PATIENCE: (**see** "calmness") composure; constancy; endurance; equanimity; forbearance; fortitude; imperturbability; indulgence; leniency; lenity; longanimity; long-suffering; magnanimity; moderation; passiveness; passivity; perseverance; persistence; persistency; poise; resignation; restraint; self-possession; steadfastness; submission; submissiveness; sufferance; tolerance; toleration

PATOIS: (**see** "speech") cant; dialect; jargon

PATRIARCH: chief; ecclesiast; elder; father; hierarch; leader; Nasi; pater(familias); Pope; sire; veteran

PATRIOT: Allen; chauvinist; flag-waver; Hale; jingoist; Otis; patrioteer; Revere; superzealot; zealot; PATRIOTIC(AL): (**see** "loyal") chauvinistic; devoted; liege; zealous; PATRIOTISM: Americanism; *amor patriae*; chauvinism; devotion; ethnocentrism; jingoism; loyalty; spread-eagleism; zealotry

PATRON: advocate; agent; ally; angel; backer; benefactor; boarder; buyer; champion; client; consumer; customer; defender; donor; employer; encourager; friend; grantor; guardian; guest; guide; helper; host; leader; lodger; Maecenas; partner; philanthropist; Prometheus; promoter; protector; saint; Samaritan; savior; sponsor; supporter; sympathizer; trader; upholder; user; PATRONAGE: (**see** "charity") advantage; aegis; aid; alms; assist(ance); authority; avail; benefaction; benefice; beneficence; benefit; benevolence; benison; bequest; bestowal; blessing; bonus; boon; boost; bounty; care; concession; condescension; countenance; control; dole; egis; encouragement; favor; furtherance; gain; graciousness; gift; grant; gratuity; guardianship; handsel; help; honorarium; improvement; influence; interest; kind(li)ness; largess(e); lead; legacy; leverage; liberality; lift; maintenance; munificence; preferment; privilege; prize; profit; program; protection; provision; sake; solicitude; sponsorship; superiority; support; talent; tip; trade; turn; utility; windfall

PATRONIZING: condescending; haughty; kneeling; stooping; supercilious; yielding

PATTERN: **v.** arrange; blueprint; design; devise; draw; fashion; form; guide; imitate; make; model; outline; plan; plot; program;

rule; scheme; shape; sketch; PATTERN: **n.** archetype; arrangement; attitude; average; *beau idéal*; blueprint; charcteristic; composition; configuration; conformation; constellation; convention; copy; custom; design; device; die; distribution; drawing; ethos; example; exemplar; exemplum; fiber; figure; form(at); formation; grouping; guide; idea-(l); last; map; meaning; method; modality; mode; model; mold; motif; norm; order; original; orthodoxy; outline; paradigm; paragon; phase; picture; plan; plot; precedent; principle; program; prototype; purpose; rhythm; routine; rule(r); sample; scale; semé; sequence; shape; sketch; specimen; standard; stencil; stereotype; sterling; style; syndroms; system; template; tendency; tracing; type; yardstick

PATULOUS: diffuse; distended; expanded; expanding; gaping; open; spread(ing)

PAUCITY: (**see** "lack") dearth; exiguity; fewness; insufficiency; scantiness; scarcity

PAUSE: **v.** break; cease; consider; delay; deliberate; demur; desist; dwell; halt; hesitate; hold; intermit; interrupt; linger; lull; recess; refrain; remain; repose; rest; stand; stay; stop; suspend; swell; tarry; waver; PAUSE: **n.** armistice; break; cessation; c(a)esura; deadlock; delay; deliberation; demur; *entr'acte*; gap; halt; hang; hesitation; hiatus; hitch; hold; interlude; intermission; interregnum; interruption; interval; lull; moratorium; recess; repose; respite; rest; selah; stance; stand; stay; stop(page); suspension; tarry; wait; waiver

PAVE: cover; floor; overlie; prepare; smooth; surface; tile

PAVILION: arbor; arena; auricle; banner; canopy; covering; flag; kiosk; litter; marquee; pawl; shelter; tabernacle; tent

PAW: **v.** (**see** "claw") clutch; feel; grab; handle; hug; maul; scrape; struggle; touch; PAW: **n.** (**see** "claw") dupe; foot; hand; maul; tool

PAWL: catch; click; detent; ratchet; tongue

PAWN: **v.** deposit; gage; guarantee; hazard; hypothecate; lend; pignorate; pledge; risk; stake; wager; PAWN: **n.** chessman; dupe; earnest; gage; guaranty; hazard; hostage; hypothecation; impignoration; loan; man; pledge; risk; security; stake; wager

PAY: **v.** (see "compensate") ante; defray; discharge; engage; expend; give; grant; hire; indemnify; liquidate; recompense; reimburse; remit; remunerate; rent; requite; return; reward; satisfy; settle; shell out; spend; tip; treat; yield; PAY(MENT): **n.** adjustment; alleviation; allowance; annuity; ante; balance; balm; benefit; charge; clearance; compensation; defrayal; deposit; earnings; emolument; employ; expenditure; fee; fine; gain; gift; hire; honorarium; indemnity; interest; liquidation; money; outlay; output; penalty; perquisite; profit; rate; recompense; remittance; remuneration; reprisal; requital; retribution; return; reward; salary; solatium; stipend(ium); subsidy; support; tax; tip; toll; treat; tribute; wage(s); wager; PAYABLE: (in) arrears; compensable; compensative; compensatory; due; outstanding; owing; paying; profitable

PEACE: (see "calm") accord; agreement; amity; calmness; conciliation; concord; contentment; freedom; harmony; hush; lull; nirvana; order; pacification; patience; pax; quiescence; quiet(ness); reconciliation; repose; rest; security; serenity; silence; stillness; tranquility; PEACEFUL or PEACEABLE: (see "calm") affable; amiable; amicable; appeasing; composed; conciliating; conciliatory; concordant; congenial; cool; easy(going); friendly; genial; gentle; halcyon; harmonious; henotic; irenic(al); mild; neighborly; nirvanic; nonbelligerent; nonviolent; oasitic; pacific(atory); pacifistic; pastoral; patient; placid; quiescent; quiet; restful; serene; smooth; sober; steady; still; tempean; tranquil; unaggressive; unagitated; undisturbed; unmartial; unmilitary; unruffled; untroubled; unwarlike; PEACEFULNESS: amiability; amicability; calmness; nonviolence; pacification; placability; serenity; tranquility; tranquilization

PEACEMAKER: conciliator; intercessor; mediator; pacificator; pacifier; palliator; placater; tranquilizer

PEAK: (see "climax") acme; alp; apex; apogee; bloom; capstone; cone; crag; crest; crown; culmination; cusp; Everest; finial; floodtide; height; high noon; hill; knob; maximum; meridian; perfection; pinnacle; piton; point; promontory; spike; spire; summit; superlative; top; tor; ultimate; zenith

PEAKED: (see "pale") anemic; drawn; pointed; sallow; sickly; thin; tired; wan; watery; weak; worn

PEAL: boom; clap; echo; resound; ring; roar; thunder; toll

PEARLY: beautiful; clear; iridescent; limpid; lustrous; margaritaceous; nacreous; opalescent; opaline; pearlescent; pellucid; precious; rare; shining; translucent

PEART: (see "active") agile; alert; brisk; clever; conscious; flourishing; frisky; live(ly); quick; smart; spry

PEASANT: boor; carl(e); churl; collie; cotter; countryman; farmer; fellah; hind; husbandman; laborer; peon; rustic; ryot; swain; tiller; toiler

PECK: **v.** bite; carp; dab; eat; kiss; nag; nibble; nip; pick; scold; tease; PECK: **n.** kiss; measure; nip; smack

PECULATE: see "steal"

PECULIAR: (see "abnormal") aberrant; anomalous; atypic(al); bizarre; characteristic; curious; distinctive; eccentric; erratic; exceptional; exclusive; extraordinary; grotesque; heterogeneous; idiocratic; idiosyncratic; individual; odd(ball); oddish; *outré*; particular; queer; querulous; rare; singular; special; specific; strange; uncommon; unconventional; unique; unusual; whimsical; PECULIARITY: (see "abnormality") bizarrerie; caprice; characteristic; distinctiveness; eccentricity; habit; haecceity; idiasm; idiocrasy; idiosyncrasy; individuality; kink; mannerism; oddity; partiality; particularity; quiddity; quirk; singularity; squint; tic; trait; trick; uniquity; vagary; way; whim(sicality)

PEDANT: formalist; pedagogue; precisionist; prig; purist; scholar; teacher; tutor

PEDDLE: advertise; circulate; hawk; huckster; meddle; piddle; pitch; retail; sell; traffic; trifle; vend

PEDESTAL: base; foot; foundation; gaine; leg; stand; support

PEDUNCLE: crus; knot; pedicel; petiole; stalk; stem

PEEL: **v.** bark; decorticate; desquamate; excoriate; exfoliate; exuviate; flake; flay; hull; husk; pare; remove; skin; strip; uncover; undress; PEEL(ING): **n.** bark; coat(ing); decortication; desquamation; ecdysis; excoriation; exfoliation; flake; hull;

husk; layer; rind; shovel; skin; PEELING: **a.** deciduous; desquamative; desquamatory; exfoliative; exuvial

PEEP: cheep; chirp; cry; emerge; eye; glance; glimpse; look; peek; peer; protrude; pry; pule; see; spy; view; PEEPER: observer; Peeping Tom; scopophiliac; viewer; *voyeur*; PEEPING: **a.** scopophilic; voyeuristic; PEEPING: **n.** scopophilia; voyeurism

PEER: **v.** (**see** "peep") gape; gaze; look; peek; squint; stare; view; PEER: **n.** coeval; confrere; contemporary; earl; equal; juror; lord; match; noble(man)

PEERLESS: (**see** "perfect") eminent; excellent; immutable; incommensurable; incomparable; majestic; matchless; *ne plus supra*; *ne plus ultra*; optimum; paramount; preeminent; sovereign; supereminent; superexcellent; superlative; supreme; ultimate; unequaled; unsurpassable

PEEVE: **v.** (**see** "annoy") bother; chafe; exasperate; fret; irk; irritate; nettle; provoke; stir; vex; PEEVE: **n. see** "grudge; PEEVISH: acidulous; atrabilarious; atrabiliar; atrabilious; bilious; bitter; captious; carping; caustic; choleric; churlish; complaining; contentious; crabbed; crabby; cranky; cross; crusty; disgruntled; fault-finding; fractious; fretful; grouchy; gruff; grumbling; grumpy; huffy; ill-natured; irascible; irritable; moody; morose; nettled; obstinate; opposing; opposite; perverse; pettish; petulant; piqued; quarrelsome; querulous; restive; snappish; snappy; sour; spleeny; splenetic; sulky; surly; testy; touchy; ugly; waspish; whining; PEEVISHNESS: crankiness; crossness; disgruntlement; distemper; irascibility; irritability; moroseness; morosity; petulance; pique; protervity; quarrelsomeness; querulousness

PEG: **v.** attach; bind; bolt; confine; fasten; fix; grade; hammer; hold; hustle; identify; nail; notch; pierce; pin; plod; plug; restrict; spike; strike; throw; PEG: **n.** bolt; degree; dowel; grade; hob; knag; knob; leg; level; perch; pin; piton; plug; pretext; reason; spike; step; stump; support; tee; throw; tooth

PELF: booty; gain; loot; lucre; money; riches; spoils; wampum; wealth

PELLET: ball; bolus; bullet; granule; mass; pill; shot; stone; wad

PELLICLE: coating; crust; cuticle; film; layer; membrane; scum; skin

PELLUCID: (**see** "clear") bright; comprehensible; crystal(line); diaphanous; intelligible; iridescent; limpid; patent; pleasing; pure; shining; translucent; transparent

PELT: **v.** assail; beat; beset; hail; hurl; hurry; pepper; speed; stone; whack; PELT: **n.** bark; fur; hide; peel(ing); rind; skin; speed; whack

PELTRY: furs; hides; pelts; refuse; rubbish; skins; trash

PEN: **v.** cage; compose; confine; coop; corral; dam; enclose; imprison; incarcerate; indite; inscribe; restrain; restrict; shut; write; PEN: **n.** cage; confine; coop; corral; cote; crib; dam; enclosure; field; fold; hutch; jail; lockup; paddock; prison; quill; stall; stir; sty; stylus; writing

PENALIZE: (**see** "discipline") amerce; chasten; chastise; correct; disadvantage; fine; forfeit; handicap; incarcerate; jail; mulct; punish; redress; restrict; revenge; sentence; PENALTY: amercement; cain; chastenment; chastisement; correction; cost; demerit; deprivation; disadvantage; discipline; doom; expiation; fine; forfeit(ure); handicap; imprisonment; incarceration; Nemesis; penance; punishment; redress; reprisal; requital; restriction; retaliation; retribution; revenge; sentence; suffering; vengeance; PENAL: castigatory; corrective; disciplinary; expiatory; penitentiary; punitive; reformative; reformatory; retributive; retributory

PENDING: abeyant; during; hanging; imminent; impending; in abeyance; *in fieri*; open; pendant; pendent; pendular; pendulous; provisional; suspended; tabled; undecided; undetermined; unsettled; until; waiting; PENDANT: aglet; bob; chandelier; earring; flag; tab; tag; tail; tassel; PENDENCY: abeyance; imminence; imminency; indecision; indetermination; pendulation; pendulosity; suspension

PENETRATE: absorb; affect; bore; comprehend; cut; delve; detect; diffuse; dig; discern; drill; enter; explore; fathom; force; imbue; impenetrate; impregnate; infest; infiltrate; insert; interpenetrate; intromit; invade; move; ooze; osmose; overrun; pass; perceive; percolate; perforate; permeate; pervade; pierce; probe; punch; puncture;

reach; riddle; saturate; search; seep; shove; sink; soak; stab; steep; stick; strike; traverse; understand; PENETRATING: acute; astute; boring; clever; deadly; deep; discerning; gimlety; impressive; incisive; keen; knowing; mordant; osmotic; penetrative; performing; permeable; perspicacious; pervading; piercing; piquant; poignant; pointing; quick; sagacious; sharp; shrewd; shrill; stabbing; subtle; trenchant; wise; PENETRATION: acuteness; comprehension; depth; discernment; entrance; entry; exploration; grasp; infiltration; ingress(ion); insertion; intellect; intelligence; intromission; invasion; judgment; penetrativeness; perception; perforation; perspicacity; probe; puncture; sagacity; search; trespass; understanding; wisdom

PENITENT: **a.** apologetic; broken; chastened; chastised; contrite; cringing; crushed; disciplined; humble(d); kneeling; mournful; regretful; remorseful; repentant; rueful; scrupulous; sorrowful; PENITENT: **n.** repenter; ruer; PENITENCE: attrition; compunction; contrition; penance; regret; remorse; repentance; rue; scruples; sorrow

PENMAN: author; calligrapher; chirographer; clerk; composer; scribe; writer; PENMANSHIP: calligraphy; chirography; hand(writing); writing

PENNANT: award; banner; burgee; championship; color; device; emblem; ensign; flag; gonfalon; guidon; jack; oriflamme; pennon; prize; sign(al); standard; streamer; symbol

PENNILESS: (**see** "poor") bankrupt; fundless; impecunious; indigent; insolvent; landless; moneyless; penceless; resourceless; *sans le sou*; unmoneyed; unprosperous; PENNILESSNESS: bankruptcy; impecuniosity; insolvency; mendicancy

PENSIVE: (**see** "thoughtful") absorbed; cogitable; cogitabund; cogitative; contemplative; engrossed; meditative; melancholic; musing; occupied; reflective

PENTACLE: hexagon; medal; pentagram; pentalpha; star; symbol; talisman

PENURY: (**see** "poverty") destitution; distress; indigence; indigency; lack; need; penuriousness; pinch; privation; scantiness; straits; want; PENURIOUS: (**see** "stingy") bankrupt; barren; close; frugal; fundless;

grasping; illiberal; impecunious; indigent; lacking; mean; miserly; moneyless; near; needy; niggardly; parsimonious; penceless; penniless; poor; resourceless; scanty; stinting; tight

PEOPLE(S): adults; ancestors; ancestry; aristocrats; aristoi (pl.); assemblage; assembly; beings; bourgeois(ie); caste; citizenry; citizens; clan; class; commonalty; community; constituency; country; crew; crowd; demos; domain; electorate; ethnics; family; fold; folks; followers; herd; *hoi polloi*; *Homo sapiens*; humanity; humankind; humans; individuals; inhabitants; kin(dred); kinfolk; kingdom; labor; laity; life; Lumpenproletariat; man(kind); mass(es); menagerie; mob; mortals; multitude; nation(ality); nobility; personnel; persons; plebeians; populace; population; *profanum vulgus*; proletariat; rabble; race; relation; relatives; residents; retainers; servants; society; souls; state; subjects; throng; tribe; universality; voters; workers; world

PEP: (**see** "energy" and "zest") dash; éclat; fire; ginger; go; initiative; liveliness; nettle; pluck; spice; spirit; spunk; vigor; vim; voltage; wattage

PEPPER: **v.** attack; batter; beat; dot; pelt; shower; thrash; PEPPER: **n.** ara; ava; capsicum; cayenne; condiment; kava; pimiento; spice; PEPPERY: abrupt; angry; choleric; excitable; fiery; hasty; hot (-tempered); irascible; passionate; piquant; pungent; snappish; spicy; spirited; stinging; touchy; zestful

PERCEIVE: (**see** "see") appreciate; apprehend; behold; comprehend; cotton; descry; detect; discern; discover; distinguish; divine; espy; feel; grasp; identify; know; locate; mind; note; notice; observe; penetrate; realize; recognize; remark; savvy; scent; sensate; sense; smell; spot; understand; view; PERCEIVABLE *or* PERCEPTIBLE: apperceivable; appreciable; ascertainable; aware; cognitional; cognitive; cognizable; cognoscible; cognoscitative; comprehensible; computable; discernible; essential; figurable; intelligible; measurable; minimal; objective; observable; obvious; palpable; percipient; persipicacious; ponderable; recognizable; seeing; sensible; tangible

PERCENTAGE: (**see** "advantage") cut; favor; number; odds; part; per centum; quota; ratio; ration; share

PERCEPTION: acumen; apperception; appreciation; apprehension; awareness; clairvoyance; cognition; cognizance; comprehension; concept(ion); consciousness; contemplation; cryptesthesia; discernment; ear; grasp; heed; hyperesthesia; idea; image; impression; insight; intelligence; judgment; knowledge; observation; penetration; perceptiveness; percipience; percipiency; perspicacity; reaction; recognition; sagacity; seeing; sensation; sense; sensibility; tact; understanding; wit; PERCEPTIVE: acuminous; appercipient; appreciative; apprehensive; aware; clairvoyant; clearheaded; clear-sighted; cognitional; cognitive; conscious; discerning; heedful; hyperesthetic; imaginative; intelligent; keen; knowing; observant; palpable; penetrating; percipient; perspicacious; piercing; precise; prehensile; quick; reactive; refined; sagacious; seeing; sensible; sensitive; sentient; sharp; subtle; sympathetic; tactile; telepathic; trenchant; understanding; witty

PERCH: **v.** alight; land; light; occupy; rest; roost; set(tle); sit; PERCH: **n.** aerie; bar; eminence; height; measure; nest; peg; pole; rod; roost; seat; station

PERCOLATE: brew; diffuse; drain; drip; enliven; exude; filter; go; leach; meet; melt; ooze; osmose; penetrate; permeate; run; seep; sieve; sift; soak; spread; strain; transude; trickle

PERDITION: bowwows; damnation; death; demolition; destruction; downfall; fall; Hell; loss; misery; oblivion; overthrow; ruin; wreck

PEREGRINE: (**see** "roving") alien; falcon: foreigner; hawk; peripatetic; rover; sojourner; wanderer

PEREMPTORY: (**see** "absolute") arbitrary; assertive; austere; coercive; commanding; compulsory; confident; decisive; dictatorial; dogmatic; exacting; firm; harsh; haughty; imperative; imperious; inexorable; inflexible; masterful; obstinate; oppressive; positive; relentless; resolute; rigid; rigorous; self-assured; stern; strict; unsparing; urging

PERENNIAL: (**see** "enduring") continual; recurrent

PERFECT: **v.** complete; consummate; educate; elaborate; end; expand; finalize; finish; improve; plan; ripen; unfold; PERFECT-(ED): **a.** absolute; accomplished; accurate; blameless; complete(d); conclusive; consummate; correct; crowning; educated; entire; errorless; exact; excellent; exemplary; expert; exquisite; faithful; faultless; final; finished; flawless; fleckless; great; holy; hotsy-totsy; ideal; immaculate; immutable; impeccable; impeccant; incommensurable; incomparable; indefectible; infallible; inimitable; intact; integral; inviolate; irreproachable; matchless; mature(d); model; *ne plus supra*; *ne plus ultra*; O.K.; optimum; paramount; peerless; plenary; pluperfect; preeminent; proficient; pure; quadrate; refined; right(eous); saintly; sheer; simple; sinless; sole; sound; sovereign; spotless; stainless; supereminent; superexcellent; superior; superlative; supreme; total; transcendent; unblemished; undefiled; unequaled; unequivocal; unflawed; unmitigated; unparalleled; unqualified; unrivaled; unspoiled; unsurpassable; unsurpassed; utter; valid; whole; PERFECTION: accomplishment; accuracy; acme; *beau idéal*; bloom; consummation; contemplation; correctness; culmination; excellence; exemplarity; expertise; fare-thee-well; faultlessness; flawlessness; finality; ideal(ity); immaculacy; impeccabliity; incomparability; indefectibility; inerrancy; infallibility; maturity; merit; peak; perfectibilism; perfectibility; proficiency; refinement; ripeness; saintliness; scrupulosity; spotlessness; unerringness; virtue; virtuosity; wholeness; PERFECTIONIST: perfectibilian; perfectibilist; perfectibilitarian; *précieuse*; precisian; precisionist; purist

PERFIDY: (**see** "deceit") apostasy; betrayal; deception; defection; dishonesty; disloyalty; faithlessness; infidelity; treachery; treason; PERFIDIOUS: (**see** "deceitful") disloyal; faithless; false; treacherous; treasonable; treasonous; tyrannical; tyrannous; untrustworthy; venal

PERFORATE: bore; drill; eat; enter; erode; excavate; grid; indent; penetrate; pierce; pit; prick; punch; puncture; riddle; sieve; stab; PERFORATION: aperture; hole; penetration; puncture; stab; tresis

PERFORM: (**see** "do") accomplish; achieve; act(uate); consummate; discharge; effect; enact; end; execute; exercise; fill; finish; fulfill; function; gain; handle; implement; keep; play; ply; practice; present; produce; prosecute; provide; reach; serve; show; transact; work; PERFORMER: actor; agent; artist(e); doer; executor; mime; musician; operator; player; stager; star; talent; PERFORMANCE: accomplishment; achievement; act(ivity); administration; audition; behavior; capacity; caper; do; efficiency; entertainment; exercise; exhibition; feat; fulfillment; function; implementation; officiation; play; power; practice; presentation; production; program; pursuit; recital; recitation; show; speed; stunt; transaction; work

PERFUNCTORY: (see "apathetic") administrative; cursory; indifferent; mechanical; unenthusiastic

PERFUME: aroma; atmosphere; attar; aura; bouquet; cologne; essence; fragrance; incense; odor; quality; redolence; scent; smell; spice; sweetness

PERHAPS: belike; haply; liable; likely; maybe; mayhaps; peradventure; perchance; possibly; probably

PERIL: (see "danger") Charybdis; crisis; exposure; hazard; insecurity; instability; jeopardy; perilousness; pitfall; risk; snare; threat; trap; venture; PERILOUS: (see "dangerous") destructive; dread(ful); explosive; hazardous; Icarian; insecure; instable; jeopardous; malign(ant); risky; shaky; tottery; unstable; venturesome; weak(ened)

PERIMETER: (see "periphery") ambit; border; boundary; bounds; circuit; circumference; edge; limits; lip; outline; outside; outskirts; rim; skirt

PERIOD: bound; cessation; circle; circuit; conclusion; continuance; cycle; date; day; decade; division; dot; duration; end; eon; epoch; era; hour; interval; length; life; limit; point; race; season; sentence; session; shift; *siècle*; space; span; spell; stadium; stage; stop; stretch; term(ination); time; track; year; PERIODIC(AL); **a.** alternate; alternating; annual(ly); cyclic(al); daily; eral; etesian; fitful; frequent; hourly; intermittent; monthly; often; quarterly; recurrent; recurring; regular(ly); rhythmic(al); seasonable; seasonal; serial; weekly; yearly; PERIODICAL: **n.** bulletin; journal; magazine; monthly; newspaper; organ; paper; publication; weekly

PERIPATETIC: **a.** ambulatory; Aristotelian; itinerant; nomadic; pedestrian; peregrine; rambling; roving; vagabond; vagrant; walking; wandering; PERIPATETIC: **n.** Aristotelian; gypsy; itinerant; nomad; pedestrian; peregrine; rambler; rover; vagabond

PERIPHERAL: circumferential; confined; distal; distant; external; marginal; peripheric; skirting; surface; PERIPHERY: ambit; border; boundary; bounds; circuit; circumference; edge; edging; end; environs; externality; fringe; limit(s); lip; margin; outline; outside; perimeter; rim; skirt; space; suburbs; surface

PERISH: (see "die") consume; decay; decrease; deteriorate; evaporate; expire; melt; rot; shrivel; spoil; vaporize; waste; wither; PERISHABLE: caducous; consumable; deciduous; ephemeral; evanescent; fleeting; fugacious; impermanent; mortal; nonpermanent; spoilable; transitory; unendurable; unpermanent; volatile; PERISHABLENESS: caducity; evanescence; fugacity; perishability; volatility

PERMANENT: (see "eternal") abiding; amaranthine; changeless; chronic; constant; continual; continuing; continuous; durable; enduring; fadeless; fast; firm; fixed; immarcescible; immutable; imperishable; indefaceable; indelible; indestructible; indissoluble; ineffaceable; ineradicable; inerasable; inextirpable; invariable; irradicable; irremovable; irreversible; irrevocable; lasting; nonperishable; perdurable; perdurant; perpetual; persistent; sessile; settled; solid; stable; steadfast; unalterable; unchangeable; unchanging; uneradicable; unerasable; PERMANENCE or PERMANENCY: durability; duration; enduringness; eternality; fixedness; fixity; immarcescibleness; immutability; imperishability; indissolubility; ineffaceability; irrevocability; perdurance; perduration; persistence; persistency; stability; steadfastness; unalterability; unchangeableness

PERMEATE: animate; diffuse; disseminate; drench; fill; fire; imbue; impregnate; infest; infiltrate; interpenetrate; invade; osmose; overrun; pass; penetrate; pervade; reek; saturate; seep; spread; steep

PERMIT: **v.** (see "allow") acquiesce; admit; allot; appoint; approve; authorize; bear; brook; charter; commission; concede; consent; countenance; credit; empower; endorse; endure; entitle; favor; franchise; give; grant; indulge; justify; leave; legalize; let; license; ordain; order; pass; patent; sanction; suffer; tolerate; vouchsafe; warrant; PERMIT **n.** or PERMISSION: acquiescence; admittance; allowability; allowance; appointment; authority; authorization; charter; commission; concession; consent; countenance; credit; endorsement; entitlement; faculty; favor; fiat; franchise; grace; grant; indulgence; justification; *laissez-passer*; leave; legalization; liberty; license; pass(port); patent; permissibility; permittance; privilege; sanction; sufferance; ticket; tolerance; toleration; visa; warrant(y); PERMISSIVE *or* PERMITTED: admissible; allowed; authorized; discretionary; elective; empowering; enabling; facultative; indulgent; innocent; lawful; legitimate; licensed; licit; official; optional; overindulgent; permissible; sanctionative; sanctioned; tolerant; tolerative; undemanding; unprohibited; unsuppressed; warranted

PERNICIOUS: (**see** "bad") baleful; baneful; deadly; deleterious; destructive; detrimental; evil; fatal; foul; harmful; hurtful; inimical; injurious; insalubrious; lethal; malign(ant); mischievous; noisome; noxious; obnoxious; painful; pestiferous; pestilent(ial); poisonous; ruinous; sinister; toxic; unhealthful; unhealthy; unsafe; unsalubrious; unwholesome; virulent

PERPENDICULAR: abrupt; erect; plumb; precipitous; sheer; standing; steep; upright; vertical; walking

PERPETUATE: classicize; commemorate; commit; deify; endure; eternalize; historicize; historify; immortalize; preserve; sanctify; PERPETUAL: (**see** "eternal") constant; continual; diuturnal; everlasting; immortal; incessant; perennial; permanent; persistent; sempiternal; unceasing; undying; unwaning; PERPETUATION: commemorization; deification; eternalization; historicity; immortalization; perpetuality; perpetuity; preservation; PERPETUITY: diuturnity; duration; endlessness; eternality; eternity; permanence; permanency; perpetuation

PERPLEX: amaze; annoy; astonish; baffle; balk; befog; befool; befuddle; beset; bewilder; bother; complicate; confound; confuse; corner; daze; deceive; delude; disconcert; dissemble; distract; disturb; dum(b)-found; dupe; embarrass; embrangle; entangle; faze; floor; flurry; fool; harass; hoodwink; interweave; involve; irk; misguide; mislead; mystify; nonplus; obfuscate; obscure; plague; pose; pother; puzzle; rattle; snarl; stagger; stump; tangle; trick; trouble; upset; worry; vex; PERPLEXED: (**see** "puzzled") anxious; asea; bewildered; bewitched; complicated; confused; disconcerted; distracted; distraught; entangled;

intricate; knotted; nonplussed; troubled; PERPLEXING: (**see** "puzzling") bewildering; dilemmatic; disconcerting; enigmatic-(al); inexplicable; perplexful; PERPLEXITY: agitation; anxiety; astonishment; bafflement; bewilderment; bugbear; care; complication; crisis; cruciality; crux; cul-de-sac: deep water; difficulty; dilemma; disorder; doubt; embarrassment; embranglement; embroilment; enigma; entanglement; exigency; fix; fog; headache; imbroglio; impasse; intricacy; issue; jam; knot; labyrinth; mess; morass; mystery; nut; ogre; pickle; plight; poser; predicament; puzzle-(ment); quagmire; quandary; question; riddle; scrape; situation; stalemate; strait; tangle; task; trouble; uncertainty; wonder

PERQUISITE: appanage; bonus; bribe; due; fee; gain; gift; gratuity; honorarium; income; influence; power; prerogative; privilege; profit(s); reward; right; salary; tip

PERSECUTE: (**see** "oppress") abuse; afflict; aggrieve; annoy; bait; beset; chase; crucify; distress; dragoon; harass; hound; hunt; maltreat; molest; pester; punish; pursue; rag; ride; torment; trouble; tyrannize; vex; victimize; worry; wrong; PERSECUTOR: Procrustean; tormentor; Torquemada; tyrant; PERSECUTION: (**see** "oppression") aggression; annoyance; crucifixion; harassment; maltreatment; molestation; pain; prosecution; punishment; rack; torment; tyranny; vexation

PERSEVERE: (**see** "continue") abide; endure; haunt; insist; keep; last; perpetuate; perseverate; persist; prevail; protract; remain; stay; stick; subsist; sustain; urge; wear; PERSEVERANCE: constancy; continuance; continuancy; continuation; determination; endurance; grit; guts; perpetuation; persistence; persistency; pertinacity; pluck; power; prolongation; protraction; resolution; stamina; steadfastness; stick-to-itiveness; strength; stubbornness; tenacity

PERSIFLAGE: badinage; banter; chaffing; flippancy; flippery; frivolity; mockery; pleasantry; raillery; ridicule; satire

PERSIST: (**see** "continue") perdure; persevere; prevail; prolong; subsist; PERSISTENT: (**see** "stubborn") assiduous; chronic; continuing; demanding; determined; diligent; dogged; enduring; frequent; hectic; importunate; indefatigable; indomitable; inveterate; lingering; obstinate; perdurant; perpetual; persevering; pertinacious; pressing; prolonged; recurrent; sedulous; solicitous; tenacious; tireless; unfailing; unflagging; unremitting; untiring; unweariable; unwearying

PERSON(S) *or* PERSONAGE: (**see** "people") article; being(s); bigwig; body; boy; brother; chap; character; child; *dramatis personae* (pl.); existent; fellow; figure; girl; head; heart; human; individual; jerk; life; man; member; mortal; nibs; one; peer; personality; presence; propositus; psyche; self; sister; someone; specimen; soul; subject; thing; unit; woman

PERSONALITY: character; disposition; ego-(ity); entity; heart; individual(ity); likability; likeableness; person(eity); psyche; self(hood); selfness; soul; temperament

PERSONATE: act; anthropomorphize; ape; assume; embody; feign; imitate; impersonate; mimic; personalize; personify; portray; represent; simulate; typify; zoomorphize; PERSONATION: anthropomorphism; anthropomorphization; embodiment; impersonation; incarnation; personification; prosopopoeia

PERSONIFY: (**see** "personate") anthropomorphize; apostrophize; embody; incarnate; personalize; zoomorphize; PERSONIFIED: embodied; incarnate; personalized

PERSONNEL: crew; employees; faculty; force; hands; members; men; organization; payroll; people; roster; staff; workers

PERSPECTIVE: appearance; capacity; configuration; difference; expectation; interrelation; opinion; panorama; proportion; prospect; rationale; scale; scene; scope; slant; view(point); vista

PERSPICACIOUS *or* PERSPICUOUS: acute; astute; clear; discerning; explicit; keen; knowledgeable; lucid; penetrating; sagacious; sharp; shrewd; PERSPICACITY: acumen; acuteness; clarity; clearness; comprehensibility; discernment; explicitness; insight; intelligence; keenness; knowledge; lucidity; penetration; perspicuity; sagacity; sharpness; shrewdness

PERSPIRE: egest; excrete; exudate; ooze; secrete; sweat; transpire; PERSPIRATION: diaphoresis; effort; egesta (pl.); excreta(pl.); excretion; exudate; exudation; sudation; sudor; swear; transpiration

PERSUADE: actuate; allure; beckon; coax; condition; convince; discipline; dispose; drive; educate; entice; exhort; expostulate; gain; get; impel; incite; incline; induce; influence; interest; lead; lure; move; overcome; prevail; prove; reason; seduce; stimulate; tease; tempt; toll; train; urge; vamp; win; PERSUASIVE: (**see** "encouraging") alluring; convincing; enticing; exhortative; expostulatory; impelling; inciting; influential; luring; moving; prevailing; stimulating; teasing; tempting; PERSUASION: (**see** "inclination") allure(ment); drive; enticement; exhortation; expostulation; incitement; inducement; influence; interest; lure; prevailment; seduction; stimulation; urge

PERT: alive; arch; bold; brash; brisk; chic; chipper; cocky; crisp; dapper; daring; discourteous; disrespectful; exuberant; fiery; flippant; forward; fresh; frisky; frivolous; haughty; hubristic; impertinent; impudent; insolent; irreverent; jaunty; lively; mischievous; nimble; officious; presuming; presumptuous; sassy; saucy; smart; spright(ly); spry; trim; vivacious; PERTNESS: arrogance; assumption; boldness; brazenness; disrespect; flippancy; forwardness; frivolousness; haughtiness; hubris; impertinence; impudence; insolence; liveliness; presumption; pretention; pride; sassiness; sauciness; sprightliness; vivacity

PERTAIN: (**see** "apply") appertain; bear; belong; concern; fit; refer; regard; relate; touch; PERTINENT: *ad rem*; anent; applicable; apposite; appropriate; apropos; apt; belonging; categorical; commensurate; competent; congruent; congruous; connected; felicitous; fit(ting); germane; happy; legal; material; opportune; orthodox; pat; proper; proportional; proportionate; related; relative; relevant; sanctioned; timely; valid; PERTINENCE *or* PERTINENCY: (**see** "application") aproposity; competency; congruency; relation(ship); relevance; relevancy; timeliness

PERTINACIOUS: (**see** "firm") dogged; importunate; tough; unyielding

PERTINENCE: **see** under "pertain"

PERTURB: **see** "disturb;" PERTURBED: **see** "uneasy;" PERTURBATION: (**see** "fear") agitation; alarm; anxiety; commotion; discomposure; distress; disturbance; dread; flurry; furor; horror; terror; trepidation; trouble; turbulence; uneasiness; uproar; worry

PERUSE: con(sider); examine; inspect; look; observe; read; scan; scrutinize; search; study; survey

PERVADE: compenetrate; concentrate; diffuse; drench; extend; fill; imbue; infiltrate; infuse; fuse; penetrate; permeate; overspread; saturate; spread

PERVERSE: (see "stubborn") awry; balky; churlish; contentious; contrary; contrawise; corrupt; crabbed; cranky; cross(-grained); disagreeable; distorted; dogged; erring; factious; forward; fractious; froward; grouchy; headstrong; improper; incorrect; intractable; irregular; mulish; obdurate; obstinate; peevish; petulant; seditious; sour; sulky; ungovernable; unnatural; unreasonable; unruly; untoward; wayward; wicked; willful; wrongheaded; wry; PERVERSITY: see "stubbornness"

PERVERT: (see "degrade") corupt; misapply; misconstrue; misdirect; misinterpret; poison; subvert; twist; wrench

PESSIMIST: (see "cynic") curmudgeon; dismal Jimmy; grouch; melancholiac; misanthropist; PESSIMISM: (see "cynicism") despair; gloom; melancholia; miserabilism; *Weltschmerz*; PESSIMISTIC: (see "gloomy" and "morose") cynical; derisive; despairing; disbelieving; distrustful; faultfinding; gloomy; grouchy; ironical; melancholy; misanthropic-(al); misogynic; misogynous; sarcastic; sardonic; satirical; sneering

PEST: annoyance; ant; bane; curse; flea; fly; infliction; insect; nudnick; nuisance; pestilence; plague; scourge; tick; trouble; vermin; PESTILENCE: calamity; destruction; disease; epidemic; (the) Four Horsemen; plague; scourge; PESTILENT(IAL): annoying; contagious; deadly; destructive; fatal; harmful; infectious; inflictive; injurious; irritating; malign(ant); mischievous; pernicious; toxic; vexatious; vexing; virulent

PESTER: (see "annoy") badger; bedevil; devil; harass; molest; nag; peeve; rib; tantalize; vex; worry

PESTLE: brayer; grinder; masher; mixer; muller; pulverizer

PET: v. (see "caress") baby; coddle; coo; cosset; court; cuddle; dally; dandle; embrace; favor; fondle; hug; humor; indulge; kiss; love; neck; nuzzle; pamper; pat; stroke; sulk; PET: n. anger; cade; canine; cat; dog; favorite; feline; huff; miff; offense; peeve; peevishness; sulk(iness); umbrage

PETITION: v. (see "appeal") ask; beg; call; entreat; importune; invoke; obsecrate; plead; pray; propose; request; solicit; sue; supplicate; vote; PETITION: n. (see "appeal") call; complaint; desire; entreaty; importunity; invocation; obsecration; plea; prayer; proposal; request; solicitation; suffrage; suit; supplication; urge; PETITIONER: appellant; applicant; candidate; orator; oratrix (fem.); supplicant; supplicator

PETRIFY: (see "frighten") affright; amaze; astonish; astound; awe; benumb; calcify; confuse; cow; daze; deaden; dumbfound; fossilize; freeze; gorgonize; harden; lapidify; paralyze; rigidify; scare; shock; stun; stupefy; thrill; torpify; PETRIFYING: (see "frightening") frightful; paralyzing; petrescent; petrifactive; petrific; stony

PETTISH: (see "petulant") fretful; gruff; huffy; irascible; irritable; peevish; spleeny; splenetic; testy; waspish

PETTY: (see "cheap") abject; beggarly; childish; contemptible; despicable; frivolous; futile; harsh; ignoble; inconsiderable; insignificant; jerkwater; lilliputian; little; meager; measly; meticulous; minor; minute; narrow(-minded); niggling; nugatory; paltry; parochial; parsimonious; pettifogging; picayune; picayunish; piddling; poor; puny; scurvy; shabby; shallow; shoestring; slight; secondary; small(-minded); subordinate; trifling; trivial; ungenerous; unimportant; PETTINESS: littleness; meanness; parochialism; parochiality; parvanimity; shabbiness; triviality

PETULANT: captious; choleric; crabbed; crabby; cranky; cross; fretful; huffy; irascible; irritable; peevish; pert; pettish; querulous; snappish; snappy; spleeny; splenetic; surly; testy; touchy; waspish

PHANTASM: (see "dream") apparition; *bête noire*; bogey; bugbear; deception; delusion; eidolon; fancy; fantasy; fetch; figment; ghost; illusion; image; phantasm(a); phantasmata (pl.); phantom; phenomenon; revenant; specter; spirit; spook; vision; will-of-the-wisp; wraith; PHANTASY: see "fantasy"

PHANTOM: (see "phantasm") semblance; shade

PHASE: (see "angle") appearance; aspect; aura; chapter; condition; division; era; face; facet; form; guise; interim; interval; look; moment; part; pattern; period; point; portion; position; posture; shade; shape; side; stadium; stage; state; step; subdivision; transition; turn

PHENOMENON: development; event; experience; fact; image; impression; manifestation; marvel; miracle; object; phantasm; phantom; phenomena (pl.); process; prodigy; reality; sight; wonder

PHILANTHROPIC(AL): (see "benevolent") beneficent; charitable; compassionate; eleemosynary; generous; humane; humanitarian; kind; liberal; sympathetic

PHILIPPIC: (see "tirade") invective; satire; screed

PHILOSOPHY: attitude; belief; calmness; concepts; conviction; credo; creed; doctrine; equanimity; inquiry; investigation; ism; methodology; principles; school; *scientia scientiarum*; system; tenet; theoretic; theory; thought; wisdom; PHILOSOPHER: Bacon; Hegel; Hume; Kant; *philosophe*; philosophess (fem.); philosophizer; physiologizer; physiologue; Plato; rationalist; sage; savant; Socrates; Spinoza; theoretician; theorician; theorist; theorizer; Zeno; PHILOSOPHIC-(AL); calm; cogitated; collected; composed; cool; erudite; impassive; imperturbable; oracular; patient; phlegmatic; prudent; rational; reflective; sage; sapient; scholarly; sedate; serene; stoic(al); studious; temperate; theoretical; thoughtful; tranquil; unruffled

PHLEGMATIC(AL): (see "calm") aloof; apathetic; cold; composed; cool; dull; heavy; impassive; imperturbable; indifferent; inert; inexcitable; languid; lymphatic; moody; morose; passive; placid; slow; sluggish; stoic(al); stolid; tardy; undemonstrative; unfeeling; unruffled

PHOBIA: see "fear"

PHONETIC: (see "oral") spoken; vocal; voiced

PHOTO(GRAPH): cut; film; flash; image; likeness; mug (shot); picture; plate; portrait; shot; snap(shot); tintype

PHRASE: v. couch; describe; express; group; put; style; term; utter; word; write PHRASE: n. catchword; clause; descrip-tion; diction; epigram; expression; idiom; maxim; motto; phraseology; slogan; term; PHRASEOLOGY: diction; language; parlance; syntax; thought; wording

PHYLACTERY: amulet; charm; reminder

PHYSIC: v. clean; cure; drug; heal; purgate; purge; remedy; relieve; treat; PHYSIC: n. aperient; cathartic; cure; drug; laxative; medicine; pill; purgative; purge; remedy

PHYSICAL: actual; bodily; carnal; concrete; constitutional; corpor(e)al; external; fleshy; hylic; lusty; material(istic); mechanical; natural; palpable; physiological; ponderable; real; scientific; sensible; somal; somatic; substantial; tangible; true; vigorous; visible; vital

PHYSICIAN: cardiologist; consultant; curer; doctor; fixer; healer; medic; mediciner; mender; obstetrician; oculist; pillroller; practitioner; psychiatrist; restorer; surgeon

PHYSICIST: hylozoist; materialist; naturalist; scientist

PHYSIOGNOMY: (see "face") appearance; aspect; configuration; expression; features; mien; posture; silhouette; visage

PHYSIQUE: (see "posture") appearance; build; carriage; constitution; form; habit(us); makeup; musculature; physicality; physiognomy; stance; state; stature; strength; vigor

PICK: v. (see "choose") collect; cull; cut; detach; eat; elect; gather; glean; grab; grasp; harvest; indent; loosen; name; nibble; ope; peck; penetrate; pierce; pilfer; pluck; prefer; reap; rob; screen; seek; seize; select; separate; steal; take; PICK: n. best; choice; elect; election; elite; gathering; gleaning; grab(s); grasp; harvest; opt(ion); plectrum; preference; seizure; selection; tool

PICKET: bullet; fence; guard; marker; pale; paling; patrol; peg; pole; post; sentinel; sentry; soldiers; stake; tether; watchman

PICKLE: v. brine; corn; cure; marinate; preserve; soak; souse; vinegar; PICKLE: n. brine; difficulty; dilemma; fix; jam; mess; plight; predicament; quandary; scrape; strait; trouble

PICNIC: clambake; cookout; entertainment; excurson; frolic; junket; outing; party

PICTURE: **v.** (**see** "draw") delineate; depict-(ure); describe; design; engrave; exhibit; fashion; illustrate; imagine; photograph; portray; represent; shoot; snap; PICTURE: **n.** configuration; copy; delineation; description; design; drawing; effigy; engraving; etching; exhibit; feature; flash; iconography; illustration; image; landscape; likeness; montage; movie; painting; panorama; pastel; pattern; photo(graph); portrait(ure); portrayal; presentation; print; profile; representation; reproduction; scene(ry); shot; similitude; situation; snap(shot); symbol; tableau; view

PICTURESQUE: alluring; artistic; beautiful; bright; charming; colorful; enticing; exotic; geoponic; graphic; lucid; pictorial; pleasant; pleasing; quaint; romantic; rural; scenic; strange; striking; unusual; vivid

PIEBALD: dappled; heterogeneous; mixed; mongrel; mottled; patched; pied; pintado; pinto; spotted; variegated

PIECE: **v.** cut; join; parcel; patch; repair; scrap; slice; splice; unite; PIECE: **n.** adjunct; amount; article; bit; chunk; coin; composition; constituent; cut; declamation; detail; example; fragment; gun; hunk; item; mind; morsel; opinion; oration; parcel; part; portion; product; scrap; section; sector; segment; shred; slice; sliver; specimen; speech; splinter; tune; unit; viewpoint; weapon; wedge

PIECEMEAL: aliquot; fractional; fractionary; fragmental; fragmentary; gradual; inching; *par pièces*; part(ly); sectional; segmental; small

PIED: **see** "piebald"

PIER: anta; berth; breakwater; buttress; dock doorpost; gatepost; groin; jetty; key; mole; pilaster; pile; pillar; post; shaft; slip; stilt; support; wharf

PIERCE: (**see** "penetrate") bore; chill; comprehend; discern; enter; gore; impale; javelin; lacerate; lance; lancinate; penetrate; perforate; poke; puncture; rend; spear; stab; stick; strike; tap; transfix; tunnel; wound; PIERCING: biting; blaring; boring; burning; cutting; gimlety; high; incisive; keen; loud; penetrating; perceptive; perforating; sharp; shrewd; shrill; strident; stridulous; tart; thorny

PIG: bacon; barrow; boar; elt; farrow; gilt; glutton; ham; hog; ingot; mold; pork(er); shoat; shote; slob; swine

PIGEON: carrier; Columbidae (pl.); cushat; dove; dupe; fantail; girl; goura; homer; homing; isabel; jacobin; nun; piper; pouter; priest; trumpeter; tumbler; turbit; victim

PIGEONHOLE: **v.** analyze; arrange; categorize; classify; defer; file; ignore; label; lose; shelve; store; systematize; PIGEONHOLE: **n.** box; compartment; cubbyhole; cubicle; hole; recess; shelf

PIGHEADED: **see** "stubborn"

PIGMENT: color; dye; lead; ochre; paint; stain; tint; umber; vermillion

PILE: **v.** (**see** "collect") accumulate; agglomerate; aggregate; amass; bank; congregate; cord; crowd; culminate; gather; heap; hoard; increase; lade; load; pyramid; rick; shock; stack; PILE: **n.** (**see** "collection") accumulation; agglomeration; aggregation; amassment; bank; battery; cache; cock; congeries; congregation; cord; cumulation; deposit; fiber; fortune; fur; gathering; hair; heap; hoard; load(s); lot(s); mass; money; mountains; pack; pillar; pole; pyramid; quantity; rack; rick; shock; slew; stack

PILFER: (**see** "steal") crib; plunder; rifle; rob

PILGRIM: crusader; immigrant; palmer; settler; traveler; voyager; wayfarer

PILL: ball; bolus; boor; dose; medicine; nuisance; pellet; pillule; pilula; remedy; tablet

PILLAGE: **v.** depredate; despoil; despoliate; devastate; flay; forage; foray; harass; harry; loot; maraud; pluck; plunder; prey; purloin; raid; ransack; ravage; reave; rifle; rob; sack; spoil; spoliate; steal; strip; PILLAGE: **n.** banditry; booth; brigandage; depredation; despoliation; devastation; foraging; foray; harassment; havoc; loot; plunder; rapine; ravagement; robbery; sacking; spoils; spoliation; theft; waste; PILLAGER: **see** "bandit"

PILLAR: beam; benefactor; bolster; column; pad; pedestal; pier; pole; post; prop; shaft; stanchion; support(er); tower

PILOT: **v.** coach; conduct; control; direct; escort; execute; guide; handle; lead; manage; operate; steer; PILOT: **n.** aviator; cicerone; controller; director; executor; flyer; guide;

helmsman; leader; manager; operator; pioneer; scout; trailblazer

PIN: **v.** attach; bind; confine; enclose; establish; fasten; fix; hold; identify; join; peg; rivet; secure; transfix; PIN: **n.** badge; bolt; brooch; cotter; dowel; fastener; feather; fid; nail; nog; ornament; peg; post; skewer; trifle

PINCH: **v.** (**see** "steal") afflict; arrest; choke; compress; confine; constrict; cram; cramp; extort; harass; impinge; narrow; nip; oppress; scrimp; squeeze; stint; straiten; tweak; vellicate; vex; wring; PINCH: **n.** (**see** "crisis") arrest; cramp; difficulty; distress; emergency; hardship; impact; juncture; nip; pain; pang; pass; plight; pressure; push; rub; shortage; squeeze; stint; strain; strait; stress; theft; vicissitude

PINE: (**see** "grieve") ache; droop; fade; flag; hunger; languish; long; thirst; tire; waste; wish; wither; yearn

PINGUID: adipose; fat(ty); fertile; oily; oleaginous; rich; unctuous

PINK: **v.** color; perforate; puncture; scallop; stab; PINK: **a.** angered; carnation; coral; excited; moved; smart; stylish; PINK: **n.** flower

PINNACLE: (**see** "acme") apex; climax; crest; culmination; épi; finial; peak; spire; summit; top; turret; zenith

PIONEER: (**see** "beginner") pathfinder; pilot; trailblazer

PIOUS: (**see** "holy") commendable; consecrated; devoted; devotional; devout; dutiful; good; holier-than-thou; leal; loyal; religiose; religious; reverent; sainted; saintly; sanctified; sanctimonious; virtuous; zealous

PIPE: **v.** carry; cry; play; whistle; PIPE: **n.** briar; brier; chimney; cinch; conduit; dudeen; eolina; flue; flute; flageolet; hooka(h); note; oboe; sound; trachea; tube

PIQUANT: biting; bright; burning; caustic; clever; fascinating; foreign; keen; lively; peppery; pleasing; provocative; pungent; racy; risqué; salty; saucy; savory; sharp; smart; spicy; spirited; stimulating; strange; strong; tart; teasing; trenchant; zestful; zesty; PIQUANCY: causticity; cleverness; enthusiasm; keenness; liveliness; piquantness; pungency; raciness; relish; sauciness; sharpness; spice; spirit; stimulation; tartness; trenchancy; vigor; vivacity; zest

PIQUE: **v.** (**see** "irritate") agitate; anger; annoy; displease; excite; goad; nettle; offend; provoke; rouse; ruffle; stimulate; sting; vex; PIQUE: **n.** (**see** "anger") acrimony; agitation; annoyance; chafing; displeasure; dudgeon; exasperation; fret; grudge; huff(iness); inflammation; ire; irritation; nettling; offense; pain; perturbation; prick; provocation; resentment; rousing; ruffling; sting; umbrage; vexation; wrath

PIRATE: **v. see** "steal;" PIRATE: **n.** Blackbeard; buccaneer; corsair; freebooter; infringer; picaroon; privateer; robber

PISTOL: arm; Colt; dag; derringer; firearm; gat; gun; handgun; iron; joker; Mauser; revolver; rod; roscoe; short arm; six-shooter; wag; weapon

PISTON: knob; plug; plunger; valve

PIT: abyss; blemish; cave; cavern; cavity; chasm; core; crater; defect; dent; depression; dint; enclosure; excavation; fovea; grave; gulf; Hell; hole; hollow; honeycomb; imperfection; indentation; lacuna; match; mine; pockmark; puncture; seed; shaft; stone; sump; well; PITTED: alveolate; faced; foveate; lacunal; lacunar; matched; pockmarked; punctured; scrobiculate

PITCH: **v.** advertise; buck; cast; decrease; dip; direct; erect; fall; fix; fling; hurl; incline; pave; peddle; plunge; regulate; roll; sell; set; sling; slope; sprawl; tell; throw; tilt; toss; wallow; PITCH: **n.** advertisement; angle; ascent; boost; cast; declivity; degree; depth; descent; dip; extent; fall; fling; grade; harmony; height; inclination; intensity; intonation; key; level; plunge; recommendation; resin; sap; sling; slope; strain; stress; tar; tone; toss; tune

PITCHER: ballplayer; container; crock; cruse; ewer; gorge; jar; jug; olla; olpe; prochoos; tosser; vessel

PITEOUS: (**see** "pitiful") compassionate; merciful

PITFALL: (**see** "snare") ambush; artifice; danger; decoy; error; gin; inveiglement; lure; maelstrom; springe; stratagem; subterfuge; temptation; trap

PITH: (**see** "kernel") center; cone; crux; embodiment; essence; extract; force; gist; grain; heart; importance; interior; jet; marrow; meat(iness); medulla; middle;

nub; nucleus; pulp; quintessence; sap; solidity; substance; vigor; weightiness; PITHY: (**see** "terse") aphoristic; apothegmatic; brief; cogent; concentrated; concise; condensed; epigrammatic(al); forceful; gnomic(al); heady; laconic(al); meaty; sententious; short; substantial; taut; terse; vigorous

PITTANCE: (**see** "bit") allowance; alms; charity; crust; dole; gift; mite; scantling; song; trifle

PITTED: **see** under "pit"

PITY: **v.** commiserate; condole; grieve; lament; regret; rue; sorrow; sympathize; PITY: **n.** charity; clemency; commiseration; compassion; condolence; consideration; empathy; generosity; grace; grief; humanity; kindness; lamentation; mercy; quarter; regret(s); remorse; ruth; sorrow; sympathy; tears; PITIFUL *or* PITIABLE: abject; afflicted; bad; *chétif*; commiserable; compassionate; contemptible; defenseless; deplorable; despicable; dismal; distressing; doleful; lamentable; mean; melancholy; merciful; miserable; moving; paltry; pathetic; piteous; plaintive; sad; squalid; teary; tender; touching; wretched; PITILESS: (**see** "cruel") cruelhearted; despiteful; devilish; diabolical; dispiteous; ferocious; hard(hearted); impiteous; implacable; inexorable; malevolent; malicious; mean; merciless; obdurate; paltry; puny; relentless; revengeful; ruthless; savage; stony; tyrannical; tyrannous; unfeeling; unmerciful; unpitying

PIVOT: **v.** (**see** "revolve") focus; hinge; rotate; slue; swing; swivel; turn; wheel; PIVOT: **n.** axle; center; cruciality; focus; hinge; hub; joint; junction; swivel; turn

PIXIE: (**see** "fairy") elf; goblin; imp; prankster; rascal; rogue; sprite

PLACABLE: **see** "peaceful" and "quiet"

PLACARD: ad(vertisement); affiche; announcement; bill; broadside; handbill; notice; poster; sign; tag

PLACATE: (**see** "calm") appease; conciliate; forgive; label; mollify; oil; pacify; please; smooth; soothe

PLACE: **v.** allocate; appoint; arrange; assign; base; categorize; class(ify); deposit; direct; dispose; distribute; establish; estimate; fix; house; identify; imbed; implant; inaugurate; induct; install; instil; invest; lay; locate; lodge; mount; order; pigeonhole; pinpoint; plant; pose; position; put; quarter; rank; reckon; recognize; repose; set(tle); situation; space; spot; station; store; vest; PLACE: **n.** abode; accommodation; appointment; area; arrangement; assignment; atmosphere; base; basis; category; city; coign of vantage; deposit; disposition; distribution; district; environment; environs; establishment; farm; field; fortress; habitation; home(stead); house; importance; installation; job; lieu; locale; locality; location; loci (pl.); locus; lodge; lookout; nest; niche; office; patio; plot; point; position; post; *pou sto*; premises; quarters; ranch; rank; region; rendezvous; repose; resort; scene; seat; second; section; site; situation; situ(s); space; sphere; spot; square; station; status; stead; step; store; street; territory; town; tract; tryst; vantage (point); village; where

PLACID: (**see** "calm") complacent; composed; cool; easy(going); equable; even; gentle; meek; mild; pacific; peaceful; phlegmatic; placable; quiet; restful; serene; smooth; smug; suant; tranquil; undisturbed; uneventful; unhasty; unhurried; unruffled

PLAGUE: **v.** (**see** "afflict") annoy; badger; beset; bother; burden; chafe; curse; distress; disturb; dun; eat; fret; gall; gnaw; grill; hamper; handicap; harass; harry; hector; infest; nag; overrun; pain; pester; scourge; tease; torment; trouble; try; twit; vex; worry; PLAGUE: **n.** abomination; affliction; annoyance; blight; bother(ation); calamity; disease; distress; epidemic; harassment; illness; infection; infestation; nuisance; outbreak; pain; pest(ilence); scourge; torment; trouble; wear; worry; vexation; PLAGUING: annoying; besetting; bothersome; calamitous; distressing; galling; grilling; impetigious; infested; overrun; pestilent(ial); pestilentious; plagued; plaguey; verminous; vexatious; vexed

PLAIN: **a.** (**see** "clear") apparent; artless; ascetic; austere; backward; bald; bare; blunt; candid; chaste; clean; coarse; common; comprehensible; countrified; country; crude; definite; democratic; distinct; downright; drear(y); dry; dull; even; evident; exoteric; explicit; express(ive); flat; flush; frank; frugal; graphic; guileless; homely; homespun; indubitable; inelaborate; inelegant; inferior; ingenuous; innocent; inornate; intelligible; legitimate; level; literal; lucid; manifest; marked; mere; nondescript; notable; obvious; open; ordinary; ostensible;

overt; palpable; patent; pellucid; perspicacious; point-blank; prominent; pronounced; pure (and simple); recognizable; rustic; salient; self-evident; self-explanatory; severe; simple; smooth; Spartan; striking; transparent; ugly; unadorned; unadulterated; unalluring; unappealing; unattractive; uncomplicated; undecorated; undisguised; undiversified; undramatic; unelaborate; unelegant; unembellished; unembroidered; unequivocal; unflavored; ungarnished; unungilded; uniform; unluxurious; unmagical; unmagnified; unmistakable; unmysterious; unobstructed;unornamented;unprepossessing; unpretentious; unsophisticated; unspectacular; unvariegated; unvarnished; vivid; well-defined; PLAIN: **n.** down; heath; llano; lowland; prairie; savannah; steppe; upland; veldt; wold

PLAINTIFF: accuser; appellant; complainant; complainer; prosecutor; suer

PLAINTIVE: (**see** "doleful") cross; discontented; elegiac; fretful; funereal; lugubrious; melancholic; melancholy; moanful; mournful; pathetic; peevish; piteous; pitiful; querulous; reedy; sad(dened); sorrowful; wistful; woeful

PLAITED: braided; folded; interwoven; kilted; knitted; pleated; twisted;

PLAN: **v.** aim; appropriate; arrange; blueprint; budget; calculate; chart; cogitate; concert; conspire; contemplate; contrive; delineate; depict; design; destine; detail; devise; diagram; draft; draw; ettle; figure; form(ulate); hatch; ideate; intend; intrigue; map; methodize; model; ordain; outline; picture; plant; plot; prearrange; precogitate; preconceive; predestine; predetermine; prefigure; premeditate; preordain; prepare; prepend; project; propose; scheme; sketch; shape; systematize; undertake; PLAN: **n.** aim; arrangement; blueprint; cabal; calculation; chart; cogitation; concept(ion); concoction; conspiracy; contemplation; contrivance; coup; course; delineation; design; device; diagram; draft; drawing; enterprise; extrapolation; fabric; form(at); form of action; formula; formulation; framework; game; idea; intention; intrigue; itinerary; lay(out); map; method; model; outline; pattern; picture; plat; plot; prearrangement; preconception; premeditation; problem; procedure; program; project; proposal; purpose; racket; regimen; representation; rule; schedule; schema; schemata (pl.); scheme; setup; sketch; stratagem; strategy; style;

system; table; tack; tactic(s); timetable; undertaking; way; PLANNED: **see** "arranged"

PLANE: **a.** even; flat; flush; level; sanded; shaven; smooth; PLANE: **n.** aircraft; facet; grade; surface; tool; tree

PLANET: earth; globe; Jupiter; luminary; Mars; Mercury; Neptune; Pluto; Saturn; Uranus; Venus; world

PLANT: **v.** abandon; bury; colonize; conceal; cultivate; establish; fix; hide; imbed; implant; inoculate; insert; place; populate; prearrange; seed; set(tle); sow; PLANT: **n.** factory; flora (pl.); flower; herb; mill; plot; pose; scheme; shop; shrub; tree; vegetable

PLAQUE: badge; brooch; deposit; disk; film; medal; memorial; ornament; patch; plate; slab; spot; tablet

PLASMA: blood; juice; lymph; milk; protoplasm; quartz; sera (pl.); serum; whey

PLASTIC: **a.** adaptable; ambivalent; amenable; changeable; compressible; constructive; creative; developmental; docile; ductile; elastic; erratic; fickle; fictile; flexible; formative; formulative; governable; impressionable; inconstant; influenceable; labile; malleable; manageable; mobile; moldable; molded; mutable; nascent; organic; pliable; pliant; pluripotent; resilient; sculptural; smooth; soft; suave; submissive; supple; susceptible; teachable; tractable; unctuous; unsettled; unstable; unsteady; vacillating; variable; waxy; yielding; PLASTIC: **n.** bakelite; lucite; resin; rubber; vinylite; PLASTICITY: adaptability; creativity; ductility; elasticity; impressionability; malleability; resiliency; suitability; suppleness; susceptibility; tractability; yield

PLATE: armor; base; china; collection; denture; disc(us); dish; disk; film; food; glass; grid; illustration; lamina; layer; lithograph; paten; patina; plaque; platter; print; scute; sheet; slab; slice; surface; teeth; tile; utensil

PLATEAU: dish; downs; highland; level; mesa; milestone; plain; platform; point; porch; region; salver; shelf; state; summit; table(land); terrace; upland

PLATFORM: base; basis; dais; deck; design; estrade; floor(ing); forum; grounds; *haut pas*; lectern; ledge; lyceum; oration; pattern; plan; plateau; podium; position; principle(s);

ramp; rostrum; scaffold; scheme; shelf; stand; state; surface; terrace

PLATITUDE: banality; bromide; cliché; commonplace; inanity; insipidity; shibboleth; staleness; triteness; truism

PLATOON: coterie; division; formation; group; set; soldiers; squad; subdivision; team; unit; volley

PLATTER: (see "plate") dish; disk; hat; lanx; record(ing); trencher

PLAUSIBLE: acceptable; affable; agreeable; believable; colorable; credible; creditable; likely; oily; popular; probable; reasonable; specious; suitable; trustworthy; PLAUSIBILITY: acceptability; affability; agreeability; believability; credibility; creditability; probability; suitability; trustworthiness

PLAY: **v.** act; amuse; bet; caper; contend; cooperate; dally; dart; disport; divert; emphasize; entertain; execute; exercise; exploit; feign; flirt; flutter; frisk; frolic; function; gamble; gambol; game; imitate; impersonate; jest; joke; kid; manipulate; mock; operate; participate; perform; ply; practice; pun; range; revel; rollick; romp; run; skip; sport; stake; toy; trifle; wager; wield; wreak; PLAY: **n.** act(ion); activity; amusement; antic; artifice; caper; comedy; contest; coup; dalliance; dallying; deal; diversion; drama; emphasis; employment; enactment; entertainment; exercise; exhibition; farce; feat; flirtation; freedom; frolic; fun; gambol; game; jest; joke; leeway; looseness; maneuver; margin; melodrama; move(ment); movie; operation; pantomime; pastime; performance; *pièce de théâtre*; prank; pun; recreation; revel; romp; room; scenario; scene; scope; show; skit; slack(ness); sport(iveness); stratagem; stroke; theatrical; tragedy; wager; PLAYFUL: animated; arch; buoyant; convivial; coy; cute; debonair; facetious; frisky; frivolous; frolicsome; gamesome; gay; humorous; impish; jesting; jocose; jocular; jolly; jovial; kittenish; lively; merry; mischievous; prankish; revelrous; roguish; romping; scampish; sportful; sportive; sprightly; PLAYFULNESS: archness; banter; facetiosity; frivolity; impishness; jocosity; jocularity; joviality; revelry; roguery; roguishness; sportiveness

PLAYER(S): (see "actor") cast; *corps dramatique*; *dramatis personae*

PLAYFUL: **see** after "play"

PLAYTHING: (**see** "toy") bauble; doll; trifle; trinket

PLAYWRIGHT: dramatist; dramaturge

PLEA: advocation; alibi; allegation; answer; apology; appeal; argument; blandishment; claim; contention; defense; entreaty; excuse; imploration; imprecation; invocation; justification; nolo; prayer; pretext; request; solicitation; suit; supplication; PLEAD: advocate; allege; apologize; appeal; argue; ask; beg; cite; defend; entreat; implore; imprecate; invoke; petition; pray; press; reason; show; solicit; sue; supplicate; urge; PLEADER: advocate; appellant; intercessor; lawyer; paraclete; supplicant

PLEASANT: affable; agreeable; alluring; amiable; amusing; attractive; balmy; beamish; beamy; blithe(some); bonhomous; bonny; buoyant; calm; charming; cheerful; cheering; chirpy; chirrupy; comely; comfortable; contented; cordial; cozy; cushy; delectable; delicate; delightful; dulcet; ebullient; elated; enjoyable; enlivened; enlivening; enthusiastic; enticing; eud(a)emonic; eupeptic; euphoric; exhilarant; exhilarated; exhilarating; fascinating; felicitous; friendly; gay; genial; gentle; glad(some); gleg; good (-natured); gracious; grateful; gratified; gratifying; happy; heartening; heartwarming; hearty; high; idyllic; inspired; inspirited; jocular; jocund; jolly; jovial; joyful; joyous; kind(ly); merry; mild; mirthful; nepenthean; nice; obliging; optimistic; playful; pleasing; pleasurable; pleasureful; promising; radiant; roseate; rosy; saccharine; sanguinary; sanguine; sanguinic; satisfied; satisfying; savory; seemly; smiling; sociable; social; soft; soothing; sparkling; spirited; sprightly; sunny; sympathetic; vivacious; volatile; warm; welcome; winsome; PLEASANTNESS or PLEASANTRY: affability; affableness; agreeability; agreeableness; amenity; amity; amusement; bliss; bonhom(m)ie; cheer(fulness); comfort; contentment; delectation; delight; diversion; ease; ebulliency; ecstasy; enjoyment; entertainment; eud(a)emonia; exhilaration; facetiosity; facetiousness; fascination; felicity; festivity; fun; gaiety; geniality; gladness; glee; graciousness; gratification; gusto; happiness; harmonization; harmony; heartiness; jest; jocularity; jocundity; joke; jollity; joviality; joy(fulness); joyousness; merriment; mirth(fulness); optimism; *plaisanterie*; playfulness;

pleasance; pleasure; rapture; raptus; sanguinity; sensuality; sophrosyne; sport; spirit; sprightliness; suavity; transport; urbanity; verve; vigor; vivacity; warmth; well-being; zest

PLEASE: allure; amuse; arride; attract; boost; captivate; charm; cheer; choose; comfort; console; delectate; delight; divert; elate; enchant; entertain; entice; enravish; enthral(l); entrance; exalt; exhilarate; fancy; favor; feast; felicitate; gladden; glorify; gratify; humor; indulge; invigorate; jubilate; like; luxuriate; mollify; oblige; pamper; pet; placate; prefer; regale; rejoice; revel; satiate; satisfy; soothe; suit; take; tickle; titillate; tittivate; transport; treat; want; wile; wish; PLEASING *or* PLEASED: (**see** "charming") agreeable; amiable; amicable; amusing; attractive; blissful; captivating; chic; comely; compatible; congenial; consonant; contented; corking; courteous; delectable; delicate; delicious; delighted; delightful; delightsome; diverting; divine; dreamy; ecstatic; Edenic; effective; elated; elysian; empyrean; enchanting; enjoyable; enraptured; entrancing; excellent; exhilarating; exhilarative; fair; favorable; felicitous; festive; fine; glad(ful); gladsome; gleeful; gracious; grateful; gratified; gratifying; halcyon; happy; harmonious; heavenly; ideal; idyllic; ingratiating; ingratiatory; jolly; joyful; joyous; jubilant; kind; lovely; luscious; merry; mirthful; nice; overjoyed; palatable; paradisiac(al); pellucid; personable; piquant; pleasant; prepossessing; rapturous; ravishing; refreshing; rejoicing; roseate; satisfactory; satisfied; satisfying; soothing; suited; taking; transported; unembittered; unresentful; welcome; well

PLEASURE: amusement; appreciation; bliss; cakes and ale; charm; choice; comfort; contentment; delectation; delight; desire; diversion; ease; ecstasy; enjoyment; entertainment; exultation; fancy; favor; felicity; festivity; fruition;'fun; gladness; glee; gratification; gratulation; gust(o); happiness; hilarity; inclination; indulgence; jocularity; jollity; joy; liking; love; merriment; oblectation; peace; piquancy; preference; purpose; rapture; raptus; recreation; relish; rest; satisfaction; sensuality; sophrosyne; sport; tang; titillation; tittivation; transport; will; wish; zest; PLEASURABLE: (**see** "pleasing") delectable; enjoyable; gratifying; hedonistic(al); piquant; pleasant; pleasureful; rapturous; sensual; sybaritic(al); titillating; zestful

PLEATED: creased; folded; plaited; plicate(d); *plissé*; shirred

PLEBEIAN: **see** "commoner" and "unsophisticated"

PLEBISCITE: decree; mandate; plebiscitum; referendum; tally; vote

PLEDGE: **v.** (**see** "assure") affiance; affirm; bet; betroth; bind; commit; contract; deposit; (en)gage; guarantee; hypothecate; impignorate; insure; mortgage; offer; pawn; pignorate; plight; promise; swear; toast; undertake; vow; PLEDGE: **n.** (**see** "assurance") affirmation; agreement; bail(ment); bet; bond; chattel; collateral; commitment; concession; contract; deposit; earnest; gage; guarantee; hostage; hypothecation; impignoration; insurance; mortgage; oath; obligation; offer; parole; pawn; pignoration; plight; promise; protection; security; surety; toast; token; troth; underaking; vow; wage; warrant; PLEDGED: **see** "committed"

PLENARY: absolute; complete; full; open; perfect; unqualified;

PLENTY: (**see** "abundance") adequacy; affluence; amplitude; aplenty; completeness; copiosity; copiousness; cornucopia; enough; galore; luxuriance; many; milk and honey; opulence; opulency; plenteousness; plentifulness; plen(t)itude; plethora; profusion; repletion; richness; spate; sufficiency; superfluity; PLENTIFUL: (**see** "abundant") abounding; adequate; affluent; ample; aplenty; complete; copious; cornucopian; enough; exuberant; fruitful; full: galore; generous; gobs; inexhaustible; large; lavish; liberal; lots; lush; luxuriant; numerous; opulent; overflowing; plenteous; plenitudinous; plethoric; productive; profuse; prolific; replete; rich; rife; sufficient; superabundant; superfluous; teeming; unmeasured; unstinted

PLENUM: full(ness); plethora; space

PLETHORA: (**see** "abundance") excess; floridity; fullness; hypertension; plenum; profusion; redundancy; repletion; superabundance; superfluity; turgescence

PLEXIFORM: complex; complicated; intricate; reticular; reticulate(d)

PLEXUS: brain; center; complexity; complication; core; crossing; network; rete; reticulation; synapse; system; tangle

PLIABLE *or* PLIANT: accommodating; accommodative; adaptable; amenable; complaisant; compliant; docile; ductile; educ(at)able; elastic; fictile; fingent; flexible; governable; green; helpful; inexperienced; influenceable; irresolute; limber; lissome; lithe; malleable; manageable; obedient; obliging; obsequious; plastic; raw; soft; submissive; supple; susceptible; tame; teachable; tractable; trainable; unstable; waxy; weak; workable; yielding

PLIGHT: **v.** (**see** "pledge") betroth; engage; pawn; promise; PLIGHT: **n.** (**see** "crisis") betrothal; case; condition; cross; difficulty; dilemma; engagement; exigency; fix; jam; lot; *mauvais pas*; mood; pickle; pledge; position; predicament; promise; quandary; scrape; situation; state

PLINTH: base(board); block; orlo; skirting; socle; subbase

PLOD: drag; drudge; inch; jog; labor; peg; plow; poke; proceed; slave; slog; slush; thud; toil; trudge; work

PLOT: **v.** abet; brew; cabal; chart; colleague; combine; compass; concoct; confederate; connive; conspire; contrive; delineate; design; develop; devise; diagram; draw; frame; intend; intrigue; invent; machinate; map; mark; mastermind; organize; outline; picture; plan; plat; program; project; propose; protract; scheme; sketch; study; trick; unite; PLOT: **n.** area; *association illégal*; bloc; brew; cabal; chart; clique; collusion; combination; conclave; concoction; confederacy; conjuration; connivance; conspiracy; conspiration; contrivance; coup; delineation; design; device; diagram; draft; drawing; faction; gang; graph; ground; group; intrigue; invention; junto; land; location; lot; machination; map; organization; outline; pact; parcel; party; picture; plan; plat; portion; program; project; proposal; ring; ruse; scenario; schema; set; site; sketch; story; stratagem; tract; trick; underground; union

PLUCK: **v.** cull; demolish; depilate; deplumate; dissever; fleece; free; garner; gather; glean; grab; harvest; pick; plunder; pull; remove; rive; rob; seize; select; strip; twang; twitch; vellicate; PLUCK: **n.** (**see** "courage") backbone; bravery; courageousness; daring; decision; determination; energy; firmness; fortitude; gameness; grab; grit; guts; mettle; nerve; perseverance; resolution; sand; spirit; tenacity; valor; vellication; will; PLUCKY: (**see** "bold") brave; courageous; daring;

distinct; fortuitous; game; gritty; gutty; nervy; persevering; sharp; spirited; tenacious; valorous

PLUG: **v.** (**see** "cork") advertise; boost; ca(u)lk; choke; clog; close; dam; estop; fill; grind; occlude; peg; recommend; shoot; stop; stuff; tighten; toil; work; PLUG: **n.** (**see** "cork") ad(vertisement); blow; bolt; boost; bott; bung; core; cud; dam; embolus; estoppal; filling; grind; horse; obstruction; occlusion; peg; pledget; punch; quid; shot; socket; spile; stopper; stopple; tamp(i)on; tap; wad; wedge

PLUG-UGLY: bandit; gangster; roughneck; rowdy; ruffian; thug; tough

PLUM: damson; drupe; gage; greengage; prize; prune; windfall

PLUMAGE *or* PLUME: adornment; aigret; crest; crown; dress; egret; feathers; panache; panoply; preen; pride; quill; tuft

PLUMP: blunt; bouncing; burly; buxom; chubby; corpulent; direct; distended; fat; fleshy; portly; pursy; rotund; round; sleek; stout; tidy; unqualified

PLUNDER: **v.** (**see** "pillage") depredate; despoil; loot; maraud; pluck; prey; raid; ransack; ravage; reave; rifle; rob; sack; spoil; spoliate; steal; strip; PLUNDER: **n.** boodle; booty; depredation; despoliation; freight; gains; goods; junk; loot; pillage; plunderage; profits; rapine; spoil(s); spoliation; swag; PLUNDERER: **see** "marauder"

PLUNGE: **v.** bet; dip; dive; engulf; enter; fall; force; gamble; hurry; immerse; jump; launch; leap; lunge; merse; pitch; ram; rush; shoot; sink; souse; submerge; swoop; thrust; PLUNGE: **n.** dip; dive; fall; gamble; immersion; jump; leap; lunge; pitch; ram; rush; sinking; submergence; thrust

PLUS: additional; advantage; and; extra; gain; more; over; positive; supplemental; surplus

PLUSH: (**see** "luxurious") baronial; easy; elegant; expensive; posh; rich; ritzy; sumptuous; superior; sybaritic

PLY: **v.** bend; comply; control; crease; double; employ; exercise; exert; fold; follow; handle; mold; operate; play; practice; press; run; sail; shape; solicit; steer; sue; urge; wield; work; yield; PLY: **n.** bend; bias; fold; inclination; layer; mold; thickness

POCKET: **v.** accept; appropriate; bag; conceal; enclose; hem (in); hide; keep; steal; suppress; swallow; POCKET: **n.** bag; bin; cavity; cul-de-sac; deposit; envelope; hole; hollow; interspace; lode; means; pod; pouch; purse; receptacle; recess; sac; sack; sinus; socket; space; void

POD: aril; boll; capsule; cover(ing); envelope; flock; herd; husk; pocket; pouch; sac; sack; school; shuck; silique

POEM: ballad; bucolic; composition; doggerel; elegy; epic; epode; idyll; lai; lay; limerick; madrigal; meter; ode; poesy; poetry; rhyme; rhythm; rime; sonnet; verse; POET: balladier; balladmonger; bard; idylist; laureate; lyricist; metrist; minstrel; odist; poetaster; rhymer; rimer; troubador; verse-maker; versemonger; versifier; POETIC(AL): artificial; bardic; idealized; idyllic; lyric; melic; metrical; poematic; stilted; versified; POETRY: (**see** "poem") metrification; poesy; verse; versification

POIGNANT: (**see** "pointed") acrid; acute; affecting; apt; biting; bitter; cutting; deep-felt; incisive; intense; keen; mordant; moving; painful; pathetic; penetrating; piercing; pressing; pungent; severe; sharp; stinging; touching; trenchant; urgent

POINT: **v.** (**see** "direct") acuminate; aim; angle; designate; detail; finish; focalize; focus; guide; head; hint; indicate; itemize; lay; level; locate; particularize; pilot; punctuate; sharpen; slant; smooth; spot; steer; taper; train; trim; POINT: **n.** ace; acumination; advantage; aim; angle; apex; argument; barb; benefit; bodkin; characteristic; cogency; course; crown; crux; culmination; dagger; degree; detail; direction; dot; end; essence; feature; focus; force; gist; goal; good; idea; issue; item; jot; juncture; kernel; locality; loci (pl.); locus; mark(er); matter; milestone; nail; neb; needle; object; particular(ity); peak; period; phase; pin; place; position; post; prickle; projection; proposition; punch; punctus; punto; purpose; question; score; spear; spike; spot; stage; station; step; subject; summit; tee; terminal; thesis; tine; tip; tittle; top; trait; unit; verge; vertex; way; POINTED: aciculate(d); aculeate; acuminate; acuminous; aimed; apicular; apiculate(d); brief; clear; concentrated; concise; conical; conspicuous; cuspate; detailed; epigrammatic; exact; incisive; leveled; lively; marked; meaningful; obvious; pertinent; piercing; piked; piquant; poignant; precise; pressing; punctilious;

punctual; pungent; purposeful; sharp(ened); significant; spicate; spicigerous; spiked; stimulating; stimulative; stinging; tangy; tapering; telling; terse; unmistakable; zestful

POINTLESS: (**see** "blunt") dull(ed); flat; frigid; futile; hebetudinous; impertinent; inane; incongruous; insipid; irrelevant; meaningless; obtuse; scoreless; senseless; unnecessary; unpointed; vacuous; vapid; POINTLESSNESS: futility; hebetude; inanity; ineffectuality; irrelevancy; vacuity; vapidity

POISE: **v.** balance; brace; dangle; hang; hover; librate; position; stabilize; suspend; POISE: **n.** (**see** "polish") address; adroitness; aplomb; balance; bearing; calm(ness); carriage; composure; cool(ness); courtesy; dexterity; dignity; ease; easiness; equality; equalization; equalness; equilibrium; equipoise; facility; glamo(u)r; grace; gravity; head; imperturbability; libration; manners; nonchalance; patience; perpendicularity; politeness; posture; readiness; repose; reserve; sangfroid; *savoir faire*; self-confidence; self-possession; serenity; stability; steadiness; tact; tranquility; POISED: (**see** "balanced") facile; hovering

POISON: **v.** blight; corrupt; degrade; destroy; harm; infect; kill; pervert; pollute; taint; toxify; undermine; vitiate; POISON: **n.** bane; blight; corruption; death; degradation; destruction; gall; infection; malignancy; perversion; pesticide; pestilence; pestilency; pollution; rottenness; taint; toxicity; toxin; venenation; venom; virulence; virus; POISONOUS *or* POISONED: (**see** "deadly") bad; baneful; corrupt; dangerous; deleterious; destructive; fatal; harmful; infected; infectious; killing; lethal; loathsome; malevolent; malign(ant); morbid; morbific; mortal; nauseating; noxious; obnoxious; pernicious; septic; spiteful; toxic; toxiferous; unfit; unsterile; venal; venenate; venomous; vicious; viperish; virose; virulent

POKE: bore; cram; dawdle; force; gorge; grope; hit; hook; inch; interfere; intrude; jab; jog; loiter; meddle; nose; nudge; penetrate; pierce; plod; potter; probe; prod; pry; punch; push; putter; search; shove; sock; stab; stir; thrust; trudge; urge

POLICE: **v.** administer; control; direct; discipline; govern; guard; monitor; regulate; superintend; supervise; watch; POLICE-(MAN): **n.** bobby; bull; constable; control; cop; fuzz; gendarme; guard; law(man);

monitor; officer; patrol(man); peeler; regulator; sheriff; trooper; watch(man)

POLICY: (see "principle") administration; aim; contract; course; craft(iness); decision; front; guideline; insurance; intention; management; method; objective; outlook; position; procedure; program; prudence; sagacity; shrewdness; theory; wisdom

POLISH: **v.** blacken; brighten; buff; burnish; civilize; clean; embellish; finish; freshen; furbish; glaze; grind; groom; improve; levigate; mill; neaten; perfect; ready; refine; refurbish; renew; rub; scour; scrub; shine; smooth; soften; POLISH: **n.** (see "culture") artistry; breeding; consummation; courtliness; diplomacy; education; elegance; embellishment; finesse; finish; gentility; glaze; gloss; grooming; luster; perfection; politeness; preciosity; refinement; *savoir faire*; sheen; shine; suavity; tact; urbanity; POLISHED: (see "cultured") cavalier; civil; courteous; couth; cultivated; diplomatic; educated; elegant; fine; finished; genteel; glossy; lustrous; polite; politic; refined; *soigné*; *soignée*; (fem.); shining; shiny; smooth; suave; tactful; terse; urbane

POLITE: (see "cultured") accomplished; affable; amiable; attentive; cavalier; ceremonial; Chesterfieldian; chivalrous; civil(ized); complaisant; cordial; correct; courteous; courtly; cultivated; decorous; deferent(ial); diplomatic; discreet; elegant; gallant; genteel; gentle; gentlemanly; graceful; gracious; manly; mannered; obliging; polished; politeful; politic; refined; sophisticated; suave; tactful; urbane; winsome; POLITENESS: (see "polish") affability; civility; comity; complaisance; courteousness; courtesy; courtliness; culture; decorousness; decorum; deferentiality; diplomacy; elegance; *prévenance*; refinement; suaveness; suavity; urbanity

POLITIC: (see "polite") artful; astute; canny; cautious; constitutional; crafty; cunning; diplomatic; discreet; expedient; foxy; ingenious; judicious; political; provident; prudent; sagacious; sage; shrewd; skillful; suave; tactful; wary; wily; wise; worldly-wise; POLITICAL: civil; governmental; temporal

POLITICIAN: candidate; courtier; politico; officeholder; office seeker; schemer; statesman

POLL: see "canvass"

POLLED: dehorned; hornless; pollard(ed); shaved; shaven; shorn

POLLUTE: (see "taint") defile; desecrate; poison; profane; POLLUTION: (see "poison") adulteration; contamination; corruption; defilement; degeneration; desecration; impurity; poison; profanation; septicity; taint; turbidity; uncleanliness

POLTROON: **a.** abject; cowardly; craven; dastardly; ignoble; mean; low; poltroonish; recreant; sneaky; sorry; POLTROON: **n.** coward; craven; dastard; milksop; recreant; sneak; wretch

POMMEL: (see "beat") cascable; handle; horn; knob; knot; protuberance

POMP: **v.** array; fuss; parade; pretend; show; strut; POMP: **n.** (see "show") array(ment); brilliance; cortege; *coup de théâtre*; dignity; display; elegance; exhibit(ion); flourish; form(ality); fuss; gala; glitter; glory; grandeur; grandiloquence; grandiosity; magnificence; ostentation; pageant(ry); parade; pomposity; pompousness; pretense; pretention; pretentiousness; pride; procession; ritual; spectacle; splash; splendor; state; vainglory; vanity; POMPOUS: (see "showy") august; blustering; bumptious; consequential; didactic(al); dignified; domineering; erudite; fatuous; flashy; formal; fustian; glorious; grandiloquent; grandiose; haughty; high-sounding; hoity-toity; imposing; inflated; insufferable; magisterial; magnificent; moralistic; orotund; ostentatious; pretentious; rubescent; self-assured; self-important; stilted; supercilious; theatrical; turgid; vain

POND: lagoon; lake; lochan; mere; pool; reservoir; tarn

PONDER: (see "think") appraise; brood; cogitate; consider; contemplate; deliberate; dream; evaluate; examine; excogitate; figure; judge; meditate; mull; muse; pore; prepend; question; reflect; roll; ruminate; study; weigh; wish; PONDERABLE: see "perceivable"

PONDEROUS: (see "heavy") bulky; clumsy; cumbersome; cumbrous; dull; elephantine; hefty; important; inanimate; labored; laborious; lifeless; massive; mastodonic; momentous; pedestrian; slow; uninspired; unwieldly; vast; weighty

POOL: v. accumulate; agglutinate; ante; combine; contribute; corner; stake; undercut; undermine; **POOL: n.** accumulation; agglutination; aggregation; ante; billiards; cartel; combination; corner; fund; game; group; kitty; lagoon; loch; mere; money; plashet; pond; pot; prize; puddle; reservoir; ring; stake(s); supply; tank; tarn

POOR: bad; bankrupt; bare; barren; beggarly; bereft; broke; contemptible; deficient; dejected; deprived; desolate; despicable; destitute; devoid; divested; down-and-out; down-at-heels; emaciated; empty; exhausted; feeble; flimsy; forsaken; fortuneless; fundless; half-baked; hardscrabble; humble; hungry; impecunious; impoverished; inadequate; indebted; indifferent; indigent; inefficient; inferior; insolvent; lacking; landless; lean; lost; low(ly); luckless; meager; mean; mediocre; middling; moneyless; necessitous; needy; ordinary; pale; paltry; parsimonious; penceless; penniless; penurious; pitiable; pitiful; portionless; poverty-stricken; puny; rank; reduced; resourceless; ruined; runty; *sans le sou*; scaly; scant(y); scrawny; scrubby; shabby; shoddy; sick(ly); so-so; squalid; starved; sterile; stipendless; straitened; thin; trivial; underprivileged; undesirable; unfavorable; unfortunate; unhappy; unmonied; unpretentious; unproductive; unprosperous; unscholarly; unwealthy; void; wanting; weak; worthless; wrong; **POORNESS: (see** "poverty") deprivation; immiserization; impecuniosity; impecunity; impoverishment; indigence; indigency; mendicancy; pauperism; pauperization

POP: v. assault; attack; bash; begin; blow; break; burst; clap; crack; dart; detonate; explode; hit; jump; knock; protrude; shoot; smack; snap; strike; **POP: n.** attempt; blow; break; burst; clap; clash; crack; dad; detonation; drink; effort; explosion; go; knock; report; snap; soda; try; whack

POPINJAY: coxcomb; dandiprat; dandy; fop; macaroni; parrot; woodpecker

POPPYCOCK: (see "nonsense") bosh; buncombe; bunk(um); fatuity; folderol; folly; foolishness; hokum; pish; posh; rot; stuff; trash

POPULACE *or* **POPULATION: (see** "people") commonalty; crowd; democracy; demos; inhabitants; mankind; masses; mob; multitude; proletariat; rabble; universe

POPULAR: accepted; alluring; approved; attractive; celebrated; cheap; common-(place); conventional; current; customary; demotic; easy; enchorial; epidemic; exoteric; familiar; famous; fashionable; favorite; general; hot; inexpensive; inferior; lay; likable; liked; likely; modish; notable; peoplish; plain; plausible; pleasing; plebeian; populous; praised; prevailing; prevalent; proletarian; public; stylish; topical; uncomplicated; unabstruse; vulgar; widespread; worthy; **POPULARITY: (see** "fame") approval; celebrity; esteem; favor; preference; privilege; repute; vogue

POPULOUS: (see "crowded") multitudinous; numerous; popular; teeming; thick

PORCH: colonnade; entrance(way); gallery; lanai; loggia; narthex; passage(way); piazza; portal; porte cochere; portico; stoa; stoop; veranda; vestibule

PORE: v. gaze; meditate; ponder; read; reflect; start; study; think; **PORE: n.** foramen; interstice; opening; ostiole; stoma(ta)

PORNOGRAPHY: coprology; curiosa (pl.); erotica (pl.); esoterica (pl.); facetiae (pl.)

PORRIDGE: atole; brose; broth; burgoo; gruel; hodgepodge; mush; pease; polenta; potpourri; pottage; soup; stew

PORT: bay; bearing; carriage; cove; demeanor; destination; door; gate; goal; harbor; haven; inlet; larboard; left; manner; mien; opening; portal; posture; refuge; wine

PORTAL: arch(way); door(way); entrance-(way); entry; gate(way); mouth; opening; passage(way); porch; port; postern

PORTEND: announce; anticipate; attest; augur; auspicate; betide; betoken; bode; connote; denominate; denote; designate; divine; evince; forebode; forecast; foresee; foreshadow; foreshow; foretell; hint; imply; import; indicate; intend; mark; mean; name; notify; predict; prefigure; presage; prognosticate; prophesy; shadow; show; signify; speak; specify; **PORTENT: (see** "omen") augury; auspication; betoken; denotation; divination; foreboding; forecast; foretelling; harbinger; hint; indication; marvel; ostent; presage; presentiment; prodigy; prognostication; prophecy; sign; token; warning; wonder; **PORTENTOUS: see** "ominous"

PORTION: (**see** "amount") allotment; allowance; apportion(ment); area; bit; block; cut; destiny; dividend; division; dole; doom; dose; dower(y); draft; draught; due; excerpt; fate; food; fraction; fragment; grain; half; helping; inheritance; lot; lump; morsel; parcel; part(icle); phase; piece; plot; province; quanta (pl.); quantity; quantum; quarter; quota; ration; region; sample; sampling; scrap; section; segment; selection; serving; share; side; slab; slice; some; splinter; split; stage; swatch; whack

PORTRAY: (**see** "picture") act; delineate; depict; describe; draw; enact; engrave; figure; form; give; limn; paint; represent; PORTRAIT: see "picture"

POSE: **v.** affect; affirm; assert; attitudinize; baffle; bewilder; claim; display; feign; model; mystify; nonplus; offer; perplex; place; position; posture; propound; puzzle; quiz; sit; POSE: **n.** (**see** "air") affectation; attitude; attitudinization; manner; mannerism; mask; masquerade; mien; position; posture; pretense; staginess; stance; theatricality; POSED: attitudinized; modeled; pretended; proposed; propounded; sat

POSER: (**see** "puzzle") facer; poseur; problem; question; stick(l)er

POSITION: **v.** aim; arrange; assign; fix; lay; mount; occupy; place; point; pose; prepare; ready; set; situate; spot; stand; POSITION: **n.** accommodation; affirmation; appointment; arrangement; assertion; assignment; attitude; bearing; berth; billet; business; chair; circumstance; coign (of vantage); coigne; commitment; condition; dignity; disposition; duty; echelon; employment; environment; fame; fix; footing; frontage; gradation; grade; group; halt; job; lay; level; locality; location; loci (pl.); locus; mark; métier; niche; number; occupation; office; order; orientation; outlook; part; place; point; policy; pose; post; posture; priority; privelege; proposition; rank(ing); rate; rating; responsibility; seat; sequence; setting; side; sight; situation; situs; stance; stand(ing); statement; station; stature; status; step; strength; stride; success; task; thesis; thinking; thought; ubiety; value; viewpoint; vocation; work

POSITIVE: **a.** (**see** "absolute") abstract; active; actual; affirmative; arbitrary; assertive; assured; authentic; basic; categorical; certain; clear; cocksure; concrete; confident; constant; constructive; decided; decisive; definite; definitive; distinct; dogmatic(al); downright; effective; emphatic; empirical; exact; explicit; factual; firm; genuine; healthy; incomparable; indisputable; indubitable; material; obstinate; obvious; opinionated; peremptory; philodoxic(al); plus; practical; precise; real; self-assured; sheer; substantive; sure; thetic(al); unconditional; unequivocal; unmistakable; unqualified; unquestionable; unyielding; utter; POSITIVE: **n.** absolute; absolutism; concretum; photo; unconditionality; POSITIVELY: absolutely; actually; certainly; extremely; indubitably; obviously; really; truly

POSSESS: (**see** "have") contain; control; convince; dominate; enjoy; envelop(e); get; grasp; hold; influence; keep; know; maintain; master; occupy; own; seize; surrender; take; use; POSSESSION(S): control; custody; detention; domination; enjoyment; envelopment; equipment; estate; fortune; grasp; holding; material; occupancy; occupation; ownership; mastery; means; property; resources; riches; self-control; stuff; substance; territory; use; wealth

POSSIBLE: achievable; attainable; capable; chance; chancy; conceivable; conceptible; contingent; dependent; earthly; executable; feasible; implicit; *in posse*; latent; likely; potential; practicable; practical; probable; promising; reasonable; suitable; superable; surmountable; undeveloped; POSSIBILITY: contingency; dynamis; eventuality; feasibility; likelihood; possibleness; potentia; potential(ity); practicability; probability; prospect; suitability; virtuality; way

POST: **v.** advertise; announce; assign; chair; denounce; dispatch; enter; haste; hurry; inform; mail; notify; place; position; publish; record; register; send; speed; spot; station; write; POST: **n.** assignment; barracks; berth; billet; camp; cantonment; chapter; column; courier; employment; encampment; fort; job; mail; marker; messenger; newel; office; picket; pier; pillar; place; pole; position; prop; quarter(s); settlement; spot; stake; station; support; timber; upright; xat

POSTER: affiche; bill; broadside; bulletin; card; courier; dodger; notice; notification; pictorial; picture; placard; sign; sticker

POSTERIOR: aft(er); behind; caudad; caudal; dorsal; posterioric; posticous; rear(ward); subsequent; tailward

POSTERITY: (**see** "descendants") afterwards; future; futurity; offspring; succession

POSTERN: back (door); door; entrance; gate; passage(way); portal; side

POSTPONE: adjourn; continue; defer; delay; forbear; leave; procrastinate; prorogue; protract; recess; remand; respite; retain; retard; shelve; slacken; slow; stay; subordinate; suspend; table; waive; POSTPONEMENT: (**see** "delay") adjournment; continuance; deferment; procrastination; prorogation; protraction; recess; remand; respite; retardation; slackening; stay

POSTULATE: **v.** ask; assume; claim; demand; guess; nominate; pose; posit; presuppose; require; sanction; stipulate; suppose; surmise; theorize; POSTULATE **n.** *or* POSTULATION: assumption; axiom; claim; demand; essentiality; guess; hypothesis; pose; posit; nomination; requirement; sanction; stipulation; supposition; surmise; theory; thesis; truth

POSTURE: **v.** assume; attitudinize; place; position; post; pretend; sit; stand; POSTURE: **n.** affectation; appearance; attitude; attudinization; bearing; build; carriage; demeanor; form; front; habit(us); heart; mien; mood; opinion; physique; place; post; pose; position; positure; pretense; situation; stance; stand; state; station; stature; status; theatricality

POT: aggregate; ante; bet; container; crock; crucible; cruse; deterioration; jar; jug; kettle; kitty; money; olla; pool; prize; ruin; saucepan; skillet; stake; wager

POTENT: able; affective; apposite; authoritative; brief; casual; cogent; compelling; concentrated; concise; constraining; convincing; dynamic; effective; effectual; efficacious; forceful; forcible; important; influential; instrumental; intense; irresistible; lusty; mighty; persuasive; pertinent; powerful; pregnant; puissant; sinewy; sovereign; stalwart; stiff; strong; sturdy; telling; timely; trenchant; urgent; valid; violent; virile; POTENCY: ability; authority; capacity; cogency; competence; competency; concentration; conciseness; constraint; domination; dynamism; effectiveness; efficacy; energy; force; influence; intensity; lustiness; majesty; might; potentiality; power; puissance; sovereignty; strength; trenchancy; vigor; virility; virtue; vis; vitality; wealth; worth

POTENTIAL: (**see** "latent") hidden; implicit; implied; inchoate; likely; possible; promising; quiescent

POTHER: (**see** "ado") controversy; fuss; stew; stir; turmoil

POTION: beverage; dose; draft; dram; draught; drink; drug; medicine; mixture; philter; preparation

POTPOURRI: (**see** "hodgepodge") anthology; collection; farrago; gallimaufry; jumble; medley; melange; miscellanea (pl.); miscellaneity; miscellany; mishmash; mix(ture); olio; pasticcio; porridge; salmagundi; series

POTTER: (**see** "trifle") dawdle; fiddle; fool; idle; loiter; mess; monkey; palter; putter; saunter; toy; waste

POTTERY: celadon; ceramic(s); china; delft; earthenware; glaze; porcelain; stoneware; uda; ware

POUCH: **see** "sac" and "sack"

POULTICE: compress; fomentation; plaster

POUNCE: **v.** descend; grab; grasp; jump; leap; seize; spring; swoop; POUNCE: **n.** claw; grab; grasp; jump; leap; snap; spring; swoop; talon

POUND: (**see** "beat") comminute; cram; crush; hammer; malleate; pelt; pulverize; pummel; ram; stamp; stuff; thump; triturate; whack

POUR: decant; diffuse; discharge; disembogue; emit; empty; expend; fill; flow; gush; issue; libate; radiate; rain; roll; run; shed; shower; slide; sluice; spew; spout; stream; supply; teem; vent

POURBOIRE: douceur; fee; gift; gratuity; lagniappe; tip

POUT: dwell; mope; moue; pique; protrude; sulk

POVERTY: bankruptcy; beggary; dearth; deficiency; denudation; depletion; deprivation destituteness; destitution; distress; emaciation; emptiness; exhaustion; exigency; famine; feebleness; immiserization; impecuniosity; impecunity; impoverishment; inadequacy; indigence; indigency; inferiority; insolvency; insufficiency; lack; meagerness; mendicancy; need; pass; paucity; pauperism; pauperization; penuriousness; penury; pinch; poorness; privation; rags; renunciation; *res angusta domi*; *sans le sou*; scantiness; scarcity; squalidity; squalor; starvation; strait(s); tenuity; unworth(iness); want; wolf

POWDER: **v.** abrade; bestrew; bray; comminute; cosmeticize; crumble; crush; dust; granulate; grind; pulverize; scatter; triturate; POWDER: **n.** cordite; cosmetic; drug; dust; pollen; talc(um); POWDERY: friable; pulverous; pulverulent

POWER(S): ability; absolutism; advantage; ammunition; arm(s); ascendency; attribution; authoritarianism; authority; can; capability; capacity; cogency; command; competence; competency; control; credit; defense; dint; domain; dominion; dynamis; dynamism; effectiveness; efficacy; efficiency; effort; electricity; empire; endowment; energy; faculty; force; genius; gift; glory; God; government; guns; horn; impact; impetus; influence; intensity; judgment; juggernaut; jurisdiction; machine; mailed fist; means; might; Moloch; money; muscle; nation; nerve; omnipotence; output; pep; performance; perseverance; potency; potentiality; prerogative; prestige; property; puissance; purchase; push; regency; reign; riches; right; rod; rule; sinew; solidity; stamina; steam; strength; superiority; supremacy; sway; sword; talent; tension; tyranny; union; use; vigor; vim; vitality; voltage; warrant; wealth; weight; wherewithal; POWERFUL: able; almighty; aristocratic; armipotent; athletic; authoritarian; autocratic; big; brawny; capable; cogent; compelling; competent; considerable; convincing; dictatorial; dominant; drastic; dynamic; earthshaking; effective; effectual; energetic; forceful; formidable; forte; giant; gigantic; great; hefty; Herculean; heroic(al); high; holy; important; imposing; influential; invincible; leonine; lusty; mighty; momentous; multipotent; muscular; omnipotent; plutocratic; potent; prepotent; prestigious; puissant; robust(ious); Samsonian; sinewy; stimulating; strenuous; strong; sturdy; substantial; substantious; supreme; telling; terrific; titanic; tyrannical; tyrannous; weighty; vast; vigorous; POWERFULNESS: (**see** "greatness") almightiness; omnipotence; omnipotency

POWERLESS: (**see** "helpless") feeble; impotent; impuissant; inert; nerveless; nugatory; sterile; unable; POWERLESSNESS:

brutum fulmen; helplessness; impotence; impotency; impuissance; incapacity; prostration; sterility

PRACTICAL: banausic; businesslike; capable; commonplace; down-to-earth; earthy; economic(al); efficient; empirical; existential; experienced; feasible; functional; hard (-bitten); hardheaded; level-headed; material(istic); matter-of-fact; practicable; pragmatic(al); proficient; purposeful; realistic; skillful; systematic; unromantic; unscrupulous; unsentimental; usable; useful; utile; utilitarian

PRACTICE: (**see** "custom" and "procedure") pursue; rehearse; warm up; work out; PRACTICED: **see** "versed"

PRAISE: **v.** acclaim; adore; adulate; applaud; approbate; approve; blandish; bless; boost; celebrate; clap; commend(ate); compliment; congratulate; emblazon; esteem; eulogize; exalt; extol; felicitate; fetishize; flatter; glorify; honor; hosanna; kudize; laud; laureate; lionize; lyricize; macarize; magnify; panegyrize; pean; pedestal; platitudinize; proclaim; recognize; respect; rhapsodize; salute; stellify; sympathize; worship; PRAISE: **n.** acclaim; acclamation; accolade; adoration; adulation; applause; approbation; approval; ascription; *baisemains* (pl.) blandishment; blessing; boost; bouquet; clap; commendation; complement; congratulation; dithyramb; doxology; emblazonment; encomium; esteem; eulogium; eulogy; exaltation; extolment; felicitation; flattery; glorification; glory; hallelujah; honor; hosanna; kudos; laudation; lionization; magnification; panegyric; pean; plaudit; prestige; recognition; respect; rhapsody; salute; stellification; tribute; worship; PRAISEWORTHY: (**see** "excellent") admirable; adorable; adulatory; approbatory; commendable; commendative; commendatory; complimentary; credi(ta)ble; eminent; encomiastic(al); estimable; eulogistic(al); exemplary; glorious; good; honest; honorific; idolatric; idolatrous; laudable; laudative; laudatory; meritorious; panegyric(al); perfect; praisable; preeminent; proper; recommendatory; splendid; supereminent; worthy

PRANCE: bound; caper; caracole; careen; cavort; dance; frisk; gambol; parade; pesade; spring; swagger; tittup

PRANK: **v.** (**see** "frolic") adorn; deck; horseplay; joke; PRANK: **n.** antic; caper; capriccio; dido; *échappée*; escapade; *espièglerie*; frolic; gambol; harlequinade; hijinks; horseplay; jest; joke; marlock; monkeyshine; shine; trick; vagary; whimsicality; PRANKSTER: joker; pixie; rascal; rogue; trickster

PRATE *or* PRATTLE: **see** "chatter"

PRAY: ask; beg; beseech; bid; conjure; crave; entreat; implore; importunate; invocate; invoke; petition; plead; pledge; request; solicit; sue; supplicate; vow; PRAYER: *absit omen;* adjuration; apology; appeal; ascription; ave; bene(diction); conjuration; credo; entreaty; imploration; imprecation; invocation; kyrie; litany; matin; motion; obsecration; orison; petition; plea; pledge; request; solicitation; suffrage; suit; supplication; vesper; vow; PRAYERFUL: devotional; devout; earnest; invocative; praying; precative; precatory; supplicatory

PREACH: evangelize; exhort; gospelize; lecture; sermonize; warn; PREACHER: **see** "clergyman;" PREACHMENT: discourse; exhortation; homily; hortation; lecture; preaching; sermon; warning

PRECARIOUS: (**see** "dangerous" and "uncertain") hairbreadth; hand-to-mouth; insecure; shaky; tottery; touch-and-go; uneasy; unstable

PRECAUTION: **see** "foresight"

PRECEDE: antecede; antedate; excel; forerun; herald; introduce; lead; outrank; pace; preface; proceed; publicize; scout; transcend; PRECEDING: above; aforesaid; antecedent; anterior; before; earlier; first; former; leading; over; precedent; precursory; prefatory; preliminary; prevenient; previous; principal; prior; PRECEDENCE: antecedence; lead; preference; priority; rank; right; rule; ruling; superiority; supremacy; PRECEDENT: **a.** antecedent; anterior; leading; preceding; routine; ruling; PRECEDENT: **n.** antecedent; custom; dicta (pl.); dictum; rule; ruling; sign; token

PRECEPT: (**see** "principle") act; axiom; behest; bid(ding); canon; charge; code; command(ment); direction; doctrine; example; injunction; instruction; landmark; law; mandate; maxim; order; ordinance; precedent; proverb; regulation; rule; ruling; teaching; warrant; writ

PRECINCT: **see** "area"

PRECIOUS: affected; alembicated; beloved; choice; costly; dear; esteemed; estimable; excellent; expensive; fastidious; fine; glorious; gold(en); great; hypocritical; important; inestimable; invaluable; lovable; overnice; overrefined; particular; pearly; priceless; rare; refined; select; superior; treasured; valuable; worthy

PRECIPICE: bluff; cliff; crag; danger; declivity; descent; disaster; drop; linn; pali; perpendicular(ity); slope

PRECIPITATE: **v.** accelerate; catalyze; cause; condense; deposit; descend; dispatch; drive; excite; expedite; fall; focalize; force; haste; hurl; hurry; press; provoke; quicken; rain; rouse; separate; set(tle); shoot; sleet; snow; speed; start; stimulate; subside; throw; urge; PRECIPITATE **a.** *or* PRECIPITOUS: abrupt; accelerated; dangerous; driven; expedited; expeditious; forced; full; Gadarene; hasty; headlong; headstrong; heady; impetuous; impulsive; overhanging; perpendicular; premature; quick(ened); rapid; rash; sheer; speedy; steep; sudden; PRECIPITATION: deposit; excitement; hail; haste; moisture; precipitancy; provocation; rain; sleet; snow

PRECISE: absolute; accurate; arithmetical; attentive; authentic; authoritative; careful; cautious; ceremonious; certain; clear; clocklike; close-grain(ed); conscientious; correct; definite; definitive; delicate; detailed; determinative; discriminating; discriminatory; distinct; elegant; even; exact(ing); explicit; fastidious; finicky; flat; formal; fussy; genuine; hairline; immaculate; impeccable; implicit; inflexible; keen; literal; mathematical; measured; meticulous; microscopic; minute; minutiose; minutious; neat; nice; obdurate; orthodox; overnice; painstaking; particular; pointed; prim; prompt; proper; prudent; punctilious; punctual; puritanical; rabbinic(al); refined; regular; right; rigid; rigorous; scientific; scrupulous; slavish; specific; steady; stiff; strict; surgical; thin; timely; unalterable; undeviating; unequivocal; unmistakable; unquestionable; very; watchful; PRECISION: ceremony; correctitude; correctness; definiteness; definitude; delicacy; exactitude; exactness; formality; justness; literality; minuteness; nicety; preciosity; preciseness; science; scrupulosity; sensitivity; truth; veracity

PRECISIAN: disciplinarian; drillmaster; martinet; precisionist; puritan; rigorist

PRECLUDE: avert; avoid; bar; block; close; debar; deter; estop; hinder; hold; impede; obviate; prevent; prohibit; restrain; stop; ward

PRECONCEIVE: (see "plan") dream; ideate; imagine; preimagine; premeditate; scheme; think

PRECURSOR: crier; forerunner; harbinger; herald; leader; messenger; predecessor; scout; trailblazer

PREDATORY: carnivorous; harpactophagous; plundering; predaceous; predacious; predative; rapacious

PREDESTINATION: destiny; determinism; fatalism; fate; foreknowledge; foreordination; necessarianism; necessism; preordination

PREDETERMINE: (see "destine" and "plan") foredestine; foreordain; predestine; PREDETERMINATION: foreordination; ideation; *partipris*; plan; predestination; predilection; prejudgment; prejudication

PREDICAMENT: (see "perplexity") bind; box; condition; corner; crisis; cruciality; cul-de-sac; deadlock; difficulty; dilemma; entanglement; exigency; extremity; fix; hole; horns of a dilemma; imbroglio; impasse; jam; kettle of fish; lot; maelstrom; *mauvais pas*; mess; mood; node; pass; pickle; pinch; plight; problem; puzzle; quandary; scrape; situation; spot; state; stew; strait; vortex

PREDICT: adumbrate; augur; betoken; bode; calculate; conjecture; discern; discover; divine; figure; forebode; forecast; foresee; foreshadow; foretell; guess; haruspicate; infer; locate; omen; perceive; portend; presage; prognosticate; prophesy; read; secondguess; soothsay; suppose; warn; PREDICTING or PREDICTIVE: foreboding; foreseeing; foretelling; haruspical; ominous; prognostic(ative); prophetic(al); PREDICTION: acumen; augury; bodement; chiromancy; crystallomancy; forecast; foretelling; fortune-telling; haruspication; haruspicy; insight; intuition; metagnomy; omen; presage; prognosis; prognostication; prophesy; vaticination; PREDICTOR: forecaster; fortuneteller; haruspex; Nostradamus; prognosticator; sage; seer; soothsayer

PREDISPOSE: brainwash; dispose; educate; incline; influence; pave; prejudice; prepare; sell; subject; sway; teach; tend; train;

PREDISPOSED: (see "biased"); inclined partial; prejudiced; prone; sold; subject; susceptible; tendentious; tending; PREDISPOSITION: (see "tendency") diathesis; inclination; leaning; predilection; proclivity

PREDOMINATE: (see "prevail") control; defeat; exceed; govern; hold; overawe; overcome; preponderate; reign; rule; surpass; sway; top; PREDOMINANT: absolute; ascendant; authoritative; controlling; paramount; peremptory; predominating; preponderant; preponderating; prevailing; reigning; ruling; superior; supreme; PREDOMINANCE or PREDOMINATION: (see "control") ascendancy; authority; defeat; government; majority; paramountcy; preponderancy; prevalence; rule; superiority; supremacy

PREEMINENT: above; celebrated; chief; consummate; distinguished; exalted; exceeding; excellent; first; foremost; great; main; noble; nonpareil; outstanding; over; palmary; paramount; peerless; praiseworthy; prominent; splendid; star; superior; supreme; transcendent; unequaled

PREEMPT: (see "take") sequester

PREEN: arrange; bristle; clean; curry; doll; dress; fuss; gloat; neaten; perk; plume; primp; prink; smooth; spruce; swagger; swell; trick; trim

PREFACE: **v.** begin; front; herald; introduce; open; precede; prelude; PREFACE: **n.** antecedent; *avant-propos*; beginning; blessing; exordium; foreword; front; introduction; isagoge; opening; overture; prayer; preamble; preliminary; prelude; proem; program(ma); prolegomenon; prologue; prolusion; protasis; spadework; PREFATORY: introductory; prefacial; prefatorial; preliminary; premonitory; prolegomenous; prolusory

PREFER: advance; approve; charge; choose; cull; desire; elect; exalt; fancy; favor; like; offer; opt; ordain; order; pick; present; promote; propose; purpose; raise; recommend; select; will; wish; PREFERABLE: see "advantageous" and "right"; PREFERENCE: advantage; alternative; antecedence; choice; desirability; desire; discrimination; fancy; favor(ite); inclination; like; option; pick; popularity; precedence; predilection; predisposition; preferment; prejudice; priority; privilege; promotion; selection; taste;

want; wish; PREFERRED: (**see** "esteemed") blue-eyed; chosen; fair-haired; favored; popular; predilect(ed)

PREFIGURE: (**see** "predict") augur; cogitate; determine; dream; foresee; foreshadow; foretell; imagine; indicate; shadow; signify; type; typify

PREGNANT: *enceinte*; expressive; fecund; fertile; germinal; gestating; gravid; heavy; inventive; meaningful; parous; replete; rich; significant; suggestive; teeming; tumefactive; tumescent; weighty; PREGNANCY: cyesis; enceinteship; encyesia; eucyesis; fecundity; fetation; fertility; fruitfulness; gestation; gravidation; gravidism; gravidity; meaningfulness; parturience; syllepsis; tecnogonia

PREJUDGMENT: (**see** "predetermination") prejudice

PREJUDICE: animus; bent; bias; color(ing); conatus; declination; determinant; determination; diathesis; disposition; dogmatism; enmity; fanaticism; favor; flair; hatred; illiberality; impatience; inclination; insularism; insularity; intolerance; intoleration; jaundice; jealousy; leaning; mood; narrowmindedness; narrowness; objection; outlook; parochialism; partiality; *parti pris*; penchant; peninsularity; predilection; predisposition; preference; prejudgment; prepossession; presumption; proclivity; provincialism; sectionalism; slant; slope; spite; susceptibility; sway; taste; temperament; tendency; trend; turn; unfairness; PREJUDICED: (**see** "biased") bigoted; determined; fanatic; insular; insulated; intolerant; monastic; narrow(-minded); parochial; partial; peninsular; prejudicial; provincial; sectarian; slanted; tendentious; unindifferent

PRELATE: archbishop; bishop; cardinal; chaplain; clergyman; cleric; dignitary; ecclesiastic; hierarch; pontiff; pope; primate

PRELIMINARY: **a.** (**see** "introductory") antecedent; before; exploratory; first; imperative; indispensable; initiative; introductory; liminary; precedential; preceding; precursive; precursory; prefatory; prefatorial; premonitory; previous; proemial; PRELIMINARY: **n.** (**see** "preface") condition (precedent); essential(ity); preamble; prerequisite; requirement; *sine qua non*; spadework

PRELUDE: (**see** "preface") beginning; introduction; opening; overture; preamble; proem; prolusion

PREMATURE: (**see** "before") anticipatory; early; green; hasty; hurried; inopportune; precipitate; precocious; prevenient; previous; rash; raw; sudden; unripe; unseasonable; untimely

PREMEDITATE: **see** "plan;" PREMEDITATED: (**see** "deliberate") aforethought; calculated; designed; intended; intentional; meant; planned; plotted; voluntary

PREMISE: (**see** "basis") assumption; base; beginning; condition; contingency; education; foundation; ground(s); groundwork; prelude; presupposition; proposition; PREMISES: area; buildings; campus; data (pl.); digs; estate; grounds; land

PREMIUM: **a.** (**see** "fancy") exceptional; first-class; first-rate; high; PREMIUM: **n.** agio; award; bonus; bounty; fee; gift; guerdon; lagniappe; meed; payment; prize; recompense; remuneration; requital; reward; stake; value

PREMONITION: (**see** "foretoken" and "warning") feeling; forewarning; hunch; prenotion; presentiment

PREOCCUPIED: (**see** "inattentive") absent-(minded); absorbed; abstracted; concerned; dreaming; engrossed; filled; lost; musing; oblivious; occupied; rapt; solicitous; studious; unattentive; uninquiring; unobservant; unobserving; working; PREOCCUPATION: **see** "abstraction" and "concern"

PREPARE: acclimatize; adapt; adjust; admonish; agree; alter; anticipate; arm; arrange; await; bid; brace; brew; buckle; caution; coach; compose; concoct; condition; confect; consider; construct; contemplate; contract; contrive; cook; counsel; cultivate; decoct; develop; devise; diet; discipline; dispense; dispose; do; draft; drill; edit; educate; exercise; fabricate; facilitate; fatten; fit; fix; foment; forge; fortify; gather; get; gird; grind; groom; habituate; harden; hatch; impend; instruct; introduce; inure; invest; load; make; mix; modify; organize; outline; pave; persuade; plan; plot; polish; practice; precondition; process; provide; qualify; ready; refine; rehearse; reinforce; restore; season; sketch; stipulate; stir; strengthen; study; teach; tell; toss; toughen; train; trim; unlimber;

warm up; warn; work; PREPARATORY: (see "introductory" and "preliminary") antecedent; prefatorial; PREPARED: admonished; armed; braced; conditioned; drilled; educated; *en garde*; equipped; exercised; expungatory; licensed; preconditioned; predigested; processed; readied; ready; set; toughened; trained; worked; PREPARATION: address; anticipation; arrangement; batch; brew; conception; condition; confection; consideration; contemplation; decoction; education; equipment; exercise; fabrication; fitness; medicine; mixture; preparation; preparative; preparedness; provision; purveyance; rehearsal; suspicion; tonic; training; warning

PREPOSTEROUS: (see "absurd") bizarre; fantastic(al); grotesque; nonsensical; unbelievable; unearthly

PREREQUISITE: **a. see** "preliminary;" PREREQUISITE: **n.** (see "necessity") condition precedent; essential(ity); indispensability; need(fulness); postulate; preliminary; requirement; *sine qua non*

PRESAGE: **v.** (see "forebode" and "forecast") preindicate; prognosticate; PRESAGE: **n.** (see "omen") augury; divination; foreboding; forecast(ing); foreknowledge; foreshadowing; indication; intuition; portent; prediction; prescience; presentiment; prognostic(ation); prophesy

PRESCRIBE: advise; advocate; allot; assign; command; confine; control; decree; define; designate; destine; dictate; direct; dose; enjoin; establish; fix; invalidate; medicate; ordain; order; outlaw; recommend; regulate; restrain; rule; set; specify; treat; urge; PRESCRIBED: arbitrary; authoritative; authorized; official; prescriptive; recommended; thetic(al); PRESCRIPTION: (see "dose") amount; direction; drug; preparation; ration; remedy; rule

PRESENCE: air; appearance; attendance; bearing; being; carriage; demeanor; effectiveness; here and now; hereness; manner; mien; occurrence; person; physicality; poise; posture

PRESENT: **v.** (see "give") accuse; award; bestow; cite; confer; convey; dedicate; devise; display; dispose; donate; endow; exhibit; expose; furnish; grant; introduce; offer; perform; play; pose; propound; provide; represent; show; stage; submit; supply; tender; urge; PRESENT: **a.** actual; avail-

able; contemporaneous; contemporary; current; existent; existing; here; immediate; instant; moment; nonce; now; today; visible; PRESENT: **n.** (see "gift") gratuity; handsel; offering; *status quo*; temporality; PRESENTLY: anon; consequently; current(ly); directly; forthwith; immediately; necessarily; now; shortly; soon

PRESENTATION: (see "description" and "representation") award; bestowal; bestowment; conferment; conferral; delivery; display; disposition; donation; exhibition; exposure; gift; offer; performance; show; submission; unveiling

PRESERVE: **v.** bottle; can; collect; conserve; corn; cure; deliver; dry; enshrine; fix; forbear; freeze; guard; heal; hold; keep; lock; maintain; pickle; protect; prove; rectify; relieve; remedy; rescue; reserve; restore; resuscitate; retain; salt; save; season; shield; smoke; spare; store; support; sustain; tin; treasure; treat; uphold; vindicate; PRESERVE: **n.** collection; fruit; jam; jelly; marmalade; park; reservation; reserve; sanctuary; treasury; PRESERVATION: conservation; deliverance; enshrinement; guarantee; guardianship; immortalization; maintenance; perpetuation; protection; reservation; reserve; resuscitation; safekeeping; salvation; warrant; PRESERVATIVE: alcohol; creosote; fixer; vinegar

PRESS: **v.** afflict; argue; assail; beseech; beset; clasp; coerce; commandeer; compel; compress; constrain; contend; cram; crowd; crush; depress; embrace; emphasize; entreat; exert; express; flatten; force; goad; harass; huddle; hug; importune; impress; insist; iron; jam; oppose; precipitate; prosecute; mass; sit; smooth; squash; squeeze; stamp; strain; stress; stuff; throng; thrust; tramp(le); urge; wedge; weigh; work; PRESS: **n.** (see "pressure") closet; crowd; cupboard; distress; huddle; jurnalism; multitude; newspaper; rush; serry; straits; throng; PRESSING: acute; burdensome; clamorous; coercive; critical; crying; earnest; exacting; exigent; imminent; impending; imperative; important; importunate; insistent; poignant; rushing; threatening; urgent; warm; weighty; PRESSURE: burden; coercion; compression; constraint; criticality; dispatch; distraint; distress; drive; emphasis; exaction; exigency; force; head; heat; heaviness; hurry; immediacy; imminency; impact; impetus; importance; importunacy; importunance; influence; insistence; instancy; mass; obligation; oppression; ponderosity;

press; priority; push(ing); rush; squeeze; squeezing; strain; stress; sway; tension; thrust; touch; urgency; weight; work

PRESTIGE: acceptance; accolade; ascendency; authority; bias; cachet; caste; character; class; credit; éclat; esteem; estimation; eminence; face; fame; glory; honor; influence; kudos; note; power; renown; reputation; repute; riches; standing; stature; status; supereminence; wealth; worth(iness); PRESTIGIOUS: (see "notable") eminent; esteemed; famed; famous; influential; powerful; renowned; reputable

PRESUME: (see "assume" and "presuppose") anticipate; dare (say); expect; guess; imply; postulate; pretend; suppose; surmise; take for granted; PRESUMED: (see "probable") assumed; circumstantial; implied; postulated; presumable; presumptive; presupposed; supposed; PRESUMPTION: arrogance; assumption; audacity; boldness; circumstantiality; conception; effrontery; expectation; forwardness; guess; outrecuidance; presumptuousness; presupposition; supposition; surmise; PRESUMPTIVE: apparent; a priori; arrogant; assumed; brash; due; hypothetical; Icarian; inferred; postulatory; presumed; probable; supposed; supposititious; PRESUMPTUOUS: anticipative; arrogant; assuming; audacious; bold; brash; brassy; bumptious; certain; cocksure; confident; familiar; fresh; haughty; Icarian; imperious; impertinent; impudent; insolent; nervy; nosy; overbearing; overbold; overweening; pretentious; rash; sassy; saucy; temerarious; uppish; uppity

PRESUPPOSE: (see "anticipate") assume; contemplate; dare (say); expect; pose; posit; postulate; premise; presume; surmise; PRESUPPOSITION: (see "anticipation") assumption; belief; bias; conjecture; deduction; guess; inference; opinion; postulate; postulation; predilection; premise; presumption; prolepsis; surmise

PRETEND: allege; ape; assert; assume; attitudinize; beseem; bluff; cheat; claim; cloak; color; counterfeit; deceive; disguise; dissemble; distort; fabricate; fake; falsify; feign; forge; garble; imitate; impersonate; invent; lie; mask; mime; mimic; mislead; misrepresent; offer; play; pose; posture; presume; profess; purport; queen; reckon; represent; seem; sham; simulate; venture; weave; PRETENDED: (see "affected") affectational; alleged; Barmecidal; beseeming; colored; hypocritical; illusory; ostensi-

ble; ostensive; pseudo; quasi; self-styled; simulated; so-called; soi-disant; spurious; supposed; unreal; PRETENDER: affecter; aper; bluffer; charlatan; claimant; counterfeit; cowan; deceiver; faker; four-flusher; fraud; hypocrite; idol; imitator; imposter; make-believe; mimer; mimic; mountebank; poser; poseur; poseuse (fem.); pretendant; quack(salver); shyster; snob; swindler; Tartuf(f)e; tricheur; tricheuse (fem.); trickster

PRETENSE or PRETENSION: acrobatics; act; affectation; air; alibi; apology; artifice; aspiration; assumption; attitudinization; blind; bluff; cant; charade; claim; cloak; color; color of office; copy; counterfeit; cover; deceit; deception; disguise; dissembling; dissimulation; dodge; duplicity; excuse; expediency; expedient; fabrication; face; falseness; falsification; feint; fiction; fraud; gloss; guise; hollowness; hypocrisy; illusion; imitation; insincerity; intention; make-believe; make-do; makeshift; mask; misrepresentation; ostentation; pageant(ry); performance; persiflage; playacting; plea; pomp; pose; postiche; presumptuousness; pretensiveness; pretentiousness; pretext; ruse; semblance; sham; shift; show; simulacrum; simulation; speciosity; speciousness; stratagem; subterfuge; trick; unreality; wile

PRETENTIOUS: (see "showy") affectational; affected; ambitious; artificial; arty; assuming; bombastic; conceited; conspicuous; false; Faustian; fictional; fictitious; fictive; gaudy; haughty; high(falutin); high-flown; high-flying; ostentatious; papier-mâché; pharisaic(al); pompier; pompous; presuming; presumptuous; religiose; sanctimonious; self-important; sonorous; tawdry; unnatural; vain; PRETENTIOUSNESS: blague; bombast; falsity; flummery; haughtiness; humbug; ostentation; outrecuidance; pomposity; presumptuousness; pretention; pretensiveness; sanctimony; self-importance; showiness; vanity

PRETERMIT: intermit; interrupt; neglect; omit; pass (over); suspend

PRETERNATURAL: (see "supernatural"); abnormal; exceptional; ghostly; nonnatural

PRETEXT: (see "pretense") alibi; apology; color; cover; excuse; guise; mask; plea

PRETTY: (see "beautiful") apt; attractive; bonny; charming; chic; comely; considerable; cute; dainty; delicate; excellent; fair; fetching; fine; good; graceful; handsome;

indifferent; *joli(e)*; lovely; miserable; moderate(ly); nice; pat; petite; pleasing; poor; striking; sweet; winsome

PREVAIL: (**see** "beat") actuate; avail; be; coerce; conquer; dominate; drive; exist; impose; induce; influence; master; move; obtain; overcome; persist; persuade; predominate; preponderate; reach; reign; rule; succeed; surmount; sway; triumph; win; PREVAILING *or* PREVALENT: abiding; abounding; accepted; ascendant; catholic; chronic; common; comprehensive; conquering; current; customary; demotic; dominant; efficacious; enchorial; endemic; epidemic; existing; existent; general; indigenous; living; popular; predominant; regal; regnant; reigning; rife; spread; successful; sweeping; universal; usual; victorious; widespread; PREVALENCE: ascendency; circulation; currency; existence; persistence; predominance; predomination; regnancy; universality

PREVARICATE: (**see** "lie") cavil; deviate; devise; dodge; equivocate; evade; exaggerate; fable; fabulize; falsify; fib; invent; misrepresent; misstate; palter; pettifog; quibble; tergiversate

PREVENT: (**see** "bar") anticipate; avert; balk; block; check; circumvent; contain; counteract; dam; debar; destroy; deter; estop; exclude; foil; forbid; foreclose; forestall; frustrate; gag; guard; halt; help; hinder; hold; impede; intercept; interrupt; keep; obstruct; obviate; override; paralyze; preclude; prohibit; repress; restrain; restrict; retain; scotch; screen; stop; subdue; thwart; ward; warn; PREVENTING: circumventive; precautionary; preventative; preventive; prophylactic; PREVENTION: alexiteric; antiseptic; circumvention; guard; prevent(at)ive; prophylactic; prophylaxis

PREVIOUS(LY): already; antecedent(ly); anterior; before(hand); done; earlier; erst; erstwhile; first; foregoing; former; hasty; hitherto; impatient; introductory; over; past; precedent; preceding; precursory; prefatory; preliminary; premature; preparatory; prior; quondam; ultimate(ly)

PREY: **v.** defraud; depredate; devour; dragoon; hunt; kill; loot; pillage; plunder; ravage; rob; spoil; victimize; PREY(ING): **n.** depredation; kill; loot; pillage; plunder; predacity; predation; prize; quarry; rapacity; rapine; ravagement; ravin; spoils; victim; PREYING: **a.** carnivorous; gnawing;

harpactophagous; predaceous; predative; rapacious; wasting

PRICE: (**see** "fee") amount; appraisement; bill; charge; consideration; cost; dues; duty; evaluation; expenditure; expense; fare; figure; money; outlay; rate; sacrifice; sum; tab; tariff; tax; terms; ticket; toll; valuation; value

PRICELESS: (**see** "costly") high-priced; impayable; incalculable; inestimable; invaluable; matchless; rare; rich; valuable

PRICK: (**see** "stab") impel; incite; prod; provoke; stick; stimulate; stir; urge; PRICKLE: accantha; barb; bristle; bur(r); point; prod; spicula; spicule; spine; sting; thistle; thorn; PRICKLY: acanthoid; acanthous; echinate; horrent; muricate; sensitive; spinous; spiny; stinging; thorny; vexatious

PRIDE: **v. see** "preen;" PRIDE: **n.** airs; *amour propre*; arrogance; conceit; disdain; display; ego(t)ism; esprit; *esprit de corps*; exaltation; glory; haughtiness; hauteur; horn; hubris; insolence; loftiness; lordliness; magnificence; ostentation; pique; pomposity; power; prime; self-conceit; self-esteem; self-exaltation; self-glory; self-regard; self-respect; vainglory; vanity; PRIDEFUL: (**see** "haughty") conceited; elated; fastuous; insolent; lordly; ostentatious; pompous; self-conceited; self-glorifying; self-regarding; vain(glorious)

PRIEST: (**see** "clergyman") abbe; cleric; confessor; curé; divine; domine; druid; ecclesiastic; hierophant; lama; minister; padre; pastor; presbyter; rabbi; PRIESTLY: Aaronic; clerical; ecclesiastic(al); hierarchic(al); hieratic; hierophant(ic); Levitical; pontifical; rabbinic(al); sacerdotic; sacerdot(ic)al; PRIESTHOOD: clericality; ecclesiasticism; priestianity; sacerdocy

PRIM: chic; decorous; fastidious; formal; neat; nice; *pincé*; *pincée* (fem.); posh; precise; prig(gish); prissy; proper; proud; prudish; puritanic(al); religiose; sanctimonious; schoolteachery; sedate; sissified; smug; stiff; straight-laced; trim; PRIMNESS: decorousness; fastidiousness; formality; nicety; preciosity; priggishness; prissiness; prudery; sanctimony; squeamishness; stiffness

PRIMAL: (**see** "primitive") autochthonic; fundamental; immemorial; indigenous; original; patriarchal; primeval; principal

PRIMARY: aboriginal; ancient; basic; chief; constitutional; direct; elemental; elementary; first(hand); fundamental; idiopathic; independent; initial; leading; main; original; prime(val); primitive; primordial; principal; radical; simple; underivative; underived; virgin

PRIMATE: ape; archbishop; bishop; elder; exarch; hierarch; leader; lemur; mammal; man; marmoset; monkey; patriarch; prelate

PRIME: **v.** charge; coach; fill; instruct; load; prepare; ready; stimulate; teach; PRIME: **a.** (see "primary") best; chief; choice; commercial; excellent; finest; first(-class); fresh; good; healthy; leading; main; original; primitive; vigorous; useful

PRIMER: abecedaria (pl.); abecedarium; hornbook; introduction; reader

PRIMEVAL: (see "primitive") aboriginal; ancient; antiquated; antique; distant; early; first; hoary; native; old(en); original; pristine; traditional; venerable

PRIMITIVE: **a.** aboriginal; ancient; antiquated; antique; archaic; autochthonal; autochthonic; autochthonous; axiomatic; backward; barbaric; barbarous; basic; crude; dark; earlier; early; elemental; first; fundamental; Gothic; gross; hoary; ignorant; indigenous; naïve; native; Neanderthal; nonliterate; old(en); original; patriarchal; persistent; postulational; prehistoric; primal; primary; prime(val); primogenial; primordial; pristine; quaint; retarded; rough; rude; rudimentary; savage; self-taught; self-tutored; simple; ultimate; uncivilized; uncouth; uncultured; undeveloped; unevolved; unrefined; unsophisticated; untaught; untutored; venerable; wild; PRIMITIVE: **n.** aboriginal; aborigine; native; primitiveness; primitivism; primitivity; primordial; savage

PRIMORDIAL: (see "primitive") aboriginal; ancient; antiquated; antique; crude; earliest; early; elementary; first; fundamental; hoary; native; old(en); original; primary; primeval; pristine; traditional; undeveloped; PRIMORDIUM: anlage; beginning; commencement; embryo; origin(ation); rudiment

PRIMP: (see "preen") arrange; cosmeticize; neaten; smarten

PRINCE: cardinal; chief; dauphin; king; leader; monarch; noble(man); peer; ruler; satrap; sovereign; tetrarch; PRINCELY: (see "royal") magnificent; noble; stately

PRINCIPAL: **a.** (see "chief") alpha; arch; capital; cardinal; consequential; controlling; dominant; essential; first; foremost; grand; great(est); head; highest; important; influential; leading; main; major; model; original; outstanding; paramount; preceding; predominant; preeminent; premier; prevailing; primal; primary; primate; prime; prominent; salient; superior; supreme; top; PRINCIPAL: **n.** alpha and omega; captain; chief; head; lead(er); original; principalship; star; superior; teacher

PRINCIPLE(S): alpha and omega; apothegm; assumption; axiom; basis; belief; canon; capstone; cause; character; clyssus; code; command(ment); constitution; convention; cornerstone; criteria (pl.); criterion; declaration; decree; dicta (pl.); dictum; direction; disposition; doctrine; dogma; element; endowment; essence; ethic(s); example; faculty; formula; foundation; fundament; ground (rule); guideline; honor; idea; instruction; integrity; key(note); keystone; landmark; law; Magna C(h)arta; mandate; maxim; model; mood; nature; norm; opinion; origin; philosophy; policy; postulate; prana; precept; pronouncement; purpose; principia (pl.); principium; proverb; quintessence; rectitude; regulation; rudiment; rule; sanction; saying; source; spirit; standard; statement; teaching; tenet; theme; theorem; theorum; theory; truth; PRINCIPLED: **see** "moral"

PRINT: **v.** draw; issue; picture; publish; stamp; trace; PRINT(ING): **n.** book; design; drawing; etching; figure; impression; issue; mark; photo(graph); picture; publication; stamp; tracing; vestige

PRIOR: antecedaneous; antecedent; anterior; earlier; foregoing; former; hitherto; past; precedent(ial); preceding; precursory; preferential; preliminary; previous; retroactive; superior; transcendent; PRIORITY: antecedence; anteriority; ascendancy; position; precedence; preeminence; preference; prerogative; primacy; privilege; rank; seniority; superiority; supremacy; urgency

PRISON: (see "jail")bars; bastille; brig; cage; cell; clink; coop; dungeon; imprisonment; jug; keep; limbo; pen(itentiary); pokey; quad; stir; PRISONER: captive; con(vict); *détenu; détenue* (fem.); internee; jailbird; lifer; termer

PRISSY: affected; demure; fastidious; finicky; fussy; nice(-Nelly); old-maidish; old womanish; precise; priggish; prim; proper; prudish; schoolteacherish; sissified; squeamish

PRISTINE: (**see** "primary") aboriginal; clear; early; fresh; innocent; native; new; original; primeval; primitive; pure; uncorrupted; unspoiled; unsullied; untouched; unused; unworn; virgin(al)

PRIVATE(LY): *à deux*; *a huis clos*; *à la dérobée*; backstage; cameral; chamber; civilian; closet; confidential(ly); covert(ly) delitescent; *entre nous*; esoteric; hidden; *in camera*; *in petto*; individual; *inter nos*; interior; internal; particular; personal; postern; privatim; privily; privy; restricted; retired; secluded; secret(ly); separate; sequestered; solitary; solitudinous; special; *sub rosa*; PRIVACY: hermitage; isolation; penetralia (pl.); privity; sanctuary; seclusion; secrecy; solitude

PRIVATION: absence; adversity; deprivation; destitution; exigency; hardship; indigence; indigency; loss; need; penury; pinch; poverty; squalor; strait(s); want

PRIVILEGE: advantage; benefice; beneficium; benefit; boon; character; claim; copyright; dispensation; due; emancipation; exemption; favor; franchise; freedom; grace; grant; honor; immunity; independence; indulgence; liberty; license; patent; permission; position; power; precedence; preference; prerogative; priority; prize; right; sufferance; title; tolerance; toleration; warranty

PRIZE: **v.** appraise; appreciate; award; capture; cherish; esteem; honor; love; price; rate; value; PRIZE: **n.** advantage; award; belt; bonus; booty; commendation; *cordon bleu*; cup; gem; *grand prix*; honor; jewel; laurel(s); loot; medal; meed; palm; *pièce de résistance*; plum; premium; pool; pot; privilege; reward; ribbon; showpiece; stake; swag; trophy; windfall

PROBABLE: (**see** "likely") apparent; circumstantial; credible; creditable; logical; ostensible; plausible; possible; potential; presumable; presumed; presumptive; *prima facie*; promising; rational; reasonable; supposed; verisimilar; PROBABILITY: advantage; chance; credibility; creditability; expectation; favor; hope; likelihood; logicality; odds; possibility; potentiality; presumption; prospect; supposition; vantage; verisimility

PROBATION: approval; evaluation; examination; investigation; novitiate; parole; postulancy; test(ing); trial; PROBATIONER: (**see** "novice") acousmatic; boot; cadet; novitiate; plebe; recruit; trainee

PROBE: **v.** dig; enter; examine; explore; feel; inquire; inquisit; investigate; jab; palpate; penetrate; pierce; poke; prod; measure; reconnoiter; scout; scrutinize; search; see; sift; sound (out); stick; thrust; PROBE: **n.** entrance; examination; exploration; inquest; inquiry; inquisition; investigation; jab; looksee; measure; palpation; penetration; poke; prod(ding); reconnaissance; scouting; scrutiny; search; sifting; stick; test; trial

PROBITY: (**see** "honesty") dependability; fealty; honor; integrity; justice; loyalty; principle; rectitude; reliability; sincerity; trust; uprightness

PROBLEM: (**see** "perplexity") bugbear; crisis; cruciality; crux; difficulty; dilemma; doubt; enigma; headache; issue; knot; matter; mystery; nut; ogre; poser; predicament; project; proposition; puzzle; quagmire; question; riddle; situation; subject; task; topic; trouble; uncertainty; worry; PROBLEMATIC(AL): **see** "uncertain"

PROBOSCIS: beak; lorum; neb; nib; nose; snout; trunk

PROCEED: act; advance; arise; begin; carry (on); continue; emanate; ensue; flow; fly; follow; go; issue; move; originate; pace; pass; plod; plow; precede; process; progress; result; rise; spring; stem; transact; travel; wade; wend; PROCEEDS: cash; residuals; result(s); return(s); surplus; winnings; winnowing; yield; PROCEEDING: (**see** "procession") act(ion); affair; cavalcade; ceremony; circumstance; cortege; course; deed; *démarche*; event; formation; happening; incident; maneuver; march; measure; movement; negotiation; occurrence; procedure; process; retinue; series; step; transaction; trial; PROCEDURE: (**see** "method") accouterment; approach; ceremony; course; custom; device; examination; form(ality); liturgy; management; mechanics; methodology; mode; *modus operandi*; motion; observance; order(liness); plan; policy; practice; proceeding; process; protocol; regulation; rite; ritual; rule; service; step; system; technique; tenor; test; theory; track; trade; trend; trial; usage; way

PROCESS: **v.** (**see** "proceed") complete; condition; cook; do; finish; make; manufacture; polish; prepare; prosecute; ready; refine; smooth; treat; PROCESS: **n.** action; activity; advance(ment); affair; change; condition; course; deed; design; development; emanation; experiment; extension; function; growth; issuance; mandate; maneuver; measure; mechanism; method(ology); motion; operation; order; outgrowth; phenomenon; plan; plot; procedure; proceeding; program; progress(ion); projection; reaction; refinement; response; stage; step; succession; summons; system; transformation; undertaking; warrant; writ; PROCESSION: (**see** "proceeding") cavalcade; ceremony; cortege; file; formation; group; line; litany; march; motorcade; movement; pageant(ry); parade; progression; retinue; sequence; series; set; state; stream; succession; trail; train

PROCLAIM: (**see** "announce") advertise; air; annunciate; assert; asseverate; blaze; blazon; broadcast; circulate; clarion; cry; declare; demonstrate; disseminate; divulge; exclaim; extol; glorify; herald; manifest; notify; noncupate; praise; preach; predicate; promulgate; prove; publicize; publish; resound; reveal; show; sound; speak; spread; state; swear; tell; PROCLAMATION: (**see** "announcement") annunciation; avowal; blazon; decree; edict; fiat; law; mandate; mandatum; manifesto; notice; notification; order; poster; promulgation; publication; report; revelation; statement; white paper

PROCLIVITY: (**see** "bias") bent; diathesis; disposition; inclination; leaning; predilection; predisposition; proneness; tendency; want; wish

PROCRASTINATE: (**see** "delay") defer; lag; postpone; PROCRASTINATION: (**see** "inactivity") delay; postponement

PROCURE: (**see** "get") achieve; acquire; attain; borrow; bring; buy; cause; contract (for); contrive; earn; effect; get; hire; induce; lease; manage; obtain; pick; purchase; rent; secure; win

PROD: **v.** (**see** "provoke") dig; egg; goad; incite; insist; jostle; poke; prick; probe; punch; remind; slog; stick; thrust; urge; PROD: **n.** awl; dig; gadfly; goad; incitement; needle; nudge; poke; prick; probe; punch; quirt; reminder; skewer; spur; stick; stimulant; stimulation; thrust; urging; whip

PRODIGAL: **a.** ample; extravagant; flush(ed);

lavish; liberal; lush; luxuriant; profuse; reckless; squandering; unrestrained; wasteful; PRODIGAL: **n.** (**see** "wastrel") profligate; spender; spendthrift; squanderer

PRODIGIOUS: (**see** "huge") abnormal; amazing; enormous; immense; large; monstrous; stupendous; vast

PRODUCE: **v.** accomplish; act; augment; bear; beget; breed; carry; cause; compose; compound; conceive; confect; cook; create; design; develop; dramatize; effect; emit; engender; exhibit; extend; fabricate; fashion; father; forge; form(ulate); furnish; generate; give; hatch; impart; increase; inspire; institute; issue; make; manufacture; merchandise; occupy; originate; perform; prepare; process; procreate; prolong; propagate; provoke; raise; separate; shape; show; spawn; stage; swell; yield; PRODUCE: **n.** see "product;" PRODUCER: creator; director; farmer; generator; maker; manufacturer; procreator; PRODUCING: (**see** "productive") aborning; feracious; generative; parturient; procreant; procreative; PRODUCTIVE: aborning; abundant; causative; constructive; creative; exuberant; fat; feracious; fructiferous; fructuous; fruitful; generative; helpful; imaginative; luxuriant; originative; parturient; plenteous; plentiful; procreant; procreative; profitable; prolific; prosperous; rich; teemful; teeming; uberous; yielding; PRODUCTIVENESS: creativity; fecundity; fertility; fruitfulness; productivity; prolificacy; uberty; PRODUCTION: (**see** "produt") crops; drama; edition; elongation; energy; extension; growth; harvest; outflow; output; play; produce; response; throughput; turnout; yield

PRODUCT(S): aftermath; amount; child; composition; consequence; crops; effect; effort; emolument; *fructus industriales* (pl.); *fructus naturales* (pl.); fruit(age); harvest; gain; goods; handiwork; issue; item; job; manifestation; merchandise; offspring; opus; outcome; output; performance; proceeds; produce; production; profit(s); progeny; property; realizaton; resource(s); result(s); return(s); stocks; thing(s); wealth; works; yield; young

PROEM: exordium; foreword; introduction; opening; preamble; preface; prelude; prolegomenon

PROFANE: **v.** abuse; blaspheme; curse; defile; desecrate; dishallow; pollute; unhallow; violate; vulgarize; PROFANE: **a.** blasphemous; blue; cursing; earth(l)y; foul; impious; irreverent; lay; mundane; sacrilegious; secular; sulfurous; sulphurous; temporal; ungodly; unhallowed; unsacred; unsainted; unsaintly; unsanctified; vulgar; wicked; worldly; PROFANITY: blasphemy; desecration; profanation; profaneness; sacrilege; vulgarity

PROFESS: acknowledge; admit; affirm; allege; assert; avouch; avow; claim; confess; declare; follow; observe; own; practice; pretend; proclaim; purport; state; teach; testify; witness; PROFESSION: (**see** "work") acknowledgement; admission; art; avowal; bar; bench; business; calling; craft; declaration; duty; employment; faith; law; medicine; métier; occupation; practice; protestation; religion; service; skill; task; testimony; trade; vocation; vow; PROFESSOR: **see** "instructor"

PROFICIENT: (**see** "able") accomplished; adept; adroit; advanced; apt; *au fait*; capable; competent; consummate; conversant; dext(e)rous; effective; efficient; expert; masterful; masterly; practiced; qualified: skilled; skillful; versed; PROFICIENCY; (**see** "ability") accomplishment; adeptness; competence; competency; consummation; dexterity; expertise; expertness; mastery; perfection; practice; skill(fulness); virtuosity

PROFILE: biography; configuration; contour; curve; drawing; figure; form; graph; outline; physiognomy; shape; silhouette; size; synopsis

PROFIT: **v.** advance; advantage; aid; avail; benefit; clear; further; gain; improve; increase; make; mend; net; promote; serve; use; PROFIT: **n.** acquisition; advance; advantage; aid; avail; beneficialness; benefit; boot(y); cleanup; cut; dividend(s); emolument; excess; fruit(age); furtherance; gain; gravy; improvement; income; increase; increment; interest; killing; lucre; net; percentage; proceeds; product(s); promotion; rake-off; receipts; return(s); reward; service; share(s); stride; use; value; winnings; yield; PROFITABLE: advantageous; beneficial; economic(al); expedient; fat; fructiferous; fructuous; fruitful; gainful; golden; good; helpful; lucrative; lush; opportune; moneymaking; paying; productive; prolific; prosperous; remunerating; rewarding; salutary; useful; PROFITLESS: (**see** "unprofitable") unprofited; valueless; worthless

PROFLIGATE: **a.** (**see** "lewd" and "wicked")

dissolute; excessive; extravagant; libertine; licentious; prodigal; reckless; wasteful; PROFLIGATE: **n. see** "wastrel"

PROFOUND:(**see** "deep") abstruse; abysmal; accomplished; complete; consummate; deep (-seated); discerning; erudite; exhaustive; fathomless; great; hard; heavy; inexplicable; intellectual; intense; knowledgeable; learned; mysterious; occult; penetrating; recondite; sagacious; sage; scholarly; solemn; thick; thorough(ly); wise; PROFUNDITY: abstrusity; consummation; depth; discernment; erudition; intensity; knowledge; learnedness; mystery; penetration; profoundness; sagacity; scholarliness; wisdom

PROFUSE: (**see** "excessive") abundant; bountiful; copious; cornucopian; exceeding; extra(vagant); exuberant; galore; generous; lavish; liberal; lush; luxurious; overflowing; plentiful; plethoric; prodigal; prolific; rampant; redundant; replete; spreading; superabundant; superfluous; surplus; unstinted; wasteful; PROFUSION: abundance; affluence; copiosity; cornucopia; extravagance; fullness; lavishness; opulence; opulency; plenum; plethora; prodigality; profuseness; redundance; redundancy; riot; sumptuosity; superabundance; superfluity; surplus; tumult; turbulence; wastefulness

PROGENY: (**see** "breed") child; children; clan; class; descendants; disciples; family; followers; fruit; issue; kin; offshoot; offspring; outcome; phylum; produce; products; race; scion; seed; sort; stock; strain; successors; tribe; yield; young

PROGNOSTICATE: (**see** "predict") augur; bode; diagnose; divine; forebode; forecast; foreshadow; foretell; omen; predict; presage; prophesy

PROGRAM: **v.** activate; advance; blueprint; catalog(ue); draft; fare; itemize; make; map; outline; pattern; plan; schedule; schematize; PROGRAM: **n.** agenda; agendum; bill; blueprint; booklet; card; catalog(ue); curriculum; design; draft; edict; entertainment; exhibition; list; map; menu; notice; outline; pattern; plan; playbill; policy; procedure; proclamation; project; prospectus; recital; schedule; schema (pl.); schemata; scheme; sequence; sketch; statement; syllabus; table; tariff; therapy; ticket; treatment

PROGRESS: **v.** advance; arrange; attain; contrive; control; create; develop; drift; drive; effect; enlarge; evolve; fashion; forge;

gain; grow; improve; increase; march; move; pace; proceed; push; shape; stem; step; stride; succeed; thrive; work; PROGRESS: **n.** action; advance(ment); attainment; betterment; circuit; course; development; direction; drift; drive; evolution; expedition; flow; gain; going; growth; headway; improvement; increase; journey; line; march; motion; movement; pace; procession; progression; progressivism; push; rate; rise; route; schedule; step; stride; sweep; swing; telesis; toehold; tour; trend; velocity; PROGRESSIVE: (**see** "modern") advancing; categoric(al); consecutive; increasing; moving; sequential; serial; successive

PROHIBIT: (**see** "bar") ban; block; caution; check; curb; debar; deny; enjoin; estop; exclude; forbid; hinder; inhibit; interdict; preclude; prevent; refuse; restrain; restrict; shut; stop; suppress; taboo; tabu; warn; withhold; PROHIBITED: banned; barred; blocked; checked; curbed; enjoined; estopped; excluded; forbidden; illicit; inhibited; precluded; prevented; proscribed; restrained; taboo; tabu; unlawful; PROHIBITIVE: costly; dear; inhibitory; interdictive; interdictory; proscriptive; PROHIBITION: ban; bar; embargo; estoppel; forbiddance; inhibition; injunction; interdiction; interdictum; outlawry; preclusion; proscription; restraint; restriction; suppression; taboo; tabu; veto

PROJECT: **v.** (**see** "plan") aim; beetle; bulge; calculate; carry; contrive; design; devise; direct; drive; eject; estimate; expand; extend; extrapolate; fling; hurl; intend; jet; jut; lift; map; outline; pitch; plot; point; propel; protrude; push; reach; scheme; shoot; throw; PROJECT: **n.** (**see** "plan") design; device; enterprise; extrapolation; idea; intention; job; outline; pattern; plot; problem; program; proposal; protuberance; purpose; schedule; schema; schemata (pl.); scheme; setup; task; undertaking; work; PROJECTING: beetling; conspicuous; eminent; full; gibbose; gibbous; prominent; protruding; protrusive; protuberant; raised; salient; PROJECTION: arm; barb; bulge; cam; design; ear; ejection; ell; eminence; estimation; fin; flap; jetty; jutting; knob; knot; ledge; lobe; lug; plan; promontory; prong; protrusion; protuberance; scheme; shelf; snag; spur; tab; tine; tooth; tusk; wart; wing

PROJECTILE: arrow; ball; bomb; bullet; dart; javelin; missile; pellet; rock(et); shell; shot; spear; torpedo; weapon

PROLETARIAT(E) *or* PROLETARIAN: laborer(s); masses; rabble; wage earners; worker(s)

PROLIFIC: abundant; copious; cornucopian; fecund; fertile; fruitful; generative; luxuriant; luxurious; philoprogenitive; productive; profuse; proliferous; propagative; reproductive; teeming; PROLIFICITY: cornucopia; fecundity; fertility; fruitfulness; luxuriousness; philoprogeneity; philoprogenitiveness; productivity; reproductivity

PROLIX: copious; diffuse; extended; lengthy; long(-winded); overlong; pleonastic; prolonged; protracted; protractive; repetitious; tautological; tedious; tiresome; verbose; wearisome; wordy; PROLIXITY: **see** "wordiness"

PROLOGUE: **see** "introduction"

PROLONG: continue; draw (out); endure; extend; increase; last; lengthen; persist; postpone; prorogue; protract; repeat; spin; sustain; PROLONGED: profuse; prolix; protracted; protractive; repetitious; sostenente; sostenuto; sostinente; sustaining; PROLONGATION: (**see** "continuation") continuance; continuity; duration; expansion; extension; perseverance; prolixity; prorogation; protraction; sustentation; sustention

PROMENADE: **v.** dance; display; drive; march; parade; ride; strut; swagger; walk; PROMENADE: **n.** alameda; ball; dance; display; drive; excursion; gallery; mall; march; marina; parade; party; paseo; pomp; Prado; ride; walk

PROMINENT: (**see** "leading") aquiline; blatant; capital; celebrated; chief; conspicuous; distinct; distinguished; eminent; high; important; jutting; main; manifest; notable; noticeable; notorious; obvious; outstanding; popular; preeminent; projecting; protruding; protuberant; public; renowned; salient; signal; stellar; striking; uppermost; well-known; PROMINENCE: celebrity; center (of attraction); conspicuity; conspicuousness; cynosure; distinction; eminence; eminency; emphasis; fame; hill; limelight; prestige; projection; promontory; protrusion; protuberance; salience; saliency; superiority

PROMISCUOUS: careless; casual; haphazard; heterogeneous; hybrid; indiscriminate; irregular; mingled; miscellaneous; mixed

PROMISE: **v.** agree; assure; avow; consent; contract; covenant; declare; engage; guarantee; hope; offer; pledge; plight; stipulate; swear; undertake; vow; warrant; PROMISE: **n.** agreement; assurance; avowal; commitment; committal; consent; contract; covenant; declaration; earnest; engagement; expectation; foretoken; guarantee; hope; oath; offer; parole; pledge; plight; stipulation; undertaking; vow; warrant(y); word; PROMISING: (**see** "auspicious" and "fair") apt; enterprising; likely; promiseful; up-and-coming

PROMONTORY: cape; cliff; headland; Jutland; land; mount; ness; noup; point; projection; prominence; skaw; spit

PROMOTE: (**see** "aid") abet; advance; advertise; advocate; avail; ballyhoo; benefit; boost; commend; contribute; cultivate; develop; dignify; educate; elevate; encourage; endow; enhance; equip; exalt; excite; foment; forward; foster; further; graduate; help; improve; increase; institute; launch; lobby; manage; nurse; nurture; organize; patronize; prefer; push; raise; speed; strengthen; subsidize; support; talk up; urge; PROMOTION: advancement; advertising; ballyhoo; brevet; enhancement; furtherance; furthering; graduation; preference; preferment; publicity; raise; subsidy; support; PROMOTER: abettor; encourager; entrepreneur; entrepreneuse (fem.); impresario

PROMPT: **v.** abet; activate; actuate; advise; alert; animate; assist; cue; encourage; expedite; goad; guide; impel; incite; induce; inspire; instigate; move; needle; nudge; persuade; poke; prick; prod; promote; provoke; punch; remind; rouse; spur; stimulate; suggest; tell; tempt; urge; PROMPT: **a.** or **adv.** alert; apt; animated; celeritous; early; easy; expeditious; immediate(ly); inspired; instant; keen; mercurial; moved; moving; pronto; punctual; quick; ready; soon; speedy; swift; telegraphic; vigilant; wing-footed; yare; PROMPTNESS: (**see** "speed") alacrity; celerity; expedition; promptitude; punctuality; PROMPTER: aid(er); reader; reminder

PROMULGATE: (**see** "advertise") air; announce; blazon; broadcast; circulate; declare; disseminate; emblazon; herald; issue; proclaim; pronounce; publicize; publish; sow; spread

PRONE: abed; accumbent; addicted; apt; couchant; disposed; dormant; downward; flat; horizontal; inclined; jacent; latent; leaning; level; liable; likely; lying; open; predisposed; prostrate; ready; recumbent; resting; sensitive; sleeping; supine; tending; willing; wishing; PRONENESS: (**see** "tendency") propensity

PRONG: antler; branch; fang; fork; horn; nib; peg; point; projection; tine

PRONOUNCE: affirm; articulate; announce; assert; asseverate; declaim; declare; deliver; express; proclaim; promulgate; publicize; publish; mouth; recite; say; speak; specify; state; stress; utter; voice; PRONUNCIATION: (**see** "speech") articulation; orthoepy; phonology; utterance; PRONOUNCEMENT(S): (**see** "announcement") declaration; dicta (pl.); dictamen; dictum; edict; fiat; promulgation; rule

PROOF: attestation; authentication; certification; confirmation; corroboration; credential(s); deed; demonstration; documentation; draft; evidence; ground; ordeal; reason; strength; testimony; test(ing); title; token; trial; validity; verification; voucher

PROP: **v.** bolster; brace; encourage; help; shore; sprag; strengthen; support; sustain; truss; uphold; PROP: **n.** bolster; brace; column; gib; nog; pole; rance; sprag; staff; stake; stanchion; stay; stick; stilt; support; timber; truss; underfooting; underpinning; upright

PROPAGANDA: advertising; agitprop; blurb; brainwashing; dissemination; evangelism; evangelization; information; pitch; publicity

PROPAGATE: (**see** "breed") engender; extend; graft; imbue; increase; plant; publicize; seed; sow; teach; train

PROPEL: accelerate; drive; force; gun; impel; move; oar; paddle; ply; project; push; rev; row; scull; shove; sweep; thrust; urge; PROPELLER; blade; driver; fan; fin; oar; paddle; prop; screw

PROPENSITY: (**see** "bias") bent; impulse; inclination; leaning; predilection; proneness; tendency

PROPER: (**see** "correct") acceptable; accepted; accurate; adapted; adequate; applicable; appropriate; apropos; apt; *au fait*; becoming; comely; *comme il faut*; compatible; condign; conventional; cricket; decent;

decorous; *de rigueur*; distinctive; due; exact; excellent; fair; felicitous; fit(ting); formal; good; just; kosher; lawful; legitimate; licit; meet; moral; nice; opportune; orderly; orthodox; own; peculiar; pertinent; praiseworthy; precise; prim; principled; prissy; reasonable; regular; relevant; right(ful); rightly; ritual; sanctioned; satisfactory; seasonable; sedate; seemly; sound; square; staid; standard; stiff; strict; suitable; suited; timely; well

PROPERTY: (**see** "estate") appurtenances; assets; attribute; belongings; bonds; buildings; characteristic(s); chattels; element; essence; faculty; goods; holdings; land; money; nature; ownership; peculiarity; personalia (pl.); personality; possessions; power; predicate; quality; realty; resource(s); riches; right; stocks; substance; trait; virtue; wealth

PROPHESY: auspicate; augur; bode; declare; divine; exhort; forebode; forecast; foreshadow; foretell; hariolate; portend; preach; predict; prefigure; presage; prognosticate; PROPHECY: bodement; divination; estimation; forecast; foretelling; haruspication; omen; portent; prediction; prognostication; pythonism; revelation

PROPHET: augur; auspex; haruspex; interpreter; Jeremiah; leader; Mohammed; Nostradamus; oracle; predictor; prognosticator; prophesier; revealer; seer; sibyl; soothsayer; spokesman; teacher; vaticinator; PROPHETESS: Cassandra; Debbora; Deborah; Pythian; pythoness; seeress; sibyl; soothsayer; PROPHETIC(AL): adumbrated; anticipative; apocalyptic(al); augural; auspicious; cabalistic; divinatory; farseeing; farsighted; fateful; fatidic; foretelling; incantatory; interpretative; mantic; ominous; oracular; phylacteric; portentous; predictive; presageful; presaging; prescient; prognosticative; pythonic; revelatory; sagacious; sibylline; talismanic; vatic(al); vaticinal

PROPHYLACTIC: **see** "antidote"

PROPINQUITY: affinity; approximation; association; communion; kinship; likeness; nearness; neighborhood; relationship; solidarity; togetherness; vicinity

PROPITIATE: (**see** "calm") adjust; appease; assuage; compose; conciliate; expiate; forgive; gratify; mitigate; moderate; mollify; pacify; placate; reconcile; sacrifice; satisfy; smooth; soften; soothe; tranquilize; PRO-

PITIATION: amends; apology; appeasement; atonement; conciliation; expiation; penance; reconciliation; redress; reparation; repentance; sacrifice

PROPITIOUS: (**see** "favorable") advantageous; auspicious; beneficial; benevolent; benign(ant); bright; encouraging; friendly; gracious; heartening; helpful; hopeful; kind(ly); lucky; merciful; opportune; pleasing; promising; prosperous; reassuring; right; roseate; rosy; satisfactory; timely

PROPORTION: allotment; amount; balance; commensurability; commensuration; degree; dimension; dividend; end; extent; form(at); harmony; lot; magnitude; measure; mixture; part; percentage; pro rata; quota; quantity; rate; rating; ratio; relation; shape; share; size; symmetry; PROPORTIONAL: **see** "relevant"

PROPOSE: (**see** "suggest") contrive; extend; initiate; intend; offer; petition; pose; postulate; propound; speculate; start; vote; PROPOSAL: appeal; application; bid; design; feeler; gesture; measure; motion; move; offer; outline; overture; plan; postulation; program; project; proposition; prospectus; request; schedule; scheme; suggestion; PROPOSITION: agreement; assumption; corollary; deal; formula; hypothesis; idea; lemma; particular; petition; philosopheme; plan; point; postulata (pl.); postulate; postulatum; premise; principle; problem; project; proposal; sentence; settlement; statement; subject; term(s); theme; theorem; theorum; theory; thesis; topic; understanding; undertaking

PROPOUND: **see** "propose"

PROPRIETOR: boss; landlord; lord; master; owner; proprietary

PROPRIETY: *agréments*; amenity; appropriateness; aproposity; *bienséance*; convention(ality); decency; decorum; delicacy; etiquette; fitness; grace; manners; pertinence; pertinency; relevance; relevancy; right; suitability; PROPRIETIES: *agréments*; amenities; covenances; conventionalities; decora; *les convenances*; urbanities

PROSAIC(AL): (**see** "comonplace") common; down-to-earth; dry(as dust); dull; factual; flat; humdrum; insipid; jejune; lengthy; literal(istic); long-winded; low; matter-of-fact; monotonous; ordinary; pedantic; plain; prolix; prosy; provincial; realistic; sober;

stolid; stupid; tedious; temporal; *terre à terre*; terrestrial; tiresome; unexciting; unimaginative; uninspired; uninteresting; unleavened; unpoetic(al); weary; workaday

PROSCRIBE: **see** "ban" and "prohibit"

PROSCRIPT: (**see** "ban") exile; forbid; interdict; outlaw; prohibit; proscribe; taboo; tabu; PROSCRIPTION: (**see** "ban") exile; interdict(ion); outlawry; prohibition; taboo; tabu; veto

PROSE: (**see** "writing") biography; essay; history; matter-of-factness; novel; ordinariness; plainness; romance

PROSECUTE: accuse; arraign; charge; continue; develop; follow; indict; investigate; perform; practice; press; proceed; process; pursue; study; sue; wage; PROSECUTION: arraignment; continuation; development; expansion; investigation; lawsuit; pressure; proceeding; process; pursuit; study; suit; undertaking

PROSELYTE: (**see** "beginner") conscript; convert; neophyte; recruit

PROSPECT: **v.** anticipate; develop; examine; expect; explore; face; hope; hunt; inspect; investigate; look; mine; probe; scout; search; seek; survey; PROSPECT: **n.** anticipation; aspect; expectancy; expectation; exposure; foresight; future; futurity; goal; hope; horizon; landscape; lookout; mine; outlook; panorama; possibility; probability; prognosis; promise; prospective; purview; scene; view; vision; vista; PROSPECTUS: announcement; bulletin; catalog(ue); compendium; description; design; list; outline; plan; program; schema; sketch; survey; view; vision

PROSPER: (**see** "flourish") achieve; bloom; boom; fatten; favor; gain; grow; speed; succeed; thrive; wax; zoom; PROSPERITY: achievement; advance; affluence; attainment; *bonne fortune*; boom; fare; fortune; gain; hap; in clover; luck; opulence; progress; riches; success; thrift; weal; wealth; welfare; well-being; PROSPEROUS: affluent; auspicious; blooming; booming; fat; favorable; flourishing; flush; fortunate; golden; good; halcyon; happy; healthy; lucky; lush; palmy; plush; posh; productive; profitable; propitious; rich; rosy; successful; thriving; victorious; well-fixed; well-healed; well-off; well-to-do; zooming

PROSTITUTE: (**see** "debase") bawd; call girl; camp follower; chippie; chippy; cocodette; cocotte; courtesan; demimondaine; demimonde; doxy; *fille de joie*; harlot; hetaira; hooker; hussy; hustler; *nymphe du pavé*; Paphian; party girl; *petite dame*; quean; streetwalker; strumpet; tart; tramp; trollop; whore; PROSTITUTION: corruption; debasement; harlotry; promiscuity; venality; whoredom

PROSTRATE: **v.** abase; bow; debilitate; demolish; exhaust; flatten; floor; humble; kowtow; level; overcome; overthrow; weaken; PROSTRATE: **a.** abased; abed; abject; bedfast; depressed; down; exhausted; fallen; fell; flat; floored; helpless; humble; level; low; powerless; procumbent; prone; recumbent; sick; supine; tired; PROSTRATION: abasement; collapse; exhaustion; helplessness; powerlessness; prosternation; shock; stupefaction; submission; submissiveness; supinity

PROSY: **see** "prosaic"

PROTAGONIST: (**see** "antagonist") adversary; advocate; champion; competitor; enemy; foe; hero; leader; spokesman; warrior

PROTECT: (**see** "care") administer; aid; bolster; buffer; bulwark; cherish; cover; cultivate; cushion; defend; direct; dispose; encircle; enclose; encourage; father; feed; fend; fortify; foster; guard; guide; harbor; hedge; keep; lead; mind; minister; mother; muffle; nurse; nurture; pad; palliate; preserve; prove; provide; repel; safeguard; save; screen; secure; serve; shield; shelter; support; suppress; vindicate; ward; warn; watch; PROTECTIVE: avuncular; custodial; defensive; defensory; fatherly; maternal(istic); motherly; paternal(istic); preservative; prophylactic; safeguarding; secure; sheltering; shielding; tutelary; tutorial; PROTECTION *or* PROTECTOR: aegis; ammunition; apron; armament; armour; arms; auspice(s); bastion; bib; bodyguard; bolster; breastwork; buffer; bulwark; canopy; caretaker; Cerberus; champion; chaperone; claviger; concierge; conductor; conservation; cover(age); covering; coverture; cushion; custodian; custody; custos; defense; dependence; father; fence; gloss; guarantee; guarantor; guard(ian); guardianship; guidance; guide; guns; housing; immunity; indemnity; influence; insurance; janitor; keeper; lacquer; lee; lid; mat; monitor;

mote; mother; pad; paint; palladium; parapet; pass(port); patron(age); pillow; port; preservation; preservative; proctor; prophylactic; prophlaxis; protection; rampart; redoubt; regent; safe-conduct; safeguard; safety; sanctuary; screen; seat; security; shade; shellac; shelter; shepherd; shield; superintendent; teacher; tent; tutelage; tutor; umbrella; varnish; veneer; warden; warrant; wing; wrap

PROTEIN: albumin; amine; casein; egg; fibrin; globulin; histon; legume; legumin; meat

PROTEST: **v.** (**see** "complain") affirm; appeal; argue; assert; asseverate; aver; cry; declare; demur; deny; deprecate; dissent; expostulate; fuss; grieve; inveigh; kick; mourn; object; oppose; oppugn; profess; quibble; reclaim; refuse; remonstrate; represent; repudiate; resist; shout; squeal; vow; yell; yowl; PROTEST(ATION): **n.** (**see** "complaint") acknowledgment; appeal; argument; *cri de coeur*; cry; declaration; demur; denial; deprecation; disapproval; dissent; expostulation; fuss; kick; objection; opposition; quibble; remonstrance; remonstration; shout; tirade; yell; yowl

PROTRACT: broaden; continue; defer; delay; drag; elongate; extend; lengthen; plot; postpone; procrastinate; prolong; spin; spread; stretch; widen

PROTRUDE: (**see** "bulge") beetle; emerge; extend; extrude; interfere; jut; obtrude; peep; pop; pout; project; shoot; swell; thrust; PROTRUSION *or* PROTUBERANCE: bulge; bulginess; bump(iness); bunch; eminence; excrescence; excrescency; gibbosity; gnarl; hump; hunch; jag; knob; knot; knurl; lobe; lump; nob; node; nub; projection; prominence; protuberancy; puff; salience; saliency; snag; PROTRUDING *or* PROTUBERANT: bulbous; bulging; bulgy; bumpy; conspicuous; gibbose; gibbous; jutting; obtrusive; projecting; prominent; protrusile; protrusive; salient; swollen

PROUD: abashless; arrogant; bombastic; conceited; contemptuous; dignified; disdainful; ego(t)istic(al); elated; exalted; exuberant; exultant; formal; glad; gratified; happy; haughty; high; hubristic; imperial; imperious; independent; insolent; lofty; lordly; magnificent; majestic; orgillous; orgulous; overbearing; overweening; pleased; presumptuous; prideful; satisfied; scornful; self-conceited; splendid; stately; stiff; supercilious; swollen; unabashed; unashamed; vain(glorious); vigorous

PROVE: (**see** "establish") ascertain; authenticate; check; circumstantiate; confirm; convince; corroborate; demonstrate; determine; evince; guarantee; identify; justify; manifest; persuade; proclaim; show; solve; substantiate; test; testify; try; verify; vindicate; vouch; PROVED *or* PROVEN: **see** "established;" PROVING: confirmative; confirmatory; demonstrative; justificatory; substantive; PROVABLE: (**see** "certain") noncontradictory

PROVENANCE: (**see** "origin") provenience; source

PROVENDER: (**see** "food") chow; corn; eats; feed; fodder; forage; grain; grub; hay; oats; provisions; meat; straw; viands

PROVERB: adage; aphorism; apothegm; axiom; brocard; byword; catchword; epigram; gnome; maxim; mot; motto; parable; precept; saw; saying; truism; truth; PROVERBIAL: **see** "legendary"

PROVIDE: afford; agree; appropriate; arm; arrange; bequeath; budget; cater; contribute; cure; devote; dispense; donate; endow; endue; equip; establish; feed; fit; fortify; furnish; gird; give; grant; hire; house; lend; loan; lodge; outfit; perform; plan; ply; prepare; purvey; ready; relieve; remedy; rent; rig; sell; serve; shelter; stipulate; stock; store; strengthen; supply; support; treat; yield

PROVIDENCE: (**see** "prudence") fate; fortune; God; guidance; help; thrift; PROVIDENT(IAL): careful; cautious; considerate; discreet; economical; farseeing; fateful; foresighted; forethoughtful; fortunate; frugal; heaven-sent; helpful; lucky; miraculous; opportune; prudent; saving; thoughtful; thrifty; wise

PROVINCE: action; area; bailiwick; beat; charge; circuit; colony; country; department; dependency; district; division; domain; duty; field; function; hemisphere; jurisdiction; limit; métier; office; parish; portion; precinct; realm; region; sphere; territory; tract; walk

PROVINCIAL: *borné*; bucolic; countrified; crude; insular; limited; local; narrow;

parochial; prosaic(al); restrained; rural; rustic; sectional; unpolished; unsophisitcated; vulgar

PROVISION(S); (see "provender") ammunition; cates; chow; eatables; fare; fodder; food; larder; preparation; proviso; supplies; supply; terms; viands; viatica (pl.); viaticum; victuals

PROVISIONAL: (see "temporary") *ad hoc*; circumstantial; conditional; contingent; ephemeral; evanescent; fleeting; interim; stopgap; tentative

PROVOKE: aggravate; agitate; anger; annoy; arouse; badger; bait; call; catalyze; chafe; challenge; combat; confront; dare; defy; dig; drive; egg; elicit; enrage; evince; evoke; exacerbate; exasperate; excite; fire; fret; goad; hit; impel; incense; incite; infuriate; inspire; instigate; ire; irritate; jog; jostle; kindle; lash; madden; mock; move; needle; nettle; nudge; occasion; offend; pain; peeve; perturb; pique; poke; precipitate; prick; prod; prompt; push; quicken; roll; rouse; spur; stampede; stick; stimulate; sting; stir; strike; taunt; tease; tempt; thrust; upset; urge; vex; work

PROWESS: (see "valor") boldness; excellence; gallantry

PROWL: caterwaul; gad; lurk; perambulate; rable; roam; rove; slink; sneak; steal; stray; wander

PROXIMAL: closest; immediate; nearest; next; proximate

PROXY: agent; ballot; delegate; deputy; election; factor; power of attorney; proctor; procurator; representative; sub(stitute); vicar; vice; vote

PRUDE: Comstock; Grundyite; hypocrite; prig; purist; puritan; PRUDISH: lily-white; narrow(-minded); nice-Nelly; overscrupulous; priggish; prim; prissy; pudibund; puritanical; religiose; rigid; rigorous; squeamish; standoffish; stark; stern; straight(-laced); strict; touch-me-not-ish; Victorian; PRUDERY: Comstockery; Grundyism; priggishness; primness; prissiness; pudibundity; squeamishness

PRUDENT: (see "provident") alert; careful; cautious; circumspect; cool; discreet; forehanded; frugal; heedful; judicious; penetrating; reliable; sagacious; sensible; shrewd;

solid; thrifty; wary; well-advised; wise; PRUDENCE: calculation; canniness; care; caution; circumspection; cleverness; discernment; discretion; economy; forehandedness; foresight; forethought; frugality; judgment; judiciality; judiciousness; moderation; policy; providence; reason; restraint; sagacity; self-control; shrewdness; skill; sophrosyne; temperance; thrift; vigilance; wariness; wisdom

PRUNE: abridge; cut; dress; eliminate; lop; plume; preen; prime; primp; purge; reduce; remove; retrench; shape shorten; smooth; spur; thin; trim

PRURIENT: carnal; coarse; craving; curious; dissolute; foul; gross; impure; itching; itchy; lecherous; lewd; longing; wanton

PRY: v. detach; enquire; examine; extract; fish; gaze; inquire; inspect; move; nose; open; peep; peer; prize; probe; raise; scrutinize; seek; snoop; PRY: n. lever(age); PRYING: (see "curious") inquisitorial; nosy; peeping; probing; snooping; snoopy

PSEUDO: bogus; counterfeit; fake; false; feigned; mock; sham; simulated; spurious; unreal

PSEUDONYM: alias; anonym(e); *nom de guerre*; *nom de plume*; pen name

PSYCHE: brain; personality; mind; self; soul; spirit(uality); vital; principle; wit(s); PSYCHIC: see "mental" and "supernatural"

PSYCHOLOGICAL: functional; mental; spiritual; temperamental

PSYCHOSIS: see "insanity;" PSYCHOTIC: (see "insane") hallucinatory; odd; off; mad; mani(a)c; maniacal; queer

PUBLIC: a. administrative; civic; civil; commercial; common; communal; conspicuous; exoteric; external; free; general; governmental; humanitarian; impersonal; international; known; lay; manifest; material; municipal; national; open; overt; patriotic; politic(al); popular; prominent; secular; social; societal; sovereign; universal; urbane; well-known; PUBLIC: n. audience; bourgeoisie; citizenry; commonalty; community; constituency; electorate; mankind; masses; multitude; nation; people; populace; population; proletariat; rabble; state; town

PUBLICATION: book; disclosure; divulgation; journal; newspaper; organ; pamphlet; proclamation; promulgation; writing

PUBLICITY: acclaim; advertisement; advertising; agitprop; attention; ballyhoo; circulation; disclosure; display; dissemination; éclat; exploitation; headline; ink; limelight; magnificence; notice; pageantry; promotion; promulgation; propaganda; revelation; show; space; spectacle; spotlight

PUBLISH *or* PUBLICIZE: acknowledge; advertise; air; announce; blaze; blazon; broach; broadcast; censure; circularize; circulate; communicate; cry; declare; delate; disclose; disseminate; divulge; emit; evulgate; exploit; headline; herald; impart; issue; nuncupate; print; proclaim; promote; promulgate; pronounce; propagate; reveal; spread; tell; utter; vent(ilate); voice

PUCKER: **v.** bind; bulge; constrict; contract; corrugate; crease; fold; frown; furrow; gather; perplex; purse; ruffle; shirr; wrinkle; PUCKER: **n.** agitation; anxiety; binding; bulge; corrugation; fold; furrow; gathering; perplexity; ruffle; unevenness; wrinkle; PUCKERED: bullate; drawn; gathered; puckery; sour; uneven; wrinkled

PUCKISH: **see** "impish"

PUDDLE: mess; mire; muddle; plashet; pond; pool; quagmire; sink

PUERILE: boyish; callow; childish; fatuous; feeble; foolish; green; immature; inadequate; inane; ineffectual; inexperienced; infantile; jujune; juvenile; puny; raw; shallow; silly; simple; sophomoric; trivial; unthinking; vapid; weak; youthful

PUFF: **v.** advertise; blow; bluster; boast; brag; breathe; distend; elate; emit; erupt; expand; expel; explode; extol; flam; flutter; gasp; gratify; gust; huff; inflate; open; overrate; pant; pooh; pop; praise; rouse; smoke; stuff; swell; waft; PUFF: **n.** blow; bluff; blurb; boast; braggart; breath; cake; cloud; gasp; gust; huff; inflation; pant(ing); pouf; praise; protuberance; show; smoke; swelling; waft; whiff; wind

PUG: boxer; dog; fighter; grind; nose; pugilist; temper

PUGNACIOUS *or* PUGILISTIC: (**see** "hostile") aggressive; bellicose; belligerent; fistic; truculent; vitriolic; vituperative

PUISNE: **a.** associate; insignificant; junior; lower; subordinate; PUISNE: **n.** associate; judge; junior; student; subordinate

PUISSANT: (**see** "strong") mighty; powerful; PUISSANCE: **see** "power" and "strength"

PULCHRITUDE: (**see** "beauty") attractiveness; comeliness; excellence; grace; handsomeness; loveliness

PULE: (**see** "cry") complain; peep; repine; snivel; weep; whimper; whine

PULL: **v.** attract; cheer; commit; draft; drag; draw; extract; gather; haul; heave; impel; jerk; lug; magnetize; perpetrate; pluck; rend; root; stretch; tear; tow; tug; uproot; wrench; yank; PULL: **n.** attraction; draft; drag; draw; effort; exertion; force; graft; influence; jerk; magnetism; opinion; power; tear; traction; tug; weight; wrench; yank

PULLULATE: breed; bud; germinate; increase; multiply; sprout; swarm; teem

PULP: cellulose; chyme; magma; mash; mass; mush; pap; paper; pith; tissue; writing; PULPY: macerated; magmatic; mashed; mushy; pultaceous

PULPIT: ambo; clergy; dais; desk; lectern; ministry; platform; preachers; priesthood; rostrum

PULSATE: accent; beat; oscillate; palpate; pulse; quiver; thrill; throb; thump; vibrate; waver; PULSATION *or* PULSE: accent; beat(ing); cadence; ictus; meter; oscillation; palmus; palpitation; quiver; rhythm; throb(bing); undulation; vibration; PULSATIVE *or* PULSATORY: beating; palpant; pulsatile; rhythmic; systolic; throbbing; vibrating

PULVERIZE: annihilate; atomize; bray; comminute; contriturate; crush; demolish; disintegrate; grind; levigate; micronize; mill; mull; pestle; powder; reduce; triturate; PULVERIZATION: comminution; trituration; PULVERULENT *or* PULVERIZED: comminute(d); dusty; powdered; powdery

PUMMEL: (**see** "beat") conquer; pound; thump

PUMP: **v.** aerate; draw; examine; inflate; interrogate; probe; question; quiz; raise; stimulate; test; throb; PUMP: **n.** heart; shoe; slipper; syringe

PUN: adnomination; assonance; calembour; equivoke; equivoque; *jeu de mots*; mot; paradigm; paronomasia; quibble; quip; *turlupinade*; wisecrack; witticism

PUNCH: **v.** bore; clout; cuff; drill; drive; gad; hit; paste; penetrate; perforate; pierce; poke; pound; prick; prod; pummel; puncture; push; smite; stab; stamp; strike; swat; thump; PUNCH: **n.** awl; blow; buffoon; clout; clown; cogency; cuff; drill; drink; energy; force; hole; jester; mountebank; perforation; plug; point; poke; pritchel; prod; puncture; strike; thrust; thump; tool; vigor

PUNCTILIOUS: (**see** "precise") attentive; careful; cautious; ceremonious; conscientious; exact(ing); finicky; formal; fussy; nice; observant; particular; pointed; punctual; scrupulous; stiff; strict; timely

PUNCTUAL: (**see** "precise") accurate; careful; concentrated; constant; definite; detailed; exact; faithful; loyal; pointed; regular; timely; true

PUNCTURE: (**see** "punch") destroy; gore; penetrate; perforate; pierce; prick; riddle; stab; stick

PUNDIT: authority; Brahmin; critic; guru; Nestor; pandit; sage; scholar; swami; teacher; wit

PUNGENT: acrid; acute; biting; caustic; flavorful; flavorous; heady; irritating; keen; mordant; painful; penetrating; peppery; piercing; piquant; poignant; prickling; racy; salty; sarcastic; severe; sharp; shrill; snappy; spicy; stabbing; stimulating; stinging; tangy; tart; telling; vinegary

PUNISH: (**see** "discipline") admonish; amerce; beat; cane; castigate; chasten; chastise; consume; correct; deplete; drub; fine; flagellate; flog; frap; hurt; lash; lick; mulct; penalize; rebuke; requite; restrain; retaliate; revenge; scourge; sentence; silence; smite; strike; thump; torture; vindicate; whip; wreak; PUNISHMENT: (**see** "discipline") admonishment; admonition; amercement; castigation; chastenment; chastisement; correction; downfall; expiation; fine; flagellation; flogging; grueling; infliction; judgment; lashing; lesson; Nemesis; penalization; penalty; penance; punition; purgatory; rebuke; retaliation; retribution; revenge; sentence; torture; vengeance; vindication; wrack; PUNISHING *or* PUNITIVE: (**see** "disciplinary") castigatory; correctional; cor-

rective; disciplinal; disciplinatory; discriminatory; expiatory; flagellant; hard; grueling; penal; penitentiary; punitory; retaliative; retaliatory; retributive; vindicative; vindicatory

PUNK: **a.** (**see** "bad") inferior; miserable; poor; worthless; PUNK: **n.** amadou; beginner; conch; fuel; gangster; hoodlum; jerk; kindling; nonsense; novice; ruffian; tinder; touchwood

PUNT: **v.** drive; hit; kick; pole; propel; PUNT: **n.** boat; kick; wagon

PUNY: (**see** "trivial") *chétif*; inexperienced; inferior; insignificant; petty; picayune; poor; sick(ly); skinny; slight; unskilled; weak

PUPIL abecedarian; alphabetarian; apostle; beginner; catechumen; disciple; educatee; learner; neophyte; novice; probationer; protégé; scholar; student; trainee; tyro; ward

PUPPET: Charlie McCarthy; doll; dupe; effigy; figure; Guignol; Judy; marionette; pawn; Punch; stooge; tool; underling; vassal

PURBLIND: blind; dim-sighted; dull; myopic; obtuse; shortsighted; stupid

PURCHASE: **v.** (**see** "buy") acquire; bargain; barter; employ; expend; gain; get; hire; obtain; procure; secure; PURCHASE: **n.** acquisition; advantage; bargain; booty; buy; emption; gain; procurement; property; PURCHASABLE: corrupt; salable; venal; PURCHASER: **see** "buyer"

PURE: absolute; abstract; angelic; antiseptic; archangelic; ascetic; blameless; candid; chaste; cherubic; classic(al); clean; clear; complete; continent; crystal(line); decent; decorous; demure; devout; discreet; divine; downright; entire; fair; faithful; faultless; fresh; fundamental; genuine; good; guileless; guiltless; hermetic(al); holy; homozygous; immaculate; imputrescible; incorrupt(ed); incorruptible; innocent; inviolable; inviolate; irreproachable; lucid; mere; modest; moral; neat; perfect; plain; proper; *pur et simple*; real; refined; rich; seraphic; sheer; simon-pure; simple; sincere; sober; spotless; stainless; stark; sterile; sublime; temperate; theoretic(al); thoroughbred; true; ultrapure; unadulterated; unalloyed; unblemished; unblighted; unblotted; uncontaminated; uncorrupt(ed); uncorruptible; undefiled; unmixed; unpolluted; un-soiled; unsordid; unspotted; unstained; unsullied; untainted; untarnished; un-touched; unviolated; upright; utter; vestal; virgin(al); virtuous; PURIFY: (see "cleanse") absolve; absterge; alembicate; antisepticize; atone; baptise; bleach; chasten; clarify; clean; clear; correct; defecate; de-purate; deterge; discharge; edulcorate; elimi-nate; emit; epurate; evacuate; exonerate; exorcise; expiate; expurgate; filter; fire; flush; free; lustrate; pardon; physic; purge; rectify; redeem; refine; sprinkle; spurge; sterilize; strain; wash; whiten; PURI-FICATION: ablation; ablution; abreaction; abstersion; baptism; bathing; cathartic; catharsis; cleansing; defecation; depuration; edulcoration; elimination; epuration; lustra-tion; purgative; refinement; PURITY: ascesis; chastity; cleanliness; continence; decency; decorousness; decorum; demure-ness; demurity; godliness; holiness; honor; immaculacy; incorruptibility; innocence; integrity; inviolability; maidenliness; modesty; pucelage; pudicity; sacredness; sanctification; sanctity; sanctitude; sterility; virginity; virtue

PURGATORY: Erebus; limbo; misery; punishment

PURGE: v. (see "purify") absterge; clean; discharge; eliminate; expel; fire; free; kill; physic; rid; PURGE: n. abstergent; aperient; catharsis; cathartic; cleansing; laxative; physic; purgation; purgative; purification; wash

PURIFY: see under "pure"

PURITANICAL: (see "prudish") genteel; narrow(-minded); rigid; rigorous; scrupulous; stark; stern; straight(-laced); strict; Victorian

PURITY: see under "pure"

PURLIEU(S): ambit; area; bounds; confines; environ(s); habitat; haunt; locality; neigh-borhood; parish; precinct; region; suburb(s)

PURLOIN: (see "steal") appropriate; filch; thieve

PURPLE: cardinate; empurpled; lavender; lilac; magenta; mauve; puce; regal; violet; PURPLISH: porphyrous; purpureal; pur-purean; purpureous; purpurescent; pur-purine

PURPORT: v. connote; convey; denote; imply; import; intend; mean; pretend; pro-

fess; signify; tend; PURPORT: n. connota-tion; consequence; denotation; design; drift; gist; implication; import(ance); intendment; intention; meaning; pretense; purpose; sense; significance; signification; substance; ten-dency; tenor; view; weight

PURPOSE: v. aim; aspire; choose; contem-plate; design; determine; direct; figure; impart; intend; meditate; ordain; order; plan; plot; project; propose; ween; will; wish; PURPOSE: n. (see "destiny" and "intention") aim; ambition; aspiration; ben-efit; *causa finalis*; design; desire; determina-tion; direction; dream; effect; end; expecta-tion; finality; function; goal; good; idea(l); intendment; intent(ion); meaning; object-(ive); pattern; philosophy; plan; plot; point; project; purport; resolution; resolve; result; revenance; sake; scope; significance; use; will; wish; PURPOSIVE or PURPOSE-FUL: (see "intentional") businesslike; directional; functional; premeditated; teleological; telic

PURPOSELESS: (see "aimless") amorphous; arrant; capricious; chaotic; desultory; drift-less; dysteleological; effete; empty; erratic; erring; feckless; fickle; fitful; foolish; incon-stant; indefinite; indirect; indiscriminate; intentionless; irregular; lax; loose; meaning-less; objectless; prodigal; purportless; rambling; random; senseless; shifting; soft; tumultuary; undirected; undisciplined; unintended; unpremeditated; unpurposed; unpurposeful; useless; wavering

PURSE: v. draw; knit; pucker; wrinkle; PURSE: n. ante; award; bag; billfold; bourse; burse; crumenal; finances; funds; handbag; means; money; pocketbook; porte-monnaie; pouch; prize; pucker; resources; reward; stake; treasure; wallet; wrinkle

PURSER: boucher; bursar; cashier; comp-troller; exchequer; paymaster; treasurer

PURSUE: annoy; bedevil; chase; continue; cultivate; dog; drive; ensue; expel; follow; hasten; hound; hunt; maintain; oust; per-secute; persist; plod; practice; proceed; prosecute; quest; remove; ride; run; seek; shadow; shag; stalk; tag; tail; track; trail; tread; PURSUIT: (see "occupation") ac-tivity; avocation; business; calling; caper; chase; employment; endeavor; fad; field; following; hobby; hunt; interest; métier; objective; performance; persistence; practice; prosecution; quest; trade; trail; vocation; work

PURSY: asthmatic; baggy; fat; fleshy; obese; plump; puckered; pudgy; puffy; pursed; stout; swollen; wealthy

PURVEY: (**see** "sell") assist; cater; furnish; get; offer; pander; procure; provide; provision; serve; supply

PUS: matter; maturation; suppuration

PUSH: **v.** abet; accelerate; advance; aid; assist; augment; back; boost; butt; cram; crowd; direct; drive; elevate; exert; expedite; extend; feed; force; heave; help; hoist; impel; increase; intertrude; intrude; jostle; kite; move; nudge; operate; press; proceed; prod; progress; project; promote; propel; prosecute; pump; rush; send (out); shove; slug; stick; stress; thrust; urge; PUSH: **n.** acceleration; action; advance(ment); assault; assist; boost; boot; butt; campaign; compulsion; crisis; crowd; drive; emergency; energy; enterprise; exertion; extremity; force; gang; heave; hoist; impulse; influence; intrusion; jag; jostle(ment); move; nudge; offense; operation; pinch; press; pressure; prod; progress; promotion; prosecution; rush; shove; stress; thrust; urge; PUSHING *or* PUSHY: aggressive; arrogant; bumptious; intrusive; officious; presumptuous; uppish; uppity; PUSHER: arriviste; parvenu; wheeler(-dealer)

PUSILLANIMITY: (**see** "weakness") cowardliness; PUSILLANIMOUS: (**see** "cowardly") contemptible; craven; fearful; feeble; irresolute; mean-spirited; sorry; spiritless; timid; timorous; weak; white-livered

PUT: (**see** "place") adapt; apply; assume; cram; express; focus; imbed; impose; impute; insert; install; invest; lodge; quarter; set; shove; station; subject; suppose; throw; urge

PUTATIVE: (**see** "supposed") alleged; attributed; believed; deemed; hypothesized; inferred; reputed; said; thought

PUTREFY: **see** "rot;" PUTREFACTION: corruption; decay; decomposition; disintegration; putrescence; rot(tenness); PUTRID: bad; corrupt; decomposed; depraved; diseased; fecal; fetid; foul; fusty; immoral; mephitic; obscene; offensive; polluted; putrescent; putrified; rancid; rotted; rotten; saprogenic; septic; sour; stinking; tainted; ulcerous; vicious; vile

PUZZLE: **v.** (**see** "perplex") amaze; baffle; befog; befuddle; bewilder; cap; complicate; confound; confuse; disconcert; distract; dum(b)found; embarrass; entangle; get; gripe; grope; mystify; nonplus; pose; stick; stump; tangle; wonder; PUZZLE: **n.** (**see** "perplexity") acrostic; alphagram; alphametic; alternade; ambiguity; anacrostic; anagram; antigram; arithmorem; beheadment; betagram; bewilderment; brainteaser; cancrine; berse; charade; chronogram; cipher; code; complexity; complication; confusion; conundrum; crossword; cryptogram; curtailment; decapitation; deletion; deltagram; difficulty; distraction; Double-Crostic; doubt; embarrassment; enigma; entanglement; equivoque; eteostic; facer; gammagram; halfsquare; intricacy; joke; knot; labyrinth; linkade; literatim; logogriph; magic square; maze; metagram; misgiving; mutation; mystery; obscurity; omegram; palindrome; pangrammatic (sentence); paradox; paragram; paronomasia; poser; problem; pun; puzzlement; quadade; quandary; question; quinade; quiz; rebus; reversal; riddle; secret; Sotadic (verse); sphinx; stick(l)er; tangle; teaser; telestich; transade; transbeheadment; transcurtailment; transdeletion; transposal; transposition; trinade; uncertainty; wordplay; PUZZLED *or* PUZZLING: ambiguous; ambivalent; asea; baffling; bewildering; bewitched; cabalistic; complex; complicated; confounding; confused; confusing; cryptic(al); Delphian; Delphic; disconcerted; distracted; distraught; doubtful; elliptic(al); enigmatic(al); entangled; equivocal; hidden; impenetrable; incomprehensible; inexplicable; inscrutable; intricate; involved; knotty; mixed; mysterious; mystic(al); mystifying; nonplussed; obscure; occult; paradox(i)al; perplexing; problematic(al); questionable; recondite; secret; sphinxlike; troubled; undecipherable; unfathomable; unintelligible; ununderstandable; vague

PYGMY: **a.** dwarfish; elfin; elfish; elvish; midget; pixie; pygm(a)ean; PYGMY: **n.** Achua; Akka; Batwa; Doko; dwarf; elf; gnome; midget; minim; Negrito; pixy; runt

PYRAMID: **v.** accrue; agglutinate; enlarge; heap; increase; pile; point; PYRAMID: **n.** Cheops; Khufu; heap; increase; point; spire; tent; tower; ziggurat

PYTHONIC: (**see** "huge") inspired; monstrous; oracular

PYX: binnacle; box; capsa; casket; ciborium; tabernacle; vessel

Q

QUACK: Cagliostro; charlatan; empiric; faker; humbug; imposter; medicaster; mountebank; pretender; quacksalver; sham

QUADRANGLE: campus; court(yard); enclosure; square; tetragon

QUADRATE: adapt; adjust; agree; conform; correspond; perfect; square; suit

QUADRUMANE: (see "monkey") anthropoid; ape(let); gibbon; gorilla; kra; langur; lar; lemur; maha; orang

QUADRUPED: ass; cat; cow; dog; donkey; horse; mammal

QUAFF: (see "drink") draft; guzzle; swallow; swill

QUAGGY: boggy; fenny; flabby; marshy; muddy; queachy; soft; spongy; swampy; yielding

QUAGMIRE: bog; difficulty; fen; marsh; morass; mudhole; problem; swamp; trap

QUAIL: v. (see "cower") blench; cringe; falter; fawn; flinch; hesitate; quake; quiver; recoil; shake; shiver; shrink; shudder; weaken; wince; wither; QUAIL: n. bird; colin; lowa; Massena; squealer; turnix

QUAINT: (see "bizarre") affected; antique; attractive; curious; different; droll; eccentric; elegant; exotic; fanciful; grotesque; handsome; odd(ish); old-fashioned; outré; peculiar; picturesque; pleasing; popular; pretty; proud; queer; refined; rococo; singular; strange; uncommon; unfamiliar; unreasonable; unusual; whimsical; wise

QUAKE: (see "shake") agitate; flutter; oscillate; quail; quiver; shiver; shudder; tremble; vibrate

QUALIFY: abate; adapt; alter; assuage; capacitate; certify; characterize; describe; designate; diminish; educate; entitle; equip; fit; graduate; habituate; justify; learn;

license; limit; measure (up); mitigate; moderate; modify; name; pass; prepare; quantify; ready; restrain; restrict; soften; temper; train; vary; QUALIFICATION: capacitation; capacity; condition; education; eligibility; endowment; exception; experience; expertise; expertness; fitness; graduation; habilitation; hability; learning; license; limitation; modification; need; proviso; readiness; requisite; reserve; restriction; skill; suitability; test; training; trial; virtuosity; QUALIFIED: (see "capable") able; accomplished; adept; apt; certified; competent; conditional; consummate; educated; effectual; eligible; endowed; equipped; experienced; expert; fit; licensed; likely; limited; modified; prepared; ready; registered; restricted; skilled; skillful; suitable; tested; trained; tried; QUALIFYING: (see "limiting") adjectival; adjective; limited; qualificatory; restrictive

QUALITY: aristocracy; aspect; attribute; brand; caliber; capacity; character(istic); class; color(ing); condition; difference; disposition; essence; excellence; feature; function; genius; grade; intensity; kind; make; mettle; nature; occupation; peculiarity; personality; position; profession; property; rank; reputation; resonance; skill; standard; state; status; strain; stuff; substance; superiority; texture; timbre; tone; touch; trait; virtue; way

QUALM: (see "uneasiness") apprehension; compunction; disbelief; doubt; faintheartedness; fear; misgiving; nausea; pall; pang; regret; scruple; spasm; squeamishness; throe; twinge; uncertainty; uneasiness; QUALMISH: see "queasy"

QUANDARY: (see "difficulty") bewilderment; crisis; dilemma; doubt; fix; pass; perplexity; pickle; plight; predicament; puzzle(ment); strait; uncertainty

QUANTITY: aggregate; aggregation; amount; amplitude; any; batch; bulk; bushel; crowd; dose; duration; enormity; extent; heap; heaviness; hecatomb; legion; length; load;

lot(s); magnitude; mass; mess; multitude; number; plentitude; plenty; plethora; portion; quanta(pl.); quantum; result; size; some; spate; sum; supply; total; volume; wealth; weight; welter; whole; world; worth; yield

QUARANTINE: **v.** ban; cut (off); enisle; exclude; insulate; interdict; isolate; restrain; restrict; QUARANTINE: **n.** ban; exclusion; insulation; interdiction; isolation; restraint; restriction; sanction; stoppage

QUARREL: **v.** altercate; argue; bicker; brawl; broil; caterwaul; cavil; clash; complain; contend; debate; disagree; dispute; dissent; feud; fight; fuss; jangle; miff; misunderstand; rift; row; rupture; scrap; spat; split; squabble; strive; struggle; tiff; tussle; wrangle; QUARREL: **n.** affray; altercation; argument; bicker(ing); brawl; brouhaha; caterwaul; clash; complaint; contention; contest; controversy; *démêlé*; disagreement; discord; dispute; dissention; dogfight; donnybrook; embroglio; feud; fight; fracas; fray; fuss; *mélange*; melee; misunderstanding; rift; riot; row; ruction; run-in; rupture; scene; scrap; scrape; set-to; skirmish; spat; squabble; strife; tift; tilt; tussle; words; wrangle; QUARRELSOME: *acariâtre*; adverse; aggressive; argumentative; bellicose; belligerent; boisterous; brawlsome; brawly; cantankerous; cat-and-dog; choleric; combative; contentious; discordant; disputable; disputatious; dissentious; dissident; fractious; gladiatorial; hostile; inharmonious; litigious; militant; perverse; pugnacious; querulous; refractory; ructious; termagant(ish); troublesome; turbulent; ugly; unruly; QUARRELSOMENESS: *acarirâtreté*; bellicosity; belligerency; contentiousness; pugnacity; turbulence; turbulency; unruliness

QUARRY: dupe; game; object; pigeon; prey; ravin; scapegoat; victim

QUARTER: area; billet; clemency; coin; consideration; direction; district; division; forbearance; fourth; locality; lodge; mercy; period; position; quadrant; region; section; station; sympathy; term; territory; ward

QUARTERS: (**see** "house") abode; accommodations; billet; bivouac; digs; dwelling; housing; lodge; lodgings; rooms; space

QUASH: (**see** "quell") abate; annul; cancel; crush; destroy; drop; extinguish; overthrow; spike; subdue; suppress; vacate; void

QUAVER: (**see** "quake") fear; oscillation; quiver; shake; swing; tremolo; trill; vibration; wavering

QUEASY: apprehensive; delicate; doubtful; faint(hearted); fastidious; fearful; giddy; hazardous; nauseated; nauseating; qualmish; queer; regretful; risky; sick; squeamish; ticklish; uncertain; uncomfortable; uneasy; unsettled

QUEEN: bee; belle; chieftainess; empress; goddess; monarch; ranee; rani; *reine*; sovereign; QUEENLY: gracious; haughty; majestic; noble; queenlike; regal; regnal; royal; sovereign

QUEER: **see** "disturb;" QUEER: **a.** (**see** "bizarre") astounding; curious; dippy; droll(ish); eccentric; eerie; eery; extraordinary; faint; fantastic; freakish; funny; giddy; grotesque; hipped; obsessed; odd(ish); *outré* peculiar; quaint; queasy; questionable; quixotic; ridiculous; shady; sham; singular; spurious; strange; suspicious; touched; uncommon; unconventional; unexpected; unique; unusual; whimsical

QUELL: abate; allay; arrest; assuage; beat; calm; check; conquer; cool; crush; curb; dampen; defeat; destroy; down; end; extinguish; hush; lull; moderate; mollify; overcome; overpower; overthrow; pacify; quash; quench; quiet; reduce; repress; rout; silence; slake; soothe; spike; squelch; stem; stifle; still; stop; subdue; subside; suppress; vanquish

QUENCH: (**see** "quell") allay; arrest; calm; check; cool; dampen; dash; destroy; end; extinguish; gratify; inhibit; overcome; quiet; sate; satiate; satisfy; slake; stifle; subdue; subside; suppress

QUERULOUS: (**see** "peevish") cantankerous; carping; complaining; cranky; cross; curmudgeonish; fastidious; faultfinding; fidgety; fretful; grouchy; huffy; irritable; petulant; plaintive; questioning; quibbling; touchy; unsatisfied; whimpering; whining

QUERY: **v.** ask; examine; inquire; interrogate; quest(ion); quiz; test; QUERY: **n.** (**see** "question") doubt; examination; inquiry; interrogation; probe; quest; questioning; quiz; test

QUEST: **v.** demand; examine; hunt; inquire; probe; pursue; query; quiz; search; seek;

test; QUEST: **n.** adventure; desideratum; examination; expedition; exploit; goal; grail; Holy Grail; hunt; inquiry; inquisition; investigation; journey; odyssey; probe; problem; pursuit; reconnaissance; reconnoiter; safari; search; seeking; trek; venture

QUESTION: **v.** accuse; ask; catechize; cavil; challenge; charge; consider; debate; demand; dispute; doubt; examine; grill; inquire; inquisit; interrogate; marvel; ponder; pose; probe; pump; query; quiz; reason; research; scruple; search; seek; sift; suspect; test; waver; wonder; QUESTION: **n.** catechism; challenge; chance; charge; contention; controversy; conundrum; debate; discussion; dispute; doubt; examination; inquiry; interrogation; issue; matter; mystery; nut; objection; point; poser; problem; proposition; puzzle; query; quest; quiz; search; subject; suspicion; test; topic; QUESTIONABLE: ambiguous; contentious; contingent; controversial; controvertible; cryptic(al); debatable; disputable; disputatious; disreputable; doubtful; dubious; dubitable; equivocal; fishy; hesitant; hypothetical; incredible; indecisive; indefinite; indeterminate; infamous; moot; mysterious; notorious; obscure; occult; oracular; outrageous; paradoxical; polemical; provisional; provocative; questioning; reluctant; scandalous; seamy; shadowy; shady; shaky; suspicious; unbelievable; uncertain; unclear; unconfirmed; unconvincing; undecided; undetermined; unlikely; unpromising; unreliable; unsafe; vague; QUESTIONING: catechesis; catechism; catechization; equivocation; inquest; inquiry; inquisition; probe

QUESTIONNAIRE: blank; feeler; form; inquiry; letter; probe; query; straw; survey; vote

QUIBBLE: **v.** (**see** "carp") argue; bicker; cavil; censure; complain; criticize; disparage; dodge; drum; equivocate; evade; nag; object; palter; pettifog; protest; shift; shuffle; straddle; QUIBBLE **n.** or QUIBBLING: argument; bicker(ing); cavil; chicanery; equivocation; evasion; hairsplitting; objection; protest(ation); scrupulosity; shuffling; sophistry; speciosity; QUIBBLING: **a.** (**see** "peevish") argumentative; bickering; captious; carping; casuistic; hairsplitting; querulous; questioning; sophistical; sophomoric; specious; QUIBBLER: *advocatus diaboli*; carper; caviler; devil's advocate; equivocator; hairsplitter; protester; questioner

QUICK(LY): active; acute; agile; alert; alive; animate(d); anon; apace; apt; astucious; astute; burning; celeritous; charged; darting; deft(ly); dexterous; expeditious; facile; fast; fiery; filled; fleet; Gadarene; gay; hasty; hurried; imbued; immediate(ly); impatient; impetuous; instant(aneous); intelligent; intense; keen; lissome; live(ly); living; mercurial; moving; nimble; overhasty; passionate; perceptive; perspicacious; presto; prompt(ly); rapid(ly); ready; resourceful; rushing; sensitive; sharp; shifting; skillful; slapdash; snappy; soon; speedily; speedy; sprightly; sudden; summarily; summary; swift; telegraphic; *tout de suite*; vital; volant; witty; yare; yielding; QUICKEN: (**see** "accelerate") enliven; excite; refresh; speed; stir; QUICKNESS: acumen; alacrity; astucity; celerity; deftness; dexterity; dispatch; expedition; facileness; facilitation; facility; hastiness; hurry; instantaneity; nous; perspicacity; sagacity; sensitivity; skill(fulness); speed; wit(tiness)

QUIDDITY: distinction; essence; haecceity; nature; peculiarity; oddity; quibble; trifle; whim(sicality)

QUIDNUNC: busybody; frump; gossip; newsmonger; talebearer; tattler

QUIESCENT: (**see** "quiet") arrested; asleep; calm; dormant; inactive; inert; latent; motionless; passive; placid; potential; resting; serene; silent; sleeping; stagnant; static; still; tranquil; undisturbed; unruffled; QUIESCENCE: **see** "silence" and "stagnation"

QUIET(EN) **v.** (**see** "hush") allay; calm; ease; lull; pacify; repress; settle; silence; still; soothe; tranquilize; tut; unruffle; QUIET: **a.** allayed; aphonic; calm; contented; dormant; dumb; eased; gentle; halcyon; hushed; inactive; inarticulate; level; low; lulled; mild; motionless; mousy; noiseless; numb; pacific; pacified; peaceful; placid; quiescent; relaxed; reposeful; rested; restful; retired; secluded; sedate; serene; settled; silenced; silent; soothed; speechless; still(ed); stilly; tranquilized; troubleless; undisturbed; undramatic; unexacted; unexacting; unexciting; unmolested; unruffled; voiceless; QUIET(NESS): **n.** armistice; calm(ness); contentment; dormancy; ease; hush; inactivity; latency; leisure; lull; order; pacification; passivity; peace(fulness); placidity; quiescence; quietus; repose; rest; retirement; serenity; silence; stillness; tranquility

QUIETUS: (**see** "death") acquittance; discharge; extinction; mort; release; repose; rest; settlement;

QUINTESSENCE: (**see** "essence") attar; clyssus; core; elixir; ether; extract(ion); fundamental(ity); gist; heart; pith; principle; substance

QUIP: (**see** "jest") gibe; mot; retort; sally; sarcasm; scoff; wisecrack; witticism

QUIRK: angle; bend; caprice; channel; conceit; crook; curve; equivocation; evasion; gibe; groove; mannerism; peculiarity; quibble; quip; shift; singularity; subterfuge; taunt; trait; trick; turn; twist

QUIT: (**see** "abandon") abdicate; abnegate; acquit; cease; clear; conduct; deliver; depart; desist; discharge; discontinue; drop; forsake; free; go; leave; liberate; part; release; relieve; relinquish; render; renounce; repay; requite; resign; retire; rid; scram; shoot; stop; surrender; yield; QUITTER: abdicator; abnegator; renunciator; surrenderer

QUITE: all; completely; considerable; entirely; positively; pretty; rather; totally; very; wholly

QUIVER: (**see** "quail") oscillation; vibration

QUIXOTIC: chimerical; dreamy; eccentric; fantastic; ideal(istic); imaginary; impractical; mad; queer; rash; romantic; unpractical; utopian; visionary

QUIZ: (**see** "question") examine; inquire; inquisit; mock; ridicule; test

QUONDAM: former(ly); old; once; onetime; sometime

QUOTA: (**see** "distribution") allotment; assignment; contingent; dividend; dole; estimate; extent; measure; percentage; portion; proportion; rating; ration; share; target

QUOTATION: (**see** "excerpt") cital; citation; extract; motto; paraphrase; passage; price; quote; reference; report; selection

QUOTE: **v.** adduce; cite; confirm; copy; examine; excerpt; extract; mention; name; note; notice; observe; paraphrase; recite; repeat; report; QUOTE: **n. see** "quotation"

QUOTIDIAN: commonplace; daily; diurnal; everyday; ordinary; trivial

R

RABBI: clergyman; lord; master; priest; scholar; teacher; RABBINIC(AL): **see** "particular"

RABBIT: buck; bunny; coney; Cuniculus; cony; doe; hare; hyrax; lagomorph; lapin; rodent

RABBLE: **a.** coarse; disorderly; noisy; ragtag; trashy; vulgar; RABBLE: **n.** canaille; commonalty; crowd; demos; dregs; *faex populi*; herd; heterogeneity; *hoi polloi*; horde; *ignobile vulgus*; *Lumpenproletariat*; masses; mob; multitude; populace; *profanum vulgus*; proletariat; ragtag; riffraff; scum; trash; unwashed; varletry

RABID: (**see** "mad") bawdy; crazy; eager; enthusiastic; extreme; fanatical; fierce; fiery; frantic; furious; insane; intolerant; radical; raging; rampant; unreasonable; violent; virulent; zealous

RACE: **v.** (**see** "run") compete; contest; dart; dash; drive; gallop; haste(n); hie; lope; pace; relay; span; speed; sprint; tear; trot; RACE: **n.** ancestry; breed; career; caste; channel; clan; class; clique; competition; conduit; contest; coterie; country; course; current; dart; dash; descendants; division; family; flavor; gallop; game; genus; groove; group; house; humanity; kind; line(age); man(kind); marathon; match; name; nation; order; origin; parentage; passageway; paternity; pedigree; people; period; phylum; regatta; relay; run; sept; sort; species; spring; stock; strain; stream; subspecies; taste; tribe; trot; type; variety; watercourse; RACIAL: cultural; ethnic(al); genetic; gentilic; phyletic; phylogen(et)ic; stock

RACK: **v.** (**see** "torment") afflict; agitate; excruciate; grill; harass; punish; tease; torture; wrench; RACK: **n.** agony; anguish; cloud; destruction; excruciation; frame-(work); harassment; oppression; pace; pain; pang; punishment; strain; suffering; support; torment; torture

RACKET: agitation; babel; bat; brawl; brouhaha; business; clamor; clash; clatter; commotion; confusion; din; dint; discord; disturbance; dodge; fracas; fuss; gamble; game; hubbub; imposture; loudness; noise; noisiness; occupation; perturbation; quarrel; revel; riot; scheme; scuffle; spat; squabble; stir; strife; trick; tumult; turbulence; uproar; wrangle

RACY: animated; brisk; colorful; exhilarating; fiery; flavorous; forcible; fresh; gam(e)y; lively; natural; obscene; peppery; piquant; pungent; rich; risqué; saucy; sharp; spicy; spirited; stimulating; strong; suggestive; unspoiled; vigorous; zestful

RADIATE: beam; broadcast; diffuse; disseminate; effulge; effuse; emanate; emit; gleam; glitter; glow; illuminate; shed; shine; spread; RADIANCE: beauty; brightness; brilliance; dazzlement; effulgence; effulgency; glare; glitter; glory; glow; illumination; lambency; light; luminosity; luster; pink; refulgence; resplendence; resplendency; scintillation; sheen; shimmer; shine; splendor; RADIANT: aglow; auroral; aurorean; beamy; blithe(ful); bright; brilliant; burning; dazzling; divergent; ecstatic; gleaming; glorious; glowing; golden; happy; joyful; lambent; livid; lucent; luminous; lustrous; pleased; rayonnant; resplendent; scintillating; scintillescent; shining; splendent; vigorous

RADICAL: **a.** basal; basic; capital; cardinal; drastic; extreme; forward; full; fundamental; heretical; heterodox; ingrained; inherent; innate; Jacobinic; left; liberal; organic; original; rabid; rebellious; red; revolutionary; sansculottic; sansculottish; thoroughgoing; total; ultimate; ultra; unconventional; unorthodox; visionary; vital; wild-eyed; RADICAL: **n.** (**see** "rebel") basis; extremist; firebrand; foundation; fundamentalist; Jacobin; leftist; liberal; red; revolutionary; root; sansculotte; septembrist; sign; support; surd; ultraist; Young Turk; RADICALISM: heresy; heterodoxy; Jacobinism; radicality; sansculotterie; sansculottism; ultraism

RADIUS: area; bone; compass; extent; field; ken; length; limit; orbit; range; reach; rod; scope; span; spoke; sweep; throw; width

RAFFISH: careless; cheap; common; crude; devil-may-care; disreputable; flashy; frowsy; infamous; low; rakish; rowdy; tawdry; unconventional; unkempt; vulgar; worthless

RAFFLE: chance; drawing; gamble; lottery; jumble; tangle

RAFT: aggregation; balsa; barge; catamaran; collection; float; gobs; lots; mass; mat; quantity; transport

RAG: **v.** abuse; annoy; banter; berate; censure; chaff; curse; denounce; guy; josh; jostle; kid; needle; persecute; rate; rebuke; reproach; reprove; revile; rib; ridicule; scoff; scold; taunt; tease; torment; upbraid; vituperate; RAG: **n.** cloth; newspaper; periodical; remnant; scrap; tatter; tune; RAGGED(Y): defective; dilapidated; discordant; erose; fragmentary; frayed; harsh; irregular; jagged; mean; poor; raguly; rent; rough; run-down; scrappy; scratchy; shabby; shaggy; straggling; straggly; tattered; tattery; torn; uneven; unfinished; unkempt; unpolished; worn

RAGE: **v.** (see "anger") agitate; bluster; boil; bubble; chafe; churn; cry; effervesce; erupt; explode; ferment; flare; foam; fret; fulminate; fume; rampage; rant; rave; rush; seethe; shout; splutter; spread; steam; stew; storm; RAGE: **n.** anger; conniption; craze; cry; dudgeon; eagerness; enthusiasm; excitation; excitement; fad; fashion; fervor; fit; flare; frenzy; fulmination; furor; fury; ire; madness; mania; mode; paroxysm; passion; pique; ramp(age); roar; storm; style; temper; tempest; tirade; uproar; violence; vogue; whim; wrath; RAGING: berserk; blustering; cyclonic; extraordinary; frenzied; fulminating; fuming; furibund; grim; hot; incensed; infuriated; rabid; rampant; ranting; severe; shouting; spluttering; storming; tremendous; unassuaged; uncontrolled; unpalliated; violent; wild

RAGOUT: see "hash"

RAID: **v.** assault; attack; forage; foray; harass; invade; maraud; molest; pillage; prey; steal; RAID: **n.** assault; attack; expedition; forage; foray; incursion; inroad; invasion; maraud; onset; pillage; siege; RAIDER: **see** "bandit"

RAIL: **v.** abuse; berate; censure; curse; denounce; jaw; rant; rate; rebuke; reproach; reprove; revile; scoff; scold; swear; upbraid; vituperate; RAIL: **n.** bar; bird; fence

RAILLERY: asteism; badinage; banter; chaff(ing); fun; irony; jest(ing); joking; kidding; mockery; needling; persiflage; play; pleasantry; ridicule; satire; sport

RAILROAD: **v.** expedite; frame; hurry; rush; send; transport; RAILROAD: **n.** line; track; transportation

RAIMENT: (see "clothes") apparel; array(ment); attire; clothing; costume; dress; garb; garment(s); habiliments; outfit; rags; togs; uniform; vestments; vesture

RAIN: **v.** bestow; drizzle; flood; mist; mizzle; precipitate; pour; shed; sprinkle; RAIN: **n.** cloudburst; downpour; drizzle; flood; mist; mizzle; pluviosity; precipitate; preciptation; serin; shower; spate; sprinkle

RAISE: **v.** (see "elevate") advance; aggrandize; animate; arouse; augment; awaken; boost; borrow; breed; build; cheer; climb; collect; construct; create; cultivate; educate; encourage; enhance; ennoble; erect; escalate; establish; exalt; excite; extol; flush; gather; grow; heave; heighten; hoist; honor; incite; increase; inspire; inspirit; institute; intensify; introduce; jack; jerk; jump; kick; leaven; levitate; levy; lift; lighten; magnify; muster; nourish; nurture; pinnacle; produce; promote; rear; recruit; resurrect; rise; rouse; rout; sharpen; sing; start; stimulate; stir; sublimate; summon; train; transcend; up(heave); uplift; upright; voice; RAISE: **n.** advancement; elevation; enhancement; ennoblement; escalation; increase; promotion; start; transcendency; RAISED: bred; convex; cultivated; elevated; ennobled; erected; exalted; grew; hefted; heightened; hoisted; hove; magnified; napped; produced; prominent; roused; stimulated; stirred

RAKE: **v.** attack; censure; collect; dig (out); even; gather; ransack; rub; scan; scour; scrape; scratch; search; smooth; survey; touch; RAKE: **n.** comb; debauchee; inclination; lecher; libertine; lothario; profligate; rakehell; roué; satyr; tool; RAKISH: (see "raffish") devil-may-care; licentious; wanton

RALLY: **v.** arouse; banter; collect; deride;

encourage; gather; join; joke; marshal; mass; meet; mobilize; mock; muster; organize; prevail; reassemble; recover; recuperate; ridicule; rouse; stir; strengthen; summon; taunt; twit; unite; RALLY: **n.** assembly; clambake; conclave; gathering; mass; mobilization; muster(ing); picnic; recovery; recuperation; renewal; rousing; summoning

RAM: **v.** block; butt; cram; crash; drive; fill; force; pack; plunge; pound; push; shove; strike; stuff; tamp; thrust; RAM: **n.** Aries; buck; ovine; piston; plunger; sheep; welter

RAMBLE: **v.** bellwaver; digress; diverge; drift; explore; gad; hike; meander; perambulate; peregrinate; prowl; range; roam; rove; saunter; scramble; sprawl; straggle; stray; stroll; tour; travel; trudge; wander; waver; RAMBLE: **n.** digression; drift; expedition; gad; hike; meander(ing); perambulation; peregrination; ploy; prowl; range; stroll; travel; RAMBLING: circuitous; circumambagious; curbed; desultory; devious; digressive; discursive; large; meandering; moving; parenthetical; perambulatory; peregrine; peripatetic; rampant; rolling; sprawling; spreading; winding

RAMIFICATION: (**see** "arm") branch(ing); consequence; divergence; division; embranchment; extension; fork(ing); offshoot; outgrowth; part; ramus; separation; spur; subdivision

RAMP: gangplank; incline; passage(way); platform; run(way); slope; stair(way); wall

RAMPANT: aggressive; clamorous; dominant; extravagant; exuberant; feral; fierce; impetuous; luxuriant; predominant; prevalent; profuse; rambling; rank; rearing; rife; savage; teeming; turbulent; unbridled; unchecked; unrestrained; violent; wild

RAMPART: agger; barricade; bulwark; defense; embankment; escarp(ment); fort(ification); line; mole; mound; parapet; redan; ridge; wall

RAMUS: barb; branch; division; fork; projection; ramification

RANCH: farm; hacienda; spread

RANCID: disagreeable; fetid; foul; frowsy; fusty; musty; noisome; obnoxious; odious;

offensive; putrescent; putrid; rank; rotten; smelly; sour; spoiled; stale; stinking; tainted; unclean; unpleasant

RANCOR: (**see** "hate") animosity; antagonism; antipathy; aversion; bitterness; enmity; gall; grudge; hatred; hostility; malevolence; malice; malignity; poison; spite; spleen; venom; RANCOROUS: **see** "malign"

RANDOM: (**see** "aimless") casual; chance-(wise); chancy; desultory; driftless; erratic; fitful; fortuitous; gratuitous; haphazard; indefinite; indiscriminate; purposeless; stochastic; stray; unaimed; unplanned; vagrant; wild

RANDY: coarse; disorderly; lecherous; lustful; sexy; vulgar

RANGE: **v.** (**see** "roam") array; gad; grade; graze; line; marshal; move; place; ramble; rank; rove; run; sort; spread; standardize; stray; sweep; RANGE: **n.** area; array; authority; beat; breadth; calendar; catalog-(ue); category; circulation; class(ification); compass; comprehensibility; comprehensiveness; cycle; degree; diapason; difference; direction; distance; distribution; domain; excursion; extensity; extent; field; flight; freedom; gamut; gradation; incidence; jurisdiction; ken; latitude; leeway; length; lexicon; liberty; license; line; mountains; octave; orbit; opportunity; outlook; oven; panorama; pantheon; pasturage; pasture; permission; play; power; prospect; purpose; purview; radius; rainbow; ramble; rank; rate; reach; realm; region; repertoire; resort; room; row; run; scale; scene; scope; sequence; series; size; space; span; spectrum; sphere; spread; steps; stove; stretch; sweep; swing; tier; tolerance; toleration; variance; variation; view; vocabulary; way; width

RANK: **v.** (**see** "range") arrange; classify; file; grade; identify; place; rate; score; sort; RANK: **a.** absolute; abundant; coarse; complete; corrupt; dank; dense; downright; excessive; exuberant; fertile; fetid; flagrant; foul; frank; glaring; gross; indecent; lush; luxuriant; luxurious; numerous; musty; offensive; olid; poor; rampant; rancid; rich; smelly; stinking; utter; vigorous; vulgar; wild; RANK: **n.** antecedence; arrangement; array(ment); caste; class(ification); compartment; degree; dignity; distinction; division; echelon; eminence; estate; excellence; figure file; formation; grade; grandeur; line; mark;

order; place; position; precedence; prestige; priority; privilege; procedure; range; rate; rating; row; score; seniority; series; stall; standing; station; tier

RANKLE: (see "anger") chafe; fester; gall; grate; grind; inflame; injure; irritate; pain; poison; ulcerate; vex

RANSACK: (see "loot") despoil; explore; pillage; plunder; raid; rake; ravage; rifle; rummage; sack; search; seek; snoop; spoil; strip

RANSOM: v. (see "free") deliver; emancipate; extricate; liberate; manumit; redeem; reprieve; rescue; save; RANSOM: n. see "reward"

RANT: blow; bluster; bombast; curse; declaim; discourse; fulminate; fume; rage; rail; rampage; rave; scold; spout; storm; vociferate

RAP: v. bop; box; censure; clout; criticize; cuff; knock; strike; thump; thwack; whack; RAP: n. see "blow" and "trifle"

RAPACIOUS: (see "greedy") avaricious; covetous; cruel; extortionate; feracious; grasping; mercenary; merciless; piratical; plundering; predacious; raptorial; ravenous; relentless; venal; voracious; RAPACITY: see "cupidity" and "greed"

RAPHE: joint; line; seam; suture; union

RAPID: (see "hasty") abrupt; accelerated; agile; apace; brisk; cursory; desultory; expeditious; fast; fleeting; Gadarene; hurried; precipitate; quick; speedy; superficial; swift; winged

RAPSCALLION: (see "rogue") ne'er-do-well; rascal; villain

RAPT: absorbed; abstracted; attentive; bewitched; charmed; cognizant; dreamy; enchanted; engrossed; enraptured; entranced; lost; reflective; thoughtful; transported

RAPTURE: delight; delirium; ecstasy; elation; enthusiasm; entrancement; euphoria; exaltation; extravagance; joy; love; orgasm; paroxysm; passion; raptus; rhapsody; seventh heaven; transport; RAPTUROUS: (see "elated") delirious; ecstatic; frenzied; org(i)astic; paroxysmal; passionate; rhapsodic(al)

RARE: beautiful; capital; choice; curious; dear; different; distinctive; esoteric; estimable; excellent; exceptional; exclusive; exotic; extra(ordinary); extreme; fine; incomparable; individual; infrequent; inimitable; intimate; limited; matchless; noteworthy; novel; odd; paranormal; particular; pearly; peculiar; peerless; precious; privileged; raw; recherché; remarkable; risqué; scarce; select; single; singular; slight; slim; special; specific; spectacular; strange; superlative; supernacular; supernatural; tenuous; thin; ultra; uncommon; uncustomary; underdone; unexampled; unique; unparalleled; unprecedented; unpurchasable; unusual; RARENESS: attenuation; infrequency; oddity; peculiarity; rarefaction; rarity; seldomness; subtility; subtilization; tenuity; RARITY: anomaly; extravagance; infrequency; oddity; phenomenality; prodigality; prodigy; rara avis; scarcity; tenuity; tulipe noire

RAREFIED: abstruse; attenuated; decreased; diluted; esoteric; purified; reduced; refined; tenuous; thin(ned); watered; weakened

RASCAL: (see "scamp") cad; cheat; culprit; dog; imp; Judas; knave; miscreant; pixie; prankster; rakehell; rapscallion; reprobate; ribald; robber; rogue; rowdy; ruffian; scalawag; Scapin; scaramouche; sharper; sharpster; thief; thug; tough; trickster; varlet; varmint; villain; yegg; RASCALLY: base; dishonest; false; knavish; mean; rakehell(y); trickish; tricky; unprincipled; villainous; worthless; RASCALITY: (see "baseness") scoundreldom; villainy

RASH: a. (see "reckless") adventurous; audacious; careless; disregardful; écervelé; extravagant; foolhardy; giddy; harebrained; hasty; headlong; headstrong; heady; heedless; Icarian; ill-advised; impatient; impetuous; imprudent; impulsive; incautious; inconsiderate; indiscreet; injudicious; mad(cap); precipitate; presumptuous; sudden; temerarious; thoughtless; unadvised; unthinking; unwary; venturesome; venturous; wily; RASH: n. anthema; eczema; eruption; exanthem; hives; impetigo; uredo; urticaria; RASHNESS: acrasy; assumption; audacity; carelessness; disregard; effrontery; extravagance; impetuosity; impulsivity; presumption; recklessness; temerity; thoughtlessness

RASP: abrade; creak; file; grate; grind; groan; irritate; offend; scrape; scratch

RAT(S): apostate; deserter; heel; informer;

louse; Muridae (pl.); Quisling; rodent; scab; snob; stinker; traitor; vermin

RATE: **v.** (**see** "classify") adjudge; adjudicate; adjust; analyze; apportion; appraise; assay; assess; chide; consider; count; criticize; deserve; estimate; evaluate; evalue; examine; figure; gain; jaw; judge; justify; levy; prize; rail; rank; ration; regard; reprimand; revile; scold; score; set; share; tax; test; value; RATE: **n.** account; allowance; amount; apportionment; appraisal; assessment; cess; charge; class; cost; course; curve; degree; duty; estimate; estimation; evaluation; figure; flow; gain; gait; gradation; impost; incidence; income; kind; levy; loss; pace; payment; price; proportion; range; rank; ratio; relation; scale; score; share; speed; standing; stride; tariff; tax; toll; trend; valuation; value; velocity; wage; worth

RATHER: ere; especially; instead; preferably; quite; somewhat; sooner; than

RATIFY: (**see** "approve") affirm; attest; authorize; certify; confirm; consent; corroborate; elect; endorse; establish; O.K.; pass; permit; sanction; seal; second; settle; subscribe; substantiate; uphold; validate; verify; vote

RATING: (**see** "rank" and "rate") credit; mark; score; standing

RATIO: ground; nature; odds; percentage; proportion; quotient; rate; rationale

RATION: **v.** allot; allow; apportion; appropriate; budget; deal; distribute; divide; dole; dose; equalize; limit; measure; mete; share; RATION: **n.** allotment; allowance; apportionment; appropriation; budget; deal; degree; division; dole; dosage; dose; equalization; food; helping; limit; measure; meed; percentage; portion; provisions; quote; rate; relation; serving; share

RATIONAL: Apollonian; Apollonic; Apollonistic; balanced; Cartesian; cognitive; consequential; cool; defensible; equitable; fair; fit(ting); harmonious; intellective; intellectual; intelligent; judicious; just; logical; normal; ordered; philosophical; probable; proper; rationalistic; reasonable; reasoning; restrained; right; sagacious; sane; sapient; sensible; sober; sound; tenable; thinking; thoughtful; understandable; wise

RATTLE: **v.** addle; agitate; annihilate; chatter; clatter; confuse; crepitate; discomfit; discompose; disconcert; distract; embarrass; faze; fluster; gab; rouse; upset; RATTLE: **n.** chatter; clack; clatter; confusion; crepitation; maraca; noise; rack(et); rale; sistrum; toy; uproar

RAUCOUS: cacophonous; dry; hard; harsh; hoarse; husky; loud; raucid; strident; stridulent; unmelodious

RAVAGE: **v.** annihilate; assault; consume; demolish; denudate; depauperate; deplumate; deracinate; desolate; despoil; destroy; devastate; devour; dismantle; eat; exterminate; extinguish; extirpate; harry; havoc; impoverish; loot; overrun; overthrow; pillage; plunder; ransack; raven; raze; rob; ruin; sack; spoil; spoliate; squander; strip; waste; RAVAGE: **n.** assault; demolishment; denudation; depauperation; deplumation; depredation; deracination; despoilment; despoliation; destruction; devastation; dismantlement; extermination; extinguishment; havoc; looting; overthrow; pillage; plunder; rapine; ruin; sacking; spoliation

RAVE: (**see** "rant") blow; bluster; declaim; enthuse; fulminate; fume; rage; rampage; storm; RAVING: (**see** "mad") berserk; delirious; extravagant; frantic; frenzied; fulminating; fuming; incoherent; irrational; maniac(al); rabid; wild

RAVEL: break; crumble; disentangle; disintegrate; entangle; fray; fret; involve; run; sleave; slough; untangle; untwist; unweave; unwind

RAVENOUS: (**see** "greedy") craving; devouring; edacious; ferocious; gluttonous; grasping; insatiable; lupine; miserly; preying; rapacious; voracious; wolfish

RAVINE: arroyo; clough; ditch; gap; glen; gorge; gulch; gully; gut; lin; nullah; valley; wadi; wash

RAVISH: abduct; abuse; allure; bewitch; charm; defile; deflower; despoil; enchant; enthrall; plunder; raid; rape; seduce; seize; snatch; take; violate

RAW (**see** "inexperienced") abraded; *au naturel*; bleak; callow; chafed; chilly; coarse; cold; crude; cutting; damp; earthy; green; harsh; immature; inclement; indelicate; irritated; irritating; lean; naked; new;

nipping; nippy; nude; rare; risqué; rough; rude; sharp; sore; unassimilated; unbound; uncooked; uncorrected; uncultivated; uncured; underdone; underripe; undigested; undressed; unedited; unevaluated; unfair; unhealed; unimproved; unmellowed; unprepared; unprocessed; unrefined; unripe(ned); unseasoned; unskilled; untried; unworked; unwrought; visceral; vulgar

RAY: beam; emanation; gleam; glimmer; light; particle; radiance; shaft; skate; streak trace

RAZE: demolish; deprive; destroy; devastate; dismantle; dismember; divest; effect; erase; level; obliterate; overthrow; prostrate; rescind; ruin; strip; subvert; tear (down); unrig; wreck

RAZZ: (see "ridicule") banter; chaff; deride; needle; taunt; tease; twit

REACH: v. accomplish; achieve; acquire; advene; arrive; attain; carry; come; communicate; compass; cover; deal; deliver; embrace; end; extend; find; finish; fulfill; gain; get; go; grasp; grope; hit; impress; influence; make; meet; obtain; overtake; penetrate; possess; project; run; seize; span; strain; stretch; strike; take; thrust; touch; win; REACH: n. (see "range") area; control; distance; expanse; extent; grasp; jurisdiction; ken; length; orbit; panorama; promontory; radius; scope; span; stretch; view; vista

REACT: see "feel;" REACTION: allergy; backlash; change; counteraction; feel(ing); impression; influence; kick(back); overaction; perception; process; rebound; recoil; reflex; response; return; shock; tendency; tropism; REACTIONARY: see "conservative"

REACTIVATE: (see "revive") convalesce; recrudesce; recuperate; restore; revivify; REACTIVATION: convalescence; recrudescence; recrudescency; recuperation; restoration; resuscitation; revivification

REACTOR: activator; catalyst; reagent

READ: con; decipher; discover; edit; foresee; foretell; indicate; interpret; judge; learn; measure; note; peruse; predict; recite; register; relate; scan; skim; solve; speak; study; understand; READER: anthology; book; elocutionist; lector; lecturer; pr(a)elector; primer; teacher; READABLE: comprehensible; decipherable; interesting; legible; scrutable; understandable

READY: v. see "prepare;" READY: a. adroit; aimed; alert; A-O.K.; apt; arranged; at beck and call; available; cheerful; cocked; compliant; convenient; desirous; dext(e)rous; disposed; eager; easy; en garde; enthusiastic; equipped; expectant; expeditious; facile; fit(ted); fitting; flexible; handy; inclined; liable; likely; lively; nimble; obvious; O.K.; on tap; operational; opportune; preconditioned; preinclined; prepared; prime(d); prompt; proper; quick; resourceful; right; set; simple; speedy; suitable; supplied; swift; unhesitating; unquestionable; waiting; willing; witty; yare; READINESS: alacrity; alertness; aptitude; ease; facility; interest; preparation; preparedness; promptitude; promptness; suitability; tendency

REAL: (see "authentic") absolute; actual-(ized); alive; bona fide; certain; definitive; demonstrable; factual; fair; fundamental; genuine; indisputable; inherent; intrinsic; legitimate; literal; live; living; natural; objective; occurring; official; positival; positive; pure; right; significant; sincere; substantial; substantive; sure; true; ultimate; unaffected; unpresuming; unpresumptuous; unpretended; unpretentious; unquestionable; veritable; REALISTIC: (see "practical") Cartesian; certain; down-to-earth; earthy; everyday; genuine; hard; nontheatrical; sober; tough; unfantastic; unromantic; unsensational; REALLY: absolutely; actually; genuinely; indeed; ma foi!; positively; truly; unquestionably; verily; REALITY: actual(ity); being; Dasein; existent; fact; nature; objectivity; realization; substance; substantiality; verity

REALIZE: (see "comprehend") accomplish; achieve; acquire; actualize; apprehend; complete; conceive; consider; consummate; discern; effect; execute; fulfill; gain; get; grasp; know; learn; obtain; perceive; perfect; recognize; redeem; reflect; see; seize; sense; think; understand; win; REALIZATION: accomplishment; achievement; actualization; apprehension; completion; comprehension; consummation; discernment; fruition; fulfillment; perfection; pleasure; reality; recognition; understanding

REALM: (see "region") area; control; country; department; division; domain; dominion; empire; fief; group; hemisphere; jurisdiction; kingdom; land; people; property; province; range; region; sphere; territory; world

REAM: v. bevel; bore; cheat; countersink;

deepen; enlarge; stretch; victimize; widen; REAM: **n.** lots; measure; paper

REANIMATE: cheer; enliven; liven; pep; rally; recover; recreate; recuperate; reinvigorate; resuscitate; revitalize; revivify

REAP: (**see** "gain") accumulate; acquire; collect; cut; garner; gather; glean; harvest; produce; win

REAR: **v.** boost; breed; build; construct; educate; elevate; erect; establish; foster; instruct; lift; nourish; nurse; nurture; originate; produce; raise; rise; teach; tower; train; upbring; REAR: **a.** abaft; aft(er); astern; back; behind; hind(most); posterior(ly); REAR: **n.** (**see** "rump") buttocks; *derrière*; posterior

REASON: **v.** (**see** "think") argue; conclude; consider; contemplate; contend; controvert; debate; deduce; deliberate; discourse; discuss; explain; expostulate; formulate; infer; influence; intellectualize; logicize; mediate; meditate; persuade; ponder; prove; question; ratiocinate; rationalize; review; speculate; study; talk; REASON: **n.** (**see** "reasoning") aim; argument; basis; brain; cause; comprehension; consideration; contention; dialectic; explanation; faculty; intellect; intelligence; intuition; judgment; justification; logic; mind; motive; noesis; nous; object-(ive); proof; prudence; purpose; question; ratiocination; rationale; rationality; reasonability; reasonableness; sanity; sense; subject; thinking; thought; understanding; wherefore; whyfor; wisdom; wit; REASONABLE: (**see** "rational") acceptable; accountable; agreeable; appropriate; cheap; defensible; due; equitable; fair; fit(ting); honest; inexpensive; judicious; just(ifiable); justified; legitimate; lenient; logical; middling; moderate; modest; politic; probable; proper; prudent; rationalistic; right; sane; sensible; square; tenable; tolerable; tolerant; valid; wise; REASONER: arguer; argufier; dialectician; dialectologist; logician; ratiocinator; rationalist; thinker; REASONING: apprehension; argument(ation); contemplation; debate; dialectics; intellection; logic; ratiocination; speculation; wit; REASONABLENESS; agreeability; cheapness; defensibility; equitability; fairness; honesty; justness; moderation; prudence; sanity; sense; sensibility; tolerance; wisdom

REAVE: break; deprive; despoil; pillage; plunder; remove; rend; rob; seize; tear; unravel

REBEL: **v.** arise; complain; defy; disobey; fight; insurrect; kick; mutiny; oppose; quit; resist; revolt; rise; strike; REBEL: **n.** anarch(ist); dissident; firebrand; frondeur; incendiary; insurgent; insurrectionist; malcontent; mutineer; radical; red; sanculotte; septembrist; striker; REBELLION: contumacy; defiance; disorder; disturbance; hostility; insurrection; mutiny; outbreak; putsch; resistance; revolt; revolution; sedition; treason; tumult; war(fare); REBELLIOUS: (**see** "stubborn") anarchic(al); anarchistic; disaffected; fractious; hostile; insurgent; insurrectionary; malcontent; mutinous; perverse; refractory; revolutionary; riotous; rude; seditious; treasonable; treasonous; turbulent; unyielding; wild

REBORN: redivivus; regenerated; reincarnated; renascent; revived; revivified; REBIRTH: metempsychosis; reincarnation; renaissance; renascence; revival; revivification

REBOUND: **v.** backfire; boomerang; bounce; carom; dap; echo; hop; kick; kiss; leap; react; recoil; recover; reecho; reflect; repercuss; resile; return; reverberate; ricochet; skip; spring; REBOUND: **n.** backfire; boomerang; bounce; carom; echo; hop; kick-(back); kiss; reaction; recoil; recovery; reecho; repercussion; resilience; resiliency; reverberation; ricochet; skip; spring

REBUFF: **v.** censure; check; chide; defeat; rebuke; refuse; reject; repel; repulse; slap; snub; stop; REBUFF: **n.** black eye; censure; check; chide; defeat; refusal; rejection; repellency; repulsion reversal; reverse; setback; slap; snub; tut

REBUKE: **v.** admonish; animadvert; berate; blame; castigate; censure; chasten; chastise; check; chide; criticize; disapprove; lecture; objurgate; rate; rebuff; reprehend; reprimand; reproach; reprove; repulse; scold; slap; snub; stop; tongue-lash; twit; upbraid; vituperate; REBUKE: **n.** admonishment; admonition; animadversion; castigation; censure; chastenment; chastisement; check; comeuppance; criticism; disapproval; lecture; objurgation; rebuff; reprimand; reproof; repulse; scold(ing); slap; snub; tut; REBUKING: admonishing; admonitory; castigatory; chastening; chastising; objurgatory; reprehensive

RECALCITRANT: (**see** "obstinate" and "stubborn") intractable; resistant; unmanageable

RECALL: **v.** abnegate; annul; applaud; cancel; reclaim; recollect; remember; remind; reminisce; repeal; repudiate; respond; restore; retire; retract; review; revive; revoke; summon; withdraw; **RECALL:** **n.** abnegation; annulment; applause; cancellation; encore; recision; recognition; recollection; remembrance; reminiscence; repeal; reproduction; repudiation; rescission; retraction; revival; revocation; summons; withdrawal

RECANT: (**see** "renounce") abjure; abrogate; annul; deny; disavow; disclaim; palinode; repudiate; rescind; retract; revoke; unsay; void; withdraw

RECAPITULATE: describe; rehearse; reiterate; repeat; restate; retrograde; review; sum (up); summarize; synopsize; unite

RECEDE: back (up); backfire; contract; counteract; countermarch; decline; depart; depreciate; deviate; die; diminish; draw (in); dwindle; ebb; fade; fall; go; move; pass; recoil; regress; retire; retrace; retract; retreat; retrocede; retrograde; retrogress; shrink; subside; wane; withdraw; wither; worsen

RECEIVE: accept; accommodate; acquiesce; acquire; admit; adopt; assimilate; attend; bear; believe; catch; collect; consent; contain; derive; earn; entertain; experience; gain; gather; get; glean; greet; harbor; hear; hold; imbibe; include; induct; initiate; intercept; intromit; listen; naturalize; obtain; partake; pocket; procure; reap; see; shelve; submit; suffer; support; sustain; swallow; take; undergo; welcome; yield; **RECEIVING:** receptive; recipient; **RECEIVER:** awardee; bailee; conservator; donee; receptionist; receptor; recipient

RECENT: advanced; contemporary; current; deceased; fresh; inchoate; late(ly); modern(e); near; neoteric; new; novel; topical; young

RECEPTACLE: bag; basket; bin; box; can; carton; case; chest; container; crate; envelope; hamper; hanaper; holder; pan; pot; repository; sack; safe; shelter; urn; utensil; vase; vault; vessel

RECEPTION: acceptance; acceptation; admission; apprehension; approval; assent; at home; collation; conversazione; entertainment; feast; fete; gathering; harbor; harboring; intromission; intuition; levee; ovation; party; reaction; receipt; receptivity; recipience; response; soiree; tea; treat(ment); welcome; **RECEPTIVE:** (**see** "obedient") acceptant; acceptive; elastic; entertaining; recipient; susceptible; susceptive

RECESS: alcove; armistice; bay; break; cavity; cell; cleft; continuance; corner; cove; crypt; enclosure; entr'acte; hiatus; hold; interim; intermission; interval; lull; niche; nook; opening; pause; pocket; recession; respite; rest; retreat; seclusion; sinus; suspension; **RECESSION:** abatement; armistice; declension; decline; decrescence; diminution; hiatus; lull; pause; recedence; recess; retreat; retrocession; suspension; withdrawal

RECHERCHÉ: choice; exotic; exquisite; farfetched; fine; fresh; good; new; novel; precious; rare; uncommon

RECIDIVATE: backslide; lapse; relapse; withdraw; worsen

RECIPE: directions; form(ula); instructions; method; pattern; prescription

RECIPIENT: awardee; bailee; conservator; donee; heir; legatee; receiver; receptionist; receptor

RECIPROCATE: alternate; bandy; change; cooperate; exchange; help; interchange; repay; requite; retaliate; return; share; trade; **RECIPROCAL:** (**see** "mutual") bilateral; common; cooperative; equal; opposite; synallagmatic

RECITE: communicate; count; declaim; deliver; detail; enumerate; list; mouth; narrate; orate; quote; read; recapitulate; recoil; rehearse; relate; renumerate; repeat; report; reproduce; rhetorize; say; speak; state; talk; tell; **RECITAL:** concert; discourse; enumeration; exhibition; litany; musicale; narration; narrative; performance; program; reading; recitation; recitative; rehearsal; relation; repetition; rote; story

RECKLESS: adventurous; audacious; bold; brash; careless; dangerous; daring; dashing; desperate; devil-may-care; excessive; extravagant; foolhardy; foolish; harum-scarum; hasty; headlong; heady; heedless; hell-bent; hotspur; Icarian; impetuous; improvident; imprudent; impulsive; incautious; inconsiderate; indifferent; irresponsible; mad(cap); neglectful; negligent; perdu; precipitate; prodigal; profligate; rash; regardless; *sans attention*; scatterbrained; temerarious; thoughtless; venturesome; venturous;

wasteful; wild; RECKLESSNESS: audacity; daredeviltry; desperation; extravagance; foolishness; improvidence; imprudence; neglect; negligence; prodigality; temerariousness; temerity; thoughtlessness; unwisdom; wastefulness

RECKON: (**see** "think") account; add; assign; attribute; believe; calculate; claim; class(ify); compute; conceive; conclude; consider; count; deem; depend; determine; enumerate; estimate; evaluate; expect; figure; guess; imagine; impute; judge; number; opine; place; pretend; rate; regard; rely; repute; sum (up); suppose; tally; RECKONING: addition; agreement; *agrément*; appraisal; bill; calculation; comeuppance; computation; count; date; determination; payment; penalty; post; recompense; reward; shot; tab; tale

RECLAIM: amend; fix; object; protest; recall; recondition; recover; redeem; reform; refurbish; regenerate; renew; repair; rescue; restore; resuscitate; save; subdue; take; tame; train

RECLINE: (**see** "lie") incline; lean; relax; repose; rest; RECLINING: abed; accumbent; decumbent; prone; reclinate; reclined; recumbent; relaxing; reposing; resting; supine; RECLINATION: accumbency; anaclisis; decubation; decumbency; decubitus; recumbency; supinity

RECLUSE: **a.** anchoristic; ascetic; cloistered; enisled; eremitic(al); hermitic; monastic; remote; removed; sequestered; solitary; RECLUSE: **n.** anchoret; anchorite; ascetic; cenobite; cloisterer; eremite; Essene; friar; hermit; incluse; *inclusus*; monastic; monk; nun; solitudinarian; solivagant;

RECOGNIZE: accept; accredit; acknowledge; admit; apprehend; authorize; commend; concede; correct; credit; discern; distinguish; espy; face; greet; honor; know; legalize; own; note; notice; perceive; praise; realize; remember; respect; revise; salute; sanction; see; spot; tell; RECOGNITION: acceptance; accreditation; accreditment; acknowledgment; admission; admittance; apperception; apprehension; attention; authorization; awareness; concession; credit; discernment; fame; greeting; honor; identification; legalization; memorial; monument; notice; observation; perception; plaque; recall; remembrance; salutation; salute; sanction; sense; tablet; RECOGNIZABLE: cognizable; cognoscitive; discernible; identifiable; visible

RECOIL: **v.** act; balk; blemish; boomerang; bounce; carom; defy; falter; flinch; jump; kick; quail; react; rebound; reecho; reel; reflect; repercuss; resile; retreat; return; reverberate; ricochet; shrink; shy; spurn; start; treat; wince; RECOIL: **n.** boomerang; bounce; carom; defiance; flinch; kick(back); quail; reaction; rebound; reecho; reflection; repercussion; resilience; resiliency; retreat; return; reverberation; ricochet; wince

RECOLLECT: contemplate; meditate; recall; reflect; remember; reminisce; review; RECOLLECTION: anamnesis; autobiography; concentration; contemplation; meditation; memoir(s); memory; rally; recognition; recovery; remembrance; reminiscence

RECOMMEND: advise; approve; back; commend; commit; consign; counsel; endorse; entrust; guarantee; introduce; suggest; support; vouch; RECOMMENDATION: (**see** "counsel") backing; boost; commendation; endorsement; guarantee; pitch; plug; reference; support; testimonial

RECOMPENSE: **v.** compensate; give; hire; pay; reimburse; remunerate; repay; requite; return; reward; RECOMPENSE: **n.** (**see** "salary") amends; compensation; consideration; emolument; fee; guerdon; hire; indemnification; indemnity; meed; merit; payment; quittance; reckoning; reimbursement; remuneration; repayment requital; retribution; reward; wage(s)

RECONCILE: (**see** "atone") accord; adapt; adjust; agree; appease; avert; conciliate; cure; expiate; harmonize; heal; mediate; pacify; placate; propitiate; purge; reconciliate; rectify; restore; reunite; settle; shrive; square; synchronize; syncretize; RECONCILIATORY: appeasing; conciliatory; healing; henotic; syncretistic; RECONCILIATION: (**see** "harmony") accord; amends; appeasement; atonement; eirenicon; expiation; irenicon; penance; propitiation; rapprochement; reconcilement; redemption; reparation; satisfaction; syncretism; understanding

RECONDITE: cabalistic; deep: Delphian; Delphic; difficult; erudite; esoteric; hidden; learned; mysterious; mystic(al); obscure; obtuse; occult; profound; secret; unknown; wise

RECONNOITER: examine; explore; inquire; inspect; look; perambulate; probe; scan; scout; see; spy; survey; test

RECONSIDER: see "reflect"

RECONSTRUCT: (see "renovate") reassemble; rebuild; reconstitute; recreate; reevoke; rehabilitate; reorganize

RECORD: **v.** catalog(ue); chart; chronicle; copy; docket; enroll; enscroll; enter; file; list; log; mark; note; register; remember; score; spread; tabulate; tally; tape; trace; transcribe; write; RECORD(S): **n.** account; achievement; acta (pl.); agenda (pl.); agendum; almanac; annals; archives; biography; blotter; calendar; career; catalog-(ue); chronicle; compendium; copy; course; diary; disk; docket; document(ary); entry; estreat; file; history; inscription; instrument; inventory; journal; legend; life; list; log; mark; memo(randum); memorial; minute; monument; note; notice; performance; platter; policy; register; registry; remembrance; report; roll; schedule; scroll; slate; source; tabulation; tally; tape; text; transcript(ion); writing

RECOUNT: describe; detail; enumerate; itemize; narrate; particularize; recite; reiterate; relate; report; retell; state; tell

RECOVER: amend; collect; cure; deliver; heal; gain; get; improve; mend; offset; overcome; rally; rebound; recapitulate; recapture; reclaim; recollect; recoup; recruit; recuperate; redeem; refind; regain; renew; renovate; repossess; rescue; restore; resume; retake; retrieve; revoke; salvage; win; RECOVERY: collection; convalescence; cure; deliverance; healing; reacquisition; reactivation; rebound; recapture; recoupment; recoverance; recuperation; redemption; renewal; renovation; repossession; rescue; restoration; resumption; retrieval; retrievement; return; revival; revivification; revocation; salvage; upturn

RECREANT: **a.** abject; apostate; base; cowardly; craven; dastardly; faithless; false; low; pusillanimous; renegade; tame; timid; traitorous; treacherous; undependable; unfaithful; untrue; RECREANT: **n.** apostate; backslider; betrayer; coward; craven; dastard; deserter; knave; poltroon; renegade; traitor

RECREATION: see "entertainment" and "play"

RECREMENT: dregs; dross; refuse; scoria; scum; spume

RECRUIT: **v.** assemble; conscribe; conscript; draft; enlist; gather; hire; impress; increase muster; raise; recover; refresh; reinforce; renew; repair; replenish; revive; strengthen; supply; RECRUIT: **n.** beginner; boot; draftee; enlistee; learner; neophyte; newcomer; novice; novitiate; reinforcement; rooky; selectee; soldier; trainee; tyro

RECTIFY: (see "correct") adjust; ameliorate; amend; better; emend; fix; improve; mend; purify; redress; reform; regulate; remedy; repair; restore; revise; right; straighten

RECTITUDE: (see "virtue") correctness; integrity; righteousness; uprightness

RECUPERATE: (see "recover") convalesce; RECUPERATION: convalescence; lysis; recovery; rest(oration)

RECUR: haunt; iterate; persevere; reappear; reiterate; repeat; return; revolve; RECURRENCE: cyclicality; cyclicity; iteration; periodicity; perseveration; recurrency; reiteration; revolution; RECURRING *or* RECURRENT: circular; cyclic(al); inveterate; iterative; perennial; periodic(al); reiterative; repetitive; secular

RED: bloodshot; bloody; blushing; carmine; cerise; cherry; communist; coral; crimson; erythematous; fiery; fired; flagrant; flushed; hectic; magenta; pink; radical; revolutionary; rubescent; rubicund; ruddy; rufescent; russet; REDDISH *or* REDDENED: erubescent; incarmined; incarnadine; rubescent; rubicund; rubious; rufescent; rutilant; REDNESS: erubescence; rubescence; rubicundity; ruddiness; rufescence; rufosity; russet

REDACT: compose; draft; edit; frame; pen; redo; revise; write

REDE: advise; counsel; explain; interpret; plan; relate

REDEEM: absolve; atone; clear; compensate; convert; deliver; expiate; extricate; free; fulfill; justify; liberate; offset; pay; propitiate; prove; purify; ransom; realize; reclaim; recoup; recover; redress; reform; regain; reinstate; release; repair; repossess; repurchase; rescue; restore; retrieve; salvage; satisfy; save; REDEEMABLE: convertible; justifiable; reclaimable; redemptible; redemptive; repairable; restorable; retrievable; savable; REDEMPTION: atonement; conversion; cure; deliverance; expiation; extrication; freedom; redress; reform(ation); release; rescue; restoration

REDOLENT: aromatic; balmy; balsamic; distinctive; evocative; fragrant; odoriferous; reminiscent; rich; scented; spicy; REDOLENCE: aroma; bouquet; fragrance; odor; perfume; scent; smell

REDOUBLE: ingeminate; intensify; reduplicate; reecho; reiterate; renew; repeat; reproduce; retrace

REDOUBTABLE: august; awesome; dread; fearful; fearsome; fierce; formidable; illustrious; imminent

REDRESS: (**see** "remedy") compensate; correct; counteract; cure; fix; neutralize; offset

REDUCE: abase; abate; abbreviate; abridge; allay; alleviate; analyze; assuage; break (down); cheapen; check; compel; concentrate; conciliate; condense; confine; conquer; consolidate; contract; convert; curtail; dampen; debase; debilitate; decimate; decrease; deduct; defeat; degrade; demolish; demote; deoxidize; deprive; derate; devalue; diet; digest; dilute; dim-(inish); discount; disintegrate; divest; downgrade; ease; ebb; eclipse; economize; eliminate; enervate; enfeeble; impair; learn; lessen; lick; limit; lose; lower; make; master; melt; minify; minimize; mitigate; moderate; modify; mute; narrow; overthrow; overturn; palliate; pare; peel; pejorate; play (down); plebify; pulverize; refine; resolve; restore; restrict; shade; shave; shed; shorten; shrink; shrivel; silence; skeletonize; slim; smooth; soften; soft-pedal; subdue; subject; subjugate; surmount; temper; thin; tranquilize; translate; trim; undercut; vulgarize; weaken; whittle; wither; REDUCTION: (**see** "lessening") abatement; abridgement; adaptation; alleviation; analysis; check; conquest; conversion; curtailment; cut; declension; decrease; decrement; deduction; defeat; demotion; devaluation; dilution; diminishment; disintegration; downgrading; ease; economy; effacement; elimination; loss; lowering; meiosis; miniature; minification; minimization; mitigation; moderation; palliation; pejoration; plebification; restriction; shade; shrinkage; slash; softening; subjection; subjugation; subtraction; translation; weakening; vulgarization

REDUNDANT: abundant; copious; *de trop*;

excessive; extra; exuberant; immaterial; lavish; overflowing; pleonastic; plethoric; profuse; prolix; repetitious; spare; superabundant; supererogative; supererogatory; superfluous; supernumerary; surplus; swelling; tautological; tautologous; verbose; wordy; REDUNDANCE *or* REDUNDANCY: ambage; circumlocution; copiosity; evasion; macrology; overabundance; overflow; periphrasis; pleonasm; profusion; prolixity; repetition; superabundance; supererogation; superfluity; surplus; tautology; verbiage; verboseness; verbosity; wordiness

REDUPLICATE: copy; iterate; redouble; reiterate; repeat

REECHO: resound; reverberate; REECHOING: reverberant; reverberative; reverberatory

REED: arrow; culm; grass; pipe; sley; stem; thatch; tule

REEF: atoll; bank; bar; barrier; cay; key; lode; ridge; shoal; spit; vein

REEFER: cigarette; coat; eton; jacket; midshipman; miner; oyster; smoke

REEK: **v.** emanate; emit; exhale; fume; issue; rise; smell; smoke; steam; REEK: **n.** emanation; exhalation; fog; fume; halo; issue; mist; nidor; odor; smell; smoke; steam; stink; vapor

REEL: **v.** falter; recoil; rock; roll; spin; stagger; sway; teeter; totter; waver; wheel; whirl; REEL: **n.** dance; drum; spin; spool; sway; teeter; totter; wavering; wheel; whirl(ing); winch; windlass

REESTABLISH: (**see** "restore") refound; resettle; REESTABLISHMENT: (**see** "restoration") apocatastasis; rapprochement; reacquisition; recuperation; resettlement

REFER: advert; allude; appeal; apply; ascribe; assign; attribute; charge; cite; concern; consign; consult; direct; impute; mention; pertain; point; quote; recommend; regard; relate; resort; send; submit; turn; REFERABLE: ascribable; assignable; attributable; imputable; pertinent; referential; REFERENCE(S): allusion; bibliography; commendation; credentials; denotation; manual; meaning; mention; recommendation; relation; respect; testimonial(s)

REFEREE: adjudicator; arbiter; arbitrator; judge; moderator; official; ump(ire)

REFINE: alembicate; attenuate; chasten; civilize; clarify; clean(se); concentrate; cultivate; debarbarize; defecate; depurate; domesticate; edit; educate; elevate; exalt; expurgate; file; finish; garble; groom; improve; instruct; interpret; perfect; polish; prepare; process; purify; rarefy; reduce; smelt; smooth; spiritualize; subtilize; treat; REFINED: (see "polished") alembicated; attenuated; civilized; cleansed; concentrated; courteous; cultivated; cultured; dainty; delicate; diplomatic; elegant; ethereal; exact; exalted; fastidious; gentle; mannerly; perceptive; perfected; polite; precise; rare-(fied); *recherché*; subtle; tactful; terse; unvulgar; well-bred; well-spoken; REFINEMENT: alembication; artistry; attenuation; breeding; civilization; concentration; courtesy; cultivation; culture; delicacy; diplomacy; discrimination; education; elegance; exaltation; expertise; finesse; gentility; gentleness; grace; humanization; instruction; manners; perception; perfection(ment); poise; polish; politeness; preciosity; precision; quality; rarefaction; subtlety; tact; training; virtuosity

REFLECT: (see "rebound") bend; censure; cogitate; concentrate; conclude; consider; contemplate; copy; debate; deliberate; discredit; echo; examine; excogitate; express; gather; glance; glare; ideate; imagine; imitate; meditate; mirror; muse; perpend; philosophize; ponder; pore; ratiocinate; realize; reason; recollect; reconsider; reecho; remember; repeat; reproach; resolve; rethink; return; reverberate; revolve; ruminate; shine; show; signify; skip; speculate; study; suspect; theorize; think; weigh; REFLECTIVE: (see "meditative") cogitative; deliberative; ratiocinative; ruminant; thinking; thoughtful; REFLECTION: (see "thought") aspersion; blame; censure; cogitation; contemplation; criticism; disparagement; echo; fold; ghost; idea(tion); image; imputation; introspection; likeness; meditation; perpension; ratiocination; repetition; reproach; shadow; thought

REFORM: amend; chasten; convert; correct; emend; freshen; houseclean; improve; mend; rectify; refurbish; remodel; reorganize; restore; revise; REFORMATION: conversion; emendation; housecleaning; redemption; renovation; restoration; revision

REFRACTORY: (see "stubborn;) bellicose; cantankerous; contrary; disobedient; headstrong; immune; incorrigible; insusceptible; intractable; mulish; mutinous; obstinate; perverse; rebellious; reluctant; resistant; restive; sullen; unchangeable; uncooperative; unmanageable; unresponsive; unruly; unwilling; willful

REFRAIN: v. abstain; avoid; cease; desist; forbear; leave; omit; pause; spare; stop; REFRAIN: n. abstention; aria; avoidance; burden; chorus; song

REFRESH: animate; brace; cheer; cool; encourage; energize; enliven; exhilarate; fan; fortify; freshen; invigorate; liven; quicken; recreate; refocillate; reform; regale; reinvigorate; relieve; renew; renovate; replenish; rest(ore); revive; revivify; stimulate; strengthen; vitalize; vivify; REFRESHING: animating; bracing; crisp; encouraging; enervating; enlivening; exuberant; fragrant; heartening; hearty; invigorating; nourishing; oasitic; recreating; reinvigorating; roborant; stimulating; strengthening; tonic; vigorous; zestful; REFRESHMENT(S): collation; drink; food; exhilaration; invigoration; lunch(eon); meal; oasis; reanimation; recreation; regeneration; reinvigoration; relief; repast; rest(oration); revivification; stimulation; tea; treat; vigor; vitality; zest

REFUGE: altar; anchorage; ark; asylum; church; cove; cover; covert; den; fastness; fort(ress); harbor; haven; home; lair; nest; oasis; port; protection; recourse; refreshment; relief; resource; retirement; retreat; safety; sanctuary; sanitarium; seclusion; security; shade; shadow; shelter; solitude; stronghold; umbrage

REFUND: v. indemnify; kick back; offset; rebate; recompense; reimburse; remunerate; repay; requite; restitute; restore; return; REFUND: n. indemnification; kickback; rebate; reimbursement; repayment; restitution; restoration; return

REFURBISH: (see "renew") brighten; freshen; renovate; repair; repristinate

REFUSE: v. abandon; decline; deny; disallow; disavow; disown; fail; rebuff; reject; renege; renounce; repel; repudiate; repulse; resign; revoke; spurn; withhold; REFUSE: n. (see "waste") ashes; bran; carrion; chaff; clinkers; coom(b); debris; dejecta (pl.); detritus; dregs; dross; ejecta(menta) (pl.); garbage; glumes; grounds; hulls; husks; junk; leavings; lees; litter; offal; offscourings; ort(s); rabble; rejecta(menta) (pl.); remains;

residuals; residue; residuum; rubbish; scoria (pl.); scourings; scrap(s); scum; silt; slag; sullage; trash; wash; waste; REFUSAL: abnegation; declension; denegation; disavowal; disclaimer; dismissal; negative; rebuff; rejection; renouncement; repudiation; stoppage; unwillingness

REFUTE: confute; deny; disprove; expose; invalidate; overthrow; rebut; repeal; REFUTING: anatreptic; elenc(h)tic; refutative; refutatory; REFUTATION: confutation; denial; disproof; elenchus

REGAIN: **see** "recover"

REGAL: august; baronial; grand(iose); imperial; imposing; Junoesque (fem.); kingly; magnificent; majestic; noble; purple; queenly; royal; splendid; stately; statuesque; sublime

REGALE: amuse; banquet; delight; dine; divert; entertain; feast; feed; fete; gratify; please; refresh; treat; wine

REGALIA: (**see** "finery") war paint

REGARD: **v.** admire; appreciate; approve; attend; behold; care; cherish; concern; consider; contemplate; deem; esteem; estimate; evaluate; exalt; eye; favor; figure; find; gaze; heed; honor; infer; judge; keep; love; like; look; mark; mind; note; notice; obey; observe; pertain; praise; prize; rate; reck(on); refer; relate (to); remark; respect; revere; scrutinize; see; think; treat; understand; value; view; REGARD: **n.** (**see** "admiration") affection; appreciation; approbation; approval; care; concern; consideration; cordiality; cordialness; devotedness; devotion; dignity; esteem; estimation; *estime*; exaltation; favor; gaze; glance; greetings; heed; homage; honor; look; love; motive; notice; observation; praise; relation; respect; reverence; understanding; value; warmth; worth

REGENERATE: (**see** "renew") recreate; reform

REGENT: deputy; director; governor; head; instructor; master; official; professor; ruler; superintendent; supervisor; viceroy; warden

REGIME(N): administration; course; diet; government; hygiene; measure; plan; regulation; remedy; rule; system

REGION: affairs; area; arena; beat; belt; circuit; clime; contour; country; demesne; district; division; domain; dominion; environment; experience; field; heath; hemisphere; jurisdiction; kingdom; land; locale; locality; location; milieu; orbit; part; planet; plateau; portion; position; precinct; province; purlieu; quarter; range; realm; section; sector; society; space; sphere; subdivision; terrain; territory; topography; tract; ward; world; zone

REGISTER: **v.** chart; convey; correspond; enroll; enter; impress; index; indicate; list; mark; matriculate; record; tally; REGISTER: **n.** annals; archives; blotter; book; chart; chronicle; index; list; record(s); roster; rota; table; tally; tariff

REGRESS: abate; ebb; recidivate; relapse; retrograde; retrogress; reverse; sink; withdraw; REGRESSION: abatement; ebb(ing); recession; recidivation; recidivism; relapse; retrogradation; retrogression; return; reversal; reversion; withdrawal

REGRET: **v.** bewail; cry; deplore; disappoint; grieve; lament; moan; mourn; repent; repine; rue; sorrow; trouble; worry; REGRET: **n.** (**see** "guilt") attrition; compassion; compunction; concern; conscience; contrition; cry; demur; dissatisfaction; grief; lamentation; longing; misgiving; pain; pang; penitence; pity; qualm; reluctance; remorse; repentance; repining; rue; sadness; scruple; sorrow; trouble; unease; uneasiness; woe; worry; REGRETFUL: anxious; compassionate; compunctious; contrite; crying; deplorable; deprecative; distressful; distressing; lamentable; penitent(ial); qualmish; reluctant; remorseful; repentant; repining; rueful; sad(dened); sorry; uneasy; unfortunate; woeful; REGRETTABLE: (**see** "deplorable") misfortunate; unlucky

REGULAR(LY): accustomed; authorized; clocklike; common(place); complete; congruent; consistent; conventional; correct(ly); customary; duly; equiangular; equilateral; established; familiar; first-string; fixed; frequent; full; general; habitual; harmonious; invariable; isometric; lawful(ly); methodical; metronomic(al); normal; orderly; periodic(al); precise; prevalent; proper(ly); recurrent; rhythmic(al); set(tled); shipshape; standard; stated; successive; symmetric(al); synchronous; systematic(al); thorough(ly); typical; undeviating; uniform; unmitigated; unswerving; unusual; wonted; REGULARITY: clockwork; meter; normality; normalness; order(liness); periodicity; rhythm-

(icity); synchroneity; synchronism; system; uniformity

REGULATE: adjust; arrange; check; choose; clock; conduct; control; curb; curtail; direct; dispose; fix; gauge; govern; guide; limit; manage; master; measure; methodize; moderate; monitor; order; organize; pace; prescribe; reconcile; regularize; repress; restrain; rule; set; shape; square; standardize; superintend; supervise; systematize; time; REGULATION: **see** "rule"

REHABILITATE: **see** "restore"

REHASH: **v.** redo; refurbish; renovate; restate; summarize; REHASH: **n.** *réchauffé*; renovation; restatement; summarization

REHEARSE: coach; describe; drill; enumerate; narrate; portray; practice; prepare; recapitulate; recite; recount; relate; repeat; report; retell; say; train; REHEARSAL: **see** "repetition"

REIGN: **v.** (**see** "control") exist; govern; influence; predominate; prevail; rule; REIGN: **n.** (**see** "control") authority; domination; dominion; government; influence; power; prevalence; rule; sovereignty; sway; term; REIGNING: controlling; dominant; existent; existing; governing; prevailing; prevalent; regnant; ruling

REIMBURSE: (**see** "refund") compensate; indemnify; offset; pay; recompense; recoup; remunerate; repay; requite; restore

REIN: **v.** check; control; curb; restrain; slow; stop; REIN(S): **n.** check(s); control(s); haunches; leashes; license; loins; restraint; scope; swing

REINCARNATION: metempsychosis; palingenesis

REINFORCE: bolster; combine; double; encourage; fortify; harden; increase; invigorate; prop; recruit; shore; stay; steel; strengthen; support; REINFORCEMENT: brace; food; fortification; help; invigoration; prop; recruitment; stay; succor; support

REINSTATE: rehire; reinstall; renew; replace; restore; revest

REINVIGORATE: **see** "renew"

REITERATE: drum; echo; hammer; harp;

recapitulate; reduplicate; rehearse; repeat; restate

REJECT: abhor; abjure; avoid; blackball; cancel; cashier; cast; decline; defy; deny; disallow; discard; dismiss; eject; eliminate; exclude; forsake; forswear; jilt; negate; negative; ostracize; oust; rebuff; refuse; repel; repudiate; repulse; rescind; resist; return; scorn; scout; shed; shun; spurn; veto; void; vomit; REJECTION: abdication; banishment; collapse; denial; denigration; disallowance; disavowal; disclaimer; disclamation; dismissal; elimination; exclusion; expulsion; ostracism; rebuff; recision; refusal; relegation; renunciation; repudiation; repulse; rescission; return; sack; scorn; turndown

REJOICE: celebrate; cheer; delight; elate; enrapture; exhilarate; exuberate; exult; gladden; gloat; glory; jubilate; please; revel; REJOICING: **a.** (**see** "happy") carnivalesque; exuberant; festive; jubilant; mirthful; rejoiceful; REJOICING: **n.** (**see** "happiness") celebration; cheer; delight; exuberance; exuberation; exultation; festivity; glee; glory; jubilation; mirth(fulness); rejoicement

RELAPSE: **v.** backslide; ebb; lapse; recidivate; regress; retrocede; retrograde; retrogress; sink; slip; subside; worsen; RELAPSE: **n.** backslide; declination; ebb(ing); palindromia; recidivation; recidivism; recrudescence; recurrence; regression; retrocession; RELAPSING: palindromic; recidival; recidivous; regressive; retrocessive; retrogressive

RELATE: (**see** "tell") account; affiliate; apply; concern; connect; describe; detail; enumerate; join; league; link; narrate; pertain; recite; recount; refer; regard; rehearse; report; state; touch; unite; utter; RELATED: affiliated; affirmative; agnate; agnatic; akin; allied; analogous; ancillary; applicable; apposite; associated; auxiliary; belonging; cognate; common; comparative; congeneric; congenerous; connected; consanguineous; correlative; corresponding; germane; kin(dred); leagued; material; matrilateral; matrilineal; matrilinear; near; patrilineal; patrilinear; pertaining; pertinent; relevant; satellite; satellitic; septal; synonymous; told; umbilical; RELATION: account; agnate; bond; chronicle; cognate; cognati (pl.); cognatus; congenator; congener; congeneric; connection; heir(ess); kin(dred); kinsman; kinswoman; narration; narrative; next of kin; parent; pertinence; ration; recital;

reference; relative; respect; sib(ling); story; RELATIONSHIP: affairs; affiliation; affinity; agnation; association; bond; cognate; cognati (pl.); cognation; cognatus; consanguinity; contact; dealings; filiation; footing; implication; involvement; juxtaposition; kinship; liaison; narration; narrative; reference; relative; relativity; respect; scale; standing; status; syngenesis; RELATIVE: **a.** (**see** "related") anent; applicable; approximate; comparative; corresponding; in re; pertaining; pertinent; relevant; RELATIVE: **n. see** "relation"

RELAX: abate; assuage; bask; calm; divert; ease; lessen; loosen; lull; mitigate; moderate; open; recreate; relent; relieve; remit; rest; slacken; soften; stop; unbend; unbrace; unclench; unclinch; unlax; unstrain; unstretch; weaken; RELAXED: (**see** "comfortable") abated; assuaged; dormant; eased; immobile; mitigated; moderated; placid; restful; slackened; softened; tranquil; unhurried; weakened; RELAXATION: abatement; assuagement; calm(ness); cessation; comfort; detachment; *détente*; disengagement; diversion; ease; entertainment; laxation; leisure; letup; looseness; peace-(fulness); placidity; quiet(ude); recreation; release; relief; remission; repose; rest; slack-(ening); tranquility

RELEASE: **v.** abreact; absolve; acquit; actuate; deliver; detach; discharge; disconnect; disengage; dispatch; drop; ease; emancipate; emit; except; excuse; exempt; extricate; forgive; free; initiate; liberate; loose(n); open; parole; quash; quit; relax; relent; relieve; relinquish; remise; remit; resign; rest; shed; spread; surrender; transmit; trigger; trip; unbind; unburden; uncage; unchain; unconfine; uncork; uncouple; undo; unfurl; unpen; unrestrain; untie; unwedge; unyoke; ventilate; RELEASE: **n.** absolution; acquittal; acquittance; actuation; deliverance; discharge; disengagement; ease; emancipation; excuse; exemption; extrication; freedom; freeing; initiation; liberation; loosening; outlet; parole; quash; quitclaim; relaxation; relief; relinquishment; remise; rest; salvation; surrender; trigger; unbinding; unrestraint; ventilation

RELENT: abate; bow; defer; dissolve; ease; ebb; forbear; forgive; give; melt; moderate; modify; mollify; relax; slacken; soften; submit; subside; thaw; wane; yield; RELENTLESS: fierce; hard; immovable; implacable; inexorable; inflexible; merciless;

obdurate; pitiless; rigid; rigorous; ruthless; savage; stern; strict; stringent; unyielding

RELEVANT: *ad rem*; allied; anent; applicable; apposite; appropriate; apropos; apt; associated; cognate; commensurate; competent; congruous; connected; correspondent; fit(ting); german(e); *in re*; material; pertaining; pertinent; proper; proportional; proportionate; relating; relative; suitable; RELEVANCE: applicability; aproposity; aptness; commensurability; competency; congruency; homogeneity; materiality; pertinence; proportion; relevancy; respect; suitability

RELIABLE: absolute; assured; attached; believable; certain; conclusive; consistent; decisive; dependable; devoted; faithful; incontestible; incontrovertible; indubitable; leal; loyal; positive; prudent; solid; steady; sure; tried; true; trustful; trusted; trustworthy; undeniable; undoubted; unequivocal; unquestionable; worthy; RELIABILITY: authenticity; believability; credence; credibility; credibleness; dependability; devotion; loyalty; solidity; trustability; trustfulness; trustworthiness; truth(fulness)

RELIANCE: assurance; belief; confidence; conviction; credence; credit; dependability; dependence; dependency; expectation; faith; guarantee; guardianship; hope; loyalty; mainstay; optimism; security; trust; tutelage

RELIC(S): antiques; antiquity; corpse; curio; fragment; keepsake; leavings; memento; memorial; monument; remains; remnant; residue; residuum; ruins; skeleton; souvenir; token; trace

RELIEVE: aid; allay; alleviate; assist; assuage; clear; comfort; cure; deliver; deprive; diminish; discharge; disembarrass; ease; empty; end; exonerate; extricate; free; furnish; help; improve; indemnify; lessen; lighten; loose(n); mitigate; moderate; open; quench; redress; reduce; refresh; relax; release; remedy; replace; rescue; rest; rid; right; rob; soothe; succeed; succor; sustain; temper; unburden; unlock; RELIEF: aid; alleviation; amusement; anodyne; antidote; assistance; assuagement; balm; *bon secours*; comfort; consolation; deliverance; diminishment; discharge; distraction; diversion; dole; ease; entertainment; escape; exoneration; extrication; food; freedom; help; improvement; indemnification; lessening; lightening; maintenance; mitigation; moderation; nourishment; oasis; palliation; redress; reduction; refreshment; relaxation; release; relinquishment; remedy; remission; replacement; reproval; rescue; rest; sharpness; solace; succor; support; sustenance; vividness; warmth

RELIGION(S): belief; church; clericalism; communion; credo; creed; cult; culture; deism; denomination; devotion; devotedness; devoutness; ecclesiasticism; faith; fold; godliness; observance; persuasion; pietism; piety; reverence; sanctity; sect; tenet; theology; trust; veneration; worship; RELIGIOUS: churchy; devotional; devout; divine; ecclesiastical; evangelistic; fervent; godlike; godly; Jehovistic; orthodox; pietistic-(al); pious; religiose; sacred; sacrosanct; sanctified; sanctimonious; spiritual; theopathic; zealous

RELINQUISH: abandon; abdicate; abjure; cast; cede; demit; desert; desist; disappear; disclaim; forego; forsake; forswear; leave; let; quit; part; recant; release; renounce; resign; retire; retreat; secede; separate; shed; stop; surrender; vacate; vanish; waive; withdraw; yield

RELISH: (see "enjoy") appetite; appetizer; appreciation; condiment; dash; delight; élan; enjoyment; fancy; flavor; gratification; gusto; *hors d'oeuvre*; inclination; liking; partiality; piquancy; pleasure; predilection; sauce; savor; spice; stomach; tang; taste; trace; zest

RELUCTANT: (see "averse") *à contre coeur*; adverse; afraid; backward; chary; demurring; discouraged; disinclined; grudging; hesitant; indisposed; loath; obstinate; opposed; opposing; passive; recalcitrant; refractory; remiss; resisting; shy; slack; slow; tardy; undisposed; uneager; unwilling; unwishful; wary

RELY: await; bank; base; believe; confess; confide; commit; consign; count (on); depend; entrust; expect; hang; hinge; hope; impart; lean; predicate; reckon; repose; rest; share; tell; trust; turn

REMAIN: **v.** (see "stay") abide; bide; continue; dwell; endure; exist; last; linger; lodge; lurk; outlast; outlive; pause; persist; prevail; prolong; protract; reside; rest; stand; subsist; survive; tarry; wait; REMAIN(S) **n.** or REMAINDER: arrear(s); ash(es); balance; bit; bone(s); cadaver; *caput mortuum*; corpse;

debris; detritus; dregs; dust; end(s); estate; excess; fossils; fragment(s); ghost; heel; leavings; lees; leftover(s); magma; oddment(s); offscourings; ort(s); overage; part; piece; rag; refuse; relic(s); remnant; residua (pl.); residue; residuum; rest; ruins; rump; scoria; scrapings; scraps; scum; sediment; shard; suggestion; surplus; trace; vestige; vestigia (pl.); vestigium; waste

REMARK: **v.** (see "say") annotate; assert; asseverate; comment; discern; express; gloss; heed; note; notice; observe; perceive; see; state; talk; utter; REMARK(S): **n.** advice; annotation; assertion; asseveration; comment(ary); expression; item; mot; notice; observation; oration; retort; sally; speech; statement; talk; utterance; words

REMARKABLE: (see "extraordinary") discernible; noticeable; signal; significant; uncommon

REMEDY: **v.** abate; adjust; aid; compensate; correct; cure; doctor; fix; heal; medicate; mend; neutralize; patch; physic; rectify; redress; relieve; repair; restore; reward; right; REMEDY: **n.** abatement; action; aid; alterative; antidote; antitoxin; application; arcanum; correction; corrective; counteraction; cure; dose; draught; drug; elixir; embrocation; help; herb; law; lotion; medicament; medicine; pill; placebo; preparation; prescription; redress; relief; remediation; repair; reparation; restoration; restorative; simple; specific; stimulant; stomachic; therapeutic(s); therapy; tolerance; tonic; REMEDIAL: ablative; clinical; correctional; corrective; curative; healing; herbal; lenitive; medicamentary; medicamentous; medicative; medicinal; panacean; remediable; reparable; restorative; salubrious; salutary; salutiferous; sanable; sanatory; therapeutic(al)

REMEMBER: bethink; cogitate; commemorate; consider; mark; meditate; memorialize; mention; mind; monumentalize; muse; place; recall; recite; recollect; record; reflect; reminisce; reproduce; retain; reward; think; REMEMBRANCE: commemoration; commendation; consideration; cup; curio; gift; keepsake; medal; memento; memorial; memory; monument; recall; recollection; reminder; reminiscence; reproduction; retrospect; reward; souvenir; tablet; thought; token; trophy; REMEMBERING: anamnesis; reminiscence; REMEMBERED: commemorated; memoried; memorized

REMIND: (see "remember") bug; jog; jostle; nag; nudge; REMINDER: (see "remembrance") amulet; cue; hint; memento; memo(randum); mention; note; phylactery; prod; remembrancer; souvenir; string; touch

REMINISCENCE: (see "remembrance") anamnesis; evocation; feuilleton; memorabilia (pl.); memoir(s); recall

REMISS: (see "careless") backward; delinquent; derelict; dilatory; idle; inattentive; indolent; languid; lax; lazy; lenient; loose; malfeasant; misfeasant; neglectful; negligent; shiftless; slack; slow; thoughtless; unmindful; REMISSION: abatement; abeyance; armistice; cancellation; carelessness; delinquency; deliverance; dereliction; forgiveness; idleness; inattention; indolence; laxity; laziness; looseness; malfeasance; misfeasance; negligence; pardon; recess; relaxation; relief; relinquishment; suspension

REMIT: abate; absolve; acquit; alleviate; annul; cancel; convey; defer; excuse; exonerate; forgive; forward; mitigate; moderate; pardon; pay; postpone; relax; release; remand; rend; send; transfer; transmit

REMNANT(S): (see "remains") aftertaste; rag; tab

REMODEL: see "renovate"

REMONSTRATE: (see "scold") animadvert; blame; censure; chide; criticize; deprecate; disapprove; disparage; expostulate; object; objurgate; oppose; protest; recriminate; reprimand; reproach; scoff; upbraid

REMORSE: (see "grief") compassion; compunction; contrition; distress; penitence; pity; qualm; regret; repentance; rue; self-reproach; sorrow; REMORSEFUL: (see "regretful") compunctious; contrite; penitent; rueful; sorrowful; REMORSELESS: see "cruel"

REMOTE: abroad; abstracted; accidental; afar; alien; aloof; ancient; antipodean; apart; away; chancy; devious; distant; divergent; extraneous; extringent; far(-off); forane; foreign; hoary; inaccessible; indirect; interior; irrelevant; isolated; obscure; odd; off; old; outer; outlying; out-of-the-way; outside; overseas; past; recluse; removed; secluded; secret; segregated; separate(d); slight; solitary; stale; superfluous; tramontane; transmontane; ulterior; ultimate; ultramontane; ultramundane; unconnected; unessential; unrelated; utmost; REMOTENESS: see "distance"

REMOVE: ablate; abolish; abstract; assassinate; bench; brush; cancel; cashier; castrate; change; cover; cut; dele(te); depart; deport; depose; deprive; destroy; detach; dethrone; disappear; discard; dislocate; dismiss; displace; doff; drop; eject; eliminate; emasculate; empty; eradicate; erase; evacuate; excise; export; exterminate; extirpate; extract; fire; isolate; kill; lift; lop; mitigate; move; obliterate; oust; pare; part; peel; pluck; prune; rend; replant; rescind; resect; retire; retreat; rid; rob; sack; segregate; separate; sequester; sever; shift; shunt; steal; strip; supersede; sweep; swipe; switch; tear; transfer; transplant; transport; uncouple; unhook; unhorse; uproot; upset; vacate; winnow; withdraw; wrench; REMOVAL: ablation; abolishment; abstraction; clearance; debridement; deletion; deprivation; dismissal; displacement; ejectment; elimination; eradication; erasure; evacuation; expurgation; extermination; extraction; isolation; migration; obliteration; ouster; relief; retirement; retreat; riddance; segregation; separation; sequestration; severance; shift; supersedence; supersedure; supersession; sweep; switch; transfer(ence); transferral; translation; transplantation; transportation; vacation; withdrawal

REMUNERATE: (see "compensate") recompense; reimburse; repay; satisfy; settle; REMUNERATION: bounty; compensation; emolument; fee; honorarium; pay(ment); recompense; reimbursement; requital; reward; satisfaction

REND: break; burst; chop; cleave; crack; disintegrate; divide; do; fracture; lacerate; mangle; pierce; remove; rip; rive; rupture; separate; sever; shatter; split; sunder; tear; uproot; wrench; wrest

RENDER: administer; apportion; assign; bestow; clarify; construe; contribute; deliver; depict; dispense; dissolve; distribute; echo; execute; explain; express; extract; form; furnish; give; impart; interpret; make; melt; pay; perform; play; present; provide; recite; record; reflect; repay; report; requite; restore; return; reword; save; send; specify; state; surrender; translate; transmit; try; yield

RENDEZVOUS: appointment; date; engagement; gathering; haunt; meeting (place); refuge; resort; retreat; tryst

RENEGADE: (**see** "traitor") apostate; deserter; escapee; rat; rebel; turncoat

RENEW: continue; enliven; freshen; intensify; mend; reanimate; reassume; reawaken; rebuild; recharge; recommence; recreate; recrudesce; redouble; reestablish; reform; refresh; regenerate; reinstate; reinvigorate; rejuvenate; renovate; repair; repeat; replace; replenish; repristinate; restore; resume; resuscitate; revigorate; revise; revivify

RENOUNCE: abandon; abdicate; abjure; abnegate; abrogate; apostasize; cede; concede; deny; desert; disavow; disclaim; disown; forego; forsake; forswear; give up; leave; quit; recant; refuse; reject; relinquish; remit; renege; renounce; repudiate; rescind; resign; retract; revoke; revolt; spurn; tergiversate; waive; RENUNCIATION: abjuration; abnegation; abrogation; apostasy; desertion; disavowal; disclaimer; quittance; recantation; recision; rejection; renouncement; repudiation; rescission; retraction; revocation; sacrifice; tergiversation

RENOVATE: (**see** "renew") alter; fix; make over; mend; modernize; overhaul; patch; polish; recondition; reconstruct; redo; refresh(en); refurbish; regenerate; remodel; repair; repristinate; restore; revamp; revive

RENOWN: (**see** "fame" and "honor") acclaim; distinction; eminence; kudos; luster; reputation

RENT: **v.** charge; hire; lease; let; rend; rupture; tear; RENT: **a.** hired; let; ripped; ruptured; split; torn; RENT: **n.** income; hire; hole; revenue; rip; rupture; slit; tax; tear; toll; tribute

REPAIR: (**see** "remedy" and "renovate") darn; doctor; fix; mend; modernize; overhaul; paste; patch; recondition; reconstruct; redeem; refix; regenerate; remodel; renew; replenish; repristinate; resort; restore; restyle; reword; service

REPARATION: amends; atonement; balm; compensation; damages; expiation; indemnification; indemnity; overhaul; pay(ment); propitiation; recompense; reconditioning; redress; rehabilitation; remodeling; remuneration; renovation; repair; requital; restitution; restoration; retribution; return; reward; satisfaction; service

REPARTEE: banter; humor; irony; rejoinder; reply; retort; riposte; sally; satire; wit

REPAST: (**see** "food") banquet; drink; eating; entertainment; feast; feed; lunch; meal; tiffin; treat; viands; victuals

REPAY: avenge; compensate; indemnify; meed; pay; reciprocate; recompense; refund; reimburse; remunerate; requite; retaliate; retort; return; reward; satisfy

REPEAL: **v.** (**see** "cancel") abandon; abolish; abrogate; annul; obrogate; recall; renounce; rescind; retract; revoke; void; REPEAL: **n.** abolishment; abrogation; annulment; cancellation; obrogation; recall; recision; renunciation; rescission; revocation

REPEAT: ape; battologize; cite; din; ditto; divulge; duplicate; echo; emphasize; encore; hammer; harp; imitate; ingeminate; iterate; mimic; quote; recapitulate; recite; recur; redo; redouble; reduplicate; rehearse; reiterate; replicate; reproduce; restate; retall; return; reverberate; reword; sing; summarize; tell; REPETITION: alliteration; anaphora; battology; copy; ditto; duplication; echo; emphasis; encore; ingemination; iteration; mention; perseverance; pleonasm; recapitulation; recital; redundancy; reduplication; rehearsal; reiteration; replica(tion); reproduction; reverberation; summarization; summary; tautology; verbigeration; REPETITIOUS *or* REPEATING: alliterational; alliterative; battological; echoic; frequentative; imitative; iterative; monotonous; perseverant; prolix; redundant; reduplicative; reiterative; repetitional; repetitive; replicate; routine; stereotyped; stereotypical; tautologic(al); tautologous; translating

REPEL: beat; check; discourage; disgust; disperse; fence; fend; fight; nauseate; oppose; parry; protect; rebuff; refuse; reject; repulse; resist; revolt; scatter; sicken; stop; vanquish; ward (off)

REPENT: (**see** "regret") atone; grieve; rue; REPENTANCE: (**see** "regret") atonement; contrition; grief; penitence; sadness; sorrow; REPENTANT: (**see** "regretful") contrite; penitent(ial); remorseful; rueful; sad(dened); sorry

REPETITION: **see** under "repeat"

REPINE: (**see** "grieve") complain; fret; grumble; lament; languish; moan; mope; mourn; rue; wish

REPLACE: alternate; change; displace; exchange; interchange; rearrange; reconstitute;

reconstruct; refill; refund; reinstate; relieve; remove; renew; repair; replenish; reset; restock; restore; substitute; succeed; supersede; supplant; supply

REPLENISH: (see "replace") add; fill; freshen; hire; nourish; recruit; refill; renew; restock; restore; stock

REPLETE: abounding; abundant; bloated; charged; complete; copious; fat; filled; full; glutted; gorged; lousy; rich; sated; stout; stuffed; surfeited; teeming; REPLETION: fullness; glut; plethora; profusion; satiety

REPLICA: bis; carbon (copy); copy; diminutive; duplicate; ectype; facsimile; image; painting; photo(graph); picture; reproduction; sculpture; statue

REPLY: v. agree; answer; ape; atone; conform; confute; correspond; counter(act); defend; do; echo; explain; fulfill; imitate; meet; pay; rebut; rejoin; repeat; replicate; report; resound; respond; retaliate; retort; return; reverberate; satisfy; REPLY: n. action; agreement; answer; antiphon; atonement; comeback; conformation; conformity; correspondence; counter(action); counterstatement; defense; echo; explanation; fulfillment; letter; note; payment; plea; rebuttal; rejoinder; repartee; replication; *réplique*; report; response; result; retaliation; retort; return; reverberation; satisfaction; solution; speech

REPORT: v. announce; apprise; arrive; broadcast; bruit; cable; chronicle; communicate; cover; cry; declare; describe; detail; disclose; dispatch; express; impart; inform; mention; narrate; noise; note; notify; promulgate; pronounce; publish; recite; record; relate; rumor; specify; state; talk; tell; warn; wire; write; REPORT: n. (see "noise") account; advisory; announcement; appraisal; bang; broadcast; bruit; cable; cahier; canard; card; character; chronicle; communication; cry; declaration; description; detail; dispatch; explosion; fame; findings; gossip; hearsay; information; intelligence; message; narration; narrative; news(cast); noise; note; notification; pop; pronouncement; recital; recitation; record; relation; reputation; repute; rumor; rundown; statement; story; submission; summary; survey; tale; talk; telegram; tidings; wire

REPOSE: v. compose; confide; lie; place; recline; relax; rely; reside; rest; sit; sleep; slumber; trust; REPOSE: n. calm(ness); cessation; comfort; composure; confidence;

death; ease; easiness; harmony; inactivity; intermission; laxation; leisure; pacification; peace(fulness); poise; quiescene; quiet(ude); reclination; relaxation; requiescence; respite; rest; sereneness; serenity; sleep; slumber; tranquility; trust

REPREHENSIBLE: (see "bad") blamable; censurable; condemnable; culpable; damnable; notorious; obnoxious; odious; reprovable; vicious; wicked; wrong

REPRESENT: act; betoken; delineate; depict; describe; display; draw; emblematize; exemplify; exhibit; fashion; figure; give; illustrate; imitate; limn; mimic; mirror; model; personate; picture; portray; present; produce; protest; sample; service; show; sketch; speak; symbolize; typify; warrant; REPRESENTATIVE: a. collective; emblematic(al); illustrative; model; sample; symbolic(al); typical; typifying; REPRESENTATIVE: n. agent; ambassador; champion; congressman; delegate; deputy; diplomat; emissary; envoy; legate; minister; proxy; salesman; sample; specimen; substitute; surrogate; vicar; REPRESENTATION: agency; commission; copy; delegation; delineation; depiction; description; drawing; effigy; exemplification; exhibit(ion); expostulation; guarantee; guaranty; illustration; interpretation; likeness; mimicry; mirror; model; personation; personification; picture; plan; portrait; portrayal; remonstrance; sample; sham; sketch; substitution; theme; travesty; type; typification; warranty

REPRESS: (see "check") bridle; conquer; control; crush; curb; grind down; inhibit; overcome; overpower; prevent; quell; rein; restrain; silence; stifle; subdue; suppress; swallow; tread; understate; REPRESSED: bridled; checked; controlled; crushed; curbed; inhibited; latent; restrained; silent; stifled; subdued; suppressed; REPRESSION: (see "oppression") compression; constraint; control; inhibition; lid; restraint; subjection; suppression

REPRIEVE: (see "respite") commutation; pardon; remission

REPRIMAND: v. admonish; berate; blame; censure; chasten; chastise; chew out; chide; discipline; eat out; lecture; punish; rate; rebuke; reprehend; reproach; reprove; scold; skin; slate; spank; upbraid; REPRIMAND: n. admonishment; call-down; censure; chastisement; dressing down; earful; lecture; music; punishment; rebuke; reproach; reproof; scolding; spanking; talking to; task

REPROACH: **v.** abuse; accuse; admonish; berate; blame; castigate; caution; censure; chasten; chastise; chide; condemn; criticize; discredit; disparage; objurgate; rate; rebuke; reprehend; reprimand; reprove; scold; shame; snub; stigmatize; taunt; tongue-lash; twit; vituperate; REPROACH: **n.** abuse; accusation; admonishment; admonition; bar sinister; blame; castigation; caution; censure; chastenment; chastisement; chide; condemnation; contumely; criticism; disapproval; discredit; disesteem; disgrace; disparagement; ignominy; invective; objurgation; odium; opprobrium; rebuke; reprehension; reprimand; reproof; scolding; setdown; shame; snub; spot; stigma; taunt; twit; upbraiding; vituperation

REPROBATE: **see** "dissolute", "immoral" and "scoundrel"

REPRODUCE: (**see** "duplicate") generate; photograph; portray; recite; remember; spawn; REPRODUCTION: (**see** "replica") abiogenesis; accrementition; agamogenesis; amphigony; autogenesis; carbon copy; copy; counterpart; duplicate; duplication; ectype; facsimile; photo(graph); picture; protogenesis; recall; reconstruction; record; regeneration; revival; syngamy; syngenesis; transcript(ion); REPRODUCTIVE: creative; fertile; gestational; gestative; progenitive

REPROOF: (**see** "reproach") censure; objurgation; rebuke; reprimand; scolding; setdown; snub; vituperation; REPROVE: **see** "reproach;" REPROVING: admonitory; castigatory; chastening; condemnatory; disparaging; ignominious; odious; reprehensible

REPTILE: **a.** crawling; creeping; despicable; groveling; low; malignant; mean; ophidian; reptant; reptilian; reptiloid; serpentiform; REPTILE: **n.** (**see** "snake") alligator; amphibian; crocodile; frog; knave; lizard; newt; ophidian; reptilian; snake; toad; viper; worm

REPUDIATE: abandon; abjure; abolish; abrogate; annul; cancel; countermand; debar; decline; defy; deny; desert; disaffirm; disavow; discard; disclaim; dismiss; disown; divorce; dodge; exclude; expel; leave; null-(ify); quash; recall; recant; refuse; reject; renounce; renunciate; repeal; rescind; return; reverse; revoke; spurn; vacate; void;

REPUDIATION: abandonment; abjuration; abolishment; abrogation; cancellation; countermand; denial; desertion; disaffirmance; disaffirmation; disavowal; disclamation; dismissal; divorce; exclusion; nullification; recision; refusal; rejection; renunciation; rescission; revocation; vacation; vōidance

REPUGNANT: (**see** "hateful") abominable; bitter; despicable; dirty; distasteful; fulsome; grisly; gruesome; incompatible; inconsistent; loathsome; lousy; nasty; objectionable; odious; offensive; opposed; rebarbative; repulsive; sickening; smelly; sordid; sour; squalid; squeamish; stingy; ugly; unfriendly; unpalatable; unsavory; REPUGNANCE *or* REPUGNANCY: abhorrence; antagonism; antipathy; aversion; despicability; disgust; dislike; distaste; hate; hatred; horror; hostility; incompatibility; incongruity; inconsistency; loathing; loathsomeness; odium; offense; offensiveness; opposition; repulsion; repulsiveness; revulsion; sordidness; squeamishness

REPULSE: beat; defeat; disgust; foil; rebuff; refuse; reject; repel; REPULSIVE: (**see** "hateful" and "repugnant") abominable; despicable; dirty; fulsome; greasy; grisly; gritty; loathsome; lousy; nameless; nasty; objectionable; odious; offensive; sickening; sordid; squalid; ugly; unsavory; unwholesome; REPULSION: aversion; despicability; disgust; dislike; hate; hatred; repugnance; repugnancy; repulsiveness; revulsion; sordidness; squalidity; squalor

REPUTE: (**see** "reputation") character; credit; distinction; fame; flavor; honor(ableness); odor; renown; word; REPUTED: **see** "so-called;" REPUTABLE: (**see** "honorable") dependable; estimable; prestigious; reliable; respectable; trustworthy; REPUTATION: (**see** "fame") celebrity; character; credit; distinction; éclat; esteem; estimation; flavor; glory; honor(ableness); laurels; merit; name; note; odor; prestige; renown; repute; trust; weight; word; worthiness

REQUEST: **v.** (**see** "appeal") adjure; apply; ask; beg; beseech; demand; direct; entreat; importune; invite; order; petition; plead; pray; seek; solicit; sue; supplicate; tell; REQUEST: **n.** (**see** "appeal") application; demand; direction; entreaty; invitation; order; petition; plea; prayer; rogation; solicitation; suit; supplication

REQUIRE: ask; behoove; call; claim; command; compel; crave; demand; desire; dictate; engage; enjoin; exact; force; hire; hold; impose; insist (upon); involve; lack; levy; necessitate; need; tax; want; wish; REQUIRED: (see "imperative") coercive; compelling; compulsory; deontic; *de rigueur*; essential; indispensible; lacking; mandatory; needful; obligatory; prerequisite; requisite; supposed; wanted; wanting; REQUIREMENT: command; compulsion; condition; essential(ity); exigency; indispensibility; lack; mandate; necessity; need; occasion; precedent; precondition; prerequisite; prius; requisite; *sine qua non*

REQUISITE: (see "due" and "requirement") essential; indispensable; necessary; needful

REQUITE: atone; avenge; compensate; ease; exchange; lull; pay; punish; quiet(en); quit; reciprocate; recompense; remunerate; remedy; render; repay; retaliate; return; reward; satisfy; settle; solicit; soothe; REQUITAL: see "wage"

RESCIND: abolish; abrogate; annul; cancel; discard; dissolve; lift; quash; recall; recant; reject; repeal; reverse; revoke; vacate; void

RESCUE: v. aid; deliver; emancipate; extricate; free; help; liberate; manumit; preserve; ransom; recapture; reclaim; recover; redeem; release; relieve; reprieve; retake; retrieve; revivify; salvage; save; RESCUE: n. deliverance; delivery; emancipation; extrication; freedom; help; liberation; manumission; preservation; ransom; recoverance; redemption; retaking; revivification; succor

RESEARCH: v. analyze; assay; attempt; consider; demonstrate; endeavor; examine; exercise; experience; experiment; explore; feel; inquire; investigate; ponder; practice; probe; question; scrutinize; search; study; test; try; venture; RESEARCH: n. analysis; assay; attempt; demonstration; endeavor; examination; exercise; experiment(ation); exploration; inquest; inquiry; investigation; ordeal; practice; probe; proof; quest; scrutiny; search; study; test; trial; undertaking; venture

RESEMBLANCE: affinity; agreement; analogue; analogy; appearance; approximation; assonance; caricature; copy; counterpart; duplicate; effigy; equality; equivalence; facsimile; image; likeness; match; nearness; parallel(ism); parity; photo(graph); picture; portrait; replica; representation; reproduction; ringer; semblance; shape; similarity;

simile; similitude; simulation; simulacrum; synonymity; twin; uniformity; verisimilitude; verisimility; RESEMBLE: see "simulate"

RESENTMENT: (see "hate") acrimony; anger; animosity; animus; annoyance; asperity; bad blood; bile; bitterness; choler; dander; deploration; displeasure; dudgeon; envy; gall; grudge; hatred; hostility; huff; hurt; indignation; irascibility; ire; irritation; jaundice; jealousy; offense; outrage; pique; prejudice; rancor; spleen; umbrage; vexation; wrath; RESENTFUL: belligerent; bitter; envious; hurt; jealous; mad; sore; umbrageous

RESERVE: v. cache; defer; deposit; hide; hold; keep; retain; save; spare; stock; store; withhold; RESERVE: n. ace in the hole; apathy; backlog; caution; coldness; constraint; decency; detachment; diffidence; dignity; exception; forbearance; fund; gravity; ice; inventory; log; modesty; money; poise; qualification; reservation; reservoir; resource(s); restraint; restriction; retardation; reticence; salt; savings; self-control; self-constraint; self-restraint; shyness; silence; skepticism; spare; standby; stock; storage; store; strength; supply; surplus; taciturnity; thrift; unsociability; vitality; RESERVED: aback; alone; aloof; apart; apathetic; bashful; cautious; chary; circumspect; close; cold; conditioned; cool; coy; delitescent; demure; detached; diffident; distant; egocentric; frigid; frosty; gelid; icy; incommunicable; incommunicative; indrawn; kept; modest; moodish; noncommittal; off(ish); on ice; only; passionless; phlegmatic(al); proud; remote; removed; restrained; retarded; retentive; reticent; retiring; secluded; secretive; self-restrained; sequestered; shy; silent; skeptical; stately; strange; taciturn; timid; unapproachable; unappropriated; uncommunicative; undemonstrative; unemotional; unfriendly; unsociable; withdrawn

RESERVOIR: bank; basin; cache; cavity; cistern; cupboard; depository; pond; pool; reserve; store(house); sump; supply; tank; treasure; treasury

RESIDE: (see "live") abide; bide; domicile; domiciliate; dwell; inhabit; inhere; lie; lodge; occupy; put; remain; repose; room; roost; settle; sit; sojourn; stay; stop; tenant

RESIDENCE: (see "house") abode; domicile; dwelling; establishment; habitation; home; housing; inhabitance; inhabitancy; inhabitation; lodging; mansion; occupancy; office;

residency; seat; stay; RESIDENT: **a.** dwelling; firm; fixed; indwelling; inherent; innate; present; residing; seated; RESIDENT: **n.** burgess; burgher; cit(izen); domicile; dweller; habitué; householder; inhabitant; inhabitress; lessee; occupant; tenant

RESIDUE: (**see** "waste") ash(es); cinders; dregs; excess; exudate; gum; heel; leavings; lees; orts; relics; remainder; remains; remnant; residual; residuum; rest; scum; sediment; shard; silt; slag; sludge; soot; sordes; surplus; tar

RESIGN: abandon; abdicate; abjure; acquiesce; cede; commit; consign; demit; disaffiliate; dis(a)ssociate; forego; foreswear; leave; quit; release; relegate; relinquish; renounce; retire; secede; submit; surrender; vacate; waive; withdraw; yield; RESIGNATION: abandonment; abdication; acquiescence; defeatism; disaffiliation; disaffirmation; di-(sa)ssociation; humility; obedience; obeisance; passivity; patience; relinquishment; renouncement; renunciation; retirement; submission; submissiveness; surrender; yield-(ing)

RESILIENT: (**see** "elastic" and "flexible") buoyant; live; rubbery; springy; RESILIENCE *or* RESILIENCY: (**see** "flexibility") bounce; buoyancy; elasticity; plasticity; spring(iness); temper; tone; yield

RESIST: (**see** "fight") bear; combat; contend; contest; defeat; defend; defy; disobey; face; fend; foil; frustrate; meet; oppose; prevent; refuse; reject; repudiate; repugn; rival; stand; tolerate; vie; withstand; RESISTANT: (**see** "stubborn") close-minded; disobedient; immune; incompliant; obstinate; recalcitrant; refractory; resisting; stout; sturdy; unmanageable; unresponsive; RESISTANCE: (**see** "stubbornness") defense; friction; hardness; hostility; immunity; limitation; load; rebellion; rigidity; severity; stability; stand; steadfastness; steadiness; sturdiness

RESOLUTE: (**see** "resistant" and "stubborn") bold; brave; confident; constant; decided; decisive; determined; dogged; faithful; firm; fixed; game; gritty; hard; indomitable; inflexible; intransigent; leal; loyal; manly; obstinate; peremptory; persevering; positive; resolved; rigid; stalwart; sta(u)nch; steadfast; steady; stiff; stout(hearted); sturdy; true; unbendable; unbending; uncompromising; undaunted; undismayed; unflinch-

ing; unshaken; unswerving; unwavering; valiant; RESOLUTION *or* RESOLUTENESS: analysis; boldness; bravery; certainty; confidence; constancy; courage; decision; decisiveness; deliberateness; disentanglement; doggedness; energy; fortitude; grit; guts; indomitability; loyalty; manhood; mettle; obstinacy; opinion; perseverance; pluck; proposal; purpose; resoluteness; resolve; result; sand; scheme; separation; spirit; stamina; starch; steadfastness; strength; topic; undauntedness; vigor(ousness); will

RESOLVE: **v.** adjust; amortize; analyze; clear; conclude; consummate; decide; decompose; determine; disintegrate; dispel; end; intend; lapse; liquidate; mean; pay; plan; reduce; rid; sell; separate; settle; solve; split (up); unravel; unriddle; RESOLVE: **n.** (**see** "resolution") purpose; RESOLVED: see "determined"

RESONANT: consonant; echoing; orotund; plangent; resounding; reverberatory; ringing; silvery; sonorant; sonoriferous; sonorous; tonal; tympanic; vibrant; RESONANCE: empathy; orotundity; plangency; rapport; sonority; sound; timbre; tone

RESORT: **v.** apply; go; refer; repair; try; use; RESORT: **n.** abode; aid; assemblage; beach; beat; company; den; dive; haunt; help; hotel; inn; joint; lodge; mountains; ocean; purlieu; range; recourse; refuge; resource; retreat; seashore; shift; shore; spa; throng

RESOUND: burst; celebrate; clang; detonate; echo; explode; extol; fulminate; peal; pop; proclaim; reecho; reverberate; ring; roar; RESOUNDING: (**see** "resonant") emphatic; forceful; plangent; reverberatory; ringing; roaring; unequivocal

RESOURCE(S): ammunition; assets; bag of tricks; bonds; capability; contrivance; credits; deposits; device; equipment; estate; expedience; expediency; expedient; faculty; funds; investments; machinery; makeshift; means; money; products; property; purse; reserve; resort; revenue; savings; shift; skill; stocks; stopgap; stratagem; strength; substitute; supply; surrogate; wealth

RESOURCEFUL: apt; artistic; clever; creative; cunning; endowed; fertile; imaginative; ingenious; innovative; inventive; sharp

RESPECT: **v.** (**see** "esteem") admire; adore; awe; devote; dote; face; favor; fear; front;

heed; honor; look; observe; regard; revere-
(nce); stellify; value; venerate; worship;
RESPECT(S): **n.** (**see** "esteem") admiration; adoration; approbation; awe; *baisemains* (pl.); concern; consideration; deference; deferentiality; detail; devoir; devotion; dignity; duty; fealty; fear; genuflexion;
heed; homage; honor; izzat; loyalty; notice
obedience; obeisance; obsequiousness;; obsequity; particular; prestige; regard; relevance;
reverence; stellification; value; veneration;
way; worship; worth; RESPECTED *or*
RESPECTABLE: (**see** "honorable") creditable; estimable; honored; illustrious; presentable; prestigious; reputable; time-
honored; venerable; well-beloved; RESPEC-
TABILITY: creditability; estimability;
prestige; reputability; veneration; RE-
SPECTFUL: amenable; decorous; defer-
ent(ial); honorable; obeisant; reverent(ial);
tractable; venerative

RESPIRE: breathe; exhale; inhale; live;
oxidate; suspire

RESPITE: (**see** "break") armistice; cessation;
commutation; deferment; delay; *entr'acte*;
fast; forbearance; halt; intermission; interruption; interval; lull; pause; postponement;
recess; recreation; reprieve; rest; stay; stop;
surcease; suspension; truce

RESPLENDENT: (**see** "bright") aureate;
brilliant; dazzling; effulgent; fulgid; glittering; glorious; gorgeous; grand; luminous;
lustrous; radiant; shining; splendent; splendid; splendiferous; splendorous; superb;
RESPLENDENCE: **see** "luster"

RESPOND: (**see** "answer") bid; echo; feel;
follow; react; rejoin; reply; write; RE-
SPONSE: (**see** "answer") anthem; antiphon;
echo; kick(back); letter; output; reaction;
reception; rejoinder; reply; retort; reverberation; ricochet; RESPONSIVE: amenable; antiphonal; echoic; impressionable;
liable; reactive; sensible; sensitive; subject;
susceptible; tender; tractable

RESPONSIBLE: (**see** "answerable") accountable; amenable; capable; chargeable; creditable; explainable; liable; presentable;
reliable; solvent; subject; trusted; trustworthy; RESPONSIBILITY: (**see** "duty")
accountability; amenability; ball; burden;
care; charge; domain; job; jurisdiction;
liability; load; mission; obligation; office;
onus; position; reliability; solvency; sphere;
task; trust; trustworthiness; vocation

REST: **v.** abide; base; cease; discontinue;
ease; ground; halt; idle; laze; lean; lie;
loll; nap; pause; perch; recline; refresh;
relax; rely; remain; repose; settle; sit;
sleep; slumber; stay; stop; trust; unbend;
REST: **n.** (**see** "respite") armistice; base;
caesura; calm(ness); cessation; comfort;
death; discontinuance; dormancy; ease; end;
excess; freedom; halt; immobility; immobilization; inaction; inactivity; intermission;
interval; latency; leisure; lodging; lull; nap;
pause; peace(fulness); perch; quiescence;
quiet(ude); recess; recreation; refreshment;
relaxation; release; remainder; repose; seat;
serenity; shelter; siesta; silence; sleep;
slumber; stay; stillness; stop; support;
surplus; tranquility; RESTFUL: calm; comfortable; easy; placid; quiet; relaxed; reposeful; serene; soothing; tranquil; RESTING:
abed; asleep; dead; dormant; idle; inactive; incumbent; latent; leaning; quiescent;
quiet; procumbent; sessile; sleeping; supine

RESTAURANT: bistro; cafe(teria); chop-
house; coffeehouse; diner; eatery; estaminet;
luncheonette; steakhouse; tearoom

RESTITUTION: (**see** "restoration") apocatastasis; indemnification; indemnity; reparation; repayment; reinstatement; return

RESTIVE: (**see** "restless") balky; fidgety;
fractious; impatient; inflexible; persistent;
stubborn

RESTLESS: (**see** "anxious") agitated; agitato;
annoyed; averse; changeable; changeful;
churning; discontented; disobedient; disquiet; disturbed; energetic; erethic; fidgety;
fitful; fractious; fretful; frisky; hectic; impatient; impetuous; intractable; insubordinate;
itchy; moodish; moody; mulish; mutinous;
nervous; obstinate; peeved; perverse; rattled; rebellious; recalcitrant; refractory;
reluctant; resentful; riotous; skittish; sleepless; spasmodic; splenetic; stubborn; trembling; tremulous; unceasing; uneasy; ungratified; unruly; unsettled; untranquil; wakeful; RESTLESSNESS: agitation; annoyance; anxiety; aversion; disquietude; dyspathy; dysphoria; energy; fitfulness; impatience; impetuosity; impetuousness; inquietude; insubordination; intractability; mood-
ishness; mulishness; mutiny; nervousness;
rebellion; refractoriness; sleeplessness; stir;
stubbornness; uneasiness; unruliness; wakefulness

RESTORE: cure; fix; heal; mend; reactivate;
reanimate; reawaken; recover; recreate;

rectify; redecorate; redeem; redo; reduce; reestablish; reform; refresh; refund; regain; rehabilitate; reinstate; reinstitute; reinvigorate; rejuvenate; renew; renovate; repair; repay; replace; repristinate; rescue; resettle; reshape; restitute; resuscitate; return; revive; revivify; right; save; set; stet; RESTORATION: instauration; reanimation; recession; reconstruction; redemption; reestablishment; refreshment; refurbishment; rehabilitation; reimbursement; reinstatement; reinstitution; reinvigoration; rejuvenation; rejuvenescence; renewal; reparation; repristination; restitution; resurgence; resurgency; resuscitation; revitalization; revivescence; revivification; RESTORED: reconditioned; redivivus; refurbished; reinvigorated; rejuvenated; renewed; repristinated; resuscitated; revitalized; revivified; whole; RESTORING: analeptic; invigorating; rejuvenating; rejuvenescent; restorative; resuscitative; roborant; tonic; RESTORATIVE: **see** "cure", "curable" and "remedy"

RESTRAIN: abridge; arrest; awe; bar; bate; bind; block; bottle; bridle; cage; censure; check; choke; circumscribe; coarct; confine; constrain; contract; control; cope; cramp; crib; curb; damp(en); debar; demarcate; deny; deter; discipline; dissuade; encircle; enjoin; enslave; exclude; fasten; fence; fetter; gag; grab; halt; hamper; handcuff; hinder; hold; impede; imprison; inhibit; interdict; jail; keep; lash; leash; limit; manacle; moderate; muzzle; overcome; penalize; pin; prevent; punish; quarantine; rein; repress; restrict; rivet; separate; shackle; silence; sink; snaffle; snub; squelch; stay; stem; still; stop; subordinate; suppress; temper; tether; throttle; tie; trammel; understate; withhold; RESTRAINED or RESTRAINING: Apollonian; Apollonic; Apollonistic; balanced; bound; caged; captive; circumscribed; confined; constricted; cramped; disciplined; discreet; dispassionate; harmonious; inhibited; inhibitory; low-key(ed); moderate; modest; orderly; patient; rational; restricted; restrictive; retentive; self-controlled; severe; sober; stultified; subdued; temperate; tied; uncomplaining; unemancipated; unexpansive; RESTRAINT or RESTRICTION: absentation; abstinence; bind; bit; captivity; censure; check; circumscription; circumspection; coarctation; coercion; compression; confinement; constraint; constriction; continence; control; curb; denial; deterrence; deterrent; discipline; discouragement; discretion; durance; duress; economy; embargo; extenuation; fetter(s); force; gag; golden

mean; hamper(ing); handcuffs; hindrance; impediment; inhibition; interdiction; law; limitation; manacle; measure; moderateness; moderation; monopoly; obligation; order; patience; prudence; quaratine; repression; reserve; restriction; retention; retentive; reticence; sanction; self-control; self-denial; shackle; silence; simplicity; stay; stint; taboo; tabu; temperance; tie; trammel; understatement; writ

RESTRICT: (**see** "restrain") ban; bar; bind; check; choke; circumscribe; coarct; coerce; confine; constrain; contract; cramp; crimp; curb; delimit(ate); diminish; discipline; fence; fetter; hamper; handcuff; hinder; impede; inhibit; isolate; limit; modify; narrow; number; pen; prohibit; qualify; reduce; repress; restrain; separate; stifle; stint; straiten; tie; RESTRICTED or RESTRICTIVE: abbreviated; abridged; circumscribed; circumstrictive; cloist(e)ral; cloistered; close-quarter(ed); colytic; detached; exclusive; inhibited; inhibitory; insulated; isolated; limited; parochial; peninsular; provincial; severe; sheltered; specific; strict; truncated; RESTRICTION: (**see** "restraint") ascription; censure; check; circumscription; coarctation; coercion; confinement; constraint; constriction; delimitation; disability; discrimination; disqualification; exception; exclusion; hamper(ing); inhibition; limitation; line; manacle; qualification; reduction; restraint; sanction; striction; stricture

RESULT: **v.** accrue; arise; close; conclude; effect; end; ensue; eventuate; finalize; finish; follow; grow; hap(pen); issue; occur; originate; proceed; rise; spring; terminate; RESULT(S): **n.** after effect; aftermath; child; conclusion; consequence; decision; denouement; echo; effect; effort; end; essay; event(uality); experience; finalization; fruit; fruition; happening; impact; issue; loss; outcome; proceeding; product; profit; progeny; purpose; reaction; repercussion; residual; residuum; resolution; score; sequel; sequela; sum; termination; total; training; turnout; upshot; work

RESUME: continue; epitomize; recommence; reiterate; renew; reoccupy; reopen; repeat; retake; summarize

RÉSUMÉ: abridgement; abstract; compendium; epitome; recapitulation; summary; syllabus; synopsis

RETAIL: (**see** "sell") barter; distribute;

hawk; peddle; relate; repeat; retell; trade; vend

RETAIN: absorb; assimilate; bind; clutch; continue; detail; economize; employ; engage; enjoy; grasp; hire; hold; husband; imbibe; keep; last; maintain; own; postpone; preserve; prevent; recollect; remember; reserve; save; secure; soak (up); RETAINER: employment; engagement; fee; servant

RETAINERS: adherents; attendants; claque; clique; company; cortege; crew; dependents; employees; entourage; escorts; family; followers; gang; hirelings; maintainers; mercenaries; minions; parade; procession; retinue; servants; staff; suite; tail; train

RETALIATE: see "punish" and "reciprocate;" RETALIATION: (see "penalty") comeuppance; Nemesis; punishment; reciprocation; redress; reprisal; requital; retortion; retribution; return; revenge; reward; riposte; talion; vengeance

RETARD: v. arrest; balk; blunt; brake; check; choke; clog; cramp; crawl; damp(en); dawdle; deaden; decrease; defer; delay; drag; fetter; hamper; handcuff; hinder; impede; inch; inhibit; interrupt; keep (back); lag; lengthen; lessen; obscure; obstruct; postpone; prevent; procrastinate; protract; pull; repress; restrain; slacken; slow; stop; stunt; suspend; RETARDED: arrested; backward; balked; checked; clogged; cramped; dark; decreased; delayed; fettered; hampered; handcuffed; hindered; impeded; inhibited; interrupted; kept; lessened; limited; obstructed; primitive; repressed; restrained; slackened; slowed; stunted; unrefined; RETARD(ATION): n. arrest; backwardness; check; clog; decrease; delay; doldrums; hampering; hindrance; impediment; inhibition; interruption; lag; obstacle; obstruction; postponement; procrastination; repressing; restraint; retardment; slack; slowness; slump; suppression; suspension

RETENTIVE: close; grasping; gripping; parsimonious; restrained; restraining; reticent; saving; stingy; tenacious; RETENTIVENESS: retentivity; tenacity

RETICENT: brachysyllabic; dumb; laconic; reserved; restrained; retentive; secret; silent; speechless; tacit(urn); uncommunicative; untalkative; unwordy; RETICENCE: laconism; reserve; retentiveness; retentivity; secrecy; taciturnity

RETINUE: (see "retainers") attendance; attendants; company; cortege; crew; entourage; escort; family; followers; gang; servants; staff; suite; tail; train

RETIRE: go; leave; lie; recall; recede; redeem; resign; retreat; shrink; sleep; superannuate; withdraw; RETIRED: abed; asleep; cloisteral; cloistered; closeted; emeritus; en retraite; gone; hidden; hors de combat; inactive; lone; obscured; otiose; quiet; remote; removed; reserved; secluded; secret; sequestered; sleeping; solitary; superannuated; withdrawn; RETIRING: (see "humble" and "shy") modest; reserved; sensitive; shrinking; unassertive; unassuming; RETIREMENT: (see "seclusion") ease; grass; pasturage; superannuation

RETORT: v. answer; quip; repay; reply; retaliate; return; RETORT: n. alembic; answer; crucible; mot; quip; remark; repartee; reply; retaliation; ripost(e); rise; sally; witticism

RETRACE: backtrack; backtrail; duplicate; perseverate; recall; recollect; reiterate; reminisce; repeat; retell

RETRACT: (see "withdraw") abandon; abjure; abrogate; annul; cancel; deny; disavow; disclaim; disown; forswear; gainsay; nullify; palinode; recall; recant; recede; renounce; repeal; repudiate; rescind; reverse; revoke; withdraw; RETRACTION: abandonment; abjuration; cancellation; denial; disavowal; disclaimer; nullification; palinode; recall; recantation; revocation; withdrawal

RETREAT: v. (see "withdraw") backtrack; backtrail; crawfish; escape; leave; recede; relinquish; remove; retire; retract; RETREAT: n. altar; arbor; ark; asylum; back track; den; cape; castle; citadel; cover; harbor; haven; hermitage; home; lair; nest; nook; port; privacy; recess(ion); redoubt; refuge; relinquishment; resort; retiral; retirement; retraction; retrogression; rout; safety; sanctuary; sanctum; seclusion; shade; shelter; solitude; tower; villeggiatura; withdrawal

RETRENCH: (see "curtail") abridge; clip; cut; decrease; diminish; dock; economize; eliminate; excise; lessen; obtruncate; omit; pare; prime; reduce; remove; save; shorten; truncate

RETRIBUTION: (see "penalty") compensation; correction; last judgment; Nemesis; payment; punishment; recompense; redress;

reparation; repayment; reprisal; requital; restitution; retaliation; return; revenge; reward; talion; vengeance

RETRIEVE: correct; find; recoup; recover; recruit; recuperate; refind; regain; remedy; repair; repossess; rescue; restore; revise; salvage; save

RETROACTIVE: *ex post facto*; *nunc pro tunc*; prior

RETROGRADE: **v.** backslide; decline; degenerate; deteriorate; lapse; recapitulate; recede; regress; relapse; retreat; retrogress; revert; sink; slide; slip; slow; worsen; RETROGRADE: **a.** backward; catabolic; decadent; degenerated; deteriorated; inverse; inverted; opposed; rearward; retreating; retrogressed

RETROGRESS: **see** "retrograde"

RETURN: **v.** answer; ebb; pay; react; reappear; rebound; reciprocate; recoil; recompense; recur; reelect; reflect; reject; remand; repay; reply; repudiate; requite; respond; restore; retaliate; retort; revert; revisit; revive; yield; RETURN(S): **n.** answer; dividend(s); proceeds; profit(s); reaction; reappearance; rebate; reciprocation; reciprocity; recoil; recompense; recovery; recurrence; recursion; reelection; remand; repayment; repetition; reply; response; restitution; restoration; retaliation; retort; retribution; reversion; revisit; riposte; yield(ing)

REVEAL: **(see** "air") bare; bespeak; betray; communicate; disburden; disclose; discover; display; divulge; evince; exhibit; expose; foretell; impart; inform; manifest; occasion; open; portend; promulgate; provoke; publicize; publish; show; squeal; tell; unclose; uncover; uncurtain; unmask; unscreen; unveil; unwrap; REVELATION: apocalypse; disclosure; discovery; divulgation; divulgement; divulgence; exposé; gospel; manifestation; oracle; prophecy; revealment; vision; REVELATIVE: apocalyptic; epiphanic; heuristic; revelatory; REVEALING: betraying; diaphanous; expressive; informative; informing; oracular; prophetic; talebearing; telltale

REVEL: **v.** apricate; bask; carouse; celebrate; delight; feast; luxuriate; riot; roister; royster; wallow; wassail; REVEL(RY): **n.** carnival; carousal; carousing; celebration; conviviality; delight; ecstasy; entertainment; feast; festivity; lark; merrymaking; orgy;

party; revelment; revelry; riot; saturnalia; spree; wassail; REVELROUS: **(see** "gay") loud; noisy; roistering; roisterous

REVELATION: **see** under "reveal"

REVENANT: **(see** "ghost") apparition; eidolon; gospel; oracle; phantom; specter; spirit; spook; wraith

REVENGE: **v.** afflict; avenge; chastise; discipline; penalize; punish; repay; requite; retaliate; retort; vindicate; visit; REVENGE: **n.** affliction; avengement; chastisement; discipline; Nemesis; penalty; punishment; reciprocation; redress; reprisal; requital; retaliation; retortion; retribution; riposte; satisfaction; talion; vengeance; vindication; vindictiveness; REVENGEFUL: grudgeful; malevolent; malicious; punitive; rancorous; resentful; retaliative; vengeful; vindicative; viperish; vituperative

REVENUE: annuity; assets; bonds; collection; credits; customs; duties; earning(s); excises; fruits; funds; income; interest; load; means; money; pay; proceeds; produce; profits; receipts; rentals; rents; resources; results; return(s); salary; stipend; stocks; taxes; tithes; wages; wealth; yield

REVERE: **(see** "worship") admire; adore; canonize; cherish; defer; deify; esteem; hallow; honor; idealize; idolize; love; pedestal; prize; respect; reverence; stellify; venerate; REVERENCE: **(see** "worship") admiration; adoration; awe; bow; clergyman; deference; dread; esteem; estimation; exaltation; fear; homage; honor; idealization; idolization; piety; regard; religion; respect; stellification; tetragrammation; veneration; worship; REVERENT *or* REVERENTIAL: **(see** "religious") deferential; pious; tetragrammatous; venerative; worshipful

REVERIE: abstraction; dream; fancy; fantasy; impracticality; muse; notion

REVERSE: **v.** about-face; about-turn; alter; annul; back(water); cancel; commutate; defeat; disaffirm; invert; nullify; overthrow; overturn; regress; repeal; repudiate; rescind; retract; revoke; subvert; transpose; undo; unravel; upset; vacate; void; wheel; REVERSE **n.** *or* REVERSAL: about-face; adversity; annulment; anticlimax; atavism; back(lash); backup; backwardness; bouleversement; cancellation; change; check; contrary; converse; *culbuteur*; defeat; disaffirmance; disaffirmation; hap; inversion; jolt; metathesis; misfortune; mishap; mutation; obverse; opposite; overthrow; overturning; rear; rebuff; repeal; recision; regression; repudiation; rescission; retraction; reversement; revocation; setback; shake-up; transposition; trial; turnabout; turnover; undoing; upset; version; *volte-face*; REVERSION: atavism; escheat; lapse; mutation; relapse; remainder; return; sport; throwback

REVERT: (**see** "reverse") advert; annul; escheat; invert; lapse; recur; relapse; return; revest; revoke; undo

REVIEW: **v.** analyze; commentate; consider; criticize; edit; examine; hash (over); inspect; look; ponder; reason; recapitulate; reconsider; reexamine; rehearse; restudy; retrace; speculate; study; survey; REVIEW: **n.** (**see** "survey") analysis; comment; criticism; critique; look(-see); recapitulation; reconsideration; rehearsal; revision; study

REVILE: (**see** "berate") abuse; asperse; criticize; needle; rail; scold; score; vilify

REVISE: (**see** "alter") amend; blue-pencil; change; convert; correct; edit; emend; improve; mend; modify; overhaul; patch; rearrange; recognize; reconsider; redact; reexamine; reform; remodel; renew; renovate; reorganize; repair; restore; review; REVISION: (**see** "alteration") amendment; change; conversion; correction; emendment; improvement; modification; overhaul; rearrangement; recension; redaction; reexamination; reformation; remodeling; renewal; renovation; reorganization; repair; restoration; revise

REVIVE: activate; animate; cheer; ebb; enliven; exhume; freshen; furbish; help; invigorate; perk; quicken; rally; reactivate; reanimate; reawaken; recall; recover; reexamine; refocillate; refresh; refurbish; reinforce; reinspire; reinspirit; reinvigorate; rejuvenate; rekindle; renew; renovate; repair; repristinate; restore; resurge; resuscitate; return; review; revitalize; revivificate; revivify; rouse; vivify; REVIVING: redivivus; renascent; revivescent; REVIVAL: anabiosis; reanimation; recall; recrudescence; redivivus; renaissance; renascence; renewal; repristination; reproduction; restoration; resurrection; resuscitation; revivification; risorgimento; vivification

REVOKE: abjure; abolish; abrogate; adeem; annul; cancel; countermand; nullify; reas-

sume; recall; recant; recover; renege; renounce; repeal; rescind; retract; vitiate; withdraw; REVOCATION: abolishment; abrogation; annulment; counteraction; countermand; nullification; recantation; recision; recovery; repeal; rescission; retraction; reversal; reverse; revokement; vitiation; withdrawal

REVOLT: **v.** abominate; appal(l); arise; daunt; desert; disgust; dismay; frighten; horrify; mutiny; nauseate; offend; rebel; recoil; renounce; renunciate; repel; riot; rise; scare; shock; sicken; terrify; uprise; REVOLT **n.** *or* REVOLUTION: (**see** "rebellion") anarchy; change; circuit; *coup d'état*; cycle; gyration; gyre; insubordination; insurgency; insurrection; mutiny; outbreak; overthrow; putsch; rebellion; recurrence; riot; rotation; sedition; tumult; uprising; war; REVOLUTIONARY: **see** "rebellious;" REVOLTING: (**see** "disgusting") bilious; choleric; despicable; fulsome; irascible; loathsome; nauseating; nauseous; noisome; offensive; repugnant; repulsive; revellent; revulsive; riotous; shocking; sickening

REVOLVE: circle; circulate; circumduct; circumgyrate; consider; gyrate; hinge; meditate; orbit; pirl; pirouette; pivot; ponder; reason; recur; reflect; roll; rotate; ruminate; slue; spin; swing; swivel; turn; twirl; vertiginate; wheel; whirl; REVOLUTION: **see** under "revolt"

REVOLVER: arm; Colt; firearm; gat; gun; handgun; pistol; rod; rotator; weapon

REVULSION: (**see** "nausea") repulsion; withdrawal

REWARD: **v.** atone; award; compensate; give; grant; guerdon; indemnify; pay; recompense; redress; remedy; remember; remunerate; requite; subsidize; REWARD: **n.** additament; amends; atonement; award; bonus; bounty; compensation; consideration; crown; cumshaw; cup; dividend; extra; freedom; fruit; gain; gift; gratuity; guerdon; honorarium; indemnity; lagniappe; laurels; lucre; medal; meed; money; Oscar; pay-(ment); premium; prize; profit; ransom; recompense; redress; remembrance; remuneration; reparation; requital; retribution; return; ribbon; satisfaction; subsidy; surplus; tip; utu; yield

REWORD: alter; edit; paraphrase; repeat; revise; rewrite

RHAPSODY: (**see** "rapture") bombast; ecstasy; extravagance; orgasm; raptus

RHETORIC(AL): baronial; bombastic; Ciceronian; declamatory; Demosthenean; Demosthenic; eloquent; epideictic; florid; flowery; fluent; forensic; grandiloquent; oratorical; ornate; orotund; rubescent; wordy

RHYTHM: (**see** "meter") accent; alliteration; beat; cadence; cadency; coordination; harmonization; harmony; ictus; lilt; measure; melody; modulation; music; pace; pattern; periodicity; regularity; sequence; sound; swing; symmetry; tempo; throb; time; tone; verse; RHYTHMIC(AL): cadenced; cadential; harmonious; lilting; measured; melodious; periodical; regular; swinging; symmetrical; throbbing

RIANT: (**see** "gay") jocose; jocular; jolly; jubilant; laughing; mirthful

RIB: **see** "tease"

RIBALD: base; blue; brutish; coarse; contemptible; crude; depraved; filthy; gross; indecent; irreverent; jocular; lewd; loose; obscene; off-color; offensive; racy; raffish; randy; raw; risqué; rough; rude; scabby; scabrous; scurrilous; spicy; sweaty; uncouth; vile; vulgar

RIBBON: award; band; commendation; coque; decoration; fillet; prize; reward; strip; stripe; trophy

RICH: abundant; adorned; affluent; ample; amusing; bedizened; colorful; copious; costly; daedalian; daedal(ic); exotic; expensive; fat; fecund; fertile; flourishing; flush(ed); fruitful; generous; gilt; golden; high; juicy; lavish; Lucull(i)an; lush; luxuriant; luxurious; meaningful; moneyed; opulent; ornate; plenteous; plentiful; plush(y); precious; pregnant; productive; prosperous; pure; racy; rank; redolent; replete; resourceful; savory; showy; spicy; succulent; sumptuous; superb; valuable; vivid; wealthy; weighty; RICHES *or* RICHNESS: (**see** "wealth") abundance; affluence; amplitude; cache; copiosity; copiousness; elegance; estate; fortune; gold; hoard; lucre; luxe; luxuriance; luxuriousness; luxury; means; money; opulence; opulency; pelf; plenty; possessions; power; profusion; sumptuosity; treasure; treasury; wherewithal

RICKETY: dilapidated; feeble; flimsy; frail; imperfect; rachitic; ramshackle; rattletrap; shaky; sick(ly); tenuous; tottering; tremulous; tumbledown; unsafe; unsound; unstable; weak; wobbly

RICOCHET: carom; echo; glance; rebound; skip

RID: (**see** "free") cast (off); clean(se); clear; delete; deliver; destroy; detach; disabuse; disburden; discharge; disencumber; disengage; disentangle; dislodge; dispatch; ease; eject; eliminate; eradicate; execute; expel; extricate; fire; kill; liberate; liquidate; loose(n); purge; relieve; relinquish; remove; shake; unburden; unclog; undeceive; undelude; unload; vanquish; wipe (out)

RIDDLE: **v.** corrupt; debase; explain; interpret; mystify; penetrate; perforate; permeate; perplex; pierce; puncture; puzzle; screen; sieve; sift; RIDDLE: **n.** (**see** "puzzle") ambiguity; charade; conundrum; crux; difficulty; enigma; entanglement; intricacy; labyrinth; maze; mystery; obscurity; paradox; perplexity; prize; problem; quandary; question; rebus; secret; sphinx; strait

RIDE: badger; float; harass; hector; nag; needle; obsess; oppress; overlap; override; surmount; survive; travel; tyrannize

RIDGE: arête; chine; crest; elevation; esker; hill; line; prominence; range; raphe; rib; ruga; rugae (pl.); rugosity; seam; spine; spur; wale; welt

RIDICULE: **v.** badger; banter; buffoon; burlesque; chaff; criticize; deride; gibe; guy; harass; hector; jeer; lambaste; lampoon; mime; mimic; mock; needle; pan; pillorize; pillory; quiz; rail; rally; razz; rib; ride; roast; satirize; scoff; scout; taunt; tease; twit; RIDICULE: **n.** asteism; banter; buffoonery; burlesque; chaff; derision; fun; gibe; irony; lampoon; leering; mimicry; mockery; needling; panning; pasquinade; raillery; razz; ribbing; ridiculosity; ridiculousness; riding; sarcasm; satire; scorn; taunt; teasing; travesty

RIDICULOUS: (**see** "absurd") bizarre; catachrestic; comic(al); derisible; derisive; droll; eccentric; extravagant; farcical; far-fetched; foolish; funny; grotesque; incongruous; ironic; laughable; ludicrous; nonsensical; odd; *outré*; picayune; picayunish; preposterous; *recherché*; risible; silly; strained; trifling; trivial; waggish

RIFLE: **v.** (**see** "pilfer") despoil; ransack; rob; steal; strip; RIFLE: **n.** arm; carbine; firearm; gun; Mauser; musket; weapon

RIFT: breach; break; chink; cleft; crack; cranny; crevasse; crevice; disagreement; dispute; divergence; fault; fissure; flaw; interval; lag; opening; rent; rima; separation; space; split

RIG: **v.** adjust; align; assemble; bedizen; cheat; clothe; dress; equip; fit; fix; furnish; manipulate; outfit; prepare; provide; swindle; RIG: **n.** apparatus; clothing; derrick; dress; equipage; equipment; getup; harness; machine(ry); outfit; team

RIGHT: **v.** adjust; amend; avenge; correct; cure; emend; fix; gee; justify; rectify; redress; relieve; remedy; restore; set; square; vindicate; RIGHT: **a.** or **adv.** actual; adequate; advantageous; A-O.K.; appropriate; authoritarian; authorized; conservative; correct; dexter; dextral; due; equal; equitable; exact(ly); fair; fit(ting); genuine; good; irrefutable; just; lawful; legal; legitimate; meet; meticulous; moral; nice; normal; O.K.; particular; pat; precise(ly); proper; real; reasonable; righteous; sane; scrupulous; sound; square; straight; sufficient; suitable; true; undisputed; unimpeachable; upright; veracious; warranted; well; RIGHT: **n.** advantage; appange; authority; claim; commission; concession; correctitude; correctness; droit; due; duty; entitlement; equity; excuse; faculty; fairness; favor; franchise; gee; grant; guarantee; guaranty; immunity; justice; opportunity; option; ownership; permission; permit; perquisite; possession; power; prerogative; principle; privilege; property; propriety; rank; rating; seniority; title; truth; voucher; warrant; RIGHTIST: **see** "conservative"

RIGHTEOUS: divine; equitable; good; holy; honorable; just; magnanimous; moral; principled; rectitudinous; religious; right; sanctimonious; upright; virtuous; RIGHTEOUSNESS: dharma; justification; probity; rectitude; religiosity; sanctimoniousness; sanctimony; scrupulosity; uprightness; virtue

RIGID *or* RIGOROUS: accurate; ascetic; asperous; astringent; austere; bleak; chilly; cold; constricting; cruel; dismal; dour; Draconian; drastic; erect; exact(ing); extreme; firm; fixed; flinty; formal; frightful; frigid; frozen; granitic; grave; hard; harsh; icy; immalleable; imperative; inclement; inelastic; inexorable; inflexible; inquisi-

torial; ironbound; ironfisted; ironhanded; irreducible; marble; marmoreal; mortified; mortifying; muscle-bound; obdurate; peremptory; precise; Procrustean; raw; relentless; restrained; restricted; rugged; ruthless; scrupulous; self-denying; self-disciplined; self-mortified; serious; set; severe; sharp; solid; sour; Spartanic; stark; stern; stiff; stony; stout; straight(-laced); strenuous; strict; stringent; strong; stubborn; tense; tough; unbending; unbent; unbowed; uncompliant; uncomplying; uncompromising; unpliant; unrelenting; unshakable; unsubdued; unyielding; vigorous; RIGIDITY: asceticism; astringency; austerity; bleakness; cruelty; dismality; exaction; fixity; formality; frigidity; gravity; hardness; harshness; iciness; inclemency; inelasticity; inexorability; inflexibility; mortification; obdurancy; peremptoriness; pertinacity; precision; resistance; restriction; rigidification; rigidness; rigor(ism); ruggedness; ruthlessness; scrupulosity; seriousness; setness; severity; sharpness; solidity; stiffness; stoutness; strenuosity; strictness; stringency; stubbornness; tenseness; toughness; unyieldingness; vigor

RIGOR: (**see** "austerity" and "rigidity") ardor; difficulty; exactitude; exactness; hardship; inclemency; scrupulosity; severity; sternness; stiffness; strenuosity; strictness; stringency; vicissitude; RIGOROUS: **see** "rigid"

RILE: (**see** "vex") anger; annoy; arouse; bug; harass; irritate; needle; offend; ridicule; roil

RIM: border; brim; brink; circumference; edge; flange; frame; lip; margin; outskirts; periphery; skirt; verge

RIND: bark; cortex; cover(ing); crust; epicarp; hull; husk; integument; peel(ing); shell; skin

RING: **v.** call; chime; circumnavigate; clang; clank; dial; din; echo; encircle; enclose; gird; jingle; peal; phone; repeat; resound; sound; surround; telephone; toll; RING: **n.** annulation; annulet; arena; band; bloc; cabal; call; chime; circle(t); circuit; clang; clank; clique; coterie; course; encirclement; enclosure; faction; girdle; gong; hoop; jingle; junto; knell; loop; oval; peal; pool; racecourse; rink; set; sonority; sound; spiral; tintinnabulation; toll; RINGED: annular; annulate; annulose; circumferential; circumnavigated; encircled; wedded

RINSE: absterge; bathe; cleanse; lave; sluice; wash

RIOT: **v.** attack; brawl; despoil; disturb; insurrect; mutiny; pillage; rebel; waste; RIOT: **n.** (see "rebellion") brawl; broil; carousal; commotion; confusion; disorder; dissipation; disturbance; *émeute*; excess; fracas; fray; insurrection; melee; merrymaking; mutiny; outbreak; pandemonium; pillage; profusion; revelry; row; rumbullion; tumult; turbulence; turmoil; uproar; welter; RIOTOUS: abundant; agitated; boisterous; contumacious; disloyal; disobedient; disorderly; exuberant; incendiary; inflammatory; insubordinate; insurgent; lawless; loud; luxuriant; mutinous; noisy; oppugnant; pandemoniac-(al); profligate; profuse; rebellious; recalcitrant; recusant; refractory; resistive; retractable; revolutionary; seditious; treacherous; tumultuary; tumultuous; turbulent; ungovernable; unmanageable; unrestrained; unruly; unsubmissive; violent; wanton

RIP: **v.** cleave; cut; divide; open; part; rend; rive; sever; shred; slash; split; tear; RIP: **n.** cheat; debauchee; devil; libertine; rent; rogue; roué; scamp; tear

RIPE: adult; complete; consummate; developed; experienced; fit; full(-blown); grown; late; lush; mature(d); mellow(ed); perfect-(ed); prepared; ready; suitable; RIPEN: age; bloom; develop; fit; grow; improve; mature; mellow; perfect; prepare; RIPENESS: see "maturity" and "perfection"

RIPPLE: babble; billow; cockle; comb; fret; gurgle; lap; purl; riff; ruffle; surge; undulation; wave

RISE: **v.** advance; appear; arise; ascend; begin; circulate; clamber; climb; commence; creep (up); derive; elevate; emanate; emerge; escalate; flow; gain; grow; happen; head; hop; improve; incline; increase; insurrect; intensify; issue; leap; levitate; lift; loom; mount; occur; originate; progress; prosper; raise; ramp; reach; rear; result; resurge; revolt; rocket; scale; skin; skyrocket; soar; spring; stand; start; stem; surface; surge; surmount; surpass; swell; thrive; tower; transcend; twine; vine; upspring; upswing; swell; RISE *or* RISING: **n.** acclivity; advance(ment); appearance; ascendance; ascendancy; ascension; assent; assurgency; beginning; bulge; circulation; clamber; climb; commencement; creep-(ing); derivation; emanation; emergence; escalation; flight; flow; gain; grade; gradient; growth; head; hill(top); hop; improvement; incline; increase; insurrection; intensification; issuance; leadership; leap; levitation;

lift; mastery; origin(ation); overflow; pitch; power; progress(ion); prosperity; raise; ramp; reach; resurgence; retort; revolt; scale; skyrocketing; slope; source; spring; start; stem; surge; surpassing; sway; swell-(ing); tide; towering; upgrade; upspring; upswing; RISING: **a.** ascending; ascensional; ascensive; assurgent; climbing; emanating; emerging; escalating; exceeding; growing; hopping; improving; increasing; issuing; montant; ortive; skyrocketing; surgent; surpassing; swelling; thriving; transcending

RISIBLE: (see "funny") absurd; amusing; bizarre; droll; laughable; ridiculous

RISK: **v.** (see "endanger") adventure; bet; chance; dare; expose; gamble; hazard; imperil; jeopardize; tempt; venture; wager; RISK: **n.** (see "peril") adventure; bet; chance; contingency; danger; dare; gamble; hazard; jeopardy; long shot; plight; threat; throw; venture; wager; RISKY: (see "dangerous") adventurous; bold; chancily; chancy; critical; daring; explosive; hazardous; injurious; jeopardous; ominous; parlous; perilous; precarious; queasy; questionable; speculative; uncertain; unhealthful; unhealthy; unstable; venturesome; RISKINESS: adventure; adventurousness; chanciness; jeopardy; peril(ousness); precariousness; speculation

RISQUÉ: blue; borderline; broad; daring; improper; indecent; indelicate; obscene; off-color; questionable; salacious; salty; scabrous

RITE(S) *or* RITUAL: burial; celebration; ceremonial(ism); ceremony; commencement; convention; cult; fetish; form(ality); formula; funeral; graduation; honor; incantation; liturgy; novena; observance(s); office; ovation; panoply; parade; procedure; protocol; prayer; role; sacrament; sacrum; solemnity; usage(s); wedding

RIVAL: **v.** compete; contend; cope; emulate; envy; even; excel; exert; fight; match; oppose; outshine; paragon; strive; vie; RIVAL: **n.** antagonist; comparative; competition; competitor; corrival; enemy; foe; match; Nemesis; opponent; peer; RIVALROUS: antagonistic; competing; competitive; competitory; contesting; opposing; RIVALRY: antagonism; competition; contention; emulation; envy; fight; jealousy; match; opposition; race

ROAD: agger; alley; artery; avenue; Bahn; *camino real*; course; drang; drive; estrada; harbor; highway; iter; land; pad; passage-(way); path; pike; railway; roadway; route; street; thoroughfare; track; trail; way

ROAM: err; gad; gallivant; graze; hike; meander; prowl; ramble; range; rove; run; saunter; scour; spread; squander; straggle; stray; stroll; sweep; traipse; travel; traverse; trifle; walk; wander; ROAMING: (see "roving") ambulatory; discursive; itinerant; meandering; migratory; nomadic; perambulatory; peripatetic; prodigal; vagarious; vagrant; wandering

ROAR: v. bawl; bellow; bluster; boom; bray; clamor; howl; laugh; outcry; shout; thunder; ululate; vociferate; ROAR: n. bawl; bellow; boom; bray; clamor; howl; laugh; noise; outcry; shout; thunder; vociferation

ROAST: bake; banter; broil; cook; criticize; grill; heat; lampoon; parch; ridicule; satirize; swelter

ROB: (see "steal") burglarize; depredate; deprive; despoil; fleece; hold up; pillage; pluck; purloin; reave; relieve; remove; rifle; roll; spoliate; take; ROBBING: larcenous; predaceous; predacious; predatory; ROBBERY: burglary; depredation; despoliation; holdup; larceny; pillage; piracy; plunder; predacity; spoliation; stickup; theft; ROBBER: see "bandit"

ROBE: v. apparel; array; attire; cloak; clothe; costume; dress; gown; invest; vest-(ure); ROBE: n. apparel; array; attire; cape; cloak; costume; dress; garment(s); gown; mantle; purple; toga; vestment(s)

ROBOT: see "mannikin"

ROBUST: able-bodied; athletic; brawny; firm; flourishing; full-bodied; hale; hardy; healthy; hearty; husky; lusty; masculine; muscular; powerful; robustious; rough; rude; rugged; sinewy; sound; stalwart; stark; stout; strong; sturdy; valid; vigorous; virile; well; ROBUSTNESS: athleticism; brawniness; huskiness; lustihood; lustiness; robusticity; strength; sturdiness; vigor; virility

ROCK: v. astonish; dislodge; disturb; react; reel; rool; shake; stagger; sway; swing; teeter; totter; waver; weave; ROCK: n. foundation; marble; mineral; stone; support; trap; trass; tuff; ROCKY: craggy; daft;

difficult; dizzy; flinty; hard; insensitive; obdurate; obscene; rickety; rough; rugged; shaky; steadfast; stony; stubborn; uncouth; unfeeling; unpromising; unstable; weak

ROCKET: v. arise; soar; rise; tower; zoom; ROCKET: n. firework; missile; projectile; pyrotechnic

ROD: authority; bar; cane; club; crop; cudgel; cue; ferrule; gat; gun; measure; perch; pistol; pole; power; revolver; scepter; shaft; shoot; spindle; support; stake; stem; stick; switch; twig; tyranny; wand

RODENT: a. biting; corroding; erose; gnawing; raw; spreading; RODENT: n. beaver; cavy; con(e)y; hare; hutia; mouse; muskrat; pica; porcupine; rabbit; rat; shrew; squirrel

ROGATION: litany; prayer; request; rite; supplication; worship

ROGUE(S): beggar; caitiff; cheat; devil; gamin; gamine (fem.); imp; knave; libertine; malefactor; miscreant; picaro; picaroon; pixie; prankster; rapscallion; rascal; renegade; reprobate; ribald; rip; scalawag; scamp; scant-o-grace; scapegrace; scaramouche; scoundrel; sharpster; swindler; rip; tear; vagrant; varmint; *vaurien*; vermin; villain; wag; ROGUISH: arch; clever; devilish; dishonest; *espiègle*; foxy; impish; knavish; mischievous; pawky; picaresque; playful; puckish; raffish; satanic; scampish; sly; sportive; unprincipled; waggish; wanton; wicked; ROGUISHNESS: devil(t)ry; *espièglerie*; gaminerie; knavery; knavishness; mischief; raffishness; rascality; roguery; scalawaggery; scampishness; waggishness

ROIL: disorder; disturb; irritate; muddy; rile; stir; vex; ROILY: disordered; muddy; turbid; turbulent

ROLE: business; character; cloak; clothes; direction; duty; function; impersonation; job; office; part; person; position; sphere; work

ROLL: v. begin; bolt; coil; consider; curl; elapse; enfold; envelope; extend; furl; gyrate; list; lurch; move; pass; ponder; pour; progress; revolve; rob; rock; rotate; surge; sway; swing; toss; trill; troll; trundle; turn; wallow; wheel; whirl; wind; wrap; ROLL: n. biscuit; bun; cadre; list; lurch-(ing); money; record; reverberation; roster; rota; rotation; scroll; surge; sway; trill; undulation

ROMANCE: **v.** court; exaggerate; invent; love; woo; ROMANCE: **n.** affair; *affaire; affaire d'amour*; fable; falsehood; fantasy; gest(e); glamo(u)r; love(making); novel; story; tale; ROMANTIC: ardent; cavalier; chimerical; chivalresque; chivalrous; dramatic; dreamy; emotional; enticing; exotic; fabulous; fanciful; fervent; foreign; glamorous; heroic; ideal(istic); imaginary; imaginative; melodramatic; mushy; picaresque; picturesque; poetic(al); quixotic, Romanesque; sentimental; unrealistic; utopian; visionary

ROMP: **v.** caper; frisk; frolic; gambol; lark; play; sport; ROMP: **n.** antic; caper; frisk; frolic; gambol; lark; play; rogue; runaway; scamp; sport

ROOF: canopy; cover(ing); culmination; cupola; dome; domicile; dwelling; home; house; gambrel; mansard; shelter; slate; summit; tent; tile; top; vault; ROOFLESS: alfresco; homeless; hypaethral; open-air; upaithric

ROOKIE: **see** "beginner"

ROOM(S): accommodation; apartment; area; atrium; aula; berth; capacity; cell; chamber; clearance; compartment; compass; crypt; cubicle; cubiculum; digs; expanse; extent; field; flat; hall(way); latitude; leeway; lodge; lodging; margin; occasion; opportunity; place; play; quarter(s); range; sala; salon; saloon; scope; space; suite; vault; ROOMY: (**see** "ample") baronial; broad; capacious; cavernous; comfortable; commodious; expansive; extensive; large; latitudinous; spacious; suitable; uncrowded; vast; wide

ROOST: **v.** abide; alight; land; light; live; lodge; nest; perch; settle; sit; sleep; stay; ROOST: **n.** abode; dwelling; home; house; limb; lodging; nest; perch; pole; rookery

ROOT: **v.** applaud; burrow; cheer; clap; dig; encourage; establish; fix; grub; imbed; implant; plant; set(tle); start; stem; ROOT: **n.** ancestor; base; basis; bottom; bulb; cause; cheer; core; encouragement; etymon; foundation; ground; heart; motive; origin(ation); radical; radix; reason; rhyzome; source; stem; tie; tuber

ROPE: **v.** bind; catch; curb; ensnare; fasten; inveigle; lasso; restrain; stay; swindle; tether; tie; ROPE: **n.** bight; cable; hawser;

lariat; lasso; line; marline; noose; reata; sequence; tether

ROSTER: agenda (pl.); agendum; catalog-(ue); directory; inventory; itemization; list; register; registry; roll; rota; scroll; slate; table; tariff

ROSTRUM: beak; dais; desk; platform; prow; pulpit; rostra (pl.); snout; stage; tribune

ROSY: (**see** "bright") auroral; aurorean; blooming; blushing; budding; *couleur de rose*; dandy; favorable; fine; flattering; florid; flowery; flushed; healthy; optimistic; pink; radiant; red; rosaceous; roseate; ruddy; rubicund; sanguine(ous)

ROT: **v.** contaminate; corrupt; crumble; decay; decompose; defile; degenerate; deteriorate; disintegrate; mold; necrose; pollute; putrefy; putresce; smell; sour; spoil; stink; taint; waste; ROT: **n.** breakdown; contamination; corruption; decay; decomposition; degeneration; deterioration; disease; disintegration; gangrene; mold; mortification; necrosis; nonsense; poison; pollution; putrefaction; putrescence; taint; weakness; ROTTEN *or* ROTTING: abominable; bad; carious; contaminated; corrupt; decayed; decaying; decomposed; deteriorated; dirty; disagreeable; diseased; disintegrated; fetid; foul; fusty; infected; moldy; necrotic; noisome; obnoxious; offensive; putrefactive; putrefied; putrescent; putrid; rancid; rank; smelly; sour; spoiled; stinking; tainted; unclean; unpleasant

ROTATE: alternate; birl; change; circle; circulate; circumduct; circumgyrate; circumvolve; eddy; exchange; gyrate; orbit; oscillate; pirouette; revolve; roll; rote; slue; spin; substitute; swing; swirl; turn; twirl; wheel; whirl; whiz; vertiginate; ROTATING: alternating; changing; circulating; gyrating; orbiting; oscillating; revoluble; revolving; rotary; spinning; vertiginous; ROTATION: alternation; change; circulation; circumduction; circumgyration; circumvolution; eddy; exchange; gyration; orbit; pirouette; revolution; spin; succession; swing; swirl; torque; turning; vortex; whirl

ROUÉ: debauchee; devil; libertine; rake; rip; womanizer

ROUGH: agrestic; approximate; asperate; asperous; austere; bluff; blunt; boisterous;

boorish; broken; bumpy; choppy; coarse; cobbly; crude; curt; difficult; discourteous; grained; granular; granulose; gravelly; gross; gruff; hairy; harageous; hard; harsh; hilly; hispid(ulate); hispidulous; hoarse; imperfected; impolite; inclement; indelicate; irregular; jagged; jarring; lumpy; makeshift; offensive; primitive; rank; rasping; raspy; raucous; raw; ribald; robust(i)ous; rocky; rowdy; rude; ruffled; rugged; rustic; rutted; scabrous; scratchy; seamy; severe; shaggy; slap-bang; stern; stony; stormy; sturdy; tartarly; tempestuous; trying; turbulent; unburnished; uncouth; unculled; undressed; uneven; unfine; unfinished; ungenteel; ungentle; unhewn; unpolished; unrefined; unshaped; unshorn; unsmooth(ed); unwrought; violent; wild; ROUGHNESS: asperity; austerity; bumpiness; choppiness; coarseness; crudeness; crudity; discourtesy; harshness; hispidity; imperfection; impoliteness; inclemency; inconsistency; indelicacy; inequality; irregularity; robusticity; rudeness; rusticity; scabrousness; scratchiness; severity; storminess; unevenness; unrefinement; violence

ROUND: **a.** (**see** "circular") about; ample; annular; around; bold; brisk; bulbous; complete; convex; curved; cyclic(al); cylindrical; fast; finished; gibbose; gibbous; globate; harsh; large; mellow; near; orbed; orbic(ular); outspoken; plain; plump; rich; ringed; rotund; shapely; sonorous; spherical; spheriform; spheroid(al); spiral; vigorous; ROUND: **n.** activity; bout; cartridge; circuit; course; cycle; dance; revolution; ronde; rung; series; set; shell; song; swing; tour; wheel; ROUNDNESS: circularity; globosity; orbicularity; rotundity; spheroidicity

ROUNDABOUT: **a.** (**see** "devious") ambagious; ambient; anfractuous; circuitous; circumferential; circumlocutious; circumlocutory; curving; deviating; indirect; labyrinthian; labyrinthine; meandering; serpentine; winding; ROUNDABOUT: **n.** anfractuosity; circle; circuity; circularity; circumbendibus; circumlocution; detour; indirection

ROUSE: (**see** "waken") awake(n); bestir; encourage; excite; foment; hie; incite; inflame; instigate; intensify; kindle; mount; prick; prod; provoke; raise; rally; rout; start(le); stimulate; stir; surprise; urge

ROUT: **v.** beat; chase; conquer; defeat; demoralize; disorganize; drub; lick; overpower; overthrow; overwhelm; ream; repulse; rouse; scatter; stampede; swamp; vanquish; ROUT: **n.** debacle; defeat; demoralization; disorder; disorganization; disruption; repulse; retreat; *sauve qui peut*; stampede; vanquishment

ROUTE: **v.** direct; prearrange; send; ship; ROUTE: **n.** (**see** "road") artery; circuit; course; door; entrance; itinerary; journey; line; march; pad; passage; path(way); trail; trend; trip; walk; way

ROUTINE: **a.** (**see** "commonplace") administrative; customary; cut-and-dried; executive; formal; functional; habitual; mechanical; methodical; normal; ordinary; perfunctory; periodic(al); *pro forma*; psychologic-(al); regular; repetitious; systematic; systematized; uniform; usual; ROUTINE: **n.** course; custom; form(ality); groove; habit; harness; mechanics; mechanism; method; pace; pattern; practice; precedent; procedure; rota; rote; rut; sequence; series; system; track; treadmill; wont

ROVE: (**see** "roam") gad; ramble; range; wander; ROVING: arrant; desultory; digressive; discursive; itinerant; migratory; mobile; nomadic; peregrine; peripatetic; rambling; roaming; vagrant; wandering; ROVER: freebooter; maverick; nomad; peregrine; peripatetic; pilgrim; pirate; rambler; sailor; straggler; stray; traveler; vagrant; waif; wanderer

ROW: **v.** navigate; oar; scull; ROW: **n.** alley; brawl; colonnade; fight; file; fracas; line; quarrel; rank; ruckus; ruction; sequence; squabble; street; string; succession; tier

ROWDY: **a.** (**see** "boisterous") loud; noisy; raffish; vulgar; ROWDY: **n.** blusterer; bully; hoodlum; plug-ugly; roisterer; rough; ruffian; thug; tough; ROWDYISM: **see** "boisterousness"

ROYAL: (**see** "kingly") aristocratic; august; authoritative; basilic(al); big; commanding; courtly; crown; dignified; easy; elite; exalted; excellent; famous; fine; glorious; grand; imperial; imposing; lofty; lordly; magnificent; majestic; monarchical; noble; paramount; princely; queenly; regal; ruling; stately; sovereign; splendid; sublime; superb; supreme; titled; ROYALTY: **see** "aristocrats"

RUB: **v.** abrade; annoy; brighten; buff; burnish; chafe; erase; file; fret; grate; graze; irritate; massage; polish; rake; scour; scrape; scratch; shine; smear; smooth; RUB: **n.** (**see** "difficulty") dilemma; hindrance; obstacle; roughness

RUBBISH: (**see** "waste") chaff; debris; detritus; dross; ejectamenta; garbage; hodgepodge; junk; litter; offal; refuse; rejectamenta (pl.); riffraff; rot; rubble; scoria; scoriae (pl.); scree; sewage; trash; tripe; truck

RUBE: (**see** "rustic") boor; bumpkin; clod(hopper); clown; cornball; countryman; dolt; fool; hick; yahoo

RUBICUND: (**see** "ruddy") erubescent; florid; flushed; red(dish); rosy; rubescent

RUBIGINOUS: brown(ish); ferruginous; reddish; rufous; rusty; tawny

RUBRIC: canon; category; class(ification); commandment; concept; custom; flourish; form(ula); gloss; heading; law; letter; name; paraph; rule; statute; technique; title

RUCTION: (**see** "brawl") contention; dissention; friction; rupture

RUDDY: brownish; erubescent; florid; flushed; glowing; lively; red(dish); rosy; rubescent; rubicund; rufescent; sanguine; vivid

RUDE: abrupt; abusive; artless; austere; awkward; barbarous; bitter; blunt; boisterous; bold; boorish; brusque; callow; churlish; cloddish; clodhopperish; clodhopping; clownish; clumsy; coarse; contumelious; crabbed; cross; crude; curt; dedecorous; disagreeable; discordant; discourteous; disrespectful; dour; dull; elemental; elementary; flippant; gawky; gross; green; gruff; grumpy; guileless; hard; harsh; ignorant; ill-bred; illiterate; ill-mannered; immoderate; impolite; imprecise; impudent; inelegant; inexperienced; inexpert; insolent; inurbane; loud; loutish; natural; oafish; offensive; open; peasant; philistine; profane; raw; ribald; robust; rough; rugged; rustic; sassy; saucy; savage; shaggy; short; simple; snappish; snappy; snarling; stern; stormy; stupid; sturdy; surly; unceremonious; uncivil(ized); uncourteous; uncourtly; uncouth; ungrateful; ungracious; unkind; unlearned; unmannered; unmanufactured; unmitigated; unpolished; unshaped; unskilled; unskillful; unsophisticated; unsubtle; untutored; un-

trained; vigorous; violent; vulgar; wild; yokelish; RUDENESS: awkwardness; artlessness; barbarism; brutality; callowness; cloddishness; clownishness; clumsiness; contumely; crudeness; curtness; discourteousness; discourtesy; disrespect; dullness; gaucherie; gawkishness; impudence; incivility; inelegance; insolence; inurbanity; sauciness; savagery; stupidity; ungraciousness; vulgarity

RUDIMENT: (**see** "beginning") ABC; anlage; element(al); embryo; fundamental; germ; principle; root; seed; vestige; RUDIMENTARY: (**see** "beginning") abecedarian; abecedary; abortive; basic; causal; contingent; elemental; elementary; embryonic; fragmental; fundamental; germinal; imperfect(ed); inchoate; inchoative; incipient; incomplete; initial; nascent; potential; primary; rudimental; undeveloped; vestigial

RUE: **v.** cry; deplore; disappoint; grieve; lament; regret; repent; weep; RUE: **n.** bitterness; compassion; disappointment; grief; lamentation; penitence; pity; regret; remorse; repentance; RUEFUL: depressed; despairing; dismal; doleful; lamentable; lugubrious; melancholy; mournful; penitent(ial); pitiable; pitiful; plaintive; regretful; remorseful; sad; sorrowful; sorry; woeful

RUFFIAN: (**see** "bandit", "gangster" and "tough") brute; scoundrel

RUFFLE: **v.** abrade; agitate; annoy; bluster; bristle; derange; disconcert; disturb; embarrass; fret; graze; irritate; nettle; pucker; rattle; ripple; roll; roughen; rumple; shuffle; stiffen; stir; strut; swagger; unsettle; upset; vex; wrinkle; RUFFLE: **n.** commotion; crimp; flounce; frill; pucker; ripple; ruche; rumple; skirmish; wrinkle

RUGGED: austere; chilly; coarse; hardy; harsh; ironbound; irregular; jagged; robust; rough; rude; stern; stiff; strong; sturdy; uncouth; unequal; uneven; ungentle; vigorous; weathered; wild

RUIN: **v.** bankrupt; beat; botch; bungle; collapse; crash; crumble; damn; decay; decimate; defeat; defile; deflower; demolish; denude; deprive; despoil; destroy; devastate; disintegrate; divest; doom; explode; fall; fleece; impoverish; injure; lose; overthrow; overwhelm; pillage; plunder; ravage; ravish; raze; reave; rifle; riot; rip; rob; sack; shatter; shipwreck; sink; spoil; spurn; strip; subvert; swamp; torpedo; undo; wreck; RUIN: **n.** annihilation; bane; bankruptcy;

bowwows; bungle; calamity; catastrophe; collapse; crash; damage; decay; decimation; demolishment; despoliation; destruction; deterioration; devastation; dilapidation; dishonor; doom; downfall; explosion; failure; fall; grief; havoc; holocaust; injury; labefaction; loss; overthrow; perdition; pillage; plunder; pot; relic; reversal; shipwreck; smash; sorrow; undoing; wrack; wreck(age); RUINED: desolate; destroyed; downfallen; *flambé*; flat; forlorn; gone; hopeless; *kaput*; lost; perdue; wrecked; wretched; RUINOUS: (**see** "dire") baneful; cancerous; cataclysmic(al); catastrophic(al); damnatory; destructive; disastrous; malign(ant); pernicious; undone; wrecked; RUINS: **see** "remains"

RULE: **v.** (**see** "command") administer; control; curb; decide; decree; determine; dictate; direct; dominate; execute; formulate; govern; guide; influence; judge; lead; manage; moderate; order; predominate; preponderate; preside; prevail; sway; RULE-(S): **n.** (**see** "command") administration; arithmocracy; authority; book; bylaws; canon; caveat; code; constitution; contest; convention(ality); covenant; criteria (pl.); criterion; custom; decision; decree; determination; dicta (pl.); dictamen; dictate; dictum; direction; discipline; doctrine; domination; dominion; etiquette; example; formula; government; guidance; guide; habit; helm; Hoyle; imperative; influence; injunction; law; lead(ership); mastery; maxim; measure; method(ology); model; norm; order; ordinance; power; practice; precedent; precept; predomination; prerogative; prescription; principle; procedure; pronouncement; protocol; regency; regime (n); *règlement*; regula(tion); reign; ritual; rubric; schedule; sovereignty; standard; statute; supremacy; sway; system; technique; theorem; theorum; tradition

RULER(S): ameer; archon; Atahualpa; Caesar; caliph; chief; commander; czar; despot; dictator; dynast; emir; emperor; establishment; ethnarch; gerent; government; governor; gubernator; king; lord; magister; mikado; monarch; nabob; oligarch; overlord; pantocrator; potentate; president; prince; queen; regent; shah; sovereign; sultan; tetrarch; tsar

RULING: **a.** administrative; chief; commanding; conventional; current; customary; decisive; determinant; determinative; disciplinary; doctrinal; dominating; domineering; executive; governmental; guiding; im-perative; leading; precedential; predominant; predominating; prevailing; prevalent; principal; procedural; regnal; regnant; reigning; sovereign; RULING: **n.** (**see** "decision") decree; fiat; judgment; order; statement

RUMINANT: **a.** bovine; bovoid; meditative; RUMINANT: **n.** alpaca; bison; Bos; Bovidae (pl.); bovine; camel; cow; deer; giraffe; goat; mammal; sheep; zebra

RUMINATE: (**see** "think") brew; chew; cogitate; consider; contemplate; deliberate; meditate; mull; muse; ponder; reflect; weigh

RUMOR: **v.** bruit; cry; gossip; murmur; noise; norate; say; tattle; whisper; RUMOR: **n.** bruit; canard; fame; gossip; grapevine; hearsay; inkling; intimation; murmur; noise; notoriety; report; roorback; scuttlebutt; story; talk; tattle; tidings; whisper; words

RUMP: (**see** "buttocks") beam; breech; *derrière*; end; fragment; gluteus (maximus); podex; posterior; remainder

RUN: **v.** chase; compete; conduct; consort; contest; course; dart; dash; decamp; drive; employ; escape; execute; expedite; flee; flow; fly; function; fuse; gad; gallop; go; govern; haste(n); head; hie; hightail; lope; man(age); melt; operate; pace; panic; pilot; ply; pour; propel; race; range; resort; retreat; revel; riff; roam; rush; scamper; scram; scud; speed; spread; spring; sprint; steer; stream; supervise; tear; travel; trot; use; wield; RUN: **n.** (**see** "race") brook; course; creek; dart; dash; distance; flow; gallop; lope; panic; path; range; ravel; route; scale; series; spring; stream; string; track; trip; way

RUN-DOWN: ancient; depleted; dilapidated; exhausted; squalid; tatterdemalion; uncared-for; unmaintained

RUNNER: branch; candidate; conduit; courier; horse; mat; messenger; miler; racer; rug; scarf; stolon; smuggler; supervisor; whippet

RUNT: chit; dwarf; elf; peewee; pigmy; RUNTY: **see** "short"

RUNWAY: airstrip; channel; groove; passage-(way); path(way); ramp; road; space; strip; tarmac; track; trail

RUPTURE: **v.** breach; break; burst; disrupt; feud; fracture; herniate; protrude; quarrel; split; stick; tear; RUPTURE: **n.** breach; break; disruption; feud; fracture; hernia; quarrel; rent; rhexis; rift; split; tear

RURAL: (**see** "rustic") agrarian; agrestic; agricultural; Arcadian; backwoodsy; bucolic; campestral; churlish; countrified; country; cracker-barrel; geoponic; georgic; idyllic; naïve; pastoral; peasant; provincial; simple; sylvan; uncomplicated; unsophisticated; villatic

RUSE: (**see** "trick") blind; dodge; sell; stall

RUSH: **v.** (**see** "run") attack; bang; barge; blitz; charge; dart; dash; defeat; deluge; drive; flash; flood; flush; fly; hasten; hie; hurl; hurry; hurtle; leap; outpour; overpower; overwhelm; press; race; rip; scud; shoot; speed; spurt; stampede; stave; storm; streak; surge; tear; thrust; vanquish; RUSH: **n.** attack; avalanche; blitz; burst; bustle; buzz; charge; commotion; confusion; dash; deluge; disturbance; excitement; flood; flurry; haste; hurry; land-office business; onset; outpouring; press; race; scud; spate; spurt; stampede; storm; surge; surging; tantivy; tear; tornado; torrent; tumult; whirl; whirlwind; RUSHING: Gadarene; heedless; impetuous; precipitate; precipitous; pressing; surging; torrential; tumultuous

RUST: **v.** canker; color; corrode; decay; degenerate; eat; erode; impair; oxidate; tarnish; weaken; RUST: **n.** accretion; aerugo; canker; coat(ing); corrosion; decay; degeneration; desuetude; disuse; erosion; idleness; inaction; inertia; obsolescence; oxidation; patina; verdigris

RUSTIC: (**see** "rural") agrarian; agrestic; agricultural; artless; awkward; backwoodsy; barbaric; boorish; bucolic; cloddish; clodhopperish; clodhopping; coarse; countrified; geoponic; georgic(al); hick; inelegant; pastoral; peasant; plain; rough; rude; rustical; simple; sturdy; sylvan; uncouth; unpolished; unsophisticated; untaught; yokelish; RUSTIC: **n.** backwoodsman; barbarian; boor; bucolic; bumpkin; clod(hopper); clown; cornball; countryman; dolt; eclogue; fool; hayseed; idyl; mossback; peasant; rube; simpleton; yahoo; yokel

RUSTLING: breezy; gentle; murmuring; soft; susurrous; swishing; whispering

RUT: channel; estrus; furrow; grind; groove; habit; heat; impasse; path; practice; routine; track

RUTHLESS: (**see** "tough") barbaric; hardfisted; heartless; merciless; pitiless; Procrustean; relentless; revengeful; savage; unsparing; wild

RUTILANT: (**see** "bright") gleaming; glittering; glowing; red(dish); shining

S

SABULOUS: arenaceous; dusty; floury; gritty; sandy

SAC: ascus; bag; bursa; cavity; cyst; pocket; pouch; vesicle

SACCHARINE: (see "sweet") agreeable; friendly; gentle; honeyed; pleasant; sirupy; sugary; syrupy; treacly

SACERDOTAL: churchly; clerical; ecclesiastical; priestly; sacred

SACK: v. bag; cashier; despoil; discharge; dismiss; drop; fire; jilt; loot; pillage; plunder; ravage; rob; strip; SACK: n. bag; bed; cashier; container; despoliation; destruction; discharge; dismissal; dress; havoc; poke; pouch; rejection; sherry; spoliation; wine

SACRAMENT: baptism; ceremony; communion; covenant; eucharist; form(ality); host; marriage; mass; pledge; rite; ritual; service; solemnity; symbol; token

SACRED: (see "holy") cherished; consecrated; dedicated; divine; hallow(ed); inviolable; inviolate; numinous; pious; pure; religious; revered; reverential; sacerdotal; sacramental; sacramentary; sacrosanct; sainted; sanctified; undefiled; valued; venerable; venerated; SACREDNESS: (see "holiness") consecration; inviolability; sacramentality; sacrosanctity; sanctification; sanctitude; sanctity

SACRIFICE: v. abnegate; bunt; for(e)go; give; immolate; lose; offer; renounce; resign; surrender; yield; SACRIFICE: n. abnegation; bunt; burnt offering; crucifixion; deprivation; hecatomb; immolation; loss; oblation; offering; privation; renunciation; sacrification; surrender; victim

SACRILEGE: blasphemy; desecration; impiety; profanation; profanity; SACRILEGIOUS: blasphemous; hypocritical; impious; irreverent; profane

SAD: afflicting; afflictive; atrabilarious; atra-biliar; atrabiliary; atrabilious; atrocious; bad; baleful; bitter; blue; calamitous; cheerless; crabbed; dark; defunctive; dejected; deplorable; depressed; depressing; desolate; *désolé*; despairing; despondent; dire; disconsolate; discouraged; dismal; dispirited; distressful; distressing; doleful; dolent(e); dolentissimo; dolesome; dolorific; doloroso; dolorous; downcast; drab; drear(y); dull; dumpish; elegiac; forlorn; funebr(i)ous; funereal; gloomy; glum; grave; grieved; grievous; heartbreaking; heartbroken; heartsick; heavy(hearted); hypochondriacal; hysterical; inconsolable; inconsolate; inferior; infestive; joyless; lachrymal; lachrymatory; lachrymose; lamentable; lamented; lugubrious; melancholic; melancholious; melancholy; mirthless; miserable; moody; morbid; mournful; painful; pathetic; *penseroso*; pensive; plaintive; poor; raptureless; rueful; saddened; serious; severe; somber; sombrous; sore; sorrowful; sorry; spiritless; sulky; triste; tristful; unenjoying; unfestive; unhappy; unjoyous; unrejoicing; wan; wearied; wistful; woebegone; woeful; wretched; SADNESS: affliction; bitterness; blues; cheerlessness; dejection; depression; desolation; despair; despondency; disconsolation; discouragement; dismality; dispiritedness; distress; doldrums; dolor; dreariment; dreariness; dumps; ennui; forlornity; gloom(iness); gravity; grief; heartache; heartbreak; heartsickness; hypochondriasis; hysteria; inconsolation; infestivity; joylessness; lachrymals; lamentation; languishment; lugubriosity; megrims; melancholia; melancholy; mirthlessness; misery; mournfulness; pathos; rue(fulness); sorrow(fulness); *tristesse*; unhappiness; vapors; woe; SADDEN: contrist; darken; deject; depress; discourage; dispirit; distress; grieve; pain

SAFARI: excursion; expedition; exploration; hike; hunt; journey; junket; reconnaissance; tour; trek; trip

SAFE: a. (see "unharmed") cautious; certain; *ex abundante cautela*; harmless; hazardless; impregnable; invulnerable; out of the woods; protected; reliable; riskless; secure; sure;

tame; tried; trustworthy; unassailable; un-conquerable; uncontaminated; undangerous; unharmed; unharmful; unharming; unhurt; uninjured; uninjurious; unmolested; un-precarious; SAFE: **n.** chest; coffer; cup-board; stronghold; vault; SAFETY: anchor; *anchora*; asylum; exemption; freedom; pre-servation; protection; refuge; retreat; safe-ness; salvation; sanctuary; security; surety

SAFEGUARD: (**see** "protect") defense; pal-ladium; prophylactic; prophylaxis; protec-tion; rail(ing); safety; shield; umbrella

SAG: bend; collapse; curve; decline; deflate; dip; drift; droop; drop; flag; flex; give; hang; lull; settle; sink; slacken; slouch; slump; sway; swing; wilt

SAGA; Edda; epic; legend; myth; narrative; novel; story; tale; tradition

SAGACIOUS: (**see** "wise") acute; apt; astute; brainy; cautious; circumspect; deep; dis-cerning; discreet; farsighted; intellectual; judicious; keen; penetrating; perceptive; perspicacious; prophetic; prudent; quick; rational; sage; sapient(ial); sensible; sharp (-witted); shrewd; subtle; tactful; witted; witty; SAGACITY: acuity; acumen; acute-ness; astucity; astuteness; canniness; clever-ness; discretion; farsightedness; insight; judg-ment; keenness; ken; penetration; percep-tion; perceptiveness; perceptivity; perspica-city; policy; prudence; sagaciousness; sapi-ence; sensibility; shrewdness; tact; wisdom; wit

SAGE: **a.** (**see** "wise") acuminous; discern-ing; intellectual; judicious; Nestorian; per-spicacious; philosophic(al); profound; prudent; sagacious; sane; sapient(ial); Solo-monic; wise; SAGE: **n.** herb; Nestor; philo-sopher; pundit; salvia; seasoning; Solomon; solon

SAID: **see** "spoken"

SAIL: **v.** cruise; dart; float; fly; glide; navigate; scud; skate; skim; SAIL: **n.** canvas; cruise; sheet; spinnaker

SAILOR(S): crew(men); *gens de mer*; gob; hat; jack; mariner; matelot; middy; sail; sea-farer; seaman; tar; tarpot; toty

SAINTLY: angelic; beatific; canonized; celes-tial; cherubic; heavenly; holy; pietistic; pious; religious; sacred; sacrosanct; sancti-fied; seraphic; spiritual; sublime; unprofane

SAKE: account; advantage; behalf; benefit; beverage; drink; end; good; interest; objec-tive; purpose; score

SALAAM: **v.** bend; bow; curts(e)y; genuflect; greet; kowtow; nod; salute; SALAAM: **n.** bend; bow; curts(e)y; genuflexion; greeting; kowtow; nod; obeisance; salutation; salute

SALABLE: **see** after "sale"

SALARY: allowance; compensation; emolu-ment; fee; hire; honorarium; income; money; pay(ment); recompense; remunera-tion; salt; stipend(ium); wage(s)

SALE: abalienation; alienation; auction; bar-gain; barter; bazaar; buy; change; clearance; deal; demand; disposal; distribution; ex-change; handsel; market; opening; pur-chase; trade; transaction; vendition; vendue; SALABLE: good; marketable; mercenary; merchantable; purchasable; suitable; venal; vendible

SALIENT: bounding; conspicuous; impor-tant; impressive; jetting; jumping; jutting; leaping; manifest; notable; noticeable; out-standing; principal; projecting; prominent; protuberant; rampant; roaring; saltant; signal; significant; sharp; striking

SALLOW: anemic; ashen; ashy; colorless; etiolated; gray; icteric; ischemic; jaundiced; muddy; pale; pallid; pasty; sickly; wan; yellowish

SALLY: **v.** attack; bound; burst; dash; digress; frolic; issue; leap; quip; rush; start; try; SALLY: **n.** antic; attack; bound; dash; digression; escapade; excursion; fray; frolic; jaunt; jest; joke; leap; mot; outbreak; out-burst; quip; rush; sortie; spring; start; trip; try; witticism

SALMAGUNDI: farrago; gallimaufry; hash; heterogeneity; hodgepodge; jumble; medley; malange; mishmash; mixture; olio; pot-pourri

SALON: assemblage; assembly; exhibition; hall; levee; parlor; party; reception; room; saloon; shop

SALOON: bar(room); groggery; joint; pub; salon; taproom

SALT: **v.** corn; cure; enrich; flavor; preserve; season; SALT: **n.** brine; common sense; condiment; earthiness; flavor; food; gob;

humor; keep; kern; mariner; mineral; money; pay; preserver; pungency; reserve; sailor; sal; salary; savor; sea; seaman; season(ing); sense; sharpness; skepticism; sodium chloride; taste; wit; SALTY: brackish; briny; caustic; earthy; experienced; piquant; pungent; racy; risqué; saliferous; saline; sharp; sophisticated; witty

SALTANT: dancing; jumping; leaping; salient

SALUTARY: advantageous; beneficial; bracing; corrective; curative; desirable; good; healing; healthful; healthy; hygienic; medicinal; nutritious; profitable; remedial; restorative; roborant; salubrious; sanative; sound; strengthening; therapeutic(al); tonic; useful; wholesome

SALUTE: **v.** accost; address; approve; bow; compliment; congratulate; curts(e)y; dip; genuflect; greet; hail; honor; kiss; praise; salaam; toast; wave; welcome; SALUTE: **n.** a chara; address; allocution; aloha; approval; ave; bow; compliment; congratulation; curts(e)y; dip; genuflexion; gesture; greeting; hail; kiss; praise; salaam; salutation; salvo; toast; waive; welcome

SALVAGE: (**see** "retrieve") forage; redeem; rescue; save; scrounge

SALVATION: (**see** "freedom") absolution; atonement; deliverance; extrication; liberation; manumission; Nirvana; preservation; ransom; redemption; regeneration; release; repair; reprieve; respite; safety

SALVE: **v.** (**see** "ease") allay; anoint; assuage; cure; flatter; heal; mitigate; quiet; relieve; remedy; soothe; treat; SALVE: **n.** balm; cerate; cure; ease; flattery; inunction; nard; oil; ointment; plaster; relief; remedy; treatment; unction; unguent

SAME: adequate; akin; alike; coequal; coessential; coetaneous; coeval; coextensive; cognate; commensurate; comparable; conformable; conforming; congruent; ditto; duplicate; equal; equiponderant; equivalent; even; ibidem; idem; identic(al); ilk; invariable; isometric; isonomous; just; kind; like(wise); monotonous; one; peer; repetitious; resembling; selfsame; similar; synonymous; tantamount; twin; unchanging; very; SAMENESS: (**see** "equality") accord; analogy; coequality; coetaneity; coevality; congruency; correspondence; counterpart; equality; equiponderance; equivalence; identical-

ity; likeness; monotony; oneness; repetition; resemblance; selfsameness; similarity; singleness; unanimity; uniformity; wearisomeness

SAMPLE: **v.** copy; examine; exemplify; experience; experiment; match; represent; sip; symbolize; taste; test; try; SAMPLE: **n.** archetype; *beau idéal*; bit; bite; case; copy; cut; example; excerpt; exemplar; exemplification; fragment; illustration; indication; instance; microcosm; model; parcel; part; pattern; piece; portion; prototype; replica; representation; representative; slip; sliver; specimen; splinter; swatch; taste; tasting; trial

SANCTIFY: (**see** "deify") canonize; consecrate; hallow; sacralize; stellify

SANCTIMONIOUS: (**see** "holy") devout; holier-than-thou; Pecksniffian; pharisaic(al); pietistic(al); religiose; self-righteous

SANCTION: **v.** abet; acclaim; accredit; allow; approve; authorize; commend; confirm; corroborate; countenance; countersign; enable; encourage; endorse; establish; indulge; license; maintain; pass; permit; praise; ratify; recognize; validate; vouchsafe; warrant; SANCTION: **n.** abetment; acclaim; accreditation; accreditment; allowance; amen; approbation; approval; assent; authority; authorization; coercion; commendation; confirmation; consideration; control; countenance; credit; decree; dispensation; encouragement; endorsement; esteem; favor; fiat; franchise; freedom; imprimatur; indulgence; isolation; liberty; license; penalty; permission; permit; plaudit; praise; privilege; punishment; quarantine; ratification; recognition; regard; repute; restriction; sufferage; sufferance; warrant; SANCTIONED: approved; authorized; confirmed; conventional; institutive; lawful; legal; legitimate; official; orthodox; permissive; permitted; proper; ratified; valid

SANCTITY: (**see** "holiness") beatification; consecration; deification; godliness; inviolability; purity; sacredness; saintliness

SANCTUARY: adytum; altar; *ancora salutis*; *ancora spei*; ark; asylum; church; cover; fane; harbor; haven; holy of holies; home; hospice; immunity; oasis; penetrale; preserve; protection; refuge; retreat; safety; sanctum; *sanctum sanctorum*; shelter; shrine; tabernacle; temple

SAND: beach; courage; fortitude; gravel;

grit; guts; mettle; nerve; pluck; power; resolution; sea; shore; silica; spirit; stamina; SANDY: arenaceous; arenose; gritty; nervy; plucky; sabulous; shifting; unsound; unstable

SANE: all there; competent; *compos mentis*; good; healthy; logical; lucid; normal; rational; reasonable; right; sage; sensible; sober; sound; wise; SANITY: competence; competency; equilibrium; lucidity; *mens sana*; normality; rationality; reason(ableness); sense; soundness; wholesomeness; wit(s)

SANGFROID: (**see** "coolness") aplomb; coldbloodedness; competence; equanimity; imperturbability; indifference; phlegm; unconcern

SANGUINARY: (**see** "bloody") bloodthirsty; gory; murderous

SANGUINE: (**see** "cheerful") anticipative; ardent; bloody; buoyant; certain; confident; elated; enthusiastic; euphoric; expectant; gay; gory; happy; hopeful; inspirited; optimistic; plethoric; red; ruddy; spirited; warm

SANITARY: (**see** "clean") clinical; healthful; hygienic; sterile; surgical; wholesome

SANITY: **see** under "sane"

SAP: **v.** debilitate; diminish; drain; enervate; enfeeble; exhaust; impoverish; subvert; undermine; unsettle; weaken; wreck; SAP: **n.** blood; energy; essence; fluid; fool; health; ichor; juice; lymph; pitch; pith; secretion; simpleton; trench; vigor; vitality; SAPPY: foolish; foppish; juicy; lush; mawkish; pithy; sentimental; silly; simple; succulent; vital

SAPID: engaging; palatable; piquant; savory; tasty; zestful

SAPIENT: (**see** "wise") acute; discerning; perspicacious; knowing; knowledg(e)able; sagacious; sage; sapiential; SAPIENCE: acuteness; discernment; intelligence; judgment; knowledge; perspicacity; sagacity; sageness; sense; taste; wisdom

SAPOR: flavor; gusto; piquancy; relish; sapidity; savor(iness); taste; zest

SARCASTIC: (**see** "abusive") acerb(ic); acidulous; acrimonious; Archilochian; austere; biting; caustic; contemptible; corrosive; cutting; cynical; derisive; disdainful;

edged; grim; harsh; hostile; incisive; ironic-(al); keen; mordacious; mordant; needling; painful; piercing; sardonic; sassy; satiric(al); saucy; scornful; sharp; sneering; sulfurous; trenchant; vinegary; virulent; vitriolic; SARCASM: acerbity; acrimony; aspersion; banter; causticity; censure; contempt; criticism; cynicism; derision; detraction; diatribe; disparagement; gibe; invective; irony; mordacity; needling; rebuke; ridicule; sardonicism; satire; scorn; sneer; taunt; uncourteousness; wit

SARDONIC: (**see** "abusive") acrid; biting; bitter; cynical; derisive; disdainful; dry; ironic(al); mocking; sarcastic; satiric(al); saturnine; scornful; skeptical; wry

SASH: band; belt; casement; cord; cummerbund; frame(work); gate; girdle; obi; scarf; strip

SASSY *or* SAUCY: abusive; airy; arch; arrogant; bantam; bold; brash; brazen; bumptious; cavalier; cheeky; chic; chipper; cocky; conceited; contemptuous; contumelious; despicable; dictatorial; discourteous; disdainful; disrespectful; flip(pant); forward; fresh; haughty; impertinent; impudent; insolent; irreverent; jaunty; malapert; nervy; officious; proud; rude; sarcastic; smart; smart-aleck(y); spirited; stylish; supercilious; trim; uncourteous; SASSINESS *or* SAUCINESS: abuse; arrogance; boldness; brashness; cheek; contempt(ibility); contumely; despicability; disdain; irreverence; nerve; pertness; procacity; protervity; sarcasm; sauce

SATAN: (**see** "devil") Apollyon; archfiend; Belial; fiend; Lucifer; Mephistopheles; reprobate; Satanas; tempter; SATANIC: (**see** "devilish") awful; bad; demoniac(al); derisive; diabolic(al); evil; fiendish; ghoulish; hellish; impious; impish; infernal; Luciferian; malevolent; Mephistophelean; mephitic; saturnine; vicious; wicked

SATCHEL: bag; cabas; etui; grip; handbag; reticule; sack; valise

SATE: appease; bore; cloy; cram; fatigue; flag; glut; gorge; gratify; jade; overfill; pall; satiate; saturate; stodge; stuff; surfeit; tire; SATED: blasé; crammed; fatigued; filled; flagged; full; glutted; gorged; gratified; jaded; satiated; satisfied; saturated; sophisticated; surfeited

SATELLITE: **a.** adjacent; ancillary; concomitant; dependent; dominated; related; satellitic; subordinate; subsidiary; SATEL-LITE: **n.** adherent; agent; attendant; companion; fan; follower; Luna; minion; moon; orbit; retainer; rocket; sputnik; subordinate; subsidiary; sycophant; votary

SATIATE: **see** "sate"

SATIRIZE: abuse; burlesque; caricature; censure; criticize; detract; grind; lampoon; lash; needle; pasquinade; ridicule; scourge; skin; SATIRE: abuse; burlesque; caricature; censure; criticism; cynicism; derision; diatribe; irony; humor; invective; lampoon; mockery; Pantagruelism; pasquinade; philippic; raillery; ridicule; sarcasm; sardonicism; scourge; skit; Sotadic; wit; SATIRIC(AL): abusive; biting; caustic; censorious; cutting; disdainful; dry; ironic(al); Juvenalian; Pantagruelian; poignant; sarcastic; sardonic(al); Shavian; Swiftian; taunting; witty; SATIRIST: farceur; farceuse (fem.); Pantagruelist; Pope; railleur; Shaw; sillographer; Swift; Voltaire

SATISFY: accommodate; allay; answer; appease; assure; atone; befriend; cheer; cloy; comfort; compensate; comply; content; convince; cram; cure; defray; discharge; dispel; do; exemplify; feed; fill; fulfill; glut; gorge; gratify; indemnify; jade; liquidate; meet; overfill; pacify; pall; pay; persuade; please; prove; reconcile; redeem; relieve; remedy; remunerate; repay; reward; sate; satiate; saturate; serve; settle; slake; smooth; stuff; suffice; suit; surfeit; SATISFACTION: amends; apology; atonement; comfort; complacency; content(edness); contentment; conviction; discharge; enjoyment; fulfillment; gratification; gratulation; indemnification; oblectation; penance; pleasure; reconciliation; redress; remuneration; reparation; repayment; repletion; requital; restitution; revenge; satiation; satiety; satisfyingness; stability; surfeit; vindication; SATISFACTORY, SATISFIED *or* SATISFYING: acceptable; adequate; approvable; comfortable; convinced; decent; effective; enjoyable; fair; fine; full; good; gratifying; informative; neat; passable; pleasant; pleasing; pleasurable; proper; rewarding; square; sufficient; unaspiring

SATURATE: cloy; cram; crowd; deluge; drench; fill; imbue; impenetrate; impregnate; infuse; ingrain; interpenetrate; jade; neutralize; overfill; overwhelm; penetrate; permeate; pervade; ret; sate; satiate; seethe; soak; sog; sop; steep; suffuse; surfeit; wash;

wet; SATURATION: concentration; contentment; imbibition; impregnation; infusion; intensity; interpenetration; limit; penetration; permeation; pervasion; satiation; satiety; surfeit; vividness

SATURNALIA: carnival; excesses; feast; festival; games; orgies; party; revels

SATURNINE: (**see** "devilish") dour; dull; gloomy; glum; grave; heavy; leaden; melancholic; melancholy; morbid; morose; sardonic; sluggish; somber; sullen; surly; taciturn; wry

SATYR: ape; butterfly; demon; faun; goat; libertine; roué; Silenus

SAUCE: adjunct; allemande; *béchamel*; condiment; curry; dressing; flavor; gravy; relish; sassiness; sauciness; seasoning; soy(a); tabasco; *velouté*

SAUCY: **see** "sassy"

SAUNTER: amble; bummel; dawdle; fool; idle; lag; loaf; loiter; lounge; mosey; potter; ramble; range; sashay; stray; stroll; walk

SAVAGE: **a.** angered; animal(istic); atrocious; avenging; backward; barbaresque; barbarian; barbaric; barbar(i)ous; bestial; bloody; boorish; brutal; brutish; butcherly; cannibalic; cannibalistic; crazed; crude; cruel; crushing; devastating; diabolic(al); dispiteous; enraged; fell; feral; ferine; ferocious; fiendish; fierce; Gothic; grim; gross; harsh; heathenish; impiteous; infrahuman; inhuman(e); malevolent; merciless; nonhuman; pagan; Philistinic; pitiless; Procrustean; punitive; raging; relentless; rough; rude; rugged; ruthless; Satanic(al); subhuman; tramontane; truculent; turbulent; tyrannic(al); tyrannous; unchristian; uncivil(ized); uncultured; undomesticated; unmerciful; unrefined; unrestrained; untamed; vengeful; vicious; violent; wild; yahoo; SAVAGE: **n.** aborigine; animal; barbarian; beast; brute; cannibal; heathen; pagan; primitive; yahoo; SAVAGENESS *or* SAVAGERY: anger; animalism; animality; backwardness; barbarism; barbarity; barbarousness; bestiality; bloodthirstiness; brutality; callousness; cannibalism; cannibality; cold-bloodedness; cruelty; degradation; demoralization; despitefulness; devil(t)ry; ferity; ferocity; fiendishness; fury; hardheartedness; hardness; hellishness; implacability; induration; inhumanity; malice; Philistinism; primitivity; ruthlessness; savagery; savagism; truculence; truculency; tyranny; unrestraint; vengeance; vengefulness; wickedness

SAVE: accumulate; avoid; bank; cache; can; catch; conserve; deliver; deposit; economize; eke; except; exclude; exempt; extricate; free; freeze; guard; have; help; hoard; hold; husband; keep; pare; preserve; protect; recover; redeem; reduce; rescue; reserve; retain; retrench; safeguard; salvage; scrape; scrimp; spare; stint; store; tin; underspend; SAVING: accumulative; careful; chary; close; conservative; economical; except; frugal; planned; practical; profitable; provident; prudent(ial); redeeming; reserving; sparing; stingy; stinting; thrifty; underspending; unwasteful

SAVIO(U)R: benefactor; deliverer; emancipator; liberator; messiah; preserver; redeemer

SAVOIR FAIRE: (see "ease") address; adroitness; courtesy; courtliness; diplomacy; grace; poise; posture; skill; tact(fulness)

SAVOR: v. feel; like; relish; season; smack; smell; taste; SAVOR: n. aura; feeling; flavor; odor; perfume; relish; scent; smack; smell; tang; taste; tinge; tone; SAVORY: (see "appetizing") agreeable; ambrosial; dainty; delectable; delicious; edifying; exquisite; flavorous; fragrant; good; gratifying; gustable; gustatory; luscious; mint(y); nectareous; nice; palatable; piquant; pleasant; pleasing; rich; salty; sapid; satisfying; savorous; spicy; sweet; tasteful; tasty; teasing; tempting; toothsome; wholesome

SAW: (see "maxim") adage; aphorism; axiom; cliché; epigram; gnome; motto; proverb; saying; tag; tool; wisecrack; witticism

SAY: acknowledge; advertise; affirm; air; allege; announce; annunciate; articulate; assert; asseverate; assure; aver; avouch; avow; broadcast; certify; cite; claim; comment(ate); confirm; declare; demonstrate; depose; designate; emphasize; explain; exposit; expound; express; give; inform; lecture; maintain; manifest; mention; name; nuncupate; orate; order; pledge; postulate; predicate; proclaim; profess; promulgate; pronounce; propound; protest; publicize; publish; recite; relate; repeat; report; signify; speak; specify; spread; state; suppose; swear; talk; tell; testify; utter; voice; vow; write

SAYING(S): (see "maxim") adage; ana; aphorism; apothegm; assertion; banality; bijouterie; bon mot; bromide; byword; catchword; cliché; dictum; dit; epigram; motto; pearls of wisdom; platitude; precept; proverb; saw; shibboleth; slogan; wisecrack; witticism

SCAB: apostate; blackleg; crust; eschar; mange; rot; scale; scoundrel; scurf; strikebreaker; SCABBY: contemptible; crusty; despicable; desquamative; inferior; mean; peeling; poor; scabrous; scurrilous; squalid

SCALE: v. ascend; bark; calibrate; clamber; climb; exfoliate; flake; gradate; grade; graduate; measure; mount; pare; peel; reduce; rise; rust; shell; slough; surmount; weigh; SCALE: n. balance; bract; calibration; coat(ing); covering; degree; despumation; desquamation; diapason; dimension; exfoliation; extent; film; flake; gamut; gauge; husk; incrustation; ladder; lamina; layer; patina; plate; peel; proportion; ramentum; rate; ratio; relationship; rule(r); run; rust; scab; scurf; scute; series; size; squama; standard; weight; SCALINESS: desquamation; scabrousness; squamation; squamosity; SCALY: (see "flaky") base; despicable; encrusted; furfuraceous; inferior; laminar; leprose; mean; paleiform; poor; scabrous; scurfy; scutate; squamous; stingy

SCAMP: v. cheat; scant; skimp; slight; SCAMP: n. bacalao; black sheep; cheat; culprit; dog; imp; Judas; knave; mauvais sujet; miscreant; polisson; prankster; rakehell; rapscallion; rascal; reprobate; ribald; rip; robber; rogue; roué; rowdy; ruffian; scalawag; Scapin; scaramouche; scoundrel; sharp-(st)er; thug; tough; trickster; varlet; varmint; villain; yegg

SCAMPER: (see "run") flee; fly; hasten; hie; scram; scud; speed

SCAN: (see "examine") analyze; check; eye; inspect; look; peek; rake; read; scrutinize; survey; test

SCANDALIZE: derogate; detract; embarrass; malign; offend; revile; shock; slander; traduce; vilify; SCANDAL: aspersion; defamation; derogation; detraction; discredit; disgrace; infamy; mud; obliquity; obloquy; offense; shame; slander; vilification; SCANDALOUS: atrocious; defamatory; disgraceful; disreputable; disrespectful; flagitious; flagrant; heinous; infamous; libelous; malodorous; notorious; obliquitous; obloquial; offensive; outrageous; shameful; slanderous; villainous

SCANT: **v.** limit; restrict; scamp; scrimp; slight; spare; stint; SCANT(Y): **a.** bare; barren; chary; economical; exiguous; few; frugal; inadequate; infinitesimal; insufficient; lacking; lean; little; meager; mean; naked; narrow; niggard; parsimonious; rare; skimpy; short; shy; slender; slight; small; spare; sparse; stingy; stringent; thin; threadbare; SCANTINESS: (**see** "scarcity") exiguity; frugality; parcity; paucity; sparcity; stringency

SCAR: **v.** blemish; cicatrize; disfigure; injure; mar; mark; scarify; wound; SCAR: **n.** blemish; cicatrice; cicatrix; cicatrization; cliff; crag; defect; disfigurement; flaw; injury; mark; scab; ulosis; wound

SCARCE: barely; deficient; hardly; infrequent; insufficient; rare; scant(y); sparing; sparse; thin; uncommon; wanting; SCARCITY: dearth; deficiency; exigency; exiguity; famine; fewness; hunger; inadequacy; insufficiency; lack; parcity; paucity; rareness; rarity; scantiness; scarceness; shortage; sparcity; sparsity; stringency; uncommonness; want

SCARE: **v.** abash; affright; agrise; alarm; appall; awe; browbeat; bulldoze; bully; coerce; cow; daunt; dismay; domineer; frighten; hector; horrify; intimidate; menace; overawe; panic; petrify; shock; shoo; startle; surprise; terrify; terrorize; threaten; unnerve; SCARE: **n.** affright; alarm; bugaboo; fright; intimidation; menace; panic; petrification; shock; startle; surprise; terror; threat; SCARY: alarmed; alarming; anxious; bloodcurdling; eerie; frightened; frightening; ghostly; gory; murderous; scared; spooky; startling; terrorizing; threatening; timid

SCARECROW: bugaboo; effigy; ghost; guy; *homme de paille*; malkin; ogre; ragamuffin; specter; tatterdemalion

SCATHE: **see** "damage;" SCATHELESS: **see** "unharmed"

SCATHING: blue; boiling; burning; caustic; corrosive; damaging; harmful; hurtful; mordant; sarcastic; scalding; severe; sulfurous; truculent; virulent; vitriolic; vituperative

SCATTER: bestrew; branch; broadcast; cast; circulate; clutter; deal; decentralize; derange; diffuse; disband; disburse; disgregate; dispel; dispense; disperse; disseminate; dissipate; distribute; diverge; diversify; interspace; intersperse; litter; promulgate; publish; rout; separate; sow; splatter; spread; spray; sprinkle; squander; strew; ted; waste; SCATTERED: cast; cluttered; dealt; diffuse-(d); discrete; disordered; disrupted; disseminated; distributed; disunited; infrequent; interspaced; interspersed; irregular; isolated; promulgated; rambling; random; separate-(d); sparse; sparsile; sporadic; spread; sprinkled; strewn; tossed; vagrant; wasted; SCATTERING: diaspora; diffusion; disjection; dispersion; dissemination; distribution; promulgation; sampling; scatteration; sporadicity; sprinkling

SCENARIO: libretto; outline; play; plot; screenplay; script; synopsis

SCENE: (**see** "area") action; display; episode; event; exhibition; landscape; locale; locality; location; pageant; painting; panorama; perspective; photo(graph); place; quarrel; representation; scape; setting; show; sight; site; situation; spectacle; sphere; stage; state; tabloid; theater; view; vista; SCENIC: **see** "dramatic;" SCENERY: diorama; landscape; panorama; props; set(s); setting; show; view

SCENT: **v.** aromatize; discover; feel; nose; odorize; perceive; perfume; smell; spice; SCENT: **n.** (**see** "aroma") aromaticity; aura; bouquet; cachet; effluvia (pl.); effluvium; essence; flair; fragrance; incense; inkling; intimation; musk; nidor; nose; odor; perfume; redolence; sign; smell; track; SCENTED: aromatic; balsamic; odiferous; odorous; olent; perfumed; pungent; redolent; spicy

SCEPTER: authority; baton; fasces; mace; rod; sovereignty; staff; wand

SCHEDULE: **v.** appoint; arrange; assign; catalog(ue); designate; list; register; SCHEDULE: **n.** agenda (pl.); agendum; appointments; arrangement; card; catalog-(ue); curriculum; designation; inventory; items; list; menu; plan; program(me); proposal; prospectus; record; register; roll; roster; scheme; slate; table; tabulation; tariff; time(table)

SCHEME: **v.** aim; angle; arrange; aspire; contemplate; contrive; design; devise; diagram; intrigue; machinate; manipulate; outline; plan; plot; premeditate; prepare; program; project; shape; shift; sketch; SCHEME: **n.** aim; angle; arrangement; aspiration; babel; cabal; cadre; complexity; conspiracy; contrivance; contemplation; design; device; diagram; diversion; dodge; draft; epitome; escapade; hypothesis; intrigue; knack; lark; lottery; machination; manipulation; network; plan; plot; premeditation; preparation; program; project; purpose; racket; schedule; setup; shape; shift; sketch; stratagem; strategy; system; table; tabulation; texture; theory; underplot; web

SCHISM: breach; break; disagreement; discord; disharmony; dissent(ion); disunion; disunity; diversion; diversity; division; faction; hostility; rent; rift; sect; separation; split

SCHOLAR: academe; academic(ian); academist; disciple; learner; literati (pl.); literato; literatus; pedant; philomath; polyhistor; polymath; pundit; pupil; sabora; sage; savant; student; trainee; SCHOLARLY: (**see** "learned") academic(al); bibliognostic; bookish; erudite; knowing; knowledg(e)able; learned; lettered; pedantic; philomathic(al); scholastic; studious; SCHOLARSHIP: accomplishment; aid; burse; erudition; foundation; grant; knowledge; learning; lore; scholarliness

SCHOOL: **v.** advance; coach; cultivate; discipline; drill; educate; guide; indoctrinate; instruct; inure; prepare; stabilize; teach; train; tutor; SCHOOL: **n.** academe; academy; assemblage; bevy; class; club; colegio; college; company; coterie; crowd; denomination; disciples; discipline; drove; faculty; flock; followers; gang; group; gymnasium; herd; institute; institution; lycée; lyceum; multitude; multiversity; philosophy; prep; scholasticate; sect; seminary; session; university

SCIENCE: ability; art; craft(smanship); erudition; expertise; knowledge; learning; lore; method(ology); nature; proficiency; scientism; skill(fulness); study; SCIENTIAL: able; capable; competent; expert; knowing; knowledg(e)able; proficient; SCIENTIFIC: accurate; efficient; exact; expert; skilled; skillful; sound; systematic; systematized; SCIENTIST: researcher; savant

SCINTILLA: (**see** "bit") atom; glimmer; iota; jot; particle; rag; ray; scrap; shadow; spark; tittle; trace; whit; SCINTILLATE: **see** "sparkle"

SCION: child; cutting; descendant; graft; heir; offshoot; shoot; slip; son; sprout; twig

SCOFF: belittle; blame; censure; chide; contemn; criticize; decry; deprecate; deride; despise; disapprove; disdain; disparage; fleer; flout; scorn; scout; sneer; spurn; taunt; upbraid; SCOFFER: Abderite

SCOLD: **v.** (**see** "criticize") berate; blame; castigate; censure; chafe; chastise; chew (out); chide; excoriate; hector; jaw; lambaste; lecture; nag; objurgate; peck; rag; rail; rant; rate; rebuke; reprimand; reprove; revile; scoff; tongue-lash; upbraid; vilify; vituperate; yap; SCOLD(ING): **n.** castigation; censure; chiding; excoriation; lecture; objurgation; raillery; rebuke; reproach; shrew; termagant; upbraiding; virago; vituperation; vixen

SCOOP: **v.** bail; beat; chisel; dig; dip; excavate; gouge; hollow; lade; ladle; shovel; spoon; SCOOP: **n.** beat; dipper; hollow; ladle; shovel; spoon; story

SCOPE: (**see** "range") aim; ambit; area; arena; breadth; category; compass; comprehensiveness; degree; diapason; domain; dominion; elbowroom; empire; end; extension; extent; field; franchise; freedom; gamut; ground; jurisdiction; latitude; leeway; length; lexicon; liberty; license; margin; object; opportunity; orbit; panorama; pantheon; permission; play; power; precinct; province; purpose; purview; radius; reach; realm; region; reign; rein; room; rope; size; space; spectrum; sphere; stretch; subdivision; sweep; swing; terrain; territory; tether; text; topography; tract; vent; way; width; SCOPIC: commodious; comprehensive; extensive; jurisdictional; latitudinal; latitudinous; orbital; panoramic; visual

SCORCH: blister; burn; censure; char; criticize; devastate; dry; excoriate; flay; parch; roast; scathe; score; sear; shrivel; singe; wither

SCORE: **v.** (**see** "criticize") abrade; achieve; arrange; assail; berate; blister; burn; castigate; censure; chalk; charge; count; crease; cut; enumerate; excoriate; furrow;

gain; grade; groove; grudge; list; mar; mark; notch; orchestrate; rate; reckon; record; roast; scorch; scratch; singe; tabulate; tally; win; SCORE: **n.** account; basket; behalf; consideration; count(er); cut; debt; down; excoriation; indebtedness; mark; music; notch; object; point; rank; rate; rating; reason; reckoning; run; sake; scratch; summary; tab; tally; target; twenty

SCORN: **v.** (**see** "disdain") contemn; despise; mock; scoff; SCORN: **n.** (**see** "contempt") asteism; contumely; derision; disdain; flout; gibe; opprobrium; ridicule; sauciness; sneer; sniff; taunt; SCORNFUL: (**see** "contemptible") contemptuous; contumelious; derisible; derisive; despicable; disdainful; haughty; saucy; snippy; supercilious; SCORNFULNESS: arrogance; condescension; contempt(ibility); contumely; derision; despicability; disdain; haughtiness; hauteur; mockery; opprobrium; ridicule; sauciness

SCOUNDREL: blackguard; bounder; cad; cheat; criminal; culprit; demon; devil; gamin; heel; knave; miscreant; profligate; rapscallion; rascal; rat; renegade; reprobate; rip; rogue; roué; rounder; ruffian; scamp; swindler; tear; tough; trickster; varlet; villain; wastrel; wretch

SCOUR: brighten; brush; buff; burnish; clean(se); clear; mop; polish; purge; range; rove; rub; rummage; sand; scrub; search; seek; swab

SCOURGE: **v.** (**see** "criticize") afflict; chasten; chastise; devastate; flay; flog; harry; lash; plague; punish; satirize; swinge; switch; whip; SCOURGE: **n.** affliction; bane; chastenment; chastisement; criticism; devastation; disaster; disease; evil; plague; punishment; satire

SCOUT: **v.** browse; deride; despise; dismiss; explore; flout; guide; look; mock; observe; reconnoiter; reject; ridicule; scoff; search; seek; spurn; spy; SCOUT: **n.** agent; emissary; explorer; fellow; guide; guy; lookout; messenger; pal; reconnaissance; searcher; spy; vancourier; vanguard; watchman; SCOUTING: exploration; reconnaissance; reconnoiter; search

SCOWL: frown; glare; glower; lower; moue; stare

SCRAM: decamp; elope; escape; flee; go; leave; quit; run; scat; shoo; shove; vamoose

SCRAMBLE: **v.** clamber; climb; haste; hie; jostle; jumble; mix; muss; push; ramble; scale; scram; scrabble; sprawl; spread; straggle; strive; struggle; swarm; traverse; SCRAMBLE: **n.** climb; haste; jostling; jumble; mess; mixture; muss; push; sprawl; struggle

SCRAP: **v.** abandon; battle; brawl; discard; dispose; end; fight; junk; tussle; SCRAP(S): **n.** (**see** "waste") battle; bit; bite; brawl; chip; crumb; cutting; driblet; end; fight; fracas; fragment(s); garbage; hassle; jot; junk; leftover; melee; morsel; mouthful; oddment; odds and ends; ort(s); piece; rag; remnant; row; rumpus; scantling; set-to; speck; tatter; trash; tussle; war

SCRAPE: **v.** abrade; accumulate; clean; eke; erase; expunge; gather; grate; graze; paw; rasp; roughen; rub; scratch; shave; skin; smooth; strip; tear; SCRAPE: **n.** (**see** "scrap") abrasion; difficulty; dilemma; fight; fix; fracas; graze; jam; *mauvais pas*; mess; muss; perplexity; pickle; plight; predicament; puzzle(ment); quandary; rub; scratch; SCRAPING(S): chaff; dust; earnings; fillings; leavings; offscourings; ramenta; scraps; shavings

SCRATCH: **v.** (**see** "scrape") abrade; cancel; cicatrize; claw; dig; eliminate; erase; expunge; grate; graze; groove; incise; irritate; lacerate; mar; mark; obliterate; pit; rake; rist; roughen; rub; scar(ify); score; scribble; scrub; tear; withdraw; wound; write; SCRATCH: **n.** abrasion; beginning; cancellation; cicatrix; cicatrization; clawing; groove; incision; irritation; laceration; mar; mark; pit; roughness; rub; scar; score; scrape; scribble; tear; test; trial; withdrawal; wound; zero

SCRAWNY: bony; cadaverous; gaunt; lank(y); lean; rawboned; scragged; scraggy; scranny; skeletonic; skinny; spare; thin

SCREAM: **v.** caterwaul; complain; cry; demand; protest; screak; screech; shriek; vociferate; yell; SCREAM: **n.** caterwaul; clamor; complaint; cry; demand; outburst; protest(ation); screech; shriek; vociferation; yell; SCREAMING: clamorous; stentorian; vociferous

SCREECH: **see** "scream"

SCREED: diatribe; dissertation; essay; harangue; story; tirade

SCREEN: **v.** analyze; blind; bolt; censor; clean; cloak; conceal; cover; curtain; eliminate; examine; guard; hide; inspect; mask; partition; prevent; protect; riddle; separate; shade; shelter; shield; sieve; sift; sort; strain; veil; wall; winnow; SCREEN: **n.** blind; cinema; cloak; cover(ing); grille; guard; hedge; net(ting); mask; movies; partition; pavis(e); protection; security; separation; shade; shelter; sieve; sifter; strainer; trommel; umbrella; veil; wall

SCREW: **v.** cheat; contort; crumple; fasten; spiral; squint; thread; turn; twist; SCREW: **n.** bargainer; contortion; fastener; fee; helix; hire; jack; prop(eller); spiral; twist; wage

SCRIBBLE: **v.** march; scrabble; scratch; scrawl; write; SCRIBBLE **n.** or SCRIBBLING: cacography; griffonage; hen scratch; hen track; hieroglyphic(s); mark; *pattes de mouche*; scrabble; scratch; scrawl

SCRIBE: amanuensis; author; clerk; copyist; editor; journalist; penman; reporter; scrivener; scriver; writer

SCRIMMAGE: **see** "fight"

SCRIMP: (**see** "save") eke

SCRIP: bills; bond; certificate; currency; document; list; memorandum; money; scrap

SCRIPT: alphabet; document; handwriting; letter; penmanship; scenario; type; writing

SCRIPTURE: Bible; oracle(s); gospels; synoptics; testament; text; word; writing

SCROLL: bundle; coil; convolution; design; draft; flourish; list; loop; outline; papyrus; roll; roster; schedule; streamer; testimonial; volute

SCROUNGE: browse; cadge; crowd; find; forage; hunt; look; pilfer; press; prowl; pry; salvage; scavenge(r); search; seek; sponge; wheedle

SCRUB: **v.** (**see** "scour") cancel; clean; eliminate; scratch; wash; SCRUB: **n.** bush; cancellation; dwarf; mongrel; nobody; peewee; runt; SCRUBBY: dwarfish; inferior; mean; paltry; peewee; poor; runty; shabby; short; small; stunted; undersize

SCRUFF: coating; crust; dandruff; dross; film; nape; refuse; scum; skimmings; slur

SCRUPLE: **v.** balk; demur; doubt; falter; fret; hesitate; protest; question; stick; waver; SCRUPLE: **n.** balk; coin; compunction; demur; doubt; hesitation; iota; jot; money; particle; peculiarity; penitence; protest; qualm; scrupulosity; suspicion; uncertainty; wait; wavering; SCRUPULOUS: (**see** "precise") cautious; compunctious; conscientious; correct; exact; fastidious; finical; meticulous; nice; painstaking; precise; principled; punctilious; rabbinic(al); severe; shy; staid; strict; uprig..t; SCRUPULOUSNESS: integrity; meticulosity; preciseness; precision; punctiliousness; scrupulosity; severity; strictness; uprightness

SCRUTINIZE: (**see** "see") audit; examine; explore; eye; gaze; inspect; investigate; plumb-line; probe; pry; scan; sift; study; test; weigh; SCRUTINY: **see** "examination"

SCUD: **v.** dart; flash; fly; run; sail; skim; speed; SCUD: **n.** cloud; gust; rush

SCUFFLE: **v.** (**see** "fight") scurry; wrestle; SCUFFLE: **n.** clinch; fight; fray; melee; scrimmage; shuffle; struggle; tussle

SCUM: (**see** "waste") despumation; desquamation; dirt; dross; film; foam; froth; offscouring(s); patina; rabble; refuse; residue; scoria; scoriae (pl.); scurf; silt; skin; spume

SCURRILOUS: (**see** "abusive") burning; castigating; censorious; mean; scabby; scurrile; slanderous

SCURRY: (**see** "hasten") bustle; dart; dash; flurry; flutter; haste; hie; hurry; run; rush; scour; scud; scuttle; skelter

SCURVY: **a.** base; cheap; contemptible; discourteous; low; mean; scurfy; sorry; vile; SCURVY: **n.** scorbutus

SCUTTLE: (**see** "scurry") abandon; destroy; run; sink; withdraw

SEA: billow; brine; deep; drink; expanse; flood; foam; lake; main; ocean; salt; surf; surge; wave(s)

SEAL: **v.** authenticate; close; confirm; enclose; fasten; notarize; pledge; ratify; secure; settle; shut; stamp; SEAL: **n.** assurance; authentication; cachet; closure; confirmation; die; guarantee; impression; imprimatur; otary; pledge; ratification; signet; stamp; wafer; wax

SEAM: cicatrix; cicatrization; commissure;

crease; crevice; fissure; fold; groove; hem; joint; junction; juncture; layer; line; raphe; ridge; scar; stitch; stratum; synchondrosis; union; wrinkle

SEAMAN: **see** "sailor"

SEAR: **v.** blight; braise; brand; burn; cauterize; char; cook; desiccate; dry; fire; parch; shrivel; singe; wither; SEAR: **a. see** "sere"

SEARCH: **v.** browse; comb; cull; drag; examine; expiscate; explore; feel; ferret; fine-comb; fish; forage; frisk; hunt; inquire; inspect; investigate; look; peek; perlustrate; peruse; probe; pursue; quest(ion); ransack; rummage; scan; scour; scrutinize; seek; sift; snoop; survey; SEARCH: **n.** comb; examination; expiscation; exploration; forage; frisk; hunt; inquest; inquiry; inquisition; inspection; investigation; look; peek; perlustration; probe; pursuit; quest(ion); reconnaissance; reconnoiter; scouring; scrutinization; scrutiny; seeking; survey; visit; SEARCHING: expiscatory; inquiring; inquisitive; inquisitorial; investigative; probing; scrutinous; searchful; SEARCHER: detective; disquisitor; hunter; huntsman; inquisitor; inspector; peeker; prober; querist; questioner; researcher; scrutinizer; seeker; tracer

SEASON: **v.** acclimatize; accustom; age; corn; cure; devil; discipline; drill; flavor; inure; habituate; harden; mature; prepare; ripen; salt; savor; spice; temper; time; train; weather; SEASON: **n.** autumn; estrus; fall; heat; holiday(s); interval; occasion; period; spell; spring; summer; term; tide; time; winter; SEASONING: basil; condiment; flavor(ing); mustard; oregano; relish; sage; salt; sauce; spice; thyme; SEASONABLE: (**see** "timely") auspicious; convenient; expedient; opportune; pat; pertinent; proper; right; suitable; well-timed

SEAT: **v.** establish; fit; install; locate; place; set(tle); sit; station; SEAT: **n.** abode; asana; bench; bottom; buttocks; capital; center; chair(manship); dwelling; foundation; fundament(al); house; location; membership; office; perch; pew(age); place; position; residence; rocker; sedan; sella; settee; site; sofa; stool; station; support; throne

SECEDER(S): Adullamite; Cave of Adullam; schismatic; schismatist; secessionist; splinter (group)

SECLUDE: cache; cloister; confine; cover;

exclude; hide; isolate; protect; retire; screen; secrete; sequester; shut; withdraw; SECLUDED *or* SECLUSIVE: ascetic; cloisteral; cloistered; closed-door; covert; desolate; detached; embowered; enisled; hermitic; hidden; inaccessible; inapproachable; insulated; isolated; monarchal; monastic; monkish; odd; out-of-the-way; private; recluse; remote; removed; restricted; retired; screened; secreted; sequestered; sheltered; shy; solitary; unapproachable; unfrequented; withdrawn; SECLUSION *or* SECLUSIVENESS: ascesis; closed corporation; detachment; insulation; isolation; reclusion; retiracy; retirement; sequestration; solitariness; solitude

SECOND: **v.** (**see** "aid") abet; assist; back; confirm; corroborate; encourage; endorse; forward; further; handle; promote; substitute; support; sustain; SECOND: **a.** (**see** "secondary") beta; inferior; next; other; SECOND: **n.** aide; alternate; another; assistant; backer; beta; flash; instant; jiffy; moment; next; other; subordinate; substitute; trice; twinkle; twinkling

SECONDARY: (**see** "auxiliary") accessorial; accessory; ancillary; collateral; consequential; dependent; derivational; derivative; epiphenomenal; etiological; following; incidental; inferior; minor; paltry; satellite; satellitic; second-rate; second-string; subaltern(ate); subject; subordinate; subservient; subsidiary; substandard; supplementary; tangential; tributary

SECRET: **a.** abstruse; acroamatic; *à huis clos*; anonymous; apocryphal; arcane; auricular; back-alley; backdoor; backstage; behind-the-scenes; cabalistic; chamber; clandestine; closemouthed; collusory; concealed; confidential; covert; cryptic(al); cryptogenic; enigmatic(al); epoptic; esoteric; furtive; genital; hidden; hugger-mugger; hush-hush; illicit; inmost; inner; intimate; latent; mysterious; mystic(al); obscured; occult; private; privy; recondite; reticent; retired; secluded; secretive; shrouded; sibylline; sly; sneaky; *sotto voce*; star-chamber; stealthy; stolen; surreptitious; top-drawer; unacknowledged; unavowed; undeclared; undercover; undercurrent; underground; underhand(ed); under-the-counter; under-the-table; under wraps; undivided; unlawful; unrevealed; unseen; untold; unverbalized; veiled; SECRET(S): **n.** acroama(tics); apocrypha (pl.); arcana (pl.); arcanum; *arcanum arcanorum*; cabala; conspiracy; Eleusinian mysteries; esoterica(pl.); intrigue; machination; mystery; privacy; riddle; tune; SECRETLY: *à huis clos*; *à la sourdine*; *à porte close*; confidentially; covertly; *in camera*; *in pectore*; *in petto*; *januis clausis*; *sub rosa*; *sub silentio*; SECRECY: clandestineness; clandestinity; confidentiality; covertness; discretion; esotery; furtiveness; hush-hush; invisibility; mysteriousness; mysticity; privacy; secretiveness; secretness; silence; suppression; wraps

SECRETARY: adviser; aide; amanuensis; assistant; confidant; desk; escritoire; officer; recorder

SECRETE: bank; bury; conceal; disguise; excrete; exude; hide; mask; screen; seclude; shut; SECRETION: bile; chicle; concealment; gum; hormone; insulin; juice; laap; latex; lerp; milk; resin; saliva; sap

SECRETIVE: see "secret" and "shy"

SECT: church; clan; class; cult; denomination; faction; following; group; order; party; school; SECTARIAN: **a.** (**see** "biased") denominational; parochial; partisan; SECTARIAN: **n.** bigot; dissenter; heretic; nonconformist; partisan; zealot

SECTION: (**see** "divide") area; class; component; cut(ting); division; field; fraction; fragment; group; length; member; panel; parcel; part; passage; piece; portion; profile; quarter; region; sector; segment; slice; specimen; subdivision; township; unit; SECTIONAL: disjointed; disjunctive; divisive; fractional; fragmentary; local(istic); multipartite; parochial; piecemeal; provincial; provisional; regional; segmental; segmented; subdivided

SECTOR: (**see** "section") arc; area; piece; quarter

SECULAR: agelong; centuried; cyclical; diuturnal; earthly; laic(al); lay; mundane; nonclerical; nonprofessional; nonreligious; nonsacred; profane; temporal; worldly

SECURE: **v.** affix; anchor; annex; attach; belay; bind; catch; confine; connect; effect; employ; engage; ensure; fasten; firm; fix; gain; get; guarantee; guard; hire; house; indemnify; insure; lock; moor; nail (down); pin(ion); procure; produce; protect; restrain; rivet; rope; seal; seize; sew; shield; shut; store; stow; tack; tie; tighten; SECURE: **a.** *à couvert*; assured; certain; confident; dependable; firm; formidable; free; guaranteed; guarded; impregnable; inalien-

able; inviolable; invulnerable; protected; safe; solid; sound; stout; strong; sure; tight; trustworthy; unassailable; unassailed; unconquerable; undisturbed; unlost; SECURITY: assurance; bail; bond; certainty; collateral; confidence; covenant; defense; dependability; deposit; ease; firmness; freedom; gage; guarantee; guaranty; guard; impregnability; inalienability; indemnification; independence; insurance; invulnerability; pact; peace; pledge; protection; safety; screen; shelter; stability; sureness; surety; token; unconquerability; warranty; watch

SEDATE: **v.** (**see** "calm") dose; opiate; quieten; tranquilize; SEDATE: **a.** (**see** "calm") composed; decorous; demure; placid; prim; proper; proud; quiet; serene; serious; settled; sober; solemn; staid; stiff; still; thoughtful; tranquil; unobtrusive; unruffled

SEDATIVE: (**see** "soothing") alleviator; anodyne; bromide; calmant; calmative; drug; lenitive; nervine; opiate; palliative; quietive; remedy; tranquilizer

SEDENTARY: abed; asleep; firm; fixed; immobile; lying; retired; seated; sedent; sessile; settled; sitting; sleeping; stationary; still; undisturbed

SEDIMENT: (**see** "waste") alluvium; deposit; dregs; *faex*; fecula; foots; grit; grounds; hypostasis; lees; loess; magma; precipitate; recrement; residuum; scoria; scoriae (pl.); sedimentation; settlings; silt; sludge

SEDITIOUS: (**see** "riotous") disobedient; factious; fractious; insubordinate; refractory; revolting; revolutionary; traitorous; turbulent; unruly

SEDUCE: (**see** "allure") charm; coax; corrupt; debauch; entice; induce; suggest; tempt; SEDUCTIVE: see "alluring;" SEDUCTION: allure(ment); debauchery; debauchment; enticement; seducement; temptation; SEDUCER: charmer; Circe; corrupter; debauchee; enticer; seductress; succubus; tempter; vamp(ire)

SEDULOUS: (**see** "attentive") busy; diligent; engaged; occupied; working

SEE: accompany; appreciate; apprehend; ascertain; attend; behold; call; comprehend; conduct; consider; contemplate; descry; detect; discern; discover; distinguish; divine; escort; espy; examine; expect; eye; eyewitness; feel; foresee; gape; gaze; glance; glare;

glimpse; glower; grasp; guard; heed; identify; inspect; judge; ken; know; locate; look; mark; meet; mind; notice; obey; observe; ogle; peek; peer; penetrate; perceive; pore; pry; realize; recognize; regard; remark; savvy; scan; scent; scrutinize; search; seek; sensate; sense; spot; spy; stare; study; suppose; undergo; understand; vide; view; visit; visualize; watch; welcome; witness

SEED: (**see** "sow") acorn; bean; bulb; corm; descendents; egg; embryo; fruit; germ; grain; issue; kernel; nucleus; nut; offspring; origin; ova (pl.); ovule; ovum; pit; progeny; putamen; seat; semen; source; spawn; sperm; spore; tuber; SEEDY: debilitated; decayed; dingy; disheveled; faded; frayed; mean; needy; old; ragged; rough; shabby; shopworn; spiritless; squalid; tacky; tattered; threadbare; unkempt; untidy; worn; wretched

SEEK: appeal; apply; aspire; assay; attempt; beg; begin; beseech; browse; comb; court; endeavor; entreat; essay; explore; ferret; fish; follow; hunt; inquire; look; probe; prospect; pry; pursue; ransack; request; resort (to); rummage; scout; scrounge; search; solicit; start; strive; sue; supplicate; test; try; undertake; venture; woo; SEEKER: adventurer; appellant; aspirant; assayist; beseecher; explorer; fisherman; hunter; inquirer; inquisitor; prober; prospector; pursuer; researcher; scout; searcher; student; supplicant; venturer

SEEM: ape; appear; feign; look; pretend; sound; SEEMING: apparent; disguised; evident; feigned; like; ostensible; quasi; semblable; *soi-disant*; specious; verisimilar; verisimilous; virtual

SEEMLY: agreeable; appropriate; apt; beautiful; becoming; befitting; comely; congruous; decent; decorous; due; easy; expedient; fair; fit(ting); good-looking; handsome; likely; meet; nice; personable; pleasant; pleasing; proper; suitable; timely; SEEMLINESS: **see** "grace"

SEEP: bleed; drain; drip; leak; ooze; osmose; percolate; permeate; soak; spread

SEER: crystal gazer; diviner; foreteller; fortuneteller; gazer; oracle; predictor; prophet; soothsayer; sorcerer; visionary; SEERESS: Phoebad; prophetess; sibyl

SEESAW: alternate; crossruff; oscillate; reciprocate; teeter; tilt; vacillate; waver

SEETHE: boil; bubble; churn; cook; effervesce; ferment; foam; fume; gurgle; itch; rage; rave; saturate; sizzle; soak; steam; stew; SEETHING: (**see** "mad") aboil; agitated; boiling; bubbling; churning; ebullient; effervescent; effusive; foaming; foamy; frothing; fuming; gay; gleeful; gurgling; intense; sizzling; steaming; violent; volatile; zestful

SEGMENT: arc; cantle; chapter; constituent; cut; division; fraction; fragment; item; length; link; metamere; paragraph; parcel; part; percentage; piece; portion; section; sector; share; slice; somite; telson; verse; ward; wedge

SEGREGATE: (**see** "isolate") ghettoize; separate; sequester

SEIZE: afflict; annex; apprehend; appropriate; arrest; arrogate; bag; bind; capture; carry; catch; clutch; collar; commandeer; confiscate; conquer; control; cop; descend; distrain; dominate; embargo; entrap; fasten; get; grab; grapple; grasp; grip; hent; impound; jump; land; latch; loot; lure; nab; net; overpower; plunder; possess; pounce; preempt; prehend; reave; rob; sack; sequester; snare; snatch; spring; steal; subdue; tackle; take; trap; usurp; win; yoke; SEIZURE: annexation; apoplexy; apprehension; appropriation; arrest(ment); arrogation; attack; captivity; capture; catch; clutch; confiscation; defeat; distraint; domination; embargo; entrapment; fit; grab; grasp; manucapture; nab; orgasm; overpowering; paroxysm; plundering; possession; pounce; preemption; retention; robbery; seizin; sequestration; snatch; spell; steal; stroke; tackle; taking; trapping; usurpation; winning

SELDOM: (**see** "infrequent") unoften

SELECT: **v.** call; choose; cull; decide; designate; draft; draw; elect; extract; muster; name; nominate; opt; pick; prefer; screen; separate; specify; take; tap; vote; SELECT: **a.** (**see** "choice") ace; best; chosen; clubby; cream; discriminating; elect; elite; excellent; fancy; good; premium; rare; superior; top(s); SELECTIVE: eclectic; discriminative; discriminatory; SELECTION: choice; cull; part; pick; portion; share; vote

SELF: ego; embodiment; id; identical; individual; person(ality); psyche; same; soul

SELF-CENTERED *or* SELF-CONCEITED:

(see "selfish") autotheistic; conceited; egocentric; ego(t)istic(al); individualistic; introversive; introverted; self-important; self-sufficient; vain(glorious)

SELF-CONFIDENCE: aplomb; assurance; balance; bumptiousness; cockiness; conceit; egocentricity; overconfidence

SELF-CONTROL: (see "calmness" and "poise") abnegation; abstinence; aplomb; ascesis; asceticism; automat(i)on; continence; perpendicularity; prudence; reason; restraint; self-direction; self-restraint; sophrosyne; temperance; will; wisdom

SELF-DENIAL: (see "self-control") abnegation; abstinence; ascesis; asceticism; humility; limitation; restraint; self-abnegation

SELF-ESTEEM: *amour propre*; assurance; complacency; ego(t)ism; pride; self-conceit; self-respect; vainglory; vanity

SELF-EVIDENT: aphoristic; axiomatic; clear; hypothetico-deductive; indubitable; manifest; palpable; postulational; prima facie; *res ipsa loquitur*

SELFHOOD: individualization; ipseity; personality; proprium; self-centeredness; selfishness

SELF-IMPORTANCE: conceit; consequentiality; illusionism; pomposity; pompousness; pride; pursiness; self-conceit; self-esteem

SELFISH: *alieni appetens*; apolaustic; asocial; autophilic; autotheistic; conceited; dissocial; egocentric(al); ego(t)istic(al); gluttonish; hedonic; hedonistic; intemperate; narcissan; narcissistic; narcistic; self-centered; self-conceited; self-indulgent; self-seeking; self-serving; sybaritic; unsocial; SELFISHNESS: *amour de soi*; asociality; autism; autophilia; autotheism; *après nous* (or *moi*) *le déluge*; conceit; dissociability; egocentricity; egocentrism; egomania; ego(t)ism; hedonism; introversion; iotacism; narcissism; *outrecuidance*; selfhood; selfism; self-love; self-satisfaction; self-seeking; solipsism

SELF-LOVE: see "selfishness"

SELF-RESPECT: see "pride"

SELF-RESTRAINT: abnegation; abstinence; ascesis; asceticism; continence; humility; moderation; self-abnegation; self-control;

self-denial; sobriety; sophrosyne; temperance

SELF-RIGHTEOUS: holier-than-thou; hypocritical; Pecksniffian; pharisaic(al); pietistic(al); religiose; sanctimonious

SELF-SATISFIED: (see "independent") bumptious; complacent; conceited; pompous; self-complacent; vainglorious

SELF-SEEKER: cormorant; hedonist; sybarite; sycophant

SELL: abalienate; alienate; auction; bargain; barter; betray; cant; cater; cheat; convey; convince; deceive; deed; dupe; furnish; give; gull; hawk; huckster; influence; joke; market; monger; pander; peddle; persuade; provision; purvey; push; retail; stick; supply; trade; transfer; trick; truck; vend; SELLER: coster(monger); dealer; draper; grocer; hawker; merchant; monger; peddler; pusher; salesman; trader; tradesman; trafficker; vender; vendor

SEMBLANCE: apparition; appearance; arrangement; aspect; copy; countenance; dodge; excuse; exterior; face; figure; form; gloss; guise; image; likeness; look; phantom; picture; pose; pretense; seeming(ness); shadow; shape; show; similarity; verisimilitude

SEMESTER: course; half; period; session; term

SEMPITERNAL: endless; eternal; ever(lasting); perpetual

SEND: affect; assign; cast; commit; consign; convey; delegate; deliver; depute; direct; discharge; dismiss; dispatch; drive; eject; emit; express; fire; fling; forward; freight; impart; impel; issue; hurl; launch; mail; move; ordain; order; post; project; propel; remand; remit; remove; render; route; ship; sling; telegraph; throw; toss; transfer; transmit

SENILE: (see "aged") aging; ancient; anecdotal; caducous; decrepit; doddering; feeble; infirm; old; senescent; superannuated; venerable; SENILITY: (see "age") anecdotage; anility; antiquity; caducity; childishness; decrepitude; dotage; feebleness; infirmity; senescence; seniority; superannuation; venerability

SENIOR: **a.** advanced; *aîné*; elder(ly); first; older; precedent; puisne; ranking; superior;

upper(most); SENIOR: **n.** (see "leader") dean; doyen; doyenne (fem.); elder; master; parent; principal; puisne; student; superior; SENIORITY: age; eldership; leadership; priority; privileges; rank; rating; rights; superiority

SENSATION: (see "sense") awareness; emotion; esthesia; feel(ing); kick; killer-diller; pain; perception; phenomenality; sensibility; stimulus; SENSATIONAL: arresting; astounding; emotional; exciting; extraordinary; gory; impressive; lurid; melodramatic; phenomenal; scandalous; sensationary; showy; spectacular; splashy; stunning; thrilling; wild; wonderful

SENSE: **v.** (see "feel") anticipate; apprehend; comprehend; detect; expect; grasp; judge; note; notice; perceive; realize; reason; sensate; smell; suspect; taste; understand; SENSE: **n.** acumen; apperception; appreciation; apprehension; awareness; brain(s); capacity; comprehension; connotation; consciousness; conviction; course; denotation; discernment; discretion; discrimination; emotion; esthesia; faculty; feel(ing); flair; foresight; genius; gist; grasp; gumption; hearing; import; insight; instinct; intellect; intelligence; intendment; intent; intuition; judgment; kick; knowledge; learning; meaning; mind; opinion; pain; palpation; penetration; perception; perspicacity; prudence; purport; reason(ing); recognition; sagacity; sanity; sapience; sensation; sensibility; sentience; sight; significance; smell; sophrosyne; stimulus; talent; taste; touch; trend; understanding; view; wisdom; wit(s)

SENSELESS: absurd; dull; fatuous; foolish; frigid; idiotic; inept; insensate; insensible; insipid; irrational; irrelevant; meaningless; nonsensical; pointless; purposeless; reasonless; silly; stupid; unconscious; unfeeling; unreasonable; unwise; unwitty; witless

SENSIBLE: acute; apprehensible; aware; bright; cognizant; competent; conscious; cool; discreet; intelligent; intelligible; judicious; keen; material; penetrating; perceivable; perceptible; perspicacious; persuaded; philosophic(al); politic; prudent; rational; readable; reasonable; sagacious; sage; sane; sapient; satisfied; sensitive; sharp; shrewd; subtle; understandable; wise; SENSIBILITY: (see "delicacy") aesthetics; emotion; feeling; sensitiveness; sensitivity

SENSITIVE: acute; allergic; bashful; dangerous; exquisite; fastidious; humble; hyper-

algesic; hyperesthetic; impressible; impressionable; irritable; leiodermatous; liable; meticulous; perceptive; perilous; precarious; predisposed; prone; quick; responsive; retiring; sensory; sensuous; sentient; shy; sore; subject; supersensitive; susceptible; temperamental; tender; thin-skinned; touchy; vital; waspish; SENSITIVITY: (see "delicacy") irritability; quick; sensitiveness; susceptibility; tactfulness; tenderness; touchiness

SENSUAL: animal(istic); Apician; bestial; carnal; common; earthy; epicurean; epithumetic; fleshy; gross; Hogarthian; irreligious; lecherous; lurid; luxurious; materialistic; Rabelaisian; scabrous; sensory; sensualistic; sensuous; sexual; sultry; sybaritic; temporal; unspiritual; *voluptuaire*; voluptuary; *voluptueux*; voluptuous; vulgar; worldly; SENSUALITY: carnality; concupiscence; hedonism; lechery; lusciousness; luxuriousness; luxury; pleasure; sensualism; sensuosity; sensuousness; sybaritism; *volupté*; voluptuosity; voluptuousness; worldliness; SENSUALIST: carnalist; hedonist; lecher; sybarite; voluptuary

SENSUOUS: Anacreontic; Bacchic; Dionysian; epicurean; erotic; Faustian; hedonic; hedonistic; lush; luxurious; orgiastic; sensitive; sensual(istic); sexual; sybaritic(al); voluptuous; worldly; SENSUOUSNESS: see "sensuality"

SENTENCE: **v.** condemn; decide; decree; discipline; doom; judge; penalize; punish; SENTENCE: **n.** adage; condemnation; conviction; decision; decree; doom; judgment; order; penalty; proposition; punishment; rap; stretch; term

SENTENTIOUS: aphoristic; brief; concise; curt; didactic; epigrammatic; expressive; laconic; meaningful; moralistic; pithy; short; significant; succinct; terse; wise; witty

SENTIMENT: (see "thought") belief; emotion; feeling; idea; judgment; maxim; motto; mush; notion; opinion; *pensée*; predilection; sensibility; sentimentality; toast; view; SENTIMENTAL: affected; bathetic; cloying; cloysome; dramatic(al); dreamy; emotional; frothy; goody-goody; gushy; maudlin; mawkish; melodramatic; misty-eyed; moonstruck; mushy; romantic; sirupy; sloppy; slushy; sobby; soft; soppy; soupy; sugary; sweet; syrupy; tear-jerking; tender; throbbing; treacly; SENTIMENTALISM: bathos; emotion; gushiness; hearts and flowers; maudlinism; mawkishness; molasses; romanticism; sentimentality; slop-over; sweetness; syrup; tenderness; treacle

SENTINEL *or* SENTRY: guard(ian); keeper; lookout; patrol; picket; scout; soldier; vedette; vidette; warden; watch(man)

SEPARATE: **v.** abscise; abstract; apportion; bar; beset; bifurcate; bisect; break; chop; cleave; comb; compartmentalize; cut; deal; decompose; delete; demarcate; departmentalize; detour; disaffiliate; disarticulate; disassociate; discerp; discharge; disconnect; discriminate; disengage; disentangle; disgregate; disjoin(t); dislink; dislocate; dismember; dispart; disperse; dissect; dissever; dissociate; dissolve; distinguish; distribute; disunite; divaricate; diverge; divide; divorce; eliminate; enisle; estrange; exclude; extract; fence; filter; fork; fractionalize; ghettoize; hew; intervene; isolate; mark; measure; open; osmose; part(ition); precipitate; remove; rend; resolve; retire; rip; rive; rupture; scatter; secern; seclude; segregate; sever(alize); sieve; slip; snap; sort; split; spread; strain; strip; sunder; surround; tear; thrash; thresh; unbind; unbuckle; unchain; uncombine; uncouple; undo; unhook; unjoin(t); unlink; unlock; unmix; unravel; wedge; widen; winnow; withdraw; wrench; SEPARATE(D): **a.** alone; apart; autonomous; bisected; broken; cloven; compartmentalized; cracked; departmentalized; detached; disarticulated; disassociated; discontinued; discontinuous; discrete; disembodied; disengaged; disentangled; disjoined; disjointed; dislocated; dissociated; distant; distinct; distinguished; disunited; divergent; diverging; divided; divorced; eliminated; enisled; filtered; forked; free; immaterial; independent; individual; isolated; lone(ly); open(ed); parted; particular; rent; retired; ruptured; scattered; secluded; segregated; sequestered; several; severed; shredded; single; sole; solitary; sorted; split; sporadic; spread; sundered; unaffiliated; unallied; unamalgamated; unassociated; unattached; unbound; unbuckled; unchained; uncombined; unconnected; undone; unlocked; unraveled; unrelated; widened; withdrawn; wrenched; SEPARATENESS: (**see** "separation") discreteness; divisibility; partibility; separability; severality; SEPARATING: (**see** "divisive") centrifugal; demarcative; disjunctive; dissociative; schismatic(al)

SEPARATION: (**see** "parting") abscission; alienation; bar(rier); bifurcation; boundary; breach; break; chasm; cleavage; cleft; crack; deal; decomposition; defile; deletion; demarcation; detachment; detour; dialysis; difference; disaffiliation; disarticulation; disassociation; discerption; discharge; discon-

nection; discontinuity; disengagement; disentanglement; disjunction; disjunctivity; disjuncture; dislocation; dismemberment; dispersal; dissection; disseverance; disseveration; dissociation; dissolution; distance; distinction; distinctiveness; distribution; disunion; divarication; divergence; division; divorce(ment); divulsion; elimination; estrangement; exclusion; extraction; fence; filter(ing); fissure; fork; fracture; gap; gash; hedge; incision; indentation; intervention; isolation; joint; juncture; leave(taking); opening; osmosis; parting; partition; removal; resignation; resolution; retirement; rift; rima; rip; rupture; scattering; schism; schizoidism; seam; secession; seclusion; segregation; sejunction; separateness; sequestration; severance; slit; snap; sorting; split; spread; sundering; synchondrosis; tear; wall; wedge; winnowing; withdrawal

SEPARATIST: dissenter; heretic; nonconformist; Pharisee; pilgrim; revolutionary; sectary; Zoarite

SEPT: clan; class; family; group; kin; race; seven; sib; tribe

SEPTIC: (**see** "rotten") corrupt; hectic; impure; obnoxious

SEPULCHER: coffin; grave; repository; terminus; tomb; urn; vault

SEQUEL: (**see** "consequence") aftermath; backlash; backwash; continuation; effect; repercussion; suite

SEQUENCE: (**see** "series") arrangement; cadence; caravan; cavalcade; chain; concatenation; consecution; consecutiveness; continuance; continuum; course; cycle; episode; following; gamut; gradation; method; order; pattern; procedure; procession; program; progression; range; regularity; rhythm; rope; routine; row; run; sequacity; sequel; seriality; set; straight; string; succession; suite; system; thread; time; track; train; SEQUENTIAL: alphabetical; categorical; chronologic(al); consecutive; consequent; continuous; *en suite*; numeral; ordinal; sequacious; serial; seriate; successive

SEQUESTER: (**see** "separate") appropriate; condemn; confiscate; enisle; ghettoize; hide; insulate; isolate; retire; seclude; secrete; segregate; seize; take; withdraw

SERE: arid; dead; desiccated; dried; dry;

parched; threadbare; withered; wizened

SERENADE: charivari; chivaree; house-warming; nocturne; song

SERENE: (see "calm") august; balmy; bright; clear; content; cool; dispassionate; easy; fine; halcyon; limpid; peaceful; pellucid; placid; quiet; satisfied; steady; still; tranquil; undisturbed; unflurried; unflustered; unperturbed; unruffled; untroubled; unvexed; SERENITY: (see "calmness") composure; contentment; dispassion; equanimity; imperturbability; imperturbation; limpidity; peace(ableness); peacefulness; placidity; quiet(ude); repose; *sang froid*; sereneness; tranquility

SERF: *adscriptus glebae*; *ascriptitius glebae*; colona; colonus; esne; helot; litus; menial; neif; peon; servant; slave; vassal; villein; SERFDOM: (see "slavery") bondage; helotism; helotry; peonage; serfhood; servitude; subjection; thralldom

SERIAL: (see "sequential") alphabetical; categorical; chronologic(al); consecutive; continuous; following; sequel; sequent; seriate; *seriatim*; successional; successive

SERIES: alphabet(ization); arrangement; campaign; cascade; catalog(ue); categorization; category; cavalcade; chain (reaction); concatenation; cordon; course; diapason; group-(ing); hierarchization; link(age); list; panel; periodicity; proceeding; procession; routine; run; sequence; seriality; set; span; spectrum; steps; stratification; streak; string; sweep; tour

SERIOUS: ardent; ascetic; austere; authoritative; businesslike; busy; capital; careful; climactic; consequential; critical; dangerous; decided; deep; demure; determined; devoted; devotional; devout; difficult; diligent; eager; earnest; emphatic; fated; fervent; firm; first-degree; fixed; formidable; funeral; grave; grievous; grim; heavy; high; humorless; immovable; important; importunate; intense; intent; joyless; laughterless; major; mirthless; momentous; mortuary; no-nonsense; obstinate; prayerful; profound; prudent; reliable; religious; resolute; risky; sad; sedate; sepulchral; *sérieux*; serioso; severe; significant; silent; sincere; sober; solemn; solid; somber; sombrous; staid; steady; stern; studious; thoughtful; unfunny; unhumorous; unmirthful; urgent; warm; weighty; zealous; SERIOUSNESS: (see "earnestness") ascesis; austerity; authorita-

tiveness; criticality; danger; devotedness; devotion; diligence; eagerness; fervency; gravity; grimness; intenseness; profundity; resolution; sedateness; seriosity; severity; significance; sincerity; soberness; sobriety; solemnity; thoughtfulness; weight

SERMON: discourse; dissertation; exhortation; harangue; homily; lecture; lesson; message; preachment; reproof; speech; talk; tract

SERPENT: see "snake;" SERPENTINE: ambagious; ambivalent; circuitous; devious; diabolic; guileful; indirect; meandering; serpentiform; serpentile; sinuous; snaky; sneaky; subtle; tortuous; untrustworthy; wily; winding

SERVANT: amah; attendant; bonne; boy; butler; chef; domestic; drudge; employee; factotum; flunky; gillie; handmaid(en); help; maid; man; menial; page; serf; servile; servitor; servitress; slave(y); valet; vassal

SERVE: (see "attend") accompany; administer; advance; aid; answer; assist; associate; avail; benefit; chaperone; collaborate; comply; conduct; convoy; deal; do; favor; follow; forward; foster; function; further; give; gratify; groom; guard; guide; heed; help; ladle; last; lead; maintain; mark; mind; minister; mother; nurse; obey; oblige; officiate; perform; pilot; play; promote; provide; purvey; represent; satisfy; shepherd; spend; spread; squire; steer; suffice; supply; support; tend; treat; undergo; usher; visit; wait; watch; wet-nurse; work; worship; SERVER: ladle; salver; spoon; tray; utensil; waiter

SERVICE: advantage; aid; army; assistance; attendance; avail; business; combat; devotion; dishes; duty; employment; gain; help; labor; ministration; ministry; navy; office; profit; rite(s); ritual; set; treatment; tribute; use; utility; work; worship; SERVICEABLE: see "useful" and "valuable"

SERVILE: **a.** abject; base; compliant; controlled; creeping; cringing; deferential; fawning; groveling; ignoble; imitative; instrumental; mean; menial; obsequious; oppressed; parasitical; sequacious; servient; shrinking; slavish; subject; subjugated; submissive; subordinate; subservient; sycophantic; tractable; truckling; vassal; SERVILE: **n.** see "servant;" SERVILITY: abjection; abjectness; compliance; deference; dependence; imitation; obsequiousness; obsequity;

sequacity; servitude; slavery; slavishness; submission; subservience; subserviency; sycophancy; toadyism; SERVITUDE: **see** "serfdom" and "slavery"

SESSION: assembly; assize; class; council; court; meeting; period; school; seance; semester; sitting; term; time; vestry

SET: **v.** adjust; allot; allow; apply; arbitrate; arrange; congeal; decline; decree; define; deposit; determine; establish; estimate; fire; firm; fit; fix; gel; harden; jell; lay; locate; park; perch; pit; place; plant; position; post; prepare; prescribe; put; rate; ready; regulate; settle; stabilize; station; stow; straighten; value; SET: **a.** (**see** "settled") A-O.K.; assigned; decided; determined; immovable; intentional; located; O.K.; premeditated; prepared; prescribed; ready; resolved; rigid; sessile; situated; specified; SET: **n.** adherents; aggregate; assortment; battery; bent; caste; chain; circle; claque; clique; clutch; collection; coterie; galaxy; gang; group; junto; location; retinue; series; service; society; string; suite; supporters; SETTING: (**see** "set") array; background; bed; environment; hardening; insertion; locale; milieu; *mise-en-scène*; mounting; placement; position; scene; site; situs; stage; station; trap

SETBACK: (**see** "reverse") haymaker; rebuff; trial; vexation; withdrawal

SETTLE: (**see** "set") adjust; alight; arbitrate; arrange; bench; calm; choose; clarify; clear; close; colonize; compose; compound; compromise; conclude; confirm; congeal; consolidate; decide; descend; determine; dispose; drop; end; ensconce; establish; fall; fix; install; judge; lay; lie; light; liquidate; locate; lodge; meet; moor; nest(le); occupy; park; pay; perch; plant; regulate; reside; resolve; rest; rivet; roost; rule; sag; satisfy; seat; silence; sink; sit; stabilize; station; straighten; subside; SETTLED: (**see** "set") built-up; clear-cut; decided; determined; ended; established; firm; fixed; immutable; liquidated; resolved; sedentary; sessile; solid; stable; steadfast; sure; understood; unquestionable; unswerving; SETTLEMENT: (**see** "ending") accommodation; adaptation; agreement; base; camp; colonization; colony; community; compact; composition; compromise; disposition; dregs; *fait accompli*; habitation; harmonization; installation; liquidation; location; occupation; outpost; payment; post; reconciliation; *res adjudicata*; sedentation; statement; testament; town;

understanding; village; will; SETTLER: boomer; colonist; colonizer; frontiersman; immigrant; pilgrim; squatter

SEVEN: hebdomad; heptad; sept(enary); VII

SEVER: (**see** "separate") axe; cleave; cut; detach; disarticulate; disassociate; disconnect; disengage; disjoin(t); disperse; dissociate; dissolve; distinguish; disunite; divide; divorce; hack; hatchet; part; rend; split; sunder; SEVERANCE: (**see** "separation") difference; disassociation; disconnection; disengagement; disjointure; dissociation; dissolution; divorcement; rent; split; sundering

SEVERAL: certain; different; distinct; divers-(e); few; lot(s); many; number; numerous; plural; respective; sundry; various

SEVERE: acute; afflictive; arctic; arduous; arrogant; ascetic; atrocious; austere; autocratic; blistering; censorious; cold; critical; cruel; dangerous; deadly; difficult; dire; domineering; dour; Draconian; drastic; exacting; excruciating; extreme; firm; flagrant; forbidding; frosty; fulminating; grievous; grim; grueling; hard; harsh; heinous; inclement; inexorable; inflexible; intemperate; intense; iron; lamentable; malign(ant); marked; merciless; obdurate; oppressive; plain; Procrustean; raging; rigid; rigorous; scathing; scorching; scrupulous; serious; sharp; sober; sound; stern; stiff; straight(-laced); strict; stringent; strong; taut; terrible; terrific; tough; trying; tyrannical; tyrannous; uncharitable; uncompromising; unmitigated; unpalliated; unrelenting; vehement; vicious; violent; virulent; wicked; SEVERITY: acid test; atrociousness; atrocity; austereness; austerity; crisis; criticality; cruelty; excruciation; hardness; hardship; harshness; inclemency; inexorability; inflexibility; intemperance; intensity; mercilessness; obduracy; oppression; precision; rigidity; rigor; scrupulosity; scrupulousness; seriousness; severeness; strictness; stringency; tyranny; vehemence; violence; virulence

SEW: baste; mend; patch; secure; stitch; suture; tack

SEWAGE *or* SEWER: (**see** "rubbish") cesspit; cesspool; cloaca; cloaca maxima; sluice; sough

SEX: gender; kind; SEXY *or* SEXUAL: aphrodisiac; bawdy; Cytherean; erogenic;

erogenous; erotic; erotogenic; hot; lustful; randy; suggestive; venereal; voluptuary; voluptuous; SEXINESS: aphrodisia; bawdiness; erogeneity; ero(ti)cism; erotogenesis; erotogenicity; priapism; satyriasis; voluptuosity; voluptuousness

SEXLESS: asexual; castrate(d); neuter; spayed

SHABBY: abject; beggarly; contemptible; decayed; decaying; despicable; deteriorated; dilapidated; dingy; disheveled; dishonorable; dog-eared; dowdy; down-at-heel; drab; dull; faded; frowsy; impoverished; inferior; insufficient; low; mangy; meager; mean; miserable; miserly; neglected; outworn; paltry; pitiful; poor; ragged; ratty; reduced; runty; scrubby; scurvy; seedy; shoddy; shopworn; sleazy; slovenly; soiled; sordid; squalid; stale; stingy; tacky; tagrag; tatterdemalion; threadbare; unartistic; unfair; ungenerous; untidy; wasted; worn; wretched; SHABBINESS: despicability; dinginess; dilapidation; dowdiness; impoverishment; manginess; meagerness; miserliness; seediness; squalidity; squalidness; tackiness

SHACK: cabin; hovel; hut(ch); lean-to; shanty; shed

SHACKLE: v. (see "check") bind; bridle; chain; choke; clog; curb; disable; fetter; halter; hamper; handcuff; impede; limit; pinion; restrain; restrict; rope; tie; trammel; SHACKLE: n. binder; bridle; chain(s); clevis; coupling; curb; disability; disablement; fetter(s); gyve(s); halter; hampering; handcuffs; impediment; irons; limitation; manacle(s); restraint; restriction; rope; tie; SHACKLED: see "restrained"

SHADE: v. (see "shadow") blind; color; cover; curtain; darken; dim; disguise; dull; eclipse; lower; obscure; overshadow; protect; reduce; screen; shadow; shelter; shield; tint; tone; veil; SHADE: n. blind; cast; cloud; color; cover; curtain; darkness; defect; degree; difference; dimness; eclipse; foliage; ghost; gloom; hue; leaves; nuance; obscurity; protection; reduction; retreat; screen; shadow; shelter; shield; specter; spirit; streak; stripe; suggestion; swab; tinge; tint; tone; tree(s); umbra(ge); umbrella; variation; veil; visor; SHADY: (see "suspicious") adumbral; cool; crooked; dark(ened); devious; dishonest; disreputable; dubious; elmy; hidden; penumbral; questionable; screened; shadowed; shadowy; sheltered; tricky; umbrageous; uncertain; unethical; unreliable

SHADOW: v. (see "shade") adumbrate; betoken; cloud; cover; curtain; darken; dim(inish); dog; dull; eclipse; extinguish; follow; hide; inumbrate; obscure; prefigure; protect; pursue; reduce; screen; scud; shelter; shield; shroud; stalk; symbolize; tail; trace; trail; typify; veil; SHADOW: n. (see "shade") adumbration; aura; cloud; counterpart; darkness; difference; figure; form; ghost; obscurity; outline; penumbra; phantom; prefiguration; profile; remnant; shape; shelter; silhouette; specter; symbol; trace; type; umbra(ge); vestige; SHADOWY: (see "shady") adumbral; dreamlike; dreamy; fleeting; ghostly; imaginary; indistinct; nebulous; obscure; penumbral; tenebrous; unsubstantial; vague

SHADY: see under "shade"

SHAFT: arrow; barb; beam; column; dart; excavation; flagstaff; groove; handle; lance; missile; opening; passage(way); pillar; pit; pole; ray; rod; spear; spire; stele; stem; thill; trunk; tunnel; weapon

SHAG: cormorant; dance; fiber; hair; nap; pile; thicket; wool; SHAGGY: bushy; comate; confused; hairy; harsh; hirsutal; hirsute; nappy; rough; rude; seedy; shabby; shoddy; unclear; uneven; unkempt; unpolished; unshort; woolly

SHAKE: v. agitate; arouse; bounce; brandish; clash; coerce; convulse; cower; daunt; dislodge; eject; fluctuate; flutter; force; frighten; grasp; jar; jolt; jounce; mix; move; oscillate; quake; quaver; quiver; reel; rid; rock; shed; shiver; shock; shudder; stagger; sway; swing; teeter; totter; tremble; trill; vibrate; waggle; wave(r); weaken; wobble; SHAKE: n. blow; clash; coercion; dismissal; earthquake; fluctuation; flutter; force; instant; jar; jolt; minute; quake; quaver; quiver; rattle; rock; shock; sway; swing; tremble(ment); tremor; tremulation; SHAKING or SHAKY: (see "feeble") convulsed; cowering; dangerous; faint; fearful; fluctuating; fluttery; frightened; infirm; insecure; instable; loose; nervous; palpitating; palsied; perilous; precarious; quaking; quaky; quavering; quivery; ramshackle; rattletrap; reeling; rickety; risky; rocking; rocky; shivering; shuddering; squeamish; swaying; swinging; teetering; timorous; tottering; tottery; trembling; tremorous; tremulous; unprotected; unreliable; unsafe; unsettled; unstable; unsteady; unsure; vibrating; vibratory; wambly; wavering; weak(ened); wobbling; wobbly; SHAKINESS: (see "instability") danger; fluctuation; fright; insecurity; palsy; peril; risk(iness); shiver; shudder; sway; swing; totter; waver; wobble

SHALLOW: apparent; artificial; childish; cursory; depthless; empty; foolish; frivolous; frothy; glib; hollow; idle; ignorant; inane; incondite; magazinish; narrow-minded; obvious; petty; provincial; silly; simple; slight; sophomoric; specious; superficial; tenuous; trifling; trivial; unintellectual; unprofound; SHALLOWNESS: (**see** "emptiness") artificiality; childishness; foolishness; frivolity; ignorance; inanity; simplicity; speciosity; superficiality; tenuosity; triviality

SHAM: **v.** ape; cajole; cheat; counterfeit; deceive; defraud; dissemble; dissimulate; fake; feign; hoax; humbug; imitate; malinger; mock; pretend; simulate; substitute; travesty; trick; SHAM: **a.** adulterated; apocryphal; artificial; bogus; brummagem; counterfeit; deceptive; dissimulative; factitious; faked; false; farcical; feigned; fraudulent; frivolous; imitated; phony; pretended; pseudo; simulated; spurious; substitute; SHAM: **n.** affectation; cheat; counterfeit; deceit(fulness); deception; dissemblance; dissimulation; fake(ry); falseness; falsity; farce; feint; fraud; hoax; hocus-pocus; hollowness; humbug; hypocrisy; illusion; imitation; imposture; legerdemain; pageant-(ry); pastiche; prestidigitation; pretense; representation; simulacrum; substitute; travesty; trick; *trompe-l'oeil*; wile

SHAMBLE(S): confusion; hobble; mess; ruins; shreds; shuffle; slaughterhouse; walk; wreckage

SHAME: **v.** abase; abash; degrade; discomfit; disconcert; discountenance; disgrace; dishonor; embarrass; humble; humiliate; reproach; scandalize; stigmatize; SHAME: **n.** abasement; abashment; bashfulness; chagrin; confusion; contempt; decency; degradation; derision; discomfiture; disgrace; dishonor; disrepute; embarrassment; guilt; humiliation; ignominy; indecency; infamy; modesty; mortification; odium; opprobrium; *pudeur*; pudibundity; pudicity; reproach; scandal; stigma; SHAMELESS: (**see** "brazen") arrant; barefaced; brass(y); brazenfaced; degrading; hard; immodest; impudent; outrageous; unabashed; unblushing; unscrupulous; SHAMEFUL: ashamed; bad; base; degrading; disgraceful; dishonorable; evil; gross; ignominious; indecent; infamous; inglorious; mean; offensive; outrageous; vile

SHANTY: cabin; cote; hovel; hut(ch); lean-to; shack; shed

SHAPE: **v.** adapt; adjust; alter; arrange; build; carve; cast; change; chisel; configure; conform; construct; contrive; control; create; cut; design; determine; develop; devise; direct; effect; engrave; erect; fashion; fit; forge; form(alize); formulate; frame; guide; hack; hammer; hew; loom; make; manipulate; materialize; model(ize); modify; mo(u)ld; move; outline; plan; progress; regulate; sculpt(ure); square; style; succeed; trim; work; SHAPE: **n.** appearance; aspect; *belle tournure*; build; cast; configuration; conformation; construction; contour; cut; design; fashion; figure; form(at); frame; *Gestalt*; guise; hue; incline; likeness; make-(up); mo(u)ld; morphology; outline; pattern; plan; posture; profile; sculpture; silhouette; state; structure; texture; type; SHAPELY: chiseled; curvaceous; sculpturesque; statuesque; symmetric(al); trim; well-turned; SHAPELESS: amorphous; crude; fashionless; figureless; formless; heterogeneous; misshapen; ugly; uncomposed; unformed; unmolded

SHARD: fragment; piece; potsherd; remains; residue; scale; shell

SHARE: **v.** administer; allot; allow; apportion; appropriate; assign; authorize; award; bestow; cut; deal; designate; dispense; distribute; divide; dole; earmark; give; grant; impart; limit; measure; mete; ordain; parcel; partake; participate; rate; ration; regulate; slice; split; tax; tithe; SHARE: **n.** allotment; allowance; assignment; authorization; award; bestowal; bonus; codominance; condominium; cut; deal; designation; distribution; dividend; division; dole; earning(s); finger; gift; grant; hand; interest; limit; lot; measure; melon; parcel; part-(icipation); portion; quota; quotient; rate; ration; return; reward; segment; split; tax(ation); tithe; whack

SHARK: ace; cheat(er); expert; extortioner; fish; rogue; sharpster; swindler

SHARP: (**see** "keen") acerb; acid; acrid; acuate; acute; alert; angular; biting; brilliant; brisk; clear; costly; cute; cutting; descriptive; distinct; dressy; elegant; fiery; fine; furious; gingery; graphic; harsh; impetuous; intelligent; intense; irascible; merciless; merry; narrow; nipping; nippy; peaked; penetrating; piercing; piquant; poignant; pointed; pretty; prickly; pungent;

quick-witted; raw; ready-witted; ridged; sagacious; scintillating; severe; sharpened; shrewd; sly; smart; spiked; stabbing; stiff; stringent; stylish; tangy; unblunted; undulled; vigilant; violent; wily; witty; SHARPEN: chafe; deepen; edge; exacerbate; exaggerate; excite; file; grind; heighten; hone; increase; intensify; point; raise; stimulate; strop; whet; worsen

SHARPER *or* SHARPSTER: ace; cheat(er); expert; extortioner; gyp; knave; rogue; shark; sharpie; swindler; trickster

SHATTER: break; burst; clatter; comminute; crack; crumble; dash; demolish; destroy; disintegrate; disperse; dissipate; explode; fracture; fragmentate; impair; kill; rend; rive; ruin; scatter; shiver; shred; sink; smash; splinter; split; wreck

SHAVE: **v.** cheat; crop; cut; deduct; denude; depilate; discredit; economize; graze; pare; reduce; scrape; shear; shorten; slice; strip; SHAVE: **n.** tonsure

SHEAR: cheat; clip; cut; defraud; divest; fleece; fork; part; plunder; reduce; shave; shorten; strip; trim

SHEATH: case; dress; envelope; garment; lorica; ocrea; scabbard; sleeve; spathe; theca; tube; wrap(per)

SHEATHE: bury; cancel; case; close; cover; encase; hide; invaginate; wrap

SHED: **v.** cast; desquamate; diffuse; discard; doff; drop; effuse; emit; exfoliate; exuviate; fall; flow; impart; junk; mo(u)lt; peel; pour; reduce; release; spill; slough; strip; SHED: **n.** (**see** "shanty") cote; hovel; lean-to; outbuilding

SHEEN: brightness; brilliance; fluorescence; fulguration; glare; glaze; glitter; gloss(iness); illumination; light; luminosity; luster; nitidity; phosphorescence; polish; radiance; refulgence; refulgency; scintillation; shine; splendor

SHEEPLIKE: amenable; docile; meek; ovine; sheepish; stupid; suasive; timid; yielding

SHEER: **v.** avert; deflect; deviate; divert; swerve; turn; SHEER: **n.** abrupt; absolute; arrant; cobwebby; complete; crude; diaphanous; downright; filmy; fine; flimsy; frothy; gauzy; gossamer(y); gross; mere; out-and-out; pellucid; perpendicular; positive; precipitous; pure; quite; simple; stark; steep; tenuous; thick; thin; transparent; undiluted; unmitigated; unmixed; unqualified; utter

SHEET: cover(ing); expanse; layer; ledge; linen; newspaper; page; paper; surface

SHELF: bracket; ledge; mantle(piece); reef; sandbank; shoal

SHELL: **v.** bomb(ard); husk; peel; scale; shuck; strafe; strip; SHELL: **n.** armor; arms; boat; bomb; burr; carapace; carcass; case; casing; coat; conch; cover(ing); cowry; framework; hull; husk; matrix; pod; shard; shot; skeleton; skin; wrapper

SHELTER: **v.** board; chamber; conceal; cover; defend; embosom; guard; harbor; hide; house; lodge; preserve; protect; safeguard; screen; secure; shade; shed; shield; SHELTER: **n.** abri; anchorage; ark; asylum; berth; board; cabin; cave; coat; compartment; cote; cottage; cover(ing); covert(ure); defense; dugout; guard; harbor; haven; hood; hostel; house; housing; hovel; hut; lean-to; lee; lodge; lodging; nest; niche; nook; pound; preserve; protection; quarterage; quarters; receptacle; refuge; roof; safeguard; safety; sanctuary; sanctum; screen; security; shack; shade; shed; tent; umbrage; umbrella; wickiup; windbreak; SHELTERED: **see** "protected" and "restricted"

SHEPHERD: **v.** conduct; direct; escort; guide; herd; lead; protect; safeguard; shield; tend; usher; watch; SHEPHERD: **n.** (**see** "leader") director; guide; herder; herdsman; pastor; watch(man)

SHIBBOLETH: catchword; criterion; custom; password; platitude; saying; slogan; test; truism; usage

SHIELD: **v.** avert; conceal; cover; defend; fence; forbid; guard; hide; protect; safeguard; save; screen; secure; shade; shepherd; shroud; SHIELD: **n.** aegis; apron; armor; badge; bib; buckler; cover(ing); defense; ecu; *écusson*; egis; emblem; escutcheon; fence; guard; handle; pavis(e); pelta; protection; rail(ing); safeguard; screen; scutcheon; scute; scutum; shade; shell; shelter; targe; umbrella

SHIFT: **v.** (**see** "change") alter; baffle; contrive; counter(change); deviate; dislocate; dodge; drift; evade; fend; float; fluctuate; increase; interchange; intermit; jump;

manage; metastasize; move; oscillate; reciprocate; remove; rotate; ship; shirk; shuffle; shunt; slip; stir; stray; substitute; sway; swerve; transfer; transplant; transpose; trick; vary; SHIFT: **n.** (**see** "change") alteration; camise; chemise; development; deviation; device; dislocation; diversification; diversion; dodge; evasion; extremity; fault; fluctuation; fraud; metabasis; metastasis; movement; period; removal; resource; reversal; round; shake-up; shirt; shuffle; shunt; slip; substitute; substitution; swerve; swing; tour; transfer; transition; translation; transposition; turnover; variation; wile; SHIFTY: (**see** "unreliable") elusive; evasive; fickle; greasy; lubricious; oleaginous; resourceful; serpentine; serpiginous; snaky; sneaky; tricky; unfair; unstable; SHIFTING: inefficient; moving; unstable; vagabond; vagrant; wandering

SHIFTLESS: (**see** "idle" and "lazy") inefficient

SHILLY-SHALLY: **v.** dawdle; dodge; hesitate; idle; laze; trifle; vacillate; waver; SHILLY-SHALLY: **n.** dodge; hesitation; indecision; irresolution; vacillation; waver(ing)

SHIMMER: **see** "flash" and "shine"

SHIN: anticnemion; cnemis; crus; leg; shank; tibia

SHINE: **v.** beacon; beam; buff; burnish; coruscate; dazzle; effulge; excel; flame; flare; flash; furbish; glare; glaze; gleam; glisten; glitter; gloss; glow; irradiate; phosphoresce; polish; radiate; reflect; rutilate; scintillate; sparkle; star; twinkle; SHINE: **n.** beacon; brightness; buff; burnish; chatoyance; effulgence; glare; glaze; gleam; glint; glisten(ing); glitter; gloss; glow; illumination; irradiation; liking; luster; nimbus; phosphorescence; polish; prank; radiance; radiation; rutilation; scintillation; sheen; shimmer; show; sparkle; splendor; twinkle; SHINING: adazzle; aglow; beaming; bright; brilliant; chatoyant; cheerful; cheery; dazzling; effulgent; fulgent; glaring; glary; glassy; gleaming; glossy; glowing; illuminated; incandescent; iridescent; lucent; lucid; luminous; lustrous; neat; nitid; pellucid; phosphorescent; polished; radiant; refulgent; resplendent; rutilant; scintillating; shiny; sparkling; splendorous

SHIP: **v.** (**see** "send") board; express; freight; mail; shift; transport; SHIP: **n.** argosy; bark; boat; bug; caravel; coracle; craft; doni; galiot; galleon; galley; junk; leviathan; liner; lugger; oiler; sail; scow; tartan; tub; tug; vessel; watercraft; SHIPMENT: cargo; consignment; express; freight; goods; lading; load; mail

SHIPSHAPE: arranged; neat; orderly; snug; taut; tidy; trig; trim

SHIRK: avoid; evade; fend; goldbrick; malinger; shift; shun; slack; sneak; SHIRKER: avoider; dodger; *embusqué*; evader; goldbrick; malingerer; slacker; sneak

SHIVER: **v.** (**see** "shake") chill; excite; flutter; oscillate; quail; quake; quiver; shatter; shudder; splinter; thrill; totter; tremble; trill; vibrate; SHIVER: **n.** chill; flutter; *frisson*; oscillation; quake; quiver; shudder; tremble; vibration

SHOAL: bank; bar; crowd; drove; horde; host; reef; shallow; spit

SHOCK: **v.** abash; alarm; appall; astonish; astound; awe; collide; daunt; disedify; disgust; dismay; electrify; embarrass; frighten; horrify; jar; offend; outrage; overawe; revolt; scandalize; scare; startle; stun; surprise; terrify; terrorize; unman; unnerve; SHOCK: **n.** alarm; apoplexy; blow; collision; concussion; crash; crowd; dismay; disturbance; earthquake; embarrassment; explosion; fright; heap; horror; impact; jar; jolt; mop; outrage; prostration; reaction; scare; shake; stack; stroke; stupefaction; surprise; trauma; violence; SHOCKED: abashed; aghast; appalled; astonished; astounded; disgusted; dismayed; embarrassed; frightened; jarred; offended; outraged; unedified; SHOCKING: appalling; awful; bad; damaging; dedecorous; degrading; deplorable; desperate; dreadful; disgraceful; disgusting; distressing; electrifying; embarrassing; extreme; fearful; frightening; frightful; grim; harsh; hideous; horrible; horrifying; humiliating; immodest; improper; indecent; indecorous; *infra dignitatem* (abb. infra dig.); odious; offensive; opprobrious; outrageous; painful; percussive; repellant; revolting; scandalous; startling; stunning; terrible; traumatic; ugly; vulgar

SHODDY: **see** "cheap" and "shabby"

SHOE: balmoral; base; blucher; boot; brogue; casing; clog; ferrule; loafer; moccasin; mule; oxford; pad; sabot; sandal; scuff; slipper; socket; SHOEMAKER: cobbler; crispin; soutar; souter; sutor

SHOOT: **v.** blast; cast; dart; discard; discharge; exhaust; explode; extend; fire; fling; flip; germinate; hurry; ignite; kill; launch; mature; pain; plunge; precipitate; project; protrude; pump; quit; rush; score; scud; snipe; speed; spring; spurt; squirt; SHOOT: **n.** bough; branch; bud; chit; cion; frond; growth; limb; offspring; ratoon; rod; scion; sprig; sprout; thrust; tiller; twig; twinge

SHOP: **v.** buy; hunt; market; purchase; trade; SHOP: **n.** activity; atelier; boutique; burse; business; emporium; establishment; factory; laboratory; market; mart; mill; office; plant; salon; shoppe; store; studio

SHORE: **v.** border; brace; buttress; prop; stay; support; SHORE: **n.** bank; beach; brink; coast; land; leg; marge; playa; prop; ripa; sand; seacoast; seaside; strand; waterside

SHORT: abbreviated; abrupt; bare; brief; brittle; compact; compendious; concise; condensed; crisp; cross; cryptic; curt(ailed); deciduous; decurtate; defective; deficient; diminished; diminutive; direct; dwarfed; dwarfish; ephemeral; epitomized; expeditious; friable; fugitive; imperfect; inadequate; incomplete; instantaneous; insufficient; lacking; laconic; limited; little; low; meager; momentaneous; momentary; off; quick; reduced; runty; scant(y); shy; slack; snappish; squat(ty); stubby; substandard; succinct; summary; terse; transitory; truncated; unceremonious; uncivil; underdeveloped; SHORTEN: abbreviate; abridge; apocopate; bobtail; curtail; cut; derive; diminish; dock; elide; lessen; lop; reduce; retrench; slash; syncopate; telescope; truncate; SHORTENING: (**see** "abridgement") abbreviation; apocopation; curtailment; distillation; epitome; resumé; retrenchment; synopsis; truncation

SHORTCOMING: (**see** "defect") blemish; deficiency; dereliction; deviation; fault; foible; imperfection; leeway; omission; vice

SHORTAGE: abbreviation; deficiency; deficit; drought; famine; hunger; insufficiency; lack; loss; need; ullage; underage; underdevelopment; want

SHORTHANDED: undermanned; understaffed

SHORT-LIVED: (**see** "transient") ephemeral; transitory; unenduring

SHOT: attempt; ball; BB; blast; boost; bullet; cartridge; cast; chance; charge; conjecture; delivery; discharge; dose; drink; go; guess; hypo(dermic); injection; lead; marksman; missile; opportunity; pellet; photo(graph); range; reach; rush; scope; shell; stimulus; swallow; try

SHOUT: **v.** (**see** "exclaim") bawl; bellow; call; command; cry; noise; rejoice; roar; scream; vociferate; yell; yoo-hoo; SHOUT: **n.** (**see** "exclamation") bellow; call; command; conclamation; cry; hallelujah; noise; outcry; roar; scream; vociferation; yell; yoo-hoo

SHOVE: abet; aid; boost; compel; drive; jostle; leave; peddle; propel; push; shunt; thrust

SHOVEL: hat; ladle; scoop; spade; tool

SHOW: **v.** allege; appear; array; assert; bare; brandish; come; conduct; dazzle; declare; demonstrate; disclose; display; dispose; divulge; escort; evince; exhibit; explain; expose; flash; flaunt; flourish; guide; identify; indicate; inform; instruct; justify; leave; manifest; mark; note; offer; parade; perform; play; plead; present; proclaim; produce; prove; reflect; represent; reveal; signify; stage; symbolize; teach; tender; usher; SHOW: **n.** appearance; array(ment); art; bluff; boast(ing); bravado; brilliance; burletta; ceremony; chance; cinema; circus; comedy; contest; cortege; *coup de théâtre*; cynosure; dash; dazzlement; demonstration; dignity; disclosure; display; divulgence; dodge; éclat; elaboration; elegance; enactment; excuse; exhibit(ion); exposé; exposition; extravaganza; fantasy; farce; fare; flash; floridity; flourish; form(ality); frippery; fuss; gala; gaudery; glitter; glory; gloss; grandeur; grandiloquence; grandiosity; hippodrome; hoopla; indication; legit; magnificence; magniloquence; mask; masque; minstrel; movie; opera; ornamentation; ostentation; pageant(ry); parade; performance; play; pomp(osity); pompousness; pontificality; presentation; pretense; pretention; pretentiousness; pride; procession; production; puff; ritual; ritziness; semblance; shine; showiness; spectacle; spectacle; spectacular; splash; splendor; stadium; stage; state; style; theater; theatrical; to-do; trace; tragedy; vainglory; vanity; vaunt(ing); SHOWY: actorish; actory; actressy; adorned; affected; agonistic; alien; arabesque; artificial; arty; attractive; august; aureate; aurelian; aurulent; ba⁻onial; baroque; bedizened; begemmed; bejeweled; bespangled; blatant; blustering; bombastic; bright; brilliant; brummagem; bumptious; captivating; carnivalesque; charming; cheap; *chichi*; chintzy; cinematic; circusy; claptrap; clinquant; colorful; Corinthian; dashing; dazzling; decorated; decorative; dignified; dramatic(al); dramaturgic(al); dressy; elaborate; elegant; embellished; enchanting; exotic; extraneous; extravagant; fancy; farcical; fascinating; fastidious; festooned; fiery; flamboyant; flashing; flashy; florid; flourishing; flowery; foreign; formal; frilly; fustian; garish; gaudy; gay; gorgeous; giddy; gingerbread; glamorous; glaring; glittering; glittery; glossy; golden; gorgeous; grand; grandiloquent; grandiose; haughty; histrionic; imitative; imposing; inflated; jazzy; jeweled; loud; lurid; lush; lustrous; lyric(al); magisterial; magnificent; magniloquent; majestic; megalomani(a)c; meretricious; mysterious; operatic; opulent; ornamental; ornamented; ornate; orotund; ostentatious; *outré*; overdecorated; picturesque; plush(y); pompous; pretentious; prismatic; *recherché*; resplendent; rich; ritzy; rococo; romantic; rubescent; scenic; scintillating; sensational; smart; snazzy; *soigné*; *soignée* (fem.); sonorous; spangled; specious; spectacular; splashy; splendaceous; splendid; splendorous; sportive; sporty; stagy; strange; striking; sumptuous; swank(y); tasseled; tawdry; tessellated; theatric(al); thespian; tinny; tinsel; unrestrained; vain; vaudevillian; vivid; SHOWINESS: (**see** "gaudiness") acrobatics; acrobatism; affectation; artiness; attitudinization; blatancy; cabotinage; cinematics; floridity; flourish; frilliness; histrionics; histrionism; melodramatics; orotundity; ostentation; pageantry; pomp(osity); pontificality; Sardoodledom; speciosity; theatricality; theatrics; trumpery; vanity

SHOWER: **v.** bathe; drizzle; flow; misle; mizzle; pepper; pour; rain; rush; scatter; spate; spray; sprinkle; SHOWER: **n.** abundance; bath; drizzle; flow; misle; mizzle; party; rain; rush; scattering; spate; spray; sprinkle; sprinkling

SHRED: (**see** "fragment") bit; dag; filament; part(icle); piece; rag; scrap; shaving; sliver; snip; string; strip; tag; tatter; tear; tuft; wisp

SHREW: banshee; bat; battleaxe; beldame; crone; erd; fury; hag; harpy; harridan; hellcat; Jezebel; ma(e)nad; mammal; randy; scold; spitfire; strumpet; tartar; termagant; Tisiphone; virago; vixen; witch; Xantippe

SHREWD: (**see** "careful") acuminous; acute; arch; artful; astute; biting; calculating; canny; cautious; chary; circumspect(ive); clever; crafty; cunning; cute; dangerous; deliberate; diplomatic; discerning; distressing; foxy; guarded; hard; heady; judicious; keen; knowing; knowledg(e)able; mindful; observant; parlous; penetrating; perspicacious; piercing; politic; prudent; reflective; sagacious; sapient; severe; sharp; sly; smart; stratagematic; suave; subtle; tricky; vigilant; watchful; wily; wise; SHREWDNESS: (**see** "caution") acumen; astucity; astuteness; calculation; callidity; canniness; care(fulness); circumspection; cleverness; comprehension; craft(iness); cunning; diplomacy; discernment; discrimination; foxiness; judiciousness; keenness; knowledge; mindfulness; observance; penetration; perspicacity; policy; prudence; reflection; sagacity; sapience; slyness; strategy; suavity; subtlety; trickery; vigilance; wariness; wisdom

SHRILL: acute; biting; calliopean; extravagant; high(-pitched); ill-tempered; intemperate; keen; penetrating; piercing; piping; poignant; pungent; reedy; sharp; strident; stridulous; treble; SHRILLNESS: keenness; reediness; stridency; stridor; stridulation

SHRIMP: crustacean; dwarf; peewee; prawn; shellfish

SHRINE: adytum; altar; ark; cathedral; chapel; chasse; image; mausoleum; memorial; naos; reliquary; sanctorium; sanctuary; *sanctum sanctorum*; temple; tomb

SHRINK: abate; atrophy; compact; contract; cower; curl; decrease; deflate; desiccate; diminish; disappear; dry; dwindle; evaporate; flinch; huddle; lessen; parch; quail; recede; recoil; reduce; retire; retract; shrivel; shy; telescope; vaporize; volatilize; waste; wince; withdraw; wither; wizen; wrinkle; SHRINKING: abating; bashful; coy; diminishing; humble; lessening; modest; retiring; shy; timid

SHRIVEL: (**see** "shrink") crine; dry; parch; reduce; scorch; sear; wither; wizen; wrinkle; SHRIVELED: atrophic; atrophied; dried; parched; reduced; scorched; shrunken; sear(ed); small; thin; wizened; wrinkled

SHROUD: **v.** cloud; cover; hide; lop; mask; pall; screen; shelter; trim; SHROUD: **n.** cerement; cloud; cover(ing); cowl; envelope; garment; mask; pall; screen; shelter; winding-sheet

SHRUB(S): arboret; boscage; brier; bush; foliage; frutex; herb; r(a)etem; tree; undergrowth

SHRUNKEN: (**see** "shriveled") atrophic; atrophied; wizened

SHUCK: (**see** "expose") shell; unhusk

SHUDDER: **v.** (**see** "shake") quake; quiver; shiver; tremble; SHUDDER: **n.** frisson; oscillation; quake; tremor; tremulation; vibration

SHUFFLE: **v.** change; confuse; deal; derange; drag; equivocate; juggle; jumble; manipulate; mix; move; prevaricate; quibble; scuff(le); shift; SHUFFLE: **n.** (**see** "trick") dance; jumble; scuffle; shift

SHUN: avoid; balk; cut; disdain; elude; escape; eschew; evade; flee; fly; ignore; refrain; refuse; scorn; shy; taboo

SHUNT: bypass; deflect; detour; deviate; divert; dodge; flinch; shift; shove; shuttle; sidetrack; switch; transfer

SHUT: **v.** bar; block(ade); cease; close; confine; cover; exclude; fasten; fold; hide; immure; pen; prohibit; seal; seclude; secrete; secure; stop; suspend; SHUT: **a.** barred; blockaded; blocked; closed; covered; drawn; excluded; fastened; sealed; secluded; suspended; unopen(ed)

SHY: **v.** avoid; balk; demur; dodge; evade; recoil; refuse; scruple; shrink; shun; SHY: **a.** abashed; antisocial; bashful; cautious; chary; circumspect; constrained; coy; Daphnean; demure; diffident; distant; distrustful; evasive; fearful; hesitant; hidden; humble; lacking; mim; modest; necessary; needed; pavid; recluse; reluctant; reserved; retiring; scant; secluded; sensitive; shamefaced; sheepish; short; shrinking; solitary; suspicious; timid; timorous; unassertive; unassuming; unintimate; unobtrusive; verecund; wary; wild; withdrawn; SHYNESS: bashfulness; cautiousness; circumspection; constraint; coyness; diffidence; hesitancy; humbleness; humility; modesty; sheepishness; suspicion; timidity; verecundity; wariness

SIBLING: brother; kinsman; relative; sister; twin

SIBYL: fortuneteller; oracle; prophetess; seeress; sorceress; witch

SICK(LY): (**see** "ill") aeger; ailing; *à la mort*; amort; bedfast; cachectic; cachexic; chagrined; contaminated; declining; defective; depressed; diseased; diseaseful; disgusted; disordered; faulty; fevered; feverish; indisposed; infirm; languid; leprous; macabre; maladive; malign(ant); mawkish; morbid; morbific(al); morbose; pale; pallid; pasty; pathologic(al); peaked; phthisic; prostrate; puny; queasy; sallow; streaked; suffering; tubercular; unhappy; unhealthful; unhealthy; unsound; unwholesome; upset; valetudinarian; wan; weak(ened); SICKEN: cloy; deteriorate; disgust; nauseate; surfeit; SICKENING: cloying; disgusting; insipid; mawkish; nauseating; nauseous; SICKNESS: (**see** "disease") bout; cachexia; diseasedness; disorder; fever; illness; indisposition; infirmity; malady; malignancy; mischief; morbidity; nausea; paroxysm; pathology; qualm; queasiness; seizure; sore; spell; stroke; suffering; vapors

SIDE: **v.** agree; join; support; SIDE: **n.** angle; aspect; bezel; border; division; edge; face; facet; faction; flank; lateral; latus; leaf; margin; movement; party; phase; portion; position; sect; surface; verge

SIDESTEP: see "avoid"

SIDETRACK: avert; avoid; bypass; detour; deviate; distract; divert; shunt; sidestep; switch

SIDEWAYS *or* SIDEWISE: askance; aslant; crabwise; edged; indirectly; laterally; obliquely; slyly

SIDLE: cant; deviate; edge; inch; skew; slide

SIESTA: break; doze; lull; nap; recess; rest; sleep

SIEVE: **v.** bolt; clean; filter; gossip; percolate; perforate; riddle; screen; select; separate; sift; strain; winnow; SIEVE: **n.** basket; colander; filter; mesh; screen; sifter; strainer; tamis; tattler; trommel

SIFT: analyze; bolt; clean; discuss; dissect; examine; filter; inquire; investigate; part; probe; question; screen; separate; sieve; sort; strain; winnow

SIGH: **v.** complain; grieve; groan; lament; long; moan; mourn; sob; suspirate; suspire; thirst; yearn; SIGH: **n.** complaint; groan; lament(ation); moan; sob; suspiration

SIGHT: **v.** aim; espy; eye; glimpse; look; peep; perceive; see; sense; spot; view; SIGHT: **n.** aim; exhibition; eye(ful); glimpse; judgment; look; opinion; panorama; peep; perception; scene; scenery; sense; show; spectacle; view(point); vision; vista

SIGN: **v.** affix; attract; beacon; beckon; endorse; engage; gesticulate; gesture; hire; indorse; motion; seal; signal; signify; subscribe; underwrite; wave; write; SIGN: **n.** adumbration; augury; badge; banner; beacon; beckon(ing); brand; cachet; clue; criterion; cue; description; descriptor; device; divination; earmark; emblem; ensign; escutcheon; evidence; expression; flag; footprint; forewarning; gesticulation; gesture; guide(post); harbinger; hint; index; indication; indicia (pl.); indicium; manifestation; mark; message; miracle; motion; nod; note; omen; placard; portent; poster; precedent; presage; proof; seal; segno; shingle; signal; signum; standard; stop; surmise; symbol; symptom; token; trace; type; vestige; warning; wonder; SIGNED: endorsed; indorsed; onomatous; subscribed; underwritten

SIGNAL: **v.** (**see** "sign") alarm; alert; buzz; call; flag; flare; gesture; herald; indicate; motion; nod; ring; sign(alize); signify; summon; toot; wag; warn; wave; whistle; wink; yell; SIGNAL **a.** (**see** "important") conspicuous; distinctive; eminent; famous; memorable; momentous; notable; noticeable; obvious; outstanding; prominent; remarkable; salient; significant; SIGNAL: **n.** alarm; alert; beacon; bell; buzz(er); call; cue; curfew; flag; flare; gesticulation; gesture; glare; gong; horn; impulse; indication; information; light; mark(er); motion; nod; ring; sign; symptom; target; token; toot; wag; warning; watchword; wave; whistle; wink; yell

SIGNATURE: autograph; hand; identification; inscription; John Hancock; mark; name; seal; sigil; signum; subscription; writing

SIGNIFICANT: (**see** "important") authoritative; basic; cogent; consequential; considerable; conspicuous; critical; decisive; definite; definitive; determinative; distinctive; eminent; essential; eventful; expressive; famous; fundamental; grave; great; imposing; indicative; influential; material; meaningful; meaty; memorable; momentous; notable; noticeable; outstanding; paramount; portentous; pressing; prominent; real; relevant; remarkable; salient; sensible; serious; signal;

sound; substantial; suggestive; superior; telling; true; urgent; valid; valuable; vital; weighty; SIGNIFICANCE *or* SIGNIFICATION: (**see** "importance") authoritativeness; bearing; consequence; consequentiality; conspicuity; distinction; eminency; essence; fame; gravity; import; inwardness; meaning; message; moment; sense; seriousness; significatum; size; stress; suggestiveness; token; understanding; urgency; weight(iness)

SIGNIFY: (**see** "signal") allude; announce; betoken; communicate; convey; declare; denote; express; foreshow; gesture; imply; import; indicate; inform; intimate; matter; mean; motion; portend; show; sign; speak; spell; suggest; wave; SIGNIFICATION: **see** under "significant"

SILENT: agape; aphonic; awestruck; brachysyllabic; calm; close-lipped; close-mouthed; close-tongued; conticent; dead; dumb; hushed; inactive; inarticulate; inaudible; incommunicable; incommunicative; laconic; lulled; muffled; mum; mute; noiseless; placid; quiescent; quiet; reserved; retentive; reticent; secret(ive); silentious; soft; soundless; speechless; stifled; still; subauditory; suppressed; tacit(urn); tight-lipped; tongue-tied; tranquil; unannounced; unbroached; uncommunicative; unconfiding; undeclared; unexpressed; unloquacious; unmentioned; unresponsive; unspoken; unvoiced; utterless; wordless; SILENCE: **v.** (**see** "quell" and "quiet") awe; calm; close; embarrass; hush; lull; pacify; placate; soft-pedal; squelch; stifle; still; suppress; tranquilize; SILENCE: **n.** aphony; armistic; calm; death; hush; inarticulation; inaudibleness; lull; muteness; oblivion; obmutescence; obscurity; omission; peace; placidity; quiescence; quiet(ude); rest; reticence; secrecy; squelch; soft pedal; stillness; taciturnity; tranquility; unresponsiveness; wordlessness

SILKEN *or* SILKY: delicate; effeminate; gentle; glossy; harmonious; ingratiating; insinuating; lithe; lustrous; luxurious; satiny; seric; sericeous; sleek; slick; smooth; soft; tender

SILLY: absurd; anserine; anserous; apish; asinine; brainless; childish; coddled; daft; dazed; dense; dull; dumb; empty; fatuous; feeble; foolish; frivolous; goofy; idiotic; imprudent; inane; indiscreet; injudicious; insane; insipid; irrational; namby-pamby; nonsensical; pathetic; preposterous; puerile; ridiculous; senseless; sentimental; shallow;

sickly; simple; stunned; stupefied; stupid; trifling; trivial; unreasonable; unwise; unwitty; vacuous; vapid; vertiginous; weak; witless; SILLINESS: (see "absurdity") asininity; childishness; emptiness; foolishness; frivolity; goofiness; idiocy; inanition; inanity; indiscretion; insanity; *niaiserie*; puerility; ridiculosity; shallowness; simplicity; vacuity; witlessness

SILT: alluvium; deposit; dirt; dregs; drift; lees; loess; mire; mud; ooze; residue; scum; sediment; slime; wash

SILVER: **n.** Ag; argent(um); cash; change; coins; money; plate; service; sterling; tableware; SILVER(Y): **a.** argent(iferous); argentine; argentous; clear; gray; resonant; shining; white

SIMILAR: (see "alike") akin; analogical; analogous; close; comparable; congruent; consimilar; coordinate; corresponding; duplicate; equal; equivalent; faithful; homogenous; homologous; homonymous; identical; kin; like; parallel; reciprocal; resembling; same; semblable; synonymous; SIMILARITY: analogy; comparability; congruency; duplication; equality; equivalence; parallelism; resemblance; simile; synonymity

SIMILE: analogy; comparison; metaphor; parable; similarity

SIMMER: boil; brood; bubble; ferment; seethe; stew

SIMPLE: (see "silly") absolute; artless; asinine; bare; barren; *bona fide*; bucolic; candid; casual; childish; clear; comfortable; common; credulous; crude; dense; dull; dumb; easy(going); effortless; elemental; elementary; facile; fatuous; feebleminded; folksy; foolish; frank; fundamental; guileless; gullible; half-witted; harsh; homespun; humble; idyllic; ignorant; incomplex; incomplicate; inelaborate; inexpert; informal; ingenuous; innocent; laborless; lax; light; limpid; lowly; lucid; mere; mild; modest; naïve; naked; natural; nontechnical; oafish; obvious; open; ordinary; pastoral; peaceful; placid; plain; plebeian; primary; primitive; pure; rural; rustic; sheer; single; singular; silly; slow; smooth; soft; sole; soothing; straightforward; stupid; tame; tractable; tranquil; trustful; unadorned; unaffected; unaggravated; unalloyed; unassuming; uncombined; uncomplex; uncomplicated; uncompounded; unconditional; underived; undidactic; uneducated; unembellished;

unentangled; unfussy; ungarnished; unillusioned; uninvolved; unperplexed; unpretentious; unruly; unsophisticated; untroublesome; untutored; unvarnished; SIMPLIFY: abridge; clarify; explain; informalize; streamline; SIMPLICITY: artlessness; austerity; candor; child's play; clarity; elegance; fundamental(ity); genuineness; guilelessness; homeliness; humility; ignorance; ingenuosity; ingenuousness; innocence; intelligibility; kid stuff; naïveté; neatness; plainness; precision; primitivity; restraint; stupidity; unaffectedness; unsophistication

SIMPLETON: (see "blockhead") Abderite; ass; *bon enfant*; boob(y); clown; daw; dope; dupe; fool; gaup; gawk; goose; gump; harlequin; idiot; jellyfish; loon; moron; nincompoop; ninny; nitwit; noodle; oaf; scoffer; simp; softhead

SIMULACRUM: appearance; counterfeit; effigy; icon; image; imitation; imposture; mask; phantom; semblance; sham; verisimilitude; verisimility

SIMULATE: act; affect; ape; assume; concoct; copy; counterfeit; disguise; dissemble; equivocate; fake; feign; imitate; lie; mimic; mock; pretend; prevaricate; resemble; sketch; SIMULATED: artificial; assumed; counterfeit; derivative; factitious; fictitious; imitated; mock; *soi-disant*; supposititious; verisimilar; verisimilous; SIMULATION: acting; cant; feint; fiction; hypocrisy; pretense; sanctimony; supposition; verisimilitude; verisimility

SIMULTANEOUS: (see "concurrent") conjoint; contemporary; harmonious; momentaneous; symphonic; symphonious; together; united

SIN: **v.** blaspheme; curse; err; lapse; offend; slip; transgress; violate; SIN: **n.** blasphemy; crime; delict; dereliction; depravity; error; evil; fault; guilt; immorality; iniquity; lapse; misdeed; misdemeanor; offense; peccancy; shortcoming; slip; transgression; vice; violation; wickedness; wrong; SINFUL: culpable; depraved; derelict; flagitious; heinous; iniquitous; nefarious; peccant; piacular; unheavenly; unregenerate(d); wicked; SINNER: transgressor; wrongdoer

SINCE: after; ago; as; because; for; from; hence; later; subsequently; syne; yet

SINCERE: (see "candid") aboveboard; ardent; artless; bona fide; childlike; conscientious; direct; earnest; frank; genuine; guileless; heartfelt; hearty; honest; incorruptible; ingenuous; innocent; intense; natural; nocent; open; outspoken; plain; pretenseless; pure; real; serious; simple; straightforward; straight-from-the-shoulder; true(-blue); truthful; unaffected; undesigning; undisguised; unfeigned; unsophisticated; upright; wholehearted; whole-souled; SINCERITY: (**see** "honesty") *bona fides*; *bonne foi*; conscience; consideration; feeling; genuineness; heart(iness); innocence; integrity; naturalness; probity; straightforwardness; truth; veracity; willingness; zeal

SINECURE: cinch; gravy; pipe; snap

SINFUL: **see** under "sin"

SINEW: force; leader; ligament; mainstay; muscle; nerve; power; strength; tendon; SINEWY: athletic; brawny; burly; husky; muscular; robust(ious); sound; stout; strong; sturdy; tendinous; tough; vigorous; wir(e)y

SING: call; cantillate; carol; chant; chirp; chortle; croon; descant; echo; hum; inform; intone; laud; lilt; modulate; praise; rejoice; ring; talk; tell; troll; vocalize; warble; yodel; SINGER: alto; bard; basso; canary; cantor; caroler; *chanteur*; *chanteuse* (fem.); crooner; descanter; minstrel; poet; siren; songbird; songster; songstress; soprano; vocalist; warbler

SINGLE: **a.** ace; alone; apart; azygous; celibate; discrete; distinct; exclusive; frank; honest; individual; isolated; lone; mono; odd; one; open; particular; select; separate(d); singular; sole; solitary; solo; special; sporadic; spouseless; unal; unbroken; undivided; uniform; unique; unitary; unmarried; unmatched; unusual; unwedded; wifeless; SINGLE: **n.** ace; bunt; hit; stag

SINGULAR: (**see** "odd") abnormal; bizarre; contrary; curious; different; eccentric; exceptional; extraordinary; fantastic(al); individual; isolated; oddish; particular; peculiar; quaint; queer; rare; remarkable; single; strange; striking; uncommon; unique; unusual; valuable; whimsical; SINGULARITY: (**see** "peculiarity") haecceity; individuality; particularity; specificity; unit

SINISTER: (**see** "bad") adverse; baleful; baneful; calamitous; catastrophic(al); corrupt(ive); dark; deadly; dire; disastrous; dishonest; evil; fateful; fearful; foreboding; ghastly; grim; harmful; horrendous; hurtful; inauspicious; injurious; left; left-handed; malevolent; malign(ant); morbific; mortal; ominous; pernicious; perverse; poisonous; portentous; secret; sinistrous; underhand(ed); unfavorable; unlucky; vicious; wicked; woeful

SINK: **v.** absorb; beat; bury; collapse; debase; deceive; decline; defeat; degenerate; descend; destroy; deteriorate; diminish; dip; dive; droop; drop; engulf; excavate; fail; fall; flag; immerse; kill; lessen; lower; merge; overwhelm; penetrate; relapse; restrain; retrograde; retrogress; ruin; sag; scuttle; set(tle); submerge; subordinate; subside; suppress; swamp; thrust; SINK: **n.** (**see** "basin") cesspool; den; drain; sewer

SINLESS: (**see** "innocent") holy; immaculate; impeccable; impeccant; inculpable; SINLESSNESS: (**see** "innocence") holiness; immaculacy; impeccability; impeccancy

SINNER: **see** under "sin"

SINUOUS: bending; circuitous; complex; crooked; curved; devious; erring; intricate; mazy; meandering; serpentine; slinky; snaky; tortuous; undulating; wavy; willowy; winding

SINUS: ampulla; antrum; arm; bay; bend; cavity; curve; hollow; opening; pocket; recess; sac

SIP: drink; gulp; lap; suck; sup; taste

SIRE: **v.** beget; breed; father; generate; originate; procreate; SIRE: **n.** father; horse; lord; king; male; man; master; parent; progenitor

SIREN: alarm; alert; bell; charmer; Circe; enchantress; enticer; *femme fatale*; Lorelei; lurer; mermaid; seducer; seductress; songbird; temptress; warning

SISTER: kin(swoman); nun; nurse; person; sib(ling); *soror*

SIT: abide; brood; convene; fit; hatch; incubate; lie; meet; perch; pose; press; remain; repress; rest; settle; squat; squelch; stay; suit; weigh; SITTING: *in situ*; installed; placid; seated; sedent(ary); sessile; situated

SITE: (**see** "area") locality; location; loci (pl.); locus; lot; place; position; scene; séance; seat; situation; situs; space; spot; stance

SITUATION: (see "aspect") accident; angle; appearance; arrangement; atmosphere; berth; case; circumstance; climax; complication; condition; conflict; conjecture; crisis; development; dilemma; episode; incident; instance; job; juncture; locality; location; métier; occasion; occurrence; pass; perch; picture; place; plight; pose; position; post; predicament; problem; quandary; scene; seat; session; site; spot; stand(ing); state; station; status; strait; thing; work

SIZE: amount; amplitude; area; avoirdupois; bigness; bulk; caliber; character; condition; degree; dignity; dimension(s); enormity; expanse; extent; format; gage; grandeur; growth; height; importance; intensity; jumbo; largeness; length; limit; magnitude; mass; measure(ments); might; ponderosity; power; prestige; proportion(s); quantity; scale; scope; shape; significance; space; spread; stature; stretch; vastness; volume; weight; width

SKELETON: analysis; anthropotomy; armature; body; bones; cadre; cage; draft; frame(work); outline; phytotomy; plan; remains; sketch; structure; support

SKEPTIC: agnostic; apikores; apikoros; apikorsim (pl.); aporetic; deist; disbeliever; dissenter; dissident; doubter; doubting Thomas; freethinker; giaour; heretic; infidel; latitudinarian; nullifidian; Pyrrhonist; questioner; recusant; theophobist; unbeliever; zetetic; SKEPTICAL: (see "doubtful") agnostic; aporetic; *cum grano salis*; disdainful; dissident; distrustful; distrusting; doubting; dubious; dubitable; incredulous; negativistic; negatory; Pyrrhonian; Pyrrhonic; recusant; sardonic; unbelieving; uncertain; SKEPTICISM: (see "doubt") agnosticism; disdain; dogmatism; dubiety; dubiosity; dubitation; incredulity; mistrust; negativism; negativity; Pyrrhonism; reserve; salt; sarcasm; sardonicism; skepsis; uncertainty

SKETCH: v. brief; chart; delineate; describe; design; draft; draw; figure; form; ink; limn; map; outline; paint; pencil; picture; plan; plot; portray; represent; shape; simulate; summarize; trace; SKETCH: n. adumbration; aperçu; brief; chart; compendium; composition; delineation; description; design; digest; draft; drawing; figure; form; idea; map; outline; painting; picture; plan; plot; portrayal; précis; report; representation; skit; summary; SKETCHY:

adumbral; cloudy; diagrammatic(al); slight; superficial; trivial

SKID: coast; drag; drift; drop; glide; scud; shift; skim; slide; slip; slue

SKILL: ability; address; adeptness; adroitness; ambidexterity; aptitude; art(ifice); artistry; capability; cleverness; competence; contrivance; control; coordination; craft(iness); cunning; dexterity; diplomacy; ease; education; efficiency; esthetics; expertise; expertness; facility; finesse; fluency; hability; ingeniosity; ingenuity; inventiveness; knack; knowledge; magic; method; occupation; practice; profession; proficiency; resources; *savoir faire*; subtlety; tact; technique; touch; trade; training; trick; virtuosity; wit; work; SKILLFUL *or* SKILLED: able; accomplished; adept; adroit; ambidexterous; apt; *au fait*; capable; clever; competent; consummate; daedalian; daedal(ic); delicate; dext(e)rous; diplomatic; easy; educated; experienced; expert; facile; familiar; fine; fit; good; habile; handy; hotshot; ingenious; inventive; masterful; masterly; perfect(ed); practiced; precise; proficient; resourceful; scient(ific); sciental; slick; smart; subtle; tactful; trained; versatile; versed; virtuosic; workmanlike; SKILLFULNESS: ability; accomplishment; address; adeptness; adroitness; cleverness; consummation; craftiness; delicacy; dexterity; expertise; finesse; ingenuity; mastery; precision; proficiency; stratagem; strategy; virtuosity; workmanship

SKIM: (see "skip") brush; dart; despumate; flit; fly; glance; glide; scoot; scud; skip; summarize

SKIMPY: deficient; lean; meager; mean; scant(y); skinny; thin; undernourished

SKIN: v. bark; cheat; criticize; decorticate; defeat; fell; flay; fleece; hull; husk; pare; peel; reprimand; satirize; scrape; strip; swindle; SKIN: n. bark; coat(ing); cover(ing); cuticle; derm(a); epidermis; film; fur; hide; hull; husk; integument; layer; peel(ing); pelage; pellicle; pelt; rind; surface; tegument; veneer

SKINFLINT: cheat; churl; curmudgeon; miser; niggard; rapscallion; rascal; rip

SKINNY: (see "slender") cadaverous; emaciated; lank(y); lean; macilent; malnourished; membranous; poor; skeletonic; skimpy; spare; tabescent; thin; undernourished

SKIP: bound; bypass; caper; dart; depart; detour; disregard; elide; elope; escape; flee; flit; fly; forego; frisk; gambol; glance; glide; hop; jump; leap(frog); leave; misfire; miss; neglect; omit; pass; reflect; ricochet; sashay; scoot; scud; skim; spring

SKIRMISH: **v.** battle; brawl; brush; clash; combat; conflict; encounter; engage; fight; flourish; rummage; scrimmage; spar; tilt; SKIRMISH: **n.** battle; bout; brawl; brush; clash; combat; conflict; contest; dispute; encounter; engagement; fight; flourish; fray; melee; rencontre; rout; soiree; tilt; tournament; velitation

SKIRT: border; dirndl; edge; environs; fringe; fustanella; kilt; margin; periphery; petticoat; rim; sarong; slip; SKIRTING: border(ing); circumferential; edging; enclosing; fringing; marginal; peripheral

SKIT: **v.** asperse; burlesque; caper; dance; flounce; jibe; joke; libel; parody; play; quip; satirize; sketch; SKIT: **n.** antic; burlesque; caper; dance; jibe; joke; libel; parody; play; quip; satire; sketch; squib; story

SKITTISH: (**see** "nervous") bashful; capricious; coy; doubtful; dubious; fearful; hesitant; irresponsible; shy; spookish; uncertain; undecided; unstable; wary

SKULK: conceal; couch; crawl; creep; crouch; glide; hide; lurk; malinger; shirk; slink; sneak; steal

SKULL: brain; cranium; head; mind

SKY: air; atmosphere; azure; blue; canopy; climate; empyrean; firmament; heaven(s); summit; vault; welkin; zenith

SKYLARK: **v.** carouse; fool; frolic; sport; SKYLARK: **n.** bird; lark; pipit

SLACK: **a.** backward; careless; dilatory; drooping; dull; easy; feeble; flabby; flaccid; inactive; inadequate; inattentive; indifferent; inert; lax; lazy; limber; limp; listless; loose; negligent; off; relaxed; remiss; slow; sluggish; soft; stagnant; still; tardy; unfirm; unsteady; weak; yielding; SLACK(NESS): **n.** abatement; carelessness; depression; detente; doldrums; downswing; easiness; easing; laches; laxation; letup; looseness;

loosening; misfeasance; moderation; recession; relaxation; remission; retardation; slowing; slump; unstress; weakening; SLACKEN: abate; curb; ease; lag; lay; loosen; moderate; relax; remit; retard; sag; slow; unstretch; weaken

SLAG: ash(es); cinders; clinker(s); coals; debris; dross; embers; lava; refuse; scoria

SLAM: **v.** (**see** "slap") abuse; bang; beat; blow; criticize; defeat; knock; rap; shut; slander; strike; SLAM: **n.** (**see** "slap") abuse; bang; blow; criticism; defeat; impact; knock; rap; strike

SLANDER: **v.** abuse; asperse; backbite; belie; belittle; besplatter; blacken; calumniate; criticize; decry; defame; degrade; denigrate; derogate; detract; disparage; hit; insult; knock; lampoon; libel; malign; offend; revile; slam; smear; traduce; vilify; vituperate; SLANDER: **n.** abuse; aspersion; calumniation; calumny; *coup de bec*; criticism; defamation; degradation; denigration; derogation; detraction; disparagement; excoriation; falsehood; lampoon; libel; malediction; satire; smear; tale; traducement; traduction; vilification; vituperation; SLANDEROUS: abusive; calumniatory; calumnious; defamatory; degradative; degrading; denigratory; disparaging; evil; insulting; libelous; offensive; scandalous; slanderful; vilifying

SLANG: (**see** "jargon") argot; cant; colloquialism; dialect; koine; lingo; *lingua franca*; patois; pidgin; vulgarism

SLANT: **v.** angle; bevel; drift; glance; heel; incline; lean; list; pitch; rake; skew; slope; splay; tilt; trend; turn; veer; SLANT(ED): **a.** arake; askew; atilt; awry; beveled; biased; colored; inclined; oblique; sidelong; slanting; sloped; sloping; SLANT: **n.** angle; attitude; bevel; bias; drift; glance; grade; gradient; inclination; incline; leaning; list; opinion; pitch; ramp; slope; stance; stand; tile; trend; veer(ing); view(point)

SLAP: **v.** (**see** "hit") bang; censure; criticize; cuff; insult; punish; rebuff; reprimand; slam; spank; strike; swat; SLAP: **n.** bang; blow; criticism; cuff; humiliation; insult; punish; rebuff; reprimand; slam; slapping; smack; spank(ing); swat

SLASH: (**see** "cut") butcher; chop; excoriate; expunge; hew; incise; jag; knife; lash; pare; reduce; rip; section; sever; shape; shorten; slit; tear; whip

SLATE: agenda (pl.); agendum; board; color; file; group; list; panel; plan; record; rock; roll; schedule; shale; shingle; slab; tablet; tile

SLATTERN: crone; hag; idler; mopsy; prostitute; sloven; slut; trifler; trollop

SLAUGHTER: (**see** "kill" and "carnage") occision; shamble

SLAVE: (**see** "toil" and "serf") bondman; dependent; drudge; esne; fief; helot; mancipium; odalisque; peon; servant; thrall; villein; SLAVERY: bondage; drudgery; helotism; indenture(ship); labor; moil; peonage; serfdom; serfhood; serfism; servitude; subjection; thralldom; toil; unfreedom; vassalage; ville(i)nage

SLAY: (**see** "kill") annihilate; assassinate; butcher; destroy; eradicate; erase; exterminate; fell; lynch; massacre; murder; overwhelm; shoot; slaughter; suppress; surprise

SLEAZY: cheap; flashy; flimsy; fragile; limp; shoddy; thin; tin(ny); tinsel; trashy

SLEEK: bland; crafty; elegant; fashionable; flourishing; glossy; healthy; lustrous; obsequious; oily; oleaginous; plump; satiny; shiny; silky; slick; slinky; sly; smooth; stylish; suave; svelt; unctuous; velvety; well-groomed

SLEEP: **v.** catnap; doze; drowse; dwell; flop; lodge; nap; nod; repose; rest; slumber; snooze; stay; SLEEP: **n.** (**see** "dormancy") catnap; coma; death; doze; drowse; hibernation; hypnosis; immobility; Land of Nod; latency; latescence; lethargy; nap; narcosis; night; nod; quiescence; quiet(ness); relaxation; repose; rest(ing); siesta; sluggishness; slumber; snooze; somnolence; sopor; stupor; suspension; torpidity; torpor; unconsciousness; wink; SLEEPY: (**see** "dormant") comatose; dead; drowsy; hypnotic; lethargic; narcotic; opiate; oscitant; phlegmatic; sluggish; slumbrous; somniferous; somnolent; somnorific; soporiferous; soporific; unconscious; SLEEPING: (**see** "dormant") asleep; comatose; dead; latent; lethargic; quiescent; quiet; unconscious; SLEEPINESS: **see** "drowsiness"

SLEEPER: beam; dormouse; drone; Pullman; shark; slumberer; support; tie; timber

SLEEPLESS: active; alert; insomniac; restless; wakeful; SLEEPLESSNESS: activity; insomnia; insomnolence; insomnolency; restlessness; wakefulness

SLEEVE: arm; channel; cylinder; dolman; mandrel; pipe; thimble; tube

SLENDER: (**see** "slight") abstemious; acicular; aciculate(d); capillary; delicate; feeble; fine; flimsy; frail; frugal; gracile; inadequate; insubstantial; lank(y); lean; limited; lissom(e); lithe(some); meager; minute; narrow; rare; reedy; scant(y); skinny; slim; small; *soigné; soignée* (fem.); spare; spindling; svelt(e); tenuous; thin; trim; trivial; weak; willowy; wispy; SLENDERNESS: gracility; lithesomeness; svelteness; tenuity

SLICE: **v.** (**see** "cut") carve; divide; hew; pare; reduce; section; sever; SLICE: **n.** collop; cut; division; gash; layer; part; piece; portion; reduction; section; segment; share; slab; stroke; wedge

SLICK: (**see** "smooth") bald; clever; contrived; deft; fluent; glib; glossy; ingratiating; obvious; oily; skillful; slimy; slippery; slithery; talkative

SLIDE: chute; coast; crawl; drift; flow; glide; glissade; pour; sidle; skate; skid; skim; skip; slip; slither; slue; sneak; steal; vanish; wriggle

SLIGHT: **v.** cut; disdain; disparage; disregard; disrespect; forget; ignore; neglect; omit; overlook; scan; slur; snub; SLIGHT: **a.** (**see** "slender") cursory; delicate; feeble; flimsy; frail; imperceptible; inconsiderable; insignificant; little; meager; minor; negligible; nominal; paltry; petty; puny; scant(y); sketchy; slim; small; superficial; thready; tiny; trifling; trivial; unimportant; wispy; SLIGHT: **n.** cut; denigration; detraction; discourtesy; disparagement; disregard; disrespect; humiliation; ignoration; neglect; nonobservance; omission; slam; slur; snub

SLIM: **v.** diet; reduce; slenderize; SLIM: **a.** (**see** "slender") adroit; clever; inferior; mean; svelte; worthless

SLIME: filth; ichor; mire; muck; mucus; mud; ooze; silt; sludge; SLIMY: (**see** "slippery") filthy; glairy; gluey; glutinous; gooey; miry; mucilaginous; mucous; muddy; offensive; oily; oleaginous; oozy; saponaceous; slick; slithery; unctuous; vile; viscid; viscous; vulgar

SLIMSY: **see** "flimsy"

SLINK: (**see** "skulk") crawl; creep; glide; lurk; slither; sneak; steal

SLIP: **v.** blunder; decline; decrease; deteriorate; dip; disengage; dislocate; elapse; elude; err; escape; evade; expire; fail; fault; fluff; glide; lapse; loosen; misstep; omit; pass; plunge; relapse; slide; slither; slue; steal; trip; SLIP: **n.** berth; blunder; boner; bull; chemise; cutting; declination; decline; defile; dip; dock; error; failure; fault; fluff; gaffe; garment; indiscretion; lapse; mishap; misstep; mistake; muff; omission; oversight; plunge; relapse; scion; shoot; slide; solecism; trip; twig; SLIPPERY: ambiguous; crafty; eely; elusive; evasive; fickle; glassy; glib; greasy; icy; immoral; lubricious; oily; oleaginous; oozy; shifty; sleek; slimy; slithery; sly; smooth; treacherous; tricky; uncertain; unsafe; unstable; wanton

SLIPSHOD: (**see** "careless") inaccurate; lax; loose; sloppy; unkempt; unthorough

SLIT: **v.** cleave; cleft; crack; cut; defile; gash; incise; rend; scar; sever; slash; split; sunder; SLIT: **n.** aperture; chink; cicatrix; cleft; crack; cut; fissure; gash; incision; opening; rent; scar; slash; split; vent

SLITHER: **v.** (**see** "slide") crawl; creep; glide; grovel; sidle; skid; slip; snake; SLITHER: **n.** crawl; creep; glide; grovel; rubbish; rubble; skid; slide; slip; splinter

SLIVER: (**see** "shred") splinter

SLOGAN: catchword; cry; maxim; motto; password; phrase; shibboleth; watchword; witticism

SLOPE: **v.** bevel; cant; incline; lean; pitch; raise; rise; slant; splay; tilt; tip; veer; SLOPE: **n.** acclivity; alp; bevel; cant; declension; declination; declivity; escarpment; fall; glacis; grade; gradient; inclination; incline; hill; lean(ing); peak; pitch; ramp; rise; scarp; slant; tile; tip; veer; SLOPING: acclivitous; declensional; declinatory; declivate; declivitous; leaning; oblique; pitched; slant(ing)

SLOPPY: (**see** "careless") desultory; dishevelled; dowdy(ish); drunk; effusive; emotional; gushing; haphazard; intoxicated; loose; messy; slapdash; slippery; slipshod; soft; tatterdemalion; unkempt; unmethodical; unmilitary; unthorough; untidy; SLOP-

PINESS: (**see** "carelessness") dishevelment; dowdiness; messiness; mussiness; untidiness

SLOTH: acedia; adynamia; apathy; inaction; inactivity; indolence; inertia; lassitude; laziness; leisure(li)ness; lethargy; logginess; loris; otiosity; pokiness; retardation; slothfulness; slowness; sluggishness; supinity; tardiness; torpescence; torpidity; torpor; SLOTHFUL: **see** "lazy"

SLOUGH: bayou; bog; fen; marsh; morass; swamp

SLOVEN(LY): (**see** "sloppy") careless; dishevelled; dowdy(ish); frowsy; messy; mussy; phlegmatic; prideless; ragged; raunchy; shabby; shoddy; slatternly; slipshod; slouchy; sluttish; tatterdemalion; uncultivated; undeveloped; unkempt; untidy

SLOW: **v.** belay; creep; dawdle; decelerate; delay; drowse; ease; gear down; hinder; lag; lessen; linger; moderate; poke; procrastinate; reduce; relax; retard; slacken; SLOW: **a.** apathetic; backward; behind-(hand); belated; boring; bovine; comatose; crawling; creeping; creepy; dawdling; delaying; deliberate; dilatory; dragging; draggletailed; dronish; drowsy; dull; easy; gentle; glacial; gradual; hasteless; heavy; humdrum; inactive; inching; indolent; inert; inexcitable; laborious; laggard(ly); lagging; languescent; languid; languorous; late; latent; latrede; lax; lazy; lead(en); leisurely; lentando; lentissimo; lethargic; lifeless; lingering; listless; low; lumbering; moderate; monotonous; phlegmatic; pok-(e)y; ponderous; procrastinating; relaxed; remiss; retarded; rusty; slack; sluggish; snail-paced; stolid; stupid; tame; tardy; tedious; torpescent; torpid; unenergetic; unhasty; unhurried; unprogressive; wearisome; weary; SLOWNESS: (**see** "sloth") deliberateness; dilatoriness; indolence; inertia; lassitude; leisure(li)ness; lethargy; logginess; pokiness; resolution; retardation; snail's pace; tediosity; torpescence; torpidity

SLUDGE: ice; mire; mud; ooze; paste; sediment; slime; slosh; slush

SLUE: pivot; sidle; skid; slide; slip; swing; turn; twist; veer

SLUG: **v.** (**see** "beat") bash; bat; clout; drive; fight; hit; plow; push; slap; smite; swat; SLUG: **n.** blow; bullet; clout; drink; drone; guideline; hit; larva; mollusk; nugget; shot; slap; strike; swat

SLUGGISH: (**see** "slow") adynamic; apathetic; dormant; draggletailed; dull; inactive; indolent; inert; languescent; languid; languorous; lethargic; lifeless; listless; logy; mushy; sleepy; slothful; stagnant; stolid; sullen; supine; tardigrade; tardy; torpid; unfeeling; uninspired; SLUGGISHNESS: (**see** "sloth" and "slowness") dormancy; dullness; indolence; inertia; lethargy; listlessness; logginess; oscitancy; slothfulness; torpidity; torpitude; torpor

SLUICE: channel; conduit; current; floodgate; flume; opening; sewer; spate; trough; vent

SLUMBER: **see** "idle" and "sleep"

SLUMP: depression; dip; doldrum(s); drop; panic; recession; repression; retardation; sag

SLUR: **v.** asperse; blacken; blur; calumniate; criticize; defame; defile; denigrate; dig; disparage; drag; elide; gloss; insult; malign; mask; obscure; reproach; shuffle; skim; skip; slander; slight; smear; stain; sully; traduce; vilify; SLUR: **n.** aspersion; blot; calumny; criticism; defamation; denigration; dig; disparagement; innuendo; insinuation; insult; macule; reproach; slander; slight; smear; smudge; snub; stain; stigma; vilification

SLY: arch(ful); artful; astute; cagey; canny; cautious; clandestine; clever; covert; crafty; cunning; cute; deceitful; deceptive; designing; diplomatic; disingenuous; duplicitous; elusive; foxy; furtive; guileful; hugger-mugger; illusory; ingenuous; insidious; knowing; oily; oleaginuous; roguish; *rusé; rusée* (fem.); scheming; secret(ive); serpentine; shrewd; sinuous; skillful; sleek; slick; snaky; sneaky; stealthy; strategic; strategetic; subtle; thievish; treacherous; tricky; underhand(ed); wary; wily; wise

SMACK: **v.** (**see** "hit") buss; crack; kiss; slap; snap; strike; SMACK: **n.** blow; boat; buss; cutter; dash; flavor; kiss; noise; relish; savor; slap; sloop; smattering; snap; strike; tang; taste; tincture; tinge; trace

SMALL: atomic; bantam; capillary; capsule; common; concentrated; detailed; diminished; diminutive; dinky; dwarfish; elfin; exiguous; few; fine; finitesimal; fractional; frail; humble(d); humiliated; illiberal; immature; inappreciable; incommodious; inconsiderable; inferior; infinitesimal; insignificant; intimate; junior; lessened; light; lilliputian; limited; little; lower; mean; microscopic; microsomatous; microsomic; miniature; minikin; minimal; miniscule; minor(-league); minuscular; minute; modest; molecular; nanitic; nanoid; narrow-minded; negligible; nominal; paltry; parsimonious; parvanimitous; petite; petty; pink; pint-size(d); puny; scant(y); secondary; selfish; shoestring; short; slight; submicroscopic; suboptimal; subsidiary; subsidized; substandard; teeny; tiny; toy; trifling; trivial; ultramicroscopic; undersize(d); ungenerous; unimportant; unmagnified; unsizable; wanting; wee(ny); without; young; SMALLNESS: exiguity; inferiority; infinitesimality; insignificance; meanness; miniature; negligibility; parvanimity; parvitude; triviality

SMART: **v.** burn; cut; hurt; pain; sting; SMART: **a.** acute; adroit; alert; amusing; apt; astute; bright; brilliant; chic; clever; cute; cutting; dapper; dext(e)rous; dressy; elegant; fashionable; flip; fresh; heady; intelligent; intense; keen; knowing; natty; neat; nifty; pert; posh; quick(-witted); ready; sassy; saucy; sharp; shrewd; *soigné; soignée* (fem.); spiffy; spirited; sporty; spruce; stylish; svelt(e); swanky; tidy; trained; trig; trim; witty; SMARTNESS: **see** "intellect" and "intelligence;" SMARTEN: **see** "spruce"

SMASH: **v.** bash; batter; break; collapse; crash; crush; dash; demolish; destroy; drive; fail; fall; hit; kill; mash; press; ruin; shatter; split; stave; wreck; SMASH: **n.** bankruptcy; beverage; blow; collapse; collision; crash; destruction; disaster; failure; hit; ruin; shot; success; wreck

SMEAR: anoint; begrime; blacken; blot(ch); blur; cover; criticize; daub; defame; defile; degrade; gaum; glair; malign; overspread; plaster; pollute; slime; slur; smirch; smooth; smother; smudge; soil; spot; spread; stain; sully; swish; tar; tarnish; vilify

SMELL: **v.** detect; inhale; nose; perfume; reek; savor; scent; sniff; stink; SMELL: **n.** (**see** "stink") air; aroma; atmosphere; attar; aura; bouquet; cachet; effluvia (pl.); effluvium; essence; fetidity; flare; fragrance; fume; funk; fust; mephitis; nidor; odor; olfaction; osmesis; osphrasia; osphresis; perfume; putridity; redolence; reek; savor; scent; sniff; stench; SMELLY: (**see** "stinking") overripe; ripe; rotten

SMILE: agree; approve; beam; favor; flash; grin; laugh; simper; smirk; sneer; SMIL-

ING: agreeable; beaming; cheerful; good; pleasant; subrident; subrisive; sunny

SMIRCH: (see "smear") begrime; blacken; blot; degrade; soil; stain; sully; tarnish

SMITE: (see "hit") affect; enamor; impress; kill; punish; strike

SMOKE: **v.** cure; fume; fumigate; preserve; puff; reek; smother; smudge; speed; steam; SMOKE: **n.** cigar(ette); cloud; fume; gas; puff; reek; smudge; speed; tobacco; vapor; SMOKY: blackened; cloudy; fuliginous; fumid; reeky; smudgy; suspicious; tarnished; thick

SMOOTH: **v.** allay; calm; compose; ease; edulcorate; even; facilitate; finish; gloss; grind; hone; iron (out); level; minimize; palliate; placate; plane; polish; preen; quiet; refine; sand(paper); scrape; still; tranquilize; uniformize; whet; SMOOTH: **a.** affable; amiable; amicable; bland; calm; clean; clever; *coulant*; courteous; couth; deft; easy; equitable; even; flat; flattering; fluent; flush; frictionless; friendly; glib; glossy; hyalescent; hyaline; ingratiating; legato; light; marble; mild; oily; oleaginous; placid; plane; pleasant; polished; quiet; saponaceous; satiny; serene; silken; silky; skillful; slick; slimy; slippery; slithery; sly; still; suant; suave; svelt; talkative; tranquil; unctuous; uneventful; uninterrupted; unrough; unruffled; unrumpled; urbane; velitudinous; velvet(y); SMOOTHNESS: gloss-(iness); lubricity; mellowness; mildness; oiliness; polish; saponaceousness; serenity; silkiness; stillness; svelteness; unctuosity

SMOTHER: (see "kill") choke; overcome; overlie; repress; smolder; stifle; suffocate; suppress

SMUDGE: **v.** begrime; blot; blur; daub; gaum; slur; smear; smoke; smutch; soil; spot; SMUDGE: **n.** blot; blur; dirt; gaum; grime; slur; smear; smoke; smut; smutch; soil(age); soot; splotch; spot; stain

SMUG: affected; bourgeois; complacent; contented; egocentric; neat; pedantic; pretentious; priggish; prim; proper; self-inflated; self-satisfied; sleek; trim; SMUGNESS: complacency; contentment; egocentricity; pedanticism; priggishness; primness; self-complacency; self-satisfaction

SNACK: (see "food") bit; bite; canapé; lunch; repast; share; taste; tiffin

SNAG: bar; difficulty; hindrance; impediment; knot; obstacle; protuberance; run; stub; stump

SNAIL: cerion; gastropod; helicid; helix; Mitra; mollusk; nerita; Ovula; Thais; triton; univalve; whelk

SNAKE: adder; asp; boa; coluber; dipsas; groveling; ingrate; krait; mamba; ophidia (pl.); ophidian; reptile; reptilian; serpent; villain; viper; SNAKY or SNAKELIKE: anguiform; anguineal; anguine(ous); apodal; colubrine; ophidian; reptilian; serpentiform; serpentine; sinuous; slithery; sneaky; viperish

SNAP: **v.** bite; break; burst; crackle; pop; pounce; snatch; spark(le); SNAP: **n.** bit; break; cookie; crackle; élan; morsel; pep; photo(graph); pushover; sinecure; spark; *un (bon) fromage*; SNAPPISH or SNAPPY: acute; animated; biting; blunt; brisk; crackling; crisp; cross; crusty; curt; cutting; edgy; fretful; huffy; irascible; ired; irritable; keen; lively; peevish; pettish; piquant; poignant; pointed; popping; prompt; pungent; quick; short; spicy; sudden; telling; testy; zippy

SNARE: **v.** (see "catch") ambush; decoy; enmesh; entice; insinuate; inveigle; lure; nab; seduce; tole; toll; trap; trick; waylay; SNARE: **n.** ambush; artifice; blind; cajolement; cover; danger; decoy; disguise; drum; enticement; gin; inveiglement; lure; maelstrom; mesh; net; noose; pitfall; ruse; seduction; snarl; springe; stratagem; subterfuge; temptation; trap; trick; web; wile

SNARL: **v.** (see "entangle") complicate; confuse; gnar(l); gnarr; growl; knot; tangle; SNARL: **n.** (see "entanglement") chaos; complication; confusion; discord; growl; knot; snare; tangle

SNATCH: (see "grab") erept; grasp; grip; nail; pounce; seize; snap; steal; wrest

SNEAK: couch; creep; lurch; skulk; slink; snoop; spy; steal; weasel; SNEAKY: clandestine; contemptible; cowardly; despicable; devious; dishonest; duplicitous; furtive; illicit; insidious; insincere; insinuating; Janus-faced; Januslike; low; mean; niggardly; oblique; ophidian; paltry; perfidious; reptilian; serpentine; sinister; sinuous; sly; snaky; sneaking; sneakish; snide; stealthy; surreptitious; two-faced; undercover; underground; underhand(ed); weaselly

SNEER: (**see** "scoff") deride; fleer; gibe; jibe; scorn; SNEERING: contemptible; cynical; derisive; disdainful; ironical; sarcastic; sardonic; scoffing

SNIDE: (**see** "sneaky") base; cheap; contemptible; counterfeit; crooked; devious; dishonest; insidious; insincere; insinuating; low; mean; oblique; sinister; spurious; stealthy; underhand(ed)

SNIFF: (**see** "smell") detect; disdain; find; nose; perceive; scent; scorn

SNIP: **v.** clip; cut; dock; lob; shorten; SNIP: **n.** (**see** "bit") cinch; cut; shortening

SNIVEL: (**see** "complain") cry; grumble; simper; sob; weep; whimper; whine

SNOB: arriviste; bighead; parvenu; pedant; swell; swelled head; toady; SNOBBERY _or_ SNOBBISHNESS: arrogance; _chichi_; haughtiness; hauteur; pedantry; snobbism; snootiness; SNOBBISH: arrogant; _chichi_; haughty; pedantic; proud; snooty; supercilious; uppish; upstage

SNOOP: investigate; lure; nose; peer; probe; prowl; pry; search

SNOOT _or_ SNOUT: face; front; grimace; muzzle; nose; nozzle; proboscis; promontory; rostrum

SNORE: rale; rhonchus; roar; rumble; sniff; stertor

SNOW: cocaine; firn; névé; pash; sleet; SNOWY: nival; niveous; pure; spotless; white

SNUB: **v.** check; cut; high-hat; humiliate; inhibit; rebuff; rebuke; reprove; restrain; slap; slight; snoot; suppress; upstage; SNUB: **n.** absent treatment; cut; humiliation; rebuff; rebuke; reproof; restraint; setdown; slap; slight; snoot; suppression

SNUG: close(d); close-fitting; comfortable; compact; content; cosh; cozy; easy; intimate; neat; orderly; posh; protected; safe; secure; taut; tidy; tight; trig; trim; warm; well-to-do

SO: also; as; ergo; extremely; hence; indeed; quite; sic; subsequently; then; therefore; thus; too; true; very; viz.

SOAK: **v.** dip; drench; imb(r)ue; immerse; intoxicate; irrigate; macerate; penetrate; percolate; permeate; rain; ret; satiate; saturate; sog; sop; souse; sponge; steep; submerge; water; wet; SOAK: **n.** alcoholic; boozer; drunk(ard); souse; spree; tippler

SOAP: castile; flattery; lather; sapo; suds; SOAPY: flattering; lathered; lathery; oily; oleaginous; saponaceous; suave; unctuous

SOAR: arise; ascend; boom; flit; float; fly; glide; increase; mount; raise; rise; sail; tower; transcend; wing; zoom

SOB: (**see** "cry") moan; pule; sigh; simper; snivel; wail; weep; whimper

SOBER: abstemious; abstentious; abstinent; ascetic; calm; collected; continent; cool; dispassionate; grave; humble; moderate; peaceful; quiet; rational; realistic; reasonable; restrained; sad; sane; sedate; self-controlled; serious; severe; solemn; somber; sparing; staid; steady; subdued; temperate; tempered; thoughtful; unfunny; unhumorous; unpretentious; unruffled; wise; SOBERNESS: abstinence; ascesis; asceticism; continence; moderation; restraint; sobriety; temperance

SOBRIQUET: agname; alias; appellation; epithet; handle; hypocoristic; nickname

SO-CALLED: alleged; pretended; pseudo; quasi; _soi-disant_; supposed; would-be

SOCIAL **a.** or SOCIABLE: affable; affected; agreeable; amadelphous; club(b)able; clubbish; clubby; communal; community; companionable; convivial; cooperative; cordial; formal; forthcoming; friendly; genial; gracious; gregarious; hospitable; human; jolly; jovial; kind(ly); merry; pleasant; public; tribal; urbane; SOCIAL: **n.** caste; clan; party; tea; SOCIABILITY: affability; agreeableness; conviviality; cordiality; friendliness; gregariousness; hospitableness; hospitality; joviality; sociality; urbanity

SOCIETY: acquaintances; association; bund; church; class; club; community; companionship; company; confraternity; corporation; elite; ethos; family; fellowship; folk; fraternity; gentry; group; lodge; mankind; _monde_; order; party; smart set; sorority; union

SOCKET: cavity; hollow; mortise; opening; orbit; outlet; pan; pod; receptacle; space; tube

SOD: clod; country; dirt; divot; grass; humus; land; lawn; peat; soil; sward; turf

SODDEN: bloated; damp; doughy; dull; heavy; humid; inert; moist; mushy; saturated; soaked; soggy; sordid; spiritless; spongy; swampy; torpid; unimaginative; wet

SOFT: (see "easy") balmy; bland; clement; comfortable; compassionate; compressible; cozy; cushy; delicate; downy; dulcet; effeminate; effete; emollient; emulsive; feeble; fleecy; fleshy; fluffy; foolish; gentle; half-witted; idle; impressionable; kind; lenient; lenitive; limp; low; malleable; massless; meek; mellow; merciful; mild; mitigatory; mollescent; mollifying; namby-pamby; nonalcoholic; palliative; perishable; pianissimo; plastic; pliable; pliant; sentimental; silken; silky; slack; smooth; suggestible; sweet; tender; tolerant; unhard(y); unmanly; velvety; waxy; weak; yielding; SOFTEN: assuage; break; edulcorate; enervate; humanize; humble; intenerate; lessen; macerate; mellow; melt; mitigate; moderate; modify; mollify; mute; palliate; polish; refine; relax; relent; smooth; subdue; tame; temper; thaw

SOGGY: (see "sodden") damp; doughy; heavy; humid; mushy; saturated; spongy; swampy; wet

SOIL: **v.** befoul; begrime; beslime; besmear; besmirch; corrupt; daub; defile; dirty; disgrace; foul; mess; pollute; smirch; smudge; spoil; spot; stain; sully; SOIL: **n.** country; dirt; earth; glebe; grime; ground; humus; land; loam; marl; sod; soot; SOILED: see "faded"

SOJOURN: abide; delay; dwell; live; lodge; peregrinate; reside; stay; stop; tarry; tenant; vigil; wait

SOLACE: **v.** allay; alleviate; assuage; calm; cheer; comfort; console; ease; entertain; hearten; lighten; mitigate; relieve; smooth; soften; soothe; SOLACE: **n.** (see "cheer") alleviation; calm; comfort; consolation; ease; entertainment; mitigation; relaxation; relief; solacement

SOLDER: braze; cement; fuse; join; repair; unite; weld

SOLDIER: Anzac; cadet; cavalryman; chasseur; combatant; dragoon; follower; GI; leader; poilu; private; sepoy; veteran; warrior; worker; SOLDIERLY: heroic; martial; military; warlike

SOLE: (see "solitary") alone; lone(ly); mere; one; only; single; solo; stag; unique; unmarried; unmatched; unshared

SOLECISM: (see "blunder") boner; breach; error; gaff(e); impropriety; lapse; slip

SOLEMN: (see "sober") august; awe-inspiring; ceremonial; ceremonious; devout; dignified; dire(ful); dispassionate; dread; formal; funereal; gloomy; grave; important; imposing; impressive; melancholy; memorable; momentous; reverential; ritualistic; sacred; sad; sedate; serious; sermonic; somber; stately; sublime; weighty; SOLEMNITY: ceremonialism; ceremoniousness; ceremony; dignity; formality; gloom; gravity; impressiveness; moment; ritual; sedateness; solemnitude; somberness; stateliness; sublimity; weightiness

SOLICIT: adjure; advertise; allure; apply; ask; attract; beg; beseech; bid; canvas(s); circulate; count; crave; curry; debate; discuss; drum (up); entice; entreat; examine; favor; implore; importune; incite; induce; inquire; investigate; invite; invoke; lure; petition; plead; poll; provoke; request; require; seek; serve; spark; sue; supplicate; tout; treat; urge; woo; SOLICITATION: advertisement; allurement; bill; canvass; dun; entreaty; importunity; incitement; invitation; invocation; petition; plea; request; statement; supplication; SOLICITUDE: anxiety; assiduity; care; caution; concern; desire; disquietude; fear; heed; uneasiness; SOLICITOUS: adjuratory; apprehensive; assiduous; benign; beseeching; cautious; concerned; eager; fatherly; fearful; implorative; inquiring; investigative; invocative; jealous; kind; motherly; pleading; supplicative; uneasy; worried

SOLID: adamantine; close; compact; concentrated; dense; durable; entire; excellent; firm; fixed; granitic; hard; immovable; impassable; intact; lasting; massive; massy; material; meaty; monolithic; permanent; physical; ponderable; prudent; real; reliable; rigid; secure; serious(-minded); set; sound; stable; steadfast; sterling; stocky; stout; strong; sturdy; substantial; tight; unanimous; unblemished; unbroken; uninterrupted; unrotten; unyielding; valid; weighty; whole

SOLIDIFY: cake; concretize; consolidate; dehydrate; desiccate; dry; evaporate; freeze; harden; jell; set; stiffen; strengthen; unite; SOLIDIFICATION: concretization; consolidation; evaporation; gelation; hardening; strengthening; union; SOLIDITY: (see "weightiness") compactness; concentration; consolidation; density; immovability; power; rigidity; solidarity; thickness; union; unshakableness; volume; weight

SOLITARY: alone; aloof; companionless; deserted; desolate; enisled; hermitic; individual; isolated; ivory-towered; lone(ly); only; reclusive; secluded; separate(d); sequestered; single; sole; solitudinarian; solo; unfrequented; unique

SOLO: a. (see "solitary") alone; individual; monophonic; monophous; single; stag; unaccompanied; SOLO: n. aria; flight; self; song

SOLON: congressman; lawmaker; legislator; representative; sage; senator; statesman

SOLUTION: answer; bath; breach; break; denouement; detection; discovery; disruption; explanation; interpretation; key; liquid; severance; solute; tincture

SOLVE: (see "analyze") answer; clear; decide; decipher; decrypt; detect; diagnose; diagnosticate; discover; dissolve; do; explain; figure; identify; interpret; prove; resolve; settle; translate; undo; unfold; unravel; unriddle; work

SOLVENT: acetone; alcohol; diluent; menstruum; plasticizer; thinner; vehicle; water

SOMBER: (see "sad") dark; depressing; funereal; gloomy; grave; gray; lenten; melancholy; sacred; serious; sombrous

SOME: about; any; lots; many; one; part; piece; portion; quantity; several; undetermined; unspecific

SOMETIME: erstwhile; former(ly); occasion(ally); often; once; quondam

SON: boy; child; disciple; fils; Fitz; heir; lad; Mac; male; native; sibling; youth

SONG: air; anthem; aria; arietta; ballad; canticle; canzona; canzone(t); carol; chanson; chant; descant; ditty; hymn; lay; lullaby; lyric(s); madrigal; melisma; melody; melos; motet; psalm(ody); refrain; rondeau; rondo; round(elay); strain; SONGFUL: ariose; lyric(al); melodic(al); melodious; sonorous

SONOROUS: full; melodious; noisy; resonant; rich; songful; tuneful; vibrant

SOON: afresh; again; anew; anon; assuredly; by and by; certainly; early; erelong; forthwith; immediate(ly); prompt(ly); quick(ly); readily; reasonable; shortly; speedily; sudden(ly); thence; willingly

SOOT: coom; dirt; grime; smut; SOOTY: black; dusty; fuliginous; grimy; smutted; soiled; stained

SOOTHE: (see "calm") allay; alleviate; appease; assuage; becalm; calm; compose; conciliate; console; ease; flatter; lull; mollify; pacify; palliate; placate; quiet; reassure; reconcile; relieve; salve; sedate; smooth; soften; still; tranquilize; SOOTHING: (see "calm") anodyne; anodynic; anodynous; antiphlogistic; assuasive; balmy; bland; calmative; calming; conciliative; conciliatory; demulcent; downy; dulcet; emollient; hesychastic; hushed; lenitive; malactic; mitigatory; mollifying; narcotic; nepenthean; palliative; placative; placatory; pleasant; sedative; sirupy; smooth; soft(ening); still; supple; sweet; syrupy; tranquilizing; treacly

SOOTHSAYER: (see "prophet") augur; auspex; Chaldean; divine(r); haruspex; mantis; oracle; prognosticator; pythonist; seer; wizard

SOP: (see "bribe") concession; placebo

SOPHISM: elenchus; fallacy; paralogism; sophistry; speciosity

SOPHISTICATED: adulterated; alembicated; aware; blasé; complex; jaded; knowing; knowledg(e)able; polished; precocious; suave; subtle; worldly; world-weary

SOPOR: carus; coma; hypnosis; lethargy; sleep; slumber; stupor; SOPORIFIC: a. anodynic; anodynous; dull; hypnotic; narcotic; opiate; sleepy; somniferous; stuporous; SOPORIFIC: n. anodyne; hypnotic; lethargic; narcotic; opiate

SORCERER: alchemist; conjurer; haruspex; mage; magi (pl.); magician; necromancer; sortileger; thaumaturge; thaumaturgist; warlock; wizard; SORCERESS: Circe; lamia; pythoness; Usha; SORCERY: charm; conjuration; diablerie; diabolism; enchantment; exorcism; incantation; magic;

necromancy; sortilege; spell; thaumaturgy; theurgy; witchcraft; witchery; wizardry

SORDID: (**see** "base") abject; avaricious; cheap; contemptible; covetous; degraded; dirty; diseased; foul; gam(e)y; grubby; ignoble; low; mean; menial; mercenary; muddy; niggardly; scurrilous; seamy; seedy; sluttish; sodden; squalid; titillating; venal; vile

SORE: **a.** abscessed; aching; acute; angered; annoyed; bitter; cankerous; chafed; distressing; grievous; infected; inflamed; mad; nettled; painful; peeved; sensitive; tender; vexed; SORE: **n.** abrasion; abscess; affliction; boil; bruise; canker; disease; fester; infection; inflammation; lesion; pustule; sickness; trouble; ulcer; wound

SORROW: **v.** (**see** "grieve") cry; lament; moan; rue; wail; weep; SORROW: **n.** (**see** "grief") agony; anguish; bale; care; commiseration; compassion; compunction; contrition; damage; distress; dole; dolor; grief; harm; heartache; lamentation; mischief; misery; misfortune; penitence; pity; regret; remorse; repentance; rue; sadness; sympathy; torment; *tristesse*; unhappiness; woe; SORROWFUL: (**see** "sad") anguished; commiserable; compassionate; contrite; desolate; *désolé*; disconsolate; doleful; dolent(e); dolentissimo; dolorific; doloroso; dolorous; forgiving; forlorn; griefful; grievous; heartbreaking; heartrending; joyless; lamentable; lamented; lugubrious; melancholy; mournful; penitent; pitiable; plaintive; rueful; saddened; *triste*; woeful

SORRY: (**see** "sad") base; contemptible; contrite; despicable; dismal; gloomy; grieved; grievous; insignificant; lamentable; mean; melancholy; mournful; paltry; penitent; petty; pitiful; poor; regretful; rueful; scrubby; shabby; shoddy; small; squalid; trifling; unfit; worn-out; worthless; wretched

SORT: **v.** alphabetize; arrange; assort; blend; catalogue; categorize; classify; collate; collocate; comb; compartmentalize; concinnate; cull; dispose; distribute; file; grade; group; identify; individualize; match; orchestrate; pigeonhole; rank; rate; screen; segregate; select; separate; sift; strain; systematize; type; SORT: **n.** character; class; disposition; fashion; grade; group; ilk; individual; kidney; kind; lot; manner; nature; quality; species; strain; stripe; thing; type; way

SORTIE: attack; foray; fray; mission; raid; safari; sally; trip

SORTILEGE: augury; divination; enchantment; lot; sorcery; witchcraft; witchery

SO-SO: (**see** "average") *comme ci comme ça*; *couci-couci*; fair; indifferent; intermediate; mediocre; medium; middle; middling; passable; small; tolerable; trifling

SOT: (**see** "drunkard") bibber; tippler; toper

SOUGH: **v.** sigh; moan; murmur; rustle; whiz; SOUGH: **n.** channel; drain; moan; sewer; sigh

SOUL: *âme*; anima; atman; being; ego; élan; essence; exemplification; fervor; inspiration; intellect; leader; life; mind; nature; person(ality); personification; pneuma; psyche; quintessence; self; spirit; wit(s)

SOUND: **v.** appear; Babelize; bong; buzz; echo; fathom; go; plumb; proclaim; noise; reverberate; ring; seem; signal; strike; summon; utter; voice; SOUND: **a.** brawny; cogent; complete; correct; durable; entire; firm; genuine; good; hale; hard; hardy; healthy; husky; important; intact; legal; level-headed; logical; lusty; muscular; orderly; orthodox; perfect; prime; proper; reliable; robust; safe; same; secure; severe; solid; stable; stalwart; sterling; straight; strong; sturdy; substantial; unblemished; unbruised; undamaged; unhurt; unimpaired; uninjured; unspeculative; valid; vigorous; weighty; whole(some); SOUND: **n.** audio; Babelism; Babelization; bay; bong; cacophony; confusion; discordance; dissonance; earshot; echo; hearing; import; klop; noise; portent; resonance; reverberation; strait; tone; tune; SOUNDNESS: brawniness; correctitude; correctness; durability; firmness; hardihood; hardness; health(iness); importance; integrality; integrity; level-headedness; orthodoxy; solidarity; solidity; solidness; solvency; strength; validity; weight

SOUP: bisque; bouillabaisse; broth; chowder; consommé; gazpacho; liquid; pottage; puree; stock; vichyssoise

SOUR: **v.** acidify; addle; curdle; deteriorate; exacerbate; ferment; impair; rot; spoil; SOUR: **a.** acerb(ic); acetose; acetous; acid(ic); acidulent; acidulous; acrid; astringent; bad; cold; cynical; disagreeable; disenchanted; distasteful; dour; dry; embittered; glum; grumpy; hard; harsh; infestive; irritable; mirthless; morbific; morbose; peevish; putrid; querulous; rotten; sharp; sore; spoiled; sullen; surly; tart; unkind; unoptimistic; unpleasant; unsanguine; unsweet; vinegary; wrong; wry; SOURNESS: acerbity; acidification; acidity; discontent; downness; infestivity; irritability; mirthlessness; moroseness; morosity; peevishness; querulousness; surliness; tartness

SOURCE: (see "origin") author; bed; beginning; bibliography; book; cause; derivation; emanation; etiology; father; font; foundation; fount(ain); fountainhead; genesis; germ; incipience; instigation; lead; lineage; mainspring; mine; model; nerve; nest; nidus; ore; prime mover; provenance; provenience; quarter; records; region; rise; root; seed; spawn; spring; staple; start; stock; substance; supplier; territory; text; well(spring)

SOUTH: auster; Dixie; SOUTHERN or SOUTHERLY: austral; meridional; torrid

SOUVENIR: (see "curio") bibelot; keepsake; knickknack; memento; memory; recollection; relic; remembrance; token; trinket

SOVEREIGN: a. absolute; authoritative; autonomous; dominant; effective; excellent; free; highest; imperial; independent; kingly; leading; paramount; potent; predominant; princely; queenly; regal; royal; ruling; self-governing; superior; superlative; supreme; unmitigated; unrestricted; unsurpassed; utter; SOVEREIGN: n. see "king;" SOVEREIGNTY: authority; autonomy; control; dominion; dynasty; empery; freedom; imperialism; independence; jurisdiction; kingship; lordship; power; sovranty; state; superiority; supremacy; sway; throne

SOW: arouse; begin; broadcast; disseminate; distribute; foment; germinate; implant; plant; promulgate; scatter; seed; strew

SPA: Baden; bath; Ems; Évian; resort; spring(s)

SPACE: v. arrange; divide; extend; open; place; separate; SPACE: n. accommodations; area; berth; blank; capacity; clearance; concourse; distance; duration; expanse; extent; firmament; headroom; hiatus; housing; interstice; interval; lacuna; Lebensraum; leeway; limit; linage; lines; margin; niche; pace; period; place; pocket; quarters; range; rift; room; runway; site; span; speed; spell; step; stretch; term; territory; tide; time;

universe; volume; zone; SPACIOUS: (see "ample") baronial; capacious; cavernous; commodious; comprehensive; copious; expansive; huge; large; magnitudinous; rangy; roomy; scopious; vast; voluminous; wide; SPACIOUSNESS: amplitude; breadth; capacity; comprehensibility; copiosity; expansiveness; magnitude; roominess; vastity; vastness; volume; width

SPADE: v. delve; dig; grub; shovel; SPADE: n. card; shovel; tool

SPAN: v. arch; bestride; bridge; encompass; measure; space; spread; straddle; stretch; surround; transverse; SPAN: n. arch; area; bridge; diapason; distance; era; extent; gamut; generation; girder; measure; pair; period; reach; roof; series; space; spread; stretch; team; time; transept; transverse; truss; yoke

SPANGLE: v. adorn; begem; bejewel; caparison; decorate; diamondize; glisten; glitter; ornament; sparkle; SPANGLE: n. adornment; ornament; sequin; star; SPANGLED: adorned; begemmed; bejeweled; caparisoned; clinquant; decorated; diamondized; ornamented

SPANK: cane; chasten; chastise; criticize; discipline; flog; paddle; paddywhack; punish; reprimand; slap; strike; tan; thrash; SPANKING: brisk; dashing; distinctive; fresh; good; large; lively; merry; quick; stout; unusual; vigorous

SPAR: v. box; contend; fight; quarrel; skirmish; stall; tilt; wrangle; SPAR: n. barite; beam; boom; gaff; mast; mineral; pole; rafter; rung; sprit; tilt; timber; tournament; yard

SPARE: v. avoid; economize; exempt; favor; forbear; free; give; preserve; refrain; relieve; save; SPARE: a. additional; barren; bony; chary; extra; free; gaunt; lank(y); lean; mean; meager; parsimonious; reserve; scant(y); scrawny; skeletal; slender; slim; sparse; stingy; superfluous; thin

SPARK: v. activate; actuate; begin; catalyze; cause; coruscate; court; flash; gleam; glint; glisten; glitter; incite; scintillate; shimmer; spangle; sparkle; stimulate; twinkle; woo; SPARK: n. arc; catalyst; coruscation; ember; fire; flash; gleam; glint; glistening; iota; light; jot; scintilla(tion); trace; twinkle; vestige

SPARTAN(IC): austere; brave; frugal; hardy; heroic; plain; rigid; severe; stoic(al); strict; unluxurious

SPASM: agitation; burst; clonicity; clonus; colic; contraction; convulsion; eddy; fit; flurry; flutter; grip; jerk; orgasm; outburst; paroxysm; qualm; seizure; tetany; tic; tonus; SPASMODIC(AL): clonic; convulsive; intermittent; orgasmic; paroxysmal; spasmatic; spastic; tonic

SPAT: bicker; gaiter; quarrel; row; tiff

SPATE: abundance; flood; flow; freshet; overabundance; overflow; rush; sluice

SPATTER: begrime; defame; scatter; slosh; spit; splash; spoil; spot; sprinkle; spurt; sully

SPAWN: **v.** breed; engender; father; generate; germinate; impregnate; produce; reproduce; seed; yield; SPAWN: **n.** germ; offspring; ova (pl.); ovum; seed; source

SPEAK: accost; address; announce; annunciate; appeal; argue; articulate; ask; asseverate; augur; babble; bark; blab(ber); bruit; cackle; carp; chat(ter); chin; colloquialize; commune; communicate; confab(ulate); confer; converse; coze; declaim; declare; deliver; depict; descant; describe; dilate; discourse; discuss; dissert; divulge; drivel; enunciate; explain; expound; express; gab-(ble); give; gobble; gossip; greet; hail; harp; hobnob; indicate; instruct; intonate; jaw; labialize; lecture; lisp; maunder; moot; mouth; narrate; orate; palaver; parley; prate; prattle; phonate; preach; prelect; proclaim; pronounce; rant; rave; read; reason; recite; recount; relate; remark; represent; reveal; say; schmooze; sermonize; signal; signify; sound (off); spiel; spout; state; talk; teach; tell; testify; utter; verbalize; visit; vocalize; voice; yak; yap; SPEAKING: **see** "speech;" SPEAKER: advocate; announcer; annunciator; audio; barker; chair-(man); cicerone; collocutor; *conférencier*; conversation(al)ist; declaimer; declamator; elocutionist; instructor; lecturer; locutor; orator; preacher; pronouncer; rhetorician; sermonizer; spieler; spokesman; talker; teacher; verbalizer; vocalizer

SPEAR: **v.** bayonet; catch; gig; gore; harpoon; impale; lance; pierce; shoot; SPEAR: **n.** assegai; bayonet; fork; gig; halberd; harpoon; lance; pike; prong; shoot; spike; sprout; staff; stalk; tine; weapon

SPECIAL: (**see** "rare") appropriate; characteristic; dear; definite; definitive; detailed; determinate; different; distinctive; exceptional; extra(ordinary); individual; intimate; limited; marked; noteworthy; particular; peculiar; privileged; single; specific; spectacular; superior; technical; typical; ultra; uncommon; unique; SPECIALTY: distinction; expertise; forte; métier; particularity; rarity; talent; technology; *tour de force*; training; work

SPECIES: category; class; division; folk; form; genre; genus; group; humanity; kind; race; sort; variety

SPECIFIC: categorical; concrete; definite; definitive; determinative; exact; explicit; express; only; outspoken; particular; peculiar; precise; restricted; sole(ly); special; specificative; unambiguous; unequivocal; unique

SPECIFY: ask; assign; decree; define; describe; express; fix; mention; order; prescribe; proscribe; request; set; stipulate

SPECIMEN: (**see** "example") case; cast; copy; individual; instance; item; model; person; piece; representation; sample; slide; standard; swab; swatch; type; unit

SPECIOUS: (**see** "showy") apparent; beguiling; casuistical; colorable; credible; deceptive; empty; facile; false; garish; gaudy; idle; likely; ostensible; plausible; presumable; probable; sophistical; superficial; syllogistic(al); vain

SPECK: bit; blemish; dot; flaw; iota; jot; mite; mote; particle; point; spot; stain; whit; SPECKLED: dotted; mottled; pied; polka-dotted; spotted; stippled; variegated

SPECTACLE: blowout; curiosity; display; drama; exhibit(ion); extravaganza; glass; high jinks; lens; pageant(ry); party; scene; show; sight; spectacular; view; whoop-de-do

SPECTACULAR: (**see** "grand") sensational; swashbuckling

SPECTATOR: **see** "witness"

SPECTER: (**see** "ghost") apparition; bogey; eidolon; fetch; manes (pl.); phantasm; phantom; shade; shadow; spirit; spook; vision; wraith; SPECTRAL: (**see** "ghostly") eerie; ghastly; scary; spooky

SPECTRUM: afterimage; apparition; array; blue; colors; green; indigo; light; orange; range; red; sequence; series; sphere; violet; yellow

SPECULATE: bet; conjecture; contemplate; diagnose; foresee; foreshadow; gamble; guess; hypothesize; meditate; muse; operate; philosophize; ponder; prognosticate; reason; reflect; review; study; suppose; surmise; theorize; think; trade; weigh; SPECULATION: conjecture; contemplation; diagnosis; examination; guess; hypothesis; investigation; observation; philosophy; prognosis; prognostication; reasoning; reflection; study; surmise; theoretics; thought

SPEECH: address; allocution; alphabetics; alphabetism; altiloquence; Americanese; argot; argument; articulation; assertion; babble; balderdash; bavardage; bombast; cackle; cant; causerie; chatter; Choctaw; colloquialism; colloquy; communication; confabulation; conference; conversation; Creole; declamation; declaration; descant; dialect; dialog; diction; discourse; discussion; disquisition; dissertation; drivel; elocution; enunciation; exhortation; exophasia; explanation; flatulence; gab(ble); gasconade; gibber(ish); glottology; gossip; grandiloquence; grandiosity; harangue; homily; hortation; idiom; instruction; intonation; jabber; jargon; kompology; language; lecture; lingo; *lingua franca*; linguistics; lip; locution; maundering; message; monologue; narration; oration; parlance; parley; patois; peroration; phonation; phonetics; phonology; phraseology; prate; prattle; preaching; prelection; proclamation; pronunciation; prose; reading; recital; recitation; recitative; remark(s); ruralism; rusticism; screed; sermon; slang; soliloquy; sonant; splutter; statement; talk; tattle; thesis; tirade; tongue; tract; treatise; twaddle; utterance; verbalism; vernacular; villagism; vocalization; whisper; words; yap

SPEECHLESS: (see "silent") agape; dumb; mute; reticent; taciturn; unvocal; unvoluble; utterless

SPEED: v. accelerate; accentuate; advance; burn (up); dash; drive; expedite; fare; fly; hasten; hie; hurry; move; precipitate; prosper; quicken; race; run; rush; smoke; succeed; tear; whirl; whisk; whizz; SPEED-(INESS): n. acceleration; accentuation; activity; alacrity; *aussitôt dit, aussitôt fait*; capacity; celerity; deftness; dispatch; drive;

expedition; expeditiousness; gait; haste; hurry; impetus; momentum; pace; performance; progress; promptitude; quickness; rapidity; rate; rush; smoke; stuff; swiftness; tempo; time; urgency; velocity; walk; SPEEDY *or* SPEEDILY: accelerated; accentuated; adept; alacritous; burning; celeritous; dashing; direct; expeditious; expeditive; fast(-moving); flying; Gadarene; nimble; posthaste; precipitous; prompt; racing; raking; rapid(ly); ready; rushing; short; soon; sudden; swift(ly); urgent; velocious; willing

SPELL: v. ask; compose; comprehend; consider; decipher; discover; form; hint; mean; phoneticize; signify; teach; understand; write; SPELL: n. attack; bewitchment; bout; charm; conjuration; enchantment; evocation; fascination; fit; illness; incantation; influence; magic; orgasm; period; seizure; sickness; sorcery; space; spasm; sway; turn; witchcraft; witchery

SPEND: blow; consume; deplete; disburse; dissipate; drain; emit; employ; endure; exert; exhaust; expend; lose; pass; pay; scatter; serve; squander; use; utilize; waste; while; SPENT: consumed; dead; disbursed; done; drained; effete; evanid; exhausted; expended; fatigued; lost; squandered; tired; used; utilized

SPENDTHRIFT: (see "wastrel") prodigal; scattergood; waster

SPHERE: ambit; area; arena; ball; beat; business; circuit; class; compass; country; cycle; direction; domain; dominion; ellipse; field; globe; influence; jurisdiction; ken; kingdom; métier; milieu; orb(it); order; path; place; plant; province; purview; radius; range; reach; realm; region; responsibility; role; scene; scope; space; spectrum; spheroid; star; sweep; territory; SPHERIC(AL): cylindrical; discoid; globate; globose; globular; orbicular; orbital; orotund; rotund; round; spheriform; spheroid(al); spheroidical

SPHINX: enigma; monster; moth; puzzle; ruins

SPICE: v. excite; flavor; please; season; tempt; SPICE: n. aroma; balm; bouquet; clove; condiment; dash; flavor(ing); ginger; mace; mull; nutmeg; pepper; perfume; piquancy; redolence; relish; salt; season-(ing); tang; zest; SPICY: aromatic; balmy;

exciting; flavored; fragrant; gingery; juicy; peppery; piquant; provocative; pungent; racy; redolent; sharp; spiced; spirited; tangy; titillating; witty; zestful

SPICULE: (**see** "spike") barb; needle; prickle; rod; sclerite; shoot; spine; spire; splinter; thorn

SPIGOT: cock; dossil; faucet; nozzle; outlet; pipe; plug; spile; spout; tap; vent

SPIKE: **v.** fortify; impale; increase; pierce; quash; stab; still; suppress; SPIKE: **n.** antler; barb; ear; horn; maximum; nail; needle; peak; point; prickle; spadix; spicule; spine; splinter; thorn; tine; SPIKED: eared; sharp; spicate; spicigerous

SPILL: divulge; escape; extend; fall; leak; overflow; pour; shed; slop; splash; tell; tumble; wash; waste

SPIN: birl; gyrate; narrate; pass; pirouette; prolong; protract; reel; revolve; stretch; tell; turn; twirl; vertiginate; weave; whirl

SPINDLE: axis; axle; bobbin; hasp; mandrel; newel; pin; rod; shaft; spool; stalk; stem

SPINE: acantha; acicula; axis; axon; back-(bone); chine; courage; fin; needle; nettle; prickle; quill; rachis; ridge; spicule; spinosity; spirit; strength; thorn; vertebra; SPINY *or* SPINOUS: acanthaceous; acanthoid; acanthological; acanthous; acicular; aciculate-(d); barbed; bristling; nettlesome; pointed; prickly; sharp; spicose; spicular; spiculate; spiculiferous; spiculose; spinelike; spinose; thorny; SPINELESS: (**see** "spiritless") invertebrate

SPIRAL: **a.** (**see** "circular") circuling; cochleate; coiled; coiling; convolute(d); corkscrew; curving; helical; helicoid; round; screwy; spherical; volute(d); whorled; winding; SPIRAL: **n.** acceleration; circle; circumvolution; coil; curlicue; helix; loop; spirality; spring; volute; whorl; winding

SPIRE: curl; flèche; peak; pinnacle; pyramid; spicule; spike; steeple; summit; tower; whorl

SPIRIT(S): alcohol; ambition; angel; animation; animus; ardor; attitude; backbone; bravery; *brio*; character; cheerfulness; cleverness; courage; dash; desire; determination; disposition; ebullience; ebulliency; ecstasy; élan; elemental; elixir; energy; enterprise; enthusiasm; esprit; *esprit de corps*; essence; euphoria; exuberance; familiar; feeling; fire; gallantry; genie; getup; ghost; ginger; go-(-ahead); grit; guts; hardihood; haunt; heart; humor; intelligence; intent; intrepidity; life; liquor; liveliness; meaning; metal; mettle; mind; mood; morale; nerve; nous; pep(per); phantasm; phantasma(ta); pluck; pneuma; principle; resolution; sand; soul; specter; spine; spiritedness; spook; spunk; stamina; temper(ament); tenacity; tendency; valor; verve; vigor; vim; vitality; vivacity; wit(s); wittiness; wraith; zeal; zest; SPIRITED: active; animated; ardent; assiduous; athirst; avid; bold; brisk; burning; dashing; desirous; eager; ecstatic; elated; energetic; enterprising; enthusiastic; fanatical; fervent; fervid; fevered; feverish; fiery; forceful; forcible; game; gamy; gingery; happy; hardy; hot; impassioned; insatiable; intense; intrepid; jaunty; keen; lively; nervous; passionate; peppery; peppy; plucky; racy; rapturous; ravenous; red(-hot); sassy; saucy; slashing; spiritful; spiritual; spruce; spunky; vehement; vigorous; vivacious; voracious; zealous; zestful

SPIRITLESS: adenoid(al); amort; apathetic; clodded; cold; comatose; cowardly; crass; dead; dejected; depressed; desiccated; dispirited; dry; dull; exanimate; faint; feckless; flat; gray; heavy; inanimate; inert; invertebrate; lackadaisical; lackluster; languescent; languorous; lethargic; lifeless; listless; mild; milky; puling; pusillanimous; sad; seedy; sodden; soggy; spineless; stolid; stupid; tame; timorous; torpid; unenthusiastic; unimaginative; unquickened; unspirited; vapid; waning; wooden

SPIRITUAL: angelic; celestial; clever; devout; divine; elevated; ethereal; holy; incorporeal; inner; intellectual; inward; mental; pastoral; psychic(al); pure; religious; sacred; spirited; sublime; superior; supermundane; supernatural; supersensory; supersensual; unearthly; unfleshy; unphysical; witty; SPIRITUAL-ITY: church; clergy; devotion; ethereality; holiness; incorporeality; incorporeity; purity; sacredness; unearthliness; unfleshliness; unworldliness

SPIT: **see** "expectorate"

SPITE: envy; grudge; hatred; ill will; malevolence; malice; meanness; perversity; rancor; spleen; ungenerosity; venom; vindictiveness; SPITEFUL: abusive; cattish; catty; dispiteous; envious; hostile; malevolent; malicious; malign(ant); mean; poisonous;

rancorous; splenetic(al); venemous; vengeful; venomous; vindicative; SPITEFULNESS: envy; malevolence; maliciousness; malignity; meanness; poison; rancor; spleen; ungenerosity; venom; vindicativeness

SPLAY: bevel; carve; expand; flan(ge); open; slant; slope; spread; widen

SPLEEN: (see "anger") depression; emotion; grudge; hatred; ire; malevolence; melancholy; milt; passion; spite

SPLENDID: aurelian; aureate; baronial; bravissimo; bright; brilliant; distinguished; effulgent; embellished; eminent; excellent; fine; flashing; florid; gallant; glorious; gold(en); gorgeous; grand; illustrious; imposing; kingly; lustrous; luxurious; magnificent; nice; nifty; opulent; ornate; posh; praiseworthy; preeminent; princely; queenly; radiant; rattling; refulgent; regal; resplendent; screaming; shining; shiny; showy; slashing; splendaceous; splendiferous; splendorous; startling; stately; sublime; sumptuous; superb; SPLENDOR: beam; brightness; dazzlement; éclat; effulgence; gleam; glitter; glory; glow; gold; kingliness; luster; luxuriousness; luxury; magnificence; majesty; pomp; princeliness; queenliness; resplendence; resplendency; shine; sublimity; sumptuosity; sumptuousness; superbity

SPLICE: attach; bind; fasten; fix; glue; graft; join; marry; solder; tie; unite; wed; weld

SPLINTER: v. rive; secede; separate; shatter; shiver; split; SPLINTER: n. chip; faction; fragment; sliver; split

SPLIT: v. apportion; bisect; break; burst; change; chap; cleave; crack; cut; dissent; divide; dole; fissure; fork; mark; part; rend; rive; roughen; rupture; separate; sever; shatter; slit; smash; splinter; tear; SPLIT: a. bifurcate(d); bipartisan; bipartite; bisected; cleft; cloven; dichotomous; dimidiate; schismatic(al); SPLIT: n. bifurcation; breach; break; change; cleavage; cleft; crack; deviation; dichotomy; disagreement; disparity; dissidence; disunion; diversion; dividend; division; faction; fission; fissure; fork; fracture; parting; rent; rift; rive; schism; separation; severance; share; slit; splinter; tear; variance

SPOIL: v. addle; baby; besplatter; botch; bungle; coddle; confound; corrupt; curdle; decay; deface; defile; deprive; destroy;

impair; indulge; injure; kill; loot; mar; pamper; pervert; pillage; plunder; putrefy; rancidify; rob; rot; ruin; sour; strip; tarnish; turn; vitiate; wreck; SPOIL(S): n. booty; loot; pelf; pillage; plunder; prize; spoliation; swag; wreckage

SPOKE: baluster; bar; obstruction; pin; radii (pl.); radius; ray; rod; rung; stake

SPOKEN: addressed; announced; annunciated; argued; articulated; asked; asseverated; babbled; blabbed; chattered; communicated; conferred; conversed; declaimed; declared; depicted; described; discussed; divulged; enunciated; explained; expounded; expressed; greeted; hailed; imparted; informed; instructed; intoned; lectured; mentioned; mouthed; narrated; oral; orated; parole; prated; prattled; preached; proclaimed; pronounced; recited; recounted; related; remarked; revealed; said; stated; testified; told; uttered; verbalized; vocalized; voiced

SPOKESMAN: (see "leader") advocate; agent; announcer; attorney; chair(man); champion; cicerone; hierophant; lawyer; minister; orator; preacher; prolocutor; prophet; protagonist; representative; speaker; sponsor

SPONGE: v. bathe; cadge; cancel; clean(se); delete; efface; erase; freshen; moisten; mooch; obliterate; soak; sop; swab; wash; wipe; SPONGE: n. ascones (pl.); dressing; drunkard; pad; parasite; Porifera; poriferan; sycon; Sycones; SPONGY: absorbent; bibulous; elastic; light; mushy; pithy; porous; saturated; soft; soggy; springy; swampy; SPONGER: see "chiseler"

SPONSOR: (see "back") angel; backer; endorser; godparent; guarantor; insurer; leader; patron; protector; spokesman; subscriber; surety; teacher; SPONSORSHIP: aegis; auspice(s); egis; guarantee; guardianship; leadership; patronage; protection; protectorship; support; tutelage

SPONTANEOUS: (see "impromptu") accidental; ad-libbed; automatic; autonomic; careless; extemporary; free; impulsive; indeterminate; indigenous; instinctive; involuntary; mechanical; naïve; native; natural; offhand; reflex; self-acting; unavoidable; unbidden; uncontrived; uncontrollable; unforced; unplanned; unpremeditated; unprompted; unrehearsed; untaught; voluntary; willing; SPONTANEITY: see "extemporization"

SPOOKY: (see "eerie") ghostly; haunting; jittery; nervous; odd; peculiar; phantasmagorical; scary; skittish; spookish; weird

SPOON: bail; club; dip; ladle; neck; nestle; pet; scoop; troll; woo

SPORADIC: (see "infrequent") isolated; random; separate; single

SPORT: v. amuse; dally; display; frolic; gambol; hunt; jest; mock; play; romp; spree; toy; trifle; SPORT: n. amusement; bon vivant; chap; companion; dalliance; derision; diversion; divertissement; fellow; fun; game; golf; high jinks; horseplay; hunting; jest; mirth; mockery; mocking; mutation; pastime; play; pleasantry; polo; recreation; SPORTIVE or SPORTY: (see "playful") fast; flashy; frolicsome; gay; jaunty; larkish; loose; loud; playsome; rakish; showy; smart

SPOT: v. blemish; blot; blotch; detect; discolor; discover; disfigure; disgrace; dot; espy; find; fix; fleck; focus; identify; locate; mark; mottle; note; notice; observe; place; position; post; recognize; see; smudge; soil; speck(le); stain; stud; sully; taint; SPOT: n. area; berth; billet; bit; blemish; blot; blotch; defect; discoloration; disfiguration; disfigurement; disgrace; dot; fault; fish; fix; flaw; fleck; locality; location; macula(tion); mark; mottle; niche; particle; pimple; place; position; post; predicament; site; situation; speck(le); splatter; sprinkle; stain; station; stigma; taint; SPOTTED: blemished; blotchy; damaged; dapple(d); espied; macular; maculate; maculose; marked; mottled; noted; patchy; piebald; pied; punctate(d); puncticular; punctiform; seen; speckled; spotty; sullied; tarnished; uneven; variegated

SPOTLESS: blameless; clean; holy; immaculate; irreproachable; pure; speckless; unblemished; unflecked; unmarked; unmarred; unspotted; unstained; unsullied; untarnished

SPOUSE: consort; fere; helpmate; husband; mate; uxor; wife

SPOUT: v. declaim; emit; jet; mouth; orate; speak; spray; spurt; stream; utter; SPOUT: n. chute; conduit; gargoyle; geat; gut(ter); jet; lip; mouth; nozzle; outlet; pipe; spile; stream; trough

SPRAWL: see "spread"

SPRAY: atomize; branch; drizzle; foam; fog; mizzle; nebulize; scatter; sparge; spatter; spout; spread; sprinkle; spume; strew; wet

SPREAD: v. announce; anoint; blazon; branch; bray; broadcast; bruit; cast; circulate; coat; cover; decentralize; delate; deploy; develop; diffuse; dilate; disperse; disseminate; distribute; divaricate; diversify; enhance; enlarge; enter; escalate; expand; expatiate; extend; fan; flan; flare; flow; gape; grow; herald; increase; interpenetrate; irradiate; lengthen; magnify; metastasize; multiply; noise; norate; ooze; open; overlay; overrun; paint; part; penetrate; percolate; plaster; proclaim; proliferate; prolong; promulgate; propagate; protract; publish; radiate; rage; ramify; range; reach; record; release; reproduce; rumor; run; scatter; scrawl; seed; seep; separate; serve; set; slather; smear; sow; splay; sprawl; spray; stretch; strew; superimpose; swell; unfold; unfurl; wander; widen; SPREAD: a. amplified; augmented; branched; cast; covered; delated; developed; dilated; distended; distributed; divaricate; enhanced; enlarged; escalated; expanded; extended; flanged; flowing; increased; inflated; intumescent; lengthened; magnified; metastasized; open; patulous; run; running; scattered; seeded; sown; splayed; stretched; swollen; unfolded; unfurled; widened; SPREAD: n. area; banquet; butter; circulation; coat; compass; contagion; cover(ing); decentralization; diapason; diaspora; difference; diffusion; dilation; dispersion; display; dissemination; distance; distribution; divarication; divergence; diversity; expanse; expansion; feast; gamut; gap; gape; increase; irradiation; jam; jelly; meal; octave; oleo; opening; paint; proliferation; promulgation; propagation; radiation; ramification; ranch; range; reach; reproduction; scope; size; span; SPREADING: divergent; expanded; patulous; radial; scrawling; serpiginous; sprawling; widening

SPREE: (see "party") antic; bacchanal(ian); bat; binge; blow(out); bout; brannigan; carousal; drunk; frolic; jag; lark; orgy; rampage; revelry; shinding; shindy; soak; splurge; tear; toot; wassail

SPRIGHTLY: active; agile; airy; animate(d); antic; balletic; blithe(ful); blithesome; bright; brisk; bubbling; buoyant; clear; crisp; effervescent; exuberant; fresh; frolicsome; gay; jaunty; lively; mercurial; mirthful; new; perky; pert; pleasant; quick;

roguish; sharp; smart; spirited; sportive; spry; vivacious; zestful; SPRIGHTLI-NESS: *allégresse*; buoyance; buoyancy; buoyantness; exuberance; gaiety; lightheartedness; liveliness; piquancy; vivacity; zest

SPRING: **v.** appear; arise; begin; bounce; bound; commence; dart(le); derive; disclose; emanate; emerge; extend; flow; glow; issue; jump; leap; originate; pounce; proceed; recoil; result; rise; saltate; salute; seep; shoot; split; spread; sprout; start; stem; strain; SPRING: **n.** beginning; bounce; bound; buoyancy; cause; coil; commencement; elasticity; font; fount(ain); geyser; helix; inception; initiation; jump; lavant; leap; motive; onset; recoil; resilience; resiliency; sally; saltation; season; source; spa; start; tension; well

SPRINKLE: asperge; baptise; bedew; bedrop; diversify; dot; dredge; drench; drizzle; flour; hose; intersperse; mizzle; nebulize; purify; rain; sand; scatter; sow; sparge; splash; splatter; spot; spout; spray; strew; wet

SPRITE: Ariel; brownie; demon; elf; fairy; fay; genie; genius; ghost; goblin; gremlin; imp; jinne; kelpy; nix(ie); pixie; pixy; puck; shade; spirit; undine

SPROUT: **v.** bud; burgeon; expand; germinate; grow; pullulate; shoot; spring (up); SPROUT: **n.** bud; burgeoning; chit; expansion; germination; growth; offshoot; outgrowth; pullulation; scion; shoot; sprouting

SPRUCE: **v.** clean; comb; freshen; groom; neaten; preen; smarten; tidy; tit(t)ivate; trim; SPRUCE: **a.** active; clean; dapper; fresh; natty; neat; smart; smug; *soigné*; *soignée* (fem.); trig; trim

SPRY: active; agile; alive; brisk; chipper; crisp; gay; hearty; jaunty; live(ly); nimble; peart; perky; pert; playful; quick; sportive; sprightly; vigorous; vivacious; zestful

SPUME: foam; froth; lather; lava; scum; suds; yeast

SPUNK: amadou; ambition; backbone; brass; courage; determination; fire; gall; grit; guts; liveliness; mettle; nerve; passion; pluck; resolution; sand; spirit; tinder; touchwood; will

SPUR: **v.** animate; bestir; catalyze; cause; dig;

drive; elate; goad; impel; incite; induce; instigate; motivate; move; persuade; precipitate; press; prick; provoke; prune; stimulate; stir; trim; urge; SPUR: **n.** brace; branch; calcar; catalysis; catalyst; edge; force; goad; incentive; instigation; motivation; motive; need; offshoot; osteophyte; outgrowth; persuasion; prick(le); projection; provocation; rowel; siding; stimulation; stimulus; strut; stud; urge; urging

SPURIOUS: (**see** "artificial") adulterate(d); apocryphal; bastard; bogus; casuistic; counterfeit; deceitful; deceptive; erroneous; extraneous; fake(d); false; falsified; feigned; fictitious; forged; fraudulent; funny; hollow; illegitimate; illogical; illusory; imitation; inauthentic; meretricious; phony; pinchbeck; pretended; pseudepigraphic(al); pseudepigraphous; pseudo(logical); sham; simulated; simulative; snide; sophistical; specious; tin(sel)

SPURN: conspue; decline; disapprove; disdain; flout; kick; refuse; reject; repel; repudiate; return; scorn; trample; tread (upon)

SPURT: burst; gush; haste; jet; spatter; spout; spray; spring; squirt

SPY: **v.** descry; discover; examine; explore; inform; inspect; instigate; look; notice; observe; peek; peer; probe; pry; scout; see; seek; watch; SPY: **n.** agent; André; Caleb; emissary; examiner; informer; inspector; investigator; scout; watcher

SQUABBLE: **see** "dispute"

SQUALID: back-alley; contemptible; crude; degraded; dingy; dirty; feculent; filthy; mangy; mean; ordurous; run-down; scabrous; seedy; shabby; sordid; worn

SQUALL: **v.** blow; cry; gust; mewl; scream; storm; SQUALL: **n.** blow; bluster; commotion; cry; gale; gust; mewl; rain; storm; wind

SQUANDER: dissipate; misspend; misuse; roam; scatter; spend; wander; waste

SQUARE: **v.** adjust; agree; balance; conform; correct; equal; equate; even; fix; jibe; match; quadrate; regulate; settle; shape; stabilize; straighten; suit; tally; true; SQUARE: **a.** correct; dependable; equable; equal(ed); even; fair; honest; just; legal; legitimate; matched; quadratic; satisfactory;

settled; stable; straightforward; substantial; tetragonal; true; SQUARE: **n.** area; centare; check(er); court; plaza; quad(rangle); unsophisticate

SQUASH: **v.** crush; disconcert; mash; press; squeeze; squelch; suppress; SQUASH: **n.** cushaw; cymling; game; pepo; zucchini

SQUEAL: (**see** "inform" and "yelp") complain; cry; protest

SQUEAMISH: afraid; careful; cautious; cold; distant; fastidious; finical; finicky; hypercritical; nauseated; overcareful; particular; prissy; prudish; qualmish; queasy; sanctimonious; scrupulous; squeamy; SQUEAMISHNESS: (**see** "disgust") fear; prudery; qualmishness

SQUEEZE: choke; compress; condense; constrain; crowd; crush; eke; embrace; extort; extract; force; grip; hug; jam; oppress; pinch; press; stifle; tighten; wring

SQUINT: **v.** (**see** "peer") deviate; SQUINT-(ING): **n.** bent; deviation; esotropia; exotropia; *louchement*; strabismus; trend; SQUINTING: **a.** louche; strabismic

SQUIRE: **v.** accompany; attend; conduct; escort; guard; usher; SQUIRE: **n.** armorbearer; attendant; beau; escort; gallant; guard; judge; lawyer; lover

SQUIRM: **see** "writhe"

STAB: **v.** attempt; cut; dagger; drive; hit; hurt; gig; gore; impale; injure; knife; knive; lance; lancinate; pain; pierce; punch; puncture; slit; spit; split; stick; strike; thrust; try; wound; STAB: **n.** attempt; cut; go; goring; hurt; injury; job; knifing; pain; pang; pierce; poke; slit; stitch; thrust; trial; try; wound(ing)

STABILIZE: adjust; balance; ballast; correct; even; firm; fix; level; maintain; poise; protect; regulate; rigidify; set(tle); steady; strengthen; tauten; thicken; trim; STABLE: **a.** adjusted; balanced; constant; correct; enduring; even; fast; firm; fixed; homeostatic; immobile; immobilized; immutable; inexpugnable; irreversible; irrevocable; lasting; level; permanent; poised; regulated; rigid; sessile; set(tled); sound; stagnant; static; steady; strong; tranquil; unchangeable; unchanging; STABLE: **n.** barn; byre; mew; stall; STABILITY: balance; ballast; constancy; correctness; endurability; equilib-

rium; firmness; fixity; homeostasis; permanence; permanency; poise; resistance; rigidity; stabilization; steadfastness; steadiness; strength; weight; STABILIZER: balance; corrective; protection; protective

STACK: **v.** (**see** "pile") arrange; load; shock; STACK: **n.** chimney; cord; heap; pile; rick; scintle; shock

STADIUM: arena; course; field; oval; period; phase; stadia (pl.); stage; track

STAFF: ballow; bar; cane; club; crew; cudgel; family; mace; officers; organization; personnel; pole; prop; reed; retinue; rod; rung; shaft; spar; stick; support; wand

STAGE: **v.** arrange; contrive; dramatize; enact; play; present; produce; show; STAGE: **n.** apron; arena; boards; center; condition; dais; degree; drama; era; forum; gradation; grade; leg; legit; moment; part; period; phase; platform; point; portion; process; proscenium; pulpit; range; rostrum; scaffold; scene; shelf; show; span; state; station; step; theater; STAGY *or* STAGED: (**see** "showy") affected; arranged; artificial; assumed; contrived; dramatic; histrionic; manipulated; melodramatic; operated; planned; rigged; theatric(al); STAGINESS: (**see** "showiness") acrobatics; cabotinage; histrionicism; histrionics; melodrama-(tics); sardoodledom; theatricality; theatrics

STAGGER: alternate; amaze; doubt; guess; hesitate; lurch; nonplus; perplex; reel; rock; shake; startle; stumble; surprise; sway; titubate; totter; tremble; trip; vacillate; vibrate; weave; welter

STAGNATION: arrest; calm(ness); death; dullness; quiescence; standstill; status; torpidity; torpor; STAGNANT: **see** "unchanging"

STAID: (**see** "calm") complacent; composed; cool; correct; decorous; demure; earnest; fixed; grave; proper; sedate; serious; settled; sober; solemn; steady

STAIN: **v.** blemish; blot; blotch; color; corrupt; defile; discolor; disgrace; dishonor; dye; imbue; maculate; mark; smirch; smudge; soil; speck; spot; stigmatize; sully; taint; tarnish; tinge; tint; STAIN: **n.** bar sinister; blemish; blot; blotch; cast; corruption; discoloration; disgrace; dishonor; dye; macula(tion); mark; pigment; sign; smirch; smudge; speck; spot; stigma(ta);

taint; tarnish; tincture; tinge; tint; STAIN-
LESS: **see** "immaculate"

STAIR: degree; escalator; flight; ladder;
riser; rung; stage; step(s); stile; sty; tread

STAKE: **v.** ante; back; bet; fasten; hazard;
mark; pawn; play; risk; support; venture;
vie; wager; STAKE: **n.** ante; bet; boundary;
fastener; interest; kitty; mark; palisade; peg;
pile; pole; post; pot; prize; risk; rod; stob;
venture; wager

STALE: airless; ancient; banal; bare; close;
common(place); dry; dull; flat; flavorless;
frowsy; fusty; hackneyed; hoary; insipid;
jejune; motionless; mo(u)ldy; musty; obsolete; old; platitudinous; remote; sandy;
stagnant; stereotyped; tasteless; threadbare; tight; trite; unaired; unventilated;
vapid; worn

STALEMATE: (**see** "check") blind alley;
block; check; crisis; cul-de-sac; dead center;
deadlock; dilemma; draw; impasse

STALK: **v.** dog; follow; haunt; hound; kill;
march; prey; pursue; shadow; stride; strut;
tail; STALK: **n.** (**see** "stem") cane; caulis;
culm; handle; pedestal; pedicel; peduncle;
petiole; reed

STALL: **v.** check; delay; divert; evade; mire;
pretend; spar; stop; STALL: **n.** blind;
booth; check; compartment; cot; counter;
crib; loge; manger; mew; pew; pretense;
rank; ruse; seat; stand; station; stop(page)

STAMINA: (**see** "strength") constitution;
courage; grit; guts; might; muscle; perseverance; power; sand; staying power; vigor;
vim; vitality

STAMMER: **v.** faffle; falter; haw; hem;
hesitate; stumble; stutter; STAMMER: **n.**
psellism; stutter(ing)

STAMP: **v.** adjudge; brand; cancel; categorize;
crush; designate; distinguish; emboss; engrave; eradicate; erase; exterminate; extinguish; form; impose; impress; imprint;
incuse; inscribe; justify; kill; mark; mold;
notarize; pound; print; pulverize; sanction;
seal; stigmatize; strike; trace; tread; STAMP:
n. appearance; blend; brand; character;
design(ation); die; effect; form; impression;
imprint; kind; label; mark; mold; nature;
pattern; pestle; postage; postmark; print;
seal; sort; stigma(ta); strike; tenor; touch;
type

STAMPEDE: **v.** demoralize; disorganize;
fly; panic; riot; rout; run; rush; STAM-
PEDE: **n.** breakaway; collapse; debacle;
demoralization; disorganization; disruption;
flight; panic; riot; rout; run; rush

STANCH *or* STAUNCH: **v.** check; extinguish;
quell; steady; stem; STANCH: **a. see**
"staunch"

STAND: **v.** abide; arise; bear; brook; endure;
halt; permit; remain; resist; rise; suffer;
support; tolerate; treat; undergo; wait;
STAND: **n.** attitude; base; case; counter;
desk; easel; frame; growth; halt; platform;
position; posture; resistance; shelf; stall;
stance; state; station; situation; stop; support; table; tabouret; tripod; trivet; way

STANDARD: **a.** appropriate; authentic; basic;
canonical; classic(al); consuetudinary; conventional; correct; customary; enduring;
ethical; exemplary; familiar; first-rate;
historical; ideal; masterly; normal; orthodox;
primal; prime; proper; pure; recognized;
regular; reliable; sanctioned; statutable;
statutory; textbookish; traditional; typic(al);
uniform; valuable; vintage; well-established;
STANDARD: **n.** amenities; axiom; banner;
beau idéal; canon; civilities; classic; colors;
comparison; convenances; conventions;
criteria(pl.); criterion; decree; denominator;
emblem; ensign; example; ga(u)ge; gonfalon;
grade; idea(l); jack; law; level; mark; masterpiece; mean; measure; method; modality;
model; norm; opus; par; pattern; pole; principle; proprieties; rule(r); sign; specimen;
stand; test; touchstone; trophy; truth; type;
unit; weight; yardstick; STANDARDIZE:
calibrate; even; gauge; regulate; set; type;
weigh

STANDING: **a.** continuing; durable; erect;
established; fixed; immovable; intact; lasting;
motionless; permanent; perpendicular;
remaining; settled; stagnant; statant; stationary; upright; vertical; STANDING: **n.**
achievement; antecedence; class(ification);
credibility; credit; degree; duration; estate;
esteem; estimation; height; hierarchy; honor;
influence; location; merit; perpendicular(ity);
position; posture; power; precedence; prestige; rank; rating; renown; reputation;
repute; situation; stature; status; trustworthiness; verticality

STANDOFFISH: (**see** "aloof") cool; coy;
haughty; reserved; uncordial; unfriendly

STANDPATTER: **see** "conservative"

STAPLE: center; commodity; core; fiber; goods; item; loop; mart; material; nail; substance

STAR(S): ace; actor; asterisk; badge; comet; constellation; decoration; destiny; *étoile*; fame; fortune; galaxy; goal; headliner; hexagram; luminary; meteor; nova; orb; ornament; pentacle; performer; planet; principal; sphere; sun; world; STARRY: astral; astrean; astriferous; astronomical; starlike; stellar; stellate; stelliform; uranic; visionary

STARCH: **v.** rigidify; stiffen; strengthen; STARCH: **n.** amyl(um); backbone; casava; energy; farina; formality; sago; vitality; STARCHY: amyloid; farinaceous; formal; precise; prim; proud; rigid; stiff

STARE: (**see** "see") gape; gawk; gaze; glare; goggle; leer; look; ogle; peer; vigil; watch

STARK: arrant; bare; barren; bleak; blunt; complete; crude; desolate; empty; extreme; fair; firm; fixed; harsh; inclement; naked; pure; rigid; robust; set; severe; sheer; simple; stiff; stormy; stout; strict; strong; stubborn; sturdy; tense; ugly; unadorned; unbending; utter(ly); very; vigorous; windy

START: **v.** (**see** "kindle") actuate; awaken; begin; catalyze; catapult; cause; commence; create; dart; flow; found; frame; initiate; institute; introduce; issue; jerk; jump; leap; make; move; organize; originate; plan; plant; propose; propound; provoke; raise; record; rouse; seed; sow; spurt; tee off; trigger; vitalize; START: **n.** (**see** "birth") advantage; beginning; bound; commencement; fit; foundation; incipience; incipiency; introduction; jerk; jump; kickoff; movement; onset; opening; origin; outburst; outset; provocation; sally

STARTLE: (**see** "alarm") arouse; awaken; awe; daunt; disturb; electrify; excite; frighten; rouse; scare; shock; stir; surprise; STARTLING: awe-inspring; awesome; bizarre; electrifying; fantastic(al); frightful; galvanic; odd; screaming; shocking; splendid; strong; stunning; surprising; terrible; terrifying

STARVE: affamish; choke; die; extinguish; famish; hunger; limit; perish; suffer; suppress; underfeed; STARVATION: famine; famishment; hunger; inedia; penury; poverty; underfeeding; undernourishment; undernutrition; want; wolf

STATE: **v.** (**see** "say") opine; utter; voice; STATE: **n.** aspect; attitude; authority; barony; body politic; Caesar; case; character; circumstance; civitas; command; commonalty; commonweal; commonwealth; condition; country; crisis; democracy; development; dignity; dilemma; dominion; dukedom; eminence; empire; estate; estre; *état*; excitement; government; growth; kingdom; lot; magnificence; mode; monarchy; mood; nation; nature; occupation; pass; plight; position; posture; predicament; process; queendom; rank; realm; rule; situation; stage; stand(ing); station; (the) *res publica*; temperament; way; weal

STATELY: (**see** "exalted") aloof; august; baronial; ceremonious; courtly; dignified; elevated; eminent; erect; formal; grandiloquent; grand(iose); haughty; imperial; imperious; imposing; impressive; Junoesque (fem.); lofty; magnificent; majestic; marmoreal; noble; palatial; perpendicular; pompous; Praxitelean; princely; proud; regal; royal; sculpturesque; solemn; statuesque; stiff; sublime; tall; togated; unapproachable; STATELINESS: aloofness; courtliness; dignity; eminence; grandeur; grandiosity; grandness; hauteur; impressiveness; loftiness; magnificence; majesty; nobility; perpendicularity; pride; regality; royalty; solemnity; sublimity

STATEMENT: account(ing); affidavit; allegation; allegatum; allegement; announcement; assertion; asseveration; bill; brochure; constatation; decision; declaration; decree; deposition; dicta (pl.); dictum; enunciation; explanation; memo(randum); narration; narrative; observation; pamphlet; postulation; precis; presentation; proclamation; profession; program; proposition; recital; recitation; remark; report; ruling; say-so; speech; story; theorem; thesis; utterance; verbality; words; writing

STATESMAN: (**see** "solon") politician

STATIC: (**see** "stable") stationary; undynamic

STATION: **v.** assign; garrison; locate; perch; place; post; set(tle); STATION: **n.** assignment; degree; depot; duty; establishment; facility; fort(ress); function; garrison; grade; habitat; halt; installation; level; location; occupation; office; outpost; perch; place(ment); point; position; post; posture; range; rank; seat; setting; settlement; ship; situation; spot; stage; stall; stand(ing); state; stop; terminal; terminus; work

STATIONARY: (**see** "calm") arrested; fixed; immobile; immovable; inactive; motionless; permanent; quiescent; rigid; sedentary; serene; sessile; set(tled); stable; standing; static; still; unchanging; unruffled

STATISTICS: **see** "facts"

STATUE: acrolith; bust; doll; effigy; figure; figurine; icon; ikon; image(ry); likeness; memorial; sculpture

STATURE: (**see** "standing") height; posture

STATUS: (**see** "state") cachet; cast; class-(ification); condition; degree; eminence; footing; level; position; posture; prestige; quality; rank(ing); rating; recognition; repute; situation; standing; station; stature

STATUTE: act; bill; canon; decree; edict; law; order; ordinance; regulation; rubric; rule; ukase

STAUNCH *or* STANCH: faithful; loyal; steadfast; strong; substantial; true; watertight

STAVE: **v.** bash; crush; hurry; rush; shatter; smash; STAVE: **n.** lag; pole; slat; stanza; stap; strip

STAY: **v.** abide; allay; appease; await; bide; block; brace; calm; cease; check; comfort; continue; curb; delay; depend; dwell; endure; exist; fix; guy; halt; hinder; hold; lag; last; linger; live; lodge; lurk; outlast; outlive; pacify; pause; persist; postpone; prevail; prevent; prolong; prop; protract; reinforce; remain; reside; rest; restrain; roost; sleep; slow; stand; stick; stop (over); strengthen; subsist; support; survive; suspend; sustain; table; tarry; visit; wait; STAY: **n.** brace; check; continuance; curb; delay; halt; hindrance; hold; persistence; postponement; reinforcement; restraint; sojourn; stand(still); stop; subsistence; survival; tarry; visit; wait

STEAD: advantage; avail; lieu; place; room; service; vice

STEADY *or* STEADFAST: calm; consistent; constant; continual; continuing; continuous; controlled; cool; dependable; diligent; disciplined; enduring; equable; even; faithful; firm; fixed; immutable; imperturbable; incessant; irreversible; irrevocable; lasting; loyal; patient; periodic(al); perpetual; persevering; persistent; *rangé*; *rangée* (fem.); regular; reliable; resolute; restrained; rocky; secure; self-possessed; sober; solid; stab(i)le; staid; sta(u)nch; steadying; strong; sure; thoughtful; tranquil; true(blue); truehearted; undeviating; unfaltering; unflinching; unfluctuating; unflustered; unhesitating; unhurried; uniform; uninterrupted; unremittent; unremitting; unremoved; unruffled; unshaken; unswerving; untremulous; unvarying; upright; STEADFASTNESS: **see** "loyalty"

STEAL: abstract; adopt; appropriate; borrow; burglarize; cop; couch; crib; defalcate; defraud; depredate; deprive; despoil; embezzle; entice; extort; extract; filch; fleece; forage; forge; glide; grab; hijack; hoist; hold up; lift; loot; misapply; misappropriate; misbeget; mulct; nail; peculate; pilfer; pillage; pinch; plagiarize; pluck; plunder; prowl; purloin; reave; relieve; remove; rifle; rob; roll; rustle; scrounge; slip; smuggle; snatch; snitch; spoliate; swipe; take; thieve; tiptoe; STEALING: **a.** burglarious; larcenous; thieving; thievish; STEALING: **n.** abstraction; appropriation; defalcation; embezzlement; forgery; larceny; malversation; misappropriation; peculation; plagiarism; plagiary; stealth; subtraction; theft; thieving

STEALTHY: *à la dérobée*; backhanded; cabalistic; catfooted; catty; cautious; clandestine; cunning; duplicitous; *en tapinois*; foxy; furtive; illicit; Machiavellian; noiseless; roundabout; secret(ive); serpentine; sinuous; skulking; sly; snaky; sneaky; stolen; surreptitious; tricky; underground; underhand(ed)

STEAM: **v.** boil; burn; evaporate; exhale; reek; smoke; sweat; vaporize; STEAM: **n.** effluvium; exhalation; fog; fume; gas; mist; power; smoke; stufa; tension; vapor

STEED: charger; cob; horse; nag; palfrey; pegasus; stallion

STEEL: **v.** acclimate; acclimatize; discipline; drill; encourage; enure; harden; inure; train; STEEL: **n.** courage; damascus; damask; hardness; invar; sword; Toledo

STEEP: **v.** bathe; brew; imbrue; immerse; infuse; macerate; moisten; ret; soak; wet; STEEP: **a.** abrupt; acclivitous; arduous; costly; dear; declivitous; elevated; excessive; exorbitant; expensive; extreme; headlong; high; incredible; lofty; perpendicular; precipitous; sheer; stiff; tall

STEEPLE: flèche; minaret; spire; tower

STEER: **v.** conn; control; direct; drive; govern; guide; helm; lead; manage; manipulate; pilot; ply; rule; stem; wend; STEER: **n.** bovine; bullock; ox

STEM: **v.** arouse; arrest; check; contain; flow; halt; hold; issue; progress; rise; spring; stanch; steer; stop; STEM: **n.** axis; base; bind; body; cane; caulis; culm; handle; leg; pedicel; pedestal; peduncle; petiole; prow; reed; rod; spindle; stalk; stick; stock; straw; trunk

STENCH: (**see** "smell") fetor; mephitis; nidor; odor(ant); putridity; rot(tenness); stink

STEP: act(ion); advance(ment); course; dance; degree; *démarche*; distance; echelon; foot-(hold); footprint; gait; grade; ladder; maneuver; movement; notch; pace; pass; place; plateau; point; procedure; progress; rank; rung; stage; stair; stile; stride; tread

STEREOTYPE: **see** "pattern"

STERILE: abortive; arid; aseptic; bare; barren; clean; deficient; destitute; dry; effete; exiguous; fallow; flat; fruitless; functionless; germless; impotent; impregnable; incompetent; inconceivable; ineffective; ineffectual; jejune; pure; unbelievable; uncreative; undemonstrative; unfertile; unfruitful; unproductive; vain

STERLING: **see** "excellent"

STERN: (**see** "strict") abaft; aft; astringent; austere; cruel; direct; dour; exact(ing); extreme; flinty; forboding; gloomy; grim; hard; harsh; inexorable; inflexible; inhospitable; obdurate; oppressive; relentless; resolute; rigid; rigorous; scrupulous; severe; stark; steadfast; stout; straight; stringent; sturdy; unbending; uncompromising; unfeeling; uninviting; unkind; unrelenting; unsympathetic; unyielding; STERNNESS: **see** "severity"

STEW: **v.** boil; broil; fret; itch; seethe; simmer; steep; swelter; worry; STEW: **n.** burgoo; confusion; difficulty; haricot; heterogeneity; impasse; itching; matelote; mixture; olio; olla (podrida); potpourri; predicament; ragout; swivet

STEWARD: agent; bailiff; bursar; chamberlain; curator; custodian; director; factor; guardian; majordomo; manager; manciple; procurator; purser; purveyor; reeve; seneschal; treasurer

STICK: **v.** adhere; agglutinate; apply; attach; baffle; balk; bind; cheat; cleave; cling; cohere; conform; conglutinate; defraud; endure; fix; glue; gore; hew; hold; impale; jam; last; lodge; nonplus; overcharge; paste; pierce; puncture; puzzle; stay; stump; wedge; STICK: **n.** adherence; agglutination; bar; bat; baton; branch; cane; coherence; conglutination; cudgel; fagot; goad; pole; rod; staff; stem; wand; STICKING *or* STICKY: adherent; adherescent; adhering; adhesive; agglutinant; agglutinating; coherent; cohesive; gluey; glutinous; gummous; gummy; humid; moist; mucilaginous; ropy; tacky; tenacious; unpleasant; viscid; viscous; STICKINESS: adherence; adhesiveness; coherence; cohesion; glutinosity; gumminess; tackiness; tenacity; viscosity

STICK-TO-ITIVENESS: adhesiveness; gluiness; importunity; perseverance; pertinacity; steadfastness; tenacity; willingness

STIFF: arduous; austere; bullish; cold; conventional; cool; crowded; difficult; drunk; exacting; expensive; firm; forceful; formal; frigid; frozen; hard; heavy; inflexible; mechanical; muscle-bound; pervaded; pompous; prim; proper; proud; pugnacious; punctilious; resolute; rigescent; rigid; rugged; rusty; severe; sharp; slow; solid; starchy; stark; steep; stern; stilted; stout; strict; strong; stubborn; taut; tense; thick; trig; unbending; uncomplying; unfriendly; unyielding; uphill; vigorous; violent; viscous; wooden; STIFFEN: ankylose; benumb; bolster; brace; constrict; coossify; gel; harden; immobilize; inspissate; ossify; ruffle; set; solidify; stabilize; starch; strengthen; support; tauten; thicken; tighten; toughen; train

STIFLE: (**see** "choke" and "constrain") conceal; damp(en); gag; hinder; mute; restrain; silence; stunt; suppress

STIGMATIZE: (**see** "stain") blame; brand; censure; defame; denigrate; denounce; discredit; flagellate; mark; taint; tarnish; STIGMA: bar sinister; blame; blemish; blot; brand; defect; disgrace; dishonor; mark; odium; onus; shame; spot; stain; symptom; taint; tarnish

STILL: **v.** (**see** "calm") allay; appease; arrest; assuage; becalm; check; gag; hush; lull; mute; overcome; pacify; quiet(en); restrain;

settle; silence; soothe; squelch; suppress; STILL: **a.** or **adv.** (**see** "calm") always; but; dormant; dull; dumb; even; ever; halcyon; hushed; immobile; impassive; inactive; inarticulate; inert; inoperative; motionless; mum; mute(d); nevertheless; noiseless; notwithstanding; obmutescent; pacific; peaceful; placid; quiescent; quiet(ly); sedentary; serene; silenced; silent; silentious; soft; stationary; stilled; taciturn; tranquil; unperturbed; unruffled; yet; STILLNESS: calmness; immobility; lifelessness; quiescence; quietude; serenity; tranquility

STIMULATE: actuate; animate; arouse; awaken; catalyze; elate; encourage; energize; enliven; evoke; excite; fan; feed; fertilize; fire; foment; fuel; galvanize; glow; goad; impel; incite; inflame; initiate; innervate; innerve; inspire; inspirit; instigate; invigorate; kindle; liven; massage; pep (up); pique; precipitate; prick(le); prime; provoke; pump; ready; rouse; spark; spur; sting; stir; thrill; tickle; tingle; titillate; tittivate; trigger; urge; vibrate; waken; whet; STIMULATING *or* STIMULATIVE: accelerative; animating; aspirational; brisk; catalytic; electric; electrifying; galvanic; heartening; hypodermic; incendiary; incisive; inspirational; inspiring; inspiriting; nutty; piquant; poignant; powerful; promptive; provocative; psychagogic; pungent; spicy; stimulatory; stimulogenous; titillating; tittivating; tonic; STIMULATION *or* STIMULUS: alcohol; attraction; catalyst; catalytic; coffee; fan; feeling; force; goad; hypodermic; incendiary; incentive; incitement; influence; inoculation; invigoration; invitation; liquor; lure; massage; motive; piquancy; prod; provocation; quirt; refreshment; reinvigoration; restorative; sensation; shot in the arm; spark; spur; stimulant; stimulativeness; sting; thrill; thrust; tickle; tingle; titillation; tittivation; tonic; trigger; urge; vibration; whip; STIMULATOR: accelerant; accentuator; agitator; catalyst; catalytic; elixir; fillip; flagellant; gadfly; incendiary; incentive; precipitator; propulsor; provocateur; shot; spur; stimulant; stimulus; tonic; whip; STIMULANT: alcohol; coffee; goad; incitement; liquor; motive; needle; nudge; prick; prod; provocation; spur; stimulus; tea; thrust; urge; whip

STING: burn; cheat; excite; gall; goad; hurt; nettle; overcharge; pain; prick; smart; stick; tang; tingle; touch; STINGING: acid; acidulous; acrimonious; aculeate; biting; blistering; burning; caustic; hot; incisive; keen; mordant; painful; penetrat-

ing; peppery; piquant; poignant; pointed; scathing; scorching; sharp; withering

STINGY: avaricious; cheap; cheeseparing; close(fisted); covetous; curmudgeonly; extortionate; frugal; grasping; greedy; grudging; illiberal; ironfisted; meager; mean; mercenary; miserly; narrow-fisted; near; niggardly; parsimonious; penny-pinching; penurious; petty; pinchpenny; retentive; scant(y); sparing; stinting; tight(fisted); ungenerous; ungiving; STINGINESS: avarice; avariciousness; covetousness; frugality; greed; illiberality; miserliness; parsimoniousness; parsimony; penury; thrift; ungenerosity

STINK: (**see** "odor" and "smell") effluvia(pl.); effluvium; fetidity; fetidness; fetor; mephitis; nidor; putridity; reek; stench; to-do; STINKING *or* STINKY: bad; effluvial; fetid; foul; fulsome; fusty; graveolent; ill-smelling; improper; malodorous; mephitic; musty; nasty; nidorous; noisome; noxious; odorous; offensive; olid; pestilent(ial); putrid; rancid; rank; repulsive; rotten; scandalous; smelly

STINT: **v.** bound; confine; limit; restrain; restrict; save; scant; scrimp; spare; STINT: **n.** chare; chore; duty; frugality; job; limitation; operation; restraint; restriction; task; work

STIPEND: allowance; compensation; expense; fee; hire; honorarium; income; pay; pension; prebend; salary; salt; screw; sum; wage

STIPULATE: agree; contract; covenant; demand; itemize; name; particularize; postulate; promise; provide; require; specify; STIPULATION: (**see** "condition") agreement; clause; contract; covenant; if; provision; proviso; requirement

STIR: **v.** activate; actuate; agitate; arouse; awaken; budge; bustle; buzz; carouse; catalyze; disturb; elate; evoke; excite; exert; fuss; fuze; goad; incite; influence; instigate; mix; move; pique; prod; provoke; quicken; rally; rouse; roust; shake; spur; stimulate; tingle; urge; waken; STIR: **n.** (**see** "commotion") activation; ado; agitation; blather; brouhaha; bustle; buzz; excitement; exertion; flurry; fuss; impression; instigation; jail; move(ment); pother; prison; prod; rally; restlessness; stimulation; tingle; to-do; urge

STITCH: **v.** ache; baste; embroider; fasten; join; sew; suture; STITCH: **n.** ache; crick;

pain; pang; punto; seam; stab; stuture; thread; throe

STOCK: **v.** breed; equip; furnish; hoard; keep; plant; prepare; preserve; provide; replenish; reserve; seed; sow; store; supply; STOCK: **n.** accumulation; animals; bond; breed; butt; cache; capital; cattle; certificate; confidence; descendants; descent; equipment; faith; family; funds; goods; handle; hoard; inventory; larder; line(age); machinery; materials; merchandise; plant; principal; race; reserve; share(s); soup; source; stem; store; supplies; supply; surplus; treasure; treasury; trunk; wares

STOCKADE: barrier; bulwark; enclosure; étape; fence; fort(ress); pen; redoubt

STOCKY: burly; chunky; compact; dumpy; fat; firm; gross; large; obese; plump; pursy; pyknic; short; solid; squat; stout; stub(by); sturdy; thick(set)

STOIC(AL): dispassionate; impassive; imperturbable; indifferent; philosophic(al); phlegmatic; resolute; Spartanic; stolid; undemonstrative; unmovable; unmoved; Zenonian

STOLID: adamant; anserine; asinine; boorish; bovine; brutish; cloddish; deadpan; dull; heavy; impassive; opinionated; spiritless; stubborn; unexcited; unperturbed; wooden; STOLIDITY: asininity; bovinity; dullness; heaviness; impassiveness; impassivity; imperturbability; imperturbation; indifference; phlegm; woodenness

STOMACH: **v.** abide; allow; brook; disgust; endure; let; nauseate; permit; STOMACH: **n.** abdomen; appetite; belly; craw; desire; gorge; inclination; maw; paunch; pouch; rumen

STONE: **v.** pelt; lapidate; throw; STONE: **n.** adamant; boulder; calculus; cenotaph; cobbles; concrete; diamond; flint; gem; granite; gravel; jewel; lapis; marble; marker; mineral; ore; pebble; pit; rock; sand; seed; slate; trap; STONY: adamant; difficult; hard; lapideous; lithic; malevolent; Niobean; pebbly; petrous; pitiless; rocky

STOOL: bench; crock; decoy; defecation; dung; dupe; feces; hassock; ottoman; seat; stand; stooge; stump; support; tabouret

STOOP: **v.** bend; bow; condescend; couch; crouch; debase; decline; degrade; deign;

descend; flex; humble; hunch; incline; kneel; kowtow; lean; overcome; submit; tilt; STOOP: **n.** bend; concession; condescension; flexure; gallery; hunch; kowtow; kyphosis; loggia; piazza; porch; submission

STOP: **v.** abort; arrest; avast; baffle; balk; block; break; catch; cease; check(mate); choke; circumvent; clog; close; consider; cork; cut; deactivate; defeat; defer; delay; desist; die; discontinue; ease; end; fail; finish; foil; freeze; frustrate; halt; hesitate; hold; impede; inactivate; intercept; interrupt; kill; leave; lodge; nip; nonplus; obstruct; occlude; oppilate; pause; plug; prevent; quit; recess; relinquish; rest; restrain; retard; scotch; secure; shut; sojourn; stall; stanch; stand; stem; stopper; strangle; stymie; suffocate; surcease; suspend; throttle; thwart; trap; wait; withhold; STOP(PAGE): **n.** armistice; arrest(ation); arrestment; balk; barrier; block(age); break; cessation; check-(mate); closedown; closing; congestion; cutoff; dam; deactivation; deadlock; delay; discontinuance; discontinuation; end; entanglement; extinction; failure; finish; frustration; halt; hiatus; hitch; hold; impediment; inactivation; intermission; jam; obstacle; obstruction; obturation; occlusion; oppilation; pause; period; plug; quiescence; quietude; recess; rest; retardation; shutdown; sojourn; stall; stand(still); stasis; station; stay; suffocation; suppression; surcease; suspension; throttle; throttling; tie(-up); wait

STOPGAP: expedient; make-do; makeshift; resort; resource; shift; substitute

STOPPER: arrestant; bung; check; cork; pad; plug; shutoff; spile; stopple; tap; wad

STORE: **v.** accumulate; bank; cache; collect; cram; deposit; fill; furnish; heap; hide; hoard; hold; house; husband; keep; load; lodge; pack; place; provide; reserve; save; secrete; secure; stint; stock; stow; supply; thesaurize; treasure; STORE: **n.** abundance; accumulation; bank; bin; boutique; budget; cache; cash; collection; fund; heap; hoard; larder; mart; mine; outlet; pack; post; repertoire; repository; reserve; shop(pe); source; stint; stock; supplies; supply; thesaurus; treasure; treasury

STOREHOUSE *or* STORAGE PLACE: ambry; argosy; armory; arsenal; attic; bank; barn; bin; cache; cupboard; depository; depot; entrepôt; étape; godown; granary; larder; magazine; mine; repertorium; repertory; repository; reserve; reservoir; safe; silo; storeroom; supply; vault; warehouse

STORM: **v.** afflict; attack; besiege; blow; bluster; bombard; burst; flood; fulminate; fume; hail; rage; rain; ramp(age); rant; rush; sleet; snow; surprise; trouble; STORM: **n.** agitation; assault; attack; blast; blizzard; blow; bluster; commotion; convulsion; crisis; cyclone; disturbance; flood; fulmination; gale; gust; hail; hurricane; monsoon; orage; outbreak; outburst; paroxysm; rage; rain; rampage; sleet; snow; squall; stink; tempest; tornado; turbulence; turmoil; twister; typhoon; violence; vortex; whirlwind; wind; STORMY: afflicted; agitated; angry; blustery; cyclonic; fulmin(e)ous; inclement; passionate; procellous; rough; rugged; stark; tempestuous; troubled; troublesome; troublous; turbulent; unruly; wild; windy; STORMINESS: inclemency; tempestivity; tempestuousness; turbulence; turbulency

STORY: account; allegory; analogy; anecdote; article; canard; chronicle; conte; dissertation; epic; essay; étage; fable; falsehood; feature; fib; fiction; floor; gag; history; hoax; iliad; information; jeremiad; legend; libretto; lie; lore; myth; narration; narrative; novel; odyssey; offer; opera; parable; philosophy; play; plot; proposition; recital; record; relation; report; romance; roorback; saga; scenario; screed; skit; statement; tale; thesis; tier; tradition; treatise; version; writing; yarn

STOUT: august; bold; brave; chubby; corpulent; courageous; durable; energetic; fat; firm; fleshy; forceful; full-bodied; healthy; heavy; husky; implacable; large; liparous; lusty; obese; orbicular; plentitudinous; plethoric; plump; portly; powerful; proud; pursy; pyknic; large; replete; resolute; rigid; robust; rotund; solid; stalwart; stanch; stark; stern; strong; sturdy; thick; tough; two-fisted; two-handed; valiant; vigorous; STOUTNESS: chunkiness; corpulence; embonpoint; firmness; fortitude; plethora; ponderosity; portliness; robusticity; thickness; toughness

STOW: (**see** "store") arrange; cache; cram; fill; hide; house; lade; load; lodge; pack; place; reserve; save; set; steeve

STRAGGLER: deserter; maverick; nomad; rover; stray(away); tramp; vagabond; waif

STRAIGHT: **a.** accurate; candid; clean; collinear; correct; direct; distortionless; erect; even; fair; flush; frank; honest; lineal; neat; parallel; perpendicular; ramrod; regular; right; rigid; sequential; severe; smooth; straightforward; true; unbent; uncluttered; undeviated; undeviating; undiluted; uninterrupted; unmixed; unmodified; unwaved; upright; vertical; virtuous; STRAIGHT: **n.** sequence; STRAIGHTEN: adjust; align; aline; compose; correct; extend; rectify; set; square; trim; unbend

STRAIGHTFORWARD: aboveboard; artless; candid; clearcut; direct; forthright; frank; homespun; honest; ingenuous; naïve; natural; open(ly); outspoken; practical; precise; pretenseless; rectitudinous; scrupulous; simple; sincere(ly); square; straightaway; unaffected; undeviating; unmannered; unpretentious; unsophisticated; upright; upstanding

STRAIN: **v.** clean; compress; constrict; exaggerate; exert; exude; filter; force; fray; fret; heave; ooze; overdo; overtax; overwork; percolate; reach; retch; sieve; sift; slave; spring; stress; stretch; strive; tax; tighten; toil; trickle; work; wrench; STRAIN: **n.** anxiety; breed; brunt; burden; coercion; convulsion; drain; effort; exertion; heat; line; melody; overtaxing; overwork; pitch; race; slavery; song; stock; stress; tax; tension; tenterhooks; toil; torque; torture; tune; weight; work; STRAINED: (**see** "farfetched") distorted; excessive; forced; weakened; wrenched; STRAINER: colander; filter; screen; seine; sieve; streak; tamis; trace

STRAIT(S): area; channel; difficulty; isthmus; juncture; narrows; neck; pass; phare; pinch; poverty; rigor; sound; trial

STRAND: **v.** beach; isolate; leave; maroon; STRAND: **n.** bank; beach; coast; cordage; fiber; filament; ply; ripa; rope; sand; shore; string; thread

STRANGE: abnormal; alien; amazing; anomalous; astounding; atypic(al); awesome; bizarre; cold; crazy; curious; distant; eccentric; eerie; erratic; exceptional; exotic; extraordinary; fantastic(al); fascinating; foreign; funny; glamorous; grotesque; heathen; inappropriate; ineffable; inexplicable; irregular; irrelevant; mysterious; mystic(al); new; novel; odd; outlandish; outré; outside; peculiar; picturesque; piquant; preternatural; psychotic; puzzling; quaint; queer; rare; remote; reserved; singular; startling;

striking; surprising; tramontane; unaccountable; unaccustomed; uncanny; unco; uncustomary; unexplicable; unfamiliar; unfrequented; unhabituated; unique; unknown; unnatural; unusual; unversed; wonderful; wondrous; STRANGER: alien; auslander; carpetbagger; foreigner; ger; inconnu; intruder; *novus homo*; outlander; outsider; tramontane; transient; ultramontane; unknown

STRANGLE: check; choke; clog; garrote; hamper; hinder; impede; interfere; obstruct; repress; smother; stifle; stop; suffocate; suppress; throttle; thwart

STRAP: **v.** beat; bind; constrain; constrict; fasten; flog; punish; strop; STRAP: **n.** band; fastener; latigo; leash; leather; ligature; rope; strop; thong

STRATAGEM: artifice; coup; cunning; dodge; finesse; knack; maneuver; plan; play; plot; ploy; ruse; scheme; shift; skill(fulness); subterfuge; trap; trick; wile; STRATEGY: course; method; plan; strategics; tactic(s)

STRATIFIED: **see** "layered"

STRATUM: bed; deposit; division; group; layer; lode; seam; strata (pl.)

STRAW: culm; farthing; fig; omen; sign; snap; stalk; stem; trifle

STRAY: **v.** (**see** "roam") deviate; divagate; divaricate; fall; gad; meander; shift; sin; skid; tumble; turn; veer; wander; STRAY: **a.** (**see** "odd") incidental; occasional; unwanted; STRAY: **n.** aberrant; deserter; maverick; nomad; rover; straggler; stranger; strayaway; tramp; vagabond; waif

STREAK: **v.** dash; line; lineate; mark; rush; striate; stripe; STREAK: **n.** brand; bridle; dart; dash; layer; line; mark; seam; series; shade; strain; stream; stria(tion); strip(e); thread; touch; trace; trait; vein; STREAKED: grizzled; linear(istic); lineate; lined; sick; streaky; striated; striped; upset; veined

STREAM: **v.** channel; drift; emit; exude; flood; flow; flux; pour; run; tide; trail (out); STREAM: **n.** arroyo; bourn(e); branch; brook; burn; cascade; channel; creek; current; downpour; effusion; flood; floss; flow; flux; fork; line; outpouring; ply; tide; torrent; vein; water

STREET: alley; artery; avenue; block; calle;

drive(way); *gade*; highway; iter; land; park(way); place; road(way); *rue*; stem; terrace; thoroughfare; via; way

STRENGTH: ability; ambition; amperage; arm; asset(s); authority; backbone; basis; beef; brawn(iness); cohesion; complement; concentration; constitution; courage; doughtiness; durability; duration; dynamism; effectiveness; efficiency; endurance; energy; force; forte; fortitude; get-up-and-go; gradation; grit; guts; horsepower; influence; integrity; intensity; kilowattage; lustihood; main; means; might; muscle; nourishment; permanency; perseverance; physique; position; potency; power; productiveness; productivity; profoundness; puissance; reinforcement; reserve; resources; robusticity; sand; sinew; soundness; spine; stability; stamina; staying power; steadfastness; sthenia; strenuosity; support; sustenance; tenacity; thew(s); toughness; vehemence; velocity; vigor; vim; violence; virility; virtue; vis; vitality; voltage; volume; wattage; weight; will(power); STRENGTHEN: affirm; aid; anneal; arm; assure; attest; augment; aver; avouch; bolster; brace; buttress; chasten; check; confirm; corroborate; countersign; develop; discipline; educate; encourage; endorse; energize; enhance; enrich; enure; establish; evidence; exercise; fortify; gird; guarantee; harden; hearten; heighten; help; improve; increase; intensify; invigorate; lace; man; mend; munify; notarize; nourish; nurture; prepare; promote; raise; ratify; reassure; recruit; refresh; reinforce; remedy; rise; seal; season; second; solidify; spike; stabilize; stamp; starch; steady; stiffen; support; sustain; swear; temper; testify; tighten; toughen; train; underbrace; undergird; uphold; validate; vitalize; STRENGTHENING: bracing; corroborative; corroboratory; invigorating; reinforcing; roborant; tonic; underbraced

STRENUOUS: (**see** "severe") active; arduous; breathless; eager; energetic; exacting; fervent; hard; Herculean; intense; loud; lusty; mighty; onerous; powerful; rigid; rigorous; rough; strong; tough; vigorous; violent; zealous

STRESS: **v.** accent(uate); emphasize; heighten; highlight; italicize; press; underline; STRESS: **n.** (**see** "strain") accent(uation); beat; brunt; convulsion; emphasis; heat; impetus; importance; intensity; load; pressure; significance; strain; tension; urgency; vehemence; vigor; violence; volume; weight

STRETCH: **v.** amplify; distend; draw; eke; elongate; enlarge; exaggerate; expand; extend; lengthen; lie; protract; pull; reach; run; span; spin; spread; strain; tighten; widen; STRETCH: **n.** distension; elasticity; elongation; exaggeration; expanse; expansion; extent; length(ening); limit; period; protraction; pull; reach; roll; run; scope; sentence; size; space; span; spread; strain; stride; tautness; tension; term; time; trick; width

STRICT: (**see** "severe") accurate; ascetic; astingent; austere; complete; conscientious; cruel; disciplinary; Draconian; exact(ing); extreme; firm; fixed; flinty; forbidding; hard; harsh; grim; inclement; inexorable; inflexible; inhospitable; inquisitorial; intransigent; nice; obdurate; onerous; oppressive; orthodox; overscrupulous; pharisaical; precise; proper; prudish; puritanic(al); relentless; resolute; right; rigid; rigoristic; rigorous; rough; ruthless; scrupulous; Spartan(ic); stark; stern; straight(-laced); stringent; strong; thorough; true; tyrannical; tyrannous; unbending; uncompromising; unfeeling; unkind; unrelenting; unsparing; unswerving; unyielding; vigorous; STRICTNESS: (**see** "severity") ascesis; austereness; austerity; correctitude; exactness; intransigence; obduracy; preciseness; precisianism; precision; puritanism; rigidity; rigor(ism); scrupulosity; scrupulousness; sternness; stringency; tyranny

STRICTURE: **see** "restriction"

STRIDE: advance(ment); distance; march; movement; position; progress(ion); stalk; step; stretch; walk

STRIDENT: blatant; cacophonous; discordant; dissonant; grating; hard; harsh; hoarse; loud; noisy; raucous; rough; shrill; stridulous; uneven

STRIFE: battle; clash; combat; competition; conflict; contention; contest; crusade; difficulty; disaster; discord; dissention; feud; fight; hostility; mutiny; quarrel; rebellion; revolt; riot; spat; struggle; tumult; turmoil; unpeace; violence; war(fare)

STRIKE: **v.** (**see** "hit") bash; bat; bean; beat; buffet; bump; clash; clout; conk; dele(te); discover; drum; expunge; fan; flog; kick; penetrate; percuss; pierce; pound; pummel; punch; ram; rap; slam; slug; smite; sock; spank; stroke; swat; thrust; thump; wallop; whack; wham; STRIKE: **n.** buffet; bump;

clout; conk; impact; kick; percussion; stoppage; walkout; STRIKING: arresting; arrestive; astounding; attractive; brilliant; colorful; colory; conspicuous; daring; dashing; dramatic; eminent; extraordinary; gripping; impressive; interesting; new; notable; noticeable; notorious; novel; obvious; outstanding; percussive; pretty; prominent; remarkable; salient; showy; signal; strange; stunning; surprising; telling; vivid; wonderful

STRING: cable; chain; condition; control; cord; dominion; drove; filament; leash; line; ribbon; rope; row; sequence; series; set; stretch; succession; tendon; thread; tie; torsade; train; twine; wire

STRINGENT: (**see** "severe") binding; bitter; close; compulsory; drawing; rigid; rigorous; rough; sharp; stern; strict; tight

STRIP: **v.** bare; decorticate; defoliate; defrock; denudate; denude; depilate; deplume; deprive; despoil; devastate; disarm; disassemble; disembellish; dismantle; disrobe; divest; expose; fillet; flay; fleece; glean; hull; loot; pare; peel; pick; pluck; plunder; ransack; ravage; reap; remove; reveal; rob; scrape; separate; skin; spoil; strake; uncover; undress; welt; STRIP: **n.** band; fillet; lath; ribbon; skin; slat; stave; stripe; STRIPPING: decortication; defoliation; denudation; desquamation; dismantlement; divestiture; ecdysis; excoriation; exfoliation; peeling; skinning; uncovering; undressing

STRIPE: band; bar; chevron; class; design; fillet; ilk; insigne; insignia (pl.); kidney; kind; line; ribbon; ridge; shade; sort; streak; striation; type; variety; vein; wale; weal; welt; wheal

STRIVE: (**see** "contend") aim; attempt; battle; clamber; climb; combat; compete; contest; cope; crusade; devote; drill; emulate; endeavor; ensue; essay; exert; fight; follow; labor; oppose; preach; pull; quarrel; rival; scramble; strain; struggle; teach; test; toil; try; tussle; vie; work; wrestle

STROKE: **v.** caress; fondle; massage; pet; soothe; strike; swish; touch; STROKE: **n.** apoplexy; beat; blow; caress; coup; dint; effort; feat; hit; ictus; impact; mark; massé; movement; shock; success; swish; touch

STROLL: **v.** amble; bummel; gander; perambulate; promenade; ramble; range; roam; rove; saunter; straggle; walk; wander;

STROLL: **n.** deambulation; perambulation; promenade; ramble; saunter; walk

STRONG: Achillean; adamantine; ardent; athletic; Atlantean; brawny; brisk; bull-headed; bully; castellated; cogent; compelling; concentrated; Cyclopean; Dionysian; doughty; earthshaking; effective; efficient; emphatic; enduring; energetic; extreme; fere; firm; forceful; great; hale; hard(y); harsh; healthy; hefty; Herculean; high-voltage; husky; important; impregnable; indomitable; intense; invincible; iron; leonine; lusty; malign(ant); manful; massive; mighty; muscular; native; numerous; potent; powerful; puissant; putrid; rank; resolute; restless; robust(ious); rotten; rugged; Samsonian; Samsonistic; secure; severe; sinewy; smelly; solid; sound; stable; stalwart; sta(u)nch; stark; steadfast; steady; sthenic; stout; strapping; strenuous; sturdy; superphysical; sure; tenacious; thewy; titanic; tough; two-fisted; two-handed; unassailable; unbending; uncompromising; unconquerable; undiminished; unexhausted; unfatiguing; untirable; untired; unweakened; unwearied; urgent; vigorous; virile; virulent; wealthy; weighty; wieldy; wild; wiry; zealous

STRONGHOLD: (**see** "castle") bastion; blockhouse; breastwork; bulwark; citadel; donjon; fastness; fort(ress); fortification; garrison; keep; muniment; redan; redoubt; refuge; safe

STRUCTURE: accomplishment; anatomy; architecture; arrangement; babel; bones; building; cadre; carpentry; components; configuration; conformation; economy; edifice; fabrication; feature; form(at); framework; lineament; makeup; meat; organ-(ization); scheme; skeleton; stroma; support; system; texture; tissue; work; STRUCTURAL: anatomical; constitutional; constructional; edificial; organic; skeletal; skeletonic; systemic; tectonic; textural

STRUGGLE: **v.** (**see** "contend") agonize; aim; clamber; climb; combat; contest; cope; debate; endeavor; fight; founder; haul; heave; hobble; justle; labor; paw; pull; quarrel; scramble; strive; toil; try; tug; vie; wrestle; writhe; STRUGGLE: **n.** agony; aim; clamber; colluctation; contention; contest; effort; endeavor; exertion; fight; hassle; pull; scramble; strife; sword; throe(s); tug (-of-war); war(fare)

STRUT: **see** "swagger"

STUBBORN: absonant; adamant(ine); balky; bellicose; bulldog(ged); bulldoggish; bull-doggy; calculated; callous; cantankerous; chronic; close-minded; cold-blooded; cold-hearted; confirmed; contemptuous; contrary; contumacious; contumelious; cross-grained; crotchety; dedolent; defiant; despotic; determined; dictatorial; difficult; disdainful; disobedient; dogged; dogmatic(al); emotional; enduring; *entêté*; firm; fixed; flint-hearted; flinty; fractious; game; glassy; hard(-boiled); hardened; hardhearted; hard-shell(ed); harsh; headstrong; hidebound; immalleable; immovable; impassive; impenitent; impertinent; impiteous; implacable; impregnable; incompliant; inconsiderate; indifferent; indocile; indomitable; inductile; indurate(d); indurative; inexorable; inexpiable; inflexible; insensible; insensitive; insubordinate; insusceptible; intractable; intransient; inured; inveterate; iron-(bound); ironclad; irreconcilable; maverick; monolithic; muleheaded; mulish; noncompliant; obdurate; obstinate; obtuse; opinionated; oppositious; ornery; pachydermatous; peremptory; perseverant; persevering; persistent; pertinacious; perverse; pervicacious; pigheaded; rebellious; recalcitrant; refractory; reluctant; renitent; resistant; resolute; resolved; restive; restrictive; right; rigid; rigorous; rude; rugged; sta(u)nch; stiff-necked; stony; strong(-minded); sulky; sullen; superior; tenacious; thick(ened); thick-skinned; tough; unaffected; unalterable; unamenable; unassailable; unbudgeable; unbudging; unchangeable; uncompliant; uncompromising; unconquerable; uncontrollable; uncooperative; unfeeling; unmanageable; unmoved; unmoving; unreasonable; unreconcilable; unreconstructed; unregenerate(d); unremitting; unrepentant; unresponsive; unruly; unshakable; unswerving; unsympathetic; unteachable; untoward; unwavering; unwillful; unwilling; unyielding; STUBBORNNESS: adamancy; balkiness; bullheadedness; cantankerousness; contrariety; contrariness; contumaciousness; contumacy; contumely; cross-grainedness; crotchiness; cussedness; defiance; determination; disobedience; fixedness; friction; hardness; impenitence; impenitency; incompliance; indifference; induration; inflexibility; insensibility; insensitivity; intractability; intractableness; intransigence; mulishness; noncompliance; obduracy; obstinacy; opposition; persistency; pertinacity; perseverance; perverseness; perversity; pigheadedness; recalcitrance; renitency; resistance; rudeness; toughness; unbudgeability; unwillingness; wilfulness

STUCK: caught; fast(ened); fixed; frozen; glued; mired

STUD: boss; horse; knob; nail; prop; rivet; scantling; spur; support; upright

STUDENT: academician; academist; beginner; cadet; candidate; coed; colleger; collegian(er); collegiate; collegienne (fem.); disciple; educatee; learner; plebe; puisne; pupil; recruit; scholar; scholastic; trainee; tyro; undergraduate

STUDIO: atelier; laboratory; office; room; shop; study; workshop

STUDY: **v.** analyze; bone; con(sider); contemplate; debate; deliberate; design; devise; endeavor; examine; experiment; eye; gaze; investigate; learn; look; lucubrate; meditate; muse; plan; plot; ponder; pore; prepare; prosecute; reason; reflect; research; scan; speculate; test; think; watch; weigh; STUDY: **n.** absorption; abstraction; analysis; application; atelier; concentration; contemplation; curriculum; deliberation; den; discipline; endeavor; examination; exercise; inventory; investigation; learning; library; lucubration; meditation; monograph; office; paper; plan; prosecution; purpose; reason(ing); reflection; research; room; self-enrichment; sketch; speculation; studio; subject; training; STUDIOUS: (**see** "bookish") analytical; assiduous; clerkly; contemplative; diligent; investigative; meditative; thoughtful

STUFF: **v.** choke; chuck; clutter; cram; crowd; distend; expand; fill; gorge; gormandize; insert; overeat; pack; pad; plug; poke; press; ram; sate; satiate; stodge; stow; surfeit; thrust; tuck; wad; STUFF: **n.** character; cloth(ing); commodity; copy; crop; equipment; essence; fabric; folderol; material; matter; merchandise; money; nonsense; paste; possessions; potion; quality; speed; structure; substance; supplies; texture; timber; STUFFED: copious; gorged; gormandized; packed; replete; sated; satiated; surfeited

STUFFY: close; crammed; dry; dull; heavy; ill-humored; narrow; provincial; self-righteous; stale; stiff; stodgy; sullen; thick; uninteresting

STUMBLE: (**see** "trip") blunder; err; fall; falter; lurch; mispronounce; stagger; stammer; titubate; totter

STUN: amaze; anesthetize; astonish; astound; benumb; besot; bewilder; blunt; confound; confuse; daze; dazzle; deaden; dope; drown; drug; dull; flabbergast; numb; overwhelm; pall; paralyze; perplex; petrify; shock; stupefy; surprise; wither; STUNNING: astonishing; astounding; attractive; beautiful; dazzling; deafening; fine; first-rate; good-looking; grand; handsome; horrifying; impressive; sensational; shocking; startling; strange; striking; stupefying; surprising; wonderful

STUNT: **v.** arrest; atrophy; choke; cramp; crowd; dwarf; retard; sap; showoff; stifle; stint; suppress; weaken; STUNT: **n.** acrobatics; act; feat; forte; gag; joke; performance; prestidigitation; sting; *tour de force*; trick; STUNTED: arrested; atrophied; checked; cramped; crowded; dwarfed; retarded; scrub(by); small; undergrown; weakened

STUPEFY: (**see** "stun") amaze; anesthetize; astonish; astound; benumb; besot; bewilder; blunt; daze; dazzle; deaden; dope; drug; dull; flabbergast; gorgonize; intoxicate; maze; muddle; numb; overwhelm; pall; paralyze; petrify; shock; STUPEFIED: **see** "aghast"

STUPENDOUS: (**see** "monstrous") awesome; marvelous; prodigious

STUPID: Abderian; addlebrained; addlepated; anserine; anserous; asinine; baboonish; batty; blank; blockheaded; blockish; blunt; Boeotian; boring; bovine; brutish; childish; chuckleheaded; claybrained; cloddish; clodpated; clumsy; crass; dense; dimwitted; doltish; dreary; dull; dull-witted; dumb; empty; fatheaded; fatuous; flat; foolish; footless; gaumless; half-baked; half-cocked; half-cracked; half-witted; heavy; hebetate; hebetudinous; idiotic; ignorant; imbecile; imbecilic; imperceptive; inane; inanimate; inept; insensate; insensible; insensitive; irrational; loutish; meaningless; moronic; nonsensical; nutty; oafish; obtuse; opaque; oscitant; pinheaded; purblind; rank; senseless; sheeplike; silly; simple(minded); sluggish; stolid; stuprous; thickheaded; thickskulled; thoughtless; torpid; unimaginative; unintelligent; unsmart; unthinking; vacuous; void; witless; STUPIDITY: absurdity; baboonery; *balourdise*; *bêtise*; crassitude; dumbness; fatuity; hebetation; hebetude; idiocy; ignorance; imbecility; impercipience; inanity; ineptitude; insanity; insipience; irrationality; lunacy; meaninglessness; moronity; nonsense; obtuseness; obtusity; oscitancy; senselessness; simple-mindedness; slowness; stolidity; stubbornness; stupidity; stupor; thoughtlessness; torpidity; torpor; witlessness

STUPOR: anesthesia; anesthetic; apathy; asphyxia; catalepsy; coma; daze; faint; hypnosis; insensibility; intoxication; lethargy; mazement; narcosis; numbness; sopor; stupefaction; swoon; syncope; torpor; trance; STUPOROUS: anesthetic; apathetic; cataleptic; comatose; hypnotic; insensible; lethargic; narcose; narcotic; opiate; somniferous; soporific; stupefactive; stuporose; unconscious

STURDY: athletic; brawny; enduring; firm; hale; hardy; hearty; lusty; muscular; powerful; pyknic; resistant; resolute; roborant; robust(ious); rough; rude; rugged; rustic; solid; sound; stalwart; stocky; stout; strong; substantial; thickset; unswerving; vigorous; yeomanly

STY: boil; hordeolum; pen; piggery; pimple; pustule; quat; rising; shed

STYLE: v. call; designate; dress; entitle; fashion; form; name; stylize; term; title; STYLE: n. appearance; art; attitude; characteristic; cry; custom; designation; diction; distinction; dress; expression; fad; fashion; form(alism); genre; graver; individuality; manner; mode; name; order; pattern; pen; rage; shape; stylus; taste; technique; title; ton; tool; trend; type; vehicle; vogue; work; STYLED: called; designated; entitled; formed; informed; named; titled; yclept; STYLISH: a la mode; *bon ton*; chic; dapper; dashing; doggy; dressy; elegant; fashionable; fastidious; genteel; jaunty; modish; natty; nice; nifty; patterned; posh; *recherché*; sassy; sharp; sleek; smart; *soigné*; *soignée* (fem.); suave; swanky; tasteful; well-groomed; STYLISHNESS: *bon ton*; *dernier cri*; elegance; fashionableness; gentility; mode; nattiness; posh; suavity; taste

STYMIE: balk; block; check; defeat; deter; impede; stop; thwart

SUAVE: (see "stylish") affable; bland; *coulant*; diplomatic; genial; genteel; gracious; ingratiating; mannered; modish; oily; oleaginous; pleasant; polite; politic; silky; sleek; smooth; soapy; soft-spoken; *soigné*; *soignée* (fem.); sophisticated; svelte; unctuous; urbane; SUAVITY: agreeableness; attractiveness; amenity; diplomacy; fra-

grance; geniality; mildness; oiliness; pleasantness; polish; propriety; unctuosity; urbanity

SUBDIVISION: arrondissement; department; development; group; paragraph; part; phase; portion; proportion; quantity; ramification; unit; ward

SUBDUE: (see "defeat") awe; beat; break; calm; censor; charm; conquer; cow; crush; curb; daunt; depress; dim; down; dull; eclipse; flatter; K.O.; lick; master; outdo; outfight; outfox; outsmart; overcome; overmaster; overmatch; overwhelm; pacify; quash; quell; reduce; repress; rout; sober; soften; subjugate; subordinate; suppress; surmount; tame; tread; underplay; vanquish; win; SUBDUED: (see "restrained") mild; unviolent

SUBJECT: v. (see "defeat") conquer; enthrall; experience; expose; predispose; subjugate; submit; sustain; take; undergo; SUBJECT: a. accountable; answerable; apt; chargeable; content; disposed; liable; likely; obedient; open; predisposed; prone; servile; subservient; susceptible; SUBJECT: n. basis; cause; citizen; follower; ground; issue; item; liege; motive; point; problem; proposition; propositus; protégé; question; reason; servant; study; subordinate; subservient; substance; text; theme; topic; vassal

SUBJECTION: (see "oppression") repression; tyranny; yoke

SUBJECTIVE: emotional; fanciful; illusory; imaginary; imaginative; inner; intellectual; introspective; pectoral; personal; psychic; psychological; psychosomatic; spiritual

SUBJOIN: (see "add") affix; annex; append; attach; unite

SUBJUGATE: (see "defeat") beat; break; conquer; cow; crush; depress; enslave; lick; master; overawe; overcome; overwhelm; subdue; subject; tame

SUBLIME: divine; ecstatic; elevated; eminent; empyreal; empyrean; exalted; excellent; good; grand; great; happy; heavenly; high; ideal; intellectual; joyous; lofty; magnanimous; magnificent; majestic; noble; notable; outstanding; rapturous; solemn; spiritual; stately; supreme; transcendent; SUBLIMITY: divinity; ecstasy; elevation; eminence; empyrean; exaltation; grandeur; grandiloquence; grandiosity; happiness; heaven; joy-

(ousness); magnanimity; magnificence; majesty; nobility; rapture; raptus; solemnity; stateliness; transport

SUBMIT: abide; acquiesce; allow; bear; bend; bow; break; brook; capitulate; cede; comply; cringe; defer; genuflect; give; let; lower; obey; offer; permit; present; receive; refer; relent; render; resign; soften; subdue; succumb; suffer; suggest; supply; surrender; truckle; yield; SUBMISSION: acquiescence; allowance; capitulation; compliance; deference; obedience; permission; prostration; reception; resignation; report; servitude; slavishness; sufferance; surrender; vail; yield(ing); SUBMISSIVE: (see "subservient") amenable; cringing; deferential; fawning; genuflectory; humble; menial; obedient; obsequious; penitent; predisposed; resigned; servile; slavish; subject; tame; teachable; tractable; truckling; unerect; yielding; SUBMISSIVENESS: acquiescence; amenability; deferentiality; fatalism; genuflexion; humbleness; humility; inertia; obsequiousness; obsequity; patience; receptivity; resignation; susceptibility; surrender; tractability

SUBNORMAL: deficient; dwarfish; lacking; low(er); smaller; subliminal; suboptimal; substandard; undersize(d)

SUBORDINATE(D): a. (see "below") adjective; adjunct; adverbial; ancillary; auxiliary; beneath; down(ward); inferior; lower; menial; neath; nether; puisne; satellite; satellitic; secondary; second-string; servile; slow; subalternate; subject; submissive; subservient; subsidiary; tangential; under(lying); undermost; underneath; vassal; SUBORDINATE: n. aide; ancilla(ry); assistant; auxiliary; cog(wheel); employee; inferior; lieutenant; minion; parergon; protégé; satellite; scrub; second fiddle; second-string; servile; slave; subaltern(ate); subalternation; subalternity; subordination; subserviency; subservient; subsidiary; substitute; vassal

SUBSCRIBER: see "backer"

SUBSERVIENT: a. (see "submissive") cringing; fawning; menial; ministerial; obedient; obeisant; obsequious; oily; servile; slavish; subalternate; subject; subordinate; subsidiary; sycophantic; truckling; unctuous; unemancipated; SUBSERVIENT: n. see "subordinate"

SUBSIDE: (see "ease") abate; decrease; descend; die; dim(inish); ebb; fall; languish; lapse; lower; precipitate; recede; relapse; set(tle); sink; slacken; slow; stop; tranquilize; wane

SUBSIDIARY: a. (see "contingent") accessory; adjuvant; ancillary; auxiliary; contributory; derivative; minor; satellite; satellitic; secondary; segmental; segmentary; subordinate; subservient; succursal; supplemental; supplementary; tangential; tributary; SUBSIDIARY: n. (see "assistant") auxiliary; branch; child; client; collateral; contingent; dependent; derivative; disciple; hanger-on; minion; retainer; satellite; sponger; subordinate; subservient; tributary; vassal

SUBSIDY: addition; aid; allowance; annuity; bonus; bounty; bribe; endowment; gift; grant; gratuity; indemnity; money; payment; pension; premium; reward; subvention; support; tribute

SUBSIST: be; board; continue; eat; exist; fare; feed; hold; live; maintain; obtain; persist; remain; reside; succor; survive

SUBSTANCE: aspect; basis; characteristic; compound; constituent; content; corporality; corporeity; element; entity; essence; estate; factor; fiber; flesh; form; gist; ground(s); heart; import; ingredient; intent; majority; mass; material(ity); matter; meat; mixture; nature; part; possessions; property; quality; reality; resource(s); riches; sense; staple(s); subject; substratum; sum; tenor; texture; wealth; weight; worth(iness); SUBSTANTIAL: abundant; corporeal; essential; firm; formidable; full-bodied; fundamental; great; heavy; important; lasting; massive; material; meaty; plenteous; plentiful; ponderable; real; solid; square; substantive; true; wealthy; wearing; weighty; well-to-do; SUBSTANTIALITY: corporeality; corporeity; heaviness; massiveness; massivity; physicality; solidarity; solidity; weightiness

SUBSTANTIATE: (see "prove") validate; verify; vouch

SUBSTANTIVE: a. (see "substantial") categorematic; firm; lasting; self-contained; solid; SUBSTANTIVE: n. entity; noun; pronoun

SUBSTITUTE: v. alternate; change; commute; exchange; interchange; replace; supersede; supplant; swap; trade; SUBSTITUTE: a. cheaper; ersatz; *faute de mieux*; inferior; secondary; shoddy; standby;

SUBSTITUTE: **n.** alternate; alternative; backup; bench warmer; change; commutation; deputy; ersatz; expedient; follower; heir; helper; Hobson's choice; *locum tenens;* means; proxy; *quid pro quo*; relief; replacement; resource; second; standby; stand-in; stopgap; sub; succedaneum; successor; surrogate; understudy; vice; SUBSTITUTED: changed; exchanged; replaced; substitutional; substitutionary; substitutive; succedaneous; supplanted; SUBSTITUTION: change; exchange; replacement; shift; surrogation; trade; vicariousness

SUBTERFUGE: (**see** "trick") artifice; blind; chicane; deception; duplicity; evasion; excuse; fraud; prestidigitation; pretense; ruse; shift; stratagem

SUBTERRANEAN: abysmal; chthonic; dark; hidden; nether; plutonic; secret; sunk; underneath

SUBTILE *or* SUBTLE: airy; alembicated; artful; cautious; crafty; delicate; devious; elusive; ethereal; gradual; imperceptible; ingenious; insidious; intangible; perceptive; rarefied; refined; skillful; sly; sophisticated; tactful; tenuous; underhand(ed); unobtrusive; wary; wily; witty

SUBTRACT: **see** "deduct"

SUBURB(AN): **a.** rural; urban; SUBURB(S): **n.** *banlieue(x)*; environ(s); faubourg; outskirts; purlieu(s); suburbia; town; vicinity

SUBVENTION: (**see** "subsidy") aid; bounty; endowment; grant

SUBVERT: (**see** "corrupt") alienate; confute; defeat; demolish; destroy; extinguish; gainsay; honeycomb; infiltrate; invert; overset; overthrow; overturn; pervert; raze; ruin; sabotage; sap; supersede; supplant; suppress; topple; undermine; unhorse; upset; weaken

SUCCEED: accomplish; achieve; acquire; arrange; arrive; attain; click; conquer; control; contrive; create; effect; ensue; fashion; flourish; follow; forge; gain; get; go; guide; happen; manipulate; move; obtain; occur; pass; prevail; procure; progress; prosper; prove; reach; realize; reap; relieve; replace; shape; supplant; triumph; win; work; SUCCESS: accomplishment; achievement; attainment; control; éclat; fame; find; flourish; fortune; gain; hit; killing; luck; position; progress; prosperity; realization; smash; *succès fou*; thrift; triumph; wealth;

wow; SUCCESSFUL: affirmative; famed; famous; favorable; fortunate; happy; lucky; prosperous; thrifty; triumphant

SUCCESSIVE: alphabetical; arow; categorical; consecutive; hereditary; repetitive; sequacious; sequential; serial; seriate; subsequential; succedent; SUCCESSION: alternance; alternation; catenation; chain; consecution; course; descendants; dynasty; genealogy; generation; inheritance; line; march; order; parade; posterity; progression; rotation; row; sequacity; sequence; series; string; subsequence; successivity; successorship; SUCCESSOR(S): (**see** "substitute") descendant; follower; heir; progeny; relief; replacement; substitution; surrogate

SUCCINCT: blunt; brief; close-fitting; compact; compressed; concise; crisp; curt; laconic; pithy; sententious; short(ened); terse; witty

SUCCOR: **v.** aid; assist; help; nurse; nurture; relieve; serve; SUCCOR: **n.** (**see** "assistance" and "food") reinforcement(s); rescue; secours; subsistence; substance; sustenance

SUCCULENT: delicious; fresh; juicy; lush; nutritive; pappy; rich; sappy; tender

SUCCUMB: bow; capitulate; cease; collapse; defer; die; fail; fall; lose; sag; sink; submit; surrender; wilt; yield

SUCK: absorb; devitalize; draw; drink; engulf; exhaust; imbibe; lap; lick; nurse; suckle; SUCKING: paratrophic; young

SUCTION: absorption; draw; exhaust; intake

SUDDEN(LY): **a.** or **adv.** alert; *à l'improviste*; abrupt; early; expeditious; extemporaneous; extemporary; fast(-moving); hasty; headlong; imminent; mushroomlike; precipitate; precipitous; presto; quick(ly); rapid; rash; snap(py); soon; subitaneous; swift(ly); unexpected(ly); unforeseen; unprepared

SUDS: barm; beer; bubbles; foam; froth; lather; scum; soap(suds); yeast

SUE: appeal; ask; beg; claim; court; entreat; follow; implore; petition; plead; ply; pray; prosecute; seek; solicit; woo

SUFFER: abide; ache; acquiesce; admit; agonize; allow; bear; bide; bleed; brave; brook; continue; droop; encounter; endure; experience; feel; gain; grieve; hurt; know;

labor; languish; learn; let; meet; pain; permit; realize; receive; sample; see; smart; stand; starve; stomach; subject; submit; support; sustain; test; tolerate; twinge; undergo; use; writhe; SUFFERING: **a.** (**see** "painful") ill; sick; SUFFERING: **n.** ache; affliction; agony; calamity; cost; cruciation; distress; evil; excruciation; extremity; grief; grievance; hurt; illness; languishment; pain; pang; rack; resignation; sickness; torment; torture; trial; tribulation; SUFFERABLE: (**see** "tolerable") bearable

SUFFICE: (**see** "serve") appease; do; last; satisfy

SUFFICIENT: abundant; adequate; ample; bastant; commensurate; competent; decent; due; enough; enow; equipollent; equiponderant; fair; fine; fit(ting); full; good; meet; passable; plenteous; plentiful; plenty; proper; resourceful; satisfactory; satisfying; suitable; SUFFICIENCY: (**see** "adequacy") ability; adequateness; capacity; confidence; competence; competency; satisfaction; suitability

SUFFIX: (**see** "add") affix; attach; subjoin

SUFFOCATE: asphyxiate; burke; choke; die; garrote; impede; smother; stifle; stop; strangle

SUFFRAGE: approval; assent; ballot; consensus; franchise; petition; prayer; sanction; voice; vote

SUFFUSE: bathe; blush; color; cover; flush; imbue; infuse; overspread; pour; saturate; spill; spread; wash; wrap

SUGAR: biose; ketose; sucrose

SUGGEST: adumbrate; advise; allude; connote; cue; denote; evoke; hint; implicate; imply; import; indicate; insinuate; inspire; intimate; invite; mention; moot; name; offer; proffer; prompt; propose; propound; recommend; seduce; shadow; speak; submit; summon; tempt; whisper; SUGGESTION: advice; allusion; cast; clue; color; connotation; cue; dash; denotation; design; evocation; hair; hint; hue; idea; implication; inkling; innuendo; insinuation; insinuendo; intimation; invitation; litigation; motion; notion; offer; opinion; overtone; plan; proffer; project; prompting; proposal; proposition; prospect(us); reminder; scheme; shade; shadow; smattering; soupçon; suspicion; tang; technique; tinge; tip; touch;

trace; umbrage; whisker; whisper; wrinkle; SUGGESTIVE: connotative; evocative; expressive; indicative; insinuative; meaningful; off-color; pregnant; provocative; racy; reminiscent; risqué; seminal; significant

SUICIDE: *felo-de-se*; self-destruction; SUICIDAL: brash; deadly; destructive; fatal; foolish; lethal; rash; self-destructive

SUIT: **v.** accommodate; adapt; adjust; agree; attire; become; befit; cause; costume; count; dress; fit; square; SUIT: **n.** action; agreement; appeal; attire; case; clothing; costume; courtship; dress; entreaty; habit; harmony; outfit; petition; prosecution; request; series; set; supplication; trial; wooing; SUITABLE: acceptable; adaptable; adap(ta)tive; a-dapted; adequate; applicable; apposite; appropriate; apropos; apt; becoming; befitting; calculated; comely; commensurate; comfortable; condign; congruent; congruous; consonant; convenient; creditable; decorous; desirable; due; equal; expedient; felicitous; fit(ted); fitting; handy; ideal; idoneous; level; likely; meet; open; opportune; pat; pertinent; plausible; presentable; proper; qualified; relative; relevant; right; seasonable; seemly; semblable; sufficient; suited; timely; usable; SUITABILITY: (**see** "fitness") adaptability; adaptitude; appropriateness; aproposity; aptness; compatibility; creditability; decency; expediency; fitness; idoneity; opportuneness; patness; plausibility; propriety; qualification; rightness; sufficiency; timeliness

SUITE: chain; company; convoy; cortege; escort; followers; furniture; group; retinue; rooms; sequel; series; set; staff; string; train

SUITOR: admirer; amoroso; appellant; beau; flame; litigant; lover; petitioner; pleader; steady; swain; sweetheart; wooer

SULK: cry; frown; grieve; huff; mope; moue; pet; pout; scowl; SULKY: **a.** (**see** "sullen") doggish; grouchy; inactive; pettish; sluggish; SULKY: **n.** carriage; gig; perambulator; plow

SULLAGE: (**see** "waste") drainage; dross; mud; refuse; scoria; sewage; silt

SULLEN: atrabiliar; churlish; crabbed; crabby; cross; dismal; doggish; dour; gloomy; glowering; glum; grim; grouchy; grumpy; ill-humored; irascible; lowering; melancholy; moody; morose; obstinate; peevish;

pettish; pouty; refractory; sad; saturnine; somber; sour; splenetic; stubborn; sulky; surly; unsociable; vinegary; SULLENNESS: churlishness; dismality; gloom; irascibility; melancholy; moodiness; morosity; peevishness; sadness; saturninity; spleen; surliness; unsociability

SULTRY: burning; close; coarse; damp; dank; hot; humid; lurid; miasmic; moist; muggy; oppressive; passionate; scabrous; sensual; sexy; stifling; still; stuffy; sulfurous; sweltering; torrid; tropical; voluptuous

SUM: **v.** add; cast; figure; foot; number; recap; total; SUM: **n.** (**see** "amount") addition; aggregate; complement; entirety; epitome; figure; gist; height; limit; mint; money; number; price; purse; quantity; recapitulation; result(ant); stipend; substance; summation; summit; total(ity); whole

SUMMARIZE: abbreviate; abridge; abstract; add; brief; digest; embody; epitomize; recap(itulate); synopsize; tabulate; typify; SUMMARY: **a.** abbreviated; abridged; abstracted; brief; concise; cursory; desultory; drumhead; elliptic(al); fast; hasty; immediate; informal; speedy; quick(ly); succinct; superficial; tabulate; terse; SUMMARY: **n.** abbreviation; abridgement; abstract; account; addition; breviary; breviate; brief; capsule; compend(ium); conclusion; conspectus; digest; epitome; pandect; précis; prospectus; recap(itulation); restatement; résumé; schema; schemata (pl.); score; summarization; summation; syllabus; synopsis; table; tabulation; truncation; view; wrap-up

SUMMIT: acme; apex; apogee; arete; cap; climacteric; climacterium; climax; comb; completion; consummation; crest; crown; culmination; elevation; end; height; high tide; meridian; mountain; noon; peak; pinnacle; point; ridge; roof; spire; sum; tip; top(gallant); vertex; zenith

SUMMON: arouse; bid; call; cite; command; conjure; convene; convoke; entreat; evocate; evoke; gesture; hail; implore; incite; invite; invoke; muster; order; raise; rally; recall; signal; subpoena; suggest; wave; whistle

SUMPTUOUS: (**see** "grand" and "rich") luxurious; magnificent; opulent; superb

SUN: **v.** apricate; bask; illume; irradiate; luxuriate; shine; SUN: **n.** climate; day; glory; luminary; parhelion; power; Sol; splendor;

star; SUNNY: **see** "cheerful" and "optimistic"

SUNDER: break; cleave; disunite; divide; part; rend; rive; separate; sever; split

SUNSET: crepuscle; curfew; decline; dusk; evening; nightfall; sunglow; twilight

SUPERABUNDANCE: (**see** "excess") flood; gob(s); lot(s); overflow; plenty; plethora; redundance; redundancy; superfluity; surplus

SUPERANNUATED: (**see** "old") aged; anile; antiquated; antique; decrepit; disqualified; passé; retired; senescent; senile

SUPERB: (**see** "elegant") extra; fine; golden; gorgeous; graceful; grand; majestic; posh; rich; royal; stately; sumptuous; superfine; super(ior); ultra

SUPERFICIAL: casual; cursory; depthless; desultory; external; facile; fleeting; flimsy; formal; glib; hasty; idle; incondite; light; one-dimensional; partial; passing; sciolistic; shallow; sketchy; skin-deep; sophomoric; specious; summary; surface; surficial; tenuous; SUPERFICIALITY: flimsiness; inanity; shallowness; sketchiness; speciosity; tenuosity; triviality; veneer

SUPERFINE: (**see** "elegant") choice; deluxe; excellent; extra(ordinary); luxurious; nice; plush; posh; prime; rich; superb; superior

SUPERFLUOUS: (**see** "excessive") copious; *de trop*; elaborate; exaggerated; exceeding; exorbitant; extra(vagant); extreme; flooded; flooding; frilly; gaudy; gingerbread; immoderate; improvident; incredible; inexhaustible; inordinate; intemperate; irrational; lavish; luxurious; melodramatic; needless; nimious; nonessential; ostentatious; over(flowing); prodigal; profligate; profuse; rampant; rash; reckless; recrementitious; redundant; showy; spare; superabundant; supererogatory; surplus; thick; uncommon; unending; unreasonable; unrestrained; wasteful; wild; SUPERFLUITY: (**see** "excess") bountifulness; copiosity; copiousness; enthusiasm; exaggeration; excessiveness; excrescence; exorbitance; extravagance; flood; frill; furbelow; gingerbread; grandiosity; immoderation; improvidence; intemperance; magnificence; nimiety; ornamentation; ostentation; over(flowing); plethora; prodigality; profligacy; rampancy; redundance; superabundance; superflux; unreasonableness; unrestraint; wantonness; waste(fulness)

SUPERHUMAN: divine; extrahuman; extraordinary; gigantic; Herculean; supernatural; uncanny

SUPERINTEND: (see "supervise") boss; conduct; control; direct; guide; lead; nurse; oversee; regulate; SUPERINTENDENT: see "superior" and "supervisor"

SUPERIOR: **a.** above; antidemocratic; aristocratic; best; better; capital; chief; distinguished; dominant; eminent; excellent; exceptional; fine(r); finest; first-class; first-rate; five-star; foremost; formidable; Grade A; grander; greater; haughty; high-class; higher; high-grade; high-level; important; lordly; magisterial; magistratical; master; meritorious; noted; outstanding; over(most); palmy; paramount; plushy; precedent(ial); predominant; preeminent; preferable; prepotent; ruling; seeded; significant; snobbish; sovereign; spiritual; supercilious; supereminent; supernal; supernatural; superordinary; superordinate; surpassing; unyielding; upper; useful; valuable; victorious; SUPERIOR: **n.** (see "leader") boss; chief; director; employer; overseer; sovereign; supervisor; teacher; victor; SUPERIORITY: advantage; conspicuity; dominance; domination; dominion; *dominium directum*; edge; eminence; excellence; haughtiness; hauteur; lead; majority; mastership; mastery; meliority; odds; precedence; predominance; predomination; preeminence; preponderance; preponderation; prominence; quality; sovereignty; success; superciliousness; supereminence; supremacy; transcendence; victory; worth(iness)

SUPERLATIVE: **a.** (see "superior") cardinal; choice; consummate; eminent; exaggerated; excellent; excessive; exquisite; greatest; highest; incomparable; leading; peak; peerless; pluperfect; prepotent; signal; sovereign; supernal; supreme; transcendent; ultra; unsurpassed; utmost; SUPERLATIVE: **n.** acme; peak; supereminence; supernaculum; utmost

SUPERNATURAL: abnormal; charismatic; dark; divine; earthly; eerie; excessive; extrahuman; extraphysical; extrasensory; extreme; ghostly; hyperphysical; incorporeal; magic; marvelous; metaphysical; miracular; miraculous; mystic(al); numinous; obscure; occult; paraphysical; parapsychological; preternatural; psychic; secret; spectral; superhuman; superior; supermundane; supernormal; supranormal; transcendent(al); unknowable; unknown; weird

SUPERSEDE: annul; defer; displace; follow; forbear; omit; override; replace; substitute; supplant; void

SUPERSTITION: (see "fear") idolatry

SUPERVISE: boss; chaperone; conduct; control; counsel; direct; discipline; educate; engineer; guide; inspect; instruct; invigilate; lead; manage; nurse; oversee; proctor; regulate; scrutinize; superintend; survey; teach; train; SUPERVISORY: disciplinary; instructive; managerial; proctorial; supervisorial; surveillant; SUPERVISOR: (see "leader") boss; chairman; chaperone; chief; director; employer; engineer; guide; head; instructor; manager; master; monitor; proctor; regent; superintendent; superior; surveillant; teacher; trainer; warden; SUPERVISION: chairmanship; chaperonage; invigilation; mastery; oversight; proctorship; superintendence; surveillance; survey

SUPINE: abed; abject; apathetic; horizontal; inactive; indifferent; indolent; inert; languid; lazy; lethargic; listless; otiose; prone; prostrate; recumbent; servile; slothful; sluggish; torpid

SUPPLANT: see "displace"

SUPPLE: adaptable; agile; complacent; complaisant; compliant; easy; flexible; fluent; gracile; limber; lissom(e); lithe(some); nimble; obsequious; pliable; pliant; responsive; soft; submissive; yielding; SUPPLENESS: ease; elasticity; flexibility; gracility; lissomeness; litheness; lithesomeness; submission

SUPPLEMENT: **v.** (see "add") displace; eke; implement; substitute; supplant; SUPPLEMENT: **n.** (see "appendix") addenda (pl.); addendum; additament; addition; adjunct; annex(ation); annexion; pendant; postscript; sequel; SUPPLEMENTAL or SUPPLEMENTARY: accessorial; accessory; additional; addititious; adjunctive; adjuvant; adminicular; adscititious; ancillary; associated; auxiliary; complemental; complementary; consequential; contributory; corollary; corroborative; equivalent; resulting; succenturiate; supervenient

SUPPLICATE: (see "beg") abjure; appeal; ask; beseech; conjure; crave; entreat; implore; importune; petition; plead; pray; request; sue; SUPPLICATION: adjuration; appeal; ave; entreaty; imploration; importunity; imprecation; litany; obsecration; petition; plea; prayer; request; rogation; solicitation; suit

SUPPLY: **v.** accommodate; aid; cater; contribute; donate; dose; endue; equip; feed; fertilize; fill; fulfill; furnish; give; help; lend; loan; occupy; outfit; participate; pour; prescribe; provide; relieve; replace; serve; stock; vouchsafe; SUPPLY *or* SUPPLIES: **n.** accumulation; affluence; aid; amount; arms; arsenal; bank; cache; cash; feed; food; fund(s); goods; grist; help; inventory; items; maintenance; material(s); mine; mint; ordnance; pool; provisions; quantity; relief; reserves; reservoir; resources; riches; spate; stock; store(s); storehouse; stream; stuff; succession; support; wad; warehouse; wares; wealth

SUPPORT: **v.** abet; accompany; adopt; advocate; aid; anchor; applaud; approve; assist; attend; back; base; bear; board; bolster; boost; brace; bracket; buoy; buttress; carry; champion; comfort; corroborate; countenance; countersign; convey; cushion; defend; embolden; embrace; encourage; endorse; endure; espouse; fasten; favor; feed; fire; follow; freshen; fuel; further; gird; grubstake; guard; help; hold; invigorate; join; keep; lace; maintain; patronize; pin; prepare; preserve; promote; prop; provide; recommend; refresh; reinforce; sanction; second; shore; side; spike; sponsor; stake; stand; steel; stiffen; strengthen; subsidize; substantiate; suffer; suggest; supply; sustain; tie; tolerate; transmit; transport; truss; undergird; underlay; underlie; underpin; underprop; uphold; vote (for); SUPPORT: **n.** abetment; accompaniment; adminicle; adoption; advocacy; aid; alimentation; alimony; applause; approval; assistance; auxiliary; backer; backing; base(ment); basis; behalf; benefit; benison; board; bolster; bones; boost; brace; bracket; buttress; champion; clientele; comfort; cooperation; cornerstone; corroboration; countenance; cradle; crutch; cushion; defense; encouragement; endorsement; espousal; fastener; favor; following; furtherance; girder; girdle; guard; help; interest; invigoration; keep; lacing; leg; limb; livelihood; living; maintenance; means; mounting; patron(age); peg; preparation; profit; promotion; proof; prop; rack; radical; railing; recommendation; refreshment; reinforcement; rest; rib; rock; sanction; second; shore; side; skeleton; spike; spine; sponsorship; stay; stead; steel; stiffening; strength(ening); structure; strut; subsidy; subsistence; substantiation; sustainment; sustenance; sustentation; tenon; tie; trestle; truss; tutelage; underfooting; underlayment; underpinning; underprop; vindica-

tion; wing; SUPPORTER: (**see** "backer" and "follower") booster; devotee; guarantor; insurer; pillar; rooter; underwriter; zealot; SUPPORTIVE *or* SUPPORTING: adminicular; aiding; alimentative; auxiliary; bearing; cooperative; corroborative; corroboratory; helpful; helping; sustaining; sustentacular; sustentative

SUPPOSE: (**see** "think") apprehend; assume; believe; conceive; conjecture; consider; deduce; deem; divine; expect; fancy; guess; hypothecate; hypothesize; imagine; infer; judge; opine; postulate; predicate; presume; see; speculate; surmise; suspect; take; theorize; trow; ween; SUPPOSED: academic; alleged; assumed; attributed; believed; conditional; conjectural; deemed; designed; expected; hypothesized; hypothetical; imagined; inferred; intended; permitted; presumptive; pretended; probable; putative; reputed; required; said; *soi-disant*; suppositional; suppositi(ti)ous; suppositive; suspected; theoretic(al); thought; understood; SUPPOSITION: assumption; conception; conjecturality; conjecture; deduction; divination; expectation; forgery; guess(work); hypothesis; if; postulation; postulatum; presumption; principle; probability; speculation; surmise; suspicion; tenet; theory; thought; understanding

SUPPRESS: (**see** "defeat") annihilate; ban; check; choke; conceal; crush; cushion; deaden; de-emphasize; disperse; dissolve; down; extinguish; inhibit; interdict; kill; muffle; murder; mute; overcome; overpower; overwhelm; prohibit; quash; quell; repress; restrain; sink; slay; smother; snub; spike; squash; starve; stop; strangle; stunt; subdue; subordinate; throttle; weaken; withhold; SUPPRESSION: (**see** "defeat") annihilation; ban; check; de-emphasis; dissolution; extinction; inhibition; interdiction; prohibition; repression; restraint; retardation; stoppage; strangulation

SUPPURATE: abscess; fester; maturate; SUPPURATION: abscess; festering; gangrene; matter; maturation; pus

SUPREME: absolute; capital; celestial; chief; crowning; crucial; dominant; eminent; excellent; faultless; final; first; flawless; foremost; glorious; grand; great(est); high(est); *hors concours*; imperial; important; incomparable; inimitable; last; loftiest; lofty; matchless; mighty; nonpareil; Olympian; outstanding; palmy; paramount; peerless; perfect; powerful; predominant; preeminent;

preponderant; prime; principal; *sans pareil*; signal; significant; sovereign; stellar; sublime; supereminent; superlative; surpassing; transcendent(al); ultimate; unequalable; unequaled; unexampled; unparalleled; unrivaled; unsurpassable; unsurpassed; utmost; vital; SUPREMACY: ascendancy; authority; dominance; domination; dominion; eminence; excellence; grandeur; grandiosity; masterdom; mastery; might; perfection; power; precedence; predominance; predomination; preeminence; preeminency; preponderance; primacy; priority; signality; sovereignty; supremeness; suzerainty; transcendence; transcendency

SURCEASE: abatement; cessation; ease; end; respite; rest; stop

SURE: (see "certain") actual; assured; authentic; confident; constant; convinced; enduring; established; everlasting; fast; firm; genuine; indubitable; ineluctable; inevitable; inexhaustible; infallible; positive; real; reliable; safe; secure; set(tled); stable; steadfast; steady; strong; true; undoubtable; unerring; unfailing; unfaltering; unflagging; unquestionable

SURETY: adpromissor; assurance; bail; bond; bondsman; certainty; confidence; fact; guarantee; guaranty; hostage; mortgage; pledge; recognizance; safety; security; sponsor; sureness; voucher

SURFACE: (see "superficial") appearance; exterior(ity); facet; finish; ground; outside; pavement; periphery; plate; platform; sheet; side; skin; veneer·

SURFEIT: cloy; disgust; glut; gorge; jade; overfill; overflow; oversupply; pall; sate; satisfy; saturate; sicken; stuff; SURFEITED: blasé; cloyed; complete; jaded; replete; sated; satiated; saturated; sickened; stuffed

SURGE: v. arise; billow; gush; gust; heave; ripple; rise; roll; rush; soar; swell; toss; undulate; wave; SURGE: n. billow(s); gush; heave; increase; ripple; rolling; sweep; swell(ing); tide; undulation; variation; wave(s)

SURLY: abrupt; acrimonious; bearish; boorish; brusque; churlish; crabbed; crabby; cross; crusty; discourteous; dour; glum; grouchy; gruff; grum(py); haughty; ill-humored; ill-natured; intractable; irritable; morose; peevish; pert; pettish; rude; sassy; saucy; short; snappish; snarling; sour;

sullen; testy; touchy; uncivil; unkind; vinegary; SURLINESS: see "irritability"

SURMISE: v. (see "guess") assume; believe; conjecture; deduce; deem; extrapolate; fancy; gather; hypothesize; imagine; infer; opine; presume; scent; smell; suppose; suspect; theorize; think; SURMISE: n. assumption; belief; conclusion; conjecture; deduction; extrapolation; guess; hypothesis; inference; opinion; peradventure; presumption; sign; supposition; suspicion; theory; thought; trace

SURMOUNT: (see "defeat") ascend; beat; cap; climax; climb; conquer; crown; lick; master; overcome; prevail; ride; rise; rout; scale; subdue; surpass; top; vanquish; vault

SURNAME: agnomen; appellation; cognomen; cognomination; eponym; family name; *nom de famille*; patronym(ic)

SURPASS: (see "exceed") beat; cap; defeat; eclipse; excel; extend; head; lead; outdo; outmatch; outmeasure; outnumber; outpace; outpull; outrank; outreach; outrival; outrun; outscore; outshine; outsmart; outstrip; outvie; outweigh; overshadow; overstep; overtop; preponderate; surmount; top; tower; transcend; SURPASSING: dominant; exceeding; excelling; overriding; preponderating; superior; towering; transcendent

SURPLUS: (see "excess") copiosity; copiousness; extra; gain; glut; over(age); overflow; overmeasure; plus; redundance; redundancy; remainder; reserve; rest; spare; superabundance; surplusage

SURPRISE: v. alarm; amaze; ambush; astonish; astound; awe; baffle; bewilder; bowl (over); capture; confound; daze; disconcert; discover; electrify; find; flabbergast; floor; overwhelm; rouse; seize; shock; start(le); storm; stun; stupefy; waylay; SURPRISE: n. alarm; amazement; ambush; astonishment; awe; bewilderment; blow; bombshell; capture; dazzlement; shock; start; stupefaction; wonder; SURPRISING *or* SURPRISED: (see "strange") agape; amazed; amazing; astonished; astounding; baffling; bewildering; overwhelming; shocking; startling; stunning; stupefying; unforewarned; unlooked-for

SURRENDER: v. abandon; abdicate; abnegate; accede; capitulate; cede; commit; comply; deliver; entrust; forego; forsake;

give (in); give up; grant; leave; quit; relax; relinquish; remise; remit; renounce; resign; sacrifice; submit; succumb; waive; withdraw; yield; SURRENDER: **n.** abandonment; abdication; abnegation; accession; capitulation; capture; cession; collapse; compliance; deliverance; fall; grant; relinquishment; remission; renunciation; resignation; submission; yield(ing)

SURREPTITIOUS: backdoor; cabalistic; cladestine; covert; deceptive; duplicitous; furtive; secret; serpentine; slithery; sly; snaky; stealthy; undercover; underhand(ed)

SURROUND: beset; besiege; block(ade); box; circle; circumfuse; circumscribe; compass; cover; embosom; embrace; encase; encircle; enclose; encompass; envelop; environ; fence; gird(le); hedge; hem; hold; invest; possess; ring; separate; swathe; wrap; SURROUNDING: **a.** ambient; besetting; circumambient; circumferential; circumjacent; circumscribed; circumvallate; encapsulated; encompassing; enveloping; investing; ringed; wrapped; SURROUNDING(S): **n.** alentours; ambience; circumfusion; circumjacencies; circumscription; circumvention; confines; context; entourage; environment; environs; milieu; *mise-en-scène*; periphery; suburbs; zone

SURVEILLANCE: **see** "survey"

SURVEY: **v.** appraise; ascertain; consider; determine; espy; estimate; evaluate; examine; inspect; investigate; look; map; measure; oversee; perlustrate; plan; plot; poll; probe; prospect; review; scan; scrutinize; search; see; study; supervise; traverse; view; SURVEY: **n.** appraisal; brief; capsule; compendium; condensation; conspectus; description; epitome; estimation; evaluation; examination; glimpse; inspection; investigation; look; look-see; measurement; once-over; panel; panorama; perlustration; plan; poll; probe; prospect(us); questionnaire; recension; reconnaissance; report; review; scrutinization; scrutiny; search; study; supervision; surveillance; surveyal; surveyance; synopsis; view; vista

SURVIVE: abide; continue; endure; exist; last; live; outlast; outlive; outwear; persist; remain; ride; stand; stay; sustain; wear; weather; SURVIVAL: continuation; continuity; echo; endurance; remain(s); survivance; sustenance; trace; vestige

SUSCEPTIBLE: **(see** "sensitive") easy; impressible; impressionable; liable; malleable; open; plastic; pliable; predisposed; prone; reactive; responsive; subject; tendentious; tender; weak; SUSCEPTIBILITY: delicacy; impressibility; impressionability; liability; malleability; plasticity; predilection; predisposition; sensitivity; tendentiousness; tenderness; weakness

SUSPECT: anticipate; believe; distrust; doubt; feel; hesitate; imagine; misdoubt; mistrust; question; scent; smell; suppose; surmise; think

SUSPEND: adjourn; await; call; cease; check; continue; debar; defer; delay; desist; disconnect; discontinue; eject; exclude; halt; hang; hinder; hold; intermit; interrupt; levitate; oust; poise; postpone; pretermit; reprieve; reserve; retard; shelve; shunt; sling; stay; stop; swing; table; withhold; SUSPENSION: abeyance; abeyancy; armistice; cessation; cloture; continuance; delay; emulsion; exclusion; halt; intermission; interruption; lull; moratorium; peace; pendulosity; pretermission; quiet; recess; remission; reprieve; respite; rest; retardation; stop(page); truce; vacation; withdrawal; SUSPENDED: abeyant; halted; pendant; pensile; slung; stopped; suspensory; tabled

SUSPICIOUS: accusatory; conjectural; distrustful; doubtful; dubious; equivocal; fishy; hesitant; incredulous; incriminatory; inquisitorial; jealous; leery; *louche*; querulent(ial); questionable; skeptical; suspected; umbrageous; wary; wise; SUSPICION: apprehension; dash; distrust; doubt; dubiety; fear; hesitancy; hesitation; hint; incredulity; inkling; intimation; jealousy; mistrust; shade; soupçon; suggestion; surmise; touch; trace; umbrage; uneasiness; wariness

SUSTAIN: **(see** "support") confirm; contend; corroborate; endure; establish; experience; favor; feed; hold; live; mention; nourish; prolong; receive; stay; subject; suffer; survive; undergo; SUSTAINING: aiding; bread-and-butter; nourishing; nutritious; strengthening; supporting; supportive; sustentacular; sustentative; SUSTENANCE: **(see** "food") aliment(ation); endurance; living; maintenance; means; nourishment; nutriment; refreshments; strength; support; sustentation; sustention; upkeep

SUTURE: **v.** sew; stitch; SUTURE: **n.** joint; junction; line; raphe; seam; stitch; synarthrosis; synchondrosis; union

SWAB: (see "clean") epaulet; lout; lubber; malkin; mop; specimen

SWAG: boodle; booty; loot; plunder; spoils

SWAGGER: **v.** brag; bristle; flourish; hector; prance; preen; sashay; strut; swash(buckle); swing; SWAGGER: **n.** arrogance; bounce; bravado; cockiness; fanfaronade; flamboyance; gasconade; liveliness; panache; pose; rodomontade; verve; SWAGGERER: braggadocio; bravado; gasconade; rodomontade; swashbuckler; SWAGGERING: blustering; blusterous; blustery; bullying; fashionable; jaunty; swashbuckling; thrasonical

SWAIN: beau; boy; Damon; flame; gallant; lad; lover; peasant; rustic; shepherd; squire; suitor; youth

SWALLOW: (see "drink") absorb; accept; appropriate; believe; bolt; comprehend; consume; devour; displace; down; eat; endure; englut; engulf; grasp; gulp; imbibe; ingest; ingurgitate; overwhelm; quaff; receive; repress; sip; swamp; toss

SWAMP: **v.** (see "defeat") beat; deluge; destroy; engulf; flood; inundate; overpower; overwhelm; ruin; sink; submerge; swallow; SWAMP: **n.** bog; fen; marsh; mire; morass; quagmire; slough; SWAMPY: deluginous; fenny; found(e)rous; miry; paludal; paludous; palustral; sodden; soggy; spongy; uliginous; waterlogged

SWANK(Y): (see "rich") lush; luxurious; ostentatious; plush(y); posh; smart

SWAP: bandy; barter; change; exchange; substitute; trade

SWARD: grass; green(sward); lawn; sod; turf

SWARM: **v.** abound; amass; burgeon; climb; collect; congregate; cover; crowd; flock; herd; hover; jam; mass; migrate; mob; mount; move; overflow; pack; pour; pullulate; shin; sweep; teem; throng; SWARM: **n.** aggregation; amassment; army; assemblage; bevy; collection; colony; congregation; crowd; emigration; flock; gathering; herd; hive; horde; host; migration; mob; multitude; nest; number; pack; press; quantity; school; shoal; sweep; throng; SWARMING: abounding; alive; burgeoning; bustling; crowding; pullulating; pushing; replete; rife; teeming; thronging

SWASTIKA: cross; fylfot; gammadion; hakenkreuz; tetraskelion

SWATHE: bandage; bind; clothe; cover; dress; envelop; support; surround; swaddle; tape; wrap

SWAY: **v.** (see "swing") affect; brandish; command; control; deflect; divert; dominate; give; govern; hang; influence; lurch; nod; oscillate; pend; rock; roll; rule; say; seesaw; shimmy; stagger; swag; tilt; toss; totter; vacillate; veer; wave(r); weave; SWAY: **n.** ascendancy; authority; command; control; dominance; domination; dominion; fluctuation; force; government; influence; lurch; oscillation; potency; power; pressure; rule; sag; shimmer; sovereignty; strength; superiority; swing; tilt; toss; vacillation; veer(ing); waver

SWEAR: accuse; adjure; affirm; afflict; anathematize; asseverate; attest; aver; beshrew; blaspheme; condemn; curse; damn; denounce; depone; depose; doom; emphasize; excommunicate; execrate; fulminate; harass; impede; invoke; maledict; objurgate; pledge; promise; proscribe; rail; rant; stress; testify; threaten; vilify; SWEARING: adjuration; affirmation; asseveration; attestation; averment; blasphemy; damnation; deposition; execration; imprecation; invocation; malediction; objurgation; profanity; promise; testimony

SWEAT: **v.** bleed; drudge; excrete; extort; exude; fleece; labor; languish; ooze; overwork; perspire; slave; steam; swelter; toil; work; SWEAT: **n.** (see "perspiration") drudgery; labor; slavery; sudor; toil; work

SWEEP: **v.** brush; clean; clear; collect; cover; destroy; drift; drive; dust; graze; oar; range; reach; remove; scour; spread; swarm; swoop; trail; win; SWEEP: **n.** capture; clearance; course; drift; drive; extent; graze; ken; movement; oar; orb; progress; range; reach; removal; scope; series; space; spread; swarm; trail; wash; wave; SWEEPING: absolute; all-inclusive; broad; complete; comprehensive; extensive; general; indiscriminate; swarming; wholesale; wide

SWEET: **a.** agreeable; attractive; captivating; charming; cherubic; cloying; darling; dear; dolce; dolcissimo; dulcet; easy; engaging; enticing; even; fetching; fragrant; friendly; gentle; honeyed; lovely; loving; melodious; moderate; musical; nectareous; nice; personable; pleasant; pleasing; pretty; saccharine; savory; sirupy; smooth; soft; sticky; sugared; sugary; tender; treacly; unsoured; wholesome; winning; winsome; SWEET(S): **n.** beloved; candy; cates; confection; darling; dear;

dessert; fondant; honey; molasses; pastry; sugar; sweetmeats; syrup; treacle; SWEET-NESS: amiability; fragrance; saccharinity; sentimentality; sweetheart; syrup; treacle

SWEETHEART: Adonis; Aphrodite; beloved; *bon ami*; *bonne amie* (fem.); beau; beaux (pl.); cherie; darling; dear; dreamboat; dulcinea; fellow; flame; friend; girl(friend); inamorata (fem.); inamorato; lad; ladylove; love(r); lovey-dovey; man (friend); mistress; suitor; sweet(ie); sweetness; turtledove; valentine; well-beloved

SWELL: **v.** augment; billow; bloat; blow; bulge; dilate; distend; enlarge; expand; extend; ferment; grow; hypertrophy; increase; inflate; intensify; intumesce; pout; preen; protrude; puff; rise; strut; stuff; surge; tumefy; tumesce; SWELL: **a.** (**see** "swollen") fashionable; grand; great; posh; pretty; stylish; tip-top; tumescent; turgescent; turgid; wonderful; SWELL(ING): **n.** blain; bloating; bulge; crescendo; dila(ta)tion; distension; dropsy; edema; enlargement; expansion; increase; inflation; intumescence; knot; lump; node; phyma; protrusion; protuberance; protuberation; surge; tumefaction; tumescence; tumidity; turgescence; turgidity; turgidness; turgor; undulation; SWELLED: see "swollen"

SWELTER: fret; languish; oppress; perspire; roast; stew; sweat; SWELTERING: **see** "humid"

SWERVE: (**see** "deviate") bend; cut; deflect; depart; detour; digress; diverge; meander; sheer; shift; turn; veer; waver; yaw

SWIFT(LY): (**see** "hasty") abrupt; alert; apace; celeritous; expeditious; fast; fleet-(ing); fleet-foot(ed); flighty; Gadarene; headlong; heedless; hurried; mercurial; meteoric; prompt; quick(silver); raking; rapid; ready; speedy; sudden; summary; telegraphic; transient; winged; SWIFT-NESS: acceleration; alacrity; celerity; expedition; fleetingness; heedlessness; hurry; promptitude; promptness; rapidity; speed SWIM: abound; bathe; crawl; dip; float; overflow; reel; teem; SWIMMER: Leander; naiad; natator; SWIMMING: natant; natatory

SWINDLE: see "cheat;" SWINDLER: (**see** "fraud") charlatan; cheat(er); *chevalier d'industrie*; cozener; embezzler; fake(r); finagler; harpy; imposter; knave; mounte-

bank; pretender; quack(salver); rogue; shark; sparp(st)er; Tartuffe; thief

SWING: **v.** accomplish; alternate; curve; dangle; fluctuate; hang; hinge; influence; manage; oscillate; pend(ulate); pivot; ply; rock; roll; rotate; shake; shift; slue; suspend; swagger; sway; swivel; turn; undulate; veer; wag; wave(r); wheel; wield; SWING: **n.** activity; arc; course; license; lilt; progress-(ion); range; rein; rotation; round; scope; SWINGING: dangling; fluctuating; hanging; oscillating; pendant; pendular; pendulous; suspended; undulating

SWIPE: (**see** "steal") rub; strike; wipe

SWITCH: **v.** beat; cane; change; divert; exchange; flog; lash; shift; shunt; strike; substitute; swap; swing; trade; whip; SWITCH: **n.** birch; cane; exchange; hair; rod; shift; shunt; sprig; spur; substitute; swap; twig; trade

SWIVEL: hinge; pilot; pivot; swing; traverse; turn

SWOLLEN: billowed; bloated; boastful; bombastic; bulbous; bulged; bulging; dilated; distended; dropsical; edematous; enlarged; expanded; gravid; gross; hypertrophic; hypertrophied; incrassate; increased; inflated; intumescent; overflowing; paunchy; pneumatic; pompous; pregnant; protuberant; proud; puffed; puffy; stuffed; swaggering; swelled; tumefacient; tumefactive; tumescent; tumid; turgescent; turgid

SWOON: (**see** "faint") fade; float

SWOOP: alight; dart; descend; drop; grab; grasp; pounce; seize; souse; sweep

SWORD: bayonet; bilbo; blade; brand; claymore; control; cutlass; dirk; épée; estoc; Excalibur; foil; force; kukri; pata; power; rapier; saber; scimitar; struggle; Toledo; yataghan; war

SYBARITE: epicure; glutton; hedonist; sensualist; voluptuary

SYCOPHANT: accuser; defamer; fawner; flatterer; flunky; informer; hanger-on; leech; menial; minion; parasite; slanderer; slave; spaniel; sponge(r); subservient; talebearer; toady; yes-man

SYLLABUS: abridgement; abstract; aperçu;

breviary; compend(ium); digest; epitome; list; outline; précis; summary; synopsis; table

SYLPH: **see** "fairy"

SYMBOLIZE: agree; allegorize; concur; emblematize; embody; harmonize; identify; reflect; represent; sample; summarize; typify; SYMBOL: (**see** "emblem") allegory; attribute; badge; button; character; creed; descriptor; ensign; figure; gesture; ideogram; insigne; insignia (pl.); logogram; mark; motif; om; palm; picture; sign; star; token; type; SYMBOLIC(AL): algebraic; allegorical; allusive; emblematic(al); figurative; hieroglyphic; metaphoric(al); pathognom(on)ic; representative; schematic; token; typic(al)

SYMMETRY: accord; agreement; arrangement; balance; beauty; conformity; correspondence; equipoise; equivalence; evenness; form; harmony; orchestration; order; proportion; regularity; rhythm; SYMMETRIC(AL): balanced; commensurable; congruent; corresponding; equal; even; proportional; regular; rhythmic(al); round; spherical

SYMPATHY: accord; affinity; alliance; altropathy; altruism; association; benevolence; charity; clemency; comfort; commiseration; compassion; condolence; congeniality; consent; consolation; empathy; feeling; friendship; geniality; harmony; heart; help; inspiration; interest; kindness; love; loyalty; mercy; mutuality; pathos; pity; relationship; relief; ruth; solace; sop; symmetry; tenderness; tolerance; toleration; unity; SYMPATHETIC: altruistic; approving; charitable; chickenhearted; compassionate; condolatory; congenial; consonant; empathetic; favorable; favoring; friendly; genial; human(e); infectious; kind(ly); largehearted; merciful; philanthropic(al); pigeonhearted; Samaritan; simpatico; softhearted; tender; tolerant; understanding; warm; SYMPATHIZE: (**see** "understand") comfort; empathize; pity; solace

SYMPOSIUM: banquet; collection; discussion; gathering; meeting; party

SYMPTOM: ache; alarm; badge; clew; criteria (pl.); criterion; evidence; fever; forerunner; indication; mark; note; pain; sign; stigma; token; trace; warning

SYNONYMOUS: **see** "like"

SYNOPSIS: abridgement; abstract; aperçu; brief; compend(ium); condensation; conspectus; digest; epitome; outline; précis; summary; syllabus; table

SYRUP: glucose; honey; maple; molasses; sentimentality; sorghum; sweetness; treacle

SYSTEM: arrangement; chain; class(ification); combination; complex; cosmos; cult; design; division; economy; frame(work); gauge; grid; group; ism; labyrinth; machine(ry); medium; method; mode; network; order(liness); organism; organization; philosophy; plan; plexus; procedure; process; program; regime(n); regularity; religion; reticulation; ritual; rule; schedule; scheme; sequence; structure; syntax; theory; web; whole; works; SYSTEMATIC(AL): alphabetical; arranged; businesslike; cosmic; designed; methodical; orderly; organized; planned; practical; procedural; regular; scientific; symmetric(al); systematized; taxonomic(al); SYSTEMATIZE: (**see** "classify") alphabetize; file; methodize; scientize

T

TAB: a(i)glet; appendage; bill; check; cost; extension; flap; grip; label; latchet; pan; price; projection; remnant; strap; strip; stub; tag; tongue

TABERNACLE: church; habitation; kirk; meetinghouse; sanctuary; temple; tent

TABLE: **v.** catalog(ue); delay; feed; index; list; postpone; tabulate; TABLE: **n.** bench; board; canon; catalog(ue); chart; counter; desk; fare; food; index; meal; register; roll; roster; rostrum; rota; schedule; scheme; sitting; stand; statement; synopsis; tableau; tablet; tabouret; tabulation; tariff

TABLEAU: arrangement; image; list; picture; portrait; scene; table

TABLET: leaf; lozenge; medicine; memorial; pad; paper; pastille; pill; plaque; sheet; slab; slate; table; troche

TABOO or TABU: **v.** anathematize; ban; bar; censure; condemn; damn; debar; embargo; exclude; hinder; interdict; outlaw; prevent; prohibit; proscribe; restrain; shun; veto; TABOO or TABU: **n.** ban; bar; censure; condemnation; convention; embargo; exclusion; exile; hindrance; interdiction; prevention; prohibition; proscription; restraint; veto

TACIT: agreed; implicit; implied; indicated; inferred; oral; silent; understood; unsaid; unspoken; wordless

TACITURN: close; curt; dour; dumb; laconic; monosyllabic; mum; mute; reserved; reticent; sententious; silent; speechless; still; uncommunicative; untalkative; unvocal; unvoluble

TACK: **v.** add; angle; annex; append; attach; base; connect; drive; hammer; hitch; jibe; join; laveer; link; nail; secure; tie; TACK: **n.** adhesiveness; brad; course; method; nail; path; stickiness; TACKY: adhesive; dowdy; frowsy; ragged; seedy; sticky

TACKLE: **v.** approach; attack; grab; grapple; grasp; seize; try; TACKLE: **n.** attack; equipment; gear; grab; grapple; grasp; outfit; paraphernalia; player; pulley; rigging; stop; tools; yoke

TACT: ability; acumen; acuteness; address; aptness; care; caution; circumspection; cleverness; consideration; delicacy; delicatesse; diplomacy; discernment; discretion; discrimination; finesse; intelligence; judgment; penetration; perception; perspicacity; poise; politeness; prudence; refinement; *savoir faire*; sensitivity; sharpness; skill-(fulness); taste; touch; TACTFUL: acuminous; adroit; careful; cautious; circumspect(ive); considerate; consummate; delicate; diplomatic; discreet; discriminating; fitting; penetrating; perspicacious; polite; politic; prudent; refined; sensitive; sharp; skillful; suave; tasteful; thoughtful; TACTLESS: awkward; blunt; clumsy; gauche; impolite; impolitic; inapt; inconsiderate; indiscreet; inept; maladroit; rude; thoughtless; undiplomatic; untactful; TACTLESSNESS: gaucherie; inaptitude; incaution; inconsideration; indiscretion; ineptitude; maladroitness; rudeness; thoughtlessness

TACTIC(S): (**see** "course") method; plan; strategy

TAG: **v.** append; brand; dog; follow; hound; hunt; identify; join; label; tail; ticket; trail; TAG: **n.** (**see** "tab") cliché; flap; frazzle; game; identification; label; loop; mark(er); projection; rag; remnant; saw; stub; tail; tassel; tatter; ticket; trail; vestige

TAIL: **v.** dog; follow; hound; hunt; scout; seek; shadow; tag; trail; TAIL: **n.** appendage; buttocks; cauda; caudal appendage; coccyx; conclusion; dregs; end; extremity; foot; pendant; rear; residuum; retinue; scut; shadow; stalk; trail; train; TAILLESS: acaudal; acaudate; anurous; ecaudate

TAILOR: **v.** adapt; fashion; fit; make; style; trim; TAILOR: **n.** draper; *maestro-sastre*; sartor

617

TAINT: **v.** befoul; blemish; contaminate; corrupt; debase; deduct; defile; deprave; discolor; disgrace; dishonor; infect; mark; poison; pollute; rot; soil; sour; spot; stain; sully; tarnish; vitiate; TAINT: **n.** blemish; cloud; contamination; corruption; defilement; disgrace; dishonor; infection; maculation); mark; poison; pollution; reproach; stain; tarnish; vitiation; TAINTED: bad; contaminated; corrupt(ed); damaged; decayed; discolored; diseased; fetid; infected; marked; poisoned; polluted; putrid; rancid; rank; rotted; rotten; septic; soiled; sour; stained; vitiated

TAKE: abduct; abstract; accept; accommodate; accompany; accroach; acquire; adopt; appropriate; arrest; assume; bag; bear; believe; borrow; captivate; capture; carry; catch; charm; cheat; choose; collar; commandeer; comprehend; conduct; confiscate; contract; co-opt(ate); cop; defeat; delight; draw; drink; eat; embezzle; endure; escort; extort; gain; get; grab; grasp; grip; guide; have; hog; kidnap; lead; nap; occupy; photograph; pick; pillage; pocket; preempt; purloin; reach; receive; remove; rob; seize; select; sequester; snatch; spheterize; steal; subtract; suppose; swallow; swindle; tote; undergo; understand; usurp; win; withdraw; withstand

TALE: account; anecdote; canard; cock-and-bull story; conte; fable; fabula; fabulae (pl.); falsehood; fiction; geste; legend; lie; myth; narrative; novel; recital; report; saga; slander; story; sum; total; yarn

TALENT(S): (**see** "ability") accomplishment(s); adeptness; adroitness; aptitude; art(istry); bent; capacity; dexterity; direction; draft; endowment; expertise; field; flair; forte; genius; gift; hability; head; ingeniosity; inventiveness; knack; performer; power; skill(fulness); trait; vein; virtuosity; wisdom; wit

TALISMAN: (**see** "charm") amulet; fetish; grigri; periapt; phylactery; relic; symbol; token; TALISMANIC: **see** "magical"

TALK: (**see** "speak") address; articulation; babble(ment); banter; blather; buzz; chat-(ter); chinning; chitchat; chitter-chatter; colloquy; communication; confabulation; conference; conversation; crack; descant; dialect; discourse; discussion; drivel; gossip; language; lecture; lingo; meeting; mention; oration; oratory; palaver; parlance; prattle; reasoning; rejoinder; repartee; reply;

report; riposte; rumor; sermon; speech; spiel; talkfest; verbiage; words; TALKATIVE: articulate; babblative; buzzy; chattering; chatty; chitchatty; communicable; communicative; communicatory; conversable; discoursive; discursive; explanatory; fluent; garrulous; glib(-tongued); gossipy; logorrheic; loquacious; mouthy; multi-loquacious; multiloquent; prolix; unreticent; verbose; vocative; vociferant; vociferous; voluble; wordy; TALKATIVENESS: chattiness; flatulence; fluency; *flux de bouche*; *flux de paroles*; *furor loquendi*; garrulity; garrulousness; glibness; logomania; logorrhea; loquaciousness; loquacity; multiloquence; verbomania; verbosity; volubility; windiness; wordiness

TALKER: (**see** "speaker") colloquist; confabulator; conversant; conversationalist; exponent; orator

TALL: altitudinous; elevated; eminent; exaggerated; high; improbable; lofty; long; statuesque; towering

TALLY: **v.** agree; balance; complement; correspond; count; equal; gibe; jibe; list; match; reckon; record; register; score; square; suit; tabulate; total; TALLY: **n.** census; count; counterpart; goal; list; match; notch; number; point; register; run; score; touchdown; vote

TAME: **v.** break; civilize; control; cultivate; discipline; domesticate; domesticize; drill; gentle; humble; master; overcome; soften; subdue; subjugate; train; TAME(D): **a.** amenable; benign(ant); broken; civil(ized); controlled; cultivated; disciplined; docile; domesticated; domesticized; *domitae naturae*; drilled; dull; flat; gentle; harmless; harnessed; inert; insipid; meek; mild; milky; obedient; overcome; plastic; pliant; spiritless; subdued; subjugated; submissive; timid; timorous; tractable; trained; uninteresting; TAMENESS: benignancy; civility; civilization; complaisance; control; docility; domesticality; domestication; domesticity; gentility; gentleness; harmlessness; meekness; mildness; obedience; timidity; tractability

TAMPER: alter; bribe; experiment; interfere; machinate; manipulate; meddle; mess; molest; plot; snoop; tinker; torment; weaken

TAN: **v.** beat; chastise; discipline; tar; whip; TAN: **a.** (**see** "tawny") bronze; buff; *café-au-lait*; dun; ecru; sunburned; tanned

TANG: bite; characteristic; flavor; nip; odor; savor; smattering; suggestion; taste; trace; zest; TANGY: (see "appetizing") biting; flavorful; nippy; racy; savory; spicy; tasty; zestful

TANGIBLE: (see "material") palpable; real; tactile

TANGLE: v. coil; confuse; derange; embroil; entrap; interlock; intertwine; interweave; involve; jumble; knot; mat; maze; perplex; shag; sleave; snare; snarl; trap; twist; weave; TANGLE: n. argument; bewilderment; coil; conflict; confusion; derangement; embroilment; jumble; jungle; mat; maze; morass; muddle; perplexity; shag; snare; snarl; thicket; trap; twist(ing)

TANTALIZE: (see "tease") allure; annoy; charm; excite; harass; plague; provoke; tempt; tickle; torment; vex; worry

TANTRUM: anger; caprice; fit; huff; miff; outburst; paroxysm; pet; rage; snit; spell

TAP: v. connect; dance; designate; drain; draw; drum; name; open; percuss; pierce; puncture; rap; select; strike; touch; TAP: n. bar; cock; dance; faucet; nut; plug; puncture; rap; spigot; spile; strike; touch

TAPER: acuminate; diminish; ebb; lessen; narrow; sharpen; TAPERING: acuminate; acuminous; conical; diminishing; fusiform; sharp; spired; wedged

TAPESTRY: arras; cloth; curtain; dosser; fabric; tapis; textile

TAR: (see "sailor") asphalt; pitch

TARDY: (see "late") behind(hand); belated; comatose; delayed; detained; dilatory; indolent; lagging; lethargic; overdue; procrastinative; remiss; slow; sluggish

TARGET: aim; bird; bull's-eye; butt; center; date; device; fall guy; goal; mark; nark; object(ive); patsy; quota; score; signal

TARNISH: v. begrime; besmirch; blemish; corrode; corrupt; deteriorate; dim(inish); discolor; disfigure; disgrace; dishonor; dissipate; dull; injure; rust; smudge; soil; spoil; spot; stain; sully; taint; vitiate; TARNISH: n. aerugo; blemish; debasement; deterioration; patina; rust; soil; stain; verdigris

TARRY: (see "delay") abide; bide; dally; dawdle; detain; idle; lag; linger; loiter; procrastinate; remain; retard; saunter; slack(en); sojourn; stay; wait

TART: a. acerb(ic); acid; acrid; acrimonious; biting; blunt; caustic; curt; cutting; painful; pert; piercing; piquant; pungent; sassy; saucy; severe; sharp; sour; vinegary; TART: n. cake; doxy; flan; prostitute

TASK: amount; assignment; burden; business; chare; charge; chore; deed; devoir; difficulty; drudgery; duty; employment; enterprise; feat; function; job; labor; métier; mission; objective; office; onus; position; problem; project; reprimand; responsibility; stint; toil; undertaking; vocation; work

TASKMASTER: (see "disciplinarian") martinet; overseer; Simon Legree

TASTE: v. degustate; drink; eat; feel; flavor; partake; relish; sample; savor; sip; smack; sup; test; undergo; TASTE: n. appetite; appreciation; aptitude; bit; bite; degustation; discernment; genius; gustation; gusto; heart; inclination; judgment; liking; palate; partiality; penchant; predilection; preference; race; relish; sample; sapidity; sapor; savor; sip; smack; snack; style; tact; tang; tooth; zest; TASTY or TASTEFUL: (see "appetizing") aesthetic(al); appealing; apt; artistic; attractive; beautiful; chaste; cultivated; cultured; dainty; delicate; delicious; discriminating; discriminative; elegant; esthetic(al); exquisite; fastidious; fine; fit; flavorable; flavorful; flavorous; fruity; gustatory; gustful; luscious; neat; nice; palatable; pleasant; pleasing; racy; relishing; sapid; savory; tactful; toothsome; yummy

TASTELESS: banal; dull; flat; garish; gaudy; inartistic; overdecorated; showy; tawdry; tin(ny); trashy; trumpery; uninteresting; unleavened; unsavory; unseasoned; vapid; vulgar; watery; TASTELESSNESS: banality; gaudiness; insipidity; vapidity; vulgarity

TATTERED: (see "worn") broken-down; disrupted; ragged; shattered; squalid; threadbare

TATTLE: blab(ber); blurb; chatter; divulge; gossip; inform; jabber; prate; prattle; snitch; talk; tell; TATTLER or TATTLETALE: blab; gossip(er); informer; quidnunc; telltale

TAUNT: v. (see "tease") challenge; deride;

gibe; insult; jeer; jibe; mock; needle; offend; provoke; quip; rag; rally; reproach; ridicule; scoff; sneer; tantalize; twit; upbraid; TAUNT: **n.** challenge; derision; gibe; insult; jeer; jibe; mock; offense; provocation; quip; reproach; ridicule; scoff; sneer; twit

TAUT: (**see** "tight") disciplined; drawn; firm; formal; high-strung; nervous; severe; snug; stiff; stretched; strict; tense; tidy; trim

TAVERN: alehouse; bar; cabaret; grogshop; inn; pub; roadhouse; saloon; tap(room)

TAWDRY: (**see** "cheap") coarse; flamboyant; flashy; florid; garish; gaudy; gingerbread; gross; loud; phony; pretentious; showy; tasteless; tin(ny); tinsel; trashy; vulgar

TAWNY: bronze; buff; *café-au-lait*; dun; dusty; ecru; fulvid; fulvous; olive; rubiate; swart(hy); tan(ned); tigrine

TAX: **v.** accuse; assess; burden; charge; exact; fine; lade; levy; load; overburden; overdo; overreach; rate; strain; tire; tithe; TAX: **n.** assessment; burden; capitation; cess; charge; customs; duty; exaction; excise; fee; fine; imposition; impost; levy; load; ratal; rate; scat; scot; stent; strain; tailage; tariff; tithe; toll; tribute

TEA: beverage; Bohea; cambric; cha; gathering; hyson; kat; lunch(eon); meal; pekoe; reception; refreshments; soiree; tiffin; tisane; yerba

TEACH: adapt; advance; advise; alter; brainwash; coach; conduct; counsel; cultivate; demonstrate; direct; discipline; dissemble; drill; edify; educate; enlighten; exhort; explain; exposit; expound; familiarize; fit; govern; guide; imbue; impart; implant; impregnate; inculcate; indoctrinate; influence; inform; initiate; instruct; inure; lecture; manipulate; monitor; move; nurture; preach; prepare; prime; school; shift; show; stabilize; suit; train; tutor; TEACHABLE: (**see** "changeable") amenable; apt; childlike; compliant; correctible; corrective; corrigible; disciplinable; docible; docile; ductile; dutiful; educa(ta)ble; elastic; facile; fitting; flexible; gentle; governable; influenceable; innocent; instructible; malleable; manipula(ta)ble; naïve; obedient; plastic; pliable; pliant; soft; submissive; tame; tensile; tractable; treatable; trusting; yielding; TEACHER(S): academic(ian); archididascalos; archididascalus; coach; conductor;

counsel(lor); didact(ician); disciplinarian; docent; doctor; educator; explainer; expounder; guide; guru; indoctrinator; instructor; lecturer; maestro; master; mentor; monitor; pedagog(ue); pedantocrat; preacher; preceptor; precisian; principal; pro; prof(essor); professoriat(e); scholarch; scholastic; schooldame; schoolmarm; schoolmaster; schoolmistress; scribe; sponsor; trainer; tutor

TEACHING(S): (**see** "knowledge") curriculum; demonstration; didacticism; didactics; doctrine; education; enlightenment; evangel(ism); explanation; instruction; instructorship; knowledge; message; pedagogics; pedagogism; pedagogy; precept; propaedeutics; punditry; schooling; teachership; tuition; tutelage

TEAM: **v.** collaborate; cooperate; group; join; marry; match; pair; yoke; TEAM: **n.** brace; collaboration; cooperation; crew; eleven; gauge; group; match; nine; outfit; pair; set; span; side; squad; yoke

TEAR: **v.** cleave; dilacerate; disarticulate; discerp; disjoin(t); dismember; disrupt; divide; fly; fracture; jag; lacerate; lancinate; laniate; mangle; part; race; remove; rend; rent; rip; rive; run; rupture; rush; separate; sever; shatter; shred; slash; slit; sunder; wrench; TEAR: **n.** binge; disarticulation; discerption; dismemberment; divulsion; flurry; laceration; lag; rend; rent; rip; rive; rupture; rush; shred; slash; slit; snag; split; spree; toot

TEARFUL: (**see** "sad") crying; lachrymal; lachrymatory; lachrymose; maudlin; mawkish; moist; saddened; sorrowful; teary; weeping

TEASE: allure; anger; annoy; attract; badger; baffle; bait; banter; beg; bother; chaff; challenge; charm; chide; coax; cross; deride; devil; displease; distress; disturb; entice; exasperate; excite; fascinate; fret; gall; gibe; goad; harass; harry; hector; importune; incite; insult; inveigle; invite; irk; irritate; jeer; jibe; josh; lure; mock; nag; needle; offend; pester; pique; plague; prompt; provoke; quip; rag; rally; reproach; rib; ride; ridicule; scoff; sneer; solicit; suggest; tantalize; taunt; tempt; tickle; torment; trouble; try; twit; vex; wheedle; woo; worry

TECHNIQUE: (**see** "mechanics" and "procedure") handling; method; rubric; treatment; wrinkle

TEDIOUS: (**see** "dull") boresome; boring; dreary; drowsy; everlasting; fatiguing; flat; humdrum; indefinite; irksome; long (-winded); monotonous; peevish; prolonged; protracted; slow; stupid; tiresome; uninteresting; vexatious; wearied; weariful; wearisome; weary; TEDIUM: (**see** "dullness") boredom; ennui; fatigue; monotony; tediousness

TEEM: abound; burgeon; crowd; flock; mob; overflow; pack; pour; pullulate; swarm; throng; TEEMING: abounding; alive; burgeoning; bustling; fertile; pregnant; pullulating; replete; rife; thronging

TEETH: dentures; grinders; ivory; lowers; plate; tusk; uppers

TELESCOPE: **v.** abridge; coalesce; collapse; combine; compress; condense; fold; TELESCOPE: **n.** glass; lens

TELL: acquaint; advise; annunciate; apprise; articulate; ascertain; asseverate; blab(ber); communicate; declare; describe; detail; direct; disclose; divulge; enumerate; enunciate; explain; express; impart; inform; manifest; mention; mouth; narrate; notify; order; own; recite; recognize; recount; relate; report; request; reveal; say; speak; squeal; state; talk; unbosom; utter; verbalize; warn; TELLING: authoritative; cogent; convincing; decisive; definitive; effective; effectual; efficacious; expressive; forceful; important; impressive; pertinent; pointed; potent; powerful; pungent; revealing; revelant; sound; striking; timely; valid; weighty

TEMERARIOUS: (**see** "bold") brash; cheeky; foolhardy; nervy; presumptuous; rash; reckless; venturesome; TEMERITY: (**see** "boldness") audacity; brass; cheek; effrontery; gall; guts; nerve; offense; offensiveness; rashness; recklessness; venture-(someness)

TEMPER: **v.** adapt; adjust; allay; alloy; anneal; attune; bland; compound; dilute; harden; mitigate; mix; moderate; modify; moisten; qualify; season; soften; strengthen; toughen; TEMPER: **n.** anger; blood; calm-(ness); character; composure; dander; disposition; equanimity; feeling; hardness; humor; makeup; mettle; mood; nature; outburst; passion; personality; rage; resiliency; tantrum; tendency; tiff; tone; trend; vein; TEMPERAMENT: calm(ness); character; complexion; composure; condition; constitution; courage; crasis; disposition; equanimity; feeling; hardness; humor; mood; nature; passion; personality; propensity; sensibility; state; TEMPERAMENTAL: capricious; constitutional; excitable; fickle; high-strung; impatient; impetuous; irritable; mercurial; psychological; quicksilver; sensitive; testy; tricky; uncertain; unstable; unsteady; volatile; waspish

TEMPERANCE: abnegation; composure; consistency; equability; measure; mediocrity; moderation; restraint; self-control; self-restraint; sobriety; sophrosyne; TEMPERATE: abstemious; abstinent; Apollonian; Apollonic; Apollonistic; calm; constitutional; continent; dispassionate; equable; mild; moderate; phlegmatic; restrained; self-controlled; self-restrained; sober; tempered; undemonstrative; TEMPERATENESS: abstemiousness; abstention; abstinence; moderation; self-control; self-restraint; sobriety

TEMPEST: blast; excitement; gale; hurricane; monsoon; orage; rage; stir; storm; tumult; turmoil; uproar; wind; TEMPESTUOUS: **see** "stormy"

TEMPLE: cathedral; church; edifice; huaca; mosque; naos; synagogue; tabernacle; wat

TEMPO: activity; beat; ictus; motion; pace; presto; pulse; rate; rhythm; speed; time

TEMPORAL: (**see** "common") chronological; civil; laic(al); political; temporary; terrestrial; transient; transitory; worldly

TEMPORARY: *ad hoc*; *ad interim*; brief; conditional; deciduous; ephemeral; ephemerous; episodic(al); evanescent; fleeting; impermanent; interim(istic); limited; momentary; mundane; nisi; passing; provisional; stopgap; substitute; temporal; tentative; timely; topical; transient; transitional; transitory; TEMPORARINESS: ephemerality; impermanence; impermanency; momentariness; temporality; topicality; transiency

TEMPT: (**see** "tease") allure; attract; bait; charm; court; decoy; draw; entice; fascinate; incite; induce; inveigle; invite; lure; persuade; prompt; provoke; risk; solicit; suggest; taunt; venture; wheedle; woo; TEMPTING: alluring; attractive; enticing; fascinating; inciting; inviting; luring; persuasive; provocative; provoking; seductive; sirenic(al); TEMPTATION: allure(ment);

attraction; enticement; fascination; lure; seduction; test(ing); trial

TENACIOUS: (see "stubborn") adhesive; bulldog(ged); bulldoggish; bulldoggy; cohesive; fast; gluey; glutinous; gummy; obstinate; persistent; retentive; sticky; strong; tough; viscous; TENACITY: adherence; adhesiveness; clinginess; cohesiveness; grit; guts; inveteracy; mettle; nerve; obstinacy; persistency; pluck; retentiveness; retentivity; sand; stickiness; stick-to-itiveness; strength; toughness; viscosity

TENANT: dweller; inhabitant; lessee; lodger; occupant; renter; sharecropper; villein

TEND: (see "protect") administer; aid; baby-sit; bend; care; conduce; cultivate; direct; dispose; father; feed; foster; gravitate; guard; incline; lead; lean; mind; minister; mother; nurse; nurture; protect; provide; serve; shield; swing; verge; wait; watch

TENDENCY: aim; appetence; appetency; aspiration; bent; bias; conatus; conducement; current; course; diathesis; direction; disposition; drift; drive; flair; flow; genius; goal; habit; idiosyncrasy; impulse; inclination; instinct; intimation; leaning; line; motion; movement; nisus; object; predilection; predisposition; proclivity; proneness; propensity; purpose; readiness; reflex; run; scope; sense; set; slant; spirit; stream; susceptibility; temper(ament); tenor; thought; tide; tone; trait; trend; turn; twist; vein; voyage; way; wind

TENDER: v. bid; give; offer; present; proffer; TENDER: a. acute; affectionate; amatory; benevolent; chickenhearted; clement; compassionate; considerate; cordial; delicate; emotional; fond; fragile; gentle; green; hyperalgesic; immature; impressionable; kind; lenient; loving; mellow; merciful; mild; moving; pathetic; responsive; sensitive; silken; soft(hearted); solicitous; sore; succulent; susceptible; sympathetic; tame; thoughtful; ticklish; touching; warm-(hearted); weak; yielding; young; youthful; TENDER: n. bid; boat; money; offer; TENDERNESS: affection; benevolence; clemency; compassion; delicacy; fondness; fragility; gentleness; hyperalgesia; hyperesthesia; kindness; leniency; love; mercy; mildness; sensitivity; softness; sympathy; tenuity; warmheartedness; weakness

TENET: (see "belief") creed; doctrine; dogma; formula; method; philosophy; principle

TENOR: character; course; drift; effect; import; intent; mood; nature; note; procedure; purport; stamp; substance; tendency; tone; transcript; trend; voice

TENSE: edgy; firm; frenetic; hard; hectic; high-strung; jittery; nervous; rapt; rigid; stiff; stretched; taut; tight; tired; tonic; unrelaxed; TENSENESS or TENSION: (see "rigor") coercion; drive; fanteeg; fatigue; heat; intensity; nervousness; power; pressure; rigidity; steam; strain; stress; stretch; tautness; tonicity; unrest

TENT: abode; canopy; canvas; cover(ing); dwelling; habitation; lodge; marquee; shelter; teepee

TENTACLE: arm; feeler; hair; palp; process; tendril

TENTATIVE: (see "temporary" and "uncertain") unconfirmed

TENUITY: faintness; feebleness; indigence; indigency; meagerness; poverty; rarity; slenderness; thinness; TENUOUS: delicate; diaphanous; filmy; fine; flimsy; gossamer(y); hazy; infirm; insignificant; meager; rare; sheer; slender; slim; subtle; thin; vague; weak

TENURE: see "holding"

TERGIVERSATE: apostatize; desert; equivocate; lie; renounce; retreat; shift; shuffle

TERM: v. see "name;" TERM(S): n. agreement; article; boundary; concord; condition; contract; course; cycle; denomination; descriptor; division; duration; end; expression; finish; footing; interim; interval; limit; month; name; period; price; proposition(s); provision(s); quarter; rhema; season; semester; sentence; session; space; state-(ment); stretch; tenure; time; word; year

TERMAGANT: crone; scold; shrew; virago; vixen

TERMINAL: a. concluding; conclusive; dying; ending; final; last; limiting; terminatory; ultimate; TERMINAL: n. depot; end(ing); extremity; finality; finial; outlet; point; pole; station; terminus

TERMINATE: (see "end") cease; close; cut; determine; die; discharge; dissolve; expire; finish; fire; halt; kill; result; sack; set(tle); stop; suspend; TERMINATION: (see "end") amen; discharge; discontinuance; discontinuation; expiration; finish; finis; suffix; term

TERMINOLOGY: (see "name") nomenclature; orismology; words

TERRACE: balcony; bank; berm(e); dais; deck; embankment; gallery; level; plain; plateau; porch; portico; street; way

TERRESTRIAL: earthbound; earth(l)y; geal; global; human; mundane; prosaic; temporal; worldly(-wise); worldwide

TERRIBLE: alarming; apocalyptic(al); appalling; astounding; awesome; awful; bad; calamitous; cataclysmal; cataclysmic; destructive; difficult; dire; disastrous; disreputable; dreadful; extreme; fearful; fell; formidable; frightening; frightful; ghastly; great; grim; horrible; horrific; imposing; intense; laborious; misfortunate; outrageous; overwhelming; portentous; punk; redoubtable; shocking; terrific; terrifying; troublesome; ugly; wicked

TERRIFIC: (see "huge" and "terrible") astounding; excellent; gorgeous; grand; magnificent; marvelous; overpowering; powerful; severe; shattering; superb; tremendous

TERRIFY: affright; agrise; appall; cow; daunt; deter; electrify; frighten; galvanize; intimidate; menace; panic; petrify; scare; TERRIFYING: (see "frightful" and "terrible") dismayful; gorgonesque; Gorgonian; hair-raising; hideous; menacing; scary; terrorful

TERRITORY: (see "area") arena; authority; branch; country; demesne; department; district; division; dominion; empire; field; franchise; ground; imperium; jurisdiction; land(scape); place; possession; precinct; province; realm; region; sphere; subdivision; terrain; terrene; topography; tract

TERROR: affright; alarm; anxiety; apprehension; *bête noir*; bugbear; consternation; dread; fear; fright; nightmare; scourge; terribleness; threat; worry; TERRORIST: alarmist; firebrand; goon; Jacobin; rebel

TERSE: abbreviated; aphoristic; axiomatic; brachysyllabic; brief; brusque; compact; compendious; concise; crisp; curt; epigrammatic(al); exact; laconic(al); monosyllabic; neat; pithy; poignant; pointed; polished;

postulational; refined; sententious; short; succinct; summary; Tacitean; telegrammatic; telegraphic; trenchant; unwordy

TEST: v. analyze; ascertain; assay; determine; essay; evaluate; examine; exercise; experiment; explore; inquire; inspect; palpate; probe; prove; quiz; rehearse; run; scrutinize; shakedown; taste; try; TEST: n. analysis; assay; audition; criteria (pl.); criterion; crucible; dry run; essay; examination; exercise; experiment; inquiry; inspection; inventory; norm; oral; ordeal; procedure; qualification; quiz; rehearsal; run; scratch; scrutiny; shakedown; standard; temptation; touchstone; trial; try(out); TESTED: see "experienced"

TESTAMENT: affirmation; Bible; book; convention; credo; creed; disposition; evidence; scripture; testamentum; will; witness

TESTIFY: adjure; affirm; allege; assert; asseverate; assure; attest; aver; avow; certify; cite; claim; confess; declare; depone; depose; display; evince; maintain; manifest; plead; probate; profess; prove; recite; reveal; say; show; speak; swear; state; vouch; witness

TESTIMONY: acknowledgment; affidavit; affirmation; allegation; attestation; authentication; data (pl.); declaration; deposition; evidence; profession; proof; symbol; witness; TESTIMONIAL: affidavit; appreciation; commendation; decoration; endorsement; evidence; medal; plaudit; recommendation; symbol; token; tribute; warrant; word

TESTY: (see "crabby") caustic; choleric; cranky; cross; exasperated; fretful; ill-humored; impatient; irascible; irritable; nervous; peevish; pettish; petulant; temperamental; vinegary; waspish

TETHER: v. bind; confine; fasten; leash; limit; restrain; tie; TETHER: n. bond; chain; leash; limit; range; restraint; rope; scope; tie

TEXT: book; copy; manuscript; matter; passage; scope; script; source; subject; theme; topic; verse; version; work; writing

TEXTILE: cloth; cotton; denim; fabric; fiber; filament; flannel; goods; linen; rayon; silk; woolen; worsted; yarn

TEXTURE: arrangement; character(istic); consistency; essence; fabric; fiber; grain; nap; nature; quality; scheme; shape; size; structure; substance; wale; weave; web; woof

THANK: **v.** acknowledge; appreciate; credit; gladden; THANK(S): **n.** appreciation; grace; gramercy; gratitude; THANKFUL: appreciative; glad; grateful; gratified; obliged; pleased; THANKFULNESS: appreciation; gratefulness; gratification; gratitude; gratulation

THANKLESS: (**see** "ungrateful") unappreciated; unappreciative; unthankful

THAW: (**see** "melt") unbend; unfreeze

THEATER: area; arena; boards; cinema; drama; house; legit; movie; odeon; odeum; opera; playhouse; plays; scene; sphere; THEATRIC(AL) (**see** "showy") artificial; dramatic; dramaturgic(al); factitious; histrionic; melodramatic; meretricious; operatic; pompous; stagy; thespian; unreal; vivid

THEFT: abstraction; burglary; embezzlement; larceny; pilfering; pillage; piracy; plagiarism; purloining; removal; robbery; stealing; taking; thievery

THEME: article; discourse; essay; exercise; issue; item; leitmotif; leitmotiv; material; matter; melody; message; motif; note; paper; point; principle; problem; proposition; question; representation; subject; tema; text; theorum; thesis; topic

THEORIZE: (**see** "guess") hypothesize; philosophize; postulate; propose; speculate; THEORY: (**see** "philosophy") assumption; belief; concept(ion); conjecture; doctrine; dogma; formula; frame of reference; fundament; hypothesis; idea(l); ism; knowledge; philosopheme; plan; policy; postulata (pl.); postulate; postulatum; presumption; presupposition; principle; procedure; proposition; schemata (pl.); scheme; speculation; supposition; surmise; system; theoretic; theorum; thesis; viewpoint; THEORETIC(AL): academic; closet; conjectural; contemplative; fictitious; hypothetical; ideal; impractical; intellectual; platonic; postulatory; presumptive; putative; quodlibetic; speculative; suppositional; supposititious; THEORIST: doctrinaire; dogmatist; egghead; idealogue; ideologist; visionary

THERAPY: cure; dose; drug(s); medicine; physiatrics; program; therapeutics; treatment

THEREFORE: accordingly; because; consequently; ergo; hence; since; so; then; thence

THESIS: affirmation; article; assumption; contention; discourse; dissertation; essay; monograph; opinion; paper; philosophy; position; postulate; proposition; statement; story; theme; theory; treatise; writing

THESPIAN: (**see** "theatrical") actor; actress; mime; player; trouper

THICK: burly; calloused; chummy; close; clumped; clustered; coagulated; compact; concentrated; condensed; consolidated; crammed; crass; crowded; deep; dense; distilled; dull; excessive; frequent; gross; grumous; heavy; hoarse; husky; hyposensitive; massed; numerous; obtuse; populous; profound; roily; sheer; solid; stiff; stocky; stolid; stratified; stuffy; stupid; swarming; teeming; turbid; undilute(d); utter; viscous; THICKEN: blur; broaden; cake; clabber; clot; clump; cluster; coagulate; concentrate; confirm; congeal; curdle; dry; firm; freeze; gather; gel; harden; increase; inspissate; intensify; jell; lump; mass; obscure; press; set; solidify; stick; stiffen; THICKNESS: body; concentration; diameter; extent; firmness; layer; mass; ply; solidarity; solidity; stratum; viscosity; volume; voluminousness; width

THICKET: boscage; bosk; brake; brush; bushes; chaparral; clump; coppice; copse; covert; grove; growth; hedge; jungle; morass; shag; spinny; tangle; tussock; wood(s)

THIEF: bandit; burglar; crook; depredator; embezzler; fagin; felon; filcher; hijacker; larcenist; peculator; picaroon; pickpocket; pilferer; pirate; plunderer; THIEVISH: burglarious; furtive; larcenous; mercurial; sly; stealthy; sticky-fingered; thieving; THIEVERY: **see** "theft"

THIN: **v.** attenuate; dilute; extenuate; lessen; rarefy; reduce; scamp; skimp; slenderize; slim; water; weaken; THIN(NED): **a.** attenuated; bony; cachectic; cachexic; cadaverous; delicate; dilute(d); dim; emaciated; fine; flimsy; fragile; frail; gaunt; hairline; inadequate; lank(y); lathy; lean; lessened; little; malnourished; meager; poor; precise; rare(fied); reedy; scant(y); scantily; scrimpy; sheer; skeletal; skeletonic; skimpy; skinny; slender; slight; slim; spare; sparse; tenuous; thinnish; thready; transparent; unsatisfying; unsubstantial; washy; watery; weak; THINNESS: emaciation; fragility; insubstantiality; macilency; malnourishment; malnutrition; meagerness; slenderness; tenuity

THING(S): (see "gadget") accomplishment; act; affair(s); article; being; business; circumstance; complication; deed; entity; essence; fear; gear; goods; idea; item; matter; notion(s); noun; object; obsession; particle; phobia; possession(s); product; traps

THINK: analyze; appraise; apprehend; assume; believe; brood; calculate; cerebrate; chew over; cogitate; compute; conceive; conceptualize; conclude; concoct; conjecture; consider; contemplate; contrive; decide; deliberate; design; devise; distinguish; divine; dwell (on); esteem; estimate; evolve; examine; excogitate; expect; fancy; fathom; feel; figure; guess; hold; hope; hypothesize; ideate; imagine; infer; intellectualize; intend; invent; judge; lucubrate; meditate; mull; muse; opine; perpend; plan; ponder; pore; preconceive; prefigure; premeditate; project; propose; purpose; question; ratiocinate; rationalize; reason; recall; reckon; recollect; reflect; regard; remember; repute; reveal; revolve; ruminate; scheme; speculate; study; suppose; suspect; trow; understand; ween; weigh; wish; THINKER: brain; computer; contemplator; intellect(ual); mind; philosopher; ponderer; speculator; theorist; wit; THINKING: a.(see "thoughtful") cogitative; conceptualistic; contemplative; intellectual; meditative; rational; ruminant; ruminative; THINKING: n. (see "thought") alogism; conceptualization; dereism; knowledge; position; reason(ing); speculation; understanding

THIRST: anadipsia; craving; desire; dipsomania; longing; polydipsia; wish; yen; THIRSTY: arid; avid; craving; desirous; dry; eager; keen; parched; wishful

THONG: knout; lash; leash; quirt; romal; strap; string; thread; whip

THORN: arrow; beard; briar; hook; irritation; jag; prickle; projection; sarcasm; shaft; spear; spike; stob; trouble; vexation; THORNY: (see "spiny") brambly; difficult; hard; irritating; prickly; tough; vexatious

THOROUGH: (see "complete") *gung ho*; well-done; THOROUGHGOING: (see "absolute" and "out-and-out") all-out; arrant; deep-dyed; double-dyed; enthusiastic; hearty; sheer; unreserved

THOUGHT: analysis; apprehension; attention; belief; brainwork; care; cerebration; cogitation; concentration; concept(ion);

conceptualization; conjecture; consideration; contemplation; deliberation; discourse; drift; estimation; excogitation; expectation; fancy; guess; hope; idea(l); ideation; imagination; inference; intellection; intellectualization; intent(ion); intuition; judgment; knowledge; lucubration; meditation; mentation; message; mind; muse; musing; notion; opinion; *pensée*; pensiveness; perception; philosophy; phrase; pitch; plan; ponderation; position; prefiguration; premeditation; reason(ing); reckoning; recollection; reflection; regard; rumination; sense; sentiment; speculation; study; supposition; thinking; understanding; view; wish

THOUGHTFUL: absorbed; acute; brainy; calculating; calculative; circumspect; cogitable; cogitabund; cogitative; conceptualistic; considerate; contemplative; cool; deliberate; deliberative; engrossed; grave; heedful; intellectual; intelligent; introspective; inventive; keen; meditative; mindful; museful; musing; nomothetic; occupied; penetrating; pensive; perspicacious; philosophic(al); politic; provident; prudent; purposeful; quick; rapt; rational; reasonable; reasoned; reflective; sad; sagacious; sensible; sharp; shrewd; sober; solemn; speculative; studious; tender; thinking; unhurried; wise

THOUGHTLESS: abstracted; careless; frivolous; giddy; heedless; hoity-toity; improvident; imprudent; impulsive; inattentive; incogitable; incogitant; incogitative; inconsiderate; indeliberate; indifferent; insensate; neglectful; negligent; rash; reckless; stupid; unmindful; unthoughtful; THOUGHTLESSNESS: carelessness; folly; frivolity; giddiness; improvidence; imprudence; inattention; incogitability; incogitance; incogitancy; indifference; recklessness; stupidity; unthoughtfulness

THOUSAND: chiliad; mil(le); millenial; millenniary; millennium

THRALL: see "slave"

THRASH: beat; belabor; belt; cane; consider; drub; drudge; drum; flail; flog; flourish; lace; lambaste; lick; paddle; paddywhack; pepper; pound; separate; spank; strike; tan; thump; trounce; wave; whip; vanquish

THREAD: cord; course; fiber; filament; line; lisle; reeve; sequence; stamen; strand; thong; twine; wire; yarn

THREADBARE: banal; barren; common-

(place); deteriorated; hackneyed; jejune; mean; napless; scanty; seedy; sere; shabby; stale; stereotyped; tatterdemalion; thin; trite; vapid; worn

THREATEN: comminate; dare; endanger; expose; hector; imperil; intimidate; menace; portend; venture; wheedle; THREAT: anathema; club; commination; dare; denunciation; epithet; intimidation; menace; minacity; notice; peril; risk; sword of Damocles; terror; thunder; THREATENED *or* THREATENING: comminatory; dangerous; denunciatory; endangered; epithetic; fateful; fraught; imminent; imperiled; inauspicious; menaced; menacing; minacious; minatorial; minatory; ominous; prognostic; portentous; sinister; threatful; thundering; troublesome; ugly

THREE: ter; *tria*; triad; trin(ary); trine; trinity; trio; trivalent; THREEFOLD: ternary; trinal; trinary; triple(d)

THRENODY: dirge; elegy; lament(ation); requiem

THRESH: beat; best; flail; harvest; hull; pound; separate; thrash; win(now)

THRESHOLD: (see "beginning") boundary; door(way); end; entrance; eve; gate; horizon; outset; route; sill; verge

THRIFT: accumulation; caution; conservation; economy; forehandedness; fortune; frugality; growth; husbandry; miserliness; parcity; providence; prudence; reserve; saving(s); stinginess; success; THRIFTY: cautious; conservative; economical; forehanded; frugal; housewifely; meager; *ménager*; provident; prudent; saving; scanty; sparing; stingy

THRILL: v. affect; charm; enchant; excite; flush; please; quiver; shiver; stir; throb; tingle; touch; transfix; tremble; vibrate; THRILL: n. bang; boot; charge; enchantment; enthrallment; excitement; flush; frisson; kick; pleasure; quiver; throb(bing); tingle; tingling; transfixion; tremor; vibration; THRILLING: breathless; breathtaking; electric; exciting; galvanic; hair-raising; intense; moving; throbbing; vibrating

THRIVE: advance; batten; boom; enlarge; enrich; fatten; flourish; grow; improve; increase; luxuriate; progress; prosper; succeed; wax

THROAT: fauces; gorge; gula; gullet; hatch; inlet; maw; neck; passage; pharynx; trachea; voice

THROB: v. (see "beat") ache; oscillate; pain; palpitate; pulsate; stab; thrill; undulate; vibrate; THROB: n. ache; ictus; pain; pang; pulsation; stab; stitch; throe; undulation; vibration; THROBBING: painful; palpitant; pulsatile; pulsating; stabbing; thrilling

THROE(S): (see "difficult") ache; anguish; disorder; distress; pain; pang; rack; regret; spasm; stitch; struggle

THRONE: asana; cathedra; chair; king; seat; sovereign(ty)

THRONG: v. (see "gather") agglutinate; aggregate; amass; congregate; crowd; jam; mass; meet; press; swarm; teem; THRONG: n. (see "mob") agglutination; aggregation; amassment; army; assemblage; clutch; congregation; crew; crowd; gathering; hecatomb; horde; host; jam; mass; meeting; multitude; press; school; shoal; swarm

THROUGH: across; among; by; diagonal; done; during; ended; final; finished; into; over; past; per; via; washed-up; with

THROW: v. abandon; advance; build; cast; catapult; chuck; construct; deliver; dislodge; dispatch; eject; emit; exert; fling; heave; hurl; impel; launch; peg; pelt; pitch; precipitate; project; propel; sling; thrust; toss; unseat; wing; THROW: n. cover(ing); fling; pitch; quilt; risk; scarf; spread; toss; wrap

THRUST: v. cram; dart; dig; drift; drive; eject; enter; extend; fill; fire; fling; hurl; intrude; jab; kick; overcome; pack; penetrate; pierce; plunge; poke; probe; prod; propel; protrude; push; ram; reach; shear; shove; sink; stab; strike; throw; THRUST: n. assault; attack; drift; drive; energy; entry; fling; intrusion; jab; kick; lunge; onset; penetration; plunge; punch; shoot; shove; stab; strain; stress; strike; stroke; velocity; venture; vigor; volley

THUG: (see "bandit") gangster; killer

THUMB: digit; handle; phalanx; pollex

THUMP: advertise; advocate; bang; beat; conquer; cudgel; drive; endorse; force; hammer; hit; knock; pound; punch; punish; strike; thrash; whip

THUNDER: boom; energy; force; fulmination; noise; roar; roll; rumble; strength; threat; violence; THUNDERING: booming; dangerous; foudroyant; fulminant; fulminating; fulmin(e)ous; loud; mighty; threatening; thundrous; tonitruant; tonitruous

THUS: consequently; ergo; hence; sic; so; yet

THWART: (see "foil") baffle; balk; block; check; clash; contravene; curb; defeat; disable; frustrate; hamper; handicap; hinder; impede; impinge; interrupt; obstruct; oppose; prevent; quarrel; spite; stop; stymie

TICKET: v. book; characterize; classify; label; list; mark; price; schedule; tag; TICKET: n. ballot; card; *carte d'entrée*; cost; coupon; ducat; label; license; list; note; pass; permit; plan; price; program; schedule; slate; slip; stub; summons; tag; tax; token; voucher

TICKLE: amuse; annoy; awaken; divert; excite; pinch; please; provoke; stimulate; tease; tingle; titillate; tittivate; torment; vellicate

TIDBIT: bit; bite; *bonne bouche*; delicacy; eatable; kickshaw; morceau; morsel

TIDE: chance; current; decrease; ebb; fall; flood; flow; holiday; increase; neap; opportunity; overflow; rise; season; space; stream; swing; time; wave

TIDING(S): advice; ·evangel; event; gospel; happening; intelligence; message; news; report; rumor; slogan; word

TIDY: (see "neat") comely; decent; fair; healthy; large; natty; ordered; orderly; plump; precise; *rangé*; *rangée* (fem.); smart; smug; *soigné*; *soignée* (fem.); spruce; systematic; taut; trim

TIE: v. attach; band; bind; connect; constrain; couple; draw; equal(ize); fasten; fix; hitch; ligate; link; marry; moor; rivet; rope; secure; strap; tack; tether; truss; unite; TIE: n. ascot; attachment; band; beam; bind; bond; brace; connection; coupling; cravat; dead heat; draw; equality; hitch; knot; ligation; ligature; linchpin; link; neutralization; nexus; obligation; relation; restraint; rivet; root; rope; sleeper; stalemate; standoff; toss-up

TIFF: (see "brawl") anger; bout; fit; huff; outburst; quarrel; snit; spat; temper

TIGHT: cheap; close; compact; compressed; constant; constrained; dense; drunk(en); exacting; faithful; firm; fixed; full; impervious; intoxicated; miserly; narrow; rigid; secure; smooth; snug; solid; stingy; stretched; strict; taut; tense; trying; TIGHTEN: choke; contract; crank; draw; improve; lace; smooth; squeeze; straighten; stretch; tauten; wind; wrench

TILL: v. cultivate; farm; plant; plow; prepare; seed; toil; TILL: n. box; drawer; tray; TILLABLE: arable; cultivatable; farmable; fertile

TILLER: cultivator; farmer; handle; helm; husbandman; lever; plowman; sapling; shoot

TILT: burst; cant; careen; dip; duel; heel; incline; joust; lean; list; pitch; rush; seesaw; slant; slope; sway; tip

TIMBER: beam; character; forest; logs; lumber; material(s); stuff; trees; wood(s)

TIMBRE: (see "tone") character; clang; pitch; quality; resonance; ring; sonority; sound

TIME: v. see "clock;" TIME: n. age; appointment; beat; cadence; chronology; clock; cycle; date; duration; end; eon; epoch; era; event; future; generation; ictus; interim; interval; leisure; length; lilt; limit(ation); occasion; opportunity; meter; moment; past; period; present; rhythm; season; sentence; sequence; session; span; speed; spell; stretch; succession; tempo; tense; term; tide; turn

TIMELESS: (see "everlasting") ageless; changeless; dateless; eternal; hourless; immemorial; in perpetuity; intemporal; interminable; unending; unrestricted; TIMELESSNESS: (see "eternity") indefinitude; infinity; perpetuality; perpetuity

TIMELY: abreast; advanced; advantageous; apposite; appropriate; auspicious; contemporary; current; early; expedient; fresh; happy; late; lucky; meet; modern(istic); new; novel; now; opportune; pat; present-day; prompt; proper; propitious; providential; recent; relevant; seasonable; seasonably; seasonal; suitable; tempestive; temporary; timeous; topical; up-to-date

TIMEPIECE: chronometer; clock; horologe; hourglass; sundial; watch

TIMID: (**see** "bashful") afraid; chary; chicken-hearted; chicken-livered; cowardly; craven; effeminate; faint(hearted); fearful; fearsome; frightened; gentle; henny; hesitant; humble; irresolute; maidenly; mild; modest; mousy; overawed; pavid; pusillanimous; retiring; scary; sheepish; shrinking; shy; soft(hearted); tentative; timorous; tremulous; trepid; undaring; unheroic; unimpressive; weak; TIMIDITY: bashfulness; doubt; dubiety; dubitation; fear; effeminacy; faintheartedness; faintness; fearfulness; hesitation; indecision; inferiority (complex); irresolution; mousiness; pusillanimity; shyness; vacillation; weakness

TIMING: (**see** "pace") coordination

TIMOROUS: (**see** "timid") tremulous

TIN: **v.** can; coat; preserve; TIN(NY): **a.** base; inferior; spurious; tawdry; TIN: **n.** metal; stannum

TINDER: amadou; explosive; fuel; kindling; punk

TINGE: **v.** affect; dye; color; imbue; impregnate; influence; modify; pink; shade; stain; streak; taint; tincture; tint; touch; TINGE: **n.** cast; color; complexion; dash; dye; hue; nuance; shade; smack; stain; streak; taint; tint; tone; touch; trace

TINGLE: **v.** (**see** "stimulate") burn; excite; glow; prick(le); sting; stir; thrill; tickle; tinkle; vibrate; TINGLE: **n.** frisson; glow; stimulation; sting; stir; tickle; vibration

TINSEL: **see** "trashy"

TINT: (**see** "tinge") blush; color(ation); dye; hue; nuance; shade; stain; tone

TINY: diminutive; dwarf(ish); itsy-bitsy; itty-bitty; lilliputian; little; microscopic; miniature; minute; peewee; petite; small; submicroscopic; teeny; ultramicroscopic; wee

TIP: **v.** bribe; cant; careen; cue; dip; dunk; heel; incline; lean; list; lurch; oil; overturn; palm; slant; slope; tap; tilt; toe; topple; touch; upset; TIP: **n.** acme; apex; baksheesh; bonus; bribe; cue; douceur; edge; end; extremity; gift; gratuity; hint; incline; insinuation; lagniappe; offering; oil; perquisite; point; pourboire; ransom; summit; terminal; terminus; tilt; tribute; *Trinkgeld*

TIPSY: (**see** "drunk") askew; groggy; merry; unsteady; wobbly

TIRADE: fulmination; harangue; invective; philippic; protest; rage; screed; speech

TIRE: bore; burden; debilitate; defeat; deplete; disgust; distress; drain; enervate; exhaust; fag; fatigue; irk; jade; labor; overcome; overdo; overwork; pall; sap; sate; satiate; strain; tax; tucker; weaken; weary; worry; TIRED: (**see** "fatigued") beat; blown; bushed; dead; debilitated; dilapidated; drained; exhausted; footsore; hackneyed; overweary; overworked; run-down; unrefreshed; unrelaxed; unrested; weary; worked

TIRELESS: exhaustless; fast-stepping; indefatigable; perpetual; sustained; unending; unflagging; unweariable; TIRELESSNESS: indefatigability; inexhaustibility

TIRESOME: (**see** "dull") annoying; boresome; boring; bromidic; drear(y); exhausting; fatiguing; irritating; monotonous; tedious; wearied; wearisome; weary; TIRESOMENESS: (**see** "fatigue") dreariness; dullness; exhaustion; irritation; monotony; tedium; wearisomeness

TISSUE: bast; fabric; fat; fiber; flesh; material; meat; membrane; muscle; net; tela; texture; web

TITANIC: (**see** "huge") colossal; earthshaking; enormous; gigantic; monstrous; powerful; strong; towering; vast

TITLE: (**see** "name") appellation; appellative; book; caption; championship; claim; cognomen; deed; degree; denomination; designation; epithet; ground; heading; headline; honorific; inscription; justification; label; mark; muniment; ownership; predicate; proof; rank; reason; right; rubric; term; titulus; work

TITTLE: (**see** "bit") atom; gossip; hair; jot; mite; part(icle); point; whisker; whisper; whit

TITUBATE: reel; stagger; stumble; totter

TOADY: **v.** apple-polish; cower; cringe; fawn; kowtow; TOADY: **n.** apple-polisher; cringer; flunkey; lackey; leech; minion; parasite; pawn; sycophant; toadeater; yes-man

TOAST: **v.** brown; celebrate; crisp; drink; dry; parch; roast; tan; warm; TOAST: **n.** bread; greeting; pledge; skoal; TOAST-MASTER: *arbiter bibendi*; ceremoniarius; emcee; officiator

TOBACCO: burley; capa; caporal; knaster; latakia; Vuelta; weed

TOE: (**see** "obey") dactyl; digit; phalanx

TOGETHER: accompanying; along; associated; bound; bundled; coincidental(ly); collected; concerted; conjoined; conjointly; consecutively; *en banc*; *en masse*; grouped; holus-bolus; jointly; massed; mutually; *pari passu*; reciprocal(ly); simultaneous(ly); *tête-à-tête*; unanimous(ly); unisonant; unisonous; united; unsegregated; unseparated; *vis-à-vis*; with; TOGETHERNESS: association; communion; concentricity; concert; cooperation; *esprit de corps*; *gung ho*; mutuality; omneity; oneness; propinquity; simultaneity; solidarity; team spirit; unanimity

TOGGERY *or* TOGS: (**see** "clothes") clothing; dress; garb; gear

TOIL: **v.** drudge; exert; grind; hammer; labor; plod; plug; slave; strain; till; travail; work; TOIL: **n.** (**see** "work") activity; drudgery; exertion; fatigue; grind; labor; pains; slavery; sweat; travail; trouble

TOKEN: **a.** minimal; perfunctory; simulated; TOKEN: **n.** amulet; badge; bit; characteristic; emblem; evidence; expression; fare; feature; gesture; index; indication; keepsake; mark; memento; memorial; omen; part; password; pawn; pledge; portent; precedent; reminder; script; sign(ification); souvenir; symbol; tessera; ticket

TOLD: **see** "spoken"

TOLERABLE: acceptable; allowable; bearable; endurable; fair(ish); indifferent; liv(e)able; middling; moderate; passable; satisfactory; so-so; sufferable; supportable

TOLERATE: abide; accept; adapt; allow; bear; brook; condone; endure; forbear; go; habituate; let; pass; permit; recognize; resist; stand; stomach; submit; suffer; support; undergo; vouchsafe; TOLERANT: agnostic-(al); benevolent; benign(ant); broad-minded; elastic; enduring; forbearing; indulgent; latitudinarian; lenient; magnanimous; peaceable; placable; submissive; tractable; TOL-

ERANCE *or* TOLERATION: abidance; acclimation; acclimatization; adaptation; allowance; benevolence; endurance; fortitude; habituation; indulgence; laissez-faire; latitude; latitudinarianism; leeway; liberality; license; magnanimity; margin; maximum; stamina; sufferance; sympathy

TOLL: cess; charge; compensation; duty; exaction; excise; fare; fee; impost; knell; levy; rate; rent; ring; sound; tailage; tax; tithe; tribute

TOMB: catacomb; cenotaph; crypt; grave; lair; mastaba; monument; vault

TOMBOY: gamine; *garçon manqué*; garçonne; hoyden; romp; TOMBOYISH: gamine; hoydenish; rompish

TOMFOOLERY: **see** "nonsense"

TOMORROW: mañana; morning; morrow

TONE: accent; attitude; balance; cadence; character; clang; color; energy; expressiveness; feel; harmony; health; hue; inflection; key; modulation; mood; notes; pitch; quality; resiliency; resonance; ring; savor; shade; sonority; sound; spirit; style; temper; timbre; tint; tonicity; tonus; trend; vigor

TONGUE: abuse; abusiveness; dialect; flap; glossa; glossae (pl.); glossus; idiom; language; lingua; linguae (pl.); lorriker; projection; speech; tab; utterance; voice

TONIC: **a.** astringent; bracing; healthy; invigorating; refreshing; restorative; roborant; stimulating; TONIC: **n.** astringent; bracer; catalyst; elixir; fillip; invigoration; pep; pick-me-up; pop; remedy; restorative; roborant; soda; stimulant; stimulation; vigor; vitalizer

TOO: additional; also; and; besides; else; excessive(ly); extravagantly; extremely; likewise; moreover; over(ly); then; very

TOOL(S): agent; apparatus; appliance; cat's-paw; device; dupe; enginery; gadget(ry); gear; implement; instrument; machine; mechanism; outfit; paraphernalia; pawn; puppet; rat; rebel; utensil; utility

TOOTH: appetite; canine; cog; dens; fang; incisor; liking; molar; projection; taste; tusk; TOOTH-SHAPED: dentate; denticulate(d); dentiform; serrate(d); TOOTH-

LESS: edentate; edentulous; futile; ineffective

TOP: **v.** (**see** "defeat") beat; best; cap; çlear'; climax; cover; crest; crown; dominate; excel; outdo; surmount; surpass; win; TOP(S): **n.** (**see** "choice") acme; A-one; apex; apogee; best; cap; climax; consummation; cover; crest; crown; culmination; dome; excellence; head; lid; maximum; meridian; peak; pinnacle; point; ridge; roof; summit; surface; tip; topmost; topnotch; toy; tuft; vertex; zenith

TOPER: **see** "drunk(ard)"

TOPIC: (**see** "theme") gambit; ground; head(ing); issue; item; material; matter; point; problem; proposition; question; subject; text; themata (pl.); theorum; thesis; TOPICAL: current; local; temporary; thematic; timely; useful

TOPPLE: **see** "fall"

TOPSY-TURVY: askew; awry; cockeyed; confused; disordered; inverted; upset; upside-down

TORCH: arsonist; cresset; firebug; flare; flash(light); guidance; incendiary; lamp; lantern; light; pyromaniac

TORMENT: **v.** (**see** "tease") afflict; agitate; agonize; badger; bait; crucify; devil; distress; disturb; dragoon; excoriate; excruciate; fret; grill; harass; harrow; lacerate; molest; persecute; pester; plague; punish; rack; rage; tickle; torture; trouble; vex; worry; TORMENT: **n.** (**see** "rack") affliction; agony; anguish; bale; calamity; cruciation; crucifixion; distress; excruciation; fire and brimstone; harassment; hell(fire); oppression; pain; persecution; plague; punishment; purgatory; scourge; sorrow; suffering; torture; woe; TORMENTER: (**see** "persecutor") pest; plague

TORPID: apathetic; comatose; dormant; dull; hypnotic; indifferent; lackadaisical; lethargic; nonchalant; phlegmatic(al); pococurante; sleepy; sluggish; sodden; somnolent; stagnant; stolid; stupid; stuporous; torporific; TORPOR: acedia; apathy; coma; dormancy; dullness; hypnosis; indifference; lackadaisy; lethargy; nonchalance; phlegm; sleep; sloth(fulness); sluggishness; slumber; somnolence; stagnation; stolidity; stupefaction; stupidity; stupor; torpidity; torpitude

TORRENT: (**see** "stream") cascade; current; downpour; flood; flow; flux; outpouring; river; rush; spate; tide

TORRID: afire; ardent; arid; burning; dry; fired; hot; parched; parching; passionate; scorched; scorching; sultry; tropical

TORTOISE: chelonian; emyd; terrapin; Testudinata (pl.); testudo; turtle

TORTUOUS: (**see** "devious") serpentine; sinuate; sinuous; snaky

TORTURE: **v.** afflict; coerce; cruciate; crucify; distort; excruciate; flay; martyr; punish; torment; TORTURE: **n.** abuse; affliction; anguish; coercion; cruciation; crucifixion; cruelty; distress; excruciation; martyrdom; martyrization; pain; punishment; rack; strain; suffering; torment; work

TOSS: (**see** "throw") agitate; bandy; brandish; buffet; concoct; consume; debate; discard; fling; flip; flounce; heave; hurl; interject; jettison; mix; pitch; punish; roll; stagger; surge; swallow; sway; tumble; vibrate; wave; wobble

TOTAL: **v.** (**see** "add") cast; complete; compute; figure; foot (up); number; reckon; summarize; tabulate; tally; TOTAL: **a.** absolute; aggregate; all(-out); complete; dead; full(-scale); *in toto*; out-and-out; overall; perfected; summatory; thoroughgoing; totalistic; totalitarian; *tout à fait*; utter; whole; TOTAL: **n.** aggregate; all; amount; entirety; recapitulation; sum(mation); summarization; tabulation; tally; whole; TOTALITY: absoluteness; entirety; integrality; mutuality; omneity; oneness; sum; system; totalitarianism; unanimity; universality

TOTEM: emblem; figure; pole; token; xat

TOTTER: capitulate; fall; oscillate; reel; rock; shake; shimmy; stagger; sway; vacillate; waver; weaken; wobble

TOUCH: **v.** abut; adjoin; affect; approach; border; brush; cheat; contact; disturb; feel; get; graze; handle; impinge; impress; meddle; meet; nick; palpate; pertain; relate; scratch; shave; verge; TOUCH: **n.** (**see** "trace") contact; dash; defect; feel; knack; mark; mention; modicum; palpation; pressure; quantity; reminder; responsiveness; scintilla; sensitiveness; shade; skill; smattering; soupçon; stamp; stroke; tact; temperament; tincture; tinge; trait; vein; vestige; weakness; TOUCHING: abutting; affecting; against; attingent; concerning; co(n)terminous; contiguous; moving; pathetic; pitiful; poignant; sad; tactual; tangent(ial); tender; TOUCHY: (see "sensitive") choleric; crabbed; crabby; doubtful; irascible; irksome; nervous; oversensitive; peppery; precarious; reactive; snappish; sore; temperamental; tender; ticklish; uncertain

TOUGH: **a.** (see "stubborn") adamant; aggressive; brutal; crustaceous; firm; hard; hard-boiled; hardened; hardfisted; hard-handed; hardy; harsh; inured; knotty; menacing; militant; powerful; puzzling; realistic; robust; rocky; rough; rowdy(ish); ruffianly; ruthless; severe; sinewy; steely; stiff; stout; strong; sturdy; tenacious; thorny; threatening; untender; unyielding; weatherbeaten; wiry; withy; TOUGH: **n.** bandit; bully; desperado; hoodlum; plugugly; rascal; roughneck; rowdy; ruffian; thug; toughie; TOUGHEN: discipline; drill; exercise; harden; inure; season; strengthen; taw; temper; train; TOUGHNESS: hardness; severity; sinewiness; strength; tenacity

TOUR: (see "journey") circuit; drive; excursion; expedition; itinerary; itineration; peregrination; pilgrimage; promenade; round; safari; series; shift; turn; visit; TOURIST: see "traveler"

TOURNAMENT: contest; event; joust; match; meet; series; tourney

TOW: see "drag"

TOWER: **v.** arise; elevate; fly; loom; mount; overshadow; overtop; rear; rise; soar; surge; surpass; TOWER: **n.** Babel; campanile; citadel; cupola; dome; donjon; fortress; pillar; rondel; sanctuary; spire; steeple; tor(rion); turret; TOWERING: (see "tall") excessive; gigantic; imposing; overweening; overwhelming; surging; surpassing

TOWN: citizenry; city; electorate; hamlet; metropolis; municipality; public; village; TOWNSHIP: area; deme; district; subdivision; TOWN(S)MAN: burgher; cit(izen); oppidan; resident; urbanite

TOXIN: (see "poison") bane; ricin; venom; virus

TOY: **v.** amuse; dally; fondle; pet; philander; play; sport; trifle; TOY: **a.** see "imitation;" TOY: **n.** bauble; doll; geegaw; imitation; kickshaw; knickknack; model; plaything; trifle; trinket; tuft

TRACE: **v.** ascertain; copy; delineate; develop; dog; draw; examine; follow; hound; hunt; mark; outline; record; sketch; smell; sniff; stamp; track; train; TRACE: **n.** bit; cast; clew; echo; evidence; footprint; fossil; gleam; glint; hairbreadth; hint; impression; indication; line; mark; memento; memorial; particle; path; ray; record; relic; relish; remains; remnant; scent; scintilla; show; sign; sketch; smattering; smell; sniff; soupçon; spark; spoor; strain; streak; suggestion; surmise; survival; suspicion; symptom; tang; tincture; tinge; token; touch; track; trail; vestige; vestigia (pl.); whisker; whisper

TRACK: (see "hunt" and "trace") course; evidence; footprint; mark; method; orbit; path; procedure; rail(s); road; run; rut; scent; sequence; slot; spoor; trail; turf; vestige; wake

TRACT: area; book(let); dissertation; essay; leaflet; lot; pamphlet; parcel; part; plot; quarter; region; sector; stretch; territory; tractate; tractus; treatise; zone

TRACTABLE: (see "obedient" and "pliant") gentle; tame; treatable; unvicious

TRADE: **v.** barter; buy; deal; exchange; interchange; job; market; merchandise; negotiate; reciprocate; sell; specialize; substitute; swap; traffic; transact; TRADE: **n.** art; barter(ing); business; clientele; coarse; commerce; commutation; craft; custom; deal; exchange; habit; industry; interchange; job; market(ing); mercantilism; merchandise; métier; mode; negotiation; occupation; patronage; practice; procedure; profession; pursuit; reciprocation; sale(s); skill; substitution; swap; transaction; work; TRADER *or* TRADESMAN: (see "merchant") agent; artisan; broker; craftsman; dealer; draper; jobber; monger; salesman; shopkeeper; storekeeper; wholesaler

TRADITION: acceptation; attitude; belief(s); characteristics; code; convention; custom(s); doctrine; epic; ethos; folklore; habits; heritage; information; institution(s); knowledge; learning; legacy; legend; lineage; lore; method; mores; myth; practice(s); principle(s); rule(s); standing; style; usage(s);

wisdom; TRADITIONAL: accepted; ancestral; atavistic; characteristic; conventional; cultural; customary; habitual; historical; legendary; orthodox(ical); prescriptive; traditionalistic; tralatitious; unwritten; venerated; veteran

TRADUCE: (**see** "defame") betray; violate

TRAFFIC: **v.** (**see** "trade") sell; specialize; transact; travel; wander; TRAFFIC: **n.** (**see** "trade") commerce; dealings; sales; transport(ation); travel

TRAGEDY: **see** "calamity;" TRAGIC(AL): calamitous; deplorable; dreadful; fearful; horrible; lamentable; melancholy; woeful

TRAIL: **v.** (**see** "hunt" and "trace") dog; drag; foil; follow; hound; lag; sweep; traipse; trudge; TRAIL: **n.** (**see** "track") abature; aftermath; footprint; line; path(way); pug; route; scent; slot; spoor; sweep; train

TRAIN: **v.** (**see** "teach") aim; breed; coach; coeducate; command; control; direct; discipline; dominate; drill; educate; equip; handle; level; manage; nurture; prepare; protract; ready; rear; school; tame; TRAIN: **n.** arrangement; caravan; cavalcade; chain; cortege; court; dress; disposition; file; following; line; method; process; retainers; retinue; sequel; sequence; series; set; suite; tail; trail; way; TRAINED: aimed; bred; broken; disciplined; drilled; educated; equipped; formed; inured; leveled; prepared; professional; reared; *rompu*; *rompue* (fem.); schooled; shaped; tamed; taught; TRAINING: (**see** "education") apprenticeship; breeding; discipline; rearing; traineeship; upbringing

TRAIT: (**see** "peculiarity") characteristic; criterion; denominator; direction; feature; function; haecceitas; haecceity; hallmark; item; knack; mark; particularity; point; quality; talent; tendency; touch; view; way

TRAITOR: apostate; backslider; betrayer; defector; deserter; escapee; escaper; expatriate; heretic; Iscariot; Judas; knave; Modred; rat; rebel; recalcitrant; recreant; renegade; seducer; snake; tergiversator; turncoat; turntail; viper; TRAITOROUS: disloyal; duplicitous; faithless; false; heretic; Iscariotic-(al); perfidious; treacherous; treasonable

TRAMMEL: (**see** "hinder") bridle; confine; enmesh; gag; hamper; handicap; impede; muzzle

TRAMP: **v.** bum; hike; hobo; pad; peregrinate; press; step; stroll; travel; tread; trounce; trudge; walk; wander; TRAMP: **n.** beggar; bohemian; bum; gaberlunzie; hiker; hobo; nomad; picaro; prostitute; rogue; sponger; steamer; vagabond; vagrant

TRAMPLE: (**see** "oppress") override; pad; ride; spurn; step (on); tyrannize; vanquish

TRANCE: absorption; abstraction; coma; daze; ecstasy; fit; hypnosis; mazement; rapture; raptus; seizure; somnolence; swoon; transport; unconsciousness

TRANQUIL: (**see** "calm") agreeable; easy; equal; equanimous; even; gentle; lenient; lown; mild; pacific; peaceable; peaceful; placid; pleasant; quiet; relaxed; restful; serene; smooth; soft; solacing; stable; steady; still; subdued; tame; undisturbed; unrestrained; unruffled; unworrying; TRANQUILITY: (**see** "calmness") agreeableness; balance; calm; ease; easiness; equality; equanimity; gentility; harmony; indolence; leniency; mildness; peaceableness; peacefulness; pleasantry; quiet(ness); quietude; serenity; smoothness; stillness

TRANSACT: accomplish; act; barter; conduct; deal; do; effect; exchange; execute; merchandise; negotiate; perform; perpetuate; prosecute; sell; swap; trade; traffic; treat; work; TRANSACTION: act(ion); actus; adjustment; affair; barter; business; compact; compromise; covenant; deal; deed; doing; event; exchange; happening; matter; occurrence; passage; proceeding; purchase; sale; step; swap; trade; undertaking

TRANSCEND: cap; climb; elevate; exceed; excel; outdo; outstrip; raise; rise; soar; surmount; surpass; TRANSCENDENT: excelling; exquisite; surpassing

TRANSCRIPT(ION): apograph; arrangement; carbon; copy; duplicate; record; replica; reproduction; tape; tenor; translation; writing

TRANSFER: **v.** alien; barter; carry; cede; change; consign; convey; deed; depart; depute; exchange; give; grant; leave; let; migrate; move; pass; remove; send; shift; swap; trade; transport; TRANSFER: **n.** carryover; consignment; conveyance; deed; exchange; grant; move; removal; sale; shift; swap; ticket; token; trade; transference; translation

TRANSFIX: affix; allure; charm; enchant; fasten; hold; hypnotize; impale; nail; pierce; pin; spear; stab; thrill; transpierce

TRANSFORM: (see "change") alter; convert; fashion; metamorphose; modify; renovate; shift; transfigure; transmogrify; transmutate; transmute; transplant; turn; TRANSFORM-ATIVE: metamorphic; permutative; trans-forming; transmutative; TRANSFORMA-TION: (see "change") conversion; evalua-tion; metamorphism; metamorphosis; per-mutation; process; renovation; transfigura-tion; transmogrification; transmutation

TRANSGRESS: break; cross; disobey; err; fault; infract; infringe; offend; sin; trespass; violate; TRANSGRESSION: break; crime; delict; delinquency; disobedience; error; fault; immorality; impropriety; infraction; infringement; malconduct; malfeasance; misfeasance; moral turpitude; offense; sin; tort; trespass; unconformity; violation; wrong(doing); TRANSGRESSOR: (see "criminal") offender; wrongdoer

TRANSIENT: (see "brief") deciduous; ema-nant; ephemeral; ephemerous; evanescent; fleeting; flighty; fugitive; immaterial; imper-manent; momentary; passing; preterient; short-lived; temporal; temporary; transitory; vanishing; TRANSIENCY: ephemerality; transitoriness; TRANSIENTS: flotsam and jetsam

TRANSIT: change; conveyance; journey; passage; transition; transportation

TRANSITION: (see "transformation") change; development; evolution; fall; flux; movement; passage; rise; segue; shift

TRANSITORY: (see "transient") episodic; evanescent; fleet(ing); fly-by-night; flying; occasional; passing; temporal; temporary; transitorial; volatile

TRANSLATE: adapt; change; convert; con-vey; decipher; decode; explain; interpret; move; paraphrase; read; reduce; render; reproduce; transcribe; transfer; transform; transmute; transport; TRANSLATION: adaptation; conversion; conveyance; expla-nation; move; paraphrase; phrase; pony; removal; rendering; rendition; reproduction; shift; transcription; transfer; transformation; transition; transmutation; version

TRANSMIT: bear; carry; communicate; con-duct; convey; deliver; disseminate; emit;

enclose; give; hand (down); impart; influ-ence; mail; metastasize; pass; phone; post; remit; send; throw; tote; traject; transfer; wire; write; TRANSMISSION: conduc-tance; conduction; conveyance; deliverance; delivery; message; metastasis; passage; tra-jection; transfer; transmittance; transporta-tion

TRANSMUTE: (see "change") alchemize

TRANSPARENT: amorphous; clear; colorless; crystal(line); diaphanous; fragile; frank; glassy; guileless; hyaline; intelligible; limpid; lucent; lucid; luminous; lustrous; obvious; open; patent; pellucid; perspicacious; sheer; thin; translucent; transpicuous; vitreous; vitrescent; TRANSPARENCY: clarity; clearness; crystallinity; diaphaneity; lim-pidity; perspicacity; translucence; trans-lucency; transpicuity; vitrescence; white

TRANSPIRE: (see "occur") excrete; exhale; exude; perspire

TRANSPORT: v. (see "transfer") banish; bear; carry; convey; delight; deliver; deport; emigrate; enrapture; exile; inflame; move; pass; rapt; ship; translate; transmit; trans-plant; truck; TRANSPORT: n. delight; rapture; raptus; ship; vessel; TRANS-PORTED: borne; carried; delighted; en-raptured; impassioned; moved; rapt; ridden; TRANSPORTATION: banishment; car-riage; change; conveyance; deportation; emigration; journey(age); passage; ride; ticket; traffic; train; transit(ion); transplanta-tion; truck

TRANSPOSE: see "change"

TRAP: v. ambush; catch; confine; corner; ensnare; entangle; gin; hold; incarcerate; intrigue; pen; snare; stop; tangle; tree; waylay; TRAP: n. ambush; artifice; bunker; carriage; creel; drum; gin; incarceration; inveiglement; nail; net; pit(fall); plot; ruse; snare; spider web; springe; stratagem; toil(s); web; weir; wile(s); TRAPPINGS: see "furnishings"

TRASH: (see "waste") ashes; balderdash; claptrap; debris; dejecta; detritus; dirt; dross; ejecta(menta) (pl.); fatras; filth; flummadiddle; fragments; garbage; junk; leavings; money; muck; nonsense; offal; quackery; refuse; reject(amenta); riffraff; rubbish; scourings; scraps; scum; stuff; tripe; trumpery; waste; TRASHY: cheap; claptrap; flimsy; paltry; poor; riffraff;

substandard; tawdry; tinny; tin(sel); trifling; trumpery; worthless

TRAVEL: **v.** advance; associate; aviate; cover; depart; drive; fly; follow; gallivant; globetrot; go; itinerate; jet; journey; motor; move; mush; pass; peregrinate; proceed; ride; roam; run; safari; tour; traffic; tramp; traverse; trek; visit; voyage; wend; TRAVEL: **n.** circuit; course; excursion; expedition; globe-trot(ting); itinerary; itineration; journey; locomotion; locomotivity; move; passage; peregrination; pilgrimage; ride; safari; tour; traffic; transportation; trek; trip; voyage; TRAVELER(S): globe-trotter; itinerant; motorist; nomad; passenger; peregrinator; piepoudre; pilgrim; tourist; tramp; transient; viator; visitor; voyager; wayfarer; TRAVELING: ambulatory; discursive; errant; itinerant; locomotive; nomadic; perambulatory; peripatetic; portable

TRAVERSE: advance; course; cover; cross; deny; examine; ford; go; move; pass; patrol; penetrate; range; rebut; refute; span; survey; travel

TRAVESTY: burlesque; caricature; disguise; imitation; lampoon; makeup; mimic; parody; representation; satire; sham

TRAY: board; hod; salver; server

TREACHEROUS: arrant; dirty; disaffected; dishonorable; disloyal; disobedient; duplicitous; faithless; false(hearted); fickle; infamous; insidious; Iscariotic(al); malign(ant); mutinous; perfidious; Punic; rascally; rebellious; recreant; seditious; traitorous; treasonable; treasonous; unfaithful; unreliable; unscrupulous; unstable; untrustworthy; untrue; venomous; viperish; TREACHERY: (**see** "disloyalty") betrayal; duplicity; *fides Punica*; perfidy; Punic faith; treason; triplicity

TREAD: **v.** (**see** "walk") beat; conquer; follow; press; pursue; repress; stamp; subdue; trample; TREAD: **n.** crush; dance; foot(fall); footprint; pace; pad; sole; stamp; step; tire; trample; walk

TREASON: betrayal; duplicity; lese majesty; perfidy; prodition; treachery; TREASONOUS: **see** "treacherous"

TREASURE: **v.** appreciate; cache; cherish; collect; esteem; evaluate; hoard; keep; love; prize; recognize; store; value; TREASURE: **n.** cache; coin; gems; hoard; money; preserve; prize; riches; store; wealth; TREA-

SURER: bursar; chamberlain; comptroller; exchequer; quaestor; TREASURY: bank; burse; cache; chest; coffer; exchequer; fisc; funds; gold; hoard; money; purse; riches; stock; store(house); thesaurus; valuables; value; vault; wealth

TREAT: **v.** administer; amuse; argue; arrange; attend; bargain; care (for); comment; confer; cure; deal; delight; discuss; doctor; dose; entertain; explain; feast; handle; manage; manipulate; medicate; negotiate; nurse; parley; prescribe; process; provide; refine; regale; regard; relieve; satisfy; serve; tend; use; write; TREAT: **n.** amusement; *bonne bouche*; delicacy; delight; entertainment; reception; welcome; TREATMENT: action; administration; behavior; conduct; discipline; dosage; handling; management; manner; medicament(s); medication; medicine; reception; remedy; technique; therapeusis; therapeutics; therapy; training; usage; use; welcome

TREATISE: account; book; catholicon; discourse; disquisition; dissertation; encyclopedia; essay; exegesis; exposition; pandect; story; tale; thesis; tract(ate); writing

TREATY: agreement; arrangement; cartel; compact; mise; negotiation; pact; protocol

TREBLE: acute; high-pitched; shrill; threefold; triple; triplicate

TREE: **v.** (**see** "trap") catch; corner; TREE(S): **n.** arbor(etum); arbustum; boscage; copse; forest; lineage; pedigree; timber; wood(s)

TRELLIS: arbor; espalier; lattice(work); pergola

TREMBLE: **v.** agitate; dodder; fear; jar; quake; quaver; shake; shiver; shudder; teeter; thrill; throb; vibrate; wobble; TREMBLE **n.** or TREMOR: agitation; jar; quaver; quiver(ing); shake; throb; tremblement; tremulation; vibration; TREMBLING: atremble; doddering; fearful; quaking; quavering; quavery; quivering; quivery; shaky; shivering; shuddering; throbbing; tremorous; tremulant; tremulous; vibrating

TREMENDOUS: (**see** "huge") alarming; dreadful; gigantic; leviathan; prodigious; terrific; terrifying; titanic; vast

TREMOR: **see** under "tremble"

TREMULOUS: (**see** "trembling") agitated; aspen; nervous; palpitating; quaky; quavering; quavery; quivering; rickety; shaking; shaky; shivery; timorous; tremando; tremulant; vibrating; wavering

TRENCH: canyon; cut; ditch; excavation; foss(e); furrow; gulley; leat; mote; sap; scrobicula

TRENCHANT: acrid; acute; biting; brief; brisk; caustic; clear-cut; cogent; concise; crisp; critical; cutting; impressive; intense; keen; mordant; penetrating; perceptive; poignant; pointed; sectorial; severe; sharp; short; sour; vinegary; vivid

TREND: (**see** "tendency") approach; bandwagon; belief; bent; course; current; curve; direction; drift; flow; ground swell; inclination; indication; intimation; leaning; line; motion; movement; route; sense; slant; squint; stream; temper; tenor; thought; tide; tone; vein; vogue; wind

TRESPASS: **v.** encroach; entrench; err; impinge; infringe; interlope; invade; molest; offend; poach; sin; transgress; TRESPASS: **n.** breach; encroachment; impingement; incursion; infringement; misfeasance; molestation; offense; transgression; TRESPASSER: encroacher; interloper; invader; misfeasor; poacher; sinner; transgressor

TRIAD: three; trinary; trine; trinity; trio; trivalent

TRIAL: ache; affliction; agony; analysis; annoyance; assay; attempt; audition; calvary; competition; contest; controversy; cross; *crucis experimentum*; demonstration; dry run; effort; endeavor; endurance; essay; exam(ination); experience; experiment; hardship; hearing; heat; judgment; lawsuit; limit; ordeal; pain; pang; procedure; proceeding; proof; rehearsal; sample; scratch; scrutiny; setback; shakedown; strain; temptation; test; tribulation; tryout; vexation; visitation

TRIANGULAR: deltoid(al); pyramidal; pyriform; trigonal

TRIBE: assemblage; assembly; band; category; clan; class; family; genre; group; horde; nation; phratry; race; sept; sib; village

TRIBULATION: **see** "suffering"

TRIBUNAL: (**see** "court") asembly; bar; bench; forum; seat

TRIBUTE: blackmail; bribe; commendation; duty; encomium; gift; homage; honor; impost; money; offering; ovation; praise; ransom; rent(al); service; tariff; tax; testimonial; tip; toll

TRICK: **v.** (**see** "fool") cajole; cheat; cozen; deceive; decorate; defraud; delude; do; dodge; dupe; elude; ensnare; entrap; finagle; flam; gloss; gull; hoax; inveigle; jockey; juggle; maneuver; manipulate; mousetrap; outwit; preen; pretend; stall; swindle; take (in); trap; victimize; wangle; work; TRICK-(ERY) **n.** or TRICKINESS: art(ifice); *blague*; blind; caper; characteristic; charlatanry; chicane(ry); connivance; conniving; contrivance; coup; cozenage; craft(iness); cunning; custom; deceit; deception; defraudation; delusion; design; device; dexterity; dido; dodge; double-dealing; doubleness; duplicity; elusion; entrapment; escamotage; evasion; excuse; expedient; feat; feint; finery; finesse; forgery; fourberie; fraud; gag; gambit; game; gloss; guild; habit; hankypanky; high jinks; hoax; hocus-pocus; horseplay; illusion; imposture; ingenuity; insincerity; intrigue; inveiglement; invention; jest; joke; knack; legerdemain; pretense; pretension; Machiavellianism; machination; maneuver; misrepresentation; mountebankery; ornament; palmistry; peculiarity; pettifoggery; phonous bolonus; plan; plot; prank; prestidigitation; pretense; pretension; racket; roguishness; ruse; scheme; sham; shift(iness); skill; skullduggery; sleight (of hand); slipperiness; sophistry; sortilege; stall; stratagem; stretch; stunt; suavity; subterfuge; subtlety; swindle; tomfoolery; turn; wile; wiliness; TRICKY: (**see** "deceitful") artful; captious; changeable; circuitous; crafty; deceptive; delusive; devious; dishonest; disingenuous; duplicitous; elusive; foxy; fraudulent; illusive; impish; ingenious; ingenuous; insidious; insincere; intricate; inventive; oily; oleaginous; pretentious; quirky; roguish; serpentine; shifty; shrewd; skillful; slippery; sly; snaky; sneaky; snide; stratagemic(al); subtle; ticklish; tortuous; tricksome; uncertain; unfair; unreliable; wily

TRICKLE: drip; drop; emit; flow; ooze; osmose; percolate; seep

TRIED: dependable; faithful; known; reliable; tested; true; trustworthy

TRIFLE: **v.** dally; dawdle; diddle-daddle; fiddle-faddle; fidget; flirt; fool; idle; loiter; manipulate; mess; monkey; nibble; palter; piffle; potter; putter; tamper; toy; waste;

TRIFLE(S): **n.** bagatelle; bauble; bibelot; bit; bonbon; doodad; fico; fiddlestick; fig; flotsam and jetsam; flummadiddle; folderol; gaud; geegaw; gimcrack; hair; inconsequence; inconsequentia (pl.); insignificance; insubstantiality; iota; jot; kickshaw; knickknack; laugh; minutia; minutiae (pl.); molehill; negligibility; nihility; nothing(ness); nugacity; *nugae canorae* (pl.); particle; *peu de chose*; piffle; pin; plaything; *quelque chose*; quiddling; *rien*; song; straw; sublety; thingumbob; toy; trace; trinket; trivia (pl.); triviality; vain; vanity; whim-wham; TRIFLER: boulevardier; *flâneur*; *flâneuse* (fem.); idler; unessential; TRIFLING: airy; banal; childish; common(place); contemptible; decipient; flippant; foolish; frivolous; funny; hackneyed; heedless; humble(d); immomentous; inadequate; inane; inconsequential; indifferent; insignificant; light; little; nambypamby; negligible; no-account; nogood; nominal; nugacious; nugatory; paltry; pettifogging; petty; picayune; picayunish; piffling; puerile; ridiculous; shallow; silly; small-scale; trivial; two-bit; unimportant; wishy-washy; TRIFLINGNESS: desipience; desipiency; frivolity; heedlessness; negligibility; triviality; unimportance

TRIG: (**see** "neat") formal; prim; stiff

TRIGGER: **v.** actuate; initiate; release; start; stimulate; trip; TRIGGER: **n.** catch; lever; release; sear; start; stimulus

TRILL: quaver; roll; shake; sing; tremble; tremolo; twirl; vibrate; warble

TRIM: **v.** adjust; adorn; beautify; chastise; cheat; clip; condition; cut; decorate; defeat; defraud; economize; edge; fashion; finish; fit; fix; hack; lop; pare; perk; point; prepare; prune; reduce; remove; shave; shroud; smooth; spruce; spur; stabilize; swindle; tailor; thrash; tidy; TRIM: **a.** (**see** "neat") primp; saucy; shipshape; slender; svelte; taut; tidy; trig

TRINKET(S): (**see** "trifle") bagatelle; bibelot; bijou(terie); charm; dido; dingus; doodad; doohickey; gadget; gaud; geegaw; kickshaw; *objet d'art*; ornament; *peu de chose*; *quelque chose*; tahli; thingumbob; whim-wham

TRIP: **v.** caper; dance; err; fail; fall; frisk; halt; hop; jaunt; ramble; run; sally; skip; slip; stagger; stumble; TRIP: **n.** (**see** "journey") blunder; course; dance; distance; error; expedition; failure; fall; hegira; jaunt; junket; mistake; peregrination; safari; sally; skip; stumble; tour; trek

TRIPLE: cubed; hit; ternary; ternate; third; threefold; treble(d); trichotomous; trinal; trine; trinitarian

TRISTFUL: (**see** "sad") gloomy; melancholy; saddened; sorrowful; *triste*

TRITE: ancient; archaic; banal; bare; beaten; bromidic; cliché; common(place); corny; dull; flat; frayed; hackneyed; hoary; jejune; old(-fashioned); passé; pedestrian; platitudinous; pompier; rusty; shopworn; stale; stereotyped; stereotypical; threadbare; twice-told; vapid; wornout; TRITENESS: banality; bathos; bromide; jejunity; pedestrianism; stereotype; truism; vapidity

TRITURATE: bray; bruise; grind; masticate; pulverize; rub; thrash

TRIUMPH: **v.** (**see** "conquer") achieve; boast; exult; flourish; prevail; win; TRIUMPH: **n. see** "victory;" TRIUMPHANT: conquering; elated; exultant; joyous; jubilant; prevailing; triumphal; triumphing; victorious

TRIVIAL: banal; childish; common(place); delicate; feeble; flimsy; futile; gimcrack; hairsplitting; inconsequential; inconsiderable; inferior; insignificant; insubstantial; knickknacky; leger; light; little; marginal; mean; mediocre; minor; minute; nominal; ordinary; paltry; petty; piperly; poor; puny; shallow; silly; slight; small; thin; trifling; unimportant; vain; weak; worthless; TRIVIALITY: banality; bauble; gimcrack; inconsequentia (pl.); inconsequentiality; inferiority; insubstantiality; marginalia (pl.); minutiae (pl.); mouse; nugacity; trifle; trivia (pl.)

TROD: **see** "trudge"

TROOP: **v.** assemble; associate; consort; march; mingle; move; parade; throng; TROOP(S): **n.** army; band; battery; brigade; collection; crowd; company; horde; march; number; parade; party; regiment; soldiers; squad; throng

TROPHY: (**see** "award") crown; cup; flag; garland; keepsake; laurel(s); medal; memorial; Oscar; palm; patch; prize; reward; ribbon; scalp; spoils; standard; token; wreath

TROPICAL: **see** "torrid"

TROT: canter; dance; hasten; hurry; jog; pace; run

TROUBLE: **v.** (**see** "annoy") afflict; bedevil; beset; bother; discommode; discompose; distress; disturb; haunt; impose; inconvenience; inflict; obsess; perpetrate; perplex; plague; pother; torment; vex; wreak; TROUBLE: **n.** ado; adversity; affliction; ailment; annoyance; bedevilment; besetment; bother(ation); care; caution; chagrin; coil; cumbrance; deep water; difficulty; disease; disorder; dissatisfaction; distress; disturbance; effort; encumbrance; exertion; fireworks; grief; hindrance; hot water; illness; imposition; infliction; labor; mischief; obstruction; pain(s); perplexity; perturbation; pickle; plague; plight; punishment; sickness; sore(ness); toil; torment; uneasiness; unrest; vexation; woe; worry; TROUBLED: afflicted; agitated; bedeviled; bothered; discouraged; diseased; distressed; disturbed; fretful; ill(-humored); inconvenienced; obsessed; perplexed; sad; solicitous; stormy; tormented; troublous; turbulent; uneasy; vexatious; vexed; TROUBLESOME: (**see** "difficult") arduous; boisterous; bothersome; burdensome; damaging; discommodious; distressing; disturbing; hard; harmful; Herculean; ill; importunate; infestive; laborious; lamentable; nasty; noisy; obstreperous; outrageous; perplexing; pesky; pesterous; pestiferous; pestilent(ial); plaguesome; recalcitrant; refractory; terrible; threatening; turbulent; ugly; uneasy; unruly; vexatious; wearisome; wicked

TROUBLEMAKER: **see** "mischief-maker"

TROUGH: basin; channel; chute; conduit; container; depression; groove; gut(ter); hod; manger; spout; strake

TRUANT: bum; escapee; hobo; micher; straggler; tramp; trivant; vagabond; vagrant

TRUCE: (**see** "armistice") break; breather; cease-fire; cessation; desition; discontinuance; interruption; lull; quiet(ude); recess; respite; rest; surrender; suspension; withdrawal

TRUCK: **v.** barter; cart; move; sell; trade; traffic; transport; TRUCK: **n.** cart; dolly; lorry; produce; rubbish; wagon; van; vehicle; waste

TRUCKLE: bend; bow; cringe; curtsy; kneel; knuckle; kowtow; submit; yield

TRUCULENT: (**see** "savage") bellicose; belligerent; deadly; military; pugnacious; vitriolic; vituperative

TRUDGE: hike; march; pace; plod; slog; tramp; trod; walk

TRUE: accurate; actual; alined; complete; confirmed; constant; correct; decent; dependable; devoted; essential; exact; fair; faithful; firm; fitting; genuine; germane; honest; honorable; ideal; inherent; intrinsic; just; legal; legitimate; loyal; moral; noble; nonfictional; objective; official; orthodox; proper; real; right(ful); sincere; square; sta(u)nch; steadfast; steady; straight; strict; substantial; trustworthy; typical; unassailable; unexaggerated; unfeigned; unvarnished; upright; valid; veracious; veritable; very; virtuous; worthy; TRULY: amen; duly; indeed; legally; really; rightly; verily; yea

TRUISM: (**see** "witticism") axiom; banality; bromide; cliché; maxim; moral; motto; platitude; quip; saw; saying; wisecrack

TRUMPERY: **a.** cheap; despicable; gaudy; poor; showy; tasteless; tawdry; tin(ny); trashy; trumped-up; worthless; TRUMPERY: **n.** (**see** "nonsense") bric-a-brac; paraphernalia (pl.); tin; triviality; twaddle

TRUMPET: **v.** advertise; announce; blare; blow; herald; proclaim; promulgate; utter; TRUMPET: **n.** bugle; clarion; cornet; horn; lure

TRUNK: body; bole; box; caber; chest; coffer; locker; luggage; stem; stock; torso

TRUST: **v.** bank; believe; confide; credit; depend; esteem; expect; hope; rely; rest; TRUST: **n.** assurance; belief; care; cartel; combination; confidence; corner; corporation; credence; credit; custody; dependence; esteem; faith; group; hope; interest; obligation; monopoly; reliance; syndicate; TRUSTY, TRUSTED *or* TRUSTWORTHY: authentic; authoritative; calculated; dependable; esteemed; faithful; firm; inerrable; inerrant; infallible; innocent; leal; loyal; official; predictable; regular; reliable; secure; sound; sta(u)nch; tried; true(-blue); trusting; yeomanly; TRUSTWORTHINESS: **see** "reliability"

TRUTH: accuracy; actuality; affirmation;

axiom; certainty; certitude; deed; enlightenment; eternities (pl.); exactitude; exactness; fact; fealty; fidelity; genuineness; honesty; knowledge; nonfiction; platitude; postulation; precision; principle; probity; reality; reliability; rightness; sincerity; standard; truism; truthfulness; veracity; verification; verisimilitude; verities (pl.); verity; *vraisemblance*; TRUTHFUL: accurate; actual; candid; genuine; honest; point-blank; precise; reliable; sincere; trustworthy; veracious; veridical; TRUTHFULNESS: accuracy; candidness; honestness; honesty; precision; reliability; truth; veracity; veridicality

TRY: **v.** afflict; aim; assay; aspire; attempt; beset; demonstrate; endeavor; essay; ettle; exact; examine; experiment; hear; investigate; judge; ply; prove; put; rack; risk; say; stab; strive; struggle; tackle; tax; tease; test; undertake; use; venture; TRY: **n.** attempt; endeavor; experiment; go; opportunity; stab; struggle; test; trial; turn; undertaking; venture; whack; whirl

TUB: **see** "vat"

TUBE: bouch; bronchus; cylinder; duct; hose; main; pipe; straw; tunnel

TUCK: close; cover; cram; eat; enclose; fit; fold; hide; insert; lap; pleat; stuff; wrap

TUFT: (**see** "fragment") feather; whisk; wisp

TUG: **v.** contend; drag; draw; haul; labor; pull; struggle; toil; tow; yank; TUG: **n.** boat; chain; drag; draw; effort; haul; pull; rope; strap; struggle; yank

TUMBLE: **v.** (**see** "fall") collapse; drop; fail; flop; leap; overthrow; roll; stumble; topple; toss; trip; TUMBLE: **n.** collapse; disarray; disorder; downfall; drop; failure; fall; flop; heap; leap; mess; overthrow; roll; spill; stumble; tousle

TUMID: (**see** "swollen") bulging; bombastic; edematous; hypertrophic; pneumatic; protuberant; turgid

TUMOR: adenoma; cancer; cheloid; growth; keloid; moro; neoplasm; phyma; swelling; wart; wen; yaw

TUMULT: agitation; Babel(ism); bouleversement; brouhaha; coil; combustion; commotion; confusion; din; disorder; disturbance; emotion; ferment; fight; fray; hubbub; hurly-burly; hurry; maelstrom; paroxysm;

profusion; rabblement; revolt; riot; rush; struggle; *Sturm und Drang*; turbulence; turmoil; uproar; violence; welter; whirl(pool); whirlwind; TUMULTUOUS: **see** "disorderly;" TUMULTUARY: aimless; haphazard; irregular; riotous; undisciplined

TUNE: **v.** adapt; adjust; attune; correspond; fix; harmonize; set; syntonize; TUNE: **n.** (**see** "music") accompaniment; agreement; air; amount; approach; aria; attitude; course; extent; intonation; key; lilt; melisma; melody; modulation; sonance; song; strain; syntonization; theme; TUNEFUL: (**see** "melodious") assonant; chantant; harmonious; homophonous; musical; rhythmic(al); syntonic; syntonous; unisonant

TUNIC: acton; blouse; camisa; chiton; coat; garment; integument; jacket; mantle; overblouse; palla; shirt; smock; stole; surcoat; toga; waist

TUNNEL: **see** "tube" and "undermine"

TURBID: cloudy; confused; dark; dense; dirty; disturbed; dull; feculent; filthy; foul; grimy; impure; muddy; murky; nebulous; obscure; opaque; polluted; roily; swollen; thick; unclean; unsettled

TURBULENT: agitated; brawling; disordered; disorderly; disturbed; mad; manic; nervous; noisy; restless; revolutionary; riotous; stormy; tempestuous; termagant; tumultous; unpeaceable; unpeaceful; unplacable; unquiet; unsettled; violent; wild; TURBULENCE: (**see** "uproar") havoc; perturbation; riot; tumult

TURF: cess; divot; grass; green; ground; peat; plot; sod; sward; track

TURGID: (**see** "swollen") bloated; bombastic; distended; hypertrophic; inflated; pompous; tumid

TURMOIL: (**see** "hassle" and "tumult") commotion; destruction; disquiet(ude); havoc; hell; helter-skelter; unrest; uproar

TURN: **v.** (**see** "revolve") alter; bend; change; circle; crank; decline; depend; deviate; digress; dip; eddy; go; gyrate; hang; hinge; oscillate; pirouette; pivot; pronate; reverse; revert; revolve; rotate; shift; slant; slue; sour; spin; supinate; swerve; swing; swirl; twist; veer; wheel; whirl; wind; TURN: **n.** alteration; bent; change; circle; circumduction; clinamen; course; curve; deflection;

deviation; dip; go; gyration; modification; movement; opportunity; oscillation; pirouette; pivot; pronation; reversal; reverse; reversion; revolution; roll; rotation; shift; slue; spell; stretch; supination; swing; talent; tendency; time; tour; trend; trick; twist; veer; wheel; whirl; TURNING: about-face; bend; crisis; deviation; flexure; gyration; reversal; rotation; shift(ing); veering; *volte-face*

TURNCOAT: apostate; deserter; rat; renegade; traitor

TURRET: lathe; minaret; spire; tourelle; tower

TURTLE: arrau; Caretta; chelonian; cooter; emyd; jurara; terrapin; Testudinata (pl.); tortoise

TUSK: fang; incisor; ivory; projection; razor; tenon; tooth

TUTOR: (**see** "teach" and "teacher") coach; docent; governess; instructor; mentor; pedagog(ue); trainer

TWADDLE: babble; chatter; claptrap; drivel; fustian; gabble; nonsense; rot; talk; wishwash

TWANG: nasality; pang; plunk; pungency; sound; twangle; twank; twinge

TWIG: branch; child; cion; offshoot; rod; scion; shoot; slip; switch; withe

TWILIGHT: candlelight; crepuscle; darkness; dusk; evening; gloaming; gloom; indefiniteness; indistinctness; nightfall; semidarkness

TWIN: **a.** binary; coupled; didymous; dioscuric; double; dual; duplicate; dyadic; gemel; identical; jumelle; matching; mated; parallel; similar; .two; TWIN(S): **n.** *alter ego*; brace; carbon; copy; counterpart; couplet; dual; duo; duplex; duplicate; identical; pair; sibling(s); two

TWINE: (**see** "twist") cord; string; tangle; thread

TWINGE: ache; pain; pang; prickling; qualm; shoot; stab; stitch; throe; tic; twitch

TWINKLE: blink; flash; flicker; gleam; glint; glitter; scintillate; shine; sparkle; wink; TWINKLING: flashing; gleaming; instant; momentary; scintillating; scintillescent; sparkling

TWIRL: **v.** (**see** "twist") circle; coil; dance; rotate; spin; turn; vertiginate; wave; whirl; TWIRL: **n.** (**see** "twist") circle; convolution; curl; dance; gyration; rotation; slue; spin; twistification

TWIST: **v.** bend; coil; contort; convolute; curl; curve; deflect; deviate; distort; entwine; gnarl; gyrate; interlace; interweave; intort; pervert; plait; scriggle; skew; slue; squirm; tangle; torture; tweak; twine; twirl; vertiginate; vine; volutate; warp; wind; worm; wreathe; wrest; wring; writhe; TWIST: **n.** contortion; convolution; curl; curve; dance; deflection; deviation; distortion; eccentricity; gimmick; gyration; idiosyncrasy; intortion; joke; kick; perversion; rotation; sinuosity; slue; tortuosity; twirl; twistification; TWISTED: atwist; contorted; curled; interlaced; intertwined; interwoven; intorted; meandering; serpentine; sinuous; tangled; tortile; tortuous; vertiginous; vined; volute(d); wound; wreathed

TWIT: (**see** "josh") banter; blame; deride; gibe; joke; needle; reproach; ridicule; taunt; tease; upbraid

TWITCH: **v.** fibrillate; jerk; pluck; pull; stab; tug; tweak; twinge; vellicate; yank; TWITCH: **n.** contraction; fasciculation; fibrillation; hitch; pant; pinch; stab; tic; tug; twinge; vellication

TWITTER: chirp; flutter; giggle; quiver; titter

TWO: brace; couple; couplet; duality; duplex; dyad; pair; span; team; tway; twins; yoke

TYCOON: baron; industrialist; leader; nabob; plutocrat; shogun; VIP

TYPE: **v.** assort; classify; determine; identify; mark; prefigure; print; represent; typify; TYPE: **n.** assortment; brand; breed; caste; character; class(ification); description; exemplar; exemplum; form; genre; ilk; impression; kidney; kind; make; mask; model; mold; nature; pattern; prefiguration; representation; representative; shape; sign; sort; species; specimen; stamp; standard; stripe; style; token; variety

TYPICAL: characteristic; classic(al); collective; distinctive; emblematic; exemplary; fair; general; model; prefigurative; quintessential; regular; representative; symbolic(al); symptomatic; true; typic; usual; TYPICAL-

ITY: classicality; exemplarity; quintessentiality; typicalness; typification

TYRANT: autocrat; commissar; despot; dictator; exploiter; hector; intimidator; martinet; Nero; oligarch; oppressor; overlord; satrap; TYRANNY: absoluteness; absolutism; autocracy; despotism; oppression; rod; ruffian; sword; TYRANNOUS: **see** "oppressive;" TYRANNIZE: **see** "oppress" and "trample"

TYRO: (**see** "beginner") abecedarian; amateur; learner; neophyte; novice

U

UBIQUITOUS: (**see** "everywhere") omnipresent

UGLY: bad; base; crude; cruel; dangerous; deformed; dire; disagreeable; disorderly; displeasing; evil; frightening; frightful; grisly; grotesque; gruesome; hideous; homely; horrible; horrific; horrifying; ill-natured; in(a)-esthetic; inelegant; leprous; non(a)esthetic; offensive; plain; quarrelsome; repugnant; repulsive; rough; rude; surly; terrible; threatening; troublesome; unadorned; un(a)esthetic; unappealable; unappealing; unbeauteous; unbeautified; unbeautiful; uncharming; undecorative; unelegant; unhandsome; unlovable; unlovely; unornamental; unpicturesque; unprepossessing; unpretty; unsightly; unstylish

ULCER: boil; carbuncle; lesion; pustule; sore

ULTERIOR: (**see** "hidden") concealed; further; furtive; latent; obscure; obstruse; remote; unavowed

ULTIMATE: **a.** absolute; basic; concluding; conclusive; crowning; dernier; earliest; elemental; ending; eventual; extreme; farthest; final; fundamental; furthest; greatest; intrinsic; last; maximal; maximum; original; primary; primitive; real; remote; sheer; supreme; terminal; ultra; unmitigated; utmost; ULTIMATE: **n.** absolute; apotheosis; extreme; maximum; ULTIMATUM: demand; offer; order; ultimate

ULTRA: A-one; best; beyond; fanatical; forward; radical; superior; superlative; top; ultimate; uncompromising

ULULATE: bellow; cry; howl; lament; roar; wail

UMBER: brown; burnt; chestnut; dusky; shadowy

UMBRAGE: animosity; annoyance; antipathy; aversion; bitterness; darkness; disesteem; dislike; displeasure; dissatisfaction; enmity; foliage; grudge; hate; hatred; hint; huff; indication; ire; malice; offense; overshadowing; pique; rancor; refuge; resentment; shade; shadow; shelter; spite; suggestion; suspicion

UMPIRE: arbiter; judge; mediator; negotiator; referee; ump

UNABLE: **see** "incapable"

UNABRIDGED: complete; comprehensive; cyclopedic(al); encyclopedic(al); full; *in extenso*; unbowdlerized; uncensored; uncut; unexpurgated

UNACCEPTABLE: disliked; unorthodox; unreceivable; unsanctioned; unwanted

UNACCUSTOMED: (**see** "strange") unhabituated; unused

UNACKNOWLEDGED: (**see** "unofficial") ownerless; unowned

UNADORNED: austere; bald; bare; barren; inornate; naked; native; nude; plain; sheer; stark; ugly; unbeauteous; unbeautiful; undecorated; unembellished; unornamented; utter

UNADULTERATE(D): clear; frank; genuine; plain; pure; simon-pure; true; uncorrupt(ed); unmingled; unmixed; unsophisticated

UNAFFECTED: **see** "calm" and "indifferent"

UNAFRAID: bold; brave; fearless; unaffrighted; unappalled; unapprehensive; unawed; unfrightened; unterrified; unterrifying

UNAIDED: **see** "alone"

UNALIKE: **see** "dissimilar"

UNALTERABLE: (**see** "unchangeable") unexcepted

UNAMBIGUOUS: (**see** "clear") univocal; unquestionable

UNAMBITIOUS: see "lazy"

UNAMUSING: (see "dull") unfunny

UNANIMOUS: agreed; agreeing; concordant; consentient; harmonious; mutual; one; solid; unisonant; universal; UNANIMITY: accord; concord(ance); consension; consensus; consentience; harmony; mutuality; solidity; union; universality

UNANNOUNCED: (see "silent") unadvertised; unheralded; unproclaimed; unpublicized; unpublished

UNAPPEALING: banal; drear(y); dull; impersonable; in(a)esthetic; insipid; plain; somber; subfusc(ous); trite; ugly; unattractive; unbeauteous; unbeautiful; uninviting; untempting

UNAPPEASABLE: avenging; gluttonous; immitigable; implacable; inappeasable; inflexible; intractable; irreconcilable; rancorous; relentless; remorseless; ruthless; unassuageable; unmitigable; untamable; unyielding; vindicative; voracious

UNAPPRECIATED: unapplauded; unpraised; unrecognized; unsung; unthanked

UNAPPROACHABLE: see "uppish"

UNAPPROVED: see "unauthorized" and "unorthodox"

UNASHAMED: abashless; proud; unabashed

UNASKED: unsolicited; unsought

UNASSISTED: see "alone"

UNASSUMING: bashful; diffident; humble; modest; open; plain; retiring; shy; simple

UNATTACHED: alone; bachelor; celibate; discrete; disjoin(t)ed; isolated; lone; loose; single; stag; uncommitted; unescorted; unmarried; unwedded

UNATTAINABLE: (see "idealistic") inaccessible; uncatchable; un-come-at-able; unreachable

UNATTEMPTED: unessayed; untested; untried

UNATTENDED: (see "alone") unescorted

UNATTENTIVE: see "preoccupied"

UNATTRACTIVE: (see "unappealing") uninviting; untempting

UNAUTHORIZED: apocryphal; contraband; counterfeit; illegal; illicit; proscriptive; spurious; unapproved; unauthoritative; unlawful; unofficial; unorthodox; unsanctioned

UNAVOIDABLE: accidental; certain; essential; indubitable; inevitable; invincible; unescapable; unevadable; unpremeditated

UNAWARE: careless; forgetful; ignorant; incognizant; insensible; nescient; oblivious; subconscious; unacquainted; unapprised; unconscious; uninformed; unknowing; unmindful; unwary; UNAWARENESS: incognizance; incognoscibility; oblivion; subconsciousness; unconsciousness

UNBALANCE: astasia; confusion; derangement; disequilibration; disequilibrium; disproportion; dyscrasia; imbalance; instability; lopsidedness

UNBEARABLE: (see "unendurable") insufferable; intolerable; unsustainable

UNBEATEN: unbent; unbowed; undefeated; unexcelled; unsubdued; unsurpassed; untrod; UNBEATABLE: invincible; unconquerable; unexcelled; unsurpassed

UNBECOMING: dishonorable; disreputable; immodest; impertinent; improper; inappropriate; inapt; incongruous; indecent; indecorous; unbeauteous; unseemly; unsuitable; untoward

UNBELIEVABLE: fantastic(al); implausible; improbable; inconceivable; incredible; incredulous; insupposable; preposterous; prodigious; thin; unconceivable; uncreditable; uncredited; unlikely; unplausible; unsubstantial; unswallowable; unthinkable; untrusted

UNBELIEVER: agnostic; aporetic; atheist; disbeliever; doubter; doubting Thomas; heretic; infidel; kaffir; latitudinarian; miscreant; nihilist; pagan; skeptic; UNBELIEVING: aporetic; atheistic; disbelieving; doubting; heretical; heterodox; incredulous; skeptical; unorthodox

UNBEND: condescend; extend; melt; relax; repose; rest; slacken; straighten; thaw; unflex; vouchsafe

UNBIASED: see "fair" and "impartial"

UNBIND: see "untie"

UNBLEMISHED: see "pure"

UNBOUNDED: see "unlimited"

UNBOWED: see "unbroken"

UNBRIDLED: crapulous; incontinent; intemperate; rampageous; rampant; riotous; unbroken; unchecked; uncontrolled; ungovernable; ungoverned; unmanageable; unrestrained

UNBROKEN: complete; contiguous; continuous; entire; intact; inviolate(d); regular; single; smooth; unbowed; unbridled; undivided; uninterrupted; unplowed; unriven; unsubdued; unsubsided; untamed; unviolate(d); whole; wild; UNBREAKABLE: adamantine; immarcescible; immarcessible; immutable; imperishable; indestructible; infrangible; intact; inviolable; inviolate; invulnerable; irrefrangible

UNBROTHERLY: unfraternal

UNBURDEN: confide; disclose; disembosom; ease; empty; free; relieve; reveal; rid; shed; unbosom; unload; unpack; unweigh

UNBURNABLE: apyrous; asbestine; asbestos; incombustible; inflammable; noncombustible; nonflammable

UNCANNY: bizarre; eerie; mysterious; queer; superhuman; unco; weird

UNCEASING: see "constant"

UNCENSORED: see "unexpurgated"

UNCEREMONIOUS(LY): abrupt; impromptu; informal; offhand; rude; sly(ly)

UNCERTAIN: *ambigendi locus*; ambiguous; ambivalent; amphibolic; chanceful; chancy; changeable; changing; conditional; contingent; critical; dangerous; dim; disputable; doubtful; dubious; dubitable; enigmatic(al); equivocal; erratic; erring; faltering; fickle; fitful; flickering; fluffy; halting; hazardous; hesitant; hovering; impredicable; improbable; inconclusive; inconsistent; indefinite; indefinitive; indeterminate; indistinct; inexplicit; insecure; irregular; muddy; nebulous; penumbral; perilous; possible; precarious; problematic(al); questionable; reserved; risky; shaky; skeptical; slippery; temperamental; tentative; tottering; touchy; un-

clear; unconcerned; unconfident; undecided; unformalized; unmathematical; unpredictable; unreliable; unsettled; unstable; unsteady; unsure; vacillating; vague; vatical; visionary; wandering; wavering; whimsical; wobbly; UNCERTAINTY: (see "doubt") ambiguity; ambivalence; amphibologism; demur; doubtfulness; dubiety; dubiosity; dubiousness; dubitation; fluctuation; flux; gamble; incertitude; indefinability; indefinitude; indetermination; inexactitude; irresolution; mistrust; precariousness; problem; question; skepticism; suspicion

UNCHALLENGED: (see "undisputed") uncontested; unfought

UNCHANGEABLE: (see "rigid") abiding; absolute; adamant(ine); changeless; constant; continuing; durable; enduring; fast; firm; fixed; immarcescible; immarcessible; immutable; imperishable; implacable; imprescriptible; inalienable; inalterable; incommutable; inconvertible; indestructible; indomitable; inexorable; infinite; intractable; invariable; irreducible; irreversible; irrevocable; lasting; monolithic; obstinate; permanent; perpetual; stable; stout; strong; stubborn; tough; unalterable; unamendable; UNCHANGED: intact; pristine; sedentary; sessile; static; stationary; unaltered; unconverted; uncut; unexpurgated; unregenerate(d); unrepentant; unreformable; unretouched; unshifted; untempered; UNCHANGING: (see "eternal") ceaseless; changeless; consistent; constant; fixed; immarcescible; immarcescible; immobile; indomitable; intractable; invariable; invariant; stable; stagnant; static; stationary; unaltered; uniform; universal; unmodified

UNCHECKED: (see "unrestrained") rampant; unbridled; unbroken; uncurbed; unextirpated; ungovernable; ungoverned; unhindered; untamed; wild

UNCIVIL: (see "rude") barbaric; barbarous; bluff; blunt; boorish; discourteous; disrespectful; gruff; haughty; ill-mannered; impolite; savage; vulgar; UNCIVILIZED: (see "barbarian") barbaric; barbarous; brutish; discourteous; feral; Gothic; inhuman(e); primitive; rude; savage; unchristian; uncouth; uncultivated; uncultured; wild

UNCLASSIFIED: (see "mixed") ungraded; UNCLASSIFIABLE: acategorical; amorphous; heterogeneous

UNCLEAN: dirty; excrementitious; filthy;

foul; immund; impure; maculate(d) muddled; muddy; obscene; nasty; polluted; putrid; repulsive; septic; slimy; soiled; squalid; sullied; unbathed; unscoured; unscrubbed; unwashed; vile; wicked; UNCLEANLINESS: acatharsia; dirt; feculence; filth; immundity; impurity; maculacy; nastiness; obscenity; pollution; putrefaction; putridity; repulsivity; squalor; wickedness

UNCLEAR: (see "ambiguous", "uncertain" and "vague") clouded; cloudy; confused; flat; incoherent; indistinct; indistinguishable; inexplicit; loose; opaque; shaggy; undistinct

UNCLOSE: (see "open") disclose; reveal; unwrap

UNCLOTHE: divest; strip; tirl; uncover; undress

UNCO: bizarre; eerie; strange; uncanny; unknown; weird

UNCOMFORTABLE: (see "uneasy") disconcerting; unlivable

UNCOMMON: choice; curious; exceptional; extraordinary; great; individual; infrequent; interesting; large; odd(ish); outstanding; peculiar; piquant; quaint; rare; *recherché*; scant; singular; special; strange; unco; uncustomary; unusual

UNCOMMUNICATIVE: dumb; laconic; mute; obmutescent; reserved; reticent; retired; silent; speechless; taciturn; unvoluble; unwordy

UNCOMPLETE(D): crude; unbuilt; undone; unended; unexecuted; unfinished; unpolished

UNCOMPLICATED: (see "simple") unentangled; uninvolved

UNCOMPLIMENTARY: antagonistic; derogatory; disparaging; dyslogistic; unflattering; ungracious

UNCOMPROMISING: devoted; dyed-in-the-wool; extreme; firm; grim; hard-shell; inflexible; intractable; intransigent; recalcitrant; rigid; severe; strict; strong; ultra; unmovable; unyielding; wholehearted

UNCONCERN: apathy; disinterest(edness); indifference; inertia; insouciance; nonchalance; passivity; reluctance; UNCONCERNED: apathetic; calm; careless; disinterested; free; indifferent; insensible; insouciant; lackadaisical; open; passive; phlegmatic; pococurante; reluctant; serene; uninterested; unsolicitous

UNCONDITIONAL or UNCONDITIONED: (see "absolute" and "raw") inconceivable; infinite; plenary; unknowable; unreserved; unrestrained

UNCONFORMABLE: see "unconventional"

UNCONGENIAL: asocial; disagreeable; discordant; discourteous; incompatible; incongruous; inharmonious; uncivil; ungregarious; unharmonious; unsociable; unsuitable

UNCONQUERABLE: absolute; Achillean; formidable; impregnable; indefeasible; indefeatable; indomitable; inexpugnable; insuperable; insurmountable; intractable; invincible; invulnerable; irrepressible; unassailable; unbeatable; undefeatable; unsurmountable; unsurpassable; unswerving; unvanquishable; unyielding; UNCONQUERABLENESS: indomitability; inexpugnability; insuperability; invincibility; unconquerability

UNCONSCIOUS: (see "stuporous") anesthetized; asleep; comatose; ignorant; insensate; insensible; nonconscious; senseless; unaware; unconscient; unknowable; unknown; unplanned; UNCONSCIOUSNESS: anesthesia; coma; ignorance; insensibility; narcosis; senselessness; sleep; stupor

UNCONSERVATIVE: see "extreme" and "unconventional"

UNCONSTRAINED: see "free"

UNCONTROLLED or UNCONTROLLABLE: (see "free") disobedient; intractable; paroxysmal; rampant; refractory; unbounded; unbridled; unchecked; unconfined; unconstrained; uncoordinated; ungoverned; unguided; unmanageable; unrestrainable; unrestrained; unruly; unsupervised; untrained; wild

UNCONVENTIONAL: abnormal; anomalous; atypic(al); beatnik; bizarre; Bohemian; capricious; curious; *dégagé*; easy; eccentric; erratic; extreme; far-out; free; heretical; heterodox; informal; irregular; odd; off-(-center); peculiar; quaint; queer; raffish; singular; strange; uncommon; unconformable; unconservative; uncultured; unethical; unorthodox; unusual; way-out; wayward;

whimsical; wild; wrong; UNCONVEN-
TIONALITY: Bohemianism; heterodoxy;
unconventionalism; unorthodoxy; wildness

UNCONVINCING: (see "unbelievable")
doubtful; dubious; fishy; implausible; questionable

UNCORRECTED: rampant; unadjusted;
undisciplined; ungovernable; unrefined;
unreformed; untrained; wild

UNCOUTH: agrestic; awkward; baboonish;
barbaric; barbarous; boorish; clownish;
clumsy; desolate; gauche; gawky; graceless;
incondite; indecorous; indelicate; odd; outlandish; plebeian; provincial; rough; rude;
rustic; solitary; unbeseeming; unchivalrous;
uncomfortable; uncourtly; uncultivated;
unfamiliar; ungainly; unpleasant; unrefined;
vulgar; UNCOUTHNESS: babbittry; baboonery; barbarism; barbarity; gaucherie;
indecorum; rudeness; rusticity

UNCOVER: bare; dig; disclose; divest; exhume; expose; ferret out; find; hunt; open;
probe; reveal; strip; unbare; uncap; uncase;
uncowl; undress; unearth; unfold; unlid;
unmantle; unsheathe; UNCOVERED:
(see "open" and "naked") bare(headed);
exposed; uncapped; undraped; undressed;
unmantled; unsheathed; unveiled

UNCRITICAL: favorable; naïve; pleased;
unexacting

UNCTION: absorption; oil; ointment; salve;
unctuousness; unguent; UNCTUOUS:
bland; fatty; greasy; hypocritical; oily;
oleaginous; pinguid; plastic; salvy; sleek;
slick; smooth; soapy; soothing; suave; wily

UNCULTIVATED: arid; barbaric; barbarous; barren; fallow; raw; rough(hewn);
sloven(ly); uncivilized; uncouth; uncultured;
undeveloped; unplowed; unpolished; unrefined

UNCULTURED: (see "uncouth") backward;
barbaric; barbarous; brutish; gross; ignorant;
illiterate; philistine; philistinic; primitive;
rough; rude; uncultivated; uneducated;
unrefined; wild

UNCUT: rough; unpruned; untrimmed; whole

UNDAMAGED: scatheless; sound; unassailed;
unharmed; unhurt; unimpaired; unscarred;
unscathed; whole

UNDAUNTED: bold; brave; fearless; intrepid;
sta(u)nch; Spartan; unblenched; unblenching; unbloodied; undashed; undauntable;
undefeated; undespairing; undiscouraged;
undismayed; unflinching; unvanquished

UNDECIDED: (see "doubtful") abeyant;
ambivalent; dilemmatic; disabused; hesitant;
inconstant; irresolute; open(-minded); pendant; pending; shaky; shy; uncertain;
uncrystallized; under advisement; undetermined; unformed; unhoodwinked; unresolved; unsettled; unstable; vacillating;
vacillatory; volatile; wavering

UNDECORATED: see "plain" and "unadorned"

UNDEFEATED: (see "undaunted") unvanquished

UNDEFILED: (see "pure") clean; clear;
immaculate; intemerate; inviolable; sterile;
uncorrupted; unpolluted; unspoiled; unstained; unsullied; untainted

UNDEMONSTRABLE or UNDEMON-
STRATIVE: anapodictic; apathetic; aseptic; calm; composed; indemonstrable; indifferent; lackadaisical; laconic; lazy; nonchalant; phlegmatic; phlegmatous; reserved;
restrained; stoic(al); stolid

UNDENIABLE: (see "clear") conceded;
excellent; *flagrante delicto*; incontestable;
incontrovertible; indisputable; indubitable;
red-handed; unquestionable

UNDER: below; beneath; buried; down;
inferior; less; lower; neath; nether; sotto;
subaltern(ate); subjacent; subordinate; substratal; substrative; underlying; underneath;
within

UNDERDONE: impartial; incomplete; rare;
raw; underacted; undercooked

UNDERESTIMATE: see "undervalue"

UNDERGO: bear; brook; endure; experience;
feel; pass; permit; stand; subject; suffer;
survive; sustain; take; taste; tolerate

UNDERGROUND: chthonian; secret; stealthy; submundane; subterranean; subter-
restrial; underfoot; underhand(ed); underneath

UNDERHAND(ED): clandestine; covered;
covert; deceitful; devious; dishonest; dis-

ingenuous; duplicitous; filthy; foxy; funny; furtive; hugger-mugger; left-handed; Machiavellian; oblique; secret; serpentine; shorthanded; sinister; sly; snaky; sneaky; snide; stealthy; subtle; surreptitious; tricky; underground; undermanned; unfair; unobtrusive; vile; wily; UNDERHANDEDNESS: chicanery; clandestinity; deceitfulness; deviousness; duplicity; sinisterity; sneakiness; stealth; surreption; trickery

UNDERLINE: see "emphasize" and "underscore"

UNDERLING: (see "assistant") employee; minion; puppet; slave; subaltern(ate); subordinate; vassal

UNDERLYING: beneath; fundamental; implicit; innate; subjacent; substantive; substratal; substrative; subtending; under(neath)

UNDERMINE: bore (from within); cave; cripple; demoralize; erode; excavate; impair; knife; sap; subvert; thwart; tunnel; weaken

UNDERRATE: (see "lower") undercut; underestimate; underprice; undervalue

UNDERSCORE: (see "emphasize") heighten; stress; underdraw; underline

UNDERSTAND: accept; appreciate; apprehend; comprehend; conceive; consider; cotton; decipher; decode; dig; discern; emphasize; fathom; feel; follow; get; grasp; have; infer; interpret; ken; know; learn; perceive; realize; recognize; regard; savvy; see; sense; solve; sympathize; translate; unfold; unravel; UNDERSTANDING: a. apperceptive; clearheaded; empathetic; empathic; intimate; intuitive; keen; kind; perceptive; percipient; sympathetic; tolerant; UNDERSTANDING: n. accord; agreement; adjustment; apperception; apprehension; comprehension; conception; contract; discouragement; empathy; entente; faculty; grasp; harmony; head; implication; insight; intellect; intelligence; intent; interpretation; intuition; inwit; judgment; kindness; knowledge; learning; meaning; mind; perception; perspicacity; realization; reason; reconciliation; signification; sympathy; uptake; UNDERSTANDABLE: (see "clear") comprehensible; conceivable; conceptible; concludable; fathomable; gatherable; graspable; interpretable; translatable; UNDERSTOOD: agreed; appreciated; apprehended; assumed; comprehended; connotative; dis-

cerned; felt; grasped; implicate; implicit; implied; inferred; interpreted; perceived; realized; recognized; sensed; supposed; tacit

UNDERTAKE: accept; agree; attempt; begin; contract; covenant; do; embark; engage; essay; guarantee; postulate; promise; try; venture; UNDERTAKING: act(ivity); aval; avowal; beginning; business; crusade; effort; emprise; enterprise; job; mood; project; obligation; occupation; risk; task; trouble; venture; work

UNDERTOW: current; eddy; riptide; vortex

UNDERVALUE: (see "lower") underestimate; underprice; underprize; underrate

UNDERWRITE: abet; back; confirm; finance; foot; guarantee; insure

UNDESERVED or UNDESERVING: desertless; indign; unearned; unjustified; unmeritable; unmerited; unwarranted; unworthy

UNDESIRABLE: (see "bad") egregious; evil; flagrant; inappropriate; inexpedient; inopportune; objectionable; rejected; unenviable; unwanted; unwished

UNDETERMINED: (see "doubtful") abeyant; dubious; equivocal; immense; indefinite; pending; uncertain; undecided; unfathomed; unsettled; unsounded; vague

UNDEVELOPED: barren; crude; elementary; embryonic; fallow; immature; incipient; latent; nascent; primitive; primordial; quiescent; raw; rough; rudimentary; sloven(ly); uncultivated; underripe; undisciplined; uneducated; unevolved; unexpanded; unexploited; unmined; unquarried; unripened; untrained; unused; untaught; unwrought

UNDEVIATING: (see "regular") correct; direct; reliable; true; unswerving

UNDIGNIFIED: infra dignitatem (abb. infra dig.); tactless; undiplomatic

UNDILUTED: all; entire; neat; pure; raw; rough; thick; unmitigated; unqualified

UNDIMINISHED: unabated; unlessened; unshortened; whole

UNDINE: gnome; nix(ie); nymph; sylph

UNDIPLOMATIC: (see "tactless") impolitic; undignified

UNDISCIPLINED: (see "aimless" and "unrestrained") amok; coltish; gamine; haphazard; hoydenish; raw; tomboyish; tumultuary; unchastened; unchastised; uncompelled; uncorrected; unenforced; unreformed; unruly; untaught; untrained; wild

UNDISCOURAGED: see "undaunted"

UNDISGUISED: (see "frank" and "open") genuine; gross; raw; rough; undissembled

UNDISPUTED: (see "certain") unchallenged; uncontested; uncontradicted; undenied; unfought

UNDISTINGUISHED: see "obscure"

UNDISTURBED: (see "indifferent") undistracted; unperturbed; unworried

UNDIVIDED: (see "whole") all; common; entire; impartible; imparticipable; impartite; single; total; unbroken

UNDO: annul; cancel; destroy; dissolve; kill; loose(n); open; resolve; ruin; separate; solve; unbutton; undress; unfasten; unmake; unman; unravel; unroll; untie; unwind; upset; UNDONE: lost; opened; rare; ruined; unachieved; unfastened; unfinished; unperformed; unraveled; untied; UNDOING: cancellation; defeasance; destruction; labefaction; loosening; reversal; ruin; unfastening

UNDOMESTICATED: feral; unbroken; undisciplined; untamed; wild

UNDONE: see under "undo"

UNDOUBTED: (see "unquestionable") authentic; certain; official; positive; sure; undoubtable

UNDRAPED: see "undressed"

UNDRESS: see "unclothe;" UNDRESSED: bare; déshabillé; disarranged; disrobed; en déshabillé; naked; nude; rough; unclothed; uncovered; undone; undraped; unrigged; unrobed

UNDULATING: flickering; fluctuating; rippling; rolling; scalloped; vibrating; wavy; UNDULATION: flicker; heave; pulsing; surge; surging; swell(ing); tremolo; vibration; wave; waviness

UNDULY: all-out; excessively; overweening

UNDYING: agelong; amaranthine; ceaseless; changeless; continual; continuous; endless; eternal; everlasting; immarcescible; immarcessible; immortal; immutable; incessant; indestructible; interminable; lasting; permanent; perpetual; timeless; unceasing; unending; unremitting

UNEARTH: delve; detect; dig; discover; disinter; examine; exhume; expose; find; probe; root; uncover; uproot

UNEARTHLY: bizarre; celestial; chthonian; eerie; fantastic; heavenly; hellish; ideal; miraculous; preposterous; preternatural; spiritual; supernatural; unworldly; weird

UNEASY: afraid; alarmed; all-overish; anxious; apprehensive; awkward; choppy; disconcerting; disturbed; doubtful; dubious; dysphoric; embarrassed; erethic; fearful; fidgety; frightened; gêné; indisposed; leery; perturbed; restless; shaken; squeamish; suspicious; timid; troubled; uncertain; uncomfortable; unquiet; unsettled; unstable; upset; worried; UNEASINESS: agitation; alarm; anxiety; apprehension; awkwardness; cold feet; compunction; disbelief; discomposure; disquiet(ude); dissatisfaction; distress; distrust; doubt; dread; dubiety; dyspathy; dysphoria; embarrassment; faintheartedness; fear; fright; gêne; hesitation; inquietude; instability; malaise; misgiving; pall; pang; penitence; perturbation; premonition; qualm; quandary; queasiness; regret; remorse; restlessness; scruple; solicitude; spasm; squeamishness; suspicion; throe; trouble; twinge; uncertainty; unrest; worry

UNEDUCATED: (see "ignorant") benighted; callow; crude; dumb; green; illiterate; rude; simple; undisciplined; unenlightened; unprepared; untamed; untaught; untrained; wild

UNEMOTIONAL: (see "calm" and "impassive") antiseptic; blasé; hard-boiled; intellectual; unfeeling; unimpassioned

UNEMPLOYED: free; idle; inactive; lazy; otiose; retired; unengaged; unoccupied

UNENDING or UNENDED: (see "undying") ageless; agelong; boundless; ceaseless; changeless; continual; continuous; endless; egregious; eternal; everlasting; extravagant; incessant; interminable; perpetual; stintless; timeless; unceasing; unexpired; unremitting; unrestrained; unrestricted

UNENDURABLE: insufferable; insupportable; intolerable; unbearable; unbrookable; unsustainable; UNENDURING: caducous; deciduous; ephemeral; fragile; short-lived; transient; transitory

UNENLIGHTENED *or* UNENLIGHTENING: (**see** "ignorant") backward; benighted; heathen; pagan; uneducated; unilluminated; uninformed; uninstructed; untaught; untrained

UNENTERTAINING: (**see** "dull") unamusing; unfunny

UNENTHUSIASTIC: **see** "perfunctory"

UNENVIOUS: (**see** "generous") ungrudging; unjealous

UNEQUAL: different; disparate; disproportionate; dissimilar; inadequate; incommensurable; inegalitarian; inequalitarian; inequitable; insufficient; intemperate; irregular; odd; rugged; unbalanced; uneven; unfair; unjust; unlike; variable; wanting; UNEQUALED: incommensurable; incomparable; matchless; *ne plus ultra*; nonpareil; peerless; transcendent(al); uneven; unmatchable; unmatched; unparagoned; unparalleled; unprecedented; unrivaled; unsurpassed; untranscended; variable; UNEQUALITY **see**: "inequality"

UNEQUIVOCAL: (**see** "unquestionable") certain; clear; direct; emphatic; forceful; perfect; point-blank; resounding

UNESCAPABLE: (**see** "inescapable") inevitable; unavoidable; unevadable

UNESSENTIAL: (**see** "nonessential") dispensable; extraneous; insubstantial; supererogatory; unimportant

UNEVEN: alop; asperate; asperous; asymmetric(al); disparate; disproportionate; dissimilar; dissymmetric(al); diverse; erose; erratic; fluctuating; frayed; harsh; hilly; inadequate; inequal; inequitable; irregular; odd; ragged; rough; rugged; shaggy; spasmodic; spotty; tattered; unequal; unfair; unlevel(ed); unproportionate; unproportioned; unsymmetric(al); variable

UNEVENTFUL: **see** "commonplace"

UNEXAGGERATED: **see** "true"

UNEXCITABLE: (**see** "calm") sedate; UN-

EXCITING: blah; bland; boring; common(place); flat; placid; prosaic(al); quiet; tame; throbless

UNEXPANDED: **see** "undeveloped"

UNEXPECTED: accidental; extemporaneous; rare; sudden; supervenient; temporary; unannounced; unanticipated; undevised; unforeseen; unheralded; unhoped-for; unlooked-for; unknown; unperceived; unplanned; unsuspected

UNEXPLAINED: inscrutable; insoluble; irresolute; questionable; unaccounted (for); unresolved

UNEXPLORED: uncharted; undetermined; unfathomed; uninvestigated; unplumbed; unsounded; wild

UNEXPRESSED: implicit; implied; inarticulate(d); tacit; unspoken; unuttered; unvocalized

UNEXPURGATED: unabridged; unbowdlerized; uncensored; uncut; unedited

UNFADING: amaranthine; immarcescible; immortal; permanent; undying

UNFAIR: (**see** "unjust") biased; devious; dishonest; disproportionate; excessive; foul; inequitable; partial; prejudiced; tricky; underhand(ed); unfavorable; wrong(ful)

UNFAITHFUL: (**see** "disloyal") apostate; false; inaccurate; recreant; tyrannous; untrustworthy; UNFAITHFULNESS: apostasy; disloyalty; falsity; improbity; inaccuracy; infidelity; perfidy; recreancy; traitorousness; treachery; tyranny; untrustworthiness

UNFAMED: humble; lowly; unnoticed

UNFAMILIAR: (**see** "strange") exotic; foreign; heathen; inconversant; odd; pagan; quaint; unaccustomed; uncanny; uncommon; unknown

UNFASHIONABLE: bad; deformed; ill; old-fashioned; out(moded); passé; unmodish; vulgar

UNFASTEN: detach; loose(n); open; unbuckle; unclasp; undo; unhitch; unhook; unpin; untie

UNFATHOMED: cosmic; ethereal; immense;

impenetrated; impervious; infinite; soundless; undetermined; unsounded; vast; wide

UNFAVORABLE: (**see** "undesirable") contrary; damaging; derogatory; detrimental; disadvantageous; disagreeable; disparaging; dyslogistic; foul; ill-omened; inauspicious; inclement; low; ominous; opposed; oppressive; portentous; prejudicial; sinister; sinistrous; unadvantageous; undesirable; unfair; unjust; unpopular; unprepossessing; unpropitious; wrong

UNFEELING: analgesic; anesthetic; apathetic; brutal; callous; cold(-blooded); coldhearted; comatose; cruel; dull; emotionless; fell; feral; hard(hearted); impassible; impenitent; impervious; impiteous; implacable; incompassionate; indurate; indurative; insensate; insensitive; insentient; matter-of-fact; obdurate; obtuse; oppressive; sentimentless; staid; stoic(al); stolid; torpid; unaffectionate; uncompassionate; unemotional; unenervated; unimpressionable; unmoved; unpassionate; unresponsive; unstirred; unsusceptible; unsympathetic; unyielding

UNFETTERED: (**see** "free") unbound; ungagged; unlimited; untrammeled

UNFINISHED: (**see** "uncompleted") left; undone

UNFIT: blemished; bungled; bungling; crippled; deficient; denatured; disabled; disqualified; *hors de combat*; impertinent; impotent; improper; inadequate; inappropriate; inapt; incapable; incompetent; ineffectual; inefficient; inept; inexpert; insufficient; lacking; maladroit; sorry; unable; unexemplary; unhealthy; unqualified; unskilled; unskillful; unsound; unsuitable; unsuited; untimely; wanting; wrong

UNFLATTERING: accurate; blunt; candid; frank; open; unbeauteous

UNFOLD: bloom; blossom; deploy; develop; disclose; display; elaborate; evolute; evolve; expand; open; perfect; plan; plot; reveal; spread; unfurl; unroll; unwrap

UNFORGIVABLE: inexcusable; inexpiable; irremissible; unpardonable; UNFORGIVING: impenitent; implacable; relentless; uncondoned

UNFORESEEABLE *or* UNFORESEEN: (**see** "unexpected") chance; incalculable; lucky; undivined; unguessed; unimagined; un-

perceived; unpredicted; unprophetic; unsuspected

UNFORMED: (**see** "undecided") embryonic; immature; unformulated

UNFORTUNATE: (**see** "calamitous" and "unlucky") deplorable; evil; fortuneless; hapless; ill-fared; ill-fated; impoverished; inapt; infelicitous; inopportune; lamentable; misadventurous; poor; regrettable; unfelicitous; unpropitious; unsuccessful; unsuitable; untoward

UNFOUNDED: (**see** "untrue.") baseless; groundless; illusive; inaccurate

UNFREQUENTED: alone; isolated; lone(ly); solitary; untraveled; wild

UNFRIENDLY: adverse; alien; alone; antagonistic; asocial; averse; belligerent; chill(y); cold; conflicting; contrary; cool; disaffected; formal; frosty; hostile; icy; ill-mannered; inhospitable; inimical; malevolent; malign(ant); opposed; oppugnant; rancorous; repugnant; savage; standoffish; unamiable; uncivil(ized); uncongenial; uncordial; unfavorable; ungregarious; unhospitable; unneighborly; unsympathetic; wild

UNFRIGHTENED: **see** "unafraid"

UNFRUITFUL: acarpous; barren; fallow; fruitless; infertile; sterile; unproductive; unprofitable

UNFURL: disclose; display; loosen; open; release; spread; unfold; unroll; unwind

UNGAINLY: angular; angulous; awkward; clumsy; coarse; gauche; gawky; inept; inexpert; loggy; stupid; ugly; unexpert; unwieldly; weedy; wooden

UNGENEROUS: **see** "illiberal"

UNGODLY: blasphemous; desecrating; heathenish; impious; indecent; irreligious; irreverent; outrageous; pagan; profane; sacrilegious; sinful; terrible; unconsecrated; undevout; undivine; unhallowed; unholy; unsanctified; unsanctimonious; wicked; UNGODLINESS: blasphemy; impiety; irreligiosity; irreverence; profanity; sacrilege; unholiness; wickedness

UNGOVERNED: (**see** "wild") undisciplined; unruled; unruly

UNGRATEFUL: boorish; crude; curt; disagreeable; distasteful; gruff; harsh; ingrateful; repellant; rough; severe; thankless; unappreciated; uncongenial; UNGRATEFULNESS: ingratitude; thanklessness

UNGUARDED: (see "unprotected") open; unguided; unled; unpiloted; unshepherded

UNGUENT: cerate; chrism; nard; ointment; pomade; salve

UNGULATA: cow; deer; horse; ruminant; swine; tapir; ungulate

UNHAMPERED: (see "direct") clear; cloudless; unimpeded; unrestrained

UNHAPPY: (see "sad") agitated; anhedonic; awkward; dejected; disagreeable; disconsolate; dismal; dissatisfied; distressed; distressing; disturbed; drear(y); dysphoric; inept; infelicitous; melancholy; miserable; mournful; painful; unappeased; undelighted; undelightful; unfortunate; unpleasant; unsatisfied; wretched; UNHAPPINESS: anhedonia; distress; dolor; dysphoria; grief; infelicity; melancholy; misery; misfortune; sadness; sorrow; undelight; unrest; woe; worry; wretchedness

UNHARMED: hale; intact; safe; scatheless; sound; unbattered; unblemished; unbroken; unbruised; undamaged; undefaced; unhurt; unimpaired; uninjured; unmarked; unmarred; unmolested; unravaged; unravished; unscarred; unscathed; untouched; unwounded; unwronged; whole

UNHARMONIOUS: (see "inharmonious") cacophonic; cacophonous; discordant; disharmonious; disputatious; dissentient; dissentious; dissident; dissonant; harsh; rough; strident

UNHEALABLE: insanable; intractable; raw

UNHEALTHFUL or UNHEALTHY: bad; dangerous; diseased; diseaseful; inimical; injurious; insalubrious; insalutary; insanitary; malignant; morbid; morbific; noxious; pathological; pernicious; risky; septic; sick(ly); unsound; unwholesome; weak

UNHEEDING or UNHEEDED: absent(ly); absent-minded; deaf; impercipient; oblivious; unaware; unlooked at; unmindful; unnoticed; unobservant(ly); unobserved

UNHOLY: (see "ungodly") carnal; common;

godless; profane; terrible; unconsecrated; undivine; unhallowed; unorthodox; unsanctified; unsanctimonious; unspiritual; wicked

UNHONORED: unacknowledged; unesteemed; unlaureled; unrespected; unsung

UNHORSE: free; overthrow; topple; unseat; upset

UNHURT: see "unharmed"

UNIDENTIFIED: alias; incognita (fem.); incognito; unrecognized

UNIFIED: (see "united") integrated; together; UNIFYING: afferent; cementatory; centralizing; centripetal; consolidating; integrative; UNIFICATION: (see "union") consolidation; ensemble; integration

UNIFORM: a. alike; changeless; comparable; consistent; consonant; constant; equable; equal; equiform; even; harmonious; homogeneous; homologous; invariable; isogenous; level; like; monolithic; regular; similar; single; stable; standard; steady; symmetrical; synonymous; unanimous; unchanging; undifferentiated; unvaried; UNIFORM: n. garb; livery; panoply; suit; UNIFORMITY: constancy; continuity; equability; equanimity; homogeneity; isogeny; level(ness); monolithism; monotony; resemblance; sameness; semblance; similitude; unanimity; uniformness

UNIFY: (see "unite") orchestrate

UNIMAGINATIVE or UNIMAGINED: frigid; insipid; jejune; limited; monotonous; pedantic; pedestrian; pointless; practical; prosaic(al); sodden; spiritless; torpid; undreamed; unfancied; unleavened; wooden

UNIMPAIRED: (see "unharmed") hale; sound; undamaged; unhurt; whole

UNIMPEDED: (see "unhampered") free; open; unstayed

UNIMPORTANT: (see "inferior") dispensible; inconsequential; insignificant; insubstantial; irrelevant; lightweight; low(-level); minor(-league); one-horse; slight; small(-scale); trifling; trivial; two-bit; unessential; unimpressive; UNIMPORTANCE: see "insignificance"

UNIMPRESSED: see "bored;" UNIMPRESSIVE: (see "timid") unimposing

UNINHABITED: (see "wild") unpeopled; unpopulated; unsettled

UNINJURED: (see "unharmed") unravaged; unscarred; unwounded

UNINSPIRED: (see "dull") dry as dust; pedantic; pedestrian; prosaic(al); unelevated; unexalted; unfired; unoriginal

UNINTELLECTUAL: see "ignorant;" UNINTELLIGENT: brutish; dull; dumb; fatuous; foolish; idiotic; ignorant; inane; obscure; simple; unwise; witless; UNINTELLIGIBLE: abstruse; incomprehensible; puzzling; unfathomable; unununderstandable

UNINTENTIONAL or UNINTENDED: (see "accidental") inadvertent; purposeless; undeliberate; undesigned; unmeant; unpremeditated; unpurposed

UNINTERESTING or UNINTERESTED: (see "dull") apathetic; banal; barren; boring; bromidic; comatose; common(place); dingdong; disinterested; ho-hum; humdrum; immature; inattentive; incurious; indifferent; insipid; jejune; lackadaisical; languid; languorous; prosaic(al); routine; sterile; tedious; unenquiring; uninvolved; unremarkable; unstimulating; vapid; workaday

UNINVITING: (see "unappealing") untempting

UNINVOLVED: see "simple"

UNION: (see "fusion") accord; accretion; adherence; affinity; agglutination; alliance; amalgam(ation); anastomosis; association; cementation; club; coadunation; coalescence; coalition; coherence; colligation; combination; concord(ance); concert; concrescence; confederacy; confederation; confluence; conjugation; conjunction; conjuncture; connection; connectivity; consolidation; consortion; copulation; ensemble; ensign; federation; flag; harmony; integration; joint(ure); junction; juncture; knot; lamination; league; liaison; ligature; link(age); lodge; marriage; merger; oneness; raphe; rapprochement; seam; solidity; suture; synchondrosis; syncretism; synoecism; unanimity; unification; unit(ion); unitization; unity; whole

UNIQUE: alone; apart; bizarre; characteristic; choice; eccentric; exceptional; isolated; lone; matchless; nonpareil; notable; odd; one; only; original; quaint; queer; rare; segregated; separated; single; sole; special; strange; sui generis; uncommon; unequal(ed); unexampled; unprecedented; unusual; UNIQUENESS: eccentricity; isolation; oddity; phoenixity; unica (pl.); unicity; unicum; uniquity

UNIT: ace; amount; being; chapter; chorus; combination; component; digit; district; entity; existent; individual; integer; link; module; molecule; monad; number; object; one; organism; part(icle); person; piece; point; portion; principle; residue; singularity; specimen; subdivision; subsistent; substantive; syllable; thing; word

UNITARY: integrative; monadic; monadological; monistic

UNITE or UNIFY: (see "fuse" and "join") accrete; add; adhere; agglutinate; ally; amalgamate; associate; bind; blend; catenate; cement; centralize; coadunate; coagment; coalesce; coalite; coapt; cohere; colleague; colligate; combine; commerge; commingle; concatenate; concentrate; concert; concrete; concur; confederate; conjoin; conjugate; connect; consociate; consolidate; conspire; cooperate; embody; fasten; federate; fix; graft; harmonize; incorporate; inosculate; integrate; laminate; link; marry; merge; mix; nail; orchestrate; organize; recapitulate; relate; solder; solidify; suture; syncretize; synoecize; synthesize; tie; unitize; wed; weld; yoke; UNITED: (see "fused" and "joined") agglutinated; allied; amalgamative; associated; blended; cemented; centralized; coadunate; coadunative; coalesced; coherent; colligated; combined; concatenated; concordant; concrete; conjoint; conjugate; conjunct; connected; consentaneous; consentient; consociated; consolidated; federated; harmonious; incorporated; integrated; joint; laminated; married; merged; mixed; one; syncretic; syncretistic; undetached; unified; unisonous; unitive; wedded

UNITY: accord; affinity; allness; concert; entity; harmony; identity; integrality; integration; omneity; one(ness); singularity; sympathy; syncretism; totality; unanimity; unification; uniformity; union(ization)

UNIVERSAL: a. all-around; all-including; all-inclusive; altogether; boundless; broad; catholic; common; complete; comprehensive; connotative; cosmic; cosmopolitan; consolidated; detailed; ecumenical; embracive; encyclic; encyclopedic(al); entire; epidemic; everywhere; far and near; far-reaching; general; generic; grand; impersonal; inclusive; indefinite; infinite; intensive; invariant; liberal; macrocosmic; omnipresent; pandemic; panharmonic; peregrine; prevalent; sweeping; synoptic; thoroughly; throughout; total; transcendental; ubiquitous; unanimous; unchanging; unexcluding; unexclusive; unlimited; whole; wide-ranging; widespread; wide-spreading; UNIVERSAL: **n.** abstraction; concept; exemplar; law; moral; principle; trait; UNIVERSALITY: catholicity; infinity; universalness

UNIVERSITY: **see** "college"

UNJUST: biased; dishonest; exorbitant; foul; hard; inequal; inequitable; one-sided; oppressive; partial; unequal; unfair; unilateral; unwarranted; wrong(ful); UNJUSTIFIABLE *or* UNJUSTIFIED: gratuitous; illegal; illegitimate; iniquitous; injudicious; undeserved; unlawful; unmerited; unright-(ful); unwarranted; unworthy; wrong

UNKEMPT: blowsy; careless; dirty; disheveled; disorderly; dowdy; frowsy; lax; moth-eaten; patchy; ragged(y); rough; ruffled; seedy; shaggy; slack; slatternly; slipshod; squalid; tousled; unclean; uncombed; ungroomed; untidy

UNKIND: brutal; cruel; *désobligeant*; disgracious; disobliging; fell; hard; harsh; inconsiderate; inhuman(e); rigorous; severe; ungracious; UNKINDNESS: brutality; cruelty; harshness; inconsideration; ingratitude; inhumanity; severity; ungraciousness; ungratefulness; unkindness

UNKNOWN: **a.** alias; alien; imponderable; incalculable; incognito; incondite; indeterminate; inexplicable; inexpressible; inglorious; recondite; strange; supernatural; unanswerable; unascertained; unbeknown; uncharted; unchristened; unexpected; unfamiliar; unidentified; unnamed; unrecognizable; unrecognized; unrenowned; unsuspected; UNKNOWN: **n.** imponderabilia (pl.)

UNLADYLIKE: gamine; hoydenish; improper; tomboyish

UNLAWFUL: contraband; criminal; extralegal; felonious; illegal; illegitimate; illicit; irregular; lawless; malfeasant; unauthorized; under-the-counter; unjustified

UNLEARNED: (**see** "ignorant") natural; uneducated; unschooled; untaught; untrained; unversed

UNLEAVENED: azymous; banal; pedestrian; tedious; trite; unimaginative

UNLED: **see** "leaderless"

UNLESS: but; except(ing); last; nisi; save; than

UNLIKE: (**see** "opposite") alien; anomalous; antipathic; different; disparate; dissimilar; distinct; diverse; heterogeneous; incongruous; irrelevant; odd; sundry; unequal; unmatched

UNLIKELY: but; except(ing); improbable; lest; nisi; save; than; unprobable

UNLIMITED: bottomless; boundless; countless; endless; free; illimitable; immeasurable; immeasured; immense; immensurate; imponderable; incalculable; incomprehensible; indefinite; inexhaustible; infinite; innumerable; interminable; nonrestrictive; numberless; perpetual; plenipotent(ial); plenipotentiary; termless; unbounded; uncircumscribed; unconfined; undefined; unfathomable; unfettered; unimpeded; unmeasurable; unmeasured; unrestricted; untrammeled; vast; wide; world-wide

UNLOAD: deliver; disburden; discard; discharge; disemburden; disencumber; disgorge; drop; dump; eject; jettison; relieve; remove; rid; sell; trade

UNLOCK: disclose; discover; free; interpret; ope; open; release; solve; undo; unfasten

UNLUCKY: calamitous; disastrous; evil; fey; hapless; ill(-boding); ill-fated; ill-omened; ill-starred; inauspicious; infaust; inopportune; jinxed; luckless; misadventurous; miserable; misfortunate; regrettable; ruined; unfortunate; unpropitious; untoward

UNMANAGEABLE: (**see** "stubborn") disobedient; intractable; recalcitrant; refractory; uncontrollable; uncontrolled; undisciplined; unrestrained; unruly; wild

UNMANNERED *or* UNMANNERLY: (**see** "coarse" and "rude") discourteous; impolite; mannerless; straightforward; unaffected

UNMARRED: (**see** "unharmed") unblemished; unbroken; undefaced; unhurt; uninjured; unmarked; whole

UNMARRIED: celibate; single; sole; unhusbanded; unmatched; unmated; unwedded; widowed

UNMASCULINE: (**see** "feminine") effeminate; girlish; unmanful; unmanlike; unmanly; womanly

UNMATCHED: azygous; celibate; odd; single; unmarried; unmated; unpaired

UNMENTIONED: **see** "omitted"

UNMERCIFUL: (**see** "merciless") excessive; extreme; harsh; impiteous; severe

UNMERITED: erroneous; indign; undeserved; unearned; unwarranted; unworthy; wrong

UNMINDFUL: (**see** "inattentive") abstracted; carefree; careless; disregardful; forgetful; neglectful; negligent; oblivious; remiss; slack; unaware; ungrateful; unobservant; unobserving; unvigilant; unwatchful

UNMISTAKABLE: (**see** "clear") certain; clear-cut; cut-and-dried; decisive; definite; definitive; distinct; downright; express; frank; incontrovertible; manifest; obvious; outspoken; patent; pointed; pronounced; undisguised

UNMITIGATED: (**see** "sheer" and "undiluted") arrant; bald; barefaced; consummate; downright; out-and-out; stark; ultimate

UNMIXED: (**see** "unadulterated") pureblood; purebred; raw; sheer; unassimilated; unblended; undiversified; unmingled; UNMIXABLE: immiscible; incompatible; unassimilable

UNMODIFIED: **see** "unchanged"

UNMOLESTED: (**see** "safe") unharmed; unhurt; uninjured; unplundered

UNMOURNED: **see** "unsung"

UNMOVED _or_ UNMOVABLE: apathetic; calm; dead; dispassionate; firm; flinty; immovable; indifferent; inert; inexorable; obstinate; recalcitrant; resolute; serene; stubborn; unaffected; unbudgeable; undisturbed; unimpressed; unpassionate

UNMUSICAL: arrhythmic(al); cacophonic; cacophonous; discordant; harsh; inharmonious; strident; unharmonious

UNNAMED: (**see** "unknown") alias; anonymous; incognita (fem.); incognito; innominate; pseudonymous; undubbed; unchristened; undesignated; unidentified; unmarked; unsigned; unspecified

UNNATURAL: (**see** "strange") abnormal; abominable; adventitious; adventive; artificial; contrived; illegitimate; irregular; perverse; uncanny

UNNEEDED _or_ UNNECESSARY: gratuitous; inessential; needless; nonessential; superfluous; uncalled-for; unnecessitated; unneedful; unobliged; unrequired; unrequisite; unwanted; useless

UNNERVE: (**see** "weaken") denervate; unman; upset

UNNOTICED: (**see** "unseen") impercipient; unobserved

UNOBJECTIVE: blind; subjective; unclinical;

UNOBLIGED: (**see** "unnecessary") uncommitted; undogmatic(al)

UNOBSERVANT: astigmatic; impercipient; inattentive; incurious; nonobservant; unperceiving; unperceptive; unpercipient; unseeing; UNOBSERVED: (**see** "unseen") unnoticed; unremarked

UNOCCUPIED: (**see** "idle") empty; otiose; unowned; unpossessed; untenanted

UNOFFICIAL: contraband; informal; offhand; officious; offstage; unacknowledged; unauthorized; unorthodox; unsanctioned

UNOPPOSED: unfought; unresisted

UNORGANIZED: acosmic; messy; slovenly; unassorted; unoriented; unsorted

UNORIGINAL: artificial; copied; counterfeit; derivative; tangential; unimaginative; uninspired

UNORTHODOX: heretical; heterodox; radical; unacknowledged; unapproved; uncanonical; unconventional; unholy; unofficial; unsanctioned; UNORTHODOXY: heresy; heterodoxy; unconventionality

UNPAID: (**see** "due") unrecompensed; unremunerated; unsalaried

UNPAIRED: alone; azygous; odd; single; uncoupled; unmarried; unmatched; unmated; unwedded

UNPARALLELED: A-one; epochal; exceptional; momentous; *ne plus ultra*; superior; supreme; unequaled; unmatched; unrivaled; unsurpassed

UNPARDONABLE: inexcusable; inexpiable; irremissible; unforgivable; wrong

UNPERFORMED: **see** "uncompleted"

UNPERTURBED: (**see** "indifferent") calm; carefree; happy; unbothered; undisturbed; unworried

UNPIERCED: imperforate; intact; unpenetrated; whole

UNPLANNED: **see** "unexpected"

UNPLEASING *or* UNPLEASANT: bad; beastly; bilious; brutal; crude; disagreeable; displeasing; evil; fiendish; ghastly; gummy; hairy; objectionable; offensive; painful; plutonian; plutonic; rough; rugged; troublesome; uncomfortable; undelightful; undesirable; unhappy; unpalatable; unsavory; vile; UNPLEASANTNESS: (**see** "disagreement") disagreeableness; disamenity; displeasure; dissatisfaction; pain; pang; suffering; undelight; unhappiness; unpleasure

UNPOLISHED: agrestic; boorish; coarse; crude; gauche; gross; ill-mannered; inurbane; ragged; rough; tattered; unburnished; uncivilized; uncouth; uncultivated; uncultured; unhewn; unrefined

UNPOPULAR: **see** "unfavorable"

UNPREDICTABLE: ambivalent; capricious; chameleonic; errant; fickle; incalculable; uncertain; unforeknowable; unreckonable; vagarious; whimsical

UNPREJUDICED: (**see** "impartial") cosmopolitan; equitable; fair(-minded); free; honest; indifferent; judicious; just; unbiased; uninfluenced; unjaundiced; unprepossessed

UNPREMEDITATED: accidental; *brevi manu*; extemporaneous; hasty; headlong; impromptu; undesigned; unintentional

UNPREPARED: caught short; ill-prepared; inexperienced; raw; unaltered; unavoidable; uncooked; uneducated; unequipped; unexpected; unfurnished; unprovided; unready; untrained

UNPRETENTIOUS: (**see** "plain") unsophisticated

UNPRODUCTIVE: arid; bare; barren; dry; fallow; idle; nonproductive; poor; sterile; unfruitful; unprofitable; unremunerative; unrewarding; untilled; useless; vain

UNPROFITABLE: arid; barren; dry; fallow; fruitless; frustraneous; idle; infructuous; inutile; poor; profitless; sterile; unlucrative; unproductive; unprofited; unremunerative; unrewarding; useless; vain

UNPROMISING: (**see** "dubious") unlikely

UNPROTECTED: (**see** "defenseless") unfenced; unguarded; unshielded; unsupported

UNPROVED: alleged; assumed; inexperienced; undocumented; unestablished; unproven; unsubstantiated; untested; untried

UNPUBLISHED: unedited; unpromulgated; unpronounced; unpublicized

UNPUNISHED: unatoned; unchastened; unchastised; undisciplined; unexpiated; unwhipped

UNQUALIFIED: absolute; all-embracing; bald; categoric(al); complete; consummate; direct; disabled; disbarred; disqualified; explicit; genuine; helpless; impotent; incapable; incompetent; ineligible; inexpert; maladroit; out-and-out; plenary; plump; sheer; straight-out; straight-way; sweeping; thoroughgoing; unable; undiluted; unfit(ted); unreserved; unrestricted; unsatisfactory; utter; wrong

UNQUESTIONABLE: (**see** "clear") actual; authentic; certain; conceded; conclusive; critical; crucial; decisive; definite; definitive; distinct; exact; explicit; final; hands-down; immutable; implacable; implicit; incontestible; incontrovertible; indisputable; indubitable; official; positive; sure; unchallenged; undisputable; undisputed; undoubtable; undoubted; unequivocal; unmistakable; unprovocative; UNQUESTIONED: (**see** "undisputed") unchallenged

UNRAVEL: disentangle; feaze; interpret; ope; open; resolve; reverse; separate; solve; undecipher; undo; untie; unwind

UNREAL: affected; artificial; Barmecidal; baroque; chaotic; chimerical; counterfeit; delusive; disembodied; dramatic; false; fantastic; fictitious; Gothic; grotesque; histrionic; illusional; illusive; illusory; imaginary; impalpable; imperceptible; incorporeal; insubstantial; intangible; melodramatic; *papier-mâché*; phantasmagoric(al); phantasmal; phantom; platonic; pretentious; staged; stagy; strange; supersensible; theatric(al); unlifelike; unrealistic; unsubstantial; Utopian; visionary; whimsical; UNREALISM: ideality; unreality; unsubstantiality

UNREASONABLE: (see "stubborn") absonant; absurd; crackbrained; crackpot; extravagant; extreme; fatuous; illogical; immoderate; inappropriate; incongruous; inordinate; insane; irrational; paralogical; paralogistic; perverse; preposterous; quaint; rabid; radical; rash; reckless; senseless; unconscionable; unreasoned; UNREASONABLENESS: extravagance; illogicality; incoherence; insanity; irrationality; unsoundness; UNREASONED: (see "unthinking") unreasonable

UNRECOGNIZED: (see "unsung") unprofessed; unrealized

UNREFINED: (see "uncultured") barbaric; barbarous; brutal; brutish; coarse(-grained); crass; crude; dreadful; earthy; graceless; gross; inelegant; offensive; primitive; raw; ribald; rude; rustic; savage; troglodytic; ugly; uncouth

UNREGRETTED: unlamented

UNREGULATED: (see "disorderly") chaotic; messy; uncontrolled; undisciplined; ungoverned; unmanaged; unmanned

UNRELATED: accidental; arbitrary; discrete; disjointed; dissociate(d); extraneous; extrinsic; heterogeneous; impertinent; inapplicable; inapposite; incidental; intercalary; interpolated; irrelevant; parenthetical; separate(d); tangential; unakin; unallied; unconnected

UNRELIABLE: (see "tricky") changeable; contradictious; devious; duplicitous; feckless; queasy; shaky; shiftless; shifty; ticklish; tottery; treacherous; uncertain; unconscionable; undependable; unfair; unscrupulous; untrustworthy; untrusty; villainous; wobbly; UNRELIABILITY: duplicity; unconscionableness; unscrupulosity; villainy

UNRESERVED: (see "unrestrained") all-out; entire; exuberant; frank; full; hearty; open; outspoken; thoroughgoing; unconditional; unqualified

UNRESPECTABLE: (see "disrespectable") bad; disreputable

UNREST: (see "disquiet") disorder; ferment; nervousness; tautness; tenseness; trouble; turmoil; worry

UNRESTRAINED: absolute; apod(e)ictic(al); bizarre; boisterous; bold; clamorous; crazy; deictic; demonstrative; desolate; ebullient; effervescent; effusive; emotional; epideictic; exaggerative; exhibitive; expressive; extravagant; exuberant; fanciful; fantastic(al); fierce; flamboyant; foolish; frank; free(hand); hog-wild; hysterical; immoderate; immodest; impertinent; incontinent; indiscriminate; inordinate; insane; intemperate; jazzy; lavish; lawless; lax(ative); limitless; loose; lyric; mad; manic; mandlin; mawkish; mobile; movable; open; outpouring; *outré*; overflowing; passionate; plenary; plenipotent(ial); probative; prodigal; promiscuous; psychotic; rampant; released; rhapsodic; scaturient; self-indulgent; senseless; sentimental; showy; sovereign; spontaneous; theatrical; tumultuary; unburdened; unchastened; unchastised; uncontrollable; uncontrolled; uncurbed; undampened; undisciplined; unembarrassed; unhampered; uninhibited; unlicensed; unlimited; unpunished; unreal; unreserved; unstinted; unyoked; vehement; wanton; wild

UNRESTRICTED: (see "unrestrained") free; mobile; movable; open; plenary; plenipotent(ial); sovereign; unending; unlimited; unzoned

UNREVEALED (see "hidden") cached; concealed; *in pectore*; *in petto*; secret; shrouded; veiled

UNREWARDING: see "unprofitable"

UNRIPE: (see "raw") green; immature; undeveloped; verdant

UNRIVALED: incomparable; peerless; nonpareil; supreme; unequaled; unparalleled

UNROLL: develop; discover; display; evolve; exhibit; open; reveal; spread; uncoil; unfurl; unshroud; unveil; unwind

UNRUFFLED: (see "calm") cool; even; halcyon; imperturbable; indifferent; jaunty; nonchalant; placid; quiet; sedate; serene; smooth; steady; still; unaffected; unflustered; uniform; unshaken

UNRULY: boisterous; contentious; difficult; disobedient; feral; fractious; headstrong; intractable; lawless; mutinous; noisy; obstinate; quarrelsome; rampageous; rampant; recalcitrant; recusant; refractory; ructious; stormy; stubborn; tempestuous; troublesome; turbulent; unbridled; uncontrollable; uncontrolled; undisciplinable; undisciplined; ungovernable; unguided; unmanageable; unsupervised; vexatious; violent; wanton; wild; willful;

UNSAFE: (see "dangerous") hot; Icarian; shaky; tottering; unassured; unreliable; unsecured; unsound

UNSAID: see "unspoken"

UNSALABLE: unmerchantable

UNSANCTIONED: (see "unofficial") illicit; unacceptable; unauthorized; unorthodox

UNSANITARY: see "insanitary"

UNSATIATED: gluttonous; hungry; unextinguished; unquelled; unquenched

UNSATISFACTORY: (see "unsound") bad; disappointing; dissatisfactory; failing; lame; measly; poor; suboptimal; substandard; unqualified; wrong

UNSATISFIED: disstatisfied; insatiated; querulous; unappeased; unassuaged; unatoned; unfulfilled; unhappy; unquenched; unsatiated

UNSCRUPULOUS: (see "dishonest") bowelless; brazen; duplicitous; Machiavellian; shameless; treacherous; unprincipled; UNSCRUPULOUSNESS: dishonesty; shamelessness; treachery; unscrupulosity

UNSEASONABLE: abnormal; ill-timed; improper; inappropriate; inexpedient; inopportune; malapropos; untimely; unusual; UNSEASONED: green; immature; inexperienced; raw; untimely; untrained

UNSEAT: (see "unhorse") depose; displace; overthrow; remove; upset

UNSEEMLY: (see "unbecoming") immodest; improper; inappropriate; indecent; indecorous; solecistic; unbecoming; undecorous; unseasonable

UNSEEN: (see "hidden") undescried; undetected; undiscerned; uneyed; unnoted; unnoticed; unobserved; unperceived; unrecognized; unremarked; unviewed; unwitnessed

UNSELFISH: altruistic; charitable; chivalrous; generous; magnanimous; philanthropic-(al); selfless; UNSELFISHNESS: altropathy; altruism; charity; chivalry; consideration; devotion; generosity; magnanimity; philanthropy; selflessness

UNSETTLED: abeyant; agitated; anchorless; deranged; disrupted; disturbed; doubtful; drifting; erratic; helmless; inconstant; insecure; instable; itinerant; maddened; nomadic; pendant; pending; precarious; queasy; rattletrap; resolute; rudderless; shaky; tottering; undecided; undetermined; uninhabited; unpaid; unplanted; unpopulated; unquiet; unresolved; unstable; vagrant; variable; wavering; wobbly

UNSHAKABLE: (see "firm") adamant; grounded; impregnable; inflexible

UNSHEATHE: bare; draw; remove; uncover; unfurl

UNSIGHTLY: see "ugly"

UNSIGNED: anonymous; blank; pseudonymous; unidentified

UNSKILLED or UNSKILLFUL: amateurish; awkward; bungling; butcherly; clumsy; feckless; gauche; green; ignorant; inapt; inept; inexperienced; inexpert; maladroit; puisne; raw; rusty; unartful; uneducated; unpracticed; unproficient; untrained; UNSKILLFULNESS: amateurishness; gaucherie; inaptitude; maladroitness

UNSOCIABLE: antisocial; asocial; awkward; backward; bashful; clannish; detached; discordant; incompatible; inharmonious; inhospitable; isolated; moronic; reserved; shy; solitary; solitudinarian; troglodytic; uncompanionable; uncongenial; unfriendly; ungregarious; withdrawn

UNSOLVABLE: inextricable; inscrutable; insoluble; unexcogitable

UNSOPHISTICATED: artless; bucolic; candid; countrified; folksy; frank; genuine; guileless; homespun; inexperienced; ingenuous; innocent; naïve; natural; native; open; pastoral; plain; plebeian; practical; pure; rough-hewn; rural; rustic; shy; simple (minded); specious; straightforward; unadulterated; unpretentious; unworldly; verdant

UNSOUGHT: see "unwanted"

UNSOUND: (**see** "illogical") bad; corrupt; crazy; dangerous; demented; disappointing; diseased; evil; false; fragile; insane; invalid; psychotic; sandy; shaky; sick(ly); tottering; unacceptable; unhealthful; unhealthy; unorthodox; unreliable; unsafe; unsatisfactory; unwholesome; weak; wobbly

UNSPARING: free; generous; hard; liberal; literal; procrustean; profuse; relentless; ruthless

UNSPEAKABLE: (**see** "bad") execrable; *horribile dictu*; indescribable; indicible; ineffable; inerrable; inexpressive; nefandous; nefarious; objectionable; unmentionable; unreportable; unutterable; utterless; vile

UNSPIRITUAL: (**see** "unholy") carnal; common; godless

UNSPOKEN: inarticulate; obmutescent; secret; silent; speechless; tacit; unarticulated; uncommunicated; unexpressed; unrelated; unsaid; unstated; unuttered; unverbalized; unvocalized; wordless

UNSPOTTED: **see** "unsullied"

UNSTABLE *or* UNSTEADY: alterable; astatic; ataxic; changeable; drunk(en); emotional; erratic; faithless; fickle; fitful; fluctuating; inconstant; indeterminate; infirm; insecure; instable; insurmountable; irregular; irresponsible; jerky; jumpy; labile; loose; mercurial; movable; mutable; nervy; oscillating; precarious; protean; quavering; quavery; quicksilver; risky; rocky; shaky; skittish; temperamental; tipsy; titubant; trembling; tremulous; unbalanced; uncertain; undermined; undulating; unequable; unfirm; unfixed; unjustified; unsafe; unsettled; unsteadfast; vacillating; vague; variable; vertiginous; volatile; voluble; wavering; weak; wobbly

UNSTAINED: **see** "unsullied"

UNSTATED: (**see** "unspoken") unrecited

UNSTOPPABLE: inextinguishable; insatiable; unextinguishable; unquenchable

UNSTUDIED: (**see** "unthinking") casual; impromptu; natural; offhand; random; unaffected; unexamined; unlearned; unweighed

UNSUBDUED: (**see** "unbroken") feral; undefeated; vicious; wild

UNSUBSTANTIAL: (**see** "airy") aerial; cloud-built; diaphanous; empty; ethereal; footless; frivolous; imaginary; inane; insignificant; lacking; paper; *papier-mâché*; pointless; shadowy; shallow; thin; trifling; trivial; unbelievable; unreal; vacant; visionary; UNSUBSTANTIALITY: aeriality; airiness; diaphaneity; emptiness; ethereality; frivolity; inanity; pointlessness; shadowiness; shallowness; triviality

UNSUCCESSFUL: (**see** "vain") fruitless; hapless; hopeless; ill-fared; ill-fated; *manqué*; unfortunate; unproductive; unprofitable

UNSUITABLE *or* UNSUITED: (**see** "untimely") *à propos de rien*; disagreeable; discordant; fantastic(al); gauche; impertinent; improper; inapplicable; inappropriate; inapt; incompatible; incongruent; incongruous; inconvenient; inept; infelicitous; inharmonious; unbecoming; unbefitting; uncongenial; unfit(ting); unmeet; unsatisfactory; unseemly; untidy; UNSUITABILITY: inaptitude; inconcinnity; incongruity; ineptitude; infelicity; maladjustment; maladroitness; misalliance; unsuitableness

UNSULLIED: clean; fresh; immaculate; new; pristine; pure; spotless; unblemished; unspotted; unstained; untainted; untarnished

UNSUNG: unhymned; unlamented; unmourned; unpraised; unrecognized; unwept

UNSUPERVISED: rampant; uncontrolled; undirected; undisciplined; unguided; untaught; untrained; wild

UNSUPPORTED: open; unbuttressed; undemonstrated; undocumented; unpropped; unproved; unsubstantiated

UNSURE: **see** "uncertain"

UNSURPASSED: (**see** "unequaled") unexcelled

UNSYMPATHETIC: brutal; brutish; cruel; glassy; hard(ened); harsh; heartless; icy; ill-disposed; impervious; unfeeling; unreceptive; unresponsive; unwavering; unyielding

UNTAINTED: (**see** "untouched") pure; sterile; uncontaminated

UNTAMED: barbaric; barbarous; callous; *ferae naturae*; feral; ferine; ferocious; fierce; rambunctious; savage; unbroken; undisciplined; unfettered; unsubdued; vicious; wild

UNTANGLE: **see** "extricate"

UNTAUGHT: (**see** "untrained") ignorant; naïve; natural; spontaneous; unbred; undisciplined

UNTEACHABLE: indocile; intractable; opinionated; stubborn

UNTHINKABLE: extraordinary; incogitable; inconceivable; incredible; thoughtless; unimaginable; unspeakable; UNTHINKING: automatic; careless; casual; feckless; glib; heedless; inattentive; incogitant; inconsiderate; mechanical; puerile; rash; stupid; thoughtless; uncritical; unexamining; unideaed; unmindful; unmotivated; unphilosophic(al); unpremeditated; unreflecting; unreflective; unreliable; unstudied; unthought; vacant; vacuous

UNTHOUGHT: see "unthinking"

UNTIDY: bedraggled; careless; dirty; disheveled; disorderly; dowdy; draggled; draggletailed; frumpy; littered; messy; rough; seedy; sloppy; slovenly; tatterdemalion; unfastidious; unfit; ungroomed; unkempt; unpresentable; unsuitable; UNTIDINESS: dishevelment; dowdiness; seediness; sloppiness; slovenliness; unkemptness;

UNTIE: clear; detach; disclose; disengage; disentangle; dissolve; divorce; free; liberate; loose(n); open; resolve; solve; unbind; unfasten; unfold; unknot

UNTIMELY: anachronous; impracticable; impractical; improper; inappropriate; inauspicious; inconvenient; inexpedient; inopportune; intempestive; malapropos; premature(ly); undue; unexpedient; unfavorable; unpropitious; unpunctual; unseasonable; unsuitable; unsuited

UNTIRING: endless; everlasting; fatigueless; indefatigable; prolonged; protracted; sustained; tireless; unflagging; unswerving; unwearying

UNTOLD: boundless; countless; great; immeasurable; immense; incalculable; innumerable; limitless; numberless; secret; unarticulated; unbreathed; uninformed; unnumbered; unrehearsed; unrevealed; unverbalized; unvocalized; vast; wide

UNTOUCHABLE: exempt; inviolable; invulnerable; sacrosanct; unaffected; unequated; UNTOUCHED: free; insensible; intact;

new; pristine; pure; unaffected; unblemished; unharmed; uninjured; unreached; untainted; untarnished

UNTRAINED: green; ignorant; illiterate; inexperienced; inexpert; nescient; raw; unbred; unbroken; uncultured; undisciplined; uneducated; unseasoned; untaught; untutored

UNTREATED: raw; uncared-for; unmedicated

UNTRIED: (**see** "unattempted") callow; green; immature; inexperienced; inexpert; raw; unexercised; unfledged; unproved; untested; unused; unventured

UNTRIMMED: (**see** "uncut") unpruned

UNTROD(DEN): trackless; unfooted; untraversed; unused

UNTRUE: counterfeit; dishonest; disloyal; fabulous; false; fictitious; lying; mendacious; mythological; spurious; suppositious; unfair; unfaithful; unfounded; wrong; UNTRUTHFUL: **see** "false;" UNTRUTHFULNESS: dishonesty; duplicity; inaccuracy; inveracity; mendacity

UNTRUSTWORTHY: (**see** "dishonest" and "uncertain") disingenuous; flattering; limber; meanspirited; shaky; treacherous; unreliable; wobbly

UNTUTORED: **see** "untrained"

UNTWIST: disentangle; feaze; free; loose(n); straighten; unclasp; uncoil; unravel; untangle; unwind; unwreathe

UNUNITED: apart; disarticulated; disassembled; discrete; disunited; separate(d)

UNUSABLE: (**see** "useless") afunctional; inapplicable; inutile; unapplicable; unconsumable; uneatable; UNUSED: (**see** "untried") inoperative; unexpended; unexploited; untapped

UNUSUAL: abnormal; anomalistic; anomalous; bizarre; curious; different; distinct; ectopic; eerie; esoteric; exceptional; exotic; extraordinary; fantastic(al); funny; grotesque; heteromorphic; heteromorphous; irregular; notable; novel; odd; *outré*; paranormal; peculiar; phenomenal(istic); rare; *recherché*; remarkable; singular; spanking; strange; unaccustomed; uncommon; unhabituated; unique; unlike; unseasonable; weird; UNUSUALNESS: abnormality; bizarrerie; exoticism; grotesquerie; irregularity; oddity; peculiarity; phenomenality; singularity; uniquity; unusuality; whimsicality

UNUTTERABLE: (see "unspeakable") indescribable; ineffable; inenarrable; inexpressible

UNVARYING: (see "dull") constant; fixed; monotonous; plain; steady; unchanging; unfluctuating; uniform; uninterrupted

UNVEIL: (see "expose") display; divulge; exhibit; introduce; reveal; show; uncurtain; unfurl; unmask; unsheathe

UNVERIFIED: unapproved; unsubstantiated; unvouched

UNVOICED: secret; silent; stifled; surd; tacit; unarticulated; unuttered; unvocalized

UNWANTED: *de trop*; faulty; nonessential; objectionable; superfluous; unasked; undesirable; undesired; uninvited; unnecessary; unsought; unwelcome; unwished(-for)

UNWARLIKE: (see "peaceful") nonbelligerent; pacific

UNWEARIED: (see "strong") indefatigable; unfatiguing; untiring

UNWELCOME: *de trop*; distasteful; *non grata*; unacceptable; unaccepted; ungreeted; unwanted; unwished(-for)

UNWELL: (see "sick") ailing

UNWHOLESOME: bad; banal; corrupt; decayed; deleterious; detrimental; diseased; ill; immoral; inimical; insalubrious; loathsome; malign(ant); morbid; noisome; noxious; offensive; pathological; pernicious; poisonous; putrescent; putrid; repulsive; rotten; sick(ly); unhealthful; unhealthy; unsound

UNWIELDLY: (see "awkward") impractical; inconvenient; involved; ungainly; unhandy

UNWILLING: (see "stubborn") adverse; averse; disinclined; grudging; indisposed; involuntary; loath; obstinate; refractory; reluctant; UNWILLINGNESS: (see "stubbornness") aversion; disinclination; nolition; refusal; reluctance; reluctancy; reluctation; repugnance

UNWIND: (see "unroll") disengage; uncoil; undo

UNWISE: amiss; foolhardy; foolish; ill-advised; ill-judged; impolitic; impracticable; imprudent; indiscreet; inexpedient; injudicious; insipient; rash; reckless; senseless; silly; thoughtless; undiscerning; unintelligent; untimely; weakened; witless

UNWONTED: rare; uncommon; unused; unusual

UNWORLDLY: (see "spiritual") unearthly; unsophisticated

UNWORRIED: see "unperturbed"

UNWORTHY: bad; base; contemptible; derogatory; despicable; dishonorable; indign; inglorious; poor; unbecoming; undeserving; unentitled; unfit; unjustified; unmeritable; unmerited; unmeritorious; unseemly; worthless

UNWRAP: see "unfold"

UNWRINKLED: ironed; smoothed; unfurrowed

UNWRITTEN: blank; customary; nuncupative; oral; parol(e); tacit; traditional; unentered; unpenned; unrecorded; unregistered

UNYIELDING: (see "stubborn") adamant(ine); determined; dogged; firm; flinty; game; glassy; grim; hard(-shelled); harsh; headstrong; immalleable; impregnable; indomitable; inductile; inflexible; intractable; iron(bound); ironclad; obstinate; perseverant; persevering; persistent; pertinacious; perverse; pigheaded; recalcitrant; resistant; resolute; resolved; right; rigid; rigorous; severe; sta(u)nch; stern; stiff; strong; superior; tenacious; tough; unalterable; unassailable; uncompromising; unremitting; unshakable; unswerving; unsympathetic; unwavering

UP: above; atop; over; supra; upon

UPBRAID: (see "scold") criticize; reprimand; reprove; tongue-lash

UPHEAVAL: (see "convulsion") agitation; cataclysm; change; commotion; disorder; earthquake; explosion; labefaction; orogeny; overthrow

UPKEEP: conditioning; expenses; living; maintenance; means; support; sustenance; sustentation

UPLAND: country; down; inland; interior; mesa; plain; plateau; ridge

UPLIFTING: (**see** "inspiring") inspirational; inspirative; inspiriting; instigative

UPON: above; astride; atop; on(to); over; superior

UPPER: above; advanced; high(er); innermost; senior; superior; top; UPPERMOST: first; foremost; highest; loftiest; senior; superior; supreme; top(most)

UPPISH: (**see** "haughty") arrogant; assuming; elated; offish; presumptuous; pretentious; proud; pushing; pushy; snobbish; snooty; unapproachable; uppity

UPRIGHT: **a.** chivalrous; conscientious; correct; erect; fair; grand; honest; honorable; incorrupt; just; moral; noble(-minded); orthograde; orthostatic; perpendicular; punctilious; rectitudinous; right(eous); rigid; scrupulous; standing; steadfast; straight(forward); true; trustworthy; uprighteous; vertical; virtuous; UPRIGHT: **n.** mast; perpendicular(ity); pole; UPRIGHTNESS: honesty; incorruption; integrity; perpendicularity; probity; rectitude; scrupulosity; scrupulousness; uprighteousness; veridicality; verticality

UPRISING: acclivity; ascent; *coup d'état*; insurgence; insurgency; insurrection; mutiny; overthrow; putsch; rebellion; revolt; riot

UPROAR: (**see** "confusion" and "tumult") ado; Babel(ism); bedlam; brouhaha; callithump; charivari; clamor; commotion; conclamation; confusion; din; disorder; disturbance; excitement; fracas; furor; hubbub; hurly-burly; moil; noise; pandemonium; racket(ry); riot; roar; shindy; storm; tempest; tintamar(re); turbulence; turmoil

UPROOT: deracinate; destroy; eradicate; exterminate; extirpate; pull; tear; UPROOTED: (**see** "displaced") deracinated; eradicated; exterminated; extirpate; lumpen

UPSET: **v.** capsize; careen; defeat; derange; disarrange; discompose; disconcert; dismay; disparage; frazzle; interrupt; keel; overturn; subvert; tip; unhorse; unnerve; unseat;

upturn; UPSET: **a.** disordered; ill; indisposed; sick; tipped; uneasy; unhorsed; unseated; upturned; worried; UPSET: **n.** careen; bouleversement; derangement; overthrow; overturn; upside-downness

UPSHOT: conclusion; effect; essence; gist; limit; outcome; result

UPSTANDING: (**see** "upright") straightforward

UPSTART: *arrivé*; *arrivist(e)*; *hesterni quirites*; Johnny-come-lately; mushroom; *nouveau riche*; *novus homo*; parvenu; snip; snob

UP-TO-DATE: **see** "modern"

UPWARD: anabatic; ascending; ascensional; ascensive; assurgent; greater; higher

URBANE: bland; civil; cordial; courteous; courtly; mannerly; polished; polite; politic; refined; sophisticated; suave; svelte

URCHIN: arab; boy; brat; child; gamin; guttersnipe; hedgehog; imp

URGE: **v.** abet; adjure; advocate; animate; argue; ask; beg; beseech; coax; conjure; demand; desire; drive; egg; encourage; entice; export; fillip; force; goad; hasten; hie; high-pressure; impel; implicate; implore; importune; incite; inculcate; induce; insist; instigate; nudge; petition; pledge; plot; ply; poke; pray; precipitate; press; prick; prod; push; request; rouse; sic; solicit; spur; stimulate; stir; supplicate; URGE: **n.** animation; desire; drive; encouragement; exhortation; fillip; force; goad; impulse; incentive; libido; lust; passion; push; spur; stimulation; wish; yen

URGENT: acute; cogent; compelling; critical; crying; dangerous; demanding; dire; exacting; exigent; extreme; hot; immediate; imminent; imperative; imperious; important; importunate; impressing; insentient; insistent; menacing; momentous; necessary; necessitous; persistent; pertinacious; poignant; pressing; required; rushing; serious; solicitous; strained; straitened; stressing; vehement; vital; URGENCY: criticality; danger; desperation; exigency; extremity; imminence; importunity; impulse; insistence; instancy; pressingness; pressure; priority; seriousness; vehemence

USABLE: (**see** "available" and "practical") consumable; consumptible; expendable;

feasible; functional; instrumental; open; practicable; suitable; useful; utile; utilitarian

USAGE(S): advantage; ceremony; consuetude; custom(s); experience; familiarity; form; habit; law; manner; method; mode; mores (pl.); practice; prescription; procedure; rites; technique; tradition; treatment; use; utility; way; wont; world

USE: **v.** accustom; apply; attack; avail; consume; decrease; deplete; eat; employ; engage; enjoy; enlist; harness; hire; inure; invoke; involve; manage; manipulate; observe; occupy; partake; pass; practice; run; spend; treat; utilize; wear; wield; work; USE(S): **n.** ability; advantage; applicability; application; avail; benefit; capability; convenience; custom; demand; deployment; destination; disposition; employment; end; esteem; exercise; exercitation; exploration; form; function; habit; liking; manner; method; necessity; object; observance; power; practice; profit; purpose; service; treatment; usage; usefulness; utility; utilization; USEFUL: able; advantageous; beneficial; effective; effectual; efficacious; efficient; empirical; expedient; feasible; functional; good; helpful; materialistic; multipurpose; opportune; polyfunctional; practicable; practical; profitable; remunerative; serviceable; suitable; superior; tenable; utile; utilitarian; valuable; viable; yeoman; USEFULNESS: efficacy; efficiency; feasibility; functionality; practicability; use; utility

USELESS: abortive; afunctional; bootless; disabled; empty; footless; fruitless; functionless; futile; futureless; helpless; *hors de combat*; idle; incapacitated; ineffective; ineffectual; inefficacious; inefficient; inept; inutile; needless; nonfunctional; nugatory; null; otiose; out; purposeless; sterile; unavailing; uncooperative; unhelpful; unnecessary; unproductive; unserviceable; unusable; unutile; vain; valueless; void; worthless; USELESSNESS: futility; helplessness; idleness; incapacity; ineffectuality; inutility; loss; otiosity; sterility; waste

USER: beneficiary; consumer; partaker; utilizer

USHER: **v.** (**see** "direct") attend; escort; introduce; seat; show; USHER: **n.** attendant; conductor; doorkeeper; escort; guide; herald; precursor; tiler

USUAL: (**see** "customary") common(place); conventional; customarily; habitual; ordinary; prevailing; prevalent; public; regular; traditional; wonted; USUALNESS: conventionality; habit(uality); prevalence; tradition

USURP: appropriate; arrogate; assimilate; assume; condemn; confiscate; encroach; exact; forfeit; grab; hold; impinge; occupy; oppress; override; seize; sequester; take; trample; wreak; wrest

UTILITY: advantage; avail; benefit; convenience; device; expediency; favor; implement; profit; service(ableness); tool; usableness; use(fulness)

UTILIZE: (**see** "use") capitalize; domesticate; harness

UTMOST: best; distant; end; extent; extreme; fare-thee-well; fare-you-well; farthest; final; fullest; greatest; highest; largest; last; limital; maximum; nth; outside; remote; superlative; ultimate; utter(most)

UTOPIA: Eden; heaven; ideal; Zion; UTOPIAN: chimerical; Edenic; heavenly; ideal(istic); impractical; visionary

UTTER: **v.** (**see** "speak") articulate; breathe; broach; couch; exclaim; express; frame; give; offer; phonate; pronounce; relate; trumpet; voice; UTTER: **a.** absolute; complete; consummate; crude; entire; excessive; exorbitant; extravagant; extreme; fair; full; gross; incarnate; mere; moot; out-and-out; perfect; pluperfect; positive; peremptory; pure; quite; remote; sheer; sovereign; stark; thorough; total; ugly; unconditional; unmitigated; unspeakable; unusual; utmost; uttermost; whole; UTTERLY: absolutely; altogether; assuredly; completely; entirely; fully; positively; quite; sheer; stark; thick; total(ly); wholly; UTTERANCE: articulation; chorus; descant; expression; observation; speech; tongue

V

VACANT: abandoned; absent; bare; barren; blank; carefree; deserted; destitute; disengaged; dull; empty; expressionless; foolish; free; idle; inane; null; open; silly; studied; stupid; unemployed; unfilled; unoccupied; unthinking; vacuous; vague; void; wanting; VACANCY: abandonment; barrenness; blank; chasm; emptiness; gap; idleness; inanity; leisure; opening; space; vacuity; vacuum; void

VACATE: annul; cancel; depart; leave; move; retire; VACATION: annulment; furlough; holiday; intermission; leave; recess; respite; rest; spell; stop; suspension

VACILLATE: fluctuate; hesitate; oscillate; seesaw; sway; teeter; totter; wag; wave(r); wiggle; wiggle-waggle; wobble; VACILLATING: **see** "wavering" and "weak;" VACILLATION: (**see** "indecision") feebleness

VACUOUS: dull; empty; hollow; inane; insubstantial; stupid; vain; VACUITY: (**see** "vacancy") hollowness; inanity; monotony; stupidity; void

VACUUM: cavity; emptiness; gap; hole; hollow; pocket; space; vacuity; void

VAGABOND: **a.** homeless; idle; irregular; itinerant; loose; nomadic; peripatetic; prowling; roaming; roving; truant; unsettled; unstable; unsteady; wandering; VAGABOND: **n.** arab; beggar; Bohemian; bum; casual; derelict; drifter; flotsam and jetsam (pl.); gaberlunzie; gypsy; hobo; idler; itinerant; loafer; lorel; nomad; peregrine; peripatetic; picaro; rascal; rodney; rogue; rover; scamp; straggler; temporizer; tramp; truant; vagrant; wanderer; wastrel; VAGABONDISH: Bohemian; nomadic; picaresque; VAGABONDAGE: nomadism; vagabondia

VAGRANT: **a.** (**see** "vagabond") azygous; circumforaneous; itinerant; masterless; peregrine; peripatetic; random; roving; vagrom; VAGRANT: **n.** (**see** "vagabond") beachcomber; flotsam and jetsam; itinerant; pere-grine; peripatetic; undesirable; unfortunate; waif; wanderer

VAGARY: **see** "whim"

VAGUE: abstract; acategorical; aerial; ambiguous; amorphous; amphibolic; amphibological; clouded; cloudy; confused; cryptic; dark; diaphanous; dim; doubtful; dreamlike; dreamy; dubious; dubitable; elusive; equivocal; filmy; fuzzy; hazy; illogical; imprecise; inconcrete; indecisive; indefinable; indefinite; indescribable; indeterminable; indeterminate; indistinct; inexpert; inexplicable; insubstantial; intangible; *in nubibus*; nebulous; nubilous; obscure; primitive; shadowy; sibylline; sketchy; tenuous; uncertain; unclear; undefinable; undefined; unexplicit; unfixed; unsettled; vacant; vaporous; VAGUENESS: abstraction; aeriality; ambiguity; cloudiness; dimness; dubiety; dubiosity; equivocality; illogicality; imprecision; indefinitude; insubstantiality; intangibility; nebulosity; obscurity; vaporosity

VAIN: abortive; baseless; boastful; bombastic; conceited; dandyish; desperate; dogmatic; ego(t)istical; empty; flatulent; foolish; foppish; frivolous; fruitless; frustraneous; futile; hollow; hopeless; hubristic; idle; improbable; ineffectual; inflated; nugatory; null; officious; ostentatious; otiose; overweening; pedantic; pompous; pragmatic(al); pretentious; profitless; proud; rodomontade; self-centered; self-conceited; shallow; showy; silly; theatrical; trifling; trivial; unavailing; unimportant; unprofitable; unreal; unrewarded; unsatisfying; unsubstantial; unsuccessful; useless; vainglorious; valueless; vapid; visionary; worthless

VAINGLORY: boastfulness; bombast; conceit; gasconade; ostentation; parade; pomp(osity) pompousness; rodomontade; self-exaltation; self-glorification; show; theatrics; vanity

VALE: adieu; dale; dell; dingle; earth; farewell; glen; valley

VALEDICTION: adieu; farewell; good-bye; speech

VALET: attendant; Crispin; equerry; flunky; helper; lackey; man; servant; squire

VALIANT: (see "brave") bold; chivalric; chivalrous; excellent; gallant; intrepid; noteworthy; resolute; stalwart; stout(hearted); valorous

VALID: actual; authentic; authoritative; authorized; binding; certified; cogent; convincing; effective; efficacious; efficient; fair; genuine; good; healthy; just(ifiable); justful; lawful; legal; legitimate; licensed; licit; logical; objective; official; powerful; real; reasonable; registered; robust; sanctioned; sealed; solid; sound; strong; substantial; telling; true; weighty; VALIDATE: attest; authenticate; authorize; confirm; notarize; prove; ratify; register; sanction; seal; substantiate; test; VALIDITY: authority; cogency; force; justness; proof; soundness; strength; weight

VALLEY: canyon; dale; dell; depression; dingle; glen; gorge; gulch; hollow; hoya; ravine; swale; trough; vale

VALOR: (see "chivalry") arete; boldness; bravery; courage(ousness); dash; fearlessness; fortitude; gallantry; grit; guts; hardihood; heroism; integrity; intrepidity; manliness; nerve; nobility; pluck; prowess; spunk; virtue; VALOROUS: (see "brave") bold; courageous; dauntless; doughty; fortitudinous; gallant; heroic; intrepid; noble; stout; valiant; virtuous

VALUE: **v.** adjudge; adjudicate; admire; analyze; appraise; appreciate; approve; assay; assess; cherish; comprehend; compute; discriminate; esteem; evaluate; examine; figure; heed; judge; love; perceive; prize; rate; realize; reckon; recognize; regard; respect; treasure; VALUE(S): **n.** (see "worth") appraisal; approval; assessment; carat; comprehension; cost; denomination; discrimination; esteem; ethos; figure; importance; judgment; love; merit; number; par; price; principles; prize; rate; rating; realization; recognition; regard; respect; sterling; treasure; utility; virtue; weight; VALUABLE: admirable; classic; costly; esteemed; estimable; inestimable; meritorious; priceless; rare; respectable; serviceable; significant; singular; sumless; superior; treasured; useful; vital; weighty; worthy

VALUELESS: (see "worthless") baff; miserable; nugatory; tin(ny); trashy; trifling; vain

VALVE: check; cock; faucet; outlet; regulator; tap

VAMPIRE: bat; bloodsucker; Dracula; extortionist; *femme fatale*; flirt; ghoul; incubus; lamia; mercenary; siren; sorceress; succubus; temptress

VAN: dray; fore(front); front; head; lead; lorry; truck

VANDAL: defacer; destroyer; looter; pillager; plunderer; rioter; robber; spoiler

VANE: blade; fan; feather; flag; pennon; weathercock

VANISH: beat (down); cease; depart; die; disappear; dissolve; evanesce; evaporate; fade; flee; fly; lose; melt; pass; recede; relinquish; run; sink; vaporize; volatize; VANISHING: (see "fleeting") diaphanous; ephemeral; ethereal; evanescent; flying; unsubstantial; vaporous; vapory; volatile

VANITY: *amour-propre*; arrogance; conceit; display; ego(t)ism; emptiness; falsity; flatulence; folly; futility; gaud; hollowness; hubris; knickknack; ostentation; otiosity; pomposity; pretention; pretentiousness; pride; self-importance; self-love; sham; show; trifle; vainglory; worthlessness

VANQUISH: (see "beat") conquer; control; defeat; overpower; override; overthrow; rout; subdue; trample; triumph

VANTAGE: (see "superiority") coign (of vantage)

VAPID: banal; bland; blank; dead; dull; flat; flavorless; inane; insipid; jejune; lifeless; mild; pointless; shopworn; spiritless; stale; tame; tasteless; trite; uninteresting

VAPOR(S): bubble; cloud; effluvium; evaporation; exhalation; fog; fume; gas; haze; hysteria; idea; miasma; mist; moisture; nervousness; neurosis; notion; phantasm; rack; reek; smoke; spray; steam; VAPORIZE: see "evaporate;" VAPOROUS: clouded; cloudy; ethereal; filmy; foggy; indistinct; miasmic; misty; moist; steamy; unreal; unsubstantial; vague; vain; vaporific; vapory; volatile

VARIED: altered; changed; deranged; differed; diverse; diversified; manifold; mosaic; multifarious; multiform; variant; variegated; VARIABLE: aberrant; alterable; ambivalent; bivalent; capricious; chameleonic; changeable; different; fickle; fitful; flexible; inconstant; irresolute; mercurial; mobile; mutable; plastic; protean; quicksilver; restless; shifting; shifty; uneven; unsettled; unstable; unsteady; vagrant; variant; versatile; wavering; VARIATION: (see "difference") aberration; adaptation; alteration; change; deviation; dimension; diversification; inflection; latitude; leeway; maneuver; modification; mutation; nuance; permutation; shade; shift(ing); surge; tolerance; turning; variability; variance; veer(ing); warp

VARIEGATE: **v.** dapple; diversify; enliven; fleck; mottle; speckle; spot; vary; VARIEGATE(D): **a.** checked; checkered; chimerical; dappled; diverse; diversified; heterogeneous; iridescent; kaleidoscopic; menald; motley; opalescent; parti-colored; piebald; pied; pinto; prismatic; skewbald; speckled; spotted; tessellate(d); variant; varied; VARIEGATION: diversification; iridescence; mosaic; tessellation

VARIETY: assortment; brand; change; class-(ification); difference; diversification; diversity; division; form; genre; genus; grab bag; heterogeneity; intermixture; kidney; kind; medley; melange; miscellaneity; miscellany; mixture; multifariousness; multiformity; multiplicity; numerousness; phylum; race; sort; species; stock; strain; stripe; style; subspecies; tribe; variation; versatility

VARIOUS: (see "variable") different; divers-(e); heterogeneous; manifold; many; multifarious; multiple; multiplex; multiplicious; mutable; numerous; protean; several; sundry

VARNISH: **v.** adorn; conceal; cover; embellish; excuse; furbish; gloss; paint; palliate; polish; refurbish; shellac; VARNISH: **n.** (see "veneer") concealment; cover; enamel; gloss; japan; lacquer; shellac; veneer

VARY: see "diversify; VARYING: see "diverse" and "unstable;" VARIATION: see under "varied"

VASSAL: (see "slave") bondsman; dependent; feudatory; helot; liegeman; puppet; retainer; serf; servant; subject; tenant; thrall; underling; villein

VAST: (see "huge") big; boundless; broad; Brobdingnagian; colossal; comprehensive; cosmic; Cyclopean; cyclopedic; elephantine; enorm(ous); extensive; extreme; Gargantuan; global; grand(iose); great; Herculean; illimited; immeasurable; immense; imponderable; inexhaustible; infinite; large; leviathan; magnitudinous; mighty; monstrous; numerous; scopious; spacious; titanic; unbounded; uncircumscribed; unlimited; unrestrained; unrestricted; untold; wide; worldwide; VASTNESS *or* VASTITUDE: colossality; comprehensiveness; enormity; enormousness; expanse; globality; immeasurability; immensity; indefinitude; infinitude; magnitude; vastity

VAT: bac; barrel; caldron; cistern; keel; pit; tank; tub; vessel

VATICINATOR: oracle; predictor; prognosticator; prophet

VAULT: (see "leap") arch(way); canopy; cave; cavern; ceiling; cellar; chamber; concameration; crater; crypt; curvet; fornix; heaven(s); roof; safe; sky; tomb; VAULTED: arched; concave; cupolar; curved; domed; roofed

VAUNT: (see "boast") brag; crow; vapor

VEER: **v.** alter; deflect; detour; dip; drift; drop; shift; slue; stray; sway; swerve; turn; wander; wear; yaw; VEER: **n.** see "shift"

VEGETABLE: herb; legume; plant; VEGETATION: flora; herbage; listlessness

VEHEMENT: ardent; colorful; eager; emphatic; energetic; fervent; fervid; fierce; firm; furious; hearty; heated; hot; impassioned; impetuous; insistent; intense; lively; loud; passionate; potent; profound; pronounced; rancorous; severe; showy; strenuous; strong; truculent; urgent; violent; vivid; wild; zealous; VEHEMENCE: ardor; emphasis; enthusiasm; fervor; fierceness; fire; firmness; force; fury; heat; impetuosity; intensity; passion; profoundness; strength; vigor; violence; vividness; zeal(otry)

VEHICLE: (see "carriage") agency; agent; binder; car; carrier; channel; conveyance; device; diluent; excipient; form; means; medium; outlet; style; work

VEIL: **v.** blur; cloak; cloister; conceal; cover; curtain; disguise; enclose; fog; hide; muffle;

obscure; pretend; screen; withhold; wrap; VEIL: **n.** caul; cloak; cloistered life; cover(ing); curtain; disguise; film; fog; mesh; net; obscuration; pall; pretense; screen(ing); scrim; smoke; velum; VEILED: blurred; chiaroscuro; cloaked; cloistered; concealed; curtained; disguised; hidden; incognito; muffled; obscured; penumbral; screened; *sfumato*; tenebrous; velate

VEIN: bent; cava; cavity; channel; crevice; current; direction; fettle; fissure; humor; lane; lode; manner; mood; shade; strain; streak; stream; stria; stripe; style; talent; tenor; tinge; touch; trait; tributary; variegation

VELLICATE: nip; pinch; pluck; tickle; titillate; twitch

VELLUM: manuscript; membrane; paper; parchment; skin

VELOCITY: (**see** "speed") amount; strength

VENAL: bought; bribed; corrupt; hired; mercenary; paid; poisonous; salable; sordid; vendable

VEND: (**see** "sell") auction; barter; hawk; peddle; trade; VENDOR: (**see** "seller") merchant; peddler; trader; trafficker; vender

VENEER: **v.** (**see** "varnish") coat; cover; enamel; overlay; polish; VENEER; **n.** coat-(ing); cover(ing); enamel; gloss; lac; layer; overlay; polish; pretense; shell; shellac; surface; varnish

VENERATE: (**see** "worship") admire; adore; esteem; honor; love; prize; regard; respect; revere; value; VENERABLE: (**see** "ancient") aged; august; benevolent; classic; esteemed; good; grave; hoary; honorable; old(en); patriarch(al); respectable; respected; revered; reverential; sacred; sage; seasoned; serious; superannuated; time-worn; veteran; vintage; wise; worthy; VENERATION: adoration; awe; benevolence; cultism; devotion; dulia; esteem; honor; respect; reverence; sacredness; worship

VENEREAL: (**see** "sexual") aphrodisiac; Cytherean

VENGEANCE: (**see** "hatred") avengement; Nemesis; punishment; recrimination; reprisal; retaliation; retribution; revenge; wrack

VENOM: bane; blight; enmity; gall; hate; malevolence; malice; malignity; poison; rancor; resentment; spite; toxin; virulence; virus; VENOMOUS: baneful; envenomed; malign(ant); mischievous; poisoned; poisonous; spiteful; toxic; viperish; virulent

VENT: **v.** air; broach; disclose; eject; emit; expel; express; pour; promulgate; publish; reveal; run; say; utter; VENT: **n.** aperture; bung; egress; escape; flue; hole; meatus; opening; outlet; spiracle; window; VENTILATED: advertised; aerated; aired; disclosed; exposed; freshened; oxygenated

VENTURE: **v.** attempt; brave; chance; dare; embark; endanger; endeavor; essay; experiment; explore; gamble; hazard; imperil; invest; jeopardize; peril; plunge; presume; pretend; prospect; risk; speculate; stake; tempt; test; threaten; try; undertake; wage; VENTURE: **n.** attempt; chance; courage; dare; endeavor; enterprise; essay; excursion; experiment; gamble; hazard; investment; jeopardy; peril; plunge; project; risk; speculation; stake; test; threat; trial; try; undertaking; VENTURESOME: **see** "hazardous"

VERACIOUS: (**see** "true") accurate; direct; honest; reliable; sincere; truthful; veritable; VERACITY: **see** "truthfulness"

VERANDA: balcony; gallery; lanai; loggia; patio; piazza; porch; portico; pyal; stoa; stoop

VERB: rhema; vocable; word; VERBAL: (**see** "oral") lingual; literal; *ore tenus*; spoken; talkative; verbatim; verbose; vocal; wordy; written

VERBATIM: (**see** "literal") textual; verbal; word-for-word

VERBIAGE: diction; prolixity; redundancy; verbosity; wordage; wordiness; wording; words

VERBOSE: loquacious; prolix; talkative; tedious; verbal; voluble; wordy; VERBOSENESS: (**see** "wordiness") loquacity; prolixity; talkativeness; verbosity; volubility

VERDANT: fresh; green; raw; springlike; unripe; unsophisticated; vernal; youthful

VERDICT: (**see** "decision") determination; judgment; outcome; vote

VERDIGRIS: crust; deposit; film; patina; pigment; rust

VERGE: approach; border; boundary; bounds; brim; brink; circumference; edge; fringe; horizon; impingement; limit; margin; point; range; rim; rod; scope; skirt; staff; threshold; top; touch

VERIFY: affirm; attest; audit; authenticate; check; confirm; correct; document; establish; evidence; examine; justify; prove; ratify; see; substantiate; support; test; validate; view; witness; VERIFIED: (see "established") attested; audited; authenticated; confirmed; documented; seen; substantiated; tested; validated; viewed; witnessed; VERIFICATION: (see "examination") affirmation; averment; documentation; substantiation

VERILY: amen; assuredly; certainly; confidentially; indeed; positively; really; truly; truthfully; yea

VERISIMILITUDE: likelihood; likeness; possibility; probability; similarity; truth; verity

VERITABLE: actual; authentic; genuine; real; VERITY: actuality; fact; faithfulness; honesty; reality; truth(fulness); veracity; veritability

VERMIFORM: flexible; long; sinuous; slender; thin; vermicular; winding; wormlike

VERNACULAR: **a.** common; indigenous; local; native; vulgar; VERNACULAR: **n.** argot; cant; dialect; idiom; jargon; language; lingo; patois; patter; slang

VERNAL: fresh; green; springlike; youthful; verdant

VERSATILE: accomplished; adept; all-around; ambidextrous; capable; changeable; clever; diversified; erudite; facile; familiar; handy; inconstant; many-sided; multiskilled; polygraphic; proficient; skilled; skillful; trained; variable; versed

VERSE: division; jingle; limerick; line; meter; metrification; poem; poesy; poetry; rhyme; rime; rondel; speech; stanza; stave; stich; strophe; text; versification; writing; VERSIFIER: bard; poet(aster); rhymer; rhymester; rimer

VERSED: accomplished; acquainted; adept; aware; clever; erudite; familiar; practiced; proficient; skilled; skillful; trained; versatile; well-read

VERSION: account; adaptation; arrangement; aspect; copy; description; edition; form; impression; interpretation; issue; printing; production; rendition; report; side; story; text; translation; turning; variant

VERTEBRA: (see "spine") backbone; chine; segment; spondyl

VERTEX: acme; apex; crown; keystone; point; summit; top; zenith

VERTICAL: erect; orthograde; orthostatic; perpendicular; plumb; standing; straight; upright; VERTICALITY: erectness; perpendicularity; plumbness

VERTIGO: confusion; dinus; disequilibrium; dizziness; giddiness; instability; staggers

VERVE: (see "vitality") animation; aptitude; bounce; dash; élan; energy; enthusiasm; feeling; force; life; liveliness; pep(per); spirit; swagger; talent; vigor; vivacity; zest; zip

VERY: absolutely; actual; exact; exceedingly; extremely; famously; genuine; identical; particular; precise; pretty; quite; real; same; selfsame; sheer; so; spanking; special; thoroughly; très; true; truly; unqualified; utter(ly); veritable

VESICLE: bladder; bleb; blister; cavity; cyst; hollow; sac

VESSEL: (see "ship") barrel; bowl; cask; container; diota; disk; keg; mug; pan; pot; receptacle; urn; utensil

VEST: **v.** array; attire; dress; encompass; endow; furnish; garb; give; grant; place; robe; surround; VEST: **n.** cassock; garment; jacket; waistcoat

VESTAL: chaste; pure; virginal

VESTIBULE: anteroom; cavity; entrance-(way); entry; foyer; hall; lobby; narthex; passage(way); porch

VESTIGE: dregs; echo; evidence; footprint; footstep; fragment; gleam; glint; lees; mark; memorial; print; relic; remainder; remains;

residual; residuum; rudiment; sediment; shadow; shred; sign; silt; spark; stamp; survival; tag; tatter; tincture; token; trace; track; twinkle; whisker; whisper

VESTMENT: alb; cassock; chasuble; clothing; covering; dress; ephod; frock; garb; garment; gremial; habiliment; habit; robe; scapular; uniform

VETERAN: **a.** (**see** "venerable") seasoned; VETERAN: **n.** ex-serviceman; grognard; old hand; oldster; patriarch; patrician; pro(fessional)

VETO: **v.** annul; cancel; deny; forbid; interdict; kill; negate; negative; nullify; override; prohibit; quash; rescind; taboo; VETO: **n.** annulment; cancellation; denial; forbiddance; interdiction; negation; prohibition; quash; recision; rescission; taboo

VEX: (**see** "annoy") afflict; anger; batter; belabor; bug; distress; disturb; embitter; exercise; fret; harass; irritate; itch; needle; perplex; persecute; pique; pother; roil; wear; weary; worry; VEXATION: affliction; agitation; anger; annoyance; besetment; chafe; chagrin; discomfit; displeasure; distress; disturbance; embitterment; fret; grief; harassment; impatience; irritation; itch; misery; mortification; nuisance; pain; perplexity; persecution; pique; pother; soreness; trouble; uneasiness; worry; VEXATIOUS *or* VEXED: (**see** "annoying") aching; afflictive; aggravating; choleric; disordered; distressing; disturbing; grilling; harassing; impatient; nasty; pesky; pestiferous; pestilent(ial); petulant; provoking; restive; roiled; ructious; tedious; troubled; troublesome; unquiet; wearful; wicked

VIABLE: **see** "living"

VIAL: amp(o)ule; bottle; cruet; phial

VIAND(S): (**see** "food") cates; chow; eats; fare; grub; provisions; victuals

VIATOR: (**see** "traveler") motorist; tourist; voyager; wayfarer

VIBRATE: agitate; alternate; beat; brandish; fluctuate; jar; oscillate; palpitate; quaver; quiver; resonate; shake; shiver; swing; thrill; throb; tirl; toss; tremulate; trill; undulate; wave(r); VIBRANT *or* VIBRATORY: animated; lively; oscillant; oscillating; pulsing; resonant; resounding; shaking; shivering; sonorous; throbbing; tremulant; trem-

ulous; trilling; undulant; undulatory; vibratile; vibrating; vigorous

VICAR: altarist; clergyman; curate; deputy; pastor; priest; proxy; representative; substitute; vice-regent

VICE: blemish; corruption; crime; defect; depravity; evil; failing; fault; flagitiousness; flaw; harmfulness; ill; immorality; imperfection; iniquity; lust(fulness); place; shortcoming; sin; stead; taint; vileness; wickedness

VICINITY: (**see** "habitat") area; locale; locality; nearness; neighborhood; parish; precinct; province; proximity; way

VICIOUS: (**see** "bad") assaultive; barbaric; barbarous; diseased; egregious; feral; flagitious; flagrant; infamous; iniquitous; intense; malevolent; malicious; malign(ant); morbid; nefarious; reprehensible; reprobate; savage; spiteful; unruly; vile; villainous; wicked; wild; VICIOUSNESS: barbarity; egregiousness; ferity; flagitiousness; flagrancy; malevolence; maliciousness; malignity; morbidity; reprehension; savagery; spitefulness; wickedness; wildness

VICISSITUDE: **see** "difficulty"

VICTIM: boob; butt; cat's-paw; cold turkey; cully; dupe; goat; gull; laughingstock; loser; mark; martyr; nark; prey; quarry; sacrifice; sap; scapegoat; schlemiel; underdog; VICTIMIZE: **see** "cheat"

VICTOR: champion; conqueror; master; subjugator; superior; vanquisher; winner; VICTORY: achievement; advantage; ascendency; award; conquest; defeat; mastery; ovation; palm; prevailment; subjugation; success; superiority; supremacy; triumph; win

VICTUALS: **see** "food"

VIE: compete; contend; contest; emulate; hazard; jostle; match; rival; run; stake; strive; struggle; wager

VIEW: **v.** (**see** "see") behold; examine; eye; glimpse; inspect; look; observe; ogle; peek; regard; scan; scrutinize; sight; survey; VIEW: **n.** aim; angle; appearance; aspect; belief; concept(ion); diagram; examination; expectation; faith; glimpse; idea; inspection; judgment; ken; look; mind; object; opinion; outlook; panorama; peek; perspective; perspectivity; prospect; regard; religion; representation; scape; scene; scheme; scope; scrutiny; sight; sketch; summary; survey; tenet; viewpoint; vista

VIEWPOINT: (**see** "view") angle; attitude; frame of reference; scope; tenet; theory

VIGIL: care; gaze; observation; patrol; sight; sleeplessness; sojourn; stare; stay; wakefulness; watchfulness; VIGILANT: agog; alert; attentive; avid; aware; careful; cautious; Cerberean; circumspect; heedful; jealous; keen; observant; prudent; sharp; shrewd; sleepless; wakeful; wary; watchful; zealous; VIGILANCE: **see** "heedfulness"

VIGOR(OUSNESS): ardor; capacity; dash; drive; élan; emphasis; energy; enthusiasm; esprit; exertion; force(fulness); gusto; health; impetuosity; intensity; life; liveliness; lust-(iness); might (and main); paunch; pep(per); pepperiness; potency; power; sap; soundness; spirit; stamina; sthenia; strength; thrust; validity; vehemence; verve; vim; vir; vitality; vivacity; voltage; wattage; zest; zip; VIGOROUS: (**see** "bracing") active; animated; athletic; burly; chipper; cogent; *con spirito*; cyclonic(al); dashing; dynamic(al); energetic; florid; florishing; forceful; forcible; fresh; gymnastic; hale; hammer and tongs; hard; healthy; husky; juicy; live(ly); lush; lusty; mighty; pepful; pepperish; peppy; potent; powerful; proud; puissant; refreshing; robust(ious); slashing; spirited; spry; stark; stiff; stout; strenuous; strong; sturdy; torrential; two-fisted; undegenerate; unwilted; unwithered; vehement; virile; vital; wholesome; youthful; zealous

VILE: (**see** "bad") abhorrent; abject; abominable; awful; base; beggarly; brutal; brutish; common; contaminated; contemptible; corrupt; crusty; degenerate; degraded; depraved; despicable; disgusting; egregious; evil; filthy; flagitious; flagrant; foul; groveling; humiliating; ignominious; immoral; impure; infamous; inferior; insanitary; lousy; low; mean; nasty; obscene; odious; paltry; poor; profligate; putrid; repulsive; shocking; slimy; sordid; unhealthy; unsanitary; vicious; villainous; vulgar; vulturine; vulturous; wicked; wrong

VILIFY: abuse; asperse; berate; blacken; calumniate; censure; condemn; curse; damn; defame; degrade; denigrate; denounce; disparage; libel; lower; malign; rebuke; revile; slander; smear; traduce; upbraid; vituperate

VILLAGE: aldea; burg; dorp; dump; hamlet; kraal; microcosm; mir; municipality; settlement; thorp; town; tribe

VILLAIN(OUS) **a.** (**see** "cowardly") bad; criminal; dastardly; felonious; mean; miscreant; rapscallion; unconscionable; unprincipled; unscrupulous; vicious; vile; wicked; wretched; VILLAIN: **n.** (**see** "rogue" and "traitor") badman; blackguard; boor; criminal; culprit; delinquent; evildoer; felon; Iago; knave; malefactor; meanie; miscreant; offender; outlaw; profligate; rapscallion; rascal; reprobate; rounder; ruffian; scamp; scapegrace; scoundrel; sinner; snake; transgressor; vagabond; viper; vulture; wretch; wrongdoer; VILLAINY: cowardliness; criminality; depravity; flagitiousness; knavery; miscreancy; viciousness; villainousness; wickedness

VILLATIC: countrified; rural; rustic

VILLEIN: carl; churl; esne; helot; peasant; peon; serf; slave; thrall; villager

VINCULUM: band; bond; brace; frenum; union

VINDICATE: absolve; acquit; assist; avenge; clear; confirm; defend; exculpate; excuse; exonerate; extenuate; justify; maintain; perceive; protect; prove; revenge; right; substantiate; support; sustain; uphold; VINDICATION: absolution; acquittal; compurgation; defense; exculpation; exoneration; justification; proof; revenge; satisfaction; substantiation; support

VINDICTIVE: (**see** "revengeful") grudgeful; malevolent; malicious; rancorous; resentful; unforgivable; vengeful; wrathful

VINE: cipo; grape; hop; ivy; liana; liane; trumpet

VIOLATE: (**see** "defile") abuse; betray; breach; break; contravene; debauch; desecrate; dishonor; err; fracture; harm; impinge; infringe; offend; pollute; profane; ravish; traduce; transgress; VIOLATION: abuse; betrayal; breach; break; contravention; crime; desecration; disturbance; encroachment; error; impingement; infraction; infringement; interruption; invasion; irreverence; misdeed; offense; profanation; rape; ravishment; sin; traduction; transgression; trespass; vice

VIOLENT: abnormal; abnormous; acute;

bestial; bloody; crimson; cyclonic(al); disordered; disorderly; disturbed; emotional; excited; extreme; fanatical; fierce; forcible; frantic; frenzied; furious; great; hammer and tongs; hard; heady; hot; impetuous; impulsive; intemperate; intense; irate; loud; mad; maniac(al); raging; rampant; rebellious; riotous; ruthless; savage; seething; severe; sharp; stiff; stormy; strong; tempestuous; torrential; tumultuous; turbulent; unnatural; unreal; vehement; vivid; volcanic; wild; VIOLENCE: barbarity; ferocity; fervor; force (and arms); foul play; furiousness; fury; impetuosity; impetuousness; injury; intensity; mailed fist; mania; passion; rampancy; severity; strength; strife; tempestuousness; thunder; tumult; turbulence; vehemence

VIPER: (**see** "snake") adder; asp; boa; cerastes; ophidian; serpent; villain

VIRAGO: barge; fury; rullion; scold; shrew; termagant; vixen; Xantippe

VIRGIN(AL): **a.** chaste; first; fresh; gentle; initial; innocent; maiden(ly); modest; native; new; primary; pristine; pure; unadulterated; undefiled; unspoiled; unsullied; untapped; untouched; VIRGIN: **n.** damsel; lass; madonna; maid(en); *virgo intacta*

VIRTU: antique; artistry; curio; *objet d'art*; relic

VIRTUE: arete; character; chastity; courage; decency; dharma; energy; excellence; fidelity; goodness; grace; honesty; honor; innocence; integrity; merit; morality; potency; probity; property; purity; quality; rectitude; righteousness; sainthood; sanctitude; sanctity; strength; uprightness; valor; value; virtuousness; worth; VIRTUOUS: chaste; decent; efficacious; excellent; exemplary; good; holy; honorable; innocent; meritorious; moral; pure; rectitudinous; religious; righteous; sainted; saintly; sanctified; seraphic; straight; upright; virginal

VIRULENT: acrimonious; bitter; deadly; harsh; hostile; malign(ant); noxious; poison(ous); rabid; severe; strong; toxic; venomous; VIRULENCE: acrimony; bitterness; hatred; hostility; ill will; malignancy; poison; rabidity; strength; toxicity; venom(ousness)

VIRUS: bacteria (pl.); bacterium; disease; germ; microorganism; poison; toxin; venom

VISAGE: appearance; aspect; cast; countenance; face; features; front; guise; look; map; mug; physiognomy; puss; semblance

VISCID *or* VISCOUS: (**see** "sticky") adhesive; gluey; glutinous; stiff

VISE: clamp; pincher; tool; winch

VISIBLE: apparent; available; conspicuous; discernible; discoverable; external; macroscopic; manifest; obvious; ocular; open; patent; perceptible; present; recognizable; seen; temporal; visual

VISION: (**see** "imagination") apparition; awareness; chimera; concept(ion); discernment; dream; eye(sight); fancy; fantasy; foresight; hallucination; ghost; glance; glimpse; illusion; image; mirage; object; peek; percipience; perception; perspicacity; phantasm; phantom; prospect; revelation; shadow; sight; specter; spirit; survey; view; wraith; VISIONARY: **a.** (**see** "fantastic") aerial; airy(-fairy); chimerical; delusional; delusive; doctrinaire; dogmatic(al); dreamy; fanciful; fantastic; far-fetched; fey; heterodox; ideal(istic); illusionary; illusory; imaginary; impractical; insane; irresponsible; ivory-tower; Laputan; mad; mythical; non-realistic; notional; phantom; platonic; platonistic; poetic(al); quixotic(al); radical; romantic; starry(-eyed); theoretical; translunary; unpractical; unreal(istic); unsubstantial; utopian; wild(-eyed); VISIONARY: **n.** doctrinaire; dogmatist; dreamer; enthusiast; fantasist; fantast; idealist; idealogue; ideologist; philosopher; radical; romancer; romanticist; seer; theorist; Utopian

VISIT: **v.** afflict; attend; avenge; benefit; bless; call; chat; frequent; go; haunt; impose; inspect; minister; punish; see; sojourn; stay; stop; travel; VISIT: **n.** call; chat; search; sojourn(ment); stay; stop; travel; visitation; VISITOR: caller; guest; sojourner; tourist; traveler; visitant

VISTA: (**see** "view") outlook; panorama; perspective; prospect; scape; scent; sight

VISUALIZE: (**see** "imagine") conceive; envision; fancy; foresee; perceive; picture; see; VISUAL: **see** "visible"

VITAL: animate(d); cordial; energetic; essential; exigent; fatal; flourishing; fresh; fundamental; imperative; important; indispensible; invigorating; live(ly); living; mortal; necessary; organic; pivotal; requisite;

sensitive; zetetic; VITALITY: (see "vigor") bounce; drive; *élan vital*; endurance; energy; force; juice; life; liveliness; pep(per); resiliency; sap; snap; starch; strength; verve; vim; vitalness

VITIATE: cancel; contaminate; corrupt; debase; defile; deprave; impair; injure; invalidate; pervert; pollute; spoil; taint; tarnish; void

VITREOUS: glassy; hard

VITUPERATE: see "vilify;" VITUPERATION: abuse; blame; censure; invective; railing; rebuke; reproof; scolding; truculency; vilification

VIVACITY: (see "vigor") animation; brilliance; brio; dash; élan; fire; genius; gusto; life; liveliness; longevity; pep(per); pertness; snap; sparkle; spiritedness; sprightliness; verve; vivaciousness; zest; zip

VIVID: active; acute; animated; bright; brilliant; clean-cut; clear; colorful; colory; distinct; eidetic; extravagant; flashing; fresh; garish; glowing; graphic; intense; keen; lifelike; live(ly); lucid; overdecorated; picturesque; piquant; poignant; precise; quick; real; rich; sharp; showy; slashing; spirited; sprightly; striking; strong; telling; trenchant; vehement; vibrant; visual

VIXEN: (see "virago") fox; scold; shrew

VOCABULARY: diction(ary); glossary; language; lexicon; *lexis*; nomenclature; onomasticon; range; speech; synonymicon; talk; terminology; terms; wordbook; wordstock; words

VOCAL: articulate; clamorous; elegant; expressive; fluent; fluid; glib; intonated; oral; outspoken; parol; phonetic; resounding; sonant; spoken; tacit; talkative; verbal; vocalic; voiced; voluble; VOCALIZE: (see "speak") articulate; enunciate; phonate; pronounce; sing; speak; talk; utter; VOCALIZATION: articulation; enunciation; phonation; pronunciation; speech; talk; utterance

VOCATION: (see "work") field; occupation; walk; VOCATIONAL: banausic; materialistic; occupational; professional; training; working

VOCIFEROUS: (see "loud") blatant; boisterous; clamorous; noisy; outspoken; strident;

talkative; vociferant; VOCIFEROUSNESS: (see "talkativeness") vociferance

VOGUE: bug; custom; fad; fashion; favor; fever; hobby; insanity; intensity; madness; mania; mode; passion; popularity; rage; style; trend; whim

VOICE: **v.** announce; articulate; divulge; emit; express; give; mouth; pronounce; rumor; say; sound; speak; state; talk; tell; utter; vocalize; vociferate; VOICE: **n.** accent; alto; articulation; bass; choice; expression; intonation; key; mouth; opinion; option; preference; rumor; soprano; sound; speech; suffrage; talk; tenor; throat; tone; tongue; utterance; vocalization; vociferation; vote; wish; VOICED: articulated; enunciated; phonated; said; sonant; sonic; sounded; stated; told; uttered; vocalized; vociferated

VOICELESS: aphonetic; dumb; inarticulate; inaudible; mute; silent; spirate; surd; tongue-tied

VOID: **v.** abolish; annul; bare; cancel; clear; discharge; leave; null(ify); quash; rescind; vacate; veto; VOID: **a.** bare; barren; blank; deserted; destitute; devoid; empty; hollow; idle; ineffective; ineffectual; lacking; leisured; noneffective; nugatory; null; *nullius juris*; unemployed; unoccupied; useless; vacant; vacuous; vain; wanting; VOID: **n.** absence; abyss; barrenness; emptiness; hollowness; lack; nothingness; nugacity; nullity; vacancy; vacuum; want

VOLATILIZE: atomize; evaporate; exhale; vaporize; VOLATILE: airy; buoyant; capricious; changeable; ebullient; elastic; evanescent; explosive; fickle; filmy; fitful; flighty; flying; frivolous; fugitive; gaseous; giddy: imponderable; irresolute; light(hearted); mercurial; quicksilver; subtle; temperamental; transitory; vague; vaporous; volant; volcanic

VOLITION: choice; conation; decision; desire; determination; election; preference; will; wish

VOLLEY: broadside; burst; discharge; emission; fire; flight; fusillade; group; salvo

VOLUBLE: (see "talkative") fickle; fluent; glib(-tongued); loquacious; revolving; rotating; unstable; vocal; wordy

VOLUME: (see "amount") aggregate; album;

amplitude; audio; book; bulk; capacity; compass; cubage; dimensions; document; extent; intensity; loudness; magnitude; mass; number; quantity; roll; scroll; size; solidity; space; strength; tome; vastity; vastness

VOLUMINOUS: (see "large") bulky; encyclopedic(al); full; numerous; swelling

VOLUNTARY: choice; compliant; deliberate; disposed; free; gratuitous; honorary; intended; intentional; spontaneous; uncompelled; unconstrained; unforced; volent; volitional; voluntative; volunteer; willful; willing

VOLUNTEER: see "offer"

VOLUPTUOUS: (see "sensuous" and "worldly;") VOLUPTUARY: see "sensualist"

VOLUTE: (see "spiral") scroll-shaped

VOMIT: discharge; disgorge; empty; gush; heave; regurgitate; retch; VOMITING: disgorgement; emesis; hyperemesis; nausea; nauseousness; regurgitation; retching

VORACIOUS: avid; eager; edacious; esurient; famished; gluttonous; greedy; hungry; immoderate; insatiable; rapacious; ravening; ravenous

VORTEX: eddy; gyre; maelstrom; predicament; swirl; tornado; whirlpool; whirlwind; wind

VOTARY: addict; adherent; admirer; aficionada (fem.); aficionado; believer; buff; devotee; disciple; enthusiast; fan; fiend; follower; ite; minion; worshiper

VOTE: v. authorize; ballot; choose; decide; declare; determine; dispose; elect; name; nominate; petition; propose; ratify; score; select; tally; voice; VOTE: n. ballot; confidence; determination; entreaty; franchise; opinion; petition; plebiscite; referendum; suffrage; tally; ticket; verdict; voice; wish

VOUCH: abet; affirm; assure; attest; aver; back; endorse; guarantee; indorse; insure;

maintain; prove; sponsor; substantiate; support; testify; uphold; verify; vouchsafe; warrant; VOUCHER: bill; certificate; chit; credential; endorser; guarantor; note; proof; receipt; release; statement; support; warrantor

VOUCHSAFE: accord; allow; award; bestow; concede; condescend; deign; favor; give; grant; let; permit; stoop; supply; yield

VOW: v. consecrate; declare; dedicate; devote; pledge; profess; promise; protest; swear; wish; VOW: n. assertion; asseveration; claim; declaration; dedication; oath; pledge; prayer; profession; promise; wish

VOYAGE: (see "journey") expedition; exploration; safari; trek; trip; tour; undertaking; VOYAGER: see "traveler"

VULGAR: base; boisterous; boorish; cheap; coarse; common(place); crass; crude; customary; disgusting; disreputable; dirty; earthy; Falstaffian; filthy; flashy; frowsy; garish; general; gross; gutty; Hogarthian; ignoble; ill-bred; ill-mannered; immoral; indecent; indelicate; infamous; irreverent(ial); lewd; low(-minded); lurid; mean; nasty; obscene; odious; offensive; overdecorated; plebeian; popular; profane; public; Rabelaisian; raffish; rakish; randy; ribald(rous); rowdy(dowdy); rude; scurrile; scurrilous; slimy; sordid; tabloid; tawdry; unconventional; uncouth; uncultivated; unkempt; unrefined; unurbane; vernacular; vile; visceral; VULGARITY: (see "coarseness") commonness; crassness; crudeness; earthiness; flashiness; indecency; indelicacy; irreverence; lewdness; nastiness; obscenity; profanity; ribaldry; rowdiness; rudeness; scurrility; sordidness; vulgarization

VULNERABLE: (see "liable") assailable; assaultable; attackable; criticizable; exposed; open; unguarded; VULNERABILITY: (see "liability") weakness

VULPINE: alopecoid; artful; crafty; cunning; foxy; sly; wily

VULTURE: buzzard; condor; harpy; papa; urubu; villain

W

WACKY: (see "crazy") batty; disordered; erratic; foolish; insane; irrational

WAD: (see "stuff") amount; bundle; line; lump; mass; money; pack; pad; pellet; plug; stopper; tuft; wealth

WADE: ford; plodge; plug; proceed

WAFER: biscuit; cake; candy; cookie; cracker; disk; host; lamina; scale; seal

WAFT: **v.** blow; carry; convey; signal; smell; transmit; transport; WAFT: **n.** beckoning; breath; gust; odor; puff; smell; whiff

WAG: see "shake" and "wit;" WAGGISH: arch; comic; espiègle; frolicsome; good-humored; humorous; impish; impy; jocular; jolly; mischievous; roguish; sportive; witty; WAGGISHNESS: archness; espiéglerie; frolicsomeness; good humor; impishness; jocularity; mischief; roguery; roguishness; wit

WAGE(S): compensation; earnings; emolument; fee; gain; hire; honorarium; income; lucre; pay(ment); perquisite; profit; rate; recompense; remuneration; requital; salary; salt; screw; stipend

WAGER: **v.** ante; bet; gamble; hazard; lay; pledge; risk; stake; venture; vie; WAGER: **n.** ante; bet; gamble; hazard; pledge; pot; prize; risk; stake; venture

WAIF: castaway; foundling; gaberlunzie; gamin; strafe; stray; unfortunate; vagrant; wanderer

WAIL: **v.** (see "lament") bawl; caterwaul; complain; deplore; howl; keen; mewl; moan; sob; ululate; weep; yammer; WAIL: **n.** caterwaul; complaint; howl; keen; lament-(ation); moan; sob; ululation; weep(ing); yammer; WAILING: plangorous; ululant

WAIT: **v.** abide; attend; await; bide; defer; delay; expect; halt; hang (around); hold; hope; linger; loiter; keep; pause; recess; remain; serve; sojourn; stand; stay; tarry; tend; WAIT: **n.** ambush; armistice; break; delay; intermission; interval; pause; recess; sojourn; stay; tarry

WAITER: attendant; garçon; lackey; maître d'hôtel; salver; servant; steward; tray

WAIVE: abandon; cede; defer; dismiss; dispense; disregard; excuse; forego; forsake; postpone; refrain; relinquish; renounce; repudiate; resign; surrender; yield

WAKEN: actuate; arouse; awake(n); bestir; encourage; enkindle; excite; fire; foment; hie; incite; inflame; instigate; intensify; kindle; prick; prod; provoke; raise; rally; rouse; rout; start(le); stimulate; stir; surprise; urge; wake

WALE: grain; mark; rib; ridge; streak; stripe; weal; welt; wheal

WALK: **v.** amble; ambulate; behave; circumambulate; conduct; deambulate; gad; hike; hoof; limp; mush; navigate; pace; parade; pedestrianize; pedestrinate; perambulate; peregrinate; plod; promenade; ramble; sashay; saunter; step; stride; stroll; strut; tramp; travel; traverse; tread; WALK: **n.** association; alameda; allée; amble; ambulation; avenue; beat; behavior; conduct; course; distance; field; gad; gait; haunt; hike; hoof; limp; navigation; pace; parade; paseo; passage(way); path(way); perambulation; peregrination; plod; prado; promenade; province; ramble; round(s); route; sashay; saunter; speed; status; step; stride; stroll; strut; tramp; travel; traverse; tread; WALKING: afoot; ambulant; ambulatory; à pied; deambulatory; itinerant; passant; pedestrian; peripatetic; rambling; sauntering; strolling; strutting; traveling

WALL: **v.** border; bound; confine; enclose; fence; immure; incarcerate; partition; separate; WALL: **n.** barrier; cliff; defense; enclosure; fence; immurement; levee; parapet; partition; rampart; side

673

WALLOW: **v.** billow; flounder; grovel; languish; launch; luxuriate; pitch; revel; roll; sprawl; surge; toss; welter; WALLOW-(ING) **n.** degeneration; degradation; floundering; groveling; mudhole; volutation; welter

WAMPUM: (**see** "money") peag(e); roanoke; se(a)wan; shells

WAN: anemic; ashen; ashy; bloodless; dim; etiolated; faded; faint; feeble; languid; lifeless; livid; low; lusterless; pale; pallid; sickly; watery

WAND: baguet; baton; caduceus; cane; mace; pointer; pole; rod; scepter; staff; stick; verge

WANDER: circulate; circumambulate; cruise; depart; deviate; digress; divagate; diverge; err; expatiate; gad; itinerate; meander; moon; move; perambulate; peregrinate; prowl; ramble; range; rave; roam; rove; saunter; spread; stray; stroll; swerve; traffic; traipse; travel; traverse; veer; WANDERER: Arab; floater; gadabout; itinerant; meanderer; nomad; Odysseus; peregrinator; peregrine; rambler; rover; straggler; traveler; truant; vagabond; vagrant; WANDERING: **a.** abroad; afield; aimless; amiss; arrant; away; circumambulatory; delirious; *dépaysé*; desultory; deviating; devious; digressive; discursive; errant; erratic; erring; erroneous; floating; footloose; fugitive; lost; meandering; migratory; nomadic; Odyssean; off; perambulatory; peripatetic; roving; straying; trailing; traveling; traversing; uncertain; vagabond(ish); vagarious; vagrant; winding; WANDERING: **n.** circumambulation; divagation; errantry; expiation; fugitivity; itineration; odyssey; perambulation; peregrination; peregrinism; peregrinity; shift; traveling; vagabondage; vagabondism

WANE: abate; decay; decline; decrease; dim(inish); dip; dwindle; ebb; fade; flag; lessen; peter; sag; wilt; WANING: **a.** declinatory; decreasing; decrescent; dwindling; ebbing; fading; flagging; lessening; sagging; WANING: **n.** abatement; declension; declination; decrease; decrescence; diminishment; diminution; dwindle; fading; flagging; recession

WANT: **v.** ache; covet; crave; desiderate; desire; fail; hanker; like; long; miss; necessitate; need; opine; pine; require; thirst; wish; yearn; WANT: **n.** absence; ache; dearth; defect; deficiency; depletion; desiderata (pl.); desideratum; desideria (pl.);

destitution; distress; emptiness; exigency; exiguity; failure; famine; hunger; inadequacy; indigence; insufficiency; lack; necessity; need; pang; penury; pinch; poverty; privation; requirement; scarcity; starvation; thirst; wish; yearn(ing); WANTING: absent; deficient; deserted; desiderative; destitute; inadequate; incomplete; lacking; necessitous; needing; poor; short; shy; void; wishing; yearning

WANTON: capricious; contrary; cruel; deliberate; depraved; disregardful; extravagant; free; frolicsome; heedless; immoral; impish; inhuman(e); insolent; intended; lascivious; lavish; lecherous; lewd; licentious; loose; lustful; malicious; merciless; playful; prodigal; rakish; rampant; rank; reckless; refractory; sensual; sportive; unchaste; undisciplined; unrestrained; unruly; untoward; wayward; wild

WAR(FARE): (**see** "battle") combat; conflict; contest; crusade; feud; (the) Four Horsemen; hostility; operations; riot; strife; struggle; WARLIKE: bellicose; belligerent; brave; combative; embattled; hostile; martial; militant; military; soldierly

WARBLE: carol; chirp; sing; trill; yodel

WARD: **v.** avert; block; care; defend; deflect; fence; fend; guard; keep; parry; protect; repel; safeguard; watch; WARD: **n.** area; block; care; corridor; custody; district; division; guard; heir; keeping; minor; parish; precinct; protection; quarter(s); room; watch

WARDEN: curator; custodian; gateman; guard(ian); head; keeper; porter; ranger; regent; superintendent; superior; warder; watch(man)

WARDER: bulwark; guard; keeper; mace; staff; stronghold; warden; watchman

WARDROBE: almirah; ambry; apparel; armory; bedroom; cabinet; closet; clothes; clothespress; clothing

WAREHOUSE: depot; *entrepôt*; étape; godown; mart; storage(room); store(room)

WARINESS: **see** under "wary"

WARLIKE: **see** under "war"

WARM: affectionate; alive; amorous; angry; ardent; brisk; calid; clement; comfortable;

cordial; emotional; enthusiastic; excited; fervent; feverish; flushed; genial; genuine; glowing; gracious; grateful; heated; hospitable; hot; humid; intense; intimate; irascible; lively; mild; muggy; natural; passionate; sincere; smug; summerlike; sympathetic; tender; tepid; toasty; uncooled; zealous; WARMING: **a.** calefacient; calefactory; calescent; WARMING: **n.** calefaction; calescence; WARMTH: affection; anger; animation; ardency; ardor; calefaction; calor; cordiality; cordialness; élan; emotion; empressement; energy; enthusiasm; excitement; fervency; fervor; fever; fire; flush; geniality; glow; graciosity; graciousness; heat; hospitality; intensity; irritation; life; passion; regard; temperature; vehemence; zeal(otry)

WARN: (**see** "caution") admonish; advise; alert; apprise; arouse; awaken; command; counsel; cry (havoc); exhort; flag; foretoken; forewarn; hend; inform; intimate; notify; precondition; previse; prohibit; protect; report; reprehend; sermonize; signal; summon; threaten; ward; WARNING: (**see** "caution") admonition; advice; alarm; alert; augury; beacon; bell; blinker; buzzer; caveat; counsel; example; exhortation; flag; foretoken; homily; hortation; light; lighthouse; monition; notice; omen; portent; prediction; premonition; presentiment; prevision; sign; signal; siren; summons; symptom; threat; tocsin

WARP: **v.** bend; bias; buckle; contort; contract; damage; deflect; distort; falsify; flex; influence; mar; misinterpret; pervert; shrivel; sway; torture; turn; twist; vine; weave; wind; wrinkle; WARP: **n.** aberration; bias; buckling; contortion; damage; distortion; foundation; perversion; twist; variation; warpage; wrinkle

WARRANT: **v.** approve; assure; attest; authorize; certify; commission; covenant; guarantee; insure; justify; pledge; represent; sanction; secure; vouch; WARRANT(Y): **n.** appointment; approval; assurance; attestation; authorization; berat; certificate; commission; covenant; declaration; document; foundation; grant; guarantee; guaranty; insurance; justification; pledge; plevin; preservation; protection; right; sanction; security; voucher; writ

WARREN: hutch; rabbitry; tenement

WARRIOR: cavalryman; combatant; dragoon; fighter; GI; infantryman; jingo(ist); marine; sailor; soldier; spahi; veteran

WARSHIP: battleship; cutter; flattop; frigate; galleon; submarine

WART: ecphyma; excrescence; growth; papilloma; projection; sycoma; tumor; verruca vulgaris

WARY: alert; cagy; canny; careful; cautious; chary; circumspect; cunning; discreet; economical; foxy; guarded; hesitant; leery; provident; prudent; scrupulous; sly; watchful; wise; WARINESS: (**see** "prudence") caution; circumspection; discretion; distrust; foxiness; hesitancy; leeriness; watchfulness

WASH: **v.** bathe; bleach; clean(se); cover; deterge; drench; drift; erode; flow; hose; launder; lave; leach; mundify; obliterate; overlay; overspread; purge; purify; rinse; saturate; suffuse; tint; tub; WASH: **n.** ablution; alluvium; bath; cleansing; dregs; eddy; erosion; laundry; lotion; purge; refuse; silt; sweep; WASHING: ablution; bathing; laundry; lavage; lotion; rinse; rinsing; showering; tubbing

WASTE: **v.** abuse; atrophy; attenuate; consume; decay; demolish; deplete; despoil; destroy; devastate; diminish; dissipate; drain; dwindle; eat; elapse; emanate; empty; enfeeble; erode; exhaust; expend; exploit; fritter; idle; loose; loot; pillage; macerate; misuse; neglect; pass; pine; potter; ravage; riot; rot; ruin; sack; shrink; spend; spill; spoil; squander; wear; wither; WASTE: **n.** accumulation; alluvium; ash(es); bones; bran; briss; *capita mortua* (pl.); *caput mortuum*; carrion; chaff; cinder(s); clinkers; cobs; coom(b); cullage; culls; damage; debris; decay; decrement; dejecta (pl.); deposit; depreciation; desert; desolation; despumation; desquamation; destruction; detritus; dilapidation; diminution; dirt; draff; drainage; dregs; driblets; droppings; dross; dung; dust; effluvium; egesta; ejecta(menta); erosion; excess; excrement; excreta; excretion; exhaust; expanse; exploitation; exudate; exuviate; faex; feces; fecula; feculence; film; filth; foam; foots; fragments; froth; garbage; garble; glumes; grit; grounds; havoc; heel; hulls; husk; hypostasis; impurity; junk; leavings; lees; lint; litter; loess; loot; loss; magma; muck; mud; neglect; oddments; offal; offscouring(s); ort(s); particles; patina; peltry; pieces; precipitate; prodigality; rabble; recrement; refuse; rejecta(menta); relics; remainder; remains; remnants; residuals; residue; residuum; rest; rot; rubbish; ruin; Sahara; scales; scobs; scoria; scoriae (pl.); scourings; scrap(s);

scree; screenings; scruff; scum; sediment-(ation); settlings; sewage; shards; sile; silt; slag; sludge; smut; soot; sordes; sordor; spoils; spume; stive; stools; stour; stretch; stuff; sullage; surplus; trash; tripe; trivia (pl.); truck; trumpery; uselessness; vestige; wash; wastage; wear; wilderness; wilds; WASTED: atrophic; atrophied; desolate; deteriorated; devastated; emaciated; empty; eroded; gaunt; haggard; idle; lank(y); pinched; poor; ravaged; skinny; spare; squandered; tabescent; treeless; uncultivated; weak; wild

WASTEFUL: careless; consumptive; costly; extravagant; improvident; imprudent; incautious; incompetent; lavish; prodigal; profligate; spendthrifty; thriftless; uneconomic(al); unthrifty; WASTEFULNESS: carelessness; extravagance; improvidence; imprudence; incautiousness; incompetence; incompetency; lavishness; prodigality; profligacy; superfluity; unthrift(iness)

WASTELAND: barrenness; desert; desolation; moor; Sahara; sand; swamp; waste; wilderness

WASTREL: dissolute; good-for-nothing; outcast; prodigal; profligate; rounder; scattergood; spender; spendthrift; squanderer; vagabond; vagrant; waif; waster

WATCH: v. (see "see") chaperone; check; clock; cover; descry; eye; follow; gaze; guard; hark; heed; investigate; invigilate; look; mark; mind; monitor; observe; police; protect; scout; shield; spy; start; supervise; survey; tend; WATCH: n. chaperonage; chaperone; guard(ian); horologe; invigilation; lookout; monitor; observation; police; scout; scrutiny; sentinel; sentry; surveillance; timepiece; wakefulness; watchman; WATCHFUL: alert; attentive; aware; careful; cautious; Cerberean; circumspect; discerning; heedful; observant; open-eyed; ready; sleepless; surveillant; vigilant; wakeful; wary; wide-awake; WATCHFULNESS: (see "caution") weather eye; WATCHER or WATCHMAN: (see "watch") Cerberus; chaperone; custodian; flagman; guard(ian); keeper; lookout; observer; scout; sentinel; sentry; superintendent; surveillant; viewer; warden; warder; watchdog

WATCHTOWER: beacon; lighthouse; lookout; mirador

WATCHWORD: catchword; countersign; cry; motto; password; shibboleth; signal; slogan

WATER: v. dilute; flood; hose; irrigate; moisten; soak; spray; sprinkle; wet; WATER: n. Adam's ale; aqua; eau; HOH: irrigation; lake; ocean; pond; pool; river; sea; stream; tide; WATERY: aqueous; boggy; humid; hydrated; hydrogenous; hydrous; ichorous; moist; pallid; serous; soggy; thin; vapid; washy; weak; wet; wishy-washy; WATERINESS: aquosity; humidity; moistness; sogginess; WATERLESS: anhydrous; arid; dehydrated; desiccated; dry; inspissated; sublimated

WATERWAY: canal; channel; river; strait; stream

WAVE: v. billow; brandish; falter; flag; flap; float; flourish; fluctuate; flutter; gesture; greet; motion; oscillate; ripple; sag; shake; signal; signify; sink; surge; sway; swell; swing; toss; twirl; undulate; vacillate; vibrate; waver; WAVE: n. advance; billow; breaker; comber; curve; flutter; gesture; greeting; increase; motion; movement; oscillation; ripple; sea(s); sign; signal; surf; sway; sweep; swell; swing; tide; undulation; vacillation; vibration; WAVY: curving; flexing; flexuous; ondoyant; ondy; rolling; sinuate; sinuous; undulant; undular; undulating; undulatory; undulous; wavering

WAVERING: see "uncertain"

WAX: v. become; enrich; gain; grow; increase; polish; WAX: n. cere; cerumen; fat; grease; gum; oil; pela; polish; resin; suet; WAXY: adhesive; ceral; impressible; impressionable; plastic; pliable; soft; viscid; waxlike; yielding

WAY: action; activity; advance; alley; artery; aspect; avenue; behavior; career; category; channel; characteristic; course; decision; description; design; device; direction; distance; district; existence; fashion; feature; form; habit; highway; idiosyncrasy; iter; journey; kind; lane; life; locality; manner; means; method; mode; movement; neighborhood; objective; opening; opportunity; passage(way); path; peculiarity; plan; possibility; practice; procedure; process; progress(ion); quality; range; respect; road; route; scheme; scope; sort; stand; state; street; style; system; thoroughfare; track; trail; train; trait; via; vicinity; wont

WAYFARER: (see "traveler") itinerant; nomad; passenger; pilgrim; tourist; tramp; transient; visitor; voyager

WAYLAY: ambush; assail; attack; beset; intercept; seize; stop; surprise; trap

WAYWARD: capricious; contrary; delinquent; depraved; disobedient; errant; erratic; fickle; froward; headstrong; intractable; lawless; malfeasant; perverse; refractory; stubborn; unpredictable; unruly; unsteady; untoward; wanton; willful

WEAKEN: (see "subvert") abate; attenuate; castrate; cripple; curtail; damage; debile; debilitate; decay; decline; decompose; decrease; degrade; degress; dehydrate; denervate; denudate; denude; desiccate; destroy; devitalize; diminish; disable; disembowel; divest; drain; dwindle; ebb; emasculate; enervate; enfeeble; etiolate; eviscerate; exhaust; extenuate; fade; fail; fatigue; harm; honeycomb; hurt; impair; incapacitate; infiltrate; jade; lessen; lower; mar; minimize; prostrate; quail; quaver; reduce; refine; relax; retrogress; rot; sap; shake; shrink; sink; soften; strain; strip; subside; suck; suppress; tamper; thin; tire; underemphasize; undermine; understress; unman; unnerve; unstrengthen; upset; wane; water; wear; WEAK(ENED): adynamic; anemic; anile; asthenic; attenuated; barren; bedridden; boneless; burned-out; burnt-out; cachectic; damaged; decadent; decrepit; deficient; degenerate(d); delicate; devitalized; dilute; dim(med); disabled; effete; enervated; enfeebled; etiolated; exhausted; faint; feckless; feeble; flabby; flat; foolish; forceless; fragile; frail; fruitless; gripless; gritless; gutless; hypodynamic; idle; impaired; impotent; impuissant; inapt; ineffective; ineffectual; inefficient; infirm; invertebrate; irresolute; lame; languid; lifeless; light; maladive; milk-and-water; old; outmoded; out-of-date; peccable; phthisic(al); pliable; powerless; puny; purposeless; sapless; shaky; sick(ly); simple; slack; soft; spent; stagnant; strained; subpotent; susceptible; thin; tired; tubercular; tuckered; underpowered; understrength; undervitalized; undynamic; unemphatic; unfortified; unfruitful; unhealthful; unhealthy; unimpressive; unmanful; unmanly; unmasculine; unprolific; unsound; unstable; unsteady; unsupported; unwise; vacillating; valetudinarian; vulnerable; wan; watered; watery; wavering; wearied; wearisome; winded; wishy-washy; worn(-out)

WEAKNESS: adynamia; asthenia; atony; attenuation; cachexia; cowardice; cowardliness; debilitation; debility; decadence; decrepitude; defect; delicacy; depletion; devitalization; disability; dyspnea; effeminacy; enervation; enfeeblement; ennui; exhaustion; *faiblesse*; faintness; fatigue; fault; fear; feebleness; flaw; flesh; foible; frailty; helplessness; hole; hypodynamia; hypokinesia; hypokinesis; imbecility; impairment; impotence; impotency; impuissance; inability; inanition; incapacitation; incapacity; infirmity; irritation; lackadaisy; languishment; languor; lassitude; lethargy; lifelessness; listlessness; marasmus; monotony; overstrain; powerlessness; puniness; pusillanimity; susceptibility; tedium; tenderness; tenuity; tiredness; tiresomeness; toil; touch; vacillation; vulnerability; weariness; wearisomeness

WEAL: happiness; health; prosperity; state; stripe; success; wale; wealth; welfare; well-being; welt

WEALTH: abundance; accumulation; affluence; assets; bonds; capital; chattels; estate; fortune; funds; Golconda; gold; goods; land; lucre; luxuriance; luxury; material; means; mine; money(bags); opulence; pelf; plenty; possessions; power; profusion; property; prosperity; riches; silver spoon; stock(s); substance; success; supply; treasure; treasury; wads; wampum; weal; wherewithal; WEALTHY: abundant; affluent; excessive; flush; heeled; loaded; lush; luxuriant; luxurious; moneyed; opulent; profuse; purse-proud; pursy; rich; solid; strong

WEAN: accustom; alienate; detach; estrange; reconcile; withdraw; WEANING: ablaction; withdrawal

WEAPON(S): arm(s); armamentaria (pl.); armament(s); artillery; claw; club; dagger; dirk; fowling piece; gat; gun; implement; iron; knife; lance; matériel; piece; pistol; rifle; rod; snee; spear; spur; sword; talon

WEAR: **v.** abrade; abrase; bear; cavitate; chafe; consume; corrode; decay; deteriorate; diminish; eat; erode; exhaust; fray; fret; gall; gnaw; grind; have; impair; last; lessen; macerate; pass; rub; rust; show; tire; use; vex; wash; waste; worry; WEAR: **n.** abrasion; attrition; clothes; clothing; corrosion; costume; decay; detrition; diminution; durability; erosion; fashion; friction; impairment; rub; rust; use; vogue; wash; waste

WEARY: **v.** (see "annoy") bore; droop; exhaust; fag; fatigue; flag; irk; jade; languish; long; pall; pine; tire; tucker; weaken; WEARY **a.** *or* WEARIED: apathetic; blasé; bored; burnt-out; disinterested; effete; exhausted; fagged; fatigued; flagged; footsore; impatient; irked; jaded; palled; sad;

sated; satiated; spent; surfeited; tedious; tired; tiresome; tuckered; undazzled; unimpressed; uninterested; unraptured; WEARISOME: (see "wearied") arduous; boring; burdensome; dree; dry; dull; exhaustive; fatiguesome; fatiguing; hard; heavy; humdrum; insipid; irksome; laborious; monotonous; stupid; tedious; tiresome; troublesome; tuckered

WEAVE: braid; careen; devise; entwine; fashion; interlace; knit; make; mat; oscillate; plait; produce; reel; rock; spin; stagger; sway; waver

WEB: (see "entanglement") complexity; fabric; gossamer; maze; net; scheme; snare; structure; tela; texture; tissue; warp

WED: (see "marry") bind; couple; espouse; hitch; join; tie; unite; wive

WEDGE: (see "cram") breach; chock; coign; cotter; cuneus; gib; jam; key; obstruction; pie; piece; quoin; separation; shim; slice; sliver

WEE: baby; diminutive; early; lilliputian; little; microscopic; minute; petite; small; teeny; tiny; ultramicroscopic; young

WEED: v. (see "eradicate") cull; cultivate; extirpate; hoe; WEED: n. cigar; darnel; dock; growth; plantain; tare; tobacco

WEEK: cycle; hebdomad; sennet; sennight

WEEN: (see "think") believe; conceive; expect; fancy; imagine; purpose; suppose

WEEP: (see "cry") bewail; blubber; boohoo; complain; grieve; keen; lament; mewl; moan; mourn; ooze; sob; sorrow; wail; yammer

WEIGH: (see "think") ascertain; balance; bear; burden; consider; counterbalance; depress; determine; encumber; evaluate; examine; influence; judge; measure; militate; muse; perpend; poise; ponder; stress; study; WEIGHT: avoirdupois; ballast; bulk; burden; consequence; corpulence; corpulency; credibility; credit; encumbrance; evaluation; force; gravitation; gravity; handicap; heaviness; heft; impact; importance; incubus; influence; judgment; load; mass(iveness); massivity; measure; obesity; opinion; perpension; ponderability; ponderance; ponderosity; ponderousness; power; pressure; prestige; pull; quantity; scale; size;

standard; strength; stress; thought; troy; value; worth; WEIGHTY: burdensome; corpulent; cumbersome; cumbrous; earnest; forceful; grave; gravid; grievous; heavy; hefty; important; influential; massive; massy; momentous; obese; onerous; ponderable; ponderous; powerful; significant; solemn; solid; strong; substantial; telling; valuable; worthy; WEIGHTINESS: authoritativeness; authority; avoirdupois; dignity; gravity; heaviness; importance; ponderability; ponderosity; significance; solemnity; solidity; strength; value; worth

WEIR: barrier; dam; net; seine; trap

WEIRD: (see "odd") awesome; awful; bizarre; cabalistic; creepy; eerie; eldritch; ghostly; grotesque; incantatory; mysterious; queer; spooky; strange; supernatural; talismanic; uncanny; unco; unearthly; unusual; wild

WELCOME: (see "greet") a. acceptable; *accueillant*; agreeable; *bienvenu*; cordial; good; pleasing; unscorned; WELCOME: n. *accueil*; bienvenue; glad hand; greeting; hospitality; open arms; ovation; reception; salutation; treat(ment)

WELD: see "unite"

WELFARE: aid; future; good; happiness; health; progress; prosperity; sele; success; weal; well-being

WELKIN: air; atmosphere; firmament; heaven; sky; vault

WELL: v. flow; gush; issue; pour; rise; seep; spurt; WELL: a. acceptable; adequate; advisable; bien; cured; desirable; fortunate; gay; good; gratified; hale; healed; healthy; lucky; pleasing; proper; right; sane; satisfactory; sound; WELL: n. cavity; excavation; fo(u)nt; fountain; hole; pit; reservoir; shaft; spring

WELT: border; confusion; edge; fringe; hem; ridge; strip; swelling; turmoil; wale; weal; wheal

WELTER: grovel; languish; roll; slue; toss; tumble; twist; wallow; writhe

WEND: alter; change; depart; direct; go; pass; proceed; shift; turn; travel

WEST: Occident; sunset; WESTERN: American; declining; European; Hesperian; Occidental; westerly

WET: **v.** anoint; bedew; dampen; deluge; douse; drench; humidify; immerse; moisten; saturate; shower; soak; souse; spray; sprinkle; water; WET: **a.** asop; bedewed; clammy; crazy; damp; dank; humid; misguided; moist(ened); moisty; rainy; soaked; soppy; soupy; undried; watery; wrong; WETNESS: aquosity; humectation; humidity; moistness; moisture; saturation

WHACK: (**see** "strike") bang; defeat; thwack

WHALE: beluga; blue; cachalot; cetacean; cete; graso; mammal; rorqual; sperm

WHARF: berth; dock; jetty; key; landing; levee; marina; pier; quay

WHEAL: mark; ridge; stripe; swelling; wale; weal; welt; whelk; urticaria

WHEEDLE: allure; bam; blandish; cajole; charm; coax; court; draw; entice; flatter; humor; induce; inveigle; lure; seduce; tempt; threaten

WHEEL: **v.** alter; circle; curve; gyrate; hinge; pivot; reel; reverse; revolve; roll; rotate; spin; spiral; sway; swing; turn; twirl; whirl; WHEEL: **n.** bicycle; bike; caster; circle; cycle; disk; helm; leader; pulley; round; sphere; spiral; sprocket

WHEEZE: **v.** gasp; puff; WHEEZE: **n.** device; dodge; gag; gasp; joke; puff; rale; trick; WHEEZY: asthmatic; panting; phthisic(al); phthisicky; short-breathed

WHELP: child; chit; cub; dog; pup(py); rib; ridge; rogue; youngster

WHEN: altogether; as; enough; though; whereas; whereupon; while

WHEREWITHAL: ability; goods; guts; means money; nerve; power; riches; wealth

WHET: animate; arouse; edge; egg; excite; grind; hone; incite; inspire; kindle; provoke; quicken; rouse; sharpen; smooth; spur; stimulate; sting; stir

WHIFF: **v.** exhale; fan; inhale; savor; smack; smell; waft; WHIFF: **n.** gust; hint; instant; intimation; jiffy; odor; pouf; puff; savor; smack; smell; waft; wind

WHILOM: erst; former(ly); once; quondam; sometime

WHIM(SICALITY) *or* WHIMS(E)Y: (**see** "caper") bizarrerie; boutade; caprice; captiousness; chimera; crotchet; desire; eccentricity; fad; fancy; fantasque; fantasticality; fantasticalness; folly; freak; haecceity; humor; idea; idiosyncrasy; impulse; madness-mania; megrim(s); mood; notion; oddity; passion; peculiarity; puckishness; quiddity; quirk; roguery; roguishness; singularity; temper; thing; vagary; vanity; vogue; whimsicalness; winch; WHIMSICAL: (**see** "fickle") capricious; captious; crotchety; droll; episodic(al); erratic; fanciful; fancy; fluky; freakish; haphazard; impish; irregular; irresponsible; notional; notionless; notiony; odd(ish); puckish; quaint; queer; roguish; singular; skittish; strange; uncertain; unpredictable; vagarious; whims(e)y

WHIMPER: (**see** "complain") bleat; cry; mewl; protest; pule; sniff; wail; whine; yammer

WHIMS(E)Y *or* WHIMSICAL: **see** under "whim"

WHINE: (**see** "complain") beat; cry; grumble; mewl; pule; snivel; wail; whimper; yammer

WHIP: **v.** (**see** "beat") abuse; arouse; bind; castigate; chastise; defeat; flagellate; flog; fustigate; hasten; lash; punish; tan; thrash; thump; thwack; whisk; WHIP: **n.** cat; cat-o'-nine-tails; crop; knout; lash; quirt; rod; stick; stroke

WHIRL: **v.** (**see** "spin") circle; gyrate; pirouette; speed; WHIRL: **n.** eddy; gorge; gyration; maelstrom; pirouette; rotation; rush; spin; try; turmoil; turn; vertigo; vortex

WHIRLPOOL: Charybdis; confusion; eddy; gorge; gurge; maelstrom; riptide; swirl; tumult; vortex

WHISPER: **v.** hint; murmur; siffilate; WHISPER: **n.** (**see** "hint") murmur; undertone; WHISPERING: (**see** "murmuring") susurration

WHIT: ace; atom; bit; breath; ghost; grain; iota; jot; mite; particle; scintilla; scrap; scruple; speck; tittle

WHITE *or* WHITISH: alabaster; albescent; albino(tic); ashen; blonde; candent; candescent; Caucasian; chalky; chaste; colorless; fair; hoar(y); honorable; innocent; ivory; light; niveous; pale; pallid; silvery; snowy;

transparent; wan; WHITEN: albify; blanch; bleach; etiolate; pale; palliate

WHITTLE: carve; cut; diminish; make; pare; reduce; remove; shape; trim; wear

WHIZ: **v.** buzz; hiss; hum; purr; speed; whir; WHIZ(ZER): **n.** (**see** "expert") bargain; corker; deal; live wire; wizard

WHOLE: **a.** absolute; all; complete; concentrated; defectless; *en bloc; en masse;* entire(ly); exclusive; extensive; full; gross; healed; healthy; impartite; inclusive; intact; integral; large; livelong; maiden; overall; perfect; plenary; pure; quite; sound; total; unbroken; uncrippled; uncut; undamaged; undeformed; undivided; unhurt; unimpaired; unmarred; unmotivated; untorn; unviolated; well; WHOLE: **n.** aggregrate; all; ensemble; entirety; integer; integral; mass; organization; solidum; sum; system; total(ity); union; unit; unity; WHOLENESS: (**see** "totality") developedness; integrality; integrity; oneness; totality

WHOLEHEARTED: absolutely; enthusiastic; freely; fully; hearty; implicit; unquestionable; unrestrained; unrestricted; zestful

WHOLESALE: abundant; bulk; extensive; gobs; indiscriminate; large; lots; massive; sweeping; unrestrained; unrestricted; wide

WHOLESOME: (**see** "healthful") beneficial; cautionary; clear-cut; curative; good; healthy; prudent; remedial; restorative; salubrious; salutary; salutiferous; sanative; savory; sound; sweet; vigorous

WHOOP: boast; boom; call; cheer; crow; cry; halloo; hoopoe; hoot; praise; pursue; shout; urge; utter; vaunt; yell

WHORL: cochlea; coil; spiral; turn; volution

WICKED: abhorrent; abominable; atrocious; Babylonian; bad; base; blasphemous; caitiff; criminal; cruel; cursed; dangerous; dark; depraved; devilish; diabolic(al); disgraceful; disreputable; dissolute; evil; excellent; execrable; fell; flagitious; flagrant; foul; ghoulish; guilty; hateful; heinous; hellish; ill; immoral; impious; improper; infamous; iniquitous; intractable; irreligious; licentious; Machiavellian; malevolent; malicious; malign(ant); mean; Mephistophelian; mischievous; nefarious; nefast; notorious; odious; offensive; outrageous; piacular; profane; profligate; reprehensible; risqué; roguish;

satanic(al); satanized; saturnine; scandalous; severe; sinful; sinister; terrible; troublesome; unclean; ungodly; unhallowed; unholy; unjust; unprincipled; unrighteous; unvirtuous; vexatious; vicious; vile; villainous; viperish; viperous; wrong; WICKEDNESS: (**see** "evil") abomination; Belial; debasedness; debasement; diablerie; enormity; flagitiousness; immorality; infamy; iniquity; licentiousness; misdeed; naughtiness; rascality; sinfulness; sinisterity; turpitude; uncleanliness; ungodliness; unholiness; vice; viciousness; villainy

WICKET: arch; door(way); entrance; gate-(way); hoop; loophole; window

WIDE: (**see** "broad") all-inclusive; ample; amplificated; comprehensive; dilatable; dila(ta)tive; dilated; distended; elastic; expandable; expansive; extended; extensive; far-flung; far-reaching; general; illimitable; intensive; magnitudinous; panoramic; roomy; spacious; vast; widespread; WIDEN: broaden; dilate; enlarge; expand; extend; grow; overspread; ream; splay; spread; WIDESPREAD: abounding; acceptable; catholic; common(place); comprehensive; copious; diffuse(d); ecumenical; endemic; epidemic; far-reaching; general; international; liberal; national; pandemic; peregrine; peregrinic; popular; predominant; prevalent; regnal; regnant; rife; teeming; universal; unlimited; unrestricted; worldwide

WIDE-AWAKE: **see** "alert"

WIDTH: amplitude; beam; breadth; comprehension; comprehensiveness; expansiveness; extensivity; extent; fullness; greatness; largeness; length; liberality; magnitude; measurement; scope; spaciousness; thickness

WIELD: brandish; command; control; direct; employ; exercise; exert; flourish; govern; handle; manage; manipulate; play; ply; rule; run; show; sway; swing; use; wreak

WIFE: bride; consort; *feme covert; femme couverte;* fere; frau; helpmate; mate; partner; rib; spouse; uxor

WIG: dignitary; hair; peruke; postiche; switch; tete; toupee

WIGWAM: cabin; hogan; hut; lodge; pueblo; tent; te(e)pee; wickiup

WILD: abandoned; amok; angry; animal-

(istic); barbaric; barbarous; beastly; berserk; bestial; boisterous; brutal(ized); corybantic; desirous; desolate; destructive; dissolute; dithyrambic; eager; emotional; enthusiastic; erratic; exaggerated; excited; extravagant; fantastic; feral; ferocious; fey; fierce; frantic; frenetic(al); frenzied; giddy; haywire; heathenish; hysterical; impassioned; impulsive; incoherent; inordinate; insane; intemperate; intractable; irrational; licentious; loose; mad; maniac(al); native; natural; overanxious; overwhelming; pagan; passionate; prodigal; rabid; random; raging; raving; rebellious; reckless; riotous; rough; rude; rugged; savage; shy; stormy; strong; tempestuous; turbulent; unassuaged; unbranded; unbroken; uncharted; uncivilized; unconquered; uncontrolled; unconventional; uncultivated; undisciplined; undomesticated; unexplored; ungovernable; ungoverned; unguided; unhandled; uninhabited; unmapped; unrestricted; unrestrained; unruly; unsubdued; unsupervised; untamable; untamed; untrained; violent; visionary; wasteful; WILDNESS: animality; barbarity; bestiality; confusion; ferity; mania; savageness; savagery; savagism; turbulence; turbulency; uncontrol; unruliness; wilderness

WILDCAT: **a.** illegitimate; irresponsible; unreliable; unsound; ununionized; WILDCAT: **n.** balu; bobcat; chaus; eyra; lynx

WILE: art(ifice); deceit(fulness); deception; fraud; feint; guile; machination; ruse; snare; stratagem; toy; trick(ery); whimsicality

WILL: **v.** behest; bequeath; choose; command; decree; demise; desire; devise; direct; elect; endow; entrust; intend; leave; ordain; order; prefer; purpose; transmit; wish; WILL: **n.** (**see** "bequest") ambition; appetite; backbone; behest; choice; command; courage; decision; design; desire; determinant; determination; disposal; disposition; faculty; fire; gall; goal; grit; guts; inclination; intellect; intent(ion); liking; mettle; mind; nerve; passion; pleasure; pluck; power; purpose; resolution; sand; self-control; self-direction; settlement; spirit; spunk; testament; volition; wish

WILLFUL: flinthearted; hardhearted; headstrong; intentional; obstinate; perverse; premeditated; resolute; self-determined; self-willed; stubborn; ungovernable; unruly; voluntary

WILLING: agreeable; amenable; available; compliant; convenient; disposed; eager; fain; favorable; flexible; free; inclined; lief; obedient; persevering; prone; ready; receptive; steadfast; tenacious; unforced; usable; voluntary; WILLINGLY: cheerfully; freely; gladly; lief(ly); noncompulsorily; readily; voluntarily; WILLINGNESS: amenability; compliance; eagerness; fairness; heart; inclination; perseverance; pertinacity; readiness; receptivity; sincerity; steadfastness; stick-to-itiveness; tenacity; tractability; zeal(ousness)

WILLOWY: delicate; flexible; graceful; lissom(e); pliant; reedy; slender; supple; svelt

WILLY-NILLY: ambivalent; cyclonic; fickle; fluctuating; helpless; inevitable; *nolens volens*; uncertain; vacillating

WILT: (**see** "decline") sag

WILY: (**see** "sly") arch; artful; astute; clever; crafty; cunning; designing; foxy; insidious; politic; serpentine; snaky; sneaky; sticky; subtle; tricky

WIN: achieve; acquire; attain; beat; best; captivate; capture; carry; conquer; defeat; drub; earn; gain; get; have; hit; obtain; overcome; overtake; prevail; reach; score; secure

WINCE: cringe; flinch; quail; recoil; reel; shrink; shy

WIND: **v.** bend; bind; coil; crank; crook; curl; curve; encircle; enlace; enmesh; entangle; entwine; insinuate; intertangle; interweave; intort; involve; loop; meander; mingle; tighten; turn; twine; twist; undulate; vine; warp; weave; wrap; wreathe; WIND: **n.** auster; bise; blast; blow; bora; boreas; breath; breeze; chinook; flatulence; flatus; foehn; gale; gas; gust; hurricane; intimation; leste; levanter; mistral; Notus; odor; pampero; ponente; samiel; Santa Ana; sarsar; scent; simoon; sirocco; solano; squall; storm; strength; tebbad; tempest; tendency; tornado; trend; twister; typhoon; waterspout; whirlwind; zephyr

WINDFALL: advantage; bonus; boon; chance; fortune; gain; gift; godsend; gravy; luck; manna; vail

WINDING: **a.** aberrant; ambagious; anfractuous; apostrophic; astray; bending; circuitous; crazy; crooked; curved; curving; desultory; deviant; deviated; deviating; devious; digressive; discursive; divaricative; excursive;

flexuous; furtive; indirect ingenuous; intransigent; labyrinthian; labyrinthine; mazy; meandering; meandrous; mysterious; oblique; off course; out-of-the-way; parenthetic-(al); perverse; purposeless; rambling; random; reeling; roundabout; roving; serpentine; shifting; shifty; sinful; sinister; sinuate; sinuous; sly; snaky; snide; spide; spiral; staggering; stealthy; straying; subtle; tangential; tortuous; treacherous; tricky; turning; underhanded; unfair; unscrupulous; wandering; WINDING: **n.** aberrance; aberration; ambage; anfractuosity; circuity; circumbendibus; contortion; convolution; deflection; departure; detour; deviance; deviant; deviation; digression; divagation; divergence; diversion; drift(age); eccentricity; errancy; error; excursion; flexuosity; indirection; intortion; intransigence; meandering; sinuation; sinuosity; torque; torsion; tortuosity; treachery; trickery; turning; underhandedness; unfairness; uscrupulosity; variant; veering; wandering

WINDOW: aperture; casement; dormer; eye; fenestra; fenestration; opening; oriel; pane; sash; slot

WINE (**see** "regale") Asti; intoxicant; Médoc; Moselle; negus; sack; *sève*; *vin*; vino; vintage; vinum

WING: **v.** aviate; dispatch; flex; fly; sail; WING: **n.** adjunct; ala; alae (pl.); alette; alula; annex; arm; division; ell; extension; faction; flank; flight; pennon; pinion; projection; sail; squadron; want; WINGED: alate; elevated; flown; pennate; rapid; swift

WINK: **v.** bat; blink; connive; disregard; flash; flicker; glance; gleam; ignore; nap; nic(ti)-tate; overlook; signal; twinkle; twitch; WINK: **n.** blink; flash; flicker; glance; gleam; instant; moment; nap; nictitation; signal; sparkle; tic; twinkle; twitch

WINNER: ace; champ(ion); conqueror; earner; faceman; first; high; medalist; victor; WINNING: **see** "attractive" and "winsome"

WINNOW: analyze; assort; blow; bolt; delete; disperse; eliminate; fan; fly; glean; remove; scatter; screen; select; separate; sieve; sift; stir

WINSOME: agreeable; attractive; blithe; bonny; captivating; charming; cheerful; chic; gay; gracious; lovable; personable; pleasant; pleasing; pretty; winning

WINTRY: boreal; brumal; cheerless; chilling; cold; hibernal; hiemal; icy; inclement; sleety; snowy; stormy; winterish

WIPE: abolish; annihilate; cancel; clean; delete; dry; effect; erase; exhaust; expunge; exterminate; mob; obliterate; rub; swab

WISDOM: acumen; astuteness; brains; depth; discernment; discretion; discrimination; experience; farsightedness; gnosis; information; insight; instinct; intelligence; judgment; judiciality; knowledge; learning; lore; perpendicularity; perspicacity; philosophy; policy; prescience; profundity; prudence; rationality; reason(ableness); sagaciousness; sagacity; sageness; sanity; sapience; sapiency; sense; sententiousness; shrewdness; skill(fulness); subtlety; understanding; wit

WISE: acuminous; advantageous; alert; aphoristic; apothegmatic; astucious; astute; brainy; bright; calculating; cautious; circumspect; cognizant; crafty; deep; desirable; discerning; discreet; dicriminating; enlightened; equitable; erudite; farseeing; farsighted; gnomic(al); good; hep; impartial; informed; instructed; intellectual; intelligent; judgmatic(al); judicious; keen; knowing; knowledgeable; learned; logical; Nestorian; oracular; orphic; penetrating; perceptive; perspicacious; philosophic(al); politic; profound; prophetic(al); prudent; quick; rational; reasonable; sagacious; sage; sane; sapient(ial); sensible; sententious; sharp (-witted); shrewd; smar; Solomonian; Solomonic; sound; subtle; tactful; witty

WISH: **v.** (**see** "desire") aspire; covet; crave; hanker; long; repine; vote; vow; want; will; yearn; WISH: **n.** (**see** "desire") pleasure; WISHFUL: **see** "desirable"

WISHY- WASHY: banal; diluted; feeble; flat; forceless; inane; insipid; jejune; namby-pamby; pale; sickly; thin; unimpressive; vapid; vaporous; void; watery; weak

WISP: (**see** "fragment") tuft; whisk

WIT(S): ability; acumen; alertness; Aristophanes; astuteness; *bel esprit*; brain; brevity; brilliance; causticity; coruscation; drollery; esprit; facetiosity; facetiousness; fun; grain; *homme d'esprit*; humor; ingeniosity; ingenuity; inspiration; intellect; intelligence; inventiveness; irony; jocularity; judgment; memory; mind; mordacity; *nugae canore* (pl.); perception; percipience; persiflage; persifleur; reason(ing); repartee; sagacity; *sal Atticus*;

salt; sanity; sarcasm; satire; sense; sharpness; skill; soul; subtlety; talent; thinker; wag; whimsicality; wisdom; WITTY: acuminate; acuminous; Aristophanic; bright; brilliant; caustic; clever; compact; concise; droll; epigrammatic(al); facetious; funny; humorous; ingenious; intelligent; jocose; jocular; laconic; mercurial; perceptive; pithy; quick; ready; sage; satirical; scintillating; scintillescent; sharp; smart; spiritual; subtle; terse; waggish; WITTINESS: facetiosity; humor; jocularity; perception; percipience; *plaisanterie*; scintillation; waggishness; WITTICISM: (see "maxim") adage; aphorism; apothegm; bijouterie; *bon mot*; coruscation; epigram; facetiae (pl.); facetiosity; gag; *jeu d'esprit*; *jeu de mots*; jocosity; joke; laconicism; mot; *mot pour rire*; motto; paronomasia; poem; pun; quip; retort; sally; saw; saying; truism; *turlupinade*; wisecrack

WITCH: banshee; charmer; enchantress; hag; Hecate; hex; lamia; necromancer; pythoness; sibyl; siren; sorceress; vampire; WITCHCRAFT: charm; devil(try); enchantment; magic; necromancy; sorcery; sortilege; spell; witchery

WITH: accompanying; against; along; among; beside; between; by; for; notwithstanding; over; plus; through; upon; visiting; within

WITHDRAW: abandon; abdicate; abjure; abrogate; avoid; backtrack; backtrail; cancel; concede; crawfish; decamp; deduct; deny; depart; deport; desert; detach; disavow; disclaim; disown; distract; divert; eliminate; empty; escape; evacuate; exhaust; expatriate; forsake; forswear; gainsay; go; leave; nullify; quit; recall; recant; recede; recidivate; relinquish; remove; renounce; repudiate; rescind; resign; retire; retract; retreat; reverse; revoke; scratch; secede; siphon; subduct; substract; subtract; surrender; take; unsay; withhold; WITHDRAWN: (see "shy^v") antisocial; overdrawn; WITHDRAWAL: abandonment; abdication; abrogation; back track; cancellation; deduction; denial; departure; desertion; detachment; disavowal; disclaimer; discontinuance; discontinuation; diversion; elimination; escape; evacuation; exhaustion; nullification; quittance; recantation; recession; recidivation; relinquishment; removal; renouncement; renunciation; repudiation; resignation; retirement; retraction; retreat; reversal; revocation; revulsion; scratch; secession; seclusion; separation; setback; subduction; substraction; subtraction; surrender

WITHER: age; atrophy; decay; die; droop; drop; fade; flag; languish; paralyze; quail; sear; senesce; shrink; shrivel; stun; waste; wilt; wizen; wrinkle; WITHERED: (see "dry") sapless; wizened

WITHIN: *ab intra*; autogenous; during; encircled; endogenous; esoteric; herein; in(doors); indwelling; inner; inside; internal(ly); into; intramural; inward(ly); under

WITHOUT: *ab extra*; beyond; exempt; external(ly); lacking; minus; outdoors; outside; outwardly; unless

WITHSTAND: abide; bear; best; bide; brook; confront; contain; contend; contest; defy; endure; face; forbear; oppose; persist; take; tolerate; vie; wear

WITLESS: see "crazy"

WITNESS: **v.** (see "see") attest; behold; betoken; look; observe; subscribe; testify; vouch; watch; WITNESS: **n.** attendant; attestation; attestator; attester; beholder; bystander; confirmation; deponent; evidence; observation; observer; onlooker; proof; spectator; teste; testimony; viewer; voucher; watcher

WITTICISM: see under "wit;" WITTY: see under "wit"

WIZARD: adept; authority; conjurer; diviner; Druid; enchanter; expert; go-getter; hotshot; fiend; live wire; mage; magi (pl.); magician; magus; necromancer; prestidigitator; sage; seer; shaman; sorcerer

WIZEN: age; desiccate; dry; shrink; shrivel; wither

WOBBLE: see "shake"

WOE: affliction; agony; anathema; anguish; bale; bane; calamity; curse; disease; distress; dole; dolor; grief; heartache; illness; misery; misfortune; pain; pang; sadness; sickness; sorrow; torture; tribulation; trouble; unhappiness; WOEFUL: afflicted; crestfallen; dejected; deplorable; desolate; dilapidated; disconsolate; downcast; forlorn; melancholy; miserable; paltry; pitiful; sad; sorrowful; sorry; threnodic; unhappy; woebegone; wretched

WOLF: coyote; famine; lobo; poverty; roué; starvation; WOLFISH: ferocious; gluttonous; lupine; ravenous; wolflike;

WOMAN: dam; dame; dish; doll; dowager; enchantress; female; femineity; feminie (pl.); feminity; femme; hausfrau; housewife; lady; madam; matriarch; matron; mesdames (pl.); milady; mistress; mother; paramour; princess; queen; señora; señorita; shrew; virago; wife; womankind; WOMANHOOD: feminality; femineity; feminie; femininity; matronage; matronhood; matronliness; motherhood; muliebrity; womanity; womanliness; womenfolks; womenkind; WOMANLY: **see** "unmasculine"

WONDER: **v.** doubt; marvel; meditate; muse; ponder; puzzle; question; speculate; WONDER: **n.** admiration; amazement; astonishment; awe; bewilderment; curiosity; fascination; marvel; perplexity; phenomenon; portent; prodigy; rarity; stupefaction; surprise; wonderment

WONDERFUL: admirable; amazing; astonishing; astounding; dandy; excellent; exciting; extraordinary; fine; good; grand; great; ineffable; jim-dandy; marvelous; miraculous; mirific; phenomenal; stupenduous; surprising; swell; unexpected; unique; unspeakable; wondrous

WONT: custom; habit; practice; tradition; usage; use

WOO: address; beg; court; entreat; implore; importune; invite; plead; seek; solicit; spark; sue

WOOD(S): forest; fuel; grove; sylva; timber; trees; WOODED: arboraceous; arboreal; arborescent; WOODY: ligneous; lignescent; pithy; sylvan; xyloid; WOODEN: awkward; clumsy; deadpan; expressionless; firm; hard; inflexible; lifeless; rigid; sedate; solid; spiritless; stiff; stolid; stupid; tense; ungainly; unmovable

WOOF: element; fabric; filling; material; texture; thread; weft

WOOL: abb; angora; down; fiber; fleece; fur; hair; merino; yarn; WOOLLY: blurry; confused; downy; flocculent; flocculose; indistinct; lanate; laniferous; lanose; lanuginous; soft; tosy; warm

WORD(S): account; assertion; command; countersign; description; dictionary; discourse; epithet; expression; gospel; idiom; information; language; lexicon; *lexis*; maxim; message; name; neologism; news; nomenclature; phrase(ology); pledge; promise; prov-erb; remark; report; repute; rhema; rumor; signal; speech; talk; term; testament; thesaurus; utterance; verbiage; vocable; vocabulary; wordage; word-stock

WORDBOOK: dictionary; lexicon; libretto; nomenclature; onomasticon; synonymicon; vocabulary

WORDY: babbling; chattering; circumlocutious; copious; diffuse; effusive; fluent; garrulous; glib; grandlioquent; logorrheic; loquacious; noisy; palaverous; pleonastic; profuse; prolix; protracted; redundant; repetitious; rhetorical; talkative; tautological; verbal; verbose; vocal; voluble; windy; WORDINESS: (**see** "verboseness") affluence; catalogia; circumlocution; *copia verborum*; diffusion; effusion; facundity; fluency; garrulity; glibness; logorrhea; loquaciousness; loquacity; macrology; officialese; periphrasis; pleonasm; prolixity; redundancy; talkativeness; tautology; verbalism; verbality; verbiage; verbigeration; verbomania; verbosity; volubility; voluminosity; windiness

WORK: **v.** achieve; arrang; cajole; contrive; create; dig; drag; drudge; effect; embroider; excite; execute; exert; exploit; fag; fashion; ferment; forge; function; grind; grub; guide; hammer; knuckle down; labor; maneuver; manipulate; move; operate; perform; plug; press; produce; progress; provoke; run; serve; shape; slave; strive; succeed; sweat; toil; trick; use; WORK: **n.** accomplishment; achievement; act(ion); activity; application; art; assignment; barricade; book; business; calling; chore; craft; deed; drudgery; duty; effect; effort; elbow grease; employment; endeavor; energy; erg; ergon; exercise; exertion; exploitation; fatigue; force; function; game; grind; hobby; job; karma; labor; management; material; métier; mission; moil; occupation; opus; pains; performance; pressure; production; profession; pursuit; result; service; skill; slavery; structure; style; sweat; task; toil; trade; use; vehicle; vocation; workmanship

WORKER, WORKMAN *or* WORKMEN: artificer; artisan; craftsman; creator; crew; doer; follower; force; gang; hand(s); handcraftsman; handyman; journeyman; laborer; mate(y); mechanic; men; navvy; operator; opificer; peon; slave; smith; soldier; toiler

WORKMANSHIP: art(isanship); artistry;

craftsmanship; expertise; handicraft; manufacture; skill(fulness); virtuosity; work

WORKS: books; deeds; factory; insides; machine(ry); mechanism; mill; plant; shop

WORKSHOP: atelier; establishment; lab-(oratory); plant; studio

WORLD: affairs; career; cosmos; creation; domain; earth; experience; globe; group; humanity; infinity; kingdom; life; macrocosm; mankind; manners; microcosm; multitude; nature; people; planet; public; quantity; realm; region; society; sphere; universe; usage; vale; WORLDLY: bestial; carnal; cosmic; earth(l)y; fashionable; fleshy; global; hedonic; human; intramundane; laic; lustful; luxurious; mondain(e); mortal; mundane; profane; secular; sensual; sensuous; sophisticated; subastral; subcelestial; sublunary; temporal; terrene; terrestrial; uncelestial; universal; unspiritual; voluptuous; wanton; WORLDLINESS: carnality; fleshiness; lust; mundaneness; mundanity; secularism; secularity; sensuality; temporality; universality; WORLDWIDE: ecumenical; global; pandemic; planetary; prevalent

WORM: v. crawl; creep; extract; inch; insinuate; wriggle; writhe; WORM: n. annelid; ess; fluke; grub; larva; leech; lurg; maggot; naid; nema(tode); wretch

WORN: abraded; attrite; bare; broken-down; burned-out; burnt-out; consumed; debilitated; depleted; dilapidated; disreputable; dissipated; dog-eared; eaten; effete; eroded; erose; exhausted; fatigued; frayed; hackneyed; impaired; jaded; magged; passé; seedy; shabby; shelfworn; shot; spent; stale; tattered; threadbare; tired; trite; unwearable; used; vapid; wasted; weathered; weatherworn; worm-eaten; worn-out

WORRY: v. (see "annoy") badger; bait; bother; care; cark; gnaw; harass; harry; importune; nag; scold; stew; tantalize; torment; vex; wear; weary; WORRY: n. (see "annoyance") anxiousness; care; difficulty; distress; fantod(s); fear; nightmare; problem; torment; trouble; vexation; worriment; WORRYING: or WORRIED: afraid; annoyed; anxious; apprehensive; disconcerted; distressed; fazed; fearful; perplexed; preoccupied; puzzled; tense; vexed

WORSE: see "bad;" WORSEN: damage; decline; degenerate; deteriorate; disimprove; exacerbate; impair; lessen; retard; retro-

grade; retrogress; tragedize; WORSENING: a. declinatory; deteriorating; exacerbative; retrograde; retrogressive; WORSENING: n. declination; deterioration; exacerbation; retrogression

WORSHIP: v. admire; adore; adulate; canonize; commune; defer; deify; devote; esteem; exalt; fetichize; hallow; honor; idolize; love; obey; observe; pedestal; praise; prize; respect; revere(nce); serve; stellify; venerate; WORSHIP: n. admiration; adoration; adulation; church; cultism; cultus; deference; devotion; discipline; dulia; esteem; exaltation; hierurgy; homage; honor; idolatry; latria; liturgy; observation; piety; regard; religion; respect; reverence; service; stellification; veneration; WORSHIPER: see "votary"

WORST: beat; best; conquer; defeat; foil; master; outdo; overcome; overmaster; overthrow; quell; rout; subjugate; vanquish

WORTH: appreciation; candor; character; cost; credit; estimation; excellence; goodness; honesty; honor; importance; integrity; manhood; merit; morality; nobility; nobleness; price; rectitude; regard; reliability; riches; righteousness; salability; sincerity; stability; use(fulness); utility; valor; value; venerability; virtue; wealth

WORTHINESS: see under "worthy"

WORTHLESS: abject; ambsace; barren; base; brassy; cheap; cheesy; chétif; contemptible; crummy; despicable; empty; feckless; flimsy; fustian; futile; hollow; idle; ignoble; impotent; incompetent; ineffective; ineffectual; inoperative; insignificant; inutile; invalid; junky; lacking; lazy; low; mean; miserable; nugatory; paltry; petty; piddling; piperly; profitless; profligate; putrid; raca; rascally; scurvy; sterile; stramineous; tin(ny); trashy; trifling; trivial; undeserving; ungainful; unimportant; unproductive; unreliable; useless; vain; valueless; vile

WORTHY: admirable; chivalrous; commendable; condign; considerable; creditable; decent; dependable; desirable; eligible; esteemed; estimable; excellent; exemplary; fair; fitting; generous; gentle; good; heroic; honest; honorable; important; laudable; laudatory; meritorious; noble; notable; noted; reliable; rich; salable; true; valuable; venerable; virtuous; weighty; worthwhile; WORTHINESS: (see "fitness") desirability; desirableness; importance; reputation; veneration

WOUND: **v.** bruise; contuse; cut; damage; gall; gash; harm; hurt; injure; lacerate; maim; mutilate; offend; pierce; scathe; shoot; slash; stab; sting; touch; traumatize; WOUND: **n.** blow; bruise; contusion; cut; damage; detriment; distress; gash; harm; hurt; injury; laceration; lesion; slash; slit; sore; stab; trauma(tism); vulnus

WRACK: destruction; downfall; eelgrass; kelp; punishment; ruin; seaweed; vengeance; wreck(age)

WRAITH: (**see** "ghost") apparition; doppelganger; specter; spirit; vision

WRANGLE: **v.** (**see** "argue") arguify; altercate; bicker; brawl; debate; dispute; ergotize; quarrel; spar; WRANGLE: **n. see** "quarrel"

WRAP: **v.** bundle; clothe; coil; conceal; enclose; encompass; envelope; fold; furl; hide; involve; lap; obscure; parcel; suffuse; surround; swaddle; swathe; veil; vine; wind; WRAP: **n.** boa; carton; cover(ing); envelope; hull; husk; kimono; overcoat; package; paper; peignoir; scarf; shawl; skin; throw; wrapping

WRATH: (**see** "anger") animosity; choler; condemnation; exasperation; fury; indignation; ire; irritation; rage; resentment; WRATHFUL: (**see** "angry") Achillean; vindicative

WREATH: anadem; bay; chaplet; coronet; crown; festoon; garland; laurel; lei; trophy; WREATHE: contort; intort; twist; vine; wind; writhe

WRECK: (**see** "destroy" and "ruin") damage; demolishment; desolation; dilapidation; sabotage; wreckage; WRECKAGE: flotsam; flotsam and jetsam; shambles

WRENCH: **v.** distort; force; injure; jerk; pervert; pull; snatch; sprain; strain; tear; tighten; twist; wrest; wring; yank; WRENCH: **n.** distortion; jerk; pull; spanner; sprain; strain; tear; tool; twinge; twist; yank

WREST: change; deflect; distort; elicit; extort; force; move; pull; rend; tear; twist; wrench; wring; yark; WRESTLE: combat; debate; grapple; scuffle; squirm; struggle; tussle; wiggle

WRETCH: caitiff; outcast; pariah; rogue; roué; scoundrel; skunk; sufferer; victim

WRETCHED: (**see** "miserable") abject; abominable; abysmal; afflicted; base; calamitous; contemptible; crude; damnable; dejected; deplorable; despicable; detestable; distressed; dreadful; execrable; forlorn; gaunt; grievous; inefficient; lamentable; meager; mean; odious; outworn; paltry; poor; sad; shabby; sick(ly); sorry; squalid; unfortunate; unhappy; woeful; worthless

WRING: **see** "squeeze"

WRINKLE: **v.** contract; corrugate; crease; crimp; draw; fold; furl; furrow; line; muss; pucker; WRINKLE: **n.** angle; blemish; corrugation; crease; crimp; fault; fold; furrow; hint; line; method; pucker; rick; ridge; ruga; rugae (pl.); rugosity; seam; suggestion; technique; WRINKLED: corrugated; creased; furrowed; lined; puckered; rugate(d); rugose; rugous; seamed; wrinkly

WRIT: breve; capias; deed; document; habeas corpus; judgment; mandamus; mandate; mandatum; order; precept; process; scripture; sentence; subpoena; summons

WRITE: author; autograph; compose; depict; dictate; draft; express; indite; inscribe; mark; pen; pencil; prosify; publish; record; rhapsodize; scrawl; scribble; scribe; scrive; sign; transcribe; type; WRITER: allegorist; annalist; author; belle-lettrist; belletrist; cacographer; calligrapher; calligraphist; chronicler; columnist; communicator; composer; contributor; correspondent; dramatist; dramaturge; editor(ialist); epistolarian; essayist; exegete; exegetist; hack; historian; historiographer; inkslinger; interpreter; journalist; lampoonist; lawyer; litterateur; memorialist; novelist; penman; playwright; poet; prosaist; prosateur; rhetorician; romancer; satirist; scribbler; scribe; scriver; scrivener; WRITING(S) account; advertisement; almanac; anecdote; annal(s); announcement; answer; anthology; anti-novel; apograph; article; autobiography; *belles lettres*; bible; bibliography; book(let); breviary; brief; brochure; bulletin; cahier; calligraphy; cameo; casebook; catalog(ue); chirography; chronicle; circular; commemoration; communication; compilation; composition; contribution; corpus; declaration; decree; delineation; diary; directory; discourse; disquisition; dissertation; document(ary); dodger; draft; editorial; encyclopedia; epic; epigram; epigraph; epilogue; epistle; epitaph; essay; étude; excerpt(s); exegesis; explanation; exposition; fable; fantasia; fiction; folio; garland; graffiti (pl.); graffito;

hand; history; inscription; instrument; interpretation; introduction; irony; item; journal(ism); judgment; knowledge; lampoon; leaflet; ledger; legend; letter; libretto; literature; log; longhand; magazine; magnum opus; mail; manual; manuscript; masterpiece; memo(randum); memorial; message; monograph; narration; narrative; newspaper; note; notebook; notice; novel-(la); novelette; ode; opera; opinion; opus; pamphlet; paper; penmanship; penny dreadful; periodical; play; poem; poetry; pornography; poster; potboiler; proclamation; prologue; prose; prospectus; publication; record(ation); register; repertory; report; rescript; romance; saga; satire; scenario; screed; script(ure); scrivening(s); shorthand; skit; sonata; squib; stanza; statement; storiation; story; summary; symposium; telegram; text(book); theme; thesis; tirade; tome; topic; tract(ate); transcript-(ion); treatise; verse; vignette; volume; white paper; words; work; write-up; yarn

WRITHE: agonize; contort; extricate; squirm; twist; wrench; wriggle; wring

WRONG: **v.** abuse; betray; cheat; defraud; dishonor; harm; hurt; injure; malign; oppress; violate; WRONG: **a.** all wet; amiss; askew; awry; bad; cockeyed; criminal; damaging; delinquent; disadvantageous; dishonest; erroneous; evil; false; faulty; guilty; harmful; immoral; improper; inadequate; inappropriate; inapt; incorrect; inequitable; injurious; insane; mistaken; off; oppressive; poor; rank; sinful; sour; unconventional; unethical; unfair; unfit(ted); unjust; unmerited; unpardonable; unqualified; unright; unsatisfactory; unsuitable; untrue; venal; villainous; wicked; WRONG: **n.** abuse; betrayal; crime; defraudation; delinquency; derelict(ion); dishonor; error; evil; falsity; fault; fraud; grievance; harm; hurt; ill(-doing); immorality; impropriety; inaccuracy; iniquity; injury; injustice; malefaction; malfeasance; malignity; misdeed; misdemeanor; misfeasance; mistake; misunderstanding; oppression; sin; tort; transgression; turpitude; unfairness; unjustness; unright(fulness); untruth; venality; vice; villainy; violation; wickedness; WRONGFUL: **see** "unjust" and "wrong"

WRONGDOING: (**see** "misconduct") malpractice; misbehavior; WRONGDOER: (**see** "criminal") offender; sinner; transgressor

WRY: askew; bent; contorted; crooked; distorted; humorous; oblique; perverse; sardonic; saturnine; twisted; warped; wrongheaded

Y

YAP: bark; chatter; gab; scold; yammer; yelp

YARD: area; compound; court; enclosure; gaff; garden; garth; grounds; lawn; measure; patio; pound; quad(rangle); spar; YARD-STICK: (see "standard") criterion; ruler; touchstone

YARN: abb; anecdote; chat; conversation; exaggeration; fabrication; fib; fleece; genappe; narration; narrative; saga; spiel; story; tale; thread; wool; worsted

YAW: **v.** deviate; gape; steer; yawn; zigzag; YAW: **n.** blister; tumor; zigzag

YAWN: **v.** dehisce; gape; open; oscitate; part; split; yaw; YAWN: **n.** cavity; chasm; dehiscence; dullness; gape; gaping; opening; oscitation; tedium; yaw; YAWNING: cavernous; gaping; open; oscitant; patulous

YEARN: **v.** (see "want") ache; burn; consume; crave; desire; dream; hanker; long; pain; pang; pant; pine; sigh; wish; YEARN(ING): **n.** (see "desire") compassion; homesickness; lovesickness; nostalgia; wishfulness; wistfulness

YEAST: barm; ferment; leaven; rising

YELL: **v.** bawl; bellow; call; cheer; complain; cry; howl; protest; roar; scream; screech; shout; shriek; ululate; utter; whoop; yammer; yap; YELL: **n.** bellow; call; cheer; complaint; cry; howl; protest(ation); roar; scream; screech; shout; shriek; ululation; whoop; yammer; yap; yelp

YELLOW(ISH): amber; aureate; citreous; citrine; cowardly; craven; dishonorable; favel; flavescent; flavous; flaxen; fulvous; golden; icterine; jaundiced; jaune; jealous; lemon; luteous; lutescent; mean; olive; saffron; sallow; sandy; straw; tan; xanthic xanthous; yellowy

YELP: (see "yell") bark; cry; kiyi; squeal; yap; yawp; yip

YEN: (**see** "want") appetite; craving; desire; drive; hanker; longing; lust; passion; urge; yearn(ing)

YES: accord; affirmation; affirmative; agreement; assent; aye; concurrence; indeed; *ja*; sure; true; truly

YET: again; also; besides; but; e'en; even; finally; henceforth; hitherto; however; nevertheless; notwithstanding; still; though

YIELD: **v.** accede; accommodate; acknowledge; acquiesce; afford; aggregate; agree; bear; bend; bestow; bow; capitulate; cause; cede; comply; concede; consent; defer; discharge; emit; follow; forego; furnish; give; grant; hear; impart; knuckle under; lose; occasion; pay; produce; quit; recite; relent; relinquish; render; resign; retire; return; sag; sanction; soften; submit; suffer; surrender; YIELD(ING): **n.** accommodation; acquiescence; aggregate; amount; capacity; capitulation; cession; complaisance; compliance; concession; crop(s); flexibility; malleability; obedience; output; outturn; pay; plasticity; proceeds; product(s); profit(s); quantity; resignation; resiliency; result(s); return(s); revenue; submission; succumbence; succumbency; surrender; turnout; yieldance; YIELDING: **a.** accommodating; acquiescent; adaptable; agreeable; amenable; capitulatory; complaisant; compliant; craven; cringing; ductile; dutiful; facile; fingent; flexible; irresistible; kind; limber; malleable; marshy; obedient; plastic; pliable; pliant; quaggy; ready; resigned; resilient; soft; spongy; submissive; supple; susceptible; teachable; tender; timid; tractable; unresistant; weak

YOKE: (**see** "unite") bond; brace; cangue; couple; harness; pair; pillory; repression; subjection; subjugation; team; union

YOKEL: boor; bumpkin; countryman; hayseed; hick; lout; plowboy; rustic

YONDER: thence; there; thither; yon

YORE: ago; antiquity; before; eld; erst; formerly; past

YOUNG: **a.** adolescent; diminutive; early; fey; fresh; green; immature; impubic; inconabular; inexperienced; junior; juvenile; little; new; premature; puerile; puisne; small; suckling; unbearded; unpracticed; vernal; youthful; wee; YOUNG: **n. see** "offspring;" YOUNGSTER: adolescent; babe; baby; boy; child; chit; colt; filly; kid; lad; moppet; pup(py); tad; tot; whelp; yo(u)nker; youth; YOUNGER: inferior; junior; puisne; youthful

YOUTH: adolescent; Aladdin; boy; boyhood; bud; damsel; girl; girlhood; gossoon; hobbledehoy; juvenile; lad; lass(ie); maid(en); minor; miss; puberty; pubescence; salad days; stripling; teenager; youngling; youngster; yo(u)nker; YOUTHFUL: adolescent; beardless; boyish; budding; callow; childish; early; fresh; girlish; green; hebetic; inexperienced; juvenile; kittenish; maiden(ish); maidenly; nealogic; neanic; puerile; vernal; vigorous; virginal; youngling; young(ish); YOUTHFULNESS: adolescence; boyishness; girlishness; juniority; juvenility; *le bel âge*; minority; nonage; puberty; pubescence

Z

ZANY: (**see** "crazy") antic; buffoon; clown; comic; fool; jester; madcap; Merry-Andrew; simpleton; toady

ZEAL: ardency; ardor; assiduity; calenture; concentration; dash; dedication; desire; devotement; devotion; diligence; eagerness; earnestness; ebullience; ebulliency; élan; emotion; energy; enthusiasm; faithfulness; fanaticism; feeling; ferment; fervency; fervidity; fervor; fidelity; fire; flame; force; ginger; glow; gusto; heart(iness); heat; hustle; industry; intensity; love; loyalty; nerve; passion; pep(per); pressure; rabidity; rapture; raptus; rush; sedulity; soul; spirit; stir; strain; tension; vehemence; verve; vigor; vivacity; voracity; warmth; zealotism; zealotry; zest; zip; ZEALOUS: active; animated; ardent; assiduous; burning; crusading; dedicated; devoted; devout; diligent; dithyrambic; eager; ebullient; emotional; energetic; enraptured; enterprising; enthusiastic; evangelical; evangelistic; extreme; fanatic(al); fervent; feverish; fierce; fiery; fired; forceful; frantic; glowing; great; heated; high-spirited; hot(-blooded); igneous; impassioned; inflammable; intense; jealous; keen; loving; loyal; passionate; perfervid; pious; pushful; pushy; rabid; rapturous; religious; romantic; sanguine; sedulous; sentimental; shining; strong; torrid; vehement; vigilant; vigorous; vivacious; volcanic; warm; zestful

ZEALOT: buff; bigot; devotee; disciple; enthusiast; fan(atic); hustler; partisan; superzealot; votary; ZEALOTISM: (**see** "zeal") zealotry; zealousness

ZENITH: acme; apex; apogee; cap; climax; crest; crown; culmination; heavens; height; noon; peak; pinnacle; point; prime; sky; summit; top

ZEPHYR: aura; breeze; wind

ZERO: blank; cipher; nadir; naught; nihility; nil; nobody; none; nonentity; nothing; nought; ought; void

ZEST: (**see** "vigor" and "zeal") appetite; appetizer; ardor; dash; eagerness; edge; élan; energy; enjoyment; enthusiasm; fervor; fever; fire; flavor; ginger; glee; gusto; initiative; keenness; kick; mettle; nerve; pep(per); piquancy; rapture; raptus; relish; sapidity; savor; spice; spirit; sting; tang; taste; twang; verve; vim; vitality; zealotry; zip; ZESTFUL: (**see** "zealous") breezy; edged; enjoyable; flavorful; gingery; gleeful; keen; piquant; racy; rapturous; relishing; sapid; spicy; spirited; tangy; wholehearted

ZIGZAG: **v.** deviate; slue; swerve; tack; yaw; ZIGZAG: **a.** askew; awry; erratic; oblique; sinuous,

ZIP: (**see** "zest") élan; energy; hiss; pep(per); snap; vim

ZONE: **v.** (**see** "divide") encircle; ZONE: **n.** area; band; belt; berth; circuit; clime; district; division; dominion; girdle; isle; latitude; layer; longitude; precinct; quarter; region; ring; section; sector; space; territory; tract; ward